THE COMPLETE WORKS OF WILLIAM SHAKESPEARE

VOLUME VI

A NOTE TO THE READER

For each work in this set the editors have provided supplementary material that will help the reader better understand the work as both a play to be performed and a literary work.

In his general Foreword, Joseph Papp brings Shakespeare alive as he has for the audiences at his productions. The reader is also acquainted with the theater in which the plays were originally performed.

More detailed information precedes the text of each work: an Introduction places the work in context and discusses its structure and action, and performance notes give a director's view of the problems presented by the characters and themes of each work as interpreted in previous productions.

Each work is followed by a brief record of what is known about the original publication and performance and an attempt to date them; textual departures from the copy text; and an extensive essay on Shakespeare's sources. There are also suggestions for further reading on each work.

THE COMPLETE WORKS OF WILLIAM SHAKESPEARE

VOLUME VI

TIMON OF ATHENS

TITUS ANDRONICUS

THE TEMPEST

THE WINTER'S TALE

HENRY VIII

THE COMPLETE POEMS AND SONNETS

BANTAM BOOKS

Toronto • New York • London • Sydney • Auckland

THIS EDITION CREATED BY
QUALITY PAPERBACK BOOK CLUB

A Bantam Book / published by arrangement
with Scott, Foresman and Company

PRINTING HISTORY
Scott, Foresman edition published/January 1980
Bantam edition, with newly edited text and substantially
revised, edited, and amplified notes, introductions, and
other materials, published/February 1988
Valuable advice on staging matters has been
provided by Richard Hosley.
Collations checked by Eric Rasmussen.
Additional editorial assistance by Claire McEachern

Cover and display type designed by Charlotte Staub.

Published simultaneously in the United States and Canada.

Bantam Books are published by Bantam Books,
a division of Bantam Doubleday Dell Publishing Group, Inc.
Its trademark, consisting of the words "Bantam Books"
and the portrayal of a rooster, is Registered in U.S. Patent
and Trademark Office and in other countries. Marca Registrada.
Bantam Books, 666 Fifth Avenue, New York, NY 10103.
Printed in the United States of America.

Foreword

It's hard to imagine, but Shakespeare wrote all of his plays with a quill pen, a goose feather whose hard end had to be sharpened frequently. How many times did he scrape the dull end to a point with his knife, dip it into the inkwell, and bring up, dripping wet, those wonderful words and ideas that are known all over the world?

In the age of word processors, typewriters, and ballpoint pens, we have almost forgotten the meaning of the word "blot." Yet when I went to school, in the 1930s, my classmates and I knew all too well what an inkblot from the metal-tipped pens we used would do to a nice clean page of a test paper, and we groaned whenever a splotch fell across the sheet. Most of us finished the school day with ink-stained fingers; those who were less careful also went home with ink-stained shirts, which were almost impossible to get clean.

When I think about how long it took me to write the simplest composition with a metal-tipped pen and ink, I can only marvel at how many plays Shakespeare scratched out with his goose-feather quill pen, year after year. Imagine him walking down one of the narrow cobblestoned streets of London, or perhaps drinking a pint of beer in his local alehouse. Suddenly his mind catches fire with an idea, or a sentence, or a previously elusive phrase. He is burning with impatience to write it down—but because he doesn't have a ballpoint pen or even a pencil in his pocket, he has to keep the idea in his head until he can get to his quill and parchment.

He rushes back to his lodgings on Silver Street, ignoring the vendors hawking brooms, the coaches clattering by, the piteous wails of beggars and prisoners. Bounding up the stairs, he snatches his quill and starts to write furiously, not even bothering to light a candle against the dusk. "To be, or not to be," he scrawls, "that is the—." But the quill point has gone dull, the letters have fattened out illegibly, and in the middle of writing one of the most famous passages in the history of dramatic literature, Shakespeare has to stop to sharpen his pen.

Taking a deep breath, he lights a candle now that it's dark, sits down, and begins again. By the time the candle has burned out and the noisy apprentices of his French Huguenot landlord have quieted down, Shakespeare has finished Act 3 of *Hamlet* with scarcely a blot.

Early the next morning, he hurries through the fog of a London summer morning to the rooms of his colleague Richard Burbage, the actor for whom the role of Hamlet is being written. He finds Burbage asleep and snoring loudly, sprawled across his straw mattress. Not only had the actor performed in *Henry V* the previous afternoon, but he had then gone out carousing all night with some friends who had come to the performance.

Shakespeare shakes his friend awake, until, bleary-eyed, Burbage sits up in his bed. "Dammit, Will," he grumbles, "can't you let an honest man sleep?" But the playwright, his eyes shining and the words tumbling out of his mouth, says, "Shut up and listen—tell me what you think of *this*!"

He begins to read to the still half-asleep Burbage, pacing around the room as he speaks. ". . . Whether 'tis nobler in the mind to suffer the slings and arrows of outrageous fortune—"

Burbage interrupts, suddenly wide awake, "That's excellent, very good, 'the slings and arrows of outrageous fortune,' yes, I think it will work quite well. . . ." He takes the parchment from Shakespeare and murmurs the lines to himself, slowly at first but with growing excitement.

The sun is just coming up, and the words of one of Shakespeare's most famous soliloquies are being uttered for the first time by the first actor ever to bring Hamlet to life. It must have been an exhilarating moment.

Shakespeare wrote most of his plays to be performed live by the actor Richard Burbage and the rest of the Lord Chamberlain's men (later the King's men). Today, however, our first encounter with the plays is usually in the form of the printed word. And there is no question that reading Shakespeare for the first time isn't easy. His plays aren't comic books or magazines or the dime-store detective novels I read when I was young. A lot of his sentences are complex. Many of his words are no longer used in our everyday speech. His profound thoughts are often condensed into poetry, which is not as straightforward as prose.

Yet when you hear the words spoken aloud, a lot of the language may strike you as unexpectedly modern. For Shakespeare's plays, like any dramatic work, weren't really meant to be read; they were meant to be spoken, seen, and performed. It's amazing how lines that are so troublesome in print can flow so naturally and easily when spoken.

I think it was precisely this music that first fascinated me. When I was growing up, Shakespeare was a stranger to me. I had no particular interest in him, for I was from a different cultural tradition. It never occurred to me that his plays might be more than just something to "get through" in school, like science or math or the physical education requirement we had to fulfill. My passions then were movies, radio, and vaudeville—certainly not Elizabethan drama.

I was, however, fascinated by words and language. Because I grew up in a home where Yiddish was spoken, and English was only a second language, I was acutely sensitive to the musical sounds of different languages and had an ear for lilt and cadence and rhythm in the spoken word. And so I loved reciting poems and speeches even as a very young child. In first grade I learned lots of short nature verses—"Who has seen the wind?," one of them began. My first foray into drama was playing the role of Scrooge in Charles Dickens's *A Christmas Carol* when I was eight years old. I liked summoning all the scorn and coldness I possessed and putting them into the words, "Bah, humbug!"

From there I moved on to longer and more famous poems and other works by writers of the 1930s. Then, in junior high school, I made my first acquaintance with Shakespeare through his play *Julius Caesar.* Our teacher, Miss McKay, assigned the class a passage to memorize from the opening scene of the play, the one that begins "Wherefore rejoice? What conquest brings he home?" The passage seemed so wonderfully theatrical and alive to me, and the experience of memorizing and reciting it was so much fun, that I went on to memorize another speech from the play on my own.

I chose Mark Antony's address to the crowd in Act 3,

scene 2, which struck me then as incredibly high drama. Even today, when I speak the words, I feel the same thrill I did that first time. There is the strong and athletic Antony descending from the raised pulpit where he has been speaking, right into the midst of a crowded Roman square. Holding the torn and bloody cloak of the murdered Julius Caesar in his hand, he begins to speak to the people of Rome:

> If you have tears, prepare to shed them now.
> You all do know this mantle. I remember
> The first time ever Caesar put it on;
> 'Twas on a summer's evening in his tent,
> That day he overcame the Nervii.
> Look, in this place ran Cassius' dagger through.
> See what a rent the envious Casca made.
> Through this the well-belovèd Brutus stabbed,
> And as he plucked his cursèd steel away,
> Mark how the blood of Caesar followed it,
> As rushing out of doors to be resolved
> If Brutus so unkindly knocked or no;
> For Brutus, as you know, was Caesar's angel.
> Judge, O you gods, how dearly Caesar loved him!
> This was the most unkindest cut of all . . .

I'm not sure now that I even knew Shakespeare had written a lot of other plays, or that he was considered "timeless," "universal," or "classic"—but I knew a good speech when I heard one, and I found the splendid rhythms of Antony's rhetoric as exciting as anything I'd ever come across.

Fifty years later, I still feel that way. Hearing good actors speak Shakespeare gracefully and naturally is a wonderful experience, unlike any other I know. There's a satisfying fullness to the spoken word that the printed page just can't convey. This is why seeing the plays of Shakespeare performed live in a theater is the best way to appreciate them. If you can't do that, listening to sound recordings or watching film versions of the plays is the next best thing.

But if you do start with the printed word, use the play as a script. Be an actor yourself and say the lines out loud. Don't worry too much at first about words you don't immediately understand. Look them up in the footnotes or a dictionary, but don't spend too much time on this. It is more profitable (and fun) to get the sense of a passage and sing it out. Speak naturally, almost as if you were talking to a friend, but be sure to enunciate the words properly. You'll be surprised at how much you understand simply by speaking the speech "trippingly on the tongue," as Hamlet advises the Players.

You might start, as I once did, with a speech from *Julius Caesar,* in which the tribune (city official) Marullus scolds the commoners for transferring their loyalties so quickly from the defeated and murdered general Pompey to the newly victorious Julius Caesar:

> Wherefore rejoice? What conquest brings he home?
> What tributaries follow him to Rome
> To grace in captive bonds his chariot wheels?
> You blocks, you stones, you worse than senseless
> things!
> O you hard hearts, you cruel men of Rome,
> Knew you not Pompey? Many a time and oft
> Have you climbed up to walls and battlements,
> To towers and windows, yea, to chimney tops,
> Your infants in your arms, and there have sat
> The livelong day, with patient expectation,
> To see great Pompey pass the streets of Rome.

With the exception of one or two words like "wherefore" (which means "why," not "where"), "tributaries" (which means "captives"), and "patient expectation" (which means patient waiting), the meaning and emotions of this speech can be easily understood.

From here you can go on to dialogues or other more challenging scenes. Although you may stumble over unaccustomed phrases or unfamiliar words at first, and even fall flat when you're crossing some particularly rocky passages, pick yourself up and stay with it. Remember that it takes time to feel at home with anything new. Soon you'll come to recognize Shakespeare's unique sense of humor and way of saying things as easily as you recognize a friend's laughter.

And then it will just be a matter of choosing which one of Shakespeare's plays you want to tackle next. As a true fan of his, you'll find that you're constantly learning from his plays. It's a journey of discovery that you can continue for the rest of your life. For no matter how many times you read or see a particular play, there will always be something new there that you won't have noticed before.

Why do so many thousands of people get hooked on Shakespeare and develop a habit that lasts a lifetime? What can he really say to us today, in a world filled with inventions and problems he never could have imagined? And how do you get past his special language and difficult sentence structure to understand him?

The best way to answer these questions is to go see a live production. You might not know much about Shakespeare, or much about the theater, but when you watch actors performing one of his plays on the stage, it will soon become clear to you why people get so excited about a playwright who lived hundreds of years ago.

For the story—what's happening in the play—is the most accessible part of Shakespeare. In *A Midsummer Night's Dream*, for example, you can immediately understand the situation: a girl is chasing a guy who's chasing a girl who's chasing another guy. No wonder *A Midsummer Night's Dream* is one of the most popular of Shakespeare's plays: it's about one of the world's most popular pastimes—falling in love.

But the course of true love never did run smooth, as the young suitor Lysander says. Often in Shakespeare's comedies the girl whom the guy loves doesn't love him back, or she loves him but he loves someone else. In *The Two Gentlemen of Verona*, Julia loves Proteus, Proteus loves Sylvia, and Sylvia loves Valentine, who is Proteus's best friend. In the end, of course, true love prevails, but not without lots of complications along the way.

For in all of his plays—comedies, histories, and tragedies—Shakespeare is showing you human nature. His characters act and react in the most extraordinary ways—and sometimes in the most incomprehensible ways. People are always trying to find motivations for what a character does. They ask, "Why does Iago want to destroy Othello?"

The answer, to me, is very simple—because that's the way Iago is. That's just his nature. Shakespeare doesn't explain his characters; he sets them in motion—and away they go. He doesn't worry about whether they're likable or not. He's interested in interesting people, and his most fascinating characters are those who are unpredictable. If you lean back in your chair early on in one of his plays, thinking you've figured out what Iago or Shylock (in *The Merchant of Venice*) is up to, don't be too sure—because that great judge of human nature, Shakespeare, will surprise you every time.

He is just as wily in the way he structures a play. In *Macbeth,* a comic scene is suddenly introduced just after the bloodiest and most treacherous slaughter imaginable, of a guest and king by his host and subject, when in comes a drunk porter who has to go to the bathroom. Shakespeare is tickling your emotions by bringing a stand-up comic onstage right on the heels of a savage murder.

It has taken me thirty years to understand even some of these things, and so I'm not suggesting that Shakespeare is immediately understandable. I've gotten to know him not through theory but through practice, the practice of the *living* Shakespeare—the playwright of the theater.

Of course the plays are a great achievement of dramatic literature, and they should be studied and analyzed in schools and universities. But you must always remember, when reading all the words *about* the playwright and his plays, that *Shakespeare's* words came first and that in the end there is nothing greater than a single actor on the stage speaking the lines of Shakespeare.

Everything important that I know about Shakespeare comes from the practical business of producing and directing his plays in the theater. The task of classifying, criticizing, and editing Shakespeare's printed works I happily leave to others. For me, his plays really do live on the stage, not on the page. That is what he wrote them for and that is how they are best appreciated.

Although Shakespeare lived and wrote hundreds of years ago, his name rolls off my tongue as if he were my brother. As a producer and director, I feel that there is a professional relationship between us that spans the centuries. As a human being, I feel that Shakespeare has enriched my understanding of life immeasurably. I hope you'll let him do the same for you.

Joseph Papp

Joseph Papp gratefully acknowledges the help of Elizabeth Kirkland in preparing this Foreword.

The Playhouse

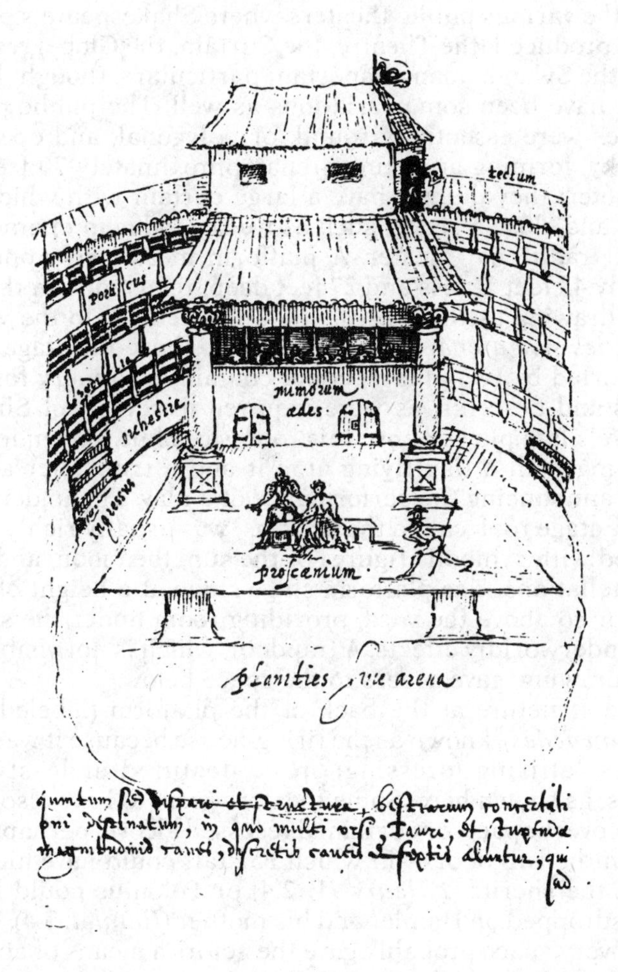

This early copy of a drawing by Johannes de Witt of the Swan Theatre in London (c. 1596), made by his friend Arend van Buchell, is the only surviving contemporary sketch of the interior of a public theater in the 1590s.

From other contemporary evidence, including the stage directions and dialogue of Elizabethan plays, we can surmise that the various public theaters where Shakespeare's plays were produced (the Theatre, the Curtain, the Globe) resembled the Swan in many important particulars, though there must have been some variations as well. The public playhouses were essentially round, or polygonal, and open to the sky, forming an acting arena approximately 70 feet in diameter; they did not have a large curtain with which to open and close a scene, such as we see today in opera and some traditional theater. A platform measuring approximately 43 feet across and 27 feet deep, referred to in the de Witt drawing as the *proscaenium,* projected into the yard, *planities sive arena*. The roof, *tectum,* above the stage and supported by two pillars, could contain machinery for ascents and descents, as were required in several of Shakespeare's late plays. Above this roof was a hut, shown in the drawing with a flag flying atop it and a trumpeter at its door announcing the performance of a play. The underside of the stage roof, called the heavens, was usually richly decorated with symbolic figures of the sun, the moon, and the constellations. The platform stage stood at a height of 5½ feet or so above the yard, providing room under the stage for underworldly effects. A trapdoor, which is not visible in this drawing, gave access to the space below.

The structure at the back of the platform (labeled *mimorum aedes*), known as the tiring-house because it was the actors' attiring (dressing) space, featured at least two doors, as shown here. Some theaters seem to have also had a discovery space, or curtained recessed alcove, perhaps between the two doors—in which Falstaff could have hidden from the sheriff (*1 Henry IV,* 2.4) or Polonius could have eavesdropped on Hamlet and his mother (*Hamlet,* 3.4). This discovery space probably gave the actors a means of access to and from the tiring-house. Curtains may also have been hung in front of the stage doors on occasion. The de Witt drawing shows a gallery above the doors that extends across the back and evidently contains spectators. On occasions when action "above" demanded the use of this space, as when Juliet appears at her "window" (*Romeo and Juliet,* 2.2 and 3.5), the gallery seems to have been used by the actors, but large scenes there were impractical.

The three-tiered auditorium is perhaps best described by Thomas Platter, a visitor to London in 1599 who saw on that occasion Shakespeare's *Julius Caesar* performed at the Globe:

> The playhouses are so constructed that they play on a raised platform, so that everyone has a good view. There are different galleries and places [*orchestra, sedilia, porticus*], however, where the seating is better and more comfortable and therefore more expensive. For whoever cares to stand below only pays one English penny, but if he wishes to sit, he enters by another door [*ingressus*] and pays another penny, while if he desires to sit in the most comfortable seats, which are cushioned, where he not only sees everything well but can also be seen, then he pays yet another English penny at another door. And during the performance food and drink are carried round the audience, so that for what one cares to pay one may also have refreshment.

Scenery was not used, though the theater building itself was handsome enough to invoke a feeling of order and hierarchy that lent itself to the splendor and pageantry onstage. Portable properties, such as thrones, stools, tables, and beds, could be carried or thrust on as needed. In the scene pictured here by de Witt, a lady on a bench, attended perhaps by her waiting-gentlewoman, receives the address of a male figure. If Shakespeare had written *Twelfth Night* by 1596 for performance at the Swan, we could imagine Malvolio appearing like this as he bows before the Countess Olivia and her gentlewoman, Maria.

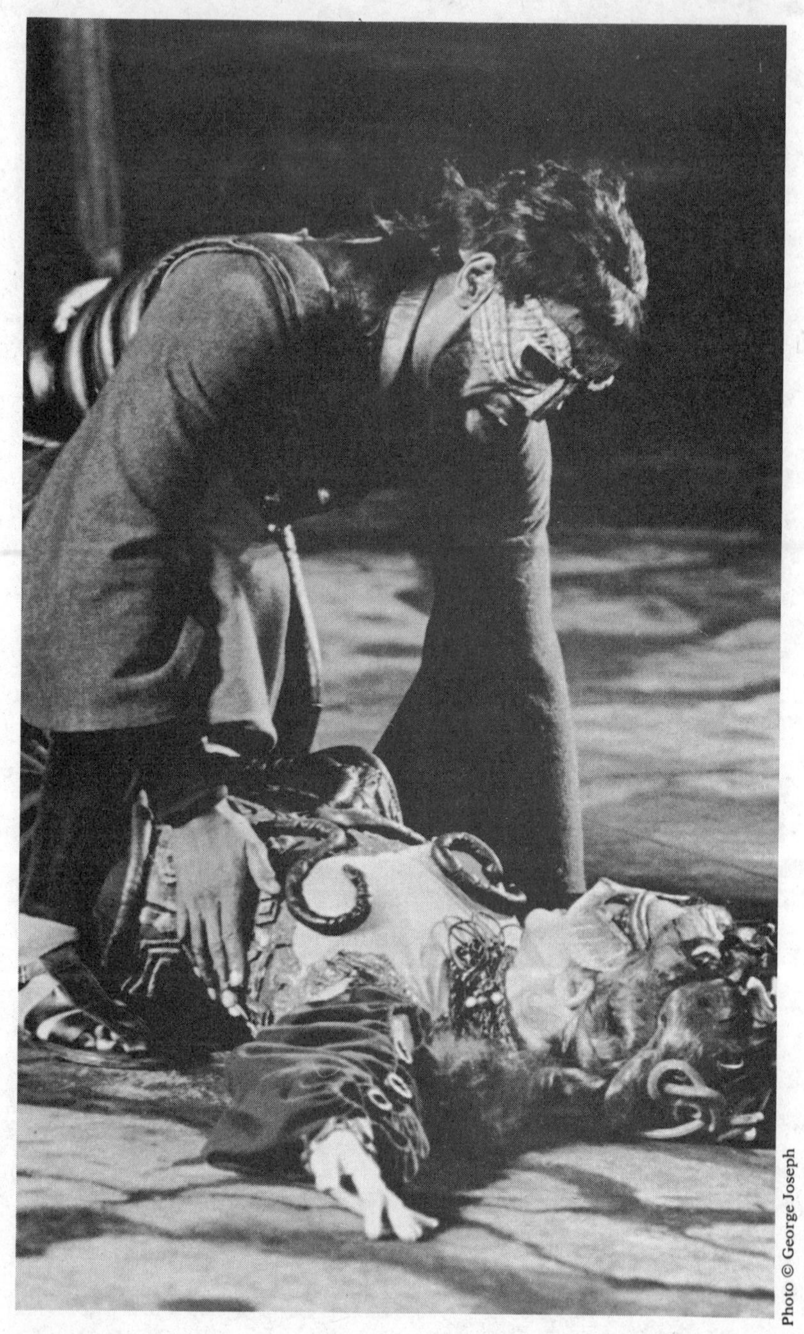

Photo © George Joseph

Timon of Athens, with Shepperd Strudwick (center) as Timon, directed by Gerald Freedman in 1971 at the Delacorte Theater in Central Park.

TIMON
— OF —
ATHENS

TIMON OF ATHENS

Foreword

Timon of Athens is a dark and cynical play, not often performed on the stage today. It has an affinity with *Troilus and Cressida* because it's about corruption and bitterness, and possibly with *King Lear* because it concerns ingratitude. In a way, Timon could be seen as a preliminary sketch of Lear, someone driven by the madness of sorrow back to his most basic earthbound self. He goes from being a man who has everything—wealth, prestige, friends, and flatterers—to a man who digs in the earth and utters stunningly savage curses against humanity: "O blessèd breeding sun, draw from the earth / Rotten humidity; below thy sister's orb / Infect the air!" There's a primitive quality to Timon's retreat to the cave, his digging, and his guttural cursing that works powerfully in the theater.

Joseph Papp

Joseph Papp gratefully acknowledges the help of Elizabeth Kirkland in preparing this Foreword.

Introduction

Timon of Athens is Shakespeare's most relentless study in misanthropy. It expresses with *King Lear* a moral outrage at human depravity, but refuses to soften anger with compassionate tears. The protagonist learns little other than bitterness from his encounters with avarice and ingratitude. In its mordant vision of human folly, *Timon of Athens* resembles a number of other Roman or classical plays. As in *Julius Caesar, Titus Andronicus, Coriolanus,* and *Troilus and Cressida,* the dominant mood is one of enervation and futility. Political conflicts end in stalemate or a victory for opportunists; the populace and their leaders are fickle and craven; private virtues of noble men must yield to crass considerations of statecraft. Banishment or self-exile is too often the reward of those who have given their lives to public service. Shakespeare's misanthropic vision in *Timon of Athens* is, then, integral to his portrayal of humanity's political and social nature in the ancient classical world. This is a world to which Shakespeare turned often during his writing career, especially during the period from about 1601 to 1608, when he was engaged primarily in writing tragedies. As a group, the Roman and classical plays tend to differ from the great tragedies of evil (*Hamlet, Othello, King Lear, Macbeth*) in that the classical plays naturally make less use of a Christian perspective and focus instead on a sardonic and dispiriting view of life's tragic absurdity. Even in *Antony and Cleopatra,* where Shakespeare offers us an ennobling dream of greatness to offset the worldly failure of his protagonists, the arena of human conflict remains pitiless and disillusioning. *Timon of Athens* offers no compensatory vision; it is bleak to the end, unwavering in its denial.

Timon of Athens appears to have been written between 1605 and 1608, and is often grouped with *King Lear* (c. 1605) on grounds of stylistic and thematic similarity. For its chief source it uses Thomas North's translation of Plutarch's *The Lives of the Noble Grecians and Romans,* a source also for *Julius Caesar, Antony and Cleopatra, Coriolanus,* and parts of other plays. *Timon of Athens* also makes use, through intermediary versions, of the dialogue called *Ti-*

mon, or *The Misanthrope,* by the Greek satirist Lucian. The play may not have been produced; the text, not printed until the 1623 Folio, appears to have been taken from the author's unfinished manuscript, with contradictory uncanceled lines (see Timon's will, 5.4.70–73), unresolved discrepancies as to the amount of money Timon gives or requests, and passages of half-versified prose. Whatever the exact date and circumstance of composition, the play certainly belongs to the period of Shakespeare's most unsparing portrayal of human villainy and corruption.

Like *Troilus and Cressida, Timon of Athens* defies the conventional categories of tragedy, comedy, and history. Generically, the play stands chiefly between tragedy and satire in its preoccupation with dying and sterility. The play is tragic in portraying a fall from greatness, satiric in exposing an unfeeling society. Satire is potentially comic as well, and we are invited to laugh sardonically at the hypocrisies of Timon's fair-weather friends. The play is also a history, drawn from historical sources, as its Folio title, *The Life of Timon of Athens,* suggests. We ought to see or read it with the expectations not simply of tragedy but also of satire and ironic history.

As a genre, in fact, the play most resembles those works that the Painter and the Poet wish to offer Timon himself: a "moral painting" and a "satire against the softness of prosperity" (1.1.95 and 5.1.32–33). Such a genre is deliberately old-fashioned, reminiscent of medieval morality plays and of the "hybrid" morality plays of the 1570s and '80s like Thomas Lupton's *All for Money* (c. 1577) or Thomas Lodge and Robert Greene's *A Looking Glass for London and England* (1587–1591), which inveigh against usury and the neglect of military heroes. John Marston's later quasi-morality, *Histriomastix* (c. 1599), proclaims the decline of civilization through worldly insolence. Ben Jonson's *Volpone* (1605–1606), though "comical" rather than "tragical" in its satire, similarly castigates human greed. The *Parnassus* trilogy (1598–1603), a series of three mordantly satirical plays written to be acted by students at Cambridge, indulges in a massive venting of spleen against a philistine culture. *Timon of Athens* follows this tradition of social satire, derived from both English and classical models. Like most satire of the 1600s, both dramatic and nondramatic, it is crabbed in style, features a railing protagonist, and denounces through exaggerated caricature an ugly array of types representing a broad social spectrum. Choice of the satiric morality play as a generic model accords well with the play's acerbic view of decadence and "softness."

Human greed, with which *Timon of Athens* is so occupied, lends itself readily to satiric treatment. Avarice does not seem terrifying at first, like the spiritual sins of envy or prideful ambition as portrayed in *Othello* and *Macbeth;* instead, it is disgusting, ludicrous, and incredibly tenacious. Avarice is after all one of the Deadly Sins and is often referred to in medieval commentary as the pivotal Sin, the *radix malorum,* or root of all evils. Although less vivid in its manifestation than pride or envy, greed is insidious and all-embracing. We see its corrupting effects in Timon's friends. Those who sponge off him and then desert him are quick to return when he is rumored to have found gold in his exile. Greed is also self-deceiving. Many are the excuses offered for failing to come to Timon's aid: one friend rates Timon as a bad credit risk, another happens to be short of ready cash at the moment, a third insists that Timon's generosity to him wasn't as great as people suppose, and so on. No wonder Timon feels he must devise for such hypocrites a suitable comeuppance, consisting of a farewell banquet in which their crass expectations are rewarded with a mocking litany of curses and a dinner of water and stones.

Appropriately for this satirical depiction of human greed, the characters are virtually all types or social abstractions in a generic portrayal of avarice. Several represent the crafts and professions, and are abstractly labeled as such: the Poet, the Painter, the Jeweler, the Merchant. Others are "flattering lords" or "false friends" or "thieves." Seldom in Shakespeare do we find so many characters without proper names. They are depersonalized, and we are distanced from them. Apemantus is another type, a "churlish philosopher," recognizable in all his appearances by this one feature; we learn little about him other than that he professes to scoff at worldliness with a scabrous wit derived in part from legends about Diogenes the Cynic philosopher and other devotees of an extravagantly simple mode of life. Timon himself becomes a type in his conversion to misanthropy, "infected," as Apemantus says, by "A poor unmanly melancholy sprung / From change of fortune" (4.3.205–206). Apemantus' remark appeals to a view of personality as governed by "humors" or dominant traits such as melancholy or irascibility, which are generated by imbalance in the body of the four "humors," blood, phlegm, bile, and black bile. Images of disease, prominent throughout the play, are often derived from such "humorous" imbalances. The imagery also associates character types, as in Jonson's *Volpone,* with various beasts: the lion, the fox, the ass, the wolf, the bear, and most of all the dog. By means of such techniques, Shakespeare portrays those whom Timon comes to despise with a seemingly intentional onesidedness; the caricatures of avarice are vivid and amusing, with little allowance for subtlety or change. The plot too is, by Shakespeare's standard, unusually lacking in complication: Timon discovers the ingratitude and graspingness of his fellow creatures and retires from a world he can no longer tolerate, breathing upon it his dying curse. The dramatic tension of this uneventful story lies instead in Timon's own tortured spiritual saga, in the painful process of realization, in the revulsion, the refusal to compromise, the spurning even of honest friendship, the bitter renunciation and longing for oblivion. Alcibiades, too, is a complex character, offering as he does the alternatives of vengeful action against an ungrateful world or of successful conciliation; the debate between Alcibiades and Timon is an essential part of Timon's working toward total rejection of hope. The true drama is thus inner, and is increasingly contrasted with a static and superficial society toward which we are asked to feel revulsion and finally indifference.

There are no villains in *Timon of Athens,* only weak and foolish men. What is depressing about greed, in fact, is its insidious normality. Those who desert Timon have many prudent arguments on their side. After all, his original generosity is excessive and reckless. If his friends take advantage of him, they can at least say they have tried to warn him. Even a fool can see what lies in store. Much of Timon's wealth goes into drunken and gluttonous debauchery, into "feasts, pomps, and vainglories" (1.2.247–248). Timon does not know how to use prosperity wisely, and even his loyal servants deplore the "riot" (2.2.3). He is deaf to the friendly counsel of his steward, Flavius. For one who is so openhanded, Timon is surprisingly churlish with his creditors. And is he not presumptuous to assume that his friends will come to his aid when such vast sums are needed? Are they to be blamed for not emulating his prodigal decline into poverty? Clearly Timon expects too much. We readily though sadly perceive, as do all Timon's friends, that commerce is a god worshiped by all; need he be so shocked at this? As bystanders, we share with Timon's choric servants the certainty that his large requests for help will be refused. And yet, no matter how stupid or blind Timon may be, the desertion of him is still monstrous. Timon differs from us chiefly in being an idealist, in expecting that men will repay kindness with gratitude. We know, as do Timon's sympathetic servants, that most men are not like that.

Timon thus tears himself apart in a rage at what we consider the way of the world. We find his misanthropy intemperate, and yet we cannot help being moved by his sweeping indictment of human pettiness and inhumanity. Timon's furor carries him beyond satire. He is, like Lear, all the more clear-sighted for being near to madness. Wisdom and folly exchange places, as Apemantus' friend the Fool has already pointed out (2.2.99–120). In Timon's nearly mad vision beggars and lords are interchangeable, distinguished only by wealth and position. Love of gold, he sees, inverts everything decent in human life, making "Black white, foul fair, wrong right, / Base noble, old young, coward valiant" (4.3.29–30). Thieves and whores are at least more honest than their counterparts in everyday life, the respectable citizens of Athens and their wives, and so Timon mockingly rewards the thieves and insults the hypocrites. Yet Timon also inveighs furiously against women and all sexuality in a way that suggests feelings of betrayal. Though women occupy virtually no place in Timon's life, he himself has sought to displace women by serving as the generous source of comfort for all his friends—a self-created and narcissistic role that is destined to collapse into self-hatred and dread of all human feeling. His curse embraces the cosmos as well as humanity, inverting all semblance of hierarchical order: obedience must turn to rebellion, fidelity to incontinence, virginity to lasciviousness. "Degrees, observances, customs, and laws" must "Decline to your confounding contraries" (4.1.19–20). Clothing and cosmetics must be stripped away, as in *King Lear,* so that humanity's monstrosity may be revealed for what it truly is

Three persons, Apemantus, Alcibiades, and Flavius, serve as chief foils to Timon in his estrangement from humanity. Apemantus the Cynic, who first taught Timon to rail at greed, now counsels him to find stoic contentment in renunciation of desire, or, conversely, to thrive as a flatterer by preying on those who have undone him (4.3.200–234). Alcibiades, the military commander banished by an ungrateful Athenian Senate for presuming to beg the life of one who had rashly shed blood in a quarrel, offers Timon the example of revenge against his enemies; subsequently, he offers Athens the olive branch with the sword, making "war breed peace" (5.4.83), in an accommodating move that is important for the conclusion of the play and its final mitigating tone. Timon, although resembling both men as railer and as victim of ingratitude, rejects their counsels as too politic, too worldly. His stand is unflinching, absolute, so lacking in compromise that his sole choice can be to curse, die, and hope for oblivion. Only Flavius, his steward, offers brief consolation. Flavius comes to him, like Kent to King Lear, offering love and service in exile. Flavius even speaks in paradoxes reminiscent of *King Lear,* calling Timon "My dearest lord, blest to be most accurst, / Rich only to be wretched" (4.2.43–44). These are precious words, showing that humanity is not utterly irredeemable. Still, this consolation is evidently too late to offset the nightmarish truth that Timon has learned. Timon experiences little of the compassionate love that comes to Lear in his madness, but he at least faces the bleakness of human existence with unbending honesty.

Timon of Athens in Performance

Timon of Athens onstage suffered the fate of many of Shakespeare's late plays: neglect, followed by adaptation in an attempt to remedy its presumed defects. Not until the mid-nineteenth century was it often seen in anything like its original form. The reasons are not hard to imagine: the bitter misanthropy and caustic satire, the ambiguity as to genre, the distasteful presentation of women (which means, among other things, there are no adequate roles for lead actresses), and above all the absence of romantic interest. No performance is recorded as having occurred during Shakespeare's lifetime, and the text is sufficiently unfinished that we cannot safely assume his company ever acted it. The first certain theatrical event of any kind, in fact, was the performance of Thomas Shadwell's *The History of Timon of Athens, the Man-hater,* at the theater in Dorset Garden in 1678. Thomas Betterton played Timon; his wife (Mary Sanderson) and Mrs. Shadwell (Anne Gibbs) took the roles of two new female characters, Evandra and Melissa. With music by Henry Purcell and a new love plot, the play enjoyed quite a success.

Shadwell's adaptation adroitly supplies the conflicts of love and honor, so necessary to Restoration heroic drama, that Shakespeare had somehow neglected to provide. The two women in Timon's life are Melissa, a coquettish gold digger, and Evandra, his selfless and devoted mistress—both of them Restoration stereotypes. Melissa, when we first see her with her maid Chloe as she makes herself up for a visit from Timon, is flirtatiously trying to balance the attentions of two men, the wealthy Timon and the powerful Alcibiades. She naturally drops Timon when he falls into financial ruin, but then, hearing of his having found gold, seeks him out at his cave. Fittingly, she is rejected by Timon and then by Alcibiades, whom she has also jilted in his time of banishment. Melissa is thus a much-expanded counterpart of Shakespeare's Phrynia and Timandra, suitably punished for her infidelities and heartlessness. Evandra, who embodies the selfless qualities of Shakespeare's loyal steward, Flavius, is contrasted to Melissa in every way. Evandra remains loyal to Timon even when he leaves her for Melissa; she offers all her wealth to assist him in his financial difficulties, follows him into exile after he churlishly turns down her offer of help, and, when Timon despairingly commits suicide, takes her own life rather than outlive him.

Flavius meanwhile is replaced by a self-seeking steward called Demetrius, who warns Timon of impending ruin but is interested only in his own survival. Alcibiades becomes the heroic foe of tyranny and friend of democracy, no doubt with some application to the politics of the 1670s and especially to the high-handed tactics of Charles II and his Catholic brother, later James II. The story of the two added women not only provides love interest but a unified plot, required by neoclassical ideas of form. Shadwell boasted that he had made Shakespeare's original "into a play," though he granted, as his age was ready to do, that Shakespeare's genius provided the main strength of the work, however much it needed to be rescued from oblivion by added refinements. Shadwell managed in fact to save a number of Shakespeare's scenes, including the one in which Timon is approached by the Painter, the Poet, the Jeweler, and the Merchant (1.1), and the colloquy between Timon and Apemantus (4.3).

Shadwell's *Timon* did remarkably well. It was absent from the stage only in nine of the years between 1678 and 1745. After Betterton, Barton Booth was the outstanding Timon of the era. Although Shakespeare's text seems to have been briefly revived in Dublin in 1761, Shadwell's adaptation continued on into the late eighteenth century in a slightly modified version by James Love in 1768 and another by Thomas Hull in 1786.

A script prepared by Richard Cumberland for a production by actor-manager David Garrick at the Theatre Royal, Drury Lane, in 1771, made use of some Shadwell as well, but developed the conflict of selfish and selfless love in a new and, if possible, more sentimental direction. This version replaces Melissa and Evandra with Evanthe, Timon's virtuous daughter. She receives the attentions of three men, of whom two, Lucius and Lucullus, are interested only in her inheritance. They meet their just reward when Lucullus' buried money is found in the woods by Timon and when Lucius' house in Athens is looted by Alcibiades' troops intent upon revenging the wrongs done to Timon. Evanthe's true love is Alcibiades himself, a man of sterling honor who would never dream of keeping mistresses. When Evanthe is delivered to Alcibiades by the Athenian elders as a hostage, he escorts her to Timon's cave and receives a parental blessing on their marriage just before Timon expires on the steps of the ruined Temple of Faunus. Poetic justice having been richly served, virtue is triumphant.

George Lamb began the movement back to Shakespeare's text in a version presented at Drury Lane in 1816, with Edmund Kean as Timon, though even here Cumberland's approach of administering fit punishment to the grasping Lucius and Lucullus is retained, while Alcibiades' whores are left out in the interest of "refinement of manners." The cuts are heavy, but most of what is left is Shakespeare's. Not until actor-manager Samuel Phelps's productions at the Sadler's Wells Theatre in 1851 and 1856 do we hear of a genuine and successful revival. Phelps was attracted to the scenic possibilities of *Timon*'s classical setting, as he had been in his *The Winter's Tale* (1845) and was to be in his *Pericles* (1854), among others. Phelps provided Greek interiors, classical landscapes, and a stirring march of Alcibiades and his army to Athens. The production ran for forty nights in late 1851 and was among Phelps's greatest successes. Yet it did less well in his revival of 1856.

Theater managers of the late nineteenth and early twentieth centuries continued to deal uncertainly with the conflicting demands of scenic realism and restoration of Shakespeare's text. Charles Calvert produced out a version in 1871 in Manchester, England, at the Prince's Theatre, from which Phrynia and Timandra were excluded, but which added an array of dancing sequences to the banqueting scenes (1.2 and 3.6). In Calvert's production, Timon recovers his sanity under the care of his servants and dies in their arms, reconciled with humanity. Frank Benson's production of the play at Stratford-upon-Avon on Shakespeare's birthday, in 1892, emphasized the contrast between the magnificence of Timon's fortune and his subsequent "sour misery." Although Benson claimed to "love the play and the part," his *Timon* was not a success. J. H.

Leigh produced the play in London at the Court Theatre in 1904, and Frederick Warde toured America with it in 1910. Robert Atkins produced it at the Old Vic in 1922.

William Bridges-Adams seems to have been the first to address the bitterness of *Timon* in modern terms, at the Picture House, the temporary home of the Shakespeare Festival Theatre in Stratford-upon-Avon, in 1928, and since that time *Timon* has enjoyed a modest revival of interest. A young Tyrone Guthrie directed the Norwich Players at the Maddermarket Theatre in 1931, and then again some twenty-one years later, in 1952, at the Old Vic, with settings by Tanya Moiseiwitsch. For Nugent Monck's production at London's Westminster Theatre in 1935, Benjamin Britten, then aged twenty-one, provided a musical score that captured a modern sense of disillusionment. The play has readily lent itself to modern dress, as in the Birmingham Repertory Theatre's version of 1947. Michael Benthall directed the Old Vic's third *Timon* in 1956, with Ralph Richardson in the title role.

At Stratford, Canada, in 1963, Peter Coe and Michael Langham produced a modern-dress *Timon* that flashily emphasized the play's disillusioned cynicism. Apemantus was a jaded newspaper reporter with a cigarette constantly dangling from his lips; Timon hosted his banquet, which featured a jazz combo playing Duke Ellington music, in a red brocade dinner jacket. John Schlesinger's production at Stratford-upon-Avon in 1965 was more traditional in its decor but nonetheless deeply persuasive in its denunciation of sham and hypocritical friendship; as Timon (Paul Scofield) moved from an initial exuberant innocence to an appalling rage, "the excess of his misanthropy," as critic Robert Speaight noted, "was also the measure of his growth." At Ashland, Oregon, in 1978, director Jerry Turner returned to an aggressively modern idiom. Timon's flatterers and hangers-on were Texas tycoons in white three-piece suits and ten-gallon hats, amid a set that displayed the vulgar ostentation of a love of wealth. Alcibiades and his whores in Act 4, conversely, were guerrilla fighters with automatic weapons and camouflage outfits. The set articulated the doubleness of Turner's vision by literally turning itself inside out on a revolving platform stage; a decadently sybaritic civilization revealed at its back or underside a skeleton of anarchy and revolution.

Timon's deep cynicism has obviously challenged contemporary actors and directors and intrigued modern audiences. Richard Pasco, at The Other Place in Stratford-upon-Avon in 1980, was secretive and withdrawn as Timon in Ron Daniels's Kabuki-like production of the play in which the vibrant portrait of Timon's aristocratic Athens gave way after the intermission to a bare stage with a single tree. Jonathan Pryce's Timon, in the BBC television version directed by Jonathan Miller in 1981, revealed the strain and compulsive quality of his initial generosity and optimism, thus granting his emotional trajectory clarity and coherence.

Without doubt, the most significant modern production of *Timon* was a French version directed by Peter Brook in Paris in 1974. Brook staged the play in the shell of an abandoned Victorian theater, in an area of the orchestra with the audience around it in bleachers. The scarred backstage walls and the cavity that had formerly held the stage became part of the play's dispiriting vision, prompting *The New York Times*'s reviewer to remark: "Every spectator at once knows that he is sitting inside a symbol of the decline of the West." Brook's production memorably proved that *Timon,* even though it will never be a major work in its unfinished form, can enlist the sympathy of today's audiences by its compelling vision of protest against complacent wealth and venality.

TIMON
OF
ATHENS

The Actors' Names

TIMON OF ATHENS
LUCIUS *and* LUCULLUS, *two flattering lords*
SEMPRONIUS, *another flattering lord*
VENTIDIUS, *one of Timon's false friends*
APEMANTUS, *a churlish philosopher*
ALCIBIADES, *an Athenian captain*
[PHRYNIA, TIMANDRA, *mistresses of Alcibiades*
AN OLD ATHENIAN]
Certain SENATORS [*and* LORDS]
[FLAVIUS, *steward to Timon*]
POET, PAINTER, JEWELER, [*and*] MERCHANT
FLAMINIUS, *one of Timon's servants*
[LUCILIUS, *another*]
SERVILIUS, *another*
CAPHIS,
PHILOTUS' [SERVANT],
TITUS' [SERVANT],
HORTENSIUS' [SERVANT],
[ISIDORE'S SERVANT,
Two of] VARRO'S [SERVANTS], *several servants to usurers* [*Timon's creditors*]
[A PAGE
A FOOL
Three STRANGERS
Two MESSENGERS]
Certain THIEVES [*or* BANDITTI]
CUPID [*and*] *certain* MASKERS [*as Amazons*]

With divers other Servants and Attendants, [*other Lords, Officers, Soldiers*]

[SCENE: *Athens, and the neighboring woods*]

1.1

Enter Poet, Painter, Jeweler, and Merchant, at several doors. [The Poet and Painter form one group, the Jeweler and Merchant another.]

POET Good day, sir.
PAINTER I am glad you're well.
POET
I have not seen you long. How goes the world? 3
PAINTER
It wears, sir, as it grows.
POET Ay, that's well known. 4
But what particular rarity? What strange, 5
Which manifold record not matches? See, 6
Magic of bounty, all these spirits thy power 7
Hath conjured to attend! I know the merchant.
PAINTER
I know them both. Th' other's a jeweler.
MERCHANT [*To the Jeweler*]
O, 'tis a worthy lord!
JEWELER Nay, that's most fixed. 10
MERCHANT
A most incomparable man, breathed, as it were, 11
To an untirable and continuate goodness. 12
He passes. 13
JEWELER I have a jewel here—
MERCHANT
O, pray, let's see 't. For the Lord Timon, sir?
JEWELER
If he will touch the estimate. But for that— 16
POET [*Reciting to himself*]
"When we for recompense have praised the vile,

1.1. Location: Athens. Timon's house.
s.d. several separate **3 long** for a long time. **How . . . world** i.e., how are you doing? (But the Painter quibbles on the literal sense.) **4 wears** decays. **grows** ages **5 rarity** unusual occurrence. **strange** strange event **6 Which . . . matches** i.e., which all recorded history cannot equal **7 Magic of bounty** i.e., the remarkable attractive power of generosity. **spirits** i.e., beings, persons (spoken of as if they were spirits conjured by magic) **10 worthy lord** i.e., Timon. **fixed** certain **11 breathed** inspired; or trained through exercise **12 untirable** inexhaustible. **continuate** habitual **13 passes** surpasses **16 touch the estimate** offer or meet the price

It stains the glory in that happy verse 18
Which aptly sings the good."

MERCHANT [*Looking at the jewel*] 'Tis a good form. 19

JEWELER And rich. Here is a water, look ye. 20

PAINTER [*To the Poet*]
You are rapt, sir, in some work, some dedication 21
To the great lord.

POET A thing slipped idly from me. 22
Our poesy is as a gum which oozes
From whence 'tis nourished. The fire i' the flint
Shows not till it be struck; our gentle flame
Provokes itself and like the current flies 26
Each bound it chafes. What have you there? 27

PAINTER
A picture, sir. When comes your book forth?

POET
Upon the heels of my presentment, sir. 29
Let's see your piece. [*He examines the painting.*]

PAINTER 'Tis a good piece.

POET
So 'tis. This comes off well and excellent.

PAINTER
Indifferent.

POET Admirable! How this grace 33
Speaks his own standing! What a mental power 34
This eye shoots forth! How big imagination 35
Moves in this lip! To th' dumbness of the gesture 36
One might interpret. 37

PAINTER
It is a pretty mocking of the life. 38
Here is a touch; is 't good?

POET I will say of it,

18 happy felicitous, matching truthful praise to a worthy object
19 form shape, appearance. (Refers to the jewel.) **20 water** luster
21 dedication (Such works were customarily dedicated to great noblemen.) **22 idly** casually **26 Provokes itself** i.e., is self-generating
26–27 flies . . . chafes seeks escape from the riverbanks that confine it
29 Upon . . . presentment as soon as I have presented it (to Lord Timon, in hopes of obtaining his patronage) **33 Indifferent** i.e., not bad. **this grace** i.e., of the person in the picture **34 Speaks . . . standing** conveys the dignity of its subject **35 big** largely **36–37 To . . . interpret** i.e., the very gestures depicted are eloquent **38 mocking** mirroring

It tutors nature. Artificial strife 40
Lives in these touches, livelier than life.

Enter certain Senators.

PAINTER How this lord is followed!
POET
The senators of Athens. Happy man!
PAINTER Look, more!
[*The Senators pass over the stage, and exeunt.*]
POET
You see this confluence, this great flood of visitors.
[*He shows his poem.*]
I have in this rough work shaped out a man
Whom this beneath world doth embrace and hug 47
With amplest entertainment. My free drift 48
Halts not particularly, but moves itself 49
In a wide sea of tax. No leveled malice 50
Infects one comma in the course I hold, 51
But flies an eagle flight, bold and forth on, 52
Leaving no tract behind. 53
PAINTER How shall I understand you? 54
POET I will unbolt to you. 55
You see how all conditions, how all minds, 56
As well of glib and slippery creatures as
Of grave and austere quality, tender down 58
Their services to Lord Timon. His large fortune,
Upon his good and gracious nature hanging, 60
Subdues and properties to his love and tendance 61
All sorts of hearts; yea, from the glass-faced flatterer 62

40 Artificial strife the striving of art to surpass nature **47 this beneath world** i.e., the world itself, beneath the sphere of the moon **48 entertainment** welcome. **drift** design **49 Halts not particularly** doesn't concern itself with criticizing anyone individually **50 tax** censure. **leveled** aimed, as a gun is aimed at a particular object **51 comma** i.e., detail **52 forth on** straight on **53 tract** track, trace **54 How . . . you** what do you mean **55 unbolt** unlock, disclose **56 conditions** ranks, temperaments **58 tender down** tender, offer **60 hanging** providing attractive adornment, like rich clothes **61 properties** appropriates. **tendance** tending on him (also in l. 85) **62 glass-faced** showing in his look, as by reflection, the looks of his patron

To Apemantus, that few things loves better
Than to abhor himself—even he drops down
The knee before him and returns in peace 65
Most rich in Timon's nod. 66

PAINTER I saw them speak together.

POET
Sir, I have upon a high and pleasant hill
Feigned Fortune to be throned. The base o' the mount 69
Is ranked with all deserts, all kind of natures, 70
That labor on the bosom of this sphere 71
To propagate their states. Amongst them all 72
Whose eyes are on this sovereign lady fixed
One do I personate of Lord Timon's frame, 74
Whom Fortune with her ivory hand wafts to her, 75
Whose present grace to present slaves and servants 76
Translates his rivals.

PAINTER 'Tis conceived to scope. 77
This throne, this Fortune, and this hill, methinks,
With one man beckoned from the rest below,
Bowing his head against the steepy mount 80
To climb his happiness, would be well expressed 81
In our condition.

POET Nay, sir, but hear me on. 82
All those which were his fellows but of late— 83
Some better than his value—on the moment 84
Follow his strides, his lobbies fill with tendance, 85
Rain sacrificial whisperings in his ear, 86

65 returns departs **66 in Timon's nod** for having been acknowledged by Timon **69 Feigned** imagined, supposed **70 ranked . . . deserts** filled with the ranks of all degrees of merit **71 this sphere** i.e., the earth **72 propagate** enlarge. **states** fortunes **74 personate** represent. **frame** mold, nature **75 ivory** white. **wafts** beckons, waves **76–77 Whose . . . rivals** i.e., Fortune, whose gracious favor transforms his (Timon's) rivals immediately into slaves and servants **77 to scope** to the purpose **80 Bowing his head** i.e., bending forward with the effort. **steepy** steep **81 his happiness** i.e., to his good fortune **81–82 would . . . condition** would find a striking parallel in the human condition **82 hear me on** hear me speak further **83 but of late** only recently **84 better . . . value** his superiors. **on the moment** immediately **85 his . . . tendance** fill the anterooms of his house with their attentive presence **86 sacrificial whisperings** whispers of sacrifices made in his honor, or whispers offered with reverential deference as a sacrifice is offered

Make sacred even his stirrup, and through him 87
Drink the free air.

PAINTER Ay, marry, what of these? 88

POET
When Fortune in her shift and change of mood
Spurns down her late beloved, all his dependents, 90
Which labored after him to the mountain's top
Even on their knees and hands, let him slip down,
Not one accompanying his declining foot.

PAINTER 'Tis common.
A thousand moral paintings I can show 95
That shall demonstrate these quick blows of Fortune's
More pregnantly than words. Yet you do well
To show Lord Timon that mean eyes have seen 98
The foot above the head. 99

Trumpets sound. Enter Lord Timon, addressing himself courteously to every suitor; [*a Messenger from Ventidius talking with him; Lucilius and other servants following*].

TIMON Imprisoned is he, say you?

MESSENGER
Ay, my good lord. Five talents is his debt, 101
His means most short, his creditors most strait. 102
Your honorable letter he desires 103
To those have shut him up, which failing 104
Periods his comfort.

TIMON Noble Ventidius! Well, 105

87 stirrup i.e., as they help him to his horse **87–88 through . . . air** seem to breathe the free air only through his bounty **88 marry** (A mild oath, originally "By Mary.") **90 Spurns down** kicks or thrusts down **95 moral paintings** allegorical depictions **98 mean eyes** i.e., of men of low degree **99 The foot . . . head** i.e., highest fortune tumbling headlong downward by the turn of Fortune's wheel; or perhaps the foot of Fortune poised over the head of the once-prosperous man **101 talents** units of money today worth $2000 or more. (But Shakespeare was evidently uncertain about the *talent's* value as he wrote this play. *Talents* is also a Biblical term; see, for example, Matthew 25:14–29.) **102 short** limited. **strait** severe, exacting **103 Your . . . letter** a letter from your honor **104 those** those who **104–105 which failing Periods** the lack of which puts an end to

I am not of that feather to shake off 106
My friend when he must need me. I do know him 107
A gentleman that well deserves a help,
Which he shall have. I'll pay the debt and free him.

MESSENGER Your lordship ever binds him. 110

TIMON
Commend me to him. I will send his ransom;
And being enfranchised, bid him come to me. 112
'Tis not enough to help the feeble up,
But to support him after. Fare you well. 114

MESSENGER All happiness to your honor! *Exit.*

Enter an Old Athenian.

OLD ATHENIAN
Lord Timon, hear me speak.

TIMON Freely, good father. 116

OLD ATHENIAN
Thou hast a servant named Lucilius.

TIMON I have so. What of him?

OLD ATHENIAN
Most noble Timon, call the man before thee.

TIMON
Attends he here or no? Lucilius!

LUCILIUS [*Coming forward*] Here, at your lordship's service.

OLD ATHENIAN
This fellow here, Lord Timon, this thy creature, 122
By night frequents my house. I am a man
That from my first have been inclined to thrift,
And my estate deserves an heir more raised 125
Than one which holds a trencher.

TIMON Well, what further? 126

OLD ATHENIAN
One only daughter have I, no kin else
On whom I may confer what I have got.
The maid is fair, o' the youngest for a bride, 129

106 feather i.e., disposition (as in "birds of a feather") **107 know him** know him to be **110 binds him** i.e., to grateful obligation
112 enfranchised set free **114 But** i.e., but one must continue
116 Freely readily, gladly. **father** (Respectful term of address to an old man.) **122 creature** dependent, hanger-on **125 more raised** of higher social position **126 holds a trencher** i.e., serves at table, handling wooden dishes **129 o' the . . . bride** just of marriageable age

And I have bred her at my dearest cost 130
In qualities of the best. This man of thine
Attempts her love. I prithee, noble lord, 132
Join with me to forbid him her resort; 133
Myself have spoke in vain.

TIMON The man is honest.

OLD ATHENIAN Therefore he will be, Timon. 136
His honesty rewards him in itself;
It must not bear my daughter. 138

TIMON Does she love him?

OLD ATHENIAN She is young and apt. 140
Our own precedent passions do instruct us 141
What levity's in youth.

TIMON [*To Lucilius*] Love you the maid?

LUCILIUS
Ay, my good lord, and she accepts of it. 143

OLD ATHENIAN
If in her marriage my consent be missing,
I call the gods to witness, I will choose
Mine heir from forth the beggars of the world
And dispossess her all. 147

TIMON How shall she be endowed 148
If she be mated with an equal husband? 149

OLD ATHENIAN
Three talents on the present; in future, all. 150

TIMON
This gentleman of mine hath served me long;
To build his fortune I will strain a little,
For 'tis a bond in men. Give him thy daughter. 153
What you bestow, in him I'll counterpoise, 154
And make him weigh with her.

OLD ATHENIAN Most noble lord, 155
Pawn me to this your honor, she is his. 156

130 bred . . . cost brought her up and educated her at great expense **132 Attempts** tries to win **133 her resort** access to her **136 Therefore he will be** i.e., he will be if we forbid him to see my daughter **138 bear my daughter** carry off my daughter into the bargain **140 apt** easily wooed, impressionable **141 precedent** former **143 accepts of** accepts **147 all** wholly **148 How . . . endowed** what dowry will she be given **149 an equal husband** one of equal estate **150 on the present** immediately **153 bond** obligation. **in** among **154 counterpoise** match, counterbalance **155 weigh with her** be equal to her in estate **156 Pawn . . . honor** if you'll pledge your word of honor to do as you have said

TIMON
My hand to thee; mine honor on my promise.

LUCILIUS
Humbly I thank your lordship. Never may
That state or fortune fall into my keeping 159
Which is not owed to you! 160

Exeunt [*Lucilius and Old Athenian*].

POET [*Presenting his poem*]
Vouchsafe my labor, and long live your lordship! 161

TIMON
I thank you; you shall hear from me anon. 162
Go not away.—What have you there, my friend?

PAINTER
A piece of painting, which I do beseech 164
Your lordship to accept. [*He presents his painting.*]

TIMON Painting is welcome.
The painting is almost the natural man; 166
For since dishonor traffics with man's nature, 167
He is but outside; these penciled figures are 168
Even such as they give out. I like your work, 169
And you shall find I like it. Wait attendance 170
Till you hear further from me.

PAINTER The gods preserve ye!

TIMON
Well fare you, gentleman. Give me your hand;
We must needs dine together.—Sir, your jewel 173
Hath suffered under praise.

JEWELER What, my lord, dispraise? 174

TIMON
A mere satiety of commendations. 175
If I should pay you for 't as 'tis extolled,
It would unclew me quite.

JEWELER My lord, 'tis rated 177

159 That i.e., any **160 owed to you** acknowledged to be from you **161 Vouchsafe** deign to accept **162 anon** shortly **164 piece** example, specimen **166 the natural man** man as he truly is, not what he pretends to be **167 traffics** deals (improperly) **168 He is but outside** i.e., he becomes a mere outward appearance. **penciled** painted **169 Even . . . out** exactly as they appear **170 Wait** remain in **173 needs** necessarily, of course **174 suffered under praise** been overwhelmed by praise. (But the Jeweler misunderstands.) **175 mere** utter **177 unclew** unwind, i.e., ruin

As those which sell would give; but you well know 178
Things of like value differing in the owners
Are prizèd by their masters. Believe 't, dear lord, 180
You mend the jewel by the wearing it.

[He presents a jewel.]

TIMON Well mocked. 182

MERCHANT
No, my good lord, he speaks the common tongue 183
Which all men speak with him.

Enter Apemantus.

TIMON Look who comes here. Will you be chid? 185

JEWELER We'll bear, with your lordship. 186

MERCHANT He'll spare none.

TIMON
Good morrow to thee, gentle Apemantus!

APEMANTUS
Till I be gentle, stay thou for thy good morrow— 189
When thou art Timon's dog, and these knaves honest. 190

TIMON
Why dost thou call them knaves? Thou know'st them not.

APEMANTUS Are they not Athenians?

TIMON Yes.

APEMANTUS Then I repent not. 194

JEWELER You know me, Apemantus?

APEMANTUS Thou know'st I do. I called thee by thy 196
name. 197

TIMON Thou art proud, Apemantus.

APEMANTUS Of nothing so much as that I am not like Timon.

TIMON Whither art going?

178 As . . . give at a price which merchants would pay, i.e., at cost **180 prizèd . . . masters** valued as their owners are respected; i.e., the gem will increase in value because Timon will wear it **182 mocked** performed **183 common tongue** general opinion **185 Will you be chid** are you prepared to be scolded **186 We'll . . . lordship** i.e., we'll put up with it if your lordship can **189–190 Till . . . honest** i.e., you must wait for my "good morrow" until I have become free of satirical sharpness and until men are free of the faults I criticize, something as likely to happen as Timon changing places with his dog **194 repent not** don't regret what I said **196–197 thy name** i.e., knave

APEMANTUS To knock out an honest Athenian's brains.
TIMON That's a deed thou'lt die for.
APEMANTUS Right, if doing nothing be death by the law. 204
TIMON How lik'st thou this picture, Apemantus?
APEMANTUS The best, for the innocence. 206
TIMON Wrought he not well that painted it?
APEMANTUS He wrought better that made the painter, and yet he's but a filthy piece of work.
PAINTER You're a dog. 210
APEMANTUS Thy mother's of my generation. What's she, if I be a dog? 211
TIMON Wilt dine with me, Apemantus?
APEMANTUS No. I eat not lords. 214
TIMON An thou shouldst, thou'dst anger ladies. 215
APEMANTUS O, they eat lords. So they come by great bellies. 216
TIMON That's a lascivious apprehension. 218
APEMANTUS So thou apprehend'st it. Take it for thy labor.
TIMON How dost thou like this jewel, Apemantus?
APEMANTUS Not so well as plain dealing, which will not cost a man a doit. 222
TIMON What dost thou think 'tis worth?
APEMANTUS Not worth my thinking.—How now, poet?
POET How now, philosopher?
APEMANTUS Thou liest.
POET Art not one?
APEMANTUS Yes.
POET Then I lie not.
APEMANTUS Art not a poet?
POET Yes.

204 doing nothing i.e., since there are no honest Athenians, I will be doing nothing. **death by the law** subject to the death penalty. (Athenians have no brains; therefore to knock out their brains is to do nothing.) **206 innocence** innocuous character, inability to do harm (as real life can) **210 dog** (*Cynic* is derived from the Greek for "dog.")
211 generation species **214 eat not lords** do not consume the substance of great men. (But in his next speech Apemantus gives the phrase a sexual meaning.) **215 An** if **216 come by** acquire **218 apprehension** (1) interpretation (2) seizure, grasp (with a bawdy suggestion in the idea of seizing physically) **222 doit** half a farthing, coin of slight value

APEMANTUS Then thou liest. Look in thy last work, 233
where thou hast feigned him a worthy fellow. 234

POET That's not feigned. He is so.

APEMANTUS Yes, he is worthy of thee, and to pay thee for thy labor. He that loves to be flattered is worthy o' the flatterer. Heavens, that I were a lord!

TIMON What wouldst do then, Apemantus?

APEMANTUS E'en as Apemantus does now: hate a lord with my heart.

TIMON What, thyself?

APEMANTUS Ay.

TIMON Wherefore?

APEMANTUS That I had no angry wit to be a lord.—Art 245
not thou a merchant?

MERCHANT Ay, Apemantus.

APEMANTUS Traffic confound thee, if the gods will not! 248

MERCHANT If traffic do it, the gods do it.

APEMANTUS Traffic's thy god, and thy god confound thee!

Trumpet sounds. Enter a Messenger.

TIMON What trumpet's that?

MESSENGER
'Tis Alcibiades and some twenty horse, 253
All of companionship. 254

TIMON
Pray, entertain them; give them guide to us. 255
[*Exeunt some attendants.*]
[*To his guests.*] You must needs dine with me. Go not you hence
Till I have thanked you.—When dinner's done,
Show me this piece.—I am joyful of your sights. 258

Enter Alcibiades, with the rest.

233 Then thou liest (because poets are supposed to feign) **234 him** i.e., Timon **245 That . . . lord** i.e., that in becoming a lord I had forfeited the angry wit that only an independent philosopher can enjoy
248 Traffic confound may business or trade ruin **253 horse** horsemen **254 of companionship** belonging to the same party
255 entertain them show them hospitality. **give them guide** show them in **258 of your sights** to see you

Most welcome, sir!

APEMANTUS So, so, there! Aches contract 259
And starve your supple joints! That there should be 260
Small love amongest these sweet knaves, and all
This courtesy! The strain of man's bred out 262
Into baboon and monkey.

ALCIBIADES
Sir, you have saved my longing, and I feed 264
Most hungerly on your sight.

TIMON Right welcome, sir! 265
Ere we depart, we'll share a bounteous time 266
In different pleasures. Pray you, let us in. 267
Exeunt [*all except Apemantus*].

Enter two Lords.

FIRST LORD What time o' day is 't, Apemantus?

APEMANTUS Time to be honest.

FIRST LORD That time serves still. 270

APEMANTUS The most accursèd thou, that still omitt'st it. 271

SECOND LORD Thou art going to Lord Timon's feast?

APEMANTUS Ay, to see meat fill knaves and wine heat fools.

SECOND LORD Fare thee well, fare thee well.

APEMANTUS Thou art a fool to bid me farewell twice.

SECOND LORD Why, Apemantus?

APEMANTUS Shouldst have kept one to thyself, for I mean to give thee none.

FIRST LORD Hang thyself!

APEMANTUS No, I will do nothing at thy bidding. Make thy requests to thy friend.

SECOND LORD Away, unpeaceable dog, or I'll spurn thee 283 hence!

APEMANTUS I will fly, like a dog, the heels o' the ass. 285
[*Exit*.]

259 So, so, there well, well, look at that (i.e., all the bowing and scraping) **260 starve** destroy **262 strain** race, stock. **bred out** degenerated **264 saved** anticipated and thus prevented **265 hungerly on your sight** hungrily on the sight of you **266 depart** part company **267 different** various. **in** enter **270 still** always **271 most** i.e., more. **omitt'st** fail to take advantage of **283 unpeaceable** quarrelsome, incessantly barking. **spurn** kick **285 fly** flee

FIRST LORD
He's opposite to humanity. Come, shall we in 286
And taste Lord Timon's bounty? He outgoes 287
The very heart of kindness. 288

SECOND LORD
He pours it out. Plutus, the god of gold,
Is but his steward. No meed but he repays 290
Sevenfold above itself; no gift to him
But breeds the giver a return exceeding
All use of quittance.

FIRST LORD The noblest mind he carries 293
That ever governed man.

SECOND LORD
Long may he live in fortunes! Shall we in?

FIRST LORD I'll keep you company. *Exeunt.*

✤

1.2

Hautboys playing loud music. A great banquet served in, [Flavius and others attending]; and then enter Lord Timon, the states, the Athenian Lords, [Alcibiades, and] Ventidius (which Timon redeemed from prison). Then comes, dropping after all, Apemantus, discontentedly, like himself.

VENTIDIUS Most honored Timon,
It hath pleased the gods to remember my father's age
And call him to long peace. 3
He is gone happy and has left me rich. 4
Then, as in grateful virtue I am bound
To your free heart, I do return those talents, 6
Doubled with thanks and service, from whose help
I derived liberty. [*He offers money.*]

286 opposite to (1) antagonistic to (2) the reverse of **287 outgoes** surpasses **288 heart** essence **290 meed** merit; or gift **293 use of quittance** usual rates of repayment with interest

1.2. Location: A banqueting room in Timon's house.
s.d. Hautboys oboelike instruments. **states** i.e., rulers of the state, senators. **dropping** i.e., "dropping in," arriving casually. **like himself** not in finery **3 long peace** eternal rest **4 gone** died **6 free** generous

TIMON O, by no means,
Honest Ventidius. You mistake my love.
I gave it freely ever, and there's none
Can truly say he gives if he receives. 12
If our betters play at that game, we must not dare 13
To imitate them. Faults that are rich are fair. 14
VENTIDIUS A noble spirit!
[*They all stand ceremoniously looking at Timon.*]
TIMON
Nay, my lords, ceremony was but devised at first
To set a gloss on faint deeds, hollow welcomes, 17
Recanting goodness, sorry ere 'tis shown; 18
But where there is true friendship, there needs none. 19
Pray, sit. More welcome are ye to my fortunes
Than my fortunes to me. [*They sit.*]
FIRST LORD
My lord, we always have confessed it. 22
APEMANTUS
Ho, ho, confessed it? Hanged it, have you not? 23
TIMON
O, Apemantus, you are welcome.
APEMANTUS No,
You shall not make me welcome.
I come to have thee thrust me out of doors.
TIMON
Fie, thou'rt a churl. You've got a humor there 27
Does not become a man; 'tis much to blame. 28
They say, my lords, *Ira furor brevis est,* but yond 29
man is ever angry. Go, let him have a table by himself, 30

12 gives . . . receives (Cf. Acts 20:35: "It is more blessed to give than to receive.") **13 betters** superiors. **at that game** i.e., taking in wealth while seeming to be generous **14 that are rich** i.e., in those who are rich. **fair** i.e., excused by their wealth **17 set a gloss on** give a speciously fair appearance to **18 Recanting goodness** generosity that takes back what it has offered **19 there needs none** there is no need for ceremony **22 confessed it** acknowledged the truth of what you say **23 Hanged it** i.e., killed it instead. (Apemantus replies with a jesting allusion to the saying, "Confess and be hanged.") **27 churl** surly person. **humor** disposition **28 Does** that does **29 Ira furor brevis est** wrath is a brief madness. (Horace's *Epistles,* 1.2.62.) **30 ever** always

for he does neither affect company nor is he fit for 't, 31
indeed.

APEMANTUS Let me stay at thine apperil, Timon. I come 33
to observe; I give thee warning on 't.

TIMON I take no heed of thee. Thou'rt an Athenian,
therefore welcome. I myself would have no power; 36
prithee, let my meat make thee silent. 37

APEMANTUS I scorn thy meat; 'twould choke me, for I 38
should ne'er flatter thee. O you gods, what a number 39
of men eats Timon, and he sees 'em not! It grieves me
to see so many dip their meat in one man's blood; and 41
all the madness is, he cheers them up too. 42
I wonder men dare trust themselves with men.
Methinks they should invite them without knives; 44
Good for their meat, and safer for their lives. 45
There's much example for 't. The fellow that sits next
him, now parts bread with him, pledges the breath of 47
him in a divided draft, is the readiest man to kill 48
him. 'T has been proved. If I were a huge man, I 49
should fear to drink at meals,
Lest they should spy my windpipe's dangerous notes. 51
Great men should drink with harness on their throats. 52

TIMON [*Toasting a Lord who drinks to him*]
My lord, in heart! And let the health go round. 53

SECOND LORD
Let it flow this way, my good lord. 54

31 affect (1) like (2) seek, aim at **33 thine apperil** your peril, risk **36 would . . . power** do not wish the power (to silence you) **37 meat** food **38–39 for I . . . thee** (Apemantus implies that Timon's food is to reward flatterers; Apemantus, being none, would choke on it.) **41 one man's blood** (Possible allusion to the Last Supper; the *fellow* in ll. 46–49, who shares food and drink only to betray his host, is like Judas.) **42 all . . . too** the most mad aspect of his behavior is that he encourages them **44 without knives** (Refers to the Renaissance custom of guests bringing their own knives.) **45 Good . . . meat** i.e., without knives, the guests would eat less food **47 parts** shares. **pledges the breath** i.e., drinks to the health **48 a divided draft** a cup that they share **49 huge** great in rank and wealth **51 windpipe's . . . notes** indications on my throat of where my windpipe is (and hence where it might be slit) as the head is thrown back. (The *windpipe* also suggests a bagpipe capable of *notes* or musical sounds.) **52 harness** armor **53 in heart** heartily. **health** toast, and the cup **54 flow** circulate

APEMANTUS Flow this way? A brave fellow! He keeps 55
his tides well. Those healths will make thee and thy 56
state look ill, Timon. 59
Here's that which is too weak to be a sinner: 58
Honest water, which ne'er left man i' the mire. 59
This and my food are equals; there's no odds. 60
Feasts are too proud to give thanks to the gods. 61

Apemantus' grace.

Immortal gods, I crave no pelf. 62
I pray for no man but myself.
Grant I may never prove so fond 64
To trust man on his oath or bond,
Or a harlot for her weeping,
Or a dog that seems a-sleeping,
Or a keeper with my freedom, 68
Or my friends, if I should need 'em.
Amen. So fall to 't. 70
Rich men sin, and I eat root. [*He eats and drinks.*]
Much good dich thy good heart, Apemantus! 72

TIMON Captain Alcibiades, your heart's in the field 73
now.

ALCIBIADES My heart is ever at your service, my lord.

TIMON You had rather be at a breakfast of enemies than 76
a dinner of friends. 77

ALCIBIADES So they were bleeding new, my lord, 78
there's no meat like 'em. I could wish my best friend
at such a feast.

APEMANTUS Would all those flatterers were thine enemies then, that then thou mightst kill 'em—and bid
me to 'em! 83

FIRST LORD Might we but have that happiness, my lord,

55 brave fine. (Said ironically.) **56 tides** times, seasons (with quibbling reference to *flow* of tides) **57 state** (1) physical condition (2) fortune, estate **58 a sinner** an incentive to sin **59 i' the mire** i.e., in trouble **60 there's no odds** there's nothing to choose between them **61 Feasts** i.e., partakers of fine feasts **62 pelf** property, possessions **64 fond** foolish **68 keeper** jailer **70 fall to 't** i.e., begin to eat **72 dich** may it do. (Originally a contraction of "d' it ye" in the phrase "much good do it you.") **73 field** battlefield **76 of** consisting of **77 of** among **78 So** provided that **83 to 'em** i.e., to eat them

that you would once use our hearts, whereby we 85
might express some part of our zeals, we should think 86
ourselves forever perfect. 87

TIMON O, no doubt, my good friends, but the gods
themselves have provided that I shall have much help
from you. How had you been my friends else? Why
have you that charitable title from thousands, did not 91
you chiefly belong to my heart? I have told more of 92
you to myself than you can with modesty speak in 93
your own behalf; and thus far I confirm you. O you 94
gods, think I, what need we have any friends if we 95
should ne'er have need of 'em? They were the most
needless creatures living, should we ne'er have use for 97
'em, and would most resemble sweet instruments 98
hung up in cases, that keeps their sounds to themselves.
Why, I have often wished myself poorer, that I
might come nearer to you. We are born to do benefits;
and what better or properer can we call our own than 102
the riches of our friends? O, what a precious comfort
'tis to have so many, like brothers, commanding one 104
another's fortunes! O, joy's e'en made away ere 't can 105
be born! Mine eyes cannot hold out water, methinks. 106
To forget their faults, I drink to you. 107

[*He weeps, and drinks a toast.*]

APEMANTUS Thou weep'st to make them drink, Timon.

SECOND LORD [*To Timon*]
Joy had the like conception in our eyes,
And at that instant like a babe sprung up. 109

APEMANTUS
Ho, ho! I laugh to think that babe a bastard. 111

THIRD LORD [*To Timon*]
I promise you, my lord, you moved me much. 112

85 use our hearts make trial of our love **86 zeals** love **87 forever perfect** completely happy **91 charitable title** beloved name. **from** from among **92 told** (1) recited (2) counted **92–93 of you** i.e., concerning your deservings **94 confirm you** endorse your claim to be my worthy friends **95 what** why **97 needless** useless **98 instruments** musical instruments **102 properer** more fittingly **104 commanding** having at their disposal **105 made away** destroyed, i.e., turned to tears **106 born** i.e., expressed **107 To . . . faults** i.e., to mask my weakness in giving way to tears **109 sprung up** (1) leaped from the womb (2) welled up like a spring of tears **111 bastard** i.e., illegitimate, without genuine source. (Refers to the guests' tears.) **112 promise** assure

APEMANTUS Much! *Sound tucket* [*within*]. 113
TIMON What means that trump?

Enter Servant.

How now? 114

SERVANT Please you, my lord, there are certain ladies most desirous of admittance.
TIMON Ladies? What are their wills?
SERVANT There comes with them a forerunner, my 118 lord, which bears that office to signify their pleasures. 119
TIMON I pray, let them be admitted. [*Exit Servant.*]

Enter Cupid.

CUPID
Hail to thee, worthy Timon, and to all
That of his bounties taste! The five best senses
Acknowledge thee their patron, and come freely
To gratulate thy plenteous bosom. Th' ear, 124
Taste, touch, and smell, pleased from thy table rise;
They only now come but to feast thine eyes. 126

TIMON
They're welcome all. Let 'em have kind admittance.
Music, make their welcome!
[*Cupid summons the maskers.*]

FIRST LORD
You see, my lord, how ample you're beloved. 129

[*Music.*] *Enter a masque of Ladies* [*as*] *Amazons, with lutes in their hands, dancing and playing.*

APEMANTUS Hoyday! 130
What a sweep of vanity comes this way!
They dance? They are madwomen.
Like madness is the glory of this life 133
As this pomp shows to a little oil and root. 134

113 Much (An expression of contemptuous disbelief; playing on *much* in the previous line.) **s.d. tucket** trumpet call **114 trump** trumpet blast **118 forerunner** herald, messenger **119 which** who. **office** function. **pleasures** wishes **124 gratulate** greet, salute. **plenteous bosom** generous heart **126 They** i.e., the maskers. **only now come but** come only **129 ample** amply **130 Hoyday** (Exclamation denoting surprise; a variety of "heyday.") **133 Like** similar, equal. **glory** vain-glory **134 As . . . root** i.e., in the same way as this splendid feast appears when compared with the mere necessities of life

We make ourselves fools to disport ourselves 135
And spend our flatteries to drink those men 136
Upon whose age we void it up again 137
With poisonous spite and envy. 138
Who lives that's not depravèd or depraves? 139
Who dies that bears not one spurn to their graves 140
Of their friends' gift? 141
I should fear those that dance before me now
Would one day stamp upon me. 'T has been done;
Men shut their doors against a setting sun. 144

The Lords rise from table, with much adoring of Timon; and to show their loves each singles out an Amazon, and all dance, men with women, a lofty strain or two to the hautboys, and cease.

TIMON
You have done our pleasures much grace, fair ladies,
Set a fair fashion on our entertainment, 146
Which was not half so beautiful and kind. 147
You have added worth unto 't and luster,
And entertained me with mine own device. 149
I am to thank you for 't. 150

FIRST LADY
My lord, you take us even at the best. 151

APEMANTUS Faith, for the worst is filthy and would not 152
hold taking, I doubt me. 153

TIMON
Ladies, there is an idle banquet attends you; 154
Please you to dispose yourselves. 155

135 disport entertain **136–138 And . . . envy** and lavish our flatteries in drinking the healths of those upon whom, when they are old, we cast up our surfeit in poisonous spite and malice **139 depravèd** vilified, slandered. **depraves** slanders **140 spurn** injury, insult **141 gift** giving **144 s.d. hautboys** oboelike instruments **146 Set . . . on** given grace and elegance to **147 was not** i.e., before your arrival was not. **kind** gracious **149 with . . . device** (The masque appears to have been designed by Timon to surprise his guests; or, he acknowledges that it was designed especially for him.) **150 am to** am under obligation to **151 take . . . best** i.e., praise us most generously **152 the worst** i.e., the worst part of you. (An obscene suggestion.) **152–153 would . . . taking** i.e., (1) would not warrant notice (2) is too rotten with venereal disease **153 doubt me** fear **154 idle** trifling, slight **155 dispose yourselves** take your places

ALL LADIES Most thankfully, my lord.
Exeunt [*Cupid and Ladies*].

TIMON Flavius!

FLAVIUS
My lord?

TIMON The little casket bring me hither.

FLAVIUS Yes, my lord. [*Aside*.] More jewels yet?
There is no crossing him in 's humor; 160
Else I should tell him well, i' faith I should, 161
When all's spent, he'd be crossed then, an he could. 162
'Tis pity bounty had not eyes behind, 163
That man might ne'er be wretched for his mind. *Exit*. 164

FIRST LORD Where be our men?

SERVANT Here, my lord, in readiness.

SECOND LORD
Our horses!

Enter Flavius [*with the casket*].

TIMON O my friends, I have one word
To say to you. Look you, my good lord,
I must entreat you honor me so much 169
As to advance this jewel; accept it and wear it, 170
Kind my lord. [*He offers a jewel.*]

FIRST LORD
I am so far already in your gifts—

ALL So are we all.

Enter a Servant.

SERVANT
My lord, there are certain nobles of the Senate
Newly alighted and come to visit you.

TIMON
They are fairly welcome. [*Exit Servant.*]

FLAVIUS I beseech your honor, 176
Vouchsafe me a word; it does concern you near. 177

160 humor frame of mind **161 well** plainly **162 crossed** (1) wishing to have his debts canceled (2) thwarted (as in l. 160). **an** if **163 bounty** generosity. **had not eyes behind** i.e., is not able to be more cautious **164 for his mind** on account of his generous inclinations **169 you honor** you to honor **170 advance** make more worthy; i.e., by possessing it **176 fairly** sincerely **177 near** closely

TIMON
Near? Why then, another time I'll hear thee.
I prithee, let's be provided to show them entertainment.

FLAVIUS [*Aside*] I scarce know how.

Enter another Servant.

SECOND SERVANT
May it please your honor, Lord Lucius,
Out of his free love, hath presented to you
Four milk-white horses trapped in silver. 183

TIMON
I shall accept them fairly. Let the presents 184
Be worthily entertained. [*Exit Servant.*]

Enter a third Servant.

How now? What news? 185

THIRD SERVANT Please you, my lord, that honorable gentleman, Lord Lucullus, entreats your company tomorrow to hunt with him and has sent your honor two brace of greyhounds. 189

TIMON
I'll hunt with him; and let them be received,
Not without fair reward. [*Exit Servant.*]

FLAVIUS [*Aside*] What will this come to?
He commands us to provide, and give great gifts,
And all out of an empty coffer;
Nor will he know his purse, or yield me this, 194
To show him what a beggar his heart is,
Being of no power to make his wishes good. 196
His promises fly so beyond his state 197
That what he speaks is all in debt; he owes
For every word. He is so kind that he now
Pays interest for 't; his land's put to their books. 200
Well, would I were gently put out of office
Before I were forced out!
Happier is he that has no friend to feed

183 trapped in silver in silver-mounted trappings **184 fairly** graciously **185 Be worthily entertained** given the reception they deserve **189 brace** pair **194 purse** financial situation. **yield me this** grant me opportunity **196 Being of** i.e., the desires of his heart having **197 state** estate **200 put . . . books** i.e., mortgaged to those whom he has befriended with gifts

Than such that do e'en enemies exceed. 204
I bleed inwardly for my lord. *Exit.*

TIMON [*To the Lords*] You do yourselves
Much wrong, you bate too much of your own merits.— 206
Here, my lord, a trifle of our love. [*He offers a gift.*]

SECOND LORD
With more than common thanks I will receive it.

THIRD LORD O, he's the very soul of bounty!

TIMON And now I remember, my lord, you gave good 210
words the other day of a bay courser I rode on. 'Tis 211
yours because you liked it.

THIRD LORD
O, I beseech you, pardon me, my lord, in that. 213

TIMON
You may take my word, my lord: I know no man
Can justly praise but what he does affect. 215
I weigh my friends' affection with mine own. 216
I'll tell you true, I'll call to you. 217

ALL LORDS O, none so welcome.

TIMON
I take all and your several visitations 219
So kind to heart, 'tis not enough to give. 220
Methinks I could deal kingdoms to my friends
And ne'er be weary. Alcibiades,
Thou art a soldier, therefore seldom rich.
It comes in charity to thee; for all thy living 224
Is 'mongst the dead, and all the lands thou hast
Lie in a pitched field. 226

ALCIBIADES Ay, defiled land, my lord. 227

204 Than . . . exceed i.e., than he that feeds so-called "friends" who, by consuming his wealth, outdo his enemies in ruining him **206 bate . . . of** belittle too much **210–211 gave good words** spoke favorably **211 bay courser** dark brown horse with black mane and tail **213 pardon . . . that** i.e., forgive my declining the offer; my mentioning the horse was not meant as a hint **215 but . . . affect** a thing unless he likes and desires it **216 weigh . . . with** give equal weight to . . . as compared with **217 call to** call on; or, perhaps, appeal to in time of need **219 all . . . several** your joint and individual **220 kind** kindly. **'tis . . . give** there isn't enough wealth in my possession to match my wish to be generous **224 It . . . thee** i.e., giving to you is an act of real charity. **living** (1) existence (2) property, wealth **226 pitched field** battlefield **227 defiled** (1) with a quibble on *pitched;* cf. *Ecclesiasticus* 13:1: "He that toucheth pitch shall be defiled" (2) arrayed with files or rows of soldiers

FIRST LORD We are so virtuously bound—
TIMON And so am I to you.
SECOND LORD So infinitely endeared—
TIMON All to you. [*To servants.*] Lights, more lights! 231
FIRST LORD
The best of happiness, honor, and fortunes
Keep with you, Lord Timon! 233
TIMON Ready for his friends. 234
Exeunt lords [*and all but Apemantus and Timon*].
APEMANTUS What a coil's here! 235
Serving of becks and jutting-out of bums! 236
I doubt whether their legs be worth the sums 237
That are given for 'em. Friendship's full of dregs.
Methinks false hearts should never have sound legs. 239
Thus honest fools lay out their wealth on curtsies. 240
TIMON
Now, Apemantus, if thou wert not sullen,
I would be good to thee.
APEMANTUS No, I'll nothing; for if I should be bribed too, there would be none left to rail upon thee, and then thou wouldst sin the faster. Thou giv'st so long, Timon, I fear me thou wilt give away thyself in paper 246 shortly. What needs these feasts, pomps, and vain- 247 glories?
TIMON Nay, an you begin to rail on society once, I am 249 sworn not to give regard to you. Farewell, and come 250 with better music. *Exit.*
APEMANTUS So.
Thou wilt not hear me now; thou shalt not then.
I'll lock thy heaven from thee. 254
O, that men's ears should be
To counsel deaf, but not to flattery! *Exit.*

231 All to you i.e., the obligation is entirely mine; or, all mine is yours **233 Keep** dwell, remain **234 Ready for** ready to assist **235 coil** fuss **236 Serving of becks** bowing **237 legs** (1) limbs (2) bows, curtsies **239 have sound legs** i.e., be disguised by the outwardly healthy appearance of sound legs able to make bows **240 curtsies** (1) bows (2) courtesies **246 I fear me** I fear. **paper** bonds, promises to pay **247 What needs** what necessity is there for **249 an** if **250 give regard to** take notice of **254 thy heaven** i.e., my saving advice

2.1 *Enter a Senator* [*with papers in his hand*].

SENATOR
And late, five thousand. To Varro and to Isidore 1
He owes nine thousand, besides my former sum,
Which makes it five-and-twenty. Still in motion 3
Of raging waste? It cannot hold; it will not. 4
If I want gold, steal but a beggar's dog 5
And give it Timon, why, the dog coins gold.
If I would sell my horse and buy twenty more
Better than he, why, give my horse to Timon—
Ask nothing, give it him—it foals me straight 9
And able horses. No porter at his gate, 10
But rather one that smiles and still invites 11
All that pass by. It cannot hold. No reason 12
Can sound his state in safety.—Caphis, ho! 13
Caphis, I say!

Enter Caphis.

CAPHIS Here, sir. What is your pleasure?

SENATOR
Get on your cloak and haste you to Lord Timon.
Importune him for my moneys. Be not ceased 16
With slight denial, nor then silenced when 17
"Commend me to your master" and the cap 18
Plays in the right hand, thus, but tell him 19
My uses cry to me; I must serve my turn 20
Out of mine own. His days and times are past, 21
And my reliances on his fracted dates 22
Have smit my credit. I love and honor him, 23

2.1. Location: Athens. A Senator's house.
1 late lately **3–4 Still . . . waste** perpetually and ceaselessly squandering **4 hold** hold out, last (also in l. 12) **5 steal but** I need only steal **9 foals me straight** at once yields me foals, i.e., more horses (as gifts) **10 And able horses** i.e., and what's more they are full-grown horses, not literally foals. **porter** i.e., one who sternly denies entrance **11 still** constantly **12 reason** rational inquiry **13 sound . . . safety** by sounding the depth of Timon's financial position find it to be safe **16 ceased** silenced, put off **17 slight** negligent, offhand **17–19 when . . . thus** i.e., when he offers fair greetings and flattering gestures in lieu of real payment **20 uses** needs **21 days and times** i.e., dates for repayment of his loans **22 fracted** broken (by failure to meet payments on notes due) **23 smit** smitten, hurt

But must not break my back to heal his finger.
Immediate are my needs, and my relief
Must not be tossed and turned to me in words, 26
But find supply immediate. Get you gone.
Put on a most importunate aspect,
A visage of demand, for I do fear
When every feather sticks in his own wing 30
Lord Timon will be left a naked gull, 31
Which flashes now a phoenix. Get you gone. 32

CAPHIS I go, sir.

SENATOR [*Giving him bonds*]
Ay, go, sir. Take the bonds along with you
And have the dates in compt.

CAPHIS I will, sir.

SENATOR Go. *Exeunt.* 35

✤

2.2

Enter steward [*Flavius*] *with many bills in his hand.*

FLAVIUS
No care, no stop! So senseless of expense 1
That he will neither know how to maintain it 2
Nor cease his flow of riot, takes no account 3
How things go from him nor resumes no care 4
Of what is to continue. Never mind 5
Was to be so unwise to be so kind. 6
What shall be done? He will not hear till feel. 7
I must be round with him, now he comes from hunting. 8
Fie, fie, fie, fie!

26 tossed and turned i.e., bandied back as in tennis **30 When . . . wing** i.e., when everything is in the hands of its rightful possessor **31 gull** (1) unfledged bird (2) dupe **32 Which flashes now** who now showily displays himself as. **phoenix** mythical bird, one of a kind, i.e., rare and precious creature **35 in compt** reckoned

2.2. Location: Athens. Before Timon's house.
1 senseless unaware, regardless **2 know** learn **3 riot** reveling **4–5 resumes . . . continue** makes no provision for continuing **5–6 Never . . . kind** never was there a mind so unwise in being so kind, so determined to be stupidly generous **7 till feel** until he suffers feelingly **8 round** plainspoken

Enter Caphis [*and the Servants of*] *Isidore and Varro.*

CAPHIS
Good even, Varro. What, you come for money? 10
VARRO'S SERVANT Is 't not your business too?
CAPHIS It is. And yours too, Isidore?
ISIDORE'S SERVANT It is so.
CAPHIS Would we were all discharged! 14
VARRO'S SERVANT I fear it. 15
CAPHIS Here comes the lord.

Enter Timon and his train [*with Alcibiades*].

TIMON
So soon as dinner's done we'll forth again, 17
My Alcibiades.—With me? What is your will?
CAPHIS [*Presenting a bill*]
My lord, here is a note of certain dues. 19
TIMON Dues? Whence are you?
CAPHIS Of Athens here, my lord.
TIMON Go to my steward.
CAPHIS
Please it your lordship, he hath put me off
To the succession of new days this month. 24
My master is awaked by great occasion 25
To call upon his own, and humbly prays you 26
That with your other noble parts you'll suit 27
In giving him his right.
TIMON Mine honest friend,
I prithee but repair to me next morning. 29
CAPHIS
Nay, good my lord—
TIMON Contain thyself, good friend.
VARRO'S SERVANT
One Varro's servant, my good lord—
ISIDORE'S SERVANT
From Isidore; he humbly prays your speedy payment.

10 Good even (A greeting used any time after noon.) **14 discharged** paid **15 fear it** i.e., am apprehensive about our being paid **17 forth** go forth **19 dues** debts **24 To . . . month** from one day to another all month **25 awaked** i.e., forced **26 his own** i.e., that which he has lent you **27 with . . . parts** in conformity to your other noble qualities **29 repair** come

CAPHIS
If you did know, my lord, my master's wants— 33

VARRO'S SERVANT
'Twas due on forfeiture, my lord, six weeks and past. 34

ISIDORE'S SERVANT
Your steward puts me off, my lord, and I
Am sent expressly to your lordship.

TIMON Give me breath.— 37
I do beseech you, good my lords, keep on; 38
I'll wait upon you instantly.
[*Exeunt Alcibiades and Lords.*]
[*To Flavius.*] Come hither. Pray you, 39
How goes the world, that I am thus encountered
With clamorous demands of broken bonds
And the detention of long-since-due debts 42
Against my honor?

FLAVIUS Please you, gentlemen, 43
The time is unagreeable to this business.
Your importunacy cease till after dinner, 45
That I may make his lordship understand 46
Wherefore you are not paid.

TIMON Do so, my friends.— 47
See them well entertained. [*Exit.*]

FLAVIUS Pray, draw near. *Exit.* 48

Enter Apemantus and Fool.

CAPHIS Stay, stay, here comes the Fool with Apemantus.
Let's ha' some sport with 'em. 50

VARRO'S SERVANT Hang him! He'll abuse us. 51

ISIDORE'S SERVANT A plague upon him, dog!

VARRO'S SERVANT How dost, Fool?

APEMANTUS Dost dialogue with thy shadow?

VARRO'S SERVANT I speak not to thee.

33 wants needs **34 on forfeiture** on penalty of forfeiting the security for it if not paid on the date prescribed **37 breath** breathing space, time to breathe **38 keep on** go ahead without me **39 wait . . . instantly** be with you in a moment **42 the detention** the charge of withholding payment **43 Against my honor** contrary to my honorable reputation **45 importunacy** persistent demands **46 That** so that **47 Wherefore** why **48 entertained** received, treated. **draw near** come this way. (Said to Timon, or possibly to the creditors' servants, who, however, decide to remain.) **50 ha'** have **51 abuse** vilify

APEMANTUS No, 'tis to thyself. [*To the Fool.*] Come away. 56
ISIDORE'S SERVANT [*To Varro's Servant*] There's the fool 57
hangs on your back already. 58
APEMANTUS No, thou stand'st single; thou'rt not on him 59
yet. 60
CAPHIS [*To Isidore's Servant*] Where's the fool now? 61
APEMANTUS He last asked the question. Poor rogues 62
and usurers' men, bawds between gold and want!
ALL THE SERVANTS What are we, Apemantus?
APEMANTUS Asses.
ALL THE SERVANTS Why?
APEMANTUS That you ask me what you are, and do not
know yourselves. Speak to 'em, Fool.
FOOL How do you, gentlemen?
ALL THE SERVANTS Gramercies, good Fool. How does 70
your mistress?
FOOL She's e'en setting on water to scald such chickens 72
as you are. Would we could see you at Corinth! 73
APEMANTUS Good! Gramercy.

Enter Page.

FOOL Look you, here comes my mistress' page.
PAGE [*To the Fool*] Why, how now, captain? What
do you in this wise company?—How dost thou,
Apemantus?
APEMANTUS Would I had a rod in my mouth, that I 79
might answer thee profitably. 80
PAGE Prithee, Apemantus, read me the superscription 81
of these letters. I know not which is which.
[*He shows two letters.*]

56 'tis to thyself i.e., you (Varro's servant) speak to yourself when you say "fool" **57–58 There's . . . already** i.e., you (Varro's servant) have been labeled fool already. (See l. 56.) **59–60 No . . . yet** i.e., no, you (Isidore's servant), a fool, are standing by yourself; you're not on the back of Varro's servant yet **61 Where's . . . now** i.e., whose back is labeled fool now **62 He** he who (i.e., Caphis, who has now been called a fool like the others) **70 Gramercies** many thanks **72 She's . . . scald** (Allusion to the sweating-tub treatment for venereal disease, a disease that causes loss of hair just as a chicken loses its feathers through scalding. The Fool also implies that they are fools deserving to be plucked.) **73 Corinth** a city noted for its brothels; hence, a brothel or the district for such houses **79 rod** stick (to use for a beating) **80 profitably** to your profit (by teaching you a lesson) **81 superscription** address

APEMANTUS Canst not read?
PAGE No.
APEMANTUS There will little learning die then that day thou art hanged. This is to Lord Timon, this to Alcibiades. Go, thou wast born a bastard and thou'lt die a bawd.
PAGE Thou wast whelped a dog and thou shalt famish 89 a dog's death. Answer not; I am gone. *Exit.*
APEMANTUS E'en so thou outrunn'st grace. Fool, I will 91 go with you to Lord Timon's.
FOOL Will you leave me there?
APEMANTUS If Timon stay at home.—You three serve 94 three usurers?
ALL THE SERVANTS Ay. Would they served us! 96
APEMANTUS So would I—as good a trick as ever hangman served thief.
FOOL Are you three usurers' men?
ALL THE SERVANTS Ay, Fool.
FOOL I think no usurer but has a fool to his servant; my mistress is one, and I am her fool. When men come to borrow of your masters, they approach sadly and go away merry, but they enter my mistress' house merrily and go away sadly. The reason of this?
VARRO'S SERVANT I could render one. 106
APEMANTUS Do it then, that we may account thee a whoremaster and a knave; which notwithstanding, thou shalt be no less esteemed.
VARRO'S SERVANT What is a whoremaster, Fool?
FOOL A fool in good clothes, and something like thee. 'Tis a spirit; sometimes 't appears like a lord, sometimes 112 like a lawyer, sometimes like a philosopher, with two stones more than 's artificial one. He is very often like 114 a knight; and generally, in all shapes that man goes

89 whelped born. **famish** die **91 E'en so** precisely so. **thou outrunn'st grace** you run away from profitable teaching and God's grace
94 If . . . home i.e., while Timon remains at home, a fool is there. **You three** do you three **96 Would** we wish **106 one** (Implies that the Fool's mistress's house is a bawdy house, where men come merrily but leave diseased and poorer.) **112 spirit** i.e., one that can assume various shapes **114 stones** testicles. **than 's** than his, the philosopher's. **artificial one** i.e., the philosopher's stone, supposed to change other metals into gold

up and down in from fourscore to thirteen, this spirit walks in.

VARRO'S SERVANT Thou art not altogether a fool.

FOOL Nor thou altogether a wise man. As much foolery as I have, so much wit thou lack'st.

APEMANTUS That answer might have become Apemantus. 121

ALL THE SERVANTS Aside, aside! Here comes Lord Timon.
[*They stand aside.*]

Enter Timon and Steward [*Flavius*].

APEMANTUS Come with me, Fool, come.

FOOL I do not always follow lover, elder brother, and 125
woman; sometimes the philosopher. 126
[*Exeunt Apemantus and Fool.*]

FLAVIUS [*To Servants*]
Pray you, walk near. I'll speak with you anon. 127
Exeunt [*Servants*].

TIMON
You make me marvel wherefore ere this time 128
Had you not fully laid my state before me, 129
That I might so have rated my expense 130
As I had leave of means.

FLAVIUS You would not hear me. 131
At many leisures I proposed—

TIMON Go to! 132
Perchance some single vantages you took 133
When my indisposition put you back,
And that unaptness made your minister 135
Thus to excuse yourself.

FLAVIUS O my good lord, 136
At many times I brought in my accounts,

121 become been fitted for **125–126 lover . . . woman** i.e., various sorts of persons proverbially connected with folly; an *elder brother* is the oldest son, one who will inherit property and hence worth cultivating **127 walk near** remain nearby. **anon** shortly **128 wherefore** why **129 fully . . . state** completely detailed my financial position **130 rated** i.e., estimated and regulated **131 As . . . means** as my means permitted **132 leisures** times when you were free. **proposed** conferred, conversed **133 single vantages** occasional opportunities **135–136 that . . . yourself** i.e., my disinclination to listen on those occasions served as your excuse thereafter for remaining silent. (*Made your minister* means "became your agent or means.")

Laid them before you. You would throw them off
And say you found them in mine honesty. 139
When for some trifling present you have bid me
Return so much, I have shook my head and wept; 141
Yea, 'gainst th' authority of manners prayed you 142
To hold your hand more close. I did endure
Not seldom, nor no slight checks, when I have 144
Prompted you in the ebb of your estate 145
And your great flow of debts. My lovèd lord,
Though you hear now too late, yet now's a time; 147
The greatest of your having lacks a half 148
To pay your present debts.

TIMON Let all my land be sold.

FLAVIUS
'Tis all engaged, some forfeited and gone, 151
And what remains will hardly stop the mouth 152
Of present dues. The future comes apace; 153
What shall defend the interim? And at length
How goes our reckoning?

TIMON
To Lacedaemon did my land extend. 156

FLAVIUS
O my good lord, the world is but a word.
Were it all yours to give it in a breath,
How quickly were it gone!

TIMON You tell me true.

FLAVIUS
If you suspect my husbandry of falsehood, 160
Call me before th' exactest auditors
And set me on the proof. So the gods bless me, 162
When all our offices have been oppressed 163
With riotous feeders, when our vaults have wept 164

139 found . . . honesty i.e., found warrant for believing the books properly kept in knowing me to be honest **141 Return so much** give as in repayment a large gift **142 'gainst . . . manners** contrary to what good manners dictated **144 checks** rebukes **145 in** in regard to **147 yet . . . time** i.e., late as it is, it is necessary that you be made acquainted with it **148 The greatest . . . having** your total wealth at a most optimistic reckoning **151 engaged** mortgaged **152–153 stop . . . Of** satisfy **153 dues** debts. **apace** quickly **156 Lacedaemon** Sparta **160 husbandry** management, stewardship **162 set . . . proof** put me to the test **163 offices** rooms, especially the kitchen and pantries **164 vaults** wine cellars

With drunken spilth of wine, when every room 165
Hath blazed with lights and brayed with minstrelsy,
I have retired me to a wasteful cock 167
And set mine eyes at flow.

TIMON Prithee, no more.

FLAVIUS
Heavens, have I said, the bounty of this lord!
How many prodigal bits have slaves and peasants 170
This night englutted! Who is not Timon's? 171
What heart, head, sword, force, means, but is Lord
Timon's? 172
Great Timon, noble, worthy, royal Timon!
Ah, when the means are gone that buy this praise,
The breath is gone whereof this praise is made.
Feast-won, fast-lost; one cloud of winter showers, 176
These flies are couched. [*He weeps.*]

TIMON Come, sermon me no further. 177
No villainous bounty yet hath passed my heart; 178
Unwisely, not ignobly, have I given.
Why dost thou weep? Canst thou the conscience lack 180
To think I shall lack friends? Secure thy heart. 181
If I would broach the vessels of my love 182
And try the argument of hearts by borrowing, 183
Men and men's fortunes could I frankly use 184
As I can bid thee speak.

FLAVIUS Assurance bless your thoughts! 186

TIMON
And in some sort these wants of mine are crowned, 187
That I account them blessings; for by these 188
Shall I try friends. You shall perceive how you 189
Mistake my fortunes; I am wealthy in my friends.—
Within there! Flaminius! Servilius!

165 spilth spilling **167 retired . . . cock** withdrawn to sit beside the wastefully flowing faucet of a barrel **170 bits** morsels **171 is not** i.e., does not profess himself to be **172 means** financial resources **176 fast-lost** (1) lost in time of fast (2) lost quickly and for good **177 are couched** hide themselves (to avoid Timon's requests for help). **sermon** lecture **178 villainous bounty** generosity that I am ashamed of **180 conscience** faith, or judgment **181 Secure** set at ease **182 broach** tap, open **183 try . . . hearts** test protestations of love **184 frankly** as freely **186 Assurance . . . thoughts** may your hopes prove well founded **187 sort** manner, sense. **crowned** given a special dignity **188 That** so that **189 try** test

Enter three Servants [*Flaminius, Servilius, and another*].

SERVANTS My lord? My lord?
TIMON I will dispatch you severally: [*To Servilius*] you 193
to Lord Lucius; [*To Flaminius*] to Lord Lucullus you—
I hunted with his honor today; [*To the other*] you to
Sempronius. Commend me to their loves, and, I am
proud, say, that my occasions have found time to use 197
'em toward a supply of money. Let the request be fifty 198
talents.
FLAMINIUS As you have said, my lord.
[*Exeunt Servants.*]
FLAVIUS [*Aside*] Lord Lucius and Lucullus? Humh!
TIMON Go you, sir, to the senators,
Of whom, even to the state's best health, I have 203
Deserved this hearing. Bid 'em send o' th' instant 204
A thousand talents to me.
FLAVIUS I have been bold—
For that I knew it the most general way— 206
To them to use your signet and your name, 207
But they do shake their heads, and I am here
No richer in return.
TIMON Is 't true? Can 't be?
FLAVIUS
They answer, in a joint and corporate voice, 210
That now they are at fall, want treasure, cannot 211
Do what they would, are sorry; you are honorable,
But yet they could have wished—they know not—
Something hath been amiss—a noble nature
May catch a wrench—would all were well—'tis pity. 215
And so, intending other serious matters, 216
After distasteful looks and these hard fractions, 217

193 severally separately **197 occasions** needs. **time** opportunity **198 toward** for **203 to . . . health** i.e., for my services in behalf of the state's welfare. (Cf. 4.3.93–96, where Alcibiades refers to Timon's sword and fortune offered in the defense of Athens.) **204 o' th' instant** at once **206 For that** because. **general** comprehensive, or customary (?) **207 signet** signet ring and seal, token of authority **210 corporate** united **211 at fall** at low ebb. **want** lack **215 catch a wrench** be wrenched away from its true bent **216 intending** turning their attention to, or pretending (?) **217 hard** harsh. **fractions** broken sentences

With certain half-caps and cold-moving nods 218
They froze me into silence.

TIMON You gods, reward them!
Prithee, man, look cheerly. These old fellows 220
Have their ingratitude in them hereditary.
Their blood is caked, 'tis cold, it seldom flows; 222
'Tis lack of kindly warmth they are not kind; 223
And nature, as it grows again toward earth, 224
Is fashioned for the journey dull and heavy.
Go to Ventidius. Prithee, be not sad.
Thou art true and honest—ingeniously I speak— 227
No blame belongs to thee. Ventidius lately
Buried his father, by whose death he's stepped
Into a great estate. When he was poor, 230
Imprisoned, and in scarcity of friends, 231
I cleared him with five talents. Greet him from me. 232
Bid him suppose some good necessity 233
Touches his friend, which craves to be remembered
With those five talents. That had, give 't these fellows 235
To whom 'tis instant due. Ne'er speak or think
That Timon's fortunes 'mong his friends can sink.

FLAVIUS [*Aside*] I would I could not think it.
That thought is bounty's foe; 239
Being free itself, it thinks all others so. *Exeunt.* 240

✤

218 half-caps i.e., salutations halfheartedly given. **cold-moving** chilling **220 cheerly** cheerful **222 caked** congealed **223 'Tis . . . kind** it is lack of natural warmth that makes them not generous (with pun on *kind,* natural, of humankind) **224 earth** i.e., the grave **227 ingeniously** frankly **230–232 When he was poor,** etc. (These lines echo Matthew 25:34–37 when Jesus discusses the Last Judgment.) **231 scarcity** need **232 cleared** freed **233 good** genuine **235 That had** when you have that. **these fellows** to these fellows **239 That . . . foe** i.e., the naive assumption that friends will remain true in hard times is the undoing of the bounteous impulse **240 free** generous

3.1

[Enter] Flaminius, waiting to speak with a lord, [Lucullus,] from his master. Enter a Servant to him.

LUCULLUS' SERVANT I have told my lord of you. He is coming down to you.

FLAMINIUS I thank you, sir.

Enter Lucullus.

LUCULLUS' SERVANT Here's my lord.

LUCULLUS [*Aside*] One of Lord Timon's men? A gift, I warrant. Why, this hits right; I dreamt of a silver basin 6
and ewer tonight.—Flaminius, honest Flaminius, you 7
are very respectively welcome, sir. [*To Servant.*] 8
Fill me some wine. [*Exit Servant.*] And how does
that honorable, complete, free-hearted gentleman of 10
Athens, thy very bountiful good lord and master?

FLAMINIUS His health is well, sir.

LUCULLUS I am right glad that his health is well, sir. And what hast thou there under thy cloak, pretty Flaminius?

FLAMINIUS Faith, nothing but an empty box, sir, which, in my lord's behalf, I come to entreat your
honor to supply; who, having great and instant occa- 18
sion to use fifty talents, hath sent to your lordship to 19
furnish him, nothing doubting your present assistance 20
therein.

LUCULLUS La, la, la la! "Nothing doubting," says he?
Alas, good lord! A noble gentleman 'tis, if he would 23
not keep so good a house. Many a time and often I ha' 24
dined with him and told him on 't, and come again to 25
supper to him of purpose to have him spend less, and 26
yet he would embrace no counsel, take no warning by 27
my coming. Every man has his fault, and honesty is 28
his. I ha' told him on 't, but I could ne'er get him from 't.

3.1. Location: Athens. Lucullus' house.
6 hits right accords perfectly **7 ewer** pitcher. **tonight** last night
8 respectively respectfully **10 complete** accomplished **18 supply** fill
18–19 instant occasion urgent need **20 nothing** not at all. **present** immediate **23 'tis** he is **24 keep . . . house** be so lavish in his entertaining **25 on 't** of it **26 of** on **27 by** from **28 honesty** liberality

Enter [*Lucullus'*] *Servant, with wine.*

LUCULLUS' SERVANT Please your lordship, here is the wine.

LUCULLUS Flaminius, I have noted thee always wise. Here's to thee. [*He offers a toast.*]

FLAMINIUS Your lordship speaks your pleasure. 34

LUCULLUS I have observed thee always for a towardly 35 prompt spirit—give thee thy due—and one that 36 knows what belongs to reason, and canst use the time 37 well if the time use thee well. Good parts in thee! [*To* 38 *Servant.*] Get you gone, sirrah. [*Exit Servant.*] Draw nearer, honest Flaminius. Thy lord's a bountiful gentleman; but thou art wise, and thou know'st well enough, although thou com'st to me, that this is no time to lend money, especially upon bare friendship, 43 without security. Here's three solidares for thee. 44 [*He gives a tip.*] Good boy, wink at me, and say thou 45 sawst me not. Fare thee well.

FLAMINIUS
Is 't possible the world should so much differ, 47
And we alive that lived? Fly, damnèd baseness, 48
To him that worships thee! [*He throws the money back.*]

LUCULLUS Ha? Now I see thou art a fool, and fit for thy master. *Exit Lucullus.*

FLAMINIUS
May these add to the number that may scald thee! 52
Let molten coin be thy damnation, 53
Thou disease of a friend and not himself! 54
Has friendship such a faint and milky heart
It turns in less than two nights? O you gods! 56
I feel my master's passion. This slave 57

34 Your . . . pleasure it pleases your lordship to say so **35–36 towardly prompt** quick to meet another's thoughts, well-disposed **37–38 canst . . . thee well** can make the most of an opportunity when it presents itself **38 parts** qualities **43 bare** mere **44 solidares** small coins. (A term invented by Shakespeare, evidently.) **45 wink** shut the eyes **47–48 so . . . lived** i.e., change so much in our lifetime **52 scald** i.e., roast in hell **53 Let . . . damnation** i.e., may you be punished in hell by having molten metal poured down your throat **54 Thou . . . himself** you who are no true friend at all, but only a diseased resemblance **56 It turns** that it sours like milk (with quibble on the idea of *turn* as in "turncoat") **57 feel . . . passion** i.e., feel angry on my master's behalf, share his anger and his suffering **57–58 slave Unto his honor** person slavishly devoted to his own dignity. (Said ironically.)

Unto his honor has my lord's meat in him. 58
Why should it thrive and turn to nutriment
When he is turned to poison? 60
O, may diseases only work upon 't! 61
And, when he's sick to death, let not that part of nature
Which my lord paid for be of any power
To expel sickness, but prolong his hour! *Exit.*

✤

3.2 *Enter Lucius, with three Strangers.*

LUCIUS Who, the Lord Timon? He is my very good friend and an honorable gentleman.

FIRST STRANGER We know him for no less, though we 3 are but strangers to him. But I can tell you one thing, my lord, and which I hear from common rumors: now 5 Lord Timon's happy hours are done and past, and his estate shrinks from him.

LUCIUS Fie, no, do not believe it! He cannot want for 8 money.

SECOND STRANGER But believe you this, my lord, that not long ago one of his men was with the Lord Lucullus to borrow so many talents, nay, urged extremely 12 for 't, and showed what necessity belonged to 't, and 13 yet was denied.

LUCIUS How?

SECOND STRANGER I tell you, denied, my lord.

LUCIUS What a strange case was that! Now, before the gods, I am ashamed on 't. Denied that honorable man? There was very little honor showed in 't. For my own part, I must needs confess, I have received some small kindnesses from him, as money, plate, jewels, and suchlike trifles, nothing comparing to his; yet had he 22 mistook him and sent to me, I should ne'er have de- 23 nied his occasion so many talents.

58 meat i.e., food of a feast **60 When . . . poison** when his behavior is so poisonous **61 work upon 't** thrive upon it, *my lord's meat in him*

3.2. Location: Athens. A public place.
3 for no less to be no less than you say **5 which** one which **8 want for** lack **12 urged extremely** begged insistently **13 what . . . to 't** how necessary it was **22 his** i.e., Lucullus' receiving of generosity
23 mistook . . . me i.e., mistakenly sent to me, who owe him less

Enter Servilius.

SERVILIUS See, by good hap, yonder's my lord. I have 25
sweat to see his honor. [*To Lucius.*] My honored lord— 26

LUCIUS Servilius? You are kindly met, sir. Fare thee
well. Commend me to thy honorable virtuous lord,
my very exquisite friend. [*He starts to go.*] 29

SERVILIUS May it please your honor, my lord hath
sent—

LUCIUS Ha? What has he sent? I am so much endeared 32
to that lord; he's ever sending. How shall I thank him,
think'st thou? And what has he sent now?

SERVILIUS He's only sent his present occasion now, my 35
lord, requesting your lordship to supply his instant 36
use with so many talents. 37

LUCIUS
I know his lordship is but merry with me;
He cannot want fifty—five hundred—talents. 39

SERVILIUS
But in the meantime he wants less, my lord.
If his occasion were not virtuous, 41
I should not urge it half so faithfully.

LUCIUS
Dost thou speak seriously, Servilius?

SERVILIUS Upon my soul, 'tis true, sir.

LUCIUS What a wicked beast was I to disfurnish myself 45
against such a good time, when I might ha' shown 46
myself honorable! How unluckily it happened that I 47
should purchase the day before for a little part, and 48
undo a great deal of honor! Servilius, now before the 49
gods, I am not able to do—the more beast, I say—I
was sending to use Lord Timon myself, these gentle- 51

25 hap fortune **25–26 I have sweat** i.e., I have been hurrying
29 exquisite sought after **32 endeared** obliged **35 occasion** need
36–37 supply . . . use provide for his immediate need **39 He cannot . . . talents** (Probably an indication of Shakespeare's uncertainty over the value of this currency; see also *so many* above in ll. 12, 24, and 37.)
41 were not virtuous were due to a fault instead of a virtue, i.e., generosity **45–46 disfurnish . . . time** leave myself unprepared for such an excellent opportunity **47–49 that I . . . honor** i.e., that I just yesterday laid out a sum of money in a small investment and thus made it impossible now to acquire a great honor by helping Timon **51 use** borrow from

men can witness; but I would not for the wealth of 52
Athens I had done 't now. Commend me bountifully
to his good lordship, and I hope his honor will con- 54
ceive the fairest of me, because I have no power to be 55
kind. And tell him this from me: I count it one of my
greatest afflictions, say, that I cannot pleasure such an 57
honorable gentleman. Good Servilius, will you befriend me so far as to use mine own words to him?

SERVILIUS Yes, sir, I shall.

LUCIUS I'll look you out a good turn, Servilius. 61

Exit Servilius.

True, as you said, Timon is shrunk indeed; 62
And he that's once denied will hardly speed. *Exit.* 63

FIRST STRANGER Do you observe this, Hostilius?

SECOND STRANGER Ay, too well.

FIRST STRANGER Why, this is the world's soul, 66
And just of the same piece 67
Is every flatterer's sport. Who can call him his friend
That dips in the same dish? For, in my knowing, 69
Timon has been this lord's father 70
And kept his credit with his purse, 71
Supported his estate; nay, Timon's money
Has paid his men their wages. He ne'er drinks
But Timon's silver treads upon his lip. 74
And yet—O, see the monstrousness of man
When he looks out in an ungrateful shape!— 76
He does deny him, in respect of his, 77
What charitable men afford to beggars.

THIRD STRANGER
Religion groans at it.

FIRST STRANGER For mine own part,
I never tasted Timon in my life, 80

52 would not do not wish **54–55 conceive the fairest** think the best **55 because** i.e., even though **57 pleasure** satisfy, please **61 look you out** seek occasion to do you **62 shrunk** brought low **63 speed** prosper **66 soul** real essence, vital principle **67 just . . . piece** exactly the same (i.e., cut from the same piece of cloth) **69 dips . . . dish** (Alludes to Judas' betrayal of Christ; see Matthew 26:23.) **70 father** i.e., patron **71 kept his** i.e., maintained Lucius'. **his purse** i.e., Timon's wealth **74 treads** presses **76 looks out** appears **77 He . . . his** i.e., Lucius denies Timon an amount that equals, in comparison with Lucius' total wealth **80 tasted Timon** i.e., sampled Timon's liberality

Nor came any of his bounties over me 81
To mark me for his friend; yet I protest,
For his right noble mind, illustrious virtue, 83
And honorable carriage, 84
Had his necessity made use of me, 85
I would have put my wealth into donation 86
And the best half should have returned to him, 87
So much I love his heart. But I perceive
Men must learn now with pity to dispense,
For policy sits above conscience. *Exeunt.* 90

✤

3.3 *Enter a third Servant* [*of Timon's*] *with Sempronius, another of Timon's friends.*

SEMPRONIUS
Must he needs trouble me in 't? Hum! 'Bove all others? 1
He might have tried Lord Lucius or Lucullus;
And now Ventidius is wealthy too,
Whom he redeemed from prison. All these
Owe their estates unto him.
SERVANT My lord,
They have all been touched and found base metal, 7
For they have all denied him.
SEMPRONIUS How? Have they denied him?
Has Ventidius and Lucullus denied him?
And does he send to me? Three? Humh!
It shows but little love or judgment in him.
Must I be his last refuge? His friends, like physicians,
Thrive, give him over. Must I take th' cure upon me? 14
He's much disgraced me in 't. I'm angry at him,
That might have known my place. I see no sense for 't 16

81 came . . . me was I the recipient of any of his generosity **83 For** because of **84 carriage** conduct **85 made use of me** i.e., sought my aid **86 put . . . donation** i.e., made a gift of my wealth **87 returned** i.e., gone to its proper place, where it belongs **90 policy** self-interest

3.3. Location: Athens. Sempronius' house.
1 Must . . . me does he have to involve me **7 touched** (Metaphor derived from testing metals with a touchstone to see if they are gold.) **14 Thrive . . . over** i.e., thrive on his wealth, but now give him up as beyond help **16 That . . . place** who should have acknowledged my position (among his friends). **sense** reason

But his occasions might have wooed me first; 17
For, in my conscience, I was the first man 18
That e'er receivèd gift from him.
And does he think so backwardly of me now 20
That I'll requite it last? No! 21
So it may prove an argument of laughter 22
To th' rest, and I 'mongst lords be thought a fool.
I'd rather than the worth of thrice the sum
He'd sent to me first, but for my mind's sake; 25
I'd such a courage to do him good. But now return, 26
And with their faint reply this answer join:
Who bates mine honor shall not know my coin. 28

Exit.

SERVANT Excellent! Your lordship's a goodly villain. 29
The devil knew not what he did when he made man
politic; he crossed himself by 't, and I cannot think but 31
in the end the villainies of man will set him clear. 32
How fairly this lord strives to appear foul! Takes vir- 33
tuous copies to be wicked, like those that under hot 34
ardent zeal would set whole realms on fire. 35
Of such a nature is his politic love.
This was my lord's best hope; now all are fled,
Save only the gods. Now his friends are dead, 38
Doors that were ne'er acquainted with their wards 39
Many a bounteous year must be employed 40
Now to guard sure their master. 41
And this is all a liberal course allows: 42
Who cannot keep his wealth must keep his house. 43

Exit.

17 But his occasions i.e., but that he, in his need **18 in my conscience** to my knowledge **20 think . . . me** (1) think I am so backward (2) think of me last **21 requite** repay **22 argument of** subject for **25 but . . . sake** if only in recognition of my good feeling toward him **26 courage** desire **28 Who bates** whoever abates, detracts from **29 goodly** proper. (Said ironically.) **31 politic** cunning. **crossed** foiled (by making man his rival in treachery) **32 set him clear** i.e., make even the devil look innocent **33 How fairly** with what a plausible appearance of virtue **33–35 Takes . . . fire** i.e., how this lord models himself on the virtuous for wicked purposes, like religious bigots who for zealous purposes would burn down whole kingdoms **38 Now** now that **39 wards** bolts, locks **40 Many** for many **41 guard sure** i.e., protect from arrest for debt **42 liberal** generous **43 keep . . . keep** preserve . . . stay inside

3.4

Enter [*two of*] *Varro's Men, meeting* [*Titus' Servant and*] *others, all* [*being servants of*] *Timon's creditors, to wait for his coming out. Then enter Lucius'* [*Servant*] *and Hortensius'* [*Servant*].

VARRO'S FIRST SERVANT
Well met. Good morrow, Titus and Hortensius.
TITUS' SERVANT
The like to you, kind Varro.
HORTENSIUS' SERVANT Lucius! 2
What, do we meet together?
LUCIUS' SERVANT Ay, and I think
One business does command us all;
For mine is money.
TITUS' SERVANT So is theirs and ours.

Enter Philotus' [*Servant*].

LUCIUS' SERVANT
And Sir Philotus too!
PHILOTUS' SERVANT Good day at once. 6
LUCIUS' SERVANT Welcome, good brother.
What do you think the hour?
PHILOTUS' SERVANT Laboring for nine. 8
LUCIUS' SERVANT
So much?
PHILOTUS' SERVANT Is not my lord seen yet?
LUCIUS' SERVANT Not yet. 9
PHILOTUS' SERVANT
I wonder on 't. He was wont to shine at seven. 10
LUCIUS' SERVANT
Ay, but the days are waxed shorter with him. 11
You must consider that a prodigal course
Is like the sun's,
But not, like his, recoverable. I fear 14
'Tis deepest winter in Lord Timon's purse;

3.4. Location: Athens. Timon's house.
2 like same **6 at once** to one and all **8 Laboring for** moving toward **9 much** i.e., late **10 was . . . shine** used to be up **11 are waxed** have grown **14 But . . . recoverable** i.e., the sun will return from its wintry path, but Timon cannot recover (since his funds are not *recoverable*)

That is, one may reach deep enough and yet
Find little.

PHILOTUS' SERVANT I am of your fear for that. 17

TITUS' SERVANT
I'll show you how t' observe a strange event. 18
Your lord sends now for money?

HORTENSIUS' SERVANT Most true, he does.

TITUS' SERVANT
And he wears jewels now of Timon's gift,
For which I wait for money. 21

HORTENSIUS' SERVANT It is against my heart. 22

LUCIUS' SERVANT Mark how strange it shows:
Timon in this should pay more than he owes,
And e'en as if your lord should wear rich jewels 25
And send for money for 'em. 26

HORTENSIUS' SERVANT
I'm weary of this charge, the gods can witness. 27
I know my lord hath spent of Timon's wealth, 28
And now ingratitude makes it worse than stealth. 29

VARRO'S FIRST SERVANT
Yes, mine's three thousand crowns. What's yours?

LUCIUS' SERVANT Five thousand, mine.

VARRO'S FIRST SERVANT
'Tis much deep, and it should seem by th' sum 32
Your master's confidence was above mine, 33
Else surely his had equaled. 34

Enter Flaminius.

TITUS' SERVANT One of Lord Timon's men.

LUCIUS' SERVANT Flaminius? Sir, a word. Pray, is my lord ready to come forth?

FLAMINIUS No, indeed, he is not.

TITUS' SERVANT We attend his lordship. Pray signify so much. 39

FLAMINIUS I need not tell him that. He knows you are too diligent. [*Exit.*] 41

17 am of share **18 observe** i.e., analyze **21 For . . . money** i.e., while I wait for the money used to buy those jewels **22 heart** wish, feeling **25–26 e'en . . . for 'em** i.e., it's just as though your master should both wear the jewels Timon gave him and simultaneously demand the money that paid for those jewels **27 charge** commission **28 spent** made use **29 stealth** theft **32 much deep** very great **33 mine** my master's **34 his had equaled** i.e., my master's loan would have equaled in amount your master's **39 attend** are waiting for **41 diligent** i.e., officious

Enter steward [*Flavius*] *in a cloak, muffled.*

LUCIUS' SERVANT
Ha! Is not that his steward muffled so?
He goes away in a cloud. Call him, call him. 43
TITUS' SERVANT [*To Flavius*] Do you hear, sir?
VARRO'S SECOND SERVANT [*To Flavius*] By your leave, sir.
FLAVIUS
What do ye ask of me, my friend?
TITUS' SERVANT
We wait for certain money here, sir.
FLAVIUS Ay, 47
If money were as certain as your waiting,
'Twere sure enough.
Why then preferred you not your sums and bills 50
When your false masters eat of my lord's meat? 51
Then they could smile and fawn upon his debts,
And take down th' interest into their gluttonous maws. 53
You do yourselves but wrong to stir me up. 54
Let me pass quietly.
Believe 't, my lord and I have made an end; 56
I have no more to reckon, he to spend. 57
LUCIUS' SERVANT Ay, but this answer will not serve. 58
FLAVIUS
If 'twill not serve, 'tis not so base as you,
For you serve knaves. [*Exit.*]
VARRO'S FIRST SERVANT How? What does his cashiered 61
worship mutter?
VARRO'S SECOND SERVANT No matter what; he's poor,
and that's revenge enough. Who can speak broader 64
than he that has no house to put his head in? Such 65
may rail against great buildings. 66

43 in a cloud (1) muffled (2) in a state of confusion and ignominy
47 certain certain sums of. (But Flavius puns bitterly in the next line on the sense of "reliable," "predictable.") **50 preferred** presented **51 eat** ate. (Pronounced *et.*) **53 th' interest** i.e., the food and drink they consumed as though it were interest on the loans **54 do yourselves but** only do yourselves **56 made an end** severed our relationship **57 reckon** keep account of **58 serve** do. (But Lucius punningly replies in the sense of "act as servant.") **61 cashiered** dismissed. (*His cashiered worship* is offered sardonically as if it were a title of dignity.) **64 broader** (1) more freely (2) more in the open, abroad **65–66 Such . . . buildings** i.e., a man who is houseless and out of service, like Flavius, has nothing to lose and can inveigh against injustice and inequality

Enter Servilius.

TITUS' SERVANT O, here's Servilius. Now we shall know some answer.

SERVILIUS If I might beseech you, gentlemen, to repair 69
some other hour, I should derive much from 't. For 70
take 't of my soul, my lord leans wondrously to discon- 71
tent. His comfortable temper has forsook him; he's 72
much out of health and keeps his chamber. 73

LUCIUS' SERVANT
Many do keep their chambers are not sick, 74
And if it be so far beyond his health, 75
Methinks he should the sooner pay his debts
And make a clear way to the gods.

SERVILIUS Good gods! 77

TITUS' SERVANT
We cannot take this for answer, sir.

FLAMINIUS (*Within*) Servilius, help! My lord, my lord!

Enter Timon, in a rage.

TIMON
What, are my doors opposed against my passage?
Have I been ever free, and must my house
Be my retentive enemy, my jail? 82
The place which I have feasted, does it now,
Like all mankind, show me an iron heart?

LUCIUS' SERVANT Put in now, Titus. 85

TITUS' SERVANT My lord, here is my bill.

LUCIUS' SERVANT Here's mine.

HORTENSIUS' SERVANT And mine, my lord.

BOTH VARRO'S SERVANTS And ours, my lord.

PHILOTUS' SERVANT All our bills.

TIMON
Knock me down with 'em! Cleave me to the girdle! 91

LUCIUS' SERVANT Alas, my lord—

TIMON Cut my heart in sums!

TITUS' SERVANT Mine, fifty talents.

69 repair return **70 derive** benefit **71 take 't . . . soul** i.e., believe I speak sincerely **72 comfortable temper** cheerful disposition **73 keeps** stays in **74 are** who are **75 if . . . health** if his condition is so far from good health **77 make . . . gods** i.e., pay all his debts to smooth his way to heaven **82 retentive** confining **85 Put in** i.e., make your claim
91 Knock, Cleave (Timon puns on *bills* as weapons.) **girdle** belt

TIMON Tell out my blood! 95
LUCIUS' SERVANT Five thousand crowns, my lord.
TIMON
Five thousand drops pays that. What yours? And yours?
VARRO'S FIRST SERVANT My lord—
VARRO'S SECOND SERVANT My lord—
TIMON
Tear me, take me, and the gods fall upon you! 100
Exit Timon.
HORTENSIUS' SERVANT Faith, I perceive our masters may throw their caps at their money. These debts 102 may well be called desperate ones, for a madman owes 103 'em. *Exeunt.*

Enter Timon [*and Flavius*].

TIMON
They have e'en put my breath from me, the slaves. 105
Creditors? Devils!
FLAVIUS My dear lord—
TIMON What if it should be so? 108
FLAVIUS My lord—
TIMON
I'll have it so. My steward!
FLAVIUS Here, my lord.
TIMON
So fitly? Go, bid all my friends again, 111
Lucius, Lucullus, and Sempronius—all.
I'll once more feast the rascals.
FLAVIUS O my lord,
You only speak from your distracted soul;
There's not so much left to furnish out 115
A moderate table.
TIMON Be it not in thy care. Go, 117
I charge thee, invite them all. Let in the tide
Of knaves once more. My cook and I'll provide.
Exeunt.

✤

95 Tell out count out by the drop **100 the gods fall upon you** i.e., may the gods attack you as with an army **102 throw . . . at** i.e., give up hope of recovering **103 desperate** (1) unlikely to be recovered (2) resulting from desperate madness **105 e'en . . . me** left me breathless **108 What . . . so** i.e., suppose I give it a try. (Timon has thought of the mock banquet he will serve in 3.6.) **111 fitly** conveniently **115 furnish out** supply **117 Be . . . care** don't you worry about it

3.5

Enter three Senators at one door, Alcibiades meeting them, with attendants.

FIRST SENATOR [*To another Senator*]
My lord, you have my voice to 't. 1
The fault's bloody; 2
'Tis necessary he should die.
Nothing emboldens sin so much as mercy.
SECOND SENATOR Most true. The law shall bruise 'em. 5
ALCIBIADES
Honor, health, and compassion to the Senate! 6
FIRST SENATOR Now, Captain?
ALCIBIADES
I am an humble suitor to your virtues;
For pity is the virtue of the law, 9
And none but tyrants use it cruelly.
It pleases time and fortune to lie heavy 11
Upon a friend of mine, who in hot blood 12
Hath stepped into the law, which is past depth 13
To those that without heed do plunge into 't. 14
He is a man, setting his fate aside, 15
Of comely virtues;
Nor did he soil the fact with cowardice— 17
An honor in him which buys out his fault— 18
But with a noble fury and fair spirit,
Seeing his reputation touched to death, 20
He did oppose his foe;
And with such sober and unnoted passion 22
He did behave his anger, ere 'twas spent, 23
As if he had but proved an argument. 24
FIRST SENATOR
You undergo too strict a paradox, 25

3.5. Location: Athens. The Senate House.
1 voice to 't vote in favor of it (the death sentence under consideration) **2 fault's bloody** crime involved bloodshed **5 'em** i.e., all such offenders **6 compassion to the Senate** i.e., may the Senate have compassion **9 virtue** chief merit, essence **11–12 lie . . . Upon** oppress **13 stepped into** incurred the penalties of **13–14 past depth To** over the heads of **15 setting . . . aside** excluding his ill-fated action **17 fact** deed **18 buys out** redeems **20 touched to death** fatally threatened **22 unnoted** so well under control as to be unobservable **23 behave** control **24 but . . . argument** only been testing a philosophical proposition **25 undergo** undertake

Striving to make an ugly deed look fair.
Your words have took such pains as if they labored
To bring manslaughter into form and set quarreling 28
Upon the head of valor—which indeed 29
Is valor misbegot, and came into the world
When sects and factions were newly born.
He's truly valiant that can wisely suffer
The worst that man can breathe, 33
And make his wrongs his outsides, 34
To wear them like his raiment, carelessly, 35
And ne'er prefer his injuries to his heart, 36
To bring it into danger.
If wrongs be evils and enforce us kill, 38
What folly 'tis to hazard life for ill! 39

ALCIBIADES
My lord—

FIRST SENATOR You cannot make gross sins look clear. 40
To revenge is no valor, but to bear. 41

ALCIBIADES
My lords, then, under favor, pardon me 42
If I speak like a captain.
Why do fond men expose themselves to battle, 44
And not endure all threats? Sleep upon 't, 45
And let the foes quietly cut their throats
Without repugnancy? If there be 47
Such valor in the bearing, what make we 48
Abroad? Why then, women are more valiant 49
That stay at home, if bearing carry it, 50
And the ass more captain than the lion, the felon
Loaden with irons wiser than the judge, 52

28 bring . . . form make manslaughter appear orderly, or according to form **28–29 set . . . of** make quarreling the highest kind of, or subdivision of **29 which** i.e., quarreling, duelling **33 breathe** i.e., speak (as also in l. 61) **34 his outsides** merely external circumstance **35 raiment** clothing. **carelessly** without anxiety **36 prefer** present **38 kill** to kill **39 'tis** this is, i.e., this code that obliges one to repay evil with violence. **for ill** in a bad cause **40 clear** innocent **41 to bear** i.e., bearing insults calmly is true valor **42 under favor** by your leave **44 fond** foolish **45 Sleep** i.e., why do they not sleep **47 repugnancy** resistance **48 the bearing** i.e., putting up with insults. **make** do **49 Abroad** away from home **50 bearing** putting up with insults (with a pun on "childbearing" and perhaps on "supporting the man in sexual intercourse") **52 Loaden with irons** weighed down with shackles

If wisdom be in suffering. O my lords,
As you are great, be pitifully good. 54
Who cannot condemn rashness in cold blood?
To kill, I grant, is sin's extremest gust, 56
But in defense, by mercy, 'tis most just. 57
To be in anger is impiety,
But who is man that is not angry? 59
Weigh but the crime with this.

SECOND SENATOR You breathe in vain.

ALCIBIADES In vain? His service done
At Lacedaemon and Byzantium
Were a sufficient briber for his life.

FIRST SENATOR What's that?

ALCIBIADES
Why, I say, my lords, he's done fair service 66
And slain in fight many of your enemies.
How full of valor did he bear himself
In the last conflict, and made plenteous wounds!

SECOND SENATOR
He has made too much plenty with 'em. 70
He's a sworn rioter; he has a sin that often 71
Drowns him and takes his valor prisoner.
If there were no foes, that were enough 73
To overcome him. In that beastly fury
He has been known to commit outrages
And cherish factions. 'Tis inferred to us 76
His days are foul and his drink dangerous.

FIRST SENATOR
He dies.

ALCIBIADES Hard fate! He might have died in war.
My lords, if not for any parts in him— 79
Though his right arm might purchase his own time 80
And be in debt to none—yet, more to move you,

54 pitifully good good by showing mercy **56 sin's extremest gust** the relish of extremest sin. (*Gust* means outburst, indulgence.) **57 by mercy** by a merciful interpretation of law **59 not** i.e., never **66 fair** excellent **70 made . . . 'em** i.e., used them as an excuse for an excess of riotous pleasure (playing on *plenty, plenteous*) **71 sworn rioter** inveterate debauchee. **a sin** i.e., drunkenness **73 If** even if. **foes** accusers **76 cherish factions** encourage dissension and conspiracy. **inferred** alleged **79 parts** admirable traits **80 his right . . . time** i.e., his ability in war should obtain his freedom and let him live out his natural life

Take my deserts to his and join 'em both; 82
And, for I know your reverend ages love 83
Security, I'll pawn my victories, all 84
My honors, to you, upon his good returns. 85
If by this crime he owes the law his life,
Why, let the war receive 't in valiant gore, 87
For law is strict, and war is nothing more.

FIRST SENATOR
We are for law. He dies; urge it no more,
On height of our displeasure. Friend or brother, 90
He forfeits his own blood that spills another. 91

ALCIBIADES
Must it be so? It must not be. My lords,
I do beseech you, know me.

SECOND SENATOR How?

ALCIBIADES Call me to your remembrances.

THIRD SENATOR What?

ALCIBIADES
I cannot think but your age has forgot me.
It could not else be I should prove so base 98
To sue and be denied such common grace. 99
My wounds ache at you.

FIRST SENATOR Do you dare our anger?
'Tis in few words, but spacious in effect: 101
We banish thee forever.

ALCIBIADES Banish me?
Banish your dotage, banish usury,
That makes the Senate ugly.

FIRST SENATOR
If after two days' shine Athens contain thee,
Attend our weightier judgment. 106

82 to in addition to **83 for** because **84 Security** (1) safety (2) collateral for a loan (using a financial metaphor found also in *purchase, pawn, good returns,* etc.) **85 upon . . . returns** as a pledge that he will make a good return on your investment in him, i.e., fight bravely in war **87 let . . . gore** i.e., let him pay his debt by bleeding as a soldier **90 On . . . our** on pain of our highest **91 another** i.e., another's **98 else be** otherwise be (that). **prove** i.e., be considered **99 To sue** as to request **101 spacious in effect** of great import (with quibble on the spacious world to which Alcibiades is banished) **106 Attend . . . judgment** expect our more severe sentence

And, not to swell our spirit, 107
He shall be executed presently. *Exeunt* [*Senators*]. 108

ALCIBIADES
Now the gods keep you old enough
That you may live
Only in bone, that none may look on you!— 111
I'm worse than mad. I have kept back their foes,
While they have told their money and let out 113
Their coin upon large interest, I myself
Rich only in large hurts. All those for this? 115
Is this the balsam that the usuring Senate 116
Pours into captains' wounds? Banishment!
It comes not ill; I hate not to be banished. 118
It is a cause worthy my spleen and fury, 119
That I may strike at Athens. I'll cheer up
My discontented troops and lay for hearts. 121
'Tis honor with most lands to be at odds. 122
Soldiers should brook as little wrongs as gods. *Exit.* 123

✤

3.6

[*Music. Tables and seats set out; servants attending.*] *Enter divers friends* [*of Timon*] *at several doors.*

FIRST LORD The good time of day to you, sir.
SECOND LORD I also wish it to you. I think this honorable lord did but try us this other day. 3
FIRST LORD Upon that were my thoughts tiring when 4
we encountered. I hope it is not so low with him as he 5
made it seem in the trial of his several friends.

107 spirit anger **108 presently** immediately **111 Only in bone** i.e., mere skeletons **113 told** reckoned. **let** lent **115 hurts** injuries **116 balsam** balm, medicine **118 It . . . ill** it is not such a bad thing after all **119 worthy** worthy of **121 lay for hearts** endeavor to win their affection **122 'Tis . . . odds** it's honorable to be at variance with a country (and its political leaders) in most instances **123 brook . . . gods** endure insults as little as the gods do

3.6. Location: Athens. A banqueting room in Timon's house.
s.d. several separate **3 did but try** was only testing us **4 tiring** preying, feeding, i.e., busily engaged **5 encountered** met. **it is . . . him** his financial situation is not so desperate

SECOND LORD It should not be, by the persuasion of his 7
new feasting.
FIRST LORD I should think so. He hath sent me an earnest inviting, which many my near occasions did urge 10
me to put off; but he hath conjured me beyond them, 11
and I must needs appear. 12
SECOND LORD In like manner was I in debt to my importunate business, but he would not hear my excuse. 13
I am sorry, when he sent to borrow of me, that my
provision was out. 16
FIRST LORD I am sick of that grief too, as I understand 17
how all things go. 18
SECOND LORD Every man here's so. What would he
have borrowed of you?
FIRST LORD A thousand pieces. 21
SECOND LORD A thousand pieces?
FIRST LORD What of you?
SECOND LORD He sent to me, sir— Here he comes.

Enter Timon and attendants. [*Music plays.*]

TIMON With all my heart, gentlemen both! And how
fare you?
FIRST LORD Ever at the best, hearing well of your lordship.
SECOND LORD The swallow follows not summer more
willing than we your lordship.
TIMON [*Aside*] Nor more willingly leaves winter, such
summer birds are men.—Gentlemen, our dinner will
not recompense this long stay. Feast your ears with 33
the music awhile, if they will fare so harshly o' the 34
trumpet's sound. We shall to 't presently.
FIRST LORD I hope it remains not unkindly with your
lordship that I returned you an empty messenger.
TIMON O, sir, let it not trouble you.

7 persuasion evidence **10 inviting** invitation. **many . . . occasions** my many urgent necessities or business **11 conjured . . . them** summoned me so urgently as to overcome my previous commitments **12 needs** necessarily **13 in debt to** obligated to **16 provision was out** resources were exhausted **17–18 as . . . go** particularly as I now understand the state of affairs. (Perhaps hinting at Timon's seeming ability to entertain lavishly again.) **21 pieces** i.e., gold coins **33 stay** delay **34 they . . . o'** they (your ears) will deign to feast on such rough fare as

SECOND LORD My noble lord—
TIMON Ah, my good friend, what cheer?

The banquet brought in.

SECOND LORD My most honorable lord, I am e'en sick 41
of shame that when your lordship this other day sent
to me I was so unfortunate a beggar. 43
TIMON Think not on 't, sir.
SECOND LORD If you had sent but two hours before—
TIMON Let it not cumber your better remembrance.— 46
Come, bring in all together.
SECOND LORD All covered dishes! 48
FIRST LORD Royal cheer, I warrant you. 49
THIRD LORD Doubt not that, if money and the season
can yield it.
FIRST LORD How do you? What's the news?
THIRD LORD Alcibiades is banished. Hear you of it?
FIRST AND SECOND LORDS Alcibiades banished?
THIRD LORD 'Tis so, be sure of it.
FIRST LORD How? How?
SECOND LORD I pray you, upon what? 57
TIMON My worthy friends, will you draw near?
THIRD LORD I'll tell you more anon. Here's a noble feast 59
toward. 60
SECOND LORD This is the old man still. 61
THIRD LORD Will 't hold? Will 't hold? 62
SECOND LORD It does; but time will—and so— 63
THIRD LORD I do conceive. 64
TIMON Each man to his stool, with that spur as he 65
would to the lip of his mistress. Your diet shall be in 66
all places alike. Make not a city feast of it, to let the 67
meat cool ere we can agree upon the first place; sit, sit. 68
[*They sit.*] The gods require our thanks.

You great benefactors, sprinkle our society with

41 e'en quite **43 so . . . beggar** so unfortunate as to be out of ready reserves **46 cumber . . . remembrance** trouble your happier thoughts, memories **48 covered** (Implies particularly elegant fare.) **49 Royal** fit for royalty **57 what** what ground **59 anon** soon **60 toward** imminent **61 old man still** man we once knew **62 hold** last **63 will** i.e., will tell **64 conceive** understand **65 that spur** the same eagerness **66 diet** food **66–67 in . . . alike** the same wherever you sit to eat **67 city feast** formal occasion, with seating by rank **68 first place** place of honor

thankfulness. For your own gifts, make yourselves praised; but reserve still to give, lest your deities be 72 despised. Lend to each man enough, that one need not lend to another; for, were your godheads to borrow of men, men would forsake the gods. Make the meat be beloved more than the man that gives it. Let no assembly of twenty be without a score of villains. If there sit twelve women at the table, let a dozen of them be—as they are. The rest of your fees, O gods—the senators 79 of Athens, together with the common tag of people— 80 what is amiss in them, you gods, make suitable for destruction. For these my present friends, as they are 82 to me nothing, so in nothing bless them, and to nothing are they welcome.

Uncover, dogs, and lap!

[*The dishes are uncovered and seen to contain warm water and stones.*]

SOME SPEAK What does his lordship mean?

SOME OTHERS I know not.

TIMON

May you a better feast never behold,
You knot of mouth-friends! Smoke and lukewarm water 89
Is your perfection. This is Timon's last, 90
Who, stuck and spangled with your flatteries, 91
Washes it off and sprinkles in your faces
Your reeking villainy.

[*He throws the water in their faces.*]

Live loathed and long,
Most smiling, smooth, detested parasites,
Courteous destroyers, affable wolves, meek bears,
You fools of fortune, trencher-friends, time's flies, 96
Cap-and-knee slaves, vapors, and minute-jacks! 97

72 reserve still always hold back something **79 fees** i.e., what is held in fee from you, your gifts or benefactions (?) or, those who hold their lives in fee from you (?) **80 tag** rabble **82 For** as for **89 knot** company, crowd. **mouth-friends** friends in words only. **Smoke** i.e., steam, "hot air" **90 Is your perfection** suits you perfectly **91 stuck and spangled** bespattered and decorated **96 trencher-friends** friends only while being fed. **time's flies** fair-weather insects **97 Cap-and-knee slaves** men obsequious with their caps and curtsies. **vapors** substanceless creatures. **minute-jacks** mannikins that strike a bell on the outside of a clock; hence, time-servers

Of man and beast the infinite malady 98
Crust you quite o'er! What, dost thou go?
Soft! Take thy physic first! Thou too, and thou! 100
Stay, I will lend thee money, borrow none.
[*He assaults them and drives them out.*]
What, all in motion? Henceforth be no feast
Whereat a villain's not a welcome guest.
Burn, house! Sink, Athens! Henceforth hated be
Of Timon, man, and all humanity! *Exit.* 105

Enter the Senators, with other Lords, [*returning*].

FIRST LORD How now, my lords?
SECOND LORD Know you the quality of Lord Timon's 107
fury?
THIRD LORD Push! Did you see my cap? 109
FOURTH LORD I have lost my gown.
FIRST LORD He's but a mad lord, and naught but hu- 111
mors sways him. He gave me a jewel th' other day, 112
and now he has beat it out of my hat. Did you see my
jewel? [*They search for their belongings.*]
THIRD LORD Did you see my cap?
SECOND LORD Here 'tis.
FOURTH LORD Here lies my gown.
FIRST LORD Let's make no stay.
SECOND LORD
Lord Timon's mad.
THIRD LORD I feel 't upon my bones.
FOURTH LORD
One day he gives us diamonds, next day stones.
Exeunt the Senators [*etc.*].

✣

98 the infinite malady every loathsome disease **100 Soft** i.e., wait a minute. **physic** medicine **105 Of** by **107 quality** occasion **109 Push** pshaw **111–112 humors** caprice

4.1 *Enter Timon.*

TIMON

Let me look back upon thee. O thou wall
That girdles in those wolves, dive in the earth
And fence not Athens! Matrons, turn incontinent! 3
Obedience fail in children! Slaves and fools, 4
Pluck the grave wrinkled Senate from the bench
And minister in their steads! To general filths 6
Convert o' th' instant, green virginity! 7
Do 't in your parents' eyes. Bankrupts, hold fast;
Rather than render back, out with your knives
And cut your trusters' throats! Bound servants, steal! 10
Large-handed robbers your grave masters are, 11
And pill by law. Maid, to thy master's bed! 12
Thy mistress is o' the brothel. Son of sixteen,
Pluck the lined crutch from thy old limping sire; 14
With it beat out his brains! Piety, and fear, 15
Religion to the gods, peace, justice, truth, 16
Domestic awe, night rest, and neighborhood, 17
Instruction, manners, mysteries, and trades, 18
Degrees, observances, customs, and laws, 19
Decline to your confounding contraries, 20
And yet confusion live! Plagues, incident to men, 21
Your potent and infectious fevers heap
On Athens, ripe for stroke! Thou cold sciatica, 23
Cripple our senators, that their limbs may halt 24
As lamely as their manners! Lust and liberty 25
Creep in the minds and marrows of our youth, 26

4.1. Location: Outside the walls of Athens.
3 fence (1) enclose (2) defend. **incontinent** lascivious **4 Obedience fail** let obedience fail **6 general filths** common prostitutes **7 green** young **10 trusters'** of those who have trusted you, your creditors. **Bound** indentured **11 Large-handed** rapacious **12 pill** pillage. **to** go to **14 lined** stuffed, padded **15 fear** religious awe **16 Religion to** veneration of **17 Domestic awe** respect for the seniors of a household. **neighborhood** neighborliness **18 mysteries** crafts **19 Degrees** established ranks of society **20 confounding contraries** opposites that reduce all to chaos **21 yet** i.e., in spite of this dissolution, still let **23 cold** chilling, or caused by chill. **sciatica** nerve pain in hip and leg **24 halt** limp **25 liberty** licentiousness **26 marrows** soft tissues filling the cavities of bone (thought of as the source of vitality and strength)

That 'gainst the stream of virtue they may strive 27
And drown themselves in riot! Itches, blains, 28
Sow all th' Athenian bosoms, and their crop 29
Be general leprosy! Breath infect breath,
That their society, as their friendship, may 31
Be merely poison! Nothing I'll bear from thee 32
But nakedness, thou detestable town!
[*He strips off his garments.*]
Take thou that too, with multiplying bans! 34
Timon will to the woods, where he shall find
Th' unkindest beast more kinder than mankind.
The gods confound—hear me, you good gods all—
Th' Athenians both within and out that wall!
And grant, as Timon grows, his hate may grow
To the whole race of mankind, high and low!
Amen. *Exit.*

✤

4.2 *Enter steward* [*Flavius*], *with two or three Servants.*

FIRST SERVANT
Hear you, Master Steward, where's our master?
Are we undone, cast off, nothing remaining?
FLAVIUS
Alack, my fellows, what should I say to you?
Let me be recorded by the righteous gods, 4
I am as poor as you.
FIRST SERVANT Such a house broke?
So noble a master fall'n? All gone, and not
One friend to take his fortune by the arm 7
And go along with him?
SECOND SERVANT As we do turn our backs
From our companion thrown into his grave,

27 stream current **28 blains** blisters **29 Sow** fall like seed in
31 society associating with one another **32 merely** entirely **34 bans** curses

4.2. Location: Athens. Timon's house.
4 be recorded by say in the hearing of **7 his fortune** i.e., Timon in his misfortune

So his familiars to his buried fortunes 11
Slink all away, leave their false vows with him
Like empty purses picked; and his poor self,
A dedicated beggar to the air, 14
With his disease of all-shunned poverty,
Walks, like contempt, alone. More of our fellows. 16

Enter other Servants.

FLAVIUS
All broken implements of a ruined house.

THIRD SERVANT
Yet do our hearts wear Timon's livery; 18
That see I by our faces. We are fellows still,
Serving alike in sorrow. Leaked is our bark, 20
And we, poor mates, stand on the dying deck, 21
Hearing the surges threat. We must all part 22
Into this sea of air.

FLAVIUS Good fellows all,
The latest of my wealth I'll share amongst you. 24
Wherever we shall meet, for Timon's sake,
Let's yet be fellows. Let's shake our heads and say, 26
As 'twere a knell unto our master's fortunes, 27
"We have seen better days." Let each take some.
[*He gives them money.*]
Nay, put out all your hands. Not one word more. 29
Thus part we rich in sorrow, parting poor.
[*Servants*] *embrace, and part several ways.*
O, the fierce wretchedness that glory brings us!
Who would not wish to be from wealth exempt,
Since riches point to misery and contempt? 33
Who would be so mocked with glory, or to live
But in a dream of friendship,
To have his pomp and all what state compounds 36

11 his familiars . . . fortunes those close to him when he was fortunate, now perceiving his ruin **14 dedicated . . . air** beggar having nothing and nowhere to go **16 like contempt** as if he were contemptibility itself **18 livery** uniform worn by male household servants (here used metaphorically) **20 bark** sailing vessel **21 mates** (1) fellows (2) mates of a vessel. **dying** i.e., sinking **22 surges** waves **24 latest** last remnant **26 yet** still. **shake our heads** (in sorrow) **27 knell** tolling of a bell, announcing a death or other misfortune **29 put out all** all put out **33 point to** tend to **36 what state compounds** that which constitutes dignity and splendor

But only painted, like his varnished friends? 37
Poor honest lord, brought low by his own heart,
Undone by goodness! Strange, unusual blood, 39
When man's worst sin is he does too much good!
Who then dares to be half so kind again?
For bounty, that makes gods, do still mar men. 42
My dearest lord, blest to be most accurst, 43
Rich only to be wretched, thy great fortunes
Are made thy chief afflictions. Alas, kind lord!
He's flung in rage from this ingrateful seat
Of monstrous friends,
Nor has he with him to supply his life, 48
Or that which can command it. 49
I'll follow and inquire him out.
I'll ever serve his mind with my best will; 51
Whilst I have gold, I'll be his steward still. *Exit.*

✣

4.3 *Enter Timon, in the woods* [*with a spade*].

TIMON
O blessèd breeding sun, draw from the earth
Rotten humidity; below thy sister's orb 2
Infect the air! Twinned brothers of one womb,
Whose procreation, residence, and birth
Scarce is dividant, touch them with several fortunes, 5
The greater scorns the lesser. Not nature, 6
To whom all sores lay siege, can bear great fortune 7
But by contempt of nature. 8
Raise me this beggar, and deny 't that lord; 9

37 But only nothing more than **39 blood** nature **42 bounty** generosity **43 to be** only to be **48 Nor . . . life** nor has he anything to maintain himself with **49 that . . . it** i.e., money **51 serve his mind** execute his wishes

4.3. Location: Woods and cave, near the seashore; in front of Timon's cave.

2 Rotten humidity rot-causing damp. **thy sister's** i.e., the moon's
5 dividant separate, divisible. **touch** if you test. **several** different
6 The and the result is that the **6–8 Not . . . nature** i.e., human nature, which suffers so many afflictions, cannot experience good fortune without scorning fellow creatures who are less fortunate **9 Raise me** raise. (*Me* is a colloquial usage meaning something like "believe me.")

The senator shall bear contempt hereditary, 10
The beggar native honor. 11
It is the pasture lards the brother's sides, 12
The want that makes him lean. Who dares, who dares 13
In purity of manhood stand upright
And say "This man's a flatterer"? If one be,
So are they all, for every grece of fortune 16
Is smoothed by that below. The learnèd pate 17
Ducks to the golden fool. All's obliquy; 18
There's nothing level in our cursèd natures 19
But direct villainy. Therefore, be abhorred
All feasts, societies, and throngs of men!
His semblable, yea, himself, Timon disdains. 22
Destruction fang mankind! Earth, yield me roots! 23
[*He digs.*]
Who seeks for better of thee, sauce his palate 24
With thy most operant poison! [*He finds gold.*] What
is here? 25
Gold? Yellow, glittering, precious gold?
No, gods, I am no idle votarist. 27
Roots, you clear heavens! Thus much of this will make 28
Black white, foul fair, wrong right,
Base noble, old young, coward valiant.
Ha, you gods! Why this? What this, you gods? Why, this
Will lug your priests and servants from your sides,
Pluck stout men's pillows from below their heads. 33
This yellow slave
Will knit and break religions, bless th' accurst, 35

10 bear contempt hereditary receive contempt as though he were born low **11 native honor** (will receive) honor as though born great **12–13 It is . . . lean** i.e., it is the inheritance and possessing of pasture that makes one brother fat, the lack (want) that makes him, the younger brother, lean. (The Folio reads *leave* for *lean,* which could mean that the younger brother has to leave in search of riches elsewhere.) **lards** that fattens. **want** lack (of good pasture) **16 grece** step **17 smoothed** assiduously prepared. **pate** head **18 Ducks** bows obsequiously. **golden** rich. **All's obliquy** i.e., all's deviating from the right **19 level** direct. (The contrary to *obliquy.*) **22 His semblable** i.e., his own kind, his own image **23 fang** seize **24 sauce** stimulate, tickle **25 operant** active, potent **27 no idle votarist** no trifler in my vows (of leading a spare existence) **28 clear** pure **33 Pluck . . . heads** i.e., expedite the death of healthy men by pulling the pillows from beneath their heads as they sleep (supposedly a way of throttling them) **35 knit . . . religions** knit men together in religious harmony and then break that harmony apart

Make the hoar leprosy adored, place thieves 36
And give them title, knee, and approbation 37
With senators on the bench. This is it
That makes the wappened widow wed again; 39
She whom the spital house and ulcerous sores 40
Would cast the gorge at, this embalms and spices 41
To th' April day again. Come, damnèd earth, 42
Thou common whore of mankind, that puts odds 43
Among the rout of nations, I will make thee 44
Do thy right nature. (*March afar off.*) Ha? A drum?
Thou'rt quick, 45
But yet I'll bury thee. Thou'lt go, strong thief, 46
When gouty keepers of thee cannot stand.
[*He buries the gold.*]
Nay, stay thou out for earnest. [*He keeps some gold.*] 48

Enter Alcibiades, with drum and fife, in warlike manner, and Phrynia and Timandra.

ALCIBIADES What art thou there? Speak.

TIMON
A beast, as thou art. The canker gnaw thy heart
For showing me again the eyes of man!

ALCIBIADES
What is thy name? Is man so hateful to thee
That art thyself a man?

TIMON
I am Misanthropos and hate mankind. 54
For thy part, I do wish thou wert a dog, 55
That I might love thee something.

ALCIBIADES I know thee well, 56
But in thy fortunes am unlearned and strange. 57

36 hoar white-skinned. **place** give recognized status and high office to **37 knee** the bended deferential knee **39 makes** enables. **wappened** worn out **40 spital house** house for the diseased (cf. hospital) **41 cast the gorge** vomit **41–42 this . . . again** i.e., money enables the diseased old woman to embalm herself with cosmetics to look April-like and marriageable **42 damnèd earth** i.e., gold **43–44 puts . . . nations** causes strife among various peoples **45 Do . . . nature** i.e., cause strife, according to your true nature. **quick** (1) swift to act (2) alive **46 go** be able to walk **48 for earnest** as an installment or pledge **s.d. drum and fife** i.e., soldiers playing drum and fife **54 Misanthropos** hater of mankind **55 For thy part** as for you **56 something** somewhat, a little **57 unlearned and strange** uninformed and ignorant

TIMON
I know thee too; and more than that I know thee
I not desire to know. Follow thy drum; 59
With man's blood paint the ground gules, gules. 60
Religious canons, civil laws, are cruel; 61
Then what should war be? This fell whore of thine 62
Hath in her more destruction than thy sword,
For all her cherubin look.

PHRYNIA Thy lips rot off! 64

TIMON
I will not kiss thee; then the rot returns
To thine own lips again.

ALCIBIADES
How came the noble Timon to this change?

TIMON
As the moon does, by wanting light to give. 68
But then renew I could not, like the moon; 69
There were no suns to borrow of. 70

ALCIBIADES Noble Timon, what friendship may I do thee?

TIMON None, but to maintain my opinion.

ALCIBIADES What is it, Timon?

TIMON Promise me friendship, but perform none. If 74
thou wilt not promise, the gods plague thee, for thou 75
art a man! If thou dost perform, confound thee, for 76
thou art a man! 77

ALCIBIADES
I have heard in some sort of thy miseries. 78

TIMON
Thou sawst them when I had prosperity.

ALCIBIADES
I see them now. Then was a blessèd time.

TIMON
As thine is now, held with a brace of harlots. 81

59 not desire do not desire **60 gules** (Heraldic name for "red.") **61 canons** rules, laws **62 fell** deadly **64 cherubin** angelic. **Thy lips** may thy lips **68 wanting** lacking **69 renew** become new again (with a quibble on the idea of renewing a loan) **70 suns** (punning on *sons*, i.e., men) **74–77 If . . . a man** i.e., may the gods plague you for being a man whether you perform your promises or don't even make promises **78 I . . . sort** i.e., I have heard something **81 brace** pair (with a quibble on the meaning "clamp," one that holds Alcibiades in its grip)

TIMANDRA
Is this th' Athenian minion whom the world 82
Voiced so regardfully?
TIMON Art thou Timandra?
TIMANDRA Yes. 83
TIMON
Be a whore still. They love thee not that use thee;
Give them diseases, leaving with thee their lust. 85
Make use of thy salt hours. Season the slaves 86
For tubs and baths; bring down rose-cheeked youth 87
To the tub-fast and the diet.
TIMANDRA Hang thee, monster!
ALCIBIADES
Pardon him, sweet Timandra, for his wits
Are drowned and lost in his calamities.—
I have but little gold of late, brave Timon,
The want whereof doth daily make revolt 92
In my penurious band. I have heard and grieved 93
How cursèd Athens, mindless of thy worth,
Forgetting thy great deeds, when neighbor states,
But for thy sword and fortune, trod upon them— 96
TIMON
I prithee, beat thy drum and get thee gone.
ALCIBIADES
I am thy friend and pity thee, dear Timon.
TIMON
How dost thou pity him whom thou dost trouble?
I had rather be alone.
ALCIBIADES
Why, fare thee well. Here is some gold for thee.
[*He offers gold.*]
TIMON Keep it. I cannot eat it.

82 Athenian minion darling of Athens **83 Voiced** spoke of. **regardfully** respectfully **85 leaving** while they are leaving **86 salt** lecherous. **Season the slaves** i.e., pickle and spice the villains as if preparing them for the pickling tub; make them ready **87 tubs and baths** (Allusion to the treatments for venereal diseases, as also in *tub-fast* and *diet* in the next line.) **92 want** lack. **make revolt** provoke mutiny **93 penurious** poverty-stricken **96 But . . . fortune** (A suggestion of Timon's history as a great military leader, for which Athens ought to be grateful.) **trod** would have trod

ALCIBIADES
When I have laid proud Athens on a heap—
TIMON
Warr'st thou 'gainst Athens?
ALCIBIADES Ay, Timon, and have cause.
TIMON
The gods confound them all in thy conquest, 105
And thee after, when thou hast conquered!
ALCIBIADES Why me, Timon?
TIMON That by killing of villains 108
Thou wast born to conquer my country. 109
Put up thy gold. Go on—here's gold—go on. 110
[*He offers gold*.]
Be as a planetary plague, when Jove 111
Will o'er some high-viced city hang his poison 112
In the sick air. Let not thy sword skip one.
Pity not honored age for his white beard;
He is an usurer. Strike me the counterfeit matron; 115
It is her habit only that is honest, 116
Herself's a bawd. Let not the virgin's cheek
Make soft thy trenchant sword; for those milk paps, 118
That through the window bars bore at men's eyes, 119
Are not within the leaf of pity writ, 120
But set them down horrible traitors. Spare not the babe, 121
Whose dimpled smiles from fools exhaust their mercy; 122
Think it a bastard, whom the oracle
Hath doubtfully pronounced thy throat shall cut, 124
And mince it sans remorse. Swear against objects; 125
Put armor on thine ears and on thine eyes,

105 confound destroy **108–109 That . . . country** (Timon evidently applauds the deed but not the doer. His words are obscure and the text may be corrupt.) **110 Put up** put away **111 planetary plague** (Allusion to the belief in the malignant influence of planets.) **112 high-viced** extremely vicious **115 Strike me** i.e., strike. **counterfeit** pretending respectability **116 habit** costume, outward appearance. **honest** chaste **118 trenchant** sharp. **milk paps** nipples **119 window bars** i.e., latticework of her bodice (?) **120 Are . . . writ** i.e., are not written down on the list of those to whom pity is to be shown **121 traitors** i.e., betrayers of men **122 exhaust** draw forth **124 doubtfully** ambiguously. **thy . . . cut** will cut your throat. (However, the phrase can also be ambiguously reversed.) **125 mince** slash, cut in small pieces. **sans** without. **Swear against objects** bind yourself by oath against objections (to your cruelty)

Whose proof nor yells of mothers, maids, nor babes, 127
Nor sight of priests in holy vestments bleeding,
Shall pierce a jot. There's gold to pay thy soldiers.
Make large confusion; and, thy fury spent, 130
Confounded be thyself! Speak not, begone.

ALCIBIADES
Hast thou gold yet? I'll take the gold thou givest me,
Not all thy counsel. [*He takes gold.*]

TIMON
Dost thou or dost thou not, heaven's curse upon thee! 134

PHRYNIA AND TIMANDRA
Give us some gold, good Timon. Hast thou more?

TIMON
Enough to make a whore forswear her trade,
And to make whores, a bawd. Hold up, you sluts, 137
Your aprons mountant. [*He throws gold into their aprons.*] You are not oathable, 138
Although I know you'll swear—terribly swear
Into strong shudders and to heavenly agues— 140
Th' immortal gods that hear you. Spare your oaths;
I'll trust to your conditions. Be whores still; 142
And he whose pious breath seeks to convert you,
Be strong in whore, allure him, burn him up. 144
Let your close fire predominate his smoke, 145
And be no turncoats. Yet may your pains six months 146
Be quite contrary. And thatch your poor thin roofs 147
With burdens of the dead—some that were hanged, 148
No matter; wear them, betray with them. Whore still; 149

127 Whose proof the tested strength of which armor. **nor yells** neither the yells **130 large confusion** wholesale destruction **134 Dost . . . not** whether you do or not **137 to . . . bawd** i.e., to make a bawd retire from turning women into whores **138 mountant** (A heraldic coinage, with sexual suggestion; see also *erection* in l. 166.) **oathable** to be believed on your oath **140 strong** violent. **agues** feverish shivers **142 your conditions** what you are, your characters **144 Be . . . whore** be resolute in whoring. **burn him up** (1) inflame him with desire (2) infect him with venereal disease **145 Let . . . smoke** i.e., let your secret and disease-carrying passion overcome his pious professions **146–147 Yet . . . contrary** i.e., may you suffer intense pain for six months (?) (Perhaps *six months* is simply an arbitrary figure, or alludes to the early symptoms of syphilis.) **147–148 thatch . . . dead** i.e., cover your balding heads (caused by venereal disease) with wigs made of the hair of corpses **149 betray with them** i.e., use these wigs to create false beauty to betray more men

Paint till a horse may mire upon your face. 150
A pox of wrinkles!

PHRYNIA AND TIMANDRA Well, more gold. What then? 151
Believe 't that we'll do anything for gold.

TIMON Consumptions sow 153
In hollow bones of man; strike their sharp shins,
And mar men's spurring. Crack the lawyer's voice, 155
That he may nevermore false title plead,
Nor sound his quillets shrilly. Hoar the flamen, 157
That scolds against the quality of flesh 158
And not believes himself. Down with the nose, 159
Down with it flat; take the bridge quite away
Of him that, his particular to foresee, 161
Smells from the general weal. Make curled-pate
ruffians bald, 162
And let the unscarred braggarts of the war
Derive some pain from you. Plague all,
That your activity may defeat and quell
The source of all erection. There's more gold. 166
[*He gives gold.*]
Do you damn others and let this damn you,
And ditches grave you all! 168

PHRYNIA AND TIMANDRA
More counsel with more money, bounteous Timon.

TIMON
More whore, more mischief first. I have given you
earnest. 170

150 mire upon bog down in. (Timon sardonically urges so thick a cosmetic covering that even a horse would become mired.) **151 A pox of wrinkles** i.e., may you be plagued with wrinkles **153 Consumptions sow** plant wasting diseases such as syphilis. (Addressed to Phrynia and Timandra.) **155 spurring** i.e., riding (here used as a sexual metaphor) **157 quillets** quibbles. **Hoar the flamen** whiten (with leprosy) the priest (with a pun on *hoar, whore*) **158 quality of flesh** fleshly desire **159 And . . . himself** i.e., and doesn't practice what he preaches. **Down . . . nose** (An effect of syphilis.) **161 his . . . foresee** in order to look out for his own interests **162 Smells . . . weal** (1) loses the scent of the common good (2) stinks above the common crowd. **curled-pate** curly-headed **166 erection** advancement (with bawdy pun) **168 grave** enclose in the grave (with a pun on "ditches" and "damming" continued from l. 167) **170 whore** whoring. **mischief** destruction. **earnest** earnest money, token payment

ALCIBIADES
Strike up the drum towards Athens. Farewell, Timon.
If I thrive well, I'll visit thee again.
TIMON
If I hope well, I'll never see thee more. 173
ALCIBIADES I never did thee harm.
TIMON
Yes, thou spok'st well of me.
ALCIBIADES Call'st thou that harm?
TIMON
Men daily find it. Get thee away and take 176
Thy beagles with thee.
ALCIBIADES We but offend him. Strike! 177
[*Drum beats.*] *Exeunt* [*Alcibiades, Phrynia, and Timandra*].
TIMON
That nature, being sick of man's unkindness, 178
Should yet be hungry! [*He digs.*] Common mother, thou 179
Whose womb unmeasurable and infinite breast
Teems and feeds all, whose selfsame mettle 181
Whereof thy proud child, arrogant man, is puffed 182
Engenders the black toad and adder blue,
The gilded newt and eyeless venomed worm, 184
With all th' abhorrèd births below crisp heaven
Whereon Hyperion's quickening fire doth shine: 186
Yield him who all thy human sons do hate, 187
From forth thy plenteous bosom, one poor root!
Ensear thy fertile and conceptious womb; 189
Let it no more bring out ingrateful man!
Go great with tigers, dragons, wolves, and bears; 191
Teem with new monsters, whom thy upward face 192

173 If I hope well if my hopes are realized **176 find it** i.e., find it harmful to be spoken well of **177 beagles** i.e., beagle hounds, fawning followers—the prostitutes **178 That** to think that. **sick of** sickened by, surfeited with **179 Common mother** i.e., the earth **181 Teems** abundantly bears offspring. **mettle** spirit, essence (with a pun on *metal;* the words were virtually interchangeable) **182 Whereof** with which **184 eyeless venomed worm** the blindworm (wrongly supposed poisonous) **186 Hyperion's** i.e., the sun's. **quickening** life-giving **187 who . . . hate** who hates all your human offspring **189 Ensear** dry up. **conceptious** fertile **191 Go great** be pregnant **192 upward** upturned

Hath to the marbled mansion all above 193
Never presented! [*He finds a root.*] O, a root! Dear thanks!—
Dry up thy marrows, vines, and plow-torn leas, 195
Whereof ingrateful man with liquorish drafts 196
And morsels unctuous greases his pure mind, 197
That from it all consideration slips— 198

Enter Apemantus.

More man? Plague, plague!

APEMANTUS
I was directed hither. Men report
Thou dost affect my manners and dost use them. 201

TIMON
'Tis, then, because thou dost not keep a dog,
Whom I would imitate. Consumption catch thee! 203

APEMANTUS
This is in thee a nature but infected, 204
A poor unmanly melancholy sprung
From change of fortune. Why this spade? This place?
This slavelike habit and these looks of care? 207
Thy flatterers yet wear silk, drink wine, lie soft,
Hug their diseased perfumes, and have forgot 209
That ever Timon was. Shame not these woods
By putting on the cunning of a carper. 211
Be thou a flatterer now and seek to thrive
By that which has undone thee. Hinge thy knee
And let his very breath whom thou'lt observe 214
Blow off thy cap. Praise his most vicious strain 215
And call it excellent. Thou wast told thus. 216

193 the marbled . . . above i.e., the heavens **195 marrows** i.e., marrow in the earth's bones, denoting her fecundity. **plow-torn leas** plowed-up pastureland **196 liquorish drafts** sweet, alcoholic drinks **197 unctuous** fatty, oily. **greases his pure mind** makes greasy and vile his once-pure mind **198 That** so that. **consideration** reflection, rationality; regard for others, or for other things than sensual **201 affect** put on **203 would** i.e., would in that case. **Consumption catch thee** may a wasting illness lay hold on you **204 but infected** i.e., not inborn and philosophical but induced by misery and hence shallow **207 habit** garment **209 perfumes** perfumed mistresses **211 putting . . . carper** assuming the manner and profession of a Cynic **214 observe** bow obsequiously before **215 strain** quality **216 Thou . . . thus** i.e., you were spoken to flatteringly in exactly this manner

Thou gav'st thine ears, like tapsters that bade welcome, 217
To knaves and all approachers. 'Tis most just
That thou turn rascal; hadst thou wealth again,
Rascals should have 't. Do not assume my likeness.

TIMON
Were I like thee, I'd throw away myself.

APEMANTUS
Thou hast cast away thyself, being like thyself—
A madman so long, now a fool. What, think'st 223
That the bleak air, thy boisterous chamberlain, 224
Will put thy shirt on warm? Will these mossed trees, 225
That have outlived the eagle, page thy heels 226
And skip when thou point'st out? Will the cold brook, 227
Candied with ice, caudle thy morning taste 228
To cure thy o'ernight's surfeit? Call the creatures
Whose naked natures live in all the spite 230
Of wreakful heaven, whose bare unhousèd trunks, 231
To the conflicting elements exposed,
Answer mere nature; bid them flatter thee. 233
O, thou shalt find—

TIMON A fool of thee. Depart. 234

APEMANTUS
I love thee better now than e'er I did.

TIMON
I hate thee worse.

APEMANTUS Why?

TIMON Thou flatter'st misery.

APEMANTUS
I flatter not, but say thou art a caitiff. 237

TIMON Why dost thou seek me out?

APEMANTUS To vex thee.

TIMON
Always a villain's office or a fool's.
Dost please thyself in 't?

217 ears i.e., attention. **like . . . welcome** i.e., like barkeeps who welcome all comers indiscriminately **223–225 think'st . . . warm** (Alludes to the practice of having a servant warm one's garment by the fire.) **226 page thy heels** i.e., follow you obediently **227 skip . . . out** jump to fulfill your command **228 Candied** crystalline. **caudle . . . taste** i.e., provide you with a caudle, a hot spiced drink **230 in** exposed to **231 wreakful** vengeful. **trunks** i.e., bodies **233 Answer** cope with, contend with. **mere** stark, unrelieved **234 of** in **237 caitiff** wretch

APEMANTUS Ay.

TIMON What, a knave too? 241

APEMANTUS

If thou didst put this sour cold habit on 242
To castigate thy pride, 'twere well, but thou 243
Dost it enforcedly. Thou'dst courtier be again
Wert thou not beggar. Willing misery 245
Outlives incertain pomp, is crowned before: 246
The one is filling still, never complete, 247
The other at high wish. Best state, contentless, 248
Hath a distracted and most wretched being, 249
Worse than the worst, content. 250
Thou shouldst desire to die, being miserable.

TIMON

Not by his breath that is more miserable. 252
Thou art a slave whom Fortune's tender arm
With favor never clasped but bred a dog. 254
Hadst thou, like us from our first swathe, proceeded 255
The sweet degrees that this brief world affords
To such as may the passive drudges of it 257
Freely command, thou wouldst have plunged thyself 258
In general riot, melted down thy youth 259
In different beds of lust, and never learned 260
The icy precepts of respect, but followed
The sugared game before thee. But myself— 262
Who had the world as my confectionary, 263

241 a knave too i.e., a fool and a villain to boot (since it is villainous to take pleasure in vexing others) **242 habit** disposition **243 'twere well** it would be a commendable thing **245–246 Willing . . . before** deliberately chosen poverty outlasts the life of insecure ceremony and wealth, and is sooner crowned with spiritual reward **247 The one** i.e., incertain pomp. **is filling still** is never satisfied **248 at high wish** at the height of contentment **248–250 Best . . . content** being at the height of prosperity without contentment means a wretched existence, worse than being at the bottom of prosperity with contentment **252 Not . . . miserable** i.e., not when he who speaks (Apemantus) is more to be pitied than I **254 but bred** i.e., but whom Fortune bred **255 swathe** swaddling clothes. **proceeded** passed through (like a student taking an academic degree) **257–258 To such . . . command** i.e., to those who have the world and its sycophants at command **259 riot** debauchery
260 different various **262 sugared game** sweet-tasting quarry **263 my confectionary** maker of sweetmeats just for me; a place where such sweetmeats are stored

The mouths, the tongues, the eyes, and hearts of men
At duty, more than I could frame employment, 265
That numberless upon me stuck, as leaves 266
Do on the oak, have with one winter's brush 267
Fell from their boughs and left me open, bare 268
For every storm that blows—I to bear this, 269
That never knew but better, is some burden. 270
Thy nature did commence in sufferance; time 271
Hath made thee hard in 't. Why shouldst thou hate men? 272
They never flattered thee. What hast thou given?
If thou wilt curse, thy father, that poor rag, 274
Must be thy subject, who in spite put stuff 275
To some she-beggar and compounded thee 276
Poor rogue hereditary. Hence, begone! 277
If thou hadst not been born the worst of men, 278
Thou hadst been a knave and flatterer.

APEMANTUS
Art thou proud yet?

TIMON Ay, that I am not thee. 280

APEMANTUS I, that I was no prodigal.

TIMON I, that I am one now.
Were all the wealth I have shut up in thee, 283
I'd give thee leave to hang it. Get thee gone. 284
That the whole life of Athens were in this! 285
Thus would I eat it. [*He eats a root.*]

APEMANTUS [*Offering food*] Here, I will mend thy feast.

TIMON
First mend my company: take away thyself.

APEMANTUS
So I shall mend mine own by th' lack of thine.

TIMON
'Tis not well mended so; it is but botched. 289

265 At duty subservient to my wishes. **frame** provide with **266 stuck** having stuck **267 winter's brush** gust of wintry wind **268 Fell** fallen. **open** exposed **269 I . . . this** that I should bear this **270 That . . . better** who have known only better fortune **271 sufferance** suffering, poverty **272 hard in 't** hardened to it **274 rag** i.e., wretch **275 in spite** out of malice **275–276 put stuff To** fornicated with **276 compounded** begot **277 hereditary** by right of inheritance **278 worst** lowest in station **280 yet** still **283 shut up** contained **284 hang it** i.e., hang yourself **285 That** I wish that **289 botched** badly mended (since you remain in your own company)

If not, I would it were. 290

APEMANTUS What wouldst thou have to Athens? 291

TIMON

Thee thither in a whirlwind. If thou wilt,
Tell them there I have gold. Look, so I have.

[*He shows his gold.*]

APEMANTUS

Here is no use for gold.

TIMON The best and truest,
For here it sleeps and does no hirèd harm.

APEMANTUS Where liest anights, Timon? 296

TIMON Under that's above me. Where feed'st thou 297
adays, Apemantus? 298

APEMANTUS Where my stomach finds meat; or, rather, where I eat it.

TIMON Would poison were obedient and knew my mind!

APEMANTUS Where wouldst thou send it?

TIMON To sauce thy dishes. 304

APEMANTUS The middle of humanity thou never knewest, but the extremity of both ends. When thou wast
in thy gilt and thy perfume, they mocked thee for too 307
much curiosity; in thy rags thou know'st none, but art 308
despised for the contrary. There's a medlar for thee. 309
Eat it. [*He gives a fruit.*]

TIMON On what I hate I feed not.

APEMANTUS Dost hate a medlar?

TIMON Ay, though it look like thee. 313

APEMANTUS An thou'dst hated meddlers sooner, thou 314
shouldst have loved thyself better now. What man
didst thou ever know unthrift that was beloved after 316
his means? 317

290 If . . . were i.e., even if you don't think things are made worse by having yourself for a companion, I wish you did (since I'd prefer to see you unhappy); or, even if it's only a botched job, I'd still prefer to see you get away from here (?) **291 What . . . have** what would you have me convey. (But Timon caustically jests in a more literal sense of the phrase.) **296 anights** at night **297 that's** that which is **298 adays** by day **304 sauce** flavor **307 gilt** fine trappings **308 curiosity** fastidiousness, refinement **309 medlar** fruit like a small brown-skinned apple, eaten when nearly decayed; used here, as often, for the sake of a quibble on *meddler,* with sexual suggestion **313 like thee** i.e., in a state of decay, or as one who meddles **314 An thou'dst** if thou hadst **316 unthrift** to be unthrifty **316–317 after his means** (1) after his wealth was gone (2) according to his means

TIMON Who, without those means thou talk'st of, didst thou ever know beloved?
APEMANTUS Myself.
TIMON I understand thee: thou hadst some means to 321 keep a dog. 322
APEMANTUS What things in the world canst thou nearest compare to thy flatterers?
TIMON Women nearest. But men—men are the things themselves. What wouldst thou do with the world, Apemantus, if it lay in thy power?
APEMANTUS Give it the beasts, to be rid of the men.
TIMON Wouldst thou have thyself fall in the confusion 329 of men and remain a beast with the beasts? 330
APEMANTUS Ay, Timon.
TIMON A beastly ambition, which the gods grant thee t' attain to! If thou wert the lion, the fox would beguile thee. If thou wert the lamb, the fox would eat thee. If thou wert the fox, the lion would suspect thee when peradventure thou wert accused by the ass. If thou 336 wert the ass, thy dullness would torment thee, and still thou livedst but as a breakfast to the wolf. If thou wert 338 the wolf, thy greediness would afflict thee, and oft thou shouldst hazard thy life for thy dinner. Wert thou the unicorn, pride and wrath would confound thee 341 and make thine own self the conquest of thy fury. Wert thou a bear, thou wouldst be killed by the horse. Wert thou a horse, thou wouldst be seized by the leopard. Wert thou a leopard, thou wert germane to the lion, 345 and the spots of thy kindred were jurors on thy life; all 346 thy safety were remotion and thy defense absence. 347 What beast couldst thou be that were not subject to a

321–322 thou . . . dog i.e., even in your poverty you were able to keep a dog, and it loved you (since all creatures love only in return for favors) **329–330 in . . . men** i.e., in the destruction of mankind you've just wished for **336 peradventure** by chance **338 livedst** wouldst live **341 unicorn** (A legendary creature, supposedly caught by being goaded into charging a tree and embedding its horn in the tree trunk.) **345 germane** akin, related **346 the spots . . . life** i.e., the crimes of those closely related to you would bring down a sentence of death upon you (with a pun on *spots* meaning "leopard's spots" and "stains, crimes") **346–347 all . . . remotion** your only safety would consist in your constantly going from place to place

beast? And what a beast art thou already, that seest
not thy loss in transformation! 350

APEMANTUS If thou couldst please me with speaking to 351
me, thou mightst have hit upon it here. The common- 352
wealth of Athens is become a forest of beasts.

TIMON How, has the ass broke the wall, that thou art 354
out of the city?

APEMANTUS Yonder comes a poet and a painter. The 356
plague of company light upon thee! I will fear to catch
it, and give way. When I know not what else to do, I'll 358
see thee again.

TIMON When there is nothing living but thee, thou
shalt be welcome. I had rather be a beggar's dog than
Apemantus.

APEMANTUS
Thou art the cap of all the fools alive. 363

TIMON
Would thou wert clean enough to spit upon!

APEMANTUS
A plague on thee! Thou art too bad to curse.

TIMON
All villains that do stand by thee are pure. 366

APEMANTUS
There is no leprosy but what thou speak'st.

TIMON If I name thee.
I'll beat thee, but I should infect my hands. 369

APEMANTUS
I would my tongue could rot them off!

TIMON
Away, thou issue of a mangy dog! 371
Choler does kill me that thou art alive;
I swoon to see thee.

APEMANTUS
Would thou wouldst burst!

350 in transformation in being changed into a beast · **351–352 If . . . here** if it were possible for anything you say to please me, what you've just said (comparing men with beasts) would be pleasing **354 How** what is this **356 Yonder . . . painter** (In fact, they do not appear until 5.1; this line may give evidence of an incompletely revised manuscript.) **358 give way** (I will) leave **363 cap** acme, summit **366 by** compared to **369 I'll** I would **371 issue** offspring

TIMON Away, thou tedious rogue!
I am sorry I shall lose a stone by thee.
[*He throws a stone at Apemantus.*]
APEMANTUS Beast!
TIMON Slave!
APEMANTUS Toad!
TIMON Rogue, rogue, rogue!
I am sick of this false world, and will love naught
But even the mere necessities upon 't. 381
Then, Timon, presently prepare thy grave. 382
Lie where the light foam of the sea may beat
Thy gravestone daily. Make thine epitaph,
That death in me at others' lives may laugh. 385
[*To the gold.*] O thou sweet king-killer and dear divorce
Twixt natural son and sire! Thou bright defiler 387
Of Hymen's purest bed! Thou valiant Mars! 388
Thou ever young, fresh, loved, and delicate wooer,
Whose blush doth thaw the consecrated snow 390
That lies on Dian's lap! Thou visible god, 391
That solderest close impossibilities 392
And mak'st them kiss; that speak'st with every tongue
To every purpose! O thou touch of hearts! 394
Think thy slave, man, rebels, and by thy virtue 395
Set them into confounding odds, that beasts 396
May have the world in empire!
APEMANTUS Would 'twere so!
But not till I am dead. I'll say thou'st gold; 398
Thou wilt be thronged to shortly.
TIMON Thronged to?
APEMANTUS Ay.
TIMON
Thy back, I prithee.
APEMANTUS Live, and love thy misery. 400

381 But even except **382 presently** immediately **385 That** in order that. **in** through **387 natural** i.e., born in the course of nature **388 Hymen** god of marriage. **Mars** i.e., as the adulterous lover of Venus **390 blush** i.e., reddish glow of gold **391 Dian** Diana, goddess of the hunt and patroness of chastity **392 close** tightly together. **impossibilities** things apparently incapable of being united **394 touch** touchstone **395 virtue** power **396 Set . . . odds** set men at self-destroying conflict with one another **398 thou'st** thou hast **400 Thy back** i.e., show me your back

TIMON
Long live so, and so die! I am quit. 401

APEMANTUS
More things like men! Eat, Timon, and abhor them. 402
Exit Apemantus.

Enter the Banditti.

FIRST BANDIT Where should he have this gold? It is 403
some poor fragment, some slender ort of his remain- 404
der. The mere want of gold and the falling-from of his 405
friends drove him into this melancholy.

SECOND BANDIT It is noised he hath a mass of treasure. 407

THIRD BANDIT Let us make the assay upon him. If he 408
care not for 't, he will supply us easily. If he covetously
reserve it, how shall 's get it? 410

SECOND BANDIT True, for he bears it not about him.
'Tis hid.

FIRST BANDIT Is not this he?

BANDITTI Where?

SECOND BANDIT 'Tis his description.

THIRD BANDIT He. I know him.

BANDITTI Save thee, Timon. 417

TIMON Now, thieves?

BANDITTI
Soldiers, not thieves.

TIMON Both too, and women's sons. 419

BANDITTI
We are not thieves, but men that much do want. 420

TIMON
Your greatest want is, you want much of meat. 421
Why should you want? Behold, the earth hath roots;
Within this mile break forth a hundred springs;
The oaks bear mast, the briers scarlet hips. 424
The bounteous huswife Nature on each bush
Lays her full mess before you. What? Why want? 426

401 quit rid (of Apemantus) **402 them** i.e., the bandits **403 should he have** can he have obtained **404 ort** fragment **405 mere** utter
407 noised rumored **408 assay** trial, test (as one would test gold ore for its content) **410 shall 's** shall we **417 Save** God save **419 Both too** both **420 want** (1) lack (2) desire **421 Your . . . meat** i.e., your greatest deficiency is that you crave such rich food (as Timon goes on to explain)
424 mast acorns. **hips** fruit of the rosebush **426 mess** food, meal

FIRST BANDIT
We cannot live on grass, on berries, water,
As beasts and birds and fishes.

TIMON
Nor on the beasts themselves, the birds and fishes;
You must eat men. Yet thanks I must you con 430
That you are thieves professed, that you work not
In holier shapes; for there is boundless theft
In limited professions. [*He gives gold.*] Rascal thieves, 433
Here's gold. Go, suck the subtle blood o' the grape 434
Till the high fever seethe your blood to froth, 435
And so scape hanging. Trust not the physician; 436
His antidotes are poison, and he slays
More than you rob. Take wealth and lives together. 438
Do villainy, do, since you protest to do 't, 439
Like workmen. I'll example you with thievery. 440
The sun's a thief, and with his great attraction 441
Robs the vast sea. The moon's an arrant thief, 442
And her pale fire she snatches from the sun.
The sea's a thief, whose liquid surge resolves 444
The moon into salt tears. The earth's a thief,
That feeds and breeds by a composture stolen 446
From general excrement. Each thing's a thief.
The laws, your curb and whip, in their rough power
Has unchecked theft. Love not yourselves. Away! 449
Rob one another. There's more gold. Cut throats.
All that you meet are thieves. To Athens go,
Break open shops; nothing can you steal
But thieves do lose it. Steal less for this I give you, 453
And gold confound you howsoe'er! Amen. 454

430 thanks . . . con I must offer you thanks **433 limited** regulated, legal (with a play on *boundless,* l. 432, as the opposite of *limited*) **434 subtle** (1) delicate (2) treacherous in its influence **435 high fever** (induced by intoxication). **seethe** boil **436 scape hanging** i.e., avoid execution by dying of excess drinking, using a natural substance **438 Take . . . together** i.e., murder your robbery victims **439 protest** profess **440 example you with** give you instances of **441 attraction** power to draw up **442 arrant** notorious **444 resolves** melts, dissolves. (Alludes to the belief that the moon draws moisture from the air and deposits it in the sea, thus creating the effect of tides.) **446 composture** compost, manure **449 Has unchecked** provide opportunity for unlimited **453–454 Steal . . . howsoe'er** if you steal less because of my giving you this gold, may gold destroy you no matter what happens

THIRD BANDIT He's almost charmed me from my profession by persuading me to it.

FIRST BANDIT 'Tis in the malice of mankind that he thus advises us, not to have us thrive in our mystery. 457 458

SECOND BANDIT I'll believe him as an enemy, and give over my trade. 459

FIRST BANDIT Let us first see peace in Athens. There is no time so miserable but a man may be true. 461 462

Exeunt Thieves.

Enter the steward [*Flavius*] *to Timon.*

FLAVIUS O you gods!
Is yond despised and ruinous man my lord? 464
Full of decay and failing? O monument 465
And wonder of good deeds evilly bestowed! 466
What an alteration of honor has desp'rate want made!
What viler thing upon the earth than friends,
Who can bring noblest minds to basest ends!
How rarely does it meet with this time's guise, 470
When man was wished to love his enemies! 471
Grant I may ever love, and rather woo
Those that would mischief me than those that do!— 473
He's caught me in his eye. I will present 474
My honest grief unto him, and as my lord
Still serve him with my life.—My dearest master!

TIMON
Away! What art thou?

FLAVIUS Have you forgot me, sir?

TIMON
Why dost ask that? I have forgot all men.
Then, if thou grant'st thou'rt a man, I have forgot thee.

FLAVIUS An honest poor servant of yours.

457 the malice of i.e., his hating of **458 mystery** trade **459 as** as I would **461–462 Let . . . true** i.e., let's not rush into reformation, at least not until there is peace in Athens; besides, there will always be time to repent **464 ruinous** brought to ruin **465 failing** weakness, downfall **465–466 monument . . . wonder** astonishing memorial. **evilly bestowed** wrongly bestowed on the wicked **470–471 How . . . enemies** i.e., how perfectly does the commandment to love one's enemies suit this degenerate age (since one's supposed friends are the ones that do greatest harm) **473 Those . . . do** i.e., those who openly profess themselves to be my enemies rather than those who, professing friendship, actually do the greater harm **474 caught . . . eye** seen me

TIMON Then I know thee not.
I never had honest man about me, I; all
I kept were knaves, to serve in meat to villains. 483
FLAVIUS The gods are witness,
Ne'er did poor steward wear a truer grief
For his undone lord than mine eyes for you.
[*He weeps.*]

TIMON
What, dost thou weep? Come nearer, then. I love thee
Because thou art a woman and disclaim'st
Flinty mankind, whose eyes do never give 489
But thorough lust and laughter. Pity's sleeping. 490
Strange times, that weep with laughing, not with
weeping!

FLAVIUS
I beg of you to know me, good my lord,
T' accept my grief, and whilst this poor wealth lasts
To entertain me as your steward still. 494
[*He offers money.*]

TIMON Had I a steward
So true, so just, and now so comfortable? 496
It almost turns my dangerous nature mild. 497
Let me behold thy face. Surely, this man
Was born of woman.
Forgive my general and exceptless rashness, 500
You perpetual-sober gods! I do proclaim 501
One honest man—mistake me not, but one;
No more, I pray—and he's a steward.
How fain would I have hated all mankind, 504
And thou redeem'st thyself! But all, save thee,
I fell with curses. 506
Methinks thou art more honest now than wise,
For by oppressing and betraying me
Thou mightst have sooner got another service; 509
For many so arrive at second masters
Upon their first lord's neck. But tell me true—
For I must ever doubt, though ne'er so sure—

483 serve in meat serve food **489 Flinty** hardhearted. **give** give forth tears **490 But thorough** except through **494 entertain** receive, employ **496 comfortable** comforting **497 dangerous** savage **500 exceptless** making no exception **501 perpetual-sober** eternally grave and sedate **504 fain** gladly **506 fell** cut down **509 service** position

Is not thy kindness subtle, covetous,
A usuring kindness, and, as rich men deal gifts,
Expecting in return twenty for one?

FLAVIUS
No, my most worthy master, in whose breast
Doubt and suspect, alas, are placed too late. 517
You should have feared false times when you did feast.
Suspect still comes where an estate is least. 519
That which I show, heaven knows, is merely love, 520
Duty, and zeal to your unmatchèd mind,
Care of your food and living; and believe it, 522
My most honored lord,
For any benefit that points to me, 524
Either in hope or present, I'd exchange 525
For this one wish: that you had power and wealth
To requite me by making rich yourself. 527

TIMON
Look thee, 'tis so. Thou singly honest man, 528
Here, take. [*He offers gold.*] The gods out of my misery
Has sent thee treasure. Go, live rich and happy,
But thus conditioned: thou shalt build from men, 531
Hate all, curse all, show charity to none,
But let the famished flesh slide from the bone
Ere thou relieve the beggar. Give to dogs
What thou deniest to men. Let prisons swallow 'em,
Debts wither 'em to nothing. Be men like blasted woods, 536
And may diseases lick up their false bloods!
And so farewell and thrive.

FLAVIUS
O, let me stay
And comfort you, my master.

TIMON
If thou hat'st curses,
Stay not; fly, whilst thou art blest and free.
Ne'er see thou man, and let me ne'er see thee.
Exit [*Flavius; Timon retires to his cave*].

517 suspect suspicion **519 still** always **520 merely** purely **522 Care of** concern for. **living** maintenance **524 For** as for. **points to me** appears in prospect for me **525 in hope** in the future **527 requite** repay **528 singly** (1) uniquely (2) earnestly **531 thus conditioned** upon this condition. **from** away from **536 Be men** let men be. **blasted** withered

5.1

Enter Poet and Painter. [*Timon enters at some point to watch them from his cave.*]

PAINTER As I took note of the place, it cannot be far where he abides.

POET What's to be thought of him? Does the rumor hold for true that he's so full of gold?

PAINTER Certain. Alcibiades reports it. Phrynia and Timandra had gold of him. He likewise enriched poor straggling soldiers with great quantity. 'Tis said he gave unto his steward a mighty sum.

POET Then this breaking of his has been but a try for 9 his friends?

PAINTER Nothing else. You shall see him a palm in Ath- 11 ens again, and flourish with the highest. Therefore 'tis not amiss we tender our loves to him in this supposed 13 distress of his. It will show honestly in us and is very 14 likely to load our purposes with what they travail for, 15 if it be a just and true report that goes of his having. 16

POET What have you now to present unto him?

PAINTER Nothing at this time but my visitation. Only I will promise him an excellent piece.

POET I must serve him so too, tell him of an intent that's 20 coming toward him. 21

PAINTER Good as the best. Promising is the very air o' 22 the time; it opens the eyes of expectation. Performance is ever the duller for his act, and but in the plainer 24 and simpler kind of people the deed of saying is quite 25 out of use. To promise is most courtly and fashionable. 26 Performance is a kind of will or testament which argues a great sickness in his judgment that makes it.

Enter Timon from his cave.

5.1. Location: The woods. Before Timon's cave. The scene is virtually continuous; Timon may well remain visible to the audience.
9 breaking bankruptcy. **try** test **11 a palm** a dignitary (probably referring to Psalm 92:12: "The righteous man shall flourish like a palm") **13 we tender** that we should offer **14 show honestly** appear to be seemly or worthy **15 load our purposes** i.e., crown our efforts. **travail** labor **16 goes of his having** is current about his wealth
20 intent project **21 coming toward** intended for **22 Good as the best** i.e., that's perfect. **air** style **24 for his act** for its being completed. **but in** excepting among **25 deed of saying** actions fulfilling words or promises **26 use** fashion

TIMON [*Aside*] Excellent workman! Thou canst not paint a man so bad as is thyself.

POET I am thinking what I shall say I have provided for 31 him. It must be a personating of himself, a satire 32 against the softness of prosperity, with a discovery of 33 the infinite flatteries that follow youth and opulency.

TIMON [*Aside*] Must thou needs stand for a villain in 35 thine own work? Wilt thou whip thine own faults in other men? Do so, I have gold for thee.

POET Nay, let's seek him.
Then do we sin against our own estate 39
When we may profit meet and come too late.

PAINTER True.
When the day serves, before black-cornered night, 42
Find what thou want'st by free and offered light. 43
Come.

TIMON [*Aside*]
I'll meet you at the turn. What a god's gold, 45
That he is worshiped in a baser temple 46
Than where swine feed!
'Tis thou that rigg'st the bark and plow'st the foam, 48
Settlest admirèd reverence in a slave. 49
To thee be worship, and thy saints for aye 50
Be crowned with plagues, that thee alone obey!
Fit I meet them. [*He comes forward.*] 52

POET Hail, worthy Timon!

PAINTER Our late noble master!

TIMON
Have I once lived to see two honest men? 55

POET Sir,
Having often of your open bounty tasted, 57
Hearing you were retired, your friends fall'n off, 58

31 provided planned **32 personating of himself** i.e., representation of his case **33 discovery** disclosure **35 needs** necessarily. **stand for** serve as a model for **39 estate** worldly well-being **42 black-cornered night** night which darkens as in corners **43 free and offered light** the light of day, freely offered to all **45 at the turn** i.e., trick for trick in a cheating game **46 a baser temple** i.e., the human body **48 rigg'st the bark** sets the ship's sail **49 admirèd . . . slave** wondering awe in a slave for his master **50 thy saints** may your saints. **aye** ever **52 Fit** it is fit that **55 once** actually **57 open** generous **58 were retired** had withdrawn. **fall'n off** estranged

Whose thankless natures—O abhorrèd spirits!
Not all the whips of heaven are large enough—
What, to you,
Whose starlike nobleness gave life and influence 62
To their whole being? I am rapt, and cannot cover 63
The monstrous bulk of this ingratitude
With any size of words.

TIMON
Let it go naked; men may see 't the better.
You that are honest, by being what you are
Make them best seen and known.

PAINTER He and myself 68
Have traveled in the great show'r of your gifts 69
And sweetly felt it.

TIMON Ay, you are honest men.

PAINTER
We are hither come to offer you our service.

TIMON
Most honest men! Why, how shall I requite you? 72
Can you eat roots and drink cold water? No.

BOTH
What we can do we'll do to do you service.

TIMON
You're honest men. You've heard that I have gold;
I am sure you have. Speak truth; you're honest men.

PAINTER
So it is said, my noble lord, but therefor 77
Came not my friend nor I.

TIMON
Good honest men! [*To the Painter*.] Thou draw'st a counterfeit 79
Best in all Athens. Thou'rt indeed the best;
Thou counterfeit'st most lively.

PAINTER So-so, my lord. 81

62 Whose . . . influence i.e., whose nobility of character was of such power as to influence men's destinies. (An astrological metaphor.) **63 rapt** i.e., overwhelmed **68 them** i.e., the ungrateful men you condemn, or ungrateful acts **69 traveled** walked (with a suggestion also of "worked, travailed," as one would labor for a patron) **72 requite** repay **77 therefor** for that reason **79 counterfeit** picture, likeness (with quibble on the idea of "fraudulence") **81 So-so** passably

TIMON
E'en so, sir, as I say. [*To the Poet.*] And for thy fiction, 82
Why, thy verse swells with stuff so fine and smooth 83
That thou art even natural in thine art. 84
But for all this, my honest-natured friends,
I must needs say you have a little fault.
Marry, 'tis not monstrous in you, neither wish I 87
You take much pains to mend.

BOTH Beseech your honor 88
To make it known to us.

TIMON You'll take it ill.

BOTH Most thankfully, my lord.

TIMON Will you, indeed?

BOTH Doubt it not, worthy lord.

TIMON
There's never a one of you but trusts a knave 93
That mightily deceives you.

BOTH Do we, my lord?

TIMON
Ay, and you hear him cog, see him dissemble, 95
Know his gross patchery, love him, feed him, 96
Keep in your bosom; yet remain assured 97
That he's a made-up villain. 98

PAINTER I know none such, my lord.

POET Nor I.

TIMON
Look you, I love you well. I'll give you gold;
Rid me these villains from your companies, 100
Hang them or stab them, drown them in a draft, 101
Confound them by some course, and come to me, 102
I'll give you gold enough.

BOTH Name them, my lord, let's know them.

82 fiction any creative writing; here, poetry (with connotation of "lying") **83 swells . . . smooth** (1) is elegantly styled and adorned (2) is a vainglorious concoction of specious fabrication **84 thou . . . thine art** (1) your art is able to triumph over nature in verisimilitude (2) you're a born fool and a liar in your art **87 monstrous** unnatural **88 mend** remedy **93 There's . . . but** i.e., each of you **95 cog** cheat **96 patchery** knavery **97 Keep** keep him **98 made-up** utter, complete **100 Rid me** if you'll rid **101 draft** privy, cesspool **102 Confound** destroy. **course** means

TIMON
You that way and you this, but two in company; 105
Each man apart, all single and alone,
Yet an archvillain keeps him company.
[*To one.*] If where thou art two villains shall not be, 108
Come not near him. [*To the other.*] If thou wouldst
not reside 109
But where one villain is, then him abandon.—
Hence, pack! There's gold. You came for gold, ye slaves. 111
[*To one.*] You have work for me; there's payment. Hence! 112
[*To the other.*] You are an alchemist; make gold of that. 113
Out, rascal dogs!

Exeunt [*Poet and Painter, beaten out by Timon, who retires to his cave*].

Enter steward [*Flavius*] *and two Senators.*

FLAVIUS
It is in vain that you would speak with Timon;
For he is set so only to himself 116
That nothing but himself which looks like man
Is friendly with him.

FIRST SENATOR Bring us to his cave. 118
It is our part and promise to th' Athenians 119
To speak with Timon.

SECOND SENATOR At all times alike
Men are not still the same. 'Twas time and griefs 121
That framed him thus. Time with his fairer hand
Offering the fortunes of his former days,
The former man may make him. Bring us to him, 124
And chance it as it may.

FLAVIUS Here is his cave.— 125
Peace and content be here! Lord Timon! Timon!
Look out, and speak to friends. Th' Athenians,

105 You . . . company (Timon riddlingly suggests that if the two of them stand apart from one another with no one else around, each has an *archvillain*—himself—to keep him company.) **108 shall not be** are not to be **109 him** i.e., the other one **111 pack** be off **112 there's payment** i.e., here's a beating or a thrown stone **113 that** i.e., a beating or a thrown stone **116 set . . . himself** so self-absorbed **118 friendly with** congenial to **119 our . . . promise** the part we have promised to undertake **121 still** always **124 The former . . . him** may turn him into his former self **125 chance it** let it happen

By two of their most reverend Senate, greet thee.
Speak to them, noble Timon.

Enter Timon out of his cave.

TIMON
Thou sun that comforts, burn! Speak and be hanged!
For each true word a blister, and each false
Be as a cauterizing to the root o' the tongue,
Consuming it with speaking!

FIRST SENATOR Worthy Timon—

TIMON
Of none but such as you, and you of Timon. 134

FIRST SENATOR
The senators of Athens greet thee, Timon.

TIMON
I thank them, and would send them back the plague,
Could I but catch it for them.

FIRST SENATOR O, forget
What we are sorry for ourselves in thee. 138
The senators with one consent of love 139
Entreat thee back to Athens, who have thought
On special dignities which vacant lie
For thy best use and wearing.

SECOND SENATOR They confess
Toward thee forgetfulness too general gross; 143
Which now the public body, which doth seldom 144
Play the recanter, feeling in itself 145
A lack of Timon's aid, hath sense withal 146
Of its own fail, restraining aid to Timon, 147
And send forth us to make their sorrowed render, 148
Together with a recompense more fruitful
Than their offense can weigh down by the dram— 150
Ay, even such heaps and sums of love and wealth
As shall to thee blot out what wrongs were theirs 152

134 Of . . . Timon i.e., we are worthy of nothing better than being punished by one another **138 What . . . thee** those wrongs that we regret having done you **139 consent** unanimous voice **143 general gross** evident to everyone **144 public body** state **145 Play the recanter** i.e., change its mind and apologize **146 Timon's aid** aid to Timon. (But suggesting also "aid to be given by Timon to Athens.") **withal** in addition **147 fail** failing. **restraining** in withholding **148 sorrowed** sorrowful. **render** rendering, i.e., of their apologies **150 can . . . dram** can outweigh under the most scrupulous measurement **152 theirs** of their making

And write in thee the figures of their love, 153
Ever to read them thine.

TIMON You witch me in it, 154
Surprise me to the very brink of tears.
Lend me a fool's heart and a woman's eyes,
And I'll beweep these comforts, worthy senators. 157

FIRST SENATOR
Therefore, so please thee to return with us, 158
And of our Athens, thine and ours, to take
The captainship, thou shalt be met with thanks,
Allowed with absolute power, and thy good name 161
Live with authority. So soon we shall drive back 162
Of Alcibiades th' approaches wild, 163
Who, like a boar too savage, doth root up
His country's peace.

SECOND SENATOR And shakes his threatening sword
Against the walls of Athens.

FIRST SENATOR Therefore, Timon—

TIMON
Well, sir, I will; therefore I will, sir; thus:
If Alcibiades kill my countrymen,
Let Alcibiades know this of Timon,
That Timon cares not. But if he sack fair Athens
And take our goodly agèd men by the beards,
Giving our holy virgins to the stain 172
Of contumelious, beastly, mad-brained war, 173
Then let him know, and tell him Timon speaks it
In pity of our agèd and our youth,
I cannot choose but tell him that I care not,
And let him take 't at worst—for their knives care not, 177
While you have throats to answer. For myself, 178
There's not a whittle in th' unruly camp 179
But I do prize it at my love before 180

153 figures (1) representations (2) numbers written in a ledger
154 Ever . . . thine i.e., to provide a perpetual record of the Athenians' love for you. **witch** bewitch **157 beweep these comforts** weep gratefully at these comforting tidings **158 so** if it **161 Allowed** vested
162 Live with continue to exercise **163 Of . . . wild** the savage attacks of Alcibiades **172 stain** pollution **173 contumelious** insolent
177 take 't at worst interpret what I say in the worst manner possible; or, (let Alcibiades' troops) do their worst destruction **178 answer** suffer the consequences **179 whittle** small clasp-knife **180 prize** value. **at** in. **before** above

The reverend'st throat in Athens. So I leave you
To the protection of the prosperous gods, 182
As thieves to keepers.

FLAVIUS [*To Senators*] Stay not; all's in vain. 183

TIMON
Why, I was writing of my epitaph;
It will be seen tomorrow. My long sickness
Of health and living now begins to mend,
And nothing brings me all things. Go, live still; 187
Be Alcibiades your plague, you his,
And last so long enough!

FIRST SENATOR We speak in vain. 189

TIMON
But yet I love my country and am not 190
One that rejoices in the common wrack, 191
As common bruit doth put it.

FIRST SENATOR That's well spoke. 192

TIMON
Commend me to my loving countrymen—

FIRST SENATOR
These words become your lips as they pass thorough
them. 194

SECOND SENATOR
And enter in our ears like great triumphers 195
In their applauding gates.

TIMON Commend me to them, 196
And tell them that, to ease them of their griefs,
Their fears of hostile strokes, their aches, losses,
Their pangs of love, with other incident throes 199
That nature's fragile vessel doth sustain 200
In life's uncertain voyage, I will some kindness do them:
I'll teach them to prevent wild Alcibiades' wrath. 202

FIRST SENATOR [*To the Second Senator*]
I like this well. He will return again.

182 prosperous causing prosperity **183 keepers** jailers **187 nothing** oblivion, death **189 last . . . enough** remain in that state as long as possible **190 yet** still **191 wrack** destruction **192 bruit** rumor **194 become** grace, do credit to. **thorough** through **195 triumphers** those coming in triumph **196 applauding gates** i.e., gates crowded with applauding citizens **199 incident throes** naturally occurring agonies **200 nature's . . . vessel** i.e., the body **202 prevent** frustrate, forestall (with a quibble on "anticipate")

TIMON
I have a tree, which grows here in my close, 204
That mine own use invites me to cut down, 205
And shortly must I fell it. Tell my friends, 206
Tell Athens, in the sequence of degree 207
From high to low throughout, that whoso please
To stop affliction, let him take his haste,
Come hither ere my tree hath felt the ax,
And hang himself. I pray you, do my greeting.
FLAVIUS [*To Senators*]
Trouble him no further. Thus you still shall find him.
TIMON
Come not to me again. But say to Athens,
Timon hath made his everlasting mansion 214
Upon the beachèd verge of the salt flood, 215
Who once a day with his embossèd froth 216
The turbulent surge shall cover. Thither come,
And let my gravestone be your oracle. 218
Lips, let four words go by and language end! 219
What is amiss, plague and infection mend!
Graves only be men's works and death their gain!
Sun, hide thy beams! Timon hath done his reign.
Exit Timon [*into his cave*].
FIRST SENATOR
His discontents are unremovably
Coupled to nature. 224
SECOND SENATOR
Our hope in him is dead. Let us return
And strain what other means is left unto us
In our dear peril.
FIRST SENATOR It requires swift foot. *Exeunt.* 227

204 close enclosure **205 use** need **206 fell** cut **207 in . . . degree** in order of social rank **214 everlasting mansion** i.e., grave **215 verge . . . flood** boundary or margin of the sea. (See 5.4.66.) **216 Who** whom or which, i.e., Timon or his grave, his *everlasting mansion* (l. 214), both of which the foaming tide will cover daily. **his** its. **embossèd** foaming
218 oracle source of wisdom **219 four words** i.e., few words
224 Coupled to nature integrally part of him **227 dear** costly, dire. **foot** i.e., action

5.2 *Enter two other Senators, with a Messenger.*

THIRD SENATOR
Thou hast painfully discovered. Are his files 1
As full as thy report?
MESSENGER I have spoke the least. 2
Besides, his expedition promises 3
Present approach. 4
FOURTH SENATOR
We stand much hazard if they bring not Timon. 5
MESSENGER
I met a courier, one mine ancient friend, 6
Whom, though in general part we were opposed, 7
Yet our old love made a particular force 8
And made us speak like friends. This man was riding
From Alcibiades to Timon's cave
With letters of entreaty which imported 11
His fellowship i' the cause against your city, 12
In part for his sake moved.

Enter the other Senators [from Timon].

THIRD SENATOR Here come our brothers. 13
FIRST SENATOR
No talk of Timon; nothing of him expect.
The enemies' drum is heard, and fearful scouring 15
Doth choke the air with dust. In, and prepare. 16
Ours is the fall, I fear, our foe's the snare. *Exeunt.* 17

✤

5.2. Location: Before the walls of Athens.
1 painfully discovered revealed unsettling news (?) or reconnoitered with painstaking effort (?). **files** military ranks **2 spoke the least** given the lowest estimate **3 expedition** speed **4 Present** immediate **5 stand much hazard** are at great risk. **they** i.e., the senators who were sent to Timon **6 one mine ancient friend** a former friend of mine **7 Whom** on whom. **in general part** on public issues **8 particular** personal **11 imported** (1) concerned, had to do with (2) importuned **12 fellowship** partnership **13 In . . . moved** undertaken or initiated partly on his (Timon's) behalf **15 scouring** hurrying along, aggressive movement **16 In** let us go in **17 Ours . . . snare** our part, I fear, is to fall, our foe's part is to set the trap

5.3 *Enter a Soldier in the woods, seeking Timon.*

SOLDIER
By all description this should be the place.
Who's here? Speak, ho! No answer? What is this?
[*He finds a rude tomb.*]
"Timon is dead, who hath outstretched his span.
Some beast read this; there does not live a man." 4
Dead, sure, and this his grave. What's on this tomb
I cannot read. The character I'll take with wax. 6
[*He makes a wax impression.*]
Our captain hath in every figure skill, 7
An aged interpreter, though young in days.
Before proud Athens he's set down by this, 9
Whose fall the mark of his ambition is. *Exit.* 10

✤

5.4 *Trumpets sound. Enter Alcibiades with his powers before Athens.*

ALCIBIADES
Sound to this coward and lascivious town 1
Our terrible approach. *Sounds a parley.* 2

The Senators appear on the walls.

Till now you have gone on and filled the time

5.3. Location: The woods. Seemingly near Timon's cave, but also at the edge of the sea; see 5.1.214–217 and 5.4.66. A rude tomb is seen.
4 Some . . . man i.e., whoever reads this will be a beast, since all men are beasts **6 I cannot read** (Suggests there is another inscription in another language, perhaps Latin, or that this scene shows signs of incomplete revision and hence apparent inconsistency.) **The . . . wax** I'll take an impression of the inscription in wax **7 every figure** all kinds of writing **9 Before . . . this** by this time he has laid siege to proud Athens **10 Whose fall** the fall of which. **mark** goal

5.4. Location: Before the walls of Athens. Appearances *on the walls* are presumably located in the gallery, above, to the rear of the stage.
s.d. powers armed forces **1 Sound** proclaim **2 terrible** terrifying
s.d. parley trumpet call to a negotiation

With all licentious measure, making your wills 4
The scope of justice. Till now myself and such 5
As slept within the shadow of your power 6
Have wandered with our traversed arms and breathed 7
Our sufferance vainly. Now the time is flush, 8
When crouching marrow in the bearer strong 9
Cries of itself, "No more!" Now breathless wrong 10
Shall sit and pant in your great chairs of ease,
And pursy insolence shall break his wind 12
With fear and horrid flight.

FIRST SENATOR Noble and young, 13
When thy first griefs were but a mere conceit, 14
Ere thou hadst power or we had cause of fear,
We sent to thee, to give thy rages balm,
To wipe out our ingratitude with loves 17
Above their quantity.

SECOND SENATOR So did we woo 18
Transformèd Timon to our city's love
By humble message and by promised means. 20
We were not all unkind, nor all deserve
The common stroke of war.

FIRST SENATOR These walls of ours 22
Were not erected by their hands from whom
You have received your grief; nor are they such
That these great tow'rs, trophies, and schools should
fall 25
For private faults in them.

SECOND SENATOR Nor are they living 26
Who were the motives that you first went out. 27

4 all licentious measure every kind of licentious behavior **4–5 making . . . justice** equating justice with your wills **6 slept** i.e., dwelled **7 traversed arms** arms inactive or folded. (A term in military drill.) **7–8 breathed Our sufferance** voiced our sufferings **8 flush** at flood, ripe **9 crouching marrow** latent resolution and might **10 of itself** of its own accord. **breathless wrong** wrongdoers who are frightened into breathlessness **12 pursy** short-winded. **break his wind** pant for breath (perhaps suggesting also to void air from the bowels in fright) **13 horrid** terrified **14 griefs** grievances. **conceit** fancy, imagined scheme of action **17–18 loves . . . quantity** offers of friendship exceeding the quantity of your grievances **20 means** terms **22 common** indiscriminate **25 trophies** monuments. **schools** public buildings **26 private** personal. **them** i.e., those from whom you have received your injuries **27 motives . . . out** instigators that prompted your banishment

Shame, that they wanted cunning, in excess 28
Hath broke their hearts. March, noble lord,
Into our city with thy banners spread.
By decimation and a tithèd death— 31
If thy revenges hunger for that food
Which nature loathes—take thou the destined tenth,
And by the hazard of the spotted die 34
Let die the spotted.

FIRST SENATOR All have not offended. 35
For those that were, it is not square to take 36
On those that are, revenge. Crimes, like lands, 37
Are not inherited. Then, dear countryman, 38
Bring in thy ranks, but leave without thy rage. 39
Spare thy Athenian cradle and those kin 40
Which in the bluster of thy wrath must fall
With those that have offended. Like a shepherd
Approach the fold and cull th' infected forth, 43
But kill not all together.

SECOND SENATOR What thou wilt,
Thou rather shalt enforce it with thy smile
Than hew to 't with thy sword.

FIRST SENATOR Set but thy foot 46
Against our rampired gates and they shall ope, 47
So thou wilt send thy gentle heart before 48
To say thou'lt enter friendly.

SECOND SENATOR Throw thy glove, 49
Or any token of thine honor else, 50
That thou wilt use the wars as thy redress
And not as our confusion, all thy powers 52
Shall make their harbor in our town till we 53
Have sealed thy full desire.

ALCIBIADES [*Throwing a glove*] Then there's my glove. 54

28 Shame . . . excess i.e., an excess of shame for their lack of cunning in statecraft **31 decimation, tithèd death** selection of every tenth to die. (The two phrases mean the same thing.) **34 die** (Singular of *dice;* with a play on the verb *die.*) **35 the spotted** the corrupt, wicked (with a play on the spots on the dice) **36 square** just **37 are** are now alive **37–38 like . . . not** are not like lands **39 without** outside **40 thy Athenian cradle** Athens, your birthplace **43 cull . . . forth** pick out the tainted **46 hew** cut **47 rampired** barricaded. **ope** open **48 So** if only **49 Throw** if you will throw **50 token** pledge **52 confusion** overthrow. **powers** armed forces **53 make their harbor** have safe lodging **54 sealed** satisfied, ratified

Descend, and open your unchargèd ports. 55
Those enemies of Timon's and mine own
Whom you yourselves shall set out for reproof 57
Fall, and no more; and, to atone your fears 58
With my more noble meaning, not a man 59
Shall pass his quarter or offend the stream 60
Of regular justice in your city's bounds 61
But shall be remedied to your public laws 62
At heaviest answer.

BOTH 'Tis most nobly spoken. 63

ALCIBIADES Descend, and keep your words. 64
[*The Senators descend, and open the gates.*]

Enter [*Soldier as*] *a Messenger* [*with a wax tablet*].

SOLDIER
My noble general, Timon is dead,
Entombed upon the very hem o' the sea; 66
And on his gravestone this insculpture, which 67
With wax I brought away, whose soft impression
Interprets for my poor ignorance.

ALCIBIADES (*Reads the epitaph*)
"Here lies a wretched corpse, of wretched soul bereft. 70
Seek not my name. A plague consume you wicked
caitiffs left! 71
Here lie I, Timon, who, alive, all living men did hate.
Pass by and curse thy fill, but pass and stay not here thy
gait." 73
These well express in thee thy latter spirits. 74
Though thou abhorredst in us our human griefs,
Scornedst our brains' flow and those our droplets which 76

55 unchargèd ports unattacked gates **57 set out for reproof** pick out for punishment **58 atone** appease, make "at one" **59 man** i.e., soldier of mine **60 pass his quarter** leave his assigned duty area **60–61 offend . . . justice** violate the norms set by established law **62 But . . . remedied** without being remanded **63 At heaviest answer** to receive severest punishment **64 s.d. open the gates** (Presumably, the *gates* are a door in the tiring-house facade representing here the *walls* of Athens; the gallery above is *on the walls*.) **66 hem** i.e., edge, shore **67 insculpture** inscription **70–73 Here . . . gait** (Of these two inscriptions, both found in Plutarch, Shakespeare would presumably have deleted one, since they contradict one another.) **71 caitiffs** wretches **73 gait** journey **74 latter spirits** recent sentiments **76 brains' flow** i.e., tears

From niggard nature fall, yet rich conceit 77
Taught thee to make vast Neptune weep for aye 78
On thy low grave, on faults forgiven. Dead
Is noble Timon, of whose memory
Hereafter more. Bring me into your city,
And I will use the olive with my sword, 82
Make war breed peace, make peace stint war, make each 83
Prescribe to other as each other's leech. 84
Let our drums strike. [*Drums.*] *Exeunt.*

77 niggard nature parsimonious human nature (unable to produce quantities of tears to compete with the sea). **conceit** imagination, fancy
78 Neptune the god of the sea in Roman mythology. **aye** ever **82 olive, sword** (Symbols of peace and war.) **83 stint** stop **84 leech** physician

Date and Text

Timon of Athens first appeared in the First Folio of 1623. The text seems to have been based on an unusually early draft of the author's papers, with manifest inconsistencies still present that would have been straightened out in a final draft. A more controversial hypothesis is that joint authorship (with Thomas Middleton) contributed to the discrepancies about the value of money and the like. The play seems to have been a last-minute substitution in the Folio, to replace *Troilus and Cressida* when for some reason (probably copyright difficulties) that play had to be removed from its original position following *Romeo and Juliet*. The Folio editors possibly had not intended to use *Timon* at all. The manuscript used by the printers seems to have been copied over in places by a second hand, as though the manuscript was too illegible for the printer to use.

Dating of the play is unusually difficult. In its unfinished state the play was probably never acted, and therefore left no trace until it was registered for publication on November 8, 1623. Stylistically it seems close to the late tragedies. Its pessimism reminds us of *King Lear,* and its use of Plutarch suggests *Antony and Cleopatra*. Theories of multiple authorship were once common and have been recently reasserted (see above on Middleton), but have not won general agreement.

Textual Notes

These textual notes are not a historical collation, either of the early folios or of more recent editions; they are simply a record of departures in this edition from the copy text. The reading adopted in this edition appears in boldface, followed by the rejected reading from the copy text, i.e., the First Folio. Only major alterations in punctuation are noted. Changes in lineation are not indicated, nor are some minor and obvious typographical errors.

Abbreviations used:
F the First Folio
s.d. stage direction
s.p. speech prefix

Copy text: the First Folio.

The Actors' Names [F lists also Varro and Lucius as "Seruants to Vsurers," and the order of names has been changed for Apemantus and Ventidius]

1.1. s.d. Merchant Merchant, and Mercer **23 gum** Gowne **oozes** vses **27 chafes** chases **43 man** men **50 tax** wax **77 conceived to scope.** conceyu'd, to scope **92 hands** hand **slip** sit **116 s.p. [and subsequently] Old Athenian** Oldm **160 s.d. Exeunt** Exit **184 s.d. Enter Apemantus** [after l. 182 in F] **222 cost** cast **227 s.p. Apemantus** pe **234 feigned** fegin'd **259 there!** their **286 Come** Comes **287 taste** raste **296 s.p. First Lord** [not in F]

1.2. s.d. [and elsewhere] Ventidius Ventigius **30 ever** verie **105 O, joy's e'en** Oh ioyes, e'ne **107 To forget their faults,** to forget their Faults. **113 s.d. Sound tucket** [F continues: "Enter the Maskers of Amazons with Lutes in their hands, dauncing and playing"] **114 s.d. Enter Servant** [after "How now?" in F] **120 s.d. Enter Cupid** [F continues: "with the Maske of Ladies"] **124 Th' ear** There **125 and smell** all **129 s.p. First Lord** Luc **s.d.** [see notes at ll. 113 and 120 above] **144 s.d. singles** single **151 s.p. First Lady** 1 Lord **167 s.d. Enter Flavius** [at l. 176 in F] **181 s.p. Second Servant** Ser **211 rode** rod **213 s.p. Third Lord** 1. L

2.1. 34 Ay, go, sir. I go sir? **35 in compt** in. Come

2.2. 1 s.p. [and elsewhere] Flavius Stew **4 resumes** resume **11 s.p. [and elsewhere] Varro's Servant** Var **13 s.p. [and elsewhere] Isidore's Servant** Isid **41 broken** debt, broken **64 s.p. [and elsewhere] All the Servants** Al [or All] **75, 104 mistress'** Masters **81 s.p. Page** Boy **96 Ay. Would** I would **132 proposed** propose **139 found** sound **160 of** or **191 Flaminius** Flauius

3.1. s.d. Enter enters **1 s.p. [and elsewhere] Lucullus' Servant** Ser

3.2. 27 s.p. [and elsewhere] Lucius Lucil

3.3. 5 Owe Owes **23 I 'mongst** 'mong'st

3.4. s.d. Men man **1 s.p. [and elsewhere] Varro's First Servant** Var. man **2 s.p. [and elsewhere] Titus' Servant** Tit **Hortensius' Servant** Hort **3 s.p. [and elsewhere] Lucius' Servant** Luci **6 s.p. Philotus' Servant** Phil **14 recoverable. I fear** recouerable, I feare: **15–16 purse; / That is,** purse, that is: **45 s.p. [and elsewhere] Varro's Second Servant** 2. Varro **88 s.p. Hortensius' Servant** 1. Var **89 s.p. Both Varro's Servants** 2. Var **112 Sempronius** Sempronius Vllorxa

3.5. 18 An And **23 behave** behooue **51 lion** Lyon? **felon** fellow **52 judge,** Iudge? **53 suffering.** suffering, **66 Why, I** Why **70 'em** him **85 honors** Honour

3.6. 1 s.p. First Lord 1 [and so throughout scene] **19 here's** heares **54 s.p. First and Second Lords** Both **80 tag** legge **87 s.p. Others** other **91 with your** you with **115 s.p. Third Lord** 2 **116 s.p. Second Lord** 3

4.1. 8 fast; fast **9 back,** backe; **13 Son** Some

4.3. 10 senator Senators **12 pasture** Pastour **13 lean** leaue **41 at, this** at. This **88 tub-fast** Fubfast **119 bars** Barne **124 thy** the **135 s.p. [and throughout scene] Phrynia and Timandra** Both **158 scolds** scold'st **187 thy human** the humane **206 fortune** future **225 mossed** moyst **254 clasped** claspt. **255 swathe, proceeded** swath proceeded, **257 drudges** drugges **258 command** command'st **287 my** thy **402 them** then **414 s.p. [and throughout scene] Banditti** All **439 villainy** Villaine **462 s.d. Exeunt** Exit **479 grant'st** grunt'st **man, I** man. I **497 mild** wilde **514 A** If not a

5.1. 5–6 Phrynia and Timandra Phrinica and Timandylo **50 worship** worshipt **66 go naked; men** go, / Naked men **70 men** man **115 in vain** vaine **125 chance** chanc'd **146 sense** since **147 its own fail** it owne fall **181 reverend'st** reuerends

5.2. 1 s.p. [and throughout scene] Third Senator 1 **5 s.p. [and throughout scene] Fourth Senator** 2 **14 s.p. First Senator** 3

5.4. 27 out. out, **28 Shame . . . excess** Shame that they wanted, cunning in excesse **55 Descend** Defend **65 s.p. Soldier** Mes

Shakespeare's Sources

Shakespeare certainly made use of a brief passage from the "Life of Marcus Antonius" in Thomas North's English translation (from the French of Jacques Amyot) of the first-century Greek biographer Plutarch's *The Lives of the Noble Grecians and Romans* (1579). This passage is a digression used to illustrate Antonius' embittered withdrawal to an Egyptian island after his defeat at Actium, in which he compares himself to the famous misanthrope of Athens, Timon. As Plutarch reports Timon's story, citing Plato and Aristophanes as his sources, Timon is a hater of mankind because he has been victimized by deception and ingratitude. Timon shuns all company but that of young Alcibiades and occasionally that of Apemantus. When asked by Apemantus why he favors this youth, Timon replies that he knows Alcibiades will some day do great mischief to the Athenians. On another occasion, Timon mounts a public rostrum and invites his Athenian listeners to come hang themselves on a fig tree growing in his yard before he cuts it down (see 5.1.204–211). When Timon dies he is buried upon the seashore (5.1.213–217). Plutarch transcribes two epitaphs, one by the poet Callimachus and one by Timon himself, both of which appear virtually word for word in Shakespeare's play (5.4.70–73). (Shakespeare probably meant to cancel one, for dramatically they are inconsistent with one another.) Plutarch thus provides Shakespeare not only with several incidents in the life of Timon but with the link connecting Timon, Alcibiades, and Apemantus. The twenty-eighth novel in William Painter's *The Palace of Pleasure* (1566) retells the events narrated by Plutarch but without adding any new information.

Oddly, Shakespeare seems to have absorbed little from Plutarch's "Life of Alcibiades," though that account does tell how the general leaves Athens in disgrace and sides with her enemies but ultimately relents when he sees that the Athenians are sorry for the injury they have done him. Alcibiades is a handsome young man and fond of women; his concubine Timandra buries him. Despite these scattered hints, however, Plutarch's "Life of Alcibiades" provides no basis for Shakespeare's plot.

The comedy of Timon by Aristophanes, to which Plutarch alludes, has not survived. Nor has Plato's description. Apparently these accounts were based on a historical figure of fifth-century Athens, Timon the son of Echecratides. Allusions to him in classical literature are common enough to suggest that his name had become synonymous with misanthropy. The fullest surviving classical record of this tradition is a dialogue by Lucian of Samosata (c. A.D. 125–180) called *Timon*, or *The Misanthrope*. No English translation was available in Shakespeare's lifetime, but he could have read Lucian in Italian, Latin, or French translation.

The dialogue begins as Timon, impoverished and abandoned by his fair-weather friends, calls upon Zeus to punish such injustice. Zeus hears this diatribe and learns from Hermes the sad tale of Timon's victimization by his ungrateful fellow beings. Aware that he has been neglectful of this case, Zeus orders Hermes to descend with Plutus (Riches) and restore Timon to prosperity. Although Plutus fears he will be treated improvidently as before, Zeus is insistent. Plutus (personifying Riches) confesses to Hermes, as they descend, how he (i.e., wealth) deceives humanity. Hermes and Plutus find Timon digging, accompanied by Poverty, Toil, Endurance, and other such allegorical companions. Poverty and his fellows are reluctant to leave Timon, for they know he has been happier with them than in his former days; and Timon too protests he wants nothing to do with prosperity. Still, the will of the gods must be obeyed, and Timon discovers treasure where he is digging.

Just as he mordantly predicts, opportunists now seek him out. One is Gnathonides the flatterer, a former recipient of Timon's hospitality who only recently has repaid that kindness by offering Timon a noose. Another, Philiades, once received from Timon a farm as a dowry for his daughters, but has spurned Timon in his poverty; now he makes a pretense of offering money, knowing Timon not to be in need. A third petitioner is the orator Demea, whose debt Timon once paid to obtain his release from jail; now, having insulted Timon in his poverty, Demea comes with a fulsome and patently fictitious decree he has composed in Timon's honor. Fourth is Thrasicles, a hypocritical philosopher who preaches self-denial but drinks to excess, and who professes to come now not for his own benefit but for those to whom he will gladly distribute Timon's new wealth. Timon drives them off one by one and then resorts to throwing stones at the ever-increasing crowd of flatterers. (This parade of villains, and their satirical discomfiture, bear an interesting resemblance to Aristophanes' *The Birds*.)

Many details here are suggestive of Shakespeare's play and are not in Plutarch: Timon's generosity to friends (including the payment of a debt and the providing of a marriage dowry), his friends' ungrateful response when he is in need, the finding of gold in the ground followed by the reappearance of his former friends, the insincere offer of money, the flattering composition in praise of Timon. The personified abstractions are parablelike, as in Shakespeare's play. Yet verbal parallels between Shakespeare and Lucian are tenuous at best. Probably Shakespeare knew some later version based on Lucian. Renaissance works inspired by Lucian are not hard to find, but none seems to be the direct source for Shakespeare. He is not likely to have known an Italian play called *Timone* of Matteo Maria Boiardo (c. 1487).

More suggestive of Shakespeare's play is an English academic play written at Cambridge (c. 1581–1600, or perhaps c. 1609–1610?) and preserved in the Dyce manuscript. (The editor Alexander Dyce first published this Elizabethan manuscript in 1842.) In this version, Timon's servant Laches warns against the effects of prodigality. When one friend, Eutrapelus, experiences financial trouble, Timon gives him five talents. Laches is driven out by Timon, but returns disguised as a soldier to serve his master. At a final banquet, Timon mocks his guests with stones painted to resemble artichokes. When he finds gold, Timon's false mistress shows her readiness to take it. Even a farcical comic subplot reminds us that Shakespeare's *Timon* contains an unrelated and perhaps vestigial Fool scene. Yet this academic play may have been written after Shakespeare's play, though surely not based on it (since *Timon* was not published until 1623 and apparently was never acted), and the likeliest explanation for the similarities is a common source. Perhaps Shakespeare knew and used a play now lost.

Apemantus does not have a prominent role in any of the versions here discussed, though he is mentioned in Plutarch.

Apemantus bears a resemblance to many satirical railers and crabbed philosophers in Renaissance literature, such as Diogenes in John Lyly's play of *Campaspe* (1584) and Jaques in Shakespeare's *As You Like It.*

The Lives of the Noble Grecians and Romans Compared Together by . . . Plutarch

Translated by Thomas North

FROM THE LIFE OF MARCUS ANTONIUS

Antonius, he[1] forsook the city and company of his friends and built him a house in the sea by the isle of Pharos[2] upon certain forced mounts which he caused to be cast into the sea,[3] and dwelt there as a man that banished himself from all men's company, saying that he would lead Timon's life because he had the like wrong offered him that was afore offered unto Timon, and that for the unthankfulness of those he had done good unto, and whom he took to be his friends, he was angry with all men and would trust no man.

This Timon was a citizen of Athens that lived about the war of Peloponnesus,[4] as appeareth by Plato and Aristophanes' comedies, in the which they mocked him, calling him a viper and malicious man unto mankind to shun all other men's companies but the company of young Alcibiades—a bold and insolent youth, whom he would greatly feast and make much of, and kissed him very gladly. Apemantus, wondering at it, asked him the cause what[5] he meant to make so much of that young man alone and to hate all others. Timon answered him: "I do it," said he, "because I know that one day he shall do great mischief unto the Athenians."

This Timon sometimes would have Apemantus in his company, because he was much like of[6] his nature and con-

1 **Antonius, he** Antonius 2 **isle of Pharos** (in the harbor of Alexandria, Egypt) 3 **upon . . . sea** (i.e., Antonius built his house out over the water on piers driven into the sea bottom. Timon similarly took refuge from society at the edge of the sea.) 4 **about the war of Peloponnesus** about the time of the prolonged war in the fifth century B.C. between the Athenian empire and the Spartan league, described by Thucydides 5 **cause what** reason why 6 **like of** alike in

ditions[7] and also followed him in manner of life. On a time[8] when they solemnly celebrated the feasts[9] called *Choae* at Athens (to wit, the feasts of the dead where they make sprinklings and sacrifices for the dead) and that they two then feasted together by themselves, Apemantus said unto the other: "O, here is a trim[10] banquet, Timon!" Timon answered again: "Yea," said he, "so [11] thou wert not here."

It is reported of him also that this Timon on a time (the people being assembled in the marketplace about dispatch of some affairs) got up into the pulpit for orations where the orators commonly use[12] to speak unto the people; and, silence being made, every man listening to hear what he would say because it was a wonder to see him in that place, at length he began to speak in this manner: "My lords of Athens, I have a little yard in my house where there groweth a fig tree, on the which many citizens have hanged themselves. And because I mean to make some building upon the place, I thought good to let you all understand it that, before the fig tree be cut down, if any of you be desperate,[13] you may there in time go hang yourselves."

He died in the city of Hales and was buried upon the seaside. Now it chanced so that the sea getting in, it compassed his tomb round about, that no man could come to it; and upon the same was written this epitaph:

> Here lies a wretched corpse, of wretched soul bereft.
> Seek not my name. A plague consume you wicked
> wretches left!

It is reported that Timon himself, when he lived, made this epitaph. For that which is commonly rehearsed[14] was not his, but made by the poet Callimachus:

> Here lie I, Timon, who, alive, all living men did hate.
> Pass by and curse thy fill, but pass and stay not here
> thy gate.[15]

Many other things could we tell you of this Timon, but this little shall suffice at this present.

7 conditions disposition, cast of mind **8 On a time** once **9 feasts** religious festival **10 trim** fine, spruce **11 so** provided **12 use** are accustomed **13 desperate** in despair **14 rehearsed** recited **15 gate** journey

---

Text based on *The Lives of the Noble Grecians and Romans Compared Together by That Grave, Learned Philosopher and Historiographer, Plutarch of Chaeronea. Translated out of Greek into French by James Amyot . . . and out of French into English by Thomas North. . . . Thomas Vautroullier . . . 1579.* Whether Shakespeare read this edition or one of the subsequent editions of 1595 and 1603 (the 1603 text was reprinted in 1612) is not certain, but the differences are minor.

Further Reading

Bayley, John. "The Big Idea: *Timon of Athens.*" *Shakespeare and Tragedy*. London: Routledge and Kegan Paul, 1981. Bayley holds that *Timon* is a play that did not fully engage Shakespeare in its emotional possibilities but only in its aesthetic challenge; nonetheless, behind its impersonal and schematic structure the play uncovers a tragic dimension in Timon's poignant unsuitability for his role either as generous lord or misanthrope.

Bradbrook, M. C. *The Tragic Pageant of "Timon of Athens."* Cambridge: Cambridge Univ. Press, 1966. Rpt. in *Shakespeare, the Craftsman*. London: Chatto and Windus, 1969. Bradbrook sees *Timon* as a work of profound and disturbing power, representing Shakespeare's formal response to the demands of the indoor theater he was writing for in 1609. The play is written in an experimental dramatic style based on the example of symbolic court pageants: Timon is a role rather than a character, and the play develops emblematically, not psychologically.

Burke, Kenneth. "*Timon of Athens* and Misanthropic Gold." *Language as Symbolic Action*. Berkeley and Los Angeles: Univ. of California Press, 1966. Using insights derived from both Freud and Marx, Burke explores the unity of the play's design. He examines how Shakespeare's rhetorical strategies are marshaled to reveal Timon's maturation and organize the tragic potential of his nature.

Campbell, Oscar James. *"Timon of Athens." Shakespeare's Satire*. London and New York: Oxford Univ. Press, 1943. Campbell asserts that *Timon* is not a tragedy but rather a tragical satire. The play's construction and concerns are satiric, and while Timon's fate suggests the structure of tragedy, his alienation and death are not presented as the suffering of a noble heart but caricatured as the inevitable result of an ignoble and irrational misanthropy.

Ellis-Fermor, Una Mary. *"Timon of Athens." Review of English Studies* 18 (1942): 270–283. Rpt. in *Shakespeare the Dramatist and Other Papers*, ed. Kenneth Muir. London: Methuen, 1961. In an influential and provocative essay,

Ellis-Fermor argues that *Timon* is unfinished even in conception. Shakespeare never succeeds in creating a Timon completely responsive to the play's theme or in relating him to the social circumstances that should give rise to action. Nonetheless, if the play is flawed and incomplete, Ellis-Fermor holds, it is a play "such as a great artist might leave behind him."

Empson, William. "Timon's Dog." *The Structure of Complex Words*. London: Chatto and Windus; New York: New Directions, 1951. Empson explores both the play and the nature of metaphor itself in examining the insistent but multivalent use of "dog" in the play. Characters refer to dogs both as symbols of flattery and of cynicism, and this becomes for Empson a means to gauge the paradoxical nature and tone of the misanthropy shared by Apemantus and Timon.

Fly, Richard D. "Confounding Contraries: The Unmediated World of *Timon of Athens*." *Shakespeare's Mediated World*. Amherst, Mass.: Univ. of Massachusetts Press, 1976. For Fly, *Timon* resists all formal and thematic impulses toward wholeness, leaving characters and episodes disturbingly isolated and polarized. The play's disjunctions and discontinuities seem to Fly to be central to the tragedy of Timon who, like the play itself, is unable to discover any possible synthesis or fusion.

Foakes, R. A. "Shakespeare's Later Tragedies." In *Shakespeare 1564–1964: A Collection of Modern Essays by Various Hands,* ed. Edward A. Bloom. Providence, R.I.: Brown Univ. Press, 1964. Foakes understands *Timon* and the other late tragedies as fundamentally different from Shakespeare's major tragedies. Morally diminished and aesthetically distanced, the heroes of the later tragedies are alienated from the audience, becoming not, as in the major tragedies, embodiments of values sanctioned by the play, but characters who, like Timon, are presented critically rather than empathetically.

Handelman, Susan. "*Timon of Athens:* The Rage of Disillusion." *American Imago* 36 (1979): 45–68. In a suggestive psychoanalytic reading of the play, Handelman locates Timon's misanthropy and alienation in his unwillingness to mourn, and his consequent inability to replace, the infantile love object: "one's own body and that of the nurturant mother." This, for Handelman, explains the absence of women in the play and Timon's disabling isolation and rage.

Hazlitt, William. *"Timon of Athens." Characters of Shakespear's Plays.* London: 1817; rpt. London: Oxford Univ. Press, 1966. Hazlitt praises the intensity and unity of *Timon,* which he finds to be "as much a satire as a play." It is "the only play of our author in which spleen is the predominant feeling of the mind." Only Flavius disrupts the "general picture of selfish depravity."

Johnson, Samuel. *"Timon of Athens."* In *Johnson on Shakespeare,* ed. Arthur Sherbo. *The Yale Edition of the Complete Works of Samuel Johnson,* vol. 8. New Haven and London: Yale Univ. Press, 1968. Though he finds the play to be often obscure, Dr. Johnson considers *Timon* a powerful "domestic tragedy." Its characters, he finds, are "various and exact" and its incidents "natural." He concludes that the play "offers a very powerful warning" against an excessive generosity that "buys flattery, but not friendship."

Kahn, Coppélia. "'Magic of Bounty': *Timon of Athens,* Jacobean Patronage, and Maternal Power." *Shakespeare Quarterly* 38 (1987): 34–57. Psychoanalytic theories of male subjectivity, anthropological studies of gifts and gift-giving, and a historical consideration of the structure and function of patronage in Renaissance England provide Kahn with a rich series of contexts for her suggestive reading of *Timon* as a play that disturbingly explores anxieties produced by social and psychological dependency.

Kernan, Alvin B. "Tragic Satire." *The Cankered Muse: Satire of the English Renaissance.* New Haven, Conn.: Yale Univ. Press, 1959. Kernan argues that in placing the satirist at the center rather than at the margins of the play, Shakespeare in *Timon* offers a penetrating analysis of the satiric vision itself. Timon's rage has a moral force behind it, born not of envy but of agonized self-knowledge; nonetheless, Shakespeare reveals the ultimate failure of the satiric sense of life, as Timon in killing himself exposes satire's compulsive negation.

Knights, L. C. *"Timon of Athens."* In *The Morality of Art: Essays Presented to G. Wilson Knight by his Colleagues and Friends,* ed. D. W. Jefferson. London: Routledge and Kegan Paul, 1969. Though the play clearly does involve a satirical attack on the deforming power of money, Knights argues that Timon's misanthropy results more directly from his rage at the destruction of his idealized sense of self. Stripped of external supports for his ego-ideal, Timon is left with nothing but a vision of an evil world that reflects in part a social reality but also Timon's self-contempt.

Muir, Kenneth. "*Timon of Athens* and the Cash-Nexus." *The Singularity of Shakespeare and Other Essays.* New York: Barnes and Noble, 1977. In an essay first published in 1947, Muir finds that the play's bitterness rests in Shakespeare's growing awareness that money has become the basis of authority in the increasingly capitalistic world of seventeenth-century England. The social order of the play is "divorced from morality" and power is "animated entirely by self-interest."

Soellner, Rolf. *"Timon of Athens": Shakespeare's Pessimistic Tragedy.* Columbus, Ohio: Ohio State Univ. Press, 1979. Soellner's extended study of the play finds its characterization, imagery, and structure informed by a powerful tragic impulse released by its overriding pessimism. Soellner's reading of *Timon* is supplemented with chapters on aspects of its social and intellectual backgrounds, discussions of the play's date, source, and original theatrical circumstances, and a useful appendix by Gary Jay Williams tracing the history of *Timon* onstage from 1816 to 1978.

Titus Andronicus, with Moses Gunn as Aaron and Olympia Dukakis as Tamora, directed by Gerald Freedman in 1967 at the Delacorte Theater in Central Park.

TITUS ANDRONICUS

TITUS ANDRONICUS

Foreword

Titus Andronicus is a revenge tragedy, extremely gory and violent. Titus himself, a beleaguered old man, reminds me of King Lear: he is subjected to unspeakable horrors, one after another, until he loses his sanity. But unlike Lear, Titus does get his revenge, and it is as gruesome and grotesque as the initial crime of the rape and mutilation of his daughter, Lavinia. Though the violence and gore in this play are overpowering, there's something audiences find gratifying in the story of one man's revenge against the people who have injured him. It's an old theme, even a primitive one, but we also see it in modern films where Rambo-esque acts of violence are carried out in the name of rightful revenge.

I think one of the most interesting characters in the play is the black man, Aaron the Moor, who is Tamora's lover. Though he's unquestionably diabolical, he's also treated with a great deal of understanding. Shakespeare put a tremendous spirit into him. For example, I love the moment in Act 4, scene 2, when Aaron stands up with his (and Tamora's) newly born son and says, "He dies upon my scimitar's sharp point / That touches this my firstborn son and heir!" There's something paternal and protective about his fierce defense of his baby boy that balances his evildoing elsewhere.

Titus Andronicus is a painful play to experience in the theater, because it's hard to watch violence being piled on violence and to see Titus beset by sorrow, grief, and finally the madness of revenge. But I've actually produced the play twice, once in the church on Manhattan's Lower East Side where I started, and later in Central Park. The production in the church had Roscoe Lee Browne as Aaron the Moor, Colleen Dewhurst as Tamora, Queen of the Goths, and a host of other actors. It was quite an event.

What's difficult about putting this play on the stage is that its pure goriness can become comic. The sight of Lavinia walking around with two stumps for hands and her tongue cut out, and Titus with his stump of a hand, and the baking of the human pies at the end, can make the audience laugh because it all seems so "gross." There isn't really enough psychological underpinning to the play to prevent the laughter, which can make it a challenge to perform.

Joseph Papp

Joseph Papp gratefully acknowledges the help of Elizabeth Kirkland in preparing this Foreword.

Introduction

Titus Andronicus has drawn some unusually harsh criticism. Ben Jonson singled it out, in his Induction to *Bartholomew Fair* (1614), as a play loved by ignorant audiences for its bombastic rhetoric. T. S. Eliot called it "one of the stupidest and most uninspired plays ever written." Others have argued that it was not Shakespeare's at all, or that it was his perfunctory revision of an old play by Christopher Marlowe, Thomas Kyd, Robert Greene, or George Peele, or an early experimental work, or even a burlesque of the revenge play then in vogue. Early it surely was; it appeared in quarto in 1594 as played by Derby's, Pembroke's, and Sussex's men, and could well have been written in 1590 or even before. The allusion in theater owner and manager Philip Henslowe's *Diary* for January 24, 1594, to a new production by Sussex's men of "Titus & Ondronicus" could refer to a new play or one newly revised or newly acquired by the company. Shakespeare's *Titus Andronicus* was widely separated in time from the great tragedies; *Romeo and Juliet* is the only other tragedy (excluding the English history plays) of the decade preceding 1599, and it probably followed *Titus Andronicus* by five years or so. Unquestionably *Titus Andronicus* does fall short of the expectations we normally bring to Shakespearean tragedy. Such a judgment compares the play, however, with the greatest dramas of the English language. Probably its most serious critical liability is that it continually reminds us of the later Roman plays and of *Hamlet* and *King Lear*. By any other dramatist the play would not seem so imperfect as it seems when assigned to Shakespeare. *Titus Andronicus* was an early success onstage, and has shown its timeless theatrical appeal in a brilliant production at Stratford-upon-Avon starring Sir Laurence Olivier in 1955.

Titus Andronicus is studded with bookish references to classical authors—another likely indication of early date. No other tragedy, perhaps no other Shakespearean play, reveals such direct evidence of youthful learning. Some of its many untranslated Latin phrases are schoolboys' favorites, such as the *"Integer vitae"* of Horace that is immediately recognized by Chiron. "I read it in the grammar long ago," he says (4.2.23). Classical allusions compare the chief characters of the play with Aeneas and Dido, Queen of Carthage; Hector, King Priam, and Queen Hecuba of Troy; Ajax and Odysseus among the Greeks; Hercules, Prometheus, Orpheus, Coriolanus, Semiramis (the siren Queen of Assyria), Pyramus, Cornelia (the mother of the Gracchi), Actaeon, and others. Yet these learned references are far from being a mere display of youthful learning; through a controlled and self-conscious artistry they enable us to explore a tragic world whose moral dimensions are defined in terms of classical literary models. Especially significant are the references to victims of rape and vengeance: Virginia the Roman, killed by her father Virginius to save her from rape; the chaste Lucrece, ravished by Tarquin; Philomel, raped and deprived of her tongue by Tereus, whose name she then reveals by weaving the information into a tapestry; and Procne, her sister and the wife of Tereus, who avenges Philomel by serving Tereus' son Itys to him in a meal.

Ovid's *Metamorphoses* gave Shakespeare his source for many of the legends, especially that of Tereus, Philomel, and Procne. Seneca's *Thyestes* offered him in dramatic form a similar tale of vengeance, in which two sons are slain and served to their parent in a grisly banquet. Shakespeare appears to have used a chapbook called *The History of Titus Andronicus;* the only extant printed copy is from the eighteenth century, but it may give a reliable version of the original. Some scholars believe that one or even two plays about Titus may have existed prior to Shakespeare's and that we can deduce their contributions to his work by examining two later continental plays derived from them: *Tragoedia von Tito Andronico* (German, 1620) and *Aran en Titus* (Dutch, 1641). Possibly one of these earlier plays was the "Tittus & Vespacia" entered in Henslowe's *Diary* for April 11, 1592, as acted by Lord Strange's men. Even if Shakespeare used such prose and dramatic sources, however, he also knew well the Ovidian and Senecan originals that had inspired them. Elizabethan revenge tragedy, containing some Senecan influences (though those Senecan elements should not be overstressed), was a strongly formative influence, especially Kyd's *The Spanish Tragedy* (c. 1587). The phenomenal recent stage successes of Marlowe had left their mark: Titus' killing of his son Mutius recalls *Tamburlaine, Part II,* and Aaron's Vice-like boasting of wanton villainy recalls *The Jew of Malta*. Shakespeare's reading in Virgil is evident not only in repeated references to the tragic love story of Dido and Aeneas but in his choice of the name Lavinia (*Aeneid,* Book 7 ff.).

As this sizable list of influences suggests, Shakespeare's first tragedy remains close to its models. Although the play anticipates several motifs in the later tragedies—the ingratitude of Rome toward its honored general as in *Coriolanus,* Roman political factionalism as in *Julius Caesar,* infirm old age confronted by human bestiality as in *King Lear*—*Titus Andronicus* is the kind of revenge play one might expect of a gifted young playwright in the early 1590s. The successful models for tragic writing in those years were Kyd and Marlowe; Greene, Peele, and others paid these two the flattery of imitation. So to an extent did Shakespeare. We can best understand *Titus Andronicus* if we view it as a revenge play in the sensational vein of Shakespeare's immediate predecessors, with generous additions of Ovidian pathos. We should not look in *Titus Andronicus* for that humane and compassionate wisdom we expect in mature Shakespearean tragedy; as a revenge play, *Titus Andronicus* focuses on violence and horror, and its mood is one of revulsion. The style too requires some adjustment in our expectations. Owing much to Kyd, Marlowe, and Ovid, it is replete with rhetorical figures and classical allusions in the manner of Shakespeare's Ovidian poems from the early 1590s, *Venus and Adonis* and *The Rape of Lucrece*. Even if its "early" features are manifest, the style works to good dramatic effect in highly wrought scenes, as when Titus pleads for justice to the unresponsive senators (3.1.1–47), or lays a trap for Tamora and her sons under the guise of his supposed madness (5.2). The seeming incongruity of violent action and elaborately refined metaphor, as in Titus' florid lament for Lavinia's mutilation (3.1.65 ff.), is not, as Eugene Waith has shown (*Shakespeare Survey* 10 [1957], 39–49), without its purpose, for it evokes pathos on behalf of gruesome suffering in a deliberately Ovidian manner, abstracting and generalizing human torment. As in Ovid, the interest is not in moralizing lessons but in the "transforming power of intense states of emotion."

Violence is an enduring feature of *Titus Andronicus*, and its function must be understood if the play is not to be dismissed as merely hyperbolical in its bloodshed. We are constantly aware of ritual human sacrifice, murder, and maiming, as in Titus' sentencing of Tamora's son Alarbus and his slaying of his own son Mutius, the massacre by Tamora's sons of Bassianus and their ravishing of Lavinia, the subsequent execution of two of Titus' sons wrongfully accused of Bassianus' murder, the cutting off of Titus' hand, the feeding to Tamora of her sons' bodies ground into a fine paste, and still more. Savage mutilation is characteristic of many of these atrocities, especially in the lopping off of hands and tongue. The play's climax is, in the manner of revenge tragedy, a spectacle of blood, with the deaths in rapid succession of Lavinia, Tamora, Titus, and Saturninus. These multiple slaughters cause revulsion in some viewers, such as T. S. Eliot, but to others the violence reveals a pattern and offers its own ethical stance on vengeance. Although we do not sense in this early play the same controlled perspective on human evil as in *Hamlet*, for example, we see that Shakespeare is intensely aware of the conflict between order and disorder. In the final scenes, Aaron the Moor is caught and sentenced to execution, Tamora and Saturninus are slain, Titus' brother Marcus appeals to Roman justice for vindication on the grounds that his family had no alternative, and Titus' last remaining son Lucius vows as the new emperor to "heal Rome's harms and wipe away her woe" (5.3.148). Even if this resolution does not fully satisfy the ethical dilemmas with which the play began, it reveals Shakespeare's disinclination to allow the fulfillment of private vengeance to be the play's ultimate concern. Shakespeare is interested throughout in the ethical problems generated by revenge, and the play's relentless horror may be a commentary on the self-defeating nature of a revenge code.

The first part of *Titus Andronicus* functions to give the avenger a motive for his bloody course of action. Ironically, Titus is himself responsible for setting in motion the events that will overwhelm him. His family, the Andronici, are the first to practice vengeance, a fact that diminishes the sympathy they might later have been able to enjoy as victims and exiles. In fact it is Lucius, ultimately to become the restorer of political stability, who first demands the ritual slaying of a captive Goth, Tamora's son Alarbus, to appease the spirits of the Andronici slain in battle. Such a demand is understandable in terms of family honor, but it is also vengeful and pagan. Despite the Romans' claim to be superior to the barbarians they fight (see 1.1.379, for example), their acts too often do not justify that claim to moral superiority. This irony is complete when the Gothic Queen Tamora and her sons plead for godlike mercy. As Tamora's son Chiron bitterly observes, "Was never Scythia half so barbarous" (1.1.131).

Equally violent and unnatural is Titus' slaying of his own son Mutius for assisting in the abduction of Titus' daughter, Lavinia. This tragic error stems, like the first, from Titus' narrow sense of family honor. Titus has unwisely refused the imperial crown, bestowing it instead on the treacherous Saturninus, and has promised Lavinia as bride to the new emperor despite her prior betrothal to Saturninus' virtuous rival and brother, Bassianus. When Titus' sons and Bassianus are driven to the expedient of abducting the lady, Titus cannot endure the shame of his violated promise and so kills Mutius in the ensuing melee. Yet for this sacrifice on behalf of the Emperor, Titus receives only ingratitude and hostility. Moreover, he has taught Tamora and her sons to seek vengeance.

Once the Andronici become the victims of Tamora and her supporters, they gain in sympathy. They suffer unspeakable atrocities. Hunted down by jeering sadists who amuse themselves through rape and mutilation, the Andronici band together in mutual tribulation and selflessly attempt to ease one another's agony. They discover Rome to be a "wilderness of tigers" (3.1.54) in which the law blindly condemns Titus' innocent sons for the murder of Bassianus. Still, Titus has committed the first barbarism and turns increasingly to barbarism in his desire for vengeance. Because the Andronici are too much like their enemies, the prevailing mood as in most revenge plays is more ironic than tragic. There is no strong sense (despite the capture of Aaron) that moral order is restored along with political order. The Andronici are vindicated, and they have gained some wisdom through suffering, but they are still the avengers who gave the first offense.

Titus Andronicus displays many conventions of the revenge play found earlier in *The Spanish Tragedy*. The avenger, Titus, is a man of high position conscientiously serving the state, like Kyd's Hieronimo, who discovers that the state itself is too corrupt to give him justice in his family wrong. The evildoers are members of the Emperor's family, protected by their royal connection. Private and public interests clash, and public welfare is the loser. The avenger has difficulty proving the identity of the villains, but finds an ingenious way at last (through Lavinia's writing in the sand). Once he becomes the avenger, like Hieronimo, Titus grows as remorseless and canny as his enemies. He becomes a menace to public order, uttering enigmatic threats and blazoning forth the injustices of the state. Verging on true madness, he also employs madness as a cloak for his Machiavellian intrigues. His plotting succeeds in duping Queen Tamora into allowing him to arrange his gruesome banquet. The drama ends, like *The Spanish Tragedy,* in a kind of play-within-the-play, as Tamora's two sons take the roles of Rape and Murder, Tamora Revenge, and Titus the cook. Playacting turns deadly earnest with a rapid succession of slaughters. Titus and Lavinia, like Hieronimo and Bel-Imperia, do not outlive their act of vengeance.

This conventional pattern embraces revenge as self-justifying. As in *The Spanish Tragedy,* where the choric Revenge controls the action for his own sinister purposes and welcomes the suffering of innocents or the collapse of governments as grist for his mill, *Titus Andronicus* portrays a world in which the avenger can act seemingly only through violence. Even Lavinia and Titus' young grandson endorse plotting and murder. Titus practices cunning toward his enemies, vowing to "o'erreach them in their own devices" (5.2.143). Our attention is increasingly drawn to the artistry of the "devices" on both sides. The machinations of Aaron and Tamora demand ingenuity in return. An eye must pay for an eye; the punishment must fit the crime. To be sure, Titus and his family do struggle to understand the moral nature of their universe. "If any power pities wretched tears, / To that I call," prays Titus, lifting his mangled hand toward heaven and imploring divine assistance (3.1.208–209). Repeatedly the Andronici ask if a divine justice exists, if it cares about savagery among humans, and if that justice will assist the defenseless. "O heavens," asks Marcus, "can you hear a good man groan / And not relent, or not compassion him?" (4.1.125–126). Why should such terrible evils afflict the human race "Unless the gods delight in tragedies?" (l. 62). Marcus seeks the identities of his niece's ravishers, hoping that Lavinia will be able to "display at last / What God will have discovered for revenge" (ll. 75–76). Is revenge to be God's or humanity's? In part at least, Marcus sees himself and his family as agents of divine justice, like Hamlet, though Titus' own errors will also require his own destruction. Yet even these questionings about the cosmos are a part of the revenge tradition, for Hieronimo in *The Spanish Tragedy* implores the gods in similar terms. Titus, for all his pleas to the heavens, is ultimately the avenger in a revenge play. He does not, like Hamlet, submit himself to what he takes to be the will of providence and wait for whatever opportunity heaven will provide. Titus swears an oath of revenge and proceeds with the most gruesome acts imaginable. In his death there is no talk of reconciliation between divine and human will. As the moment of climax approaches, revenge is seen to be a force from hell, from the "infernal kingdom," while true justice is employed "with Jove in heaven" (5.2.30; 4.3.40). Titus is a protagonist suited to a play in which revenge proceeds by its own pitiless rules, in which brutality is the dominant fact of life, and in which violence is the only apparent means of redress. Divine ideas of justice mock humanity's blind attempts at self-governance without offering reassurance and direction.

As a tragedy of evil, then, *Titus Andronicus* illuminates the nature of that evil more than it attempts to transcend evil through human nobility, as in the later tragedies. This distinctive quality is made especially manifest by the play's outward resemblance to *King Lear*. Titus is old, infirm of judgment, and victimized by his own decision to relinquish power to a person whose villainy he does not comprehend. He is, as Lear says of himself, certainly more sinned against than sinning. Titus approaches madness and generalizes in his grief about the omnipresence of murder and ingratitude in nature (3.2.52–78). His reflections on human injustice suggest the inversion of appearance and reality ("Grief has so wrought on him / He takes false shadows for true substances," (ll. 79–80), a motif of illusion that reappears in the allegorical play-within-the-play. Queen Tamora reveals an innate viciousness and sexual depravity like that of Goneril and Regan. Aaron the Moor, perhaps the first of Shakespeare's gloating Vice-like villains, resembles Edmund in *King Lear* as well as Richard III, Don John (in *Much Ado about Nothing*), and Iago (in *Othello*). *Titus Andronicus* shows us, in embryonic form and close to their sources, many of Shakespeare's later tragic themes and methods.

Aaron the Moor is the most vital character in this early play. Like the Vice of the morality play or like Marlowe's stage Machiavel, Aaron takes delight in pure evil and displays his cunning for the admiration of the audience. Evil to him is "sport," "wit," "stratagem," and above all "policy" (5.1.96; 2.3.1; 2.1.104). His malice encompasses all humanity, and proceeds from no motive other than the sinister pleasure he takes in devising plots. When he is finally captured, Aaron boasts triumphantly of the extent and variety of his cruel accomplishments:

> Even now I curse the day—and yet, I think,
> Few come within the compass of my curse—
> Wherein I did not some notorious ill,
> As kill a man, or else devise his death,
> Ravish a maid, or plot the way to do it,
> Accuse some innocent and forswear myself,
> Set deadly enmity between two friends,
> Make poor men's cattle break their necks,
> Set fire on barns and haystacks in the night
> And bid the owners quench them with their tears.
> Oft have I digged up dead men from their graves
> And set them upright at their dear friends' door,
> Even when their sorrows almost was forgot.
> (5.1.125–137)

Through its depiction of evil as both comic and diabolical, this portrait gives us a vivid insight into the origins of one type of Shakespearean villain.

The seemingly attractive side to Aaron, his fiercely protective instincts toward his bastard son born of Tamora, is part of the central evil of this play: pride of family turning to violent revenge. His black complexion, and that of his son, is equated with barbarism, pagan atheism (Aaron scoffs at those who believe in God), and diabolism. Through him, and through Tamora and her kindred, naked evil is rendered with a terrifying brilliance. As a revenge play *Titus Andronicus* is theatrically effective. To be appreciated properly, it should be seen or read in these terms rather than with the expectations we bring to *King Lear*. Shakespeare here presents barbarism and civilization as polar opposites, but he refuses to equate Rome with civilization and he allows Titus at last no escape from the barbarism that he himself sets in motion. No tragic self-awareness grows out of Titus' humiliation, as it does in *King Lear,* no regret other than for having relinquished power to Saturninus. Instead of tragic self-awareness we are left with an overpowering impression of humanity's potential for brutality. This vision is unameliorated. The constant reminder of a better world of justice and compassion merely serves to heighten the play's ironic and futile sense of wasted goodness.

Titus Andronicus in Performance

Titus Andronicus was popular enough in Shakespeare's day to have elicited a sour comment from Ben Jonson, who was appalled at the success of what he took to be a bloody and sensational piece of dramatic fluff. "He that will swear *Jeronimo* or *Andronicus* are the best plays yet," wrote Jonson in his Induction to *Bartholomew Fair* in 1614, "shall pass unexcepted at here as a man whose judgment shows it is constant, and hath stood still these five-and-twenty or thirty years." Evidently *Titus Andronicus* had become, like Thomas Kyd's *The Spanish Tragedy* (i.e., *Jeronimo*), a byword for the kind of old-fashioned violent action and hyperbole that Jonson wished more than anything to avoid.

Other evidence indicates that Shakespeare's play did well in the late sixteenth and early seventeenth centuries. Theater-owner Philip Henslowe recorded a performance on January 23, 1594, by the Earl of Sussex's men acting probably at the Rose Theatre and other performances later that year by the Lord Admiral's and Lord Chamberlain's men in combination at the Newington Butts theater. A private performance took place in January 1596 at the manor of Sir John Harington of Exton. Quarto editions of the play appeared in 1594, 1600, and 1611, all of them suggesting recent performance by the Earl of Pembroke's and Sussex's men, the Lord Chamberlain's men, or the King's men. The evidence of performance by combined troupes is testimony to the play's very large casting requirements: even with the doubling of roles that must have occurred, as many as twenty-seven actors are required, especially for the crowded first scene.

Titus Andronicus seems to have been "acted now and then" after 1660 by His Majesty's players, according to the testimony of the prompter John Downes. Such an old warhorse as *Titus* could not, however, hope to escape the adapter's hands, and the play appeared in 1678 as *Titus Andronicus, or The Rape of Lavinia,* altered by Edward Ravenscroft and acted at the Theatre Royal, Drury Lane.

The play was revived sometime around 1686 and gradually became a staple of the theater's repertory. In the early eighteenth century James Quin took the part of Aaron which he played regularly until 1724, and, with some added lines and stage business, made it the star role of the play. As Ravenscroft recasts the story, Aaron is a dominating figure even in the very first scene. (Shakespeare brings him onstage, so that his baleful presence is felt from the start, but gives him no lines.) Aaron's last major scene (5.1), in which he defies his Goth captors and boasts of his villainies, is transferred to the conclusion of the cannibalistic banquet as a fitting climax to that gory display. Aaron is revealed rear stage, by the drawing of a curtain, on the rack and refusing at first to talk, having been brought to justice by an avenging Goth whose wife nursed Aaron's child and has been murdered for her pains. The drawing of a curtain similarly reveals the bodies of Demetrius and Chiron "in chains, in bloody linen"; their dismembered heads and hands, hanging up against the wall, answer in a grimly suitable gesture of reciprocity the fate suffered by Andronicus and Lavinia. Before Tamora is slain in the play's bloody catastrophe, she stabs the black child sired by Aaron. The death of Aaron by fire occupies the final moments of an adaptation clearly designed to highlight his monstrosity. (It was also intended to illustrate, by topical analogy, the dangers of treachery and perjury that had recently come to light in the Popish Plot of 1678.)

A play with so much onstage violence was certain to encounter resistance from audiences in the later eighteenth and the nineteenth centuries, and *Titus Andronicus* was seldom seen in any guise during this time. N. H. Bannister staged it at Philadelphia's Walnut Street Theatre in 1839, though taking care to assure his audience that "every expression calculated to offend the ear has been studiously avoided." In the judgment of the critic for the *Sunday Dispatch,* Bannister succeeded in turning *Titus* "into a beautiful play." In 1849, the American black actor Ira Aldridge, who had been successfully acting in England for almost twenty-five years, added Aaron to his repertory of Moorish and black roles that included Othello and Zanga the Moor in Edward Young's *The Revenge*—a part also taken earlier by Quin. In a version of the play that he prepared along with

C. A. Somerset, Aldridge provided English audiences with their one opportunity in the entire nineteenth century to see *Titus Andronicus*. Aldridge's adaptation, like Ravenscroft's, was notable for the added prominence it bestowed on Aaron. Aldridge went well beyond Ravenscroft in an attempt to make the play palatable to his spectators, elevating Aaron into a noble figure and defender of his child (who is stolen from him), removing the rape and mutilation of Lavinia, presenting Tamora as chaste and her sons as dutiful, and allowing only Saturninus to remain a villainous figure. Reviewers were impressed with Aldridge's performance and his adaptation (one reviewer was amazed that he provided "a play not only presentable but actually attractive"), while Shakespeare's original play was dismissed as not fit to be seen onstage. After 1860, when Aldridge acted *Titus* for a final time in Glasgow, the play disappeared from the nineteenth-century stage.

When Robert Atkins produced *Titus Andronicus* at the Old Vic in 1923, then, it had not been seen even in adaptation for over sixty years and not at all in Shakespeare's original form since the 1660s. This courageous revival, by a disciple of the visionary theatrical reformer William Poel, filled its apron stage (devoid of the realistic scenery that had dominated nineteenth-century productions) with spectacle and pageantry. Atkins's stage, by approximating the conditions of the Elizabethan theater, encouraged a rediscovery of the visual effects to which Shakespeare's script pays particular attention: the triumphal procession and jockeying for political advantage in the opening scene, the pit dug for the Andronici in Act 2, scene 3, the mutilations, the grisly banquet.

Twentieth-century spectators have been more ready than their predecessors to confront theatrical images of physical horror, though those images obviously require something more than the mere exploitation of grotesquerie and sensationalism. A production in 1953 by the Marlowe Society in Cambridge, England, emphasized the play's violence, and yet, as the reviewer for *The Times* noted, the production also "found amidst the brutalities more than one note of beauty and pathos." Peter Brook's striking production at Stratford-upon-Avon in 1955, with Laurence Olivier as Titus, Anthony Quayle as Aaron, and Vivien Leigh as Lavinia, explored the theatrical language of violence in a way that rendered it both formally abstract and deeply moving. Brook, taking the view that *Titus Andronicus* is unavoidably "about the most modern of emotions—about violence, hatred, cruelty, pain"—encased the severed hands in baskets and presented the mutilated Lavinia with her arms wrapped in gauze and with scarlet streamers flowing from her mouth and wrists. The scenery, costuming, and music contributed to an effect at once stylized and ominous. Brook cut and rearranged the text to heighten the visual statement.

Joseph Papp has introduced large audiences to *Titus Andronicus* at the New York Shakespeare Festival, first in 1956 at the Emmanuel Presbyterian Church (with Colleen Dewhurst as Tamora and Roscoe Lee Browne as Aaron under Frederick Rolf's direction), and then with great success eleven years later in a production directed by Gerald Freedman at the Delacorte Theater in Central Park. Freedman, like Peter Brook, chose to represent the blood and gore—which any audience must recognize as theatrically contrived—by means of visual impressions and nonliteral staging. The actors were attired in half-masks and long, priestlike robes. In the banquet scene, the victims of the climactic slaughter were enveloped in red cloth that unwound to reveal black shrouds beneath. Musicians appeared onstage among the play's characters, part of an emphasis throughout on breaking theatrical illusion in favor of ritual and symbolic motifs. The costumes, rather than being realistically antique, suggested something nonspecific in time, part of what Freedman called "our inherited primitive consciousness."

Attempts to heighten rather than formalize the play's violence are perhaps unavoidable in a modern theater so readily fascinated with cruelty. Kenneth Tynan and Peter Myers produced a thirty-minute version as part of a program of one-act plays at the Irving Theatre in London in 1951, removing Aaron entirely but still focusing on the carnage. A production by Douglas Seale at the Center Stage in Baltimore, in 1967, invoked the terrors of Mussolini and the fascists to make its point about holocaust. Christopher Martin's 1972 production at the CSC Repertory in New York left out much of the play except the mutilations. The

BBC television version in 1985, directed by Jane Howell, focused the violence through the eyes of Titus' grandson, young Lucius. Wearing steel-rimmed spectacles, Lucius is seen repeatedly in close-up reacting to the brutality of the world around him. Another way of dealing with the violence has been to shorten the play radically and pair it with something quite different in a double bill, as in the Tynan-Myers version of 1951, the Old Vic's production of 1957 (which shared the spotlight with a reduced *The Comedy of Errors*), and John Barton's version at Stratford-upon-Avon in 1981 (paired with *The Two Gentlemen of Verona*). This pairing device suggests a desire to juxtapose and thus neutralize (or perhaps, more grimly, associate) the play's shocking violence with something strikingly opposite to it.

At its best, however, as in the productions of Brook and Freedman, in director Brian Bedford's restrained and intelligent emphasis on the rituals that seek to control the play's appalling savagery (Stratford, Canada, 1978), in the Bristol New Vic's 1978 version directed by Adrian Noble that created the effect of watching the horrifying action in a bear pit, or even in Barton's truncated text, modern theater has shown a way to see the violence of *Titus Andronicus* in artistic perspective, through the medium of theatrical self-awareness. To the extent that Shakespeare's play deals with the inadequacy of both verbal and visual language to express the tragic condition of humanity, the vivid stage images of this play offer a moving commentary on art's ability—or inability—to communicate meaning. Few plays of Shakespeare offer as detailed stage directions as *Titus Andronicus,* calling for the use of the whole Elizabethan theater—senators entering aloft, elaborate processions, the laying of Alarbus' coffin into the tomb (probably the trapdoor), the sights and sounds of hunting, a fatal pit (the trapdoor again), Lucius' son with his Ovid, Lavinia guiding her staff with her mouth and her stumps to write in the sand, Aaron on a ladder, Titus above at his study door, two banquets, and of course the mutilations. The modern theater has made some rich discoveries of a visual language in this play that show it to be worthy, however early and imperfect, of Shakespeare's genius.

TITUS ANDRONICUS

[*Dramatis Personae*

SATURNINUS, *son of the late Emperor of Rome, and afterward declared Emperor*
BASSIANUS, *his brother*

TITUS ANDRONICUS, *a noble Roman, general against the Goths*
LUCIUS, QUINTUS, MARTIUS, MUTIUS, *his sons*
LAVINIA, *his daughter*
YOUNG LUCIUS, *a* BOY, *Lucius' son*
MARCUS ANDRONICUS, *tribune of the people, and Titus' brother*
PUBLIUS, *Marcus' son*
SEMPRONIUS, CAIUS, VALENTINE, *Titus' kinsmen*

TAMORA, *Queen of the Goths, afterward Empress of Rome*
ALARBUS, DEMETRIUS, CHIRON, *her sons*
AARON, *a Moor, her lover*
NURSE

A Roman CAPTAIN
MESSENGER *to Titus*
CLOWN
AEMILIUS, *a noble Roman*
GOTHS
A Roman LORD
A ROMAN

Senators, Tribunes, Judges, Goths, Soldiers, Attendants, a Child of Aaron and Tamora

SCENE: *Rome, and the country near it*]

1.1

[Flourish.] Enter the tribunes and senators aloft; and then enter [below] Saturninus and his followers at one door, and Bassianus and his followers [at the other,] with drums and trumpets.

SATURNINUS

Noble patricians, patrons of my right,
Defend the justice of my cause with arms;
And, countrymen, my loving followers,
Plead my successive title with your swords. 4
I am his firstborn son that was the last
That ware the imperial diadem of Rome. 6
Then let my father's honors live in me,
Nor wrong mine age with this indignity. 8

BASSIANUS

Romans, friends, followers, favorers of my right,
If ever Bassianus, Caesar's son,
Were gracious in the eyes of royal Rome, 11
Keep then this passage to the Capitol, 12
And suffer not dishonor to approach
The imperial seat, to virtue consecrate, 14
To justice, continence, and nobility; 15
But let desert in pure election shine, 16
And, Romans, fight for freedom in your choice.

[Enter] Marcus Andronicus, [aloft,] with the crown.

1.1. Location: Rome. Before the Capitol. The tomb of the Andronici is provided onstage, possibly as a large property backstage or at a trap door.
s.d. aloft i.e., probably in the gallery, rearstage above the tiring-house, looking down on the main stage. **followers** (including soldiers; see *Exeunt soldiers* at ll. 55 s.d. and 59 s.d.). **drums** drummers. **trumpets** trumpeters **4 successive title** title to the succession **6 ware** wore **8 age** seniority **11 Were gracious** found favor and acceptance **12 Keep** guard, defend **14 consecrate** consecrated **15 continence** restraint **16 pure election** free choice, i.e., of the Roman citizens. (Bassianus urges the Romans to let merit, or *desert,* prevail, rather than inherited right.)

MARCUS
Princes, that strive by factions and by friends
Ambitiously for rule and empery, 19
Know that the people of Rome, for whom we stand
A special party, have by common voice 21
In election for the Roman empery
Chosen Andronicus, surnamèd Pius 23
For many good and great deserts to Rome.
A nobler man, a braver warrior,
Lives not this day within the city walls.
He by the Senate is accited home 27
From weary wars against the barbarous Goths,
That with his sons, a terror to our foes, 29
Hath yoked a nation strong, trained up in arms. 30
Ten years are spent since first he undertook
This cause of Rome, and chastisèd with arms
Our enemies' pride. Five times he hath returned
Bleeding to Rome, bearing his valiant sons
In coffins from the field. 35
And now at last, laden with honor's spoils,
Returns the good Andronicus to Rome,
Renownèd Titus, flourishing in arms.
Let us entreat, by honor of his name 39
Whom worthily you would have now succeed, 40
And in the Capitol and Senate's right,
Whom you pretend to honor and adore, 42
That you withdraw you and abate your strength,
Dismiss your followers, and, as suitors should,
Plead your deserts in peace and humbleness.

19 empery rule (as emperor) **21 A special party** i.e., a representative group specially chosen. (As a tribune, Marcus Andronicus has been elected by the *people of Rome,* l. 20, the plebeians, to represent their rights.) **23 Chosen** i.e, nominated. **Pius** dutiful, patriotic **27 accited** summoned **29 That** who, i.e., Titus **30 yoked** subdued **35 field** (The first quarto follows with three and one-half lines deleted from the second and third quartos and the Folio because they are inconsistent with ll. 96–147 below and probably represent a canceled first draft that the printer of the first quarto mistakenly included: "and at this day / To the monument of the Andronici, / Done sacrifice of expiation, / And slain the noblest prisoner of the Goths.") **39–40 by . . . succeed** i.e., by the honorable name of him you choose as worthy candidate **42 pretend** assert, profess

SATURNINUS
How fair the tribune speaks to calm my thoughts! 46
BASSIANUS
Marcus Andronicus, so I do affy 47
In thy uprightness and integrity,
And so I love and honor thee and thine,
Thy noble brother Titus and his sons,
And her to whom my thoughts are humbled all, 51
Gracious Lavinia, Rome's rich ornament,
That I will here dismiss my loving friends,
And to my fortunes and the people's favor
Commit my cause in balance to be weighed.
Exeunt soldiers [*of Bassianus*].
SATURNINUS
Friends, that have been thus forward in my right,
I thank you all and here dismiss you all,
And to the love and favor of my country
Commit myself, my person, and the cause.
[*Exeunt the soldiers of Saturninus.*]
Rome, be as just and gracious unto me
As I am confident and kind to thee. 61
Open the gates and let me in.
BASSIANUS
Tribunes, and me, a poor competitor. 63
[*Flourish.*] *They* [*Saturninus and Bassianus*] *go up into the Senate House.*

Enter a Captain.

CAPTAIN
Romans, make way! The good Andronicus,
Patron of virtue, Rome's best champion,
Successful in the battles that he fights,
With honor and with fortune is returned

46 fair courteously, gently **47 affy** trust **51 all** entirely **61 confident** without suspicion **63 poor competitor** rival of lower rank. (Bassianus is younger brother and thus not in the direct line of inheritance.)
s.d. go up (The *gates* mentioned in l. 62 are presumably a door in the facade of the tiring-house, rearstage, below the gallery. Saturninus and Bassianus presumably exit through this door and ascend inside the tiring-house to the gallery or Senate House, where they reappear with the tribunes and senators.)

From where he circumscribèd with his sword 68
And brought to yoke the enemies of Rome. 69

Sound drums and trumpets, and then enter two of Titus' sons, [Martius and Mutius]; and then two men bearing a coffin covered with black; then two other sons [Lucius and Quintus]; then Titus Andronicus; and then Tamora, the Queen of Goths, and her three sons [Alarbus,] Chiron, and Demetrius, with Aaron the Moor, and others as many as can be. Then set down the coffin, and Titus speaks.

TITUS
Hail, Rome, victorious in thy mourning weeds! 70
Lo, as the bark that hath discharged his freight 71
Returns with precious lading to the bay
From whence at first she weighed her anchorage, 73
Cometh Andronicus, bound with laurel boughs,
To re-salute his country with his tears,
Tears of true joy for his return to Rome.
Thou great defender of this Capitol, 77
Stand gracious to the rites that we intend!
Romans, of five-and-twenty valiant sons,
Half of the number that King Priam had, 80
Behold the poor remains, alive and dead.
These that survive let Rome reward with love;
These that I bring unto their latest home, 83
With burial amongst their ancestors. 84
Here Goths have given me leave to sheathe my sword. 85
Titus, unkind and careless of thine own, 86
Why suffer'st thou thy sons, unburied yet,

68 circumscribèd restrained **69 s.d. Titus Andronicus** (Titus may enter drawn in a chariot; he refers to his chariot in l. 250.) **70 weeds** garments **71 bark** sailing vessel. **his** its **73 anchorage** i.e., anchor **77 Thou** i.e., Jupiter Capitolinus **80 King Priam** King of Troy at the time of its fall; he had fifty sons **83 latest** final **84 With** i.e., let Rome reward with **85 Here . . . sword** i.e., the defeated Goths have been so good as to let me put up my weapons. (Said ironically; the Goths had no choice.) **86 unkind** deficient in natural feeling

To hover on the dreadful shore of Styx? 88
Make way to lay them by their brethren.
They open the tomb.
There greet in silence, as the dead are wont,
And sleep in peace, slain in your country's wars!
O sacred receptacle of my joys,
Sweet cell of virtue and nobility,
How many sons hast thou of mine in store,
That thou wilt never render to me more!

LUCIUS
Give us the proudest prisoner of the Goths,
That we may hew his limbs, and on a pile
Ad manes fratrum sacrifice his flesh 98
Before this earthy prison of their bones,
That so the shadows be not unappeased, 100
Nor we disturbed with prodigies on earth. 101

TITUS
I give him you, the noblest that survives,
The eldest son of this distressèd queen.

TAMORA [*Kneeling*]
Stay, Roman brethren! Gracious conqueror, 104
Victorious Titus, rue the tears I shed,
A mother's tears in passion for her son; 106
And if thy sons were ever dear to thee,
O, think my son to be as dear to me!
Sufficeth not that we are brought to Rome 109
To beautify thy triumphs, and return 110
Captive to thee and to thy Roman yoke,
But must my sons be slaughtered in the streets
For valiant doings in their country's cause?
O, if to fight for king and commonweal 114
Were piety in thine, it is in these.
Andronicus, stain not thy tomb with blood! 116

88 Styx river surrounding Hades across which souls might not cross until they had received proper burial **98 Ad manes fratrum** to the departed spirits of (our) brothers **100 shadows** shades, ghosts **101 prodigies** omens, portents of ill **104 s.d. Kneeling** (In a drawing of Act 1 of *Titus,* done in about 1595 by Henry Peacham, Tamora's sons are also shown kneeling.) **106 passion** grief **109 Sufficeth not** doesn't it suffice **110 return** i.e., accompany your return **114 commonweal** commonwealth **116 tomb** family tomb

Wilt thou draw near the nature of the gods?
Draw near them then in being merciful.
Sweet mercy is nobility's true badge.
Thrice noble Titus, spare my firstborn son.

TITUS [*Raising her*]
Patient yourself, madam, and pardon me. 121
These are their brethren, whom your Goths beheld 122
Alive and dead, and for their brethren slain
Religiously they ask a sacrifice.
To this your son is marked, and die he must
T' appease their groaning shadows that are gone.

LUCIUS
Away with him! And make a fire straight, 127
And with our swords, upon a pile of wood,
Let's hew his limbs till they be clean consumed. 129
Exeunt Titus' sons with Alarbus.

TAMORA
O cruel, irreligious piety!

CHIRON
Was never Scythia half so barbarous. 131

DEMETRIUS
Oppose not Scythia to ambitious Rome. 132
Alarbus goes to rest, and we survive
To tremble under Titus' threatening look.
Then, madam, stand resolved, but hope withal 135
The selfsame gods that armed the Queen of Troy 136
With opportunity of sharp revenge
Upon the Thracian tyrant in his tent
May favor Tamora, the Queen of Goths—
When Goths were Goths and Tamora was queen—
To quit the bloody wrongs upon her foes. 141

Enter the sons of Andronicus again [*with their swords bloody*].

121 Patient calm **122 their brethren** i.e., the brothers of those who have been slain **127 straight** at once **129 clean** wholly **131 Scythia** a region north of the Black Sea; its people were notorious for their savagery **132 Oppose** compare **135 withal** besides **136 Queen of Troy** Hecuba, wife of Priam, who after the fall of Troy was carried to Greece as a slave; there she found occasion to avenge the death of her son Polydorus by killing the two sons of the murderer, Polymnestor, King of Thrace **141 quit** requite

LUCIUS

See, lord and father, how we have performed
Our Roman rites. Alarbus' limbs are lopped,
And entrails feed the sacrificing fire,
Whose smoke, like incense, doth perfume the sky.
Remaineth naught but to inter our brethren
And with loud 'larums welcome them to Rome. 147

TITUS

Let it be so, and let Andronicus
Make this his latest farewell to their souls. 149

Sound trumpets, and lay the coffin in the tomb.

In peace and honor rest you here, my sons;
Rome's readiest champions, repose you here in rest,
Secure from worldly chances and mishaps!
Here lurks no treason, here no envy swells,
Here grow no damnèd drugs; here are no storms, 154
No noise, but silence and eternal sleep.
In peace and honor rest you here, my sons!

Enter Lavinia.

LAVINIA

In peace and honor live Lord Titus long;
My noble lord and father, live in fame!
Lo, at this tomb my tributary tears 159
I render for my brethren's obsequies, 160
And at thy feet I kneel, with tears of joy [*Kneeling*]
Shed on this earth for thy return to Rome.
O, bless me here with thy victorious hand,
Whose fortunes Rome's best citizens applaud!

TITUS

Kind Rome, that hast thus lovingly reserved
The cordial of mine age to glad my heart! 166
Lavinia, live; outlive thy father's days

147 'larums trumpet calls **149 s.d. the coffin** (Although there is presumably more than one dead son, the staging may have relied on one coffin for economy.) **154 drugs** poisonous plants **159 tributary** paid in tribute **160 obsequies** acts performed in honor of the dead
166 cordial restorative; or comfort, pleasure

And fame's eternal date, for virtue's praise! 168

[*She rises.*]

[*Marcus Andronicus speaks from above where he is accompanied by Saturninus, Bassianus, other tribunes, etc.*]

MARCUS

Long live Lord Titus, my belovèd brother,
Gracious triumpher in the eyes of Rome!

TITUS

Thanks, gentle tribune, noble brother Marcus.

MARCUS

And welcome, nephews, from successful wars,
You that survive, and you that sleep in fame!
Fair lords, your fortunes are alike in all, 174
That in your country's service drew your swords;
But safer triumph is this funeral pomp
That hath aspired to Solon's happiness, 177
And triumphs over chance in honor's bed. 178
Titus Andronicus, the people of Rome,
Whose friend in justice thou hast ever been,
Send thee by me, their tribune and their trust,
This palliament of white and spotless hue, 182
And name thee in election for the empire 183
With these our late-deceasèd emperor's sons.
Be *candidatus* then, and put it on, 185
And help to set a head on headless Rome.

[*A white cloak is brought to Titus.*]

TITUS

A better head her glorious body fits
Than his that shakes for age and feebleness.
What should I don this robe and trouble you? 189
Be chosen with proclamations today,

168 date duration **174 your . . . all** i.e., you who are alive and you who are dead share a similar fame and good fortune in your victory **177 aspired** risen. **Solon's happiness** i.e., the happiness defined by Solon (a Greek sage and lawgiver): that no man may be called happy until after his death **178 chance** the vicissitude of existence. **honor's bed** an honorable grave **182 palliament** gown or cloak **183 in election** i.e., as a candidate **185 candidatus** (Literally, one clad in white; a candidate.) **189 What** why

Tomorrow yield up rule, resign my life,
And set abroad new business for you all? 192
Rome, I have been thy soldier forty years,
And led my country's strength successfully,
And buried one-and-twenty valiant sons,
Knighted in field, slain manfully in arms,
In right and service of their noble country. 197
Give me a staff of honor for mine age,
But not a scepter to control the world.
Upright he held it, lords, that held it last.

MARCUS
Titus, thou shalt obtain and ask the empery. 201

SATURNINUS
Proud and ambitious tribune, canst thou tell? 202

TITUS Patience, Prince Saturninus.

SATURNINUS Romans, do me right.
Patricians, draw your swords, and sheathe them not
Till Saturninus be Rome's emperor.
Andronicus, would thou were shipped to hell
Rather than rob me of the people's hearts!

LUCIUS
Proud Saturnine, interrupter of the good
That noble-minded Titus means to thee!

TITUS
Content thee, Prince. I will restore to thee
The people's hearts, and wean them from themselves. 212

BASSIANUS
Andronicus, I do not flatter thee,
But honor thee, and will do till I die.
My faction if thou strengthen with thy friends,
I will most thankful be; and thanks to men
Of noble minds is honorable meed. 217

TITUS
People of Rome, and people's tribunes here,
I ask your voices and your suffrages. 219
Will ye bestow them friendly on Andronicus?

192 abroad i.e., on foot **197 In . . . of** serving the just cause of **201 obtain and ask** i.e., obtain simply by asking **202 canst thou tell** i.e., that's what you think **212 from themselves** i.e., from their present intention **217 meed** reward **219 voices** votes. **suffrages** votes

TRIBUNES
To gratify the good Andronicus
And gratulate his safe return to Rome, 222
The people will accept whom he admits.

TITUS
Tribunes, I thank you, and this suit I make:
That you create our emperor's eldest son, 225
Lord Saturnine, whose virtues will, I hope,
Reflect on Rome as Titan's rays on earth, 227
And ripen justice in this commonweal.
Then, if you will elect by my advice,
Crown him and say, "Long live our emperor!"

MARCUS
With voices and applause of every sort,
Patricians and plebeians, we create
Lord Saturninus Rome's great emperor,
And say, "Long live our Emperor Saturnine!"
[*Saturninus is crowned. A long flourish till they come down.*]

SATURNINUS
Titus Andronicus, for thy favors done
To us in our election this day,
I give thee thanks in part of thy deserts, 237
And will with deeds requite thy gentleness. 238
And, for an onset, Titus, to advance 239
Thy name and honorable family,
Lavinia will I make my empress,
Rome's royal mistress, mistress of my heart,
And in the sacred Pantheon her espouse. 243
Tell me, Andronicus, doth this motion please thee? 244

TITUS
It doth, my worthy lord, and in this match
I hold me highly honored of Your Grace. 246
And here in sight of Rome to Saturnine,
King and commander of our commonweal,
The wide world's emperor, do I consecrate
My sword, my chariot, and my prisoners,

222 gratulate salute, rejoice in **225 create** i.e., elect **227 Titan's** (Helios, the sun god, was a descendant of the Titans.) **237 in** as **238 gentleness** nobleness **239 onset** beginning **243 Pantheon** Roman temple dedicated to all the gods **244 motion** proposal **246 of** by

Presents well worthy Rome's imperious lord. 251
Receive them, then, the tribute that I owe,
Mine honor's ensigns humbled at thy feet. 253
[*A tribute is laid at Saturninus' feet.*]

SATURNINUS
Thanks, noble Titus, father of my life!
How proud I am of thee and of thy gifts
Rome shall record, and when I do forget
The least of these unspeakable deserts, 257
Romans, forget your fealty to me.

TITUS [*To Tamora*]
Now, madam, are you prisoner to an emperor,
To him that for your honor and your state
Will use you nobly and your followers.

SATURNINUS [*Aside*]
A goodly lady, trust me, of the hue
That I would choose, were I to choose anew.—
Clear up, fair Queen, that cloudy countenance.
Though chance of war hath wrought this change
of cheer, 265
Thou com'st not to be made a scorn in Rome.
Princely shall be thy usage every way.
Rest on my word, and let not discontent 268
Daunt all your hopes. Madam, he comforts you
Can make you greater than the Queen of Goths. 270
Lavinia, you are not displeased with this?

LAVINIA
Not I, my lord, sith true nobility 272
Warrants these words in princely courtesy. 273

SATURNINUS
Thanks, sweet Lavinia. Romans, let us go.
Ransomless here we set our prisoners free.
Proclaim our honors, lords, with trump and drum.
[*Flourish. Saturninus starts*
to leave, attended.]

BASSIANUS [*Seizing Lavinia*]
Lord Titus, by your leave, this maid is mine.

251 imperious imperial **253 ensigns** tokens **257 unspeakable** inexpressible **265 cheer** countenance **268 Rest** rely **270 Can** who can **272 sith** since **273 Warrants** justifies

TITUS
How, sir? Are you in earnest then, my lord?

BASSIANUS
Ay, noble Titus, and resolved withal
To do myself this reason and this right.

MARCUS
Suum cuique is our Roman justice. 281
This prince in justice seizeth but his own.

LUCIUS
And that he will and shall, if Lucius live.

TITUS
Traitors, avaunt! Where is the Emperor's guard? 284
Treason, my lord! Lavinia is surprised! 285

SATURNINUS
Surprised? By whom?

BASSIANUS
By him that justly may
Bear his betrothed from all the world away.

MUTIUS
Brothers, help to convey her hence away,
And with my sword I'll keep this door safe.

[*Exeunt Bassianus, Marcus, Lucius, Quintus, and Martius, with Lavinia.*]

TITUS [*To Saturninus*]
Follow, my lord, and I'll soon bring her back.

MUTIUS [*Guarding the door*]
My lord, you pass not here.

TITUS
What, villain boy?
Barr'st me my way in Rome? [*He stabs Mutius.*]

MUTIUS
Help, Lucius, help! 292
[*He dies.*]

[*During the fray, exeunt Saturninus, Tamora, Demetrius, Chiron, and Aaron.*]

[*Enter Lucius.*]

281 Suum cuique to each his own **284–285 Traitors . . . surprised** (Evidently Saturninus, starting to leave, has not quite realized what has happened, and his guard, accompanying him, has been caught napping.) **avaunt** begone. **surprised** taken **292 s.d. During . . . Aaron** (Evidently Saturninus, realizing he has been dishonored by the seizure of Lavinia and having decided in any case that he prefers Tamora, ll. 262–263, decides to make her his forthwith.)

LUCIUS [*To Titus*]
My lord, you are unjust; and more than so,
In wrongful quarrel you have slain your son.

TITUS
Nor thou, nor he, are any sons of mine. 295
My sons would never so dishonor me.
Traitor, restore Lavinia to the Emperor.

LUCIUS
Dead, if you will, but not to be his wife,
That is another's lawful promised love. [*Exit*.] 299

Enter aloft the Emperor [Saturninus] *with Tamora and her two sons and Aaron the Moor.*

SATURNINUS
No, Titus, no. The Emperor needs her not,
Nor her, nor thee, nor any of thy stock.
I'll trust by leisure him that mocks me once; 302
Thee never, nor thy traitorous haughty sons,
Confederates all thus to dishonor me.
Was none in Rome to make a stale 305
But Saturnine? Full well, Andronicus,
Agree these deeds with that proud brag of thine
That saidst I begged the empire at thy hands.

TITUS
O monstrous! What reproachful words are these?

SATURNINUS
But go thy ways; go, give that changing piece 310
To him that flourished for her with his sword. 311
A valiant son-in-law thou shalt enjoy,
One fit to bandy with thy lawless sons, 313
To ruffle in the commonwealth of Rome. 314

TITUS
These words are razors to my wounded heart.

295 Nor neither. (Also in l. 301.) **299 s.d. Exit** (Lucius may take Mutius' body with him and return with it at l. 341, but the presence of the dead body onstage from l. 299 to 341 would not be an inappropriate horror.) **302 by leisure** with caution, barely **305 Was . . . stale** was there no one in Rome to be made a laughingstock **310 changing piece** fickle wench **311 flourished . . . sword** brandished his sword to obtain her **313 bandy** brawl **314 ruffle** swagger

SATURNINUS

And therefore, lovely Tamora, Queen of Goths,
That like the stately Phoebe 'mongst her nymphs 317
Dost overshine the gallant'st dames of Rome,
If thou be pleased with this my sudden choice,
Behold, I choose thee, Tamora, for my bride,
And will create thee Empress of Rome.
Speak, Queen of Goths, dost thou applaud my choice?
And here I swear by all the Roman gods,
Sith priest and holy water are so near,
And tapers burn so bright, and everything
In readiness for Hymenaeus stand, 326
I will not re-salute the streets of Rome,
Or climb my palace, till from forth this place
I lead espoused my bride along with me.

TAMORA

And here in sight of heaven to Rome I swear,
If Saturnine advance the Queen of Goths,
She will a handmaid be to his desires,
A loving nurse, a mother to his youth.

SATURNINUS

Ascend, fair Queen, Pantheon. Lords, accompany
Your noble emperor and his lovely bride,
Sent by the heavens for Prince Saturnine,
Whose wisdom hath her fortune conquerèd. 337
There shall we consummate our spousal rites. 338

Exeunt omnes [*except Titus*].

TITUS

I am not bid to wait upon this bride. 339
Titus, when wert thou wont to walk alone,
Dishonored thus, and challengèd of wrongs? 341

Enter Marcus and Titus' sons [*Lucius, Quintus, and Martius*].

MARCUS

O Titus, see, O, see what thou hast done!
In a bad quarrel slain a virtuous son.

317 Phoebe (One of the names of the moon goddess.) **326 Hymenaeus** god of marriage **337 Whose . . . conquerèd** i.e., whose wise choice to be my queen has overcome her ill fortune of being conquered in battle **338 s.d. omnes** all **339 bid** invited **341 challengèd** accused

TITUS

No, foolish tribune, no; no son of mine,
Nor thou, nor these, confederates in the deed
That hath dishonored all our family.
Unworthy brother, and unworthy sons!

LUCIUS

But let us give him burial as becomes, 348
Give Mutius burial with our brethren.

TITUS

Traitors, away! He rests not in this tomb.
This monument five hundred years hath stood,
Which I have sumptuously re-edified. 352
Here none but soldiers and Rome's servitors 353
Repose in fame, none basely slain in brawls.
Bury him where you can. He comes not here.

MARCUS

My lord, this is impiety in you.
My nephew Mutius' deeds do plead for him;
He must be buried with his brethren.

MARTIUS

And shall.

QUINTUS Or him we will accompany.

TITUS

"And shall"? What villain was it spake that word?

MARTIUS

He that would vouch it in any place but here. 361

TITUS

What, would you bury him in my despite? 362

MARCUS

No, noble Titus, but entreat of thee
To pardon Mutius and to bury him.

TITUS

Marcus, even thou hast struck upon my crest,
And, with these boys, mine honor thou hast wounded.
My foes I do repute you every one. 367
So trouble me no more, but get you gone.

348 becomes is fitting **352 re-edified** rebuilt **353 servitors** armed defenders **361 vouch** maintain. **any place but here** i.e., anywhere but in this sacred place **362 in my despite** in despite of me **367 repute** think of

QUINTUS
He is not with himself. Let us withdraw. 369

MARTIUS
Not I, till Mutius' bones be burièd.
The brother [*Marcus*] *and the sons kneel.*

MARCUS
Brother, for in that name doth nature plead—

MARTIUS
Father, and in that name doth nature speak—

TITUS
Speak thou no more, if all the rest will speed. 373

MARCUS
Renownèd Titus, more than half my soul—

LUCIUS
Dear Father, soul and substance of us all—

MARCUS
Suffer thy brother Marcus to inter 376
His noble nephew here in virtue's nest,
That died in honor and Lavinia's cause.
Thou art a Roman; be not barbarous.
The Greeks upon advice did bury Ajax, 380
That slew himself, and wise Laertes' son
Did graciously plead for his funerals.
Let not young Mutius, then, that was thy joy,
Be barred his entrance here.

TITUS
Rise, Marcus, rise.
[*They rise.*]
The dismal'st day is this that e'er I saw,
To be dishonored by my sons in Rome!
Well, bury him, and bury me the next.
They put him [*Mutius*] *in the tomb.*

LUCIUS
There lie thy bones, sweet Mutius, with thy friends,

369 not with himself i.e., distracted **373 if . . . speed** if all is to succeed; or, possibly, if you remaining sons do not wish to be slain like Mutius **376 Suffer** permit **380 advice** deliberation. **Ajax** Greek hero of the Trojan War who went mad because the armor of Achilles was awarded to Odysseus, slew a flock of sheep deludedly thinking them Greeks, and later committed suicide in shame; he was refused burial until *Laertes' son,* l. 381, Odysseus, successfully pleaded for his funeral rites

Till we with trophies do adorn thy tomb. 389

They all kneel.

ALL

No man shed tears for noble Mutius;

He lives in fame that died in virtue's cause. 391

[*They rise.*] *Exeunt all but Marcus and Titus.*

MARCUS

My lord, to step out of these dreary dumps, 392

How comes it that the subtle Queen of Goths

Is of a sudden thus advanced in Rome?

TITUS

I know not, Marcus, but I know it is—

Whether by device or no, the heavens can tell. 396

Is she not then beholding to the man 397

That brought her for this high good turn so far?

MARCUS

Yes, and will nobly him remunerate. 399

[*Flourish.*] *Enter the Emperor* [*Saturninus*], *Tamora, and her two sons, with* [*Aaron*] *the Moor, at one door. Enter at the other door Bassianus and Lavinia, with others,* [*Lucius, Martius, and Quintus*].

SATURNINUS

So, Bassianus, you have played your prize. 400

God give you joy, sir, of your gallant bride!

BASSIANUS

And you of yours, my lord! I say no more,

Nor wish no less; and so I take my leave.

SATURNINUS

Traitor, if Rome have law or we have power, 404

Thou and thy faction shall repent this rape. 405

389 trophies memorials **s.d. They all kneel** (Some editors think it unlikely that Titus joins his sons in kneeling or in saying ll. 390–391, but Titus has relented and is not without feeling for the son he has slain.) **391 s.d. Exeunt** (Perhaps the sons go off in order to accompany Bassianus' entry at 399, or they may simply stand aside.) **392 dumps** melancholy **396 device** scheming **397 beholding** beholden **399 Yes . . . remunerate** (Said sarcastically; Tamora will show her gratitude in physical ways.) **400 played your prize** played and won your bout (as in fencing) **404 we** I. (The royal plural; also at ll. 410–411, etc.) **405 rape** forcible seizure

BASSIANUS
"Rape" call you it, my lord, to seize my own,
My true-betrothèd love and now my wife?
But let the laws of Rome determine all;
Meanwhile am I possessed of that is mine. 409

SATURNINUS
'Tis good, sir. You are very short with us,
But if we live we'll be as sharp with you.

BASSIANUS
My lord, what I have done, as best I may
Answer I must, and shall do with my life.
Only thus much I give Your Grace to know:
By all the duties that I owe to Rome,
This noble gentleman, Lord Titus here,
Is in opinion and in honor wronged, 417
That, in the rescue of Lavinia,
With his own hand did slay his youngest son
In zeal to you, and highly moved to wrath
To be controlled in that he frankly gave. 421
Receive him, then, to favor, Saturnine,
That hath expressed himself in all his deeds
A father and a friend to thee and Rome.

TITUS
Prince Bassianus, leave to plead my deeds. 425
'Tis thou, and those, that have dishonored me. 426
Rome and the righteous heavens be my judge
How I have loved and honored Saturnine! [*He kneels.*]

TAMORA [*To Saturninus*]
My worthy lord, if ever Tamora
Were gracious in those princely eyes of thine,
Then hear me speak indifferently for all; 431
And at my suit, sweet, pardon what is past.

SATURNINUS
What, madam? Be dishonored openly,
And basely put it up without revenge? 434

TAMORA
Not so, my lord. The gods of Rome forfend 435

409 that that which **417 opinion** reputation **421 controlled** opposed, restrained. **in . . . gave** i.e., in his free bestowal of Lavinia on Saturninus **425 leave to plead** cease pleading **426 those** those sons of mine **431 indifferently** impartially **434 put it up** put up with it **435 forfend** forbid

I should be author to dishonor you! 436
But on mine honor dare I undertake 437
For good Lord Titus' innocence in all,
Whose fury not dissembled speaks his griefs. 439
Then at my suit look graciously on him;
Lose not so noble a friend on vain suppose, 441
Nor with sour looks afflict his gentle heart.
[*Aside to Saturninus.*] My lord, be ruled by me. Be won
at last;
Dissemble all your griefs and discontents.
You are but newly planted in your throne;
Lest then the people, and patricians too,
Upon a just survey take Titus' part
And so supplant you for ingratitude,
Which Rome reputes to be a heinous sin,
Yield at entreats; and then let me alone. 450
I'll find a day to massacre them all
And raze their faction and their family,
The cruel father and his traitorous sons
To whom I suèd for my dear son's life,
And make them know what 'tis to let a queen
Kneel in the streets and beg for grace in vain.—
[*Aloud.*] Come, come, sweet Emperor. Come,
Andronicus.
Take up this good old man, and cheer the heart 458
That dies in tempest of thy angry frown.

SATURNINUS
Rise, Titus, rise. My empress hath prevailed.

TITUS [*Rising*]
I thank Your Majesty, and her, my lord.
These words, these looks, infuse new life in me.

TAMORA
Titus, I am incorporate in Rome, 463
A Roman now adopted happily, 464
And must advise the Emperor for his good.
This day all quarrels die, Andronicus.

436 author agent **437 undertake** assert, vouch **439 Whose . . . griefs** whose unconcealed anger gives testimonial to his grievances **441 vain suppose** idle supposition **450 at entreats** to entreaty. **let me alone** leave it to me **458 Take up** raise from kneeling **463 am incorporate in** have been admitted to the fellowship of **464 happily** fortunately

And let it be mine honor, good my lord,
That I have reconciled your friends and you.
For you, Prince Bassianus, I have passed
My word and promise to the Emperor
That you will be more mild and tractable.
And fear not, lords, and you, Lavinia;
By my advice, all humbled on your knees,
You shall ask pardon of His Majesty. 474
[*Lucius, Martius, Quintus, and Lavinia kneel.*]

LUCIUS
We do, and vow to heaven and to His Highness
That what we did was mildly as we might,
Tend'ring our sister's honor and our own. 477

MARCUS [*Kneeling*]
That, on mine honor, here do I protest.

SATURNINUS [*Turning away*]
Away, and talk not! Trouble us no more.

TAMORA
Nay, nay, sweet Emperor, we must all be friends.
The tribune and his nephews kneel for grace;
I will not be denied. Sweet heart, look back.

SATURNINUS
Marcus, for thy sake and thy brother's here,
And at my lovely Tamora's entreats,
I do remit these young men's heinous faults.
Stand up. [*The Andronici rise.*]
Lavinia, though you left me like a churl,
I found a friend, and sure as death I swore
I would not part a bachelor from the priest. 489
Come. If the Emperor's court can feast two brides,
You are my guest, Lavinia, and your friends.
This day shall be a love-day, Tamora. 492

TITUS
Tomorrow, an it please Your Majesty 493
To hunt the panther and the hart with me,
With horn and hound we'll give Your Grace *bonjour*. 495

474 s.d. Lucius . . . kneel (Perhaps Bassianus kneels also, though his pardon seems to have been assured at l. 469.) **477 Tend'ring** having regard for **489 part** depart **492 love-day** day appointed to settle disputes **493 an** if **495 bonjour** good morning

SATURNINUS

Be it so, Titus, and gramercy too. 496

Exeunt. Sound trumpets. Manet
[Aaron the] Moor.

496 gramercy great thanks **s.d. Manet** he remains onstage. (The Folio has Aaron exit with the rest and re-enter. The tomb of Act 1 is possibly concealed by a curtain backstage.)

2.1

AARON

Now climbeth Tamora Olympus' top, 1
Safe out of fortune's shot, and sits aloft,
Secure of thunder's crack or lightning flash, 3
Advanced above pale envy's threatening reach. 4
As when the golden sun salutes the morn
And, having gilt the ocean with his beams,
Gallops the zodiac in his glistering coach 7
And overlooks the highest-peering hills, 8
So Tamora.
Upon her wit doth earthly honor wait, 10
And virtue stoops and trembles at her frown.
Then, Aaron, arm thy heart and fit thy thoughts
To mount aloft with thy imperial mistress,
And mount her pitch whom thou in triumph long 14
Hast prisoner held, fettered in amorous chains
And faster bound to Aaron's charming eyes 16
Than is Prometheus tied to Caucasus. 17
Away with slavish weeds and servile thoughts! 18
I will be bright, and shine in pearl and gold,
To wait upon this new-made empress.
To wait, said I? To wanton with this queen,
This goddess, this Semiramis, this nymph, 22
This siren that will charm Rome's Saturnine
And see his shipwreck and his commonweal's.
Holla! What storm is this? 25

Enter Chiron and Demetrius, braving.

2.1. Location: Scene continues. Aaron remains onstage.
1 Olympus home of the Greek gods **3 of** from **4 envy's** hate's, malice's **7 Gallops** i.e., gallops through **8 overlooks** looks down on from on high **10 wit** wisdom, intelligence. **wait** attend **14 pitch** height to which a falcon soars before descending on its prey. (The image of *mounting* has sexual connotations also.) **16 charming** exerting a magic spell **17 Prometheus** Titan who stole fire from the chariot of the sun and gave it to man; as punishment, Zeus fastened him to a mountain in the Caucasus and sent a vulture to feast on his liver **18 weeds** garments **22 Semiramis** mythical Queen of Assyria, famous for her cruelty and lust **25 s.d. braving** defying (each other)

DEMETRIUS

Chiron, thy years wants wit, thy wits wants edge 26
And manners, to intrude where I am graced, 27
And may, for aught thou knowest, affected be. 28

CHIRON

Demetrius, thou dost overween in all, 29
And so in this, to bear me down with braves. 30
'Tis not the difference of a year or two
Makes me less gracious or thee more fortunate;
I am as able and as fit as thou
To serve, and to deserve my mistress' grace,
And that my sword upon thee shall approve, 35
And plead my passions for Lavinia's love.

AARON [*Aside*]

Clubs, clubs! These lovers will not keep the peace. 37

DEMETRIUS

Why, boy, although our mother, unadvised, 38
Gave you a dancing-rapier by your side, 39
Are you so desperate grown to threat your friends? 40
Go to! Have your lath glued within your sheath 41
Till you know better how to handle it.

CHIRON

Meanwhile, sir, with the little skill I have,
Full well shalt thou perceive how much I dare.

DEMETRIUS

Ay, boy, grow ye so brave? *They draw.*

AARON [*Coming forward*] Why, how now, lords?
So near the Emperor's palace dare ye draw 46
And maintain such a quarrel openly?
Full well I wot the ground of all this grudge. 48
I would not for a million of gold
The cause were known to them it most concerns,

26 wants lack. **edge** sharpness, incisiveness **27 graced** honored, favored **28 affected** loved **29 overween** arrogantly presume
30 braves threats **35 approve** prove **37 Clubs, clubs** (A cry summoning the apprentices of London to join in or suppress a riot or rebellion.)
38 unadvised ill-advisedly **39 a dancing-rapier** an ornamental weapon worn in dancing **40 to** as to **41 Go to** (An expression of impatience.)
lath counterfeit stage weapon of wood **46 So . . . palace** (It was usually against the law to draw a sword in the presence of the King or near his royal residence. See also l. 64.) **48 wot** know

Nor would your noble mother for much more
Be so dishonored in the court of Rome.
For shame, put up.

DEMETRIUS Not I, till I have sheathed 53
My rapier in his bosom, and withal 54
Thrust those reproachful speeches down his throat
That he hath breathed in my dishonor here.

CHIRON

For that I am prepared and full resolved,
Foul-spoken coward, that thunderest with thy tongue
And with thy weapon nothing dar'st perform!

AARON Away, I say!
Now, by the gods that warlike Goths adore,
This petty brabble will undo us all. 62
Why, lords, and think you not how dangerous
It is to jet upon a prince's right? 64
What, is Lavinia then become so loose,
Or Bassianus so degenerate,
That for her love such quarrels may be broached 67
Without controlment, justice, or revenge? 68
Young lords, beware! And should the Empress know
This discord's ground, the music would not please. 70

CHIRON

I care not, I, knew she and all the world. 71
I love Lavinia more than all the world.

DEMETRIUS

Youngling, learn thou to make some meaner choice. 73
Lavinia is thine elder brother's hope.

AARON

Why, are ye mad? Or know ye not in Rome
How furious and impatient they be,
And cannot brook competitors in love? 77
I tell you, lords, you do but plot your deaths
By this device.

53 put up sheathe your swords **54 withal** besides **62 brabble** quarrel, brawl **64 jet** encroach **67 broached** begun, set flowing **68 controlment** restraint **70 ground** basis (with a pun on the musical meaning "bass upon which a melody is constructed") **71 knew she** if she knew **73 meaner** of lower degree **77 brook** endure

CHIRON Aaron, a thousand deaths
Would I propose to achieve her whom I love. 80
AARON
To achieve her? How?
DEMETRIUS Why makes thou it so strange? 81
She is a woman, therefore may be wooed;
She is a woman, therefore may be won;
She is Lavinia, therefore must be loved.
What, man, more water glideth by the mill
Than wots the miller of, and easy it is 86
Of a cut loaf to steal a shive, we know. 87
Though Bassianus be the Emperor's brother,
Better than he have worn Vulcan's badge. 89
AARON [*Aside*]
Ay, and as good as Saturninus may.
DEMETRIUS
Then why should he despair that knows to court it 91
With words, fair looks, and liberality?
What, hast not thou full often struck a doe
And borne her cleanly by the keeper's nose? 94
AARON
Why, then, it seems some certain snatch or so 95
Would serve your turns.
CHIRON Ay, so the turn were served. 96
DEMETRIUS
Aaron, thou hast hit it.
AARON Would you had hit it too! 97
Then should not we be tired with this ado.
Why, hark ye, hark ye, and are you such fools
To square for this? Would it offend you then 100
That both should speed? 101

80 propose be ready to meet **81 Why . . . strange** why do you act so surprised **86 wots** knows **87 shive** slice **89 Vulcan's badge** i.e., cuckold's horns, alluding to the public shame to which he was exposed by his wife Venus' affair with Mars **91 knows** knows how. **court it** play the wooer **94 cleanly by** clean past, without being observed **95 snatch** sudden or quick catch (with a probable bawdy pun) **96 serve your turns** answer your purposes (with sexual suggestion that is underscored in Chiron's reply) **97 hit it . . . hit it** hit the nail on the head . . . scored sexually **100 square** quarrel **101 speed** succeed

CHIRON
Faith, not me.
DEMETRIUS Nor me, so I were one. 102
AARON
For shame, be friends, and join for that you jar. 103
'Tis policy and stratagem must do 104
That you affect, and so must you resolve 105
That what you cannot as you would achieve, 106
You must perforce accomplish as you may. 107
Take this of me: Lucrece was not more chaste 108
Than this Lavinia, Bassianus' love.
A speedier course than lingering languishment 110
Must we pursue, and I have found the path.
My lords, a solemn hunting is in hand; 112
There will the lovely Roman ladies troop.
The forest walks are wide and spacious,
And many unfrequented plots there are, 115
Fitted by kind for rape and villainy. 116
Single you thither then this dainty doe, 117
And strike her home by force, if not by words. 118
This way, or not at all, stand you in hope.
Come, come, our empress, with her sacred wit 120
To villainy and vengeance consecrate, 121
Will we acquaint withal what we intend; 122
And she shall file our engines with advice, 123
That will not suffer you to square yourselves, 124
But to your wishes' height advance you both.
The Emperor's court is like the house of Fame, 126
The palace full of tongues, of eyes, and ears;

102 so so long as **103 join . . . jar** conspire to obtain what you're quarreling over **104 policy** contrivance, craft **105 That** that which. **affect** desire **106–107 That . . . may** that if you can't do this in the way you'd prefer, you must necessarily accomplish it as best you can, by whatever means **108 Lucrece** a chaste Roman lady ravished by Tarquin, as told in Shakespeare's poem *The Rape of Lucrece* **110 languishment** love distress **112 solemn** ceremonial **115 plots** i.e., plots of ground **116 by kind** by nature **117 Single** single out (as in hunting) **118 home** effectually, thoroughly, to the desired place (with sexual suggestion) **120 sacred** i.e., consecrated (to villainy) **121 consecrate** dedicated **122 withal** with **123 file our engines** sharpen our devices **124 square yourselves** quarrel with one another **126 house of Fame** residence of rumor. (Described in Ovid and in Chaucer's *Hous of Fame;* see also Virgil, *Aeneid,* 4.179–190.)

The woods are ruthless, dreadful, deaf, and dull.
There speak and strike, brave boys, and take your turns;
There serve your lust, shadowed from heaven's eye,
And revel in Lavinia's treasury.

CHIRON

Thy counsel, lad, smells of no cowardice.

DEMETRIUS

Sit fas aut nefas, till I find the stream 133
To cool this heat, a charm to calm these fits,
Per Stygia, per manes vehor. *Exeunt.* 135

✤

2.2

Enter Titus Andronicus and his three sons [*and Marcus*], *making a noise with hounds and horns.*

TITUS

The hunt is up, the morn is bright and gray, 1
The fields are fragrant, and the woods are green.
Uncouple here, and let us make a bay, 3
And wake the Emperor and his lovely bride,
And rouse the Prince, and ring a hunter's peal, 5
That all the court may echo with the noise.
Sons, let it be your charge, as it is ours,
To attend the Emperor's person carefully.
I have been troubled in my sleep this night,
But dawning day new comfort hath inspired. 10

Here a cry of hounds, and wind horns in a peal. Then enter Saturninus, Tamora, Bassianus, Lavinia, Chiron, Demetrius, and their attendants.

Many good morrows to Your Majesty!

133 Sit fas aut nefas be it right or wrong **135 Per . . . vehor** I am carried through the Stygian regions, through the realm of the shades. (Adapted from Seneca's *Hippolytus*.)

2.2. Location: The grounds of the Emperor's palace.
1 gray cold, sunless light of early morning **3 Uncouple** unleash the hounds. **make a bay** keep up a deep, prolonged barking **5 ring a hunter's peal** blow a peal on the hunting horns (to set the dogs going) **10 s.d. cry** deep barking. **wind** blow

Madam, to you as many and as good.
I promisèd Your Grace a hunter's peal.

SATURNINUS
And you have rung it lustily, my lords— 14
Somewhat too early for new-married ladies.

BASSIANUS
Lavinia, how say you?

LAVINIA I say no;
I have been broad awake two hours and more.

SATURNINUS
Come on, then, horse and chariots let us have,
And to our sport. [*To Tamora.*] Madam, now shall ye see
Our Roman hunting.

MARCUS I have dogs, my lord,
Will rouse the proudest panther in the chase 21
And climb the highest promontory top.

TITUS
And I have horse will follow where the game 23
Makes way and run like swallows o'er the plain. 24

DEMETRIUS [*To Chiron*]
Chiron, we hunt not, we, with horse nor hound,
But hope to pluck a dainty doe to ground. *Exeunt.*

✣

2.3 *Enter Aaron alone* [*with a bag of gold*].

AARON
He that had wit would think that I had none,
To bury so much gold under a tree
And never after to inherit it. 3
Let him that thinks of me so abjectly
Know that this gold must coin a stratagem 5
Which, cunningly effected, will beget

14 lustily heartily **21 Will** that will. **chase** hunting ground **23 horse will** horses that will **24 run** (The first quarto's *runs* is possible, in parallel to *Makes,* but the verb probably applies to the *horse* rather than to the *game.*)

2.3. Location: A forest near Rome. A pit is provided in the stage, presumably at a trap door, and near it some representation of an elder tree.
3 inherit possess **5 coin** fabricate (with a pun on the literal meaning)

A very excellent piece of villainy.
And so repose, sweet gold, for their unrest 8
That have their alms out of the Empress' chest. 9
[*He hides the gold.*]

Enter Tamora alone to the Moor.

TAMORA
My lovely Aaron, wherefore look'st thou sad,
When everything doth make a gleeful boast? 11
The birds chant melody on every bush,
The snake lies rollèd in the cheerful sun, 13
The green leaves quiver with the cooling wind
And make a checkered shadow on the ground.
Under their sweet shade, Aaron, let us sit,
And whilst the babbling echo mocks the hounds,
Replying shrilly to the well-tuned horns
As if a double hunt were heard at once,
Let us sit down and mark their yellowing noise; 20
And after conflict such as was supposed
The wandering prince and Dido once enjoyed, 22
When with a happy storm they were surprised 23
And curtained with a counsel-keeping cave, 24
We may, each wreathèd in the other's arms,
Our pastimes done, possess a golden slumber,
Whiles hounds and horns and sweet melodious birds
Be unto us as is a nurse's song
Of lullaby to bring her babe asleep.

AARON
Madam, though Venus govern your desires,
Saturn is dominator over mine. 31
What signifies my deadly-standing eye, 32
My silence, and my cloudy melancholy, 33
My fleece of woolly hair that now uncurls
Even as an adder when she doth unroll

8–9 for . . . chest i.e., to discomfit those who will find this gold taken from Tamora's treasure chest **11 boast** display **13 rollèd** coiled **20 yellowing** baying **22 prince** i.e., Aeneas, who, taking shelter from a storm with Dido in a cave during a hunt, made love to her **23 happy** fortunate **24 curtained with** concealed by. **counsel-keeping** secret-keeping **31 Saturn . . . mine** i.e., Saturn, as the dominant planet in my horoscope, governs my temperament and makes it cold and sullen (unlike Venus' effect, which is amorous) **32 deadly-standing** fixed with a death-dealing stare **33 cloudy** gloomy

To do some fatal execution?
No, madam, these are no venereal signs. 37
Vengeance is in my heart, death in my hand,
Blood and revenge are hammering in my head.
Hark, Tamora, the empress of my soul,
Which never hopes more heaven than rests in thee,
This is the day of doom for Bassianus:
His Philomel must lose her tongue today, 43
Thy sons make pillage of her chastity
And wash their hands in Bassianus' blood.
Seest thou this letter? Take it up, I pray thee, 46
[*Giving her a letter*]
And give the King this fatal-plotted scroll.
Now question me no more; we are espied.
Here comes a parcel of our hopeful booty, 49
Which dreads not yet their lives' destruction.

Enter Bassianus and Lavinia.

TAMORA
Ah, my sweet Moor, sweeter to me than life!

AARON
No more, great Empress. Bassianus comes.
Be cross with him, and I'll go fetch thy sons 53
To back thy quarrels, whatsoe'er they be. [*Exit.*]

BASSIANUS
Who have we here? Rome's royal empress,
Unfurnished of her well-beseeming troop? 56
Or is it Dian, habited like her, 57
Who hath abandonèd her holy groves
To see the general hunting in this forest?

TAMORA
Saucy controller of my private steps! 60
Had I the power that some say Dian had,

37 venereal erotic, Venus-like **43 Philomel** (An allusion to the story in Ovid's *Metamorphoses* of Philomela, raped by her brother-in-law, Tereus; cf. 2.4.26 below. He cut out her tongue so that she could not disclose his villainy. She succeeded in weaving the account of her misfortune in a tapestry.) **46 Take it up** take it **49 parcel** part. **hopeful** hoped-for **53 Be cross** pick a quarrel **56 Unfurnished . . . troop** unprovided with a suitable escort **57 Dian** Diana, huntress and goddess of chastity. (Here used sarcastically.) **habited** dressed **60 Saucy controller** impudent critic, censurer

Thy temples should be planted presently 62
With horns, as was Actaeon's, and the hounds 63
Should drive upon thy new-transformèd limbs, 64
Unmannerly intruder as thou art!

LAVINIA

Under your patience, gentle Empress, 66
'Tis thought you have a goodly gift in horning, 67
And to be doubted that your Moor and you 68
Are singled forth to try experiments.
Jove shield your husband from his hounds today!
'Tis pity they should take him for a stag.

BASSIANUS

Believe me, Queen, your swarthy Cimmerian 72
Doth make your honor of his body's hue,
Spotted, detested, and abominable. 74
Why are you sequestered from all your train,
Dismounted from your snow-white goodly steed,
And wandered hither to an obscure plot,
Accompanied but with a barbarous Moor,
If foul desire had not conducted you?

LAVINIA

And, being intercepted in your sport,
Great reason that my noble lord be rated 81
For sauciness. [*To Bassianus.*] I pray you, let us hence,
And let her joy her raven-colored love; 83
This valley fits the purpose passing well. 84

BASSIANUS

The King my brother shall have notice of this.

LAVINIA

Ay, for these slips have made him noted long. 86
Good king, to be so mightily abused! 87

TAMORA

Why have I patience to endure all this?

62 presently immediately **63 Actaeon's** (An allusion to the story of Actaeon, who was transformed into a stag by Diana and killed by his own hounds as punishment for having watched her and her nymphs at their bath.) **64 drive** rush **66 Under your patience** i.e., if you will allow my saying so **67 horning** cuckolding **68 doubted** suspected, feared **72 Cimmerian** i.e., of black complexion. (The Cimmerii in the *Odyssey* live in perpetual darkness.) **74 Spotted** smirched **81 rated** berated, chidden **83 joy** enjoy **84 passing** surpassingly **86 slips** offenses. **noted** notorious, stigmatized **87 abused** deceived

Enter Chiron and Demetrius.

DEMETRIUS
How now, dear sovereign and our gracious mother,
Why doth Your Highness look so pale and wan?

TAMORA
Have I not reason, think you, to look pale?
These two have 'ticed me hither to this place. 92
A barren detested vale you see it is;
The trees, though summer, yet forlorn and lean,
Overcome with moss and baleful mistletoe; 95
Here never shines the sun; here nothing breeds,
Unless the nightly owl or fatal raven. 97
And when they showed me this abhorrèd pit,
They told me here at dead time of the night
A thousand fiends, a thousand hissing snakes,
Ten thousand swelling toads, as many urchins, 101
Would make such fearful and confusèd cries
As any mortal body hearing it
Should straight fall mad or else die suddenly.
No sooner had they told this hellish tale
But straight they told me they would bind me here
Unto the body of a dismal yew
And leave me to this miserable death.
And then they called me foul adulteress,
Lascivious Goth, and all the bitterest terms 110
That ever ear did hear to such effect;
And had you not by wondrous fortune come,
This vengeance on me had they executed.
Revenge it, as you love your mother's life,
Or be ye not henceforth called my children.

DEMETRIUS
This is a witness that I am thy son.
Stab him [*Bassianus*].

CHIRON
And this for me, struck home to show my strength.
[*He also stabs Bassianus, who dies.*]

92 'ticed enticed **95 Overcome** overgrown **97 fatal** ominous
101 urchins hedgehogs **110 Goth** (A quibble; pronounced somewhat like *goat,* symbolic of lechery.)

LAVINIA

Ay, come, Semiramis, nay, barbarous Tamora, 118
For no name fits thy nature but thy own!

TAMORA

Give me the poniard. You shall know, my boys,
Your mother's hand shall right your mother's wrong.

DEMETRIUS

Stay, madam, here is more belongs to her. 122
First thresh the corn, then after burn the straw. 123
This minion stood upon her chastity, 124
Upon her nuptial vow, her loyalty,
And with that painted hope braves your mightiness; 126
And shall she carry this unto her grave?

CHIRON

An if she do, I would I were an eunuch. 128
Drag hence her husband to some secret hole
And make his dead trunk pillow to our lust.

TAMORA

But when ye have the honey ye desire,
Let not this wasp outlive, us both to sting. 132

CHIRON

I warrant you, madam, we will make that sure.—
Come, mistress, now perforce we will enjoy
That nice-preservèd honesty of yours. 135

LAVINIA

O Tamora! Thou bearest a woman's face—

TAMORA

I will not hear her speak. Away with her!

LAVINIA

Sweet lords, entreat her hear me but a word.

DEMETRIUS [*To Tamora*]

Listen, fair madam. Let it be your glory
To see her tears, but be your heart to them
As unrelenting flint to drops of rain.

LAVINIA

When did the tiger's young ones teach the dam?

118 Semiramis (See note to 2.1.22.) **122 belongs to her** that is to be her portion **123 corn** grain **124 minion** hussy, wench. **stood upon** preened herself upon **126 painted** specious, unreal **128 An if** if **132 outlive** survive. **sting** i.e., do harm to (us) **135 nice** fastidiously. **honesty** chastity

O, do not learn her wrath; she taught it thee! 143
The milk thou suck'st from her did turn to marble; 144
Even at thy teat thou hadst thy tyranny. 145
Yet every mother breeds not sons alike;
[*To Chiron.*] Do thou entreat her show a woman's pity.

CHIRON
What, wouldst thou have me prove myself a bastard?

LAVINIA
'Tis true, the raven doth not hatch a lark.
Yet have I heard—O, could I find it now!— 150
The lion, moved with pity, did endure
To have his princely paws pared all away. 152
Some say that ravens foster forlorn children 153
The whilst their own birds famish in their nests; 154
O, be to me, though thy hard heart say no,
Nothing so kind, but something pitiful! 156

TAMORA
I know not what it means. Away with her! 157

LAVINIA
O, let me teach thee! For my father's sake,
That gave thee life when well he might have slain thee,
Be not obdurate; open thy deaf ears.

TAMORA
Hadst thou in person ne'er offended me,
Even for his sake am I pitiless.
Remember, boys, I poured forth tears in vain
To save your brother from the sacrifice,
But fierce Andronicus would not relent.
Therefore away with her, and use her as you will—
The worse to her, the better loved of me.

LAVINIA
O Tamora, be called a gentle queen,
And with thine own hands kill me in this place!
For 'tis not life that I have begged so long;
Poor I was slain when Bassianus died.
[*She clutches Tamora imploringly.*]

143 learn teach **144 thou suck'st** that you sucked **145 hadst thy tyranny** gained your cruelty **150 find it** find it true **152 paws** claws **153 forlorn** abandoned (by other birds) **154 birds** chicks **156 Nothing . . . pitiful** i.e., not so kind as the raven, but still showing some pity **157 it** i.e., pity

TAMORA
What begg'st thou, then? Fond woman, let me go. 172

LAVINIA
'Tis present death I beg, and one thing more 173
That womanhood denies my tongue to tell: 174
O, keep me from their worse-than-killing lust,
And tumble me into some loathsome pit,
Where never man's eye may behold my body!
Do this, and be a charitable murderer.

TAMORA
So should I rob my sweet sons of their fee.
No, let them satisfy their lust on thee.

DEMETRIUS
Away! For thou hast stayed us here too long.

LAVINIA
No grace, no womanhood? Ah, beastly creature!
The blot and enemy to our general name! 183
Confusion fall— 184

CHIRON
Nay, then I'll stop your mouth. [*To Demetrius.*] Bring thou her husband.
This is the hole where Aaron bid us hide him.
[*Demetrius and Chiron throw the body of Bassianus into the pit; then exeunt Demetrius and Chiron, dragging off Lavinia.*]

TAMORA
Farewell, my sons. See that you make her sure. 187
Ne'er let my heart know merry cheer indeed
Till all the Andronici be made away. 189
Now will I hence to seek my lovely Moor,
And let my spleenful sons this trull deflower. [*Exit.*] 191

Enter Aaron, with two of Titus' sons [*Quintus and Martius*].

AARON
Come on, my lords, the better foot before. 192

172 Fond foolish **173 present** immediate **174 denies** forbids **183 our general name** i.e., women's reputation **184 Confusion** destruction **187 sure** safe, incapable of revenge **189 made away** murdered **191 spleenful** lustful. **trull** whore, slut **192 better foot before** best foot forward

Straight will I bring you to the loathsome pit
Where I espied the panther fast asleep.

QUINTUS
My sight is very dull, whate'er it bodes.

MARTIUS
And mine, I promise you. Were it not for shame,
Well could I leave our sport to sleep awhile.
[*He falls into the pit.*]

QUINTUS
What, art thou fallen? What subtle hole is this,
Whose mouth is covered with rude-growing briers
Upon whose leaves are drops of new-shed blood
As fresh as morning dew distilled on flowers?
A very fatal place it seems to me. 202
Speak, brother. Hast thou hurt thee with the fall?

MARTIUS
O brother, with the dismal'st object hurt 204
That ever eye with sight made heart lament!

AARON [*Aside*]
Now will I fetch the King to find them here,
That he thereby may have a likely guess
How these were they that made away his brother.
Exit.

MARTIUS
Why dost not comfort me and help me out
From this unhallowed and bloodstainèd hole?

QUINTUS
I am surprisèd with an uncouth fear. 211
A chilling sweat o'erruns my trembling joints;
My heart suspects more than mine eye can see.

MARTIUS
To prove thou hast a true-divining heart,
Aaron and thou look down into this den
And see a fearful sight of blood and death.

QUINTUS
Aaron is gone, and my compassionate heart
Will not permit mine eyes once to behold
The thing whereat it trembles by surmise. 219

202 fatal ill-omened **204 object** sight **211 surprisèd** overcome. **uncouth** strange **219 by surmise** even to imagine

O, tell me who it is! For ne'er till now
Was I a child to fear I know not what.

MARTIUS

Lord Bassianus lies berayed in blood, 222
All on a heap, like to a slaughtered lamb,
In this detested, dark, blood-drinking pit.

QUINTUS

If it be dark, how dost thou know 'tis he?

MARTIUS

Upon his bloody finger he doth wear
A precious ring that lightens all this hole, 227
Which like a taper in some monument 228
Doth shine upon the dead man's earthy cheeks 229
And shows the ragged entrails of this pit. 230
So pale did shine the moon on Pyramus 231
When he by night lay bathed in maiden blood. 232
O brother, help me with thy fainting hand—
If fear hath made thee faint, as me it hath—
Out of this fell devouring receptacle, 235
As hateful as Cocytus' misty mouth. 236

QUINTUS [*Offering to help*]

Reach me thy hand, that I may help thee out,
Or, wanting strength to do thee so much good, 238
I may be plucked into the swallowing womb
Of this deep pit, poor Bassianus' grave.
I have no strength to pluck thee to the brink.

MARTIUS

Nor I no strength to climb without thy help.

QUINTUS

Thy hand once more; I will not loose again
Till thou art here aloft or I below.
Thou canst not come to me—I come to thee.

[*He falls in.*]

222 berayed in defiled by **227 ring** (Presumably the carbuncle, which was believed to emit light.) **228 monument** tomb **229 earthy** clay-colored, pale **230 ragged entrails** i.e., rough interior **231 Pyramus** the lover of Thisbe, who killed himself in the mistaken supposition that she was dead. (See *A Midsummer Night's Dream,* 1.2, 3.1, and 5.1.) **232 maiden** i.e., that of an unmarried person. (Pyramus, who dies first, lies in his own blood, not that of Thisbe, though she soon joins him in death.) **235 fell** savage **236 Cocytus** one of the rivers of Hades—the river of lamentations **238 wanting** lacking

Enter the Emperor [*Saturninus, with attendants*], *and Aaron the Moor.*

SATURNINUS
Along with me! I'll see what hole is here, 246
And what he is that now is leapt into it.
[*He speaks into the pit.*]
Say, who art thou that lately didst descend
Into this gaping hollow of the earth?

MARTIUS [*From within the pit*]
The unhappy sons of old Andronicus,
Brought hither in a most unlucky hour
To find thy brother Bassianus dead.

SATURNINUS
My brother dead! I know thou dost but jest.
He and his lady both are at the lodge
Upon the north side of this pleasant chase; 255
'Tis not an hour since I left them there.

MARTIUS
We know not where you left them all alive,
But, out alas! Here have we found him dead. 258

Enter Tamora, [*Titus*] *Andronicus, and Lucius.*

TAMORA Where is my lord the King?

SATURNINUS
Here, Tamora, though grieved with killing grief.

TAMORA
Where is thy brother Bassianus?

SATURNINUS
Now to the bottom dost thou search my wound. 262
Poor Bassianus here lies murderèd.

TAMORA
Then all too late I bring this fatal writ,
The complot of this timeless tragedy, 265
And wonder greatly that man's face can fold 266
In pleasing smiles such murderous tyranny.
She giveth Saturnine a letter.

246 Along come along **255 chase** hunting ground **258 out alas** alas. (*Out* intensifies the interjection.) **262 search** probe **265 complot** plot. **timeless** untimely **266 fold** hide, enfold

SATURNINUS (*Reads the letter*)
"An if we miss to meet him handsomely, 268
Sweet huntsman—Bassianus 'tis we mean—
Do thou so much as dig the grave for him.
Thou know'st our meaning. Look for thy reward
Among the nettles at the elder tree
Which overshades the mouth of that same pit
Where we decreed to bury Bassianus.
Do this, and purchase us thy lasting friends." 275
O Tamora, was ever heard the like?
This is the pit, and this the elder tree.
Look, sirs, if you can find the huntsman out
That should have murdered Bassianus here. 279

AARON [*Finding the gold*]
My gracious lord, here is the bag of gold.

SATURNINUS [*To Titus*]
Two of thy whelps, fell curs of bloody kind, 281
Have here bereft my brother of his life.—
Sirs, drag them from the pit unto the prison!
There let them bide until we have devised
Some never-heard-of torturing pain for them.
[*Martius and Quintus are dragged out of the pit, and Bassianus' body is raised.*]

TAMORA
What, are they in this pit? O wondrous thing!
How easily murder is discoverèd!

TITUS [*Kneeling*]
High Emperor, upon my feeble knee
I beg this boon, with tears not lightly shed,
That this fell fault of my accursèd sons—
Accursèd if the fault be proved in them—

SATURNINUS
If it be proved? You see it is apparent. 292
Who found this letter? Tamora, was it you?

TAMORA
Andronicus himself did take it up. 294

TITUS
I did, my lord, yet let me be their bail.

268 An if if. **handsomely** conveniently **275 purchase** win **279 should** was to **281 kind** nature **292 apparent** evident **294 take** pick

For, by my fathers' reverend tomb, I vow 296
They shall be ready at Your Highness' will
To answer their suspicion with their lives. 298

SATURNINUS
Thou shalt not bail them. See thou follow me.
Some bring the murdered body, some the murderers.
Let them not speak a word—the guilt is plain;
For, by my soul, were there worse end than death,
That end upon them should be executed.

TAMORA
Andronicus, I will entreat the King.
Fear not thy sons; they shall do well enough. 305

TITUS [*Rising*]
Come, Lucius, come. Stay not to talk with them. 306
[*Exeunt bearing the dead body of Bassianus;
Martius and Quintus under guard*].

✤

2.4 *Enter the Empress' sons with Lavinia, her hands cut off, and her tongue cut out, and ravished.*

DEMETRIUS
So, now go tell, an if thy tongue can speak,
Who 'twas that cut thy tongue and ravished thee.

CHIRON
Write down thy mind, bewray thy meaning so, 3
An if thy stumps will let thee play the scribe.

DEMETRIUS
See how with signs and tokens she can scrawl.

CHIRON
Go home, call for sweet water, wash thy hands. 6

DEMETRIUS
She hath no tongue to call, nor hands to wash;
And so let's leave her to her silent walks.

CHIRON
An 'twere my cause, I should go hang myself. 9

296 fathers' forefathers' **298 their suspicion** the suspicion they are under **305 Fear not** fear not for **306 them** i.e., Martius and Quintus

2.4. Location: The forest still.
3 bewray reveal **6 sweet** perfumed **9 cause** case

DEMETRIUS

If thou hadst hands to help thee knit the cord. 10

Exeunt [*Chiron and Demetrius*].

[*Wind horns.*] *Enter Marcus from hunting.*
[*Lavinia flees from him.*]

MARCUS

Who is this? My niece, that flies away so fast?
Cousin, a word. Where is your husband? 12

[*He sees her injuries.*]

If I do dream, would all my wealth would wake me! 13
If I do wake, some planet strike me down, 14
That I may slumber an eternal sleep!
Speak, gentle niece. What stern ungentle hands
Hath lopped and hewed and made thy body bare
Of her two branches, those sweet ornaments
Whose circling shadows kings have sought to sleep in, 19
And might not gain so great a happiness 20
As half thy love? Why dost not speak to me? 21
Alas, a crimson river of warm blood,
Like to a bubbling fountain stirred with wind,
Doth rise and fall between thy rosèd lips,
Coming and going with thy honey breath.
But, sure, some Tereus hath deflowered thee 26
And, lest thou shouldst detect him, cut thy tongue. 27
Ah, now thou turn'st away thy face for shame!
And notwithstanding all this loss of blood,
As from a conduit with three issuing spouts,
Yet do thy cheeks look red as Titan's face 31
Blushing to be encountered with a cloud.
Shall I speak for thee? Shall I say 'tis so?
O, that I knew thy heart, and knew the beast, 34
That I might rail at him to ease my mind!
Sorrow concealèd, like an oven stopped, 36

10 s.d. Wind horns blow hunting horns (offstage. The stage direction is from the Folio.) **12 Cousin** kinswoman **13 would . . . me** i.e., I would give all my wealth to have this be only a bad dream **14 strike me down** exert its baleful influence on me **19 shadows** i.e., protection, shelter **20–21 And . . . thy love** i.e., and could find nowhere any happiness half so great as having your love **26 Tereus** i.e., the ravisher of Philomela; see note to 2.3.43 **27 detect** expose **31 Titan's** the sun god's **34 thy heart** i.e., what is in your mind **36 stopped** closed too long, plugged up

Doth burn the heart to cinders where it is.
Fair Philomela, why, she but lost her tongue,
And in a tedious sampler sewed her mind; 39
But, lovely niece, that means is cut from thee.
A craftier Tereus, cousin, hast thou met,
And he hath cut those pretty fingers off
That could have better sewed than Philomel.
O, had the monster seen those lily hands
Tremble like aspen leaves upon a lute
And make the silken strings delight to kiss them,
He would not then have touched them for his life!
Or had he heard the heavenly harmony
Which that sweet tongue hath made,
He would have dropped his knife and fell asleep,
As Cerberus at the Thracian poet's feet. 51
Come, let us go and make thy father blind,
For such a sight will blind a father's eye.
One hour's storm will drown the fragrant meads; 54
What will whole months of tears thy father's eyes?
Do not draw back, for we will mourn with thee.
O, could our mourning ease thy misery! *Exeunt.*

✣

39 tedious sampler laboriously contrived embroidered cloth or tapestry. (See note to 2.3.43.) **51 Cerberus . . . feet** (According to legend, Orpheus' sweet singing charmed even Cerberus, three-headed dog guarding the entrance to Hades.) **54 meads** meadows

3.1

Enter the judges and senators [*and tribunes*] *with Titus' two sons bound, passing over the stage to the place of execution, and Titus going before, pleading.*

TITUS

Hear me, grave fathers! Noble tribunes, stay!
For pity of mine age, whose youth was spent
In dangerous wars whilst you securely slept;
For all my blood in Rome's great quarrel shed; 4
For all the frosty nights that I have watched; 5
And for these bitter tears which now you see
Filling the agèd wrinkles in my cheeks,
Be pitiful to my condemnèd sons,
Whose souls is not corrupted as 'tis thought.
For two-and-twenty sons I never wept, 10
Because they died in honor's lofty bed.

[*Titus*] *Andronicus lieth down and the judges pass by him.* [*Titus weeps.*]

For these, tribunes, in the dust I write
My heart's deep languor and my soul's sad tears. 13
Let my tears stanch the earth's dry appetite; 14
My sons' sweet blood will make it shame and blush. 15

[*Exeunt all but Titus.*]

O earth, I will befriend thee more with rain
That shall distill from these two ancient urns 17
Than youthful April shall with all his showers.
In summer's drought I'll drop upon thee still; 19
In winter with warm tears I'll melt the snow,
And keep eternal springtime on thy face,
So thou refuse to drink my dear sons' blood. 22

Enter Lucius, with his weapon drawn.

O reverend tribunes! O gentle, agèd men!
Unbind my sons, reverse the doom of death, 24

3.1. Location: Rome. A street.
4 my blood i.e., the blood of my sons **5 watched** stayed awake **10 two-and-twenty** (Compare 1.1.79, 195.) **13 languor** grief **14 stanch** satisfy **15 shame** be ashamed **17 urns** i.e., eyes **19 still** continually **22 So** so long as **24 doom** sentence

And let me say, that never wept before,
My tears are now prevailing orators.

LUCIUS

O noble Father, you lament in vain.
The tribunes hear you not. No man is by,
And you recount your sorrows to a stone.

TITUS

Ah, Lucius, for thy brothers let me plead.
Grave tribunes, once more I entreat of you—

LUCIUS

My gracious lord, no tribune hears you speak.

TITUS

Why, 'tis no matter, man. If they did hear,
They would not mark me; if they did mark,
They would not pity me; yet plead I must,
And bootless unto them. 36
Therefore I tell my sorrows to the stones,
Who, though they cannot answer my distress,
Yet in some sort they are better than the tribunes,
For that they will not intercept my tale. 40
When I do weep, they humbly at my feet
Receive my tears and seem to weep with me;
And, were they but attirèd in grave weeds, 43
Rome could afford no tribunes like to these. 44
A stone is soft as wax, tribunes more hard than stones;
A stone is silent and offendeth not,
And tribunes with their tongues doom men to death.
[*He rises.*]
But wherefore stand'st thou with thy weapon drawn?

LUCIUS

To rescue my two brothers from their death,
For which attempt the judges have pronounced
My everlasting doom of banishment. 51

TITUS

O happy man! They have befriended thee.
Why, foolish Lucius, dost thou not perceive
That Rome is but a wilderness of tigers?
Tigers must prey, and Rome affords no prey

36 bootless in vain **40 For that** because. **intercept** interrupt **43 grave weeds** sober garments **44 afford** provide **51 doom** sentence

But me and mine. How happy art thou then
From these devourers to be banishèd!
But who comes with our brother Marcus here?

Enter Marcus with Lavinia.

MARCUS
Titus, prepare thy agèd eyes to weep,
Or if not so, thy noble heart to break.
I bring consuming sorrow to thine age.

TITUS
Will it consume me? Let me see it, then.

MARCUS
This was thy daughter.

TITUS Why, Marcus, so she is.

LUCIUS Ay me, this object kills me! 64

TITUS
Fainthearted boy, arise, and look upon her. 65
Speak, Lavinia. What accursèd hand
Hath made thee handless in thy father's sight?
What fool hath added water to the sea,
Or brought a faggot to bright-burning Troy?
My grief was at the height before thou cam'st,
And now, like Nilus, it disdaineth bounds. 71
Give me a sword, I'll chop off my hands too, 72
For they have fought for Rome, and all in vain;
And they have nursed this woe in feeding life; 74
In bootless prayer have they been held up,
And they have served me to effectless use.
Now all the service I require of them
Is that the one will help to cut the other.
'Tis well, Lavinia, that thou hast no hands,
For hands to do Rome service is but vain.

LUCIUS
Speak, gentle sister. Who hath martyred thee? 81

MARCUS
O, that delightful engine of her thoughts, 82

64 object i.e., object of sight **65 arise** (Evidently Lucius has collapsed or fallen to his knees in grief.) **71 Nilus** the Nile **72 Give** i.e., if you will give **74 they . . . life** i.e., in sustaining Lavinia, my hands have merely prolonged her days to suffer this misery **81 martyred** mutilated **82 engine** instrument

That blabbed them with such pleasing eloquence, 83
Is torn from forth that pretty hollow cage
Where, like a sweet melodious bird, it sung
Sweet varied notes, enchanting every ear!

LUCIUS
O, say thou for her, who hath done this deed?

MARCUS
O, thus I found her, straying in the park,
Seeking to hide herself, as doth the deer
That hath received some unrecuring wound. 90

TITUS
It was my dear, and he that wounded her 91
Hath hurt me more than had he killed me dead;
For now I stand as one upon a rock
Environed with a wilderness of sea,
Who marks the waxing tide grow wave by wave,
Expecting ever when some envious surge 96
Will in his brinish bowels swallow him. 97
This way to death my wretched sons are gone;
Here stands my other son, a banished man,
And here my brother, weeping at my woes;
But that which gives my soul the greatest spurn 101
Is dear Lavinia, dearer than my soul.
Had I but seen thy picture in this plight,
It would have madded me; what shall I do
Now I behold thy lively body so? 105
Thou hast no hands to wipe away thy tears,
Nor tongue to tell me who hath martyred thee.
Thy husband he is dead, and for his death 108
Thy brothers are condemned, and dead by this. 109
Look, Marcus! Ah, son Lucius, look on her!
When I did name her brothers, then fresh tears
Stood on her cheeks, as doth the honey-dew 112
Upon a gathered lily almost withered.

83 blabbed uttered **90 unrecuring** incurable **91 dear** (with a familiar pun on *deer*, l. 89) **96 Expecting ever when** continually awaiting the moment when. **envious** spiteful **97 his** its **101 spurn** stroke, kick **105 lively** living, actual (as contrasted with her picture) **108 husband he** husband **109 by this** by now **112 honey-dew** sweet dewlike substance, or the dew itself

MARCUS
Perchance she weeps because they killed her husband;
Perchance because she knows them innocent.
TITUS
If they did kill thy husband, then be joyful,
Because the law hath ta'en revenge on them.
No, no, they would not do so foul a deed;
Witness the sorrow that their sister makes.
Gentle Lavinia, let me kiss thy lips;
Or make some sign how I may do thee ease. 121
Shall thy good uncle, and thy brother Lucius,
And thou, and I, sit round about some fountain, 123
Looking all downwards to behold our cheeks
How they are stained, like meadows yet not dry
With miry slime left on them by a flood?
And in the fountain shall we gaze so long
Till the fresh taste be taken from that clearness, 128
And made a brine pit with our bitter tears? 129
Or shall we cut away our hands, like thine?
Or shall we bite our tongues, and in dumb shows 131
Pass the remainder of our hateful days?
What shall we do? Let us that have our tongues
Plot some device of further misery, 134
To make us wondered at in time to come.
LUCIUS
Sweet Father, cease your tears, for at your grief
See how my wretched sister sobs and weeps.
MARCUS
Patience, dear niece. Good Titus, dry thine eyes.
TITUS
Ah, Marcus, Marcus! Brother, well I wot 139
Thy napkin cannot drink a tear of mine, 140
For thou, poor man, hast drowned it with thine own. 141
LUCIUS
Ah, my Lavinia, I will wipe thy cheeks.

121 do thee ease bring you comfort, relief **123 fountain** spring
128 taken removed, destroyed. **clearness** i.e., of the pure water
129 And made i.e., and the spring made **131 bite** bite out. **dumb shows** mute pageants, as in dramatic action without dialogue
134 device dramatic representation **139 wot** know **140 napkin** handkerchief **141 drowned** i.e., saturated

TITUS
Mark, Marcus, mark! I understand her signs.
Had she a tongue to speak, now would she say
That to her brother which I said to thee.
His napkin, with his true tears all bewet,
Can do no service on her sorrowful cheeks.
O, what a sympathy of woe is this, 148
As far from help as Limbo is from bliss! 149

Enter Aaron the Moor alone.

AARON
Titus Andronicus, my lord the Emperor
Sends thee this word: that if thou love thy sons,
Let Marcus, Lucius, or thyself, old Titus,
Or any one of you, chop off your hand
And send it to the King. He for the same
Will send thee hither both thy sons alive, 155
And that shall be the ransom for their fault. 156

TITUS
O gracious Emperor! O gentle Aaron!
Did ever raven sing so like a lark,
That gives sweet tidings of the sun's uprise?
With all my heart I'll send the Emperor my hand.
Good Aaron, wilt thou help to chop it off?

LUCIUS
Stay, Father, for that noble hand of thine,
That hath thrown down so many enemies,
Shall not be sent. My hand will serve the turn.
My youth can better spare my blood than you,
And therefore mine shall save my brothers' lives.

MARCUS
Which of your hands hath not defended Rome 167
And reared aloft the bloody battle-ax,
Writing destruction on the enemy's castle?
O, none of both but are of high desert.

148 sympathy agreement, sharing **149 Limbo** region bordering hell, where were confined the souls of those barred from heaven through no fault of their own, such as good men who lived before the Christian era or who died unbaptized **155 Will . . . alive** (Aaron's secret double meaning may be, "will send to you here, you being alive, both your sons.") **156 that** (Secretly, *that* may refer to the sons being sent here—dead.) **167 Which . . . hands** i.e., has either of you a hand that

My hand hath been but idle; let it serve
To ransom my two nephews from their death.
Then have I kept it to a worthy end.

AARON
Nay, come, agree whose hand shall go along,
For fear they die before their pardon come.

MARCUS
My hand shall go.

LUCIUS By heaven, it shall not go!

TITUS
Sirs, strive no more. Such withered herbs as these
Are meet for plucking up, and therefore mine. 178

LUCIUS
Sweet Father, if I shall be thought thy son, 179
Let me redeem my brothers both from death.

MARCUS
And, for our father's sake and mother's care,
Now let me show a brother's love to thee.

TITUS
Agree between you. I will spare my hand. 183

LUCIUS Then I'll go fetch an ax.

MARCUS But I will use the ax.

Exeunt [*Lucius and Marcus*].

TITUS
Come hither, Aaron. I'll deceive them both.
Lend my thy hand, and I will give thee mine. 187

AARON [*Aside*]
If that be called deceit, I will be honest,
And never whilst I live deceive men so;
But I'll deceive you in another sort,
And that you'll say, ere half an hour pass.

He cuts off Titus' hand.

Enter Lucius and Marcus again.

TITUS
Now stay your strife. What shall be is dispatched.

178 meet fit **179 shall** am to **183 spare** (In a virtuous deception, Titus uses a double meaning for *spare*; ostensibly he means "save from being cut off," but secretly he means "do without.") **187 Lend . . . mine** (Another pun, on *hand*: "Give me your assistance, and I'll give you my hand.")

Good Aaron, give His Majesty my hand.
Tell him it was a hand that warded him 194
From thousand dangers. Bid him bury it.
More hath it merited; that let it have.
As for my sons, say I account of them
As jewels purchased at an easy price,
And yet dear too, because I bought mine own. 199

AARON
I go, Andronicus, and for thy hand
Look by and by to have thy sons with thee. 201
[*Aside.*] Their heads, I mean. O, how this villainy
Doth fat me with the very thoughts of it! 203
Let fools do good, and fair men call for grace;
Aaron will have his soul black like his face. *Exit.*

TITUS [*Kneeling*]
O, here I lift this one hand up to heaven
And bow this feeble ruin to the earth.
If any power pities wretched tears,
To that I call! [*To Lavinia, who kneels.*] What, wouldst thou kneel with me?
Do, then, dear heart, for heaven shall hear our prayers,
Or with our sighs we'll breathe the welkin dim 211
And stain the sun with fog, as sometimes clouds
When they do hug him in their melting bosoms. 213

MARCUS
O brother, speak with possibility, 214
And do not break into these deep extremes.

TITUS
Is not my sorrow deep, having no bottom?
Then be my passions bottomless with them. 217

MARCUS
But yet let reason govern thy lament. 218

TITUS
If there were reason for these miseries, 219

194 warded guarded **199 dear** expensive. **because . . . own** because I am buying back what was mine to begin with **201 Look** expect **203 fat** fatten, feed **211 breathe . . . dim** make cloudy the sky with our sighs. **welkin** sky **213 melting** i.e., dissolving into teardroplike rain **214 speak with possibility** speak of things possible. **with** within the bounds of **217 be my passions** let my passionate expressions of grief be **218–219 reason . . . reason** rationality . . . necessity

Then into limits could I bind my woes.
When heaven doth weep, doth not the earth o'erflow?
If the winds rage, doth not the sea wax mad,
Threat'ning the welkin with his big-swoll'n face?
And wilt thou have a reason for this coil? 224
I am the sea. Hark how her sighs doth blow! 225
She is the weeping welkin, I the earth.
Then must my sea be movèd with her sighs,
Then must my earth with her continual tears
Become a deluge overflowed and drowned,
Forwhy my bowels cannot hide her woes, 230
But like a drunkard must I vomit them.
Then give me leave, for losers will have leave
To ease their stomachs with their bitter tongues. 233

Enter a Messenger, with two heads and a hand.

MESSENGER
Worthy Andronicus, ill art thou repaid
For that good hand thou sent'st the Emperor.
Here are the heads of thy two noble sons,
And here's thy hand in scorn to thee sent back—
Thy grief their sports, thy resolution mocked, 238
That woe is me to think upon thy woes 239
More than remembrance of my father's death.
[*He sets down the heads and hand, and exit.*]

MARCUS
Now let hot Etna cool in Sicily, 241
And be my heart an ever-burning hell!
These miseries are more than may be borne.
To weep with them that weep doth ease some deal, 244
But sorrow flouted at is double death.

LUCIUS
Ah, that this sight should make so deep a wound,
And yet detested life not shrink thereat! 247

224 coil noise, fuss **225 her** i.e., Lavinia's **230 Forwhy** because. **bowels** (Supposed to be the seat of compassion.) **her** their, my bowels' **233 ease their stomachs** relieve their resentments (with a play on *vomit*) **238 sports** entertainment **239 That** so that **241 Etna** volcanic mountain on the island of Sicily (which will, compared to Marcus' burning heart, seem cool) **244 some deal** somewhat **247 shrink** i.e., slip away

That ever death should let life bear his name, 248
Where life hath no more interest but to breathe! 249
[*Lavinia kisses Titus.*]

MARCUS
Alas, poor heart, that kiss is comfortless
As frozen water to a starvèd snake. 251

TITUS
When will this fearful slumber have an end? 252

MARCUS
Now, farewell, flattery! Die, Andronicus. 253
Thou dost not slumber. See thy two sons' heads,
Thy warlike hand, thy mangled daughter here,
Thy other banished son with this dear sight 256
Struck pale and bloodless, and thy brother, I,
Even like a stony image, cold and numb.
Ah, now no more will I control thy griefs! 259
Rend off thy silver hair, thy other hand
Gnawing with thy teeth, and be this dismal sight
The closing up of our most wretched eyes. 262
Now is a time to storm. Why art thou still?

TITUS Ha, ha, ha!

MARCUS
Why dost thou laugh? It fits not with this hour.

TITUS
Why, I have not another tear to shed.
Besides, this sorrow is an enemy,
And would usurp upon my watery eyes
And make them blind with tributary tears. 269
Then which way shall I find Revenge's cave?
For these two heads do seem to speak to me,
And threat me I shall never come to bliss
Till all these mischiefs be returned again 273
Even in their throats that hath committed them.
Come, let me see what task I have to do.

248 bear his name i.e., still be called life **249 Where . . . breathe** i.e., where virtually nothing remains of life except the drawing of breath **251 starvèd** i.e., benumbed with cold **252 fearful slumber** i.e., dreadful nightmare **253 flattery** comforting deception **256 dear** grievous **259 control** try to restrain **262 closing up** closing in death **269 tributary tears** tears paid as tribute (to sorrow, the usurping enemy) **273 mischiefs** evils, injuries

You heavy people, circle me about, 276
That I may turn me to each one of you
And swear unto my soul to right your wrongs.
[*They form a circle about Titus, and he pledges each.*]
The vow is made. Come, brother, take a head,
And in this hand the other will I bear.
[*They pick up the two heads, and give the hand to Lavinia.*]
And, Lavinia, thou shalt be employed:
Bear thou my hand, sweet wench, between thy teeth.
As for thee, boy, [*To Lucius*] go get thee from my sight;
Thou art an exile, and thou must not stay.
Hie to the Goths and raise an army there.
And if ye love me, as I think you do,
Let's kiss and part, for we have much to do.
[*They kiss.*] *Exeunt* [*Titus, Marcus, and Lavinia*].

LUCIUS
Farewell, Andronicus, my noble father,
The woefull'st man that ever lived in Rome.
Farewell, proud Rome, till Lucius come again!
He loves his pledges dearer than his life. 291
Farewell, Lavinia, my noble sister.
O, would thou wert as thou tofore hast been! 293
But now nor Lucius nor Lavinia lives
But in oblivion and hateful griefs.
If Lucius live, he will requite your wrongs
And make proud Saturnine and his empress
Beg at the gates, like Tarquin and his queen. 298
Now will I to the Goths and raise a power 299
To be revenged on Rome and Saturnine. *Exit Lucius.*

✤

276 heavy sorrowing **291 He . . . life** i.e., his vows are more important to him than his life, or he loves his family, left behind in Rome as hostages to fortune, more than his life **293 tofore** heretofore, formerly **298 Tarquin** Tarquinius Superbus, seventh king of Rome, who, because his son had raped a Roman lady, Lucretia, was banished and his kingdom overthrown; a republic was then established **299 power** army

3.2

A banquet [*set out*]. *Enter* [*Titus*] *Andronicus, Marcus, Lavinia, and the boy* [*young Lucius*].

TITUS
So, so. Now sit, and look you eat no more
Than will preserve just so much strength in us
As will revenge these bitter woes of ours.
Marcus, unknit that sorrow-wreathen knot. 4
Thy niece and I, poor creatures, want our hands 5
And cannot passionate our tenfold grief 6
With folded arms. This poor right hand of mine
Is left to tyrannize upon my breast, 8
Who, when my heart, all mad with misery, 9
Beats in this hollow prison of my flesh,
Then thus I thump it down. [*He beats his breast.*]
[*To Lavinia.*] Thou map of woe, that thus dost talk
in signs, 12
When thy poor heart beats with outrageous beating,
Thou canst not strike it thus to make it still.
Wound it with sighing, girl, kill it with groans; 15
Or get some little knife between thy teeth
And just against thy heart make thou a hole,
That all the tears that thy poor eyes let fall
May run into that sink and, soaking in, 19
Drown the lamenting fool in sea-salt tears. 20

MARCUS
Fie, brother, fie! Teach her not thus to lay
Such violent hands upon her tender life.

TITUS
How now, has sorrow made thee dote already? 23
Why, Marcus, no man should be mad but I.
What violent hands can she lay on her life?
Ah, wherefore dost thou urge the name of hands,
To bid Aeneas tell the tale twice o'er 27

3.2. Location: Rome. Titus' house.
s.d. banquet a light repast, here set out on stage as the scene begins, with appropriate furniture allowing for sitting **4 sorrow-wreathen knot** arms folded in a conventional expression of grief **5 want** lack **6 passionate** express passionately **8 tyrannize** i.e., by beating **9 Who** which **12 map** picture **15 Wound it with sighing** (Each sigh was believed to cost the heart a drop of blood.) **19 sink** receptacle **20 fool** (Here a term of pity or endearment.) **23 dote** be foolish **27 Aeneas** (See *Aeneid*, 2.2.)

How Troy was burnt and he made miserable?
O, handle not the theme, to talk of hands,
Lest we remember still that we have none. 30
Fie, fie, how franticly I square my talk, 31
As if we should forget we had no hands
If Marcus did not name the word of hands!
Come, let's fall to; and, gentle girl, eat this.
Here is no drink! Hark, Marcus, what she says;
I can interpret all her marytred signs.
She says she drinks no other drink but tears,
Brewed with her sorrow, mashed upon her cheeks. 38
Speechless complainer, I will learn thy thought;
In thy dumb action will I be as perfect 40
As begging hermits in their holy prayers. 41
Thou shalt not sigh, nor hold thy stumps to heaven,
Nor wink, nor nod, nor kneel, nor make a sign, 43
But I of these will wrest an alphabet
And by still practice learn to know thy meaning. 45

BOY [*Weeping*]
Good grandsire, leave these bitter deep laments!
Make my aunt merry with some pleasing tale.

MARCUS
Alas, the tender boy, in passion moved, 48
Doth weep to see his grandsire's heaviness.

TITUS
Peace, tender sapling! Thou art made of tears, 50
And tears will quickly melt thy life away.
Marcus strikes the dish with a knife.
What dost thou strike at, Marcus, with thy knife?

MARCUS
At that that I have killed, my lord: a fly.

TITUS
Out on thee, murderer! Thou kill'st my heart.
Mine eyes are cloyed with view of tyranny.
A deed of death done on the innocent

30 still continually **31 square** shape, regulate **38 mashed** mixed with hot water in a mash, as for brewing **40 action** gesture. **perfect** thoroughly acquainted **41 As . . . prayers** i.e., as hermits are with the subject of their prayerful meditation **43 wink** close the eyes **45 still** continual **48 passion** sorrow **50 made of tears** (See Genesis 3:16: "In sorrow thou shalt bring forth children." Like a sapling, the child is soft, unformed.)

Becomes not Titus' brother. Get thee gone!
I see thou art not for my company.

MARCUS
Alas, my lord, I have but killed a fly.

TITUS
"But"? How if that fly had a father and mother?
How would he hang his slender gilded wings 61
And buzz lamenting doings in the air! 62
Poor harmless fly,
That, with his pretty buzzing melody,
Came here to make us merry! And thou hast killed him.

MARCUS
Pardon me, sir. It was a black ill-favored fly, 66
Like to the Empress' Moor. Therefore I killed him.

TITUS O, O, O!
Then pardon me for reprehending thee,
For thou hast done a charitable deed.
Give me thy knife. I will insult on him, 71
Flattering myself as if it were the Moor 72
Come hither purposely to poison me.—
There's for thyself, and that's for Tamora!
[*He takes the knife and strikes.*]
Ah, sirrah! 75
Yet I think we are not brought so low
But that between us we can kill a fly
That comes in likeness of a coal black Moor.

MARCUS
Alas, poor man! Grief has so wrought on him
He takes false shadows for true substances.

TITUS
Come, take away. Lavinia, go with me. 81
I'll to thy closet and go read with thee 82
Sad stories chancèd in the times of old. 83
Come, boy, and go with me. Thy sight is young,
And thou shalt read when mine begin to dazzle. 85
Exeunt.

61 he i.e., the father **62 buzz . . . doings** tell sad stories **66 ill-favored** ugly **71 insult on** exult over **72 Flattering . . . if** deluding myself into believing **75 sirrah** (Ordinary term of address to inferiors.) **81 take away** clear the table. (The "banquet" and furniture are removed from the stage as the scene ends.) **82 closet** private room **83 chancèd** that occurred **85 dazzle** become dazzled, unable to see

4.1 *Enter Lucius' son, and Lavinia running after him, and the boy flies from her, with his books under his arm. Enter Titus and Marcus.*

BOY

Help, grandsire, help! My aunt Lavinia
Follows me everywhere, I know not why.
Good uncle Marcus, see how swift she comes.
Alas, sweet aunt, I know not what you mean.
[*He drops his books.*]

MARCUS

Stand by me, Lucius. Do not fear thine aunt.

TITUS

She loves thee, boy, too well to do thee harm.

BOY

Ay, when my father was in Rome she did. 7

MARCUS

What means my niece Lavinia by these signs?

TITUS

Fear her not, Lucius. Somewhat doth she mean. 9

MARCUS

See, Lucius, see how much she makes of thee;
Somewhither would she have thee go with her.
Ah, boy, Cornelia never with more care 12
Read to her sons than she hath read to thee 13
Sweet poetry and Tully's *Orator*. 14
Canst thou not guess wherefore she plies thee thus? 15

BOY

My lord, I know not, I, nor can I guess,
Unless some fit or frenzy do possess her;
For I have heard my grandsire say full oft,
Extremity of griefs would make men mad,
And I have read that Hecuba of Troy 20
Ran mad for sorrow. That made me to fear,
Although, my lord, I know my noble aunt

4.1. Location: Rome. Titus' garden.
7 when . . . Rome i.e., when my father was here to protect me **9 Somewhat** something **12 Cornelia** the mother of the Gracchi brothers, the two most famous tribunes in Roman history. (Her success in educating her sons was highly regarded.) **13 Read** gave instruction **14 Tully's Orator** Cicero's treatise on rhetoric, *De Oratore* **15 plies** importunes **20 Hecuba** (See 1.1.136 and note.)

Loves me as dear as e'er my mother did,
And would not but in fury fright my youth— 24
Which made me down to throw my books and fly,
Causeless, perhaps. But pardon me, sweet aunt,
And, madam, if my uncle Marcus go, 27
I will most willingly attend your ladyship.

MARCUS Lucius, I will. 29

[*Lavinia turns over with her stumps the books that young Lucius has let fall.*]

TITUS

How now, Lavinia? Marcus, what means this?
Some book there is that she desires to see.
Which is it, girl, of these?—Open them, boy.
[*To Lavinia.*] But thou art deeper read and better skilled;
Come and take choice of all my library,
And so beguile thy sorrow till the heavens
Reveal the damned contriver of this deed.—
Why lifts she up her arms in sequence thus? 37

MARCUS

I think she means that there were more than one
Confederate in the fact. Ay, more there was; 39
Or else to heaven she heaves them for revenge.

TITUS

Lucius, what book is that she tosseth so? 41

BOY

Grandsire, 'tis Ovid's *Metamorphoses;*
My mother gave it me.

MARCUS For love of her that's gone,
Perhaps, she culled it from among the rest.

TITUS

Soft, so busily she turns the leaves!
Help her.
What would she find? Lavinia, shall I read?
This is the tragic tale of Philomel, 49
And treats of Tereus' treason and his rape; 50

24 but in fury except in madness **27 go** i.e., come with us. (See l. 11.) The boy doesn't want to be alone with his mad aunt. **29 Lucius** i.e., young Lucius, the boy **37 in sequence** one after the other **39 fact** deed **41 tosseth** turns the pages of **49–50 Philomel, Terreus** (Cf. 2.3.43, note.)

And rape, I fear, was root of thy annoy. 51

MARCUS

See, brother, see! Note how she quotes the leaves. 52

TITUS

Lavinia, wert thou thus surprised, sweet girl,
Ravished and wronged as Philomela was,
Forced in the ruthless, vast, and gloomy woods? 55
See, see!
Ay, such a place there is, where we did hunt—
O, had we never, never hunted there!—
Patterned by that the poet here describes, 59
By nature made for murders and for rapes.

MARCUS

O, why should nature build so foul a den,
Unless the gods delight in tragedies?

TITUS

Give signs, sweet girl—for here are none but friends—
What Roman lord it was durst do the deed.
Or slunk not Saturnine, as Tarquin erst, 65
That left the camp to sin in Lucrece' bed?

MARCUS

Sit down, sweet niece. Brother, sit down by me.
[*They sit.*]
Apollo, Pallas, Jove, or Mercury 68
Inspire me, that I may this treason find!
My lord, look here. Look here, Lavinia.
He writes his name with his staff,
and guides it with feet and mouth.
This sandy plot is plain; guide, if thou canst, 71
This after me. I have writ my name 72
Without the help of any hand at all.
Cursed be that heart that forced us to this shift! 74
Write thou, good niece, and here display at last
What God will have discovered for revenge. 76
Heaven guide thy pen to print thy sorrows plain,

51 annoy injury **52 quotes** examines **55 vast** desolate **59 Patterned by that** on the pattern of that which **65 Or . . . Saturnine** or was it Saturnine who slunk. **Tarquin** (See notes at 2.1.108 and 3.1.298.) **erst** once **68 Pallas** Minerva, Athene **71 plain** level **72 after me** following my example **74 shift** expedient **76 will** wishes to. **discovered** revealed, uncovered

That we may know the traitors and the truth!
She takes the staff in her mouth, and guides it with her stumps, and writes.
O, do ye read, my lord, what she hath writ?

TITUS
"*Stuprum.* Chiron. Demetrius." 80

MARCUS
What, what! The lustful sons of Tamora
Performers of this heinous, bloody deed?

TITUS
Magni Dominator poli, 83
Tam lentus audis scelera? Tam lentus vides? 84

MARCUS
O, calm thee, gentle lord, although I know
There is enough written upon this earth
To stir a mutiny in the mildest thoughts
And arm the minds of infants to exclaims. 88
My lord, kneel down with me; Lavinia, kneel;
And kneel, sweet boy, the Roman Hector's hope. 90
[*All kneel.*]
And swear with me—as, with the woeful fere 91
And father of that chaste dishonored dame,
Lord Junius Brutus sware for Lucrece' rape— 93
That we will prosecute by good advice 94
Mortal revenge upon these traitorous Goths,
And see their blood or die with this reproach. 96
[*They rise.*]

TITUS
'Tis sure enough, an you knew how. 97
But if you hunt these bear whelps, then beware:
The dam will wake an if she wind ye once. 99

80 Stuprum violation, rape **83–84 Magni . . . vides?** Ruler of the mighty heavens, are you so slow to see and hear the crimes that are committed? (Derived from Seneca, *Hippolytus,* 671–672.) **88 exclaims** exclamations **90 the Roman Hector's hope** i.e., the hope and future of Lucius, whose deeds compare with those of Hector in Troy **91 fere** spouse, husband **93 Brutus** (After Sextus Tarquinius had raped Lucretia—see 2.1.108 and Shakespeare's *Rape of Lucrece*—Junius Brutus led the Romans to expel the Tarquin dynasty; see also 3.1.298 and *Julius Caesar,* 2.1.53–54.) **sware** swore **94 by good advice** after careful deliberation, planning **96 reproach** disgrace, infamy **97 an** if **99 dam** mother. **an if** if. **wind** scent

She's with the lion deeply still in league, 100
And lulls him whilst she playeth on her back,
And when he sleeps will she do what she list. 102
You are a young huntsman, Marcus. Let alone, 103
And come, I will go get a leaf of brass, 104
And with a gad of steel will write these words, 105
And lay it by. The angry northern wind 106
Will blow these sands like Sibyl's leaves abroad, 107
And where's our lesson then? Boy, what say you?

BOY

I say, my lord, that if I were a man,
Their mother's bedchamber should not be safe 110
For these base bondmen to the yoke of Rome. 111

MARCUS

Ay, that's my boy! Thy father hath full oft
For his ungrateful country done the like. 113

BOY

And, uncle, so will I, an if I live.

TITUS

Come, go with me into mine armory.
Lucius, I'll fit thee, and withal my boy 116
Shall carry from me to the Empress' sons
Presents that I intend to send them both.
Come, come. Thou'lt do my message, wilt thou not?

BOY

Ay, with my dagger in their bosoms, grandsire.

TITUS

No, boy, not so. I'll teach thee another course.
Lavinia, come. Marcus, look to my house.
Lucius and I'll go brave it at the court. 123

100 still always **102 list** choose, please **103 young** inexperienced. **Let alone** let it alone, be wary **104 leaf** sheet **105 gad** stylus, spike **106 lay it by** i.e., put it in safekeeping, where the words will be preserved, unlike the writing in the sand **107 Sibyl's leaves** (The Cumaean Sibyl, an inspired woman, wrote her prophecies on leaves which she placed at the entrance to her cave. Those wishing to consult them had to do so before they were scattered by the wind.) **110–111 Their . . . Rome** i.e., no place of hiding will be held sacred in my seeking to destroy these men who cravenly thrive under the yoke of Rome's tyranny **113 done the like** i.e., fought against tyranny **116 fit thee** provide you with what you need. **withal** in addition **123 brave it** put on a good show, cut a bold figure

Ay, marry, will we, sir, and we'll be waited on. 124
Exeunt [*Titus, Lavinia, and young Lucius*].

MARCUS
O heavens, can you hear a good man groan
And not relent, or not compassion him? 126
Marcus, attend him in his ecstasy, 127
That hath more scars of sorrow in his heart 128
Than foemen's marks upon his battered shield,
But yet so just that he will not revenge.
Revenge the heavens for old Andronicus! *Exit.* 131

✤

4.2

Enter Aaron, Chiron, and Demetrius, at one door, and at the other door young Lucius and another, with a bundle of weapons and verses writ upon them.

CHIRON
Demetrius, here's the son of Lucius.
He hath some message to deliver us.

AARON
Ay, some mad message from his mad grandfather.

BOY
My lords, with all the humbleness I may,
I greet your honors from Andronicus—
[*Aside*] And pray the Roman gods confound you both! 6

DEMETRIUS
Gramercy, lovely Lucius. What's the news? 7

BOY [*Aside*]
That you are both deciphered, that's the news, 8
For villains marked with rape.—May it please you,
My grandsire, well advised, hath sent by me 10

124 marry (A mild interjection equivalent to "Indeed!"; originally an oath, "by the Virgin Mary.") **be waited on** i.e., demand attention **126 compassion** have compassion for **127 ecstasy** madness **128 That** who **131 Revenge the heavens** may the heavens take revenge

4.2. Location: Rome. The Emperor's palace.
s.d. another (Presumably an attendant of Lucius, bearing the weapons and verses; see l. 16, stage direction.) **6 confound** destroy **7 Gramercy** many thanks **8 deciphered** detected **10 well advised** having considered carefully

The goodliest weapons of his armory
To gratify your honorable youth, 12
The hope of Rome; for so he bid me say.
And so I do, and with his gifts present
Your lordships, that, whenever you have need,
You may be armèd and appointed well. 16
[*His attendant presents the bundle.*]
And so I leave you both—[*Aside*] like bloody villains.
Exit [*with attendant*].

DEMETRIUS
What's here? A scroll, and written round about? 19
Let's see:
[*Reads.*] "*Integer vitae, scelerisque purus,* 20
Non eget Mauri iaculis, nec arcu." 21

CHIRON
O, 'tis a verse in Horace; I know it well.
I read it in the grammar long ago. 23

AARON
Ay, just; a verse in Horace; right, you have it. 24
[*Aside.*] Now, what a thing it is to be an ass!
Here's no sound jest! The old man hath found their guilt, 26
And sends them weapons wrapped about with lines
That wound, beyond their feeling, to the quick. 28
But were our witty empress well afoot, 29
She would applaud Andronicus' conceit. 30
But let her rest in her unrest awhile.— 31
And now, young lords, was 't not a happy star
Led us to Rome, strangers, and more than so,
Captives, to be advancèd to this height?
It did me good before the palace gate

12 gratify grace, please **16 appointed** equipped **19 round about** all around **20–21 Integer . . . arcu** (The opening lines of perhaps the best known of the Odes of Horace, l. 22: "He who is spotless in life and free of crime needs not the Moorish bow and arrow.") **23 grammar** i.e., Latin grammar book. (William Lilly's grammar book, containing this passage, was widely used in Elizabethan England.) **24 just** precisely **26 Here's no sound jest** (Said ironically to mean its opposite: Here's a splendid joke indeed.) **28 beyond their feeling** i.e., far beyond the capacity of Demetrius and Chiron to be sensitive to the injury. **to the quick** i.e., to the very life **29 witty** clever. **afoot** up and about, i.e., not in childbed (as we soon learn) **30 conceit** design **31 her unrest** i.e., her labor of delivery

To brave the tribune in his brother's hearing. 36

DEMETRIUS
But me more good to see so great a lord
Basely insinuate and send us gifts. 38

AARON
Had he not reason, Lord Demetrius?
Did you not use his daughter very friendly?

DEMETRIUS
I would we had a thousand Roman dames
At such a bay, by turn to serve our lust. 42

CHIRON
A charitable wish, and full of love!

AARON
Here lacks but your mother for to say amen.

CHIRON
And that would she, for twenty thousand more. 45

DEMETRIUS
Come, let us go and pray to all the gods
For our belovèd mother in her pains. 47

AARON
Pray to the devils. The gods have given us over. 48
Trumpets sound [*within*].

DEMETRIUS
Why do the Emperor's trumpets flourish thus?

CHIRON
Belike for joy the Emperor hath a son. 50

DEMETRIUS
Soft, who comes here?

Enter Nurse, with a blackamoor child [*in her arms*].

NURSE Good morrow, lords.
O, tell me, did you see Aaron the Moor?

36 To . . . hearing i.e., to taunt Marcus in Titus' presence **38 insinuate** ingratiate himself by flattery **42 At such a bay** cornered thus (as in hunting) **45 for . . . more** i.e., to pray for 20,000 more Roman *dames*, or ladies, to be ravished **47 pains** i.e., labor pains. (Tamora is being delivered of a child sired by Aaron; see ll. 29–31 above.) **48 Pray . . . over** (Said perhaps to Demetrius and Chiron, or as a mocking aside.) **50 Belike** probably

AARON

Well, more or less, or ne'er a whit at all, 53

Here Aaron is; and what with Aaron now? 54

NURSE

O gentle Aaron, we are all undone!

Now help, or woe betide thee evermore!

AARON

Why, what a caterwauling dost thou keep! 57

What dost thou wrap and fumble in thy arms?

NURSE

O, that which I would hide from heaven's eye,

Our empress' shame and stately Rome's disgrace!

She is delivered, lords, she is delivered.

AARON To whom? 62

NURSE I mean she is brought abed.

AARON

Well, God give her good rest! What hath he sent her? 64

NURSE A devil.

AARON

Why, then she is the devil's dam. A joyful issue! 66

NURSE

A joyless, dismal, black, and sorrowful issue! 67

Here is the babe, as loathsome as a toad

Amongst the fair-faced breeders of our clime.

The Empress sends it thee, thy stamp, thy seal, 70

And bids thee christen it with thy dagger's point.

AARON

Zounds, ye whore, is black so base a hue? 72

[*To the child.*] Sweet blowze, you are a beauteous
blossom, sure. 73

DEMETRIUS Villain, what hast thou done?

53–54 more . . . Aaron is (Punning on *more* and *Moor,* l. 52, with sardonic humor, Aaron suggests that whether he is addressed as Aaron the Great or the Less or by no title at all, he is who he is.) **57 keep** keep up **62 To whom** (Aaron plays on *delivered,* l. 61, in the sense of "handed over or transferred to another person," though he of course knows that the Nurse means "delivered of a child.") **64 God . . . rest** (Again Aaron jestingly pretends to misinterpret *brought abed,* l. 63, in its literal sense.) **66 dam** mother. **issue** result **67 issue** i.e., child **70 thy stamp, thy seal** i.e., bearing your imprint **72 Zounds** by His (Christ's) wounds **73 blowze** red-cheeked one. (Usually addressed to a wench or slattern; here an affectionately abusive term for the child.)

AARON That which thou canst not undo.
CHIRON Thou hast undone our mother.
AARON Villain, I have done thy mother. 77
DEMETRIUS
And therein, hellish dog, thou hast undone her.
Woe to her chance, and damned her loathèd choice! 79
Accurst the offspring of so foul a fiend! 80
CHIRON It shall not live.
AARON It shall not die.
NURSE
Aaron, it must. The mother wills it so.
AARON
What, must it, Nurse? Then let no man but I
Do execution on my flesh and blood.
DEMETRIUS
I'll broach the tadpole on my rapier's point. 86
Nurse, give it me. My sword shall soon dispatch it.
AARON [*Taking the child and drawing his sword*]
Sooner this sword shall plow thy bowels up.
Stay, murderous villains, will you kill your brother?
Now, by the burning tapers of the sky
That shone so brightly when this boy was got, 91
He dies upon my scimitar's sharp point
That touches this my firstborn son and heir!
I tell you, younglings, not Enceladus 94
With all his threatening band of Typhon's brood, 95
Nor great Alcides, nor the god of war 96
Shall seize this prey out of his father's hands.
What, what, ye sanguine, shallow-hearted boys! 98
Ye white-limed walls! Ye alehouse painted signs! 99
Coal black is better than another hue
In that it scorns to bear another hue;

77 done i.e., had sexual intercourse with (playing on *undone* in the previous line) **79 chance** luck. **damned** damned be **80 Accurst** accursed be **86 broach** impale **91 got** begotten **94 Enceladus** one of the giants who rose against the gods and were defeated by them; Enceladus was buried under Mount Etna in Sicily **95 Typhon** a terrible monster who attacked the gods and was flung into Tartarus **96 Alcides** Hercules, a descendant of Alcaeus **98 sanguine** red-cheeked (as distinguished from black-complexioned) **99 white-limed** whitewashed. (The image is of a fair exterior hiding darkness within.) **alehouse painted signs** i.e., cheap painted imitations of men

For all the water in the ocean
Can never turn the swan's black legs to white,
Although she lave them hourly in the flood. 104
Tell the Empress from me, I am of age
To keep mine own, excuse it how she can. 106

DEMETRIUS
Wilt thou betray thy noble mistress thus?

AARON
My mistress is my mistress, this myself, 108
The vigor and the picture of my youth.
This before all the world do I prefer;
This maugre all the world will I keep safe, 111
Or some of you shall smoke for it in Rome. 112

DEMETRIUS
By this our mother is forever shamed.

CHIRON
Rome will despise her for this foul escape. 114

NURSE
The Emperor in his rage will doom her death.

CHIRON
I blush to think upon this ignomy. 116

AARON
Why, there's the privilege your beauty bears. 117
Fie, treacherous hue, that will betray with blushing
The close enacts and counsels of thy heart! 119
Here's a young lad framed of another leer. 120
Look how the black slave smiles upon the father,
As who should say, "Old lad, I am thine own." 122
He is your brother, lords, sensibly fed 123
Of that self blood that first gave life to you, 124
And from that womb where you imprisoned were

104 lave wash. **flood** stream **106 excuse . . . can** i.e., no matter how she may wish to explain away the circumstance by getting rid of the evidence **108 this myself** i.e., this child is a part of myself **111 maugre** in spite of **112 smoke** i.e., suffer. (The metaphor is from burning at the stake.) **114 escape** escapade, outrageous transgression **116 ignomy** ignominy, shame **117 Why . . . bears** i.e., blushing is one of the benefits of your fair complexion. (Said ironically; Aaron prefers a hue that cannot incriminate itself.) **119 close enacts** secret purposes **120 framed** made. **leer** countenance, complexion **122 As . . . say** as if saying, as if one might say **123 sensibly** manifestly, or as a creature endowed with feeling (?) **124 Of** by. **self** same

He is enfranchisèd and come to light.
Nay, he is your brother by the surer side, 127
Although my seal be stampèd in his face. 128

NURSE
Aaron, what shall I say unto the Empress?

DEMETRIUS
Advise thee, Aaron, what is to be done, 130
And we will all subscribe to thy advice. 131
Save thou the child, so we may all be safe. 132

AARON
Then sit we down, and let us all consult.
My son and I will have the wind of you; 134
Keep there. Now talk at pleasure of your safety.
[*They sit.*]

DEMETRIUS [*To the Nurse*]
How many women saw this child of his?

AARON
Why, so, brave lords! When we join in league
I am a lamb; but if you brave the Moor,
The chafèd boar, the mountain lioness, 139
The ocean swells not so as Aaron storms.
[*To the Nurse.*] But say again, how many saw the child?

NURSE
Cornelia the midwife and myself,
And no one else but the delivered Empress.

AARON
The Empress, the midwife, and yourself.
Two may keep counsel when the third's away.
Go to the Empress, tell her this I said. *He kills her.*
Wheak, wheak!— 147
So cries a pig preparèd to the spit. 148

DEMETRIUS
What mean'st thou, Aaron? Wherefore didst thou this?

AARON
O Lord, sir, 'tis a deed of policy. 150

127 surer i.e., mother's **128 seal be stampèd** (See line 70 above; the child bears the imprint of the father in his looks.) **130 Advise thee** consider **131 subscribe** agree **132 so** so long as **134 have . . . you** i.e., remain at a safe distance and stay downwind of you (as in hunting, so as not to be scented by the game) **139 chafèd** enraged **147 Wheak** (Aaron mimics her dying cry.) **148 preparèd to the spit** i.e., being spitted for roasting **150 policy** prudent action

Shall she live to betray this guilt of ours,
A long-tongued babbling gossip? No, lords, no.
And now be it known to you my full intent.
Not far, one Muliteus my countryman 154
His wife but yesternight was brought to bed; 155
His child is like to her, fair as you are.
Go pack with him, and give the mother gold, 157
And tell them both the circumstance of all, 158
And how by this their child shall be advanced
And be receivèd for the Emperor's heir,
And substituted in the place of mine,
To calm this tempest whirling in the court;
And let the Emperor dandle him for his own.
Hark ye, lords, you see I have given her physic, 164
[*Pointing to the Nurse*]
And you must needs bestow her funeral. 165
The fields are near, and you are gallant grooms. 166
This done, see that you take no longer days, 167
But send the midwife presently to me. 168
The midwife and the nurse well made away,
Then let the ladies tattle what they please.

CHIRON
Aaron, I see thou wilt not trust the air
With secrets.

DEMETRIUS For this care of Tamora,
Herself and hers are highly bound to thee.
Exeunt [*Demetrius and Chiron, bearing off the Nurse's body*].

AARON
Now to the Goths, as swift as swallow flies,
There to dispose this treasure in mine arms 175
And secretly to greet the Empress' friends.
Come on, you thick-lipped slave, I'll bear you hence,
For it is you that puts us to our shifts. 178
I'll make you feed on berries and on roots,
And feed on curds and whey, and suck the goat,

154–155 one . . . wife the wife of a certain Muliteus, a fellow countryman of mine **157 pack** make a deal **158 the circumstance of all** the full details **164 physic** medicine **165 bestow** provide, furnish **166 grooms** fellows **167 days** time **168 presently** at once **175 dispose** dispose of **178 shifts** stratagems, tricks

And cabin in a cave, and bring you up 181
To be a warrior and command a camp.
Exit [*with the child*].

✤

4.3

Enter Titus, old Marcus, [*his son Publius,*] *young Lucius, and other gentlemen* [*Sempronius, Caius,*] *with bows; and Titus bears the arrows with letters on the ends of them.*

TITUS
Come, Marcus, come. Kinsmen, this is the way.
Sir boy, let me see your archery.
Look ye draw home enough, and 'tis there straight. 3
Terras Astraea reliquit; 4
Be you remembered, Marcus, she's gone, she's fled. 5
Sirs, take you to your tools. You, cousins, shall
Go sound the ocean and cast your nets;
Happily you may catch her in the sea. 8
Yet there's as little justice as at land. 9
No; Publius and Sempronius, you must do it;
'Tis you must dig with mattock and with spade,
And pierce the inmost center of the earth.
Then, when you come to Pluto's region, 13
I pray you, deliver him this petition.
Tell him it is for justice and for aid,
And that it comes from old Andronicus,
Shaken with sorrows in ungrateful Rome.
Ah, Rome! Well, well, I made thee miserable
What time I threw the people's suffrages 19
On him that thus doth tyrannize o'er me.
Go, get you gone, and pray be careful all,

181 cabin lodge

4.3. Location: Rome. A public place.
3 home to the full extent (of the bow) **4 Terras Astraea reliquit** Astraea (the goddess of justice) has abandoned the earth. (From Ovid, *Metamorphoses,* 1.150.) **5 Be you remembered** remember **8 Happily** haply, perhaps **9 there's** i.e., there in the sea there is **13 Pluto's region** the underworld, ruled over by Pluto **19 What time** when

And leave you not a man-of-war unsearched.
This wicked emperor may have shipped her hence, 23
And, kinsmen, then we may go pipe for justice. 24

MARCUS
O Publius, is not this a heavy case, 25
To see thy noble uncle thus distract? 26

PUBLIUS
Therefore, my lords, it highly us concerns
By day and night t' attend him carefully,
And feed his humor kindly as we may, 29
Till time beget some careful remedy. 30

MARCUS
Kinsmen, his sorrows are past remedy. 31
Join with the Goths, and with revengeful war
Take wreak on Rome for this ingratitude, 33
And vengeance on the traitor Saturnine.

TITUS
Publius, how now? How now, my masters?
What, have you met with her? 36

PUBLIUS
No, my good lord, but Pluto sends you word,
If you will have Revenge from hell, you shall.
Marry, for Justice, she is so employed, 39
He thinks, with Jove in heaven, or somewhere else,
So that perforce you must needs stay a time. 41

TITUS
He doth me wrong to feed me with delays.
I'll dive into the burning lake below 43
And pull her out of Acheron by the heels. 44
Marcus, we are but shrubs, no cedars we,
No big-boned men framed of the Cyclops' size, 46

23 her i.e., Justice, the goddess Astraea. (In his madness, Titus imagines that Saturninus may ship Astraea out of the country in an armed naval vessel, a *man-of-war*.) **24 pipe** whistle, i.e., look in vain **25 heavy case** sad situation **26 distract** distracted, crazed **29 feed his humor** humor him **30 careful** showing and requiring care **31 remedy** (In the first quarto, this word is followed by a catch word *But* at the foot of the page that is not repeated in the first line of the next page, possibly suggesting an omission in the text.) **33 wreak** vengeance **36 her** i.e., Justice **39 for** as for **41 stay a time** wait awhile **43 burning lake** i.e., Phlegethon, the burning river of the underworld **44 Acheron** a river in the underworld **46 Cyclops** one-eyed giants in Homer's *Odyssey* (9)

But metal, Marcus, steel to the very back,
Yet wrung with wrongs more than our backs can bear.
And sith there's no justice in earth nor hell, 49
We will solicit heaven and move the gods
To send down Justice for to wreak our wrongs. 51
Come, to this gear. You are a good archer, Marcus. 52
He gives them the arrows.
"Ad Jovem," that's for you; here, *"Ad Apollinem"*; 53
"Ad Martem," that's for myself; 54
Here, boy, "to Pallas"; here, "to Mercury"; 55
"To Saturn," Caius—not "to Saturnine"!
You were as good to shoot against the wind. 57
To it, boy! Marcus, loose when I bid. 58
Of my word, I have written to effect; 59
There's not a god left unsolicited.

MARCUS
Kinsmen, shoot all your shafts into the court.
We will afflict the Emperor in his pride.

TITUS
Now, masters, draw. [*They shoot.*] O, well said, Lucius! 63
Good boy, in Virgo's lap! Give it Pallas. 64

MARCUS
My lord, I aim a mile beyond the moon; 65
Your letter is with Jupiter by this.

TITUS Ha, ha!
Publius, Publius, what hast thou done?
See, see, thou hast shot off one of Taurus' horns. 69

MARCUS
This was the sport, my lord: when Publius shot,
The Bull, being galled, gave Aries such a knock 71

49 sith since **51 for to** to **52 gear** business **53–54 Ad Jovem, Ad Apollinem, Ad Martem** to Jove, to Apollo, to Mars **55 Pallas** Minerva, Athene **57 You . . . wind** you would do as much good shooting against the wind (as you would in appealing to Saturninus) **58 loose** let fly, discharge **59 Of** on **63 said** done **64 in Virgo's lap** in the constellation of the Virgin (the zodiacal sign representing Astraea, having fled from earth). **Give it Pallas** i.e., shoot the arrow labeled "Pallas" there **65 a mile . . . moon** (Marcus' literal meaning is intended to humor Titus' madness, but his expression also means "wild conjecture, far wide of the mark," thus commenting on the madness of their proceedings.) **69, 71 Taurus, Aries** the Bull, the Ram; signs of the zodiac **71 galled** slightly wounded

That down fell both the Ram's horns in the court; 72
And who should find them but the Empress' villain? 73
She laughed, and told the Moor he should not choose 74
But give them to his master for a present. 75

TITUS
Why, there it goes. God give his lordship joy! 76

Enter the Clown, with a basket, and two pigeons in it.

News, news from heaven! Marcus, the post is come.—
Sirrah, what tidings? Have you any letters?
Shall I have justice? What says Jupiter?

CLOWN Ho, the gibbet maker? He says that he hath 80 taken them down again, for the man must not be 81 hanged till the next week.

TITUS But what says Jupiter, I ask thee?

CLOWN Alas, sir, I know not Jupiter. I never drank with him in all my life.

TITUS Why, villain, art not thou the carrier? 86

CLOWN Ay, of my pigeons, sir; nothing else.

TITUS Why, didst thou not come from heaven?

CLOWN From heaven! Alas, sir, I never came there. God forbid I should be so bold to press to heaven in my young days. Why, I am going with my pigeons to the tribunal plebs, to take up a matter of brawl betwixt my 92 uncle and one of the Emperal's men. 93

MARCUS [*To Titus*] Why, sir, that is as fit as can be to serve for your oration; and let him deliver the pigeons to the Emperor from you.

TITUS [*To Clown*]
Sirrah, come hither. Make no more ado, 97

72 horns i.e., signs of being a cuckold, bestowed by Aaron on the Emperor **73 villain** i.e., Aaron, both servant and villain in the modern sense **74–75 should . . . But** must **76 there it goes** (A hunting cry of encouragement.) **s.d. Clown** rustic **80 gibbet maker** (The Clown seems to have heard "Jupiter" as "gibbeter.") **81 them** i.e., the gallows. **must not be** is not to be **86 carrier** postman. (But the Clown answers in the sense of "one who carries things.") **92 tribunal plebs** i.e., *tribunus plebis,* tribune of the plebs. **take up** settle amicably **93 Emperal's** (Malapropism for *emperor's.*) **97 Sirrah** (In the early texts, this line is preceded by four lines that appear to be a first draft of ll. 102–103: "TITUS Tell me, can you deliver an oration to the Emperor with a grace? CLOWN Nay, truly, sir, I could never say grace in all my life.")

But give your pigeons to the Emperor.
By me thou shalt have justice at his hands.
Hold, hold; meanwhile here's money for thy charges. 100
[*He gives money.*]
Give me pen and ink.
Sirrah, can you with a grace deliver up a supplication?

CLOWN Ay, sir.

TITUS [*Writing and handing him a supplication*] Then here is a supplication for you. And when you come to him, at the first approach you must kneel, then kiss his foot, then deliver up your pigeons, and then look for your reward. I'll be at hand, sir; see you do it bravely. 109

CLOWN I warrant you, sir. Let me alone. 110

TITUS
Sirrah, hast thou a knife? Come, let me see it.
[*He takes the knife and gives it to Marcus.*]
Here, Marcus, fold it in the oration,
For thou hast made it like an humble suppliant.— 113
And when thou hast given it to the Emperor,
Knock at my door and tell me what he says.

CLOWN God be with you, sir. I will. *Exit.*

TITUS Come, Marcus, let us go. Publius, follow me.
Exeunt.

✤

4.4

Enter Emperor [*Saturninus*] *and Empress* [*Tamora*] *and her two sons* [*and others, including guards*]. *The Emperor brings the arrows in his hand that Titus shot at him.* [*The Emperor and Empress sit.*]

SATURNINUS
Why, lords, what wrongs are these! Was ever seen
An emperor in Rome thus overborne, 2

100 charges expenses **109 bravely** handsomely, stylishly **110 Let me alone** leave it to me **113 For . . . suppliant** (A puzzling and perhaps corrupt line. Titus may mean that Marcus has made the supplication seem humble enough, even though it conceals a knife.)

4.4. Location: Rome. Before or in the palace.
2 overborne oppressed

Troubled, confronted thus, and, for the extent 3
Of equal justice, used in such contempt?
My lords, you know, as know the mightful gods,
However these disturbers of our peace
Buzz in the people's ears, there naught hath passed
But even with law against the willful sons 8
Of old Andronicus. And what an if
His sorrows have so overwhelmed his wits?
Shall we be thus afflicted in his wreaks, 11
His fits, his frenzy, and his bitterness?
And now he writes to heaven for his redress.
See, here's "to Jove," and this "to Mercury,"
This "to Apollo," this to the god of war—
Sweet scrolls to fly about the streets of Rome!
What's this but libeling against the Senate
And blazoning our unjustice everywhere? 18
A goodly humor, is it not, my lords? 19
As who would say, in Rome no justice were.
But if I live, his feignèd ecstasies 21
Shall be no shelter to these outrages;
But he and his shall know that justice lives 23
In Saturninus' health, whom, if he sleep, 24
He'll so awake as he in fury shall 25
Cut off the proud'st conspirator that lives.

TAMORA

My gracious lord, my lovely Saturnine,
Lord of my life, commander of my thoughts,
Calm thee, and bear the faults of Titus' age,
Th' effects of sorrow for his valiant sons,
Whose loss hath pierced him deep and scarred his heart;
And rather comfort his distressèd plight
Than prosecute the meanest or the best 33
For these contempts. [*Aside*.] Why, thus it shall become

3 extent exercise **8 even** conformable **11 wreaks** revengeful acts **18 blazoning** making public **19 humor** whim, caprice **21 ecstasies** fits of madness **23 his** i.e., the Andronici **23–25 justice . . . shall** i.e., justice in Rome depends on Saturninus' thriving, and, if justice be asleep, Saturninus will so rouse him to fury that he will. (The use of male pronouns for justice is unusual; see 4.3.4–5 and 23. Possibly the text should read *she* in ll. 24–25, or the pronouns may refer to Saturninus.) **33 the meanest or the best** those of low or high station

High-witted Tamora to gloze with all. 35
But, Titus, I have touched thee to the quick;
Thy lifeblood out, if Aaron now be wise, 37
Then is all safe, the anchor in the port.

Enter Clown.

How now, good fellow, wouldst thou speak with us?
CLOWN Yea, forsooth, an your mistress-ship be emperial.
TAMORA Empress I am, but yonder sits the Emperor.
CLOWN 'Tis he. [*He kneels.*] God and Saint Stephen give you good e'en. I have brought you a letter and a couple 43 of pigeons here. *He* [*Saturninus*] *reads the letter.*
SATURNINUS
Go, take him away and hang him presently. 45
CLOWN How much money must I have? 46
TAMORA Come, sirrah, you must be hanged.
CLOWN Hanged! By 'r Lady, then I have brought up a 48 neck to a fair end. *Exit* [*guarded*].
SATURNINUS
Despiteful and intolerable wrongs!
Shall I endure this monstrous villainy?
I know from whence this same device proceeds.
May this be borne?—as if his traitorous sons,
That died by law for murder of our brother,
Have by my means been butchered wrongfully!
Go, drag the villain hither by the hair.
Nor age nor honor shall shape privilege. 57
For this proud mock I'll be thy slaughterman,
Sly frantic wretch, that holp'st to make me great 59
In hope thyself should govern Rome and me. 60

Enter nuntius, Aemilius.

What news with thee, Aemilius?
AEMILIUS
Arm, my lords! Rome never had more cause.

35 High-witted clever. **gloze** deceive with smooth talk **37 Thy lifeblood out** once your lifeblood is spilled. **wise** i.e., wise enough to keep silent about the baby **43 good e'en** good afternoon or evening **45 presently** at once **46 must I** am I to **48 By 'r Lady** by Our Lady, the Virgin Mary **57 shape privilege** make for exemption **59 holp'st** helped **60 s.d. nuntius** messenger

The Goths have gathered head, and with a power 63
Of high-resolvèd men bent to the spoil 64
They hither march amain under conduct 65
Of Lucius, son to old Andronicus,
Who threats in course of this revenge to do
As much as ever Coriolanus did. 68

SATURNINUS
Is warlike Lucius general of the Goths?
These tidings nip me, and I hang the head
As flowers with frost or grass beat down with storms.
Ay, now begins our sorrows to approach.
'Tis he the common people love so much;
Myself hath often heard them say,
When I have walkèd like a private man, 75
That Lucius' banishment was wrongfully, 76
And they have wished that Lucius were their emperor.

TAMORA
Why should you fear? Is not your city strong?

SATURNINUS
Ay, but the citizens favor Lucius
And will revolt from me to succor him.

TAMORA
King, be thy thoughts imperious, like thy name. 81
Is the sun dimmed, that gnats do fly in it?
The eagle suffers little birds to sing
And is not careful what they mean thereby, 84
Knowing that with the shadow of his wings
He can at pleasure stint their melody; 86
Even so mayst thou the giddy men of Rome. 87
Then cheer thy spirit, for know, thou Emperor,
I will enchant the old Andronicus
With words more sweet and yet more dangerous
Than baits to fish or honey-stalks to sheep, 91

63 gathered head raised an army. **power** armed force **64 bent to the spoil** intent on plunder **65 amain** forcefully, swiftly. **conduct** command **68 Coriolanus** an early Roman hero turned enemy of Rome, about whom Shakespeare wrote one of his later tragedies **75 walkèd . . . man** i.e., gone in disguise among the commoners, like Henry V or the Duke in *Measure for Measure* **76 wrongfully** wrongfully imposed **81 imperious** imperial **84 careful** full of concern **86 stint** stop **87 giddy** changeable in opinion and allegiance **91 honey-stalks** clover. (Too much clover can make sheep ill.)

Whenas the one is wounded with the bait, 92
The other rotted with delicious feed. 93

SATURNINUS
But he will not entreat his son for us.

TAMORA
If Tamora entreat him, then he will;
For I can smooth and fill his agèd ears 96
With golden promises, that were his heart
Almost impregnable, his old ears deaf,
Yet should both ear and heart obey my tongue.
[*To Aemilius.*] Go thou before to be our ambassador.
Say that the Emperor requests a parley
Of warlike Lucius, and appoint the meeting 102
Even at his father's house, the old Andronicus.

SATURNINUS
Aemilius, do this message honorably,
And if he stand on hostage for his safety, 105
Bid him demand what pledge will please him best. 106

AEMILIUS
Your bidding shall I do effectually. *Exit.*

TAMORA
Now will I to that old Andronicus
And temper him with all the art I have 109
To pluck proud Lucius from the warlike Goths.
And now, sweet Emperor, be blithe again
And bury all thy fear in my devices.

SATURNINUS
Then go successantly, and plead to him. *Exeunt.* 113

✤

92 Whenas when **93 rotted** afflicted by the rot, a liver disease in sheep
96 smooth flatter **102 Of** with **105 stand** insist **106 demand** request
109 temper work upon **113 successantly** at once

5.1 [*Flourish.*] *Enter Lucius with an army of Goths, with drums and soldiers.*

LUCIUS

Approvèd warriors and my faithful friends, 1
I have receivèd letters from great Rome 2
Which signifies what hate they bear their emperor
And how desirous of our sight they are.
Therefore, great lords, be as your titles witness,
Imperious, and impatient of your wrongs,
And wherein Rome hath done you any scath 7
Let him make treble satisfaction.

A GOTH

Brave slip, sprung from the great Andronicus, 9
Whose name was once our terror, now our comfort,
Whose high exploits and honorable deeds
Ingrateful Rome requites with foul contempt,
Be bold in us. We'll follow where thou lead'st, 13
Like stinging bees in hottest summer's day
Led by their master to the flowered fields, 15
And be avenged on cursèd Tamora. 16

ALL THE GOTHS

And as he saith, so say we all with him.

LUCIUS

I humbly thank him, and I thank you all.
But who comes here, led by a lusty Goth? 19

Enter a Goth, leading of Aaron with his child in his arms.

ANOTHER GOTH

Renownèd Lucius, from our troops I strayed
To gaze upon a ruinous monastery, 21
And as I earnestly did fix mine eye
Upon the wasted building, suddenly 23

5.1. Location: Near Rome.
s.d. drums drummers **1 Approvèd** put to proof, tried **2 letters** a letter **7 scath** injury **9 slip** offspring, scion **13 bold** confident **15 their master** (Bees were thought to be led by a king bee.) **16 cursèd Tamora** (The play permits us to speculate as to why Tamora was not popular in her own country.) **19 lusty** valiant **21 ruinous** decayed **23 wasted** ruined

I heard a child cry underneath a wall.
I made unto the noise, when soon I heard 25
The crying babe controlled with this discourse: 26
"Peace, tawny slave, half me and half thy dam! 27
Did not thy hue bewray whose brat thou art, 28
Had nature lent thee but thy mother's look,
Villain, thou mightst have been an emperor.
But where the bull and cow are both milk white,
They never do beget a coal black calf.
Peace, villain, peace!"—even thus he rates the babe— 33
"For I must bear thee to a trusty Goth,
Who, when he knows thou art the Empress' babe,
Will hold thee dearly for thy mother's sake."
With this, my weapon drawn, I rushed upon him,
Surprised him suddenly, and brought him hither
To use as you think needful of the man. 39

LUCIUS
O worthy Goth, this is the incarnate devil
That robbed Andronicus of his good hand!
This is the pearl that pleased your empress' eye,
And here's the base fruit of her burning lust.— 43
Say, walleyed slave, whither wouldst thou convey 44
This growing image of thy fiendlike face? 45
Why dost not speak? What, deaf? Not a word?
A halter, soldiers! Hang him on this tree,
And by his side his fruit of bastardy.

AARON
Touch not the boy. He is of royal blood.

LUCIUS
Too like the sire for ever being good. 50
First hang the child, that he may see it sprawl—
A sight to vex the father's soul withal.
Get me a ladder.

[*A ladder is brought, which Aaron is made to ascend.*]

AARON Lucius, save the child,

25 made unto approached **26 controlled** calmed **27 slave** (Used affectionately; as also in *brat*, l. 28, and *villain*, ll. 30 and 33.) **dam** mother **28 bewray** reveal **33 rates** chides **39 use . . . man** deal with the man as you think fit **43 fruit** i.e., the baby **44 walleyed** glaring **45 image** likeness **50 for ever being** ever to be

And bear it from me to the Empress.
If thou do this, I'll show thee wondrous things
That highly may advantage thee to hear.
If thou wilt not, befall what may befall,
I'll speak no more but "Vengeance rot you all!"

LUCIUS

Say on. An if it please me which thou speak'st, 59
Thy child shall live, and I will see it nourished. 60

AARON

An if it please thee! Why, assure thee, Lucius,
'Twill vex thy soul to hear what I shall speak;
For I must talk of murders, rapes, and massacres,
Acts of black night, abominable deeds,
Complots of mischief, treason, villainies, 65
Ruthful to hear, yet piteously performed. 66
And this shall all be buried in my death
Unless thou swear to me my child shall live.

LUCIUS

Tell on thy mind. I say thy child shall live.

AARON

Swear that he shall, and then I will begin.

LUCIUS

Who should I swear by? Thou believest no god.
That granted, how canst thou believe an oath?

AARON

What if I do not? As, indeed, I do not.
Yet, for I know thou art religious 74
And hast a thing within thee callèd conscience,
With twenty popish tricks and ceremonies
Which I have seen thee careful to observe,
Therefore I urge thy oath. For that I know 78
An idiot holds his bauble for a god 79
And keeps the oath which by that god he swears,
To that I'll urge him. Therefore thou shalt vow
By that same god, what god soe'er it be,
That thou adorest and hast in reverence,

59 An if if **60 nourished** cared for **65 Complots** conspiracies
66 Ruthful lamentable, pitiable. **piteously** in a way to excite pity
74 for because **78 urge** insist on. **For that** because **79 bauble** fool's stick

To save my boy, to nourish and bring him up,
Or else I will discover naught to thee.

LUCIUS
Even by my god I swear to thee I will.

AARON
First know thou, I begot him on the Empress.

LUCIUS
O most insatiate and luxurious woman! 88

AARON
Tut, Lucius, this was but a deed of charity
To that which thou shalt hear of me anon. 90
'Twas her two sons that murdered Bassianus;
They cut thy sister's tongue, and ravished her,
And cut her hands, and trimmed her as thou sawest.

LUCIUS
O detestable villain! Call'st thou that trimming?

AARON
Why, she was washed and cut and trimmed, and 'twas
Trim sport for them which had the doing of it. 96

LUCIUS
O barbarous, beastly villains, like thyself!

AARON
Indeed, I was their tutor to instruct them.
That codding spirit had they from their mother, 99
As sure a card as ever won the set; 100
That bloody mind I think they learned of me,
As true a dog as ever fought at head. 102
Well, let my deeds be witness of my worth.
I trained thy brethren to that guileful hole 104
Where the dead corpse of Bassianus lay;
I wrote the letter that thy father found,
And hid the gold within that letter mentioned,
Confederate with the Queen and her two sons;
And what not done, that thou hast cause to rue,
Wherein I had no stroke of mischief in it?

88 luxurious lecherous **90 To** compared to **96 Trim** fine (with a play on *trimmed,* ll. 93–95) **99 codding** lustful **100 set** game **102 as . . . head** as ever went for the bear's head (in bearbaiting) **104 trained** lured

I played the cheater for thy father's hand, 111
And when I had it, drew myself apart
And almost broke my heart with extreme laughter.
I pried me through the crevice of a wall 114
When, for his hand, he had his two sons' heads,
Beheld his tears, and laughed so heartily
That both mine eyes were rainy like to his;
And when I told the Empress of this sport,
She swoonèd almost at my pleasing tale,
And for my tidings gave me twenty kisses.

A GOTH

What, canst thou say all this and never blush?

AARON

Ay, like a black dog, as the saying is. 122

LUCIUS

Art thou not sorry for these heinous deeds?

AARON

Ay, that I had not done a thousand more.
Even now I curse the day—and yet, I think,
Few come within the compass of my curse—
Wherein I did not some notorious ill,
As kill a man, or else devise his death,
Ravish a maid, or plot the way to do it,
Accuse some innocent and forswear myself,
Set deadly enmity between two friends,
Make poor men's cattle break their necks,
Set fire on barns and haystacks in the night
And bid the owners quench them with their tears.
Oft have I digged up dead men from their graves
And set them upright at their dear friends' door,
Even when their sorrows almost was forgot,
And on their skins, as on the bark of trees,
Have with my knife carvèd in Roman letters,
"Let not your sorrow die, though I am dead."

111 cheater (1) deceiver (2) escheater, one designated to take care of property forfeited to the crown **114 pried me** peered **122 like a black dog** ("To blush like a black dog" is a proverb with ironic meaning, as here; at 4.2.117–119, Aaron is proud that, being black, he cannot blush.)

But I have done a thousand dreadful things 141
As willingly as one would kill a fly,
And nothing grieves me heartily indeed
But that I cannot do ten thousand more.

LUCIUS
Bring down the devil, for he must not die
So sweet a death as hanging presently. 146
[*Aaron is brought down.*]

AARON
If there be devils, would I were a devil,
To live and burn in everlasting fire,
So I might have your company in hell
But to torment you with my bitter tongue!

LUCIUS
Sirs, stop his mouth, and let him speak no more.
[*Aaron is gagged.*]

Enter Aemilius.

A GOTH
My lord, there is a messenger from Rome
Desires to be admitted to your presence. 153

LUCIUS Let him come near.
Welcome, Aemilius. What's the news from Rome?

AEMILIUS
Lord Lucius, and you princes of the Goths,
The Roman Emperor greets you all by me;
And, for he understands you are in arms, 158
He craves a parley at your father's house,
Willing you to demand your hostages,
And they shall be immediately delivered.

A GOTH What says our general?

LUCIUS
Aemilius, let the Emperor give his pledges
Unto my father and my uncle Marcus,
And we will come. March away. [*Flourish. Exeunt.*]

✤

141 But i.e., but why go on with this recital. (Sometimes emended to *Tut,* as in the second quarto.) **146 presently** immediately **153 Desires** who desires **158 for** since

5.2 *Enter Tamora and her two sons, disguised.*

TAMORA
Thus, in this strange and sad habiliment, 1
I will encounter with Andronicus
And say I am Revenge, sent from below
To join with him and right his heinous wrongs.
Knock at his study, where they say he keeps 5
To ruminate strange plots of dire revenge.
Tell him Revenge is come to join with him
And work confusion on his enemies. 8

They knock, and Titus [*above*] *opens his study door.*

TITUS
Who doth molest my contemplation?
Is it your trick to make me ope the door,
That so my sad decrees may fly away 11
And all my study be to no effect?
You are deceived, for what I mean to do,
See here, in bloody lines I have set down,
And what is written shall be executed.
[*He shows a paper.*]

TAMORA
Titus, I am come to talk with thee.

TITUS
No, not a word. How can I grace my talk,
Wanting a hand to give it action? 18
Thou hast the odds of me; therefore no more. 19

TAMORA
If thou didst know me, thou wouldst talk with me.

TITUS
I am not mad; I know thee well enough.
Witness this wretched stump, witness these crimson lines, 22
Witness these trenches made by grief and care, 23

5.2. Location: Rome. The court of Titus' house.
1 sad habiliment somber garments **5 keeps** dwells **8 confusion** destruction **11 sad decrees** solemn resolutions **18 Wanting . . . action** lacking a hand to provide suitable gesture by way of support **19 odds of** advantage over **22 crimson** i.e., bloody (as in l. 14) **23 trenches** i.e., wrinkles

Witness the tiring day and heavy night,
Witness all sorrow, that I know thee well
For our proud empress, mighty Tamora.
Is not thy coming for my other hand?

TAMORA

Know, thou sad man, I am not Tamora;
She is thy enemy, and I thy friend.
I am Revenge, sent from th' infernal kingdom
To ease the gnawing vulture of thy mind
By working wreakful vengeance on thy foes. 32
Come down and welcome me to this world's light;
Confer with me of murder and of death.
There's not a hollow cave or lurking-place,
No vast obscurity or misty vale 36
Where bloody murder or detested rape
Can couch for fear, but I will find them out, 38
And in their ears tell them my dreadful name,
Revenge, which makes the foul offender quake.

TITUS

Art thou Revenge? And art thou sent to me
To be a torment to mine enemies?

TAMORA

I am. Therefore come down and welcome me.

TITUS

Do me some service ere I come to thee.
Lo, by thy side where Rape and Murder stands.
Now give some surance that thou art Revenge: 46
Stab them, or tear them on thy chariot wheels,
And then I'll come and be thy wagoner,
And whirl along with thee about the globe.
Provide thee two proper palfreys, black as jet, 50
To hale thy vengeful wagon swift away 51
And find out murderers in their guilty caves;
And when thy car is loaden with their heads, 53
I will dismount, and by thy wagon wheel
Trot like a servile footman all day long,
Even from Hyperion's rising in the east 56

32 wreakful vengeful **36 obscurity** place of darkness and desolation **38 couch** lie hidden **46 surance** assurance **50 proper** excellent, handsome. **palfreys** horses **51 hale** pull **53 car** chariot **56 Hyperion's** the sun god's

Until his very downfall in the sea;
And day by day I'll do this heavy task,
So thou destroy Rapine and Murder there. 59

TAMORA
These are my ministers, and come with me.

TITUS
Are they thy ministers? What are they called?

TAMORA
Rape and Murder, therefore callèd so
'Cause they take vengeance of such kind of men. 63

TITUS
Good Lord, how like the Empress' sons they are,
And you, the Empress! But we worldly men 65
Have miserable, mad, mistaking eyes.
O sweet Revenge, now do I come to thee,
And if one arm's embracement will content thee,
I will embrace thee in it by and by. [*Exit above.*]

TAMORA
This closing with him fits his lunacy. 70
Whate'er I forge to feed his brainsick humors 71
Do you uphold and maintain in your speeches,
For now he firmly takes me for Revenge;
And, being credulous in this mad thought,
I'll make him send for Lucius his son,
And whilst I at a banquet hold him sure,
I'll find some cunning practice out of hand 77
To scatter and disperse the giddy Goths
Or at the least make them his enemies.
See, here he comes, and I must ply my theme.

[*Enter Titus below.*]

TITUS
Long have I been forlorn, and all for thee.
Welcome, dread Fury, to my woeful house. 82
Rapine and Murder, you are welcome too.
How like the Empress and her sons you are!

59 So provided that **63 of . . . men** i.e., upon rapists and murderers **65 worldly** mortal **70 closing** agreeing **71 forge** invent. **humors** moods, whims **77 practice** plot. **out of hand** on the spur of the moment **82 Fury** (The Furies were primeval beings devoted to avenging certain crimes, especially against the ties of kinship.)

Well are you fitted, had you but a Moor. 85
Could not all hell afford you such a devil?
For well I wot the Empress never wags 87
But in her company there is a Moor;
And, would you represent our queen aright,
It were convenient you had such a devil. 90
But welcome as you are. What shall we do?

TAMORA
What wouldst thou have us do, Andronicus?

DEMETRIUS
Show me a murderer, I'll deal with him.

CHIRON
Show me a villain that hath done a rape,
And I am sent to be revenged on him.

TAMORA
Show me a thousand that hath done thee wrong,
And I will be revengèd on them all.

TITUS [*To Demetrius*]
Look round about the wicked streets of Rome,
And when thou find'st a man that's like thyself,
Good Murder, stab him; he's a murderer.
[*To Chiron.*] Go thou with him, and when it is thy hap 101
To find another that is like to thee,
Good Rapine, stab him; he is a ravisher.
[*To Tamora.*] Go thou with them, and in the Emperor's
court
There is a queen, attended by a Moor;
Well shalt thou know her by thine own proportion,
For up and down she doth resemble thee. 107
I pray thee, do on them some violent death;
They have been violent to me and mine.

TAMORA
Well hast thou lessoned us; this shall we do.
But would it please thee, good Andronicus,
To send for Lucius, thy thrice-valiant son,
Who leads towards Rome a band of warlike Goths,
And bid him come and banquet at thy house,
When he is here, even at thy solemn feast, 115

85 fitted i.e., fitted out to resemble the Empress **87 wags** moves about **90 were convenient** would be fitting **101 hap** chance **107 up and down** i.e., from top to toe **115 solemn** stately

I will bring in the Empress and her sons,
The Emperor himself, and all thy foes,
And at thy mercy shall they stoop and kneel,
And on them shalt thou ease thy angry heart.
What says Andronicus to this device?

TITUS [*Calling*]
Marcus, my brother! 'Tis sad Titus calls.

Enter Marcus.

Go, gentle Marcus, to thy nephew Lucius;
Thou shalt inquire him out among the Goths.
Bid him repair to me and bring with him 124
Some of the chiefest princes of the Goths.
Bid him encamp his soldiers where they are.
Tell him the Emperor and the Empress too
Feast at my house, and he shall feast with them.
This do thou for my love; and so let him,
As he regards his agèd father's life.

MARCUS
This will I do, and soon return again. [*Exit.*]

TAMORA
Now will I hence about thy business
And take my ministers along with me.

TITUS
Nay, nay, let Rape and Murder stay with me,
Or else I'll call my brother back again
And cleave to no revenge but Lucius. 136

TAMORA [*Aside to her sons*]
What say you, boys? Will you abide with him
Whiles I go tell my lord the Emperor
How I have governed our determined jest? 139
Yield to his humor, smooth and speak him fair, 140
And tarry with him till I turn again. 141

TITUS [*Aside*]
I knew them all, though they supposed me mad,
And will o'erreach them in their own devices—
A pair of cursèd hellhounds and their dam!

124 repair come **136 but Lucius** i.e., but that which Lucius and his army can provide **139 governed . . . jest** managed the jest we determined on **140 smooth . . . fair** flatter and humor him **141 turn** return

DEMETRIUS
Madam, depart at pleasure. Leave us here.

TAMORA
Farewell, Andronicus. Revenge now goes
To lay a complot to betray thy foes. 147

TITUS
I know thou dost; and, sweet Revenge, farewell.
[*Exit Tamora.*]

CHIRON
Tell us, old man, how shall we be employed?

TITUS
Tut, I have work enough for you to do.
Publius, come hither! Caius and Valentine!

[*Enter Publius, Caius, and Valentine.*]

PUBLIUS What is your will?

TITUS Know you these two?

PUBLIUS
The Empress' sons, I take them—Chiron, Demetrius.

TITUS
Fie, Publius, fie! Thou art too much deceived.
The one is Murder, and Rape is the other's name;
And therefore bind them, gentle Publius.
Caius and Valentine, lay hands on them.
Oft have you heard me wish for such an hour,
And now I find it. Therefore bind them sure, 160
And stop their mouths if they begin to cry. [*Exit.*] 161
[*Publius, Caius, and Valentine lay hold on Chiron and Demetrius.*]

CHIRON
Villains, forbear! We are the Empress' sons.

PUBLIUS
And therefore do we what we are commanded. 163
Stop close their mouths; let them not speak a word.
[*They gag and bind the two sons.*]
Is he sure bound? Look that you bind them fast.

Enter Titus Andronicus with a knife, and Lavinia with a basin.

147 complot conspiracy **160 sure** securely **161 cry** cry out **163 therefore** for that very reason

TITUS

Come, come, Lavinia. Look, thy foes are bound.
Sirs, stop their mouths. Let them not speak to me,
But let them hear what fearful words I utter.
O villains, Chiron and Demetrius!
Here stands the spring whom you have stained with
mud, 170
This goodly summer with your winter mixed.
You killed her husband, and for that vile fault
Two of her brothers were condemned to death,
My hand cut off and made a merry jest;
Both her sweet hands, her tongue, and that more dear
Than hands or tongue, her spotless chastity,
Inhuman traitors, you constrained and forced.
What would you say if I should let you speak?
Villains, for shame. You could not beg for grace. 179
Hark, wretches, how I mean to martyr you. 180
This one hand yet is left to cut your throats,
Whiles that Lavinia 'tween her stumps doth hold 182
The basin that receives your guilty blood.
You know your mother means to feast with me,
And calls herself Revenge, and thinks me mad.
Hark, villains, I will grind your bones to dust,
And with your blood and it I'll make a paste, 187
And of the paste a coffin I will rear, 188
And make two pasties of your shameful heads, 189
And bid that strumpet, your unhallowed dam,
Like to the earth swallow her own increase. 191
This is the feast that I have bid her to,
And this the banquet she shall surfeit on;
For worse than Philomel you used my daughter,
And worse than Procne I will be revenged. 195

170 spring i.e., Lavinia **179 for shame . . . grace** i.e., your colossal shame would not let you beg for mercy, would choke your plea **180 martyr** torture, kill cruelly **182 Whiles that** while **187 paste** dough **188 coffin** pie crust (probably also suggesting the container in which they will be buried) **189 pasties** meat pies **191 Like to the earth** i.e., just as the earth devours all her children when they have died. **increase** offspring **195 worse than Procne** (An allusion to Procne's revenge on Tereus for raping her sister Philomel; cf. 2.3.43, note. She killed her son Itys and served his flesh to Tereus, his father. In Seneca's *Thyestes,* Atreus similarly sets before Thyestes a dish of his own children's flesh.)

And now prepare your throats. Lavinia, come.
He cuts their throats.
Receive the blood, and when that they are dead,
Let me go grind their bones to powder small,
And with this hateful liquor temper it, 199
And in that paste let their vile heads be baked.
Come, come, be everyone officious 201
To make this banquet, which I wish may prove
More stern and bloody than the Centaurs' feast. 203
So, now bring them in, for I'll play the cook
And see them ready against their mother comes. 205
Exeunt [*bearing the dead bodies*].

✤

5.3

Enter Lucius, Marcus, and the Goths [*with Aaron prisoner, and an attendant bearing his child*].

LUCIUS
Uncle Marcus, since 'tis my father's mind
That I repair to Rome, I am content. 2

A GOTH
And ours with thine, befall what fortune will. 3

LUCIUS
Good uncle, take you in this barbarous Moor, 4
This ravenous tiger, this accursèd devil.
Let him receive no sustenance. Fetter him
Till he be brought unto the Empress' face 7
For testimony of her foul proceedings. 8
And see the ambush of our friends be strong; 9
I fear the Emperor means no good to us.

199 temper blend, mix **201 officious** busy **203 Centaurs' feast** i.e., the wedding feast of Pirithous and Hippodamia to which the Lapithae invited the Centaurs, fabulous creatures, half men and half horses. (The Centaurs attempted to carry off the women but were slaughtered by their hosts.) **205 against** by the time that

5.3. Location: The scene appears to take place in a court in Titus' house; in the opening lines Lucius speaks as if he and his soldiers have just arrived in Rome.
2 repair return **3 ours with thine** i.e., our intentions are in agreement with yours **4 in** i.e., into Titus' house; see l. 123 **7 unto** before **8 of** regarding **9 ambush** forces lying in wait to attack

AARON

Some devil whisper curses in my ear
And prompt me that my tongue may utter forth
The venomous malice of my swelling heart!

LUCIUS

Away, inhuman dog, unhallowed slave!
Sirs, help our uncle to convey him in.

[*Exeunt Goths, with Aaron.*]
Sound trumpets [*within*].

The trumpets show the Emperor is at hand.

Enter Emperor [*Saturninus*] *and Empress* [*Tamora*], *with* [*Aemilius,*] *tribunes,* [*senators*], *and others.*

SATURNINUS

What, hath the firmament more suns than one? 17

LUCIUS

What boots it thee to call thyself a sun? 18

MARCUS

Rome's emperor, and nephew, break the parle. 19
These quarrels must be quietly debated.
The feast is ready which the careful Titus 21
Hath ordained to an honorable end,
For peace, for love, for league, and good to Rome.
Please you therefore draw nigh and take your places.

SATURNINUS Marcus, we will.

[*A table is brought in. The company sit down.*]

Trumpets sounding, enter Titus like a cook, placing the dishes, and Lavinia with a veil over her face, [*young Lucius, and others*].

TITUS

Welcome, my gracious lord; welcome, dread Queen;
Welcome, ye warlike Goths; welcome, Lucius;
And welcome, all. Although the cheer be poor, 28
'Twill fill your stomachs. Please you eat of it.

SATURNINUS

Why art thou thus attired, Andronicus?

17 What . . . than one i.e., two suns cannot occupy the same heavenly sphere, and Rome cannot have two kings at once **18 boots** avails **19 break the parle** cease the dispute **21 careful** full of sorrows; assiduous **28 cheer** fare

TITUS
Because I would be sure to have all well
To entertain Your Highness and your empress.

TAMORA
We are beholding to you, good Andronicus. 33

TITUS
An if Your Highness knew my heart, you were. 34
My lord the Emperor, resolve me this: 35
Was it well done of rash Virginius 36
To slay his daughter with his own right hand
Because she was enforced, stained, and deflowered?

SATURNINUS It was, Andronicus.

TITUS Your reason, mighty lord?

SATURNINUS
Because the girl should not survive her shame, 41
And by her presence still renew his sorrows. 42

TITUS
A reason mighty, strong, and effectual;
A pattern, precedent, and lively warrant
For me, most wretched, to perform the like.
Die, die, Lavinia, and thy shame with thee,
And with thy shame thy father's sorrow die!
[*He kills Lavinia.*]

SATURNINUS
What hast thou done, unnatural and unkind? 48

TITUS
Killed her for whom my tears have made me blind.
I am as woeful as Virginius was,
And have a thousand times more cause than he
To do this outrage, and it now is done.

SATURNINUS
What, was she ravished? Tell who did the deed.

TITUS
Will 't please you eat? Will 't please Your Highness feed?

TAMORA
Why hast thou slain thine only daughter thus?

33 beholding beholden **34 were** would be **35 resolve** answer **36 Virginius** Roman centurion who, according to Livy, killed his daughter to prevent her from being raped (rather than killing her afterward to preserve her honor, as told here to accord with Titus' story. The latter version was also current in the Renaissance.) **41 Because** in order that **42 still** continually **48 unkind** unnatural

TITUS

Not I; 'twas Chiron and Demetrius.
They ravished her and cut away her tongue,
And they, 'twas they that did her all this wrong.

SATURNINUS

Go fetch them hither to us presently. 59

TITUS

Why, there they are, both bakèd in this pie,
Whereof their mother daintily hath fed,
Eating the flesh that she herself hath bred.
'Tis true, 'tis true; witness my knife's sharp point.

He stabs the Empress.

SATURNINUS

Die, frantic wretch, for this accursèd deed!

[*He kills Titus.*]

LUCIUS

Can the son's eye behold his father bleed?
There's meed for meed, death for a deadly deed! 66

[*He kills Saturninus. A great tumult, during which Marcus, Lucius, and others go aloft.*]

MARCUS

You sad-faced men, people and sons of Rome,
By uproars severed, as a flight of fowl
Scattered by winds and high tempestuous gusts,
O, let me teach you how to knit again
This scattered corn into one mutual sheaf, 71
These broken limbs again into one body.

A ROMAN LORD

Let Rome herself be bane unto herself, 73
And she whom mighty kingdoms curtsy to,
Like a forlorn and desperate castaway,
Do shameful execution on herself,
But if my frosty signs and chaps of age, 77
Grave witnesses of true experience,
Cannot induce you to attend my words. 79

59 presently at once **66 meed for meed** measure for measure **s.d. A great . . . aloft** (In ll. 130–134, Marcus and Lucius offer to throw themselves down from where they are speaking.) **71 corn** grain **73 s.p. A Roman Lord** (Perhaps Aemilius; compare his speech at ll. 137 ff.) **bane** poison, death **77 But if** if. **frosty signs** i.e., white hair. **chaps** wrinkles **79 attend** listen to

[*To Lucius.*] Speak, Rome's dear friend, as erst our ancestor, 80
When with his solemn tongue he did discourse
To lovesick Dido's sad-attending ear 82
The story of that baleful burning night
When subtle Greeks surprised King Priam's Troy.
Tell us what Sinon hath bewitched our ears, 85
Or who hath brought the fatal engine in
That gives our Troy, our Rome, the civil wound. 87
My heart is not compact of flint nor steel, 88
Nor can I utter all our bitter grief,
But floods of tears will drown my oratory
And break my utterance, even in the time
When it should move ye to attend me most
And force you to commiseration.
Here's Rome's young captain. Let him tell the tale,
While I stand by and weep to hear him speak.

LUCIUS

Then, gracious auditory, be it known to you
That Chiron and the damned Demetrius
Were they that murderèd our emperor's brother,
And they it were that ravishèd our sister.
For their fell faults our brothers were beheaded, 100
Our father's tears despised, and basely cozened 101
Of that true hand that fought Rome's quarrel out 102
And sent her enemies unto the grave;
Lastly, myself unkindly banishèd, 104
The gates shut on me, and turned weeping out
To beg relief among Rome's enemies,
Who drowned their enmity in my true tears
And oped their arms to embrace me as a friend.
I am the turned-forth, be it known to you, 109
That have preserved her welfare in my blood 110
And from her bosom took the enemy's point, 111

80 erst formerly, once. **our ancestor** i.e., Aeneas **82 sad-attending** seriously listening **85 Sinon** the crafty Greek who persuaded the Trojans to take the wooden horse (the *fatal engine*) into their city **87 civil** incurred in civil strife **88 compact** composed **100 fell** savage, cruel **101 and basely cozened** and he was basely cheated **102 fought . . . out** fought to the finish in behalf of Rome's cause **104 unkindly** unnaturally **109 turned-forth** exile **110 in** by **111 from . . . point** took in my own bosom the sword's point aimed at her, Rome's, bosom

Sheathing the steel in my adventurous body.
Alas, you know I am no vaunter, I;
My scars can witness, dumb although they are, 114
That my report is just and full of truth.
But soft, methinks I do digress too much,
Citing my worthless praise. O, pardon me,
For when no friends are by, men praise themselves.

MARCUS
Now is my turn to speak. Behold the child:
[*Pointing to the child in the arms of an attendant*]
Of this was Tamora deliverèd,
The issue of an irreligious Moor,
Chief architect and plotter of these woes.
The villain is alive in Titus' house,
And as he is to witness, this is true.
Now judge what cause had Titus to revenge
These wrongs unspeakable, past patience, 126
Or more than any living man could bear.
Now have you heard the truth. What say you, Romans?
Have we done aught amiss, show us wherein, 129
And from the place where you behold us pleading
The poor remainder of Andronici
Will hand in hand all headlong hurl ourselves,
And on the ragged stones beat forth our souls, 133
And make a mutual closure of our house. 134
Speak, Romans, speak, and if you say we shall,
Lo, hand in hand, Lucius and I will fall.

AEMILIUS
Come, come, thou reverend man of Rome,
And bring our emperor gently in thy hand,
Lucius our emperor; for well I know
The common voice do cry it shall be so.

ALL
Lucius, all hail, Rome's royal emperor!

MARCUS [*To attendants*]
Go, go into old Titus' sorrowful house
And hither hale that misbelieving Moor

114 dumb . . . are (The scars are dumb mouths, giving mute testimony.)
126 patience endurance **129 Have we** if we have **133 ragged** rough, rugged **134 closure** conclusion, death

To be adjudged some direful slaughtering death
As punishment for his most wicked life.
[*Exeunt attendants. Marcus, Lucius, and the others come down.*]

ALL
Lucius, all hail, Rome's gracious governor!

LUCIUS
Thanks, gentle Romans. May I govern so
To heal Rome's harms and wipe away her woe!
But, gentle people, give me aim awhile, 149
For nature puts me to a heavy task.
Stand all aloof, but, uncle, draw you near
To shed obsequious tears upon this trunk.— 152
O, take this warm kiss on thy pale cold lips,
[*Kissing Titus*]
These sorrowful drops upon thy bloodstained face,
The last true duties of thy noble son!

MARCUS [*Kissing Titus*]
Tear for tear, and loving kiss for kiss,
Thy brother Marcus tenders on thy lips.
O, were the sum of these that I should pay
Countless and infinite, yet would I pay them!

LUCIUS [*To young Lucius*]
Come hither, boy. Come, come, and learn of us
To melt in showers. Thy grandsire loved thee well.
Many a time he danced thee on his knee,
Sung thee asleep, his loving breast thy pillow;
Many a story hath he told to thee,
And bid thee bear his pretty tales in mind
And talk of them when he was dead and gone.

MARCUS
How many thousand times hath these poor lips,
When they were living, warmed themselves on thine!
O, now, sweet boy, give them their latest kiss. 169
Bid him farewell; commit him to the grave;
Do them that kindness, and take leave of them. 171

BOY [*Kissing Titus*]
O grandsire, grandsire! Ev'n with all my heart
Would I were dead, so you did live again!—

149 give me aim bear with me, give me encouragement
152 obsequious mourning **169 latest** last **171 them** i.e., the lips

O Lord, I cannot speak to him for weeping.
My tears will choke me if I ope my mouth.

[*Enter attendants with Aaron.*]

A ROMAN
You sad Andronici, have done with woes. 176
Give sentence on this execrable wretch
That hath been breeder of these dire events.

LUCIUS
Set him breast-deep in earth and famish him;
There let him stand and rave and cry for food.
If anyone relieves or pities him,
For the offense he dies. This is our doom. 182
Some stay to see him fastened in the earth.

AARON
Ah, why should wrath be mute and fury dumb?
I am no baby, I, that with base prayers
I should repent the evils I have done.
Ten thousand worse than ever yet I did
Would I perform, if I might have my will.
If one good deed in all my life I did,
I do repent it from my very soul.

LUCIUS
Some loving friends convey the Emperor hence,
And give him burial in his father's grave. 192
My father and Lavinia shall forthwith
Be closèd in our household's monument.
As for that ravenous tiger, Tamora,
No funeral rite nor man in mourning weed,
No mournful bell shall ring her burial;
But throw her forth to beasts and birds to prey. 198
Her life was beastly and devoid of pity,
And being dead, let birds on her take pity. 200

Exeunt, [*bearing the dead bodies*].

176 s.p. A Roman (The speech is sometimes assigned to Aemilius.) **182 doom** decision, judgment **192 father's** (or possibly *fathers',* forefathers') **198 prey** prey upon **200 pity** (The first quarto text closes the play with this line. The second quarto and subsequent texts add the following four lines:
See justice done on Aaron, that damned Moor,
By whom our heavy haps had their beginning.
Then, afterwards, to order well the state,
That like events may ne'er it ruinate.)

Date and Text

On February 6, 1594, "a Noble Roman Historye of Tytus Andronicus" was entered in the Stationers' Register, the official record book of the London Company of Stationers (booksellers and printers), to John Danter, along with "the ballad thereof." The entry probably, though not certainly, refers to Shakespeare's play. Later in that same year, at any rate, Danter published a quarto volume with the following title:

> THE MOST LAMENTABLE Romaine Tragedie of Titus Andronicus: As it was Plaide by the Right Honourable the Earle of *Darbie,* Earle of *Pembrooke,* and Earle of *Sussex* their Seruants. LONDON, Printed by Iohn Danter, and are to be sold by *Edward White* & *Thomas Millington,* at the little North doore of Paules at the signe of the Gunne. 1594.

This text seems to have been set from Shakespeare's foul papers in an unpolished state. A second quarto appeared in 1600, adding the name of the Lord Chamberlain's company to those who had acted the play. It was set up from a slightly damaged copy of the first quarto. Although the second quarto made some improvements, these were probably by the compositor and not the author, or may have been made in a press corrected first quarto no longer extant (since we have only one copy today). A third quarto (1611), set up from the second, contributed new errors. The First Folio text of 1623 was derived from the third quarto, but with an authentic added scene (3.2) from a manuscript source and with additional stage directions that suggest a playhouse promptbook. One theory is that the copy used by the Folio printers, the third quarto, had been corrected from an annotated copy of the second quarto that had been used as a promptbook, or perhaps directly from the promptbook. Despite these improvements, the first quarto clearly remains the authoritative text except for Act 3, scene 2.

The date of *Titus* must be prior to 1594. Philip Henslowe's *Diary* records a performance of a "Titus & Ondronicus" by the Earl of Sussex's men on January 24, 1594, and indicates it was "ne" or new. This could certainly mean a new play, but it could also mean it was newly revised or newly acquired. Since the players on this occasion, Sussex's men, were listed third on the 1594 title page after Derby's and Pembroke's men, they may just have acquired *Titus*. Two allusions may point to an earlier date: *A Knack to Know a Knave* (performed in 1592) and *The Troublesome Reign of King John* (published 1591) may contain echoes of *Titus*. Stylistic considerations favor a date around 1590 or even earlier.

The authorship of *Titus* would appear at first glance to be beyond question. Although the 1594 quarto does not mention Shakespeare's name (a common omission in such early texts, especially since the author was as yet relatively unknown), Francis Meres (in his *Palladis Tamia: Wit's Treasury*, 1598, a slender volume on contemporary literature and art, valuable because it lists most of Shakespeare's plays that existed at that time) assigns the play to Shakespeare, and the Folio editors included it in the 1623 edition. Doubts began to arise, however, when Edward Ravenscroft observed in 1687 that he had been "told by some anciently conversant with the stage that it was not originally his, but brought by a private author to be acted, and he only gave some master touches to one or two of the principal parts or characters." This remark touched off a controversy that continues today; for example, J. Dover Wilson in his New Cambridge Shakespeare (1948) and J. C. Maxwell in his Arden edition (1953) still argue for the presence of Peele, in the first act especially. Nevertheless, Ravenscroft's testimonial is suspect both because it came one hundred years after the fact and because Ravenscroft himself was embarked on an adaptation of *Titus* and so might wish to denigrate the original. The efforts at assigning portions of the play to Shakespeare's contemporaries have generally been motivated by a wish to rescue Shakespeare's reputation from the violent and garish effects of this play. Most recent criticism prefers to regard the play as an interesting experiment in revenge tragedy by a young artist, with many shrewdly characteristic Shakespearean touches. The external evidence of the Elizabethan period, at any rate, is entirely on the side of awarding the play wholly to Shakespeare.

Henslowe's *Diary* records the performance of a "Tittus & Vespacia" on April 11, 1592, a "ne" play by Strange's men. Despite the similarity of the title, this play was probably on an independent subject.

Textual Notes

These textual notes are not a historical collation, either of the early quartos and the early folios or of more recent editions; they are simply a record of departures in this edition from the copy text. The reading adopted in this edition appears in boldface, followed by the rejected reading from the copy text, i.e., the quarto of 1594. Only major alterations in punctuation are noted. Changes in lineation are not indicated, nor are some minor and obvious typographical errors.

Abbreviations used:
F the First Folio
Q the quarto of 1594
s.d. stage direction
s.p. speech prefix

Copy text: the first quarto of 1594, except for 3.2, based on F.

1.1. 14 seat, to virtue consecrate, seate to vertue, consecrate [The punctuation variations from the edited text are considerable in this play and are generally not recorded in these notes.] **35 the field** [Q follows with a half line and three more lines: "and at this day, / To the Monument of that *Andronicy* / Done sacrifice of expiation, / And slaine the Noblest prisoner of the *Gothes*."] **55 s.d. Exeunt** Exit **64 s.p. Captain** [not in Q] **69 s.d. three sons** two sonnes **98 manes** manus **129 s.d. Exeunt** Exit **157 s.p. Lavinia** [not in Q] **227 Titan's** [F] Tytus **243 Pantheon** Pathan **265 chance** [F] change **281 cuique** cuiqum **300 s.p. [and elsewhere] Saturninus** Emperour **317 Phoebe** Thebe **318 gallant'st** [F] gallanst **359 s.p. Martius** Titus two sonnes speakes **s.p. Quintus** [not in Q] **361 s.p. Martius** Titus sonne speakes **369 s.p. Quintus** 3. Sonne **370 s.p. Martius** 2. Sonne [also at l. 372] **389 s.d. They all kneel** they all kneele and say **390 s.p. All** [not in Q] **391 s.d. Exeunt** Exit **392 dreary** dririe [Q] sudden [F] **399 Marcus. Yes . . . remunerate** [F; not in Q] **475 s.p. Lucius** [F; not in Q] **476 mildly** mi'd ie

2.1. 37 s.p. [and elsewhere] Aaron Moore **110 than** this

2.2. 1 morn [F] Moone **11** [Q provides a s.p.: Titus] **24 run** runnes

2.3. 13 snake [F] snakes **69 try** [F] trie thy **72 swarthy** swartie [Q] swarth [F] **88 s.p. [and elsewhere] Tamora** Queene **131 ye desire** we desire **150 heard** hard **153 Some** So me **160 ears** [F] yeares **175 their** there **180 satisfy** satisfice (?) **192 s.p. Aaron** [not in Q] **208 s.d. Exit** [at l. 207 in Q] **210 unhallowed** [F] vnhollow **222 berayed in blood** bereaud in blood [Q, with marginal correction in contemporary handwriting: "heere reau'd of lyfe"] **231 Pyramus** [F] Priamus **236 Cocytus'** Ocitus **260 s.p. [and elsewhere] Saturninus** King **276** [Q provides a s.p.: King] **291 fault** faults

2.4. 5 scrawl scrowle **11 s.p. Marcus** [not in Q] **27 him** them **30 three** their

3.1. 17 urns ruines **21 on thy** [F] out hy **67 handless** handles **146 his** her **225 blow** flow **281 employed:** imployde in these Armes [Q] employd in these things [F]

3.2 [the entire scene is missing in Q; copy text is F] **s.d. banquet** Bnaket [F] **1 s.p. [and throughout scene] Titus** An **39 complainer** complaynet **52 thy knife** knife **53 fly** Flys **54 thee** the **55 are cloyed** cloi'd **72 myself** my selfes

4.1. 1 s.p. [and throughout] Boy [F] Puer **10 s.p. Marcus** [not in Q] **19 griefs** greeues **52 quotes** coats **55 Forced** Frocd **80 s.p. Titus** [not in Q] **90 hope** hop (?) I op (?)

4.2. 15 lordships, that Lordships **51 Good** God **96 Alcides** Alciades **125 that** [F] your

4.3. 56 Saturn Saturnine, to **77 News . . . come** [assigned in Q to Clown] **96 from you** [Q follows with four lines: *Titus.* Tell mee, can you deliuer an Oration to the Em- / perour with a grace. / *Clowne.* Nay truelie sir, I could neuer say grace in all / my life.]

4.4. 5 know, as know know **48 By 'r** be **93 feed** seede **98 ears** [F] yeares **105 on** [F] in

5.1. 17 s.p. All the Goths [not in Q] **20 s.p. Another Goth** Goth **43 here's** [F] her's **53 Get me a ladder** [assigned in Q to Aaron] **113 extreme** extreanie

5.2. 18 it action [F] that accord **38 them out** the mout **49 globe** Globes **52 murderers** murder **caves** cares **56 Hyperion's** Epeons **61 they** them **65 worldly** wordlie **121 s.d.** [at l. 120 in Q] **196 s.d.** [at l. 203 in Q]

5.3. 26 gracious lord [F] Lord **36 Virginius** Viginius **125 cause** course **141 s.p. All** Marcus **142 s.p. Marcus** [no s.p. here in Q; see previous note] **144 adjudged** [F] adiudge **146 s.p. All** [not in Q] **154 bloodstained** blood slaine **163 Sung** Song **172 s.p. Boy** [F] Puer

Shakespeare's Sources

Any departures from the original text are noted with an asterisk and appear at the bottom of the page in boldface; original readings are in roman.

Although we do not today possess any work that Shakespeare could have used for his immediate source in *Titus,* we have an eighteenth-century chapbook called *The History of Titus Andronicus* that may tell us substantially what that source was like. This chapbook is similar to Shakespeare's play. According to Ralph Sargent (*Studies in Philology,* 1949), a closely related prose version, now lost, served as Shakespeare's chief source. This hypothesis is now generally accepted. Some scholars even argue that the Stationers' Register entry in 1594 to the printer John Danter for his publication of "a Noble Roman Historye of Tytus Andronicus" with "the ballad thereof" refers to just such a prose account. Of this we cannot be certain, for Danter did, after all, publish Shakespeare's play in that same year, and the ballad appears to owe some of its details to the play (though based primarily, it would seem, on the lost prose version). All in all, the existence of a prose *History of Titus* when Shakespeare wrote his play seems likely. (A ballad of "Titus Andronicus' Complaint," published in 1620 in Richard Johnson's *The Golden Garland of Princely Pleasures,* attests to the continued currency of the story in the early seventeenth century.)

The prose *History* (a modernized edition of which follows) is a fictitious medley of revenge stories inspired by Seneca and Ovid. It is set in the last days of the Roman Empire, but contains no recognizable historical characters or events. Titus Andronicus is a Roman senator who defends Rome against the Goths in a protracted ten-year struggle, losing twenty-two of his own sons in the conflict. He slays the Gothic King Tottilius in battle and captures the Queen, Attava. When Tottilius' two sons Alaricus and Abonus continue the assault on Rome, the Roman Emperor wearies of the conflict and resolves to marry Attava against the advice of his general, Andronicus. The Queen, naturally regarding Titus as an enemy, proceeds to obtain powerful positions for her own kinsmen. She succeeds in having Titus banished, but he is recalled by popular insistence. Attava has an affair with her nameless Moorish servant and has a black child by him. Discovery of the child leads to the Moor's banishment, but he too is later recalled. Attava opposes the marriage of Titus' daughter Lavinia to the Emperor's only son (by a former marriage), since she desires the possession of the empire for her own sons. The remainder of the story proceeds much as in the play, except that we do not learn what happens to Rome after Titus' death. Shakespeare's chief additions include Titus' candidacy for and rejection of the throne, the struggle between Saturninus and Bassianus, the sacrifice of Tamora's son Alarbus, and a greatly magnified role for Aaron the Moor.

Although the prose version itself made use of Ovid and Seneca, Shakespeare evidently consulted these authors directly as well. The play contains many explicit references to classical authors, most notably when Lavinia turns the pages of Ovid's *Metamorphoses* to the story of Philomela's rape (4.1). In Ovid's famous account (Book 6, 526 ff.), King Tereus of Thrace rapes Philomela, cuts out her tongue (but not her hands) to prevent her from revealing the crime, and keeps her prisoner. She nevertheless manages to weave her story into a tapestry and send it to her sister, Procne, who liberates Philomela and plots with her to serve Tereus and Procne's son Itys to him at a banquet.

A similar grisly feast takes place in Seneca's *Thyestes,* from which Shakespeare may well have drawn some particulars. Atreus, the wronged avenger, murders the two sons of Thyestes and serves them to him. As in Shakespeare's play, there are two sons rather than one. Of these two sons, one is guilty of ambition, whereas Ovid's Itys is an innocent victim. The slayer is a male avenger, not (as in Ovid) the mother of the slain victim. Senecan conventions of underworld spirits of revenge and the like are also present in the play, though they may have reached Shakespeare by way of Thomas Kyd's *The Spanish Tragedy* and other plays of the late 1580s. Both Ovid and Seneca were commonly taught in Elizabethan grammar schools, though both were also available in English translation: Ovid by Arthur Golding (1567) and Seneca by Jasper Heywood (1560). Christopher Marlowe's *Tamburlaine* and *The Jew of Malta* certainly had an influence, especially on Shakespeare's conception of Aaron the Moor.

Two continental plays about Titus, the German *Tragoedia*

von Tito Andronico (1620) and the Dutch *Aran en Titus* by Jan Vos (1641), were once thought to have been derived from an English play before 1594, which might then have served as a source for Shakespeare. In the German play the name of Titus' son Lucius is Vespasian, and this fact has caused scholars to wonder if the "Tittus & Vespacia" acted in April 1592 by the acting company known as Lord Strange's men (as mentioned in Philip Henslowe's *Diary*) was about Titus Andronicus. Lucius' part is small for such prominence in a title, however, and the prevailing opinion today is that Henslowe's play was on an independent subject.

The History of Titus Andronicus

Chapter 1

How, Rome being besieged by the barbarous Goths and being at the point to yield through famine, it was unexpectedly rescued by Andronicus, with the utter defeat of the enemy, for which he was received in triumph.

When the Roman Empire was grown to its height and the greatest part of the world was subjected to its imperial throne, in the time of Theodosius,[1] a barbarous northern people out of Swedeland, Denmark, and Gothland[2] came into Italy in such numbers under the leading of Tottilius, their king, that they overran it with fire and sword, plundering churches, ripping up women with child, and deflowering virgins in so horrid and barbarous a manner that the people fled before them like flocks of sheep.

To oppose this destroying torrent of the Goths—a barbarous people, strangers to Christianity—the Emperor raised a mighty army in Greece, Italy, France, Spain, Germany, and England, and gave battle under the passage of the Alpine mountains, but was overthrown with the loss of threescore thousand of his men, and, flying to Rome, was besieged in it by a numerous host of these barbarians, who

1 Theodosius Roman Emperor from 379 to 395 **2 Gothland** (in modern-day southern Sweden)

pressed so hard to beat down the walls and enter with a miserable slaughter of the citizens that such as could get over the river Tiber fled in a fearful manner to a distant country. The siege lasting ten months, such a famine arose that no unclean thing was left uneaten; dogs, cats, horses, rats, and mice were curious dainties.[3] Thousands died in the streets of hunger, and most of those that were alive looked more like glass[4] than living creatures. So that, being brought to the last extremity, the vulgar sort[5] came about the Emperor's palace and with piteous cries implored him either to find some means to get them food to stay[6] their fleeting lives or make the best terms he could and open the gates to the enemy.

This greatly perplexed him. The former he could not do, and the latter he knew would not only uncrown him, if he escaped with his life, but be the ruin of the Roman Empire. Yet in the greatest of this extremity he unexpectedly found relief.

Titus Andronicus, a Roman senator and a true lover of his country, hearing in Graecia, where he was governor of the province of Achaia, what straits Rome and his sovereign were brought into by the barbarous nations, got together friends and sold whatever he had of value to hire soldiers. So that with his small army he secretly marched away, and, falling upon the mighty army of the enemy (when they were drowned, as it were, in security, wine, and sleep, resolved to make a general storm the next day,[7] in which they had undoubtedly carried[8] the city), he and his sons, entering their camp and followed by the rest, made such a slaughter that the cry and confusion were exceeding great. Some changed sleep into death, others vomited wine and blood mixed together through the wounds they received; some lost heads at once, other[9] arms. Tottilius, in this confusion being awakened, had his first care to convey away his queen and two sons, who were newly come to the camp, and then labored to rally his flying men; but being desperately charged by Andronicus, he was thrown from his horse and much

3 curious dainties rare delicacies **4 like glass** i.e., emaciated, hollow **5 the vulgar sort** the commoners **6 stay** prolong **7 resolved . . . day** having determined to make a general assault on Rome the next day **8 had undoubtedly carried** would undoubtedly have won **9 other** others

wounded, many lives being lost in remounting him.[10] Whereupon, seeing the slaughter so great by the pale beams of the moon and not knowing the number of his adversaries, having caused the retreat to be sounded he fled in great confusion and left the rich spoils of his camp, the wealth of many plundered nations, to Andronicus and his soldiers; who, being expert in war, would not meddle with them that night, but stood to their arms till the morning.

Chapter 2

How in ten years' war, with the loss of two-and-twenty of his valiant sons, he won many famous battles, slew Tottilius, King of the Goths, and did many other brave exploits, etc.

The watch upon the walls of Rome, having heard a confused cry and the clashing of arms, were greatly astonished, but could not think what it should mean, for the camps of the barbarous Goths extended in a large circuit about the famous city. However, the captains of the guards advertised[1] the Emperor of it, who sent out scouts. But they, fearful of approaching too near the enemy in the night, could get certain intelligence only that they heard the groans and cries, as they thought, of dying men. However, the shades of night being dispelled and the glorious sun casting forth a cheerful light, the porters of the gate, espying three men coming towards it, and, soon after being come up, knocked[2] with great earnestness, they[3] took the courage to demand what they were and what they required.[4]

"I am," said one of them, "Andronicus, your friend, and desire admittance to speak with the Emperor, since the news I bring will no doubt be pleasing to him."

Upon this, lifting[5] up his helmet, they knew him with joy, knowing him to be a very worthy patriot, thinking he came to do them good, as he had often done in their great distress

10 remounting him getting him back on his horse

1 advertised informed **2 and, soon . . . knocked** i.e., (three men) who, soon after arriving at the gate, knocked at it **3 they** i.e., the porters of the gate **4 required** wanted **5 lifting** i.e., Andronicus lifting

when the Huns and Vandals invaded the empire some years before and were beaten out by him.

The Emperor no sooner heard he was come but he ran from his palace to meet him, and would not suffer him to kneel but embraced him tenderly as a brother, saying, "Welcome, Andronicus, in this, the time of our greatest misery! It was thy counsel I wanted, to know how to free us from this barbarous enemy, against whose force the city cannot long hold out."

"May it please Your Majesty," replied Andronicus, "let those fears be banished. The work is done to you unknown. I and my twenty-five sons and what friends and soldiers I could get have this night fallen into[6] their quarters, cut off fifty thousand of them, and their scattered remains with their king are fled."

At this the Emperor was astonished and scarce could believe it, though he very well knew the integrity of Andronicus, till his own captains came and told him the siege was raised, with a miserable[7] slaughter, but by whom they knew not, unless the enemy had fallen out among themselves, and the troops they could yet see in view were but inconsiderable. Now these were those that belonged to Andronicus, who, as soon as it was day, were in pursuit of the enemy under the command of his five-and-twenty sons.

This surprising news was no sooner spread in the city but the joy of the people was exceeding great; and when they knew who was their deliverer they went in procession and sung his praises. After that he rode in a triumphant chariot through the city, crowned with an oaken garland, the people shouting, trumpets sounding, and all other expressions and demonstrations of joy that a grateful people could afford their deliverer, in which he behaved himself so humble that he gained the love of all.

This was no sooner over but he desired the Emperor to join what forces he could with those that he had brought and speedily pursue the enemy before he could gather new strength, that he might beat him out of Italy and his other countries where he yet held strong garrisons. This was embraced as good counsel, and the senators, by the Emperor's

6 fallen into attacked **7 miserable** devastating, causing misery

mandate, assembled with joy, who chose with one consent Andronicus their general. He was not slow in mustering his forces, nor in the speedy pursuit. He found they had passed the Alps and that their army was increased by new supplies; yet he gave them battle and, charging through the thickest of their squadrons hand to hand, slew Tottilius and beat down his standard.[8] Whereupon the Goths fled and the slaughter continued for many miles, covering all the lanes and roads with the bodies of the dead. And in the pursuit he took the Queen of the Goths captive and brought her to Rome, for which signal[9] victory he had a second triumph[10] and was styled[11] the deliverer of his country. But his joy was a little eclipsed by the loss of five of his sons, who died courageously fighting in battle.

Chapter 3

How the Emperor, weary of so tedious a war, contrary to the mind[1] and persuasions of Andronicus, married the Queen of the Goths and concluded a peace; how she tyrannized, and her sons slew the prince that was betrothed to Andronicus' daughter and hid him in the forest.

The Goths, having found the pleasantness of these fruitful countries, resolved not so to give them over, but, encouraged by Tottilius' two sons, Alaricus and Abonus, sent for fresh forces and made a desolation in the Roman provinces, continuing a ten years' war, wherein the valiant Andronicus, captain-general of the empire, gained many victories over them with great effusion of blood on either side. But those barbarous people still increasing in their numbers, the Emperor desiring peace, it was agreed to, in consideration he should marry[2] Attava, Queen of the Goths, and in case he should die without issue, her sons might succeed in the empire. Andronicus opposed this very much, as did many other,[3] knowing, through the Emperor's weakness,

8 standard flag serving as the army's rallying point **9 signal** notable **10 triumph** triumphal procession **11 styled** named with an honorific title

1 mind opinion **2 he should marry** of his marrying **3 other** others

that she, being an imperious woman and of a haughty spirit, would govern him as she pleased and enslave the noble empire to strangers.[4] However, it was carried on with a high hand,[5] and great preparations were made for the royal nuptials, though with very little rejoicing among the people; for what they expected soon followed.

The Queen of the Goths, being made Empress, soon began to show her disposition according to the cruelty of her nation and temper, persuading the easy[6] Emperor to place the Goths in the places of his most trusty friends; and having, above all, vowed revenge on Andronicus, who most opposed her proceedings, she procured[7] him to be banished. But the people, whose deliverer he had been in their greatest extremity, calling to mind that and his many other good services, rose unanimously in arms and went clamoring to the palace, threatening to fire it[8] and revenge so base an indignity on the Queen if the decree which had been passed against all reason was not speedily revoked. This put her and the Emperor into such a fear* that their request was granted. And now she plotted by more private ways to bring the effects of revenge and implacable hatred about more secretly.

She had a Moor as revengeful as herself, whom she trusted in many great affairs, and was usually privy to her secrets, so far that from private dalliances she grew pregnant and brought forth a blackamoor child. This grieved the Emperor extremely, but she allayed his anger by telling him it was conceived by the force of imagination, and brought many suborned women and physicians to testify the like had often happened. This made the Emperor send the Moor into banishment, upon pain of death never to return to Rome; but her lust, and the confidence she had put in him as the main engine[9] to bring about her devilish designs, made her plot to have that decree revoked; when, having got the Emperor into a pleasant humor, she feigned herself sick, telling him withal[10] she had seen a vision which commanded her to call back the innocent Moor from banishment or she should never recover of that sickness.

*__fear__ Fears

4 strangers foreigners **5 with a high hand** with imperious exercise of power **6 easy** pliable **7 procured** caused **8 fire it** burn it down **9 engine** means **10 withal** in addition

The kind, good-natured Emperor, who could not resist her tears and entreaties, with some difficulty consented to it, provided he should be commanded to keep always out of her sight, lest the like mischance might happen as had been before. This she seemingly consented to, and he was immediately sent for, and the former familiarities continued between them, though more privately.

Andronicus, besides his sons, had a very fair and beautiful daughter named Lavinia, brought up in all singular virtues, humble, courteous, and modest, insomuch that the Emperor's only son by a former wife fell extremely in love with her, seeking her favor by all virtuous and honorable ways, insomuch that, after a long courtship, with her father and the Emperor's consent she was betrothed to him.

The Queen of the Goths, hearing this, was much enraged because from such a marriage might spring princes that might frustrate her ambitious designs, which was to make her sons emperors jointly. Wherefore she labored all she could to frustrate it by declaring what a disgrace it would be to the Emperor to marry his son to the daughter of a subject, who[11] might have a queen with a kingdom to her dowry. But, finding the prince constant,[12] she resolved to take him[13] out of the way. So it was plotted between her, the Moor, and her two sons that they should invite him to hunt in the great forest on the banks of the river Tiber and there murder him. This was effected by shooting him through the back with a poisoned arrow, which came out at his breast, of which wound he fell from his horse and immediately died. Then they digged a very deep pit in a pathway and threw him in, covering it lightly with boughs and sprinkling earth on it; and so, returning, reported they had lost the Prince in the forest, and though they had sought and called everywhere, they could not find him.

CHAPTER 4

How the wicked Moor, who had laid with the Empress and got into her favor above all others, betrayed Andronicus'

11 who he who **12 finding the prince constant** finding the Emperor firmly resolved ("The Prince" usually refers to the Emperor's son, but here it probably refers to the Emperor, i.e., "the Emperor, the prince.") **13 him** i.e., the Emperor's son

three sons and charged the Prince's murder on them, for which they were cast into a dungeon and, after their father had cut off his hand to save them, were beheaded.

The fair Lavinia no sooner heard the Prince was missing but she fell into great sorrow and lamentation, her heart misgiving her of some treachery, and thereupon she entreated her brothers to go in search of him, which they did with all speed. But, being dogged by the Moor and the Queen of Goths' two sons, they unluckily coming in the way where the pit was digged, they fell both in upon the dead body and could not, by reason of the great depth, get out. Their cruel enemies no sooner saw this but they hasted to the court and sent the guards in search of the murdered Prince, who found Andronicus' two sons with the dead body, which[1] they drew up and carried prisoners to the court, where the Moor and the other two falsely swore against them that they had often heard them threaten revenge on the Prince because he had put them to the foil[2] in a tournament at jousting. This, and the circumstances of their being found, with the vehement aggravation,[3] was a sufficient ground to the Emperor to believe, who loved his son entirely and was much grieved for his death. And though they denied it with all the protestations imaginable and pleaded their innocence, demanded the combat[4] against their accusers, which by the law of arms they ought to have been allowed, they were immediately loaden[5] with irons and cast into a deep dungeon among noisome[6] creatures, as frogs, toads, serpents, and the like, where, notwithstanding all the intercessions that were made, they continued,[7] eating the filth that they found in that place.

At last the Queen, designing to work her revenge on Andronicus, sent the Moor in the Emperor's name to tell him, if he designed[8] to save his sons from the misery and death that would ensue, he should cut off his right hand and send it to court. This the good-natured father scrupled not to do; no, nor had it been his life to ransom them, he would have freely parted with it. Whereupon, laying his hand on a

1 which i.e., the dead body and Andronicus' two sons **2 put them to the foil** defeated them **3 aggravation** accusation **4 the combat** a trial by combat **5 loaden** loaded down **6 noisome** offensive, noxious **7 continued** remained **8 designed** intended, hoped

block, he gave the wicked Moor his sword, who immediately struck it off and inwardly laughed at the villainy. Then, departing with it, he told him his sons should be sent to him in a few hours. But whilst he[9] was rejoicing with the hopes of their delivery, a hearse came to his door with guards, which made his aged heart to tremble. The first thing they presented him was his hand, which they said would not be accepted; and the next was his three sons beheaded. At this woeful sight, overcome with grief, he fainted away on the dead bodies. And when he recovered again, he tore his hoary hair, which age and his lying in winter camps for the defense of his country had made as white as snow, pouring out floods of tears; but found no pity from the hardened villains, who left him with scoffs in the midst of his woeful lamentations with his sorrowful daughter. Yet this was not all, for soon after, another to-be-deplored affliction followed, as shall in the next chapter be shown.

Chapter 5

How the two lustful sons of the Empress, with the assistance of the Moor, in a barbarous manner ravished Lavinia, Andronicus' beautiful daughter, and cut out her tongue and cut off her hands to prevent discovery; yet she did it by writing in the dust with a wand,[1] etc.

The fair and beautiful Lavinia for the loss of her lover* and brothers so basely murdered by treachery, tore her golden hair, shed floods of tears, and with her nails offered violence to that lovely face kings had adored and beheld with admiration. She shunned all company, retiring to woods and groves to utter her piteous complaints and cries to the senseless trees. When one day, being watched thither by the Moor, he gave notice of it to the Queen's two sons, who, like the wicked Elders and chaste Susanna, had a long time burned in lust, yet knew her virtues were proof against all temptations, and therefore it could not be obtained but by

***lover** Lovers

9 he i.e., Andronicus

1 wand stick

violence. So, thinking this an opportunity to serve their turns, immediately repaired to the grove, and setting the Moor to watch on the outborders, soon found her pensive and sorrowful, yet comely and beautiful in tears. When, unawares, before she saw them, like two ravenous tigers they seized the trembling lady, who struggled all she could and cried out piteously for help. And seeing what their wicked intentions bent at, she offered them her throat, desiring they would bereave her of her life but not of her honor. However, in a villainous manner, staking her down by the hair of her head and binding her hands behind her, they turned up her nakedness and forced their way into her closet of chastity, taking it by turns, the elder beginning first and the younger seconding him as they had before agreed on. And having tired themselves in satiating their beastly appetites, they began to consider how they should* come off[2] when such a villainy was discovered. Whereupon, calling the Moor to them, they asked his advice, who wickedly counseled them to make all sure, seeing they had gone thus far, by cutting out her tongue to hinder her telling tales and her hands off to prevent her writing a discovery.[3] This the cruel wretches did whilst she in vain entreated 'em to take away her life, since they had bereaved her of her honor, which was dearer to her. And in this woeful condition they left the lady, who had[4] expired for the loss of blood had not her uncle Marcus happened accidentally, soon after, to come in search of her, who, at the woeful sight overcome with sorrow, could hardly keep life in himself; yet, recovering his spirits, he bound up her wounds and conveyed her home.

Poor Andronicus' grief for this sad disaster was so great that[5] no pen can write or words express. Much ado they had to restrain him from doing violence upon himself. He cursed the day he was born to see such miseries fall on himself and family, entreating her to tell him, if she could any ways do it by signs, who had so villainously abused her. At last the poor lady, with a flood of tears gushing from her eyes, taking a wand between her stumps, wrote these lines:

***should** should should

2 come off avoid detection and punishment **3 discovery** explanation, disclosure **4 had** would have **5 that** as

The lustful sons of the proud Empress
Are doers of this hateful wickedness.

Hereupon he vowed revenge, at the hazard of his own and all their lives, comforting his daughter with this when nothing else would do.

CHAPTER 6

How Andronicus, feigning himself mad, found means to entrap the Empress' two sons in a forest, where, binding them to a tree, he cut their throats, made pies of their flesh, and served them up to the Emperor and Empress, then slew them, set the Moor quick[1] *in the ground, and then killed his daughter and himself.*

Andronicus, upon these calamities, feigned himself distracted and went raving about the city, shooting his arrows towards heaven as in defiance, calling to hell for vengeance, which mainly[2] pleased the Empress and her sons, who thought themselves now secure. And though his friends required[3] justice of the Emperor against the ravishers, yet they could have no redress, he rather threatening them if they insisted on it. So that, finding they were in a bad case and that in all probability their lives would be the next, they conspired together to prevent that mischief and revenge themselves. Lying in ambush in the forest when the two sons went a-hunting, they surprised them and, binding them to a tree, pitifully crying out for mercy though they would give none to others, Andronicus cut their throats whilst Lavinia, by his command, held a bowl between her stumps to receive the blood. Then, conveying the bodies home to his own house privately, he cut the flesh into fit pieces and ground the bones to powder and made of them two mighty pasties,[4] and invited the Emperor and Empress to dinner, who, thinking to make sport with his frantic humor, came. But when they had eat[5] of the pasties he told them what it was; and thereupon giving the watchword to

1 quick alive **2 mainly** greatly **3 required** begged **4 mighty pasties** large meat pies **5 eat** eaten

his friends, they immediately issued out, slew the Emperor's guards, and lastly the Emperor and his cruel wife after they had sufficiently upbraided them with the wicked deeds they had done. Then, seizing on the wicked Moor, the fearful villain fell on his knees, promising to discover[6] all; but when he had told how he had killed the Prince, betrayed the three sons of Andronicus by false accusation, and counseled the abuse to the fair Lavinia, they scarce knew what torments sufficient to devise for him. But at last, digging a hole, they set him in the ground to the middle alive, smeared him over with honey, and so, between the stinging of bees and wasps and starving, he miserably ended his wretched days. After this, to prevent the torments he[7] expected when these things came to be known, at his daughter's request he killed her; and so, rejoicing he had revenged himself on his enemies to the full, fell on his own sword and died.

Text based on *The History of Titus Andronicus, the Renowned Roman General. Who, after he had saved Rome by his valor, etc. Newly translated from the Italian copy printed at Rome. London: printed and sold by C. Dicey in Bow churchyard and at his wholesale warehouse in Northampton.* It is a mid-eighteenth-century text probably derived from a sixteenth-century original.

6 discover reveal, tell **7 he** i.e., Andronicus

Further Reading

Baker, Howard. "Transformations of Medieval Structure: *Titus Andronicus* and the Shakespearian Practice." *Induction to Tragedy: A Study in a Development of Form in "Gorboduc," "The Spanish Tragedy," and "Titus Andronicus,"* 1939. Rpt. New York: Russell and Russell, 1965. Baker denies that *Titus* is a Senecan tragedy. Asserting its greater dependence upon English medieval and Ovidian models, he concludes that *Titus* is an Elizabethan transformation of Ovid's story of Philomel.

Bowers, Fredson Thayer. *Elizabethan Revenge Tragedy 1587–1642,* pp. 110–118. Princeton, N.J.: Princeton Univ. Press, 1940. Bowers examines *Titus* as an example of the Elizabethan revenge play. Though Shakespeare's play follows most of the conventions of this subgenre, it departs from its models with the introduction of Aaron's unmotivated villainy, which, for Bowers, disrupts the clear moral outlines of the play.

Bradbrook, M. C. "Moral Heraldry: *Titus Andronicus, Rape of Lucrece, Romeo and Juliet.*" *Shakespeare and Elizabethan Poetry: A Study of His Earlier Work in Relation to the Poetry of the Time.* London: Chatto and Windus, 1951. For Bradbrook, *Titus* is less a play than a formal pageant. It stylizes the play's violence in its emblematic and heraldic scenes and in a rhetoric drawn from late medieval poetry of "complaint."

Brooke, Nicholas. *"Titus Andronicus." Shakespeare's Early Tragedies.* London: Methuen, 1968. Brooke's essay explores Shakespeare's use of structural and poetic techniques to manipulate our response to the play. *Titus* insists that we are appalled by the spectacle of human nobility degenerating into bestiality, but its stylization is designed to prevent us from responding sympathetically to those who are victimized.

Brower, Reuben A. "Most Lamentable Romaine Tragedie." *Hero and Saint: Shakespeare and the Graeco-Roman Heroic Tradition.* New York and Oxford: Oxford Univ. Press, 1971. Though lacking the structural unity and moral clarity of the great tragedies, *Titus,* Brower finds, initiates Shakespeare's exploration of their controlling themes of justice and human suffering. *Titus* movingly poses "the great questions: why should a noble man suffer, why are his cries for justice unheard, how is he to act?"

Danson, Lawrence N. "Introduction: *Titus Andronicus.*" *Tragic Alphabet: Shakespeare's Drama of Language.* Princeton, N.J.: Princeton Univ. Press, 1974. For Danson, Shakespeare's tragedies are plays about the difficulty of achieving truthful and effective verbal expression. This is powerfully felt in *Titus,* where Titus' need to "wrest an alphabet" from the mute Lavinia is symbolic of the task confronting both Shakespeare and his characters of finding a language able to articulate the complexities of human life.

Ettin, Andrew V. "Shakespeare's First Roman Tragedy." *ELH* 37 (1970): 325–341. Ettin denies that Rome serves as the symbol of civilization in the play. He proposes instead that Shakespeare subjects the values of Rome to intense scrutiny, raising disturbing questions about both the ethical and the literary legacy that Renaissance England inherited from Rome.

Hattaway, Michael. "*Titus Andronicus:* Strange Images of Death." *Elizabethan Popular Theatre.* London: Routledge and Kegan Paul, 1982. Hattaway examines the play as it would have been staged in Shakespeare's playhouse. He examines Shakespeare's use of theatrical space, stage emblems, music, and props, as well as his indebtedness to the theatrical techniques of contemporaries such as Thomas Kyd and Christopher Marlowe, in a play that explores not just the representation of violence but the audience's perception of it.

Hunter, G. K. "Shakespeare's Earliest Tragedies: *Titus Andronicus* and *Romeo and Juliet.*" *Shakespeare Survey* 27 (1974): 1–9. While *Titus* and *Romeo and Juliet* represent the full range of Shakespeare's tragic practice (the former possessing the bleakest view of human potential, the latter often veering toward comedy), the differences between them should not obscure important affinities. The two plays, Hunter argues, are unique among Shakespeare's tragedies as tales of cities: in each, a conflict between rival households threatens civic order; and in each, the use of a family tomb as a central stage prop emphasizes the social and personal aspects of the tragedy.

Metz, G. Harold. "The Stage History of *Titus Andronicus.*" *Shakespeare Quarterly* 28 (1977): 154–169. Contrary to critical assertions that *Titus* holds little appeal for modern audiences, Metz's overview of the play's stage history shows that the play has enjoyed a lively presence on the stage in this century with twenty-three separate productions between 1951 and 1974, including outstanding successes directed by Peter Brook (1955) and Gerald Freedman (1967).

Miola, Robert S. "*Titus Andronicus:* Rome and Romans." *Shakespeare's Rome*. Cambridge: Cambridge Univ. Press, 1983. Miola shows how deeply *Titus* is steeped in things Roman: the poetry of Virgil, Seneca, and Ovid; the Roman obsessions with exile, rebellion, civil war, blood ritual, and the code of military honor; and most of all, the inflexible Roman *pietas,* which demands that natural feeling be subordinated to public need.

Sommers, Alan. "'Wilderness of Tigers': Structure and Symbolism in *Titus Andronicus.*" *Essays in Criticism* 10 (1960): 275–289. The opposition of civilization and barbarism, of Rome and primitive nature, is for Sommers the central conflict of the play. Sommers explores the structural and symbolic patterns enforcing this opposition, in which he discovers the play's tragic meaning and Titus' tragic stature.

Spencer, T. J. B. "Shakespeare and the Elizabethan Romans." *Shakespeare Survey* 10 (1957): 27–38. Spencer's essay discusses Shakespeare's Roman plays in terms of the Elizabethan use and understanding of Roman history. *Titus,* he finds, is typical of many Elizabethan treatments of Roman history in that it offers not a true picture of a particular political situation but a generalized portrait of Roman politics and political institutions—a product, perhaps, of Shakespeare's desire "not to get it all right but to get it all in."

Waith, Eugene M. "The Metamorphosis of Violence in *Titus Andronicus.*" *Shakespeare Survey* 10 (1957): 39–49. Waith explores the relation between the raw violence enacted in

Titus and the rhetorical style in which it is written. Waith finds that Shakespeare adopts a style and a mode of characterization derived from Ovid and designed to arouse astonishment rather than terror at the spectacle of characters under extraordinary emotional stress.

Photo © George Joseph

From the 1962 New York Shakespeare Festival production of *The Tempest* with (l. to r.) Charles Durning as Stephano, John Heffernan as Trinculo, and James Earl Jones as Caliban, directed by Gerald Freedman at the Delacorte Theater in Central Park.

THE TEMPEST

THE TEMPEST

Foreword

I prefer the human, personal elements in *The Tempest* to broad symbolic interpretations. One of my favorite parts of the play is the first meeting between the young girl Miranda and the young boy Ferdinand. I enjoy watching their relationship grow until she actually proposes to him, saying, "I am your wife, if you will marry me; / If not, I'll die your maid."

Then there's the wonderful scene where the jester-comedian Trinculo encounters the deformed slave Caliban—"What have we here, a man or a fish? Dead or alive?"—and creeps under Caliban's gaberdine (a kind of cloak) to stay out of the rain. Along comes Trinculo's companion Stephano, drunk and singing. When he sees a strange monster with two extra legs (Trinculo's) sticking out from under it, he exclaims, "Four legs and two voices—a most delicate monster!" and decides to save it by giving it a drink from his bottle of sack (sherry). When this is played onstage, it's a hilarious sight gag.

The most intriguing character in the play is unquestionably Prospero, the enigmatic, fascinating Prospero. We must understand his motivations, which are difficult to uncover at first. Here is a strange man who is always using his magic to keep the plot moving: he creates a storm, engineers his daughter's meeting with Ferdinand, keeps the other shipwreck survivors lost on the island, and commands his spirit Ariel to carry out his plans. His attitude toward Caliban is one of stern cruelty, and their relationship, too, cries out for greater exploration.

Never having directed the play, it is difficult for me to evaluate Prospero's role fully, but it's clear that through him Shakespeare creates the atmosphere of magic and fantasy in which *The Tempest* is bathed.

Joseph Papp

Joseph Papp gratefully acknowledges the help of Elizabeth Kirkland in preparing this Foreword.

Introduction

Shakespeare creates in *The Tempest* an idealized world of imagination, a place of magical rejuvenation like the forests of *A Midsummer Night's Dream* and *As You Like It.* The journey to Shakespeare's island is to a visionary realm, where everything is controlled by the artist. Yet the journey is no escape from reality, for the island shows men what they are and what they ought to be. Even its location juxtaposes "real" world with idealized landscape: like Plato's New Atlantis or Thomas More's Utopia, Shakespeare's island is to be found both somewhere and nowhere. On the narrative level it is located in the Mediterranean Sea. Yet there are overtones of the New World, the Western Hemisphere, where Thomas More had situated his island of Utopia. Ariel fetches dew at Prospero's command from the "Bermudas" (1.2.230). Caliban when prostrate reminds Trinculo of a "dead Indian" (2.2.33) who might be displayed before gullible crowds eager to see such a prodigious creature from across the seas; and Caliban's god, Setebos, was, according to Richard Eden's account of Magellan's circumnavigation of the globe (in *History of Travel,* 1577), worshiped by South American natives. An inspiration for Shakespeare's story (for which no direct literary source is known) may well have been various accounts of the shipwreck in the Bermudas in 1609 of the *Sea Venture,* which was carrying settlers to the new Virginian colony. Shakespeare borrowed details from Sylvester Jourdain's *A Discovery of the Bermudas, Otherwise Called the Isle of Devils,* published in 1610, and from William Strachey's *A True Repertory of the Wreck and Redemption . . . from the Islands of the Bermudas,* which Shakespeare must have seen in manuscript since it was not published until after his death. He wrote the play shortly after reading these works, for *The Tempest* was acted at court in 1611. He may also have known or heard of various accounts of Magellan's circumnavigation of the world in 1519–1522 (including Richard Eden's shortened English version, as part of his *History of Travel,* of an Italian narrative by Antonio Pigafetta), Francis Fletcher's journal of Sir Francis Drake's circumnavigation in 1577–1580, Richard Rich's *News from Virginia* (1610), and still other potential sources of information. Shakespeare's fascination with the Western Hemisphere gave him, not the actual location of his story, which remains Mediterranean, but a state of mind associated with newness and hope. Miranda sees on the island a "new world" in which mankind appears "brave" (5.1.185); and, although her wonder must be tempered by Prospero's rejoinder that "'Tis new to thee" (l. 186) and by Aldous Huxley's still more ironic use of her phrase in the title of his satirical novel *Brave New World*, the island still endures as a restorative vision. Even though we experience it fleetingly, as in a dream, this nonexistent realm assumes a permanence enjoyed by all great works of art.

Prospero rules as the artist-king over this imaginary world, conjuring up trials to test men's intentions and visions to promote their renewed faith in goodness. To the island come an assortment of men who, because they require varied ordeals, are separated by Prospero and Ariel into three groups: King Alonso and those accompanying him; Alonso's son, Ferdinand; and Stephano and Trinculo. Prospero's authority over them, though strong, has limits. As Duke of Milan he was bookishly inattentive to political matters and thus vulnerable to the Machiavellian conniving of his younger brother Antonio. Only in this world apart, the artist's world, do his powers derived from learning find their proper sphere. Because he cannot control the world beyond his isle, he must wait for "strange, bountiful Fortune, / Now my dear lady" (1.2.179–180) to bring his enemies near his shore. He eschews, moreover, the black arts of diabolism. His is a white magic, devoted ultimately to merciful ends: rescuing Ariel from the spell of the witch Sycorax, curbing the appetite of Caliban, spying on Antonio and Sebastian in the role of Conscience. He uses Fortune's gift of delivering his enemies into his hands to forgive and restore them, not to be revenged. Such a use of power imitates the divine, though Prospero is no god. His chief power, learned from books and exercised through Ariel, is to control the elements so as to create illusion—of separation, of death, of the gods' blessing. Yet since he is a man, even this power is an immense burden. Prospero has much to learn, like those whom he controls. He must subdue his anger, his self-pity, his readiness to blame others, his domineering over Miranda. He must overcome the vengeful impulse he experiences toward those who have wronged him, and he must conquer the longing any father feels to hold on to his daughter when she is desired by another man. He does these things through his art, devising games and shows in which his angry self-pity and jealousy are transmuted into playacting scenes of divine warning and forgiveness toward his enemies and watchful parental austereness toward Miranda and Ferdinand. Prospero's responsibilities cause him to behave magisterially and to be resented by the spirits of the isle. Even Ariel longs to be free, and it is with genuine relief as well as melancholy that Prospero finally lays aside his demanding role as creative moral intelligence.

Alonso and his court party variously illustrate the unregenerate world left behind in Naples and Milan. We first see them on shipboard, panicky and desperate, their titles and finery mocked by roaring waves. Futile ambition seems destined for a watery demise. Yet death by water in this play is a transfiguration rather than an end, a mystical rebirth as in the regenerative cycle of the seasons from winter to summer. Ariel suggests as much in his song about a drowned father: "Those are pearls that were his eyes. / Nothing of him that doth fade / But doth suffer a sea change / Into something rich and strange" (1.2.402–405). Still, this miracle is not apparent at first to those who are caught in the illusion of death. As in T. S. Eliot's *The Waste Land*, which repeatedly alludes to *The Tempest*, self-blinded human beings fear a disaster that is ironically the prelude to reawakening.

Prospero creates an illusion of loss to test his enemies and to make them reveal their true selves. Only Gonzalo, no enemy at all but one who long ago aided Prospero and Miranda when they were banished from Milan, responds affirmatively. He alone notices that his garments and those of his shipwrecked companions have miraculously been left unharmed by the salt water. His ideal commonwealth (2.1.150–171), which Shakespeare drew in part from an essay by Montaigne, postulates a natural goodness in man and makes no allowance for the dark propensities of Caliban, but at least Gonzalo's cheerfulness is in refreshing contrast to the jaded sneers of some of his companions. Sebastian and Antonio react to the magic isle, as to Gonzalo's commonwealth, by cynically refusing to believe in miracles. Confident that they are unobserved, they seize the opportunity afforded by Alonso's being asleep to plot a murder and political coup. This attempt is not only despicable but madly ludicrous, for they are all shipwrecked and no longer have kingdoms over which to quarrel. Even more ironically, Sebastian and Antonio, despite their insolent belief in their self-sufficiency, are being observed. The villains must be taught that an unseen power keeps track of their misdeeds. They may revert to type when returned to their usual habitat, but even they are at least briefly moved to an awareness of the unseen (3.3.21–27). Alonso, more worthy than they though burdened too with sin, responds to his situation with guilt and despair, for he assumes that his son Ferdinand's death is the just punishment of the gods for Alonso's part in the earlier overthrow of Prospero. Alonso must be led, by Prospero's curative illusions, through the purgative experience of contrition to the reward he thinks impossible and undeserved: reunion with his lost son.

Alonso is thus, like Posthumus in *Cymbeline* or Leontes in *The Winter's Tale*, a tragicomic figure—sinful, contrite, forgiven. Alonso's son, Ferdinand, must also undergo ordeals and visions devised by Prospero to test his worth, but more on the level of romantic comedy. Ferdinand is young, innocent, and hopeful, well-matched to Miranda. From the start Prospero obviously approves of his prospective son-in-law. Yet even Prospero, needing to prepare himself for a life in which Miranda will no longer be solely his, is not ready to lay aside at least the comic fiction of parental opposition. He invents difficulties, imposes tasks of logbearing (like those assigned Caliban) and issues stern warnings against premarital lust. In the comic mode, parents are expected to cross their children in matters of the heart. As a teacher of youth, moreover, Prospero is convinced by long experience that prizes too easily won are too lightly esteemed. Manifold are the temptations urging Ferdinand to surrender to the natural rhythms of the isle and to fulfill his desire like Caliban. In place of ceremonies conducted in civilized societies by the church, Prospero must create the illusion of ceremony by his art. The marriage of Ferdinand and Miranda accordingly unites the best of both worlds: the natural innocence of the island, which teaches them to avoid the corruptions of civilization at its worst, and the higher law of nature achieved through moral wisdom at its best. To this marriage, the goddesses Iris, Ceres, and Juno bring promises of bounteous harvest, "refreshing showers," celestial harmony, and a springtime brought back to the earth by Proserpina's return from Hades (4.1.79–117). In Ferdinand and Miranda, "nurture" is wedded to "nature." This bond unites spirit and flesh, legitimizing erotic pleasure by incorporating it within a cosmic moral order.

At the lowest level of this same cosmic and moral framework are Stephano and Trinculo. Their comic scenes juxtapose them with Caliban, for he represents untutored nature whereas they represent the unnatural depths to which persons brought up in civilized society can fall. In this they resemble Sebastian and Antonio, who have learned in supposedly civilized Italy arts of intrigue and political murder. The antics of Stephano and Trinculo burlesque the conduct of their presumed betters, thereby exposing to ridicule the self-deceptions of ambitious humans. The clowns desire to exploit the natural wonders of the isle by taking Caliban back to civilization to be shown in carnivals, or by plying him with strong drink and whetting his resentment against authority. These plottings are in vain, however, for like Sebastian and Antonio the clowns are being watched. The clowns teach Caliban to cry out for "freedom" (2.2.184), by which they mean license to do as one pleases, but are foiled by Ariel as comic nemesis. Because they are degenerate buffoons, their exposure is appropriately humiliating and satirical.

In contrast with them, Caliban is almost a sympathetic character. His sensitivity to natural beauty, as in his descriptions of the "nimble marmoset" or the dreaming music he so often hears (2.2.168; 3.2.137–145), is entirely appropriate to this child of nature. He is, to be sure, the child of a witch, and is called many harsh names such as "Abhorrèd slave" and "a born devil, on whose nature / Nurture can never stick" (1.2.354; 4.1.188–189). Yet he protests with some justification that the island was his in the first place and that Prospero and Miranda are interlopers. His very existence calls radically into question the value of civilization, which has shown itself capable of limitless depravity. What profit has Caliban derived from learning Prospero's language other than, as he puts it, to "know how to curse" (1.2.367)? With instinctive cunning he senses that books are his chief enemy, and plots to destroy them first in his attempt at rebellion. The unspoiled natural world does indeed offer civilization a unique perspective on itself. In this it resembles Gonzalo's ideal commonwealth, which, no matter how laughably implausible from the cynic's point of view, does at least challenge the very assumptions upon which Western civilization is based.

The play's ending is far from perfectly stable. Antonio never repents, and we cannot be sure what the island will be like once Prospero has disappeared from the scene. Since Prospero's occupation of the island replicates in a sense the process by which he himself was overthrown, we cannot know when the cycle of revolution will ever cease. Ultimately, however, Shakespeare's play strives to celebrate humanity's highest achievement in the union of the island with the civilized world. Miranda and Ferdinand have bright hopes for the future, even if they must be qualified by Prospero's melancholic observation that the "brave new world" with "such people in it" is only "new to thee," to those who are young and not yet experienced in the world's vexations. Even Caliban may be at last reconciled to Prospero's insistent idea of a harmony between will and reason, no matter how perilously and delicately achieved. Prospero speaks of Caliban as a "thing of darkness I / Acknowledge mine," and Caliban vows to "be wise hereafter / And seek for grace" (5.1.278–279, 298–299). This synthesis suggests that the natural man within us is more contented, better understood, and more truly free when harmonized with reason.

Caliban is a part of humanity, Ariel is not. Ariel can comprehend what compassion and forgiveness would be like, "were I human" (5.1.20), and can take good-natured part in Prospero's designs to castigate or reform his fellow creature, but Ariel longs to be free in quite another sense from that meant by Caliban. Ariel takes no part in the final integration of human society. This spirit belongs to a magic world of song, music, and illusion that the artist borrows for his use but which exists eternally outside of him. Like the elements of air, earth, fire, and water in which it mysteriously dwells, this spirit is morally neutral but incredibly vital. From it the artist achieves powers of imagination, enabling him to bedim the noontide sun or call forth the dead from their graves. These visions are illusory in the profound sense that all life is illusory, an "insubstantial pageant" melted into thin air (4.1.150–155). Prospero the artist cherishes his own humanity, as a promise of surcease from his labors. Yet the artifact created by the artist endures, existing apart from time and place as does Ariel: "Then to the elements / Be free, and fare thou well!" (5.1.321–322). No doubt it is a romantic fiction to associate the dramatist Shakespeare with Prospero's farewell to his art, but it is an almost irresistible idea because we are so moved by the sense of completion and yet humility, the exultation and yet the calm, contained in this leave-taking.

The Tempest in Performance

Mark Twain once joked that Shakespeare's plays were not by Shakespeare but by another author of the same name. His joke might, with a slight alteration, be applied to the performance history of *The Tempest*. Something called *The Tempest* has never failed to delight audiences, but from the mid-seventeenth until the late eighteenth century what audiences saw was truly another play of the same name. Adaptation began shortly after Shakespeare's death, if not before. His own play had been acted before King James by Shakespeare's acting company, the King's men, on November 1, 1611, and in the winter of 1612–1613 "before the Princess' Highness the Lady Elizabeth and the Prince Palatine Elector" in honor of their betrothal. Scholars have argued, though without much evidence, that Shakespeare composed the masque in Act 4 especially for this occasion; if he did, the process of musical elaboration began early and with his own imprimatur. More likely, the short play we have, masque and all, was written to be acted in late 1611 and afterward at the Globe Theatre, at the Blackfriars playhouse, and at court when the King so wished. Dr. Simon Forman, who recorded in his journal that he saw *Cymbeline* and *The Winter's Tale* in 1611, does not mention *The Tempest*. In any event, the King's men were soon performing a fanciful reply to Shakespeare's play, by John Fletcher, called *The Sea Voyage* (1622), and in 1667 the theater in Lincoln's Inn Fields, London, staged a production of *The Tempest* as altered by William Davenant and John Dryden.

This version of *The Tempest* was a great success. Diarist Samuel Pepys saw it eight times between 1667 and 1669, more times than any other Shakespeare play he saw except *Macbeth*, and bestowed on it his warmest praise: in January of 1669 he wrote that he "could not be more pleased almost in a comedy," and later that same year he declared it "the most innocent play that ever I saw." The authors' success lay in appealing to the tastes of their age for symmetry. Davenant hit on the idea that Shakespeare's story of a young woman (Miranda) who has never seen a man could be paired with that of a young man who has never seen a woman. "By this means," wrote Davenant afterward, "those two characters of innocence and love might the more illustrate and commend each other."

The added counterplot is thus a mirror of the main plot. Long ago, the story goes, Prospero brought with him to the island the young Duke of Mantua, named Hippolito, and has kept him secluded in a remote cave where, improbably enough, he has never seen Miranda—or her sister Dorinda. When Hippolito does see Dorinda for the first time, in a scene that parallels Miranda's first encounter with Ferdinand, Hippolito's male response is to want her and all beautiful women besides, and so he quarrels with Ferdinand and is seemingly killed by him. For this offense Ferdinand is condemned to death by Prospero, until Hippolito is revived by Ariel's aid and goes on to join the other three lovers in a predictable contretemps of jealousies and misplaced affections. Caliban, meanwhile, has a sister, Sycorax, and Ariel has a fellow-spirit named Milcha. The broadly comic plot of Stephano, Trinculo, and Caliban is enlarged into a quarrel for royal supremacy between Stephano, Mustacho, and Ventoso on the one hand and Trincalo (i.e., Trinculo), Caliban, and Sycorax on the other, with pointed satirical application to the recent factionalism of England's mid-century civil war.

With its many songs, Shakespeare's *The Tempest* was an obvious candidate for operatic treatment. Thomas Shadwell's *The Tempest* (produced in 1673, published the following year) retains the plot symmetries of Davenant and Dryden, including the topical satire directed at civil strife, while adding substantially to the music and spectacle. Shadwell gives an enlarged part to Milcha so that she and Ariel can sing together and dance a saraband. At the dramatic moment when Prospero sets Ariel and then Milcha free, "both fly up and cross in the air." When Ariel sings "Come unto these yellow sands," as in Shakespeare (1.2.378–390), Milcha answers with "Full fathom five" (ll. 400–407). Together they sing an added song, "Dry those tears which are o'erflowing." The musical settings by Pietro Reggio, Matthew Locke, and Pelham Humphrey were of a high order, and the standard remained high when, later in the century, the songs were reset to music by Henry Purcell and others.

Scenic and musical splendor prevail everywhere in Shadwell's opera. It opens with an overture, a rising curtain, and the discovery of a noble arched frontispiece supported by Corinthian columns wreathed in roses. Several Cupids fly about them. The allegorical figure of Fame appears; angels hold the royal arms of England. Behind the arch lies the menacing scene, a sky darkened by storm clouds, a coast strewn with rocks, a troubled sea in continual motion. Frightful spirits fly among the terrorized sailors. When the ship begins to sink, "the whole house is darkened, and a shower of fire falls upon 'em"—presumably the sailors, not the audience. Lightning flashes and thunder sounds. Thereupon, "in the midst of the shower of fire, the scene changes. The cloudy sky, rocks, and sea vanish, and, when the lights return, discover that beautiful part of the island which was the habitation of Prospero. 'Tis composed of three walks of cypress trees. Each sidewalk leads to a cave, in one of which Prospero keeps his daughters, in the other Hippolito. The middle walk is of great depth, and leads to an open part of the island." Possibly the effect of darkness was achieved by the shutting of flats (theatrical scenery), or the removal and then return of hanging candle-fixtures, or both.

Later in the opera, according to the contemporary account of John Downes, the audience sees one of Ariel's spirits "flying away with a table furnished out with fruits, sweetmeats, and all sorts of viands, just when Duke Trinculo and his companions were going to dinner." A masque of Furies, introduced by Dryden in 1667, is much enlarged by Shadwell with allegorical figures such as Pride, Fraud, Rapine, and Murder. A concluding masque of Neptune and Amphitrite shows these sea gods, along with Oceanus and Tethys, arising "in a chariot drawn with sea-horses," while Tritons and Nereides sport at their side. A dance of twelve Tritons is followed by a scene at sunrise in which Ariel, accompanied by other spirits, flies from the sun toward the spectators and hovers in the air while speaking the last lines. In Shadwall's hands *The Tempest* has become the embodiment of the seventeenth-century courtly masque, complete with antimasque in the ludicrous antics of Stephano and Trinculo.

The Davenant-Dryden and Shadwell adaptations, or variations of them, held the stage for much of the eighteenth century. At the Theatre Royal, Drury Lane, there were over one hundred and eighty performances in the first half of the century alone. A revival of *The Tempest*—or *The Enchanted Island,* as the adaptation was also known—in 1706 included a masque composed by "the late Mr. Henry Purcell." A revival in 1712 was again a great success; according to actor-manager Colly Cibber, the production achieved "the greatest profit that in so little a time had yet been known in my memory." In 1715 Drury Lane produced a similar version "with the tempest, with scenes, machines, dances, and all the original decorations proper to the play," in response to a revival of Beaumont and Fletcher's popular *The Island Princess* at the theater in Lincoln's Inn Fields, London. When money could not be found for the Shadwell extravaganza, Davenant and Dryden's adaptation filled in. Although James Lacy claimed to produce the play at Drury Lane in 1746 "as written by Shakespeare, never acted there before," he in fact added Shadwell's elaborate masque of Neptune and Amphitrite in Act 5, and at all events the theater soon returned to Davenant and Dryden. Actor-manager David Garrick produced *The Tempest: An Opera, Taken from Shakespeare* in 1756 at Drury Lane, without Hippolito and Dorinda but with Davenant's added clowns. John Christopher Smith, a protégé of Handel, composed the opera, with some thirty-two songs, duets, and a trio for Trinculo, Stephano, and Ventoso. Sixty children presented a garland dance at the end of Act 2, and subsequently there was a pantomime of Fortunatus, or the Genii. Garrick did revive Shakespeare's play in 1757 with Henry Mossop as Prospero and Hannah Pritchard as Miranda, albeit with some heavy cutting in Act 2, scene 1, and this version enjoyed sixty-one performances before Garrick retired in 1776.

We get a clear impression of costuming and setting during this period from a contemporary engraving seemingly based on De Loutherbourg's designs for a 1777 production at Drury Lane. Ferdinand is in the powdered wig and elegant attire of an eighteenth-century gentleman, Miranda in a sweeping coiffure with outfit to match. Such costuming evidently did not seem out of keeping with the spectacle of the Davenant-Dryden-Shadwell tradition, which continued only somewhat abated. John Philip Kemble, in his 1789 revival at Drury Lane, sought "to admit in a temperate way the additions of Dryden," retaining the Hippolito-Dorinda plot though eliminating Milcha, Sycorax, Ventoso, and Mustacho. Kemble added music in 1789, including a duet for Ferdinand and Miranda, though he cut it back in subsequent years. He cast an actress as Hippolito. In staging effects, Kemble continued the focus on the shipwreck, transferring it to the beginning of Act 2 with the following directions: "The sea. A ship in a tempest. Spirits of the wind dancing. Chorus by spirits of the storm. The ship seems to founder. Ariel and all the other spirits disappear." At the play's end, Prospero waves his wand and the scene vanishes, discovering "a view of a calm sea, and the King's ship riding at anchor . . . Ariel and the spirits re-ascend into the sky." The Haymarket Theatre, not to be outdone, staged a ballet of *The Enchanted Island* in 1804 that went beyond the effects called for by Kemble. In 1806, Kemble, who had by this time moved to the Theatre Royal, Covent Garden, produced the play there, retaining the tradition of spectacular staging but reducing the operatic content. This version of the play became the standard acting version in the first third of the nineteenth century. Kemble's own performance as Prospero was well received, even though he was criticized for his controversial decision to pronounce "aches" in the Elizabethan manner as "aitches."

The Tempest offered many temptations to the theater manager predisposed toward musical and visual elaboration, and nineteenth-century managers, with their growing fondness for scenic *vraisemblance*, made few attempts to resist. Frederic Reynolds and H. R. Bishop brought out an operatic version in 1821 at Covent Garden "as altered and adapted by Dryden and Davenant." The musical score borrowed not only from Purcell but from Haydn, Mozart, Rossini, and others. William Charles Macready played Prospero and John Emery played Caliban, while most other parts were assigned to singers. The scenes included Prospero's cave, the interior of the island, a rocky part of the island, Hippolito's cave, a lake and mountains by moonlight, a volcanic mountain and lake, and finally a cave that changes to the last scene. Caliban gave the appearance of "a hairy man of the woods"; Ariel, portrayed as feminine, had painted gauze wings. The chorus singers in the finale came down from the ceiling on wires.

Macready, after playing Prospero in this 1821 production and also in Alfred Bunn's revival at Drury Lane in 1833 as "altered by Dryden and Davenant," brought out his own *The Tempest* in 1838 at Covent Garden with a restored Shakespeare text but still with a female Ariel (played by Priscilla Horton) suspended in the air while she sang and wearing a diaphanous long gown and fairy wings. Macready took out the dialogue of the first scene to allow room for a spectacular storm. When Ferdinand drew his sword on Prospero but was prevented by Prospero's spell from doing harm with it (1.2), the young man's sword was made to fly off over his head. Helen Faucit played Miranda. Macready had at last brought an end to the long reign of Davenant and Dryden, but the resort to scenic effects was destined to continue for some time.

A Covent Garden revival of 1842, again by Macready, opened with a huge sea vessel, fully rigged and manned, and tossing about on a tempestuous ocean. "The size of the ship," wrote the reviewer for *John Bull*, "and the ingenuity with which it was managed, now rising so as to discover the keel and then dipping to the level of the stage, seeming to sink into the mimic waters, rendered the effect particularly real." Samuel Phelps, at the Sadler's Wells Theatre in 1847, similarly used spectacular effects: a full-scale ship was battered in the opening storm, its mast struck by a fireball. Phelps's own performance as Prospero was widely praised, and the production itself was hailed by the reviewer for *The Times* as the "best combination of Shakespeare and scenery." Influenced by Phelps's success, the Surrey Theatre produced *The Tempest* in 1853 with "dioramic and pictorial illusion of a storm and wreck," masques, dances, and mechanical effects. Even in America the impact of Phelps was felt. William Burton's production in 1854 in New York followed Macready in restoring Shakespeare's text to the stage, but its spectacular theatrical effects were largely inspired by Phelps.

Charles Kean's *The Tempest* of 1857 at the Princess's

Theatre may have reached some sort of pinnacle in spectacular staging. The deck actually tossed and pitched during the storm scene and appeared to founder with all on board, whereupon the storm dispersed, allowing the sun to rise on the island where Prospero (Kean), accompanied by Miranda, stood on a rock and supervised the calming of the waters. In Act 3 a scene of desolation changed suddenly into a tropical paradise, with trees rising from the earth, fountains and waterfalls flowing from the rocks, and nymphs and satyrs bearing fruit and flowers. In an allegorical finale, Prospero released the spirits who had aided him in his art and then delivered the epilogue from the deck of a vessel that sailed off into the distance, leaving Ariel alone and suspended in air. A distant chorus of spirits accompanied the fall of the curtain. Throughout, Ariel took the various forms of a ball of fire, a delicate creature arising from a tuft of flowers, a water nymph on the back of a dolphin, or a spirit riding on a bat. Kean, in other words, literalized the words of Shakespeare's song, "Where the bee sucks, there suck I. / In a cowslip's bell I lie; / There I couch when owls do cry. / On the bat's back I do fly" (5.1.88–91). Little could be added in this vein by Frank Benson at the Lyceum Theatre in 1900 or by Herbert Beerbohm Tree at His Majesty's in 1904, though they certainly did their best.

The modern stage thus had a clear mandate for change: to free *The Tempest* from a spectacular tradition that was not only costly and inflexible, requiring cuts and rearrangements of the text to accommodate the scenery, but also was ready to visualize externally and superficially what Shakespeare's own theater leaves to the imagination. A return to a theater in which stage image can suggest conflicts and the characters' states of mind, rather than literalize, was long overdue.

The inevitability of the change can in fact be sensed in the last years of the nineteenth century. In part because of a tight budget, Frank Benson's production at Stratford-upon-Avon in 1891 began the movement away from lavish stage traditions of Phelps and Kean. Benson cut the opening shipwreck and in general simplified the play's staging (though he did add a fanciful entrance for Ferdinand "drawn by a silver thread, held by two tiny Cupids"). Benson's version was regularly revived over the next quarter-century, and his own performance as Caliban was enormously influential. Benson based his interpretation of the character on a book by Daniel Wilson, Professor of History and English Literature at the University of Toronto, who argued that Shakespeare's Caliban is the missing link that Darwinian evolutionary theory demands. The athletic Benson, dressed in a costume his wife described "as half-monkey, half cocoanut," climbed trees, hung upside down, and carried an actual fish.

The two significant aspects of Benson's production, the simplified staging and the emphasis upon Caliban, were to exert a significant impact upon subsequent performances of the play. William Poel and the Elizabethan Stage Society performed the play in 1897 on an open stage with limited scenery and without scene shifts. The elaborate music of the operatic *Tempest*s gave way to a simple score for pipe and tabor by Arnold Dolmetsch, leading George Bernard Shaw to rejoice in Poel's decision to "leave to the poet the work of conjuring up the isle 'full of noises, sounds, and sweet airs.' "

In 1904, Herbert Beerbohm Tree tried to recapture the visual splendor of the lavish nineteenth-century productions. "Of all of Shakespeare's works," wrote Tree, "*The Tempest* is probably the one which most demands the aid of modern stagecraft." But if his elaborate lighting effects and his extensive use of pantomime and ballet pointed back to—and brought to an end—the tradition of spectacular staging, his portrayal of Caliban as thoughtful and sensitive looked forward to the shifting emphasis of modern productions that would increasingly see Caliban as less demonic and more tragic than earlier productions allowed and would recognize Prospero's power as more problematic. Tree's version ended with a final tableau of Caliban on the shore reaching out "in mute despair" to the departing ship.

In 1914 Ben Greet brought his production, previously on tour in England and America, to London's Old Vic. Greet followed the new tradition of simplified staging, using "no special scenery" but introducing background music by Arthur Sullivan. Sybil Thorndike, who in America had played Ceres, now took the role of Ferdinand. Two years later in New York John Corbin and Louis Calvert produced the play at the Century Theater "in the manner of the Elizabethan stage." The text was presented "in its full integrity" and every effort was made to reproduce the full range of staging possibilities offered by Shakespeare's theater. Corbin criticized Poel and Greet for an impoverished conception of these possibilities, maintaining that Shakespeare's company inevitably would have dressed its actors in lavish costumes and made use of spectacular "flyings." "There is no reason to suppose," he argued, "that the public theatres would neglect an effect so striking." Though some reviewers criticized the production as merely an "archaeological experiment" devoid of any theatrical ingenuity, others praised Corbin's reconstruction for its quick pacing, which permitted "the fine full text of Shakespeare's play [to] unfold rapidly without long, tedious, disillusioning waits between scenes."

The growing effort to understand the conditions of Shakespeare's theater led William Bridges-Adams in 1919 to produce his revival at Stratford-upon-Avon as the play might have been done at court. He used a gauze drop curtain with the portraits and coats-of-arms of the Princess Elizabeth and the Elector Palatine for whose betrothal *The Tempest* had been performed at court in 1612–1613. Though the production attempted to reproduce the pageantry of the Jacobean masque, it used only a simple set of movable, bare platforms, seeking its stateliness in speech and movement.

At the Old Vic in 1930 Harcourt Williams directed John Gielgud as Prospero, Ralph Richardson as Caliban, and Leslie French as Ariel (the first male to play the role since 1734). Ten years later at the Old Vic, Gielgud again played Prospero, this time in a production by George Devine and Marius Goring. Gielgud's Prospero was anxious and ironic. Goring's Ariel, as Audrey Williamson wrote, was "not cruel, but cool and remote," while Jack Hawkins's Caliban "vividly suggested the slow groping towards humanity." In 1957 Peter Brook directed Gielgud in his third *Tempest*. Increasingly Gielgud's interpretations of Prospero, as they moved from benign serenity to brooding irritability, revealed the price Prospero pays for his power, and Brook's production continued the movement away from the innocent theatrical magic of the stage tradition and toward an exploration of the tensions and ambiguities discovered in the text. The island was dark, overgrown with vegetation, a projection of Prospero's tortured mind, and Gielgud was an embittered anchorite determined on revenge.

Brook returned to the play in 1968 at London's Roundhouse Theatre in an experimental version commissioned by Jean-Louis Barrault using French, Japanese, English, and American actors to explore the very nature of theater. Gielgud returned to *The Tempest* for a fourth time in 1974 at the National Theatre. Directed by Peter Hall, this production, like that of Bridges-Adams in 1919, conceived of the play as a Jacobean masque, but unlike the earlier production it understood the masque not as mere royal pageantry but as an expression of royal authority. Gielgud's Prospero was, in Hall's words, "a man of power, of intelligence, as shrewd and cunning and egocentric as Churchill." Costumed like the Elizabethan astrologer John Dee, Gielgud's Prospero exerted his power over a Caliban (played by Denis Quilley) who was made up to be half monster and half noble savage.

The benign magician of the early stage history of the play has given way to something more interesting and complex. In Jonathan Miller's 1970 production at London's Mermaid Theatre the play's colonial themes were explicitly explored. Basing his conception on Dominique O. Mannoni's account of the 1947 revolution in Madagascar, *La Psychologie de la Colonisation* (published in English as *Prospero and Caliban* in 1953), Miller had two black actors, Norman Beaton and Rudolph Walker, play Ariel and Caliban, clarifying the colonial parable that he found in the play. Beaton's Ariel was a noble African who successfully internalized the skills of his master, while Walker's Caliban was a demoralized and degraded slave. Miller's production ended with Ariel eagerly picking up the staff Prospero has discarded and Caliban shaking his fist in fury at the departing ship.

Derek Jarman's innovative film version, released in 1980, also explored the play's concern with subordination and mastery. Set not on an island but in the dilapidated interior of Stoneleigh Abbey in Warwickshire, the film is more gothic romance than Shakespearean romance. Heathcote Williams's Prospero is a shabby nineteenth-century aristocrat; Jack Birkett's Caliban as his butler is alternatively menacing and petulant; Karl Johnson's punk Ariel, with close-cropped hair and a white jumpsuit, is unnervingly bitter and remote, an unwilling technician for his master's experiments. Prospero's magic, which Jarman invokes with cabalistic signs and symbols and Prospero's library of occult literature, becomes a means of political and psychological domination rather than of moral renewal.

Perhaps the most remarkable modern production of *The Tempest* was one that heroically resisted the disillusionment that has characterized so many recent versions even as it recognized the play as a play of failure—the failure of the dream of perfectibility. Performed first in Milan in 1977, revived in 1982, and brought to America for the Olympic Arts Festival in Los Angeles in 1984, Giorgio Strehler's *La Tempesta* (translated into Italian by Agostino Lombardo) represented an extraordinary triumph of theatrical illusion. Prospero's relationship with Ariel was at the center of Strehler's understanding of the play, a resonant metaphor for the relationship of the director and the actor. Until the end, Ariel, a commedia dell'arte Pierrot, was attached to a wire, soaring in the air, sometimes landing nimbly on Prospero's raised finger, yet always unable to escape Prospero's will. When at last he was released, he stumbled on shaky legs, exiting through the audience. Prospero's epilogue became an apology for the limitations of his magic and for the limitations of the theater itself. As he came before the audience, the simple set suddenly disassembled, revealing the bareness and artifice of the theater's illusions. With the audience's applause, the set reformed and Ariel returned to Prospero's side. Strehler's innovative production achieved the theatrical magic that the play demands, offering thereby a profound and moving investigation of the power of theater itself. "In this *Tempest*," Strehler wrote, "we have felt the fallible, desperate, triumphant grandeur and responsibility of our profession." Strehler's *Tempest* fully allowed its audiences to feel the magic of Shakespeare's art.

THE TEMPEST

Names of the Actors

ALONSO, *King of Naples*
SEBASTIAN, *his brother*
PROSPERO, *the right Duke of Milan*
ANTONIO, *his brother, the usurping Duke of Milan*
FERDINAND, *son to the King of Naples*
GONZALO, *an honest old councillor*
ADRIAN *and* FRANCISCO, *lords*
CALIBAN, *a savage and deformed slave*
TRINCULO, *a jester*
STEPHANO, *a drunken butler*
MASTER *of a ship*
BOATSWAIN
MARINERS

MIRANDA, *daughter to Prospero*

ARIEL, *an airy spirit*
IRIS, CERES, JUNO, NYMPHS, REAPERS, [*presented by*] *spirits*

[*Other Spirits attending Prospero*]

SCENE: *An uninhabited island*

1.1 *A tempestuous noise of thunder and lightning heard. Enter a Shipmaster and a Boatswain.*

MASTER Boatswain!
BOATSWAIN Here, Master. What cheer?
MASTER Good, speak to the mariners. Fall to 't yarely, 3
or we run ourselves aground. Bestir, bestir! *Exit.*

Enter Mariners.

BOATSWAIN Heigh, my hearts! Cheerly, cheerly, my 5
hearts! Yare, yare! Take in the topsail. Tend to the Mas- 6
ter's whistle.—Blow till thou burst thy wind, if room 7
enough! 8

Enter Alonso, Sebastian, Antonio, Ferdinand, Gonzalo, and others.

ALONSO Good Boatswain, have care. Where's the Mas-
ter? Play the men. 10
BOATSWAIN I pray now, keep below. 11
ANTONIO Where is the Master, Boatswain?
BOATSWAIN Do you not hear him? You mar our labor.
Keep your cabins! You do assist the storm. 14
GONZALO Nay, good, be patient. 15
BOATSWAIN When the sea is. Hence! What cares these 16
roarers for the name of king? To cabin! Silence! Trou- 17
ble us not.
GONZALO Good, yet remember whom thou hast
aboard.
BOATSWAIN None that I more love than myself. You are
a councillor; if you can command these elements to
silence and work the peace of the present, we will not 23

1.1. Location: On board ship, off the island's coast.
3 Good i.e., it's good you've come; or, my good fellow. **yarely** nimbly
5 Cheerly cheerily **6 Tend** attend **7 Blow** (Addressed to the wind.)
7–8 if room enough as long as we have sea room enough **10 Play the men** act like men (?) ply, urge the men to exert themselves (?) **11 keep** stay **14 Keep** remain in **15 good** good fellow **16 Hence** get away
17 roarers waves or winds, or both; spoken to as though they were "bullies" or "blusterers" **23 work . . . present** bring calm to our present circumstances

hand a rope more. Use your authority. If you cannot, 24
give thanks you have lived so long and make yourself
ready in your cabin for the mischance of the hour, if it 26
so hap.—Cheerly, good hearts!—Out of our way, 27
I say. *Exit.*

GONZALO I have great comfort from this fellow. Methinks he hath no drowning mark upon him; his com- 30
plexion is perfect gallows. Stand fast, good Fate, to his 31
hanging! Make the rope of his destiny our cable, for
our own doth little advantage. If he be not born to be 33
hanged, our case is miserable. *Exeunt.* 34

Enter Boatswain.

BOATSWAIN Down with the topmast! Yare! Lower,
lower! Bring her to try wi' the main course. (*A cry* 36
within.) A plague upon this howling! They are louder
than the weather or our office. 38

Enter Sebastian, Antonio, and Gonzalo.

Yet again? What do you here? Shall we give o'er and 39
drown? Have you a mind to sink?

SEBASTIAN A pox o' your throat, you bawling, blasphemous, incharitable dog!

BOATSWAIN Work you, then.

ANTONIO Hang, cur! Hang, you whoreson, insolent noisemaker! We are less afraid to be drowned than thou art.

GONZALO I'll warrant him for drowning, though the 47
ship were no stronger than a nutshell and as leaky as
an unstanched wench. 49

24 hand handle **26 mischance** misfortune **27 hap** happen **30–31 complexion . . . gallows** appearance shows he was born to be hanged (and therefore, according to the proverb, in no danger of drowning) **33 our . . . advantage** i.e., our own cable is of little benefit **34 case is miserable** circumstances are desperate **36 Bring . . . course** sail her close to the wind by means of the mainsail **38 our office** i.e., the noise we make at our work **39 give o'er** give up **47 warrant him for drowning** guarantee that he will never be drowned **49 unstanched** insatiable, loose, unrestrained

BOATSWAIN Lay her ahold, ahold! Set her two courses. 50
Off to sea again! Lay her off!

Enter Mariners wet.

MARINERS All lost! To prayers, to prayers! All lost!
[*Exeunt Mariners.*]

BOATSWAIN What, must our mouths be cold? 53

GONZALO
The King and Prince at prayers! Let's assist them,
For our case is as theirs.

SEBASTIAN I am out of patience.

ANTONIO
We are merely cheated of our lives by drunkards. 56
This wide-chapped rascal! Would thou mightst lie
drowning 57
The washing of ten tides!

GONZALO He'll be hanged yet, 58
Though every drop of water swear against it
And gape at wid'st to glut him.
(*A confused noise within:*) "Mercy on us!"— 60
"We split, we split!"—"Farewell my wife and
children!"— 61
"Farewell, brother!"—"We split, we split, we split!"
[*Exit Boatswain.*]

ANTONIO Let's all sink wi' the King.

SEBASTIAN Let's take leave of him. *Exit* [*with Antonio*].

GONZALO Now would I give a thousand furlongs of sea
for an acre of barren ground: long heath, brown furze, 66
anything. The wills above be done! But I would fain 67
die a dry death. *Exit.*

✤

50 ahold ahull, close to the wind. **courses** sails, i.e., foresail as well as mainsail, set in an attempt to get the ship back out into open water **53 must . . . cold** i.e., must we drown in the cold sea; or, let us heat up our mouths with liquor **56 merely** utterly **57 wide-chapped** with mouth wide open **57–58 lie . . . tides** (Pirates were hanged on the shore and left until three tides had come in.) **60 at wid'st** wide. **glut** swallow **61 split** break apart **66 heath** heather. **furze** gorse, a weed growing on wasteland **67 fain** rather

1.2 *Enter Prospero* [*in his magic cloak*] *and Miranda.*

MIRANDA
If by your art, my dearest father, you have 1
Put the wild waters in this roar, allay them. 2
The sky, it seems, would pour down stinking pitch, 3
But that the sea, mounting to th' welkin's cheek, 4
Dashes the fire out. O, I have suffered
With those that I saw suffer! A brave vessel, 6
Who had, no doubt, some noble creature in her,
Dashed all to pieces. O, the cry did knock
Against my very heart! Poor souls, they perished.
Had I been any god of power, I would
Have sunk the sea within the earth or ere 11
It should the good ship so have swallowed and
The freighting souls within her.

PROSPERO
Be collected. 13
No more amazement. Tell your piteous heart 14
There's no harm done.

MIRANDA
O, woe the day!

PROSPERO
No harm.
I have done nothing but in care of thee, 16
Of thee, my dear one, thee, my daughter, who
Art ignorant of what thou art, naught knowing
Of whence I am, nor that I am more better 19
Than Prospero, master of a full poor cell, 20
And thy no greater father.

MIRANDA
More to know
Did never meddle with my thoughts.

PROSPERO
'Tis time 22

1.2. Location: The island. Prospero's cell is visible, and on the Elizabethan stage it presumably remains so throughout the play, although in some scenes the convention of flexible distance allows us to imagine characters in other parts of the island.

1 art magic **2 roar** uproar. **allay** pacify **3 pitch** a thick, viscous substance produced by boiling down tar or turpentine **4 welkin's cheek** sky's face **6 brave** gallant, splendid **11 or ere** before
13 freighting forming the cargo. **collected** calm, composed **14 amazement** consternation. **piteous** pitying **16 but** except **19 more better** of higher rank **20 full** very **22 meddle** mingle

I should inform thee farther. Lend thy hand
And pluck my magic garment from me. So,
[*Laying down his magic cloak and staff*]
Lie there, my art.—Wipe thou thine eyes. Have comfort.
The direful spectacle of the wreck, which touched 26
The very virtue of compassion in thee, 27
I have with such provision in mine art 28
So safely ordered that there is no soul—
No, not so much perdition as an hair 30
Betid to any creature in the vessel 31
Which thou heardst cry, which thou sawst sink. Sit
down, 32
For thou must now know farther.

MIRANDA [*Sitting*] You have often
Begun to tell me what I am, but stopped
And left me to a bootless inquisition, 35
Concluding, "Stay, not yet."

PROSPERO The hour's now come;
The very minute bids thee ope thine ear. 37
Obey, and be attentive. Canst thou remember
A time before we came unto this cell?
I do not think thou canst, for then thou wast not
Out three years old.

MIRANDA Certainly, sir, I can. 41

PROSPERO
By what? By any other house or person?
Of anything the image, tell me, that
Hath kept with thy remembrance.

MIRANDA 'Tis far off,
And rather like a dream than an assurance 45
That my remembrance warrants. Had I not 46
Four or five women once that tended me? 47

PROSPERO
Thou hadst, and more, Miranda. But how is it
That this lives in thy mind? What seest thou else

26 wreck shipwreck **27 virtue** essence **28 provision** foresight **30 perdition** loss **31 Betid** happened **32 Which** whom **35 bootless inquisition** profitless inquiry **37 ope** open **41 Out** fully **45–46 assurance . . . warrants** certainty that my memory guarantees **47 tended** attended, waited upon

In the dark backward and abysm of time? 50
If thou rememberest aught ere thou cam'st here, 51
How thou cam'st here thou mayst.

MIRANDA
But that I do not.

PROSPERO
Twelve year since, Miranda, twelve year since,
Thy father was the Duke of Milan and
A prince of power.

MIRANDA
Sir, are not you my father?

PROSPERO
Thy mother was a piece of virtue, and 56
She said thou wast my daughter; and thy father
Was Duke of Milan, and his only heir
And princess no worse issued.

MIRANDA
O the heavens! 59
What foul play had we, that we came from thence?
Or blessèd was 't we did?

PROSPERO
Both, both, my girl.
By foul play, as thou sayst, were we heaved thence,
But blessedly holp hither.

MIRANDA
O, my heart bleeds 63
To think o' the teen that I have turned you to, 64
Which is from my remembrance! Please you, farther. 65

PROSPERO
My brother and thy uncle, called Antonio—
I pray thee, mark me; that a brother should
Be so perfidious!—he whom next thyself 68
Of all the world I loved, and to him put
The manage of my state, as at that time 70
Through all the seigniories it was the first, 71
And Prospero the prime duke, being so reputed 72
In dignity, and for the liberal arts
Without a parallel; those being all my study,
The government I cast upon my brother

50 backward . . . time abyss of the past **51 aught** anything **56 piece** masterpiece, exemplar **59 no worse issued** no less nobly born, descended **63 holp** helped **64 teen . . . to** trouble I've caused you to remember, or put you to **65 from** out of **68 next** next to **70 manage** management, administration **71 seigniories** i.e., city-states of northern Italy **72 prime** of highest rank

And to my state grew stranger, being transported 76
And rapt in secret studies. Thy false uncle—
Dost thou attend me?

MIRANDA Sir, most heedfully.

PROSPERO
Being once perfected how to grant suits, 79
How to deny them, who t' advance and who
To trash for overtopping, new created 81
The creatures that were mine, I say, or changed 'em, 82
Or else new formed 'em; having both the key 83
Of officer and office, set all hearts i' the state
To what tune pleased his ear, that now he was 85
The ivy which had hid my princely trunk
And sucked my verdure out on 't. Thou attend'st not. 87

MIRANDA
O, good sir, I do.

PROSPERO I pray thee, mark me.
I, thus neglecting worldly ends, all dedicated
To closeness and the bettering of my mind 90
With that which, but by being so retired, 91
O'erprized all popular rate, in my false brother 92
Awaked an evil nature; and my trust,
Like a good parent, did beget of him 94
A falsehood in its contrary as great
As my trust was, which had indeed no limit,
A confidence sans bound. He being thus lorded 97
Not only with what my revenue yielded
But what my power might else exact, like one 99

76 to . . . stranger i.e., withdrew from my responsibilities as duke. **transported** carried away **79 perfected** grown skillful **81 trash** check a hound by tying a cord or weight to its neck. **overtopping** running too far ahead of the pack; surmounting, exceeding one's authority **82 creatures** dependents **82–83 or changed . . . formed 'em** i.e., either changed their loyalties and duties or else created new ones **83 key** (1) key for unlocking (2) tool for tuning stringed instruments **85 that** so that **87 verdure** vitality. **on 't** of it **90 closeness** retirement, seclusion **91–92 but . . . rate** simply because it was done in such seclusion, had a value not appreciated by popular opinion **94 good parent** (Alludes to the proverb that good parents often bear bad children; see also l. 120.) **of** in **97 sans** without. **lorded** raised to lordship, with power and wealth **99 else** otherwise, additionally

Who, having into truth by telling of it, 100
Made such a sinner of his memory 101
To credit his own lie, he did believe 102
He was indeed the Duke, out o' the substitution 103
And executing th' outward face of royalty 104
With all prerogative. Hence his ambition growing—
Dost thou hear?

MIRANDA Your tale, sir, would cure deafness.

PROSPERO
To have no screen between this part he played 107
And him he played it for, he needs will be 108
Absolute Milan. Me, poor man, my library 109
Was dukedom large enough. Of temporal royalties 110
He thinks me now incapable; confederates— 111
So dry he was for sway—wi' the King of Naples 112
To give him annual tribute, do him homage, 113
Subject his coronet to his crown, and bend 114
The dukedom yet unbowed—alas, poor Milan!— 115
To most ignoble stooping.

MIRANDA O the heavens!

PROSPERO
Mark his condition and th' event, then tell me 117
If this might be a brother.

MIRANDA I should sin
To think but nobly of my grandmother. 119
Good wombs have borne bad sons.

PROSPERO Now the condition.
This King of Naples, being an enemy
To me inveterate, hearkens my brother's suit, 122

100–102 Who . . . lie i.e., who, by repeatedly telling the lie (that he was indeed Duke of Milan), made his memory such a confirmed sinner against truth that he began to believe his own lie. **into** unto, against. **To** so as to **103 out o'** as a result of **104 And . . . royalty** and (as a result of) his carrying out all the ceremonial functions of royalty **107–108 To have . . . it for** i.e., to have no separation or barrier between his role and himself. (Antonio wanted to act in his own person, not as substitute.) **108 needs** necessarily **109 Absolute Milan** unconditional Duke of Milan **110 temporal royalties** practical prerogatives and responsibilities of a sovereign **111 confederates** conspires, allies himself **112 dry** thirsty. **sway** power **113 him** i.e., the King of Naples **114 his . . . his** Antonio's . . . the King of Naples's. **bend** make bow down **115 yet** hitherto **117 condition** pact. **event** outcome **119 but** other than **122 hearkens** listens to

Which was that he, in lieu o' the premises 123
Of homage and I know not how much tribute,
Should presently extirpate me and mine 125
Out of the dukedom and confer fair Milan,
With all the honors, on my brother. Whereon,
A treacherous army levied, one midnight
Fated to th' purpose did Antonio open
The gates of Milan, and, i' the dead of darkness,
The ministers for the purpose hurried thence 131
Me and thy crying self.

MIRANDA Alack, for pity!
I, not remembering how I cried out then,
Will cry it o'er again. It is a hint 134
That wrings mine eyes to 't.

PROSPERO Hear a little further, 135
And then I'll bring thee to the present business
Which now's upon 's, without the which this story
Were most impertinent.

MIRANDA Wherefore did they not 138
That hour destroy us?

PROSPERO Well demanded, wench. 139
My tale provokes that question. Dear, they durst not,
So dear the love my people bore me, nor set 141
A mark so bloody on the business, but 142
With colors fairer painted their foul ends. 143
In few, they hurried us aboard a bark, 144
Bore us some leagues to sea, where they prepared
A rotten carcass of a butt, not rigged, 146
Nor tackle, sail, nor mast; the very rats 147
Instinctively have quit it. There they hoist us, 148
To cry to th' sea that roared to us, to sigh

123 in . . . premises in return for the stipulation **125 presently extirpate** at once remove **131 ministers . . . purpose** agents employed to do this. **thence** from there **134 hint** occasion **135 wrings** (1) constrains (2) wrings tears from **138 impertinent** irrelevant. **Wherefore** why **139 demanded** asked. **wench** (Here a term of endearment.) **141–142 set . . . bloody** i.e., make obvious their murderous intent. (From the practice of marking with the blood of the prey those who have participated in a successful hunt.) **143 fairer** apparently more attractive **144 few** few words. **bark** ship **146 butt** cask, tub **147 Nor tackle** neither rigging (i.e., the pulleys and ropes designed for hoisting sails) **148 quit** abandoned

To th' winds whose pity, sighing back again,
Did us but loving wrong.

MIRANDA Alack, what trouble 151
Was I then to you!

PROSPERO O, a cherubin 152
Thou wast that did preserve me. Thou didst smile,
Infusèd with a fortitude from heaven,
When I have decked the sea with drops full salt, 155
Under my burden groaned, which raised in me 156
An undergoing stomach, to bear up 157
Against what should ensue.

MIRANDA How came we ashore?

PROSPERO By Providence divine.
Some food we had, and some fresh water, that
A noble Neapolitan, Gonzalo,
Out of his charity, who being then appointed
Master of this design, did give us, with
Rich garments, linens, stuffs, and necessaries, 165
Which since have steaded much. So, of his gentleness, 166
Knowing I loved my books, he furnished me
From mine own library with volumes that
I prize above my dukedom.

MIRANDA Would I might 169
But ever see that man!

PROSPERO Now I arise. 170
[*He puts on his magic cloak.*]
Sit still and hear the last of our sea sorrow. 171
Here in this island we arrived; and here
Have I, thy schoolmaster, made thee more profit 173
Than other princess' can, that have more time 174
For vainer hours and tutors not so careful. 175

MIRANDA
Heavens thank you for 't! And now, I pray you, sir—

151 loving wrong (i.e., the winds pitied Prospero and Miranda though of necessity they blew them from shore) **152 cherubin** angel **155 decked** covered (with salt tears); adorned **156 which** i.e., the smile **157 undergoing stomach** courage to go on **165 stuffs** supplies **166 steaded much** been of much use **169 Would** I wish **170 But ever** i.e., someday **171 sea sorrow** sorrowful adventure at sea **173 more profit** profit more **174 princess'** princesses. (Or the word may be *princes,* referring to royal children both male and female.) **175 vainer** more foolishly spent

For still 'tis beating in my mind—your reason
For raising this sea storm?

PROSPERO Know thus far forth:
By accident most strange, bountiful Fortune,
Now my dear lady, hath mine enemies
Brought to this shore; and by my prescience
I find my zenith doth depend upon 182
A most auspicious star, whose influence 183
If now I court not, but omit, my fortunes 184
Will ever after droop. Here cease more questions.
Thou art inclined to sleep. 'Tis a good dullness, 186
And give it way. I know thou canst not choose. 187
[*Miranda sleeps.*]
Come away, servant, come! I am ready now. 188
Approach, my Ariel, come.

Enter Ariel.

ARIEL
All hail, great master, grave sir, hail! I come
To answer thy best pleasure; be 't to fly,
To swim, to dive into the fire, to ride
On the curled clouds, to thy strong bidding task 193
Ariel and all his quality.

PROSPERO Hast thou, spirit, 194
Performed to point the tempest that I bade thee? 195

ARIEL To every article.
I boarded the King's ship. Now on the beak, 197
Now in the waist, the deck, in every cabin, 198
I flamed amazement. Sometimes I'd divide 199
And burn in many places; on the topmast,
The yards, and bowsprit would I flame distinctly, 201
Then meet and join. Jove's lightning, the precursors
O' the dreadful thunderclaps, more momentary
And sight-outrunning were not. The fire and cracks 204

182 zenith height of fortune. (Astrological term.) **183 influence** astrological power **184 omit** ignore **186 dullness** drowsiness **187 give it way** let it happen (i.e., don't fight it) **188 Come away** come **193 task** make demands upon **194 quality** (1) fellow spirits (2) abilities **195 to point** to the smallest detail **197 beak** prow **198 waist** midships. **deck** poop deck at the stern **199 flamed amazement** struck terror in the guise of fire, i.e., Saint Elmo's fire **201 distinctly** in different places **204 sight-outrunning** swifter than sight

Of sulfurous roaring the most mighty Neptune 205
Seem to besiege and make his bold waves tremble,
Yea, his dread trident shake.

PROSPERO My brave spirit!
Who was so firm, so constant, that this coil 208
Would not infect his reason?

ARIEL Not a soul
But felt a fever of the mad and played 210
Some tricks of desperation. All but mariners
Plunged in the foaming brine and quit the vessel,
Then all afire with me. The King's son, Ferdinand,
With hair up-staring—then like reeds, not hair— 214
Was the first man that leapt; cried, "Hell is empty,
And all the devils are here!"

PROSPERO Why, that's my spirit!
But was not this nigh shore?

ARIEL Close by, my master.

PROSPERO
But are they, Ariel, safe?

ARIEL Not a hair perished.
On their sustaining garments not a blemish, 219
But fresher than before; and, as thou bad'st me, 220
In troops I have dispersed them 'bout the isle. 221
The King's son have I landed by himself,
Whom I left cooling of the air with sighs 223
In an odd angle of the isle, and sitting, 224
His arms in this sad knot. [*He folds his arms.*]

PROSPERO Of the King's ship, 225
The mariners, say how thou hast disposed,
And all the rest o' the fleet.

ARIEL Safely in harbor
Is the King's ship; in the deep nook, where once 228
Thou calledst me up at midnight to fetch dew
From the still-vexed Bermudas, there she's hid; 230

205 Neptune Roman god of the sea **208 coil** tumult **210 of the mad** i.e., such as madmen feel **214 up-staring** standing on end **219 sustaining garments** garments that buoyed them up in the sea **220 bad'st** ordered **221 troops** groups **223 cooling of** cooling **224 angle** corner **225 sad knot** (Folded arms are indicative of melancholy.)
228 nook bay **230 still-vexed Bermudas** ever-stormy Bermudas. (Perhaps refers to the then-recent Bermuda shipwreck; see play Introduction. The Folio text reads "Bermoothes.")

The mariners all under hatches stowed,
Who, with a charm joined to their suffered labor, 232
I have left asleep. And for the rest o' the fleet,
Which I dispersed, they all have met again
And are upon the Mediterranean float 235
Bound sadly home for Naples,
Supposing that they saw the King's ship wrecked
And his great person perish.

PROSPERO
Ariel, thy charge
Exactly is performed. But there's more work.
What is the time o' the day?

ARIEL
Past the mid season. 240

PROSPERO
At least two glasses. The time twixt six and now 241
Must by us both be spent most preciously.

ARIEL
Is there more toil? Since thou dost give me pains, 243
Let me remember thee what thou hast promised, 244
Which is not yet performed me.

PROSPERO
How now? Moody?
What is 't thou canst demand?

ARIEL
My liberty.

PROSPERO
Before the time be out? No more!

ARIEL
I prithee,
Remember I have done thee worthy service,
Told thee no lies, made thee no mistakings, served
Without or grudge or grumblings. Thou did promise
To bate me a full year.

PROSPERO
Dost thou forget 251
From what a torment I did free thee?

ARIEL
No.

PROSPERO
Thou dost, and think'st it much to tread the ooze
Of the salt deep,
To run upon the sharp wind of the north,

232 with . . . labor by means of a spell added to all the labor they have undergone **235 float** sea **240 mid season** noon **241 glasses** i.e., hourglasses **243 pains** labors **244 remember** remind **251 bate** remit, deduct

To do me business in the veins o' the earth 256
When it is baked with frost.

ARIEL I do not, sir. 257

PROSPERO
Thou liest, malignant thing! Hast thou forgot
The foul witch Sycorax, who with age and envy 259
Was grown into a hoop? Hast thou forgot her? 260

ARIEL No, sir.

PROSPERO
Thou hast. Where was she born? Speak. Tell me.

ARIEL
Sir, in Algiers.

PROSPERO O, was she so? I must
Once in a month recount what thou hast been,
Which thou forgett'st. This damned witch Sycorax,
For mischiefs manifold and sorceries terrible
To enter human hearing, from Algiers,
Thou know'st, was banished. For one thing she did 268
They would not take her life. Is not this true?

ARIEL Ay, sir.

PROSPERO
This blue-eyed hag was hither brought with child 271
And here was left by the sailors. Thou, my slave,
As thou report'st thyself, was then her servant;
And, for thou wast a spirit too delicate 274
To act her earthy and abhorred commands,
Refusing her grand hests, she did confine thee, 276
By help of her more potent ministers
And in her most unmitigable rage,
Into a cloven pine, within which rift
Imprisoned thou didst painfully remain
A dozen years; within which space she died
And left thee there, where thou didst vent thy groans
As fast as mill wheels strike. Then was this island— 283

256 do me do for me. **veins** veins of minerals, or underground streams thought to be analogous to the veins of the human body **257 baked** hardened **259 envy** malice **260 grown into a hoop** i.e., so bent over with age as to resemble a hoop **268 one . . . did** (Perhaps a reference to her pregnancy, for which her life would be spared.) **271 blue-eyed** with dark circles under the eyes or with blue eyelids, implying pregnancy. **with child** pregnant **274 for** because **276 hests** commands **283 as mill wheels strike** as the blades of a mill wheel strike the water

Save for the son that she did litter here, 284
A freckled whelp, hag-born—not honored with 285
A human shape.

ARIEL Yes, Caliban her son.

PROSPERO
Dull thing, I say so: he, that Caliban 287
Whom now I keep in service. Thou best know'st
What torment I did find thee in. Thy groans
Did make wolves howl, and penetrate the breasts
Of ever-angry bears. It was a torment
To lay upon the damned, which Sycorax
Could not again undo. It was mine art,
When I arrived and heard thee, that made gape 294
The pine and let thee out.

ARIEL I thank thee, master.

PROSPERO
If thou more murmur'st, I will rend an oak
And peg thee in his knotty entrails till 297
Thou hast howled away twelve winters.

ARIEL Pardon, master.
I will be correspondent to command 299
And do my spriting gently. 300

PROSPERO Do so, and after two days
I will discharge thee.

ARIEL That's my noble master!
What shall I do? Say what? What shall I do?

PROSPERO
Go make thyself like a nymph o' the sea. Be subject
To no sight but thine and mine, invisible
To every eyeball else. Go take this shape
And hither come in 't. Go, hence with diligence!
Exit [*Ariel*].
Awake, dear heart, awake! Thou hast slept well.
Awake!

MIRANDA The strangeness of your story put
Heaviness in me.

PROSPERO Shake it off. Come on, 310

284 Save except. **litter** give birth to **285 whelp** offspring. (Used of animals.) **hag-born** born of a female demon **287 Dull . . . so** i.e., exactly, that's what I said, you dullard **294 gape** open wide **297 his** its **299 correspondent** responsive, submissive **300 spriting** duties as a spirit. **gently** willingly, ungrudgingly **310 Heaviness** drowsiness

We'll visit Caliban, my slave, who never
Yields us kind answer.

MIRANDA 'Tis a villain, sir,
I do not love to look on.

PROSPERO But, as 'tis,
We cannot miss him. He does make our fire, 314
Fetch in our wood, and serves in offices 315
That profit us.—What ho! Slave! Caliban!
Thou earth, thou! Speak.

CALIBAN (*Within*) There's wood enough within.

PROSPERO
Come forth, I say! There's other business for thee.
Come, thou tortoise! When? 319

Enter Ariel like a water nymph.

Fine apparition! My quaint Ariel, 320
Hark in thine ear. [*He whispers.*]

ARIEL My lord, it shall be done. *Exit.*

PROSPERO
Thou poisonous slave, got by the devil himself 322
Upon thy wicked dam, come forth! 323

Enter Caliban.

CALIBAN
As wicked dew as e'er my mother brushed 324
With raven's feather from unwholesome fen 325
Drop on you both! A southwest blow on ye 326
And blister you all o'er!

PROSPERO
For this, be sure, tonight thou shalt have cramps,
Side-stitches that shall pen thy breath up. Urchins 329
Shall forth at vast of night that they may work 330
All exercise on thee. Thou shalt be pinched

314 miss do without **315 offices** functions, duties **319 When** (An exclamation of impatience.) **320 quaint** ingenious **322 got** begotten, sired **323 dam** mother. (Used of animals.) **324 wicked** mischievous, harmful **325 fen** marsh, bog **326 southwest** i.e., wind thought to bring disease **329 Urchins** hedgehogs; here, suggesting goblins in the guise of hedgehogs **330 vast** lengthy, desolate time. (Malignant spirits were thought to be restricted to the hours of darkness.)

As thick as honeycomb, each pinch more stinging 332
Than bees that made 'em.

CALIBAN I must eat my dinner. 333
This island's mine, by Sycorax my mother,
Which thou tak'st from me. When thou cam'st first,
Thou strok'st me and made much of me, wouldst give
me
Water with berries in 't, and teach me how
To name the bigger light, and how the less, 338
That burn by day and night. And then I loved thee
And showed thee all the qualities o' th' isle,
The fresh springs, brine pits, barren place and fertile.
Cursed be I that did so! All the charms 342
Of Sycorax, toads, beetles, bats, light on you!
For I am all the subjects that you have,
Which first was mine own king; and here you sty me 345
In this hard rock, whiles you do keep from me
The rest o' th' island.

PROSPERO Thou most lying slave,
Whom stripes may move, not kindness! I have used thee, 348
Filth as thou art, with humane care, and lodged thee 349
In mine own cell, till thou didst seek to violate
The honor of my child.

CALIBAN
Oho, Oho! Would 't had been done!
Thou didst prevent me; I had peopled else 353
This isle with Calibans.

MIRANDA Abhorrèd slave, 354
Which any print of goodness wilt not take, 355
Being capable of all ill! I pitied thee,
Took pains to make thee speak, taught thee each hour
One thing or other. When thou didst not, savage,
Know thine own meaning, but wouldst gabble like

332 As thick as honeycomb i.e., all over, with as many pinches as a honeycomb has cells **333 'em** i.e., the honeycomb **338 the bigger . . . less** i.e., the sun and the moon. (See Genesis 1:16: "God then made two great lights: the greater light to rule the day, and the less light to rule the night.") **342 charms** spells **345 sty** confine as in a sty **348 stripes** lashes **349 humane** (Not distinguished as a word from *human*.) **353 peopled else** otherwise populated **354–365 Abhorrèd . . . prison** (Sometimes assigned by editors to Prospero.) **355 print** imprint, impression

A thing most brutish, I endowed thy purposes 360
With words that made them known. But thy vile race, 361
Though thou didst learn, had that in 't which good natures
Could not abide to be with; therefore wast thou
Deservedly confined into this rock,
Who hadst deserved more than a prison.

CALIBAN
You taught me language, and my profit on 't
Is I know how to curse. The red plague rid you 367
For learning me your language!

PROSPERO Hagseed, hence! 368
Fetch us in fuel, and be quick, thou'rt best, 369
To answer other business. Shrugg'st thou, malice? 370
If thou neglect'st or dost unwillingly
What I command, I'll rack thee with old cramps, 372
Fill all thy bones with aches, make thee roar 373
That beasts shall tremble at thy din.

CALIBAN No, pray thee.
[*Aside.*] I must obey. His art is of such power
It would control my dam's god, Setebos, 376
And make a vassal of him.

PROSPERO So, slave, hence! 377
Exit Caliban.

Enter Ferdinand; and Ariel, invisible, playing and singing. [*Ferdinand does not see Prospero and Miranda.*]

Ariel's Song.

ARIEL
Come unto these yellow sands,
And then take hands;

360 purposes meanings, desires **361 race** natural disposition; species, nature **367 red plague** plague characterized by red sores and evacuation of blood. **rid** destroy **368 learning** teaching. **Hagseed** offspring of a female demon **369 thou'rt best** you'd be well advised **370 answer other business** perform other tasks **372 old** such as old people suffer; or, plenty of **373 aches** (Pronounced "aitches.") **376 Setebos** (A god of the Patagonians, named in Robert Eden's *History of Travel,* 1577.) **377 s.d. Ariel, invisible** (Ariel wears a garment that by convention indicates he is invisible to the other characters.)

Curtsied when you have, and kissed 380
The wild waves whist, 381
Foot it featly here and there, 382
And, sweet sprites, bear 383
The burden. Hark, hark! 384
Burden, dispersedly [*within*]. Bow-wow. 385
The watchdogs bark.
[*Burden, dispersedly within.*] Bow-wow.
Hark, hark! I hear
The strain of strutting chanticleer
Cry Cock-a-diddle-dow.

FERDINAND
Where should this music be? I' th' air or th' earth?
It sounds no more; and sure it waits upon 392
Some god o' th' island. Sitting on a bank, 393
Weeping again the King my father's wreck,
This music crept by me upon the waters,
Allaying both their fury and my passion 396
With its sweet air. Thence I have followed it, 397
Or it hath drawn me rather. But 'tis gone.
No, it begins again.

Ariel's Song.

ARIEL
Full fathom five thy father lies.
Of his bones are coral made.
Those are pearls that were his eyes.
Nothing of him that doth fade
But doth suffer a sea change
Into something rich and strange.
Sea nymphs hourly ring his knell. 406
Burden [*within*]. Ding dong.
Hark, now I hear them, ding dong bell.

FERDINAND
The ditty does remember my drowned father. 409

380 Curtsied . . . have when you have curtsied **380–381 kissed . . . whist** kissed the waves into silence, or, kissed while the waves are being hushed **382 Foot it featly** dance nimbly **383 sprites** spirits **384 burden** refrain, undersong **385 s.d. dispersedly** i.e., from all directions, not in unison **392 waits upon** serves, attends **393 bank** sandbank **396 passion** grief **397 Thence** i.e., from the bank on which he sat **406 knell** announcement of a death by the tolling of a bell **409 remember** commemorate

This is no mortal business, nor no sound
That the earth owes. I hear it now above me. 411

PROSPERO [*To Miranda*]
The fringèd curtains of thine eye advance 412
And say what thou seest yond.

MIRANDA What is 't? A spirit?
Lord, how it looks about! Believe me, sir,
It carries a brave form. But 'tis a spirit. 415

PROSPERO
No, wench, it eats and sleeps and hath such senses
As we have, such. This gallant which thou seest
Was in the wreck; and, but he's something stained 418
With grief, that's beauty's canker, thou mightst call him 419
A goodly person. He hath lost his fellows
And strays about to find 'em.

MIRANDA I might call him
A thing divine, for nothing natural
I ever saw so noble.

PROSPERO [*Aside*] It goes on, I see, 423
As my soul prompts it.—Spirit, fine spirit, I'll free thee
Within two days for this.

FERDINAND [*Seeing Miranda*] Most sure, the goddess
On whom these airs attend!—Vouchsafe my prayer 426
May know if you remain upon this island, 427
And that you will some good instruction give
How I may bear me here. My prime request, 429
Which I do last pronounce, is—O you wonder!— 430
If you be maid or no?

MIRANDA No wonder, sir, 431
But certainly a maid.

FERDINAND My language? Heavens!
I am the best of them that speak this speech, 433
Were I but where 'tis spoken.

411 owes owns **412 advance** raise **415 brave** excellent **418 but** except that. **something stained** somewhat disfigured **419 canker** canker-worm (feeding on buds and leaves) **423 It goes on** i.e., my plan works **426 airs** songs. **Vouchsafe** grant **427 May know** i.e., that I may know. **remain** dwell **429 bear me** conduct myself. **prime** chief **430 wonder** (Miranda's name means "to be wondered at.") **431 maid or no** i.e., a human maiden as opposed to a goddess or married woman **433 best** i.e., in birth

PROSPERO [*Coming forward*] How? The best?
What wert thou if the King of Naples heard thee?

FERDINAND
A single thing, as I am now, that wonders 436
To hear thee speak of Naples. He does hear me, 437
And that he does I weep. Myself am Naples, 438
Who with mine eyes, never since at ebb, beheld 439
The King my father wrecked.

MIRANDA Alack, for mercy!

FERDINAND
Yes, faith, and all his lords, the Duke of Milan
And his brave son being twain.

PROSPERO [*Aside*] The Duke of Milan 442
And his more braver daughter could control thee, 443
If now 'twere fit to do 't. At the first sight
They have changed eyes.—Delicate Ariel, 445
I'll set thee free for this. [*To Ferdinand*.] A word, good sir.
I fear you have done yourself some wrong. A word! 447

MIRANDA [*Aside*]
Why speaks my father so ungently? This
Is the third man that e'er I saw, the first
That e'er I sighed for. Pity move my father
To be inclined my way!

FERDINAND O, if a virgin,
And your affection not gone forth, I'll make you
The Queen of Naples.

PROSPERO Soft, sir! One word more.
[*Aside*.] They are both in either's powers; but this swift
business 454
I must uneasy make, lest too light winning 455
Make the prize light. [*To Ferdinand*.] One word more: I
charge thee 456

436 single (1) solitary, being at once King of Naples and myself (2) feeble **437, 438 Naples** the King of Naples **437 He does hear me** i.e., the King of Naples does hear my words, for I am King of Naples **438 And . . . weep** i.e., and I weep at this reminder that my father is seemingly dead, leaving me heir **439 at ebb** i.e., dry, not weeping **442 son** (The only reference in the play to a son of Antonio.) **443 more braver** more splendid. **control** refute **445 changed eyes** exchanged amorous glances **447 done . . . wrong** i.e., spoken falsely **454 both in either's** each in the other's **455 uneasy** difficult **455–456 light . . . light** easy . . . cheap

That thou attend me. Thou dost here usurp 457
The name thou ow'st not, and hast put thyself 458
Upon this island as a spy, to win it
From me, the lord on 't.

FERDINAND No, as I am a man. 460

MIRANDA
There's nothing ill can dwell in such a temple.
If the ill spirit have so fair a house,
Good things will strive to dwell with 't.

PROSPERO Follow me.— 463
Speak not you for him; he's a traitor.—Come,
I'll manacle thy neck and feet together.
Seawater shalt thou drink; thy food shall be
The fresh-brook mussels, withered roots, and husks
Wherein the acorn cradled. Follow.

FERDINAND No!
I will resist such entertainment till 469
Mine enemy has more power.

He draws, and is charmed from moving.

MIRANDA O dear father, 470
Make not too rash a trial of him, for 471
He's gentle, and not fearful.

PROSPERO What, I say, 472
My foot my tutor?—Put thy sword up, traitor, 473
Who mak'st a show but dar'st not strike, thy conscience
Is so possessed with guilt. Come from thy ward, 475
For I can here disarm thee with this stick
And make thy weapon drop.

[*He brandishes his staff.*]

MIRANDA [*Trying to hinder him*] Beseech you, father!

PROSPERO
Hence! Hang not on my garments.

MIRANDA Sir, have pity!
I'll be his surety.

PROSPERO Silence! One word more 479

457 attend follow, obey **458 ow'st** ownest **460 on 't** of it **463 strive . . . with 't** i.e., expel the evil and occupy the *temple,* the body
469 entertainment treatment **470 s.d. charmed** magically prevented
471 rash harsh **472 gentle** wellborn. **fearful** frightening, dangerous; or, perhaps, cowardly **473 foot** subordinate. (Miranda, the foot, presumes to instruct Prospero, the head.) **475 ward** defensive posture (in fencing)
479 surety guarantee

Shall make me chide thee, if not hate thee. What,
An advocate for an impostor? Hush!
Thou think'st there is no more such shapes as he,
Having seen but him and Caliban. Foolish wench,
To the most of men this is a Caliban, 484
And they to him are angels.

MIRANDA My affections
Are then most humble; I have no ambition
To see a goodlier man.

PROSPERO [*To Ferdinand*] Come on, obey.
Thy nerves are in their infancy again 488
And have no vigor in them.

FERDINAND So they are.
My spirits, as in a dream, are all bound up. 490
My father's loss, the weakness which I feel,
The wreck of all my friends, nor this man's threats
To whom I am subdued, are but light to me, 493
Might I but through my prison once a day
Behold this maid. All corners else o' th' earth 495
Let liberty make use of; space enough
Have I in such a prison.

PROSPERO [*Aside*] It works. [*To Ferdinand.*] Come on.—
Thou hast done well, fine Ariel! [*To Ferdinand.*] Follow
me.
[*To Ariel.*] Hark what thou else shalt do me.

MIRANDA [*To Ferdinand*] Be of comfort. 499
My father's of a better nature, sir,
Than he appears by speech. This is unwonted 501
Which now came from him.

PROSPERO [*To Ariel*] Thou shalt be as free
As mountain winds; but then exactly do 503
All points of my command.

ARIEL To th' syllable.

PROSPERO [*To Ferdinand*]
Come, follow. [*To Miranda.*] Speak not for him.

Exeunt.

✤

484 To compared to **488 nerves** sinews **490 spirits** vital powers
493 light unimportant **495 corners else** other corners, regions
499 me for me **501 unwonted** unusual **503 then** until then, or, if that is to be so

2.1 *Enter Alonso, Sebastian, Antonio, Gonzalo, Adrian, Francisco, and others.*

GONZALO [*To Alonso*]
Beseech you, sir, be merry. You have cause,
So have we all, of joy, for our escape
Is much beyond our loss. Our hint of woe 3
Is common; every day some sailor's wife,
The masters of some merchant, and the merchant 5
Have just our theme of woe. But for the miracle, 6
I mean our preservation, few in millions
Can speak like us. Then wisely, good sir, weigh
Our sorrow with our comfort.

ALONSO Prithee, peace. 9

SEBASTIAN [*To Antonio*] He receives comfort like cold porridge. 11

ANTONIO [*To Sebastian*] The visitor will not give him 12 o'er so. 13

SEBASTIAN Look, he's winding up the watch of his wit; by and by it will strike.

GONZALO [*To Alonso*] Sir—

SEBASTIAN [*To Antonio*] One. Tell. 17

GONZALO When every grief is entertained 18
That's offered, comes to th' entertainer— 19

SEBASTIAN A dollar. 20

GONZALO Dolor comes to him, indeed. You have spoken truer than you purposed.

SEBASTIAN You have taken it wiselier than I meant you should.

GONZALO [*To Alonso*] Therefore, my lord—

2.1. Location: Another part of the island.
3 much beyond more remarkable than. **hint of** occasion for **5 masters . . . the merchant** officers of some merchant vessel and the merchant himself, the owner (or else the ship itself) **6 just** exactly **9 with** against **11 porridge** (with a pun on *peace* and *peas* or *pease*, a common ingredient of porridge) **12 visitor** one taking nourishment and comfort to the sick, i.e., Gonzalo **12–13 give him o'er** abandon him **17 Tell** keep count **18–19 When . . . entertainer** when every sorrow that presents itself is accepted without resistance, there comes to the recipient **20 dollar** widely circulated coin, the German thaler and the Spanish piece of eight. (Sebastian puns on *entertainer* in the sense of innkeeper; to Gonzalo, *dollar* suggests *dolor,* grief.)

ANTONIO Fie, what a spendthrift is he of his tongue!
ALONSO [*To Gonzalo*] I prithee, spare. 27
GONZALO Well, I have done. But yet—
SEBASTIAN He will be talking.
ANTONIO Which, of he or Adrian, for a good wager, 30
first begins to crow? 31
SEBASTIAN The old cock. 32
ANTONIO The cockerel. 33
SEBASTIAN Done. The wager?
ANTONIO A laughter. 35
SEBASTIAN A match! 36
ADRIAN Though this island seem to be desert— 37
ANTONIO Ha, ha, ha!
SEBASTIAN So, you're paid. 39
ADRIAN Uninhabitable and almost inaccessible—
SEBASTIAN Yet—
ADRIAN Yet—
ANTONIO He could not miss 't. 43
ADRIAN It must needs be of subtle, tender, and delicate 44
temperance. 45
ANTONIO Temperance was a delicate wench. 46
SEBASTIAN Ay, and a subtle, as he most learnedly de- 47
livered. 48

27 spare forbear, cease **30–31 Which . . . crow** which of the two, Gonzalo or Adrian, do you bet will speak (crow) first **32 old cock** i.e., Gonzalo **33 cockerel** i.e., Adrian **35 laughter** (1) burst of laughter (2) sitting of eggs. (When Adrian, the *cockerel,* begins to speak two lines later, Sebastian loses the bet. The Folio speech prefixes in ll. 38–39 are here reversed so that Antonio enjoys his laugh as the prize for winning, as in the proverb "He who laughs last laughs best" or "He laughs that wins." The Folio assignment can work in the theater, however, if Sebastian pays for losing with a sardonic laugh of concession.) **36 A match** a bargain; agreed **37 desert** uninhabited **39 you're paid** i.e., you've had your laugh **43 miss 't** (1) avoid saying "Yet" (2) miss the island **44 must needs be** has to be **45 temperance** mildness of climate **46 Temperance** a girl's name. **delicate** (Here it means "given to pleasure, voluptuous"; in l. 44, "pleasant." Antonio is evidently suggesting that *tender, and delicate temperance* sounds like a Puritan phrase, which Antonio then mocks by applying the words to a woman rather than an island. He began this bawdy comparison with a double entendre on *inaccessible,* l. 40.) **47 subtle** (Here it means "tricky, sexually crafty"; in l. 44, "delicate.") **47–48 delivered** uttered. (Sebastian joins Antonio in baiting the Puritans with his use of the pious cant phrase *learnedly delivered.*)

ADRIAN The air breathes upon us here most sweetly.
SEBASTIAN As if it had lungs, and rotten ones.
ANTONIO Or as 'twere perfumed by a fen.
GONZALO Here is everything advantageous to life.
ANTONIO True, save means to live. 53
SEBASTIAN Of that there's none, or little.
GONZALO How lush and lusty the grass looks! How green! 55
ANTONIO The ground indeed is tawny. 57
SEBASTIAN With an eye of green in 't. 58
ANTONIO He misses not much.
SEBASTIAN No. He doth but mistake the truth totally. 60
GONZALO But the rarity of it is—which is indeed almost beyond credit—
SEBASTIAN As many vouched rarities are. 63
GONZALO That our garments, being, as they were, drenched in the sea, hold notwithstanding their freshness and glosses, being rather new-dyed than stained with salt water.
ANTONIO If but one of his pockets could speak, would it not say he lies? 68
SEBASTIAN Ay, or very falsely pocket up his report. 70
GONZALO Methinks our garments are now as fresh as when we put them on first in Afric, at the marriage of the King's fair daughter Claribel to the King of Tunis.
SEBASTIAN 'Twas a sweet marriage, and we prosper well in our return.
ADRIAN Tunis was never graced before with such a paragon to their queen. 77
GONZALO Not since widow Dido's time. 78
ANTONIO Widow! A pox o' that! How came that "widow" in? Widow Dido!

53 save except **55 lusty** healthy **57 tawny** dull brown, yellowish **58 eye** tinge, or spot (perhaps with reference to Gonzalo's eye or judgment) **60 but** merely **63 vouched** certified **68 pockets** i.e., because they are muddy **70 pocket up** i.e., conceal, suppress; often used in the sense of "receive unprotestingly, fail to respond to a challenge." **his report** (Sebastian's jest is that the evidence of Gonzalo's soggy and sea-stained pockets would confute Gonzalo's speech and his reputation for truth telling.) **77 to** for **78 widow Dido** Queen of Carthage, deserted by Aeneas. (She was in fact a widow when Aeneas, a widower, met her, but Antonio may be amused at Gonzalo's prudish use of the term "widow" to describe a woman deserted by her lover.)

SEBASTIAN What if he had said "widower Aeneas" too?
Good Lord, how you take it! 82

ADRIAN "Widow Dido" said you? You make me study 83
of that. She was of Carthage, not of Tunis. 84

GONZALO This Tunis, sir, was Carthage.

ADRIAN Carthage?

GONZALO I assure you, Carthage.

ANTONIO His word is more than the miraculous harp. 88

SEBASTIAN He hath raised the wall, and houses too.

ANTONIO What impossible matter will he make easy
next?

SEBASTIAN I think he will carry this island home in his
pocket and give it his son for an apple.

ANTONIO And, sowing the kernels of it in the sea, bring 94
forth more islands.

GONZALO Ay. 96

ANTONIO Why, in good time. 97

GONZALO [*To Alonso*] Sir, we were talking that our gar- 98
ments seem now as fresh as when we were at Tunis at
the marriage of your daughter, who is now queen.

ANTONIO And the rarest that e'er came there. 101

SEBASTIAN Bate, I beseech you, widow Dido. 102

ANTONIO O, widow Dido? Ay, widow Dido.

GONZALO Is not, sir, my doublet as fresh as the first day 104
I wore it? I mean, in a sort. 105

ANTONIO That "sort" was well fished for. 106

GONZALO When I wore it at your daughter's marriage.

ALONSO
You cram these words into mine ears against 108
The stomach of my sense. Would I had never 109

82 take understand, respond to, interpret **83–84 study of** think about **88 miraculous harp** (Alludes to Amphion's harp with which he raised the walls of Thebes; Gonzalo has exceeded that deed by creating a modern Carthage—walls *and houses*—mistakenly on the site of Tunis.) **94 kernels** seeds **96 Ay** (Gonzalo may be reasserting his point about Carthage, or he may be responding ironically to Antonio who in turn answers sarcastically.) **97 in good time** (An expression of ironical acquiescence or amazement; i.e., "sure, right away.") **98 talking** saying **101 rarest** most remarkable, beautiful **102 Bate** abate, except, leave out. (Sebastian says, don't forget Dido; or, let's have no more talk of Dido.) **104 doublet** close-fitting jacket **105 in a sort** in a way **106 sort** (Antonio plays on the idea of drawing lots.) **108–109 against . . . sense** i.e., against my will. **stomach** appetite

Married my daughter there! For, coming thence, 110
My son is lost and, in my rate, she too, 111
Who is so far from Italy removed
I ne'er again shall see her. O thou mine heir
Of Naples and of Milan, what strange fish
Hath made his meal on thee?

FRANCISCO Sir, he may live. 115
I saw him beat the surges under him 116
And ride upon their backs. He trod the water,
Whose enmity he flung aside, and breasted
The surge most swoll'n that met him. His bold head
'Bove the contentious waves he kept, and oared
Himself with his good arms in lusty stroke 121
To th' shore, that o'er his wave-worn basis bowed, 122
As stooping to relieve him. I not doubt 123
He came alive to land.

ALONSO No, no, he's gone. 124

SEBASTIAN [*To Alonso*]
Sir, you may thank yourself for this great loss,
That would not bless our Europe with your daughter, 126
But rather loose her to an African, 127
Where she at least is banished from your eye, 128
Who hath cause to wet the grief on 't.

ALONSO Prithee, peace. 129

SEBASTIAN
You were kneeled to and importuned otherwise 130
By all of us, and the fair soul herself 131
Weighed between loathness and obedience at 132
Which end o' the beam should bow. We have lost your son, 133

110 Married given in marriage **111 rate** estimation, opinion **115 made his meal** fed himself **116 surges** waves **121 lusty** vigorous **122 that . . . bowed** i.e., that projected out over the base of the cliff that had been eroded by the surf, thus seeming to bend down toward the sea **123 As** as if. **I not** I do not **124 came . . . land** reached land alive **126 That** you who **127 rather** would rather. **loose** (1) release, let loose (2) lose **128 is banished from your eye** is not constantly before your eye to serve as a reproachful reminder of what you have done **129 Who . . . on 't** i.e., your eye, which has good reason to weep because of this, or, Claribel, who has good reason to weep for it **130 importuned** urged, implored **131–133 the fair . . . bow** i.e., Claribel herself was poised uncertainly between unwillingness to marry and obedience to her father as to which end of the scale should sink, which should prevail

I fear, forever. Milan and Naples have
More widows in them of this business' making 135
Than we bring men to comfort them.
The fault's your own.

ALONSO So is the dear'st o' the loss. 138

GONZALO My lord Sebastian,
The truth you speak doth lack some gentleness
And time to speak it in. You rub the sore 141
When you should bring the plaster.

SEBASTIAN Very well. 142

ANTONIO And most chirurgeonly. 143

GONZALO [*To Alonso*]
It is foul weather in us all, good sir,
When you are cloudy.

SEBASTIAN [*To Antonio*] Fowl weather?

ANTONIO [*To Sebastian*] Very foul. 145

GONZALO
Had I plantation of this isle, my lord— 146

ANTONIO [*To Sebastian*]
He'd sow 't with nettle seed.

SEBASTIAN Or docks, or mallows. 147

GONZALO
And were the king on 't, what would I do?

SEBASTIAN Scape being drunk for want of wine. 149

GONZALO
I' the commonwealth I would by contraries 150
Execute all things; for no kind of traffic 151
Would I admit; no name of magistrate;
Letters should not be known; riches, poverty, 153
And use of service, none; contract, succession, 154

135 of . . . making on account of this marriage **138 dear'st** heaviest, most costly **141 time** appropriate time **142 plaster** (A medical application.) **143 chirurgeonly** like a skilled surgeon. (Antonio mocks Gonzalo's medical analogy of a *plaster* applied curatively to a wound.)
145 Fowl (with a pun on *foul,* returning to the imagery of ll. 30–35)
146 plantation colonization (with subsequent wordplay on the literal meaning) **147 docks, mallows** (Weeds used as antidotes for nettle stings.) **149 Scape** escape. **want** lack. (Sebastian jokes sarcastically that this hypothetical ruler would be saved from dissipation only by the barrenness of the island.) **150 by contraries** by what is directly opposite to usual custom **151 traffic** trade **153 Letters** learning **154 use of service** custom of employing servants. **succession** holding of property by right of inheritance

Bourn, bound of land, tilth, vineyard, none; 155
No use of metal, corn, or wine, or oil; 156
No occupation; all men idle, all,
And women too, but innocent and pure;
No sovereignty—

SEBASTIAN Yet he would be king on 't.

ANTONIO The latter end of his commonwealth forgets the beginning.

GONZALO
All things in common nature should produce
Without sweat or endeavor. Treason, felony,
Sword, pike, knife, gun, or need of any engine 164
Would I not have; but nature should bring forth,
Of its own kind, all foison, all abundance, 166
To feed my innocent people.

SEBASTIAN No marrying 'mong his subjects?

ANTONIO None, man, all idle—whores and knaves.

GONZALO
I would with such perfection govern, sir,
T' excel the Golden Age.

SEBASTIAN Save His Majesty! 171

ANTONIO
Long live Gonzalo!

GONZALO And—do you mark me, sir?

ALONSO
Prithee, no more. Thou dost talk nothing to me.

GONZALO I do well believe Your Highness, and did it to minister occasion to these gentlemen, who are of such 175 sensible and nimble lungs that they always use to 176 laugh at nothing.

ANTONIO 'Twas you we laughed at.

GONZALO Who in this kind of merry fooling am nothing to you; so you may continue, and laugh at nothing still.

ANTONIO What a blow was there given!

SEBASTIAN An it had not fallen flat-long. 182

155 Bourn boundaries. **bound of land** landmarks. **tilth** tillage of soil **156 corn** grain **164 pike** lance. **engine** instrument of warfare **166 foison** plenty **171 the Golden Age** the age, according to Hesiod, when Cronus, or Saturn, ruled the world; an age of innocence and abundance. **Save** God save **175 minister occasion** furnish opportunity **176 sensible** sensitive. **use** are accustomed **182 An** if. **flat-long** with the flat of the sword, i.e., ineffectually. (Cf. "fallen flat.")

GONZALO You are gentlemen of brave mettle; you 183
would lift the moon out of her sphere if she would 184
continue in it five weeks without changing.

Enter Ariel [*invisible*] *playing solemn music.*

SEBASTIAN We would so, and then go a-batfowling. 186
ANTONIO Nay, good my lord, be not angry.
GONZALO No, I warrant you, I will not adventure my 188
discretion so weakly. Will you laugh me asleep? For I 189
am very heavy. 190
ANTONIO Go sleep, and hear us. 191
[*All sleep except Alonso, Sebastian, and Antonio.*]
ALONSO
What, all so soon asleep? I wish mine eyes
Would, with themselves, shut up my thoughts. I find 193
They are inclined to do so.
SEBASTIAN Please you, sir,
Do not omit the heavy offer of it. 195
It seldom visits sorrow; when it doth,
It is a comforter.
ANTONIO We two, my lord,
Will guard your person while you take your rest,
And watch your safety.
ALONSO Thank you. Wondrous heavy.
[*Alonso sleeps. Exit Ariel.*]
SEBASTIAN
What a strange drowsiness possesses them!
ANTONIO
It is the quality o' the climate.
SEBASTIAN Why

183 mettle temperament, courage. (The sense of *metal,* indistinguishable as a form from *mettle,* continues the metaphor of the sword.)
184 sphere orbit. (Literally, one of the concentric zones occupied by planets in the Ptolemaic astronomy.) **186 a-batfowling** hunting birds at night with lantern and *bat* or stick; also, gulling a simpleton. (Gonzalo is the simpleton, or fowl, and Sebastian will use the moon as his lantern.) **188–189 adventure . . . weakly** risk my reputation for discretion for so trivial a cause (by getting angry at these sarcastic fellows)
190 heavy sleepy **191 Go . . . us** let our laughing send you to sleep, or, go to sleep and hear us laugh at you **193 Would . . . thoughts** would shut off my melancholy brooding when they close themselves in sleep **195 omit** neglect. **heavy** drowsy

Doth it not then our eyelids sink? I find not
Myself disposed to sleep.

ANTONIO Nor I. My spirits are nimble.
They fell together all, as by consent; 204
They dropped, as by a thunderstroke. What might,
Worthy Sebastian, O, what might—? No more.
And yet methinks I see it in thy face,
What thou shouldst be. Th' occasion speaks thee, and 208
My strong imagination sees a crown
Dropping upon thy head.

SEBASTIAN What, art thou waking?

ANTONIO
Do you not hear me speak?

SEBASTIAN I do, and surely
It is a sleepy language, and thou speak'st
Out of thy sleep. What is it thou didst say?
This is a strange repose, to be asleep
With eyes wide open—standing, speaking, moving—
And yet so fast asleep.

ANTONIO Noble Sebastian,
Thou lett'st thy fortune sleep—die, rather; wink'st 217
Whiles thou art waking.

SEBASTIAN Thou dost snore distinctly; 218
There's meaning in thy snores.

ANTONIO
I am more serious than my custom. You
Must be so too, if heed me; which to do 221
Trebles thee o'er.

SEBASTIAN Well, I am standing water. 222

ANTONIO
I'll teach you how to flow.

SEBASTIAN Do so. To ebb 223
Hereditary sloth instructs me.

ANTONIO O, 224

204 consent common agreement **208 occasion** opportunity of the moment. **speaks thee** i.e., calls upon you, proclaims you usurper of Alonso's crown **217 wink'st** (you) shut your eyes **218 distinctly** articulately **221 if heed** if you heed **222 Trebles thee o'er** makes you three times as great and rich. **standing water** water that neither ebbs nor flows, at a standstill **223 ebb** recede, decline **224 Hereditary sloth** natural laziness and the position of younger brother, one who cannot inherit

If you but knew how you the purpose cherish 225
Whiles thus you mock it! How, in stripping it, 226
You more invest it! Ebbing men, indeed, 227
Most often do so near the bottom run 228
By their own fear or sloth.

SEBASTIAN Prithee, say on.
The setting of thine eye and cheek proclaim 230
A matter from thee, and a birth indeed 231
Which throes thee much to yield.

ANTONIO Thus, sir: 232
Although this lord of weak remembrance, this 233
Who shall be of as little memory
When he is earthed, hath here almost persuaded— 235
For he's a spirit of persuasion, only 236
Professes to persuade—the King his son's alive, 237
'Tis as impossible that he's undrowned
As he that sleeps here swims.

SEBASTIAN I have no hope
That he's undrowned.

ANTONIO O, out of that "no hope"
What great hope have you! No hope that way is 241
Another way so high a hope that even
Ambition cannot pierce a wink beyond, 243
But doubt discovery there. Will you grant with me 244
That Ferdinand is drowned?

SEBASTIAN He's gone.

225–226 If . . . mock it i.e., if you only knew how much you really enhance the value of ambition even while your words mock your purpose **226–227 How . . . invest it** i.e., how the more you speak flippantly of ambition, the more you in effect affirm it. **invest** clothe. (Antonio's paradox is that by skeptically stripping away illusions Sebastian can see the essence of a situation and the opportunity it presents, or that by disclaiming and deriding his purpose Sebastian shows how he values it.) **228 the bottom** i.e., on which unadventurous men may go aground and miss the tide of fortune **230 setting** set expression (of earnestness) **231 matter** matter of importance **232 throes** causes pain, as in giving birth. **yield** give forth, speak about **233 this lord** i.e., Gonzalo. **remembrance** (1) power of remembering (2) being remembered after his death **235 earthed** buried **236–237 only . . . persuade** i.e., whose whole function (as a privy councillor) is to persuade **241 that way** i.e., in regard to Ferdinand's being saved **243–244 Ambition . . . there** ambition itself cannot see any further than that hope (of the crown), but is unsure of itself in seeing even so far, is dazzled by daring to think so high. **wink** glimpse

ANTONIO Then tell me,
Who's the next heir of Naples?
SEBASTIAN Claribel.
ANTONIO
She that is Queen of Tunis; she that dwells
Ten leagues beyond man's life; she that from Naples 248
Can have no note, unless the sun were post— 249
The man i' the moon's too slow—till newborn chins
Be rough and razorable; she that from whom 251
We all were sea-swallowed, though some cast again, 252
And by that destiny to perform an act
Whereof what's past is prologue, what to come
In yours and my discharge. 255
SEBASTIAN What stuff is this? How say you?
'Tis true my brother's daughter's Queen of Tunis,
So is she heir of Naples, twixt which regions
There is some space.
ANTONIO A space whose every cubit 259
Seems to cry out, "How shall that Claribel
Measure us back to Naples? Keep in Tunis, 261
And let Sebastian wake." Say this were death 262
That now hath seized them, why, they were no worse
Than now they are. There be that can rule Naples 264
As well as he that sleeps, lords that can prate 265
As amply and unnecessarily
As this Gonzalo. I myself could make 267
A chough of as deep chat. O, that you bore 268
The mind that I do! What a sleep were this
For your advancement! Do you understand me?
SEBASTIAN
Methinks I do.
ANTONIO And how does your content 271

248 Ten . . . life i.e., it would take more than a lifetime to get there **249 note** news, intimation. **post** messenger **251 razorable** ready for shaving. **from** on our voyage from **252 cast** were disgorged (with a pun on *casting* of parts for a play) **255 discharge** performance
259 cubit ancient measure of length of about twenty inches
261 Measure us i.e., traverse the cubits, find her way. **Keep** stay. (Addressed to Claribel.) **262 wake** i.e., to his good fortune **264 There be** there are those **265 prate** speak foolishly **267–268 I . . . chat** I could teach a jackdaw to talk as wisely, or, be such a garrulous talker myself **271 content** desire, inclination

Tender your own good fortune?

SEBASTIAN I remember 272
You did supplant your brother Prospero.

ANTONIO True.
And look how well my garments sit upon me,
Much feater than before. My brother's servants 275
Were then my fellows. Now they are my men.

SEBASTIAN But, for your conscience?

ANTONIO
Ay, sir, where lies that? If 'twere a kibe, 278
'Twould put me to my slipper; but I feel not 279
This deity in my bosom. Twenty consciences
That stand twixt me and Milan, candied be they 281
And melt ere they molest! Here lies your brother, 282
No better than the earth he lies upon,
If he were that which now he's like—that's dead,
Whom I, with this obedient steel, three inches of it,
Can lay to bed forever; whiles you, doing thus, 286
To the perpetual wink for aye might put 287
This ancient morsel, this Sir Prudence, who
Should not upbraid our course. For all the rest, 289
They'll take suggestion as a cat laps milk; 290
They'll tell the clock to any business that 291
We say befits the hour.

SEBASTIAN Thy case, dear friend,
Shall be my precedent. As thou gott'st Milan,
I'll come by Naples. Draw thy sword. One stroke
Shall free thee from the tribute which thou payest, 295
And I the king shall love thee.

ANTONIO Draw together;
And when I rear my hand, do you the like
To fall it on Gonzalo. [*They draw.*]

SEBASTIAN O, but one word. 298
[*They talk apart.*]

272 Tender regard, look after **275 feater** more becomingly, fittingly **278 kibe** chilblain, here a sore on the heel **279 put me to** oblige me to wear **281 Milan** the dukedom of Milan. **candied** frozen, congealed in crystalline form. **be they** may they be **282 molest** interfere **286 thus** (The actor makes a stabbing gesture.) **287 wink** sleep, closing of eyes. **aye** ever **289 Should not** would not then be able to **290 take suggestion** respond to prompting **291 tell the clock** i.e., agree, answer appropriately, chime **295 tribute** (See 1.2.113–124.) **298 fall it** let it fall

Enter Ariel [*invisible*], *with music and song.*

ARIEL
My master through his art foresees the danger
That you, his friend, are in, and sends me forth—
For else his project dies—to keep them living.
Sings in Gonzalo's ear.

While you here do snoring lie,
Open-eyed conspiracy
His time doth take. 304
If of life you keep a care,
Shake off slumber, and beware.
Awake, awake!

ANTONIO Then let us both be sudden. 308
GONZALO [*Waking*] Now, good angels preserve the King!
[*The others wake.*]
ALONSO
Why, how now, ho, awake? Why are you drawn?
Wherefore this ghastly looking?
GONZALO What's the matter?
SEBASTIAN
Whiles we stood here securing your repose, 312
Even now, we heard a hollow burst of bellowing
Like bulls, or rather lions. Did 't not wake you?
It struck mine ear most terribly.
ALONSO I heard nothing.
ANTONIO
O, 'twas a din to fright a monster's ear,
To make an earthquake! Sure it was the roar
Of a whole herd of lions.
ALONSO Heard you this, Gonzalo?
GONZALO
Upon mine honor, sir, I heard a humming,
And that a strange one too, which did awake me.
I shaked you, sir, and cried. As mine eyes opened, 322
I saw their weapons drawn. There was a noise,
That's verily. 'Tis best we stand upon our guard, 324
Or that we quit this place. Let's draw our weapons.

304 time opportunity **308 sudden** quick **312 securing** standing guard over **322 cried** called out **324 verily** true

ALONSO
Lead off this ground, and let's make further search
For my poor son.

GONZALO Heavens keep him from these beasts!
For he is, sure, i' th' island.

ALONSO Lead away.

ARIEL [*Aside*]
Prospero my lord shall know what I have done.
So, King, go safely on to seek thy son.
Exeunt [*separately*].

✤

2.2

Enter Caliban with a burden of wood. A noise of thunder heard.

CALIBAN
All the infections that the sun sucks up
From bogs, fens, flats, on Prosper fall, and make him 2
By inchmeal a disease! His spirits hear me, 3
And yet I needs must curse. But they'll nor pinch, 4
Fright me with urchin shows, pitch me i' the mire, 5
Nor lead me, like a firebrand, in the dark 6
Out of my way, unless he bid 'em. But
For every trifle are they set upon me,
Sometimes like apes, that mow and chatter at me 9
And after bite me; then like hedgehogs, which
Lie tumbling in my barefoot way and mount
Their pricks at my footfall. Sometimes am I
All wound with adders, who with cloven tongues 13
Do hiss me into madness.

Enter Trinculo.

Lo, now, lo!
Here comes a spirit of his, and to torment me
For bringing wood in slowly. I'll fall flat.
Perchance he will not mind me. [*He lies down.*] 17

2.2. Location: Another part of the island.
2 flats swamps **3 By inchmeal** inch by inch **4 needs must** have to. **nor** neither **5 urchin shows** elvish apparitions shaped like hedgehogs **6 like a firebrand** in the guise of a will-o'-the-wisp **9 mow** make faces **13 wound with** entwined by **17 mind** notice

TRINCULO Here's neither bush nor shrub to bear off 18
any weather at all. And another storm brewing; I hear
it sing i' the wind. Yond same black cloud, yond huge
one, looks like a foul bombard that would shed his 21
liquor. If it should thunder as it did before, I know not
where to hide my head. Yond same cloud cannot
choose but fall by pailfuls. [*Seeing Caliban.*] What have
we here, a man or a fish? Dead or alive? A fish, he
smells like a fish; a very ancient and fishlike smell; a
kind of not-of-the-newest Poor John. A strange fish! 27
Were I in England now, as once I was, and had but
this fish painted, not a holiday fool there but would 29
give a piece of silver. There would this monster make 30
a man. Any strange beast there makes a man. When 31
they will not give a doit to relieve a lame beggar, they 32
will lay out ten to see a dead Indian. Legged like a
man, and his fins like arms! Warm, o' my troth! I do 34
now let loose my opinion, hold it no longer: this is no 35
fish, but an islander, that hath lately suffered by a 36
thunderbolt. [*Thunder.*] Alas, the storm is come again!
My best way is to creep under his gaberdine. There is 38
no other shelter hereabout. Misery acquaints a man
with strange bedfellows. I will here shroud till the 40
dregs of the storm be past. 41

[*He creeps under Caliban's garment.*]

Enter Stephano, singing, [*a bottle in his hand*].

STEPHANO

"I shall no more to sea, to sea,
Here shall I die ashore—"

This is a very scurvy tune to sing at a man's funeral.
Well, here's my comfort. *Drinks.*

18 bear off keep off **21 foul bombard** dirty leather jug. **his** its
27 Poor John salted fish, type of poor fare **29 painted** i.e., painted on a sign set up outside a booth or tent at a fair **30–31 make a man** (1) make one's fortune (2) be indistinguishable from an Englishman
32 doit small coin **34 o' my troth** by my faith **35 hold it** hold it in
36 suffered i.e., died **38 gaberdine** cloak, loose upper garment
40 shroud take shelter **41 dregs** i.e., last remains (as in a *bombard* or jug, l. 21)

(*Sings.*)
"The master, the swabber, the boatswain, and I, 46
The gunner and his mate,
Loved Mall, Meg, and Marian, and Margery,
But none of us cared for Kate.
For she had a tongue with a tang, 50
Would cry to a sailor, 'Go hang!'
She loved not the savor of tar nor of pitch,
Yet a tailor might scratch her where'er she did itch. 53
Then to sea, boys, and let her go hang!"

This is a scurvy tune too. But here's my comfort.
Drinks.

CALIBAN Do not torment me! O! 56

STEPHANO What's the matter? Have we devils here? Do 57 you put tricks upon 's with savages and men of Ind, 58 ha? I have not scaped drowning to be afeard now of your four legs. For it hath been said, "As proper a man 60 as ever went on four legs cannot make him give 61 ground"; and it shall be said so again while Stephano breathes at' nostrils. 63

CALIBAN This spirit torments me! O!

STEPHANO This is some monster of the isle with four legs, who hath got, as I take it, an ague. Where the 66 devil should he learn our language? I will give him 67 some relief, if it be but for that. If I can recover him 68 and keep him tame and get to Naples with him, he's a present for any emperor that ever trod on neat's 70 leather. 71

CALIBAN Do not torment me, prithee. I'll bring my wood home faster.

46 swabber crew member whose job is to wash the decks **50 tang** sting **53 tailor . . . itch** (A dig at tailors for their supposed effeminacy and a bawdy suggestion of satisfying a sexual craving.) **56 Do . . . me** (Caliban assumes that one of Prospero's spirits has come to punish him.) **57 What's the matter** what's going on here **58 put tricks upon 's** trick us with conjuring shows. **Ind** India **60 proper** handsome **61 four legs** (The conventional phrase would supply *two legs.*) **63 at'** at the **66 ague** fever. (Probably both Caliban and Trinculo are quaking; see ll. 56 and 81.) **67 should he learn** could he have learned **68 for that** i.e., for knowing our language. **recover** restore **70–71 neat's leather** cowhide

STEPHANO He's in his fit now and does not talk after 74
the wisest. He shall taste of my bottle. If he have never 75
drunk wine afore, it will go near to remove his fit. If I 76
can recover him and keep him tame, I will not take too 77
much for him. He shall pay for him that hath him, and 78
that soundly.

CALIBAN Thou does me yet but little hurt; thou wilt
anon, I know it by thy trembling. Now Prosper works 81
upon thee.

STEPHANO Come on your ways. Open your mouth. Here
is that which will give language to you, cat. Open your 84
mouth. This will shake your shaking, I can tell you, 85
and that soundly. [*Giving Caliban a drink.*] You cannot
tell who's your friend. Open your chaps again. 87

TRINCULO I should know that voice. It should be—but
he is drowned, and these are devils. O, defend me!

STEPHANO Four legs and two voices—a most delicate 90
monster! His forward voice now is to speak well of his
friend; his backward voice is to utter foul speeches and 92
to detract. If all the wine in my bottle will recover him, 93
I will help his ague. Come. [*Giving a drink.*] Amen! I 94
will pour some in thy other mouth.

TRINCULO Stephano!

STEPHANO Doth thy other mouth call me? Mercy, 97
mercy! This is a devil, and no monster. I will leave
him. I have no long spoon. 99

TRINCULO Stephano! If thou beest Stephano, touch me
and speak to me, for I am Trinculo—be not afeard—
thy good friend Trinculo.

STEPHANO If thou beest Trinculo, come forth. I'll pull

74–75 after the wisest in the wisest fashion **76 afore** before. **go near to** nearly **77 recover** restore **77–78 I will . . . much** i.e., no sum can be too much **78 He shall . . . hath him** i.e., anyone who wants him will have to pay dearly for him. **hath** possesses, receives **81 anon** presently **84–85 cat . . . mouth** (Allusion to the proverb "Good liquor will make a cat speak.") **87 chaps** jaws **90 delicate** ingenious **92 backward voice** (Trinculo and Caliban are facing in opposite directions. Stephano supposes the monster to have a rear end that can emit *foul speeches* or foul-smelling wind at the monster's *other mouth,* l. 95.) **93 If . . . him** even if it takes all the wine in my bottle to cure him **94 help** cure **97 call me** i.e., call me by name, know supernaturally who I am **99 long spoon** (Allusion to the proverb "He that sups with the devil has need of a long spoon.")

thee by the lesser legs. If any be Trinculo's legs, these are they. [*Pulling him out*.] Thou art very Trinculo indeed! How cam'st thou to be the siege of this mooncalf? Can he vent Trinculos? 106 107

TRINCULO I took him to be killed with a thunderstroke. But art thou not drowned, Stephano? I hope now thou art not drowned. Is the storm overblown? I hid me under the dead mooncalf's gaberdine for fear of the storm. And art thou living, Stephano? O Stephano, two Neapolitans scaped! [*He capers with Stephano*.] 110

STEPHANO Prithee, do not turn me about. My stomach is not constant. 115

CALIBAN
These be fine things, an if they be not spirits. 116
That's a brave god, and bears celestial liquor. 117
I will kneel to him.

STEPHANO How didst thou scape? How cam'st thou hither? Swear by this bottle how thou cam'st hither. I escaped upon a butt of sack which the sailors heaved o'erboard—by this bottle, which I made of the bark of a tree with mine own hands since I was cast ashore. 121 122 123

CALIBAN [*Kneeling*] I'll swear upon that bottle to be thy true subject, for the liquor is not earthly.

STEPHANO Here. Swear then how thou escapedst.

TRINCULO Swum ashore, man, like a duck. I can swim like a duck, I'll be sworn.

STEPHANO Here, kiss the book. Though thou canst swim like a duck, thou art made like a goose. 129
[*Giving him a drink*.]

TRINCULO O Stephano, hast any more of this?

STEPHANO The whole butt, man. My cellar is in a rock by the seaside, where my wine is hid.—How now, mooncalf? How does thine ague?

CALIBAN Hast thou not dropped from heaven?

106 siege excrement **106–107 mooncalf** monstrous or misshapen creature (whose deformity is caused by the malignant influence of the moon) **107 vent** excrete, defecate **110 overblown** blown over **115 not constant** unsteady **116 an if** if **117 brave** fine, magnificent. **bears** he carries **121 butt of sack** barrel of Canary wine **122 by this bottle** i.e., I swear by this bottle **123 since** after **129 book** i.e., bottle (but with ironic reference to the practice of kissing the Bible in swearing an oath; see *I'll be sworn* in l. 128)

STEPHANO Out o' the moon, I do assure thee. I was the man i' the moon when time was. 137

CALIBAN
I have seen thee in her, and I do adore thee.
My mistress showed me thee, and thy dog, and thy bush 139

STEPHANO Come, swear to that. Kiss the book. I will furnish it anon with new contents. Swear.
[*Giving him a drink.*]

TRINCULO By this good light, this is a very shallow 142 monster! I afeard of him? A very weak monster! The man i' the moon? A most poor credulous monster! Well 144 drawn, monster, in good sooth! 145

CALIBAN [*To Stephano*]
I'll show thee every fertile inch o' th' island,
And I will kiss thy foot. I prithee, be my god.

TRINCULO By this light, a most perfidious and drunken monster! When 's god's asleep, he'll rob his bottle. 149

CALIBAN
I'll kiss thy foot. I'll swear myself thy subject.

STEPHANO Come on then. Down, and swear.
[*Caliban kneels.*]

TRINCULO I shall laugh myself to death at this puppy-headed monster. A most scurvy monster! I could find in my heart to beat him—

STEPHANO Come, kiss.

TRINCULO But that the poor monster's in drink. An 156 abominable monster!

CALIBAN
I'll show thee the best springs. I'll pluck thee berries.
I'll fish for thee and get thee wood enough.
A plague upon the tyrant that I serve!
I'll bear him no more sticks, but follow thee,
Thou wondrous man.

TRINCULO A most ridiculous monster, to make a wonder of a poor drunkard!

137 when time was once upon a time **139 dog . . . bush** (The man in the moon was popularly imagined to have with him a dog and a bush of thorn.) **142 By . . . light** by God's light, by this good light from heaven **144–145 Well drawn** well pulled (on the bottle) **145 in good sooth** truly, indeed **149 When . . . bottle** i.e., Caliban wouldn't even stop at robbing his god of his bottle if he could catch him asleep **156 in drink** drunk

CALIBAN
I prithee, let me bring thee where crabs grow; 165
And I with my long nails will dig thee pignuts, 166
Show thee a jay's nest, and instruct thee how
To snare the nimble marmoset. I'll bring thee 168
To clustering filberts, and sometimes I'll get thee
Young scamels from the rock. Wilt thou go with me? 170

STEPHANO I prithee now, lead the way without any more talking.—Trinculo, the King and all our company else being drowned, we will inherit here.—Here, bear 173 my bottle.—Fellow Trinculo, we'll fill him by and by again.

CALIBAN (*Sings drunkenly*)
Farewell, master, farewell, farewell!

TRINCULO A howling monster; a drunken monster!

CALIBAN
No more dams I'll make for fish,
Nor fetch in firing 179
At requiring,
Nor scrape trenchering, nor wash dish. 181
'Ban, 'Ban, Ca–Caliban
Has a new master. Get a new man! 183
Freedom, high-day! High-day, freedom! Freedom, 184 high-day, freedom!

STEPHANO O brave monster! Lead the way. *Exeunt.*

✤

165 crabs crab apples, or perhaps crabs **166 pignuts** earthnuts, edible tuberous roots **168 marmoset** small monkey **170 scamels** (Possibly *seamews,* mentioned in Strachey's letter, or shellfish; or perhaps from *squamelle,* furnished with little scales. Contemporary French and Italian travel accounts report that the natives of Patagonia in South America ate small fish described as *fort scameux* and *squame.*)
173 else in addition, besides ourselves. **inherit** take possession
179 firing firewood **181 trenchering** trenchers, wooden plates **183 Get a new man** (Addressed to Prospero.) **184 high-day** holiday

3.1 *Enter Ferdinand, bearing a log.*

FERDINAND
There be some sports are painful, and their labor 1
Delight in them sets off. Some kinds of baseness 2
Are nobly undergone, and most poor matters 3
Point to rich ends. This my mean task 4
Would be as heavy to me as odious, but 5
The mistress which I serve quickens what's dead 6
And makes my labors pleasures. O, she is
Ten times more gentle than her father's crabbèd,
And he's composed of harshness. I must remove
Some thousands of these logs and pile them up,
Upon a sore injunction. My sweet mistress 11
Weeps when she sees me work and says such baseness
Had never like executor. I forget; 13
But these sweet thoughts do even refresh my labors,
Most busy lest when I do it.

Enter Miranda; and Prospero [at a distance, unseen].

MIRANDA Alas now, pray you, 15
Work not so hard. I would the lightning had
Burnt up those logs that you are enjoined to pile! 17
Pray, set it down and rest you. When this burns, 18
'Twill weep for having wearied you. My father 19
Is hard at study. Pray now, rest yourself.
He's safe for these three hours.
FERDINAND O most dear mistress, 21

3.1. Location: Before Prospero's cell.
1 sports pastimes, activities. **painful** laborious **1–2 and their . . . sets off** i.e., but the pleasure we get from those pastimes compensates for the effort **2 baseness** menial activity **3 undergone** undertaken. **most poor** poorest **4 mean** lowly **5 but** were it not that **6 quickens** gives life to **11 sore injunction** severe command **13 Had . . . executor** i.e., was never before undertaken by one of my noble rank. **I forget** i.e., I forget that I'm supposed to be working, or, I forget my happiness, oppressed by my labor **15 Most . . . it** i.e., least troubled by my labor, and most active in my thoughts, when I think of her (?) (The line may be in need of emendation.) **17 enjoined** commanded **18 this** i.e., the log **19 weep** i.e., exude resin **21 these** i.e., the next

The sun will set before I shall discharge 22
What I must strive to do.

MIRANDA If you'll sit down,
I'll bear your logs the while. Pray, give me that.
I'll carry it to the pile.

FERDINAND No, precious creature,
I had rather crack my sinews, break my back,
Than you should such dishonor undergo
While I sit lazy by.

MIRANDA It would become me
As well as it does you; and I should do it
With much more ease, for my good will is to it,
And yours it is against.

PROSPERO [*Aside*] Poor worm, thou art infected!
This visitation shows it.

MIRANDA You look wearily. 32

FERDINAND
No, noble mistress, 'tis fresh morning with me
When you are by at night. I do beseech you— 34
Chiefly that I might set it in my prayers—
What is your name?

MIRANDA Miranda.—O my father,
I have broke your hest to say so.

FERDINAND Admired Miranda! 37
Indeed the top of admiration, worth
What's dearest to the world! Full many a lady 39
I have eyed with best regard, and many a time 40
The harmony of their tongues hath into bondage
Brought my too diligent ear. For several virtues 42
Have I liked several women, never any
With so full soul but some defect in her
Did quarrel with the noblest grace she owed 45
And put it to the foil. But you, O you, 46

22 discharge complete **32 visitation** (1) visit of the sick (2) visitation of the plague, i.e., infection of love **34 by** nearby **37 hest** command. **Admired Miranda** (Her name means "to be admired or wondered at.") **39 dearest** most treasured **40 best regard** thoughtful and approving attention **42 diligent** attentive. **several** various (also in l. 43) **45 owed** owned **46 put . . . foil** (1) overthrew it (as in wrestling) (2) served as a *foil,* or contrast, to set it off

So perfect and so peerless, are created
Of every creature's best!

MIRANDA I do not know 48
One of my sex; no woman's face remember,
Save, from my glass, mine own. Nor have I seen
More that I may call men than you, good friend,
And my dear father. How features are abroad 52
I am skilless of; but, by my modesty, 53
The jewel in my dower, I would not wish
Any companion in the world but you;
Nor can imagination form a shape,
Besides yourself, to like of. But I prattle 57
Something too wildly, and my father's precepts 58
I therein do forget.

FERDINAND I am in my condition 59
A prince, Miranda; I do think, a king—
I would, not so!—and would no more endure 61
This wooden slavery than to suffer 62
The flesh-fly blow my mouth. Hear my soul speak: 63
The very instant that I saw you did
My heart fly to your service, there resides
To make me slave to it, and for your sake
Am I this patient log-man.

MIRANDA Do you love me?

FERDINAND
O heaven, O earth, bear witness to this sound,
And crown what I profess with kind event 69
If I speak true! If hollowly, invert 70
What best is boded me to mischief! I 71
Beyond all limit of what else i' the world 72
Do love, prize, honor you.

MIRANDA [*Weeping*] I am a fool
To weep at what I am glad of.

48 Of out of **52 How . . . abroad** what people look like other places **53 skilless** ignorant. **modesty** virginity **57 like of** be pleased with, be fond of **58 Something** somewhat **59 condition** rank **61 would** wish (it were) **62 wooden slavery** being compelled to carry wood **63 flesh-fly** insect that deposits its eggs in dead flesh. **blow** befoul with fly eggs **69 kind event** favorable outcome **70 hollowly** insincerely, falsely. **invert** turn **71 boded** destined for. **mischief** evil **72 what** whatever

PROSPERO [*Aside*] Fair encounter
Of two most rare affections! Heavens rain grace
On that which breeds between 'em!
FERDINAND Wherefore weep you?
MIRANDA
At mine unworthiness, that dare not offer
What I desire to give, and much less take
What I shall die to want. But this is trifling, 79
And all the more it seeks to hide itself
The bigger bulk it shows. Hence, bashful cunning, 81
And prompt me, plain and holy innocence!
I am your wife, if you will marry me;
If not, I'll die your maid. To be your fellow 84
You may deny me, but I'll be your servant
Whether you will or no.
FERDINAND My mistress, dearest, 86
And I thus humble ever.
MIRANDA My husband, then?
FERDINAND Ay, with a heart as willing 89
As bondage e'er of freedom. Here's my hand.
MIRANDA [*Clasping his hand*]
And mine, with my heart in 't. And now farewell
Till half an hour hence.
FERDINAND A thousand thousand! 92
Exeunt [*Ferdinand and Miranda, separately*].
PROSPERO
So glad of this as they I cannot be,
Who are surprised with all; but my rejoicing 94
At nothing can be more. I'll to my book,
For yet ere suppertime must I perform
Much business appertaining. *Exit.* 97

✣

79 die (probably with an unconscious sexual meaning that underlies all of ll. 77–81). **want** lack **81 bashful cunning** coyness **84 maid** handmaiden, servant. **fellow** mate, equal **86 will** desire it. **My mistress** i.e., the woman I adore and serve (not an illicit sexual partner) **89 willing** desirous **92 A thousand thousand** i.e., a thousand thousand farewells **94 with all** by everything that has happened; or *withal,* with it **97 appertaining** related to this

3.2 *Enter Caliban, Stephano, and Trinculo.*

STEPHANO Tell not me. When the butt is out, we will 1
drink water, not a drop before. Therefore bear up and 2
board 'em. Servant monster, drink to me. 3

TRINCULO Servant monster? The folly of this island! 4
They say there's but five upon this isle. We are three
of them; if th' other two be brained like us, the state 6
totters.

STEPHANO Drink, servant monster, when I bid thee.
Thy eyes are almost set in thy head. [*Giving a drink.*] 9

TRINCULO Where should they be set else? He were a 10
brave monster indeed if they were set in his tail. 11

STEPHANO My man-monster hath drowned his tongue
in sack. For my part, the sea cannot drown me. I
swam, ere I could recover the shore, five and thirty 14
leagues off and on. By this light, thou shalt be my lieu- 15
tenant, monster, or my standard. 16

TRINCULO Your lieutenant, if you list. He's no standard. 17

STEPHANO We'll not run, Monsieur Monster. 18

TRINCULO Nor go neither, but you'll lie like dogs and 19
yet say nothing neither.

STEPHANO Mooncalf, speak once in thy life, if thou
beest a good mooncalf.

CALIBAN
How does thy honor? Let me lick thy shoe.
I'll not serve him. He is not valiant.

TRINCULO Thou liest, most ignorant monster, I am in 25
case to jostle a constable. Why, thou debauched fish, 26

3.2. Location: Another part of the island.
1 out empty **2–3 bear . . . 'em** (Stephano uses the terminology of maneuvering at sea and boarding a vessel under attack as a way of urging an assault on the liquor supply.) **4 folly of** i.e., stupidity found on **6 be brained** are endowed with intelligence **9 set** fixed in a drunken stare; or sunk, like the sun **10 set** placed **11 brave** fine, splendid **14 recover** gain, reach **15 leagues** units of distance each equaling about three miles. **off and on** intermittently. **By this light** (An oath: by the light of the sun.) **16 standard** standard-bearer, ensign (as distinguished from *lieutenant,* ll. 15–17) **17 list** prefer. **no standard** i.e., not able to stand up **18 run** (1) retreat (2) urinate (taking Trinculo's *standard,* l. 17, in the old sense of "conduit") **19 go** walk. **lie** (1) tell lies (2) lie prostrate (3) excrete **25–26 in case . . . constable** i.e., in fit condition, made valiant by drink, to taunt or challenge the police

thou, was there ever man a coward that hath drunk so much sack as I today? Wilt thou tell a monstrous lie, 28 being but half a fish and half a monster?

CALIBAN
Lo, how he mocks me! Wilt thou let him, my lord?

TRINCULO "Lord," quoth he? That a monster should be such a natural! 32

CALIBAN
Lo, lo, again! Bite him to death, I prithee.

STEPHANO Trinculo, keep a good tongue in your head. If you prove a mutineer—the next tree! The poor 35 monster's my subject, and he shall not suffer indignity.

CALIBAN
I thank my noble lord. Wilt thou be pleased
To hearken once again to the suit I made to thee?

STEPHANO Marry, will I. Kneel and repeat it. I will 39 stand, and so shall Trinculo. [*Caliban kneels.*] 40

Enter Ariel, invisible.

CALIBAN
As I told thee before, I am subject to a tyrant,
A sorcerer, that by his cunning hath
Cheated me of the island.

ARIEL [*Mimicking Trinculo*]
Thou liest.

CALIBAN Thou liest, thou jesting monkey, thou!
I would my valiant master would destroy thee.
I do not lie.

STEPHANO Trinculo, if you trouble him any more in 's tale, by this hand, I will supplant some of your teeth. 48

TRINCULO Why, I said nothing.

STEPHANO Mum, then, and no more.—Proceed.

CALIBAN
I say by sorcery he got this isle;
From me he got it. If thy greatness will
Revenge it on him—for I know thou dar'st,
But this thing dare not— 54

28 sack Spanish white wine **32 natural** (1) idiot (2) natural as opposed to unnatural, monsterlike **35 the next tree** i.e., you'll hang **39 Marry** i.e., indeed. (Originally an oath: by the Virgin Mary.) **40 s.d. invisible** i.e., wearing a garment to connote invisibility, as at 1.2.377 **48 supplant** uproot, displace **54 this thing** i.e., Trinculo

STEPHANO That's most certain.

CALIBAN
Thou shalt be lord of it, and I'll serve thee.

STEPHANO How now shall this be compassed? Canst 57
thou bring me to the party?

CALIBAN
Yea, yea, my lord. I'll yield him thee asleep,
Where thou mayst knock a nail into his head.

ARIEL Thou liest; thou canst not.

CALIBAN
What a pied ninny's this! Thou scurvy patch!— 62
I do beseech thy greatness, give him blows
And take his bottle from him. When that's gone
He shall drink naught but brine, for I'll not show him
Where the quick freshes are. 66

STEPHANO Trinculo, run into no further danger. Interrupt the monster one word further and, by this hand, 68
I'll turn my mercy out o' doors and make a stockfish 69
of thee.

TRINCULO Why, what did I? I did nothing. I'll go farther
off. 72

STEPHANO Didst thou not say he lied?

ARIEL Thou liest.

STEPHANO Do I so? Take thou that. [*He beats Trinculo.*] As
you like this, give me the lie another time. 76

TRINCULO I did not give the lie. Out o' your wits and
hearing too? A pox o' your bottle! This can sack and
drinking do. A murrain on your monster, and the 79
devil take your fingers!

CALIBAN Ha, ha, ha!

STEPHANO Now, forward with your tale. [*To Trinculo.*]
Prithee, stand further off.

CALIBAN
Beat him enough. After a little time
I'll beat him too.

57 compassed achieved **62 pied ninny** fool in motley. **patch** fool
66 quick freshes running springs **68 one word further** i.e., one more
time **69 turn . . . doors** i.e., forget about being merciful. **stockfish**
dried cod beaten before cooking **72 off** away **76 give me the lie** call
me a liar to my face **79 murrain** plague. (Literally, a cattle disease.)

STEPHANO Stand farther.—Come, proceed.

CALIBAN
Why, as I told thee, 'tis a custom with him
I' th' afternoon to sleep. There thou mayst brain him,
Having first seized his books; or with a log
Batter his skull, or paunch him with a stake, 90
Or cut his weasand with thy knife. Remember 91
First to possess his books, for without them
He's but a sot, as I am, nor hath not 93
One spirit to command. They all do hate him
As rootedly as I. Burn but his books.
He has brave utensils—for so he calls them— 96
Which, when he has a house, he'll deck withal. 97
And that most deeply to consider is
The beauty of his daughter. He himself
Calls her a nonpareil. I never saw a woman
But only Sycorax my dam and she;
But she as far surpasseth Sycorax
As great'st does least.

STEPHANO Is it so brave a lass? 104

CALIBAN
Ay, lord. She will become thy bed, I warrant, 105
And bring thee forth brave brood.

STEPHANO Monster, I will kill this man. His daughter and I will be king and queen—save Our Graces!—and Trinculo and thyself shall be viceroys. Dost thou like the plot, Trinculo?

TRINCULO Excellent.

STEPHANO Give me thy hand. I am sorry I beat thee; but, while thou liv'st, keep a good tongue in thy head.

CALIBAN
Within this half hour will he be asleep.
Wilt thou destroy him then?

STEPHANO Ay, on mine honor.

ARIEL [*Aside*] This will I tell my master.

CALIBAN
Thou mak'st me merry; I am full of pleasure.

90 paunch stab in the belly **91 weasand** windpipe **93 sot** fool
96 brave utensils fine furnishings **97 deck withal** furnish it with
104 brave splendid, attractive **105 become** suit

Let us be jocund. Will you troll the catch 119
You taught me but whilere? 120

STEPHANO At thy request, monster, I will do reason, 121
any reason. Come on, Trinculo, let us sing. *Sings.* 122

"Flout 'em and scout 'em 123
And scout 'em and flout 'em!
Thought is free."

CALIBAN That's not the tune. 126

Ariel plays the tune on a tabor and pipe.

STEPHANO What is this same?

TRINCULO This is the tune of our catch, played by the
picture of Nobody. 129

STEPHANO If thou beest a man, show thyself in thy likeness. If thou beest a devil, take 't as thou list. 131

TRINCULO O, forgive me my sins!

STEPHANO He that dies pays all debts. I defy thee.
Mercy upon us!

CALIBAN Art thou afeard?

STEPHANO No, monster, not I.

CALIBAN
Be not afeard. The isle is full of noises,
Sounds, and sweet airs, that give delight and hurt not.
Sometimes a thousand twangling instruments
Will hum about mine ears, and sometimes voices
That, if I then had waked after long sleep,
Will make me sleep again; and then, in dreaming,
The clouds methought would open and show riches
Ready to drop upon me, that when I waked
I cried to dream again. 145

STEPHANO This will prove a brave kingdom to me,
where I shall have my music for nothing.

CALIBAN When Prospero is destroyed.

STEPHANO That shall be by and by. I remember the 149
story.

119 jocund jovial, merry. **troll the catch** sing the round **120 but whilere** only a short time ago **121–122 reason, any reason** anything reasonable **123 Flout** scoff at. **scout** deride **126 s.d. tabor** small drum **129 picture of Nobody** (Refers to a familiar figure with head, arms, and legs but no trunk.) **131 take 't . . . list** i.e., take my defiance as you please, as best you can **145 to dream** desirous of dreaming **149 by and by** very soon

TRINCULO The sound is going away. Let's follow it, and after do our work.

STEPHANO Lead, monster; we'll follow. I would I could see this taborer! He lays it on. 154

TRINCULO Wilt come? I'll follow Stephano.

Exeunt [*following Ariel's music*].

✤

3.3 *Enter Alonso, Sebastian, Antonio, Gonzalo, Adrian, Francisco, etc.*

GONZALO
By 'r lakin, I can go no further, sir. 1
My old bones aches. Here's a maze trod indeed
Through forthrights and meanders! By your patience, 3
I needs must rest me.

ALONSO Old lord, I cannot blame thee, 4
Who am myself attached with weariness, 5
To the dulling of my spirits. Sit down and rest. 6
Even here I will put off my hope, and keep it
No longer for my flatterer. He is drowned 8
Whom thus we stray to find, and the sea mocks
Our frustrate search on land. Well, let him go. 10

[*Alonso and Gonzalo sit.*]

ANTONIO [*Aside to Sebastian*]
I am right glad that he's so out of hope. 11
Do not, for one repulse, forgo the purpose 12
That you resolved t' effect.

SEBASTIAN [*To Antonio*] The next advantage
Will we take throughly.

ANTONIO [*To Sebastian*] Let it be tonight, 14
For, now they are oppressed with travel, they 15

154 lays it on i.e., plays the drum skillfully and energetically

3.3. Location: Another part of the island.
1 By 'r lakin by our Ladykin, by our Lady **3 forthrights and meanders** paths straight and crooked **4 needs must** have to **5 attached** seized **6 To . . . spirits** to the point of being dull-spirited **8 for** as **10 frustrate** frustrated **11 right** very. **out of hope** despairing, discouraged **12 for** because of **14 throughly** thoroughly **15 now** now that. **travel** (Spelled *trauaile* in the Folio and carrying the sense of labor as well as traveling.)

Will not, nor cannot, use such vigilance 16
As when they are fresh.

SEBASTIAN [*To Antonio*] I say tonight. No more. 17

Solemn and strange music; and Prospero on the top, invisible.

ALONSO
What harmony is this? My good friends, hark!

GONZALO Marvelous sweet music!

Enter several strange shapes, bringing in a banquet, and dance about it with gentle actions of salutations; and, inviting the King, etc., to eat, they depart.

ALONSO
Give us kind keepers, heavens! What were these? 20

SEBASTIAN
A living drollery. Now I will believe 21
That there are unicorns; that in Arabia
There is one tree, the phoenix' throne, one phoenix 23
At this hour reigning there.

ANTONIO I'll believe both;
And what does else want credit, come to me 25
And I'll be sworn 'tis true. Travelers ne'er did lie,
Though fools at home condemn 'em.

GONZALO If in Naples
I should report this now, would they believe me
If I should say I saw such islanders?
For, certes, these are people of the island, 30
Who, though they are of monstrous shape, yet note,
Their manners are more gentle, kind, than of
Our human generation you shall find
Many, nay, almost any.

PROSPERO [*Aside*] Honest lord,
Thou hast said well, for some of you there present
Are worse than devils.

16 use apply **17 s.d. on the top** at some high point of the tiring-house or the theater, on a third level above the gallery **20 kind keepers** guardian angels **21 living** with live actors. **drollery** comic entertainment, caricature, puppet show **23 phoenix** mythical bird consumed to ashes every 500 to 600 years only to be renewed into another cycle **25 want credit** lack credence **30 certes** certainly

ALONSO I cannot too much muse 36
Such shapes, such gesture, and such sound, expressing—
Although they want the use of tongue—a kind 38
Of excellent dumb discourse.

PROSPERO [*Aside*] Praise in departing. 39

FRANCISCO
They vanished strangely.

SEBASTIAN No matter, since
They have left their viands behind, for we have stomachs. 41
Will 't please you taste of what is here?

ALONSO Not I.

GONZALO
Faith, sir, you need not fear. When we were boys,
Who would believe that there were mountaineers 44
Dewlapped like bulls, whose throats had hanging at 'em 45
Wallets of flesh? Or that there were such men 46
Whose heads stood in their breasts? Which now we find 47
Each putter-out of five for one will bring us 48
Good warrant of.

ALONSO I will stand to and feed, 49
Although my last—no matter, since I feel 50
The best is past. Brother, my lord the Duke, 51
Stand to, and do as we. [*They approach the table.*] 52

Thunder and lightning. Enter Ariel, like a harpy, claps his wings upon the table, and with a quaint device the banquet vanishes.

36 muse wonder at **38 want** lack **39 Praise in departing** i.e., save your praise until the end of the performance. (Proverbial.) **41 viands** provisions. **stomachs** appetites **44 mountaineers** mountain dwellers
45 Dewlapped having a dewlap, or fold of skin hanging from the neck, like cattle **46 Wallets** pendent folds of skin, wattles **47 in their breasts** (i.e., like the Anthropophagi described in *Othello,* 1.3.146)
48 putter-out . . . one one who invests money, or gambles on the risks of travel on the condition that, if he returns safely, he is to receive five times the amount deposited; hence, any traveler **49 Good warrant** assurance. **stand to** fall to; take the risk **50 Although my last** even if this were to be my last meal **51 best** best part of life **52 s.d. harpy** a fabulous monster with a woman's face and breasts and a vulture's body, supposed to be a minister of divine vengeance. **quaint device** ingenious stage contrivance. **the banquet vanishes** i.e., the food vanishes; the table remains until l. 82

ARIEL
You are three men of sin, whom Destiny—
That hath to instrument this lower world 54
And what is in 't—the never-surfeited sea
Hath caused to belch up you, and on this island
Where man doth not inhabit, you 'mongst men
Being most unfit to live. I have made you mad;
And even with suchlike valor men hang and drown 59
Their proper selves.
[*Alonso, Sebastian, and Antonio draw their swords.*]
You fools! I and my fellows 60
Are ministers of Fate. The elements
Of whom your swords are tempered may as well 62
Wound the loud winds, or with bemocked-at stabs 63
Kill the still-closing waters, as diminish 64
One dowl that's in my plume. My fellow ministers 65
Are like invulnerable. If you could hurt, 66
Your swords are now too massy for your strengths 67
And will not be uplifted. But remember—
For that's my business to you—that you three
From Milan did supplant good Prospero;
Exposed unto the sea, which hath requit it, 71
Him and his innocent child; for which foul deed
The powers, delaying, not forgetting, have
Incensed the seas and shores, yea, all the creatures,
Against your peace. Thee of thy son, Alonso,
They have bereft; and do pronounce by me
Lingering perdition, worse than any death 77
Can be at once, shall step by step attend
You and your ways; whose wraths to guard you from— 79
Which here, in this most desolate isle, else falls 80
Upon your heads—is nothing but heart's sorrow 81

54 to i.e., as its **59 suchlike valor** i.e., the reckless valor derived from madness **60 proper** own **62 whom** which. **tempered** composed and hardened **63 bemocked-at** scorned **64 still-closing** always closing again when parted **65 dowl** soft, fine feather **66 like** likewise, similarly. **If** even if **67 massy** heavy **71 requit** requited, avenged **77 perdition** ruin, destruction **79 whose** (Refers to the heavenly powers.) **80 else** otherwise **81 is nothing** there is no way

And a clear life ensuing. 82

He vanishes in thunder; then, to soft music, enter the shapes again, and dance, with mocks and mows, and carrying out the table.

PROSPERO
Bravely the figure of this harpy hast thou 83
Performed, my Ariel; a grace it had devouring. 84
Of my instruction hast thou nothing bated 85
In what thou hadst to say. So, with good life 86
And observation strange, my meaner ministers 87
Their several kinds have done. My high charms work, 88
And these mine enemies are all knit up
In their distractions. They now are in my power;
And in these fits I leave them, while I visit
Young Ferdinand, whom they suppose is drowned,
And his and mine loved darling. [*Exit above.*]

GONZALO
I' the name of something holy, sir, why stand you 94
In this strange stare?

ALONSO O, it is monstrous, monstrous! 95
Methought the billows spoke and told me of it; 96
The winds did sing it to me, and the thunder,
That deep and dreadful organ pipe, pronounced
The name of Prosper; it did bass my trespass. 99
Therefor my son i' th' ooze is bedded; and 100
I'll seek him deeper than e'er plummet sounded, 101

82 clear unspotted, innocent **s.d. mocks and mows** mocking gestures and grimaces **83 Bravely** finely, dashingly **84 a grace . . . devouring** i.e., you gracefully caused the banquet to disappear as if you had consumed it (with puns on *grace* meaning "gracefulness" and "a blessing on the meal," and on *devouring* meaning "a literal eating" and "an all-consuming or ravishing grace") **85 bated** abated, omitted **86 So** in the same fashion. **good life** faithful reproduction **87 observation strange** exceptional attention to detail. **meaner** i.e., subordinate to Ariel **88 several kinds** individual parts **94 why** (Gonzalo was not addressed in Ariel's speech to the *three men of sin,* l. 53, and is not, as they are, in a maddened state; see ll. 105–107.) **95 it** i.e., my sin (also in l. 96) **96 billows** waves **99 bass my trespass** proclaim my trespass like a bass note in music **100 Therefor** in consequence of that **101 plummet** a lead weight attached to a line for testing depth. **sounded** probed, tested the depth of

And with him there lie mudded. *Exit.*

SEBASTIAN But one fiend at a time,
I'll fight their legions o'er.

ANTONIO I'll be thy second. 104.

Exeunt [*Sebastian and Antonio*].

GONZALO
All three of them are desperate. Their great guilt, 105
Like poison given to work a great time after,
Now 'gins to bite the spirits. I do beseech you 107
That are of suppler joints, follow them swiftly
And hinder them from what this ecstasy 109
May now provoke them to.

ADRIAN Follow, I pray you.

Exeunt omnes.

✤

104 o'er one after another **105 desperate** despairing and reckless **107 bite the spirits** sap their vital powers through anguish **109 ecstasy** mad frenzy

4.1 *Enter Prospero, Ferdinand, and Miranda.*

PROSPERO
If I have too austerely punished you, 1
Your compensation makes amends, for I
Have given you here a third of mine own life, 3
Or that for which I live; who once again
I tender to thy hand. All thy vexations 5
Were but my trials of thy love, and thou
Hast strangely stood the test. Here, afore Heaven, 7
I ratify this my rich gift. O Ferdinand,
Do not smile at me that I boast her off, 9
For thou shalt find she will outstrip all praise
And make it halt behind her.

FERDINAND I do believe it 11
Against an oracle. 12

PROSPERO
Then, as my gift and thine own acquisition
Worthily purchased, take my daughter. But
If thou dost break her virgin-knot before
All sanctimonious ceremonies may 16
With full and holy rite be ministered,
No sweet aspersion shall the heavens let fall 18
To make this contract grow; but barren hate,
Sour-eyed disdain, and discord shall bestrew
The union of your bed with weeds so loathly 21
That you shall hate it both. Therefore take heed,
As Hymen's lamps shall light you.

FERDINAND As I hope 23

4.1. Location: Before Prospero's cell.
1 austerely severely **3 a third** i.e., Miranda, into whose education Prospero has put a third of his life (?) or who represents a large part of what he cares about, along with his dukedom and his learned study (?) **5 vexations** torments **7 strangely** extraordinarily **9 boast her off** i.e., praise her so; or perhaps an error for "boast of her"; the Folio reads "boast her of" **11 halt** limp **12 Against an oracle** i.e., even if an oracle should declare otherwise **16 sanctimonious** sacred **18 aspersion** dew, shower **21 weeds** (in place of the flowers customarily strewn on the marriage bed) **23 As . . . you** i.e., as you long for happiness and concord in your marriage. (Hymen was the Greek and Roman god of marriage; his symbolic torches, the wedding torches, were supposed to burn brightly for a happy marriage, smokily for a troubled one.)

For quiet days, fair issue, and long life, 24
With such love as 'tis now, the murkiest den,
The most opportune place, the strong'st suggestion 26
Our worser genius can, shall never melt 27
Mine honor into lust, to take away 28
The edge of that day's celebration 29
When I shall think or Phoebus' steeds are foundered 30
Or Night kept chained below.

PROSPERO Fairly spoke.
Sit then and talk with her. She is thine own.
[*Ferdinand and Miranda sit and talk together.*]
What, Ariel! My industrious servant, Ariel! 33

Enter Ariel.

ARIEL
What would my potent master? Here I am.

PROSPERO
Thou and thy meaner fellows your last service 35
Did worthily perform, and I must use you
In such another trick. Go bring the rabble, 37
O'er whom I give thee power, here to this place.
Incite them to quick motion, for I must
Bestow upon the eyes of this young couple
Some vanity of mine art. It is my promise, 41
And they expect it from me.

ARIEL Presently? 42

PROSPERO Ay, with a twink. 43

ARIEL
Before you can say "Come" and "Go,"
And breathe twice, and cry "So, so,"
Each one, tripping on his toe,
Will be here with mop and mow. 47
Do you love me, master? No?

24 issue offspring **26 suggestion** temptation **27 worser genius** evil genius, or evil attendant spirit. **can** is capable of **28 to** so as to **29 edge** keen enjoyment, sexual ardor **30 or** either. **foundered** broken down, made lame. (Ferdinand will wait impatiently for the bridal night.) **33 What** now then **35 meaner fellows** subordinates **37 trick** device. **rabble** band, i.e., the *meaner fellows* of l. 35 **41 vanity** (1) illusion (2) trifle (3) desire for admiration, conceit **42 Presently** immediately **43 with a twink** in the twinkling of an eye, in an instant **47 mop and mow** gestures and grimaces

PROSPERO
Dearly, my delicate Ariel. Do not approach
Till thou dost hear me call.
ARIEL Well, I conceive. *Exit.* 50
PROSPERO
Look thou be true; do not give dalliance 51
Too much the rein. The strongest oaths are straw
To the fire i' the blood. Be more abstemious,
Or else good night your vow!
FERDINAND I warrant you, sir, 54
The white cold virgin snow upon my heart 55
Abates the ardor of my liver.
PROSPERO Well. 56
Now come, my Ariel! Bring a corollary, 57
Rather than want a spirit. Appear, and pertly!— 58
No tongue! All eyes! Be silent. *Soft music.* 59

Enter Iris.

IRIS
Ceres, most bounteous lady, thy rich leas 60
Of wheat, rye, barley, vetches, oats, and peas; 61
Thy turfy mountains, where live nibbling sheep,
And flat meads thatched with stover, them to keep; 63
Thy banks with pionèd and twillèd brims, 64
Which spongy April at thy hest betrims 65
To make cold nymphs chaste crowns; and thy broom
groves, 66
Whose shadow the dismissèd bachelor loves, 67
Being lass-lorn; thy poll-clipped vineyard; 68

50 conceive understand **51 true** true to your promise **54 good night** i.e., say good-bye to. **warrant** guarantee **55 The white . . . heart** i.e., the ideal of chastity and consciousness of Miranda's chaste innocence enshrined in my heart **56 liver** (as the presumed seat of the passions) **57 corollary** surplus, extra supply **58 want** lack. **pertly** briskly **59 No tongue** all the beholders are to be silent (lest the spirits vanish) **s.d. Iris** goddess of the rainbow, and Juno's messenger **60 Ceres** goddess of the generative power of nature. **leas** meadows **61 vetches** plants for forage, fodder **63 meads** meadows. **stover** winter fodder for cattle **64 pionèd and twillèd** undercut by the swift current and protected by roots and branches that tangle to form a barricade **65 spongy** wet **66 broom groves** clumps of broom, gorse, yellow-flowered shrub **67 dismissèd bachelor** rejected male lover **68 poll-clipped** pruned, lopped at the top, or *pole-clipped,* hedged in with poles

And thy sea marge, sterile and rocky hard, 69
Where thou thyself dost air: the queen o' the sky, 70
Whose watery arch and messenger am I, 71
Bids thee leave these, and with her sovereign grace, 72
Juno descends [*slowly in her car*].
Here on this grass plot, in this very place,
To come and sport. Her peacocks fly amain. 74
Approach, rich Ceres, her to entertain. 75

Enter Ceres.

CERES
Hail, many-colored messenger, that ne'er
Dost disobey the wife of Jupiter,
Who with thy saffron wings upon my flowers 78
Diffusest honeydrops, refreshing showers,
And with each end of thy blue bow dost crown 80
My bosky acres and my unshrubbed down, 81
Rich scarf to my proud earth. Why hath thy queen
Summoned me hither to this short-grassed green?

IRIS
A contract of true love to celebrate,
And some donation freely to estate 85
On the blest lovers.

CERES Tell me, heavenly bow,
If Venus or her son, as thou dost know, 87
Do now attend the Queen? Since they did plot
The means that dusky Dis my daughter got, 89
Her and her blind boy's scandaled company 90
I have forsworn.

IRIS Of her society 91
Be not afraid. I met her deity 92
Cutting the clouds towards Paphos, and her son 93

69 sea marge shore **70 queen o' the sky** i.e., Juno **71 watery arch** rainbow **72 s.d. Juno descends** i.e., starts her descent from the "heavens" above the stage (?) **74 peacocks** birds sacred to Juno, and used to pull her chariot. **amain** with full speed **75 entertain** receive **78 saffron** yellow **80 bow** i.e., rainbow **81 bosky** wooded. **down** upland **85 estate** bestow **87 son** i.e., Cupid. **as** as far as **89 dusky** dark. **Dis . . . got** (Pluto, or *Dis,* god of the infernal regions, carried off Persephone, daughter of Ceres, to be his bride in Hades.) **90 Her** i.e., Venus'. **scandaled** scandalous **91 society** company **92 her deity** i.e., Her Highness **93 Paphos** place on the island of Cyprus, sacred to Venus

Dove-drawn with her. Here thought they to have done 94
Some wanton charm upon this man and maid, 95
Whose vows are that no bed-right shall be paid
Till Hymen's torch be lighted; but in vain.
Mars's hot minion is returned again; 98
Her waspish-headed son has broke his arrows, 99
Swears he will shoot no more, but play with sparrows 100
And be a boy right out.

[*Juno alights.*]

CERES Highest Queen of state, 101
Great Juno, comes; I know her by her gait. 102

JUNO
How does my bounteous sister? Go with me
To bless this twain, that they may prosperous be
And honored in their issue. *They sing:* 105

JUNO
Honor, riches, marriage blessing,
Long continuance, and increasing,
Hourly joys be still upon you! 108
Juno sings her blessings on you.

CERES
Earth's increase, foison plenty, 110
Barns and garners never empty, 111
Vines with clustering bunches growing,
Plants with goodly burden bowing;

Spring come to you at the farthest
In the very end of harvest! 115
Scarcity and want shall shun you;
Ceres' blessing so is on you.

FERDINAND
This is a most majestic vision, and

94 Dove-drawn (Venus' chariot was drawn by doves.) **done** placed **95 wanton charm** lustful spell **98 Mars's hot minion** i.e., Venus, the beloved of Mars. **returned** i.e., returned to Paphos **99 waspish-headed** fiery, hotheaded, peevish **100 sparrows** (Supposed lustful, and sacred to Venus.) **101 right out** outright. **Highest . . . state** most majestic Queen **102 gait** i.e., majestic bearing **105 issue** offspring **108 still** always **110 foison plenty** plentiful harvest **111 garners** granaries **115 In . . . harvest** i.e., with no winter in between

Harmonious charmingly. May I be bold 119
To think these spirits?

PROSPERO Spirits, which by mine art
I have from their confines called to enact
My present fancies.

FERDINAND Let me live here ever!
So rare a wondered father and a wife 123
Makes this place Paradise.

Juno and Ceres whisper, and send Iris on employment.

PROSPERO Sweet now, silence!
Juno and Ceres whisper seriously;
There's something else to do. Hush and be mute,
Or else our spell is marred.

IRIS
You nymphs, called naiads, of the windring brooks, 128
With your sedged crowns and ever-harmless looks, 129
Leave your crisp channels, and on this green land 130
Answer your summons; Juno does command.
Come, temperate nymphs, and help to celebrate 132
A contract of true love. Be not too late.

Enter certain nymphs.

You sunburnt sicklemen, of August weary, 134
Come hither from the furrow and be merry. 135
Make holiday; your rye-straw hats put on,
And these fresh nymphs encounter every one 137
In country footing. 138

Enter certain reapers, properly habited. They join with the nymphs in a graceful dance, towards the end whereof Prospero starts suddenly, and speaks; after which, to a strange, hollow, and confused noise, they heavily vanish.

119 charmingly enchantingly **123 wondered** wonder-performing, wondrous **128 naiads** nymphs of springs, rivers, or lakes. **windring** wandering, winding (?) **129 sedged** made of reeds. **ever-harmless** ever-innocent **130 crisp** curled, rippled **132 temperate** chaste **134 sicklemen** harvesters, field workers who cut down grain and grass. **weary** i.e., weary of the hard work of the harvest **135 furrow** i.e., plowed fields **137 encounter** join **138 country footing** country dancing **s.d. properly** suitably. **heavily** slowly, dejectedly

PROSPERO [*Aside*]
I had forgot that foul conspiracy
Of the beast Caliban and his confederates
Against my life. The minute of their plot
Is almost come. [*To the Spirits.*] Well done! Avoid; no
more! 142

FERDINAND [*To Miranda*]
This is strange. Your father's in some passion
That works him strongly.

MIRANDA Never till this day 144
Saw I him touched with anger so distempered.

PROSPERO
You do look, my son, in a moved sort, 146
As if you were dismayed. Be cheerful, sir.
Our revels now are ended. These our actors, 148
As I foretold you, were all spirits and
Are melted into air, into thin air;
And, like the baseless fabric of this vision, 151
The cloud-capped towers, the gorgeous palaces,
The solemn temples, the great globe itself, 153
Yea, all which it inherit, shall dissolve, 154
And, like this insubstantial pageant faded,
Leave not a rack behind. We are such stuff 156
As dreams are made on, and our little life 157
Is rounded with a sleep. Sir, I am vexed. 158
Bear with my weakness. My old brain is troubled.
Be not disturbed with my infirmity. 160
If you be pleased, retire into my cell 161
And there repose. A turn or two I'll walk
To still my beating mind.

FERDINAND, MIRANDA We wish your peace. 163
Exeunt [*Ferdinand and Miranda*].

PROSPERO
Come with a thought! I thank thee, Ariel. Come. 164

142 Avoid depart, withdraw **144 works** affects, agitates **146 moved sort** troubled state, condition **148 revels** entertainment, pageant **151 baseless** without substance **153 great globe** (with a glance at the Globe Theatre) **154 which it inherit** who subsequently occupy it **156 rack** wisp of cloud **157 on** of **158 rounded** surrounded, or crowned, rounded off **160 with** by **161 retire** withdraw, go **163 beating** agitated **164 with a thought** i.e., on the instant, or summoned by my thought, no sooner thought of than here

Enter Ariel.

ARIEL
Thy thoughts I cleave to. What's thy pleasure?
PROSPERO Spirit, 165
We must prepare to meet with Caliban.
ARIEL
Ay, my commander. When I presented Ceres, 167
I thought to have told thee of it, but I feared
Lest I might anger thee.
PROSPERO
Say again, where didst thou leave these varlets?
ARIEL
I told you, sir, they were red-hot with drinking,
So full of valor that they smote the air
For breathing in their faces, beat the ground
For kissing of their feet, yet always bending 174
Towards their project. Then I beat my tabor,
At which, like unbacked colts, they pricked their ears, 176
Advanced their eyelids, lifted up their noses 177
As they smelt music. So I charmed their ears 178
That calflike they my lowing followed through 179
Toothed briers, sharp furzes, pricking gorse, and
thorns, 180
Which entered their frail shins. At last I left them
I' the filthy-mantled pool beyond your cell, 182
There dancing up to the chins, that the foul lake
O'erstunk their feet.
PROSPERO This was well done, my bird. 184
Thy shape invisible retain thou still.
The trumpery in my house, go bring it hither, 186
For stale to catch these thieves.
ARIEL I go, I go. *Exit.* 187

165 cleave cling, adhere **167 presented** acted the part of, or introduced **174 bending** aiming **176 unbacked** unbroken, unridden **177 Advanced** lifted up **178 As** as if **179 lowing** mooing **180 furzes, gorse** prickly shrubs **182 filthy-mantled** covered with a slimy coating **184 O'erstunk** smelled worse than, or, caused to stink terribly **186 trumpery** cheap goods, the *glistering apparel* mentioned in the following stage direction **187 stale** (1) decoy (2) out-of-fashion garments (with possible further suggestions of *fit for a stale* or prostitute, *stale* meaning "horse piss," l. 199, and *steal,* pronounced like *stale*)

PROSPERO
A devil, a born devil, on whose nature
Nurture can never stick; on whom my pains,
Humanely taken, all, all lost, quite lost!
And as with age his body uglier grows,
So his mind cankers. I will plague them all, 192
Even to roaring.

Enter Ariel, loaden with glistering apparel, etc.

Come, hang them on this line. 193

[*Ariel hangs up the showy finery; Prospero and Ariel remain, invisible.*] *Enter Caliban, Stephano, and Trinculo, all wet.*

CALIBAN
Pray you, tread softly, that the blind mole may
Not hear a footfall. We now are near his cell.

STEPHANO Monster, your fairy, which you say is a harmless fairy, has done little better than played the jack with us. 198

TRINCULO Monster, I do smell all horse piss, at which my nose is in great indignation.

STEPHANO So is mine. Do you hear, monster? If I should take a displeasure against you, look you—

TRINCULO Thou wert but a lost monster.

CALIBAN
Good my lord, give me thy favor still.
Be patient, for the prize I'll bring thee to
Shall hoodwink this mischance. Therefore speak softly. 206
All's hushed as midnight yet.

TRINCULO Ay, but to lose our bottles in the pool—

STEPHANO There is not only disgrace and dishonor in that, monster, but an infinite loss.

TRINCULO That's more to me than my wetting. Yet this is your harmless fairy, monster!

STEPHANO I will fetch off my bottle, though I be o'er 213
ears for my labor. 214

192 cankers festers, grows malignant **193 line** lime tree or linden **s.d. Prospero and Ariel remain** (The staging is uncertain. They may instead exit here and return with the spirits at l. 256.) **198 jack** (1) knave (2) will-o'-the wisp **206 hoodwink** cover up, make you not see. (A hawking term.) **mischance** mishap, misfortune **213–214 o'er ears** i.e., totally submerged and perhaps drowned

CALIBAN
Prithee, my king, be quiet. Seest thou here,
This is the mouth o' the cell. No noise, and enter.
Do that good mischief which may make this island
Thine own forever, and I thy Caliban
For aye thy footlicker.

STEPHANO Give me thy hand. I do begin to have bloody thoughts.

TRINCULO [*Seeing the finery*] O King Stephano! O peer! 222
O worthy Stephano! Look what a wardrobe here is for thee!

CALIBAN
Let it alone, thou fool, it is but trash.

TRINCULO Oho, monster! We know what belongs to a frippery. O King Stephano! [*He takes a gown.*] 227

STEPHANO Put off that gown, Trinculo. By this hand, I'll 228
have that gown.

TRINCULO Thy Grace shall have it.

CALIBAN
The dropsy drown this fool! What do you mean 231
To dote thus on such luggage? Let 't alone 232
And do the murder first. If he awake,
From toe to crown he'll fill our skins with pinches, 234
Make us strange stuff.

STEPHANO Be you quiet, monster.—Mistress line, is not 236
this my jerkin? [*He takes it down.*] Now is the jerkin un- 237
der the line. Now, jerkin, you are like to lose your hair 238
and prove a bald jerkin. 239

222 King . . . peer (Alludes to the old ballad beginning, "King Stephen was a worthy peer.") **227 frippery** place where cast-off clothes are sold **228 Put off** put down, or take off **231 dropsy** disease characterized by the accumulation of fluid in the connective tissue of the body **232 luggage** cumbersome trash **234 crown** head **236 Mistress line** (Addressed to the linden or lime tree upon which, at l. 193, Ariel hung the *glistering apparel.*) **237 jerkin** jacket made of leather **237–238 under the line** under the lime tree (with punning sense of being south of the equinoctial line or equator; sailors on long voyages to the southern regions were popularly supposed to lose their hair from scurvy or other diseases. Stephano also quibbles bawdily on losing hair through syphilis, and in *Mistress* and *jerkin.*) **238 like** likely **239 bald** (1) hairless, napless (2) meager

TRINCULO Do, do! We steal by line and level, an 't like Your Grace. 240

STEPHANO I thank thee for that jest. Here's a garment for 't. [*He gives a garment.*] Wit shall not go unrewarded while I am king of this country. "Steal by line and level" is an excellent pass of pate. There's another garment for 't. 245

TRINCULO Monster, come, put some lime upon your fingers, and away with the rest. 247

CALIBAN
I will have none on 't. We shall lose our time,
And all be turned to barnacles, or to apes 250
With foreheads villainous low. 251

STEPHANO Monster, lay to your fingers. Help to bear this away where my hogshead of wine is, or I'll turn you out of my kingdom. Go to, carry this. 252 253 254

TRINCULO And this.

STEPHANO Ay, and this.

[*They load Caliban with more and more garments.*]

A noise of hunters heard. Enter divers spirits, in shape of dogs and hounds, hunting them about, Prospero and Ariel setting them on.

PROSPERO Hey, Mountain, hey!

ARIEL Silver! There it goes, Silver!

PROSPERO Fury, Fury! There, Tyrant, there! Hark! Hark!

[*Caliban, Stephano, and Trinculo are driven out.*]

Go, charge my goblins that they grind their joints

240 Do, do i.e., bravo. (Said in response to the jesting or to the taking of the jerkin, or both.) **by line and level** i.e., by means of plumb line and carpenter's level, methodically (with pun on *line,* "lime tree," l. 238, and *steal,* pronounced like *stale,* i.e., prostitute, continuing Stephano's bawdy quibble). **an 't like** if it please **245 pass of pate** sally of wit. (The metaphor is from fencing.) **247 lime** birdlime, sticky substance (to give Caliban sticky fingers) **250 barnacles** barnacle geese, formerly supposed to be hatched from seashells attached to trees and to fall thence into the water; here evidently used, like *apes,* as types of simpletons **251 villainous** miserably **252 lay to** start using **253 this** i.e., the *glistering apparel.* **hogshead** large cask **254 Go to** (An expression of exhortation or remonstrance.)

With dry convulsions, shorten up their sinews 261
With agèd cramps, and more pinch-spotted make them 262
Than pard or cat o' mountain.

ARIEL Hark, they roar! 263

PROSPERO
Let them be hunted soundly. At this hour 264
Lies at my mercy all mine enemies.
Shortly shall all my labors end, and thou
Shalt have the air at freedom. For a little 267
Follow, and do me service. *Exeunt.*

✤

261 dry associated with age, arthritic (?) **convulsions** cramps
262 agèd characteristic of old age **263 pard** panther or leopard. **cat o' mountain** wildcat **264 soundly** thoroughly **267 little** little while longer

5.1 *Enter Prospero in his magic robes,* [*with his staff,*] *and Ariel.*

PROSPERO
Now does my project gather to a head.
My charms crack not, my spirits obey, and Time 2
Goes upright with his carriage. How's the day? 3

ARIEL
On the sixth hour, at which time, my lord, 4
You said our work should cease.

PROSPERO I did say so,
When first I raised the tempest. Say, my spirit,
How fares the King and 's followers?

ARIEL Confined together
In the same fashion as you gave in charge,
Just as you left them; all prisoners, sir,
In the line grove which weather-fends your cell. 10
They cannot budge till your release. The King, 11
His brother, and yours abide all three distracted, 12
And the remainder mourning over them,
Brim full of sorrow and dismay; but chiefly
Him that you termed, sir, the good old lord, Gonzalo.
His tears runs down his beard like winter's drops
From eaves of reeds. Your charm so strongly works 'em 17
That if you now beheld them your affections 18
Would become tender.

PROSPERO Dost thou think so, spirit?

ARIEL
Mine would, sir, were I human.

PROSPERO And mine shall.
Hast thou, which art but air, a touch, a feeling 21
Of their afflictions, and shall not myself,

5.1. Location: Before Prospero's cell.
2 crack collapse, fail. (The metaphor is probably alchemical, as in *project* and *gather to a head,* l. 1.) **3 his carriage** its burden. (Time is no longer heavily burdened and so can go *upright,* standing straight and unimpeded.) **4 On** approaching **10 line grove** grove of lime trees. **weather-fends** protects from the weather **11 your release** you release them **12 distracted** out of their wits **17 eaves of reeds** thatched roofs **18 affections** feelings **21 touch** sense, feeling

One of their kind, that relish all as sharply 23
Passion as they, be kindlier moved than thou art? 24
Though with their high wrongs I am struck to the quick,
Yet with my nobler reason 'gainst my fury
Do I take part. The rarer action is 27
In virtue than in vengeance. They being penitent,
The sole drift of my purpose doth extend
Not a frown further. Go release them, Ariel.
My charms I'll break, their senses I'll restore,
And they shall be themselves.

ARIEL I'll fetch them, sir.

Exit.

[*Prospero traces a charmed circle with his staff.*]

PROSPERO

Ye elves of hills, brooks, standing lakes, and groves, 33
And ye that on the sands with printless foot
Do chase the ebbing Neptune, and do fly him
When he comes back; you demi-puppets that 36
By moonshine do the green sour ringlets make, 37
Whereof the ewe not bites; and you whose pastime
Is to make midnight mushrooms, that rejoice 39
To hear the solemn curfew; by whose aid, 40
Weak masters though ye be, I have bedimmed
The noontide sun, called forth the mutinous winds,
And twixt the green sea and the azured vault 43
Set roaring war; to the dread rattling thunder 44
Have I given fire, and rifted Jove's stout oak 45
With his own bolt; the strong-based promontory 46
Have I made shake, and by the spurs plucked up 47
The pine and cedar; graves at my command

23–24 that . . . they i.e., I who am just as sensitive to suffering as they **24 kindlier** (1) more sympathetically (2) more naturally, humanly **27 rarer** nobler **33–50 Ye . . . art** (This famous passage is an embellished paraphrase of Golding's translation of Ovid's *Metamorphoses,* 7.197–219.) **36 demi-puppets** puppets of half size, i.e., elves and fairies **37 green sour ringlets** fairy rings, circles in grass (actually produced by mushrooms) **39 midnight mushrooms** mushrooms appearing overnight **40 curfew** evening bell, usually rung at nine o'clock, ushering in the time when spirits are abroad **43 the azured vault** i.e., the sky **44–45 to . . . fire** I have discharged the dread rattling thunderbolt **45 rifted** riven, split **46 bolt** lightning bolt **47 spurs** roots

Have waked their sleepers, oped, and let 'em forth
By my so potent art. But this rough magic 50
I here abjure, and when I have required 51
Some heavenly music—which even now I do—
To work mine end upon their senses that 53
This airy charm is for, I'll break my staff, 54
Bury it certain fathoms in the earth,
And deeper than did ever plummet sound
I'll drown my book. *Solemn music.*

Here enters Ariel before; then Alonso, with a frantic gesture, attended by Gonzalo; Sebastian and Antonio in like manner, attended by Adrian and Francisco. They all enter the circle which Prospero had made, and there stand charmed; which Prospero observing, speaks:

[*To Alonso.*] A solemn air, and the best comforter 58
To an unsettled fancy, cure thy brains, 59
Now useless, boiled within thy skull! [*To Sebastian and*
Antonio.] There stand,
For you are spell-stopped.—
Holy Gonzalo, honorable man,
Mine eyes, e'en sociable to the show of thine, 63
Fall fellowly drops. [*Aside.*] The charm dissolves apace, 64
And as the morning steals upon the night,
Melting the darkness, so their rising senses
Begin to chase the ignorant fumes that mantle 67
Their clearer reason.—O good Gonzalo, 68
My true preserver, and a loyal sir
To him thou follow'st! I will pay thy graces 70
Home both in word and deed.—Most cruelly 71
Didst thou, Alonso, use me and my daughter.
Thy brother was a furtherer in the act.— 73
Thou art pinched for 't now, Sebastian. [*To Antonio.*]
Flesh and blood, 74

50 rough violent **51 required** requested **53 their senses that** the senses of those whom **54 airy charm** i.e., music **58 air** song. **and** i.e., which is **59 fancy** imagination **63 sociable** sympathetic. **show** appearance **64 Fall** let fall **67 ignorant fumes** fumes that render them incapable of comprehension. **mantle** envelop **68 clearer** growing clearer **70 pay thy graces** reward your favors **71 Home** fully **73 furtherer** accomplice **74 pinched** punished, afflicted

You, brother mine, that entertained ambition,
Expelled remorse and nature, whom, with Sebastian, 76
Whose inward pinches therefore are most strong,
Would here have killed your king, I do forgive thee,
Unnatural though thou art.—Their understanding
Begins to swell, and the approaching tide
Will shortly fill the reasonable shore 81
That now lies foul and muddy. Not one of them
That yet looks on me, or would know me.—Ariel,
Fetch me the hat and rapier in my cell.

[*Ariel goes to the cell and returns immediately.*]

I will discase me and myself present 85
As I was sometime Milan. Quickly, spirit! 86
Thou shalt ere long be free.

Ariel sings and helps to attire him.

ARIEL

Where the bee sucks, there suck I.
In a cowslip's bell I lie;
There I couch when owls do cry. 90
On the bat's back I do fly
After summer merrily. 92
Merrily, merrily shall I live now
Under the blossom that hangs on the bough.

PROSPERO

Why, that's my dainty Ariel! I shall miss thee,
But yet thou shalt have freedom. So, so, so. 96
To the King's ship, invisible as thou art!
There shalt thou find the mariners asleep
Under the hatches. The Master and the Boatswain
Being awake, enforce them to this place,
And presently, I prithee. 101

ARIEL

I drink the air before me and return
Or ere your pulse twice beat. *Exit.* 103

76 remorse pity. **nature** natural feeling. **whom** i.e., who **81 reasonable shore** shores of reason, i.e., minds. (Their reason returns, like the incoming tide.) **85 discase** disrobe **86 As . . . Milan** in my former appearance as Duke of Milan **90 couch** lie **92 After** i.e., pursuing **96 So, so, so** (Expresses approval of Ariel's help as valet.) **101 presently** immediately **103 Or ere** before

GONZALO
All torment, trouble, wonder, and amazement
Inhabits here. Some heavenly power guide us
Out of this fearful country!

PROSPERO Behold, sir King, 106
The wrongèd Duke of Milan, Prospero.
For more assurance that a living prince
Does now speak to thee, I embrace thy body;
And to thee and thy company I bid
A hearty welcome. [*Embracing him.*]

ALONSO Whe'er thou be'st he or no,
Or some enchanted trifle to abuse me, 112
As late I have been, I not know. Thy pulse 113
Beats as of flesh and blood; and, since I saw thee,
Th' affliction of my mind amends, with which
I fear a madness held me. This must crave— 116
An if this be at all—a most strange story. 117
Thy dukedom I resign, and do entreat 118
Thou pardon me my wrongs. But how should Prospero 119
Be living, and be here?

PROSPERO [*To Gonzalo*] First, noble friend,
Let me embrace thine age, whose honor cannot 121
Be measured or confined. [*Embracing him.*]

GONZALO Whether this be
Or be not, I'll not swear.

PROSPERO You do yet taste
Some subtleties o' th' isle, that will not let you 124
Believe things certain. Welcome, my friends all!
[*Aside to Sebastian and Antonio.*] But you, my brace of
lords, were I so minded, 126
I here could pluck His Highness' frown upon you
And justify you traitors. At this time 128
I will tell no tales.

SEBASTIAN The devil speaks in him.

106 fearful frightening **112 trifle** trick of magic. **abuse** deceive **113 late** lately **116 crave** require **117 An . . . all** if this is actually happening. **story** i.e., explanation **118 Thy . . . resign** (Alonso made arrangement with Antonio at the time of Prospero's banishment for Milan to pay tribute to Naples; see 1.2.113–127.) **119 wrongs** wrongdoings **121 thine age** your venerable self **124 subtleties** illusions, magical powers **126 brace** pair **128 justify you** prove you to be

PROSPERO No.
[*To Antonio.*] For you, most wicked sir, whom to call brother
Would even infect my mouth, I do forgive
Thy rankest fault—all of them; and require
My dukedom of thee, which perforce I know 133
Thou must restore.

ALONSO If thou be'st Prospero,
Give us particulars of thy preservation,
How thou hast met us here, whom three hours since 136
Were wrecked upon this shore; where I have lost—
How sharp the point of this remembrance is!—
My dear son Ferdinand.

PROSPERO I am woe for 't, sir. 139

ALONSO
Irreparable is the loss, and Patience
Says it is past her cure.

PROSPERO I rather think
You have not sought her help, of whose soft grace 142
For the like loss I have her sovereign aid 143
And rest myself content.

ALONSO You the like loss?

PROSPERO
As great to me as late, and supportable 145
To make the dear loss, have I means much weaker 146
Than you may call to comfort you; for I
Have lost my daughter.

ALONSO A daughter?
O heavens, that they were living both in Naples,
The king and queen there! That they were, I wish 151
Myself were mudded in that oozy bed 152
Where my son lies. When did you lose your daughter?

PROSPERO
In this last tempest. I perceive these lords
At this encounter do so much admire 155

133 perforce necessarily **136 whom** i.e., who **139 woe** sorry **142 of . . . grace** by whose mercy **143 sovereign** efficacious **145 late** recent **145–146 supportable . . . have I** to make the deeply felt loss bearable, I have **151 That** so that **152 mudded** buried in the mud **155 admire** wonder

That they devour their reason and scarce think 156
Their eyes do offices of truth, their words 157
Are natural breath. But, howsoever you have 158
Been jostled from your senses, know for certain
That I am Prospero and that very duke
Which was thrust forth of Milan, who most strangely 161
Upon this shore, where you were wrecked, was landed
To be the lord on 't. No more yet of this,
For 'tis a chronicle of day by day, 164
Not a relation for a breakfast nor
Befitting this first meeting. Welcome, sir.
This cell's my court. Here have I few attendants,
And subjects none abroad. Pray you, look in. 168
My dukedom since you have given me again,
I will requite you with as good a thing, 170
At least bring forth a wonder to content ye
As much as me my dukedom. 172

Here Prospero discovers Ferdinand and Miranda playing at chess.

MIRANDA Sweet lord, you play me false.
FERDINAND No, my dearest love,
I would not for the world.
MIRANDA
Yes, for a score of kingdoms you should wrangle, 176
And I would call it fair play.
ALONSO If this prove 177
A vision of the island, one dear son 178
Shall I twice lose.

156 devour their reason i.e., are dumbfounded **156–158 scarce . . . breath** scarcely believe that their eyes inform them accurately what they see or that their words are naturally spoken **161 of** from **164 of day by day** requiring days to tell **168 abroad** away from here, anywhere else **170 requite** repay **172 s.d. discovers** i.e., by opening a curtain, presumably rear stage **176–177 Yes . . . play** i.e., yes, even if we were playing for twenty kingdoms, something less than the whole world, you would still contend mightily against me and play me false, and I would let you do it as though it were fair play; or, if you were to play not just for stakes but literally for kingdoms, my accusation of false play would be out of order in that your "wrangling" would be proper **178 vision** illusion

SEBASTIAN A most high miracle!

FERDINAND [*Approaching his father*]
Though the seas threaten, they are merciful;
I have cursed them without cause. [*He kneels*.]

ALONSO Now all the blessings
Of a glad father compass thee about! 182
Arise, and say how thou cam'st here.
[*Ferdinand rises*.]

MIRANDA O, wonder!
How many goodly creatures are there here!
How beauteous mankind is! O, brave new world, 185
That has such people in 't!

PROSPERO 'Tis new to thee.

ALONSO
What is this maid with whom thou wast at play?
Your eld'st acquaintance cannot be three hours. 188
Is she the goddess that hath severed us
And brought us thus together?

FERDINAND Sir, she is mortal;
But by immortal Providence she's mine.
I chose her when I could not ask my father
For his advice, nor thought I had one. She
Is daughter to this famous Duke of Milan,
Of whom so often I have heard renown
But never saw before, of whom I have
Received a second life; and second father
This lady makes him to me.

ALONSO I am hers.
But O, how oddly will it sound that I
Must ask my child forgiveness!

PROSPERO There, sir, stop.
Let us not burden our remembrances with
A heaviness that's gone.

GONZALO I have inly wept, 202
Or should have spoke ere this. Look down, you gods,
And on this couple drop a blessèd crown!

182 compass encompass, embrace **185 brave** splendid, gorgeously appareled, handsome **188 eld'st** longest **202 heaviness** sadness. **inly** inwardly

For it is you that have chalked forth the way 205
Which brought us hither.

ALONSO I say amen, Gonzalo!

GONZALO
Was Milan thrust from Milan that his issue 207
Should become kings of Naples? O, rejoice
Beyond a common joy, and set it down
With gold on lasting pillars: In one voyage
Did Claribel her husband find at Tunis,
And Ferdinand, her brother, found a wife
Where he himself was lost; Prospero his dukedom
In a poor isle; and all of us ourselves 214
When no man was his own.

ALONSO [*To Ferdinand and Miranda*] Give me your hands. 215
Let grief and sorrow still embrace his heart 216
That doth not wish you joy!

GONZALO Be it so! Amen! 217

Enter Ariel, with the Master and Boatswain amazedly following.

O, look, sir, look, sir! Here is more of us.
I prophesied, if a gallows were on land,
This fellow could not drown.—Now, blasphemy, 220
That swear'st grace o'erboard, not an oath on shore? 221
Hast thou no mouth by land? What is the news?

BOATSWAIN
The best news is that we have safely found
Our King and company; the next, our ship—
Which, but three glasses since, we gave out split— 225
Is tight and yare and bravely rigged as when 226
We first put out to sea.

ARIEL [*Aside to Prospero*] Sir, all this service
Have I done since I went.

205 chalked . . . way marked as with a piece of chalk the pathway **207 Was Milan** was the Duke of Milan **214–215 all . . . own** all of us have found ourselves and our sanity when we all had lost our senses **216 still** always. **his** that person's **217 That** who **220 blasphemy** i.e., blasphemer **221 That swear'st grace o'erboard** i.e., you who banish heavenly grace from the ship by your blasphemies. **not an oath** aren't you going to swear an oath **225 glasses** i.e., hours. **gave out** reported, professed to be **226 yare** ready. **bravely** splendidly

PROSPERO [*Aside to Ariel*] My tricksy spirit! 228

ALONSO

These are not natural events; they strengthen 229
From strange to stranger. Say, how came you hither?

BOATSWAIN

If I did think, sir, I were well awake,
I'd strive to tell you. We were dead of sleep, 232
And—how we know not—all clapped under hatches,
Where but even now, with strange and several noises 234
Of roaring, shrieking, howling, jingling chains,
And more diversity of sounds, all horrible,
We were awaked; straightway at liberty;
Where we, in all her trim, freshly beheld
Our royal, good, and gallant ship, our Master
Cap'ring to eye her. On a trice, so please you, 240
Even in a dream, were we divided from them 241
And were brought moping hither.

ARIEL [*Aside to Prospero*] Was 't well done? 242

PROSPERO [*Aside to Ariel*]

Bravely, my diligence. Thou shalt be free.

ALONSO

This is as strange a maze as e'er men trod,
And there is in this business more than nature
Was ever conduct of. Some oracle 246
Must rectify our knowledge.

PROSPERO Sir, my liege,

Do not infest your mind with beating on 248
The strangeness of this business. At picked leisure, 249
Which shall be shortly, single I'll resolve you, 250
Which to you shall seem probable, of every 251
These happened accidents; till when, be cheerful 252
And think of each thing well. [*Aside to Ariel.*] Come
hither, spirit. 253

228 tricksy ingenious, sportive **229 strengthen** increase **232 dead of sleep** deep in sleep **234 several** different, diverse **240 Cap'ring to eye** dancing for joy to see. **On a trice** in an instant **241 them** i.e., the other crew members **242 moping** in a daze **246 conduct** guide, leader **248 infest** harass, disturb. **beating on** worrying about **249 picked** chosen, convenient **250 single** i.e., by my own human powers. **resolve** satisfy, explain to **251 probable** explicable, plausible **251–252 of every These** about every one of these **252 accidents** occurrences **253 well** favorably

Set Caliban and his companions free.
Untie the spell. [*Exit Ariel.*] How fares my gracious sir?
There are yet missing of your company
Some few odd lads that you remember not. 257

Enter Ariel, driving in Caliban, Stephano, and Trinculo in their stolen apparel.

STEPHANO Every man shift for all the rest, and let no 258
man take care for himself; for all is but fortune. Corag- 259
gio, bully monster, coraggio! 260

TRINCULO If these be true spies which I wear in my 261
head, here's a goodly sight.

CALIBAN
O Setebos, these be brave spirits indeed! 263
How fine my master is! I am afraid 264
He will chastise me.

SEBASTIAN Ha, ha!
What things are these, my lord Antonio?
Will money buy 'em?

ANTONIO Very like. One of them
Is a plain fish, and no doubt marketable.

PROSPERO
Mark but the badges of these men, my lords, 270
Then say if they be true. This misshapen knave, 271
His mother was a witch, and one so strong
That could control the moon, make flows and ebbs,
And deal in her command without her power. 274
These three have robbed me, and this demidevil—
For he's a bastard one—had plotted with them 276
To take my life. Two of these fellows you
Must know and own. This thing of darkness I 278
Acknowledge mine.

257 odd unaccounted for **258 shift** provide. **for all the rest** (Stephano drunkenly gets wrong the saying "Every man for himself.") **259–260 Coraggio** courage **260 bully monster** gallant monster. (Ironical.) **261 true spies** accurate observers (i.e., sharp eyes) **263 brave** handsome **264 fine** splendidly attired **270 badges** emblems of cloth or silver worn on the arms of retainers. (Prospero refers here to the stolen clothes as emblems of their villainy.) **271 true** honest **274 deal . . . power** wield the moon's power, either without her authority or beyond her influence **276 bastard** counterfeit **278 own** recognize, admit as belonging to you

CALIBAN I shall be pinched to death.

ALONSO
Is not this Stephano, my drunken butler?

SEBASTIAN He is drunk now. Where had he wine?

ALONSO
And Trinculo is reeling ripe. Where should they 282
Find this grand liquor that hath gilded 'em? 283
[*To Trinculo.*] How cam'st thou in this pickle? 284

TRINCULO I have been in such a pickle since I saw you last that, I fear me, will never out of my bones. I shall not fear flyblowing. 287

SEBASTIAN Why, how now, Stephano?

STEPHANO O, touch me not! I am not Stephano, but a cramp.

PROSPERO You'd be king o' the isle, sirrah? 291

STEPHANO I should have been a sore one, then. 292

ALONSO [*Pointing to Caliban*]
This is a strange thing as e'er I looked on.

PROSPERO
He is as disproportioned in his manners
As in his shape.—Go, sirrah, to my cell.
Take with you your companions. As you look
To have my pardon, trim it handsomely. 297

CALIBAN
Ay, that I will; and I'll be wise hereafter
And seek for grace. What a thrice-double ass
Was I to take this drunkard for a god
And worship this dull fool!

PROSPERO Go to. Away!

ALONSO
Hence, and bestow your luggage where you found it.

SEBASTIAN Or stole it, rather.
[*Exeunt Caliban, Stephano, and Trinculo.*]

PROSPERO
Sir, I invite Your Highness and your train

282 reeling ripe stumblingly drunk **283 gilded** (1) flushed, made drunk (2) covered with gilt (suggesting the horse urine) **284 pickle** (1) fix, predicament (2) pickling brine (in this case, horse urine) **287 flyblowing** i.e., being fouled by fly eggs (from which he is saved by being pickled) **291 sirrah** (Standard form of address to an inferior, here expressing reprimand.) **292 sore** (1) tyrannical (2) sorry, inept (3) wracked by pain **297 trim** prepare, decorate

To my poor cell, where you shall take your rest
For this one night; which, part of it, I'll waste 306
With such discourse as, I not doubt, shall make it
Go quick away: the story of my life,
And the particular accidents gone by 309
Since I came to this isle. And in the morn
I'll bring you to your ship, and so to Naples,
Where I have hope to see the nuptial
Of these our dear-belovèd solemnized;
And thence retire me to my Milan, where 314
Every third thought shall be my grave.

ALONSO I long
To hear the story of your life, which must
Take the ear strangely.

PROSPERO I'll deliver all; 317
And promise you calm seas, auspicious gales,
And sail so expeditious that shall catch
Your royal fleet far off. [*Aside to Ariel.*] My Ariel, chick,
That is thy charge. Then to the elements
Be free, and fare thou well!—Please you, draw near. 322

Exeunt omnes.

✤

306 waste spend **309 accidents** occurrences **314 retire me** return
317 Take take effect upon, enchant. **deliver** declare, relate **322 draw near** i.e., enter my cell

Epilogue *Spoken by* PROSPERO.

Now my charms are all o'erthrown,
And what strength I have 's mine own,
Which is most faint. Now, 'tis true,
I must be here confined by you
Or sent to Naples. Let me not,
Since I have my dukedom got
And pardoned the deceiver, dwell
In this bare island by your spell,
But release me from my bands 9
With the help of your good hands. 10
Gentle breath of yours my sails 11
Must fill, or else my project fails,
Which was to please. Now I want 13
Spirits to enforce, art to enchant, 14
And my ending is despair
Unless I be relieved by prayer, 16
Which pierces so that it assaults 17
Mercy itself, and frees all faults. 18
As you from crimes would pardoned be, 19
Let your indulgence set me free. *Exit.* 20

Epilogue.
9 bands bonds **10 hands** i.e., applause (the noise of which would break the spell of silence) **11 Gentle breath** favorable breeze (produced by hands clapping or favorable comment) **13 want** lack **14 enforce** control **16 prayer** i.e., Prospero's petition to the audience **17 assaults** rightfully gains the attention of **18 frees** obtains forgiveness for **19 crimes** sins **20 indulgence** (1) humoring, lenient approval (2) remission of punishment for sin

Date and Text

The Tempest was first printed in the First Folio of 1623. It occupies first place in the volume and is a scrupulously prepared text from a transcript by Ralph Crane of a theater promptbook or of Shakespeare's draft after it had been annotated for production; or Crane may have provided some of the elaboration of stage directions. Shakespeare's colleagues may have placed *The Tempest* first in the Folio because they considered it his most recent complete play. The first recorded performance was at court on November 1, 1611: "Hallomas nyght was presented att Whithall before ye kinges Maiestie a play Called the Tempest." The actors were "the Kings players" (*Revels Account*). The play was again presented at court during the winter of 1612–1613, this time "before the Princes Highnes the Lady Elizabeth and the Prince Pallatyne Elector." The festivities for this important betrothal and wedding were sumptuous, and included at least thirteen other plays. Various arguments have been put forward that Shakespeare composed parts of *The Tempest,* especially the masque, for this occasion, but there is absolutely no evidence that the play was singled out for special prominence among the many plays presented, and the masque is integral to the play as it stands. Probably the 1611 production was of a fairly new play. Simon Forman, who saw *Cymbeline* and *The Winter's Tale* in 1611, does not mention *The Tempest*. He died in September of 1611. According to every stylistic test, such as run-on and hypermetric lines, the play is very late. Shakespeare probably knew Sylvester Jourdain's *A Discovery of the Bermudas,* published in 1610, and William Strachey's *A True Repertory of the Wreck and Redemption,* dated July 1610 although not published until 1625.

Textual Notes

These textual notes are not a historical collation, either of the early folios or of more recent editions; they are simply a record of departures in this edition from the copy text. The reading adopted in this edition appears in boldface, followed by the rejected reading from the copy text, i.e., the First Folio. Only major alterations in punctuation are noted. Changes in lineation are not indicated, nor are some minor and obvious typographical errors.

Abbreviations used:
F the First Folio
s.d. stage direction
s.p. speech prefix

Copy text: the First Folio. Characters' names are grouped at the heads of scenes throughout.

Names of the Actors [printed in F at the end of the play]

1.1. 8 s.d. Ferdinand Ferdinando **34 s.d. Exeunt** Exit **36 [and elsewhere] wi' the** with **38 s.d.** [at l. 37 in F]

1.2. 99 exact, like exact. Like **166 steaded much.** steeded much, **201 bowsprit** Bore-spritt **213 me. The** me the **263, 267 Algiers** Argier **284 she** he **288 service. Thou** service, thou **330 forth at** for that **377, 399 s.d. Ariel's** Ariel (or Ariell) **400 s.p. Ariel** [not in F] **385 s.d. Burden, dispersedly** [before "Hark, hark!" l. 384 in F] **387** [F provides a speech prefix, *Ar.*]

2.1. 38 s.p. Antonio Seb **39 s.p. Sebastian** Ant **232 throes** throwes

2.2. 9 mow moe **116 spirits** sprights

3.1. 2 sets set

3.2. 123 scout cout

3.3. 17 s.d. Solemn . . . invisible [after "they are fresh" in F, and followed by the s.d. at l. 19, *Enter . . . depart*] **28 me** me? **29 islanders?** Islands; **33 human** humaine **65 plume** plumbe

4.1. 9 off of **13 gift** guest **68 poll-clipped** pole-clipt **74 Her** here **110 s.p. Ceres** [not in F] **123 wife** wise **124 s.d.** [at l. 127 in F] **163 s.d. Exeunt** Exit **193 s.d. Enter . . . etc.** [after "on this line" in F] **193 them on** on them **232 Let 't** let's

5.1. 60 boiled boile **72 Didst** Did **75 entertained** entertaine **82 lies** ly **88 s.p. Ariel** [not in F] **236 horrible,** horrible. **238 her** our **249 business. At** businesse, at **250 Which . . . single** (Which shall be shortly single) **259–260 Coraggio** Corasio

Shakespeare's Sources

No direct literary source for the whole of *The Tempest* has been found. Shakespeare does seem to have drawn material from various accounts of the shipwreck of the *Sea Venture* in the Bermudas, in 1609, although the importance of these materials should not be overstated. Several of the survivors wrote narratives of the shipwreck itself and of their life on the islands for some nine months. Sylvester Jourdain, in *A Discovery of the Bermudas*, published 1610 (see the selection that follows), speaks of miraculous preservation despite the island's reputation for being "a most prodigious and enchanted place." William Strachey's letter, written in July of 1610 and published much later (1625) as *A True Repertory of the Wreck and Redemption . . . from the Islands of the Bermudas*, describes (as can be seen in the selection that follows) the panic among the passengers and crew, the much-feared reputation of the island as the habitation of devils and wicked spirits, the actual beauty and fertility of the place with its abundance of wild life (cf. Caliban's descriptions), and the treachery of the Indians they later encounter in Virginia. Shakespeare seems to have read Strachey's letter in manuscript and may have been acquainted with him. The storm scene in Chapter 4 of Laurence Twine's *The Pattern of Painful Adventures*, a major source for *Pericles*, may also have given Shakespeare material for the first scene of *The Tempest;* see the source materials in the Bantam edition of that play. Shakespeare also kept up with travel accounts of Sir Walter Ralegh and Thomas Harriot, and knew various classical evocations of a New World. The name "Setebos" came from Richard Eden's *History of Travel* (1577), translated from Peter Martyr's *De Novo Orbe* and from other travel accounts of the period. (See the Introduction to the play for the potential relevance of various journals of the circumnavigation of the globe.) All these hints are indeed suggestive, but they are scattered and relate more to the setting and general circumstance of Shakespeare's play than to the plot.

Shakespeare certainly consulted Michel de Montaigne's essay "Of the Cannibals," as translated by John Florio in

1603. Gonzalo's reverie on an ideal commonwealth (2.1.150–171) contains many verbal echoes of the essay, as can be seen in the selection that follows. Montaigne's point is that supposedly civilized persons who condemn as barbarous any society not conforming with their own are simply refusing to examine their own shortcomings. A supposedly primitive society may well embody perfect religion, justice, and harmony; civilized art can never rival the achievements of nature. The ideal commonwealth has no need of magistrates, riches, poverty, and contracts, all of which breed dissimulation and covetousness. The significance of these ideas for *The Tempest* extends well beyond the particular passage in which they are found. And Caliban himself, whose name is an anagram of "cannibal," illustrates (even though he is not an eater of human flesh) the truth of Montaigne's observation apropos of the intense and wanton cruelty he finds so widespread in so-called Western civilization: "I think there is more barbarism in eating men alive than to feed upon them being dead."

Prospero's famous valedictory speech to "Ye elves of hills, brooks, standing lakes, and groves" (5.1.33–57) owes its origin to Medea's similar invocation in Ovid's *Metamorphoses* (Book 7), which Shakespeare knew both in the Latin original and in Golding's translation: "Ye airs and winds, ye elves of hills, of brooks, of woods alone, / Of standing lakes . . ." Medea also anticipates Shakespeare's Sycorax. Medea thus provides material for the representation of both black and white magic in *The Tempest,* so carefully differentiated by Shakespeare. Ariel is part English fairy, like Puck, and part daemon. The pastoral situation in *The Tempest* is perhaps derived from Edmund Spenser's *The Faerie Queene,* Book 6 (with its distinctions between savage lust and true courtesy, between nature and art). Italian pastoral drama as practiced by Guarini and (in England) by John Fletcher may also have been an influence. The masque element in *The Tempest,* prominent as in much late Shakespeare, bears the imprint of the courtly masque tradition of Ben Jonson, Francis Beaumont, and John Fletcher. Virgil's *Aeneid* may have provided Shakespeare with a more indirect source, with its story of wandering in the Mediterranean and storm at sea, love in Carthage, the intervention of the gods, and the fulfillment of destiny in Italy.

A German play, *Die Schöne Sidea* by Jacob Ayrer, written before 1605, was once thought to have been based on an earlier version of *The Tempest* as performed by English players traveling in Germany. Today the similarities between the two plays are generally attributed to conventions found everywhere in romance.

A Discovery of the Bermudas

By Sylvester Jourdain

Any departures from the original text are noted with an asterisk and appear at the bottom of the page in boldface; original readings are in roman.

Being in ship called the *Sea Venture,* with Sir Thomas Gates, our governor, Sir George Somers, and Captain Newport, three most worthy honored gentlemen, whose valor and fortitude the world must needs take notice of, and that in most honorable designs bound for Virginia, in the height of thirty degrees of northerly latitude or thereabouts, we were taken with a most sharp and cruel storm upon the five and twentieth day of July, Anno 1609. Which did not only separate us from the residue of our fleet, which were eight in number, but, with the violent working of the seas, our ship became so shaken, torn, and leaked that she received so much water as covered two tier of hogsheads[1] above the ballast, that our men stood up to the middles with buckets, barricos,[2] and kettles to bail out the water and continually pumped for three days and three nights together without any intermission, and yet the water seemed rather to increase than to diminish. Insomuch that all our men, being utterly spent, tired, and disabled for longer labor, were even resolved, without any hope of their lives, to shut up the hatches and to have committed themselves to the mercy of the sea (which is said to be merciless) or rather to the mercy of their mighty God and redeemer (whose mercies exceed all his works), seeing no help nor hope in the apprehension of man's reason that any mother's child could escape that inevitable danger which every man had proposed and digested[3] to himself of present[4] sinking.

So that some of them, having some good and comfortable waters[5] in the ship, fetched them and drunk one to the other, taking their last leave one of the other until their more joyful and happy meeting in a more blessed world. When it pleased God, out of his most gracious and merciful providence, so to direct and guide our ship, being left to the mercy of the sea for her most advantage, that Sir George Somers, sitting upon the poop of the ship, where he sat

1 hogsheads large barrels or casks **2 barricos** kegs **3 digested** pondered **4 present** immediate **5 waters** distilled alcohol

three days and three nights together without meals' meat[6] and little or no sleep, conning[7] the ship to keep her as upright as he could (for otherwise she must needs instantly have foundered),[8] most wishedly happily descried land.

Whereupon he most comfortably encouraged the company to follow[9] their pumping and by no means to cease bailing out of the water with their buckets, barricos, and kettles, whereby they were so over-wearied, and their spirits so spent with long fasting and continuance of their labor, that for the most part they were fallen asleep in corners and wheresoever they chanced first to sit or lie. But hearing news of land, wherewith they grew to be somewhat revived, being carried with will and desire beyond their strength, every man bustled up and gathered his strength and feeble spirits together to perform as much as their weak force would permit him.

Through which weak means it pleased God to work so strongly as[10] the water was stayed[11] for that little time, which, as we all much feared, was the last period of our breathing,[12] and the ship kept from present sinking, when it pleased God to send her within half an English mile of that land Sir George Somers had not long before descried—which were the islands of the Bermudas. And there neither did our ship sink, but, more fortunately in so great a misfortune, fell in[13] between two rocks, where she was fast lodged and locked for further budging. Whereby we gained not only sufficient time, with the present help of our boat and skiff, safely to set and convey our men ashore (which were one hundred and fifty in number), but afterwards had time and leisure to save some good part of our goods and provision which the water had not spoiled, with all the tackling[14] of the ship and much of the iron about her, which were necessaries not a little available for the building and furnishing of a new ship and pinnace,[15]* which we made there for the transporting and carrying of us to Virginia.

But our delivery was not more strange in falling so oppor-

*__pinnace__ pinms

6 meals' meat food **7 conning** steering, navigating **8 foundered** been engulfed, sent to the bottom **9 follow** keep up **10 as** that **11 stayed** held back **12 the last . . . breathing** i.e., our last gasp **13 fell in** i.e., steered her way **14 tackling** ropes and pulleys **15 pinnace** a light sailing vessel used as a tender for a larger ship

tunely and happily upon the land as our feeding and preservation was beyond our hopes and all men's expectations most admirable. For the islands of the Bermudas, as every man knoweth that hath heard or read of them, were never inhabited by any Christian or heathen people, but ever esteemed and reputed a most prodigious and enchanted place, affording nothing but gusts, storms, and foul weather, which made every navigator and mariner to avoid them as Scylla and Charybdis,[16] or as they would shun the devil himself; and no man was ever heard to make for[17] the place but as[18] against their wills they have, by storms and dangerousness of the rocks lying seven leagues into the sea, suffered shipwreck. Yet did we find there the air so temperate and the country so abundantly fruitful of all fit necessaries for the sustenation and preservation of man's life, that most in a manner of all[19] our provisions of bread, beer, and victual being quite spoiled in lying long drowned in salt water, notwithstanding we were there for the space of nine months (few days over or under) not only well refreshed, comforted, and with good satiety contented but, out of the abundance thereof, provided us some reasonable quantity and proportion[20] of provision to carry us for Virginia and to maintain ourselves and that company we found there, to the great relief of them, as it fell out in their so great extremities and in respect of the shortness of time, until it pleased God that, by my lord's[21] coming thither, their store was better supplied. And greater and better provisions we might have had if we had had better means for the storing and transportation thereof. Wherefore my opinion sincerely of this island is that whereas it hath been and is still accounted the most dangerous, infortunate, and most forlorn place of the world, it is in truth the richest, healthfulest, and pleasing land (the quantity and bigness thereof considered) and merely[22] natural as ever man set foot upon.

16 Scylla and Charybdis monster and whirlpool facing each other across a narrow strait in *The Odyssey,* Book 12 **17 make for** head for **18 as** that **19 most in a manner of all** i.e., even though nearly all **20 proportion** share **21 my lord's** i.e., Sir Thomas Gates's **22 merely** utterly

[Most of the remainder of *A Discovery of the Bermudas* is taken up with a description of the island, its flora and fauna, etc., much as in William Strachey's account.]

Text based on *A Discovery of the Bermudas* [*spelled Barmudas* in the original], *Otherwise Called the Isle of Devils, by Sir Thomas Gates, Sir George Somers, and Captain Newport, with Divers Others. . . . London, Printed by John Windet . . . 1610.*

A True Repertory of the Wreck and Redemption of Sir Thomas Gates, Knight, upon and from the Islands of the Bermudas

By William Strachey

[Strachey's account is in the form of a letter, beginning as the fleet of seven ships and two pinnaces—i.e., light sailing vessels used as tenders for the larger ships—is within seven or eight days sailing of Cape Henry, Virginia, in late July of 1609.]

When on Saint James his day, July 24, being Monday, preparing for no less all the black night before, the clouds gathering thick upon us and the winds singing and whistling most unusually, which made us to cast off our pinnace, towing the same until then astern, a dreadful storm and hideous began to blow from out the northeast, which, swelling and roaring as it were by fits, some hours with more violence than others, at length did beat all light from heaven; which like an hell of darkness turned black upon us, so much the more fuller of horror as in such cases horror and fear use to[1] overrun the troubled and overmastered senses of all, which, taken up with amazement, the ears lay so sensible to the terrible cries and murmurs of the winds and distraction of our company as who was most armed[2] and best prepared was not a little shaken. . . .

For four and twenty hours the storm in a restless tumult had blown so exceedingly as we could not apprehend in our imaginations any possibility of greater violence. Yet did we still find it not only more terrible but more constant, fury added to fury and one storm urging a second more outrageous than the former, whether it so wrought upon our fears or indeed met with new forces. Sometimes shrieks[3]* in our ship amongst women and passengers not used to such hurly and discomforts made us look one upon the other with troubled hearts and panting bosoms. Our clamors drowned in the winds, and the winds in thunder.

***shrieks** strikes

1 use to habitually, characteristically **2 as who was most armed** that even that person who was most ready to protect himself **3 shrieks** (The original *strikes* is probably an error for *shrikes*.)

Prayers might well be in the heart and lips, but drowned in the outcries of the officers. Nothing heard that could give comfort, nothing seen that might encourage hope.

It is impossible for me, had I the voice of Stentor[4] and expression of as many tongues as his throat of voices, to express the outcries and miseries. . . . In which the sea swelled above the clouds and gave battle unto heaven. It could not be said to rain; the waters like whole rivers did flood in the air. And this I did still observe: that whereas upon the land, when a storm hath poured itself forth once in drifts of rain, the wind, as beaten down and vanquished therewith not long after endureth; here the glut of water, as if throttling the wind erewhile,[5] was no sooner a little emptied and qualified but instantly the winds, as having gotten their mouths now free and at liberty, spake more loud and grew more tumultuous and malignant.

What shall I say? Winds and seas were as mad as fury and rage could make them. For mine own part, I had been in some storms before. . . . Yet all that I had ever suffered gathered together might not hold comparison with this. There was not a moment in which the sudden splitting or instant oversetting of the ship was not expected.

Howbeit, this was not all. It pleased God to bring a greater affliction yet upon us, for in the beginning of the storm we had received likewise a mighty leak. And the ship . . . was grown five foot suddenly deep with water above her ballast, and we almost drowned within whilst we sat looking when to perish from above. This, imparting no less terror than danger, ran through the whole ship with much fright and amazement, startled and turned the blood and took down the braves[6] of the most hardy mariner of them all, insomuch as he that before happily felt not the sorrow of others now began to sorrow for himself when he saw such a pond of water so suddenly broken in, and which he knew could not, without present avoiding, but instantly sink him. . . .

Once, so huge a sea brake upon the poop and quarter upon us, as it covered our ship from stern to stem like a garment or a vast cloud; it filled her brim full for a while within, from the hatches up to the spar deck. This source,

4 Stentor a Greek with a voice as loud as fifty men **5 erewhile** formerly **6 braves** courage

or confluence, of water was so violent as[7] it rushed and carried the helmsman from the helm and wrested the whipstaff[8] out of his hand, which so flew from side to side that, when he would have seized[9] the same again, it so tossed him from starboard to larboard as it was God's mercy it had not split him. It so beat him from his hold and so bruised him as[10] a fresh man, hazarding in by chance, fell fair with it and, by main strength bearing somewhat up, made good his place,[11] and with much clamor encouraged and called upon others, who gave her now up, rent in pieces and absolutely lost. . . .

During all this time, the heavens looked so black upon us that it was not possible the elevation of the pole might be observed,[12] nor a star by night nor sunbeam by day was to be seen. Only upon the Thursday night, Sir George Somers, being upon the watch, had an apparition of a little round light, like a faint star, trembling and streaming along with a sparkling blaze half the height upon the mainmast and shooting sometimes from shroud to shroud, tempting[13] to settle as it were upon any of the four shrouds. And for three or four hours together, or rather more, half the night it kept with us, running sometimes along the mainyard to the very end and then returning. At which Sir George Somers called divers about him and showed them the same, who observed it with much wonder and carefulness. But upon a sudden, towards the morning watch, they lost the sight of it and knew not what way it made. The superstitious seamen make many constructions of this sea fire, which nevertheless is usual in storms—the same, it may be, which the Grecians were wont in the Mediterranean to call Castor and Pollux, of which, if one only appeared without the other, they took it for an evil sign of great tempest.[14] The Italians

7 as that **8 whipstaff** handle attached to the tiller **9 seized** i.e., secured, stopped its uncontrolled whipping about **10 as** that **11 made good his place** (Another seaman, coming on the scene by chance, manages by brute strength to secure the tiller and its handle.) **made good** supplied **12 the elevation . . . observed** to measure the elevation of the polestar above the horizon (and thereby determine latitude)
13 tempting attempting. (The phenomenon observed is St. Elmo's fire, as in *The Tempest*, 1.2.197–202.) **14 Castor and Pollux . . . tempest** (This name, taken from the twin sons of Tyndarus and Leda, was applied to St. Elmo's fire because, when the phenomenon appeared in pairs simultaneously, it was thought to signal the cessation of a storm.)

and such, who lie open to the Adriatic and Tyrrhene Sea,[15] call it a sacred body, *Corpo sancto*. The Spaniards call it Saint Elmo, and have an authentic and miraculous legend for it. Be it what it will, we laid other foundations of safety or ruin than in the rising or falling of it. Could it have served us now miraculously to have taken our height by,[16] it might have strucken amazement and a reverence in our devotions, according to the due of a miracle. But it did not light us any whit the more to our known way, who ran now (as do hoodwinked men) at all adventures,[17] sometimes north and northeast, then north and by west . . . and sometimes half the compass. . . .

It being now Friday, the fourth morning, it wanted little but that there had been[18] a general determination to have shut up hatches, and, commending our sinful souls to God, committed the ship to the mercy of the sea. Surely that night we must have done it, and that night had we then perished. But see the goodness and sweet introduction of better hope by our merciful God given unto us! Sir George Somers, when no man dreamed of such happiness, had discovered and cried[19] land. . . . But having no hope to save her by coming to an anchor in the same [some smooth water under the southeast point of the land], we were enforced to run her ashore as near the land as we could, which brought us within three quarters of a mile of shore; and, by the mercy of God unto us, making out our boats,[20] we had ere night brought all our men, women, and children—about the number of one hundred and fifty—safe into the island.

We found it to be the dangerous and dreaded island, or rather islands, of the Bermuda, whereof let me give Your Ladyship[21] a brief description before I proceed to my narration. And that the rather,[22] because they be so terrible to all that ever touched on them, and such tempests, thunders, and other fearful objects are seen and heard about them, that they be called commonly the Devil's Islands, and are feared and avoided of all sea travelers alive above any other

15 Tyrrhene Sea Tyrrhenian Sea, lying between Italy, Sicily, and Sardinia **16 to have . . . by** to have measured our latitude by. (See note 12 above.) **17 at all adventures** totally at random **18 it wanted . . . been** i.e., we were very close to. **it wanted** there lacked **19 cried** announced, called out **20 making out our boats** setting out our small ship's boats **21 Your Ladyship** the noble lady to whom the letter is written **22 rather** sooner

place in the world. Yet it pleased our merciful God to make even this hideous and hated place both the place of our safety and means of our deliverance.

And hereby also I hope to deliver the world from a foul and general error, it being counted[23] of most that they can be no habitation for men, but rather given over to devils and wicked spirits. Whereas indeed we find them now by experience to be as habitable and commodious as most countries of the same climate and situation, insomuch as, if the entrance into them were as easy as the place itself is contenting, it had long ere this been inhabited as well as other islands. Thus shall we make it appear that Truth is the daughter of Time, and that men ought not to deny everything which is not subject to their own sense.

[Strachey proceeds with a description of the islands—their climate, topography, flora and fauna, etc.]

Sure it is that there are no rivers nor running springs of fresh water to be found upon any of them. When we came first, we digged and found certain gushings and soft bubblings which, being either in bottoms or on the side of hanging ground, were only fed with rain water which nevertheless soon sinketh into the earth and vanisheth away, or emptieth itself out of sight into the sea without any channel above or upon the superficies[24] of the earth. For according as their rains fell, we had wells and pits which we digged either half full or absolute exhausted and dry; howbeit some low bottoms, which the continual descent from the hills filled full, and in those flats could have no passage away, we found to continue as fishing ponds or standing pools, continually summer and winter full of fresh water.

The shore and bays round about when we landed first afforded great store of fish, and that of divers kinds, and good. . . . We have taken also from under the broken rocks crevices[25] oftentimes greater than any of our best English lobsters, and likewise abundance of crabs, oyster, and whelks. True it is, for fish in every cove and creek we found snaules and skulles[26] in that abundance as I think no island in the world may have greater store or better fish. . . .

23 counted reckoned, supposed **24 superficies** surface **25 crevices** crayfish. (French *écrevisse.*) **26 snaules and skulles** (Identity uncertain: snails or snailfish and schools or skullfish?)

Fowl there is great store. . . . A kind of webfooted fowl there is, of the bigness of an English green plover or seamew,[27] which all the summer we saw not, and in the darkest nights of November and December (for in the night they only feed) they would come forth but not fly far from home and, hovering in the air and over the sea, made a strange hollow and harsh howling. . . . Our men found a pretty way to take them, which was by standing on the rocks or sands by the seaside and halooing, laughing, and making the strangest outcry that possibly they could. With the noise whereof the birds would come flocking to that place and settle upon the very arms and head of him that so cried, and still creep nearer and nearer, answering the noise themselves; by which our men would weigh them with their hand, and which weighed heaviest they took for the best and let the others alone, and so our men would take twenty dozen in two hours of the chiefest of them; and they were a good and well-relished fowl, fat and full as a partridge.

[Among the other adventures reported by Strachey is a conspiracy or mutiny aimed at the life of their governor, but the leaders are apprehended. Later, when they reach Virginia and find the colony of Jamestown in a perilous state, the voyagers encounter some native Indians and are surprised to discover "how little a fair and noble entreaty works upon a barbarous disposition."]

Strachey's letter, written in 1610, was published as *A True Repertory of the Wreck and Redemption of Sir Thomas Gates, Knight, upon and from the Islands of the Bermudas, His Coming to Virginia, and the Estate of the Colony Then and After under the Government of the Lord La Warre. July, 15, 1610, written by William Strachey, Esquire.* In Samuel Purchas, *Purchas His Pilgrims* (1625), Part 4, Book 9, Chapter 6, pp. 1734 ff.

---

27 seamew sea gull (perhaps to be identified with the *scamels* mentioned by Caliban in *The Tempest*, 2.2.170)

The Essays of Michael, Lord of Montaigne

Translated by John Florio

Book 1, Chapter 30: Of the Cannibals

[Montaigne begins by citing approvingly the opinion of King Pyrrhus of Greece that the so-called barbarians are often far from barbarous. "Lo, how a man ought to take heed lest he overweeningly follow vulgar opinions, which should be measured by the rule of reason and not by the common report." Montaigne cites various examples and then turns to the American Indians.]

Now, to return to my purpose, I find (as far as I have been informed) there is nothing in that nation that is either barbarous or savage, unless men call that barbarism which is not common to them. As indeed we have no other aim of truth and reason than the example and idea of the opinions and customs of the country we live in. There is ever perfect religion, perfect policy,[1] perfect and complete use of all things. They[2] are even "savage" as we call those fruits wild which nature of herself and of her ordinary progress[3] hath produced, whereas indeed they are those which ourselves have altered by our artificial devices and diverted from their common order we should rather term "savage."[4] In those[5] are the true and most profitable virtues and natural properties most lively and vigorous, which in these[6] we have bastardized, applying them to the pleasure of our corrupted taste. And if, notwithstanding, in divers fruits of those countries that were never tilled we shall find that, in respect of[7] ours, they are most excellent and as delicate unto our taste, there is no reason art should gain the point

1 There . . . policy i.e., there, in our own society as we complacently view it, is always perfect religion, perfect government **2. They** i.e., those "savage" people **3 progress** course, way **4 they are those . . . "savage"** we should instead term "savage" those things we ourselves have artificially diverted from their natural function **5 those** i.e., things made by nature **6 these** i.e., things diverted by us from their natural function **7 in respect of** in comparison with

of honor of[8] our great and puissant mother Nature. We have so much by our inventions surcharged[9] the beauties and riches of her works that we have altogether overchoked her; yet wherever her purity shineth, she makes our vain and frivolous enterprises wonderfully ashamed.

Et veniunt hederae sponte sua melius,
Surgit et in solis formosior arbutus antris,
Et volucres nulla dulcius arte canunt.

Ivies spring better of their own accord;
Unhaunted[10] plots much fairer trees afford;
Birds by no art much sweeter notes record.
[Propertius]

All our endeavors or wit cannot so much as reach to represent the nest of the least birdlet, its contexture, beauty, profit, and use, no, nor the web of a silly[11] spider. "All things," saith Plato, "are produced either by nature, by fortune, or by art. The greatest and fairest by one or other of the two first, the least and imperfect by the last."

Those nations seem therefore so barbarous unto me because they have received very little fashion from human wit[12] and are yet near their original naturality. The laws of nature do yet command them, which are but little bastardized[13] by ours, and that with such purity as I am sometimes grieved the knowledge of it came no sooner to light at what time[14] there were men that better than we could have judged of it. I am sorry Lycurgus[15] and Plato had it not, for meseemeth that, what in those nations we see by experience doth not only exceed all the pictures wherewith licentious[16] poesy hath proudly embellished the golden age and all her

8 should . . . honor of should be awarded the prize over **9 by our inventions surcharged** by means of our artificial contrivances overwhelmed **10 Unhaunted** unfrequented **11 silly** innocent, simple, tiny
12 Those . . . wit i.e., those so-called savage nations seem therefore "barbarous" to me only in the sense that they have received little fashioning from civilized intellect **13 but little bastardized** scarcely diverted from their natural function **14 at what time** when
15 Lycurgus legendary Spartan legislator whose name was applied to important social and legal reforms c. 600 B.C. **16 licentious** taking free poetic license, playing fast and loose with the truth

quaint inventions to feign[17] a happy condition of man, but also the conception and desire of philosophy. They[18] could not imagine a genuity[19] so pure and simple as we see it by experience,[20] nor ever believe[21] our society might be maintained with so little art and humane combination. It is a nation, would I answer Plato, that hath no kind of traffic,[22] no knowledge of letters,[23] no intelligence[24] of numbers, no name of magistrate,[25] nor of politic superiority,[26] no use of service,[27] of riches, or of poverty, no contracts, no successions, no dividances, no occupation but idle,[28] no respect of kindred but common,[29] no apparel but natural, no manuring of lands, no use of wine, corn,[30] or metal. The very words that import lying, falsehood, treason, dissimulations, covetousness, envy, detraction,[31] and pardon, were never heard of amongst them. How dissonant would he find[32] his imaginary commonwealth from this perfection!

Hos natura modos primum dedit.

Nature at first uprise[33]
These manners did devise.
[Virgil]

Furthermore, they live in a country of so exceeding pleasant and temperate situation that, as my testimonies[34] have told me, it is very rare to see a sick body amongst them; and they have further assured me they never saw any man there either shaking with the palsy, toothless, with eyes dropping,[35] or crooked and stooping through age.

17 all her . . . feign all of poesy's ingenious fabrications used to imagine or pretend **18 They** i.e., poesy and philosophy **19 genuity** ingenuousness, simplicity **20 by experience** i.e., by looking at the ways of so-called "savage" peoples **21 believe** believe that **22 traffic** trade **23 letters** writing **24 intelligence** knowledge, science **25 of magistrate** for a magistrate **26 politic superiority** political hierarchy **27 service** servitude **28 but idle** except leisure ones **29 no respect . . . common** no kinship ties except those held in common **30 corn** wheat. (Grains grow naturally, not by agriculture.) **31 detraction** belittling **32 How dissonant would he find** i.e., how far (from this ideal state of affairs) would he, Plato, find **33 at first uprise** at her very beginnings **34 testimonies** witnesses **35 with eyes dropping** i.e., bleary-eyed or discharging fluid

[Montaigne continues with a description of their abundance. Later in the essay he examines cannibalism in the same relativistic terms:]

I am not sorry we note the barbarous horror of such an action, but grieved that, prying so narrowly into their faults, we are so blinded in ours. I think there is more barbarism in eating men alive than to feed upon them being dead—to mangle by tortures and torments a body full of lively sense,[36] to roast him in pieces, to make dogs and swine to gnaw and tear him in mammocks[37] (as we have not only read but seen very lately, yea, and in our own memory, not amongst ancient enemies but our neighbors and fellow citizens, and, which is worse, under pretense of piety and religion) than to roast and tear him after he is dead.

Text based on *The Essays, or Moral, Politic, and Military Discourses of Lord Michael de Montaigne. . . . First written by him in French. And now done into English by . . . John Florio. Printed at London by Val. Sims for Edward Blount . . . 1603.*

36 lively sense acute feeling **37 mammocks** shreds

Metamorphoses

By Ovid

Translated by Arthur Golding

Book 7

[Medea, preparing to use her magical powers to prolong the life of Jason's father, Aeson, invokes the spirits of the unseen world.]

Ye airs and winds, ye elves of hills, of brooks, of woods alone,
Of standing lakes, and of the night, approach ye everychone! 266
Through help of whom, the crooked banks much wondering at the thing,
I have compellèd streams to run clean backward to their spring.
By charms I make the calm seas rough and make the rough seas plain,
And cover all the sky with clouds and chase them thence again.
By charms I raise and lay the winds, and burst the viper's jaw, 271
And from the bowels of the earth both stones and trees do draw.
Whole woods and forests I remove; I make the mountains shake,
And even the earth itself to groan and fearfully to quake.
I call up dead men from their graves; and thee, O lightsome Moon, 275
I darken oft, though beaten brass abate thy peril soon. 276

266 everychone everyone **271 lay** allay, cause to subside **275 lightsome** light-giving **276 though . . . soon** (Alludes to the belief that a loud noise such as that produced by beating on metal would frighten away the malign influence of an eclipse.)

Our sorcery dims the morning fair and darks the sun
at noon.

Text based on *The XV Books of P. Ovidius Naso, Entitled Metamorphoses. Translated out of Latin into English meter by Arthur Golding, Gentleman. A work very pleasant and delectable.... Imprinted at London by William Seres. 1567.*

Further Reading

Auden, W. H. "The Sea and the Mirror: A Commentary on Shakespeare's *The Tempest.*" *For the Time Being*. New York: Random House, 1944. Rpt. in *The Collected Poetry of W. H. Auden*. New York: Random House, 1945. Auden's "The Sea and the Mirror" is a poetic meditation on *The Tempest*, a sequence of imagined speeches taking up where Shakespeare's play ends. Characters declare their new knowledge of what they are: Antonio still recalcitrant, Prospero poignantly aware of his own limitations, and Caliban voicing the disturbing reality that he represents for both Prospero and the audience.

Berger, Harry, Jr. "Miraculous Harp: A Reading of Shakespeare's *Tempest.*" *Shakespeare Studies* 5 (1969): 253–283. Berger offers a complex refutation of the familiar romantic readings of the play. Focusing on Prospero's efforts at mastery in the recurring scenes in which he attempts to evoke fear, guilt, or sympathy, Berger argues that the play dramatizes the limitations of Prospero's power as well as his deep reluctance to abandon it.

Brockbank, J. Philip. "*The Tempest*: Conventions of Art and Empire." In *Later Shakespeare*, ed. John Russell Brown and Bernard Harris. Stratford-upon-Avon Studies 8. London: Edward Arnold; New York: St. Martin's, 1966. In the accounts of the wreck of the *Sea Venture* and the miraculous survival of its crew, Brockbank finds the origins of *The Tempest*'s emphasis upon providential control and moral change. For him the play celebrates the process of conversion and repentance, not in the organic metaphors of seasonal growth as in Shakespeare's pastoral plays, but in images of the mysterious, renewing action of the sea.

Coleridge, Samuel Taylor. *"The Tempest." Coleridge's Writings on Shakespeare*, ed. Terence Hawkes. New York: G. P. Putnam's Sons, 1959. In a series of lectures, Coleridge discusses the "astonishing and intuitive knowledge" of character that Shakespeare reveals in "this, almost miraculous, drama." Ariel is a spirit of the air, necessarily resenting that "he is bound to obey Prospero."

Caliban "is all earth," but Shakespeare "has raised him far above contempt." Of Prospero and Miranda Coleridge says: "I have often thought of Shakespeare as the mighty wizard himself introducing as the first and fairest pledge of his so potent art, the female character in all its charms."

Felperin, Howard. "Undream'd Shores: *The Tempest.*" *Shakespearean Romance.* Princeton, N.J.: Princeton Univ. Press, 1972. Romance, according to Felperin, is both the subject and the genre of *The Tempest.* The play tests the ability of the imagination to perfect reality, and if Prospero's magic is ultimately found unable to reconcile the idealizing impulses of romance and the resistances of history, Shakespeare's art can—in the play's ingenious combination of a fictional political action and a romantic account of a shipwreck based on historical sources.

Fiedler, Leslie A. "The New World Savage as Stranger; or, ''Tis New to Thee.'" *The Stranger in Shakespeare.* New York: Stein and Day, 1972. In a provocative reading of the play focusing on its relation to the colonizing enterprise of Renaissance Europe, Fiedler argues that Caliban's role as "a savage and deformed slave" reveals the inadequacy of the play's twin utopian hopes: Gonzalo's vision of an idealized political existence and Prospero's fantasy of innocent love.

Frey, Charles. "*The Tempest* and the New World." *Shakespeare Quarterly* 30 (1979): 29–41. Believing the play to be neither "an autonomous imaginative construct" nor "an historical document," Frey suggestively examines accounts of Sir Francis Drake's circumnavigation of the globe and records of the Jamestown settlement to explore *The Tempest*'s "peculiar merger of history and romance."

Frye, Northrop. *A Natural Perspective: The Development of Shakespeare's Comedy and Romance,* passim. New York: Columbia Univ. Press, 1965. Frye treats the late romances as a return to and culmination of the logic of the earlier romantic comedies. In *The Tempest* Frye discovers the comic movement from confusion to identity and from sterility to renewed life, lifting us out of the world of ordinary experience into a world perfected by the human imagination.

James, D. G. *The Dream of Prospero.* Oxford: Clarendon Press, 1967. James locates the play in the context of Shakespeare's own achievement in *Hamlet* and *King Lear* as well as in the intellectual and political currents of the early seventeenth century. He explores the play's complex play of tone as it reveals a world in which love and hope cannot deny the possibility of tragedy but do make it possible to bear the burden of tragic knowledge.

James, Henry. "Introduction to *The Tempest.*" In *Complete Works of Shakespeare*, 1907, ed. Sydney Lazarus Lee. Rpt. in *Henry James: Selected Literary Criticism*, ed. Morris Shapira. London: Heineman, 1963; New York: Horizon, 1964. In his introduction to *The Tempest*—one of "the supreme works of all literature"—James reflects upon the contradiction between the man who, having written the play, retires to Stratford, and the artist at the peak of his powers of expression, aware of his mastery of style and characterization.

Kermode, Frank. *"The Tempest." William Shakespeare: The Final Plays.* London: Longmans, Green, 1963. While *The Tempest*, like Shakespeare's other late plays, develops the familiar themes of repentance and renewal, its handling of this romantic material differs from the others in the neoclassic design of the plot and the philosophical and spectacular elements drawn from the masque. Above all, for Kermode, the play is strange and elusive, lacking the other romances' sustained notes of joy and rising above the ingenuities of criticism that would contain its mystery.

Kernan, Alvin B. " 'The Great Globe Itself': The Public Playhouse and the Ideal Theater of *The Tempest.*" *The Playwright as Magician: Shakespeare's Image of the Poet in the English Public Theater*. New Haven, Conn.: Yale Univ. Press, 1979. Kernan finds that in the creation and control of Prospero's island kingdom through art lie Shakespeare's strongest claims for the power of the theatrical imagination: the play is both visionary and moral, recreating in Prospero's suffering and exile the central pattern of existence.

Kott, Jan. "Prospero's Staff." *Shakespeare Our Contemporary,* trans. Boleslaw Taborski. Garden City, N.Y.: Doubleday, 1964. In Kott's dark vision of *The Tempest*, the island is not a utopian landscape but a stage on which the history of the world with its endless struggles for power is elementally enacted. Prospero's rule over Caliban's island mirrors Antonio's usurpation of Prospero's throne; Sebastian's hope to murder Alonso repeats Antonio's fratricidal desires; and the plot of Stephano, Trinculo, and Caliban to depose and murder Prospero farcically reenacts all of the grim human history that Kott sees centrally reflected in the play.

Marx, Leo. "Shakespeare's American Fable." *The Machine in the Garden: Technology and the Pastoral Ideal in America.* London and New York: Oxford Univ. Press, 1964. Marx argues that the early European travel narratives envisioning the New World either as an earthly paradise or a hideous wilderness generate the poles of *The Tempest*'s dialectical treatment of nature and civilization. The final affirmations of the play, he argues, rest on the successful mediation of this opposition, as Prospero learns both the necessity of his art to control and shape fallen nature and the limitations of his art to perfect it.

Orgel, Stephen. "New Uses of Adversity: Tragic Experience in *The Tempest.*" In *In Defense of Reading: A Reader's Approach to Literary Criticism*, ed. Reuben A. Brower and Richard Poirier. New York: E .P. Dutton, 1962; rpt. in *Essays in Shakespearean Criticism*, ed. James L. Calderwood and Harold E. Toliver. Englewood Cliffs, N.J.: Prentice-Hall, 1970. Examining the play's movement toward harmony, Orgel discovers the power and authority of the redemptive action in the experience of tragedy. Prospero leads the characters through suffering to reconciliation, not denying but transforming tragedy in the shifts of perspective achieved by his art. Even in the happy end, however, the tragic implications of human nature are not evaded as Prospero leaves the island and his magic for the imperfect world of human society.

Palmer, D. J., ed. *Shakespeare, "The Tempest": A Casebook.* London: Macmillan, 1968. Palmer's useful casebook provides extracts from William Davenant and John Dryden's Restoration adaptation of the play, comments by early critics and editors such as Nicholas Rowe, Samuel Johnson, and William Hazlitt, and modern essays, including studies by Kermode and Kott (cited above).

Peterson, Douglas L. "*The Tempest:* 'Remember, for That's My Business with You.'" *Time, Tide and Tempest: A Study of Shakespeare's Romances.* San Marino, Calif.: Huntington Library, 1973. Informed by a benign conception of time that presents Prospero with the opportunity to correct the mistakes of the past, *The Tempest,* according to Peterson, celebrates the renewing power of love. Prospero succeeds in redeeming the past and insuring the future by using the present moment to forgive rather than revenge old wrongs.

Summers, Joseph H. "The Anger of Prospero." *Dreams of Love and Power.* Oxford: Clarendon Press, 1984. Examining the various scenes in which Prospero appears irritated or angry, Summers discovers the cause in Prospero's anxiety about both his own responsibility for the past and his ability to shape the future to the happy end he desires. Only when the play's complex harmonies have been achieved and Prospero is without power is he also without anger.

Sundelson, David. "So Rare a Wonder'd Father: Prospero's *Tempest.*" In *Representing Shakespeare: New Psychoanalytic Essays,* ed. Murray M. Schwartz and Coppélia Kahn. Baltimore: Johns Hopkins Univ. Press, 1980. Rev. and rpt. in *Shakespeare's Restorations of the Father.* New Brunswick, N.J.: Rutgers Univ. Press, 1983. Sundelson brings the vocabulary and concerns of psychoanalytic criticism to *The Tempest,* locating the play's central concerns in its complex representation of fatherhood. He traces the articulated anxieties about power and sexuality and examines the process by which Prospero masters these, making possible the play's final harmony in his altruistic surrender to the desires of others.

William, David. "*The Tempest* on the Stage." In *Jacobean Theatre,* ed. John Russell Brown and Bernard Harris. Stratford-upon-Avon Studies 1. London: Edward Arnold; New York: St. Martin's Press, 1960. Sensitively attending to the play's theatrical qualities, William argues that the play in performance must resist the tendency toward visual display and sentimentality that has often obscured its strength. He charts how effective control of the play's tone, rhythm, and characterization might reveal the play's power and poignancy as its sense of triumph is tempered by an awareness of the intractable aspects of human nature that refuse to be shaped by Prospero's art.

The Winter's Tale, with Michael Moriarty as Florizel and Dixie Carter as Perdita, directed by Gladys Vaughan in 1963.

THE WINTER'S TALE

THE WINTER'S TALE

Introductory Material

Foreword by Joseph Papp

Introduction

The Winter's Tale in Performance

THE PLAY

Supplementary Material

Date and Text

Textual Notes

Shakespeare's Sources

Further Reading

Foreword

The Winter's Tale is something you tell to children at night in front of a fire—but not *just* to children, for adults are intrigued by it as well. It has a lot in common with *Pericles,* including a young girl separated from her family, a shipwreck, and a reconciliation. The great scene at the end of the play, where Hermione steps out of her statuelike frame and returns to her husband, Leontes, and her daughter, Perdita, works like a charm every time. Even though it seems so improbable, this moment stops short of melodrama because Shakespeare, as always, stays in touch with the humanity of his characters and his plays. That's what keeps him believable.

One thing in the play that many people do find unbelievable, however, is Leontes's sudden and irrational suspicion of Hermione and his best friend, Polixenes, in the first scene. It all happens so quickly that it doesn't seem to make sense. But you just have to accept Leontes for what he is. Shakespeare wasn't writing a psychological drama, he was writing a romantic play, and he isn't concerned with giving a plausible explanation for Leontes's anger. That's not the point he's making. Shakespeare needs to set the plot in motion right away, and so he achieves the buildup of Leontes's jealousy in a couple of lines.

But having said that, I do think there are quirks in people that make them suddenly react in certain ways; and I think Shakespeare knew this, too. Maybe that's what's behind Leontes's behavior. If I were directing the play, I think I would concentrate less on the *reasons* for Leontes's actions and try instead to find the mind that is capable of suddenly doubting his dearest friend and his trusted wife, seemingly without provocation.

Joseph Papp

Joseph Papp gratefully acknowledges the help of Elizabeth Kirkland in preparing this Foreword.

Introduction

The Winter's Tale (c. 1610–1611), with its almost symmetrical division into two halves of bleak tragedy and comic romance, illustrates perhaps more clearly than any other Shakespearean play the genre of tragicomedy. To be sure, all the late romances feature journeys of separation, apparent deaths, and tearful reconciliations. Marina and Thaisa in *Pericles,* Imogen in *Cymbeline,* and Ferdinand in *The Tempest,* all supposed irrecoverably lost, are brought back to life by apparently miraculous devices. Of the four late romances, however, *The Winter's Tale* uses the most formal structure to evoke the antithesis of tragedy and romance. It is sharply divided into contrasting halves by a gap of sixteen years. The tragic first half takes place almost entirely in Sicilia, whereas the action of the second half is limited for the most part to Bohemia. At the court of Sicilia we see tyrannical jealousy producing a spiritual climate of "winter / In storm perpetual"; in Bohemia we witness a pastoral landscape and a sheepshearing evoking "the sweet o' the year," "When daffodils begin to peer" (3.2.212–213; 4.3.1–3). Paradoxically, the contrast between the two halves is intensified by parallels between the two: both begin with Camillo onstage and proceed to scenes of confrontation and jealousy in which, ironically, the innocent cause of jealousy in the first half, Polixenes, becomes the jealous tyrant of the second half. This mirroring reminds us of the cyclical nature of time and the hope it brings of renewal as we move from tragedy to romantic comedy.

Although this motif of a renewing journey from jaded court to idealized countryside reminds us of *As You Like It* and other early comedies, we sense in the late romances and especially in *The Winter's Tale* a new preoccupation with humanity's tragic folly. The vision of human depravity is world-weary and pessimistic, as though infected by the gloomy spirit of the great tragedies. And because humanity is so bent on destroying itself, the restoration is at once more urgently needed and more miraculous than in the "festive" world of early comedy. Renewal is mythically associated with the seasonal cycle from winter to summer.

King Leontes's tragedy seems at first irreversible and terrifying, like that of Shakespeare's greatest tragic protagonists. He suffers from irrational jealousy, as does Othello, and attempts to destroy the person on whom all his happiness depends. Unlike Othello, however, Leontes needs no diabolical tempter such as Iago to poison his mind against Queen Hermione. Leontes is undone by his own fantasies. No differences in race or age can explain Leontes's fears of estrangement from Hermione. She is not imprudent in her conduct, like her counterpart in Robert Greene's *Pandosto* (1588), the prose romance from which Shakespeare drew his narrative. Although Hermione is graciously fond of Leontes's dear friend Polixenes and urges him to stay longer in Sicilia, she does so only with a hospitable warmth demanded by the occasion and encouraged by her husband. In every way, then, Shakespeare strips away from Leontes the motive and the occasion for plausible doubting of his wife. All observers in the Sicilian court are incredulous and shocked at the King's accusations. Even so, Leontes is neither an unsympathetic nor an unbelievable character. Like Othello, Leontes cherishes his wife and perceives with a horrifying intensity what a fearful cost he must pay for his suspicions. Not only his marriage, but his lifelong friendship with Polixenes, his sense of pride in his children, and his enjoyment of his subjects' warm regard, all must be sacrificed to a single overwhelming compulsion.

Whatever may be the psychological cause of this obsession, it manifests itself as a revulsion against all sexual behavior. Like mad Lear, Leontes imagines lechery to be the unavoidable fact of the cosmos and of the human condition, the lowest common denominator to which all persons (including Hermione) must stoop. He is persuaded that "It is a bawdy planet," in which cuckolded man has "his pond fished by his next neighbor, by / Sir Smile, his neighbor" (1.2.195–201). Leontes's tortured soliloquies are laden with sexual images, of unattended "gates" letting in and out the enemy "With bag and baggage," and of a "dagger" that must be "muzzled / Lest it should bite its master" (ll. 197, 206, 156–157). As in *King Lear,* order is inverted to disorder, sanity to madness, legitimacy to illegitimacy. Sexual misconduct is emblematic of a universal malaise: "Why, then the world and all that's in 't is nothing, / The covering sky is nothing, Bohemia nothing, / My wife is nothing" (ll. 292–294). Other characters too see the trial of Hermione as a testing of humanity's worth: if Hermione proves false, Antigonus promises, he will treat his own wife as a stable horse and will "geld" his three daughters (2.1.148). Prevailing images are of spiders, venom, infection, sterility, and the "dungy earth" (l. 158).

Cosmic order is never really challenged, however. Leontes's fantasies of universal disorder are chimerical. His wife is in fact chaste, Polixenes true, and the King's courtiers loyal. Camillo refuses to carry out Leontes's order to murder Polixenes, not only because he knows murder to be wrong but because history offers not one example of a man "that had struck anointed kings / And flourished after" (1.2.357–358). The cosmos of this play is one in which crimes are invariably and swiftly punished. The Delphic oracle vindicates Hermione and gives Leontes stern warning. When Leontes persists in his madness, his son Mamillius's death follows as an immediate consequence. As Leontes at once perceives, "Apollo's angry, and the heavens themselves / Do strike at my injustice" (3.2.146–147). Leontes paradoxically welcomes the lengthy contrition he must undergo, for it confirms a pattern in the universe of just cause and effect. Although as tragic protagonist he has discovered the truth about Hermione moments too late, and so must pay richly for his error, Leontes has at least recovered faith in Hermione's transcendent goodness. His nightmare now over, he accepts and embraces suffering as a necessary atonement.

The transition to romance is therefore anticipated to an extent by the play's first half, even though the tone of the last two acts is strikingly different. The old Shepherd signals a momentous change when he speaks to his son of a cataclysmic storm and a ravenous bear set in opposition to the miraculous discovery of a child: "Now bless thyself. Thou mett'st with things dying, I with things newborn" (3.3.110–111). Time comes onstage as Chorus, like Gower in *Pericles,* to remind us of the conscious artifice of the dramatist. He can "o'erthrow law" and carry us over sixteen years as if we had merely dreamed out the interim (4.1). Shakespeare flaunts the improbability of his story by giving Bohemia a seacoast (much to the distress of Ben Jonson), and by employing animals onstage in a fanciful way (*"Exit, pursued by a bear"*; 3.3.57 s.d.). The narrative uses many typical devices of romance: a babe abandoned to the elements, a princess brought up by shepherds, a prince disguised as a swain, a sea voyage, and a recognition scene. Love is threatened not by the internal psychic obstacle of jealousy, but by the external obstacles of parental opposition and a seeming disparity of social rank between the lovers. Comedy easily finds solutions for such difficulties by the unraveling of illusion. This comic world also properly includes clownish shepherds, coy shepherdesses, and Autolycus, the roguish peddler, whose songs help set the mood of jollity and whose machinations contribute in an unforeseen manner to the working out of the love plot. Autolycus is in many ways the presiding genius of the play's second half, as dominant a character as Leontes in the first half and one whose delightful function is to do good "against my will" (5.2.125). In this paradox of knavery converted surprisingly to benign ends, we see how the comic providence of Shakespeare's tragicomic world makes use of the most implausible and outrageous happenings in pursuit of its own inscrutable design.

The conventional romantic ending is infused, however, with a sadness and a mystery that take the play well beyond what is usual in comedy. Mamillius and Antigonus are really dead, and that irredeemable fact is not forgotten in the play's final happy moments. Conversely, in Shakespeare's most notable departure from his source, Greene's *Pandosto,* Hermione is brought back to life. All observers regard this event, and the rediscovery of Perdita, as grossly implausible, "so like an old tale that the verity of it is in strong suspicion" (5.2.29–30). The play's very title, *The Winter's Tale,* reinforces this sense of naive improbability. Why does Shakespeare stress this riddling paradox of an unbelievable reality, and why does he deliberately mislead his audience into believing that Hermione has in fact died (3.3.15–45), using a kind of theatrical trickery found in no other Shakespearean play? The answer may well be that, in Paulina's words, we must awake our faith, accepting a narrative of death and return to life that cannot ultimately be comprehended by reason. On the rational level we are told that Hermione has been kept in hiding for sixteen years, in order to bring Leontes's contrition to fulfillment. Such an explanation seems psychologically incomprehensible, however, for it casts both Hermione and her keeper Paulina in the role of sadistic punishers of the King. Instead we are drawn toward an emblematic interpretation, bearing in mind that it is more an evocative hint than a complete truth. Throughout the play, Hermione has been repeatedly associated with "Grace" and with the goddess Proserpina, whose return from the underworld, after "Three crabbèd months had soured themselves to death" (1.2.102), signals the coming of spring. Perdita, also associated with Proserpina (4.4.116), is welcomed by her father "As is the spring to th' earth" (5.1.152). The emphasis on the bond of father and daughter (rather than father and son), so characteristic of Shakespeare's late plays and especially his romances, goes importantly beyond the patriarchalism of Shakespeare's earlier plays in its exploration of family relationships. Paulina has a similarly emblematic role, that of Conscience, patiently guiding the King to a divinely appointed renewal of his joy. Paulina speaks of herself as an artist figure, like Prospero in *The Tempest,* performing wonders of illusion, though she rejects the assistance of wicked powers. These emblematic hints do not rob the story of its human drama, but they do lend a transcendent significance to Leontes's bittersweet story of sinful error, affliction, and an unexpected second happiness.

The Winter's Tale in Performance

A play that spans sixteen years, locates its action in two such widely separated places as Sicilia and Bohemia, provides landlocked Bohemia with a seacoast, divides itself more or less equally between tragedy and comedy, and brings on an allegorical figure such as Time had no hope of surviving in the Restoration and eighteenth century even if written by the immortal Shakespeare. *The Winter's Tale,* after enjoying great popularity in public and at court from 1611 (when diarist Dr. Simon Forman saw it at the Globe Theatre) until 1634 (when the King's men performed it at the palace at Whitehall for at least the fifth time), fell into neglect. It was allotted to His Majesty's servants under Thomas Killigrew in the 1660s but not acted by them. After a belated revival by Henry Giffard at the theater in Goodman's Fields, London, in 1741, in which the play was performed as an extended interval in "a concert of vocal and instrumental music," and a run at the Theatre Royal, Covent Garden, the next season, the play suffered the fate of adaption at the hands of redactors seeking to remedy its presumed manifest defects.

Mcnamara Morgan's solution, in his *The Sheep-Shearing, or Florizel and Perdita* produced, at Covent Garden in 1754, was to address systematically the problem of the violated unities of time, place, and action. He cut the first half entirely and focused instead on the romance of the two lovers, leading up to the revelation of Perdita's noble birth. The tragicomic story of Leontes and Hermione was entirely absent. Bithynia, substituted for Bohemia at the suggestion of the Shakespeare scholar Thomas Hanmer, was safely allotted a seacoast; Perdita's shepherd stepfather turned out to be Antigonus in disguise. Morgan augmented the role of Autolycus, but had the good sense to keep the sheepshearing scene reasonably intact. Dr. Thomas Arne provided music and the set.

David Garrick's *Florizel and Perdita* (Theatre Royal, Drury Lane, 1756) followed Morgan's example by beginning after the "wide gap of time" that divides Shakespeare's play in two and locating the action in one place (called Bithynia at first, Bohemia in later printed versions). Garrick was not content, however, to leave aside the story of Leontes and Hermione. To include it without seriously impairing the dramatic unities required some ingenuity. Garrick's text solves this difficulty by recalling through dialogue what took place in Sicily sixteen years before, by shipwrecking Leontes and Cleomenes on the coast of Polixenes's country (where Leontes has come in hopes of atoning for his mad jealousy), and by bringing the shipwrecked visitors to the sheepshearing. Paulina also lives now in Polixenes's kingdom, and Hermione dwells in concealment with her. Garrick's only concession to Shakespeare's first three acts, other than expository recall, is to retain the scene of Perdita's discovery on the coast with its irresistible chase by a bear. Garrick explains his modifications in a prologue that captures both eighteenth-century veneration for Shakespeare and the conviction that his genius needed to be rescued from the inanities and barbarism of his own theater:

> The five long acts, from which our three are taken,
> Stretched out to sixteen years, lay by, forsaken.
> Lest then this precious liquor run to waste,
> 'Tis now confined and bottled for your taste.
> 'Tis my chief wish, my joy, my only plan
> To lose no drop of this immortal man.

Garrick played Leontes to the memorable Hermione of Hannah Pritchard and the no less remarkable Perdita of Susannah Cibber, who sang one of the songs added (perhaps from Morgan's version) for the occasion. Autolycus, played by Richard Yates, spoke new comic material as in Morgan's version.

The Winter's Tale did well in the late eighteenth and early nineteenth centuries, though often, especially at first, in the altered guises provided for it by Garrick and Morgan. Hannah Pritchard continued to play Hermione until 1785. A succession of actresses followed Susannah Cibber as Perdita, among them Maria Macklin, Hannah Mary Pritchard, George Anne Bellamy, and Elizabeth Younge. Autolycus's augmented role attracted the comic talents of, after Yates,

Ned Shuter, E. L. Blanchard, and John Bannister, Jr. John Philip Kemble, at Drury Lane in 1802 and afterward at Covent Garden, did restore the text to something more approaching Shakespeare's, thereby delighting William Hazlitt and compensating to some degree for that critic's disappointments with staged versions of *King Lear* and other Shakespeare plays. Sarah Siddons acted Hermione in Kemble's production of 1802 and continued in the part until 1811. William Charles Macready acted Leontes at Bath in 1815, at Drury Lane in 1823, at Covent Garden in 1837 (in fact he opened his management at that theater with *The Winter's Tale,* casting Helen Faucit as Hermione), and at Drury Lane in 1843. Macready's text, like Kemble's, was no longer heavily indebted to Garrick and Morgan.

The adapted play seems to have done well in the United States. An operatic version made its appearance in 1761, and Morgan's text was performed at New York's John Street Theatre in 1795. Shakespeare's text came into its own in America with William Burton's productions at his intimate theater on Chambers Street in New York in 1851 and 1856, and then, more lavishly, in 1857 at the Broadway Theatre. Burton restored much of Shakespeare's text (including the Chorus of Time), although he also retained twenty lines that Garrick added at the end of Act 5, scene 2, and provided much stage business, especially for his role as Autolycus. Reviewers were enthusiastic about the productions even if they generally remarked more upon the scenic effects than the acting. A cutout of Mount Etna located Act 1 clearly in Sicily, and later in the act the volcano could be seen to erupt as the background to Leontes's fearful jealousy. The innocent pastoral world of Bohemia was invoked by a cottage enveloped in flowers and vines and set in a landscape of streams, meadows, and distant mountains "suffused with a roseate atmosphere of sunlight." The whole scene, according to one reviewer, was "full of that Heaven that lies about us in our infancy."

Like Burton, nineteenth-century English actor-managers were drawn to the pictorial capabilities of *The Winter's Tale,* with both good and bad results: the play's powerful stage images of discovery and reunion lent themselves to fine theatrical effects, but an overemphasis on scenic splendor hampered the movement of the play and required cutting or rearrangement. Samuel Phelps, at the Sadler's Wells Theatre in 1845 and afterward, paid particular attention to the mise-en-scène, especially in the final act. Amid classic interiors in a polychromatic style of decoration, lighting and drapery were so artfully displayed on the impressive figure of Amelia Warner as Hermione that the audience burst into applause on the removal of the curtain.

Charles Kean, at the Princess's Theatre in 1856, hit on the scheme of contrasting the Greek dress of Syracuse in the early scenes with Asiatic costuming in Bithynia (i.e., Bohemia). Convinced that ancient Syracuse had rivaled Athens in architectural splendor, Kean undertook to bring before his spectators "*tableaux vivants* of the private and public life of the ancient Greeks, at a time when the arts flourished to . . . perfection." His Syracuse of about 300 B.C. showed the fountains of Arethusa and the Temple of Minerva, a banqueting hall in the royal palace with couches for the reclining guests, musicians playing a hymn to Apollo, slaves handing out wine and garlands, and a Pyrrhic dance performed by thirty-six handsome young women in warlike garb. Hermione's dungeon in Act 2 resembled the infamous "Ear of Dionysius" where Syracusan tyrants are reputed to have abused their prisoners. The Queen faced trial in a reconstruction of the great public theater of Syracuse. A Chorus, bridging the interval between the play's two halves, was accompanied by an allegorical pageant of Time in which clouds dispersed, the Moon in her chariot sank into the ocean, and Phoebus Apollo arose in his chariot in a blaze of light. In the play's second half, a distant view of Nicaea, capital of Bithynia, could be seen beyond the rural beauties of the sheepshearing scene, and a graceful dance of shepherds and shepherdesses gave way to a celebration of Bacchus by three hundred or more writhing satyrs in wild disguise. The statue scene culminated in a torchlight procession. A young Ellen Terry played Mamillius, and she long remembered the triumphant spectacle.

Despite some outcries that Shakespeare was disappearing under the weight of so much scenery, theater managers vied with one another for new effects. F. B. Chatterton, manager at Drury Lane, produced *The Winter's Tale* in 1878 without the allegorical pageant of Time and without the bear that had so vigorously chased after Antigonus at the Princess's

Theatre, but with a Pyrrhic dance in Act 1, a frenzied Dionysiac festival in Act 4, and a trial of Hermione in the theater at Syracuse. Architectural details were painstakingly researched to produce the effect of the ancient Mediterranean world, and several newly painted scenes of Syracuse and of other classical vistas added to the verisimilar effect. Mary Anderson wowed audiences at the Lyceum Theatre in 1887 with her doubling of the matronly Hermione and the girlish Perdita, but cut the text in a way that betrayed a somewhat cavalier attitude. "No audience of these days," she said, "would desire to have *The Winter's Tale* produced in its entirety." She was especially severe in her excisions of the roguery practiced by Autolycus on the old Shepherd and his son, evidently regarding the material as overly scurrilous, and she ended the play with a couplet from *All's Well That Ends Well*. Johnston Forbes-Robertson played Leontes. The scenic splendor began in the palace of Leontes, replete with Grecian pillars and a distant landscape. An upper terrace, with marble benches and velvet drapes, accommodated much of the action. Hermione's trial took place in a Grecian hall of solid masonry; the rustic festival occurred amidst flowery banks and overarching trees. Hermione's appearance as a statue was set at the top of a flight of marble steps, enabling the magnificent Miss Anderson to descend in picturesque dignity and grace. Naturally the number of scenes had to be reduced, though Anderson expedited shifts by the use of "drops." To all this Herbert Beerbohm Tree could hardly add a great deal, though he certainly tried, at His Majesty's Theatre in 1906, rearranging the play into three acts (Sicily-Bohemia-Sicily) to facilitate his elaborate scenic ambitions.

In 1881 the company of the Royal Theatre of Saxe-Meinigen acted the play at Drury Lane in a German translation by Ludwig Tieck and August Wilhelm von Schlegel. The production was remarkable for its emphasis upon ensemble playing and its meticulous attention to textual detail. Although the Saxe-Meinigen production was enormously successful, it remained for Harley Granville-Barker, the first modern director to assert the advantages of a more flexible stage, to free the play from the static, pictorial traditions of the Victorian theater. His revolutionary production at the Savoy Theatre in 1912 employed a huge apron stage that extended halfway into the parquet, giving the impression of an Elizabethan playhouse and making possible nearly continuous action. The costumes were deliberately antiromantic and nonrealistic, and indeed the production strove to discern what is discordant and alienating in Shakespeare's play. Granville-Barker's staging, both execrated as a travesty and hailed as a major achievement, certainly anticipated the idiom of more recent years.

At London's Phoenix Theatre in 1951, Peter Brook, like Granville-Barker, used a permanent set to ensure the swift flow of the action. Eschewing the picturesque for the psychological, Brook's *The Winter's Tale* emphasized the insane world created by Leontes (John Gielgud) and the efforts of Paulina (Flora Robson) to break through the darkness of his diseased mind. The production successfully combined the symbolic and the realistic. The storm scene took place upon a cold and desolate coast: "for once," theater critic J. C. Trewin wrote, "I had no desire to laugh while Antigonus . . . fled terrified along the angry shore." After Antigonus's exit, snow began to fall heavily, and Time shivered forth to speak his chorus. As he spoke, the storm gradually diminished and the stage was slowly suffused with light; when he finished, the sun shone brightly upon the sheepshearing scene. Peter Wood, directing the play at Stratford-upon-Avon in 1960, followed Brook in his search for psychological credibility. The elegance of the court did not obscure the nightmare of sexual jealousy. Wood brilliantly used subtle physical gestures to reveal psychological states. The reviewer for *The Times* noted Leontes's "infatuated fondling of his Queen's shoulders," and in Act 1, scene 2, Mamillius suddenly clasped his father around the thighs, obviously startling Leontes (Eric Porter).

If Brook and Wood successfully probed the play's psychological substratum, recent productions have responded more directly to the theatrical possibilities suggested by Granville-Barker. In 1969 Trevor Nunn directed the play at Stratford-upon-Avon in a style that was aggressively nonrealistic. According to Christopher Morley, who designed the set (a three-sided white box forming the playing area with various small white boxes serving as furniture), the production emerged from a desire "to develop a house style in which nothing is ever literally represented." And virtually nothing was. The play began with Leontes in a rectangular box, visible through flashes of lightning, while the beginning of Time's speech was heard in the dark theater. Judi Dench doubled in the parts of Hermione and Perdita. In 1976 Nunn again directed the play, working this time with John Barton. Again, roles were revealingly doubled: most interestingly, Time and the bear were played by John Nettles. The destructive forces of nature were made an aspect of Time itself, as Nettles, wearing Time's flowing robes and carrying an abstract bear mask, stalked Antigonus, holding the mask before his face and pounding his staff once on the stage before he carried Antigonus away. Bears indeed were ubiquitous, present as a design motif on wall hangings and carpets, and in a bearskin lying on a couch. The audience was reminded that Time the implacable destroyer could not be avoided. Even in the pastoral scenes of Bohemia, a leafless tree remained onstage to qualify the play's promise of renewal. In its powerful visual images the production directly engaged the play's unreality. The shocking jealousy of Ian McKellen's Leontes seemed natural, if appalling, in this world rich in the symbolic resonances of "an old tale."

No longer wary of the play's artificiality, modern productions are prompt to call attention to the theatricality embodied in Time's bland assurance that he can leap over sixteen years, or in the self-conscious device of bringing a statue to life. A Stratford-upon-Avon production of 1986, directed by Terry Hands and starring Jeremy Irons as Leontes, concentrated visually at first on cool whites and blues for Leontes's Regency court, and then shifted into red, yellow, and orange for the scenes of rustic banqueting in the second half. A great bearskin rug on the polished floor of Leontes's palace, constantly visible with its shining eyes, became the bear that devoured Antigonus at the beginning of part two. In David Williams's production at Stratford, Canada, in the same year, a pageant of Time led off the entire performance, so that the play was seen as part of a never-ending process of aging and renewal. The statue scene (with Goldie Semple as Hermione) succeeded because the spectators were made aware that they were in the theater, with an actress practicing her craft, miming the process of bringing life to her role as any actor or actress must do with any role. Paulina's function as artist figure and as stand-in for the dramatist called attention to the way in which theater works its magic. This crucial point is easily lost when realistic scenery attempts to substitute illusion for theatrical event. The seacoast of Bohemia and its inimitable bear are phenomena of the stage, paradoxically all the more persuasive when spectators actively enlist their imaginations and become partners in the theatrical moment.

THE WINTER'S TALE

The Names of the Actors

LEONTES, *King of Sicilia*
MAMILLIUS, *young prince of Sicilia*
CAMILLO,
ANTIGONUS,
CLEOMENES,
DION, } *four Lords of Sicilia*

HERMIONE, *Queen to Leontes*
PERDITA, *daughter to Leontes and Hermione*
PAULINA, *wife to Antigonus*
EMILIA, *a lady* [*attending Hermione*]

POLIXENES, *King of Bohemia*
FLORIZEL, *Prince of Bohemia*
ARCHIDAMUS, *a lord of Bohemia*
Old SHEPHERD, *reputed father of Perdita*
CLOWN, *his son*
AUTOLYCUS, *a rogue*

[MOPSA,
[DORCAS, } *Shepherdesses.*]

[A MARINER
A JAILER
Two LADIES *attending Hermione*
Two SERVANTS *attending Leontes*
One or more LORDS *attending Leontes*
An OFFICER *of the court*
A GENTLEMAN *attending Leontes*
Three GENTLEMEN *of the court of Sicilia*
A SERVANT *of the Old Shepherd*

TIME, *as Chorus*]

Other Lords and Gentlemen, [*Ladies, Officers,*] *and Servants; Shepherds and Shepherdesses;* [*Twelve Countrymen disguised as Satyrs*]

[SCENE: *Sicilia, and Bohemia.*]

1.1 *Enter Camillo and Archidamus.*

ARCHIDAMUS If you shall chance, Camillo, to visit Bohemia on the like occasion whereon my services are now on foot, you shall see, as I have said, great difference betwixt our Bohemia and your Sicilia.

CAMILLO I think this coming summer the King of Sicilia means to pay Bohemia the visitation which he 6 justly owes him.

ARCHIDAMUS Wherein our entertainment shall shame 8 us, we will be justified in our loves; for indeed— 9

CAMILLO Beseech you—

ARCHIDAMUS Verily, I speak it in the freedom of my 11 knowledge. We cannot with such magnificence—in 12 so rare—I know not what to say. We will give you sleepy drinks, that your senses, unintelligent of our 14 insufficience, may, though they cannot praise us, as little accuse us.

CAMILLO You pay a great deal too dear for what's given freely.

ARCHIDAMUS Believe me, I speak as my understanding instructs me and as mine honesty puts it to utterance.

CAMILLO Sicilia cannot show himself overkind to Bo- 21 hemia. They were trained together in their childhoods, and there rooted betwixt them then such an affection which cannot choose but branch now. Since their 24 more mature dignities and royal necessities made separation of their society, their encounters, though not 26 personal, hath been royally attorneyed with inter- 27 change of gifts, letters, loving embassies, that they have seemed to be together though absent, shook hands as over a vast, and embraced as it were from the 30

1.1. Location: Sicilia. The court of Leontes.
6 Bohemia i.e., the King of Bohemia (also at ll. 21–22) **8–9 Wherein . . . loves** i.e., in whatever way our attempts to entertain you will shame us by falling short of your entertainment of us, we will make up for by our affection. **justified** absolved, as of spiritual sin, by faith or love
11–12 in . . . knowledge as my knowledge entitles me to speak
14 sleepy sleep-inducing. **unintelligent** unaware **21 Sicilia** the King of Sicilia **24 branch** put forth new growth, flourish (also perhaps with opposite and unconscious suggestion of "divide") **26 their society** their being together **27 personal** in person. **attorneyed** carried out by deputy **30 vast** boundless space

ends of opposed winds. The heavens continue their 31
loves!

ARCHIDAMUS I think there is not in the world either malice or matter to alter it. You have an unspeakable comfort of your young prince Mamillius. It is a gentle- 35
man of the greatest promise that ever came into my note. 37

CAMILLO I very well agree with you in the hopes of him. It is a gallant child, one that indeed physics the 39
subject, makes old hearts fresh. They that went on 40
crutches ere he was born desire yet their life to see him a man.

ARCHIDAMUS Would they else be content to die?

CAMILLO Yes, if there were no other excuse why they should desire to live.

ARCHIDAMUS If the King had no son, they would desire to live on crutches till he had one. *Exeunt.*

✤

1.2 *Enter Leontes, Hermione, Mamillius, Polixenes, Camillo.*

POLIXENES

Nine changes of the watery star hath been 1
The shepherd's note since we have left our throne 2
Without a burden. Time as long again 3
Would be filled up, my brother, with our thanks,
And yet we should for perpetuity 5
Go hence in debt. And therefore, like a cipher, 6
Yet standing in rich place, I multiply 7
With one "We thank you" many thousands more
That go before it.

LEONTES Stay your thanks awhile
And pay them when you part.

POLIXENES Sir, that's tomorrow.

31 ends . . . winds i.e., opposite ends of the earth. **The heavens** may the heavens **35 of** in the person of **37 note** observation **39–40 physics the subject** acts as a medicine to the people

1.2. Location: The same.
1 watery star moon **2 note** observation. **we** i.e., I. (The royal "we.") **3 burden** i.e., occupant **5 for perpetuity** forever **6–7 like . . . place** like a zero at the end of a number, multiplying its quantity

I am questioned by my fears of what may chance 11
Or breed upon our absence, that may blow 12
No sneaping winds at home to make us say 13
"This is put forth too truly." Besides, I have stayed 14
To tire your royalty.

LEONTES We are tougher, brother,
Than you can put us to 't.

POLIXENES No longer stay. 16

LEONTES
One sennight longer.

POLIXENES Very sooth, tomorrow. 17

LEONTES
We'll part the time between 's, then, and in that 18
I'll no gainsaying.

POLIXENES Press me not, beseech you, so. 19
There is no tongue that moves, none, none i' the world
So soon as yours could win me. So it should now,
Were there necessity in your request, although
'Twere needful I denied it. My affairs
Do even drag me homeward, which to hinder
Were in your love a whip to me, my stay 25
To you a charge and trouble. To save both, 26
Farewell, our brother.

LEONTES Tongue-tied, our Queen? Speak you.

HERMIONE
I had thought, sir, to have held my peace until
You had drawn oaths from him not to stay. You, sir,
Charge him too coldly. Tell him you are sure
All in Bohemia's well; this satisfaction 31
The bygone day proclaimed. Say this to him, 32
He's beat from his best ward.

LEONTES Well said, Hermione. 33

11–14 I am . . . truly i.e., I am anxious what may happen in Bohemia, either by chance or bred directly out of my absence; I am anxious lest biting or envious winds may be abroad that will cause me to say my fears were all too plausible **16 Than . . . to 't** than anything you can do to try me **17 sennight** sevennight, week. **Very sooth** truly **18 part the time** split the difference, i.e., divide a week in two **19 I'll no gainsaying** I will take no refusal **25 Were . . . whip** would be to make your fondness for me a punishment **26 charge** expense, burden **31–32 this . . . proclaimed** yesterday brought news to satisfy on that score (that all is well in Bohemia) **32 Say** if you say **33 ward** defensive posture. (A fencing term.)

HERMIONE
To tell he longs to see his son were strong. 34
But let him say so, then, and let him go;
But let him swear so and he shall not stay, 36
We'll thwack him hence with distaffs.
[*To Polixenes*.] Yet of your royal presence I'll adventure 38
The borrow of a week. When at Bohemia 39
You take my lord, I'll give him my commission 40
To let him there a month behind the gest 41
Prefixed for 's parting.—Yet, good deed, Leontes, 42
I love thee not a jar o' the clock behind 43
What lady she her lord.—You'll stay?

POLIXENES
No, madam. 44

HERMIONE
Nay, but you will?

POLIXENES
I may not, verily.

HERMIONE
Verily?
You put me off with limber vows; but I, 47
Though you would seek t' unsphere the stars with oaths,
Should yet say, "Sir, no going." Verily,
You shall not go. A lady's "verily" is
As potent as a lord's. Will you go yet?
Force me to keep you as a prisoner,
Not like a guest: so you shall pay your fees 53
When you depart, and save your thanks. How say you?
My prisoner or my guest? By your dread "verily,"
One of them you shall be.

POLIXENES
Your guest, then, madam.
To be your prisoner should import offending, 57
Which is for me less easy to commit
Than you to punish.

HERMIONE
Not your jailer, then,
But your kind hostess. Come, I'll question you

34 tell tell us that. **strong** a strong argument **36 he shall not stay** i.e., we wouldn't let him stay even if he wanted to **38 adventure** risk (because, as she explains, she'll undertake to repay each week with a month) **39 borrow** borrowing **40 take** capture; receive **41 let him** let him stay. **gest** time allotted for a halt in a royal progress or journey **42 good deed** i.e., in truth **43 jar** tick **44 What lady she** any lady **47 limber** limp **53 fees** payments often demanded by jailers of prisoners at the time of their release **57 import offending** imply my having offended

Of my lord's tricks and yours when you were boys.
You were pretty lordings then?

POLIXENES We were, fair Queen,
Two lads that thought there was no more behind 63
But such a day tomorrow as today,
And to be boy eternal.

HERMIONE Was not my lord
The verier wag o' the two? 66

POLIXENES
We were as twinned lambs that did frisk i' the sun
And bleat the one at th' other. What we changed 68
Was innocence for innocence; we knew not
The doctrine of ill-doing, nor dreamed
That any did. Had we pursued that life,
And our weak spirits ne'er been higher reared
With stronger blood, we should have answered heaven 73
Boldly "Not guilty," the imposition cleared 74
Hereditary ours.

HERMIONE By this we gather 75
You have tripped since.

POLIXENES O my most sacred lady,
Temptations have since then been born to 's, for
In those unfledged days was my wife a girl; 78
Your precious self had then not crossed the eyes
Of my young playfellow.

HERMIONE Grace to boot! 80
Of this make no conclusion, lest you say 81
Your queen and I are devils. Yet go on.
Th' offenses we have made you do we'll answer,
If you first sinned with us, and that with us 84
You did continue fault, and that you slipped not 85
With any but with us.

LEONTES Is he won yet? 86

63 behind to come **66 The verier wag** truly the more mischievous **68 changed** exchanged **73 stronger blood** i.e., mature sexual passions **74–75 the imposition . . . ours** i.e., excepting of course the original sin that is the condition of all mortals; or, perhaps, being freed from original sin itself (if we had continued in that pure state) **78 unfledged** not yet feathered, i.e., immature **80 Grace to boot** i.e., Heaven help me **81 Of . . . conclusion** don't follow your implied line of reasoning to its logical conclusion **84 that** if (also in l. 85) **85 fault** offense **86 Is he won yet** (Leontes has been standing aside for much of their conversation.)

HERMIONE
He'll stay, my lord.
LEONTES At my request he would not.
Hermione, my dearest, thou never spok'st
To better purpose.
HERMIONE Never?
LEONTES Never but once.
HERMIONE
What? Have I twice said well? When was 't before?
I prithee, tell me. Cram 's with praise and make 's
As fat as tame things. One good deed dying tongueless 92
Slaughters a thousand waiting upon that. 93
Our praises are our wages. You may ride 's
With one soft kiss a thousand furlongs ere
With spur we heat an acre. But to the goal: 96
My last good deed was to entreat his stay.
What was my first? It has an elder sister,
Or I mistake you. O, would her name were Grace!
But once before I spoke to the purpose. When?
Nay, let me have 't; I long.
LEONTES Why, that was when
Three crabbèd months had soured themselves to death
Ere I could make thee open thy white hand
And clap thyself my love. Then didst thou utter, 104
"I am yours forever."
HERMIONE 'Tis grace indeed.
Why, lo you now, I have spoke to the purpose twice:
The one forever earned a royal husband,
Th' other for some while a friend.
[*She gives her hand to Polixenes.*]
LEONTES [*Aside*] Too hot, too hot!
To mingle friendship far is mingling bloods. 109
I have *tremor cordis* on me. My heart dances, 110
But not for joy, not joy. This entertainment 111
May a free face put on, derive a liberty 112

92 tongueless unpraised, unsung **93 Slaughters . . . that** i.e., will inhibit many other good deeds, since they are encouraged by praise
96 heat traverse as in a race. **to the goal** to come to the point
104 clap clasp hands, plight troth **109 mingling bloods** (Sexual intercourse was thought to produce a mingling of bloods.) **110 tremor cordis** fluttering of the heart **111 entertainment** i.e., of Polixenes by Hermione **112 free face** innocent appearance

From heartiness, from bounty, fertile bosom, 113
And well become the agent. 'T may, I grant. 114
But to be paddling palms and pinching fingers,
As now they are, and making practiced smiles
As in a looking glass, and then to sigh, as 'twere
The mort o' the deer; O, that is entertainment 118
My bosom likes not, nor my brows.—Mamillius, 119
Art thou my boy?

MAMILLIUS Ay, my good lord.

LEONTES I' fecks, 120
Why, that's my bawcock. What, hast smutched thy nose? 121
They say it is a copy out of mine. Come, captain,
We must be neat; not neat, but cleanly, captain. 123
And yet the steer, the heifer, and the calf
Are all called neat.—Still virginaling 125
Upon his palm?—How now, you wanton calf? 126
Art thou my calf?

MAMILLIUS Yes, if you will, my lord.

LEONTES

Thou want'st a rough pash and the shoots that I have 128
To be full like me. Yet they say we are 129
Almost as like as eggs. Women say so,
That will say anything. But were they false
As o'erdyed blacks, as wind, as waters, false 132
As dice are to be wished by one that fixes 133
No bourn twixt his and mine, yet were it true 134
To say this boy were like me. Come, sir page,
Look on me with your welkin eye. Sweet villain! 136

113 fertile bosom i.e., generous affection **114 well . . . agent** look well in her (Hermione) who does these things **118 mort** note sounded on a horn at the death of the hunted deer **119 brows** (Alludes to cuckolds' horns, the supposed badge of men whose wives are unfaithful.) **120 I' fecks** in faith **121 bawcock** i.e., fine fellow. (French *beau coq*.) **123 not . . . cleanly** (Leontes changes the word because *neat* also means "cattle" and hence reminds him of cuckolds' horns.) **125 virginaling** touching hands, as in playing on the virginals, a keyed instrument **126 wanton** frisky **128 Thou want'st** you lack. **rough pash** shaggy head. **shoots** horns. (Another allusion to cuckolds' horns.) **129 full** fully **132 o'erdyed blacks** black garments that have been weakened by too much dye, or dyed in another color (thereby betraying a forgetfulness in the erstwhile mourner) **133–134 one . . . mine** i.e., one who intends to cheat me at dice. **bourn** boundary **136 welkin** sky-blue

Most dear'st! My collop! Can thy dam?—may 't be?— 137
Affection, thy intention stabs the center. 138
Thou dost make possible things not so held, 139
Communicat'st with dreams—how can this be?— 140
With what's unreal thou coactive art, 141
And fellow'st nothing. Then 'tis very credent 142
Thou mayst cojoin with something; and thou dost, 143
And that beyond commission, and I find it, 144
And that to the infection of my brains
And hardening of my brows.

POLIXENES What means Sicilia? 146

HERMIONE
He something seems unsettled.

POLIXENES How, my lord? 147
What cheer? How is 't with you, best brother?

HERMIONE You look
As if you held a brow of much distraction.
Are you moved, my lord?

LEONTES No, in good earnest. 150
How sometimes nature will betray its folly,
Its tenderness, and make itself a pastime 152
To harder bosoms! Looking on the lines 153
Of my boy's face, methought I did recoil 154
Twenty-three years, and saw myself unbreeched, 155
In my green velvet coat, my dagger muzzled
Lest it should bite its master and so prove,
As ornaments oft do, too dangerous.
How like, methought, I then was to this kernel,
This squash, this gentleman.—Mine honest friend, 160
Will you take eggs for money? 161

137 collop small piece of meat; i.e., of my own flesh. **dam** mother **138–143 Affection . . . something** Strong passion, your intense power pierces to the very center, the soul of man. You deal in matters normally considered fantastic; you partake of the nature of dreams. How can this be? You collaborate with unreality, and create imagined fantasies. It's all the likelier, then, that such imaginings may also become real. **144 commission** what is lawful **146 What means Sicilia** i.e., why is the King of Sicilia looking so distracted **147 something** somewhat **150 moved** angry **152 pastime** occasion for amusement **153 To harder bosoms** for persons who are less tenderhearted **154 methought** it seemed to me. **recoil** i.e., go back in memory **155 unbreeched** not yet wearing breeches **160 squash** unripe peascod or pea pod. **honest** worthy **161 take eggs for money** i.e., be imposed upon, taken advantage of, cheated. (Proverbial.)

MAMILLIUS No, my lord, I'll fight.

LEONTES

You will? Why, happy man be 's dole!—My brother, 163
Are you so fond of your young prince as we
Do seem to be of ours?

POLIXENES If at home, sir,
He's all my exercise, my mirth, my matter, 166
Now my sworn friend and then mine enemy,
My parasite, my soldier, statesman, all.
He makes a July's day short as December,
And with his varying childness cures in me 170
Thoughts that would thick my blood.

LEONTES So stands this squire 171
Officed with me. We two will walk, my lord, 172
And leave you to your graver steps. Hermione,
How thou lov'st us, show in our brother's welcome. 174
Let what is dear in Sicily be cheap. 175
Next to thyself and my young rover, he's
Apparent to my heart.

HERMIONE If you would seek us, 177
We are yours i' the garden. Shall 's attend you there? 178

LEONTES

To your own bents dispose you. You'll be found, 179
Be you beneath the sky. [*Aside.*] I am angling now,
Though you perceive me not how I give line. 181
Go to, go to! 182
How she holds up the neb, the bill to him, 183
And arms her with the boldness of a wife 184
To her allowing husband!

[*Exeunt Polixenes and Hermione.*]

Gone already! 185

163 happy . . . dole may good fortune be his lot. (Proverbial.) **166 matter** concern **170 childness** childlike ways **171 thick my blood** (Melancholy thoughts were supposed to thicken the blood.) **172 Officed** placed in particular function **174–175 How . . . cheap** (A hidden second meaning in these lines may be intentional: show just how much you love me by the way you encourage Polixenes's attentions, and thereby cheapen the most precious thing in Sicily.) **177 Apparent** heir apparent (perhaps with a suggestion too of "evident, revealed") **178 Shall 's** shall we **179 To . . . dispose you** act according to your inclinations (with more bitter double meaning, continued in *You'll be found,* i.e., found out) **181 give line** pay out line (to let the fish hook himself well) **182 Go to** (An expression of remonstrance.) **183 neb** beak, i.e., nose, mouth **184 arms her with** assumes **185 allowing** approving

Inch thick, knee-deep, o'er head and ears a forked one!— 186
Go, play, boy, play. Thy mother plays, and I 187
Play too, but so disgraced a part, whose issue 188
Will hiss me to my grave. Contempt and clamor
Will be my knell. Go, play, boy, play. There have been,
Or I am much deceived, cuckolds ere now;
And many a man there is, even at this present,
Now while I speak this, holds his wife by th' arm,
That little thinks she has been sluiced in 's absence 194
And his pond fished by his next neighbor, by
Sir Smile, his neighbor. Nay, there's comfort in 't
Whiles other men have gates and those gates opened, 197
As mine, against their will. Should all despair
That have revolted wives, the tenth of mankind 199
Would hang themselves. Physic for 't there's none. 200
It is a bawdy planet, that will strike 201
Where 'tis predominant; and 'tis powerful, think it, 202
From east, west, north, and south. Be it concluded,
No barricado for a belly. Know 't, 204
It will let in and out the enemy
With bag and baggage. Many thousand on 's 206
Have the disease and feel 't not.—How now, boy?

MAMILLIUS
I am like you, they say.

LEONTES
Why, that's some comfort.
What, Camillo there?

CAMILLO [*Coming forward*] Ay, my good lord.

LEONTES
Go play, Mamillius; thou'rt an honest man.
[*Exit Mamillius.*]
Camillo, this great sir will yet stay longer.

186 forked horned **187 play** play games. **plays** i.e., in a sexual liaison **188 Play** play a role. **issue** outcome (with a pun on the sense of "offspring" and "exit," i.e., death) **194 has been sluiced** (The water in his pond, so to speak, has been drained off by a cheating neighbor.) **197 gates** sluice gates, suggestive of the wife's chastity that has been opened and robbed **199 revolted** unfaithful **200 Physic** medicine **201 It** i.e., the cause of unchastity, the planet Venus. **strike** blast, destroy by a malign influence **202 predominant** in the ascendant. (Said of a planet.) **think it** be assured of this **204 barricado** barricade **206 bag and baggage** (with sexual suggestion, as earlier in *dagger* [l. 156], *sluiced, gates, let in and out,* etc.) **on 's** of us

CAMILLO

You had much ado to make his anchor hold.
When you cast out, it still came home.

LEONTES

Didst note it? 213

CAMILLO

He would not stay at your petitions, made
His business more material.

LEONTES

Didst perceive it? 215
[*Aside*.] They're here with me already, whispering,
rounding, 216
"Sicilia is a so-forth." 'Tis far gone 217
When I shall gust it last.—How came 't, Camillo, 218
That he did stay?

CAMILLO

At the good Queen's entreaty.

LEONTES

"At the Queen's" be 't. "Good" should be pertinent, 220
But so it is, it is not. Was this taken 221
By any understanding pate but thine?
For thy conceit is soaking, will draw in 223
More than the common blocks. Not noted, is 't, 224
But of the finer natures? By some severals 225
Of headpiece extraordinary? Lower messes 226
Perchance are to this business purblind? Say. 227

CAMILLO

Business, my lord? I think most understand
Bohemia stays here longer.

LEONTES

Ha?

CAMILLO

Stays here longer.

LEONTES

Ay, but why?

CAMILLO

To satisfy Your Highness and the entreaties
Of our most gracious mistress.

213 still continually. **came home** came back to the ship, failed to hold **215 material** important **216 They're . . . already** people are already onto my secret. **rounding** whispering, gossiping **217 a so-forth** a so-and-so, a you-know-what **218 gust** taste, i.e., hear of **220 pertinent** i.e., appropriately applied **221 so it is** as things stand. **taken** perceived **223 conceit** understanding. **soaking** i.e., very receptive **224 blocks** blockheads **225 But . . . natures** except by those of rarefied intellect. **severals** individuals **226 Lower messes** those who sit lower at table, i.e., inferior men **227 purblind** totally blind

LEONTES Satisfy? 232
Th' entreaties of your mistress? Satisfy?
Let that suffice. I have trusted thee, Camillo,
With all the nearest things to my heart, as well 235
My chamber councils, wherein, priestlike, thou 236
Hast cleansed my bosom. I from thee departed
Thy penitent reformed. But we have been
Deceived in thy integrity, deceived
In that which seems so.
CAMILLO Be it forbid, my lord! 240
LEONTES
To bide upon 't, thou art not honest; or, 241
If thou inclin'st that way, thou art a coward, 242
Which hoxes honesty behind, restraining 243
From course required; or else thou must be counted 244
A servant grafted in my serious trust 245
And therein negligent; or else a fool
That seest a game played home, the rich stake drawn, 247
And tak'st it all for jest.
CAMILLO My gracious lord,
I may be negligent, foolish, and fearful;
In every one of these no man is free,
But that his negligence, his folly, fear,
Among the infinite doings of the world
Sometimes puts forth. In your affairs, my lord, 253
If ever I were willful-negligent,
It was my folly; if industriously 255
I played the fool, it was my negligence, 256
Not weighing well the end; if ever fearful
To do a thing where I the issue doubted, 258

232 Satisfy (Leontes takes the word in a sexual sense.) **235 as well** as well as with **236 chamber councils** private affairs **240 Be it forbid** i.e., God forbid I should do such a thing **241 To bide upon 't** (1) to dwell on this matter still further, or (2) for you to insist thus on your integrity. **or** either **242 inclin'st that way** i.e., prefer being honest under ordinary circumstances **243 Which** i.e., which cowardice. **hoxes** hamstrings **244 From course required** i.e., from the direction honest inquiry must take to find the truth **245 grafted . . . trust** taken into my complete confidence. (*Grafted* means "deeply embedded," like a graft.) **247 home** i.e., for keeps, in earnest. (With perhaps a sexual double meaning, continued in *rich stake drawn.*) **drawn** won **253 puts forth** shows itself **255 industriously** willfully **256 played the fool** i.e., took some matter lightly **258 issue** outcome. **doubted** feared

Whereof the execution did cry out 259
Against the nonperformance, 'twas a fear 260
Which oft infects the wisest. These, my lord,
Are such allowed infirmities that honesty 262
Is never free of. But, beseech Your Grace,
Be plainer with me. Let me know my trespass
By its own visage. If I then deny it, 265
'Tis none of mine.

LEONTES Ha' not you seen, Camillo—
But that's past doubt; you have, or your eyeglass 267
Is thicker than a cuckold's horn—or heard— 268
For to a vision so apparent, rumor 269
Cannot be mute—or thought—for cogitation
Resides not in that man that does not think— 271
My wife is slippery? If thou wilt confess,
Or else be impudently negative 273
To have nor eyes nor ears nor thought, then say 274
My wife's a hobbyhorse, deserves a name 275
As rank as any flax-wench that puts to 276
Before her trothplight. Say 't and justify 't. 277

CAMILLO
I would not be a stander-by to hear
My sovereign mistress clouded so without
My present vengeance taken. Shrew my heart, 280
You never spoke what did become you less
Than this, which to reiterate were sin 282
As deep as that, though true.

LEONTES Is whispering nothing? 283
Is leaning cheek to cheek? Is meeting noses?

259–260 Whereof . . . nonperformance in which the completion of the task showed how wrong I was in being unwilling to undertake it
262 allowed acknowledged. **that** as **265 visage** face, i.e., plain appearance **267 eyeglass** lens of the eye **268 cuckold's horn** (A thin sheet of horn can be seen through like a lens, though a cuckold's horn is another matter.) **269 a vision so apparent** something so plainly visible
271 think i.e., think so **273 Or else** the only possible alternative to which is to **273–274 be . . . have** impudently deny that you have
274 nor eyes neither eyes **275 hobbyhorse** wanton woman **276 flax-wench** common slut. **puts to** engages in sex **277 justify** affirm
280 present immediate. **Shrew** beshrew, curse **282–283 which . . . true** i.e., to repeat which accusation would be to sin as deeply as her supposed adultery or your sinfulness in thus accusing her, even if it were true (which it isn't)

Kissing with inside lip? Stopping the career 285
Of laughter with a sigh—a note infallible
Of breaking honesty? Horsing foot on foot? 287
Skulking in corners? Wishing clocks more swift,
Hours minutes, noon midnight? And all eyes 289
Blind with the pin and web but theirs, theirs only, 290
That would unseen be wicked? Is this nothing?
Why, then the world and all that's in 't is nothing,
The covering sky is nothing, Bohemia nothing,
My wife is nothing, nor nothing have these nothings,
If this be nothing.

CAMILLO Good my lord, be cured
Of this diseased opinion, and betimes, 296
For 'tis most dangerous.

LEONTES Say it be, 'tis true. 297

CAMILLO
No, no, my lord.

LEONTES It is. You lie, you lie!
I say thou liest, Camillo, and I hate thee,
Pronounce thee a gross lout, a mindless slave,
Or else a hovering temporizer, that 301
Canst with thine eyes at once see good and evil,
Inclining to them both. Were my wife's liver
Infected as her life, she would not live 304
The running of one glass.

CAMILLO Who does infect her? 305

LEONTES
Why, he that wears her like her medal, hanging 306
About his neck, Bohemia—who, if I
Had servants true about me, that bare eyes 308
To see alike mine honor as their profits,
Their own particular thrifts, they would do that 310
Which should undo more doing. Ay, and thou, 311

285 career full gallop **287 honesty** chastity. **Horsing foot on foot** placing one's foot on that of another person and then moving the feet up and down together **289 Hours minutes** wishing hours were minutes **290 pin and web** cataract of the eye. (The lovers wish to think themselves unobserved.) **296 betimes** quickly **297 Say it be** i.e., even if it is dangerous **301 hovering** wavering **304 Infected as her life** as full of disease as is her moral conduct **305 glass** hourglass **306 like her medal** like a miniature portrait of her, worn in a locket **308 bare** bore **310 thrifts** gains **311 undo** prevent

His cupbearer—whom I from meaner form 312
Have benched and reared to worship, who mayst see 313
Plainly as heaven sees earth and earth sees heaven
How I am galled—mightst bespice a cup 315
To give mine enemy a lasting wink, 316
Which draft to me were cordial.

CAMILLO Sir, my lord, 317
I could do this, and that with no rash potion, 318
But with a lingering dram that should not work
Maliciously like poison. But I cannot 320
Believe this crack to be in my dread mistress, 321
So sovereignly being honorable. 322
I have loved thee—

LEONTES Make that thy question, and go rot! 323
Dost think I am so muddy, so unsettled, 324
To appoint myself in this vexation, sully 325
The purity and whiteness of my sheets—
Which to preserve is sleep, which being spotted
Is goads, thorns, nettles, tails of wasps—
Give scandal to the blood o' the Prince my son,
Who I do think is mine and love as mine,
Without ripe moving to 't? Would I do this? 331
Could man so blench?

CAMILLO I must believe you, sir. 332
I do, and will fetch off Bohemia for 't; 333
Provided that, when he's removed, Your Highness
Will take again your queen as yours at first,
Even for your son's sake, and thereby for sealing 336
The injury of tongues in courts and kingdoms
Known and allied to yours.

LEONTES Thou dost advise me

312 meaner form humbler station **313 benched** placed on the bench of authority. **worship** dignity, honor **315 galled** rubbed, chafed **316 lasting wink** everlasting closing of the eyes (in death) **317 were cordial** would be restorative **318 rash** quick-acting **320 Maliciously** virulently **321 crack** flaw. **dread** worthy of awe **322 sovereignly** supremely **323 Make . . . rot** i.e., if you're going to raise questions like that, may you rot in hell **324 muddy** muddle-headed **325 To . . . vexation** to ordain that I should suffer this affliction **331 ripe** ample, urgent **332 blench** swerve (from sensible conduct) **333 fetch off** do away with; or, with deliberate ambiguity, rescue (as also in *removed* in the next line) **336 sealing** silencing

Even so as I mine own course have set down.
I'll give no blemish to her honor, none.

CAMILLO My lord,
Go then, and with a countenance as clear
As friendship wears at feasts, keep with Bohemia 343
And with your queen. I am his cupbearer.
If from me he have wholesome beverage,
Account me not your servant.

LEONTES This is all.
Do 't and thou hast the one half of my heart;
Do 't not, thou splitt'st thine own.

CAMILLO I'll do 't, my lord.

LEONTES
I will seem friendly, as thou hast advised me. *Exit.*

CAMILLO
O miserable lady! But, for me,
What case stand I in? I must be the poisoner
Of good Polixenes, and my ground to do 't
Is the obedience to a master, one
Who in rebellion with himself will have
All that are his so too. To do this deed, 355
Promotion follows. If I could find example 356
Of thousands that had struck anointed kings
And flourished after, I'd not do 't; but since 358
Nor brass, nor stone, nor parchment bears not one, 359
Let villainy itself forswear 't. I must
Forsake the court. To do 't or no is certain 361
To me a breakneck. Happy star reign now! 362
Here comes Bohemia.

Enter Polixenes.

POLIXENES This is strange. Methinks
My favor here begins to warp. Not speak?— 364
Good day, Camillo.

343 keep remain in company **355 All . . . too** i.e., all who follow him similarly in rebellion against his best self and obedience to his worst self. **To do** if I do **356 If** even if **358–359 but . . . one** i.e., but since recorded history shows no instances of men who have killed a king and prospered afterwards **361 To do 't or no** i.e., either to kill Polixenes or not to kill him **362 breakneck** destruction, ruin. **Happy** propitious, favorable **364 warp** change, shrivel, grow askew (as wood warps). **Not speak** (Leontes has just passed by Polixenes without speaking.)

CAMILLO Hail, most royal sir!
POLIXENES
What is the news i' the court?
CAMILLO None rare, my lord. 366
POLIXENES
The King hath on him such a countenance
As he had lost some province and a region 368
Loved as he loves himself. Even now I met him
With customary compliment, when he,
Wafting his eyes to th' contrary and falling 371
A lip of much contempt, speeds from me, and
So leaves me to consider what is breeding 373
That changeth thus his manners.
CAMILLO I dare not know, my lord.
POLIXENES
How, dare not? Do not? Do you know, and dare not? 376
Be intelligent to me. 'Tis thereabouts, 377
For to yourself what you do know you must, 378
And cannot say you dare not. Good Camillo, 379
Your changed complexions are to me a mirror
Which shows me mine changed too; for I must be 381
A party in this alteration, finding 382
Myself thus altered with 't.
CAMILLO There is a sickness
Which puts some of us in distemper, but
I cannot name the disease; and it is caught
Of you that yet are well.
POLIXENES How? Caught of me? 386
Make me not sighted like the basilisk. 387
I have looked on thousands who have sped the better 388
By my regard, but killed none so. Camillo, 389
As you are certainly a gentleman, thereto 390

366 rare noteworthy **368 As** as if **371 Wafting . . . contrary** averting his eyes. **falling** letting fall **373 breeding** hatching **376 Do not** i.e., or do you mean you don't know **377 intelligent** intelligible. **'Tis thereabouts** it must be something of this sort, i.e., that you know and dare not tell **378–379 For . . . dare not** i.e., for in your heart, whatever it is you know, you must in fact know, and can't claim it's a matter of not daring to know **381–382 for . . . alteration** i.e., for my looks must have changed too, reflecting this change in my position **386 Of** by **387 sighted** provided with a gaze. **basilisk** a fabled serpent whose gaze was fatal **388 sped** prospered **389 regard** look **390 thereto** in addition to which

Clerklike experienced, which no less adorns 391
Our gentry than our parents' noble names, 392
In whose success we are gentle, I beseech you, 393
If you know aught which does behoove my knowledge
Thereof to be informed, imprison 't not
In ignorant concealment.

CAMILLO I may not answer. 396

POLIXENES
A sickness caught of me, and yet I well?
I must be answered. Dost thou hear, Camillo?
I conjure thee, by all the parts of man 399
Which honor does acknowledge, whereof the least
Is not this suit of mine, that thou declare
What incidency thou dost guess of harm 402
Is creeping toward me; how far off, how near;
Which way to be prevented, if to be; 404
If not, how best to bear it.

CAMILLO Sir, I will tell you,
Since I am charged in honor and by him
That I think honorable. Therefore mark my counsel,
Which must be even as swiftly followed as
I mean to utter it, or both yourself and me
Cry lost, and so good night!

POLIXENES On, good Camillo. 410

CAMILLO
I am appointed him to murder you. 411

POLIXENES
By whom, Camillo?

CAMILLO By the King.

POLIXENES For what?

CAMILLO
He thinks, nay, with all confidence he swears,
As he had seen 't or been an instrument

391 Clerklike like an educated man **392 gentry** gentlemanlike condition **393 whose success** succession from whom. **gentle** wellborn **396 ignorant concealment** concealment that would keep me ignorant, or that would proceed from pretended ignorance on your part **399 parts** obligations **402 incidency** likelihood **404 if to be** if it can be (prevented) **410 good night** i.e., this is the end **411 him** by him (Leontes); or, the one

To vice you to 't, that you have touched his queen 415
Forbiddenly.

POLIXENES O, then my best blood turn
To an infected jelly, and my name
Be yoked with his that did betray the Best! 418
Turn then my freshest reputation to
A savor that may strike the dullest nostril 420
Where I arrive, and my approach be shunned,
Nay, hated too, worse than the great'st infection
That e'er was heard or read!

CAMILLO Swear his thought over 423
By each particular star in heaven and
By all their influences, you may as well
Forbid the sea for to obey the moon 426
As or by oath remove or counsel shake 427
The fabric of his folly, whose foundation 428
Is piled upon his faith and will continue 429
The standing of his body.

POLIXENES How should this grow? 430

CAMILLO
I know not. But I am sure 'tis safer to
Avoid what's grown than question how 'tis born.
If therefore you dare trust my honesty,
That lies enclosèd in this trunk which you 434
Shall bear along impawned, away tonight! 435
Your followers I will whisper to the business, 436
And will by twos and threes at several posterns 437
Clear them o' the city. For myself, I'll put
My fortunes to your service, which are here
By this discovery lost. Be not uncertain, 440

415 vice force, as with a carpenter's tool; or, impel, tempt. (The *Vice* was a tempter in the morality play.) **418 his . . . Best** the name of him (Judas) who betrayed Christ **420 savor** stench **423 Swear . . . over** i.e., even if you should deny his suspicion with oaths **426 for to** to **427 or . . . or** either . . . or **428 fabric** edifice **428–430 whose . . . body** the foundation of which is built upon an unshaken conviction, and which will last as long as the body exists **430 standing** life, existence. **How . . . grow** i.e., how could this suspicion have arisen **434 trunk** body (with a suggestion too of a traveling trunk) **435 impawned** i.e., as a pledge of good faith **436 whisper to** secretly inform of and urge **437 posterns** rear gates **440 discovery** revelation, disclosure

For, by the honor of my parents, I
Have uttered truth, which if you seek to prove, 442
I dare not stand by; nor shall you be safer 443
Than one condemned by the King's own mouth, thereon
His execution sworn.

POLIXENES I do believe thee;
I saw his heart in 's face. Give me thy hand.
Be pilot to me, and thy places shall 447
Still neighbor mine. My ships are ready, and 448
My people did expect my hence departure
Two days ago. This jealousy
Is for a precious creature. As she's rare,
Must it be great; and as his person's mighty,
Must it be violent; and as he does conceive
He is dishonored by a man which ever
Professed to him, why, his revenges must 455
In that be made more bitter. Fear o'ershades me.
Good expedition be my friend, and comfort 457
The gracious Queen, part of his theme, but nothing 458
Of his ill-ta'en suspicion! Come, Camillo, 459
I will respect thee as a father if
Thou bear'st my life off. Hence! Let us avoid. 461

CAMILLO
It is in mine authority to command
The keys of all the posterns. Please Your Highness
To take the urgent hour. Come, sir, away. *Exeunt.*

✤

442 prove test **443 stand by** affirm publicly; stay **447–448 thy . . . mine** your official position will always be near to me **455 Professed** openly professed friendship **457–459 Good . . . suspicion** may good speed befriend me, and may my quick departure ease the predicament of the gracious Queen, who is the object of the King's suspicions but who is guiltless of them **461 avoid** depart

2.1 *Enter Hermione, Mamillius,* [*and*] *Ladies.*

HERMIONE
Take the boy to you. He so troubles me
'Tis past enduring.
FIRST LADY [*Taking Mamillius from the Queen*]
Come, my gracious lord,
Shall I be your playfellow?
MAMILLIUS
No, I'll none of you.
FIRST LADY Why, my sweet lord? 4
MAMILLIUS
You'll kiss me hard and speak to me as if
I were a baby still.—I love you better.
SECOND LADY
And why so, my lord?
MAMILLIUS Not for because 7
Your brows are blacker; yet black brows, they say,
Become some women best, so that there be not 9
Too much hair there, but in a semicircle,
Or a half-moon made with a pen.
SECOND LADY Who taught' this? 11
MAMILLIUS
I learned it out of women's faces. Pray now,
What color are your eyebrows?
FIRST LADY Blue, my lord.
MAMILLIUS
Nay, that's a mock. I have seen a lady's nose
That has been blue, but not her eyebrows.
FIRST LADY Hark ye,
The Queen your mother rounds apace. We shall
Present our services to a fine new prince
One of these days, and then you'd wanton with us, 18
If we would have you.
SECOND LADY She is spread of late
Into a goodly bulk. Good time encounter her! 20

2.1. Location: Sicilia. The royal court.
4 none of you have nothing to do with you **7 for because** because **9 so** provided **11 taught'** taught you **18 wanton** sport, play **20 Good . . . her** may she have a happy issue

HERMIONE [*Calling to her women*]
What wisdom stirs amongst you?—Come, sir, now
I am for you again. Pray you, sit by us
And tell 's a tale.
MAMILLIUS Merry or sad shall 't be?
HERMIONE As merry as you will.
MAMILLIUS
A sad tale's best for winter. I have one
Of sprites and goblins.
HERMIONE Let's have that, good sir.
Come on, sit down. Come on, and do your best
To fright me with your sprites. You're powerful at it.
MAMILLIUS
There was a man—
HERMIONE Nay, come sit down, then on.
[*Mamillius sits.*]
MAMILLIUS
Dwelt by a churchyard. I will tell it softly;
Yond crickets shall not hear it. 31
HERMIONE
Come on, then, and give 't me in mine ear.
[*They converse privately.*]

[*Enter*] *Leontes, Antigonus, Lords,* [*and others*].

LEONTES
Was he met there? His train? Camillo with him?
A LORD
Behind the tuft of pines I met them. Never
Saw I men scour so on their way. I eyed them 35
Even to their ships.
LEONTES How blest am I
In my just censure, in my true opinion! 37
Alack, for lesser knowledge! How accurst 38
In being so blest! There may be in the cup 39
A spider steeped, and one may drink, depart, 40
And yet partake no venom, for his knowledge

31 crickets i.e., the court ladies, tittering and laughing **35 scour** scurry **37 censure** judgment **38 Alack . . . knowledge** would that I knew less **39 blest** i.e., with knowledge (that causes unhappiness) **40 A spider** (The superstition referred to here is that the drinker is not poisoned by the spider in the cup unless he knows the spider to be there.)

Is not infected; but if one present
Th' abhorred ingredient to his eye, make known
How he hath drunk, he cracks his gorge, his sides, 44
With violent hefts. I have drunk, and seen the spider. 45
Camillo was his help in this, his pander.
There is a plot against my life, my crown.
All's true that is mistrusted. That false villain 48
Whom I employed was pre-employed by him.
He has discovered my design, and I 50
Remain a pinched thing, yea, a very trick 51
For them to play at will. How came the posterns 52
So easily open?

A LORD By his great authority,
Which often hath no less prevailed than so
On your command.

LEONTES I know 't too well.
[*To Hermione.*] Give me the boy. I am glad you did
not nurse him.
Though he does bear some signs of me, yet you
Have too much blood in him.

HERMIONE What is this? Sport? 59

LEONTES
Bear the boy hence; he shall not come about her.
Away with him! And let her sport herself
With that she's big with, for 'tis Polixenes
Has made thee swell thus. [*Mamillius is led out.*]

HERMIONE But I'd say he had not, 63
And I'll be sworn you would believe my saying,
Howe'er you lean to the nayward.

LEONTES You, my lords, 65
Look on her, mark her well. Be but about
To say "She is a goodly lady," and 67
The justice of your hearts will thereto add
"'Tis pity she's not honest, honorable." 69
Praise her but for this her without-door form, 70
Which on my faith deserves high speech, and straight 71

44 gorge throat **45 hefts** heavings, retchings **48 mistrusted** suspected **50 discovered** disclosed **51 pinched** tortured, ridiculous. **trick** plaything **52 play** play with **59 Sport** a joke **63 I'd** I need only **65 nayward** negative, opposite **67 goodly** attractive **69 honest** chaste **70 without-door** outward, external **71 straight** straightway, at once

The shrug, the hum or ha, these petty brands 72
That calumny doth use—O, I am out, 73
That mercy does, for calumny will sear 74
Virtue itself—these shrugs, these hums and ha's,
When you have said she's goodly, come between 76
Ere you can say she's honest. But be 't known,
From him that has most cause to grieve it should be,
She's an adulteress.

HERMIONE Should a villain say so,
The most replenished villain in the world, 80
He were as much more villain. You, my lord, 81
Do but mistake.

LEONTES You have mistook, my lady,
Polixenes for Leontes. O thou thing!
Which I'll not call a creature of thy place, 84
Lest barbarism, making me the precedent,
Should a like language use to all degrees 86
And mannerly distinguishment leave out 87
Betwixt the prince and beggar. I have said
She's an adulteress; I have said with whom.
More, she's a traitor, and Camillo is
A fedarie with her, and one that knows 91
What she should shame to know herself
But with her most vile principal, that she's 93
A bed-swerver, even as bad as those 94
That vulgars give bold'st titles, ay, and privy 95
To this their late escape.

HERMIONE No, by my life,
Privy to none of this. How will this grieve you,
When you shall come to clearer knowledge, that
You thus have published me! Gentle my lord, 99

72 brands i.e., signs, stigmas **73 out** wrong, in error **74 does** uses. (Leontes's point is that no one commits calumny by suggesting with a shrug that Hermione is unchaste; calumny attacks *virtue itself,* whereas Hermione has only the false appearance of virtue.) **76 come between** interrupt **80 replenished** full, complete **81 He . . . villain** his saying so would double his villainy **84 Which . . . place** (The King will not desecrate Hermione's exalted rank by calling her what she really is.) **86 degrees** social ranks **87 mannerly distinguishment** polite distinctions **91 fedarie** confederate, accomplice **93 principal** partner **94 bed-swerver** adulteress **95 vulgars . . . titles** common people call by the rudest names. **privy** in on the secret **99 published** proclaimed. **Gentle my** my noble

You scarce can right me throughly then to say 100
You did mistake.

LEONTES No. If I mistake
In those foundations which I build upon,
The center is not big enough to bear 103
A schoolboy's top. Away with her to prison!
He who shall speak for her is afar off guilty 105
But that he speaks.

HERMIONE There's some ill planet reigns. 106
I must be patient till the heavens look
With an aspect more favorable. Good my lords,
I am not prone to weeping, as our sex
Commonly are, the want of which vain dew
Perchance shall dry your pities; but I have
That honorable grief lodged here which burns
Worse than tears drown. Beseech you all, my lords,
With thoughts so qualified as your charities 114
Shall best instruct you, measure me; and so 115
The King's will be performed!

LEONTES Shall I be heard? 116

HERMIONE
Who is 't that goes with me? Beseech Your Highness
My women may be with me, for you see
My plight requires it.—Do not weep, good fools; 119
There is no cause. When you shall know your mistress
Has deserved prison, then abound in tears
As I come out. This action I now go on 122
Is for my better grace. Adieu, my lord. 123
I never wished to see you sorry; now
I trust I shall. My women, come, you have leave.

LEONTES Go, do our bidding. Hence!
[*Exit Queen, guarded, with Ladies.*]

A LORD
Beseech Your Highness, call the Queen again.

ANTIGONUS
Be certain what you do, sir, lest your justice

100 throughly thoroughly. **to say** by saying **103 center** earth
105 afar off indirectly **106 But . . . speaks** merely by speaking
114 qualified tempered **115 measure** judge **116 heard** i.e., obeyed
119 fools (Here, a term of endearment.) **122 come out** am released from prison **123 my better grace** my greater honor (when my name is cleared; perhaps also with a suggestion of being ennobled by suffering)

Prove violence, in the which three great ones suffer:
Yourself, your queen, your son.

A LORD For her, my lord,
I dare my life lay down and will do 't, sir,
Please you t' accept it, that the Queen is spotless
I' th' eyes of heaven and to you—I mean
In this which you accuse her.

ANTIGONUS If it prove
She's otherwise, I'll keep my stables where 135
I lodge my wife. I'll go in couples with her; 136
Than when I feel and see her no farther trust her. 137
For every inch of woman in the world,
Ay, every dram of woman's flesh is false,
If she be.

LEONTES Hold your peaces.

A LORD Good my lord— 140

ANTIGONUS
It is for you we speak, not for ourselves.
You are abused, and by some putter-on 142
That will be damned for 't. Would I knew the villain,
I would land-damn him. Be she honor-flawed, 144
I have three daughters—the eldest is eleven,
The second and the third, nine and some five— 146
If this prove true, they'll pay for 't. By mine honor,
I'll geld 'em all! Fourteen they shall not see
To bring false generations. They are co-heirs, 149
And I had rather glib myself than they 150
Should not produce fair issue.

LEONTES Cease, no more! 151
You smell this business with a sense as cold
As is a dead man's nose; but I do see 't and feel 't
As you feel doing thus, and see withal 154

135–136 I'll . . . wife (If Hermione is an adulteress, says Antigonus, then all women are no better than animals, to be penned up and guarded suspiciously.) **136 in couples** i.e., like two hounds leashed together and hence inseparable **137 Than . . . her** trust her no further than I can feel her next to me and actually see her **140 she** i.e., Hermione **142 abused** deceived. **putter-on** instigator **144 land-damn** (Meaning uncertain.) **146 some** about **149 false generations** illegitimate children. **They are co-heirs** i.e., they will share my inheritance (since I have no son to inherit all) **150 glib** castrate, geld **151 fair** legitimate **154 thus** (Leontes presumably grasps Antigonus by the arm or pinches him or tweaks his nose.) **withal** in addition

The instruments that feel.

ANTIGONUS If it be so, 155
We need no grave to bury honesty;
There's not a grain of it the face to sweeten
Of the whole dungy earth.

LEONTES What? Lack I credit? 158

A LORD
I had rather you did lack than I, my lord,
Upon this ground; and more it would content me 160
To have her honor true than your suspicion,
Be blamed for 't how you might.

LEONTES Why, what need we 162
Commune with you of this, but rather follow
Our forceful instigation? Our prerogative 164
Calls not your counsels, but our natural goodness 165
Imparts this; which if you—or stupefied 166
Or seeming so in skill—cannot or will not 167
Relish a truth like us, inform yourselves 168
We need no more of your advice. The matter,
The loss, the gain, the ordering on 't, is all 170
Properly ours.

ANTIGONUS And I wish, my liege,
You had only in your silent judgment tried it,
Without more overture.

LEONTES How could that be? 173
Either thou art most ignorant by age, 174
Or thou wert born a fool. Camillo's flight,
Added to their familiarity—
Which was as gross as ever touched conjecture, 177
That lacked sight only, naught for approbation 178
But only seeing, all other circumstances
Made up to th' deed—doth push on this proceeding. 180
Yet, for a greater confirmation—

155 instruments i.e., Leontes's fingers **158 credit** credibility
160 Upon this ground in this matter **162 we** I. (The royal "we.")
164 instigation incentive **164–166 Our prerogative . . . this** my royal prerogative is under no obligation to consult you, but rather out of natural generosity I inform you of the matter **166 or** either **167 Or . . . skill** or pretending to be stupefied out of cunning **168 Relish** savor, appreciate **170 on 't** of it **173 overture** public disclosure **174 by age** through the folly of old age **177 as gross . . . conjecture** as palpably evident as any conjecture ever touched upon and verified
178 approbation proof **180 Made up** added up. **push on** urge onward

For in an act of this importance 'twere
Most piteous to be wild—I have dispatched in post 183
To sacred Delphos, to Apollo's temple, 184
Cleomenes and Dion, whom you know
Of stuffed sufficiency. Now from the oracle 186
They will bring all, whose spiritual counsel had 187
Shall stop or spur me. Have I done well?

A LORD Well done, my lord.

LEONTES
Though I am satisfied, and need no more
Than what I know, yet shall the oracle
Give rest to the minds of others, such as he 192
Whose ignorant credulity will not
Come up to th' truth. So have we thought it good 194
From our free person she should be confined, 195
Lest that the treachery of the two fled hence 196
Be left her to perform. Come, follow us.
We are to speak in public, for this business
Will raise us all.

ANTIGONUS [*Aside*] To laughter, as I take it, 199
If the good truth were known. *Exeunt.*

✣

2.2 *Enter Paulina, a Gentleman,* [*and attendants*].

PAULINA
The keeper of the prison, call to him.
Let him have knowledge who I am. [*Gentleman goes to the door.*] Good lady, 2
No court in Europe is too good for thee;
What dost thou then in prison?

[*Enter*] *Jailer.*

Now, good sir,
You know me, do you not?

183 wild rash. **post** haste **184 Delphos** (See note at 3.1.2.) **186 Of stuffed sufficiency** abundantly qualified **187 had** having been obtained **192 he** any person (such as Antigonus) **194 Come up to** face **195 From** away from. **free** accessible **196 treachery** i.e., suspected plot to murder Leontes (see l. 47) **199 raise** rouse

2.2. Location: Sicilia. A prison.
2 Good lady (Addressed to the absent Hermione.)

JAILER For a worthy lady
And one who much I honor.

PAULINA Pray you, then,
Conduct me to the Queen.

JAILER I may not, madam.
To the contrary I have express commandment.

PAULINA
Here's ado, to lock up honesty and honor from
Th' access of gentle visitors! Is 't lawful, pray you,
To see her women? Any of them? Emilia?

JAILER So please you, madam,
To put apart these your attendants, I 13
Shall bring Emilia forth.

PAULINA I pray now, call her.—
Withdraw yourselves.

[*Gentleman and attendants withdraw.*]

JAILER And, madam,
I must be present at your conference.

PAULINA Well, be 't so, prithee. [*Exit Jailer.*]
Here's such ado, to make no stain a stain
As passes coloring.

[*Enter Jailer, with*] *Emilia.*

Dear gentlewoman, 20
How fares our gracious lady?

EMILIA
As well as one so great and so forlorn
May hold together. On her frights and griefs— 23
Which never tender lady hath borne greater— 24
She is something before her time delivered. 25

PAULINA
A boy?

EMILIA A daughter, and a goodly babe,
Lusty and like to live. The Queen receives 27
Much comfort in 't, says, "My poor prisoner,
I am innocent as you."

PAULINA I dare be sworn.

13 put apart dismiss **20 passes coloring** surpasses any justification, passes all excuse (with a pun on *coloring* in the sense of *stain* in the previous line) **23 On** in consequence of **24 Which** than which **25 something** somewhat (also in l. 55) **27 Lusty** vigorous. **like** likely

These dangerous unsafe lunes i' the King, beshrew
them! 30
He must be told on 't, and he shall. The office 31
Becomes a woman best; I'll take 't upon me. 32
If I prove honeymouthed, let my tongue blister 33
And never to my red-looked anger be 34
The trumpet any more. Pray you, Emilia,
Commend my best obedience to the Queen. 36
If she dares trust me with her little babe,
I'll show 't the King and undertake to be
Her advocate to th' loud'st. We do not know 39
How he may soften at the sight o' the child.
The silence often of pure innocence
Persuades when speaking fails.

EMILIA
Most worthy madam,
Your honor and your goodness is so evident
That your free undertaking cannot miss 44
A thriving issue. There is no lady living 45
So meet for this great errand. Please your ladyship 46
To visit the next room, I'll presently 47
Acquaint the Queen of your most noble offer,
Who but today hammered of this design, 49
But durst not tempt a minister of honor 50
Lest she should be denied.

PAULINA
Tell her, Emilia,
I'll use that tongue I have. If wit flow from 't 52
As boldness from my bosom, let 't not be doubted
I shall do good.

EMILIA
Now be you blest for it!
I'll to the Queen.—Please you, come something nearer.

JAILER
Madam, if 't please the Queen to send the babe,
I know not what I shall incur to pass it, 57
Having no warrant.

30 lunes fits of lunacy **31 on 't** of it **32 Becomes** suits **33 blister** (It was popularly supposed that lying blistered the tongue.) **34 red-looked** red-faced **36 Commend** deliver **39 to th' loud'st** as loudly as I can **44 free** generous **45 thriving issue** successful outcome **46 meet** suited. **Please** if it please **47 presently** at once **49 hammered of** formulated, conceived **50 tempt** solicit (to serve as ambassador in such a case) **52 wit** wisdom, common sense **57 to pass it** if I let it pass

PAULINA You need not fear it, sir.
This child was prisoner to the womb and is
By law and process of great Nature thence
Freed and enfranchised, not a party to
The anger of the King nor guilty of,
If any be, the trespass of the Queen.

JAILER I do believe it.

PAULINA
Do not you fear. Upon mine honor, I
Will stand betwixt you and danger. *Exeunt.*

✤

2.3 *Enter Leontes.*

LEONTES
Nor night nor day, no rest! It is but weakness
To bear the matter thus, mere weakness. If
The cause were not in being—part o' the cause,
She th' adulteress, for the harlot King 4
Is quite beyond mine arm, out of the blank 5
And level of my brain, plot-proof, but she 6
I can hook to me—say that she were gone, 7
Given to the fire, a moiety of my rest 8
Might come to me again.—Who's there?

[*Enter a*] *Servant.*

SERVANT My lord?

LEONTES How does the boy?

SERVANT
He took good rest tonight; 'tis hoped 11
His sickness is discharged.

LEONTES To see his nobleness!
Conceiving the dishonor of his mother, 13

2.3. Location: Sicilia. The royal court.
4 harlot lewd. (Originally applied to either sex.) **5–6 out . . . level** beyond the range. (Archery terms: *blank* is the center of the target or the close range needed for a direct shot at it, as in "point-blank"; *level* is the action of aiming.) **7 hook** (as with grappling hooks) **8 Given to the fire** burned at the stake (as a traitor conspiring against the King). **moiety** portion **11 tonight** last night **13 Conceiving** grasping the enormity of

He straight declined, drooped, took it deeply,
Fastened and fixed the shame on 't in himself, 15
Threw off his spirit, his appetite, his sleep,
And downright languished.—Leave me solely. Go, 17
See how he fares. [*Exit Servant.*] Fie, fie! No thought
of him. 18
The very thought of my revenges that way
Recoil upon me—in himself too mighty,
And in his parties, his alliance. Let him be,
Until a time may serve. For present vengeance,
Take it on her. Camillo and Polixenes
Laugh at me, make their pastime at my sorrow.
They should not laugh if I could reach them, nor
Shall she, within my power.

Enter Paulina [*with a baby*]; *Antigonus and Lords* [*and a Servant, trying to hold her back*].

A LORD You must not enter.

PAULINA
Nay, rather, good my lords, be second to me. 27
Fear you his tyrannous passion more, alas,
Than the Queen's life? A gracious innocent soul,
More free than he is jealous.

ANTIGONUS That's enough. 30

SERVANT
Madam, he hath not slept tonight, commanded
None should come at him.

PAULINA Not so hot, good sir.
I come to bring him sleep. 'Tis such as you,
That creep like shadows by him and do sigh
At each his needless heavings, such as you 35
Nourish the cause of his awaking. I 36
Do come with words as medicinal as true,
Honest as either, to purge him of that humor 38
That presses him from sleep.

LEONTES What noise there, ho?

15 on 't of it **17 solely** alone **18 him** i.e., Polixenes **27 be second to** aid, second **30 free** innocent **35 heavings** sighs or groans **36 awaking** inability to sleep **38 humor** distemper

PAULINA
No noise, my lord, but needful conference
About some gossips for Your Highness.

LEONTES How? 41
Away with that audacious lady! Antigonus,
I charged thee that she should not come about me.
I knew she would.

ANTIGONUS I told her so, my lord,
On your displeasure's peril and on mine,
She should not visit you.

LEONTES What, canst not rule her?

PAULINA
From all dishonesty he can. In this,
Unless he take the course that you have done—
Commit me for committing honor—trust it, 49
He shall not rule me.

ANTIGONUS La you now, you hear! 50
When she will take the rein I let her run,
But she'll not stumble.

PAULINA Good my liege, I come—
And I beseech you hear me, who professes
Myself your loyal servant, your physician,
Your most obedient counselor, yet that dares
Less appear so in comforting your evils 56
Than such as most seem yours—I say, I come 57
From your good queen.

LEONTES Good queen?

PAULINA
Good queen, my lord, good queen, I say good queen,
And would by combat make her good, so were I 61
A man, the worst about you.

LEONTES Force her hence. 62

PAULINA
Let him that makes but trifles of his eyes
First hand me. On mine own accord I'll off,

41 gossips godparents for the baby at its baptism **49 Commit** i.e., to prison **50 La . . . hear** i.e., there now, you hear how she will go on talking **56–57 in comforting . . . yours** when it comes to encouraging your evil courses than those flatterers who seem to be your most loyal servants **61 by combat** by trial by combat. **make** prove **62 worst** least manly, or lowest in rank

But first I'll do my errand. The good Queen,
For she is good, hath brought you forth a daughter—
Here 'tis—commends it to your blessing.
[*She lays down the baby.*]

LEONTES Out!
A mankind witch! Hence with her, out o' door! 68
A most intelligencing bawd!

PAULINA Not so. 69
I am as ignorant in that as you
In so entitling me, and no less honest
Than you are mad; which is enough, I'll warrant,
As this world goes, to pass for honest.

LEONTES Traitors!
Will you not push her out? [*To Antigonus.*] Give her the bastard.
Thou dotard, thou art woman-tired, unroosted 75
By thy Dame Partlet here. Take up the bastard! 76
Take 't up, I say. Give 't to thy crone.

PAULINA Forever
Unvenerable be thy hands if thou
Tak'st up the Princess by that forcèd baseness 79
Which he has put upon 't!

LEONTES He dreads his wife.

PAULINA
So I would you did. Then 'twere past all doubt
You'd call your children yours.

LEONTES A nest of traitors!

ANTIGONUS
I am none, by this good light.

PAULINA Nor I, nor any 83
But one that's here, and that's himself; for he
The sacred honor of himself, his queen's,
His hopeful son's, his babe's, betrays to slander,
Whose sting is sharper than the sword's; and will not—

68 mankind masculine, behaving like a man **69 intelligencing bawd** acting as go-between and spy (for the Queen and Polixenes) **75 woman-tired** henpecked. (From *tire* in falconry, meaning "tear with the beak.") **unroosted** driven from perch **76 Partlet** or Pertilote, a common name for a hen (as in *Reynard the Fox* and in Chaucer's "Nun's Priest's Tale") **79 by that forcèd baseness** under that wrongfully imposed name of bastard **83 by this good light** by my eyesight. (A common oath.)

For, as the case now stands, it is a curse
He cannot be compelled to 't—once remove
The root of his opinion, which is rotten
As ever oak or stone was sound.

LEONTES
A callet 91
Of boundless tongue, who late hath beat her husband
And now baits me! This brat is none of mine;
It is the issue of Polixenes.
Hence with it, and together with the dam
Commit them to the fire!

PAULINA
It is yours;
And, might we lay th' old proverb to your charge,
So like you, 'tis the worse. Behold, my lords,
Although the print be little, the whole matter
And copy of the father—eye, nose, lip,
The trick of 's frown, his forehead, nay, the valley, 101
The pretty dimples of his chin and cheek, his smiles,
The very mold and frame of hand, nail, finger.
And thou, good goddess Nature, which hast made it
So like to him that got it, if thou hast 105
The ordering of the mind too, 'mongst all colors
No yellow in 't, lest she suspect, as he does, 107
Her children not her husband's!

LEONTES
A gross hag!
And, lozel, thou art worthy to be hanged, 109
That wilt not stay her tongue.

ANTIGONUS
Hang all the husbands 110
That cannot do that feat, you'll leave yourself
Hardly one subject.

LEONTES
Once more, take her hence.

PAULINA
A most unworthy and unnatural lord
Can do no more.

LEONTES
I'll ha' thee burnt.

PAULINA
I care not.

91 callet scold **101 trick** characteristic expression. **valley** cleft of the chin (?) **105 got** begot **107 No yellow** let there be no yellow, i.e., the color of jealousy. (A chaste woman could hardly expect that her own children are illegitimate, but Paulina may be speaking hyperbolically.) **109 lozel** worthless person, scoundrel. (Addressed to Antigonus.) **110 stay** restrain

It is an heretic that makes the fire, 115
Not she which burns in 't. I'll not call you tyrant; 116
But this most cruel usage of your queen,
Not able to produce more accusation 118
Than your own weak-hinged fancy, something savors
Of tyranny and will ignoble make you,
Yea, scandalous to the world.

LEONTES On your allegiance,
Out of the chamber with her! Were I a tyrant,
Where were her life? She durst not call me so 123
If she did know me one. Away with her!

PAULINA
I pray you, do not push me; I'll be gone.
Look to your babe, my lord; 'tis yours. Jove send her
A better guiding spirit!—What needs these hands? 127
You that are thus so tender o'er his follies
Will never do him good, not one of you.
So, so. Farewell, we are gone. *Exit.*

LEONTES
Thou, traitor, hast set on thy wife to this.
My child? Away with 't! Even thou, that hast
A heart so tender o'er it, take it hence
And see it instantly consumed with fire;
Even thou and none but thou. Take it up straight.
Within this hour bring me word 'tis done,
And by good testimony, or I'll seize thy life,
With what thou else call'st thine. If thou refuse
And wilt encounter with my wrath, say so;
The bastard brains with these my proper hands 140
Shall I dash out. Go, take it to the fire,
For thou sett'st on thy wife.

ANTIGONUS I did not, sir.
These lords, my noble fellows, if they please,
Can clear me in 't.

LORDS We can. My royal liege,
He is not guilty of her coming hither.

LEONTES You're liars all.

115–116 It is . . . in 't i.e., only a heretic can be burned guiltily; an innocent person may be burned, but in that case the one who does the burning is the guilty party, having committed the heresy of loss of faith **118 Not able** you not being able **123 Where . . . life** i.e., how could she escape execution at my command **127 What . . . hands** i.e., what need is there to push me **140 proper** own

A LORD
Beseech Your Highness, give us better credit. 147
We have always truly served you, and beseech' 148
So to esteem of us; and on our knees we beg,
As recompense of our dear services 150
Past and to come, that you do change this purpose,
Which being so horrible, so bloody, must
Lead on to some foul issue. We all kneel.

LEONTES
I am a feather for each wind that blows.
Shall I live on to see this bastard kneel
And call me father? Better burn it now
Than curse it then. But be it; let it live.
It shall not neither. [*To Antigonus.*] You, sir, come
you hither,
You that have been so tenderly officious
With Lady Margery, your midwife there, 160
To save this bastard's life—for 'tis a bastard,
So sure as this beard's gray. What will you adventure 162
To save this brat's life?

ANTIGONUS Anything, my lord,
That my ability may undergo
And nobleness impose. At least thus much:
I'll pawn the little blood which I have left
To save the innocent—anything possible.

LEONTES [*Holding his sword*]
It shall be possible. Swear by this sword
Thou wilt perform my bidding.

ANTIGONUS [*His hand on the hilt*] I will, my lord.

LEONTES
Mark and perform it, seest thou; for the fail 170
Of any point in 't shall not only be
Death to thyself but to thy lewd-tongued wife,
Whom for this time we pardon. We enjoin thee,
As thou art liege man to us, that thou carry
This female bastard hence, and that thou bear it
To some remote and desert place quite out
Of our dominions, and that there thou leave it,
Without more mercy, to its own protection

147 credit belief **148 beseech'** beseech you **150 dear** loyal, heartfelt
160 Margery (A derisive term, evidently equivalent to *Partlet* in l. 76.)
162 this beard's (Probably Antigonus's.) **170 seest thou** i.e., do you hear. **fail** failure

And favor of the climate. As by strange fortune
It came to us, I do in justice charge thee,
On thy soul's peril and thy body's torture,
That thou commend it strangely to some place 182
Where chance may nurse or end it. Take it up.

ANTIGONUS [*Taking up the baby*]
I swear to do this, though a present death
Had been more merciful. Come on, poor babe.
Some powerful spirit instruct the kites and ravens
To be thy nurses! Wolves and bears, they say,
Casting their savageness aside, have done
Like offices of pity. Sir, be prosperous
In more than this deed does require!—And blessing 190
Against this cruelty fight on thy side,
Poor thing, condemned to loss! *Exit* [*with the baby*].

LEONTES No, I'll not rear 192
Another's issue.

Enter a Servant.

SERVANT Please Your Highness, posts 193
From those you sent to th' oracle are come
An hour since. Cleomenes and Dion,
Being well arrived from Delphos, are both landed,
Hasting to th' court.

A LORD So please you, sir, their speed
Hath been beyond account.

LEONTES Twenty-three days 198
They have been absent. 'Tis good speed, foretells
The great Apollo suddenly will have 200
The truth of this appear. Prepare you, lords.
Summon a session, that we may arraign 202
Our most disloyal lady; for, as she hath
Been publicly accused, so shall she have
A just and open trial. While she lives
My heart will be a burden to me. Leave me,
And think upon my bidding. *Exeunt* [*separately*].

✤

182 commend . . . place commit it to some foreign place, or as a stranger **190 more** i.e., more ways, more extent (?) **require** deserve **192 loss** destruction **193 posts** messengers **198 beyond account** i.e., unprecedented, or beyond explanation **200 suddenly** at once **202 session** trial

3.1 *Enter Cleomenes and Dion.*

CLEOMENES
The climate's delicate, the air most sweet,
Fertile the isle, the temple much surpassing 2
The common praise it bears.
DION I shall report,
For most it caught me, the celestial habits— 4
Methinks I so should term them—and the reverence
Of the grave wearers. O, the sacrifice!
How ceremonious, solemn, and unearthly
It was i' th' offering!
CLEOMENES But of all, the burst
And the ear-deafening voice o' th' oracle,
Kin to Jove's thunder, so surprised my sense 10
That I was nothing.
DION If th' event o' the journey 11
Prove as successful to the Queen—O, be 't so!—
As it hath been to us rare, pleasant, speedy,
The time is worth the use on 't.
CLEOMENES Great Apollo 14
Turn all to th' best! These proclamations,
So forcing faults upon Hermione,
I little like.
DION The violent carriage of it 17
Will clear or end the business. When the oracle,
Thus by Apollo's great divine sealed up, 19
Shall the contents discover, something rare 20
Even then will rush to knowledge. Go. Fresh horses!
And gracious be the issue! *Exeunt.*

✤

3.1. Location: Sicilia. On the way to Leontes's court.
2 isle (Shakespeare follows Greene's *Pandosto* in fictitiously placing Delphi on an island. Delphi, sometimes known as Delphos [see 2.1.184, 2.3.196, and 3.2.126], was often confused with Delos, the island birthplace of Apollo and location also of an oracle.) **4 habits** vestments **10 surprised** overwhelmed **11 event** outcome **14 is worth . . . on 't** has been well employed **17 carriage** execution, management **19 great divine** chief priest **20 discover** reveal

3.2 *Enter Leontes, Lords,* [*and*] *Officers.*

LEONTES
This sessions, to our great grief we pronounce,
Even pushes 'gainst our heart: the party tried
The daughter of a king, our wife, and one
Of us too much beloved. Let us be cleared 4
Of being tyrannous, since we so openly
Proceed in justice, which shall have due course
Even to the guilt or the purgation. 7
Produce the prisoner.

OFFICER
It is His Highness' pleasure that the Queen
Appear in person here in court. Silence!

[*Enter*] *Hermione, as to her trial,* [*Paulina, and*] *Ladies.*

LEONTES Read the indictment.

OFFICER [*Reads*] "Hermione, Queen to the worthy Leontes, King of Sicilia, thou art here accused and arraigned of high treason, in committing adultery with Polixenes, King of Bohemia, and conspiring with Camillo to take away the life of our sovereign lord the King, thy royal husband; the pretense whereof being 17 by circumstances partly laid open, thou, Hermione, contrary to the faith and allegiance of a true subject, didst counsel and aid them, for their better safety, to fly away by night."

HERMIONE
Since what I am to say must be but that
Which contradicts my accusation, and
The testimony on my part no other
But what comes from myself, it shall scarce boot me 25
To say "not guilty." Mine integrity,
Being counted falsehood, shall, as I express it,
Be so received. But thus: if powers divine
Behold our human actions, as they do,

3.2. Location: Sicilia. A place of justice, probably at court.
4 Of by **7 purgation** clearing from the accusation **17 pretense** purpose, design **25 boot** avail

I doubt not then but innocence shall make
False accusation blush and tyranny
Tremble at patience. You, my lord, best know,
Who least will seem to do so, my past life
Hath been as continent, as chaste, as true,
As I am now unhappy; which is more
Than history can pattern, though devised 36
And played to take spectators. For behold me— 37
A fellow of the royal bed, which owe 38
A moiety of the throne, a great king's daughter, 39
The mother to a hopeful prince—here standing
To prate and talk for life and honor 'fore
Who please to come and hear. For life, I prize it 42
As I weigh grief, which I would spare. For honor, 43
'Tis a derivative from me to mine, 44
And only that I stand for. I appeal 45
To your own conscience, sir, before Polixenes 46
Came to your court, how I was in your grace,
How merited to be so; since he came,
With what encounter so uncurrent I 49
Have strained t' appear thus; if one jot beyond 50
The bound of honor, or in act or will
That way inclining, hardened be the hearts
Of all that hear me, and my near'st of kin
Cry fie upon my grave!

LEONTES I ne'er heard yet
That any of these bolder vices wanted 55
Less impudence to gainsay what they did 56
Than to perform it first.

HERMIONE That's true enough,
Though 'tis a saying, sir, not due to me. 58

LEONTES
You will not own it.

36 history story, here presented in the theater. **pattern** show a similar example for **37 take** please, charm **38 which owe** who own **39 moiety** share **42 Who please** whoever chooses **42–45 For . . . stand for** as for life, I value it as I value grief, and would as willingly do without; as for honor, it is transmitted from me to my descendants, and that only I make a stand for **46 conscience** consideration, inward knowledge **49–50 With . . . thus** (I ask) by what behavior so improper I have transgressed so that I appear thus (in disgrace and on trial) **55–56 wanted Less** were more lacking in **58 due** applicable

HERMIONE More than mistress of 59
Which comes to me in name of fault, I must not 60
At all acknowledge. For Polixenes, 61
With whom I am accused, I do confess
I loved him as in honor he required; 63
With such a kind of love as might become
A lady like me; with a love even such,
So, and no other, as yourself commanded;
Which not to have done I think had been in me
Both disobedience and ingratitude
To you and toward your friend, whose love had spoke, 69
Even since it could speak, from an infant, freely
That it was yours. Now, for conspiracy, 71
I know not how it tastes, though it be dished 72
For me to try how. All I know of it
Is that Camillo was an honest man;
And why he left your court, the gods themselves,
Wotting no more than I, are ignorant. 76

LEONTES
You knew of his departure, as you know
What you have underta'en to do in 's absence.

HERMIONE Sir,
You speak a language that I understand not.
My life stands in the level of your dreams, 81
Which I'll lay down.

LEONTES Your actions are my dreams. 82
You had a bastard by Polixenes,
And I but dreamed it. As you were past all shame—
Those of your fact are so—so past all truth, 85
Which to deny concerns more than avails; for as 86
Thy brat hath been cast out, like to itself, 87

59–61 More . . . acknowledge I will not acknowledge that I am answerable for more than what may be called ordinary human faults. (Hermione insists she is not guilty of the *bolder vices* of l. 55.) **61 For** as for **63 required** deserved **69 whose love** i.e., the mutual love between Leontes and Polixenes **71 That it was yours** that this mutual love was a part of your soul. **for** as for **72 dished** served up **76 Wotting** i.e., supposing they know **81 level** aim, range **82 Your . . . dreams** i.e., you have performed what I have fantasized, and what you have done preys on my mind **85 Those of your fact** all those who do what you did **86 concerns . . . avails** may seem an understandable concern on your part but will not help **87 like to itself** as it ought to be (since it has no father)

No father owning it—which is indeed
More criminal in thee than it—so thou
Shalt feel our justice, in whose easiest passage 90
Look for no less than death.

HERMIONE Sir, spare your threats. 91
The bug which you would fright me with I seek. 92
To me can life be no commodity. 93
The crown and comfort of my life, your favor,
I do give lost, for I do feel it gone, 95
But know not how it went. My second joy
And firstfruits of my body, from his presence
I am barred, like one infectious. My third comfort,
Starred most unluckily, is from my breast, 99
The innocent milk in its most innocent mouth,
Haled out to murder; myself on every post 101
Proclaimed a strumpet; with immodest hatred 102
The childbed privilege denied, which longs 103
To women of all fashion; lastly, hurried 104
Here to this place, i' th' open air, before
I have got strength of limit. Now, my liege, 106
Tell me what blessings I have here alive
That I should fear to die? Therefore proceed.
But yet hear this; mistake me not. No life, 109
I prize it not a straw. But for mine honor,
Which I would free, if I shall be condemned
Upon surmises, all proofs sleeping else
But what your jealousies awake, I tell you
'Tis rigor and not law. Your honors all, 114
I do refer me to the oracle.
Apollo be my judge!

A LORD This your request
Is altogether just. Therefore bring forth,
And in Apollo's name, his oracle.
[*Exeunt certain Officers.*]

90–91 in whose . . . death i.e., which will impose the death sentence at least, perhaps torture also **92 bug** bugbear, bogey, imaginary object of terror **93 commodity** asset **95 give** reckon as, or give up as **99 Starred most unluckily** born under a most unlucky star **101 post** posting place for public notices **102 immodest** immoderate **103 longs** belongs, i.e., is fitting **104 all fashion** every rank **106 got . . . limit** i.e., regained my strength after having borne a child **109 No life** i.e., I do not ask for life **114 rigor** tyranny

HERMIONE
The Emperor of Russia was my father.
O, that he were alive and here beholding
His daughter's trial! That he did but see
The flatness of my misery, yet with eyes 122
Of pity, not revenge!

[*Enter Officers, with*] *Cleomenes* [*and*] *Dion.*

OFFICER [*Holding a sword*]
You here shall swear upon this sword of justice,
That you, Cleomenes and Dion, have
Been both at Delphos, and from thence have brought
This sealed-up oracle, by the hand delivered
Of great Apollo's priest, and that since then
You have not dared to break the holy seal
Nor read the secrets in 't.

CLEOMENES, DION All this we swear.

LEONTES
Break up the seals and read. 131

OFFICER [*Reads*] "Hermione is chaste, Polixenes blameless, Camillo a true subject, Leontes a jealous tyrant, his innocent babe truly begotten, and the King shall live without an heir if that which is lost be not found."

LORDS
Now blessèd be the great Apollo!

HERMIONE Praised!

LEONTES
Hast thou read truth?

OFFICER Ay, my lord, even so
As it is here set down.

LEONTES
There is no truth at all i' th' oracle.
The sessions shall proceed. This is mere falsehood.

[*Enter a Servant.*]

SERVANT
My lord the King, the King!

LEONTES What is the business?

122 flatness absoluteness **131 up** open

SERVANT

O sir, I shall be hated to report it! 143
The Prince your son, with mere conceit and fear 144
Of the Queen's speed, is gone.

LEONTES
How? Gone?

SERVANT
Is dead. 145

LEONTES

Apollo's angry, and the heavens themselves
Do strike at my injustice. [*Hermione swoons.*] How
now there?

PAULINA

This news is mortal to the Queen. Look down
And see what death is doing.

LEONTES
Take her hence.
Her heart is but o'ercharged; she will recover.
I have too much believed mine own suspicion.
Beseech you, tenderly apply to her
Some remedies for life.

[*Exeunt Paulina and Ladies, with Hermione.*]

Apollo, pardon
My great profaneness 'gainst thine oracle!
I'll reconcile me to Polixenes,
New woo my queen, recall the good Camillo,
Whom I proclaim a man of truth, of mercy;
For, being transported by my jealousies
To bloody thoughts and to revenge, I chose
Camillo for the minister to poison
My friend Polixenes; which had been done
But that the good mind of Camillo tardied 162
My swift command, though I with death and with
Reward did threaten and encourage him,
Not doing it and being done. He, most humane 165
And filled with honor, to my kingly guest
Unclasped my practice, quit his fortunes here, 167
Which you knew great, and to the hazard
Of all incertainties himself commended, 169

143 to report for reporting **144 conceit and fear** i.e., anxious concern **145 speed** fate, fortune **162 tardied** delayed **165 Not . . . done** i.e., death if he did not do it, and reward if he did **167 Unclasped my practice** disclosed my plot **169 himself commended** entrusted himself

No richer than his honor. How he glisters 170
Through my rust! And how his piety
Does my deeds make the blacker!

[*Enter Paulina.*]

PAULINA Woe the while!
O, cut my lace, lest my heart, cracking it,
Break too!

A LORD What fit is this, good lady?

PAULINA
What studied torments, tyrant, hast for me?
What wheels, racks, fires? What flaying, boiling
In leads or oils? What old or newer torture
Must I receive, whose every word deserves
To taste of thy most worst? Thy tyranny,
Together working with thy jealousies—
Fancies too weak for boys, too green and idle 181
For girls of nine—O, think what they have done,
And then run mad indeed, stark mad! For all
Thy bygone fooleries were but spices of it. 184
That thou betrayedst Polixenes, 'twas nothing;
That did but show thee, of a fool, inconstant 186
And damnable ingrateful. Nor was 't much
Thou wouldst have poisoned good Camillo's honor,
To have him kill a king—poor trespasses, 189
More monstrous standing by; whereof I reckon 190
The casting forth to crows thy baby daughter
To be or none or little, though a devil 192
Would have shed water out of fire ere done 't. 193
Nor is 't directly laid to thee, the death
Of the young Prince, whose honorable thoughts,
Thoughts high for one so tender, cleft the heart 196
That could conceive a gross and foolish sire 197
Blemished his gracious dam. This is not, no,
Laid to thy answer. But the last—O lords,

170 No richer than with no riches except. **glisters** shines **181 idle** foolish **184 spices** foretastes, samples **186 of a fool, inconstant** i.e., being a fool naturally and then inconstant into the bargain **189 To have** by having. **poor** slight **190 More . . . by** when more monstrous sins are at hand for comparison **192 or none** either none **193 shed . . . fire** wept from his fiery eyes, or while surrounded by hellfire **196 tender** young **197 conceive** apprehend that

When I have said, cry woe! The Queen, the Queen, 200
The sweet'st, dear'st creature's dead, and vengeance
  for 't
Not dropped down yet.

A LORD The higher powers forbid!

PAULINA
I say she's dead. I'll swear 't. If word nor oath
Prevail not, go and see. If you can bring
Tincture or luster in her lip, her eye,
Heat outwardly or breath within, I'll serve you
As I would do the gods. But, O thou tyrant!
Do not repent these things, for they are heavier
Than all thy woes can stir. Therefore betake thee 209
To nothing but despair. A thousand knees
Ten thousand years together, naked, fasting,
Upon a barren mountain, and still winter 212
In storm perpetual, could not move the gods
To look that way thou wert.

LEONTES Go on, go on. 214
Thou canst not speak too much. I have deserved
All tongues to talk their bitt'rest.

A LORD [*To Paulina*] Say no more.
Howe'er the business goes, you have made fault
I' the boldness of your speech.

PAULINA I am sorry for 't.
All faults I make, when I shall come to know them, 219
I do repent. Alas, I have showed too much
The rashness of a woman! He is touched
To th' noble heart. What's gone and what's past help
Should be past grief.—Do not receive affliction 223
At my petition. I beseech you, rather 224
Let me be punished, that have minded you 225
Of what you should forget. Now, good my liege,
Sir, royal sir, forgive a foolish woman.
The love I bore your queen—lo, fool again!—
I'll speak of her no more, nor of your children;
I'll not remember you of my own lord, 230

200 said finished speaking **209 woes can stir** penance can remove **212 still** always **214 To look . . . wert** to regard you **219 I make** that I make **223–224 Do . . . petition** do not afflict yourself with remorse at my urging **225 minded you** put you in mind **230 remember** remind

Who is lost too. Take your patience to you, 231
And I'll say nothing.

LEONTES Thou didst speak but well
When most the truth, which I receive much better
Than to be pitied of thee. Prithee, bring me
To the dead bodies of my queen and son.
One grave shall be for both. Upon them shall
The causes of their death appear, unto
Our shame perpetual. Once a day I'll visit
The chapel where they lie, and tears shed there
Shall be my recreation. So long as nature
Will bear up with this exercise, so long
I daily vow to use it. Come and lead me
To these sorrows. *Exeunt.*

✤

3.3 *Enter Antigonus* [*and*] *a Mariner,* [*with a*] *babe.*

ANTIGONUS
Thou art perfect then, our ship hath touched upon 1
The deserts of Bohemia?

MARINER Ay, my lord, and fear 2
We have landed in ill time. The skies look grimly
And threaten present blusters. In my conscience, 4
The heavens with that we have in hand are angry
And frown upon 's.

ANTIGONUS
Their sacred wills be done! Go, get aboard;
Look to thy bark. I'll not be long before
I call upon thee.

MARINER Make your best haste, and go not
Too far i' the land. 'Tis like to be loud weather. 10
Besides, this place is famous for the creatures
Of prey that keep upon 't.

ANTIGONUS Go thou away. 12

231 Take . . . you be patient

3.3. Location: Bohemia. The seacoast.
1 perfect certain **2 deserts of Bohemia** i.e., deserted region on the coast. (Shakespeare follows Greene's *Pandosto* in giving Bohemia a seacoast.) **4 present** immediate. **conscience** opinion **10 like** likely. **loud** stormy **12 keep upon 't** inhabit it

I'll follow instantly.

MARINER I am glad at heart
To be so rid o' the business. *Exit.*

ANTIGONUS Come, poor babe.
I have heard, but not believed, the spirits o' the dead
May walk again. If such thing be, thy mother
Appeared to me last night, for ne'er was dream
So like a waking. To me comes a creature,
Sometimes her head on one side, some another;
I never saw a vessel of like sorrow,
So filled and so becoming. In pure white robes, 21
Like very sanctity, she did approach
My cabin where I lay, thrice bowed before me,
And, gasping to begin some speech, her eyes
Became two spouts. The fury spent, anon
Did this break from her: "Good Antigonus,
Since fate, against thy better disposition,
Hath made thy person for the thrower-out
Of my poor babe, according to thine oath,
Places remote enough are in Bohemia;
There weep and leave it crying. And, for the babe 31
Is counted lost forever, Perdita, 32
I prithee, call 't. For this ungentle business 33
Put on thee by my lord, thou ne'er shalt see
Thy wife Paulina more." And so, with shrieks,
She melted into air. Affrighted much,
I did in time collect myself and thought
This was so and no slumber. Dreams are toys; 38
Yet for this once, yea, superstitiously,
I will be squared by this. I do believe 40
Hermione hath suffered death, and that
Apollo would, this being indeed the issue
Of King Polixenes, it should here be laid,
Either for life or death, upon the earth
Of its right father. Blossom, speed thee well!
[*He lays down the baby.*]

21 So . . . becoming i.e., so filled with sorrow and so attractive thus
31 for because **32 Perdita** i.e., the lost one **33 ungentle** ignoble
38 toys trifles **40 squared** directed in my course

There lie, and there thy character; there these, 46
[*He places a box and a fardel beside the baby*]
Which may, if fortune please, both breed thee, pretty, 47
And still rest thine. [*Thunder.*] The storm begins.
Poor wretch, 48
That for thy mother's fault art thus exposed
To loss and what may follow! Weep I cannot, 50
But my heart bleeds; and most accurst am I
To be by oath enjoined to this. Farewell!
The day frowns more and more. Thou'rt like to have
A lullaby too rough. I never saw
The heavens so dim by day. A savage clamor!
Well may I get aboard! This is the chase.
I am gone forever. *Exit, pursued by a bear.*

[*Enter a*] *Shepherd.*

SHEPHERD I would there were no age between ten and three-and-twenty, or that youth would sleep out the rest, for there is nothing in the between but getting wenches with child, wronging the ancientry, stealing, 61 fighting—Hark you now, would any but these boiled 62 brains of nineteen and two-and-twenty hunt this 63 weather? They have scared away two of my best sheep, which I fear the wolf will sooner find than the master. If anywhere I have them, 'tis by the seaside, browsing of ivy. Good luck, an 't be thy will! [*Seeing the child.*] 67 What have we here? Mercy on 's, a bairn, a very pretty 68 bairn! A boy or a child, I wonder? A pretty one, a very 69 pretty one. Sure some scape. Though I am not bookish, 70 yet I can read waiting-gentlewoman in the scape.

46 character writing, written account (i.e., the same as that which subsequently will serve to identify Perdita). **these** i.e., the gold and jewels found by the Shepherd, also later used to identify her **s.d. box, fardel** (The box, containing gold and jewels, is later produced by the old Shepherd and the Clown; see 4.4.758–759. They also have a *fardel,* or bundle, consisting evidently of the bearing cloth [3.3.112] and/or mantle [5.2.34] in which the babe is found.) **47 breed thee** keep you, pay for your support. **pretty** pretty one **48 And still rest thine** i.e., and still provide a heritage with what is unspent **50 To loss** to being lost. **Weep I cannot** i.e., I cannot weep as the Queen instructed me (l. 31) **61 ancientry** old people **62–63 boiled brains** addlepated youths **67 Good . . . will** i.e., may God grant me good luck in finding my sheep **68 bairn** child **69 child** i.e., female infant **70 scape** sexual escapade

This has been some stair-work, some trunk-work, 72
some behind-door-work. They were warmer that got 73
this than the poor thing is here. I'll take it up for pity.
Yet I'll tarry till my son come; he hallooed but even
now.—Whoa, ho, hoa! 76

Enter Clown.

CLOWN Hilloa, loa!

SHEPHERD What, art so near? If thou'lt see a thing to talk on when thou art dead and rotten, come hither. What ail'st thou, man?

CLOWN I have seen two such sights, by sea and by land! But I am not to say it is a sea, for it is now the sky; betwixt the firmament and it you cannot thrust a bodkin's point. 84

SHEPHERD Why, boy, how is it?

CLOWN I would you did but see how it chafes, how it rages, how it takes up the shore! But that's not to the 87 point. O, the most piteous cry of the poor souls! Sometimes to see 'em, and not to see 'em; now the ship boring the moon with her mainmast, and anon swallowed with yeast and froth, as you'd thrust a cork into 91 a hogshead. And then for the land service, to see how 92 the bear tore out his shoulder bone; how he cried to me for help and said his name was Antigonus, a nobleman. But to make an end of the ship: to see how the sea flapdragoned it! But first, how the poor souls 96 roared and the sea mocked them, and how the poor gentleman roared and the bear mocked him, both roaring louder than the sea or weather.

SHEPHERD Name of mercy, when was this, boy?

CLOWN Now, now. I have not winked since I saw these 101

72–73 stair-work . . . behind-door-work i.e., sexual liaisons under or behind the stairs or using a trunk for concealment **73 got** begot
76 s.d. Clown country fellow, rustic **84 bodkin's** needle's. (A *bodkin* can also be a dagger, awl, etc.) **87 takes up** (1) contends with, rebukes (2) swallows **91 yeast** foam **92 hogshead** large barrel. (The image is of a cork swimming in a turbulent expanse of frothing liquid.) **land service** (1) dish of food served on land (2) military service on land (as distinguished from naval service); here, the doings on land
96 flapdragoned swallowed as one would a flapdragon, i.e., a raisin or the like swallowed out of burning brandy in the game of snapdragon
101 winked closed my eyes

sights. The men are not yet cold under water, nor the bear half dined on the gentleman. He's at it now.

SHEPHERD Would I had been by, to have helped the old man!

CLOWN I would you had been by the ship side, to have helped her. There your charity would have lacked footing. 108

SHEPHERD Heavy matters, heavy matters! But look thee here, boy. Now bless thyself. Thou mett'st with things dying, I with things newborn. Here's a sight for thee; look thee, a bearing cloth for a squire's child! Look 112 thee here; take up, take up, boy. Open 't. So, let's see. It was told me I should be rich by the fairies. This is some changeling. Open 't. What's within, boy? 115

[*The Clown opens the box.*]

CLOWN You're a made old man. If the sins of your youth are forgiven you, you're well to live. Gold, all 117 gold!

SHEPHERD This is fairy gold, boy, and 'twill prove so. Up with 't, keep it close. Home, home, the next way. 120 We are lucky, boy, and to be so still requires nothing 121 but secrecy. Let my sheep go. Come, good boy, the 122 next way home.

CLOWN Go you the next way with our findings. I'll go see if the bear be gone from the gentleman, and how much he hath eaten. They are never curst but when 126 they are hungry. If there be any of him left, I'll bury it.

SHEPHERD That's a good deed. If thou mayest discern by that which is left of him what he is, fetch me to the sight of him.

CLOWN Marry, will I; and you shall help to put him i' 131 the ground.

SHEPHERD 'Tis a lucky day, boy, and we'll do good deeds on 't. *Exeunt.*

108 footing (1) foothold (2) establishment of a charitable foundation, one that would provide *charity* (l. 107) **112 bearing cloth** rich cloth or mantle in which a child was carried to its baptism **115 changeling** child left or taken by fairies **117 well to live** well-to-do **120 close** secret. **next** nearest **121–122 to be . . . secrecy** (To talk about fairy gifts would be to insure bad luck.) **still** always **126 curst** mean, fierce **131 Marry** i.e., indeed. (Originally an oath, "by the Virgin Mary.")

4.1 *Enter Time, the Chorus.*

TIME

I, that please some, try all, both joy and terror 1
Of good and bad, that makes and unfolds error, 2
Now take upon me, in the name of Time,
To use my wings. Impute it not a crime
To me or my swift passage, that I slide
O'er sixteen years and leave the growth untried 6
Of that wide gap, since it is in my power
To o'erthrow law and in one self-born hour 8
To plant and o'erwhelm custom. Let me pass
The same I am ere ancient'st order was 10
Or what is now received. I witness to 11
The times that brought them in; so shall I do 12
To th' freshest things now reigning, and make stale
The glistering of this present, as my tale 14
Now seems to it. Your patience this allowing, 15
I turn my glass and give my scene such growing 16
As you had slept between. Leontes leaving— 17
Th' effects of his fond jealousies so grieving 18
That he shuts up himself—imagine me,
Gentle spectators, that I now may be
In fair Bohemia. And remember well
I mentioned a son o' the King's, which Florizel
I now name to you; and with speed so pace 23
To speak of Perdita, now grown in grace
Equal with wondering. What of her ensues 25

4.1.
1 try test **2 that . . . error** i.e., I who make error, thus bringing joy to the bad and terror to the good, and then at last unfold or disclose error, thus bringing joy to the good and terror to the bad **6 growth untried** developments unexplored **8 law** i.e., the rule of the unity of time in a dramatic performance, normally limiting the action to twenty-four hours. **self-born** selfsame, or born of myself (since hours are the creations of Time) **10–11 ere . . . received** i.e., from the beginnings of time to the present **12 them** i.e., law and custom **14 glistering** glistening freshness **15 seems to it** seems (stale) when compared with the present **16 glass** hourglass **17 As** as if. **Leontes leaving** leaving behind Leontes for the moment **18 Th' effects . . . grieving** so grieving at the effects of his foolish jealousies **23 pace** proceed **25 Equal with wondering** as great as the wonder people feel in seeing her

I list not prophesy; but let Time's news 26
Be known when 'tis brought forth. A shepherd's daughter,
And what to her adheres, which follows after, 28
Is th' argument of Time. Of this allow, 29
If ever you have spent time worse ere now;
If never, yet that Time himself doth say 31
He wishes earnestly you never may. *Exit.*

4.2 *Enter Polixenes and Camillo.*

POLIXENES I pray thee, good Camillo, be no more importunate. 'Tis a sickness denying thee anything, a death to grant this.

CAMILLO It is fifteen years since I saw my country. Though I have for the most part been aired abroad, I 5 desire to lay my bones there. Besides, the penitent King, my master, hath sent for me, to whose feeling 7 sorrows I might be some allay—or I o'erween to think 8 so—which is another spur to my departure.

POLIXENES As thou lov'st me, Camillo, wipe not out the rest of thy services by leaving me now. The need I have of thee thine own goodness hath made. Better not to have had thee than thus to want thee. Thou, 13 having made me businesses which none without thee can sufficiently manage, must either stay to execute them thyself or take away with thee the very services thou hast done; which if I have not enough considered—as too much I cannot—to be more thank- 18 ful to thee shall be my study, and my profit therein the heaping friendships. Of that fatal country, Sicilia, prith- 20 ee, speak no more, whose very naming punishes me with the remembrance of that penitent, as thou call'st

26 list not do not care to **28 to her adheres** concerns her
29 argument subject of a story **31 yet that** i.e., yet allow that

4.2. Location: Bohemia. The court of Polixenes.
5 been aired abroad lived abroad **7 feeling** heartfelt **8 allay** means of abatement. **o'erween** am presumptuous enough **13 want** lack
18 considered i.e., rewarded **20 heaping friendships** heaping up of (your) kind services and our mutual affection

him, and reconciled king, my brother, whose loss of his most precious queen and children are even now to be afresh lamented. Say to me, when sawst thou the Prince Florizel, my son? Kings are no less unhappy, their issue not being gracious, than they are in losing 27 them when they have approved their virtues. 28

CAMILLO Sir, it is three days since I saw the Prince. What his happier affairs may be are to me unknown; but I have missingly noted he is of late much retired 31 from court and is less frequent to his princely exer- 32 cises than formerly he hath appeared.

POLIXENES I have considered so much, Camillo, and 34 with some care, so far that I have eyes under my ser- 35 vice which look upon his removedness; from whom I 36 have this intelligence, that he is seldom from the 37 house of a most homely shepherd—a man, they say, 38 that from very nothing, and beyond the imagination of his neighbors, is grown into an unspeakable estate. 40

CAMILLO I have heard, sir, of such a man, who hath a daughter of most rare note. The report of her is ex- 42 tended more than can be thought to begin from such a cottage.

POLIXENES That's likewise part of my intelligence; but, I fear, the angle that plucks our son thither. Thou shalt 46 accompany us to the place, where we will, not appear- ing what we are, have some question with the shep- 48 herd; from whose simplicity I think it not uneasy to 49 get the cause of my son's resort thither. Prithee, be my present partner in this business, and lay aside the thoughts of Sicilia.

CAMILLO I willingly obey your command.

POLIXENES My best Camillo! We must disguise our- selves. *Exit* [*with Camillo*].

27 their . . . gracious if their children behave ungraciously **28 approved** proved **31 missingly** i.e., regretfully aware of the Prince's absence
32 frequent to devoted to **34 so much** i.e., all that you say **35–36 eyes . . . removedness** spies who keep an eye on him in his absence
37 intelligence news. **from** away from **38 homely** simple
40 unspeakable i.e., beyond description **42 note** distinction **46 angle** baited fishhook. **our** (The royal "we"; also in *us,* l. 47.) **48 question** talk **49 uneasy** difficult

4.3 *Enter Autolycus, singing.*

AUTOLYCUS

When daffodils begin to peer, 1
With heigh, the doxy over the dale! 2
Why, then comes in the sweet o' the year,
For the red blood reigns in the winter's pale. 4

The white sheet bleaching on the hedge,
With heigh, the sweet birds, O, how they sing!
Doth set my pugging tooth on edge, 7
For a quart of ale is a dish for a king. 8

The lark, that tirralirra chants,
With heigh, with heigh, the thrush and the jay!
Are summer songs for me and my aunts, 11
While we lie tumbling in the hay.

I have served Prince Florizel and in my time wore three-pile, but now I am out of service. 14

But shall I go mourn for that, my dear? 15
The pale moon shines by night,
And when I wander here and there, 17
I then do most go right. 18

If tinkers may have leave to live, 19
And bear the sow-skin budget, 20
Then my account I well may give, 21
And in the stocks avouch it. 22

My traffic is sheets; when the kite builds, look to lesser 23

4.3. Location: Bohemia. A road near the Shepherd's cottage.
1 peer peep out **2 doxy** beggar's wench **4 pale** (1) paleness (2) domain, region of authority. (The image is of red blood restoring vitality to a pale complexion.) **7 set . . . on edge** i.e., whets the appetite of my thieving tooth, my taste for thieving. (To *pug* is to pull, tug.) **8 quart of ale** (To be paid for with profits from theft of sheets.) **11 aunts** i.e., whores **14 three-pile** velvet having very rich pile or nap **15 for that** i.e., for being out of service **17 wander** (i.e., as a thief) **18 most go right** i.e., live the life that is meant for me **19 live** i.e., practice their trade **20 budget** tool bag **21 my account** my account of myself **22 in . . . avouch it** i.e., affirm that I am a tinker even if I find myself sitting in the stocks, where vagabonds often end up. (Autolycus passes himself off as a tinker to mask his real calling of thief.) **23 kite** (The kite, a bird of prey, was supposed to carry off small pieces of linen with which to construct its nest, whereas Autolycus makes off with larger linen or sheets hung out to dry.)

linen. My father named me Autolycus, who, being, as 24
I am, littered under Mercury, was likewise a snapper- 25
up of unconsidered trifles. With die and drab I pur- 26
chased this caparison, and my revenue is the silly 27
cheat. Gallows and knock are too powerful on the 28
highway; beating and hanging are terrors to me. For 29
the life to come, I sleep out the thought of it. A prize, 30
a prize!

Enter Clown.

CLOWN Let me see: every 'leven wether tods; every tod 32
yields pound and odd shilling; fifteen hundred shorn,
what comes the wool to?

AUTOLYCUS [*Aside*] If the springe hold, the cock's mine. 35

CLOWN I cannot do 't without counters. Let me see; 36
what am I to buy for our sheepshearing feast? Three
pound of sugar, five pound of currants, rice—what
will this sister of mine do with rice? But my father hath
made her mistress of the feast, and she lays it on. She
hath made me four-and-twenty nosegays for the shear- 41
ers—three-man-song men all, and very good ones; 42
but they are most of them means and basses, but one 43
Puritan amongst them, and he sings psalms to horn- 44
pipes. I must have saffron to color the warden pies; 45

24 Autolycus (Like his namesake, Ulysses' grandfather, the son of Mercury, this Autolycus is an expert thief.) **who** i.e., my father **25 littered under Mercury** (1) sired by Mercury, the god of thieves (2) born when the planet Mercury was in the ascendant **26 unconsidered** left unattended, not worth thinking about **26–28 With . . . cheat** i.e., gambling and whoring have brought me to the wearing of these tattered rags, and my source of income is in cheating simpletons **28 Gallows and knock** hanging and being beaten (the hazards of being a highwayman) **29 For** as for **30 sleep . . . it** i.e., don't give a thought to punishment in the next world. **prize** booty **32 every . . . tods** every eleven sheep yield a *tod,* i.e., a bulk of wool weighing twenty-eight pounds **35 springe** snare. **cock** woodcock. (A proverbially stupid bird.) **36 counters** metal disks used in reckoning **41 made me** made. (*Me* is used colloquially.) **42 three-man-song men** singers of songs for three male voices, bass, tenor, and treble **43 means** tenors **43–45 but . . . hornpipes** i.e., except for one Puritan, who is a treble but who sings psalms even to merry dance tunes. (The Puritans were often laughed at for their pious singing.) **45 warden** made of the warden pear

mace; dates?—none, that's out of my note; nutmegs, 46
seven; a race or two of ginger, but that I may beg; four 47
pound of prunes, and as many of raisins o' the sun. 48

AUTOLYCUS O that ever I was born! [*He grovels on the ground.*]

CLOWN I' the name of me! 50

AUTOLYCUS O, help me, help me! Pluck but off these rags, and then death, death!

CLOWN Alack, poor soul! Thou hast need of more rags to lay on thee, rather than have these off.

AUTOLYCUS O sir, the loathsomeness of them offend me more than the stripes I have received, which are mighty ones and millions.

CLOWN Alas, poor man! A million of beating may come to a great matter.

AUTOLYCUS I am robbed, sir, and beaten; my money and apparel ta'en from me, and these detestable things put upon me.

CLOWN What, by a horseman or a footman? 63

AUTOLYCUS A footman, sweet sir, a footman.

CLOWN Indeed, he should be a footman by the garments he has left with thee. If this be a horseman's coat, it hath seen very hot service. Lend me thy hand; I'll help thee. Come, lend me thy hand. [*He helps him up.*]

AUTOLYCUS O, good sir, tenderly, O!

CLOWN Alas, poor soul!

AUTOLYCUS O, good sir, softly, good sir! I fear, sir, my shoulder blade is out.

CLOWN How now? Canst stand?

AUTOLYCUS [*Picking his pocket*] Softly, dear sir; good sir, softly. You ha' done me a charitable office.

CLOWN Dost lack any money? I have a little money for 76
thee. 77

AUTOLYCUS No, good sweet sir; no, I beseech you, sir.

46 out of my note not on my list **47 race** root **48 o' the sun** dried in the sun **50 I' the name of me** (An unusual and perhaps comic oath.) **63 horseman** highwayman. **footman** footpad, robber of pedestrians. (But in l. 65 the Clown uses the word to mean "attendant," who might have poor clothes.) **76–77 I have . . . thee** (The Clown reaches for his money, and might discover the robbery if Autolycus did not quickly beg him not to bother.)

I have a kinsman not past three quarters of a mile hence, unto whom I was going; I shall there have money or anything I want. Offer me no money, I pray you. That kills my heart.

CLOWN What manner of fellow was he that robbed you?

AUTOLYCUS A fellow, sir, that I have known to go about with troll-my-dames. I knew him once a servant of the Prince. I cannot tell, good sir, for which of his virtues it was, but he was certainly whipped out of the court. 85

CLOWN His vices, you would say. There's no virtue whipped out of the court. They cherish it to make it stay there; and yet it will no more but abide. 90

AUTOLYCUS Vices, I would say, sir. I know this man well. He hath been since an ape bearer, then a process server, a bailiff. Then he compassed a motion of the Prodigal Son and married a tinker's wife within a mile where my land and living lies, and, having flown over many knavish professions, he settled only in rogue. Some call him Autolycus. 92 93 95

CLOWN Out upon him! Prig, for my life, prig! He haunts wakes, fairs, and bearbaitings. 98 99

AUTOLYCUS Very true, sir. He, sir, he. That's the rogue that put me into this apparel.

CLOWN Not a more cowardly rogue in all Bohemia. If you had but looked big and spit at him, he'd have run.

AUTOLYCUS I must confess to you, sir, I am no fighter. I am false of heart that way, and that he knew, I warrant him. 106

CLOWN How do you now?

AUTOLYCUS Sweet sir, much better than I was. I can stand and walk. I will even take my leave of you and pace softly towards my kinsman's. 111

85 troll-my-dames or troll-madams (from the French *trou-madame*), a game in which the object was to *troll* balls through arches set on a board. (Autolycus uses the word to suggest women who *troll* or saunter about.) **90 no more but abide** make only a temporary stay **92 ape bearer** one who carries a monkey about for exhibition **92–93 process server** sheriff's officer who serves processes or summonses
93 compassed a motion got possession of or devised a puppet show
95 living property **98 Prig** thief **99 wakes** village festivals. (A *wake* is also a vigil for a dead person or similar ceremony.) **106 false** cowardly **111 softly** slowly

CLOWN Shall I bring thee on the way? 112

AUTOLYCUS No, good-faced sir, no, sweet sir.

CLOWN Then fare thee well. I must go buy spices for our sheepshearing. *Exit.*

AUTOLYCUS Prosper you, sweet sir! Your purse is not 116 hot enough to purchase your spice. I'll be with you at 117 your sheepshearing too. If I make not this cheat bring 118 out another, and the shearers prove sheep, let me be 119 unrolled and my name put in the book of virtue! 120

Song.

Jog on, jog on, the footpath way,
And merrily hent the stile-a; 122
A merry heart goes all the day,
Your sad tires in a mile-a. *Exit.*

✤

4.4

Enter Florizel [*in shepherd's garb, and*] **Perdita** [*in holiday attire*].

FLORIZEL

These your unusual weeds to each part of you 1
Does give a life; no shepherdess, but Flora 2
Peering in April's front. This your sheepshearing 3
Is as a meeting of the petty gods, 4
And you the queen on 't.

PERDITA Sir, my gracious lord,
To chide at your extremes it not becomes me. 6
O, pardon that I name them! Your high self,
The gracious mark o' the land, you have obscured 8

112 bring . . . way go part of the way with you **116 Prosper . . . sir** (Said to the departing Clown.) **116–117 Your . . . spice** i.e., you'll find but a cold purse to pay for your hot spices; an empty purse is a cold one. (Said after the Clown's departure.) **118–119 cheat bring out** swindle lead to **120 unrolled** taken off the roll (of rogues and vagabonds) **122 hent** take hold of (as a means of leaping over)

4.4. Location: Bohemia. The Shepherd's cottage. (See ll. 181–182, 187, etc.)

1 unusual weeds special, holiday attire **2 Flora** goddess of flowers
3 Peering . . . front peeping forth in early April **4 petty** minor
6 extremes extravagant statements **8 mark o' the land** one who is noted and used as a model by everyone

With a swain's wearing, and me, poor lowly maid, 9
Most goddesslike pranked up. But that our feasts 10
In every mess have folly, and the feeders 11
Digest it with a custom, I should blush 12
To see you so attired, swoon, I think,
To show myself a glass.

FLORIZEL I bless the time 14
When my good falcon made her flight across
Thy father's ground.

PERDITA Now Jove afford you cause!
To me the difference forges dread; your greatness 17
Hath not been used to fear. Even now I tremble
To think your father by some accident
Should pass this way as you did. O, the Fates!
How would he look to see his work, so noble,
Vilely bound up? What would he say? Or how 22
Should I, in these my borrowed flaunts, behold 23
The sternness of his presence?

FLORIZEL Apprehend
Nothing but jollity. The gods themselves,
Humbling their deities to love, have taken
The shapes of beasts upon them. Jupiter 27
Became a bull and bellowed; the green Neptune, 28
A ram and bleated; and the fire-robed god, 29
Golden Apollo, a poor humble swain, 30
As I seem now. Their transformations
Were never for a piece of beauty rarer,
Nor in a way so chaste, since my desires 33
Run not before mine honor, nor my lusts
Burn hotter than my faith.

PERDITA O, but, sir,
Your resolution cannot hold when 'tis
Opposed, as it must be, by th' power of the King.

9 wearing garb **10 pranked up** bedecked. **But that** were it not that **11 In every mess** at every table, in each group or course of dishes **12 Digest** swallow, i.e., accept. **with a custom** from habit **14 To show . . . glass** if I were to see myself in a mirror **17 difference** i.e., of rank. **forges** i.e., creates **22 bound up** i.e., covered in lowly outer garments. (The metaphor is from bookbinding.) **23 flaunts** finery **27–30 Jupiter . . . swain** (Jupiter in the guise of a bull wooed Europa, Neptune disguised as a ram deceived Bisaltis (Ovid, *Metamorphoses,* 6.117) and Apollo took the guise of a humble shepherd to enable Admetus to woo Alcestis.) **33 in a way** i.e., pursuing a purpose

One of these two must be necessities,
Which then will speak: that you must change this
purpose
Or I my life.

FLORIZEL Thou dearest Perdita, 40
With these forced thoughts, I prithee, darken not 41
The mirth o' the feast. Or I'll be thine, my fair, 42
Or not my father's. For I cannot be
Mine own, not anything to any, if 44
I be not thine. To this I am most constant,
Though destiny say no. Be merry, gentle! 46
Strangle such thoughts as these with anything 47
That you behold the while. Your guests are coming. 48
Lift up your countenance as it were the day 49
Of celebration of that nuptial which
We two have sworn shall come.

PERDITA O Lady Fortune,
Stand you auspicious!

FLORIZEL See, your guests approach.
Address yourself to entertain them sprightly, 53
And let's be red with mirth.

[Enter] Shepherd, Clown; Polixenes, Camillo [disguised]; Mopsa, Dorcas; servants.

SHEPHERD
Fie, daughter! When my old wife lived, upon
This day she was both pantler, butler, cook, 56
Both dame and servant; welcomed all, served all; 57
Would sing her song and dance her turn; now here,
At upper end o' the table, now i' the middle;
On his shoulder, and his; her face afire 60
With labor, and the thing she took to quench it 61
She would to each one sip. You are retired, 62
As if you were a feasted one and not

40 Or I my life i.e., or I will be threatened with loss of life (as Polixenes indeed threatens at ll. 436–443) **41 forced** farfetched, unnatural **42 Or** either **44 not anything** I will not be anything **46 gentle** i.e., my gentle love **47–48 Strangle . . . while** i.e., put down such thoughts by attending to matters at hand **49 as** as if **53 Address** prepare **56 pantler** pantry servant **57 dame** mistress of the household **60 On his . . . his** at one man's . . . another's **61–62 and . . . sip** and she would toast each one with the drink she took to quench the fire of her labor

The hostess of the meeting. Pray you, bid
These unknown friends to 's welcome, for it is 65
A way to make us better friends, more known. 66
Come, quench your blushes and present yourself
That which you are, mistress o' the feast. Come on,
And bid us welcome to your sheepshearing,
As your good flock shall prosper.

PERDITA [*To Polixenes*] Sir, welcome.
It is my father's will I should take on me
The hostess-ship o' the day. [*To Camillo.*] You're
welcome, sir.
Give me those flowers there, Dorcas. Reverend sirs,
For you there's rosemary and rue; these keep
Seeming and savor all the winter long. 75
Grace and remembrance be to you both, 76
And welcome to our shearing! [*Giving them flowers.*]

POLIXENES Shepherdess—
A fair one are you—well you fit our ages
With flowers of winter.

PERDITA Sir, the year growing ancient, 79
Not yet on summer's death nor on the birth
Of trembling winter, the fairest flow'rs o' the season
Are our carnations and streaked gillyvors, 82
Which some call nature's bastards. Of that kind 83
Our rustic garden's barren, and I care not
To get slips of them.

POLIXENES Wherefore, gentle maiden, 85
Do you neglect them?

PERDITA For I have heard it said 86
There is an art which in their piedness shares 87
With great creating nature.

POLIXENES Say there be;
Yet nature is made better by no mean 89

65 to 's each to his **66 more known** better acquainted **75 Seeming** outward appearance, color **76 Grace and remembrance** divine grace and remembrance after death. (Equated respectively with rue and rosemary.) **79 the year . . . ancient** i.e., when autumn arrives **82 gillyvors** gillyflowers, a kind of carnation or pink **83 nature's bastards** i.e., the result of artificial breeding. (See ll. 86–88.) **85 slips** cuttings **86 For** because **87 art** i.e., of crossbreeding. **piedness** particolor appearance. (Perdita disclaims the art of crossbreeding, since it infringes on what nature itself does so well.) **89 mean** means

But nature makes that mean. So, over that art 90
Which you say adds to nature is an art
That nature makes. You see, sweet maid, we marry
A gentler scion to the wildest stock, 93
And make conceive a bark of baser kind
By bud of nobler race. This is an art
Which does mend nature—change it, rather—but
The art itself is nature.

PERDITA So it is.

POLIXENES
Then make your garden rich in gillyvors,
And do not call them bastards.

PERDITA I'll not put
The dibble in earth to set one slip of them, 100
No more than, were I painted, I would wish 101
This youth should say 'twere well, and only therefore
Desire to breed by me. Here's flowers for you:
[*Giving them flowers*]
Hot lavender, mints, savory, marjoram, 104
The marigold, that goes to bed wi' the sun
And with him rises weeping. These are flowers
Of middle summer, and I think they are given 107
To men of middle age. You're very welcome.

CAMILLO
I should leave grazing, were I of your flock,
And only live by gazing.

PERDITA Out, alas!
You'd be so lean that blasts of January
Would blow you through and through. [*To Florizel.*]
Now, my fair'st friend,
I would I had some flow'rs o' the spring that might
Become your time of day; [*To the Shepherdesses*] and
yours, and yours,
That wear upon your virgin branches yet

90 But unless. (Polixenes's point is that the art of improving on nature is itself natural.) **93 gentler** nobler, more cultivated **100 dibble** tool for making holes in which to implant seed **101 painted** made artificially beautiful by cosmetics **104 Hot** eager, ardent, aromatic (?) (Spices were classified as hot or cold.) **107 middle summer** (Having no autumn flowers in any case [ll. 79–82], since it is too early in the season, Perdita flatters her older guests by giving them flowers appropriate to *middle age*.)

Your maidenheads growing. O Proserpina, 116
For the flow'rs now that, frighted, thou lett'st fall
From Dis's wagon! Daffodils,
That come before the swallow dares, and take 119
The winds of March with beauty; violets dim,
But sweeter than the lids of Juno's eyes
Or Cytherea's breath; pale primroses, 122
That die unmarried ere they can behold
Bright Phoebus in his strength—a malady 124
Most incident to maids; bold oxlips and 125
The crown imperial; lilies of all kinds, 126
The flower-de-luce being one. O, these I lack 127
To make you garlands of, and my sweet friend, 128
To strew him o'er and o'er!

FLORIZEL What, like a corpse?

PERDITA
No, like a bank for Love to lie and play on, 130
Not like a corpse; or if, not to be buried, 131
But quick and in mine arms. Come, take your flowers. 132
[*Giving flowers.*]
Methinks I play as I have seen them do
In Whitsun pastorals. Sure this robe of mine 134
Does change my disposition.

FLORIZEL What you do
Still betters what is done. When you speak, sweet, 136
I'd have you do it ever. When you sing,
I'd have you buy and sell so, so give alms,
Pray so; and, for the ordering your affairs,

116 Proserpina daughter of Ceres, stolen away by Pluto (*Dis*) and taken to Hades when, according to Ovid, she was gathering flowers in her garden **119 take** charm **122 Cytherea's** Venus' **124 Phoebus** the sun god **124–125 a malady . . . maids** (Young maids, suffering from green-sickness, a kind of anemia, are pale like the primrose.) **126 crown imperial** flower from the Levant, cultivated in English gardens
127 flower-de-luce fleur-de-lis. **I lack** (because the season is too late for them) **128 To . . . friend** to make garlands of them for you (Polixenes and Camillo) and for my sweet friend (Florizel) **130 Love** i.e., Cupid
131 or if or if for a corpse, that is, a living body **132 quick** alive
134 Whitsun pastorals plays (including Robin Hood plays) and English morris dances often performed at Whitsuntide, seven Sundays after Easter. (The part of Maid Marian strikes Perdita as immodest for her usual behavior.) **136 betters what is done** i.e., surpasses anything else

To sing them too. When you do dance, I wish you
A wave o' the sea, that you might ever do
Nothing but that—move still, still so,
And own no other function. Each your doing, 143
So singular in each particular, 144
Crowns what you are doing in the present deeds,
That all your acts are queens.

PERDITA O Doricles, 146
Your praises are too large. But that your youth 147
And the true blood which peeps fairly through 't
Do plainly give you out an unstained shepherd, 149
With wisdom I might fear, my Doricles,
You wooed me the false way.

FLORIZEL I think you have
As little skill to fear as I have purpose 152
To put you to 't. But come, our dance, I pray.
Your hand, my Perdita. So turtles pair, 154
That never mean to part.

PERDITA I'll swear for 'em. 155
[*They speak apart.*]

POLIXENES [*To Camillo*]
This is the prettiest lowborn lass that ever
Ran on the greensward. Nothing she does or seems
But smacks of something greater than herself,
Too noble for this place.

CAMILLO He tells her something
That makes her blood look out. Good sooth, she is 160
The queen of curds and cream.

CLOWN Come on, strike up!

DORCAS
Mopsa must be your mistress. Marry, garlic, 162
To mend her kissing with!

MOPSA Now, in good time! 163

143 Each your doing each thing you do and how you do it **144 singular** unique and peerless **146 Doricles** (Florizel's disguise name.) **147 large** lavish. **But that** were it not that **149 give you out** proclaim you to be **152 skill** reason **154 turtles** turtledoves, as symbols of faithful love **155 I'll swear for 'em** i.e., I'll be sworn they do **160 makes . . . out** makes her blush **162 mistress** i.e., partner in the dance **163 kissing** i.e., bad breath. (Dorcas jests that even garlic would improve Mopsa's breath.) **in good time** (An expression of indignation.)

CLOWN
Not a word, a word. We stand upon our manners. 164
Come, strike up! 165
[*Music.*] *Here a dance of Shepherds and Shepherdesses.*

POLIXENES
Pray, good shepherd, what fair swain is this
Which dances with your daughter?

SHEPHERD
They call him Doricles, and boasts himself 168
To have a worthy feeding; but I have it 169
Upon his own report and I believe it.
He looks like sooth. He says he loves my daughter. 171
I think so too, for never gazed the moon
Upon the water as he'll stand and read,
As 'twere, my daughter's eyes; and, to be plain,
I think there is not half a kiss to choose
Who loves another best.

POLIXENES She dances featly. 176

SHEPHERD
So she does anything—though I report it
That should be silent. If young Doricles
Do light upon her, she shall bring him that 179
Which he not dreams of.

Enter Servant.

SERVANT O master, if you did but hear the peddler at the door, you would never dance again after a tabor and 182 pipe; no, the bagpipe could not move you. He sings several tunes faster than you'll tell money. He utters 184 them as he had eaten ballads and all men's ears grew 185 to his tunes.

CLOWN He could never come better. He shall come in. 187 I love a ballad but even too well, if it be doleful matter 188 merrily set down, or a very pleasant thing indeed and 189 sung lamentably. 190

164 stand upon set store by **165 s.d. dance** (Probably a morris dance.) **168 and** i.e., and they say he **169 feeding** pasturage, lands **171 like sooth** truthful **176 another** the other. **featly** gracefully **179 light upon** choose **182 tabor** small drum **184 tell** count **185 as** as if (also in l. 208) **187 better** at a better time **188 but even too well** all too well **189 pleasant** merry **190 lamentably** mournfully

SERVANT He hath songs for man or woman, of all sizes. 191
No milliner can so fit his customers with gloves. He 192
has the prettiest love songs for maids, so without
bawdry, which is strange, with such delicate burdens 194
of dildos and fadings, "Jump her and thump her"; and 195
where some stretchmouthed rascal would, as it were, 196
mean mischief and break a foul gap into the matter, 197
he makes the maid to answer, "Whoop, do me no
harm, good man"; puts him off, slights him, with
"Whoop, do me no harm, good man."

POLIXENES This is a brave fellow. 201

CLOWN Believe me, thou talkest of an admirable con- 202
ceited fellow. Has he any unbraided wares? 203

SERVANT He hath ribbons of all the colors i' the rainbow; points more than all the lawyers in Bohemia can 205
learnedly handle, though they come to him by the
gross; inkles, caddisses, cambrics, lawns. Why, he 207
sings 'em over as they were gods or goddesses; you
would think a smock were a she-angel, he so chants to
the sleevehand and the work about the square on 't. 210

CLOWN Prithee, bring him in, and let him approach
singing.

PERDITA Forewarn him that he use no scurrilous words
in 's tunes. [*The Servant goes to the door.*]

CLOWN You have of these peddlers that have more in 215
them than you'd think, sister.

PERDITA Ay, good brother, or go about to think. 217

Enter Autolycus, singing.

191 sizes sorts **192 milliner** vendor of fancy ware and apparel, including gloves, ribbons, and bonnets **194 burdens** refrains **195 dildos and fadings** words used as part of the refrains of ballads (but with bawdy double meaning unperceived by the servant, as also in *jump her, thump her, do me no harm,* etc.) **196 stretchmouthed** widemouthed, foulmouthed **197 break . . . matter** insert some gross obscenity into the song, or act in a suggestive way **201 brave** excellent
202–203 admirable conceited wonderfully witty and clever
203 unbraided untarnished, undamaged **205 points** (1) laces for fastening clothes (2) headings in an argument **207 inkles** linen tapes. **caddisses** worsted tape used for garters. **cambrics** fine linen fabrics. **lawns** fine sheer linens **210 sleevehand** wristband. **square on 't** embroidered bosom or yoke of the garment **215 You . . . peddlers** you'll find peddlers **217 go about** intend, wish **s.d. Enter Autolycus** (Apparently he is wearing a false beard; later in this scene he removes it to impersonate a courtier to the Clown and Shepherd.)

AUTOLYCUS

Lawn as white as driven snow,
Cyprus black as e'er was crow, 219
Gloves as sweet as damask roses, 220
Masks for faces and for noses,
Bugle bracelet, necklace amber, 222
Perfume for a lady's chamber,
Golden coifs and stomachers, 224
For my lads to give their dears,
Pins and poking-sticks of steel, 226
What maids lack from head to heel,
Come buy of me, come. Come buy, come buy.
Buy, lads, or else your lasses cry.
Come buy.

CLOWN If I were not in love with Mopsa, thou shouldst take no money of me, but being enthralled as I am, it 232 will also be the bondage of certain ribbons and gloves. 233

MOPSA I was promised them against the feast, but they 234 come not too late now.

DORCAS He hath promised you more than that, or there 236 be liars. 237

MOPSA He hath paid you all he promised you. Maybe he has paid you more, which will shame you to give 239 him again. 240

CLOWN Is there no manners left among maids? Will 241 they wear their plackets where they should bear their 242 faces? Is there not milking time, when you are going 243 to bed, or kilnhole, to whistle of these secrets, but 244 you must be tittle-tattling before all our guests? 'Tis well they are whispering. Clamor your tongues, and 246 not a word more.

219 Cyprus crepe **220 sweet** i.e., perfumed (also in l. 249) **222 Bugle bracelet** bracelet of black glossy beads **224 coifs** close-fitting caps. **stomachers** embroidered fronts for ladies' dresses **226 poking-sticks** rods used for ironing and stiffening the plaits of ruffs **232–233 it will . . . bondage** it will mean the taking into custody (by means of purchase and tying up into a parcel) **234 against** in anticipation of, in time for **236–237 He . . . liars** i.e., he promised to marry you too, or else rumor is a liar **239 paid you more** i.e., made you pregnant **239–240 which . . . again** i.e., which will shame you by giving birth to his child **241–243 Will . . . faces** i.e., will they always be talking and revealing personal secrets. **plackets** slits in petticoats (with bawdy suggestion of the pudendum, as at l. 613) **244 kilnhole** fire hole of a baking oven (where maids might gossip). **whistle** whisper **246 Clamor** i.e., silence

MOPSA I have done. Come, you promised me a tawdry 248
lace and a pair of sweet gloves. 249

CLOWN Have I not told thee how I was cozened by the 250
way and lost all my money?

AUTOLYCUS And indeed, sir, there are cozeners abroad;
therefore it behooves men to be wary.

CLOWN Fear not thou, man, thou shalt lose nothing
here.

AUTOLYCUS I hope so, sir, for I have about me many
parcels of charge. 257

CLOWN What hast here? Ballads?

MOPSA Pray now, buy some. I love a ballad in print
alife, for then we are sure they are true. 260

AUTOLYCUS Here's one to a very doleful tune, how a
usurer's wife was brought to bed of twenty money-
bags at a burden, and how she longed to eat adders' 263
heads and toads carbonadoed. 264

MOPSA Is it true, think you?

AUTOLYCUS Very true, and but a month old.

DORCAS Bless me from marrying a usurer! 267

AUTOLYCUS Here's the midwife's name to 't, one Mistress Taleporter, and five or six honest wives that 269
were present. Why should I carry lies abroad?

MOPSA Pray you now, buy it.

CLOWN Come on, lay it by, and let's first see more ballads. We'll buy the other things anon.

AUTOLYCUS Here's another ballad, of a fish that appeared upon the coast on Wednesday the fourscore of 275
April, forty thousand fathom above water, and sung 276
this ballad against the hard hearts of maids. It was
thought she was a woman and was turned into a cold
fish for she would not exchange flesh with one that
loved her. The ballad is very pitiful and as true.

DORCAS Is it true too, think you?

248–249 tawdry lace cheap and showy lace, or neckerchief. (So called from St. Audrey's Fair.) **250 cozened** cheated **257 parcels of charge** valuable items **260 alife** dearly **263 at a burden** in one childbirth **264 carbonadoed** scored across and grilled **267 Bless** protect, keep **269 Taleporter** i.e., talebearer, gossip **275 fourscore** eightieth (!) **276 forty thousand fathom** 240,000 feet

AUTOLYCUS Five justices' hands at it, and witnesses more than my pack will hold. 282

CLOWN Lay it by too. Another.

AUTOLYCUS This is a merry ballad, but a very pretty one.

MOPSA Let's have some merry ones.

AUTOLYCUS Why, this is a passing merry one and goes to the tune of "Two Maids Wooing a Man." There's scarce a maid westward but she sings it. 'Tis in request, I can tell you. 288 290

MOPSA We can both sing it. If thou'lt bear a part, thou shalt hear; 'tis in three parts.

DORCAS We had the tune on 't a month ago. 294

AUTOLYCUS I can bear my part; you must know 'tis my occupation. Have at it with you. 296

Song.

AUTOLYCUS

Get you hence, for I must go
Where it fits not you to know.

DORCAS

Whither?

MOPSA

O, whither?

DORCAS

Whither?

MOPSA

It becomes thy oath full well,
Thou to me thy secrets tell.

DORCAS

Me too. Let me go thither.

MOPSA

Or thou goest to th' grange or mill. 303

DORCAS

If to either, thou dost ill.

AUTOLYCUS

Neither.

DORCAS

What, neither?

AUTOLYCUS

Neither.

282 hands signatures **288 passing** surpassingly **290 westward** in the West Country **294 on 't** of it **296 Have at it** i.e., here goes **303 Or** either. **grange** farm

DORCAS
Thou hast sworn my love to be.

MOPSA
Thou hast sworn it more to me.
Then whither goest? Say, whither?

CLOWN We'll have this song out anon by ourselves. My 309
father and the gentlemen are in sad talk, and we'll not 310
trouble them. Come, bring away thy pack after me.
Wenches, I'll buy for you both. Peddler, let's have the
first choice. Follow me, girls.
[Exit with Dorcas and Mopsa.]

AUTOLYCUS And you shall pay well for 'em.
[He follows singing.]

Song.

Will you buy any tape,
Or lace for your cape,
My dainty duck, my dear-a?
Any silk, any thread,
And toys for your head, 319
Of the new'st and fin'st, fin'st wear-a?
Come to the peddler;
Money's a meddler, 322
That doth utter all men's ware-a. *Exit.* 323

[Enter a Servant.]

SERVANT Master, there is three carters, three shepherds, three neatherds, three swineherds, that have 325
made themselves all men of hair. They call themselves 326
saultiers, and they have a dance which the wenches say 327
is a gallimaufry of gambols, because they are not in 't; 328
but they themselves are o' the mind, if it be not too
rough for some that know little but bowling, it will 330
please plentifully.

SHEPHERD Away! We'll none on 't. Here has been too

309 have this song out finish this song **310 sad** serious **319 toys** trifles **322 meddler** i.e., go-between in commercial transactions
323 utter put on the market **325 neatherds** cowherds **326 of hair** dressed in skins **327 saultiers** leapers or vaulters (with perhaps a play on *Saltiers* as a blunder for "satyrs") **328 gallimaufry** jumble
330 bowling (A more gentle sport than the vigorous satyr dancing.)

much homely foolery already.—I know, sir, we weary 333
you.

POLIXENES You weary those that refresh us. Pray, let's
see these four threes of herdsmen.

SERVANT One three of them, by their own report, sir, 337
hath danced before the King, and not the worst of the
three but jumps twelve foot and a half by the square. 339

SHEPHERD Leave your prating. Since these good men
are pleased, let them come in; but quickly now.

SERVANT Why, they stay at door, sir.
[*He goes to the door.*]

Here a dance of twelve Satyrs.

POLIXENES [*To Shepherd*]
O, father, you'll know more of that hereafter. 343
[*To Camillo.*] Is it not too far gone? 'Tis time to part
them.
He's simple and tells much. [*To Florizel.*] How now,
fair shepherd? 345
Your heart is full of something that does take
Your mind from feasting. Sooth, when I was young
And handed love as you do, I was wont 348
To load my she with knacks. I would have ransacked
The peddler's silken treasury and have poured it
To her acceptance; you have let him go,
And nothing marted with him. If your lass 352
Interpretation should abuse and call this 353
Your lack of love or bounty, you were straited 354
For a reply, at least if you make a care
Of happy holding her.

FLORIZEL Old sir, I know 356
She prizes not such trifles as these are.
The gifts she looks from me are packed and locked 358
Up in my heart, which I have given already

333 homely unpolished **337 three** threesome **339 square** foot rule **343 O . . . hereafter** (Polixenes completes the conversation he has been having with the old Shepherd during the dance.) **345 He's simple** i.e., the old Shepherd is guileless **348 handed** handled, dealt in **352 nothing marted with** done no business with **353 Interpretation should abuse** should interpret wrongly **354 were straited** would be hard-pressed **356 happy holding her** keeping her happy **358 looks** looks for

But not delivered. [*To Perdita.*] O, hear me breathe my
life 360
Before this ancient sir, who, it should seem, 361
Hath sometime loved! I take thy hand, this hand,
As soft as dove's down and as white as it,
Or Ethiopian's tooth, or the fanned snow that's bolted 364
By th' northern blasts twice o'er. [*Taking her hand.*]

POLIXENES What follows this?
How prettily the young swain seems to wash
The hand was fair before! I have put you out. 367
But to your protestation; let me hear 368
What you profess.

FLORIZEL Do, and be witness to 't.

POLIXENES
And this my neighbor too?

FLORIZEL And he, and more
Than he, and men—the earth, the heavens, and all:
That, were I crowned the most imperial monarch,
Thereof most worthy, were I the fairest youth 373
That ever made eye swerve, had force and knowledge 374
More than was ever man's, I would not prize them
Without her love; for her employ them all,
Commend them and condemn them to her service 377
Or to their own perdition.

POLIXENES Fairly offered. 378

CAMILLO
This shows a sound affection.

SHEPHERD But, my daughter,
Say you the like to him?

PERDITA I cannot speak
So well, nothing so well; no, nor mean better.

360 But not delivered i.e., but I have not confirmed it by a solemn vow before witnesses, making binding the contract. **breathe my life** i.e., pronounce eternal vows **361 this ancient sir** i.e., Polixenes **364 fanned** blown. **bolted** sifted **367 was** that was. **put you out** interrupted what you were saying **368 to your protestation** on with your public affirmation **373 Thereof most worthy** the most worthy of monarchs
374 swerve turn in my direction (out of awe and respect)
377–378 Commend . . . perdition either commend them to her service, or, failing that, condemn them to deserved destruction

By th' pattern of mine own thoughts I cut out 382
The purity of his.

SHEPHERD Take hands, a bargain! 383
And, friends unknown, you shall bear witness to 't:
I give my daughter to him and will make
Her portion equal his.

FLORIZEL O, that must be
I' the virtue of your daughter. One being dead,
I shall have more than you can dream of yet;
Enough then for your wonder. But come on: 389
Contract us 'fore these witnesses.

SHEPHERD Come, your hand;
And, daughter, yours.

POLIXENES Soft, swain, awhile, beseech you. 391
Have you a father?

FLORIZEL I have, but what of him?

POLIXENES Knows he of this?

FLORIZEL He neither does nor shall.

POLIXENES Methinks a father
Is at the nuptial of his son a guest
That best becomes the table. Pray you, once more,
Is not your father grown incapable
Of reasonable affairs? Is he not stupid 400
With age and altering rheums? Can he speak? Hear? 401
Know man from man? Dispute his own estate? 402
Lies he not bedrid, and again does nothing
But what he did being childish?

FLORIZEL No, good sir, 404
He has his health and ampler strength indeed
Than most have of his age.

POLIXENES By my white beard,
You offer him, if this be so, a wrong

382–383 By . . . of his (Perdita uses a metaphor of clothes-making to express her view that Florizel's pure thoughts must be like her own—not patterned on hers but rather perceived by her to be a model for her own.) **389 Enough . . . wonder** there will be enough then for you to wonder at **391 Soft** wait a minute **400 reasonable affairs** matters requiring the use of reason **401 altering rheums** weakening catarrhs or other diseases **402 Dispute** discuss. **estate** affairs, condition **404 being childish** when he was a child

Something unfilial. Reason my son 408
Should choose himself a wife, but as good reason
The father, all whose joy is nothing else
But fair posterity, should hold some counsel 411
In such a business.

FLORIZEL I yield all this; 412
But for some other reasons, my grave sir,
Which 'tis not fit you know, I not acquaint
My father of this business.

POLIXENES Let him know 't.

FLORIZEL
He shall not.

POLIXENES Prithee, let him.

FLORIZEL No, he must not.

SHEPHERD
Let him, my son. He shall not need to grieve
At knowing of thy choice.

FLORIZEL Come, come, he must not.
Mark our contract.

POLIXENES Mark your divorce, young sir,
[*Discovering himself*]
Whom son I dare not call. Thou art too base
To be acknowledged. Thou a scepter's heir,
That thus affects a sheephook?—Thou old traitor, 422
I am sorry that by hanging thee I can
But shorten thy life one week.—And thou, fresh piece
Of excellent witchcraft, who of force must know 425
The royal fool thou cop'st with—

SHEPHERD O, my heart! 426

POLIXENES
I'll have thy beauty scratched with briers and made
More homely than thy state.—For thee, fond boy, 428
If I may ever know thou dost but sigh
That thou no more shalt see this knack—as never 430
I mean thou shalt—we'll bar thee from succession,

408 Something somewhat. **Reason** it is reasonable that. **my son** (The disguised Polixenes seems to be speaking hypothetically, using himself as an example, but of course the application to Florizel is direct.)
411 hold some counsel be consulted **412 yield** concede **422 affects** desires, shows inclination for **425 of force** of necessity **426 thou cop'st** you deal **428 homely** (1) unattractive (2) humble. **fond** foolish
430 knack trifle, schemer

Not hold thee of our blood, no, not our kin,
Far than Deucalion off. Mark thou my words. 433
Follow us to the court.—Thou churl, for this time, 434
Though full of our displeasure, yet we free thee
From the dead blow of it.—And you, enchantment, 436
Worthy enough a herdsman—yea, him too, 437
That makes himself, but for our honor therein, 438
Unworthy thee—if ever henceforth thou 439
These rural latches to his entrance open,
Or hoop his body more with thy embraces,
I will devise a death as cruel for thee
As thou art tender to 't. *Exit.*

PERDITA Even here undone!
I was not much afeard; for once or twice
I was about to speak and tell him plainly
The selfsame sun that shines upon his court
Hides not his visage from our cottage, but
Looks on alike. Will 't please you, sir, begone? 448
I told you what would come of this. Beseech you,
Of your own state take care. This dream of mine—
Being now awake, I'll queen it no inch farther,
But milk my ewes and weep.

CAMILLO Why, how now, father?
Speak ere thou diest.

SHEPHERD I cannot speak, nor think, 453
Nor dare to know that which I know. [*To Florizel.*] O sir,
You have undone a man of fourscore three,
That thought to fill his grave in quiet, yea,
To die upon the bed my father died, 457
To lie close by his honest bones; but now
Some hangman must put on my shroud and lay me
Where no priest shovels in dust. [*To Perdita.*] O cursed
wretch,

433 Far . . . off farther off in kinship than Deucalion (the Noah of classical mythology) **434 churl** i.e., the Shepherd **436 dead** deadly. **enchantment** i.e., Perdita **437–439 him too . . . thee** worthy indeed of him (Florizel) whose behavior renders him unworthy even of you, if we were to set aside for the moment the question of the dignity of our royal house **448 alike** indifferently **453 ere thou diest** before you die of grief (?) (Although Polixenes has relented of his threat to hang the Shepherd, the Shepherd is gloomily sure it will come to a hanging, ll. 459–460.) **457 died** i.e., died on

That knew'st this was the Prince, and wouldst adven-
ture
To mingle faith with him! Undone, undone! 462
If I might die within this hour, I have lived
To die when I desire. *Exit.*

FLORIZEL [*To Perdita*] Why look you so upon me?
I am but sorry, not afeard; delayed,
But nothing altered. What I was, I am,
More straining on for plucking back, not following 468
My leash unwillingly.

CAMILLO Gracious my lord,
You know your father's temper. At this time
He will allow no speech, which I do guess
You do not purpose to him; and as hardly
Will he endure your sight as yet, I fear.
Then, till the fury of his highness settle, 474
Come not before him.

FLORIZEL I not purpose it.
I think Camillo?

CAMILLO Even he, my lord.

PERDITA
How often have I told you 'twould be thus!
How often said my dignity would last 478
But till 'twere known!

FLORIZEL It cannot fail but by
The violation of my faith; and then 480
Let nature crush the sides o' th' earth together
And mar the seeds within! Lift up thy looks. 482
From my succession wipe me, Father; I
Am heir to my affection.

CAMILLO Be advised. 484

FLORIZEL
I am, and by my fancy. If my reason 485

462 mingle faith exchange pledges **468 More . . . back** i.e., like a hound on the leash, all the more eager to go forward for having been restrained **474 his highness** his towering rage (or else *His Highness,* as a title) **478 my dignity** i.e., the new status this marriage would have offered **480 then** when that happens **482 mar the seeds within** i.e., destroy the very sources of life on earth (since all material life was thought to be derived from *seeds*) **484 affection** passionate love. **Be advised** think carefully, be receptive to wise advice **485 fancy** love

Will thereto be obedient, I have reason; 486
If not, my senses, better pleased with madness,
Do bid it welcome.

CAMILLO This is desperate, sir.

FLORIZEL
So call it, but it does fulfill my vow;
I needs must think it honesty. Camillo,
Not for Bohemia nor the pomp that may
Be thereat gleaned, for all the sun sees or
The close earth wombs or the profound seas hides 493
In unknown fathoms, will I break my oath
To this my fair beloved. Therefore, I pray you,
As you have ever been my father's honored friend,
When he shall miss me—as, in faith, I mean not
To see him any more—cast your good counsels
Upon his passion. Let myself and fortune 499
Tug for the time to come. This you may know 500
And so deliver: I am put to sea 501
With her who here I cannot hold on shore; 502
And most opportune to our need I have
A vessel rides fast by, but not prepared
For this design. What course I mean to hold
Shall nothing benefit your knowledge nor 506
Concern me the reporting.

CAMILLO O my lord, 507
I would your spirit were easier for advice 508
Or stronger for your need.

FLORIZEL Hark, Perdita.
[*To Camillo.*] I'll hear you by and by.
[*He draws Perdita aside.*]

CAMILLO [*Aside*] He's irremovable, 510
Resolved for flight. Now were I happy if
His going I could frame to serve my turn, 512
Save him from danger, do him love and honor,
Purchase the sight again of dear Sicilia
And that unhappy king, my master, whom
I so much thirst to see.

486 have reason (1) will be reasonable (2) will be sane **493 wombs** encloses, conceals **499 passion** anger **500 Tug** contend **501 deliver** report **502 who** whom **506–507 Shall . . . reporting** would not behoove you to know nor me to report **508 easier for** more open to **510 irremovable** immovable **512 frame** shape

FLORIZEL Now, good Camillo,
I am so fraught with curious business that 517
I leave out ceremony.
CAMILLO Sir, I think 518
You have heard of my poor services i' the love
That I have borne your father?
FLORIZEL Very nobly
Have you deserved. It is my father's music
To speak your deeds, not little of his care
To have them recompensed as thought on.
CAMILLO Well, my lord, 523
If you may please to think I love the King
And through him what's nearest to him, which is
Your gracious self, embrace but my direction,
If your more ponderous and settled project 527
May suffer alteration. On mine honor, 528
I'll point you where you shall have such receiving
As shall become your highness, where you may 530
Enjoy your mistress—from the whom I see
There's no disjunction to be made but by,
As heavens forfend, your ruin—marry her, 533
And, with my best endeavors in your absence, 534
Your discontenting father strive to qualify 535
And bring him up to liking.
FLORIZEL How, Camillo, 536
May this, almost a miracle, be done,
That I may call thee something more than man,
And after that trust to thee?
CAMILLO Have you thought on 539
A place whereto you'll go?
FLORIZEL Not any yet.
But as th' unthought-on accident is guilty 541
To what we wildly do, so we profess 542

517 curious demanding care **518 I leave out ceremony** (Florizel apologizes for whispering with Perdita and failing to observe proper ceremony toward Camillo.) **523 as thought on** as deservingly as in his opinion of them **527 ponderous** serious and carefully deliberated **528 suffer** permit **530 become your highness** suit your royal rank; or, suit Your Highness **533 forfend** forbid **534 with** together with **535 discontenting** discontented, displeased. **qualify** appease, pacify **536 bring . . . liking** get him to the point of approval **539 after** ever after **541–542 as . . . wildly do** just as the unexpected happening (e.g., of our being discovered by the King) is responsible for what we rashly do at this point

Ourselves to be the slaves of chance and flies 543
Of every wind that blows.

CAMILLO Then list to me.
This follows, if you will not change your purpose
But undergo this flight: make for Sicilia,
And there present yourself and your fair princess—
For so I see she must be—'fore Leontes.
She shall be habited as it becomes 549
The partner of your bed. Methinks I see
Leontes opening his free arms and weeping 551
His welcomes forth; asks thee there "Son, forgiveness!"
As 'twere i' the father's person; kisses the hands
Of your fresh princess; o'er and o'er divides him 554
Twixt his unkindness and his kindness. Th' one 555
He chides to hell, and bids the other grow
Faster than thought or time.

FLORIZEL Worthy Camillo, 557
What color for my visitation shall I 558
Hold up before him?

CAMILLO Sent by the King your father 559
To greet him and to give him comforts. Sir,
The manner of your bearing towards him, with
What you, as from your father, shall deliver— 562
Things known betwixt us three—I'll write you down,
The which shall point you forth at every sitting 564
What you must say, that he shall not perceive
But that you have your father's bosom there 566
And speak his very heart.

FLORIZEL I am bound to you.
There is some sap in this.

CAMILLO A course more promising
Than a wild dedication of yourselves
To unpathed waters, undreamed shores, most certain
To miseries enough; no hope to help you,

543 flies i.e., insignificant insects, blown about by the winds of chance **549 habited** (richly) dressed **551 free** generous, noble **554 fresh** young and beautiful **554–555 divides . . . kindness** divides his speech between his former unkindness (which he condemns) and his present intention of kindness **557 Faster** firmer; also, more swiftly **558 color** excuse, pretext **559 Hold up before** present to. **Sent** i.e., say you are sent **562 deliver** say **564 point you forth** indicate to you. **sitting** conference **566 bosom** inmost thoughts

But as you shake off one to take another; 572
Nothing so certain as your anchors, who 573
Do their best office if they can but stay you 574
Where you'll be loath to be. Besides, you know 575
Prosperity's the very bond of love, 576
Whose fresh complexion and whose heart together 577
Affliction alters.

PERDITA One of these is true: 578
I think affliction may subdue the cheek, 579
But not take in the mind.

CAMILLO Yea, say you so? 580
There shall not at your father's house these seven years 581
Be born another such.

FLORIZEL My good Camillo,
She's as forward of her breeding as she is 583
I' the rear 'our birth.

CAMILLO I cannot say 'tis pity 584
She lacks instructions, for she seems a mistress 585
To most that teach.

PERDITA Your pardon, sir; for this 586
I'll blush you thanks.

FLORIZEL My prettiest Perdita!
But O, the thorns we stand upon! Camillo,
Preserver of my father, now of me,
The medicine of our house, how shall we do?
We are not furnished like Bohemia's son,
Nor shall appear in Sicilia.

CAMILLO My lord, 592
Fear none of this. I think you know my fortunes

572 one i.e., one misery, one misfortune. **take** encounter **573 Nothing** not at all. **who** which **574–575 Do . . . to be** are doing about as well as can be hoped if they simply hold you in some hateful place (rather than allowing you to be shipwrecked and perhaps drowned)
576–578 Prosperity's . . . alters i.e., young love flourishes while things are going well, but loses its fresh complexion and strength of feeling under the test of adversity **579 subdue the cheek** make the complexion look pale and wasted **580 take in** overcome **581 your father's** (Said to Florizel, and meaning Polixenes's palace?) **these seven years** i.e., for a long time to come. (Camillo's point is that she is a nonpareil.)
583 forward . . . breeding far in advance of her lowly upbringing **584 I' the rear 'our** below me in **585 instructions** formal schooling
585–586 a mistress To most one who could teach something to most people **592 appear** appear as such

Do all lie there. It shall be so my care
To have you royally appointed as if 595
The scene you play were mine. For instance, sir,
That you may know you shall not want, one word.
[*They talk aside.*]

Enter Autolycus.

AUTOLYCUS Ha, ha, what a fool Honesty is! And Trust, his sworn brother, a very simple gentleman! I have sold all my trumpery; not a counterfeit stone, not a ribbon, glass, pomander, brooch, table book, ballad, 601 knife, tape, glove, shoe tie, bracelet, horn ring, to keep my pack from fasting. They throng who should 603 buy first, as if my trinkets had been hallowed and 604 brought a benediction to the buyer; by which means I saw whose purse was best in picture, and what I 606 saw, to my good use I remembered. My clown, who wants but something to be a reasonable man, grew so 608 in love with the wenches' song that he would not stir his pettitoes till he had both tune and words, which 610 so drew the rest of the herd to me that all their other senses stuck in ears. You might have pinched a 612 placket, it was senseless. 'Twas nothing to geld a cod- 613 piece of a purse. I could have filed keys off that hung 614 in chains. No hearing, no feeling, but my sir's song, 615 and admiring the nothing of it. So that in this time of 616 lethargy I picked and cut most of their festival purses; and had not the old man come in with a hubbub against his daughter and the King's son and scared my choughs from the chaff, I had not left a purse alive in 620 the whole army.
[*Camillo, Florizel, and Perdita come forward.*]

595 appointed equipped, outfitted **601 pomander** scent-ball. **table book** notebook **603 from fasting** i.e., from being empty **604 hallowed** made sacred, like a relic **606 best in picture** i.e., best to look at, most promising **608 wants but something** lacks one thing only (i.e., intelligence) **610 pettitoes** pig's toes; here, toes **612 stuck in ears** were occupied with their ears **613 placket** (Literally, slit in a petticoat; with bawdy suggestion.) **senseless** insensible **613–614 geld a codpiece of a purse** cut a purse loose from the pouch worn at the front of a man's breeches **615 my sir's** i.e., the Clown's **616 nothing** (1) vacuity (2) noting, tune. (*Nothing* and *noting* sounded alike in Elizabethan English.) **620 choughs** jackdaws

CAMILLO
Nay, but my letters, by this means being there
So soon as you arrive, shall clear that doubt.

FLORIZEL
And those that you'll procure from King Leontes—

CAMILLO
Shall satisfy your father.

PERDITA Happy be you!
All that you speak shows fair.

CAMILLO [*Seeing Autolycus*] Who have we here?
We'll make an instrument of this, omit
Nothing may give us aid.

AUTOLYCUS [*Aside*] If they have overheard me now, why, hanging.

CAMILLO How now, good fellow? Why shak'st thou so?
Fear not, man, here's no harm intended to thee.

AUTOLYCUS I am a poor fellow, sir.

CAMILLO Why, be so still. Here's nobody will steal that from thee. Yet for the outside of thy poverty we must 635 make an exchange. Therefore discase thee instantly— 636 thou must think there's a necessity in 't—and change 637 garments with this gentleman. Though the penny- 638 worth on his side be the worst, yet hold thee, there's 639 some boot. [*He gives money.*] 640

AUTOLYCUS I am a poor fellow, sir. [*Aside.*] I know ye well enough.

CAMILLO Nay, prithee, dispatch. The gentleman is half 643 flayed already. 644

AUTOLYCUS Are you in earnest, sir? [*Aside.*] I smell the trick on 't.

FLORIZEL Dispatch, I prithee.

AUTOLYCUS Indeed, I have had earnest, but I cannot 648 with conscience take it.

CAMILLO Unbuckle, unbuckle.
[*Florizel and Autolycus exchange garments.*]

635 the outside of thy poverty i.e., your ragged clothing **636 discase** undress **637 think** understand **638–639 pennyworth** i.e., value of the bargain **640 some boot** something in addition **643 dispatch** hurry (also in l. 647) **644 flayed** skinned, i.e., undressed **648 earnest** advance payment (playing on *in earnest* in l. 645)

Fortunate mistress—let my prophecy 651
Come home to ye!—you must retire yourself 652
Into some covert. Take your sweetheart's hat 653
And pluck it o'er your brows, muffle your face,
Dismantle you, and, as you can, disliken 655
The truth of your own seeming, that you may— 656
For I do fear eyes over—to shipboard 657
Get undescried.

PERDITA I see the play so lies
That I must bear a part.

CAMILLO No remedy.—
Have you done there?

FLORIZEL Should I now meet my father,
He would not call me son.

CAMILLO Nay, you shall have no hat. [*He gives it to Perdita.*]
Come, lady, come. Farewell, my friend.

AUTOLYCUS Adieu, sir.

FLORIZEL
O Perdita, what have we twain forgot?
Pray you, a word. [*They speak aside.*]

CAMILLO [*Aside*]
What I do next shall be to tell the King
Of this escape and whither they are bound;
Wherein my hope is I shall so prevail
To force him after, in whose company
I shall re-view Sicilia, for whose sight 670
I have a woman's longing.

FLORIZEL Fortune speed us!
Thus we set on, Camillo, to the seaside.

CAMILLO The swifter speed the better.
Exit [*with Florizel and Perdita*].

AUTOLYCUS I understand the business; I hear it. To have an open ear, a quick eye, and a nimble hand is necessary for a cutpurse; a good nose is requisite also, to smell out work for th' other senses. I see this is the time that the unjust man doth thrive. What an ex-

651–652 let . . . to ye i.e., let my prophecy that you, Perdita, will be fortunate be fulfilled for you **653 covert** secret place **655 as you can** as much as you can **655–656 disliken . . . seeming** disguise your outward appearance **657 eyes over** spying eyes **670 re-view** see again

change had this been without boot! What a boot is 679
here with this exchange! Sure the gods do this year
connive at us, and we may do anything extempore. 681
The Prince himself is about a piece of iniquity, stealing
away from his father with his clog at his heels. If I 683
thought it were a piece of honesty to acquaint the King
withal, I would not do 't. I hold it the more knavery to 685
conceal it; and therein am I constant to my profession.

Enter Clown and Shepherd [*carrying a bundle and a box*].

Aside, aside! Here is more matter for a hot brain.
Every lane's end, every shop, church, session, hang- 688
ing, yields a careful man work. [*He stands aside.*]

CLOWN See, see, what a man you are now! There is no
other way but to tell the King she's a changeling and 691
none of your flesh and blood.

SHEPHERD Nay, but hear me.

CLOWN Nay, but hear me.

SHEPHERD Go to, then. 695

CLOWN She being none of your flesh and blood, your
flesh and blood has not offended the King, and so
your flesh and blood is not to be punished by him.
Show those things you found about her, those secret
things, all but what she has with her. This being done,
let the law go whistle, I warrant you.

SHEPHERD I will tell the King all, every word, yea, and
his son's pranks too; who, I may say, is no honest
man, neither to his father nor to me, to go about to 704
make me the King's brother-in-law.

CLOWN Indeed, brother-in-law was the farthest off you
could have been to him, and then your blood had
been the dearer by I know not how much an ounce.

AUTOLYCUS [*Aside*] Very wisely, puppies!

SHEPHERD Well, let us to the King. There is that in this
fardel will make him scratch his beard. 711

679 without boot i.e., even without added payment. **What a boot** what a profit **681 connive at** look indulgently at **683 clog** encumbrance (i.e., Perdita) **685 withal** with it **688 session** court session **691 changeling** child left by the fairies **695 Go to** go ahead. (Or, an expression of impatience.) **704 go about** make it his object **711 fardel** bundle

AUTOLYCUS [*Aside*] I know not what impediment this complaint may be to the flight of my master. 713
CLOWN Pray heartily he be at' palace. 714
AUTOLYCUS [*Aside*] Though I am not naturally honest, I am so sometimes by chance. Let me pocket up my peddler's excrement. [*He takes off his false beard.*] 717 How now, rustics, whither are you bound?
SHEPHERD To the palace, an it like your worship. 719
AUTOLYCUS Your affairs there, what, with whom, the condition of that fardel, the place of your dwelling, 721 your names, your ages, of what having, breeding, and 722 anything that is fitting to be known, discover. 723
CLOWN We are but plain fellows, sir. 724
AUTOLYCUS A lie; you are rough and hairy. Let me have no lying. It becomes none but tradesmen, and they often give us soldiers the lie, but we pay them for it 727 with stamped coin, not stabbing steel; therefore they do not give us the lie. 729
CLOWN Your worship had like to have given us one, if 730 you had not taken yourself with the manner. 731
SHEPHERD Are you a courtier, an 't like you, sir?
AUTOLYCUS Whether it like me or no, I am a courtier. Seest thou not the air of the court in these enfoldings? 734 Hath not my gait in it the measure of the court? Re- 735 ceives not thy nose court odor from me? Reflect I not on thy baseness court contempt? Think'st thou, for 737 that I insinuate to toze from thee thy business, I am 738 therefore no courtier? I am courtier cap-a-pie, and one 739

713 my master i.e., Florizel **714 at'** at the **717 excrement** outgrowth of hair, beard **719 an it like** if it please **721 condition** nature **722 having** property **723 discover** reveal **724 plain** simple. (But Autolycus plays on the meaning "smooth.") **727 give . . . lie** i.e., cheat us. (But *giving the lie* also means to accuse a person to his face of lying, an affront which a soldier would repay with *stabbing steel.*) **729 give** (Autolycus punningly observes that since soldiers pay tradesmen for their wares, the tradesmen cannot be said to have *given* the lie, and so a duel is avoided.) **730 had like** was about **731 taken . . . manner** i.e., caught yourself in the act, stopped short. (The Clown observes that Autolycus has once again avoided the "giving of the lie" and its consequences in a duel by his clever equivocation. Cf. Touchstone in *As You Like It,* 5.4.) **734 enfoldings** clothes **735 measure** stately tread **737–738 for that** because **738 insinuate** pry. **to toze** in order to tease, draw out, comb out **739 cap-a-pie** from head to foot

that will either push on or pluck back thy business there. Whereupon I command thee to open thy affair. 741

SHEPHERD My business, sir, is to the King.

AUTOLYCUS What advocate hast thou to him?

SHEPHERD I know not, an 't like you.

CLOWN [*Aside to Shepherd*] "Advocate" 's the court word for a pheasant. Say you have none. 746

SHEPHERD None, sir. I have no pheasant, cock nor hen.

AUTOLYCUS
How blessed are we that are not simple men!
Yet nature might have made me as these are;
Therefore I will not disdain.

CLOWN [*To Shepherd*] This cannot be but a great courtier.

SHEPHERD His garments are rich, but he wears them not handsomely.

CLOWN He seems to be the more noble in being fantas- 755
tical. A great man, I'll warrant. I know by the picking 756
on 's teeth. 757

AUTOLYCUS The fardel there? What's i' the fardel? Wherefore that box?

SHEPHERD Sir, there lies such secrets in this fardel and box which none must know but the King, and which he shall know within this hour if I may come to the speech of him.

AUTOLYCUS Age, thou hast lost thy labor. 764

SHEPHERD Why, sir?

AUTOLYCUS The King is not at the palace. He is gone aboard a new ship to purge melancholy and air himself; for, if thou be'st capable of things serious, thou 768
must know the King is full of grief.

SHEPHERD So 'tis said, sir; about his son, that should have married a shepherd's daughter.

AUTOLYCUS If that shepherd be not in handfast, let him 772
fly. The curses he shall have, the tortures he shall feel, will break the back of man, the heart of monster.

741 open reveal **746 pheasant** (The rustics suppose that Autolycus has asked them what gift they propose to present as a bribe, as one might do to a judge in a court of law.) **755–756 fantastical** eccentric **756–757 picking on 's teeth** (A stylish affectation in Shakespeare's time.) **764 Age** old man **768 be'st capable of** know anything about **772 handfast** custody (with a play on "betrothal")

CLOWN Think you so, sir?

AUTOLYCUS Not he alone shall suffer what wit can make 776
heavy and vengeance bitter; but those that are ger- 777
mane to him, though removed fifty times, shall all 778
come under the hangman—which, though it be great
pity, yet it is necessary. An old sheep-whistling rogue, 780
a ram tender, to offer to have his daughter come into 781
grace? Some say he shall be stoned; but that death is 782
too soft for him, say I. Draw our throne into a sheep-
cote? All deaths are too few, the sharpest too easy.

CLOWN Has the old man e'er a son, sir, do you hear,
an 't like you, sir?

AUTOLYCUS He has a son, who shall be flayed alive; then,
'nointed over with honey, set on the head of a wasp's
nest; then stand till he be three-quarters and a dram 789
dead; then recovered again with aqua vitae or some 790
other hot infusion; then, raw as he is, and in the hottest day prognostication proclaims, shall he be set 792
against a brick wall, the sun looking with a southward
eye upon him, where he is to behold him with flies 794
blown to death. But what talk we of these traitorly ras- 795
cals, whose miseries are to be smiled at, their offenses
being so capital? Tell me, for you seem to be honest
plain men, what you have to the King. Being some- 798
thing gently considered, I'll bring you where he is 799
aboard, tender your persons to his presence, whisper 800
him in your behalfs; and if it be in man besides the
King to effect your suits, here is man shall do it.

CLOWN [*To Shepherd*] He seems to be of great authority. Close with him, give him gold; and though au- 804
thority be a stubborn bear, yet he is oft led by the nose
with gold. Show the inside of your purse to the outside of his hand, and no more ado. Remember—
"stoned," and "flayed alive."

776 wit ingenuity **777–778 germane** related **780 sheep-whistling** tending sheep by whistling after them **781 offer** dare **782 grace** favor **789 a dram** i.e., a small amount, a fraction **790 aqua vitae** brandy **792 prognostication** forecasting (in the almanac) **794 he** i.e., the sun **795 blown** swollen. **what** i.e., why **798 what you have to** what business you have with **798–799 Being . . . considered** i.e., (1) being a gentleman of some influence (2) if I receive a gentlemanly consideration, a bribe **800 tender your persons** introduce you **804 Close with him** accept his offer

SHEPHERD An 't please you, sir, to undertake the business for us, here is that gold I have. [*He offers money.*] I'll make it as much more and leave this young man in pawn till I bring it you.

AUTOLYCUS After I have done what I promised?

SHEPHERD Ay, sir.

AUTOLYCUS [*Taking the money*] Well, give me the moiety. 815
[*To the Clown.*] Are you a party in this business?

CLOWN In some sort, sir. But, though my case be a pitiful one, I hope I shall not be flayed out of it. 817

AUTOLYCUS O, that's the case of the shepherd's son. Hang him, he'll be made an example.

CLOWN [*To Shepherd*] Comfort, good comfort! We must to the King and show our strange sights. He must know 'tis none of your daughter nor my sister; we are gone else.—Sir, I will give you as much as this old man 824 does when the business is performed, and remain, as he says, your pawn till it be brought you.

AUTOLYCUS I will trust you. Walk before toward the seaside; go on the right hand. I will but look upon the 828 hedge and follow you. 829

CLOWN [*To Shepherd*] We are blessed in this man, as I may say, even blessed.

SHEPHERD Let's before, as he bids us. He was provided to do us good. *Exeunt* [*Shepherd and Clown*].

AUTOLYCUS If I had a mind to be honest, I see Fortune would not suffer me; she drops booties in my mouth. I am courted now with a double occasion: gold, and a 836 means to do the Prince my master good, which who knows how that may turn back to my advancement? I 838 will bring these two moles, these blind ones, aboard 839 him. If he think it fit to shore them again and that the 840 complaint they have to the King concerns him noth- 841 ing, let him call me rogue for being so far officious, for 842 I am proof against that title and what shame else be- 843 longs to 't. To him will I present them. There may be matter in it. [*Exit.*]

✣

815 moiety half **817 case** (1) cause (2) skin **824 gone else** undone otherwise **828–829 look . . . hedge** i.e., relieve myself **836 occasion** opportunity **838 turn back** redound **839–840 aboard him** i.e., to him (Prince Florizel) aboard his ship **840 shore** put ashore **841–842 nothing** not at all **843 proof against** invulnerable to

5.1 *Enter Leontes, Cleomenes, Dion, Paulina, [and] servants.*

CLEOMENES
Sir, you have done enough, and have performed
A saintlike sorrow. No fault could you make
Which you have not redeemed—indeed, paid down
More penitence than done trespass. At the last,
Do as the heavens have done, forget your evil;
With them forgive yourself.

LEONTES
Whilst I remember
Her and her virtues, I cannot forget
My blemishes in them, and so still think of 8
The wrong I did myself, which was so much
That heirless it hath made my kingdom and
Destroyed the sweet'st companion that e'er man
Bred his hopes out of.

PAULINA
True, too true, my lord.
If one by one you wedded all the world,
Or from the all that are took something good 14
To make a perfect woman, she you killed
Would be unparalleled.

LEONTES
I think so. Killed?
She I killed? I did so, but thou strik'st me
Sorely to say I did. It is as bitter
Upon thy tongue as in my thought. Now, good now, 19
Say so but seldom.

CLEOMENES
Not at all, good lady.
You might have spoken a thousand things that would
Have done the time more benefit and graced
Your kindness better.

PAULINA
You are one of those
Would have him wed again.

DION
If you would not so,
You pity not the state nor the remembrance 25
Of his most sovereign name, consider little

5.1. Location: Sicilia. The royal court.
8 in them in thinking of them, or, in comparison with them **14 the all that are** all that there are **19 good now** i.e., if you please **25 nor the remembrance** i.e., nor give consideration to the perpetuation (through bearing a child and heir)

What dangers by His Highness' fail of issue 27
May drop upon his kingdom and devour
Incertain lookers-on. What were more holy 29
Than to rejoice the former queen is well? 30
What holier than, for royalty's repair,
For present comfort and for future good,
To bless the bed of majesty again
With a sweet fellow to 't?

PAULINA There is none worthy,
Respecting her that's gone. Besides, the gods 35
Will have fulfilled their secret purposes; 36
For has not the divine Apollo said,
Is 't not the tenor of his oracle,
That King Leontes shall not have an heir
Till his lost child be found? Which that it shall
Is all as monstrous to our human reason
As my Antigonus to break his grave 42
And come again to me, who, on my life,
Did perish with the infant. 'Tis your counsel 44
My lord should to the heavens be contrary,
Oppose against their wills. [*To Leontes.*] Care not for
issue. 46
The crown will find an heir. Great Alexander
Left his to the worthiest; so his successor 48
Was like to be the best.

LEONTES Good Paulina,
Who hast the memory of Hermione,
I know, in honor, O, that ever I
Had squared me to thy counsel! Then even now 52
I might have looked upon my queen's full eyes,
Have taken treasure from her lips—

PAULINA And left them
More rich for what they yielded.

LEONTES Thou speak'st truth.

27 fail failure **29 Incertain** not knowing what to think or do (about the royal succession) **30 well** happy, at rest (in heaven) **35 Respecting** in comparison with **36 Will . . . purposes** are determined to have their secret purposes fulfilled **42 As** as for **44 'Tis your counsel** it's your advice that **46 Oppose** oppose himself. **Care not for** do not be anxious about **48 Left . . . worthiest** (When Alexander the Great died in 323 B.C., his son Alexander was yet unborn, necessitating the choice of an heir.) **52 squared me** adjusted or regulated myself

No more such wives, therefore no wife. One worse, 56
And better used, would make her sainted spirit 57
Again possess her corpse, and on this stage, 58
Where we're offenders now, appear soul-vexed,
And begin, "Why to me?"

PAULINA
Had she such power, 60
She had just cause.

LEONTES
She had, and would incense me 61
To murder her I married.

PAULINA
I should so. 62
Were I the ghost that walked, I'd bid you mark
Her eye and tell me for what dull part in 't
You chose her. Then I'd shriek, that even your ears
Should rift to hear me, and the words that followed 66
Should be, "Remember mine."

LEONTES
Stars, stars, 67
And all eyes else dead coals! Fear thou no wife;
I'll have no wife, Paulina.

PAULINA
Will you swear
Never to marry but by my free leave?

LEONTES
Never, Paulina, so be blest my spirit!

PAULINA
Then, good my lords, bear witness to his oath.

CLEOMENES
You tempt him overmuch.

PAULINA
Unless another, 73
As like Hermione as is her picture,
Affront his eye.

CLEOMENES
Good madam—

PAULINA
I have done. 75
Yet if my lord will marry—if you will, sir,
No remedy, but you will—give me the office
To choose you a queen. She shall not be so young
As was your former, but she shall be such

56–57 One . . . used i.e., if I took a new wife and treated her better **57 her** i.e., Hermione's **58 possess her corpse** i.e., return to earth (*this stage*) in Hermione's human shape **60 Why to me** i.e., why this offense to me **61 had** would have. **incense** stir up, incite **62 should so** would similarly incite you **66 rift** rive, split **67 mine** my eyes. **Stars** i.e., her eyes were stars **73 tempt** bear down on **75 Affront** confront

As, walked your first queen's ghost, it should take joy 80
To see her in your arms.

LEONTES
My true Paulina,
We shall not marry till thou bidd'st us.

PAULINA
That
Shall be when your first queen's again in breath;
Never till then. 84

Enter a Gentleman.

GENTLEMAN
One that gives out himself Prince Florizel, 85
Son of Polixenes, with his princess—she
The fairest I have yet beheld—desires access
To your high presence.

LEONTES
What with him? He comes not 88
Like to his father's greatness. His approach, 89
So out of circumstance and sudden, tells us 90
'Tis not a visitation framed, but forced 91
By need and accident. What train?

GENTLEMAN
But few, 92
And those but mean.

LEONTES
His princess, say you, with him? 93

GENTLEMAN
Ay, the most peerless piece of earth, I think,
That e'er the sun shone bright on.

PAULINA
O Hermione,
As every present time doth boast itself
Above a better gone, so must thy grave
Give way to what's seen now! [*To the Gentleman.*] Sir, you yourself
Have said and writ so, but your writing now
Is colder than that theme. She had not been 102
Nor was not to be equaled—thus your verse 103

80 walked . . . ghost if your first queen's ghost were to walk. **take joy** be overjoyed **84 s.d. Enter a Gentleman** (He is called a "Servant" in the Folio text, but his writing poetry at ll. 100–104 is more consistent with his being a courtier. Any such person at court is a servant of the king.) **85 gives out himself** reports himself to be **88 What** what retinue **89 Like to** in a manner consistent with **90 out of circumstance** without ceremony **91 framed** planned **92 train** retinue **93 mean** lowly **102 that theme** i.e., Hermione, the subject of your verses **102–103 She . . . equaled** (Presumably the poet wrote, "She has not been nor is not to be equaled.")

Flowed with her beauty once. 'Tis shrewdly ebbed 104
To say you have seen a better.

GENTLEMAN Pardon, madam.
The one I have almost forgot—your pardon!
The other, when she has obtained your eye,
Will have your tongue too. This is a creature,
Would she begin a sect, might quench the zeal
Of all professors else, make proselytes 108
Of who she but bid follow.

PAULINA How? Not women!

GENTLEMAN
Women will love her that she is a woman
More worth than any man; men, that she is
The rarest of all women.

LEONTES Go, Cleomenes.
Yourself, assisted with your honored friends,
Bring them to our embracement.

Exit [*Cleomenes with others*].

Still, 'tis strange
He thus should steal upon us.

PAULINA Had our prince,
Jewel of children, seen this hour, he had paired
Well with this lord. There was not full a month
Between their births.

LEONTES Prithee, no more, cease. Thou know'st
He dies to me again when talked of. Sure,
When I shall see this gentleman, thy speeches
Will bring me to consider that which may
Unfurnish me of reason. They are come. 123

Enter Florizel, Perdita, Cleomenes, and others.

Your mother was most true to wedlock, Prince,
For she did print your royal father off,
Conceiving you. Were I but twenty-one,
Your father's image is so hit in you, 127
His very air, that I should call you brother,
As I did him, and speak of something wildly

104 'Tis shrewdly ebbed i.e., you've egregiously gone back on your word **108 professors else** believers in other sects or deities **123 Unfurnish** deprive, divest **127 hit** exactly reproduced

By us performed before. Most dearly welcome!
And your fair princess—goddess! O! Alas,
I lost a couple that twixt heaven and earth
Might thus have stood begetting wonder as
You, gracious couple, do. And then I lost—
All mine own folly—the society,
Amity too, of your brave father, whom, 136
Though bearing misery, I desire my life 137
Once more to look on him.

FLORIZEL By his command 138
Have I here touched Sicilia, and from him
Give you all greetings that a king, at friend, 140
Can send his brother; and but infirmity, 141
Which waits upon worn times, hath something seized 142
His wished ability, he had himself 143
The lands and waters twixt your throne and his
Measured to look upon you, whom he loves— 145
He bade me say so—more than all the scepters
And those that bear them living.

LEONTES O my brother! 147
Good gentleman, the wrongs I have done thee stir
Afresh within me, and these thy offices, 149
So rarely kind, are as interpreters 150
Of my behindhand slackness. Welcome hither, 151
As is the spring to th' earth. And hath he too
Exposed this paragon to th' fearful usage—
At least ungentle—of the dreadful Neptune,
To greet a man not worth her pains, much less
Th' adventure of her person?

FLORIZEL Good my lord, 156
She came from Libya.

LEONTES Where the warlike Smalus,
That noble honored lord, is feared and loved?

136 brave noble **137 my life** i.e., to live long enough **138 him** (Redundant in modern syntax.) **140 at friend** in friendship **141 but** were it not that **142 waits . . . times** attends old age. **something** to some extent **142–143 seized . . . ability** taken away his ability (to travel) as he wishes **145 Measured** traversed **147 those . . . living** those living kings who bear scepters **149 offices** messages of good will, courteous attentions **150 rarely** exceptionally **150–151 interpreters Of** commentators on **156 adventure** hazard

FLORIZEL
Most royal sir, from thence, from him, whose daughter 159
His tears proclaimed his, parting with her. Thence, 160
A prosperous south wind friendly, we have crossed,
To execute the charge my father gave me
For visiting Your Highness. My best train
I have from your Sicilian shores dismissed,
Who for Bohemia bend, to signify
Not only my success in Libya, sir,
But my arrival and my wife's in safety
Here where we are.

LEONTES The blessèd gods
Purge all infection from our air whilst you
Do climate here! You have a holy father, 170
A graceful gentleman, against whose person, 171
So sacred as it is, I have done sin,
For which the heavens, taking angry note,
Have left me issueless; and your father's blest,
As he from heaven merits it, with you,
Worthy his goodness. What might I have been,
Might I a son and daughter now have looked on,
Such goodly things as you?

Enter a Lord.

LORD Most noble sir,
That which I shall report will bear no credit
Were not the proof so nigh. Please you, great sir,
Bohemia greets you from himself by me;
Desires you to attach his son, who has— 182
His dignity and duty both cast off— 183
Fled from his father, from his hopes, and with
A shepherd's daughter.

LEONTES Where's Bohemia? Speak.

LORD
Here in your city. I now came from him.
I speak amazedly, and it becomes 187
My marvel and my message. To your court 188

159–160 whose . . . her whose tears, as he parted with her, proclaimed her to be his daughter **170 climate** dwell, reside (in this clime) **171 graceful** full of grace, gracious **182 attach** arrest **183 dignity and duty** princely dignity and filial duty **187–188 I . . . message** i.e., I speak perplexedly as befits my perplexity and my astonishing news

Whiles he was hastening—in the chase, it seems,
Of this fair couple—meets he on the way
The father of this seeming lady and
Her brother, having both their country quitted
With this young prince.

FLORIZEL Camillo has betrayed me,
Whose honor and whose honesty till now
Endured all weathers.

LORD Lay 't so to his charge. 195
He's with the King your father.

LEONTES Who? Camillo?

LORD
Camillo, sir. I spake with him, who now
Has these poor men in question. Never saw I 198
Wretches so quake. They kneel, they kiss the earth,
Forswear themselves as often as they speak.
Bohemia stops his ears and threatens them
With divers deaths in death.

PERDITA O my poor father! 202
The heaven sets spies upon us, will not have
Our contract celebrated.

LEONTES You are married?

FLORIZEL
We are not, sir, nor are we like to be. 205
The stars, I see, will kiss the valleys first;
The odds for high and low's alike.

LEONTES My lord, 207
Is this the daughter of a king?

FLORIZEL She is,
When once she is my wife.

LEONTES
That "once," I see, by your good father's speed
Will come on very slowly. I am sorry,
Most sorry, you have broken from his liking
Where you were tied in duty, and as sorry

195 Lay . . . charge i.e., confront him with it directly **198 in question** under interrogation **202 deaths** i.e., tortures **205 like** likely **207 The odds . . . alike** i.e., Fortune is the same for the high and low (?) or perhaps, the odds of a high roll in dice are the same as those of a low roll—we are at the mercy of chance; or, the odds of a union of high and low in marriage are about the same as those of the stars kissing the valleys

Your choice is not so rich in worth as beauty, 214
That you might well enjoy her.

FLORIZEL [*To Perdita*] Dear, look up.
Though Fortune, visible an enemy, 216
Should chase us with my father, power no jot 217
Hath she to change our loves.—Beseech you, sir,
Remember since you owed no more to time 219
Than I do now. With thought of such affections, 220
Step forth mine advocate. At your request
My father will grant precious things as trifles.

LEONTES
Would he do so, I'd beg your precious mistress,
Which he counts but a trifle.

PAULINA Sir, my liege,
Your eye hath too much youth in 't. Not a month
'Fore your queen died, she was more worth such gazes
Than what you look on now.

LEONTES I thought of her
Even in these looks I made. [*To Florizel.*] But your petition
Is yet unanswered. I will to your father.
Your honor not o'erthrown by your desires, 230
I am friend to them and you. Upon which errand
I now go toward him. Therefore follow me,
And mark what way I make. Come, good my lord. 233
Exeunt.

✤

5.2 *Enter Autolycus and a Gentleman.*

AUTOLYCUS Beseech you, sir, were you present at this relation? 2

214 worth rank **216–217 Though . . . father** though Fortune were to become visible as our enemy and join my father in chasing us
219–220 since . . . now when you were no older than I am now
220 With . . . affections recalling what it was to be in love at that age
230 Your . . . desires i.e., if your chaste honor has not been overcome by sexual desire; or, if what you want in this match is compatible with your royal honor **233 way** progress

5.2. Location: Sicilia. At court.
2 relation narrative, account

FIRST GENTLEMAN I was by at the opening of the fardel, heard the old shepherd deliver the manner how he 4 found it; whereupon, after a little amazedness, we were all commanded out of the chamber. Only this, methought, I heard the shepherd say: he found the child.

AUTOLYCUS I would most gladly know the issue of it.

FIRST GENTLEMAN I make a broken delivery of the busi- 10 ness, but the changes I perceived in the King and Camillo were very notes of admiration. They seemed al- 12 most, with staring on one another, to tear the cases of 13 their eyes. There was speech in their dumbness, lan- 14 guage in their very gesture. They looked as they had 15 heard of a world ransomed, or one destroyed. A notable passion of wonder appeared in them, but the wisest beholder, that knew no more but seeing, could not say 18 if th' importance were joy or sorrow; but in the ex- 19 tremity of the one it must needs be. 20

Enter another Gentleman.

Here comes a gentleman that haply knows more.— 21 The news, Rogero?

SECOND GENTLEMAN Nothing but bonfires. The oracle is fulfilled; the King's daughter is found. Such a deal of wonder is broken out within this hour that ballad makers cannot be able to express it.

Enter another Gentleman.

Here comes the Lady Paulina's steward. He can deliver you more.—How goes it now, sir? This news which is called true is so like an old tale that the verity of it is in strong suspicion. Has the King found his heir?

THIRD GENTLEMAN Most true, if ever truth were preg- 31 nant by circumstance. That which you hear you'll 32 swear you see, there is such unity in the proofs. The

4 deliver report **10 broken** disjointed, fragmented **12 notes of admiration** (1) marks of wonderment (2) exclamation marks **13–14 cases of their eyes** eyelids **15 as** as if **18 no . . . seeing** nothing except what he could see **19 importance** import, meaning **20 of the one** of one or the other **21 haply** perhaps **31–32 pregnant by circumstance** made apparent by detailed evidence

mantle of Queen Hermione's, her jewel about the neck of it, the letters of Antigonus found with it which they know to be his character, the majesty of the creature in 36 resemblance of the mother, the affection of nobleness 37 which nature shows above her breeding, and many 38 other evidences proclaim her with all certainty to be the King's daughter. Did you see the meeting of the two kings?

SECOND GENTLEMAN No.

THIRD GENTLEMAN Then have you lost a sight which was to be seen, cannot be spoken of. There might you have beheld one joy crown another, so and in such manner that it seemed Sorrow wept to take leave of them, for their joy waded in tears. There was casting up of eyes, holding up of hands, with countenance of 48 such distraction that they were to be known by garment, not by favor. Our king, being ready to leap out 50 of himself for joy of his found daughter, as if that joy 51 were now become a loss, cries, "O, thy mother, thy mother!" then asks Bohemia forgiveness; then embraces his son-in-law; then again worries he his daughter with clipping her; now he thanks the old 55 shepherd, which stands by like a weather-bitten con- 56 duit of many kings' reigns. I never heard of such an- 57 other encounter, which lames report to follow it and undoes description to do it. 59

SECOND GENTLEMAN What, pray you, became of Antigonus, that carried hence the child?

THIRD GENTLEMAN Like an old tale still, which will have matter to rehearse though credit be asleep and not an 63 ear open. He was torn to pieces with a bear. This 64 avouches the shepherd's son, who has not only his 65 innocence, which seems much, to justify him, but a 66 handkerchief and rings of his that Paulina knows. 67

36 character handwriting **37 affection of** natural disposition to **38 breeding** rearing **48 countenance** bearing, demeanor **50 favor** features **51 if that** if **55 clipping** embracing **56–57 conduit** fountain (weeping tears) **57 of many** i.e., that has stood there during many **59 undoes . . . it** i.e., surpasses the power of language to describe it **63 rehearse** relate. **credit** belief **64 with** by **65 avouches** confirms, corroborates **66 innocence** simplemindedness (such that he would seem unable to invent such a story) **67 his** i.e., Antigonus's

FIRST GENTLEMAN What became of his bark and his followers?

THIRD GENTLEMAN Wrecked the same instant of their master's death and in the view of the shepherd; so that all the instruments which aided to expose the child were even then lost when it was found. But O, the noble combat that twixt joy and sorrow was fought in Paulina! She had one eye declined for the loss of her 75 husband, another elevated that the oracle was fulfilled. 76 She lifted the Princess from the earth, and so locks her in embracing as if she would pin her to her heart, that she might no more be in danger of losing. 79

FIRST GENTLEMAN The dignity of this act was worth the audience of kings and princes, for by such was it acted.

THIRD GENTLEMAN One of the prettiest touches of all, and that which angled for mine eyes—caught the water, though not the fish—was when, at the relation of the Queen's death, with the manner how she came to 't bravely confessed and lamented by the King, how at- 87 tentiveness wounded his daughter; till, from one sign 88 of dolor to another, she did, with an "Alas!" I would 89 fain say, bleed tears, for I am sure my heart wept blood. Who was most marble there changed color; 91 some swooned, all sorrowed. If all the world could have seen 't, the woe had been universal.

FIRST GENTLEMAN Are they returned to the court?

THIRD GENTLEMAN No. The Princess, hearing of her mother's statue, which is in the keeping of Paulina— a piece many years in doing and now newly performed 97 by that rare Italian master, Julio Romano, who, had he 98 himself eternity and could put breath into his work, would beguile Nature of her custom, so perfectly he is 100 her ape; he so near to Hermione hath done Hermione 101 that they say one would speak to her and stand in

75–76 She . . . fulfilled i.e., she wept and laughed at the same time **79 losing** being lost **87–88 attentiveness** listening to it **89 dolor** grief **91 Who . . . marble** even the most hardhearted **97 performed** completed **98 Julio Romano** Italian painter and sculptor of the sixteenth century, better known as a painter (and an anachronism in this play) **100 beguile** deprive, cheat. **custom** trade **101 ape** imitator

hope of answer—thither with all greediness of affec- 103
tion are they gone, and there they intend to sup. 104

SECOND GENTLEMAN I thought she had some great matter there in hand, for she hath privately twice or thrice a day, ever since the death of Hermione, visited that removed house. Shall we thither and with our company piece the rejoicing? 109

FIRST GENTLEMAN Who would be thence that has the benefit of access? Every wink of an eye some new grace will be born. Our absence makes us unthrifty to 112
our knowledge. Let's along. *Exeunt* [*Gentlemen*].

AUTOLYCUS Now, had I not the dash of my former life 114
in me, would preferment drop on my head. I brought the old man and his son aboard the Prince, told him I heard them talk of a fardel and I know not what. But he at that time overfond of the shepherd's daughter—so he then took her to be—who began to be much seasick, and himself little better, extremity of weather continuing, this mystery remained undiscovered. But 'tis all one to me, for had I been the finder out of this 122
secret, it would not have relished among my other dis- 123
credits.

Enter Shepherd and Clown, [*dressed in finery*].

Here come those I have done good to against my will, and already appearing in the blossoms of their fortune.

SHEPHERD Come, boy. I am past more children, but thy sons and daughters will be all gentlemen born.

CLOWN You are well met, sir. You denied to fight with me this other day because I was no gentlemen born. 131
See you these clothes? Say you see them not and think me still no gentleman born. You were best say these robes are not gentlemen born. Give me the lie, do, and 134
try whether I am not now a gentleman born.

103–104 greediness of affection eagerness born of love **104 sup** i.e., feed their hungry eyes (?) or perhaps, have a commemorative banquet (?) **109 piece** add to, augment **112 unthrifty to** passing up an opportunity to increase **114 dash** touch **122 'tis all one** it's all the same **123 relished** tasted well, suited **131 this other** the other **134 Give me the lie** accuse me to my face of lying (an insult that requires a challenge to a duel)

AUTOLYCUS I know you are now, sir, a gentleman born.
CLOWN Ay, and have been so any time these four hours.
SHEPHERD And so have I, boy.
CLOWN So you have. But I was a gentleman born before my father; for the King's son took me by the hand and called me brother; and then the two Kings called my father brother; and then the Prince my brother and the Princess my sister called my father father; and so we wept, and there was the first gentlemanlike tears that ever we shed.
SHEPHERD We may live, son, to shed many more.
CLOWN Ay, or else 'twere hard luck, being in so pre- 148
posterous estate as we are. 149
AUTOLYCUS I humbly beseech you, sir, to pardon me all the faults I have committed to your worship, and to give me your good report to the Prince my master.
SHEPHERD Prithee, son, do; for we must be gentle, now 153
we are gentlemen.
CLOWN Thou wilt amend thy life?
AUTOLYCUS Ay, an it like your good worship. 156
CLOWN Give me thy hand. I will swear to the Prince
thou art as honest a true fellow as any is in Bohemia. 158
SHEPHERD You may say it, but not swear it.
CLOWN Not swear it, now I am a gentleman? Let boors 160
and franklins say it; I'll swear it. 161
SHEPHERD How if it be false, son?
CLOWN If it be ne'er so false, a true gentleman may swear it in the behalf of his friend.—And I'll swear to
the Prince thou art a tall fellow of thy hands and that 165
thou wilt not be drunk; but I know thou art no tall fellow of thy hands and that thou wilt be drunk. But I'll swear it, and I would thou wouldst be a tall fellow of thy hands.
AUTOLYCUS I will prove so, sir, to my power. 170
CLOWN Ay, by any means prove a tall fellow. If I do not wonder how thou dar'st venture to be drunk, not

148–149 preposterous (Blunder for *prosperous.*) **153 gentle** nobly generous **156 an it like** if it please **158 honest a true** worthy an honest **160 boors** peasants **161 franklins** farmers owning their own small farms **165 tall . . . hands** brave fellow **170 my power** the best of my ability

being a tall fellow, trust me not. Hark, the kings and
the princes, our kindred, are going to see the Queen's
picture. Come, follow us. We'll be thy good masters. 175
Exeunt.

✣

5.3 *Enter Leontes, Polixenes, Florizel, Perdita, Camillo, Paulina, lords, etc.*

LEONTES
O grave and good Paulina, the great comfort
That I have had of thee!

PAULINA What, sovereign sir,
I did not well, I meant well. All my services
You have paid home. But that you have vouchsafed, 4
With your crowned brother and these your contracted
Heirs of your kingdoms, my poor house to visit,
It is a surplus of your grace which never
My life may last to answer.

LEONTES O Paulina, 8
We honor you with trouble. But we came 9
To see the statue of our queen. Your gallery
Have we passed through, not without much content
In many singularities; but we saw not 12
That which my daughter came to look upon,
The statue of her mother.

PAULINA As she lived peerless,
So her dead likeness, I do well believe,
Excels whatever yet you looked upon
Or hand of man hath done. Therefore I keep it
Lonely, apart. But here it is. Prepare 18
To see the life as lively mocked as ever 19
Still sleep mocked death. Behold, and say 'tis well.
[*Paulina draws a curtain, and discovers*]
Hermione [*standing*] *like a statue.*

175 picture i.e., likeness, painted statue

5.3. Location: Sicilia. Paulina's house.
4 home fully **8 last** last long enough. **answer** repay adequately **9 We . . . trouble** i.e., we trouble you with the demands of hospitality, though you are kind enough to call it an honor **12 singularities** rarities, curiosities **18 Lonely** isolated **19 as lively mocked** as realistically counterfeited

I like your silence; it the more shows off
Your wonder. But yet speak; first, you, my liege.
Comes it not something near?

LEONTES Her natural posture! 23
Chide me, dear stone, that I may say indeed
Thou art Hermione; or rather, thou art she
In thy not chiding, for she was as tender
As infancy and grace. But yet, Paulina,
Hermione was not so much wrinkled, nothing 28
So agèd as this seems.

POLIXENES O, not by much.

PAULINA
So much the more our carver's excellence,
Which lets go by some sixteen years and makes her
As she lived now.

LEONTES As now she might have done, 32
So much to my good comfort as it is
Now piercing to my soul. O, thus she stood,
Even with such life of majesty—warm life,
As now it coldly stands—when first I wooed her!
I am ashamed. Does not the stone rebuke me
For being more stone than it? O royal piece! 38
There's magic in thy majesty, which has
My evils conjured to remembrance and
From thy admiring daughter took the spirits, 41
Standing like stone with thee.

PERDITA And give me leave,
And do not say 'tis superstition, that
I kneel and then implore her blessing. Lady,
[*Kneeling*]
Dear Queen, that ended when I but began,
Give me that hand of yours to kiss.

PAULINA O, patience!
The statue is but newly fixed; the color's 47
Not dry.

CAMILLO
My lord, your sorrow was too sore laid on, 49
Which sixteen winters cannot blow away,

23 something somewhat **28 nothing** not at all **32 As she** as if she
38 piece work of art **41 admiring** filled with wonder. **spirits** vital
spirits **47 fixed** made fast in its color **49 sore** heavily

So many summers dry. Scarce any joy 51
Did ever so long live; no sorrow
But killed itself much sooner.

POLIXENES Dear my brother,
Let him that was the cause of this have power 54
To take off so much grief from you as he
Will piece up in himself.

PAULINA Indeed, my lord, 56
If I had thought the sight of my poor image
Would thus have wrought you—for the stone is mine— 58
I'd not have showed it.

LEONTES Do not draw the curtain.

PAULINA
No longer shall you gaze on 't, lest your fancy
May think anon it moves.

LEONTES Let be, let be.
Would I were dead but that methinks already—
What was he that did make it? See, my lord,
Would you not deem it breathed? And that those veins
Did verily bear blood?

POLIXENES Masterly done.
The very life seems warm upon her lip.

LEONTES
The fixture of her eye has motion in 't, 67
As we are mocked with art.

PAULINA I'll draw the curtain. 68
My lord's almost so far transported that
He'll think anon it lives.

LEONTES O sweet Paulina,
Make me to think so twenty years together!
No settled senses of the world can match 72
The pleasure of that madness. Let 't alone.

PAULINA
I am sorry, sir, I have thus far stirred you; but
I could afflict you farther.

51 So . . . dry i.e., and sixteen summers cannot dry up. (Camillo tells the King that he has imposed too heavy a sorrow on himself if even sixteen years' time cannot end it.) **54 him** i.e., myself (as an innocent cause, but still a cause) **56 piece up in himself** take upon himself **58 wrought** affected **67 The fixture . . . in 't** i.e., her eye, though motionless, gives the appearance of motion **68 As . . . art** in such a way that we are fooled by artistic illusion **72 No settled . . . world** no calm mind in the world

LEONTES Do, Paulina;
For this affliction has a taste as sweet
As any cordial comfort. Still methinks 77
There is an air comes from her. What fine chisel
Could ever yet cut breath? Let no man mock me,
For I will kiss her.

PAULINA Good my lord, forbear.
The ruddiness upon her lip is wet;
You'll mar it if you kiss it, stain your own
With oily painting. Shall I draw the curtain? 83

LEONTES
No, not these twenty years.

PERDITA So long could I
Stand by, a looker on.

PAULINA Either forbear, 85
Quit presently the chapel, or resolve you 86
For more amazement. If you can behold it,
I'll make the statue move indeed, descend
And take you by the hand. But then you'll think—
Which I protest against—I am assisted
By wicked powers.

LEONTES What you can make her do
I am content to look on, what to speak
I am content to hear; for 'tis as easy
To make her speak as move.

PAULINA It is required
You do awake your faith. Then all stand still.
On; those that think it is unlawful business 96
I am about, let them depart.

LEONTES Proceed.
No foot shall stir.

PAULINA Music, awake her; strike! [*Music.*] 98
'Tis time. Descend. Be stone no more. Approach.
Strike all that look upon with marvel. Come, 100
I'll fill your grave up. Stir, nay, come away,
Bequeath to death your numbness, for from him 102
Dear life redeems you.—You perceive she stirs.
[*Hermione comes down.*]

77 cordial restorative, heartwarming **83 painting** paint **85 forbear** withdraw **86 presently** immediately **96 On; those** (Often emended to *Or those.*) **98 strike** strike up **100 upon** on **102 him** i.e., death

Start not. Her actions shall be holy as
You hear my spell is lawful. Do not shun her 105
Until you see her die again, for then 106
You kill her double. Nay, present your hand. 107
When she was young you wooed her. Now in age
Is she become the suitor? [*Leontes touches her.*]

LEONTES O, she's warm!
If this be magic, let it be an art
Lawful as eating.

POLIXENES She embraces him.

CAMILLO She hangs about his neck.
If she pertain to life, let her speak too.

POLIXENES
Ay, and make it manifest where she has lived,
Or how stol'n from the dead.

PAULINA That she is living,
Were it but told you, should be hooted at
Like an old tale; but it appears she lives,
Though yet she speak not. Mark a little while.
[*To Perdita.*] Please you to interpose, fair madam. Kneel, 120
And pray your mother's blessing.—Turn, good lady;
Our Perdita is found.

HERMIONE You gods, look down
And from your sacred vials pour your graces
Upon my daughter's head!—Tell me, mine own,
Where hast thou been preserved? Where lived? How
found
Thy father's court? For thou shalt hear that I,
Knowing by Paulina that the oracle
Gave hope thou wast in being, have preserved
Myself to see the issue.

PAULINA There's time enough for that,
Lest they desire upon this push to trouble 131
Your joys with like relation. Go together, 132
You precious winners all; your exultation
Partake to everyone. I, an old turtle, 134

105–107 Do . . . double i.e., if you shun her now, you will kill her again. **then** in that case **107 double** a second time **120 madam** (Addressed to Perdita as Princess and affianced to be married.) **131–132 Lest . . . relation** lest they desire, at this stressful time, to trouble you by demanding like relation of your story **134 Partake to** share with, communicate. **turtle** turtledove

Will wing me to some withered bough and there
My mate, that's never to be found again,
Lament till I am lost.

LEONTES O, peace, Paulina! 137

Thou shouldst a husband take by my consent,
As I by thine a wife. This is a match,
And made between 's by vows. Thou hast found mine,
But how is to be questioned, for I saw her,
As I thought, dead, and have in vain said many
A prayer upon her grave. I'll not seek far—
For him, I partly know his mind—to find thee 144
An honorable husband. Come, Camillo,
And take her by the hand, whose worth and honesty 146
Is richly noted and here justified 147
By us, a pair of kings. Let's from this place.
[*To Hermione*.] What? Look upon my brother. Both your pardons,
That e'er I put between your holy looks
My ill suspicion. This' your son-in-law 151
And son unto the King, whom, heavens directing,
Is trothplight to your daughter. Good Paulina, 153
Lead us from hence, where we may leisurely
Each one demand and answer to his part
Performed in this wide gap of time since first
We were dissevered. Hastily lead away. *Exeunt.*

137 till I am lost i.e., until I die **144 For** as for **146 whose** i.e., Camillo's **147 richly noted** abundantly acknowledged. **justified** avouched **151 This'** this is **153 trothplight** betrothed

Date and Text

The Winter's Tale was first printed in the First Folio of 1623. Its text is a good one, taken evidently from Ralph Crane's transcript of Shakespeare's own well-finished draft. As in most other Crane transcriptions, the stage directions are sparse and the characters' names are grouped at the beginning of each scene. The first recorded performance was on May 15, 1611, when the quack astrologer Simon Forman saw the play at the Globe Theatre and recorded a summary of it in his commonplace book. Another performance that year at court, on November 5, is recorded in the *Revels Account,* and still another during the winter of 1612–1613. Quite possibly the play was new at the time Forman saw it. It apparently contains an allusion to the dance of ten or twelve satyrs in Ben Jonson's *Masque of Oberon,* performed at court on January 1, 1611. A 1623 entry in the *Office book* of Sir Henry Herbert, Master of the Revels, refers to *The Winter's Tale* as "an old play . . . formerly allowed of by Sir George Bucke." Bucke (or Buc) was first appointed Master of the Revels in 1610, but had occasionally licensed plays before that date during his predecessor's illness, so that the backward limit of 1610 cannot be considered absolute. Still, matters of style confirm the likelihood that Forman was seeing a new play in 1611.

Textual Notes

These textual notes are not a historical collation, either of the early folios or of more recent editions; they are simply a record of departures in this edition from the copy text. The reading adopted in this edition appears in boldface, followed by the rejected reading from the copy text, i.e., the First Folio. Only major alterations in punctuation are noted. Changes in lineation are not indicated, nor are some minor and obvious typographical errors.

Abbreviations used:
F the First Folio
s.d. stage direction
s.p. speech prefix

Copy text: the First Folio. Characters' names are grouped at the heads of scenes throughout the play.

The Names of the Actors [printed in F at the end of the play] **Archidamus** [after Autolycus in F]

1.1. 9 us, we vs: we

1.2. 104 And A **137–138 be?— / Affection, thy** be / Affection? thy **148 What . . . brother** [assigned in F to Leontes] **151–153 folly, . . . tenderness, . . . bosoms!** folly? . . . tendernesse? . . . bosomes? **158 do** do's **208 you, they** you **253 forth. In . . . lord,** forth in . . . (my Lord.) **275 hobbyhorse** Holy-Horse **386 How? Caught** How caught

2.1. 2 s.p. [and throughout scene] First Lady Lady **91 fedarie** Federarie

2.2. 32–33 me. / If . . . blister me, / If . . . blister.

2.3. 39 What Who

3.2. 10 Silence [printed in F as a s.d.] **s.d. Hermione, as to her trial . . . Ladies** [at start of scene in F, as generally with the s.d. in this play] **33 Who** Whom **99 Starred** Star'd **156 woo** woe

3.3. 64 scared scarr'd **116 made** mad

4.2. 13 thee. Thou thee, thou

4.3. 1 s.p. Autolycus [not in F] **7 on** an **10 With heigh, with heigh** With heigh **38 currants** Currence

4.4. 12 Digest it Digest **83 bastards. Of** bastards) of **98 your** you **160 out** on't **218 s.p. Autolycus** [not in F] **244 kilnhole** kill-hole **297 s.p. Autolycus** [in F, appears at l. 298] **299 Whither** Whether [and similarly throughout song] **316 cape** Crpe **355 reply, at least** reply at least, **361 who** whom **421 acknowledged** acknowledge **425 who** whom **430 see** neuer see **441 hoop** hope **470 your** my **485–486 fancy. If . . . obedient, I** fancie, if . . . obedient: I **503 our** her **614 could** would **filled** fill'd **off** of **644 flayed** fled **738 to** at **833 s.d. Exeunt** [at l. 845 in F]

5.1. 12 True [assigned in F to Leontes] **59 Where . . . appear** (Where we Offenders now appeare) **61 just** just such **75 I have done** [assigned in F to

Cleomenes] **84 s.d. Gentleman** Seruant **85 s.p. [and through l. 110] Gentleman** Ser **114 s.d. Exit** [after "us" in l. 115 in F]

5.2. 113 s.d. Exeunt Exit

5.3. 18 Lonely Louely **67 fixture** fixure

Shakespeare's Sources

Any departures from the original text are noted with an asterisk and appear at the bottom of the page in boldface; original readings are in roman.

Shakespeare based *The Winter's Tale* on Robert Greene's romantic novel called *Pandosto: The Triumph of Time* (1588), or *The History of Dorastus and Fawnia* in its running title, an abbreviated version of which follows. Shakespeare changes the names, reverses the two kingdoms of Sicilia and Bohemia, compresses the element of time, and alters the unhappy ending that afflicts King Pandosto and Queen Bellaria of Bohemia (Leontes and Hermione of Sicilia). Otherwise, the narrative outline remains intact. The story begins with the state visit of King Egistus of Sicilia (Polixenes of Bohemia) to his boyhood companion, King Pandosto of Bohemia. Queen Bellaria entertains their guest with such warmth, "oftentimes coming herself into his bedchamber to see that nothing should be amiss to mislike him," that Pandosto grows jealous. He commands his cupbearer Franion (Camillo) to murder Egistus, and the latter seems to agree but instead warns his victim to flee with him. Their hasty departure appears to confirm Pandosto's worst suspicions. He sends the guard to arrest Bellaria as she plays with her young son Garinter (Mamillius). When the Queen gives birth to a daughter in prison, the King orders the child destroyed, but relents upon the insistence of his courtiers and causes the infant to be set adrift in a small boat. The Queen nobly defends herself at her trial (in language that Shakespeare has copied in some detail). She herself requests that the oracle at Delphos be consulted. The oracle replies in words that Shakespeare has altered only slightly: "Bellaria is chaste, Egistus blameless, Franion a true subject, Pandosto treacherous, his babe an innocent; and the King shall live without an heir if that which is lost be not found." Unlike Shakespeare's Leontes, however, Pandosto is immediately stricken with remorse; and when Queen Bellaria collapses at the news of her son Garinter's death, she is truly and irrecoverably dead.

A similarly close parallel in the narrative, along with telling changes in a number of details, is characteristic of the story's second half. The babe is conveyed by a tempest to the coast of Sicilia and is discovered by an impoverished shepherd named Porrus. He and his wife Mopsa adopt the child, naming her Fawnia. By the age of sixteen, Fawnia's natural beauty rivals that of the goddess Flora. At a meeting of the farmers' daughters of Sicilia, where she is chosen mistress of the feast, Fawnia is seen by the King's son Dorastus on his way home from hawking. She counters his importunate suit with the argument that she is too lowly a match for him, but he replies that the gods themselves sometimes take earthly lovers. Her foster father, distressed by the Prince's repeated visits (though he comes in shepherd's costume), resolves to carry the jewels he found with Fawnia to the King and reveal her story, thereby escaping blame for the goings-on. Dorastus escapes with Fawnia to a ship, aided by his servant Capnio (cf. Camillo). Capnio also fulfills a role given by Shakespeare to Autolycus, for he manages to trick the shepherd Porrus into thinking he can see the King if he comes aboard Dorastus's ship. A storm drives these voyagers to Bohemia where, because of the ancient enmity between Egistus and Pandosto, they disguise themselves. Pandosto, happening to hear of Fawnia's beauty, orders her and the others to be arrested as spies and summoned to court, whereupon he falls incestuously in love with the disguised Fawnia. He promises to free the young man (who has taken the name of Meleagrus to conceal his identity) only if he will relinquish his claim to Fawnia. King Egistus meanwhile has discovered his son's whereabouts and sends ambassadors to Bohemia demanding the return of Dorastus and the execution of Fawnia, Capnio, and Porrus. Pandosto, his love for Fawnia having turned to hate, is about to comply when Porrus reveals the circumstances of Fawnia's infancy. Overjoyed to rediscover his daughter, Pandosto permits her to marry Dorastus, but then falls into a melancholy fit and commits suicide.

Shakespeare has almost entirely created some characters, such as Paulina, Antigonus, the clownish shepherd's son, and Autolycus, though Capnio does perform one of Autolycus's functions by inveigling the old shepherd aboard ship. Antigonus's journey to the seacoast of Bohemia with the infant Perdita, and his fatal exit "pursued by a bear," are Shakespearean additions. The character of Time is also added, and the shift in tone from tragedy to romance is more pronounced than in Greene. The shepherdesses at the sheepshearing are Shakespearean. The old Shepherd has a more substantial and comic role; Camillo is a stronger person than Capnio. Greene's Mopsa, the shrewish wife of old Porrus, disappears from the play. Shakespeare omits the incestuous love of Pandosto for his daughter and brings Hermione back to life. (For this motif of a statue made to breathe, he may well have recalled Ovid's account of Pygmalion in Ovid's *Metamorphoses,* Book 10.) Shakespeare's Leontes is more irrationally jealous than in Greene's account. Leontes's purgative sorrow is more intense and also more restorative than in the source; he is a truly noble and tragicomic figure, the center of a play about forgiveness and renewal.

Shakespeare may also have known Francis Sabie's *The Fisherman's Tale* (1595) and its continuation, *Flora's Fortune* (1595). From Greene's pamphlets, describing in vividly colloquial detail the life of London's underworld, Shakespeare probably derived many of Autolycus's tricks.

Pandosto: The Triumph of Time

By Robert Greene

In the country of Bohemia there reigned a king called Pandosto, whose fortunate success in wars against his foes and bountiful courtesy towards his friends in peace made him to be greatly feared and loved of all men. This Pandosto had to wife a lady called Bellaria, by birth royal, learned by education, fair by nature, by virtues famous, so that it was hard to judge whether her beauty, fortune, or virtue wan[1] the greatest commendations. These two, linked together in perfect love, led their lives with such fortunate content that their subjects greatly rejoiced to see their quiet disposition.

They had not been married long, but Fortune, willing to increase their happiness, lent them a son, so adorned with the gifts of nature as[2] the perfection of the child greatly augmented the love of the parents and the joy of their commons, insomuch that the Bohemians, to show their inward joys by outward actions, made bonfires and triumphs throughout all the kingdom, appointing jousts and tourneys for the honor of

1 wan won **2 as** that

their young prince; whither resorted not only his nobles, but also divers kings and princes which were his neighbors, willing to show their friendship they ought[3] to Pandosto and to win fame and glory by their prowess and valor. Pandosto, whose mind was fraught with princely liberality, entertained the kings, princes, and noblemen with such submiss[4] courtesy and magnifical[5] bounty that they all saw how willing he was to gratify their good wills, making a general feast for his subjects which continued by the space of twenty days, all which time the jousts and tourneys were kept to the great content both of the lords and ladies there present. This solemn triumph being once ended, the assembly, taking their leave of Pandosto and Bellaria, the young son (who was called Garinter) was nursed up in the house to the great joy and content of the parents.

Fortune, envious of such happy success, willing to show some sign of her inconstancy, turned her wheel and darkened their bright sun of prosperity with the misty clouds of mishap and misery. For it so happened that Egistus, King of Sicilia, who in his youth had been brought up with Pandosto, desirous to show that neither tract of time nor distance of place could diminish their former friendship, provided a navy of ships and sailed into Bohemia to visit his old friend and companion, who, hearing of his arrival, went himself in person and his wife Bellaria, accompanied with a great train of lords and ladies, to meet Egistus; and, espying him, alighted from his horse, embraced him very lovingly, protesting that nothing in the world could have happened more acceptable to him than his coming, wishing his wife to welcome his old friend and acquaintance. Who, to show how she liked him whom her husband loved, entertained him with such familiar courtesy as[6] Egistus perceived himself to be very well welcome. After they had thus saluted and embraced each other, they mounted again on horseback and rode toward the city, devising and recounting how being children they had passed their youth in friendly pastimes; where, by the means of the citizens, Egistus was received with triumphs and shows, in such sort that he marveled how on so small a warning they could make such preparation.

3 ought owed **4 submiss** humble **5 magnifical** munificent **6 as** that

Passing the streets thus, with such rare sights, they rode on to the palace, where Pandosto entertained Egistus and his Sicilians with such banqueting and sumptuous cheer, so royally, as they all had cause to commend his princely liberality. Yea, the very basest slave that was known to come from Sicilia was used with such courtesy that Egistus might easily perceive how both he and his were honored for his friend's sake. Bellaria, who in her time was the flower of courtesy, willing to show how unfeignedly she loved her husband by his friend's entertainment,[7] used him likewise so familiarly that her countenance bewrayed[8] how her mind was affected towards him, oftentimes coming herself into his bedchamber to see that nothing should be amiss to mislike[9] him.

This honest familiarity increased daily more and more betwixt them; for Bellaria noting in Egistus a princely and bountiful mind adorned with sundry and excellent qualities, and Egistus finding in her a virtuous and courteous disposition, there grew such a secret uniting of their affections that the one could not well be without the company of the other, insomuch that when Pandosto was busied with such urgent affairs that he could not be present with his friend Egistus, Bellaria would walk with him into the garden, where they two in private and pleasant devices would pass away the time to both their contents.

This custom still continuing betwixt them, a certain melancholy passion entering the mind of Pandosto drave him into sundry and doubtful thoughts. First, he called to mind the beauty of his wife Bellaria, the comeliness and bravery of his friend Egistus, thinking that love was above all laws and therefore to be stayed with no law; that it was hard to put fire and flax together without burning; that their open pleasures might breed his secret displeasures. He considered with himself that Egistus was a man and must needs love, that his wife was a woman and therefore subject unto love, and that where fancy forced,[10] friendship was of no force.

These and suchlike doubtful thoughts, a long time smoth-

7 by his friend's entertainment by the hospitality she showed to his friend **8 bewrayed** revealed **9 mislike** displease **10 where fancy forced** where love compelled

ering[11] in his stomach, began at last to kindle in his mind a secret mistrust, which, increased by suspicion, grew at last to a flaming jealousy that so tormented him as he could take no rest. He then began to measure all their actions and to misconstrue of their too private familiarity, judging that it was not for honest affection but for disordinate fancy, so that he began to watch them more narrowly to see if he could get any true or certain proof to confirm his doubtful suspicion. While thus he noted their looks and gestures and suspected their thoughts and meanings, they two silly[12] souls, who doubted[13] nothing of this his treacherous intent, frequented daily each other's company, which drave him into such a frantic passion that he began to bear a secret hate to Egistus and a louring[14] countenance to Bellaria; who, marveling at such unaccustomed frowns, began to cast beyond the moon,[15] and to enter into a thousand sundry thoughts which way she should offend[16] her husband; but, finding in herself a clear conscience, ceased to muse until such time as she might find fit opportunity to demand the cause of his dumps.

In the meantime, Pandosto's mind was so far charged with jealousy that he did no longer doubt, but was assured, as he thought, that his friend Egistus had entered a wrong point in his tables,[17] and so had played him false play. Whereupon, desirous to revenge so great an injury, he thought best to dissemble the grudge with a fair and friendly countenance, and so under the shape of a friend to show him the trick of a foe. Devising with himself a long time how he might best put away Egistus without suspicion of treacherous murder, he concluded at last to poison him, which opinion pleasing his humor he became resolute in his determination. And the better to bring the matter to pass he called unto him his cupbearer, with whom in secret he brake the matter, promising to him for the performance thereof to give him a thousand crowns of yearly revenues.

His cupbearer, either being of a good conscience or willing for fashion's sake to deny such a bloody request, began

11 smothering remaining hidden, like smoldering fire **12 silly** innocent **13 doubted** suspected **14 louring** scowling **15 cast beyond the moon** i.e., indulge in wild conjecture **16 which . . . offend** how she might have offended **17 tables** (The metaphor is from backgammon.)

with great reasons to persuade Pandosto from his determinate mischief, showing him what an offense murder was to the gods, how such unnatural actions did more displease the heavens than men, and that causeless cruelty did seldom or never escape without revenge. He laid before his face[18] that Egistus was his friend, a king, and one that was come into his kingdom to confirm a league of perpetual amity betwixt them; that he had and did show him a most friendly countenance; how Egistus was not only honored of his own people by obedience but also loved of the Bohemians for his courtesy; and that if now he should without any just or manifest cause poison him, it would not only be a great dishonor to his majesty and a means to sow perpetual enmity between the Sicilians and the Bohemians, but also his own subjects would repine at[19] such treacherous cruelty.

These and suchlike persuasions of Franion—for so was his cupbearer called—could no whit prevail to dissuade him from his devilish enterprise, but, remaining resolute in his determination (his fury so fired with rage as it could not be appeased with reason), he began with bitter taunts to take up[20] his man and to lay before him two baits, preferment and death, saying that if he would poison Egistus he should advance him to high dignities; if he refused to do it of an obstinate mind, no torture should be too great to requite his disobedience. Franion, seeing that to persuade Pandosto any more was but to strive against the stream, consented, as soon as opportunity would give him leave, to dispatch Egistus; wherewith Pandosto remained somewhat satisfied, hoping now he should be fully revenged of such mistrusted injuries, intending also as soon as Egistus was dead to give his wife a sop of the same sauce and so be rid of those which were the cause of his restless sorrow.

[Alone in his chamber, Franion meditates on his hard choice.]

Franion having muttered out these or suchlike words, seeing either he must die with a clear mind or live with a

18 before his face before him **19 repine at** dislike, complain about
20 take up rebuke, take up short

spotted conscience, he was so cumbered with divers cogitations that he could take no rest until at last he determined to break the matter to Egistus; but, fearing that the King should either suspect or hear of such matters, he concealed the device till opportunity would permit him to reveal it. Lingering thus in doubtful fear, in an evening he went to Egistus's lodging and, desirous to break with him of[21] certain affairs that touched the King, after all were commanded out of the chamber, Franion made manifest the whole conspiracy which Pandosto had devised against him, desiring Egistus not to account him a traitor for bewraying[22] his master's counsel but to think that he did it for conscience; hoping that although his master, inflamed with rage or incensed by some sinister reports or slanderous speeches, had imagined such causeless mischief, yet when time should pacify his anger and try[23] those talebearers but flattering parasites, then he[24] would count him as a faithful servant that with such care had kept his master's credit.

Egistus had not fully heard Franion tell forth his tale but a quaking fear possessed all his limbs, thinking that there was some treason wrought and that Franion did but shadow his craft with these false colors. Wherefore he began to wax in choler[25] and said that he doubted not Pandosto, sith[26] he was his friend, and there had never as yet been any breach of amity. He had not sought to invade his lands, to conspire with his enemies, to dissuade his subjects from their allegiance, but in word and thought he rested his[27] at all times. He knew not, therefore, any cause that should move Pandosto to seek his death, but suspected it to be a compacted knavery[28] of the Bohemians to bring the King and him at odds.

Franion, staying[29] him in the midst of his talk, told him that to dally with princes was with the swans to sing against their death,[30] and that, if the Bohemians had intended any such secret mischief, it might have been better

21 break with him of disclose his mind to Egistus concerning
22 bewraying revealing **23 try** prove **24 he** i.e., Pandosto **25 wax in choler** grow angry **26 sith** since **27 rested his** remained loyal to him, Pandosto **28 compacted knavery** conspiratorial villainy **29 staying** stopping **30 was with . . . death** i.e., was tantamount to flirting with death, like swans who, according to popular belief, sing in anticipation of (*against*) their death

brought to pass than by revealing the conspiracy; therefore His Majesty did ill to misconstrue of his good meaning, sith[31] his intent was to hinder treason, not to become a traitor; and to confirm his promises,* if it pleased* His Majesty to flee into Sicilia for the safeguard of his life, he would go with him, and if then he found not such a practice to be pretended,[32] let his imagined treachery be repaid with most monstrous torments. Egistus, hearing the solemn protestation of Franion, began to consider that in love and kingdoms neither faith nor law is to be respected, doubting[33] that Pandosto thought by his death to destroy his men and with speedy war to invade Sicilia. These and such doubts throughly weighed, he gave great thanks to Franion, promising, if he might with life return to Syracusa, that he would create him a duke in Sicilia, craving his counsel how he might escape out of the country. Franion, who having some small skill in navigation was well acquainted with the ports and havens, and knew every danger in the sea, joining in counsel with the master of Egistus's navy, rigged all their ships and, setting them afloat, let them lie at anchor to be in the more readiness when time and wind should serve.

Fortune, although blind, yet by chance favoring this just cause, sent them within six days a good gale of wind; which Franion seeing fit for their purpose, to put Pandosto out of suspicion, the night before they should sail he went to him and promised that the next day he would put the device in practice, for he had got such a forcible poison as the very smell thereof should procure sudden death. Pandosto was joyful to hear this good news, and thought every hour a day till he might be glutted with bloody revenge; but his suit had but ill success. For Egistus, fearing that delay might breed danger, and willing that the grass should not be cut from under his feet, taking bag and baggage, with the help of Franion conveyed himself and his men out of a postern[34] gate of the city, so secretly and speedily that without any suspicion they got to the seashore; where, with many a bitter curse taking their leave of Bohemia, they went aboard. Weighing their anchors and hoisting sail, they passed as fast as wind and sea would permit towards Sicilia, Egistus

*__promises__ premises [Q2, Q3] *__pleased__ please [Q2, Q3]

31 sith since **32 pretended** intended **33 doubting** fearing, suspecting **34 postern** back

being a joyful man that he had safely passed such treacherous perils.

But as they were quietly floating on the sea, so Pandosto and his citizens were in an uproar; for, seeing that the Sicilians without taking their leave were fled away by night, the Bohemians feared some treason, and the King thought that without question his suspicion was true, seeing his cupbearer had bewrayed the sum of his secret pretense.[34] Whereupon he began to imagine that Franion and his wife Bellaria had conspired with Egistus, and that the fervent affection she bare him was the only means of his secret departure; insomuch that, incensed with rage, he commanded that his wife should be carried to straight prison until they heard further of his pleasure. The guard, unwilling to lay their hands on such a virtuous princess and yet fearing the King's fury, went very sorrowfully to fulfill their charge. Coming to the Queen's lodging they found her playing with her young son Garinter, unto whom with tears doing[35] the message, Bellaria, astonished at such a hard censure and finding her clear conscience a sure advocate to plead in her case, went to the prison most willingly, where with sighs and tears she passed away the time till she might come to her trial.

But Pandosto, whose reason was suppressed with rage and whose unbridled folly was incensed with fury, seeing Franion had bewrayed his secrets and that Egistus might well be railed on but not revenged, determined to wreak all his wrath on poor Bellaria. He therefore caused a general proclamation to be made through all his realm that the Queen and Egistus had, by the help of Franion, not only committed most incestuous adultery but also had conspired the King's death, whereupon the traitor Franion was fled away with Egistus, and Bellaria was most justly imprisoned. This proclamation being once blazed[36] through the country, although the virtuous disposition of the Queen did half discredit the contents, yet the sudden and speedy passage of Egistus and the secret departure of Franion induced them[37]—the circumstances throughly considered—to think that both the proclamation was true and the King

34 bewrayed . . . pretense revealed all his secret intent **35 doing** (the guards) delivering **36 blazed** proclaimed **37 them** i.e., the people

greatly injured. Yet they pitied her case, as sorrowful that so good a lady should be crossed with such adverse fortune.

But the King, whose restless rage would admit no pity, thought that although he might sufficiently requite his wife's falsehood with the bitter plague of pinching penury, yet his mind should never be glutted with revenge till he might have fit time and opportunity to repay the treachery of* Egistus with a fatal injury. But a curst[38] cow hath oft-times short horns, and a willing mind but a weak arm; for Pandosto, although he felt that revenge was a spur to war and that envy[39] always proffereth steel, yet he saw that Egistus was not only of great puissance[40] and prowess to withstand him, but had also many kings of his alliance to aid him if need should serve, for he married to the Emperor's daughter of Russia. These and the like considerations something daunted Pandosto his[41] courage, so that he was content rather to put up a manifest injury with peace than hunt after revenge, dishonor, and loss, determining, since Egistus had escaped scot-free, that Bellaria should pay for all at an unreasonable price.

[Bellaria, in prison and prevented from defending herself against the unjust accusation, laments her high estate, which has exposed her to such infamy, and her untimely pregnancy.]

The jailer, pitying these her heavy passions, thinking that if the King knew she were with child he would somewhat appease his fury and release her from prison, went in all haste and certified Pandosto what the effect of Bellaria's complaint was, who no sooner heard the jailer say she was with child but as one possessed with a frenzy he rose up in a rage, swearing that she and the bastard brat she was big* withal should die if the gods themselves said no, thinking assuredly by computation of time that Egistus and not he was father to the child. This suspicious thought galled afresh this half-healed sore, insomuch as he could take no rest until he might mitigate his choler with a just revenge,

***of** [omitted in Q2, Q3] ***big** [omitted in Q2, Q3]

38 curst vicious (and therefore likely to attack and do harm except for its short horns) **39 envy** malice **40 puissance** might **41 Pandosto his** Pandosto's

which happened presently after. For Bellaria was brought to bed of a fair and beautiful daughter, which no sooner Pandosto heard but he determined that both Bellaria and the young infant should be burnt with fire.

His nobles, hearing of the King's cruel sentence, sought by persuasions to divert him from this bloody determination, laying before his face the innocency of the child and the virtuous disposition of his wife, how she had continually loved and honored him so tenderly that without due proof he could not nor ought not to appeach[42] her of that crime. And if she had faulted, yet it were more honorable to pardon with mercy than to punish with extremity, and more kingly to be commended of pity than accused of rigor. And as for the child, if he should punish it for the mother's offense, it were to strive against nature and justice; and that unnatural actions do more offend the gods than men; how causeless cruelty nor innocent blood never scapes without revenge. These and suchlike reasons could not appease his rage, but he rested resolute in this: that Bellaria being an adulteress, the child was a bastard, and he would not suffer that such an infamous brat should call him father.

Yet at last, seeing his noblemen were importunate upon him, he was content to spare the child's life, and yet to put it to a worser death. For he found out this device: that seeing, as he thought, it came by fortune, so he would commit it to the charge of fortune. And therefore he caused a little cockboat[43] to be provided, wherein he meant to put the babe and then send it to the mercy of the seas and the destinies. From this his peers in no wise could persuade him, but that he sent presently two of his guard to fetch the child; who, being come to the prison and with weeping tears recounting their master's message, Bellaria no sooner heard the rigorous resolution of her merciless husband but she fell down in a swoon, so that all thought she had been dead.

[Queen Bellaria, revived at last, beweeps her new misfortune and that of her child.]

Such and so great was her grief that, her vital spirits be-

42 appeach accuse **43 cockboat** small boat, often towed behind a larger vessel

ing suppressed with sorrow, she fell again down in a trance, having her senses so sotted with care that after she was revived yet she lost her memory and lay for a great time without moving as one in a trance. The guard left her in this perplexity, and carried the child to the King, who, quite devoid of pity, commanded that without delay it should be put in the boat, having neither sail nor rudder* to guide it, and so to be carried into the midst of the sea and there left to the wind and wave as the destinies please to appoint. The very shipmen, seeing the sweet countenance of the young babe, began to accuse the King of rigor[44] and to pity the child's hard fortune; but fear constrained them to that which their nature did abhor, so that they placed it in one of the ends of the boat, and with a few green boughs made a homely cabin to shroud it as they could from wind and weather. Having thus trimmed the boat, they tied it to a ship and so haled it into the main sea, and then cut in sunder the cord; which they had no sooner done but there arose a mighty tempest, which tossed the little boat so vehemently in the waves that the shipmen thought it could not continue long without sinking; yea, the storm grew so great that with much labor and peril they got to the shore.

But leaving the child to her fortunes, again to Pandosto, who, not yet glutted with sufficient revenge, devised which way he should best increase his wife's calamity. But first assembling his nobles and counselors, he called her for the more reproach into open court, where it was objected[45] against her that she had committed adultery with Egistus and conspired with Franion to poison Pandosto her husband, but, their pretense[46] being partly spied, she counseled them to fly away by night for their better safety. Bellaria, who, standing like a prisoner at the bar, feeling in herself a clear conscience to withstand her false accusers, seeing that no less than death could pacify her husband's wrath, waxed bold and desired that she might have law and justice, for mercy she neither craved nor hoped for; and that those perjured wretches which had falsely accused her to the King might be brought before her face to give in evidence. But Pandosto, whose rage and jealousy was such as

***rudder** other

44 rigor hardness of heart, cruelty **45 objected** charged **46 pretense** intent no reason nor equity could appease, told her that, for[47] her accusers, they were of such credit as their words were sufficient witness, and that the sudden and secret flight of Egistus and Franion confirmed that which they had confessed; and as for her, it was her part to deny such a monstrous crime and to be impudent in forswearing the fact, since she had passed all shame in committing the fault; but her stale countenance should stand for no coin,[48] for, as[49] the bastard which she bare[50] was served, so she should with some cruel death be requited. Bellaria, no whit dismayed with this rough reply, told her husband Pandosto that he spake upon choler[51] and not conscience, for her virtuous life had been ever such as no spot of suspicion could ever stain. And if she had borne a friendly countenance to Egistus, it was in respect he was his friend and not for any lusting affection; therefore, if she were condemned without any further proof it was rigor and not law.

The noblemen which sat in judgment said that Bellaria spake reason and entreated the King that the accusers might be openly examined and sworn, and if then the evidence were such as the jury might find her guilty (for seeing she was a prince she ought to be tried by her peers), then let her have such punishment as the extremity of the law will assign to such malefactors. The King presently made answer that in this case he might and would dispense with the law, and that the jury being once paneled they should take his word for sufficient evidence; otherwise he would make the proudest of them repent it. The noblemen, seeing the King in choler, were all whist.[52] But Bellaria, whose life then hung in the balance, fearing more perpetual infamy than momentary death, told the King if his fury might stand for a law that it were vain to have the jury yield their verdict; and therefore she fell down upon her knees and desired the King that for the love he bare to his young son Garinter, whom she brought into the world, that he would grant her a request, which was this: that it would please His

47 for as for **48 her stale countenance . . . coin** i.e., she would certainly not be honored by having her stale countenance reproduced on the royal coinage. (*Stale* suggests old, worn out, no longer attractive, and also whorelike.) **49 as** just as **50 bare** bore **51 upon choler** moved by anger **52 whist** silent

Majesty to send six of his noblemen whom he best trusted to the Isle of Delphos, there to inquire of the oracle of Apollo whether she had committed adultery with Egistus or conspired to poison him with Franion. And if the god Apollo, who by his divine essence knew all secrets, gave answer that she was guilty, she were content to suffer any torment, were it never so terrible. The request was so reasonable that Pandosto could not for shame deny it unless he would be counted of all his subjects more willful than wise. He therefore agreed that with as much speed as might be there should be certain ambassadors dispatched to the Isle of Delphos, and in the mean season[53] he commanded that his wife should be kept in close prison.

Bellaria, having obtained this grant, was now more careful[54] for her little babe that floated on the seas than sorrowful for her own mishap, for of that she doubted;[55] of herself she was assured, knowing if Apollo should give oracle according to the thoughts of the heart, yet the sentence should go on* her side, such was the clearness of her mind in this case. But Pandosto, whose suspicious head still remained in one song, chose out six of his nobility whom he knew were scarce indifferent[56] men in the Queen's behalf, and, providing all things fit for their journey, sent them to Delphos. They, willing to fulfill the King's command and desirous to see the situation and custom of the island, dispatched their affairs with as much speed as might be and embarked themselves to this voyage, which, the wind and weather serving fit for their purpose, was soon ended. For within three weeks they arrived at Delphos, where they were no sooner set on land but with great devotion they went to the temple of Apollo, and there, offering sacrifice to the god and gifts to the priest, as the custom was, they humbly craved an answer of their demand.

They had not long kneeled at the altar but Apollo with a loud voice said: "Bohemians, what you find behind the altar take, and depart." They, forthwith obeying the oracle, found a scroll of parchment wherein was written these words in letters of gold:

*__on__ one

53 mean season meantime **54 careful** worried **55 of that she doubted** i.e., she feared for the safety of her babe **56 indifferent** impartial

The Oracle

Suspicion is no proof; jealousy is an unequal judge. Bellaria is chaste, Egistus blameless, Franion a true subject, Pandosto treacherous, his babe an innocent; and the King shall live without an heir if that which is lost be not found.

As soon as they had taken out this scroll, the priest of the god commanded them that they should not presume to read it before they came in the presence of Pandosto unless they would incur the displeasure of Apollo. The Bohemian lords, carefully obeying his command, taking their leave of the priest with great reverence, departed out of the temple and went to their ships, and as soon as wind would permit them sailed toward Bohemia, whither in short time they safely arrived and, with great triumph issuing out of their ships, went to the King's palace, whom they found in his chamber accompanied with other noblemen.

Pandosto no sooner saw them but with a merry countenance he welcomed them home, asking what news. They told His Majesty that they had received an answer of the god written in a scroll, but with this charge, that they should not read the contents before they came in the presence of the King, and with that they delivered him the parchment. But his noblemen entreated him that, sith therein was contained either the safety of his wife's life and honesty or her death and perpetual infamy, that he would have his nobles and commons assembled in the judgment hall, where the Queen, brought in as prisoner, should hear the contents. If she were found guilty by the oracle of the god, then all should have cause to think his rigor proceeded of due desert; if Her Grace were found faultless, then she should be cleared before all, sith she had been accused openly. This pleased the King so that he appointed the day, and assembled all his lords and commons, and caused the Queen to be brought in before the judgment seat, commanding that the indictment should be read wherein she was accused of adultery with Egistus and of conspiracy with Franion. Bellaria, hearing the contents,[57] was no whit astonished, but made this cheerful answer:

57 the contents i.e., the King's command

"If the divine powers be privy to human actions—as no doubt they are—I hope my patience shall make fortune blush and my unspotted life shall stain spiteful* discredit.[58] For although lying report hath sought to appeach mine honor and suspicion hath intended to soil my credit with infamy, yet where virtue keepeth the fort, report and suspicion may assail but never sack.[59] How I have led my life before Egistus's coming, I appeal, Pandosto, to the gods and to thy conscience. What hath passed betwixt him and me the gods only know and I hope will presently reveal. That I loved Egistus I cannot deny; that I honored him I shame not to confess; to the one I was forced by his virtues, to the other for his dignities. But as touching lascivious lust, I say Egistus is honest, and hope myself to be found without spot. For Franion, I can neither accuse him nor excuse him, for I was not privy to his departure; and that this is true which I have here rehearsed[60] I refer myself to the divine oracle."

Bellaria had so sooner said but the King commanded that one of his dukes should read the contents of the scroll, which after the commons had heard they gave a great shout, rejoicing and clapping their hands that the Queen was clear of that false accusation. But the King, whose conscience was a witness against him of his witless fury and false suspected jealousy, was so ashamed of his rash folly that he entreated his nobles to persuade Bellaria to forgive and forget these injuries, promising not only to show himself a loyal and loving husband but also to reconcile himself to Egistus and Franion, revealing then before them all the cause of their secret flight and how treacherously he thought to have practiced his death if the good mind of his cupbearer had not prevented his purpose.

As thus he was relating the whole matter, there was word brought him that his young son Garinter was suddenly dead, which news so soon as Bellaria heard, surcharged before with* extreme joy and now suppressed with heavy sorrow, her vital spirits were so stopped that she fell down presently dead and could be never revived. This sudden sight so appalled the King's senses that he sank from his

***spiteful** spitefully ***with** which

58 shall stain spiteful discredit will eclipse spiteful slander **59 sack** plunder, despoil **60 rehearsed** recited, declared

seat in a swoon, so as he was fain[61] to be carried by his nobles to his palace, where he lay by the space of three days without speech. His commons were as men in despair, so diversely distressed. There was nothing but mourning and lamentation to be heard throughout all Bohemia—their young prince dead, their virtuous queen bereaved of her life, and their king and sovereign in great hazard. This tragical discourse of fortune so daunted them as[62] they went like shadows, not men; yet somewhat to comfort their heavy hearts, they heard that Pandosto was come to himself and had recovered his speech, who as in a fury brayed out[63] these bitter speeches:

"O miserable Pandosto! What surer witness than conscience! What thoughts more sour than suspicion! What plague more bad than jealousy! Unnatural actions offend the gods more than men, and causeless cruelty never scapes without revenge. I have committed such a bloody fact as repent I may but recall I cannot. Ah, jealousy! A hell to the mind and a horror to the conscience, suppressing reason and inciting rage; a worse passion than frenzy, a greater plague than madness. Are the gods just? Then let them revenge such brutish cruelty. My innocent babe I have drowned in the seas; my loving wife I have slain with slanderous suspicion; my trusty friend I have sought to betray, and yet the gods are slack to plague such offenses. Ah, unjust Apollo! Pandosto is the man that hath committed the fault; why should Garinter, silly[64] child, abide the pain? Well, sith the gods mean to prolong my days to increase my dolor, I will offer my guilty blood a sacrifice to those sackless[65] souls whose lives are lost by my rigorous folly."

And with that he reached at a rapier to have murdered himself, but his peers being present stayed him from such a bloody act, persuading him to think that the commonwealth consisted[66] on his safety and that those sheep could not but perish that wanted a shepherd; wishing that if he would not live for himself, yet he should have care of his subjects, and to put such fancies out of his mind, sith in sores past help salves do not heal but hurt, and in things past cure, care is a corrosive. With these and suchlike per-

61 fain obliged **62 as** that **63 brayed out** cried out **64 silly** innocent
65 sackless innocent **66 consisted** depended

suasions the King was overcome,[67] and began somewhat to quiet his mind; so that as soon as he could go abroad[68] he caused his wife to be embalmed and wrapped in lead with her young son Garinter; erecting a rich and famous sepulcher wherein he entombed them both, making such solemn obsequies at her funeral as all Bohemia might perceive he did greatly repent him of his forepassed folly; causing this epitaph to be engraven on her tomb in letters of gold:

The Epitaph

Here lies entombed Bellaria fair,
  Falsely accused to be unchaste,
Cleared by Apollo's sacred doom
  Yet slain by jealousy at last.
Whate'er thou be that passest by,
Curse him that caused this queen to die.

This epitaph being engraven, Pandosto would once a day repair to[69] the tomb and there with watery plaints[70] bewail his misfortune, coveting no other companion but sorrow nor no other harmony but repentance. But leaving him to his dolorous passions, at last let us come to show the tragical discourse of the young infant.

Who, being tossed with wind and wave, floated two whole days without succor, ready at every puff to be drowned in the sea, till at last the tempest ceased and the little boat was driven with the tide into the coast of Sicilia, where, sticking upon the sands, it rested. Fortune, minding to be wanton,[71] willing to show that as she hath wrinkles on her brows so she hath dimples in her cheeks, thought after so many sour looks to lend a feigned smile, and, after a puffing storm to bring a pretty calm, she began thus to dally. It fortuned a poor mercenary[72] shepherd that dwelled in Sicilia, who got his living by other men's flocks, missed one of his sheep, and, thinking it had strayed into the covert[73] that was hard by, sought very diligently to find that which he could not see, fearing either that the wolves or eagles had undone him (for he was so poor as a sheep was half his substance), wandered down toward the sea cliffs to see if perchance the

67 overcome prevailed upon **68 abroad** out of doors, freely about
69 repair to visit **70 watery plaints** tearful laments **71 minding to be wanton** of a mind to be fickle and playful **72 mercenary** working for wages **73 covert** sheltered spot

sheep was browsing on the sea ivy, whereon they greatly do feed; but not finding her there, as he was ready to return to his flock he heard a child cry, but knowing there was no house near, he thought he had mistaken the sound and that it was the bleating of his sheep. Wherefore, looking more narrowly, as he cast his eye to the sea he spied a little boat, from whence, as he attentively listened, he might hear the cry to come. Standing a good while in a maze,[74] at last he went to the shore and, wading to the boat, as he looked in he saw the little babe lying all alone, ready to die for hunger and cold, wrapped in a mantle of scarlet richly embroidered with gold and having a chain about the neck.

The shepherd, who before had never seen so fair a babe nor so rich jewels, thought assuredly that it was some little god, and began with great devotion to knock on his breast. The babe, who writhed with the head to seek for the pap,[75] began again to cry afresh, whereby the poor man knew that it was a child which by some sinister means was driven thither by distress of weather; marveling how such a silly[76] infant, which by the mantle and the chain could not be but born of noble parentage, should be so hardly crossed[77] with deadly mishap. The poor shepherd, perplexed thus with divers thoughts, took pity of the child and determined with himself to carry it to the King, that there it might be brought up according to the worthiness of birth, for his ability could not afford to foster it, though his good mind was willing to further it. Taking therefore the child in his arms, as he folded the mantle together the better to defend it from cold there fell down at his foot a very fair and rich purse wherein he found a great sum of gold, which sight so revived the shepherd's spirits as he was greatly ravished with joy and daunted with fear—joyful to see such a sum in his power, and fearful, if it should be known, that it might breed his further danger. Necessity wished him at the least to retain the gold, though he would not keep the child; the simplicity of* his conscience feared him from [78] such deceitful bribery. Thus was the poor man perplexed with a doubtful dilemma, until at last the covetousness of the coin overcame him; for what will not the greedy desire of gold

*of if

74 maze state of bewilderment **75 pap** breast **76 a silly** an innocent
77 crossed thwarted **78 feared him from** made him frightened of

cause a man to do? So that he was resolved in himself to foster the child and with the sum to relieve his want.

Resting thus resolute in this point, he left seeking of his sheep and, as covertly and secretly as he could, went by a byway to his house, lest any of his neighbors should perceive his carriage.[79] As soon as he was got home, entering in at the door, the child began to cry, which his wife hearing, and seeing her husband with a young babe in his arms, began to be somewhat jealous, yet marveling that her husband should be so wanton abroad sith he was so quiet at home. But, as women are naturally given to believe the worst, so his wife, thinking it was some bastard, began to crow against her goodman,[80] and taking up a cudgel (for the most master went breechless)[81] sware solemnly that she would make clubs trumps[82] if he brought any bastard brat within her doors. The goodman, seeing his wife in her majesty with her mace in her hand, thought it was time to bow for fear of blows, and desired her to be quiet, for there was none such matter; but if she could hold her peace they were made forever. And with that he told her the whole matter, how he had found the child in a little boat without any succor, wrapped in that costly mantle and having that rich chain about the neck. But at last, when he showed her the purse full of gold, she began to simper something sweetly, and, taking her husband about the neck, kissed him after her homely fashion, saying that she hoped God had seen their want and now meant to relieve their poverty, and, seeing they could get no children, had sent them this little babe to be their heir. "Take heed, in any case," quoth the shepherd, "that you be secret and blab it not out when you meet with your gossips, for, if you do, we are like[83] not only to lose the gold and jewels, but our other goods and lives." "Tush," quoth his wife, "profit is a good hatch before the door.[84] Fear not, I have other things to talk of than of this.

79 his carriage what he was carrying **80 goodman** husband **81 the most master went breechless** i.e., the person holding mastery in this household was not he who nominally wore the breeches **82 she would make clubs trumps** i.e., she would beat him with a club (playing on the metaphor of a card game) **83 like** likely **84 profit . . . door** ("To keep or set a hatch before the door" is proverbial for keeping silent. A *hatch* is a lower half-door that can be closed when the upper half is open.)

But, I pray you, let us lay up the money surely and the jewels, lest by any mishap it be spied."

[The child Fawnia, as she is named, cared for by her foster parents Porrus and Mopsa, becomes in time a beautiful young shepherdess of sixteen, sought after by many a rich farmer's son. Decked in garlands of flowers, she seems "to be the goddess Flora herself for beauty." Meantime, Egistus's only son, Dorastus, a handsome young prince of about twenty, angers his father by showing a reluctance to marry; without directly challenging his father's authority, he makes it plain that he has no taste for a marriage proposed with the daughter of the King of Denmark. When, soon afterward, Dorastus happens to encounter Fawnia, his attitude toward love and marriage is suddenly changed.]

It happened not long after this that there was a meeting of all the farmers' daughters in Sicilia, whither Fawnia was also bidden as the mistress of the feast, who, having attired herself in her best garments, went among the rest of her companions to the merry meeting, there spending the day in such homely pastimes as shepherds use. As the evening grew on and their sports ceased, each taking their leave at other, Fawnia, desiring one of her companions to bear her company, went home by the flock to see if they were well folded.[85] And as they returned it fortuned that Dorastus, who all that day had been hawking and killed store[86] of game, encountered by the way these two maids, and, casting his eye suddenly on Fawnia, he was half afraid, fearing that with Actaeon[87] he had seen Diana, for he thought such exquisite perfection could not be found in any mortal creature. As thus he stood in a maze, one of his pages told him that the maid with the garland on her head was Fawnia, the fair shepherd whose beauty was so much talked of in the court. Dorastus, desirous to see if nature had adorned her mind with any inward qualities, as she had decked her body

85 folded put into their folds or pens **86 store** a plentiful supply
87 Actaeon a hunter in Greek mythology who, because he affronted Diana, the goddess of the hunt and of virginity, by intruding on her bathing or by boasting of his skill in hunting, was changed into a stag and torn to pieces by his own hounds

with outward shape, began to question with her whose daughter she was, of what age, and how she had been trained up. Who answered him with such modest reverence and sharpness of wit that Dorastus thought her outward beauty was but a counterfeit to darken her inward qualities, wondering how so courtly behavior could be found in so simple a cottage, and cursing fortune that had shadowed wit and beauty with such hard fortune.

As thus he held her a long while with chat, Beauty, seeing him at discovert,[88] thought not to lose the vantage, but struck him so deeply with an envenomed shaft as[89] he wholly lost his liberty and became a slave to love which[90] before contemned love, glad now to gaze on a poor shepherd, who before refused the offer of a rich princess. For the perfection of Fawnia had so fired his fancy as he felt his mind greatly changed and his affections altered, cursing Love that had wrought such a change and blaming the baseness of his mind that would make such a choice; but, thinking these were but passionate toys[91] that might be thrust out at pleasure, to avoid the siren that enchanted him he put spurs to his horse and bade this fair shepherd farewell.

[Fawnia too perceives the effects of passion in herself and resolves to resist, though to no effect; she is sleepless and unable to think of anyone else but him, yet painfully aware how much Dorastus is above her in social station. Dorastus for his part is distressed to think that he loves one of such low degree and so unfit for his princely fortunes, but comes around to the view that the gods themselves do not disdain to love mortal women. "Phoebus liked Sibylla, Jupiter Io, and why not I then Fawnia?" Seeking her out in the fields, he strikes up a conversation by asking her what pleasures can possibly be found in the life of a shepherd, to which Fawnia answers with a defense of humble contentment and quiet. She sternly refuses his suggestion that she change her fortune for that of a courtly mistress, and insists that she can love Dorastus only if he becomes a shepherd.

Driven by his passion, he at length adopts her suggestion and visits her in shepherd's apparel, wryly smiling to him-

88 at discovert in an exposed position. (A hunting term.) **89 as** that
90 which (he) who **91 passionate toys** trifling passions

self at his low transformation. She is wary at first of a mere outward show of devotion, but is soon convinced by Dorastus's solemn protestations to accept and reciprocate his love. They plight their troth to each other and resolve to elope into Italy where they can live a contented life "until such time as either he could be reconciled to his father or else by succession come to the kingdom." For the time being, however, he continues to visit her in disguise as she tends her flocks, doing so with such frequency that the neighbors (who see through the disguise) begin to wonder at it and tell old Porrus what they have seen. Porrus, distraught, informs his wife that their daughter is keeping company with the King's son and is sure to lose her virginity as a result. He fears that the King will not be pleased with them if Dorastus gets Fawnia with child, and so resolves on a plan that will neither offend the King nor displease Dorastus.]

"I mean to take the chain and the jewels that I found with Fawnia and carry them to the King, letting him then to understand how she is none of my daughter, but that I found her beaten up with the water,[92] alone in a little boat, wrapped in a rich mantle wherein was enclosed this treasure. By this means, I hope the King will take Fawnia into his service, and we, whatsoever chanceth, shall be blameless." This device pleased the goodwife very well, so that they determined, as soon as they might know the King at leisure, to make him privy to this case.[93]

In the meantime, Dorastus was not slack in his affairs, but applied his matters with such diligence that he provided all things fit for their journey. Treasure and jewels he had gotten great store, thinking there was no better friend than money in a strange country. Rich attire he had provided for Fawnia, and, because he could not bring the matter to pass without the help and advice of someone, he made an old servant of his, called Capnio, who had served him from his childhood, privy to his affairs; who, seeing no persuasions could prevail to divert him from his settled determination, gave his consent, and dealt so secretly in the

92 beaten up with the water i.e., driven onto shore by the storm
93 make him . . . case disclose everything of the matter to him

cause that within short space he had gotten a ship ready for their passage. The mariners, seeing a fit gale of wind for their purpose, wished Capnio to make no delays, lest, if they pretermitted[94] this good weather, they might stay long ere they had such a fair wind. Capnio, fearing that his negligence should hinder the journey, in the nighttime conveyed the trunks full of treasure into the ship, and by secret means let Fawnia understand that the next morning they meant to depart.

She, upon this news, slept very little that night, but got up very early and went to her sheep, looking every minute when she should see Dorastus, who tarried not long for fear delay might breed danger, but came as fast as he could gallop and without any great circumstance[95] took Fawnia up behind him and rode to the haven where the ship lay, which was not three quarters of a mile distant from that place. He no sooner came there but the mariners were ready with their cockboat to set them aboard, where, being couched[96] together in a cabin, they passed away the time in recounting their old loves till their man Capnio should come.

Porrus, who had heard that this morning the King would go abroad to take the air, called in haste to his wife to bring him his holiday hose[97] and his best jacket, that he might go, like an honest substantial man, to tell his tale. His wife, a good cleanly wench, brought him all things fit, and sponged him up very handsomely, giving him the chain* and jewels in a little box, which Porrus, for the more safety, put in his bosom. Having thus all his trinkets in a readiness, taking his staff in his hand he bade his wife kiss him for good luck, and so he went towards the palace. But, as he was going, fortune, who meant to show him a little false play, prevented his purpose in this wise.

He met by chance in his way Capnio, who, trudging as fast as he could with a little coffer under his arm to the ship, and spying Porrus, whom he knew to be Fawnia's father, going towards the palace, being a wily fellow, began to doubt the worst, and therefore crossed him by* the way[98] and asked him whither he was going so early this morning.

***chain** chaines ***by** [omitted in Q1–Q3]

94 pretermitted failed to make use of **95 circumstance** ado
96 couched lodged **97 hose** trousers **98 crossed him by the way** intercepted him in his path

Porrus, who knew by his face that he was one of the court, meaning simply,[99] told him that the King's son Dorastus dealt hardly with him, for he had but one daughter who was a little beautiful, and that his neighbors told him the young Prince had allured her to folly. He went therefore now to complain to the King how greatly he was abused.

Capnio, who straightway smelt the whole matter, began to soothe* him in his talk, and said that Dorastus dealt not like a prince to spoil[100] any poor man's daughter in that sort. He therefore would do the best for him he could, because he knew he was an honest man. "But," quoth Capnio, "you lose your labor in going to the palace, for the King means this day to take the air of the sea and to go aboard of a ship that lies in the haven. I am going before, you see, to provide all things in a readiness, and, if you will follow my counsel, turn back with me to the haven, where I will set you in such a fit place as you may speak to the King at your pleasure." Porrus, giving credit to[101] Capnio's smooth tale, gave him a thousand thanks for his friendly advice and went with him to the haven, making all the way his complaints of Dorastus, yet concealing secretly the chain and the jewels. As soon as they were come to the seaside, the mariners, seeing Capnio, came aland with their cockboat, who,[102] still dissembling the matter, demanded of Porrus if he would go see the ship, who, unwilling and fearing the worst, because he was not well acquainted with Capnio, made his excuse that he could not brook the sea, therefore would not trouble him.

Capnio, seeing that by fair means he could not get him aboard, commanded the mariners that by violence they should carry him into the ship; who, like sturdy knaves, hoisted the poor shepherd on their backs and, bearing him to the boat, launched from the land.

Porrus, seeing himself so cunningly betrayed, durst not cry out, for he saw it would not prevail, but began to entreat Capnio and the mariners to be good to him and to pity his estate: he was but a poor man that lived by his labor. They, laughing to see the shepherd so afraid, made as much haste as they could and set him aboard. Porrus was no sooner in

*soothe soth

99 meaning simply speaking with innocent intent **100 spoil** despoil
101 giving credit to believing **102 who** i.e., Capnio

the ship but he saw Dorastus walking with Fawnia; yet he scarce knew her, for she had attired herself in rich apparel, which so increased her beauty that she resembled rather an angel than a mortal creature.

Dorastus and Fawnia were half astonished to see the old shepherd, marveling greatly what wind had brought him thither, till Capnio told them all the whole discourse—how Porrus was going to make his complaint to the King if by policy he had not prevented him—and therefore now, sith he was aboard, for the avoiding of further danger it were best to carry him into Italy.

Dorastus praised greatly his man's device and allowed of[103] his counsel; but Fawnia, who still feared[104] Porrus as her father, began to blush for shame that by her means he should either incur danger or displeasure.

The old shepherd, hearing this hard sentence, that he should on such a sudden be carried from his wife, his country, and kinsfolk into a foreign land amongst strangers, began with bitter tears to make his complaint, and on his knees to entreat Dorastus that, pardoning his unadvised[105] folly, he would give him leave to go home, swearing that he would keep all things as secret as they could wish. But these protestations could not prevail, although Fawnia entreated Dorastus very earnestly; but the mariners, hoisting their mainsails, weighed anchors and haled[106] into the deep, where we leave them to the favor of the wind and seas, and return to Egistus.

[Egistus discovers that his son is missing and sends out troops to search for him everywhere. They learn from a fisherman that Dorastus and Fawnia have taken ship along with Capnio and old Porrus. Porrus's wife, Mopsa, being sent for, tells of her husband's intention to tell the King of Fawnia's remarkable history because of his worry about Dorastus's overly great familiarity with Fawnia, and of Porrus's subsequent strange disappearance. Egistus falls ill with vexation and worry. Meantime Dorastus's ship weathers a severe storm and reaches the shore of Bohemia.]

103 allowed of commended, approved **104 feared** held in reverence and awe **105 unadvised** ill-considered **106 haled** proceeded under sail

Dorastus, hearing that they were arrived at some harbor, sweetly kissed Fawnia and bade her be of good cheer. When they told him that the port belonged unto the chief city of Bohemia, where Pandosto kept his court, Dorastus began to be sad, knowing that his father hated no man so much as Pandosto, and that the King himself had sought secretly to betray Egistus. This considered, he was half afraid to go on land, but that Capnio counseled him to change his name and his country until such time as they could get some other bark to transport them into Italy. Dorastus, liking this device, made his case privy to[107] the mariners, rewarding them bountifully for their pains and charging them to say that he was a gentleman of Trapolonia called Meleagrus. The shipmen, willing to show what friendship they could to Dorastus, promised to be as secret as they could or he might wish; and upon this they landed in a little village a mile distant from the city, where, after they had rested a day, thinking to make provision for their marriage, the fame of Fawnia's beauty was spread throughout all the city, so that it came to the ear of Pandosto who, then being about the age of fifty, had, notwithstanding, young and fresh affections, so that he desired greatly to see Fawnia. And, to bring this matter the better to pass, hearing they had but one man,[108] and how they rested at a very homely house,[109] he caused them to be apprehended as spies, and sent a dozen of his guard to take them. Who,[110] being come to their lodging, told them the King's message. Dorastus, no whit dismayed, accompanied with Fawnia and Capnio, went to the court (for they left Porrus to keep the stuff), who, being admitted to the King's presence, Dorastus and Fawnia with humble obeisance saluted His Majesty.

Pandosto, amazed at the singular perfection of Fawnia, stood half astonished, viewing her beauty, so that he had almost forgot himself what he had to do. At last with stern countenance he demanded their names and of what country they were and what caused them to land in Bohemia. "Sir," quoth Dorastus, "know that my name Meleagrus is, a knight born and brought up in Trapolonia, and this gentle-

107 made his case privy to divulged his secret situation to **108 man** servant **109 rested . . . house** stayed at a very humble house **110 Who** i.e., the guard

woman, whom I mean to take to my wife, is an Italian, born in Padua, from whence I have now brought her. The cause I have so small a train with me is for that, her friends unwilling to consent, I intended secretly to convey her into Trapolonia; whither, as I was sailing, by distress of weather I was driven into these coasts. Thus have you heard my name, my country, and the cause of my voyage."

Pandosto, starting from his seat as one in choler,[111] made this rough reply: "Meleagrus, I fear this smooth tale hath but small truth, and that thou coverest a foul skin with fair paintings. No doubt, this lady by her grace and beauty is of her degree more meet for a mighty prince than for a simple knight, and thou, like a perjured traitor, hast bereft her of her parents, to their present grief and her ensuing sorrow. Till, therefore, I hear more of her parentage and of thy calling I will stay[112] you both here in Bohemia."

Dorastus, in whom rested nothing but kingly valor,[113] was not able to suffer the reproaches of Pandosto but that he made him this answer: "It is not meet for a king, without due proof, to appeach[114] any man of ill behavior, nor, upon suspicion, to infer belief.[115] Strangers ought to be entertained with courtesy, not to be entreated with cruelty, lest, being forced by want to put up injuries,[116] the gods revenge their cause with rigor."

Pandosto, hearing Dorastus utter these words, commanded that he should straight be committed to prison until such time as they heard further of his pleasure; but as for Fawnia, he charged that she should be entertained[117] in the court with such courtesy as belonged to a stranger and her calling. The rest of the shipmen he put into the dungeon.

Having thus hardly[118] handled the supposed Trapolonians, Pandosto, contrary to his aged years, began to be somewhat tickled with the beauty of Fawnia, insomuch that he could take no rest, but cast in his old head a thousand new devices.

111 as one in choler like one who is angry **112 stay** keep **113 in whom . . . valor** i.e., who was nothing if not royally valiant
114 appeach accuse **115 upon . . . belief** upon mere suspicion to believe him guilty **116 lest . . . injuries** lest, those strangers being forced by their necessity to endure insults and injurious treatment
117 entertained welcomed, received **118 hardly** harshly

[The King is chagrined to find himself the victim of love's passion at his advanced age. He is loath to crave the love of another man's "concubine" and to lust after a woman who is in his custody, but he cannot resist Fawnia's beauty. Encountering her one day in a park adjoining his house, he woos her to forsake Meleagrus and perseveres when she refuses, "seeking with fair words and great promises to scale the fort of her chastity" and offering to free Meleagrus if she consents. Alone, she bewails her misfortune, while Dorastus, confined to his prison, is no less loud in his laments. Pandosto assails Fawnia once more, first with fair speeches and then with unveiled threats of force.]

While thus these two lovers[119] strove, the one to win love, the other to live in hate, Egistus heard certain news by merchants of Bohemia that his son Dorastus was imprisoned by Pandosto, which made him fear greatly that his son should be but hardly entreated.[120] Yet considering that Bellaria and he was cleared by the oracle of Apollo from that crime wherewith Pandosto had unjustly charged them, he thought best to send with all speed to Pandosto that he should set free his son Dorastus and put to death Fawnia and her father Porrus. Finding this by the advice of counsel the speediest remedy to release his son, he caused presently two of his ships to be rigged and thoroughly furnished with provision of men and victuals, and sent divers of his nobles ambassadors into Bohemia; who, willing to obey their king and receive[121] their young prince, made no delays for fear of danger, but with as much speed as might be, sailed towards Bohemia. The wind and seas favored them greatly, which made them hope of some good hap, for within three days they were landed; which Pandosto no sooner heard of their arrival but he in person went to meet them, entreating[122] them with such sumptuous and familiar courtesy that they might well perceive how sorry he was for the former injuries he had offered to their king and how willing, if it might be, to make amends.

As Pandosto made report to them how one Meleagrus, a

119 two lovers i.e., Pandosto, in love with Fawnia, and Fawnia, in love with Dorastus **120 entreated** treated **121 receive** recover **122 entreating** treating

knight of Trapolonia, was lately arrived with a lady, called Fawnia, in his land, coming very suspiciously, accompanied only with one servant and an old shepherd, the ambassadors perceived by the half what the whole tale meant, and began to conjecture that it was Dorastus, who, for fear to be known, had changed his name. But, dissembling the matter, they shortly arrived at the court, where, after they had been very solemnly[123] and sumptuously feasted, the noblemen of Sicilia being gathered together, they made report of their embassage, where they certified Pandosto that Meleagrus was son and heir to the King Egistus and that his name was Dorastus; how, contrary to the King's mind, he had privily conveyed away that Fawnia, intending to marry her, being but daughter to that poor shepherd Porrus; whereupon, the King's request was that Capnio, Fawnia, and Porrus might be murdered and put to death and that his son Dorastus might be sent home in safety.

Pandosto, having attentively and with great marvel heard their embassage, willing to reconcile himself to Egistus and to show him how greatly he esteemed his favor,* although love and fancy[124] forbade him to hurt Fawnia, yet in despite of love he determined to execute Egistus's will without mercy. And therefore he presently[125] sent for Dorastus out of prison, who, marveling at this unlooked-for courtesy, found at his coming to the King's presence that which he least doubted of,[126] his father's ambassadors; who no sooner saw him but with great reverence they honored him, and Pandosto, embracing Dorastus, set him by him very lovingly in a chair of estate.

Dorastus, ashamed that his folly was bewrayed,[127] sat a long time as one in a muse, till Pandosto told him the sum of his father's embassage; which he had no sooner heard but he was touched at the quick for the cruel sentence that was pronounced against Fawnia. But neither could his sorrow nor persuasions prevail, for Pandosto commanded that Fawnia, Porrus, and Capnio should be brought to his presence; who were no sooner come but Pandosto, having his former love turned to a disdainful hate, began to rage against Fawnia in these terms:

*__favor__ labour

123 solemnly ceremoniously **124 fancy** amorous passion
125 presently immediately **126 doubted of** feared, suspected
127 bewrayed revealed

"Thou disdainful vassal, thou currish kite, assigned by the destinies to base fortune, and yet with an aspiring mind gazing after honor, how durst thou presume, being a beggar, to match with a prince? By thy alluring looks to enchant the son of a king to leave his own country to fulfill thy disordinate lusts? O despiteful mind! A proud heart in a beggar is not unlike to a great fire in a small cottage, which warmeth not the house but burneth it. Assure thyself thou shalt die. And thou, old doting fool, whose folly hath been such as to suffer thy daughter to reach above thy fortune, look for no other meed[128] but the like punishment. But Capnio, thou which hast betrayed the King and hast consented to the unlawful lust of thy lord and master, I know not how justly I may plague thee. Death is too easy a punishment for thy falsehood, and to live, if not in extreme misery, were not to show thee equity. I therefore award that thou shalt* have thine eyes put out, and continually till* thou diest grind in a mill like a brute beast." The fear of death brought a sorrowful silence upon Fawnia and Capnio, but Porrus, seeing no hope of life, burst forth into these speeches:

"Pandosto, and ye noble ambassadors of Sicilia, seeing without cause I am condemned to die, I am yet glad I have opportunity to disburden my conscience before my death. I will tell you as much as I know, and yet no more than is true. Whereas I am accused that I have been a supporter of Fawnia's pride, and she disdained as a vile beggar, so it is that I am neither father unto her nor she daughter unto me. For so it happened that I, being a poor shepherd in Sicilia living by keeping other* men's flocks, one of my sheep straying down to the seaside, as I went to seek her I saw a little boat driven upon the shore wherein I found a babe of six days old, wrapped in a mantle of scarlet, having about the neck this chain. I, pitying the child and desirous of the treasure, carried it home to my wife, who with great care nursed it up and set it to keep sheep. Here is the chain and the jewels, and this Fawnia is the child whom I found in the boat. What she is or of what parentage I know not, but this I am assured, that she is none of mine."

Pandosto would scarce suffer him to tell out his tale but that he inquired the time of the year, the manner of the

***shalt** shall   ***till** while   ***other** others

128 meed reward

boat, and other circumstances; which when he found agreeing to his count,[129] he suddenly leapt from his seat and kissed Fawnia, wetting her tender cheeks with his tears and crying, "My daughter Fawnia! Ah, sweet Fawnia! I am thy father, Fawnia." This sudden passion of the King drave them all into a maze, especially Fawnia and Dorastus. But when the King had breathed himself awhile in this new joy, he rehearsed[130] before the ambassadors the whole matter, how he had entreated[131] his wife Bellaria for jealousy, and that this was the child whom he sent to float in the seas.

Fawnia was not more joyful that she had found such a father than Dorastus was glad he should get such a wife. The ambassadors rejoiced that their young prince had made such a choice, that those kingdoms, which through enmity had long time been dissevered, should now through perpetual amity be united and reconciled. The citizens and subjects of Bohemia, hearing that the King had found again his daughter which was supposed dead, joyful that there was an heir apparent to his kingdom, made bonfires and shows throughout the city. The courtiers and knights appointed jousts and tourneys to signify their willing minds in gratifying the King's hap.[132]

Eighteen days being passed in these princely sports, Pandosto, willing to recompense old Porrus, of[133] a shepherd made him a knight; which done, providing a sufficient navy to receive[134] him and his retinue, accompanied with Dorastus, Fawnia, and the Sicilian ambassadors, he sailed towards Sicilia, where he was most princely entertained by Egistus, who, hearing this comical[135] event, rejoiced greatly at his son's good hap, and without delay, to the perpetual joy of the two young lovers, celebrated the marriage. Which was no sooner ended but Pandosto, calling to mind how first he betrayed his friend Egistus, how his jealousy was the cause of Bellaria's death, that contrary to the law of nature he had lusted after his own daughter, moved with these desperate thoughts he fell into a melancholy fit and,

129 count account **130 rehearsed** recited, told **131 entreated** treated **132 hap** (good) fortune **133 of** from being **134 receive** hold **135 comical** ending happily, joyful to close up the comedy with a tragical stratagem,[136] he slew himself; whose death being many days bewailed of Fawnia, Dorastus, and his dear friend Egistus, Dorastus, taking his leave of his father, went with his wife and the dead corpse into Bohemia, where, after they[137] were sumptuously entombed, Dorastus ended his days in contented quiet.

Robert Greene's *Pandosto: The Triumph of Time* was published in London in 1588 (Q1), printed by Thomas Orwin for Thomas Cadman, with the running title *The History of Dorastus and Fawnia.*

A second quarto (Q2) appeared in 1592 and a third (Q3) in 1595, each a reprint of the previous. The present edition, somewhat abbreviated, is based on the first quarto. Although Shakespeare may have read one of the later quartos, the differences between the 1588 text and those of 1592 and 1595 are minor and appear to be entirely compositorial. Shakespeare appears not to have used the edition of 1607, in which Apollo's oracle reads, "the King shall die without an heir" instead of, as in the earlier texts, "the King shall live without an heir." Gathering B of the 1588 quarto is missing, and for this material the second quarto serves as the copy text; this affects the textual notes below on pp. 472 and 474.

136 stratagem device **137 they** i.e., Pandosto's remains

Further Reading

Bartholomeusz, Dennis. *"The Winter's Tale" in Performance in England and America, 1611–1976*. Cambridge and New York: Cambridge Univ. Press, 1982. Focusing on changing standards of stagecraft and fidelity to the text, Bartholomeusz's stage history traces the play in performance from its appearance on the "open stage at Whitehall" in 1611 to a production directed by John Barton and Trevor Nunn at Stratford-upon-Avon in 1976.

Draper, R. P. *"The Winter's Tale": Text and Performance*. London: Macmillan, 1985. Draper's monograph provides both an account of the rhythm and structure of the play and a consideration of four distinctive modern productions: the Royal Shakespeare Company's in 1969, 1976, and 1981, and the BBC television version directed by Jane Howell in 1980.

Egan, Robert. " 'The Art Itself Is Nature': *The Winter's Tale*." *Drama Within Drama: Shakespeare's Sense of His Art*. New York: Columbia Univ. Press, 1975. Exploring the relationship of dramatic art to the reality of experience, Egan argues that in *The Winter's Tale* Shakespeare recognizes the efficacy of drama as an agent of belief. Camillo's staging of Perdita's return and Paulina's staging of Hermione's restoration provide models of Shakespeare's own artistry that similarly work to compel faith.

Erickson, Peter. "The Limitations of Reformed Masculinity in *The Winter's Tale*." *Patriarchal Structures in Shakespeare's Drama*. Berkeley, Calif.: Univ. of California Press, 1985. Erickson sees culturally determined notions of gender shaping the action of a play that traces the replacement of a tyrannical patriarchy with a benign version capable of "including and valuing women." Nonetheless, while the regenerative movement of the play depends upon the mediation of women, their efforts can only repair, not replace, the patriarchal body politic that still insists upon "restrictive definitions of gender."

Ewbank, Inga-Stina. "The Triumph of Time in *The Winter's Tale*." *Review of English Literature* 5.2 (1964): 83–100.

Rpt. in *Shakespeare's Later Comedies: An Anthology of Modern Criticism,* ed. D. J. Palmer, Baltimore.: Penguin, 1971. Ewbank explores the ways in which the action, structure, and poetry of *The Winter's Tale* work to communicate a vital engagement with "the theme of time and change." The Chorus doesn't merely signal time's passage but serves as a "pivotal image of the Triumph of Time" in a play that resists the simplifications of conventional understanding of time "as either Revealer or Destroyer."

Felperin, Howard. " 'Tongue-tied Our Queen?': The Deconstruction of Presence in *The Winter's Tale.*" In *Shakespeare and the Question of Theory,* ed. Patricia Parker and Geoffrey Hartman. New York and London: Methuen, 1985. Felperin considers Leontes's charge of Hermione's infidelity and finds that, though we have "oracular proof" to discredit it, the jealous passion is not quite "so flimsy and fanciful" as is often assumed. Felperin's point is not to indict Hermione but to indicate how much in the play depends only upon unverifiable interpretation—by characters, audiences, and actors—of what is not represented. Through the insistent "interpretive uncertainty," the play engages "the fallen and irredeemable nature of language as a medium for defining human reality."

Foakes, R. A. "Shakespeare's Last Plays." *Shakespeare, the Dark Comedies to the Last Plays: From Satire to Celebration,* pp. 118–144. Charlottesville, Va.: Univ. Press of Virginia, 1971. The sudden and unmotivated quality of events in the play leads Foakes to see it as "a series of strange actions under an uncertain providence." He argues that finally the play is "optimistic," testifying to the benevolent purposiveness of the gods, but "it is also clear-sighted," revealing the terrifying fears and devastating losses that afflict human beings.

Frey, Charles. *Shakespeare's Vast Romance: A Study of "The Winter's Tale."* Columbia, Mo.: Univ. of Missouri Press, 1980. Believing the play unusually resistant to analysis, Frey takes a tripartite approach to "the paradoxical amalgam of coherence and vastness" at the heart of *The Winter's Tale:* first he examines theatrical and critical responses to the play, then considers various literary sources of its technique and vision, and finally he traces the play's strategies of control that lead an audience from its own isolated existence to a world of communal faith.

Frye, Northrop. "Recognition in *The Winter's Tale.*" In *Essays on Shakespeare and Elizabethan Drama in Honor of Hardin Craig,* ed. Richard Hosley. Columbia, Mo.: Univ. of Missouri Press, 1962. Rpt. in *Shakespeare's Later Comedies: An Anthology of Modern Criticism,* ed. D. J. Palmer. Baltimore: Penguin, 1971. Frye finds in the structure of the play, especially in its "double recognition scene," evidence that art itself is "part of the regenerating power of the play." The art manifested in *The Winter's Tale,* however, is not opposed to nature nor merely imitative of it, but rather belongs to its unfallen aspect and participates in its renewing powers.

Gourlay, Patricia Southard. " 'O My Most Sacred Lady': Female Metaphor in *The Winter's Tale.*" *English Literary Renaissance* 5 (1975): 375–395. Examining the roles of Hermione, Paulina, and Perdita, Gourlay traces the anxieties and hostilities that the women arouse in the play and also their creative and consoling actions. She concludes that "the women in the play embody those ambiguities of Leontes's own nature which he has feared and despised, but without which his masculine world is a wasteland."

Hartwig, Joan. "*The Winter's Tale:* 'The Pleasure of that Madness.' " *Shakespeare's Tragicomic Vision.* Baton Rouge, La.: Louisiana State Univ. Press, 1972. Focusing on the contradictions revealed in characterization, tone, and structure, Hartwig considers the "profound dislocation of fixed perceptions which Shakespeare's tragicomedy produces." The play works to suspend logic and rationality in both its characters and audience, permitting their recognition of a world of grace and wonder beyond "the limits of human possibility."

Hunter, R. G. *"The Winter's Tale." Shakespeare and the Comedy of Forgiveness.* New York: Columbia Univ. Press, 1965. Hunter sees *The Winter's Tale* as a mature example of Shakespeare's "comedy of forgiveness" in which erring humankind repents, is forgiven its sin, and is permitted to reenter an order of grace. The revelation of

Hermione testifies to Leontes's regeneration, miraculously erasing the consequence of his sin; but Mamillius remains dead, reminding Leontes and the audience that "happiness and misery, 'both joy and terror,' are human possibilities."

Matchett, William H. "Some Dramatic Techniques in *The Winter's Tale.*" *Shakespeare Survey* 22 (1969): 93–108. Focusing on the scenes of Leontes's jealousy, Antigonus's death, and the animation of the statue, Matchett examines Shakespeare's mature stagecraft, exploring "the range of Shakespeare's final control over audience response."

McDonald, Russ. "Poetry and Plot in *The Winter's Tale.*" *Shakespeare Quarterly* 36 (1985): 315–329. McDonald locates "the sources and functions" of the play's stylistic complexity in a tragicomic vision that generates "both story and style." In the play's characteristically convoluted speeches that become intelligible "only in their final clauses or movements" McDonald finds a parallel to the play world itself that only belatedly "rewards bewildered characters and spectators with understanding and happiness."

Pyle, Fitzroy. *"The Winter's Tale": A Commentary on the Structure.* New York: Barnes and Noble, 1969. Pyle, in a scene-by-scene comparison of the play with its source (Robert Greene's *Pandosto*), is concerned with the "beauty of the plotting" of *The Winter's Tale.* He resists seeing the play as a representation of divine agency, finding, rather, that it attests to the "miraculous power of the human spirit, rightly directed, to achieve the impossible."

Schanzer, Ernest. "The Structural Pattern of *The Winter's Tale.*" *Review of English Literature* 5.2 (1964): 72–82. Rpt. in *Shakespeare: A Casebook, "The Winter's Tale,"* ed. Kenneth Muir. London: Macmillan, 1968. Schanzer analyzes the shape of the play, observing that it splits into two carefully paralleled halves. Each begins with a prose scene that focuses on a harmonious relationship about to be disrupted, and each ends with a public scene fixing our attention on Hermione. These repetitions are accentuated by the Chorus, who divides the play and, in the image of the turning hourglass, "enhances our sense of the similarity of the shape and structure of the two halves."

Tayler, Edward William. "Shakespeare's *The Winter's Tale.*" *Nature and Art in Renaissance Literature.* New York: Columbia Univ. Press, 1964. Tayler focuses on the conventional division between Nature and Art as it is reflected in the language and structure of the play. The opposition of the two terms, most fully elaborated in the exchange between Florizel and Perdita in Act 4, provides Shakespeare with a means of focusing a series of ethical and social concerns, but in the final scene it "dissolves in the pageantry of the statue's descent."

Wickham, Glynne. "Romance and Emblem: A Study in the Dramatic Structure of *The Winter's Tale.*" In *The Elizabethan Theatre III,* ed. David Galloway. Hamden, Conn.: Archon, 1973. Wickham suggests that Shakespeare wrote *The Winter's Tale* with a particular event in mind: the investiture of the Prince of Wales in 1610. In adapting popular romance themes of reunion and renewal to the specific political aspirations of James's court, Shakespeare succeeds in creating a play that was "as effective an emblem for his court audience as it was an enjoyable dramatic romance for his wider public in the city of London."

Culver Pictures

A print showing Henry VIII and Anne Boleyn in a scene from *Henry VIII.*

HENRY
—VIII—

HENRY VIII

Introductory Material

Foreword by Joseph Papp

Introduction

Henry VIII in Performance

THE PLAY

Supplementary Material

Date and Text

Textual Notes

Shakespeare's Sources

Further Reading

Foreword

King John was one of Shakespeare's earliest history plays, and *Henry VIII* was one of his last. In the early play, there's a boy, Arthur, pleading for his life; in the late play, there's a woman, Katharine of Aragon, pleading for her honor. Together the plays provide a nice pair of bookends for the histories.

The courtroom scene where Queen Katharine defends herself against Henry VIII's divorce proceedings is a terrific one. The Queen, being sacrificed to Henry's need for a male heir, is dignified and eloquent. To Wolsey, she says, "Sir, / I am about to weep; but thinking that / We are a queen, or long have dreamed so, certain / The daughter of a king, my drops of tears / I'll turn to sparks of fire." And so she does, angrily accusing Wolsey of engineering the divorce. Finally, exasperated and determined, she leaves the scene of the trial, vowing never to return. It's a splendid scene.

Interestingly enough, *Henry VIII* is the only one of Shakespeare's plays I've never produced. If I were superstitious, I would say it's because the Globe Theatre burned down during a performance of *Henry VIII* in 1613. But that's not the reason; it's just that I never felt a sense of urgency about doing it. I think it would be great fun to put on, for it's full of all kinds of spectacular pageantry and ceremony, and would *look* beautiful in the theater. It's something I'd like to do in the future—Globe fires notwithstanding.

Joseph Papp

Joseph Papp gratefully acknowledges the help of Elizabeth Kirkland in preparing this Foreword.

Introduction

However much we may like to think of *The Tempest* (c. 1610–1611) as Shakespeare's farewell to his art, celebrating his retirement to Stratford in 1611 or 1612, his career was in fact not quite finished. He probably wrote *The Famous History of the Life of King Henry the Eighth* in 1613, and he evidently collaborated with the playwright John Fletcher (and possibly Francis Beaumont) in *The Two Noble Kinsmen* (1613–1616). *Henry VIII* was performed by the King's men, Shakespeare's acting company, at the Globe playhouse on June 29, 1613, as a "new" play, though perhaps it had also been performed earlier that spring at the indoors Blackfriars playhouse. During the Globe performance, small cannon (called chambers) were discharged to welcome Henry VIII and his fellow masquers to Cardinal Wolsey's house (1.4.64 ff.), accidentally setting fire to the thatch roof and burning the Globe to the ground in less than an hour. (The theater was subsequently rebuilt.) The letter reporting this incident refers to the play by the title *All Is True,* but its identification with the extant play of *Henry VIII* is virtually certain.

Not everyone has always agreed that the entire play is by Shakespeare, although doubts did not arise until the nineteenth century. Alfred Lord Tennyson was the first to suspect that much of the play is metrically non-Shakespearean. His friend James Spedding took up the suggestion in his study *Who Wrote Shakespeare's Henry VIII?* His conclusions, based on the assumption that Fletcher's mannered blank verse is generally end-stopped and much given to double or "feminine" endings, assigned only 1.1–2, 2.3–4, 3.2 (through line 204), and 5.1 to Shakespeare, attributing all the rest to Fletcher. These metrical tests have been bolstered by subsequent researchers and augmented by other methods of statistical analysis. The result is perhaps a more elaborate case for joint authorship than for most other plays of doubtful attribution. Some of the stylistic shifts noted by Tennyson are indeed discernible, as for example in the movement from the dense, elliptical grammar and compact images of the first two scenes to the conversational fluency of scenes 3 and 4.

Against these arguments, however, the case for Shakespeare's sole authorship is impressive. Although Shakespeare did apparently collaborate with Fletcher in *The Two Noble Kinsmen* during his last years, that play was excluded from the 1623 Folio, whereas *Henry VIII* was included as Shakespeare's final history play. Spedding's hypothesis of joint authorship would rob from Shakespeare several of the play's most famous scenes, such as the farewell speeches of the Duke of Buckingham, Cardinal Wolsey, and Queen Katharine, and conversely would credit Fletcher with a dramatic power not shown elsewhere. The "Fletcherian" style may well have been the result of Shakespeare's having known the work of the younger man, who became Shakespeare's heir as chief writer for the King's men. Unquestionably, Shakespeare's style did change in his later years under the influence of a sophisticated courtly audience at the indoors Blackfriars theater; the Prologue to *Henry VIII* suggests that the play was written with the more exclusive audience of Blackfriars ("The first and happiest hearers of the town") particularly in mind. Even if *Henry VIII* is a different sort of history play from *I Henry IV,* it is stylistically close to Shakespeare's late romances. The shift in texture from scenes 1 and 2 to scenes 3 and 4 makes good sense dramatically; scene 4, for example, dramatizing an evening party, is suitably conversational, whereas the dense first scene is largely expository. Neither external evidence nor tradition during Shakespeare's day links the play with Fletcher. Scholarly efforts to assign portions of the text to other authors date only from the nineteenth century, where they should be seen as part of a broader effort to reassign various parts of many other plays and thereby rescue Shakespeare from scenes presumed unworthy of his genius. The tendency to regard *Henry VIII* as defective and lacking in unity may well have been caused in part by eighteenth- and nineteenth-century productions of the play, which, although frequent and popular, treated the play as a vehicle for famous actors and actresses in the parts of Wolsey and Katharine (Thomas Betterton, John Philip Kemble, Sarah Siddons, Charles Kean, and, more recently, Sybil Thorndike, Charles Laughton, Flora Robson), and accordingly cut Act 5 and sometimes much of Act 4 along with other "extraneous" parts. Productions and criticism during the last thirty years, on the other hand, have shown *Henry VIII* to possess an impressive cohesion and to be an integral product of the late years in which Shakespeare centered his attention on romance and tragicomedy. We are safest in assuming that nineteenth-century efforts to deny Shakespeare sole authorship are now happily out of fashion, and that the Folio editors knew what they were doing when they included *Henry VIII*.

What was Shakespeare's purpose in this unexpected return to the English history play? He had set it aside fourteen years earlier, in 1599, bringing to completion in *Henry V* a series of eight plays on England's civil wars of the fifteenth century and another on the reign of King John. Why turn in 1613 to a historical subject so separated in time from that of Shakespeare's earlier interest and potentially so controversial because of its relation to the religious battle between Catholics and Protestants? Earlier generations of critics and playgoers, as we have seen, generally regarded parts of *Henry VIII* as belonging to another author or as the product of Shakespeare's presumed dotage, especially the fifth act with its apparent anticlimax following the deaths of the play's central characters, Wolsey and Katharine. More recent efforts to understand the whole of *Henry VIII* regard it as an experimental work, blending conventional genres (history, tragedy, and romance) and stressing masquelike stage effects in the opulent manner of court entertainment. Since its thematic focus is also one of courtly celebration, expressing gratitude for Queen Elizabeth's Protestant rule and wary hopes that her successor James will follow suit, the play may best be seen as a reworking of the English history play to meet the new mood of 1613. This return to a type of drama long since abandoned by Shakespeare resembles his similar fascination during his late years with the once-forgotten genre of romance.

In some ways, *Henry VIII* is deliberately unlike Shakespeare's earlier history plays and so should not be judged by their standards. The Prologue is at pains to stress that the play will contain no merriment or bawdry, no "fellow / In a long motley coat." And indeed the play is unusually lacking in a comic subplot devoted to the endearing antics of a tavern crew. To be sure, the views of the citizens are not ignored, for Queen Katharine champions their hatred of Wolsey's taxes. In the fifth act the people put in a brief appearance, crowding bumptiously forward at the christening of the Princess Elizabeth (5.4). Even here, however, the tone is one of condescending amusement at their childish eagerness to see their future queen. The common people do not provide choric commentary, as they do in *Richard III* or *Richard II*.

These factors may well reflect the increasing influence of the court on Shakespeare and the King's men. Ever since they had become the King's men in 1603, when James I came to the throne, Shakespeare's company had enjoyed a closer relationship with the throne than before. *Measure for Measure* and *Macbeth,* among other of Shakespeare's plays, seem to contain flattering allusions to the new monarch. Moreover, faced with increasing competition from the boys' acting companies, which, since reopening in 1599 after a hiatus of nearly a decade, had attracted a courtly and sophisticated clientele, Shakespeare's company acquired the lease of Blackfriars in 1608 and henceforth used this "private" theater as their winter playhouse. Shakespeare's late plays are staged with public, private, and courtly conditions of performance in mind. The late romances show the influence of Inigo Jones's lavish designs for court masques, as in *Cymbeline*'s use of machinery for celestial ascents and descents. *Henry VIII* reflects similar conditions of staging in its masquing scene (1.4), in the pageantlike trial of Katharine and the baptism of Elizabeth, and in the vision of white-robed figures dancing before the dying Katharine (4.2). This affinity to courtly entertainment should not be overstressed, for Shakespeare's company remained a public company throughout his career, and its stage was always fluidly bare of scenery when compared with Jones's ingenious devices and use of scenic perspective. Nonetheless, *Henry VIII* should be viewed as a history play for a somewhat more select audience than that of his earlier histories. The play's ornate compliments to Elizabeth have a courtly flavor. The year 1613 saw the politically important marriage of the Elector Palatine to James's daughter Elizabeth, who was often flatteringly compared with her namesake

Queen Elizabeth; and, although *Henry VIII* is not among the plays known to have been performed for this occasion, the marriage itself would have given added significance to the play.

Shakespeare's earlier histories also honor as well as examine critically the institution of monarchy, but even here *Henry VIII* provides a different emphasis. Shakespeare's earlier histories had focused on such issues as the education of a prince and on the dilemmas of power a ruler faces. *Henry VIII* is less a study of kingship and more a dramatic expression of gratitude. *Henry VIII* is not a patriotic play in a broadly popular sense. It lacks battles and triumphant oratory. It voices thanksgiving for a particular ruling family. *Henry VIII* is above all the remarkable story of Queen Elizabeth's birth. The story is certainly not without its ironies, for providence works in mysterious ways, and Elizabeth's parents were complex persons. Shakespeare's play reveals an increasing psychological interest in analysis of motive, as do other later history plays, such as John Ford's *Perkin Warbeck*. Yet the unifying impulse of the play remains the celebration of the birth of Elizabeth.

This rising action in the play is counterpointed by a series of tragic falls, which indeed seem at first to be the play's chief concern. These falls proceed in remorseless succession—Buckingham, Katharine, Wolsey. In the edifying manner of that staple of medieval tragedy, the "Fall of Princes," these deaths offer useful lessons on statecraft and personal conduct. All these characters stoically exemplify the art of holy dying. One after another, they forgive their enemies and regret such sins as they have committed, and yet they also prophesy that God's retribution will light on offenders' heads. The prevailing mood in the falls of Buckingham and Katharine is one of pity, for both are victims of the ruthless Wolsey.

Cardinal Wolsey is the most interesting character of the three and best illustrates another convention of medieval tragedy, the Wheel of Fortune. Even as he topples one victim after another, dispatching Surrey to Ireland, wheedling his way into the King's favor, reversing England's foreign policy with bewildering speed from pro-French to pro-Empire and back again, all the while amassing a vast personal fortune and negotiating for supreme power within the

Roman Church, we sense that he is preparing his own catastrophe. Fortune raises insolent worldly persons of this sort, but an overseeing power is at work and will manifest itself through the King. Wolsey, in a nobly contrite farewell, sees the moral of his fall: had he served God zealously, God would not "Have left me naked to mine enemies" (3.2.458). Wolsey knows he has ventured beyond his depth in scheming, "Like little wanton boys that swim on bladders" (l. 360). Shakespeare's appraisal of this controversial man is mixed, partly because his chief source, Raphael Holinshed's *Chronicles* (1578), incorporated both anti-Wolseyan diatribes and George Cavendish's appreciative account of Wolsey's last days. Still, the portraiture remains consistent throughout, for Wolsey is always intelligent and munificent (as in his founding of Cardinal College, later Christ Church, at Oxford) even though he employs his talents for worldly ends. His chief wrongdoing is his meddling on behalf of Rome, his finagling to gain the papacy, and, most of all, his sending of England's wealth overseas for reasons of private gain. Yet even this corrupt behavior has a function in the rising action of the story, for, had not Wolsey schemed against Queen Katharine in his plot to marry King Henry to the French Duchess of Alençon, Katharine might never have fallen to make way for Anne Bullen; and had not Wolsey given a sumptuous party to impress the court with his magnificence (1.4), Henry might never have met Queen Elizabeth's mother. Wolsey's fate is to introduce Henry to the woman whose rise will mean Wolsey's fall and the birth of a future queen. An overriding cosmic irony converts the worst intents of schemers to beneficent ends.

King Henry and Anne Bullen, who as Elizabeth's parents play the roles essential to England's bright future, are largely unaware of the great destiny they are performing. Henry especially, like Wolsey, is examined with some skepticism. His pious insistence that "conscience" alone banishes him from Katharine's bed elicits a wry observation, sotto voce, from the Duke of Suffolk: "No, his conscience / Has crept too near another lady" (2.2.17–18). As Henry neglectfully condones Wolsey's abuse of authority and credulously accepts perjured testimony against Buckingham, we catch glimpses of the whimsical tyrant whom history has revealed to us. These criticisms are muted, however, for

Henry is after all Elizabeth's father. He is not only exonerated from most wrongdoing but steps boldly forward at the play's end as champion of religious reform. Anne too is ambivalently treated. In her scene with the Old Lady (2.3), we are reminded of the all-too-apparent reasons there are for suspecting that Anne is a schemer, a high-class auctioneer of her beauty who knows that Henry will pay handsomely. An Elizabethan audience would be bound to recall her grim fate at the hands of the public executioner. Yet in her own person Anne resists these ironies. All the characters of the play, whether they stand to profit or lose by Anne's marriage, speak admiringly of her beauty and honor. Although her speeches are few, her appearances are sumptuously staged with Anne at the center of a meaningful pageant.

The religious issue is presented with a similar tact and ambiguity, for it too is both controversial and of significance to England's future. Our sympathies are charitably disposed toward Katharine, whose innocent fall is a sad price for England's larger happiness. Shakespeare refuses to associate her with the decaying order of Catholicism, as he might have done. On the other hand, Bishop Gardiner, the villain of Act 5, is undeniably a Catholic and persecutor of heretics, a dangerous man whose overthrow by Henry and the Protestant Cranmer signals the beginning of a new era in religion. Though Shakespeare tactfully omits the relationship between Katharine's divorce and the Reformation, his audience would have had little difficulty making the connection in Act 5 between Cranmer's Protestant victory and the birth of Elizabeth. These two rising actions coalesce and give perspective to the pitiable falls from greatness that have necessarily contributed to a happy and even miraculous conclusion. History and tragicomic romance fulfill a common purpose in *Henry VIII*.

Act 5 is thus central to the play's thematic concerns, despite the poor opinion in which it was held in the nineteenth century, and despite the apparently episodic way in which it introduces new characters (notably Archbishop Cranmer) and new issues. The ending confirms a pattern seen earlier in the sad stories of Buckingham and especially Wolsey, in which we mortals "outrun / By violent swiftness that which we run at, / And lose by overrunning" (1.1.141–143). Vain human striving after fame overreaches itself and brings itself down. The process is, in *Henry VIII,* not primarily a punishment for villainy, for there are no real villains here, but a curative process by which frail proud men ascend on Fortune's wheel only to discover how illusory are her rewards and how comforting are Fortune's losses that bring us to ourselves. Not a moment of ease does Wolsey enjoy until he is ruined in worldly terms. He assures Thomas Cromwell, at the moment of his fall, that "I know myself now, and I feel within me / A peace above all earthly dignities" (3.2.379–380). His fall is thus a happy fall, an instructive one for himself and others: "Mark but my fall, and that that ruined me" (l. 440). Even Katharine and her gentleman usher, Griffin, perceive a happiness in Wolsey's decline, not because it satisfies a desire for vengeance but because it offers a comforting precedent of self-discovery through suffering: "His overthrow heaped happiness upon him; / For then, and not till then, he felt himself" (4.2.64–65). To know oneself in these terms, *nosce teipsum,* is to enjoy the inestimable gift of penance and the laying aside of worldly striving. Cranmer is a suitable protagonist in Act 5 and substitute for Wolsey as the King's adviser because he cares so little for himself in a worldly sense. He is the instrument of a higher power that, having imposed various trials on members of the court for their individual and collective betterment, at last reveals a meaning in that suffering and a future happiness arising out of man's imperfect attempts to know himself. As Buckingham says earlier (2.1.124), "Heaven has an end in all."

The play when staged offers a visual contrast between ceremonial pomp and worldly loss leading to renunciation and death. The processions and public events, conveyed by unusually full stage directions, celebrate the ordered arrangement of a hierarchical society. Yet among the most powerful scenes are those of Wolsey bidding farewell to his wealth and power, and of Katharine in her isolation and approaching death. The Prologue promises to give us noble scenes, "Sad, high, and working, full of state and woe," and in this we are not disappointed. The Prologue also promises that the audience "May here find truth too"; and, despite the necessary omission of much bloodshed (we are never told directly what will become of Anne Bullen and Sir

Thomas More), the play does give a vivid account of Henry VIII's time. We "see / The very persons of our noble story / As they were living." Our impression is of great political and religious change, of splendor and richness, above all of the insecurity of worldly felicity under such a king. Theatrically the play is sumptuous, pageantlike; though it chooses not to amuse us with comedy and eschews battle scenes, it abounds in personages from history. In *Henry VIII* Shakespeare adapts the history play to his late world of romance.

Henry VIII in Performance

During a performance of *Henry VIII* on June 29, 1613, the Globe Theatre burned to the ground. The Jacobean diplomat Sir Henry Wooton, noting in a letter the play's "many extraordinary circumstances of pomp and majesty," reported that the theater was destroyed "within less than an hour" of the roof thatch catching fire from a shot fired as part of the ceremony in Act 1, scene 4. The play was performed at the rebuilt Globe in 1628 and presumably at other times before the theaters were closed by act of Parliament in 1642.

On the Restoration stage the play was unquestionably popular. The diarist Samuel Pepys judged it "a rare play" when Thomas Betterton, in the role of Henry, returned it to the stage in 1663. Pepys saw *Henry VIII* again in 1664, though he was "mightily dissatisfied," and once more in 1668, when he was "mightily pleased with the history and shows of it." In 1691, the theater historian Gerard Langbaine reported that the play "frequently appears on the present stage." It continued to be revived throughout the eighteenth century, with Barton Booth and then James Quin succeeding Betterton in the role of Henry. Booth played the King in 1727 in the spectacular version at the Theatre Royal, Drury Lane, produced to celebrate the coronation of George II. In 1744, Hannah Pritchard first played Katharine, opposite Quin as Henry in a production at the Theatre Royal, Covent Garden, and Peg Woffington took the part at Covent Garden in 1749 and again in 1751. In November of 1788 John Philip Kemble produced the play at Drury Lane, with his sister, Sarah Siddons, originating her much-admired acting of Katharine. Kemble played a minor role, a composite of Griffith and Cromwell, concentrating as director and manager on the play's scenic effects.

Largely because of the opportunities for theatrical splendor and the star roles it provides, the play became a great favorite on the nineteenth-century stage. Kemble regularly revived the play after he moved to Covent Garden in 1803, most spectacularly in 1811 in a production hailed by *The Times* as "the most dazzling stage exhibition that we have ever seen." William Charles Macready produced the play in 1837 and 1838 at Covent Garden, followed by Samuel Phelps at the Sadler's Wells Theatre in 1845, both in the usual elaborate nineteenth-century manner and with a three-act text that ended with the fall of Wolsey. In 1848, as his final appearance before he left for an American tour, Macready staged the first three acts of Shakespeare's play in a command performance for Queen Victoria and Prince Albert at Drury Lane, with Charlotte Cushman as Katharine and Phelps playing Henry. In 1848, in a revival at Sadler's Wells, Phelps restored much of the text of the play. Unquestionably the most significant production of the middle years of the century, however, was Charles Kean's magnificent *Henry VIII* at the Princess's Theatre in 1855. Splendidly emphasizing the play's pageantry and processions and with, as Kean boasted, "scrupulous attendance to historical truth in costume, architecture, and the multiplied details of action," *Henry VIII* played for one hundred nearly consecutive nights. Kean's text cut many lines to allow time for his elaborate staging, but, like Phelps, Kean performed all of Shakespeare's scenes and in their Shakespearean order.

In America the play was also successful, from the first attracting star actors to its rich parts. Lewis Hallam played Henry in New York in 1799 at the Park Theatre. In 1810 two ambitious theater managers, Thomas Cooper and Stephen Price, lured George Frederick Cooke to America, and the following year he played Cardinal Wolsey at the Park Theatre. Fanny Kemble and her father Charles played *Henry VIII* in New York while touring in 1834. Charlotte Cushman had great success as Katharine in a number of productions in the years between 1848 and her retirement from the stage in 1874; in her search for testing roles, she also acted Wolsey in 1849. Edwin Booth was a more natural Wolsey, acting the part in 1876 at the Arch Street Theatre in Philadelphia, and then to great acclaim in January 1878, in an opulent production at Booth's Theatre in New York. Helena Modjeska, opposite Otis Skinner's Henry, played Katharine "with exquisite pathos," as one reviewer remarked, at New York's Garden Theater in 1892, emerging as a worthy rival of Ellen Terry in the role.

On both sides of the Atlantic, productions exploited the opportunities the play provides for spectacular staging with large, impressive sets somewhat in the manner of grand opera. Nowhere was this potential for theatrical splendor better realized than in Henry Irving's lavish production in 1892 at the Lyceum Theatre in London, the most magnificent Shakespearean performance ever attempted by that grand master of large-scale theatrical effects. The scene at Wolsey's York Place in Act 1, scene 5, in which King Henry first meets Anne Bullen, featured an opulent banquet and then a sequence of dances, one dignified and stately, another performed in a wild manner by strangely costumed men whirling lighted torches. The first scene of Act 2 revealed the Duke of Buckingham (Johnston Forbes-Robertson), passing on his way to execution, against a beautifully detailed set of "the King's Stairs, Westminster." Katharine (Ellen Terry), at her trial, was surrounded by her maids and the sumptuously garbed supporters of her cause, while King Henry sat on his throne and listened to the advice of Cardinals Wolsey and Campeius, all amidst the Tudor Gothic magnificence of "a hall in Blackfriars." Even these scenic triumphs paled before the spectacle of Anne Bullen's coronation (4.1) in an authentic reproduction of "a street in Westminster" of the Tudor era, replete with three-storied wooden-beamed houses. At every casement appeared citizens and their wives, while below on the street (according to the journal *Dramatic Notes*) were "prentices indulging in horseplay, beggars, and street-players, the halberdiers and men-at-arms clearing the way for the attendants on Anne Boleyn [i.e., Bullen] going to her coronation." And so it went, through to the celestial vision appearing to the dying Queen Katharine, and a finale in Grey Friars Church at Greenwich, faithfully redone in the theater with ancient stained glass windows and timeworn stairs.

Staging of this kind made heavy demands on the playscript. As in opera, the sets were expensive and difficult to shift, so that scenes not fitting into the designer's decor had to be sacrificed or rearranged. The script as a whole needed to be heavily cut in order to make allowance for the ponderous and time-consuming scene changes. In any case, these alterations fit well with Irving's intentions; like most of the Victorian actor-managers, he was mainly interested in the central roles of Henry VIII, Wolsey, Katharine, and Buckingham. Performance focused on moments of high seriousness and pathos: Buckingham's farewell to the world, Wolsey's reflections on the passing of his glory, Katharine's defense at her trial and her celestial vision, and, when it was included, the play's concluding prophecy of Queen Elizabeth's reign. The eloquent speeches of these scenes were well suited to the histrionic talents of actors trained in oratorical delivery and accustomed to prominence onstage at the expense of the supporting cast.

At His Majesty's Theatre in 1910, Herbert Beerbohm Tree produced one of the last of the spectacular productions of *Henry VIII,* with a text cutting all of Act 5 and ending with a lavish ceremony of Anne's coronation. A silent film was made of five scenes from Tree's production and publicly released to wide acclaim in 1911. In 1916 he took the play to America, where it drew large and enthusiastic crowds and was praised by most reviewers for its magnificent staging. The *New York Evening Mail* headline, however, termed the evening "A Worn Echo of Another Day," and indeed a movement away from the elaborate scenic emphasis of Victorian Shakespearean production had already begun.

In 1902 Frank Benson had directed the play at Stratford-upon-Avon, with Ellen Terry as Katharine, in a production that eschewed spectacle for sentiment. Instead of emphasizing the play's pomp and processions, Benson focused on its tragic rhythms. The elegiac mode was intensified for the cast by the knowledge that Frank Rodney, playing Buckingham, was almost literally in "the last hour / Of [his] weary life," soon to die of throat cancer. Ben Greet, in 1916, directed a fast-paced production on a simple set at the Old Vic, with his usual confidence in the text to move an audience. Eight years later, the Old Vic again saw a *Henry VIII* markedly different from the slow and massive play of nineteenth-century production. Robert Atkins, a disciple of William Poel and equally committed to recovering the principles of Elizabethan staging, produced an energetic and intelligent version with a set composed of black velvet curtains and gilt arches. The most striking visual effect was the shadow of a cross thrown onto the backcloth.

Though Lewis Casson's *Henry VIII* at London's Empire Theatre in 1925, starring Sybil Thorndike as Katharine (and with a young man named Laurence Olivier as the assistant stage manager and playing a servant), attractively recalled the old scenic traditions, Terence Gray at the Cambridge Festival Theatre in 1931 energetically anticipated more modern ones. On a shiny aluminum ramp curving up to the top of the stage, characters dressed like playing-card kings and queens acted out what Gray called "a masque in the modern manner." Cardboard cutouts were used to stand in for the minor roles, and their lines were spoken by actors from the sides of the stage. In the christening scene, the set began to revolve and the baby Elizabeth, obviously a toy, was thrown into the audience.

Productions at Stratford-upon-Avon in 1949 by Tyrone Guthrie and in 1983 by Howard Davies similarly sought to undercut the pageantry, though less startlingly than Gray. Guthrie's production was marked by deliberately distracting stage business, diverting attention from the official spectacle. A duchess sneezed during Cranmer's prophecy, and, though this effect was subsequently cut, other discordant business remained. When the production was revived at the Old Vic in 1953, the year of Elizabeth II's coronation, Guthrie reduced the dislocating effects, allowing what was left to humanize rather than undermine the pageantry. Davies's 1983 production was a Brechtian political drama using a grating score by Ilona Sekacz to highlight an ironic treatment of Tudor history. The coronation procession included tailor's dummies and spoken stage directions. Set against Hayden Griffin's stage design, consisting of cutout flats, the patriotic pageantry emerged as an exercise in political legitimation unable to obscure the reality of realpolitik and human suffering.

While continuing the movement away from the scenic elaboration of the nineteenth century, other modern productions have focused more on the human drama than on the alienated politics of Davies's *Henry VIII*. In 1958 at the Old Vic, Michael Benthall directed John Gielgud as Wolsey and Edith Evans as Katharine in an often moving production that strove to preserve, as critic J. C. Trewin noted, "a balance between the personal play and the processional drama." At Stratford-upon-Avon in 1969, Trevor Nunn sought a different balance. Donald Sinden's virile Henry had an odd mixture of hard-nosed political savvy and self-deceived romanticism; Peggy Ashcroft's Katharine was at once passionate and dignified. Processions wound through the theater, but they seemed purposefully irrelevant to a production that began and ended with Henry staring out into the darkness. Kevin Billington's BBC television production (1979), with Claire Bloom superbly cast as Queen Katharine, opted for an intimate and virtually uncut performance that focused, in ways wonderfully appropriate for television's small screen, on the individual experience of loss. In 1986 the play was performed at Stratford, Ontario, in a production by Brian Rintoul that emphasized the supervisory presence of a king who was visibly trying to control the forces of history through vigilance and will. This fine production, always aware of the lines of political force and yet sensitively tracing the emotional connections between characters, found an energy and integrity in avoiding the extremes of paranoia or pageantry.

A refusal to privilege the play's visual elements and a largely ironic or disillusioned presentation of its reading of Tudor history characterize most of the all-too-infrequent productions on the modern stage. Still, it is possible that the nineteenth century perceived something vital about *Henry VIII* that we have lost. The play is in fact Shakespeare's most spectacular historical drama. The original production must have gone to extraordinary lengths to vividly enact the many processions and ceremonials in which the play abounds. No other play by Shakespeare can approach *Henry VIII* in the elaboration of stage directions asking for thrones and chairs of state, banquets, masques, ceremonial last speeches, trials, visions, council meetings, and above all rich costumes. An important irony, of course, surrounds these effects, for the splendor of worldly achievement leads inevitably to falls from power, and it is only by the enigmatic workings of providence that courtly pageantry and intrigue ultimately combine to produce a great future for England. Nevertheless, costuming and properties are essential parts of the play's complex effect. The Prologue promises matters "full of state and woe, / Such noble scenes as draw the eye to flow," and the play does not disappoint these expectations.

One staging sequence demonstrates with particular vividness the flexibility of the Shakespearean stage for which the play was originally written. In Act 5, scene 2, Thomas Cranmer, the Archbishop of Canterbury, is summoned before the King's Privy Council on charges of heresy. The King is aware of Cranmer's danger, however, and determines to witness the proceedings from *"a window above"*—i.e., the gallery at the rear of the stage in the Elizabethan playhouse, above the main acting platform. From that upper vantage, the King beholds the way Cranmer is humiliated by being kept waiting at the door, and accordingly the King conceals himself behind a curtain to observe what follows. In what is conventionally marked as scene 3 of Act 5, a council table is brought in, the councillors seat themselves, and Cranmer is called into the room. He has not in fact exited and reentered, however; he stands at the door while the scene imaginatively changes from an anteroom to the council chamber itself. Cranmer thereupon steps forward as though entering. There is no break in the action, and the King's presence all this while in the curtained space "above" confirms the theatrical continuity. Lack of scenery allows the Elizabethan stage to shift from outside to inside through an appeal to the audience's imagination; the convention is as clear and understandable to an audience as is the use of movable scenery. The swiftness and continuity of this sequence is something that the nineteenth century, with its passion for verisimilar stage effects, could not have achieved, a flexibility that is possible on the more open stage of the modern theater; but the play itself offers such a range of possibilities that we can only begin to see into its complexity when we perceive how different are the ways in which it has been offered to appreciative audiences.

HENRY
—VIII—

[*Dramatis Personae*

KING HENRY THE EIGHTH

DUKE OF BUCKINGHAM
DUKE OF NORFOLK
DUKE OF SUFFOLK
EARL OF SURREY
LORD ABERGAVENNY
LORD SANDS (*Sir Walter Sands*)
LORD CHAMBERLAIN
LORD CHANCELLOR
SIR HENRY GUILDFORD
SIR THOMAS LOVELL
SIR ANTHONY DENNY
SIR NICHOLAS VAUX

CARDINAL WOLSEY
THOMAS CROMWELL, *Wolsey's aide, later in King Henry's service*
SECRETARY *of Wolsey*
SERVANT *of Wolsey*
CARDINAL CAMPEIUS
CAPUCHIUS, *Ambassador from the Emperor Charles the Fifth*
GARDINER, *King Henry's secretary, later Bishop of Winchester*
PAGE *to Gardiner*
THOMAS CRANMER, *Archbishop of Canterbury*
BISHOP OF LINCOLN

QUEEN KATHARINE, *King Henry's wife, later divorced*
PATIENCE, *her attendant*
GRIFFITH, *her gentleman usher*
GENTLEWOMAN, } *attending*
GENTLEMAN, } *Queen Katharine*

ANNE BULLEN, *Queen Katharine's Maid of Honor, later Queen*
OLD LADY, *friend of Anne Bullen*

BRANDON
SERGEANT AT ARMS
SURVEYOR *to the Duke of Buckingham*

Three GENTLEMEN
CRIER
SCRIBE
MESSENGER *to Queen Katharine*
DOCTOR BUTTS
KEEPER *of the Council Chamber*
PORTER
Porter's MAN
GARTER KING AT ARMS

Speaker of the PROLOGUE *and* EPILOGUE

Lords, Ladies, Gentlemen, Judges, Bishops, Priests, Vergers, Lord Mayor of London and Aldermen, Common People, Attendants, Guards, Tipstaves, Halberdiers, Scribes, Secretaries, Officers, Pursuivants, Pages, Guards, Queen Katharine's Women, Musicians, Choristers, and Dancers as spirits

SCENE: *London; Westminster; Kimbolton*]

Prologue

[*Enter Prologue.*]

PROLOGUE

I come no more to make you laugh. Things now
That bear a weighty and a serious brow,
Sad, high, and working, full of state and woe, 3
Such noble scenes as draw the eye to flow,
We now present. Those that can pity here
May, if they think it well, let fall a tear;
The subject will deserve it. Such as give
Their money out of hope they may believe
May here find truth too. Those that come to see
Only a show or two, and so agree 10
The play may pass, if they be still and willing,
I'll undertake may see away their shilling
Richly in two short hours. Only they 13
That come to hear a merry, bawdy play,
A noise of targets, or to see a fellow 15
In a long motley coat guarded with yellow, 16
Will be deceived. For, gentle hearers, know 17
To rank our chosen truth with such a show
As fool and fight is, besides forfeiting
Our own brains and the opinion that we bring 20
To make that only true we now intend, 21
Will leave us never an understanding friend.
Therefore, for goodness' sake, and as you are known
The first and happiest hearers of the town, 24
Be sad, as we would make ye. Think ye see 25
The very persons of our noble story
As they were living. Think you see them great, 27
And followed with the general throng and sweat
Of thousand friends; then, in a moment, see
How soon this mightiness meets misery.

Prologue.
3 Sad . . . working serious, lofty, and exciting the emotions. **state** dignity **10 show** spectacle **13 two short hours** (A conventional period of time for a play.) **15 targets** shields **16 motley coat** pied costume of the fool. **guarded** trimmed **17 deceived** disappointed. **know** i.e., it must be acknowledged that **20 Our own brains** i.e., the labor of our brains **20–21 the opinion . . . intend** the reputation we have for presenting truthfully what we intend to play **24 first** foremost. **happiest hearers** best-qualified audience **25 sad** serious **27 great** in high position

And if you can be merry then, I'll say
A man may weep upon his wedding day. [*Exit.*]

✤

1.1

Enter the Duke of Norfolk at one door; at the other, the Duke of Buckingham and the Lord Abergavenny.

BUCKINGHAM
Good morrow, and well met. How have ye done
Since last we saw in France?
NORFOLK I thank Your Grace, 2
Healthful, and ever since a fresh admirer 3
Of what I saw there.
BUCKINGHAM An untimely ague 4
Stayed me a prisoner in my chamber when 5
Those suns of glory, those two lights of men,
Met in the vale of Andren.
NORFOLK Twixt Guînes and Ardres. 7
I was then present, saw them salute on horseback,
Beheld them when they lighted, how they clung 9
In their embracement, as they grew together; 10
Which had they, what four throned ones could have
weighed 11
Such a compounded one?
BUCKINGHAM All the whole time
I was my chamber's prisoner.
NORFOLK Then you lost
The view of earthly glory. Men might say
Till this time pomp was single, but now married
To one above itself. Each following day 16
Became the next day's master, till the last 17
Made former wonders its. Today the French, 18
All clinquant, all in gold, like heathen gods, 19
Shone down the English; and tomorrow they 20
Made Britain India—every man that stood 21

1.1. Location: London. The royal court.
2 saw i.e., saw each other **3 fresh** untired **4 what I saw there** (Norfolk's description is of the famous meeting of Henry VIII and Francis I of France in 1520. It was near Calais, at the Field of the Cloth of Gold, so called because of the magnificence of the display.) **ague** fever
5 Stayed kept **7 vale of Andren** (The name, more properly *Ardres,* appears as *Andren* in Holinshed.) **9 lighted** alighted, dismounted
10 as as if **11 Which had they** i.e., if they had grown together. **weighed** equaled in weight **16 following** succeeding **17 master** teacher, model **18 its** its own **19 clinquant** glittering **20 they** i.e., the English **21 India** i.e., seem as wealthy as the West Indies

Showed like a mine. Their dwarfish pages were
As cherubins, all gilt. The madams too, 23
Not used to toil, did almost sweat to bear
The pride upon them, that their very labor 25
Was to them as a painting. Now this masque 26
Was cried incomparable; and th' ensuing night 27
Made it a fool and beggar. The two kings,
Equal in luster, were now best, now worst,
As presence did present them; him in eye 30
Still him in praise; and being present both, 31
'Twas said they saw but one, and no discerner 32
Durst wag his tongue in censure. When these suns— 33
For so they phrase 'em—by their heralds challenged
The noble spirits to arms, they did perform
Beyond thought's compass, that former fabulous story, 36
Being now seen possible enough, got credit, 37
That *Bevis* was believed.

BUCKINGHAM O, you go far. 38

NORFOLK
As I belong to worship and affect 39
In honor honesty, the tract of everything 40
Would by a good discourser lose some life
Which action's self was tongue to. All was royal; 42
To the disposing of it naught rebelled. 43
Order gave each thing view; the office did 44
Distinctly his full function.

BUCKINGHAM Who did guide— 45
I mean, who set the body and the limbs
Of this great sport together, as you guess? 47

23 gilt (Carved statues of cherubim in churches were often gilded.) **madams** ladies **25 pride** finery. **that** so that **26 Was . . . painting** i.e., flushed them as though with cosmetics **27 cried** declared **30 As . . . them** i.e., when they appeared **30–31 him . . . praise** i.e., the one in view at the moment received the praise **32 discerner** beholder **33 Durst** dared. **censure** judgment (of one above the other) **36 that . . . story** so that stories previously thought fabulous **37 got credit** gained credibility **38 Bevis** the fourteenth-century romance *Bevis of Hampton* **39 belong to worship** am of noble rank **39–40 affect . . . honesty** i.e., love truth with honorable regard **40 tract** telling; course **42 Which . . . to** i.e., which would be best described by the event itself **43 rebelled** jarred **44–45 Order . . . function** everything appeared in its proper place, and every official performed his function without confusion **47 sport** entertainment

NORFOLK
One, certes, that promises no element 48
In such a business.
BUCKINGHAM I pray you, who, my lord? 49
NORFOLK
All this was ordered by the good discretion
Of the right reverend Cardinal of York. 51
BUCKINGHAM
The devil speed him! No man's pie is freed 52
From his ambitious finger. What had he
To do in these fierce vanities? I wonder 54
That such a keech can with his very bulk 55
Take up the rays o' the beneficial sun 56
And keep it from the earth.
NORFOLK Surely, sir,
There's in him stuff that puts him to these ends; 58
For being not propped by ancestry, whose grace
Chalks successors their way, nor called upon 60
For high feats done to the crown, neither allied 61
To eminent assistants, but spiderlike, 62
Out of his self-drawing web, 'a gives us note 63
The force of his own merit makes his way—
A gift that heaven gives for him which buys
A place next to the King.
ABERGAVENNY I cannot tell
What heaven hath given him—let some graver eye
Pierce into that—but I can see his pride
Peep through each part of him. Whence has he that?
If not from hell, the devil is a niggard,
Or has given all before, and he begins 71
A new hell in himself.
BUCKINGHAM Why the devil,

48–49 One . . . business i.e., one whose lowly origin would indicate that he lacked the capacity required for managing business of such a regal nature. **certes** certainly **51 Cardinal of York** i.e., Cardinal Wolsey **52 speed** prosper **54 fierce** extravagant **55 keech** (Literally, fat of a slaughtered animal rolled into a lump; applied to Wolsey, who was reputed to be a butcher's son.) **56 sun** i.e., King Henry **58 stuff . . . him** traits that whet him on **60 Chalks . . . way** indicates the path noble descendants are to follow **61 high feats** great deeds. **to** for **62 assistants** high officials of the crown **63 self-drawing** spun out of his own entrails. **'a . . . note** he lets us know **71 he** i.e., Wolsey

Upon this French going out, took he upon him, 73
Without the privity o' the King, t' appoint 74
Who should attend on him? He makes up the file 75
Of all the gentry, for the most part such
To whom as great a charge as little honor 77
He meant to lay upon; and his own letter, 78
The honorable board of council out, 79
Must fetch him in he papers.

ABERGAVENNY I do know 80
Kinsmen of mine, three at the least, that have
By this so sickened their estates that never 82
They shall abound as formerly.

BUCKINGHAM O, many 83
Have broke their backs with laying manors on 'em 84
For this great journey. What did this vanity 85
But minister communication of 86
A most poor issue?

NORFOLK Grievingly I think 87
The peace between the French and us not values 88
The cost that did conclude it.

BUCKINGHAM Every man,
After the hideous storm that followed, was 90
A thing inspired, and, not consulting, broke 91
Into a general prophecy: that this tempest, 92
Dashing the garment of this peace, aboded 93
The sudden breach on 't.

NORFOLK Which is budded out; 94
For France hath flawed the league and hath attached 95
Our merchants' goods at Bordeaux.

73 going out expedition, display **74 Without . . . King** without the King's being privy (to his plan) **75 file** list **77–78 To . . . upon** (i.e., the Cardinal imposed charges for defraying the expenses of the costly interview on those noblemen to whom he gave places of little honor) **78 letter** i.e., summons **79 out** not consulted **80 Must . . . papers** compels the cooperation of every person he cites. **he papers** whomever he lists **82 sickened** i.e., depleted **83 abound** thrive **84 laying . . . 'em** i.e., pawning estates for wardrobes **85 What . . . vanity** i.e., what did this extravagance accomplish **86–87 minister . . . issue** provide occasion for a conference that had little value, poor results **88 not values** is not worth **90 hideous storm** (Holinshed reports such a storm that interrupted the festivities and was taken as a prognostication.) **91 consulting** i.e., each other **92 general** common to all **93 aboded** foretold **94 on 't** of it. **is budded out** i.e., has come to pass **95 flawed** broken. **attached** seized

ABERGAVENNY Is it therefore
Th' ambassador is silenced?
NORFOLK Marry, is 't. 97
ABERGAVENNY
A proper title of a peace, and purchased 98
At a superfluous rate!
BUCKINGHAM Why, all this business 99
Our reverend cardinal carried.
NORFOLK Like it Your Grace, 100
The state takes notice of the private difference
Betwixt you and the Cardinal. I advise you—
And take it from a heart that wishes towards you
Honor and plenteous safety—that you read 104
The Cardinal's malice and his potency
Together; to consider further that 106
What his high hatred would effect wants not 107
A minister in his power. You know his nature, 108
That he's revengeful, and I know his sword
Hath a sharp edge; it's long, and 't may be said
It reaches far, and where 'twill not extend,
Thither he darts it. Bosom up my counsel; 112
You'll find it wholesome. Lo, where comes that rock 113
That I advise your shunning. 114

Enter Cardinal Wolsey, the purse borne before him, certain of the guard, and two Secretaries with papers. The Cardinal in his passage fixeth his eye on Buckingham, and Buckingham on him, both full of disdain.

WOLSEY [*To a Secretary*]
The Duke of Buckingham's surveyor, ha? 115
Where's his examination?
SECRETARY Here, so please you. 116
[*He gives a paper.*]

97 Marry (An oath, originally "by the Virgin Mary.") **98 A proper . . . peace** i.e., a fine business to give the name of peace to **99 superfluous rate** excessive price **100 carried** supervised. **Like it** may it please **104 read** interpret **106 Together** i.e., as equally strong **107–108 wants . . . power** is not without means under his control **112 Bosom up** take to heart and shut up in your bosom **113 wholesome** beneficial **114 s.d. purse** i.e., containing the great seal, pertaining to Wolsey as Lord Chancellor **115 surveyor** overseer of a household or estate **116 examination** deposition

WOLSEY
Is he in person ready?
SECRETARY Ay, please Your Grace.
WOLSEY
Well, we shall then know more, and Buckingham
Shall lessèn this big look. 119
Exeunt Cardinal and his train.
BUCKINGHAM
This butcher's cur is venom-mouthed, and I 120
Have not the power to muzzle him; therefore best
Not wake him in his slumber. A beggar's book 122
Outworths a noble's blood.
NORFOLK What, are you chafed? 123
Ask God for temperance; that's th' appliance only 124
Which your disease requires.
BUCKINGHAM I read in 's looks
Matter against me, and his eye reviled 126
Me as his abject object. At this instant 127
He bores me with some trick. He's gone to the King; 128
I'll follow and outstare him.
NORFOLK Stay, my lord,
And let your reason with your choler question 130
What 'tis you go about. To climb steep hills 131
Requires slow pace at first. Anger is like
A full hot horse who, being allowed his way, 133
Self-mettle tires him. Not a man in England 134
Can advise me like you. Be to yourself
As you would to your friend.
BUCKINGHAM I'll to the King,
And from a mouth of honor quite cry down 137
This Ipswich fellow's insolence, or proclaim 138
There's difference in no persons.
NORFOLK Be advised; 139
Heat not a furnace for your foe so hot

119 big haughty **120 butcher's cur** (Another dig at Wolsey's reputed lowly origin.) **122 book** book learning **123 blood** noble descent. **chafed** angry **124 appliance only** only remedy **126 Matter against** quarrel with **127 abject** cast-off, rejected **128 bores** undermines, cheats **130 question** debate, discuss **131 go about** intend **133 full hot** high-spirited **134 Self-mettle** his own ardent spirits **137 of honor** i.e., of a gentleman **138 Ipswich** (Wolsey's birthplace) **139 difference** distinctions in rank. **Be advised** take care

That it do singe yourself. We may outrun
By violent swiftness that which we run at,
And lose by overrunning. Know you not
The fire that mounts the liquor till 't run o'er 144
In seeming to augment it wastes it? Be advised.
I say again there is no English soul
More stronger to direct you than yourself,
If with the sap of reason you would quench
Or but allay the fire of passion.

BUCKINGHAM Sir, 149
I am thankful to you, and I'll go along
By your prescription. But this top-proud fellow, 151
Whom from the flow of gall I name not, but 152
From sincere motions, by intelligence, 153
And proofs as clear as founts in July when 154
We see each grain of gravel, I do know
To be corrupt and treasonous.

NORFOLK Say not "treasonous."

BUCKINGHAM
To th' King I'll say 't, and make my vouch as strong 157
As shore of rock. Attend. This holy fox,
Or wolf, or both—for he is equal ravenous 159
As he is subtle, and as prone to mischief
As able to perform 't—his mind and place 161
Infecting one another, yea, reciprocally,
Only to show his pomp as well in France
As here at home, suggests the King our master 164
To this last costly treaty, th' interview 165
That swallowed so much treasure and like a glass
Did break i' the wrenching.

NORFOLK Faith, and so it did. 167

BUCKINGHAM
Pray, give me favor, sir. This cunning cardinal 168
The articles o' the combination drew 169

144 mounts causes (by boiling) to rise **149 allay** temper, moderate **151 top-proud** supremely proud **152 from . . . gall** i.e., from promptings of anger **153 motions** motives. **intelligence** secret information **154 founts** springs **157 vouch** assertion, allegation **159 equal** equally **161 place** office, rank **164 suggests** incites **165 last** latest, recent. **interview** i.e., Field of the Cloth of Gold **167 wrenching** rough handling, rinsing **168 favor** attention **169 articles o' the combination** terms of the peace treaty

As himself pleased; and they were ratified
As he cried "Thus let be," to as much end 171
As give a crutch to the dead. But our count-cardinal 172
Has done this, and 'tis well; for worthy Wolsey,
Who cannot err, he did it. Now this follows,
Which, as I take it, is a kind of puppy
To th' old dam, treason: Charles the Emperor, 176
Under pretense to see the Queen his aunt—
For 'twas indeed his color, but he came 178
To whisper Wolsey—here makes visitation; 179
His fears were that the interview betwixt
England and France might through their amity
Breed him some prejudice, for from this league
Peeped harms that menaced him; privily 183
Deals with our cardinal, and, as I trow— 184
Which I do well, for I am sure the Emperor
Paid ere he promised, whereby his suit was granted
Ere it was asked—but when the way was made
And paved with gold, the Emperor thus desired
That he would please to alter the King's course 189
And break the foresaid peace. Let the King know,
As soon he shall by me, that thus the Cardinal
Does buy and sell his honor as he pleases,
And for his own advantage.

NORFOLK I am sorry
To hear this of him, and could wish he were
Something mistaken in 't.

BUCKINGHAM No, not a syllable. 195
I do pronounce him in that very shape
He shall appear in proof. 197

Enter Brandon, a Sergeant at Arms before him, and two or three of the guard.

BRANDON
Your office, Sergeant: execute it.

171 end purpose **172 count-cardinal** i.e., cardinal putting on the airs of an aristocrat **176 dam** mother (used especially of animals). **Charles** i.e., Charles V, Holy Roman Emperor, nephew of Queen Katharine, who had much to fear from an English-French alliance **178 color** pretext **179 whisper** whisper to **183 privily** secretly **184 trow** believe **189 he** i.e., Wolsey **195 Something mistaken** somewhat misunderstood **197 He . . . proof** experience shall prove him

SERGEANT Sir,
My lord the Duke of Buckingham, and Earl
Of Hereford, Stafford, and Northampton, I
Arrest thee of high treason, in the name
Of our most sovereign king.

BUCKINGHAM Lo, you, my lord,
The net has fall'n upon me! I shall perish
Under device and practice.

BRANDON I am sorry 204
To see you ta'en from liberty, to look on 205
The business present. 'Tis His Highness' pleasure
You shall to the Tower.

BUCKINGHAM It will help me nothing 207
To plead mine innocence, for that dye is on me
Which makes my whit'st part black. The will of heaven
Be done in this and all things! I obey.
O my Lord Aberga'nny, fare you well.

BRANDON
Nay, he must bear you company. [*To Abergavenny.*] The King
Is pleased you shall to the Tower, till you know
How he determines further.

ABERGAVENNY As the Duke said,
The will of heaven be done and the King's pleasure
By me obeyed!

BRANDON Here is a warrant from
The King t' attach Lord Montacute and the bodies 217
Of the Duke's confessor, John de la Car, 218
One Gilbert Perk, his chancellor—

BUCKINGHAM So, so; 219
These are the limbs o' the plot. No more, I hope?

BRANDON
A monk o' the Chartreux.

BUCKINGHAM O, Nicholas Hopkins?

BRANDON He. 221

204 device and practice stratagems and plots **205 to look on** i.e., and sorry to look on **207 nothing** not at all **217 attach** arrest **218, 219 John de la Car, Gilbert Perk** (The names are from Holinshed's account: "Master John de la Car alias de la Court, the Duke's confessor, and Sir Gilbert Perke, priest, the Duke's chancellor.") **221 Chartreux** Carthusian order

BUCKINGHAM

My surveyor is false. The o'ergreat Cardinal
Hath showed him gold; my life is spanned already. 223
I am the shadow of poor Buckingham, 224
Whose figure even this instant cloud puts on, 225
By darkening my clear sun. My lord, farewell. 226

Exeunt.

✤

1.2

Cornets. Enter King Henry, leaning on the Cardinal's shoulder, the nobles, and Sir Thomas Lovell. The Cardinal places himself under the King's feet on his right side. [*The Cardinal's Secretary attends him.*]

KING

My life itself, and the best heart of it, 1
Thanks you for this great care. I stood i' the level 2
Of a full-charged confederacy, and give thanks 3
To you that choked it. Let be called before us
That gentleman of Buckingham's. In person 5
I'll hear him his confessions justify, 6
And point by point the treasons of his master
He shall again relate. 8

A noise within, crying "Room for the Queen!" Enter the Queen [*Katharine*], *ushered by the Duke of Norfolk and* [*the Duke of*] *Suffolk. She kneels.* [*The*] *King riseth from his state, takes her up, kisses and placeth her by him.*

KATHARINE

Nay, we must longer kneel. I am a suitor.

223 spanned measured **224–226 I am . . . sun** i.e., I am the mere semblance of my former self, whose form and future hopes are obscured in this sudden cloud of affliction by the darkening of my king's favor

1.2. Location: London. The council chamber.
s.d. under . . . feet i.e., at the foot of the royal dais **1 best heart** most essential part **2 level** aim **3 full-charged confederacy** fully prepared conspiracy **5 That . . . Buckingham's** i.e., Buckingham's surveyor (1.1.115), whom Wolsey has induced to testify against his master **6 justify** prove, confirm **8 s.d. state** chair of state, raised seat with a canopy

KING
Arise, and take place by us. Half your suit
Never name to us; you have half our power.
The other moiety ere you ask is given. 12
Repeat your will and take it.

KATHARINE Thank Your Majesty. 13
That you would love yourself, and in that love
Not unconsidered leave your honor nor
The dignity of your office, is the point
Of my petition.

KING Lady mine, proceed.

KATHARINE
I am solicited, not by a few,
And those of true condition, that your subjects 19
Are in great grievance. There have been commissions 20
Sent down among 'em which hath flawed the heart 21
Of all their loyalties; wherein, although,
My good lord Cardinal, they vent reproaches
Most bitterly on you, as putter-on 24
Of these exactions, yet the King our master—
Whose honor heaven shield from soil!—even he escapes
not
Language unmannerly, yea, such which breaks
The sides of loyalty and almost appears
In loud rebellion.

NORFOLK Not "almost appears,"
It doth appear; for, upon these taxations,
The clothiers all, not able to maintain
The many to them 'longing, have put off 32
The spinsters, carders, fullers, weavers, who, 33
Unfit for other life, compelled by hunger
And lack of other means, in desperate manner
Daring th' event to th' teeth, are all in uproar, 36
And danger serves among them.

KING Taxation? 37

12 moiety half **13 Repeat your will** express your desire **19 condition** disposition (to loyalty) **20 grievance** distress. **commissions** i.e., writs authorizing a tax levy, and the agents to carry them out **21 flawed** damaged, cracked **24 putter-on** instigator **32 to them 'longing** in their employ. **put off** laid off **33 spinsters** spinners. **carders** those who comb wool for impurities. **fullers** those who beat wool to clean it **36 Daring . . . teeth** defiantly challenging the outcome **37 danger . . . them** danger is rife among them

Wherein? And what taxation? My lord Cardinal,
You that are blamed for it alike with us,
Know you of this taxation?

WOLSEY Please you, sir,
I know but of a single part in aught 41
Pertains to the state, and front but in that file 42
Where others tell steps with me.

KATHARINE No, my lord? 43
You know no more than others? But you frame 44
Things that are known alike, which are not wholesome 45
To those which would not know them and yet must 46
Perforce be their acquaintance. These exactions, 47
Whereof my sovereign would have note, they are 48
Most pestilent to the hearing, and to bear 'em
The back is sacrifice to the load. They say 50
They are devised by you, or else you suffer
Too hard an exclamation.

KING Still exaction! 52
The nature of it? In what kind, let's know,
Is this exaction?

KATHARINE I am much too venturous
In tempting of your patience, but am boldened 55
Under your promised pardon. The subjects' grief 56
Comes through commissions, which compels from each
The sixth part of his substance, to be levied 58
Without delay; and the pretense for this 59
Is named your wars in France. This makes bold mouths;
Tongues spit their duties out, and cold hearts freeze
Allegiance in them. Their curses now
Live where their prayers did, and it's come to pass
This tractable obedience is a slave 64
To each incensèd will. I would Your Highness 65

41 a single part one individual's share **42–43 front . . . me** take my place merely in the front rank with others who share the responsibility. **tell steps** keep step, march **44–46 You know . . . them** i.e., in a sense you know no more than others; but you devise measures known to all (the Council) which are so evil that men would rather not know **47 their acquaintance** i.e., known to them **48 note** knowledge **50 is sacrifice to** i.e., is bowed down under **52 exclamation** reproach **55 boldened** made bold **56 grief** grievance **58 substance** wealth **59 pretense** pretext **64 tractable** i.e., once docile **64–65 is . . . will** i.e., gives way to angry defiance

Would give it quick consideration, for
There is no primer business.

KING By my life, 67
This is against our pleasure.

WOLSEY And for me,
I have no further gone in this than by 69
A single voice, and that not passed me but 70
By learnèd approbation of the judges. If I am 71
Traduced by ignorant tongues, which neither know 72
My faculties nor person, yet will be 73
The chronicles of my doing, let me say
'Tis but the fate of place, and the rough brake 75
That virtue must go through. We must not stint 76
Our necessary actions in the fear
To cope malicious censurers, which ever, 78
As ravenous fishes, do a vessel follow
That is new trimmed, but benefit no further 80
Than vainly longing. What we oft do best,
By sick interpreters, once weak ones, is 82
Not ours, or not allowed; what worst, as oft 83
Hitting a grosser quality, is cried up 84
For our best act. If we shall stand still,
In fear our motion will be mocked or carped at, 86
We should take root here where we sit,
Or sit state-statues only.

KING Things done well, 88
And with a care, exempt themselves from fear;
Things done without example, in their issue 90
Are to be feared. Have you a precedent
Of this commission? I believe, not any. 92
We must not rend our subjects from our laws 93

67 primer more urgent **69–70 I have . . . voice** i.e., my part in this was only to cast one vote in the Council **71 approbation** approval **72 Traduced** defamed **73 faculties** qualities **75 place** high office. **brake** thicket **76 stint** stop **78 To cope** of encountering. **ever** always **80 new trimmed** newly fitted out **82 sick interpreters** i.e., those who explain our conduct out of malicious envy. **once** at one time or another. **weak** weak-witted **83 Not . . . allowed** either not credited to us, or disapproved of **84 Hitting . . . quality** being understood, or appreciated, by more vulgar natures. (The indiscriminate praise achievements less fine because their grosser minds understand them.) **86 In fear** for fear that **88 state-statues** statues of statesmen **90 example** precedent. **issue** consequences **92 Of** for **93 rend** tear

And stick them in our will. Sixth part of each? 94
A trembling contribution! Why, we take 95
From every tree lop, bark, and part o' the timber, 96
And though we leave it with a root, thus hacked,
The air will drink the sap. To every county
Where this is questioned send our letters with 99
Free pardon to each man that has denied
The force of this commission. Pray look to 't; 101
I put it to your care.

WOLSEY [*Aside to his Secretary*] A word with you.
Let there be letters writ to every shire
Of the King's grace and pardon. The grieved commons 104
Hardly conceive of me; let it be noised 105
That through our intercession this revokement
And pardon comes. I shall anon advise you 107
Further in the proceeding. *Exit Secretary.*

Enter Surveyor.

KATHARINE [*To the King*]
I am sorry that the Duke of Buckingham
Is run in your displeasure.

KING It grieves many. 110
The gentleman is learned, and a most rare speaker,
To nature none more bound; his training such 112
That he may furnish and instruct great teachers
And never seek for aid out of himself. Yet see, 114
When these so noble benefits shall prove
Not well disposed, the mind growing once corrupt, 116
They turn to vicious forms ten times more ugly
Than ever they were fair. This man so complete, 118
Who was enrolled 'mongst wonders, and when we,
Almost with ravished listening, could not find
His hour of speech a minute—he, my lady,
Hath into monstrous habits put the graces 122
That once were his, and is become as black

94 stick . . . will make them the victims of our caprice **95 trembling** causing to tremble **96 lop** branches **99 questioned** disputed **101 force** validity **104 grace** mercy. **grieved** aggrieved **105 Hardly conceive** have a bad opinion. **noised** reported, rumored **107 anon** soon **110 Is run in** has incurred **112 To . . . bound** none more indebted to nature for talents **114 out of** beyond **116 disposed** applied **118 complete** accomplished **122 habits** garments, i.e., shapes

As if besmeared in hell. Sit by us. You shall hear—
This was his gentleman in trust—of him
Things to strike honor sad.—Bid him recount
The fore-recited practices, whereof 127
We cannot feel too little, hear too much.

WOLSEY
Stand forth, and with bold spirit relate what you,
Most like a careful subject, have collected 130
Out of the Duke of Buckingham.

KING Speak freely.

SURVEYOR
First, it was usual with him—every day
It would infect his speech—that if the King
Should without issue die, he'll carry it so 134
To make the scepter his. These very words
I've heard him utter to his son-in-law,
Lord Aberga'nny, to whom by oath he menaced
Revenge upon the Cardinal.

WOLSEY Please Your Highness, note
This dangerous conception in this point.
Not friended by his wish to your high person, 140
His will is most malignant, and it stretches
Beyond you to your friends.

KATHARINE My learned lord Cardinal,
Deliver all with charity.

KING Speak on. 143
How grounded he his title to the crown
Upon our fail? To this point hast thou heard him 145
At any time speak aught?

SURVEYOR He was brought to this
By a vain prophecy of Nicholas Henton. 147

KING
What was that Henton?

SURVEYOR Sir, a Chartreux friar,
His confessor, who fed him every minute
With words of sovereignty.

KING How know'st thou this?

127 practices intrigues **130 collected** i.e., learned by spying **134 issue** offspring. **carry it so** manage affairs so as **140 Not . . . wish** his wish (that the King die childless) being ungratified **143 Deliver** tell **145 fail** i.e., dying without an heir **147 Henton** (According to Holinshed, an alias for Nicholas Hopkins; see 1.1.221.)

SURVEYOR
Not long before Your Highness sped to France,
The Duke being at the Rose, within the parish 152
Saint Lawrence Poultney, did of me demand
What was the speech among the Londoners 154
Concerning the French journey. I replied,
Men feared the French would prove perfidious,
To the King's danger. Presently the Duke 157
Said, 'twas the fear indeed, and that he doubted 158
'Twould prove the verity of certain words
Spoke by a holy monk, "that oft," says he,
"Hath sent to me, wishing me to permit
John de la Car, my chaplain, a choice hour
To hear from him a matter of some moment; 163
Whom after under the confession's seal
He solemnly had sworn that what he spoke
My chaplain to no creature living but
To me should utter, with demure confidence 167
This pausingly ensued: 'Neither the King nor 's heirs,
Tell you the Duke, shall prosper. Bid him strive
To gain the love o' the commonalty; the Duke
Shall govern England.'"

KATHARINE If I know you well,
You were the Duke's surveyor, and lost your office
On the complaint o' the tenants. Take good heed
You charge not in your spleen a noble person 174
And spoil your nobler soul. I say, take heed;
Yes, heartily beseech you.

KING Let him on.— 176
Go forward.

SURVEYOR On my soul, I'll speak but truth.
I told my lord the Duke, by the devil's illusions
The monk might be deceived, and that 'twas dangerous
For him to ruminate on this so far until
It forged him some design, which, being believed, 181

152 the Rose (A manor house belonging to Buckingham.) **154 speech** talk **157 Presently** immediately **158 doubted** feared, suspected **163 moment** importance **167 demure** grave, solemn **174 spleen** malice **176 on** go on **181 forged him** caused him to fashion. **being believed** i.e., if the Duke put faith in what the monk was telling him

It was much like to do. He answered, "Tush, 182
It can do me no damage," adding further
That, had the King in his last sickness failed, 184
The Cardinal's and Sir Thomas Lovell's heads
Should have gone off.

KING Ha? What, so rank? Aha,
There's mischief in this man.—Canst thou say further?

SURVEYOR
I can, my liege.

KING Proceed.

SURVEYOR Being at Greenwich,
After Your Highness had reproved the Duke
About Sir William Bulmer—

KING I remember
Of such a time. Being my sworn servant,
The Duke retained him his. But on; what hence? 192

SURVEYOR
"If," quoth he, "I for this had been committed,
As to the Tower, I thought, I would have played
The part my father meant to act upon 195
Th' usurper Richard, who, being at Salisbury,
Made suit to come in 's presence, which if granted,
As he made semblance of his duty, would 198
Have put his knife into him."

KING A giant traitor!

WOLSEY
Now, madam, may His Highness live in freedom, 200
And this man out of prison?

KATHARINE God mend all!

KING
There's something more would out of thee. What sayst?

SURVEYOR
After "the Duke his father," with "the knife,"
He stretched him, and, with one hand on his dagger, 204
Another spread on 's breast, mounting his eyes, 205
He did discharge a horrible oath, whose tenor

182 much like very likely **184 failed** died **192 his** as his own **195 my father** i.e., the Duke of Buckingham of Richard III's time **198 semblance** pretense. **duty** i.e., kneeling **200 may** can **204 stretched him** i.e., raised himself to his full height **205 mounting** raising

Was, were he evil used, he would outgo 207
His father by as much as a performance
Does an irresolute purpose.

KING There's his period, 209
To sheathe his knife in us. He is attached; 210
Call him to present trial. If he may 211
Find mercy in the law, 'tis his; if none,
Let him not seek 't of us. By day and night,
He's a traitor to the height. *Exeunt.* 214

✤

1.3 *Enter Lord Chamberlain and Lord Sands.*

CHAMBERLAIN
Is 't possible the spells of France should juggle 1
Men into such strange mysteries?

SANDS New customs, 2
Though they be never so ridiculous,
Nay, let 'em be unmanly, yet are followed.

CHAMBERLAIN
As far as I see, all the good our English
Have got by the late voyage is but merely 6
A fit or two o' the face; but they are shrewd ones, 7
For when they hold 'em, you would swear directly 8
Their very noses had been counselors
To Pepin or Clotharius, they keep state so. 10

SANDS
They have all new legs, and lame ones. One would take it, 11
That never see 'em pace before, the spavin 12

207 evil used badly treated **209 irresolute** unaccomplished. **period** aim, goal **210 attached** arrested **211 present** immediate **214 to the height** in the highest degree

1.3. Location: London. The royal court.
1 juggle beguile, bewitch **2 mysteries** artificial fashions **6 the late voyage** i.e., to the Field of the Cloth of Gold **7 fit . . . face** affected ways of screwing up the face into a grimace **8 hold 'em** i.e., maintain the grimaces **10 Pepin, Clotharius** kings of ancient France in the sixth and seventh centuries. **keep state** i.e., behave with an affected dignity **11 legs** mannerisms of walking and making obeisances **12 see** saw. **pace** walk. **spavin** disease of horses causing swelling of joints and lameness

Or springhalt reignèd among 'em.

CHAMBERLAIN Death, my lord! 13

Their clothes are after such a pagan cut to 't 14

That sure they've worn out Christendom.

Enter Sir Thomas Lovell.

How now? 15

What news, Sir Thomas Lovell?

LOVELL Faith, my lord,

I hear of none but the new proclamation

That's clapped upon the court gate.

CHAMBERLAIN What is 't for? 18

LOVELL

The reformation of our traveled gallants,

That fill the court with quarrels, talk, and tailors.

CHAMBERLAIN

I'm glad 'tis there. Now I would pray our monsieurs

To think an English courtier may be wise

And never see the Louvre.

LOVELL They must either— 23

For so run the conditions—leave those remnants

Of fool and feather that they got in France, 25

With all their honorable points of ignorance 26

Pertaining thereunto, as fights and fireworks, 27

Abusing better men than they can be

Out of a foreign wisdom, renouncing clean

The faith they have in tennis and tall stockings,

Short blistered breeches, and those types of travel, 31

And understand again like honest men,

Or pack to their old playfellows. There, I take it, 33

They may, *cum privilegio, "oui"* away 34

The lag end of their lewdness and be laughed at. 35

13 springhalt nervous twitching in a horse's hind legs **14 to 't** moreover, besides **15 they've . . . Christendom** they have exhausted the repertory of Christian fashions **18 clapped** placed **23 Louvre** royal palace in France, seat of the French court **25 fool and feather** i.e., folly and fashion **26 honorable . . . ignorance** i.e., what they ignorantly assume to be honorable **27 as** such as. **fireworks** i.e., whores **31 blistered** puffed. **types** emblems **33 pack** be off **34 cum privilegio** with exclusive right, immunity **34–35 oui . . . lewdness** i.e., in French manner pass the last days of their worthless lives

SANDS
'Tis time to give 'em physic, their diseases 36
Are grown so catching.

CHAMBERLAIN What a loss our ladies
Will have of these trim vanities!

LOVELL Ay, marry, 38
There will be woe indeed, lords. The sly whoresons
Have got a speeding trick to lay down ladies; 40
A French song and a fiddle has no fellow. 41

SANDS
The devil fiddle 'em! I am glad they are going,
For sure there's no converting of 'em. Now
An honest country lord, as I am, beaten
A long time out of play, may bring his plainsong 45
And have an hour of hearing, and, by 'r Lady,
Held current music too.

CHAMBERLAIN Well said, Lord Sands. 47
Your colt's tooth is not cast yet?

SANDS No, my lord, 48
Nor shall not while I have a stump.

CHAMBERLAIN Sir Thomas, 49
Whither were you a-going?

LOVELL To the Cardinal's.
Your lordship is a guest too.

CHAMBERLAIN O, 'tis true.
This night he makes a supper, and a great one, 52
To many lords and ladies. There will be
The beauty of this kingdom, I'll assure you.

LOVELL
That churchman bears a bounteous mind indeed,
A hand as fruitful as the land that feeds us; 56
His dews fall everywhere.

CHAMBERLAIN No doubt he's noble;
He had a black mouth that said other of him. 58

36 physic medicine **38 trim vanities** finely dressed but worthless dandies **40 speeding** successful. **lay down** seduce **41 fellow** equal **45 play** i.e., playing love games. **plainsong** simple chant or air **47 Held current** regarded as fashionable **48 colt's tooth** i.e., lecherousness of youth. **cast** given up **49 stump** i.e., of a tooth (with a bawdy pun) **52 makes** gives **56 fruitful** generous **58 He . . . mouth** a person must have an evil habit of speech

SANDS
He may, my lord. H'as wherewithal: in him 59
Sparing would show a worse sin than ill doctrine. 60
Men of his way should be most liberal; 61
They are set here for examples.
CHAMBERLAIN True, they are so;
But few now give so great ones. My barge stays; 63
Your lordship shall along. Come, good Sir Thomas,
We shall be late else, which I would not be, 65
For I was spoke to, with Sir Henry Guildford, 66
This night to be comptrollers.
SANDS I am your lordship's. 67
Exeunt.

✤

1.4

Hautboys. A small table under a state for the Cardinal, a longer table for the guests. Then enter Anne Bullen and divers other ladies and gentlemen as guests, at one door; at another door enter Sir Henry Guildford.

GUILDFORD
Ladies, a general welcome from His Grace
Salutes ye all. This night he dedicates
To fair content and you. None here, he hopes,
In all this noble bevy, has brought with her 4
One care abroad. He would have all as merry
As, first, good company, good wine, good welcome
Can make good people.

Enter Lord Chamberlain, Lord Sands, and [*Sir Thomas*] *Lovell.*

O my lord, you're tardy.
The very thought of this fair company
Clapped wings to me.
CHAMBERLAIN You are young, Sir Harry Guildford.

59 H'as he has. **wherewithal** necessary means **60 Sparing** frugality. **show** appear. **ill doctrine** heresy **61 way** way of life **63 stays** waits for me **65 else** otherwise **66 spoke to** asked **67 comptrollers** masters of ceremonies

1.4. Location: Westminster. A hall in York Place.
s.d. Hautboys reed instruments related to the modern oboe. **state** canopy **4 bevy** company

SANDS
Sir Thomas Lovell, had the Cardinal
But half my lay thoughts in him, some of these 11
Should find a running banquet ere they rested, 12
I think would better please 'em. By my life, 13
They are a sweet society of fair ones.

LOVELL
O, that your lordship were but now confessor
To one or two of these!

SANDS I would I were;
They should find easy penance.

LOVELL Faith, how easy?

SANDS
As easy as a down bed would afford it.

CHAMBERLAIN
Sweet ladies, will it please you sit? Sir Harry,
Place you that side; I'll take the charge of this. 20
[*The guests are shown their places at table.*]
His Grace is entering. Nay, you must not freeze;
Two women placed together makes cold weather.
My Lord Sands, you are one will keep 'em waking; 23
Pray, sit between these ladies.

SANDS By my faith,
And thank your lordship. By your leave, sweet ladies.
[*He takes a place between Anne Bullen and another lady.*]
If I chance to talk a little wild, forgive me;
I had it from my father.

ANNE Was he mad, sir?

SANDS
O, very mad, exceeding mad, in love too.
But he would bite none; just as I do now,
He would kiss you twenty with a breath. 30
[*He kisses her.*]

CHAMBERLAIN Well said, my lord. 31

11 lay secular **12 running banquet** hasty meal (with bawdy double meaning, found also perhaps in *lay,* l. 11, *confessor, easy penance,* etc.) **13 I think** i.e., which I think **20 Place you** assign places on **23 waking** i.e., lively **30 kiss you** kiss. (*You* is used colloquially to acknowledge the person addressed.) **twenty** i.e., twenty women. **with a breath** at one breath **31 said** done

So, now you're fairly seated. Gentlemen,
The penance lies on you if these fair ladies
Pass away frowning.

SANDS For my little cure, 34
Let me alone. 35

Hautboys. Enter Cardinal Wolsey and takes his state.

WOLSEY
You're welcome, my fair guests. That noble lady
Or gentleman that is not freely merry
Is not my friend. This, to confirm my welcome;
And to you all, good health! [*He drinks.*]

SANDS Your Grace is noble.
Let me have such a bowl may hold my thanks 40
And save me so much talking.

WOLSEY My Lord Sands,
I am beholding to you; cheer your neighbors. 42
Ladies, you are not merry. Gentlemen,
Whose fault is this?

SANDS The red wine first must rise
In their fair cheeks, my lord; then we shall have 'em
Talk us to silence.

ANNE You are a merry gamester, 46
My Lord Sands.

SANDS Yes, if I make my play. 47
Here's to your ladyship; and pledge it, madam, 48
For 'tis to such a thing—

ANNE You cannot show me. 49

SANDS [*To Wolsey*]
I told Your Grace they would talk anon.

Drum and trumpet. Chambers discharged.

WOLSEY What's that? 50

34 cure (1) remedy (2) cure of souls (continuing the ecclesiastical metaphor of l. 15) **35 s.d. state** chair of state **40 may** as may **42 beholding** beholden. **cheer** entertain **46 gamester** sportful, frolicsome person. (But Sands, in his reply, plays on the sense of "gambler.") **47 make my play** win my game (of love) **48 pledge it** drink in response to my toast **49 'tis . . . thing** (Sands proposes his toast in an unfinished sentence that is erotically suggestive.) **You . . . me** i.e., you can't teach me a lesson in how to drink a toast. (Anne parries the erotic suggestion of Sands by drinking to him.) **50 s.d. Chambers** small pieces of cannon (the firing of which in 1613 probably started the fire that burned down the Globe playhouse)

CHAMBERLAIN
Look out there, some of ye. [*Exit a Servant.*]

WOLSEY
What warlike voice,
And to what end, is this? Nay, ladies, fear not;
By all the laws of war you're privileged. 53

Enter a Servant.

CHAMBERLAIN
How now? What is 't?

SERVANT
A noble troop of strangers, 54
For so they seem. They've left their barge and landed,
And hither make, as great ambassadors 56
From foreign princes.

WOLSEY
Good Lord Chamberlain,
Go, give 'em welcome; you can speak the French tongue;
And, pray, receive 'em nobly and conduct 'em
Into our presence, where this heaven of beauty
Shall shine at full upon them. Some attend him.
[*Exit Chamberlain, attended.*]
All rise, and tables removed.
You have now a broken banquet, but we'll mend it.
A good digestion to you all! And once more
I shower a welcome on ye. Welcome all!

Hautboys. Enter King and others, as maskers, habited like shepherds, ushered by the Lord Chamberlain. They pass directly before the Cardinal and gracefully salute him.

A noble company! What are their pleasures?

CHAMBERLAIN
Because they speak no English, thus they prayed
To tell Your Grace that, having heard by fame 67
Of this so noble and so fair assembly
This night to meet here, they could do no less,
Out of the great respect they bear to beauty,
But leave their flocks and, under your fair conduct, 71
Crave leave to view these ladies and entreat

53 privileged i.e., entitled to immunity in the event of conflict
54 strangers foreigners **56 make** come **67 fame** report **71 fair conduct** kind permission

An hour of revels with 'em.

WOLSEY Say, Lord Chamberlain,
They have done my poor house grace, for which I pay 'em
A thousand thanks, and pray 'em take their pleasures.
Choose ladies; King and Anne Bullen.

KING
The fairest hand I ever touched! O beauty,
Till now I never knew thee! *Music. Dance.*

WOLSEY
My lord!

CHAMBERLAIN Your Grace?

WOLSEY Pray, tell 'em thus much from me:
There should be one amongst 'em, by his person,
More worthy this place than myself, to whom, 80
If I but knew him, with my love and duty
I would surrender it.

CHAMBERLAIN I will, my lord.
Whisper [*with the maskers*].

WOLSEY
What say they?

CHAMBERLAIN Such a one, they all confess,
There is indeed, which they would have Your Grace
Find out, and he will take it.

WOLSEY Let me see, then. 85
[*He comes from his chair of state.*]
By all your good leaves, gentlemen; here I'll make
My royal choice. [*He bows before the King.*]

KING [*Unmasking*] Ye have found him, Cardinal.
You hold a fair assembly; you do well, lord.
You are a churchman, or I'll tell you, Cardinal,
I should judge now unhappily.

WOLSEY I am glad 90
Your Grace is grown so pleasant.

KING My Lord Chamberlain, 91
Prithee, come hither. What fair lady's that?

80 this place i.e., this chair of state **85 it** i.e., the chair of state
90 unhappily unfavorably **91 pleasant** merry

CHAMBERLAIN
An 't please Your Grace, Sir Thomas Bullen's daughter— 93
The Viscount Rochford—one of Her Highness' women.

KING
By heaven, she is a dainty one.—Sweetheart,
I were unmannerly to take you out 96
And not to kiss you. [*He kisses Anne.*] A health, gentlemen! 97
Let it go round. [*He offers a toast.*]

WOLSEY
Sir Thomas Lovell, is the banquet ready
I' the privy chamber?

LOVELL Yes, my lord.

WOLSEY [*To the King*] Your Grace,
I fear, with dancing is a little heated.

KING
I fear, too much.

WOLSEY There's fresher air, my lord,
In the next chamber.

KING
Lead in your ladies every one.—Sweet partner,
I must not yet forsake you.—Let's be merry,
Good my lord Cardinal. I have half a dozen healths
To drink to these fair ladies, and a measure 107
To lead 'em once again; and then let's dream
Who's best in favor. Let the music knock it. 109
Exeunt, with trumpets.

✤

93 An 't if it **96 take you out** lead you out for a dance **97 health** toast **107 measure** stately dance **109 best in favor** handsomest. **knock it** strike up

2.1 *Enter two Gentlemen, at several doors.*

FIRST GENTLEMAN
Whither away so fast?
SECOND GENTLEMAN O, God save ye!
Ev'n to the hall, to hear what shall become 2
Of the great Duke of Buckingham.
FIRST GENTLEMAN I'll save you
That labor, sir. All's now done but the ceremony
Of bringing back the prisoner.
SECOND GENTLEMAN Were you there?
FIRST GENTLEMAN
Yes, indeed was I.
SECOND GENTLEMAN Pray, speak what has happened.
FIRST GENTLEMAN
You may guess quickly what.
SECOND GENTLEMAN Is he found guilty?
FIRST GENTLEMAN
Yes, truly is he, and condemned upon 't.
SECOND GENTLEMAN
I am sorry for 't.
FIRST GENTLEMAN So are a number more.
SECOND GENTLEMAN But pray, how passed it? 10
FIRST GENTLEMAN
I'll tell you in a little. The great Duke 11
Came to the bar, where to his accusations
He pleaded still not guilty and alleged 13
Many sharp reasons to defeat the law. 14
The King's attorney on the contrary
Urged on the examinations, proofs, confessions 16
Of divers witnesses, which the Duke desired
To have brought viva voce to his face; 18
At which appeared against him his surveyor,
Sir Gilbert Perk his chancellor, and John Car,
Confessor to him, with that devil monk,
Hopkins, that made this mischief.

2.1. Location: Westminster. A street.
s.d. several separate **2 the hall** i.e., Westminster Hall, where the trial was held **10 passed it** did it proceed **11 in a little** in brief **13 alleged** brought forward **14 law** i.e., case against him **16 examinations** depositions **18 viva voce** so that their voices could be heard

SECOND GENTLEMAN That was he
That fed him with his prophecies?
FIRST GENTLEMAN The same.
All these accused him strongly, which he fain 24
Would have flung from him, but indeed he could not;
And so his peers, upon this evidence,
Have found him guilty of high treason. Much
He spoke, and learnedly, for life; but all
Was either pitied in him or forgotten. 29
SECOND GENTLEMAN
After all this, how did he bear himself?
FIRST GENTLEMAN
When he was brought again to th' bar, to hear
His knell rung out, his judgment, he was stirred 32
With such an agony he sweat extremely,
And something spoke in choler, ill and hasty. 34
But he fell to himself again, and sweetly 35
In all the rest showed a most noble patience.
SECOND GENTLEMAN
I do not think he fears death.
FIRST GENTLEMAN Sure he does not;
He never was so womanish. The cause
He may a little grieve at.
SECOND GENTLEMAN Certainly
The Cardinal is the end of this.
FIRST GENTLEMAN 'Tis likely, 40
By all conjectures; first, Kildare's attainder, 41
Then deputy of Ireland, who removed, 42
Earl Surrey was sent thither, and in haste too,
Lest he should help his father.
SECOND GENTLEMAN That trick of state 44
Was a deep envious one.
FIRST GENTLEMAN At his return 45

24 which i.e., which accusations. **fain** gladly **29 Was . . . forgotten** either produced no effect or produced only ineffectual pity
32 judgment sentence **34 choler** anger. **ill** malevolent **35 fell to** recovered **40 end** cause **41 Kildare's attainder** i.e., the confiscation of estates and sentencing to death of the Earl of Kildare, Lord Lieutenant of Ireland (whom Wolsey, according to Holinshed, removed to make room for Thomas Howard, Earl of Surrey, son-in-law to Buckingham, and thereby keep Surrey in effective exile) **42 who removed** i.e., Kildare having been removed **44 father** i.e., father-in-law. **trick of state** political stratagem **45 envious** malicious

No doubt he will requite it. This is noted, 46
And generally: whoever the King favors, 47
The Cardinal instantly will find employment,
And far enough from court too.

SECOND GENTLEMAN All the commons
Hate him perniciously and, o' my conscience, 50
Wish him ten fathom deep. This duke as much
They love and dote on, call him bounteous Buckingham,
The mirror of all courtesy— 53

Enter Buckingham from his arraignment, tipstaves before him, the ax with the edge towards him, halberds on each side, accompanied with Sir Thomas Lovell, Sir Nicholas Vaux, Sir Walter Sands, and common people, etc.

FIRST GENTLEMAN Stay there, sir,
And see the noble ruined man you speak of.

SECOND GENTLEMAN
Let's stand close and behold him.

BUCKINGHAM All good people,
You that thus far have come to pity me,
Hear what I say, and then go home and lose me. 57
I have this day received a traitor's judgment,
And by that name must die. Yet, heaven bear witness,
And if I have a conscience, let it sink me, 60
Even as the ax falls, if I be not faithful!
The law I bear no malice for my death;
'T has done, upon the premises, but justice; 63
But those that sought it I could wish more Christians. 64
Be what they will, I heartily forgive 'em.
Yet let 'em look they glory not in mischief,
Nor build their evils on the graves of great men, 67
For then my guiltless blood must cry against 'em.
For further life in this world I ne'er hope,
Nor will I sue, although the King have mercies
More than I dare make faults. You few that loved me

46 requite repay **47 generally** by everybody **50 perniciously** with deadly hatred **53 mirror** i.e., paragon **s.d. tipstaves** bailiffs. **halberds** halberdiers, with long-handled weapons. **Walter** ("William" in Holinshed.) **57 lose** forget **60 sink** ruin **63 premises** evidence **64 more** better **67 Nor . . . men** i.e., nor extend their own evil careers by extinguishing the lives of noblemen. (*Evils* may suggest "hovels" or "privies.")

And dare be bold to weep for Buckingham,
His noble friends and fellows, whom to leave 73
Is only bitter to him, only dying, 74
Go with me like good angels to my end,
And, as the long divorce of steel falls on me, 76
Make of your prayers one sweet sacrifice, 77
And lift my soul to heaven.—Lead on, i' God's name!

LOVELL
I do beseech Your Grace, for charity,
If ever any malice in your heart
Were hid against me, now to forgive me frankly.

BUCKINGHAM
Sir Thomas Lovell, I as free forgive you
As I would be forgiven. I forgive all.
There cannot be those numberless offenses
'Gainst me that I cannot take peace with; no black envy 85
Shall mark my grave. Commend me to His Grace,
And if he speak of Buckingham, pray tell him
You met him half in heaven. My vows and prayers
Yet are the King's and, till my soul forsake, 89
Shall cry for blessings on him. May he live
Longer than I have time to tell his years! 91
Ever beloved and loving may his rule be!
And when old Time shall lead him to his end, 93
Goodness and he fill up one monument! 94

LOVELL
To th' waterside I must conduct Your Grace,
Then give my charge up to Sir Nicholas Vaux,
Who undertakes you to your end.

VAUX
Prepare there; 97
The Duke is coming. See the barge be ready,
And fit it with such furniture as suits 99
The greatness of his person.

BUCKINGHAM
Nay, Sir Nicholas,
Let it alone; my state now will but mock me. 101
When I came hither, I was Lord High Constable

73–74 whom . . . him i.e., the loss of whose dear company is the only cause of bitterness in death **76 divorce of steel** i.e., separation of body and soul effected by the executioner's ax **77 sacrifice** offering **85 take** make. **envy** malice **89 Yet** still. **forsake** leave my body **91 tell** count **93 Time** age **94 monument** tomb **97 undertakes** takes charge of **99 furniture** equipment **101 state** rank

And Duke of Buckingham; now, poor Edward Bohun. 103
Yet I am richer than my base accusers,
That never knew what truth meant. I now seal it, 105
And with that blood will make 'em one day groan for 't.
My noble father, Henry of Buckingham,
Who first raised head against usurping Richard, 108
Flying for succor to his servant Banister,
Being distressed, was by that wretch betrayed,
And without trial fell; God's peace be with him!
Henry the Seventh succeeding, truly pitying
My father's loss, like a most royal prince
Restored me to my honors, and out of ruins
Made my name once more noble. Now his son,
Henry the Eighth, life, honor, name, and all
That made me happy, at one stroke has taken
Forever from the world. I had my trial,
And must needs say a noble one; which makes me
A little happier than my wretched father.
Yet thus far we are one in fortunes: both
Fell by our servants, by those men we loved most—
A most unnatural and faithless service!
Heaven has an end in all. Yet, you that hear me, 124
This from a dying man receive as certain:
Where you are liberal of your loves and counsels
Be sure you be not loose; for those you make friends 127
And give your hearts to, when they once perceive
The least rub in your fortunes, fall away 129
Like water from ye, never found again
But where they mean to sink ye. All good people,
Pray for me! I must now forsake ye. The last hour
Of my long weary life is come upon me.
Farewell! And when you would say something that
is sad,
Speak how I fell. I have done; and God forgive me!
Exeunt Duke and train.

FIRST GENTLEMAN
O, this is full of pity! Sir, it calls,

103 Bohun (The Duke's family name was actually Stafford; Shakespeare follows the error in Holinshed.) **105 seal** ratify, attest to the truth of **108 raised head** gathered an army **124 end** aim **127 loose** wanting in restraint, careless **129 rub** impediment. (A term from bowls.)

I fear, too many curses on their heads
That were the authors.

SECOND GENTLEMAN If the Duke be guiltless,
'Tis full of woe. Yet I can give you inkling
Of an ensuing evil, if it fall,
Greater than this.

FIRST GENTLEMAN Good angels keep it from us!
What may it be? You do not doubt my faith, sir? 142

SECOND GENTLEMAN
This secret is so weighty, 'twill require
A strong faith to conceal it.

FIRST GENTLEMAN Let me have it;
I do not talk much.

SECOND GENTLEMAN I am confident; 145
You shall, sir. Did you not of late days hear 146
A buzzing of a separation 147
Between the King and Katharine?

FIRST GENTLEMAN Yes, but it held not; 148
For when the King once heard it, out of anger
He sent command to the Lord Mayor straight
To stop the rumor and allay those tongues 151
That durst disperse it.

SECOND GENTLEMAN But that slander, sir,
Is found a truth now, for it grows again
Fresher than e'er it was, and held for certain
The King will venture at it. Either the Cardinal,
Or some about him near, have, out of malice 156
To the good Queen, possessed him with a scruple 157
That will undo her. To confirm this too,
Cardinal Campeius is arrived, and lately, 159
As all think, for this business.

FIRST GENTLEMAN 'Tis the Cardinal;

142 faith i.e., ability to keep a secret **145 am confident** i.e., trust your discretion **146 shall** i.e., shall hear it. **late** recent **147 buzzing** rumor **148 held not** ceased; or perhaps was not believed **151 allay** restrain **156 about him near** close to him **157 possessed . . . scruple** put into his mind a doubt. (Katharine had been married to Henry's older brother, Prince Arthur, who died, still in his early teens, a year after the marriage. Such a precontract would normally invalidate a subsequent marriage with any close relative of Arthur's, but Henry's marriage to Katharine had been made possible by a papal dispensation.) **159 Cardinal Campeius** i.e., Cardinal Lorenzo Campeggio, sent from Rome to confer on the legality of the King's marriage

And merely to revenge him on the Emperor 161
For not bestowing on him at his asking
The archbishopric of Toledo, this is purposed. 163

SECOND GENTLEMAN
I think you have hit the mark. But is 't not cruel
That she should feel the smart of this? The Cardinal 165
Will have his will, and she must fall.

FIRST GENTLEMAN 'Tis woeful.
We are too open here to argue this; 167
Let's think in private more. *Exeunt.*

✤

2.2 *Enter Lord Chamberlain, reading this letter.*

CHAMBERLAIN "My lord, the horses your lordship sent for, with all the care I had, I saw well chosen, ridden, 2 and furnished. They were young and handsome, and 3 of the best breed in the north. When they were ready to set out for London, a man of my lord Cardinal's, by commission and main power, took 'em from me 6 with this reason: his master would be served before a subject, if not before the King; which stopped our mouths, sir."
I fear he will indeed. Well, let him have them.
He will have all, I think.

Enter to the Lord Chamberlain the Dukes of Norfolk and Suffolk.

NORFOLK Well met, my Lord Chamberlain.
CHAMBERLAIN Good day to both Your Graces.

SUFFOLK
How is the King employed?

CHAMBERLAIN I left him private, 14
Full of sad thoughts and troubles.

NORFOLK What's the cause? 15

161 Emperor (The Queen was the aunt of Charles V, Holy Roman Emperor and King of Spain; see 1.1.176 and note.) **163 purposed** intended **165 smart** pain **167 open** public

2.2. Location: London. The royal court.
2 ridden broken in, trained **3 furnished** equipped **6 commission** warrant. **main** great **14 private** alone **15 sad** serious

CHAMBERLAIN
It seems the marriage with his brother's wife
Has crept too near his conscience.
SUFFOLK No, his conscience
Has crept too near another lady.
NORFOLK 'Tis so.
This is the Cardinal's doing. The king-cardinal,
That blind priest, like the eldest son of Fortune, 20
Turns what he list. The King will know him one day. 21
SUFFOLK
Pray God he do! He'll never know himself else.
NORFOLK
How holily he works in all his business! 23
And with what zeal! For, now he has cracked the league
Between us and the Emperor, the Queen's great-nephew,
He dives into the King's soul and there scatters
Dangers, doubts, wringing of the conscience,
Fears, and despairs, and all these for his marriage.
And out of all these to restore the King,
He counsels a divorce, a loss of her
That, like a jewel, has hung twenty years
About his neck, yet never lost her luster;
Of her that loves him with that excellence
That angels love good men with; even of her
That, when the greatest stroke of fortune falls,
Will bless the King. And is not this course pious?
CHAMBERLAIN
Heaven keep me from such counsel! 'Tis most true
These news are everywhere; every tongue speaks 'em, 38
And every true heart weeps for 't. All that dare
Look into these affairs see this main end,
The French king's sister. Heaven will one day open 41
The King's eyes, that so long have slept upon 42
This bold bad man.
SUFFOLK And free us from his slavery.
NORFOLK We had need pray,
And heartily, for our deliverance,

20–21 blind . . . list (Alludes to Fortune, conventionally depicted as blind and turning her wheel.) **21 list** wishes **23 he** i.e., Wolsey **38 news are** (*News* was commonly considered a plural noun.) **41 The . . . sister** i.e., the Duchess of Alençon; see 3.2.85–86 **42 slept upon** been blind to

Or this imperious man will work us all
From princes into pages. All men's honors 47
Lie like one lump before him, to be fashioned 48
Into what pitch he please.

SUFFOLK For me, my lords, 49
I love him not, nor fear him; there's my creed.
As I am made without him, so I'll stand, 51
If the King please. His curses and his blessings
Touch me alike; they're breath I not believe in.
I knew him, and I know him; so I leave him
To him that made him proud, the Pope.

NORFOLK Let's in,
And with some other business put the King
From these sad thoughts that work too much upon him.
My lord, you'll bear us company?

CHAMBERLAIN Excuse me;
The King has sent me otherwhere. Besides, 59
You'll find a most unfit time to disturb him.
Health to your lordships.

NORFOLK Thanks, my good Lord Chamberlain. 61

Exit Lord Chamberlain; and the King draws the curtain and sits reading pensively.

SUFFOLK
How sad he looks! Sure he is much afflicted. 62

KING
Who's there, ha?

NORFOLK Pray God he be not angry.

KING
Who's there, I say? How dare you thrust yourselves
Into my private meditations?
Who am I? Ha?

NORFOLK
A gracious king that pardons all offenses

47 pages attendants **48 lump** i.e., lump of clay **49 pitch** height (literally, of a falcon's flight), i.e., degree of dignity. (In a mixed metaphor, the Cardinal is likened to one who reduces all men of rank to one lump, which he will refashion into creatures of whatever stature he pleases.) **51 As . . . stand** i.e., inasmuch as my rank was conferred on me by the King, not by Wolsey, I'll stand firm **59 otherwhere** elsewhere **61 s.d. curtain** (The King is probably in a "discovery space" rear stage.) **62 afflicted** troubled

Malice ne'er meant. Our breach of duty this way 68
Is business of estate, in which we come 69
To know your royal pleasure.

KING Ye are too bold.
Go to! I'll make ye know your times of business.
Is this an hour for temporal affairs, ha?

Enter Wolsey and Campeius, with a commission.

Who's there? My good lord Cardinal? O my Wolsey,
The quiet of my wounded conscience,
Thou art a cure fit for a king. [*To Campeius.*] You're
welcome,
Most learnèd reverend sir, into our kingdom.
Use us and it. [*To Wolsey.*] My good lord, have great care
I be not found a talker.

WOLSEY Sir, you cannot. 78
I would Your Grace would give us but an hour
Of private conference.

KING [*To Norfolk and Suffolk*] We are busy; go.

NORFOLK [*Aside to Suffolk*]
This priest has no pride in him?

SUFFOLK [*Aside to Norfolk*] Not to speak of.
I would not be so sick, though, for his place. 82
But this cannot continue.

NORFOLK [*Aside to Suffolk*] If it do,
I'll venture one have-at-him.

SUFFOLK [*Aside to Norfolk*] I another. 84
Exeunt Norfolk and Suffolk.

WOLSEY
Your Grace has given a precedent of wisdom 85
Above all princes, in committing freely
Your scruple to the voice of Christendom. 87
Who can be angry now? What envy reach you? 88

68 this way in this respect **69 estate** public weal **78 I . . . talker** i.e., lest my offer of hospitality be only talk, not deeds **82 sick** i.e., sick with pride. **for his place** even to gain his high office **84 have-at-him** i.e., thrust at him (Wolsey) in fencing **85 precedent** example
87 scruple doubt. **voice of Christendom** i.e., the Pope, through his representative Campeius, and the clerics and scholars of various continental universities to whom Henry submitted his problem of "conscience" **88 envy** malice

The Spaniard, tied by blood and favor to her, 89
Must now confess, if they have any goodness, 90
The trial just and noble. All the clerks— 91
I mean the learnèd ones in Christian kingdoms—
Have their free voices. Rome, the nurse of judgment, 93
Invited by your noble self, hath sent
One general tongue unto us, this good man, 95
This just and learnèd priest, Card'nal Campeius,
Whom once more I present unto Your Highness.

KING [*Embracing Campeius*]
And once more in mine arms I bid him welcome,
And thank the holy conclave for their loves. 99
They have sent me such a man I would have wished for.

CAMPEIUS
Your Grace must needs deserve all strangers' loves, 101
You are so noble. To Your Highness' hand
I tender my commission, by whose virtue,
The court of Rome commanding, you, my lord
Cardinal of York, are joined with me their servant
In the unpartial judging of this business.
[*He gives the King a document.*]

KING
Two equal men. The Queen shall be acquainted 107
Forthwith for what you come. Where's Gardiner? 108

WOLSEY
I know Your Majesty has always loved her
So dear in heart not to deny her that 110
A woman of less place might ask by law: 111
Scholars allowed freely to argue for her.

KING
Ay, and the best she shall have, and my favor
To him that does best; God forbid else. Cardinal,
Prithee, call Gardiner to me, my new secretary.
I find him a fit fellow. [*Wolsey goes to the door.*] 116

Enter Gardiner.

89 The Spaniard i.e., Charles V and his court **90 confess** concede **91 clerks** clerics, scholars **93 voices** votes **95 One general tongue** i.e., a spokesman **99 conclave** College of Cardinals **101 needs** necessarily. **strangers'** foreigners' **107 equal** impartial. **acquainted** informed **108 Gardiner** i.e., Stephen Gardiner, Wolsey's secretary; he later becomes one of the most influential members of the King's Council **110 that** that which **111 less place** lower rank **116 fit** suitable

WOLSEY [*Aside to Gardiner*]
Give me your hand. Much joy and favor to you;
You are the King's now.
GARDINER [*Aside to Wolsey*] But to be commanded
Forever by Your Grace, whose hand has raised me.
KING Come hither, Gardiner. *Walks and whispers.*
CAMPEIUS
My lord of York, was not one Doctor Pace 121
In this man's place before him?
WOLSEY Yes, he was.
CAMPEIUS
Was he not held a learnèd man?
WOLSEY Yes, surely.
CAMPEIUS
Believe me, there's an ill opinion spread, then,
Even of yourself, Lord Cardinal.
WOLSEY How? Of me?
CAMPEIUS
They will not stick to say you envied him, 126
And, fearing he would rise, he was so virtuous,
Kept him a foreign man still, which so grieved him 128
That he ran mad and died.
WOLSEY Heaven's peace be with him! 129
That's Christian care enough. For living murmurers 130
There's places of rebuke. He was a fool,
For he would needs be virtuous. That good fellow,
[*Indicating Gardiner*]
If I command him, follows my appointment; 133
I will have none so near else. Learn this, brother: 134
We live not to be gripped by meaner persons. 135
KING [*To Gardiner*]
Deliver this with modesty to the Queen. 136
Exit Gardiner.
The most convenient place that I can think of

121 Doctor Pace i.e., Richard Pace, Dean of Saint Paul's and Secretary of State, who served King Henry and Wolsey on diplomatic missions
126 stick hesitate. **envied him** i.e., were hostile toward Pace **128 Kept . . . still** kept him constantly abroad on diplomatic missions **129 died** (Pace actually died in 1536, six years after Wolsey's death.)
130 murmurers grumblers, troublemakers **133 appointment** bidding
134 none . . . else i.e., no one besides him so close to the King
135 gripped clutched at **136 Deliver . . . modesty** make this known gently

For such receipt of learning is Blackfriars; 138
There ye shall meet about this weighty business.
My Wolsey, see it furnished. O my lord,
Would it not grieve an able man to leave 141
So sweet a bedfellow? But conscience, conscience!
O, 'tis a tender place, and I must leave her. *Exeunt.*

✤

2.3 *Enter Anne Bullen and an Old Lady.*

ANNE
Not for that neither. Here's the pang that pinches:
His Highness having lived so long with her, and she
So good a lady that no tongue could ever
Pronounce dishonor of her—by my life, 4
She never knew harm-doing—O, now, after
So many courses of the sun enthroned,
Still growing in a majesty and pomp, the which 7
To leave a thousandfold more bitter than
'Tis sweet at first t' acquire—after this process, 9
To give her the avaunt! It is a pity 10
Would move a monster.

OLD LADY Hearts of most hard temper
Melt and lament for her.

ANNE O, God's will, much better
She ne'er had known pomp. Though 't be temporal, 13
Yet, if that quarrel, Fortune, do divorce 14
It from the bearer, 'tis a sufferance panging 15
As soul and body's severing.

OLD LADY Alas, poor lady!
She's a stranger now again.

ANNE So much the more 17
Must pity drop upon her. Verily,

138 such . . . learning giving a proper reception to such learned men. **Blackfriars** convent buildings in London surrendered to the crown in Henry VIII's time **141 able** vigorous

2.3. Location: London. The Queen's apartments.
4 Pronounce speak **7 Still** always **9 process** course of events **10 give . . . avaunt** bid her begone. **pity** pitiful situation **13 temporal** merely worldly prosperity, not heavenly **14 quarrel** quarreler, troublemaker **15 sufferance panging** suffering as painful **17 stranger** foreigner

I swear, 'tis better to be lowly born,
And range with humble livers in content, 20
Than to be perked up in a glistering grief 21
And wear a golden sorrow.

OLD LADY Our content
Is our best having.

ANNE By my troth and maidenhead, 23
I would not be a queen.

OLD LADY Beshrew me, I would,
And venture maidenhead for 't; and so would you, 25
For all this spice of your hypocrisy. 26
You that have so fair parts of woman on you 27
Have too a woman's heart, which ever yet 28
Affected eminence, wealth, sovereignty; 29
Which, to say sooth, are blessings; and which gifts, 30
Saving your mincing, the capacity 31
Of your soft cheveril conscience would receive 32
If you might please to stretch it.

ANNE Nay, good troth.

OLD LADY
Yes, troth, and troth. You would not be a queen?

ANNE
No, not for all the riches under heaven.

OLD LADY
'Tis strange. A threepence bowed would hire me, 36
Old as I am, to queen it. But, I pray you,
What think you of a duchess? Have you limbs
To bear that load of title?

ANNE No, in truth.

OLD LADY
Then you are weakly made. Pluck off a little; 40
I would not be a young count in your way 41
For more than blushing comes to. If your back

20 range rank. **livers** persons **21 perked up** trimmed out **23 having** possession. **troth** good faith **25 venture** risk **26 For all** in spite of. **spice** dash, touch **27 parts** qualities **28 ever yet** always **29 Affected** loved **30 sooth** truth **31 Saving your mincing** i.e., your affected coyness notwithstanding **32 cheveril** kid leather. (Used as a type of flexibility.) **36 bowed** crooked and therefore worthless; with sexual pun on "bawd," continued in *queen* (quean, whore), *bear, count* (female pudenda), *way, emballing* **40 Pluck off** come lower **41 count** (A rank below that of duke.)

Cannot vouchsafe this burden, 'tis too weak 43
Ever to get a boy.

ANNE How you do talk!
I swear again, I would not be a queen
For all the world.

OLD LADY In faith, for little England
You'd venture an emballing. I myself 47
Would for Caernarvonshire, although there 'longed 48
No more to the crown but that. Lo, who comes here?

Enter Lord Chamberlain.

CHAMBERLAIN
Good morrow, ladies. What were 't worth to know
The secret of your conference?

ANNE My good lord, 51
Not your demand; it values not your asking. 52
Our mistress' sorrows we were pitying.

CHAMBERLAIN
It was a gentle business, and becoming
The action of good women. There is hope
All will be well.

ANNE Now I pray God, amen!

CHAMBERLAIN
You bear a gentle mind, and heavenly blessings
Follow such creatures. That you may, fair lady,
Perceive I speak sincerely, and high note's
Ta'en of your many virtues, the King's Majesty
Commends his good opinion of you, and 61
Does purpose honor to you no less flowing 62
Than Marchioness of Pembroke; to which title
A thousand pound a year annual support
Out of his grace he adds.

ANNE I do not know 65
What kind of my obedience I should tender.
More than my all is nothing; nor my prayers

43 vouchsafe this burden i.e., accept this load of honors (with sexual suggestion of bearing a man) **47 emballing** investiture with the ball as a royal emblem (with sexual suggestion) **48 Caernarvonshire** an especially impoverished and barren Welsh county. **'longed** belonged **51 conference** conversation **52 Not your demand** i.e., it is not even worth your demand. **values not** is not worth **61 Commends** expresses **62 purpose** intend. **flowing** abundant **65 grace** favor

Are not words duly hallowed, nor my wishes
More worth than empty vanities; yet prayers and wishes
Are all I can return. Beseech your lordship,
Vouchsafe to speak my thanks and my obedience, 71
As from a blushing handmaid, to His Highness,
Whose health and royalty I pray for.

CHAMBERLAIN Lady,
I shall not fail t' approve the fair conceit 74
The King hath of you. [*Aside*.] I have perused her well;
Beauty and honor in her are so mingled
That they have caught the King. And who knows yet
But from this lady may proceed a gem
To lighten all this isle? [*To Anne*.] I'll to the King, 79
And say I spoke with you.

ANNE My honored lord! *Exit Lord Chamberlain.*

OLD LADY Why, this it is! See, see,
I have been begging sixteen years in court,
Am yet a courtier beggarly, nor could 84
Come pat betwixt too early and too late 85
For any suit of pounds; and you—O fate!— 86
A very fresh fish here—fie, fie, fie upon
This compelled fortune!—have your mouth filled up 88
Before you open it.

ANNE This is strange to me.

OLD LADY
How tastes it? Is it bitter? Forty pence, no. 90
There was a lady once—'tis an old story—
That would not be a queen, that would she not,
For all the mud in Egypt. Have you heard it? 93

ANNE
Come, you are pleasant.

OLD LADY With your theme, I could 94
O'ermount the lark. The Marchioness of Pembroke?
A thousand pounds a year for pure respect? 96
No other obligation? By my life,

71 Vouchsafe be so kind as **74 approve . . . conceit** confirm the good opinion **79 lighten** give light to. (Refers to Queen Elizabeth.)
84 beggarly i.e., still in need **85 pat** precisely at the opportune time **86 suit of pounds** request for money **88 compelled** unsought, forced upon one **90 Forty pence, no** i.e., I'll venture a small sum that it isn't bitter to you **93 the mud in Egypt** i.e., the wealth of Egypt resulting from its fecund land **94 pleasant** merry **96 pure** mere

That promises more thousands. Honor's train 98
Is longer than his foreskirt. By this time 99
I know your back will bear a duchess. Say,
Are you not stronger than you were?

ANNE Good lady,
Make yourself mirth with your particular fancy, 102
And leave me out on 't. Would I had no being,
If this salute my blood a jot! It faints me 104
To think what follows.
The Queen is comfortless, and we forgetful
In our long absence. Pray, do not deliver 107
What here you've heard to her.

OLD LADY What do you think me? *Exeunt.*

2.4

Trumpets, sennet, and cornets. Enter two Vergers, with short silver wands; next them two Scribes, in the habit of doctors; after them the [*Arch*] *bishop of Canterbury alone; after him the Bishops of Lincoln, Ely, Rochester, and Saint Asaph; next them, with some small distance, follows a Gentleman bearing the purse, with the great seal, and a cardinal's hat; then two Priests, bearing each a silver cross; then* [*Griffith,*] *a Gentleman Usher, bareheaded, accompanied with a Sergeant at Arms bearing a silver mace; then two Gentlemen bearing two great silver pillars; after them, side by side, the two Cardinals; two Noblemen with the sword and mace. The King takes place under the cloth of state; the two Cardinals sit under him as judges. The Queen takes place some distance*

98–99 Honor's . . . foreskirt i.e., honors to come will exceed this present gift, just as an elongated robe trailing behind is longer than the front of a skirt **102 your . . . fancy** your own private imaginings **104 salute** act upon, excite. **faints me** makes me faint **107 deliver** report

2.4. Location: London. A hall in Blackfriars.
s.d. sennet trumpet call announcing a procession. **Vergers** those who carry the verge or emblem of office; particularly, attendants on a church dignitary. **habit of doctors** i.e., furred black gowns and flat caps worn by doctors of law. **cloth of state** canopy.

from the King. The Bishops place themselves on each side the court, in manner of a consistory; below them the Scribes. The Lords sit next the Bishops. The rest of the attendants stand in convenient order about the stage.

WOLSEY
Whilst our commission from Rome is read,
Let silence be commanded.

KING
What's the need?
It hath already publicly been read,
And on all sides th' authority allowed; 4
You may then spare that time.

WOLSEY
Be 't so. Proceed.

SCRIBE
Say, "Henry, King of England, come into the court."

CRIER
Henry, King of England, come into the court.

KING Here.

SCRIBE
Say, "Katharine, Queen of England, come into the court."

CRIER
Katharine, Queen of England, come into the court.

The Queen makes no answer, rises out of her chair, goes about the court, comes to the King, and kneels at his feet; then speaks.

KATHARINE
Sir, I desire you do me right and justice,
And to bestow your pity on me; for
I am a most poor woman, and a stranger,
Born out of your dominions, having here
No judge indifferent, nor no more assurance 15
Of equal friendship and proceeding. Alas, sir, 16
In what have I offended you? What cause
Hath my behavior given to your displeasure
That thus you should proceed to put me off 19
And take your good grace from me? Heaven witness,

consistory college of cardinals **4 allowed** conceded **15 indifferent** impartial **16 equal** fair **19 put me off** discard me

I have been to you a true and humble wife,
At all times to your will conformable,
Ever in fear to kindle your dislike, 23
Yea, subject to your countenance—glad or sorry
As I saw it inclined. When was the hour
I ever contradicted your desire,
Or made it not mine too? Or which of your friends
Have I not strove to love, although I knew
He were mine enemy? What friend of mine
That had to him derived your anger did I 30
Continue in my liking, nay, gave notice
He was from thence discharged? Sir, call to mind
That I have been your wife in this obedience
Upward of twenty years, and have been blessed
With many children by you. If, in the course 35
And process of this time, you can report,
And prove it too, against mine honor aught— 37
My bond to wedlock, or my love and duty
Against your sacred person—in God's name 39
Turn me away, and let the foul'st contempt
Shut door upon me, and so give me up
To the sharp'st kind of justice. Please you, sir,
The King your father was reputed for
A prince most prudent, of an excellent
And unmatched wit and judgment. Ferdinand 45
My father, King of Spain, was reckoned one 46
The wisest prince that there had reigned by many 47
A year before. It is not to be questioned
That they had gathered a wise council to them
Of every realm, that did debate this business,
Who deemed our marriage lawful. Wherefore I humbly
Beseech you, sir, to spare me till I may
Be by my friends in Spain advised, whose counsel
I will implore. If not, i' the name of God,
Your pleasure be fulfilled!

WOLSEY You have here, lady,
And of your choice, these reverend fathers, men

23 dislike displeasure **30 derived** drawn **35 many children** (The Queen gave birth to five children, only one of whom, later Queen Mary, survived infancy.) **37 aught** anything **39 Against** toward **45 wit** intelligence **46–47 one The wisest** the very wisest

Of singular integrity and learning,
Yea, the elect o' the land, who are assembled
To plead your cause. It shall be therefore bootless 59
That longer you desire the court, as well 60
For your own quiet as to rectify 61
What is unsettled in the King.

CAMPEIUS His Grace
Hath spoken well and justly. Therefore, madam,
It's fit this royal session do proceed, 64
And that without delay their arguments
Be now produced and heard.

KATHARINE Lord Cardinal,
To you I speak.

WOLSEY Your pleasure, madam?

KATHARINE Sir,
I am about to weep; but, thinking that
We are a queen, or long have dreamed so, certain 69
The daughter of a king, my drops of tears
I'll turn to sparks of fire.

WOLSEY Be patient yet.

KATHARINE
I will, when you are humble; nay, before, 72
Or God will punish me. I do believe,
Induced by potent circumstances, that 74
You are mine enemy, and make my challenge 75
You shall not be my judge. For it is you
Have blown this coal betwixt my lord and me— 77
Which God's dew quench! Therefore I say again,
I utterly abhor, yea, from my soul 79
Refuse you for my judge, whom yet once more
I hold my most malicious foe, and think not
At all a friend to truth.

WOLSEY I do profess
You speak not like yourself, who ever yet 83
Have stood to charity and displayed th' effects 84
Of disposition gentle and of wisdom

59 bootless profitless **60 That . . . court** that you entreat the court to postpone its work **61 quiet** peace of mind **64 fit** appropriate
69 certain certainly **72 before** i.e., sooner than that (which will never be) **74 Induced** persuaded **75 make my challenge** I raise my formal objection (that) **77 blown this coal** i.e., stirred up this trouble
79 abhor protest against. (A technical term of canon law.) **83 ever yet** always **84 stood to** upheld

O'ertopping woman's pow'r. Madam, you do me wrong.
I have no spleen against you, nor injustice 87
For you or any. How far I have proceeded,
Or how far further shall, is warranted 89
By a commission from the consistory,
Yea, the whole consistory of Rome. You charge me
That I have blown this coal. I do deny it.
The King is present. If it be known to him
That I gainsay my deed, how may he wound, 94
And worthily, my falsehood, yea, as much 95
As you have done my truth! If he know
That I am free of your report, he knows 97
I am not of your wrong. Therefore in him 98
It lies to cure me, and the cure is to
Remove these thoughts from you; the which before
His Highness shall speak in, I do beseech 101
You, gracious madam, to unthink your speaking
And to say so no more.

KATHARINE My lord, my lord,
I am a simple woman, much too weak
T' oppose your cunning. You're meek and humble-
mouthed;
You sign your place and calling, in full seeming, 106
With meekness and humility; but your heart
Is crammed with arrogancy, spleen, and pride.
You have, by fortune and His Highness' favors,
Gone slightly o'er low steps and now are mounted 110
Where powers are your retainers, and your words, 111
Domestics to you, serve your will as 't please 112
Yourself pronounce their office. I must tell you, 113
You tender more your person's honor than 114
Your high profession spiritual, that again
I do refuse you for my judge, and here
Before you all appeal unto the Pope,

87 spleen malice **89 warranted** justified **94 gainsay my deed** deny my acts **95 worthily** deservedly **97 report** adverse report, accusation **98 am . . . wrong** am innocent of having wronged you **101 in** regarding **106 sign** signify, show marks of. **in full seeming** to all appearances **110 slightly** easily **111 powers . . . retainers** i.e., you command the service of people of rank **111–113 your words . . . office** i.e., your clever speeches serve your ends in any way you choose; or, your very words are immediately acted upon **114 tender more** are more concerned for

To bring my whole cause 'fore His Holiness
And to be judged by him.

She curtsies to the King, and offers to depart.

CAMPEIUS The Queen is obstinate,
Stubborn to justice, apt to accuse it, and 120
Disdainful to be tried by 't. 'Tis not well.
She's going away.

KING Call her again.

CRIER
Katharine, Queen of England, come into the court.

GRIFFITH Madam, you are called back.

KATHARINE
What need you note it? Pray you, keep your way; 126
When you are called, return. Now, the Lord help!
They vex me past my patience. Pray you, pass on.
I will not tarry; no, nor ever more
Upon this business my appearance make
In any of their courts.

Exeunt Queen and her attendants.

KING Go thy ways, Kate.
That man i' the world who shall report he has
A better wife, let him in naught be trusted
For speaking false in that. Thou art alone—
If thy rare qualities, sweet gentleness,
Thy meekness saintlike, wifelike government, 136
Obeying in commanding, and thy parts 137
Sovereign and pious else, could speak thee out— 138
The queen of earthly queens.—She's noble born,
And like her true nobility she has
Carried herself towards me.

WOLSEY Most gracious sir, 141
In humblest manner I require Your Highness 142
That it shall please you to declare, in hearing
Of all these ears—for where I am robbed and bound,
There must I be unloosed, although not there
At once and fully satisfied—whether ever I 146

120 Stubborn resistant **126 What** why. **keep your way** move on
136 government self-control, behavior **137 Obeying in commanding** i.e., combining the qualities of obedient wife and regal queen. **parts** qualities **138 else** besides. **speak thee out** declare you as you are
141 Carried borne, behaved **142 require** request **146 At . . . satisfied** given full restitution

Did broach this business to Your Highness, or
Laid any scruple in your way, which might
Induce you to the question on 't? Or ever
Have to you, but with thanks to God for such
A royal lady, spake one the least word that might 151
Be to the prejudice of her present state,
Or touch of her good person?

KING My lord Cardinal, 153
I do excuse you; yea, upon mine honor, 154
I free you from 't. You are not to be taught 155
That you have many enemies that know not
Why they are so, but, like to village curs,
Bark when their fellows do. By some of these
The Queen is put in anger. You're excused.
But will you be more justified? You ever 160
Have wished the sleeping of this business, never desired
It to be stirred, but oft have hindered, oft,
The passages made toward it. On my honor, 163
I speak my good lord Cardinal to this point, 164
And thus far clear him. Now, what moved me to 't,
I will be bold with time and your attention;
Then mark th' inducement. Thus it came; give heed to 't:
My conscience first received a tenderness,
Scruple, and prick, on certain speeches uttered
By th' Bishop of Bayonne, then French ambassador,
Who had been hither sent on the debating
A marriage twixt the Duke of Orleans and
Our daughter Mary. I' the progress of this business,
Ere a determinate resolution, he— 174
I mean the Bishop—did require a respite, 175
Wherein he might the King his lord advertise 176
Whether our daughter were legitimate,
Respecting this our marriage with the dowager, 178
Sometime our brother's wife. This respite shook 179
The bosom of my conscience, entered me,
Yea, with a spitting power, and made to tremble 181
The region of my breast, which forced such way

151 one the least a single **153 touch** sullying **154 excuse** exonerate **155 are not** do not need **160 justified** vindicated **163 passages** proceedings **164 speak** describe **174 determinate resolution** final decision **175 require** request **176 advertise** inform, confer with **178 dowager** widow **179 Sometime** formerly **181 spitting** piercing

That many mazed considerings did throng 183
And pressed in with this caution. First, methought 184
I stood not in the smile of heaven, who had 185
Commanded nature that my lady's womb,
If it conceived a male child by me, should
Do no more offices of life to 't than 188
The grave does to the dead; for her male issue
Or died where they were made, or shortly after 190
This world had aired them. Hence I took a thought 191
This was a judgment on me that my kingdom,
Well worthy the best heir o' the world, should not
Be gladded in 't by me. Then follows that 194
I weighed the danger which my realms stood in
By this my issue's fail, and that gave to me 196
Many a groaning throe. Thus hulling in 197
The wild sea of my conscience, I did steer
Toward this remedy, whereupon we are
Now present here together; that's to say,
I meant to rectify my conscience—which
I then did feel full sick, and yet not well— 202
By all the reverend fathers of the land
And doctors learned. First I began in private
With you, my lord of Lincoln. You remember
How under my oppression I did reek 206
When I first moved you.

LINCOLN Very well, my liege. 207

KING
I have spoke long. Be pleased yourself to say
How far you satisfied me.

LINCOLN So please Your Highness,
The question did at first so stagger me—
Bearing a state of mighty moment in 't, 211
And consequence of dread—that I committed 212
The daring'st counsel which I had to doubt 213

183 mazed considerings conflicting and confused thoughts **184 caution** warning **185 smile** i.e., favor **188 offices** services **190 Or** either **191 aired** given air to **194 gladded** made happy **196 By . . . fail** by my lacking a son **197 throe** pang, pain. **hulling** drifting with sails furled **202 yet** still, even now **206 oppression** distress. **reek** sweat **207 moved** mentioned the business to **211–212 Bearing . . . dread** relating to matters of the greatest consequence to the state and outcome fearful to contemplate **212–213 I committed . . . doubt** i.e., I hesitantly and with foreboding offered the best advice I could give

And did entreat Your Highness to this course
Which you are running here.

KING [*To Canterbury*] I then moved you,
My lord of Canterbury, and got your leave
To make this present summons. Unsolicited
I left no reverend person in this court,
But by particular consent proceeded
Under your hands and seals. Therefore, go on, 220
For no dislike i' the world against the person
Of the good Queen, but the sharp thorny points
Of my allegèd reasons, drives this forward.
Prove but our marriage lawful, by my life
And kingly dignity, we are contented
To wear our mortal state to come with her, 226
Katharine our queen, before the primest creature 227
That's paragoned o' the world.

CAMPEIUS So please Your Highness, 228
The Queen being absent, 'tis a needful fitness 229
That we adjourn this court till further day. 230
Meanwhile must be an earnest motion 231
Made to the Queen to call back her appeal
She intends unto His Holiness.

KING [*Aside*] I may perceive
These cardinals trifle with me. I abhor
This dilatory sloth and tricks of Rome.
My learned and well-belovèd servant, Cranmer,
Prithee, return. With thy approach, I know, 237
My comfort comes along.—Break up the court!
I say, set on. *Exeunt in manner as they entered.* 239

✤

220 Under . . . seals i.e., with your signed agreement **226 wear . . . her** (1) share the state of human existence with her till we die (2) share royal pomp with her **227 primest** most excellent **228 paragoned** set forth as a perfect model **229 needful fitness** necessary and proper action **230 further** future **231 motion** appeal, request **237 Prithee, return** (Henry apostrophizes the Protestant churchman, Thomas Cranmer, who at this time, though the play doesn't say so directly, is on the Continent collecting opinions on the King's marriage question. His return is mentioned at 3.2.401.) **239 set on** do it, proceed

3.1 *Enter Queen and her women, as at work.*

KATHARINE
Take thy lute, wench. My soul grows sad with troubles;
Sing, and disperse 'em if thou canst. Leave working. 2

GENTLEWOMAN [*Sings*]
Orpheus with his lute made trees, 3
And the mountain tops that freeze,
Bow themselves when he did sing.
To his music plants and flowers
Ever sprung, as sun and showers 7
There had made a lasting spring.

Everything that heard him play,
Even the billows of the sea,
Hung their heads, and then lay by. 11
In sweet music is such art,
Killing care and grief of heart 13
Fall asleep, or hearing, die.

Enter a Gentleman.

KATHARINE How now?

GENTLEMAN
An 't please Your Grace, the two great cardinals 16
Wait in the presence.

KATHARINE Would they speak with me? 17

GENTLEMAN
They willed me say so, madam.

KATHARINE Pray Their Graces 18
To come near. [*Gentleman goes to the door.*] What can be their business
With me, a poor weak woman, fall'n from favor?
I do not like their coming. Now I think on 't,
They should be good men, their affairs as righteous. 22
But all hoods make not monks.

Enter the two cardinals, Wolsey and Campeius.

3.1. Location: London. The Queen's apartments.
2 Leave stop **3 Orpheus** legendary musician in Greek mythology. **made trees** i.e., caused trees to bow **7 as** as if **11 lay by** subsided **13 Killing care** (so that) care that kills **16 An 't** if it **17 presence** reception room **18 willed** bade **22 their . . . righteous** i.e., the business they come on should be, like themselves, good

WOLSEY Peace to Your Highness!

KATHARINE

Your Graces find me here part of a huswife— 24

I would be all—against the worst may happen. 25

What are your pleasures with me, reverend lords?

WOLSEY

May it please you, noble madam, to withdraw

Into your private chamber, we shall give you

The full cause of our coming.

KATHARINE Speak it here.

There's nothing I have done yet, o' my conscience,

Deserves a corner. Would all other women 31

Could speak this with as free a soul as I do! 32

My lords, I care not, so much I am happy 33

Above a number, if my actions 34

Were tried by ev'ry tongue, ev'ry eye saw 'em,

Envy and base opinion set against 'em, 36

I know my life so even. If your business 37

Seek me out, and that way I am wife in, 38

Out with it boldly. Truth loves open dealing.

WOLSEY *Tanta est erga te mentis integritas, regina ser-* 40
enissima— 41

KATHARINE O, good my lord, no Latin!

I am not such a truant since my coming

As not to know the language I have lived in.

A strange tongue makes my cause more strange,
suspicious; 45

Pray, speak in English. Here are some will thank you,

If you speak truth, for their poor mistress' sake.

Believe me, she has had much wrong. Lord Cardinal,

The willing'st sin I ever yet committed 49

May be absolved in English.

WOLSEY Noble lady,

I am sorry my integrity should breed—

24 part of a huswife i.e., partially tending to household duties **25 I . . . all** i.e., I wish to be a complete housewife, in case I am divorced and forced to live alone. **against** in anticipation of **31 a corner** i.e., secrecy **32 free** innocent **33 happy** fortunate (in virtue) **34 a number** many **36 Envy** malice. **opinion** rumor **37 even** constant, upright **38 Seek . . . in** concerns me regarding my conduct as a wife **40–41 Tanta . . . serenissima** so innocent are our intentions toward you, most serene queen **45 strange** foreign **49 willing'st** most deliberate

And service to His Majesty and you—
So deep suspicion, where all faith was meant.
We come not by the way of accusation, 54
To taint that honor every good tongue blesses,
Nor to betray you any way to sorrow—
You have too much, good lady—but to know
How you stand minded in the weighty difference 58
Between the King and you, and to deliver, 59
Like free and honest men, our just opinions 60
And comforts to your cause.

CAMPEIUS Most honored madam,
My lord of York, out of his noble nature,
Zeal, and obedience he still bore Your Grace, 63
Forgetting, like a good man, your late censure
Both of his truth and him—which was too far— 65
Offers, as I do, in a sign of peace, 66
His service and his counsel.

KATHARINE [*Aside*] To betray me.—
My lords, I thank you both for your good wills.
Ye speak like honest men; pray God ye prove so!
But how to make ye suddenly an answer
In such a point of weight, so near mine honor—
More near my life, I fear—with my weak wit, 72
And to such men of gravity and learning,
In truth, I know not. I was set at work 74
Among my maids, full little, God knows, looking
Either for such men or such business.
For her sake that I have been—for I feel 77
The last fit of my greatness—good Your Graces, 78
Let me have time and counsel for my cause.
Alas, I am a woman, friendless, hopeless!

WOLSEY
Madam, you wrong the King's love with these fears.
Your hopes and friends are infinite.

KATHARINE In England
But little for my profit. Can you think, lords, 83

54 by the way for the purpose **58 minded** inclined, disposed. **difference** quarrel **59 deliver** declare **60 free** frank **63 still bore** has always borne **65 far** severe **66 in** as **72 wit** understanding **74 set** seated **77 For . . . been** for the sake of the queenly person I once was **78 fit** brief space, short spell **83 profit** benefit

That any Englishman dare give me counsel,
Or be a known friend, 'gainst His Highness' pleasure,
Though he be grown so desperate to be honest, 86
And live a subject? Nay, forsooth, my friends,
They that must weigh out my afflictions, 88
They that my trust must grow to, live not here.
They are, as all my other comforts, far hence
In mine own country, lords.

CAMPEIUS I would Your Grace
Would leave your griefs and take my counsel.

KATHARINE How, sir?

CAMPEIUS
Put your main cause into the King's protection;
He's loving and most gracious. 'Twill be much
Both for your honor better and your cause;
For if the trial of the law o'ertake ye,
You'll part away disgraced.

WOLSEY He tells you rightly. 97

KATHARINE
Ye tell me what ye wish for both—my ruin.
Is this your Christian counsel? Out upon ye!
Heaven is above all yet; there sits a judge
That no king can corrupt.

CAMPEIUS Your rage mistakes us. 101

KATHARINE
The more shame for ye! Holy men I thought ye,
Upon my soul, two reverend cardinal virtues; 103
But cardinal sins and hollow hearts I fear ye. 104
Mend 'em, for shame, my lords. Is this your comfort?
The cordial that ye bring a wretched lady, 106
A woman lost among ye, laughed at, scorned?
I will not wish ye half my miseries;
I have more charity. But say I warned ye;
Take heed, for heaven's sake take heed, lest at once 110
The burden of my sorrows fall upon ye.

86 so desperate i.e., reckless enough as **88 weigh out** compensate for **97 part away** depart **101 mistakes** misjudges **103 cardinal virtues** i.e., justice, temperance, fortitude, and prudence, constituting four of the seven virtues opposing the seven Deadly Sins **104 cardinal sins** i.e., the seven Deadly Sins **106 cordial** restorative medicine **110 at once** all at once

WOLSEY
Madam, this is a mere distraction. 112
You turn the good we offer into envy. 113

KATHARINE
Ye turn me into nothing. Woe upon ye
And all such false professors! Would you have me—
If you have any justice, any pity,
If ye be anything but churchmen's habits— 117
Put my sick cause into his hands that hates me?
Alas, he's banished me his bed already,
His love too long ago! I am old, my lords,
And all the fellowship I hold now with him
Is only my obedience. What can happen
To me above this wretchedness? All your studies 123
Make me a curse like this!

CAMPEIUS
Your fears are worse. 124

KATHARINE
Have I lived thus long—let me speak myself, 125
Since virtue finds no friends—a wife, a true one?
A woman, I dare say without vainglory,
Never yet branded with suspicion?
Have I with all my full affections
Still met the King, loved him next heaven, obeyed him, 130
Been, out of fondness, superstitious to him, 131
Almost forgot my prayers to content him,
And am I thus rewarded? 'Tis not well, lords.
Bring me a constant woman to her husband,
One that ne'er dreamed a joy beyond his pleasure,
And to that woman, when she has done most,
Yet will I add an honor: a great patience.

WOLSEY
Madam, you wander from the good we aim at. 138

KATHARINE
My lord, I dare not make myself so guilty
To give up willingly that noble title

112 mere distraction absolute frenzy **113 envy** malice **117 habits** garments **123 above** more than **123–124 All . . . this** i.e., I challenge you, in your clerical exertions, to devise a worse fate than I already have **124 worse** i.e., than your wretchedness **125 speak** describe, speak for **130 Still** always. **next** next to **131 superstitious** i.e., to the point of idolatry **138 wander from** mistake

Your master wed me to. Nothing but death
Shall e'er divorce my dignities.

WOLSEY
Pray, hear me.

KATHARINE
Would I had never trod this English earth
Or felt the flatteries that grow upon it!
Ye have angels' faces, but heaven knows your hearts.
What will become of me now, wretched lady?
I am the most unhappy woman living.
[*To her women.*] Alas, poor wenches, where are now
your fortunes?
Shipwrecked upon a kingdom where no pity,
No friends, no hope, no kindred weep for me,
Almost no grave allowed me. Like the lily
That once was mistress of the field and flourished,
I'll hang my head and perish.

WOLSEY
If Your Grace
Could but be brought to know our ends are honest, 154
You'd feel more comfort. Why should we, good lady,
Upon what cause, wrong you? Alas, our places, 156
The way of our profession, is against it;
We are to cure such sorrows, not to sow 'em.
For goodness' sake, consider what you do,
How you may hurt yourself, ay, utterly
Grow from the King's acquaintance, by this carriage. 161
The hearts of princes kiss obedience,
So much they love it; but to stubborn spirits
They swell and grow as terrible as storms.
I know you have a gentle, noble temper, 165
A soul as even as a calm. Pray, think us 166
Those we profess, peacemakers, friends, and servants.

CAMPEIUS
Madam, you'll find it so. You wrong your virtues
With these weak women's fears. A noble spirit,
As yours was put into you, ever casts 170
Such doubts, as false coin, from it. The King loves you;
Beware you lose it not. For us, if you please

154 ends intentions. **honest** honorable **156 places** official positions
161 Grow from become estranged from. **carriage** conduct **165 temper**
disposition **166 even** steadfast **170 As . . . you** such as was given to you

To trust us in your business, we are ready
To use our utmost studies in your service. 174

KATHARINE
Do what ye will, my lords, and pray forgive me
If I have used myself unmannerly; 176
You know I am a woman, lacking wit
To make a seemly answer to such persons.
Pray, do my service to His Majesty. 179
He has my heart yet, and shall have my prayers
While I shall have my life. Come, reverend fathers,
Bestow your counsels on me. She now begs
That little thought when she set footing here 183
She should have bought her dignities so dear.
Exeunt.

✤

3.2 *Enter the Duke of Norfolk, Duke of Suffolk, Lord Surrey, and Lord Chamberlain.*

NORFOLK
If you will now unite in your complaints,
And force them with a constancy, the Cardinal 2
Cannot stand under them. If you omit 3
The offer of this time, I cannot promise 4
But that you shall sustain more new disgraces
With these you bear already.

SURREY
I am joyful
To meet the least occasion that may give me
Remembrance of my father-in-law, the Duke, 8
To be revenged on him.

SUFFOLK
Which of the peers
Have uncontemned gone by him, or at least 10
Strangely neglected? When did he regard 11

174 studies efforts **176 used myself** conducted myself **179 do my service** pay my respects **183 That** who

3.2. Location: London. Antechamber to the King's apartments.
2 force urge **3–4 If . . . time** if you let this opportunity pass **8 father-in-law** i.e., Buckingham. (See 2.1.41–44 and note.) **10 uncontemned** unscorned **11 Strangely neglected** i.e., not been strangely neglected

The stamp of nobleness in any person
Out of himself?

CHAMBERLAIN My lords, you speak your pleasures. 13
What he deserves of you and me I know;
What we can do to him, though now the time
Gives way to us, I much fear. If you cannot 16
Bar his access to th' King, never attempt 17
Anything on him, for he hath a witchcraft 18
Over the King in 's tongue.

NORFOLK O, fear him not;
His spell in that is out. The King hath found 20
Matter against him that forever mars
The honey of his language. No, he's settled, 22
Not to come off, in his displeasure.

SURREY Sir, 23
I should be glad to hear such news as this
Once every hour.

NORFOLK Believe it, this is true.
In the divorce his contrary proceedings 26
Are all unfolded, wherein he appears 27
As I would wish mine enemy.

SURREY How came
His practices to light?

SUFFOLK Most strangely.

SURREY O, how, how? 29

SUFFOLK
The Cardinal's letters to the Pope miscarried, 30
And came to th' eye o' the King, wherein was read
How that the Cardinal did entreat His Holiness
To stay the judgment o' the divorce; for if 33
It did take place, "I do," quoth he, "perceive
My king is tangled in affection to
A creature of the Queen's, Lady Anne Bullen." 36

SURREY
Has the King this?

SUFFOLK Believe it.

13 Out of excepting **16 Gives way to** favors **17–18 attempt Anything on** attack, move against **20 out** finished **22 settled** fixed **23 come off** escape. **his** i.e., the King's **26 contrary** contradictory, divisive **27 unfolded** exposed **29 practices** plots **30 miscarried** went astray **33 stay** stop, delay **36 creature** dependent

SURREY Will this work?

CHAMBERLAIN

The King in this perceives him, how he coasts 38
And hedges his own way. But in this point 39
All his tricks founder, and he brings his physic 40
After his patient's death. The King already
Hath married the fair lady.

SURREY Would he had!

SUFFOLK

May you be happy in your wish, my lord,
For I profess you have it.

SURREY Now, all my joy
Trace the conjunction!

SUFFOLK My amen to 't!

NORFOLK All men's! 45

SUFFOLK

There's order given for her coronation.
Marry, this is yet but young, and may be left 47
To some ears unrecounted. But, my lords,
She is a gallant creature, and complete 49
In mind and feature. I persuade me, from her 50
Will fall some blessing to this land, which shall
In it be memorized.

SURREY But will the King 52
Digest this letter of the Cardinal's? 53
The Lord forbid!

NORFOLK Marry, amen!

SUFFOLK No, no;
There be more wasps that buzz about his nose
Will make this sting the sooner. Cardinal Campeius
Is stolen away to Rome, hath ta'en no leave,
Has left the cause o' the King unhandled, and
Is posted, as the agent of our cardinal, 59
To second all his plot. I do assure you
The King cried "Ha!" at this.

CHAMBERLAIN Now, God incense him,
And let him cry "Ha!" louder!

38–39 coasts And hedges goes a roundabout way, as by coast and hedgerow **40 physic** medicine, cure **45 Trace** follow **47 young** recent, new **49 complete** perfect, excellent **50 persuade me** am confident **52 memorized** caused to be remembered. (Refers prophetically to Queen Elizabeth.) **53 Digest** put up with, "swallow" **59 Is posted** has gone in haste

NORFOLK But, my lord,
When returns Cranmer?

SUFFOLK
He is returned in his opinions, which 64
Have satisfied the King for his divorce,
Together with all famous colleges
Almost in Christendom. Shortly, I believe,
His second marriage shall be published, and 68
Her coronation. Katharine no more
Shall be called Queen, but Princess Dowager
And widow to Prince Arthur.

NORFOLK This same Cranmer's
A worthy fellow, and hath ta'en much pain
In the King's business.

SUFFOLK He has, and we shall see him
For it an archbishop.

NORFOLK So I hear.

SUFFOLK 'Tis so.

Enter Wolsey and Cromwell.

The Cardinal!

NORFOLK Observe, observe, he's moody. 75
[*The nobles stand aside and observe.*]

WOLSEY
The packet, Cromwell, gave 't you the King? 76

CROMWELL
To his own hand, in 's bedchamber.

WOLSEY Looked he
O' th' inside of the paper?

CROMWELL Presently 78
He did unseal them, and the first he viewed
He did it with a serious mind; a heed 80
Was in his countenance. You he bade
Attend him here this morning.

WOLSEY Is he ready
To come abroad?

CROMWELL I think by this he is. 84

WOLSEY Leave me awhile. *Exit Cromwell.*

64 in his opinions having sent ahead his written opinions **68 published** proclaimed **75 moody** angry **76 packet** parcel of dispatches **78 Presently** immediately **80 heed** concern **84 this** this time

[*To himself.*] It shall be to the Duchess of Alençon,
The French king's sister; he shall marry her.
Anne Bullen? No, I'll no Anne Bullens for him;
There's more in 't than fair visage. Bullen?
No, we'll no Bullens. Speedily I wish
To hear from Rome. The Marchioness of Pembroke?

NORFOLK
He's discontented.

SUFFOLK Maybe he hears the King
Does whet his anger to him.

SURREY Sharp enough,
Lord, for thy justice!

WOLSEY [*To himself*]
The late Queen's gentlewoman, a knight's daughter, 95
To be her mistress' mistress? The Queen's queen?
This candle burns not clear; 'tis I must snuff it, 97
Then out it goes. What though I know her virtuous
And well deserving? Yet I know her for
A spleeny Lutheran, and not wholesome to 100
Our cause, that she should lie i' the bosom of
Our hard-ruled king. Again, there is sprung up 102
An heretic, an arch one, Cranmer, one
Hath crawled into the favor of the King 104
And is his oracle.

NORFOLK He is vexed at something. 105

Enter King, reading of a schedule, [*and Lovell. Wolsey stands apart, not observing the King.*]

SURREY
I would 'twere something that would fret the string, 106
The master cord on 's heart.

SUFFOLK The King, the King! 107

KING [*To himself*]
What piles of wealth hath he accumulated
To his own portion! And what expense by the hour
Seems to flow from him! How i' the name of thrift

95 late former **97 clear** bright. **snuff it** trim its wick **100 spleeny** staunch, contentious **102 hard-ruled** hard to manage **104 Hath** who has **105 s.d. schedule** scroll **106 fret** gnaw through (with a pun on the musical sense of pressing the string of a musical instrument against a "fret" or bar, continued in the play on *cord/chord*) **107 on 's** of his

Does he rake this together?—Now, my lords,
Saw you the Cardinal?

NORFOLK My lord, we have
Stood here observing him. Some strange commotion
Is in his brain. He bites his lip, and starts,
Stops on a sudden, looks upon the ground,
Then lays his finger on his temple; straight 116
Springs out into fast gait, then stops again,
Strikes his breast hard, and anon he casts 118
His eye against the moon. In most strange postures
We have seen him set himself.

KING It may well be
There is a mutiny in 's mind. This morning
Papers of state he sent me to peruse,
As I required; and wot you what I found 123
There—on my conscience, put unwittingly?
Forsooth, an inventory, thus importing 125
The several parcels of his plate, his treasure, 126
Rich stuffs and ornaments of household, which
I find at such proud rate that it outspeaks 128
Possession of a subject.

NORFOLK It's heaven's will. 129
Some spirit put this paper in the packet
To bless your eye withal.

KING If we did think 131
His contemplation were above the earth
And fixed on spiritual object, he should still
Dwell in his musings; but I am afraid
His thinkings are below the moon, not worth 135
His serious considering.

King takes his seat; whispers [*to*] *Lovell,*
who goes to the Cardinal [*Wolsey*].

WOLSEY Heaven forgive me!
Ever God bless Your Highness!

KING Good my lord,
You are full of heavenly stuff and bear the inventory
Of your best graces in your mind, the which

116 straight at once **118 anon** soon **123 wot** know **125 importing** signifying **126 several parcels** various items. **plate** precious metal, bullion **128–129 outspeaks . . . subject** describes possessions exceeding what a subject should have **131 withal** with **135 below the moon** i.e., in the mortal sphere

You were now running o'er. You have scarce time
To steal from spiritual leisure a brief span
To keep your earthly audit. Sure in that
I deem you an ill husband, and am glad 143
To have you therein my companion.

WOLSEY Sir,
For holy offices I have a time; a time
To think upon the part of business which
I bear i' the state; and nature does require
Her times of preservation, which perforce 148
I, her frail son, amongst my brethren mortal,
Must give my tendance to.

KING You have said well. 150

WOLSEY
And ever may Your Highness yoke together,
As I will lend you cause, my doing well
With my well saying!

KING 'Tis well said again,
And 'tis a kind of good deed to say well;
And yet words are no deeds. My father loved you;
He said he did, and with his deed did crown 156
His word upon you. Since I had my office,
I have kept you next my heart, have not alone 158
Employed you where high profits might come home,
But pared my present havings, to bestow 160
My bounties upon you.

WOLSEY [*Aside*] What should this mean?

SURREY [*Aside*]
The Lord increase this business!

KING Have I not made you
The prime man of the state? I pray you, tell me 163
If what I now pronounce you have found true; 164
And if you may confess it, say withal
If you are bound to us or no. What say you?

WOLSEY
My sovereign, I confess your royal graces, 167

143 ill husband unthrifty manager **148 perforce** necessarily
150 tendance attention **156 crown** i.e., fulfill (by appointing Wolsey chaplain in 1507 and Dean of Lincoln in 1509) **158 next** nearest
160 pared . . . havings reduced my own wealth **163 prime** principal
164 pronounce declare **167 graces** favors

Show'red on me daily, have been more than could 168
My studied purposes requite, which went 169
Beyond all man's endeavors. My endeavors
Have ever come too short of my desires,
Yet filed with my abilities. Mine own ends 172
Have been mine so that evermore they pointed 173
To th' good of your most sacred person and
The profit of the state. For your great graces
Heaped upon me, poor undeserver, I
Can nothing render but allegiant thanks, 177
My prayers to heaven for you, my loyalty,
Which ever has and ever shall be growing,
Till death, that winter, kill it.

KING Fairly answered.
A loyal and obedient subject is
Therein illustrated. The honor of it 182
Does pay the act of it, as, i' the contrary, 183
The foulness is the punishment. I presume 184
That, as my hand has opened bounty to you, 185
My heart dropped love, my power rained honor, more
On you than any, so your hand and heart,
Your brain, and every function of your power,
Should, notwithstanding that your bond of duty, 189
As 'twere in love's particular, be more 190
To me, your friend, than any.

WOLSEY I do profess
That for Your Highness' good I ever labored
More than mine own; that am, have, and will be— 193
Though all the world should crack their duty to you 194
And throw it from their soul, though perils did
Abound as thick as thought could make 'em and
Appear in forms more horrid—yet my duty,
As doth a rock against the chiding flood,
Should the approach of this wild river break, 199
And stand unshaken yours.

168–169 more . . . requite more than I could devise means to repay **172 filed** kept pace **173 so that** only to the extent that **177 allegiant** loyal **182 illustrated** made evident **182–183 The honor . . . it** (Cf. "Virtue is its own reward.") **184 foulness** dishonor **185 opened** granted **189 that . . . duty** i.e., your priestly vows **190 in love's particulars** in the special devotion of friendship **193 have** have been **194 crack** violate **199 break** check, hold back

KING 'Tis nobly spoken.
Take notice, lords, he has a loyal breast,
For you have seen him open 't. Read o'er this,
[*Giving him papers*]
And after, this, and then to breakfast with
What appetite you have.
Exit King, frowning upon the Cardinal [*Wolsey*]; *the nobles throng after him* [*the King*], *smiling and whispering,* [*and so exeunt*].

WOLSEY What should this mean?
What sudden anger's this? How have I reaped it? 205
He parted frowning from me, as if ruin
Leaped from his eyes. So looks the chafèd lion 207
Upon the daring huntsman that has galled him, 208
Then makes him nothing. I must read this paper— 209
I fear, the story of his anger. 'Tis so!
This paper has undone me. 'Tis th' account
Of all that world of wealth I have drawn together
For mine own ends—indeed, to gain the popedom
And fee my friends in Rome. O negligence, 214
Fit for a fool to fall by! What cross devil 215
Made me put this main secret in the packet 216
I sent the King? Is there no way to cure this?
No new device to beat this from his brains?
I know 'twill stir him strongly; yet I know
A way, if it take right, in spite of fortune 220
Will bring me off again. What's this? "To th' Pope"? 221
The letter, as I live, with all the business
I writ to 's Holiness. Nay then, farewell!
I have touched the highest point of all my greatness,
And from that full meridian of my glory 225
I haste now to my setting. I shall fall
Like a bright exhalation in the evening, 227
And no man see me more.

205 reaped i.e., deserved, incurred **207 chafèd** angry **208 galled** wounded **209 makes him nothing** destroys him (the hunter) **214 fee** pay, bribe **215 cross** perverse **216 main** weighty **220 take right** succeed **221 bring me off** let me escape **225 meridian** apex, summit **227 exhalation** i.e., any astronomical phenomenon, such as a meteor or a falling star

Enter to Wolsey the Dukes of Norfolk and Suffolk, the Earl of Surrey, and the Lord Chamberlain.

NORFOLK
Hear the King's pleasure, Cardinal, who commands you
To render up the great seal presently 230
Into our hands, and to confine yourself
To Asher House, my lord of Winchester's,
Till you hear further from His Highness.

WOLSEY Stay,
Where's your commission, lords? Words cannot carry 234
Authority so weighty.

SUFFOLK Who dare cross 'em, 235
Bearing the King's will from his mouth expressly?

WOLSEY
Till I find more than will or words to do it—
I mean your malice—know, officious lords,
I dare and must deny it. Now I feel
Of what coarse metal ye are molded—envy; 240
How eagerly ye follow my disgraces
As if it fed ye, and how sleek and wanton 242
Ye appear in everything may bring my ruin!
Follow your envious courses, men of malice!
You have Christian warrant for 'em, and no doubt 245
In time will find their fit rewards. That seal
You ask with such a violence, the King,
Mine and your master, with his own hand gave me;
Bade me enjoy it, with the place and honors,
During my life; and, to confirm his goodness,
Tied it by letters patents. Now, who'll take it? 251

SURREY
The King that gave it.

WOLSEY It must be himself, then.

SURREY
Thou art a proud traitor, priest.

WOLSEY Proud lord, thou liest!

230 presently immediately **234 commission** authorizing warrant **235 cross** oppose **240 envy** malice **242 sleek** fawning. **wanton** merry, frolicsome **245 Christian warrant** i.e., the example of other uncharitable Christians **251 letters patents** formal and public bestowing of rights or powers

Within these forty hours Surrey durst better
Have burnt that tongue than said so.

SURREY Thy ambition,
Thou scarlet sin, robbed this bewailing land 256
Of noble Buckingham, my father-in-law.
The heads of all thy brother cardinals,
With thee and all thy best parts bound together, 259
Weighed not a hair of his. Plague of your policy! 260
You sent me deputy for Ireland,
Far from his succor, from the King, from all
That might have mercy on the fault thou gav'st him; 263
Whilst your great goodness, out of holy pity,
Absolved him with an ax.

WOLSEY This, and all else
This talking lord can lay upon my credit, 266
I answer is most false. The Duke by law
Found his deserts. How innocent I was
From any private malice in his end 269
His noble jury and foul cause can witness.
If I loved many words, lord, I should tell you
You have as little honesty as honor,
That in the way of loyalty and truth 273
Toward the King, my ever royal master,
Dare mate a sounder man than Surrey can be, 275
And all that love his follies.

SURREY By my soul,
Your long coat, priest, protects you; thou shouldst feel
My sword i' the lifeblood of thee else. My lords,
Can ye endure to hear this arrogance?
And from this fellow? If we live thus tamely,
To be thus jaded by a piece of scarlet, 281
Farewell nobility! Let His Grace go forward
And dare us with his cap, like larks.

WOLSEY All goodness 283

256 Thou scarlet sin (Refers to his cardinal's cassock, described as scarlet; see 3.1.103–104. See also Isaiah 1:18.) **259 parts** qualities **260 Weighed** equaled in weight. **Plague of** a plague on. **policy** scheming **263 fault . . . him** offense you charged him (Buckingham) with **266 lay . . . credit** charge against my good name **269 From** of **273 That** I that **275 mate** rival, vie with **281 jaded** intimidated, cowed **283 dare . . . larks** dazzle us with his cardinal's hat as birds with a mirror or a piece of scarlet cloth

Is poison to thy stomach.

SURREY Yes, that goodness
Of gleaning all the land's wealth into one,
Into your own hands, Cardinal, by extortion;
The goodness of your intercepted packets
You writ to th' Pope against the King. Your goodness,
Since you provoke me, shall be most notorious.
My lord of Norfolk, as you are truly noble,
As you respect the common good, the state
Of our despised nobility, our issues, 292
Who, if he live, will scarce be gentlemen,
Produce the grand sum of his sins, the articles 294
Collected from his life. [*To Wolsey.*] I'll startle you
Worse than the sacring bell, when the brown wench 296
Lay kissing in your arms, Lord Cardinal.

WOLSEY
How much, methinks, I could despise this man,
But that I am bound in charity against it!

NORFOLK
Those articles, my lord, are in the King's hand; 300
But thus much, they are foul ones.

WOLSEY So much fairer 301
And spotless shall mine innocence arise
When the King knows my truth.

SURREY This cannot save you. 303
I thank my memory, I yet remember
Some of these articles, and out they shall. 305
Now, if you can blush and cry "Guilty," Cardinal,
You'll show a little honesty.

WOLSEY Speak on, sir;
I dare your worst objections. If I blush, 308
It is to see a nobleman want manners. 309

SURREY
I had rather want those than my head. Have at you!
First, that without the King's assent or knowledge

292 issues sons **294 articles** items of the indictment **296 sacring bell** bell rung at the most solemn portions of the Mass. (Surrey imagines a scene in which Wolsey is startled in the midst of making love by hearing the Mass bell.) **300 hand** possession **301 thus much** (I can say) this much **303 truth** loyalty **305 shall** i.e., shall come **308 objections** accusations **309 want** lack

You wrought to be a legate, by which power 312
You maimed the jurisdiction of all bishops.

NORFOLK
Then, that in all you writ to Rome, or else
To foreign princes, *"Ego et Rex meus"* 315
Was still inscribed, in which you brought the King 316
To be your servant.

SUFFOLK Then that, without the knowledge
Either of King or Council, when you went
Ambassador to the Emperor, you made bold
To carry into Flanders the great seal.

SURREY
Item, you sent a large commission 321
To Gregory de Cassado, to conclude,
Without the King's will or the state's allowance, 323
A league between His Highness and Ferrara.

SUFFOLK
That out of mere ambition you have caused 325
Your holy hat to be stamped on the King's coin.

SURREY
Then, that you have sent innumerable substance— 327
By what means got, I leave to your own conscience—
To furnish Rome, and to prepare the ways 329
You have for dignities, to the mere undoing 330
Of all the kingdom. Many more there are,
Which since they are of you, and odious,
I will not taint my mouth with.

CHAMBERLAIN O my lord,
Press not a falling man too far! 'Tis virtue.
His faults lie open to the laws; let them,
Not you, correct him. My heart weeps to see him
So little of his great self.

SURREY I forgive him.

312 wrought connived, worked. **legate** representative of the Pope
315 Ego et Rex meus my king and I. (Literally, "I and my king"; Norfolk accuses Wolsey of using the phrase in such a way as to make the King his "servant" by naming himself first, but the Latin construction requires that "ego" precede any nouns parallel with it.) **316 still** always
321 Item i.e., another item is. **large** with full power to act **323 allowance** assent **325 mere** sheer **327 innumerable substance** uncountable wealth **329 To furnish Rome** (Implies that Wolsey made gifts to Rome as bribes to obtain his own advancement.) **330 mere** utter

SUFFOLK

Lord Cardinal, the King's further pleasure is—
Because all those things you have done of late
By your power legative within this kingdom 340
Fall into the compass of a praemunire— 341
That therefore such a writ be sued against you, 342
To forfeit all your goods, lands, tenements, 343
Chattels, and whatsoever, and to be 344
Out of the King's protection. This is my charge.

NORFOLK

And so we'll leave you to your meditations
How to live better. For your stubborn answer
About the giving back the great seal to us,
The King shall know it and, no doubt, shall thank you.
So fare you well, my little good lord Cardinal.

Exeunt all but Wolsey.

WOLSEY

So farewell to the little good you bear me.
Farewell? A long farewell, to all my greatness!
This is the state of man: today he puts forth
The tender leaves of hopes; tomorrow blossoms, 354
And bears his blushing honors thick upon him; 355
The third day comes a frost, a killing frost,
And when he thinks, good easy man, full surely 357
His greatness is a-ripening, nips his root,
And then he falls as I do. I have ventured,
Like little wanton boys that swim on bladders, 360
This many summers in a sea of glory,
But far beyond my depth. My high-blown pride
At length broke under me and now has left me,
Weary and old with service, to the mercy
Of a rude stream that must forever hide me. 365
Vain pomp and glory of this world, I hate ye!
I feel my heart new opened. O, how wretched

340 legative as a papal legate **341 Fall . . . praemunire** fall within the penalties for violating a writ of praemunire, i.e., a writ by which one could be charged with appealing to a foreign court (especially a papal court) in an action involving an English subject and hence relevant to the King's court **342 sued** moved, issued **343 tenements** properties not owned outright but held for some set term **344 Chattels** personal possessions **354 tender** young **355 blushing** glowing **357 easy** easy-going **360 wanton** sportful **365 rude** rough

Is that poor man that hangs on princes' favors!
There is betwixt that smile we would aspire to,
That sweet aspect of princes, and their ruin, 370
More pangs and fears than wars or women have;
And when he falls, he falls like Lucifer,
Never to hope again.

Enter Cromwell, standing amazed.

Why, how now, Cromwell? 373

CROMWELL
I have no power to speak, sir.

WOLSEY
What, amazed 374
At my misfortunes? Can thy spirit wonder
A great man should decline? Nay, an you weep, 376
I am fall'n indeed.

CROMWELL
How does Your Grace?

WOLSEY
Why, well;
Never so truly happy, my good Cromwell.
I know myself now, and I feel within me
A peace above all earthly dignities,
A still and quiet conscience. The King has cured me,
I humbly thank His Grace, and from these shoulders,
These ruined pillars, out of pity, taken
A load would sink a navy—too much honor.
O, 'tis a burden, Cromwell, 'tis a burden
Too heavy for a man that hopes for heaven!

CROMWELL
I am glad Your Grace has made that right use of it.

WOLSEY
I hope I have. I am able now, methinks,
Out of a fortitude of soul I feel,
To endure more miseries and greater far
Than my weakhearted enemies dare offer.
What news abroad?

CROMWELL
The heaviest and the worst
Is your displeasure with the King.

WOLSEY
God bless him! 393

CROMWELL
The next is that Sir Thomas More is chosen
Lord Chancellor in your place.

370 their ruin the ruin they bring about **373 s.d.,** **374 amazed** stunned, astonished **376 an** if **393 displeasure** disgrace

WOLSEY That's somewhat sudden.
But he's a learnèd man. May he continue
Long in His Highness' favor and do justice
For truth's sake and his conscience, that his bones,
When he has run his course and sleeps in blessings,
May have a tomb of orphans' tears wept on him! 400
What more?

CROMWELL That Cranmer is returned with welcome,
Installed Lord Archbishop of Canterbury.

WOLSEY
That's news indeed.

CROMWELL Last, that the Lady Anne,
Whom the King hath in secrecy long married,
This day was viewed in open as his queen,
Going to chapel, and the voice is now 406
Only about her coronation.

WOLSEY
There was the weight that pulled me down. O Cromwell,
The King has gone beyond me! All my glories 409
In that one woman I have lost forever.
No sun shall ever usher forth mine honors,
Or gild again the noble troops that waited 412
Upon my smiles. Go get thee from me, Cromwell!
I am a poor fall'n man, unworthy now
To be thy lord and master. Seek the King;
That sun, I pray, may never set! I have told him
What and how true thou art. He will advance thee;
Some little memory of me will stir him—
I know his noble nature—not to let
Thy hopeful service perish too. Good Cromwell,
Neglect him not; make use now, and provide 421
For thine own future safety.

CROMWELL O my lord,
Must I then leave you? Must I needs forgo
So good, so noble, and so true a master?
Bear witness, all that have not hearts of iron,
With what a sorrow Cromwell leaves his lord.
The King shall have my service, but my prayers
Forever and forever shall be yours.

400 orphans' i.e., such as would be under the legal guardianship of the Lord Chancellor **406 voice** talk **409 gone beyond** overreached **412 troops** i.e., of retainers **421 make use** take advantage

WOLSEY
Cromwell, I did not think to shed a tear
In all my miseries, but thou hast forced me,
Out of thy honest truth, to play the woman. 431
Let's dry our eyes. And thus far hear me, Cromwell,
And when I am forgotten, as I shall be,
And sleep in dull cold marble, where no mention
Of me more must be heard of, say I taught thee;
Say Wolsey, that once trod the ways of glory,
And sounded all the depths and shoals of honor, 437
Found thee a way, out of his wreck, to rise in, 438
A sure and safe one, though thy master missed it.
Mark but my fall, and that that ruined me.
Cromwell, I charge thee, fling away ambition!
By that sin fell the angels; how can man, then,
The image of his Maker, hope to win by it? 443
Love thyself last; cherish those hearts that hate thee.
Corruption wins not more than honesty.
Still in thy right hand carry gentle peace 446
To silence envious tongues. Be just, and fear not.
Let all the ends thou aim'st at be thy country's,
Thy God's, and truth's; then if thou fall'st, O Cromwell,
Thou fall'st a blessèd martyr!
Serve the King, and—prithee, lead me in.
There take an inventory of all I have,
To the last penny; 'tis the King's. My robe, 453
And my integrity to heaven, is all
I dare now call mine own. O Cromwell, Cromwell!
Had I but served my God with half the zeal
I served my king, he would not in mine age
Have left me naked to mine enemies.

CROMWELL
Good sir, have patience.

WOLSEY
So I have. Farewell
The hopes of court! My hopes in heaven do dwell.
Exeunt.

431 play the woman i.e., shed tears **437 sounded** explored, fathomed **438 wreck** shipwreck **443 win** profit **446 Still** always **453 robe** i.e., clerical robe

4.1 *Enter two Gentlemen, meeting one another.*

FIRST GENTLEMAN
You're well met once again.
SECOND GENTLEMAN So are you. 1
FIRST GENTLEMAN
You come to take your stand here and behold
The Lady Anne pass from her coronation?
SECOND GENTLEMAN
'Tis all my business. At our last encounter
The Duke of Buckingham came from his trial.
FIRST GENTLEMAN
'Tis very true. But that time offered sorrow;
This, general joy.
SECOND GENTLEMAN 'Tis well. The citizens,
I am sure, have shown at full their royal minds— 8
As, let 'em have their rights, they are ever forward— 9
In celebration of this day with shows,
Pageants, and sights of honor.
FIRST GENTLEMAN Never greater,
Nor, I'll assure you, better taken, sir. 12
SECOND GENTLEMAN
May I be bold to ask what that contains,
That paper in your hand?
FIRST GENTLEMAN Yes, 'tis the list
Of those that claim their offices this day
By custom of the coronation.
The Duke of Suffolk is the first, and claims
To be High Steward; next, the Duke of Norfolk,
He to be Earl Marshal. You may read the rest.
[*He offers a paper.*]
SECOND GENTLEMAN
I thank you, sir. Had I not known those customs,
I should have been beholding to your paper. 21
But, I beseech you, what's become of Katharine,
The Princess Dowager? How goes her business?

4.1. Location: A street in Westminster.
1 You're well met i.e., I am happy to see you **8 royal minds** loyalty to the crown **9 let . . . rights** to give them due credit. **forward** i.e., eager to do **12 taken** received **21 beholding** beholden

FIRST GENTLEMAN

That I can tell you too. The Archbishop
Of Canterbury, accompanied with other
Learnèd and reverend fathers of his order,
Held a late court at Dunstable, six miles off 27
From Ampthill where the Princess lay, to which 28
She was often cited by them, but appeared not; 29
And, to be short, for not-appearance and 30
The King's late scruple, by the main assent 31
Of all these learnèd men she was divorced,
And the late marriage made of none effect; 33
Since which she was removed to Kimbolton,
Where she remains now sick.

SECOND GENTLEMAN Alas, good lady!

[*Trumpets.*]

The trumpets sound. Stand close, the Queen is
coming. *Hautboys.* 36

The Order of the Coronation.

1. *A lively flourish of Trumpets.*
2. *Then, two* Judges.
3. Lord Chancellor, *with purse and mace before him.*
4. Choristers, *singing.* Music.
5. Mayor of London, *bearing the mace. Then* Garter, *in his coat of arms, and on his head he wore a gilt copper crown.*
6. Marquess Dorset, *bearing a scepter of gold, on his head a demi-coronal of gold. With him, the* Earl of Surrey, *bearing the rod of silver with the dove, crowned with an earl's coronet. Collars of* S's.
7. Duke of Suffolk, *in his robe of estate, his coronet on his head, bearing a long white wand, as High Steward. With him, the* Duke of Norfolk, *with the rod of marshalship, a coronet on his head. Collars of* S's.

27 late recent (as also in ll. 31 and 33) **28 lay** lodged **29 cited** summoned **30 short** brief **31 main assent** general agreement **33 of none effect** void, invalid **36 close** aside **s.d. The Order of the Coronation:** (3) **Lord Chancellor** i.e., Sir Thomas More. (4) **Music** musicians (as also in l. 91). (5) **Garter** i.e., Garter King at Arms, a chief herald of the College of Arms. (6) **Collars of S's** golden chains of office made of flat, broad S-shaped links, ornately decorated.

8. *A canopy borne by four of the* Cinque Ports; *under it, the* Queen *in her robe, in her hair, richly adorned with pearl, crowned. On each side her, the* Bishops of London *and* Winchester.
9. *The old* Duchess of Norfolk, *in a coronal of gold wrought with flowers, bearing the Queen's train.*
10. *Certain* Ladies *or* Countesses, *with plain circlets of gold without flowers.*

Exeunt, first passing over the stage in order and state, and then a great flourish of trumpets.

SECOND GENTLEMAN
A royal train, believe me. These I know. 37
Who's that that bears the scepter?

FIRST GENTLEMAN
Marquess Dorset,
And that, the Earl of Surrey, with the rod.

SECOND GENTLEMAN
A bold brave gentleman. That should be
The Duke of Suffolk?

FIRST GENTLEMAN
'Tis the same: High Steward.

SECOND GENTLEMAN
And that, my lord of Norfolk?

FIRST GENTLEMAN
Yes.

SECOND GENTLEMAN [*Looking at the Queen*]
Heaven bless thee!
Thou hast the sweetest face I ever looked on.
Sir, as I have a soul, she is an angel;
Our King has all the Indies in his arms,
And more and richer, when he strains that lady. 46
I cannot blame his conscience.

FIRST GENTLEMAN
They that bear
The cloth of honor over her are four barons 48
Of the Cinque Ports. 49

(8) **Cinque Ports** barons of the Cinque Ports, a group of seaport towns (originally Dover, Hastings, Sandwich, Hythe, and Romney) situated on the southeast coast of England, in ancient times furnishing the chief parts of the English navy, in return for which they had many privileges and franchises. **in her hair** with hair loosely hanging (customary for brides) **37 train** procession **46 strains** embraces **48 cloth of honor** canopy **49 Cinque Ports** (See l. 36 s.d. and note.)

SECOND GENTLEMAN
Those men are happy, and so are all are near her. 50
I take it she that carries up the train
Is that old noble lady, Duchess of Norfolk.

FIRST GENTLEMAN
It is, and all the rest are countesses.

SECOND GENTLEMAN
Their coronets say so. These are stars indeed.

FIRST GENTLEMAN
And sometimes falling ones.

SECOND GENTLEMAN No more of that. 55
[*Exit procession.*]

Enter a third Gentleman.

FIRST GENTLEMAN
God save you, sir! Where have you been broiling? 56

THIRD GENTLEMAN
Among the crowd i' th' Abbey, where a finger
Could not be wedged in more. I am stifled
With the mere rankness of their joy.

SECOND GENTLEMAN You saw 59
The ceremony?

THIRD GENTLEMAN That I did.

FIRST GENTLEMAN How was it?

THIRD GENTLEMAN
Well worth the seeing.

SECOND GENTLEMAN Good sir, speak it to us. 61

THIRD GENTLEMAN
As well as I am able. The rich stream
Of lords and ladies, having brought the Queen
To a prepared place in the choir, fell off 64
A distance from her, while Her Grace sat down
To rest awhile, some half an hour or so,
In a rich chair of state, opposing freely 67
The beauty of her person to the people.
Believe me, sir, she is the goodliest woman
That ever lay by man; which when the people

50 all all who **55 falling** (with a sexual pun) **56 broiling** sweating **59 mere rankness** sheer exuberance **61 speak** describe **64 fell off** withdrew **67 opposing** presenting in full view

Had the full view of, such a noise arose
As the shrouds make at sea in a stiff tempest, 72
As loud, and to as many tunes. Hats, cloaks—
Doublets, I think—flew up; and had their faces 74
Been loose, this day they had been lost. Such joy
I never saw before. Great-bellied women,
That had not half a week to go, like rams 77
In the old time of war, would shake the press 78
And make 'em reel before 'em. No man living
Could say "This is my wife" there, all were woven
So strangely in one piece.

SECOND GENTLEMAN But what followed?

THIRD GENTLEMAN
At length Her Grace rose and with modest paces
Came to the altar, where she kneeled, and saintlike
Cast her fair eyes to heaven and prayed devoutly,
Then rose again and bowed her to the people;
When by the Archbishop of Canterbury
She had all the royal makings of a queen,
As holy oil, Edward Confessor's crown, 88
The rod, and bird of peace, and all such emblems
Laid nobly on her. Which performed, the choir,
With all the choicest music of the kingdom, 91
Together sung *Te Deum*. So she parted, 92
And with the same full state paced back again 93
To York Place, where the feast is held.

FIRST GENTLEMAN Sir,
You must no more call it York Place; that's past,
For since the Cardinal fell that title's lost.
'Tis now the King's, and called Whitehall.

THIRD GENTLEMAN I know it,
But 'tis so lately altered that the old name 98
Is fresh about me.

SECOND GENTLEMAN What two reverend bishops
Were those that went on each side of the Queen?

72 shrouds sail ropes **74 Doublets** close-fitting jackets **77 rams** battering rams **78 press** crowd **88 As** such as, namely **91 music** i.e., musicians **92 Te Deum** (A hymn of thanksgiving, the opening words of which are, *Te Deum laudamus*, "Thee, God, we praise.") **parted** departed **93 state** dignity **98 lately** recently

THIRD GENTLEMAN
Stokesley and Gardiner, the one of Winchester, 101
Newly preferred from the King's secretary, 102
The other, London.
SECOND GENTLEMAN He of Winchester 103
Is held no great good lover of the Archbishop's,
The virtuous Cranmer.
THIRD GENTLEMAN All the land knows that.
However, yet there is no great breach; when it comes,
Cranmer will find a friend will not shrink from him. 107
SECOND GENTLEMAN
Who may that be, I pray you?
THIRD GENTLEMAN Thomas Cromwell,
A man in much esteem with the King, and truly
A worthy friend. The King has made him Master
O' the Jewel House,
And one already of the Privy Council.
SECOND GENTLEMAN
He will deserve more.
THIRD GENTLEMAN Yes, without all doubt.
Come, gentlemen, ye shall go my way, which
Is to the court, and there ye shall be my guests.
Something I can command. As I walk thither, 116
I'll tell ye more.
BOTH You may command us, sir. *Exeunt.*

4.2 *Enter Katharine, Dowager, sick, led between Griffith, her gentleman usher, and Patience, her woman.*

GRIFFITH
How does Your Grace?

101–102 Gardiner . . . secretary (Gardiner, secretary to the King, was made Bishop of Winchester at the fall of Wolsey; he continued to act as secretary for several years.) **102 preferred** promoted **103 London** i.e., Bishop of London **107 will not** who will not **116 Something . . . command** i.e., I can provide refreshment

4.2. Location: Kimbolton Castle in Huntingtonshire. The Queen's apartments.

KATHARINE O Griffith, sick to death!
My legs like loaden branches bow to th' earth, 2
Willing to leave their burden. Reach a chair. [*She sits.*]
So; now, methinks, I feel a little ease.
Didst thou not tell me, Griffith, as thou ledst me,
That the great child of honor, Cardinal Wolsey,
Was dead?

GRIFFITH Yes, madam; but I think Your Grace,
Out of the pain you suffered, gave no ear to 't.

KATHARINE
Prithee, good Griffith, tell me how he died.
If well, he stepped before me happily 10
For my example.

GRIFFITH Well, the voice goes, madam; 11
For after the stout Earl Northumberland 12
Arrested him at York, and brought him forward,
As a man sorely tainted, to his answer, 14
He fell sick suddenly and grew so ill
He could not sit his mule.

KATHARINE Alas, poor man!

GRIFFITH
At last, with easy roads, he came to Leicester, 17
Lodged in the abbey, where the reverend abbot,
With all his convent, honorably received him; 19
To whom he gave these words, "O father Abbot,
An old man, broken with the storms of state,
Is come to lay his weary bones among ye;
Give him a little earth for charity!"
So went to bed, where eagerly his sickness
Pursued him still; and three nights after this,
About the hour of eight, which he himself
Foretold should be his last, full of repentance,
Continual meditations, tears, and sorrows,
He gave his honors to the world again,
His blessèd part to heaven, and slept in peace.

KATHARINE
So may he rest; his faults lie gently on him!

2 loaden laden, weighted down **10 happily** fittingly **11 the voice goes** i.e., people say **12 stout** brave **14 sorely tainted** grievously discredited. **answer** i.e., trial **17 roads** stages (of a journey) **19 convent** monastery

Yet thus far, Griffith, give me leave to speak him, 32
And yet with charity. He was a man
Of an unbounded stomach, ever ranking 34
Himself with princes; one that by suggestion 35
Tied all the kingdom. Simony was fair play; 36
His own opinion was his law. I' the presence 37
He would say untruths, and be ever double 38
Both in his words and meaning. He was never,
But where he meant to ruin, pitiful. 40
His promises were, as he then was, mighty;
But his performance, as he is now, nothing.
Of his own body he was ill, and gave 43
The clergy ill example.

GRIFFITH Noble madam,
Men's evil manners live in brass; their virtues
We write in water. May it please Your Highness
To hear me speak his good now?

KATHARINE Yes, good Griffith;
I were malicious else.

GRIFFITH This cardinal,
Though from an humble stock, undoubtedly
Was fashioned to much honor. From his cradle
He was a scholar, and a ripe and good one,
Exceeding wise, fair-spoken, and persuading;
Lofty and sour to them that loved him not,
But, to those men that sought him, sweet as summer.
And though he were unsatisfied in getting, 55
Which was a sin, yet in bestowing, madam,
He was most princely. Ever witness for him
Those twins of learning that he raised in you, 58
Ipswich and Oxford, one of which fell with him, 59
Unwilling to outlive the good that did it; 60
The other, though unfinished, yet so famous,
So excellent in art, and still so rising, 62

32 speak describe **34 stomach** ambition **35 suggestion** crafty dealing **36 Tied** fettered, controlled. **Simony** the selling of ecclesiastical offices **37 presence** i.e., of the King **38 double** duplicitous **40 pitiful** pitying, compassionate **43 ill** i.e., sexually depraved **55 getting** acquiring wealth **58 raised in you** built in your cities **59 Ipswich and Oxford** (Wolsey founded a college, no longer extant, at Ipswich, where he was born, and a college at Oxford that is now Christ Church.) **60 good that did** good man that founded **62 art** learning

That Christendom shall ever speak his virtue.
His overthrow heaped happiness upon him;
For then, and not till then, he felt himself, 65
And found the blessedness of being little. 66
And, to add greater honors to his age
Than man could give him, he died fearing God.

KATHARINE
After my death I wish no other herald,
No other speaker of my living actions, 70
To keep mine honor from corruption
But such an honest chronicler as Griffith.
Whom I most hated living, thou hast made me, 73
With thy religious truth and modesty, 74
Now in his ashes honor. Peace be with him!
Patience, be near me still, and set me lower.
I have not long to trouble thee. Good Griffith,
Cause the musicians play me that sad note 78
I named my knell, whilst I sit meditating
On that celestial harmony I go to.
Sad and solemn music. [*Katharine sleeps.*]

GRIFFITH
She is asleep. Good wench, let's sit down quiet,
For fear we wake her. Softly, gentle Patience. 82
[*They sit.*]

The vision. Enter, solemnly tripping one after another, six personages, clad in white robes, wearing on their heads garlands of bays, and golden vizards on their faces, branches of bays or palm in their hands. They first congee unto her, then dance; and, at certain changes, the first two hold a spare garland over her head, at which the other four make reverent curtsies. Then the two that held the garland deliver the same to the other next two, who observe the same order in their changes, and holding the garland over her head; which done, they deliver the same garland to the last two, who likewise observe the same

65 felt knew **66 little** of humble station **70 living** while alive
73 Whom he whom **74 modesty** moderation **78 note** tune **82 s.d. The vision: bays** bay leaves. **vizards** masks. **congee** make a congé, a ceremonious bow. **changes** figures in the dance

order; at which, as it were by inspiration, she makes in her sleep signs of rejoicing, and holdeth up her hands to heaven; and so in their dancing vanish, carrying the garland with them. The music continues.

KATHARINE [*Waking*]
Spirits of peace, where are ye? Are ye all gone,
And leave me here in wretchedness behind ye?

GRIFFITH
Madam, we are here.

KATHARINE It is not you I call for.
Saw ye none enter since I slept?

GRIFFITH None, madam.

KATHARINE
No? Saw you not, even now, a blessèd troop
Invite me to a banquet, whose bright faces
Cast thousand beams upon me, like the sun?
They promised me eternal happiness,
And brought me garlands, Griffith, which I feel
I am not worthy yet to wear. I shall, assuredly.

GRIFFITH
I am most joyful, madam, such good dreams
Possess your fancy.

KATHARINE Bid the music leave; 94
They are harsh and heavy to me. *Music ceases.*

PATIENCE [*To Griffith*] Do you note
How much Her Grace is altered on the sudden?
How long her face is drawn? How pale she looks,
And of an earthy cold? Mark her eyes!

GRIFFITH
She is going, wench. Pray, pray.

PATIENCE Heaven comfort her!

Enter a Messenger.

MESSENGER
An 't like Your Grace—

KATHARINE You are a saucy fellow. 100
Deserve we no more reverence?

GRIFFITH [*To Messenger*] You are too blame, 101

94 fancy imagination. **music leave** musicians cease **100 An 't like** if it please **101 too blame** too blameworthy

Knowing she will not lose her wonted greatness, 102
To use so rude behavior. Go to, kneel.

MESSENGER [*Kneeling*]
I humbly do entreat Your Highness' pardon;
My haste made me unmannerly. There is staying 105
A gentleman, sent from the King, to see you.

KATHARINE
Admit him entrance, Griffith. But this fellow
Let me ne'er see again. *Exit Messenger.*

Enter Lord Capuchius [*admitted by Griffith*].

If my sight fail not,
You should be Lord Ambassador from the Emperor, 109
My royal nephew, and your name Capuchius.

CAPUCHIUS
Madam, the same; your servant.

KATHARINE
O my lord,
The times and titles now are altered strangely
With me since first you knew me. But, I pray you,
What is your pleasure with me?

CAPUCHIUS
Noble lady,
First, mine own service to Your Grace; the next,
The King's request that I would visit you,
Who grieves much for your weakness, and by me
Sends you his princely commendations,
And heartily entreats you take good comfort.

KATHARINE
O my good lord, that comfort comes too late;
'Tis like a pardon after execution.
That gentle physic, given in time, had cured me, 122
But now I am past all comforts here but prayers.
How does His Highness?

CAPUCHIUS
Madam, in good health.

KATHARINE
So may he ever do, and ever flourish,
When I shall dwell with worms, and my poor name
Banished the kingdom!—Patience, is that letter
I caused you write yet sent away?

PATIENCE
No, madam.

102 lose forget. **wonted** accustomed **105 staying** waiting
109 Emperor i.e., Charles V **122 physic** remedy. **had** would have

KATHARINE

Sir, I most humbly pray you to deliver
This to my lord the King.

[*The letter is given to Capuchius.*]

CAPUCHIUS Most willing, madam.

KATHARINE

In which I have commended to his goodness
The model of our chaste loves, his young daughter— 132
The dews of heaven fall thick in blessings on her!—
Beseeching him to give her virtuous breeding— 134
She is young, and of a noble modest nature;
I hope she will deserve well—and a little
To love her for her mother's sake, that loved him,
Heaven knows how dearly. My next poor petition
Is that His Noble Grace would have some pity
Upon my wretched women, that so long
Have followed both my fortunes faithfully; 141
Of which there is not one, I dare avow—
And now I should not lie—but will deserve, 143
For virtue and true beauty of the soul,
For honesty and decent carriage, 145
A right good husband. Let him be a noble;
And sure those men are happy that shall have 'em.
The last is for my men—they are the poorest,
But poverty could never draw 'em from me—
That they may have their wages duly paid 'em,
And something over to remember me by. 151
If heaven had pleased to have given me longer life
And able means, we had not parted thus. 153
These are the whole contents. And, good my lord,
By that you love the dearest in this world,
As you wish Christian peace to souls departed,
Stand these poor people's friend, and urge the King
To do me this last right.

CAPUCHIUS By heaven, I will,
Or let me lose the fashion of a man! 159

132 model image. **young daughter** i.e., Mary, the only one of Katharine's many children to live to maturity; she became Queen of England (1553–1558) before her half-sister Elizabeth (1558–1603) **134 breeding** upbringing **141 both my fortunes** i.e., good and ill **143 now** i.e., on my deathbed, when true speaking is of utmost spiritual importance **145 honesty . . . carriage** chastity and proper behavior **151 over** in addition **153 able** sufficient **159 fashion** nature, characteristics

KATHARINE

I thank you, honest lord. Remember me
In all humility unto His Highness.
Say his long trouble now is passing
Out of this world. Tell him in death I blessed him,
For so I will. Mine eyes grow dim. Farewell,
My lord. Griffith, farewell. Nay, Patience,
You must not leave me yet. I must to bed;
Call in more women. When I am dead, good wench,
Let me be used with honor. Strew me over
With maiden flowers, that all the world may know 169
I was a chaste wife to my grave. Embalm me,
Then lay me forth; although unqueened, yet like 171
A queen, and daughter to a king, inter me.
I can no more. *Exeunt, leading Katharine.* 173

✤

169 maiden flowers spring flowers, symbolic of chastity. (Compare *The Winter's Tale,* 4.4.113–129.) **171 lay me forth** lay me out for burial
173 can can do

5.1 *Enter Gardiner, Bishop of Winchester, a Page with a torch before him, met by Sir Thomas Lovell.*

GARDINER
It's one o'clock, boy, is 't not?
PAGE
It hath struck.
GARDINER
These should be hours for necessities,
Not for delights; times to repair our nature
With comforting repose, and not for us
To waste these times.—Good hour of night, Sir Thomas!
Whither so late?
LOVELL
Came you from the King, my lord?
GARDINER
I did, Sir Thomas, and left him at primero 7
With the Duke of Suffolk.
LOVELL
I must to him too,
Before he go to bed. I'll take my leave.
GARDINER
Not yet, Sir Thomas Lovell. What's the matter?
It seems you are in haste. An if there be 11
No great offense belongs to 't, give your friend
Some touch of your late business. Affairs that walk, 13
As they say spirits do, at midnight, have
In them a wilder nature than the business
That seeks dispatch by day.
LOVELL
My lord, I love you, 16
And durst commend a secret to your ear 17
Much weightier than this work. The Queen's in labor, 18
They say, in great extremity, and feared 19
She'll with the labor end.
GARDINER
The fruit she goes with
I pray for heartily, that it may find
Good time, and live; but for the stock, Sir Thomas, 22
I wish it grubbed up now.
LOVELL
Methinks I could 23

5.1. Location: London. A gallery in the palace.
7 primero gambling card game **11 An if** if **13 touch** hint. **late** recent **16 dispatch** accomplishment **17 commend** entrust **18 this work** i.e., what I am involved in **19 feared** i.e., it is feared that **22 Good time** good fortune, a good delivery. **stock** trunk or main stem
23 grubbed up rooted up

Cry the amen; and yet my conscience says 24
She's a good creature and, sweet lady, does
Deserve our better wishes.

GARDINER But, sir, sir,
Hear me, Sir Thomas. You're a gentleman
Of mine own way. I know you wise, religious; 28
And, let me tell you, it will ne'er be well—
'Twill not, Sir Thomas Lovell, take 't of me—
Till Cranmer, Cromwell—her two hands—and she
Sleep in their graves.

LOVELL Now, sir, you speak of two
The most remarked i' the kingdom. As for Cromwell, 33
Besides that of the Jewel House, is made Master 34
O' the Rolls, and the King's secretary; further, sir, 35
Stands in the gap and trade of more preferments, 36
With which the time will load him. Th' Archbishop 37
Is the King's hand and tongue, and who dare speak
One syllable against him?

GARDINER Yes, yes, Sir Thomas,
There are that dare, and I myself have ventured
To speak my mind of him; and indeed this day,
Sir—I may tell it you, I think—I have
Incensed the lords o' the Council that he is— 43
For so I know he is, they know he is—
A most arch heretic, a pestilence
That does infect the land; with which they, moved, 46
Have broken with the King, who hath so far 47
Given ear to our complaint, of his great grace
And princely care foreseeing those fell mischiefs 49
Our reasons laid before him, hath commanded 50
Tomorrow morning to the Council board
He be convented. He's a rank weed, Sir Thomas, 52
And we must root him out. From your affairs
I hinder you too long. Good night, Sir Thomas.

24 Cry the amen give assent **28 way** religious faith (opposed to Protestant reform) **33 remarked** under the public eye **34–35 Master . . . Rolls** judge of the Court of Appeal **36 gap and trade** open and beaten path **37 time** course of events **43 Incensed** instigated, led to believe **46–47 with . . . King** they, moved to anger at the idea, have disclosed it to the King **49 fell** terrible, cruel **50 hath** (that) he has **52 convented** summoned

LOVELL
Many good nights, my lord. I rest your servant. 55
Exeunt Gardiner and Page.

Enter King and Suffolk.

KING
Charles, I will play no more tonight.
My mind's not on 't; you are too hard for me. 57
SUFFOLK
Sir, I did never win of you before.
KING But little, Charles,
Nor shall not, when my fancy's on my play.— 60
Now, Lovell, from the Queen what is the news?
LOVELL
I could not personally deliver to her
What you commanded me, but by her woman
I sent your message, who returned her thanks
In the great'st humbleness and desired Your Highness
Most heartily to pray for her.
KING What sayst thou, ha?
To pray for her? What, is she crying out?
LOVELL
So said her woman, and that her sufferance made 68
Almost each pang a death.
KING Alas, good lady!
SUFFOLK
God safely quit her of her burden, and 70
With gentle travail, to the gladding of
Your Highness with an heir!
KING 'Tis midnight, Charles.
Prithee, to bed, and in thy prayers remember
Th' estate of my poor queen. Leave me alone, 74
For I must think of that which company
Would not be friendly to.
SUFFOLK I wish Your Highness
A quiet night, and my good mistress will 77
Remember in my prayers.
KING Charles, good night. 78
Exit Suffolk.

55 rest remain **57 hard** good a player **60 fancy's** mind's **68 sufferance** suffering **70 God** may God. **quit** release **74 estate** condition **77–78 and my . . . Remember** and I will remember my good mistress, i.e., the Queen

Enter Sir Anthony Denny.

Well, sir, what follows?

DENNY
Sir, I have brought my lord the Archbishop,
As you commanded me.

KING Ha? Canterbury?

DENNY
Ay, my good lord.

KING 'Tis true. Where is he, Denny?

DENNY
He attends Your Highness' pleasure.

KING Bring him to us.
[*Exit Denny.*]

LOVELL [*Aside*]
This is about that which the Bishop spake. 84
I am happily come hither. 85

Enter Cranmer and Denny.

KING
Avoid the gallery. (*Lovell seems to stay.*) Ha? I have said.
Begone. 86
What? *Exeunt Lovell and Denny.*

CRANMER [*Aside*] I am fearful. Wherefore frowns he thus?
'Tis his aspect of terror. All's not well. 88

KING
How now, my lord? You do desire to know
Wherefore I sent for you.

CRANMER [*Kneeling*] It is my duty 90
T' attend Your Highness' pleasure.

KING Pray you, arise,
My good and gracious lord of Canterbury.
Come, you and I must walk a turn together;
I have news to tell you. Come, come, give me your hand.
[*Cranmer rises.*]
Ah, my good lord, I grieve at what I speak
And am right sorry to repeat what follows.
I have, and most unwillingly, of late
Heard many grievous—I do say, my lord,

84 the Bishop i.e., Gardiner **85 happily** luckily **86 Avoid** vacate
88 aspect expression **90 Wherefore** why

Grievous—complaints of you; which, being considered,
Have moved us and our Council that you shall
This morning come before us, where I know
You cannot with such freedom purge yourself 102
But that, till further trial in those charges
Which will require your answer, you must take
Your patience to you and be well contented
To make your house our Tow'r. You a brother of us, 106
It fits we thus proceed, or else no witness 107
Would come against you.

CRANMER [*Kneeling*] I humbly thank Your Highness,
And am right glad to catch this good occasion
Most throughly to be winnowed, where my chaff 110
And corn shall fly asunder. For I know 111
There's none stands under more calumnious tongues 112
Than I myself, poor man.

KING Stand up, good Canterbury!
Thy truth and thy integrity is rooted
In us, thy friend. Give me thy hand, stand up.
[*Cranmer rises.*]
Prithee, let's walk. Now, by my halidom, 116
What manner of man are you? My lord, I looked 117
You would have given me your petition that
I should have ta'en some pains to bring together
Yourself and your accusers, and to have heard you
Without endurance further.

CRANMER Most dread liege, 121
The good I stand on is my truth and honesty.
If they shall fail, I, with mine enemies,
Will triumph o'er my person, which I weigh not, 124
Being of those virtues vacant. I fear nothing 125
What can be said against me.

KING Know you not
How your state stands i' the world, with the whole
world?

102 freedom ease and completeness. **purge** excuse, clear **106 brother of us** fellow member of the Council **107 fits** is appropriate
110 throughly thoroughly **111 corn** grain **112 stands under** is the object of. **calumnious** slandering **116 by my halidom** i.e., by something sacred **117 looked** expected **121 endurance** imprisonment
124–125 which . . . vacant i.e., which I do not value if it is void of those virtues (*truth* and *honesty*) **125 nothing** not at all

Your enemies are many, and not small; their practices 128
Must bear the same proportion, and not ever 129
The justice and the truth o' the question carries 130
The due o' the verdict with it. At what ease 131
Might corrupt minds procure knaves as corrupt
To swear against you? Such things have been done.
You are potently opposed, and with a malice
Of as great size. Ween you of better luck, 135
I mean in perjured witness, than your master, 136
Whose minister you are, whiles here he lived
Upon this naughty earth? Go to, go to, 138
You take a precipice for no leap of danger
And woo your own destruction.

CRANMER God and Your Majesty
Protect mine innocence, or I fall into
The trap is laid for me!

KING Be of good cheer; 142
They shall no more prevail than we give way to. 143
Keep comfort to you, and this morning see
You do appear before them. If they shall chance,
In charging you with matters, to commit you, 146
The best persuasions to the contrary
Fail not to use, and with what vehemency
Th' occasion shall instruct you. If entreaties
Will render you no remedy, this ring
Deliver them, and your appeal to us
There make before them. [*He gives a ring.*] Look, the good man weeps!
He's honest, on mine honor. God's blest mother,
I swear he is truehearted, and a soul
None better in my kingdom. Get you gone,
And do as I have bid you. (*Exit Cranmer.*) He has strangled
His language in his tears.

Enter Old Lady.

128 small insignificant. **practices** schemes, plots **129 bear . . . proportion** be correspondingly numerous and mighty **129–131 not . . . it** i.e., the innocence of a person does not always ensure his acquittal **131 At what ease** how easily **135 Ween you of** do you expect **136 master** i.e., Christ **138 naughty** wicked **142 is** that is **143 give way to** allow **146 commit** i.e., to prison

LOVELL (*Within*) Come back! What mean you?

[*Enter Lovell, following her.*]

OLD LADY
I'll not come back. The tidings that I bring
Will make my boldness manners.—Now, good angels 159
Fly o'er thy royal head, and shade thy person
Under their blessèd wings!

KING Now, by thy looks
I guess thy message. Is the Queen delivered?
Say ay, and of a boy.

OLD LADY Ay, ay, my liege,
And of a lovely boy. The God of heaven
Both now and ever bless her! 'Tis a girl
Promises boys hereafter. Sir, your queen
Desires your visitation, and to be
Acquainted with this stranger. 'Tis as like you
As cherry is to cherry.

KING Lovell!

LOVELL Sir?

KING
Give her an hundred marks. I'll to the Queen. 170
Exit King.

OLD LADY
An hundred marks? By this light, I'll ha' more.
An ordinary groom is for such payment. 172
I will have more, or scold it out of him.
Said I for this the girl was like to him?
I'll have more, or else unsay 't; and now,
While 'tis hot, I'll put it to the issue. 176
Exit Lady [*with Lovell*].

✤

159 good angels may good angels **170 an hundred marks** i.e., about 65 pounds **172 for** suited for **176 put it to** force

5.2

Enter Cranmer, Archbishop of Canterbury,
[*pursuivants, pages, etc., attending at the door*].

CRANMER
I hope I am not too late, and yet the gentleman
That was sent to me from the Council prayed me
To make great haste. All fast? What means this? Ho! 3
Who waits there?

Enter Keeper.

Sure you know me?

KEEPER Yes, my lord,
But yet I cannot help you.

CRANMER Why?

KEEPER
Your Grace must wait till you be called for.

Enter Doctor Butts.

CRANMER So.

BUTTS [*Aside*]
This is a piece of malice. I am glad
I came this way so happily. The King
Shall understand it presently. *Exit Butts.*

CRANMER [*Aside*] 'Tis Butts, 10
The King's physician. As he passed along,
How earnestly he cast his eyes upon me!
Pray heaven he sound not my disgrace! For certain 13
This is of purpose laid by some that hate me— 14
God turn their hearts! I never sought their malice—
To quench mine honor. They would shame to make me 16
Wait else at door, a fellow councillor,
'Mong boys, grooms, and lackeys. But their pleasures

5.2. Location: London. Adjacent to the council chamber.
s.d. pursuivants messengers, subordinates (as also in l. 24). **at the door** i.e., at a stage door, as though guarding the entrance to the council chamber **3 fast** locked **10 presently** at once **13 sound** probe, search out; or speak, proclaim **14 laid** contrived as a trap **16 quench mine honor** destroy my reputation

Must be fulfilled, and I attend with patience. 19

Enter the King and Butts at a window above.

BUTTS
I'll show Your Grace the strangest sight—

KING
What's that, Butts?

BUTTS
I think Your Highness saw this many a day.

KING
Body o' me, where is it?

BUTTS
There, my lord:
The high promotion of His Grace of Canterbury,
Who holds his state at door, 'mongst pursuivants, 24
Pages, and footboys.

KING
Ha? 'Tis he, indeed.
Is this the honor they do one another?
'Tis well there's one above 'em yet. I had thought 27
They had parted so much honesty among 'em— 28
At least good manners—as not thus to suffer
A man of his place, and so near our favor, 30
To dance attendance on their lordships' pleasures, 31
And at the door too, like a post with packets. 32
By holy Mary, Butts, there's knavery!
Let 'em alone, and draw the curtain close.
We shall hear more anon.

[*They conceal themselves behind the curtain.*
Cranmer remains waiting at the door, below.]

19 s.d. at a window above (The gallery over the stage, representing a peephole through which the Council could be spied upon. The Folio text makes no scene division between this and the following scene, so that the Council would assemble under the view and in the hearing of the King; and the main stage, imagined in scene 2 to be adjacent to the council chamber, becomes in scene 3 the chamber itself.) **24 holds his state** maintains his dignity **27 one above** (Suggests Henry's role as a godlike figure.) **28 parted** shared **30 place** official position **31 dance attendance** stand waiting around **32 post** messenger. **packets** letters

5.3

A council table brought in with chairs and stools, and placed under the state. Enter Lord Chancellor; places himself at the upper end of the table on the left hand, a seat being left void above him, as for Canterbury's seat. Duke of Suffolk, Duke of Norfolk, Surrey, Lord Chamberlain, Gardiner, seat themselves in order on each side. Cromwell at lower end, as secretary. [*Keeper at the door.*]

CHANCELLOR
Speak to the business, Master Secretary.
Why are we met in council?

CROMWELL Please your honors,
The chief cause concerns His Grace of Canterbury.

GARDINER
Has he had knowledge of it?

CROMWELL Yes.

NORFOLK Who waits there?

KEEPER
Without, my noble lords?

GARDINER Yes.

KEEPER My lord Archbishop, 5
And has done half an hour, to know your pleasures.

CHANCELLOR
Let him come in.

KEEPER Your Grace may enter now.
Cranmer approaches the council table.

CHANCELLOR
My good lord Archbishop, I'm very sorry
To sit here at this present and behold 9
That chair stand empty. But we all are men,
In our own natures frail, and capable 11
Of our flesh—few are angels—out of which frailty 12
And want of wisdom, you, that best should teach us,

5.3. Location: The council chamber. Scene is continuous with the previous.
s.d. state canopy **5 Without** outside the door. (Although Cranmer seemingly has never exited, the stage has now become the room into which he has been waiting to be admitted.) **9 present** present time **11–12 capable . . . flesh** susceptible to the weaknesses of the flesh

Have misdemeaned yourself, and not a little, 14
Toward the King first, then his laws, in filling
The whole realm, by your teaching and your
chaplains'—
For so we are informed—with new opinions,
Divers and dangerous, which are heresies
And, not reformed, may prove pernicious. 19

GARDINER
Which reformation must be sudden too,
My noble lords; for those that tame wild horses
Pace 'em not in their hands to make 'em gentle, 22
But stop their mouths with stubborn bits and spur 'em
Till they obey the manage. If we suffer, 24
Out of our easiness and childish pity 25
To one man's honor, this contagious sickness,
Farewell all physic! And what follows then? 27
Commotions, uproars, with a general taint
Of the whole state, as of late days our neighbors,
The upper Germany, can dearly witness, 30
Yet freshly pitied in our memories.

CRANMER
My good lords, hitherto, in all the progress
Both of my life and office, I have labored,
And with no little study, that my teaching
And the strong course of my authority
Might go one way, and safely; and the end
Was ever to do well. Nor is there living—
I speak it with a single heart, my lords— 38
A man that more detests, more stirs against, 39
Both in his private conscience and his place, 40
Defacers of a public peace than I do.
Pray heaven the King may never find a heart
With less allegiance in it! Men that make
Envy and crooked malice nourishment
Dare bite the best. I do beseech your lordships

14 misdemeaned yourself been guilty of misconduct **19 pernicious** deadly **22 Pace . . . hands** i.e., don't lead them gently **24 manage** training, handling. **suffer** allow **25 easiness** laxness **27 physic** medicine, cure **30 upper Germany** (Refers to the Peasants' Wars, 1524; possibly to the massacre of the Anabaptists in 1535.) **38 single** honest; not given to double-dealing **39 stirs** is active **40 place** official capacity

That, in this case of justice, my accusers,
Be what they will, may stand forth face to face
And freely urge against me.

SUFFOLK Nay, my lord, 48
That cannot be. You are a councillor,
And by that virtue no man dare accuse you. 50

GARDINER
My lord, because we have business of more moment,
We will be short with you. 'Tis His Highness' pleasure,
And our consent, for better trial of you,
From hence you be committed to the Tower,
Where, being but a private man again,
You shall know many dare accuse you boldly—
More than, I fear, you are provided for. 57

CRANMER
Ah, my good lord of Winchester, I thank you;
You are always my good friend. If your will pass, 59
I shall both find your lordship judge and juror,
You are so merciful. I see your end;
'Tis my undoing. Love and meekness, lord,
Become a churchman better than ambition.
Win straying souls with modesty again; 64
Cast none away. That I shall clear myself,
Lay all the weight ye can upon my patience, 66
I make as little doubt as you do conscience 67
In doing daily wrongs. I could say more, 68
But reverence to your calling makes me modest.

GARDINER
My lord, my lord, you are a sectary, 70
That's the plain truth. Your painted gloss discovers, 71
To men that understand you, words and weakness. 72

CROMWELL
My lord of Winchester, you're a little,
By your good favor, too sharp. Men so noble, 74

48 urge make accusation **50 by that virtue** by virtue of that
57 provided prepared **59 pass** prevail **64 modesty** moderation
66 Lay . . . can i.e., no matter how hard you press **67–68 I . . . In** I have as little doubt (of my blamelessness) as you have scruples against
70 sectary follower of a heretical Protestant sect **71 painted gloss discovers** false exterior (in speech and acts) reveals **72 words** i.e., mere words **74 By . . . favor** i.e., begging your pardon

However faulty, yet should find respect 75
For what they have been. 'Tis a cruelty
To load a falling man.

GARDINER Good Master Secretary, 77
I cry your honor mercy; you may worst 78
Of all this table say so.

CROMWELL Why, my lord?

GARDINER
Do not I know you for a favorer
Of this new sect? Ye are not sound.

CROMWELL Not sound? 81

GARDINER
Not sound, I say.

CROMWELL Would you were half so honest!
Men's prayers then would seek you, not their fears.

GARDINER
I shall remember this bold language.

CROMWELL Do.
Remember your bold life too.

CHANCELLOR This is too much.
Forbear, for shame, my lords.

GARDINER I have done.

CROMWELL And I.

CHANCELLOR [*To Cranmer*]
Then thus for you, my lord: it stands agreed,
I take it, by all voices, that forthwith
You be conveyed to the Tower a prisoner,
There to remain till the King's further pleasure
Be known unto us. Are you all agreed, lords?

ALL
We are.

CRANMER Is there no other way of mercy,
But I must needs to the Tower, my lords?

GARDINER What other 93
Would you expect? You are strangely troublesome.
Let some o' the guard be ready there.

Enter the guard.

75 find be accorded **77 load** burden **78 I cry . . . mercy** I beg your pardon. **worst** with least justification **81 sound** orthodox **93 must needs to** must necessarily go to

CRANMER For me?
Must I go like a traitor thither?

GARDINER Receive him,
And see him safe i' the Tower.

CRANMER Stay, good my lords,
I have a little yet to say. Look there, my lords.
[*He shows the King's ring.*]
By virtue of that ring, I take my cause
Out of the grips of cruel men and give it 100
To a most noble judge, the King my master.

CHAMBERLAIN
This is the King's ring.

SURREY 'Tis no counterfeit.

SUFFOLK
'Tis the right ring, by heaven! I told ye all,
When we first put this dangerous stone a-rolling,
'Twould fall upon ourselves.

NORFOLK Do you think, my lords,
The King will suffer but the little finger
Of this man to be vexed?

CHAMBERLAIN 'Tis now too certain.
How much more is his life in value with him! 108
Would I were fairly out on 't!

CROMWELL My mind gave me, 109
In seeking tales and informations
Against this man, whose honesty the devil
And his disciples only envy at, 112
Ye blew the fire that burns ye. Now have at ye! 113

Enter King, frowning on them; takes his seat.

GARDINER
Dread sovereign, how much are we bound to heaven
In daily thanks, that gave us such a prince,
Not only good and wise, but most religious;
One that in all obedience makes the Church
The chief aim of his honor, and, to strengthen

100 grips clutches **108 in value with** valued by. **him** i.e., the King **109 on 't** of it (this trouble). **gave** told **112 envy at** hate **113 have at ye** i.e., on guard, watch out. (Said as one attacks an opponent.) **s.d. Enter King** (The King has presumably come down behind the scene from above. He enters on the main stage.)

That holy duty out of dear respect, 119
His royal self in judgment comes to hear
The cause betwixt her and this great offender.

KING
You were ever good at sudden commendations, 122
Bishop of Winchester. But know I come not
To hear such flattery now, and in my presence
They are too thin and base to hide offenses.
To me you cannot reach. You play the spaniel,
And think with wagging of your tongue to win me;
But whatsoe'er thou tak'st me for, I'm sure
Thou hast a cruel nature and a bloody.
[*To Cranmer.*] Good man, sit down. [*Cranmer sits.*] Now let me see the proudest
He, that dares most, but wag his finger at thee. 131
By all that's holy, he had better starve 132
Than but once think this place becomes thee not.

SURREY
May it please Your Grace—

KING No, sir, it does not please me.
I had thought I had had men of some understanding
And wisdom of my Council, but I find none.
Was it discretion, lords, to let this man,
This good man—few of you deserve that title—
This honest man, wait like a lousy footboy
At chamber door? And one as great as you are?
Why, what a shame was this! Did my commission
Bid ye so far forget yourselves? I gave ye
Power as he was a councillor to try him,
Not as a groom. There's some of ye, I see,
More out of malice than integrity,
Would try him to the utmost, had ye means,
Which ye shall never have while I live.

CHANCELLOR Thus far,
My most dread sovereign, may it like Your Grace 148
To let my tongue excuse all. What was purposed
Concerning his imprisonment was rather,
If there be faith in men, meant for his trial

119 dear respect heartfelt piety **122 sudden commendations** unrehearsed compliments **131 He** person **132 starve** die **148 like** please

And fair purgation to the world than malice, 152
I'm sure, in me.

KING Well, well, my lords, respect him.
Take him, and use him well; he's worthy of it.
I will say thus much for him: If a prince
May be beholding to a subject, I 156
Am, for his love and service, so to him.
Make me no more ado, but all embrace him.
Be friends, for shame, my lords! [*They all embrace Cranmer.*] My lord of Canterbury,
I have a suit which you must not deny me:
That is, a fair young maid that yet wants baptism;
You must be godfather and answer for her.

CRANMER
The greatest monarch now alive may glory
In such an honor. How may I deserve it,
That am a poor and humble subject to you?

KING
Come, come, my lord, you'd spare your spoons. You shall have 166
Two noble partners with you: the old Duchess of Norfolk
And Lady Marquess Dorset. Will these please you?—
Once more, my lord of Winchester, I charge you,
Embrace and love this man.

GARDINER With a true heart
And brother-love I do it. [*He embraces Cranmer.*]

CRANMER And let heaven
Witness how dear I hold this confirmation.

KING
Good man, those joyful tears show thy true heart.
The common voice, I see, is verified 174
Of thee, which says thus, "Do my lord of Canterbury
A shrewd turn, and he's your friend forever." 176
Come, lords, we trifle time away; I long
To have this young one made a Christian.
As I have made ye one, lords, one remain; 179
So I grow stronger, you more honor gain. *Exeunt.*

✣

152 purgation clearing of himself **156 beholding** beholden **166 you'd . . . spoons** (Said jestingly; spoons were a common christening gift.) **174 voice** report, opinion **176 shrewd** malicious **179 one** united in spirit

5.4 *Noise and tumult within. Enter Porter and his Man.*

PORTER You'll leave your noise anon, ye rascals! Do you 1
take the court for Paris Garden? Ye rude slaves, leave 2
your gaping. 3

ONE (*Within*) Good Master Porter, I belong to the larder. 4

PORTER Belong to the gallows, and be hanged, ye rogue!
Is this a place to roar in?—Fetch me a dozen crab tree
staves, and strong ones; these are but switches to 'em.— 7
I'll scratch your heads. You must be seeing christenings? Do you look for ale and cakes here, you rude 9
rascals?

MAN
Pray, sir, be patient. 'Tis as much impossible—
Unless we sweep 'em from the door with cannons—
To scatter 'em as 'tis to make 'em sleep
On May Day morning, which will never be. 14
We may as well push against Paul's as stir 'em. 15

PORTER How got they in, and be hanged?

MAN
Alas, I know not. How gets the tide in?
As much as one sound cudgel of four foot— 18
You see the poor remainder—could distribute,
I made no spare, sir.

PORTER You did nothing, sir. 20

MAN
I am not Samson, nor Sir Guy, nor Colbrand, 21
To mow 'em down before me; but if I spared any
That had a head to hit, either young or old,

5.4. Location: London. The palace yard.
1 leave stop. **anon** immediately **2 Paris Garden** a bear garden on the Bankside **3 gaping** shouting **4 I . . . larder** i.e., I am a servant of the palace household, in the pantry **7 to 'em** compared to them, i.e., to cudgels made of crab tree **9 ale and cakes** (Refreshments appropriate to christenings and other festivals.) **14 May Day morning** (Allusion to the custom of rising before dawn on May Day for early morning festivities.) **15 Paul's** Saint Paul's Cathedral **18 cudgel** club **20 made no spare** exercised no frugality **21 Samson** biblical character of great strength. **Sir Guy, Colbrand** (Colbrand was a legendary Danish giant slain by Guy of Warwick in the popular English romance named after its hero.)

He or she, cuckold or cuckold maker,
Let me ne'er hope to see a chine again; 25
And that I would not for a cow, God save her! 26

ONE (*Within*) Do you hear, Master Porter?

PORTER I shall be with you presently, good master puppy.—Keep the door close, sirrah.

MAN What would you have me do?

PORTER What should you do, but knock 'em down by the dozens? Is this Moorfields to muster in? Or have 32 we some strange Indian with the great tool come to 33 court, the women so besiege us? Bless me, what a fry 34 of fornication is at door! On my Christian conscience, 35 this one christening will beget a thousand; here will be father, godfather, and all together.

MAN The spoons will be the bigger, sir. There is a fel- 38 low somewhat near the door—he should be a brazier 39 by his face, for, o' my conscience, twenty of the dog 40 days now reign in 's nose; all that stand about him are 41 under the line, they need no other penance. That fire- 42 drake did I hit three times on the head, and three 43 times was his nose discharged against me; he stands there like a mortar-piece to blow us. There was a 45 haberdasher's wife of small wit near him that railed upon me till her pinked porringer fell off her head for 47 kindling such a combustion in the state. I missed the 48 meteor once and hit that woman, who cried out 49

25 chine backbone; hence a joint of beef or other meat **26 for a cow** i.e., for anything (*cow* perhaps being suggested by *chine*) **32 Moorfields** an open space outside London walls, used among other things as a training ground for the militia **33 tool** genitals. (This sentence alludes to the Elizabethan excitement over exhibited Indians.) **34–35 fry of fornication** swarm of would-be fornicators, or of bastards **38 spoons** i.e., as christening presents. (See 5.3.166.) **39 brazier** worker in brass **40–41 dog days** i.e., midsummer, when Sirius, the Dog Star, rises at about the same time as the sun **42 under the line** on the equator **42–43 firedrake** fiery dragon **45 mortar-piece** short cannon. **blow us** (1) blow us up (2) blow his nose at us **47 pinked porringer** small close-fitting cap ornamented with perforations **48 combustion** tumult. **in the state** (1) in the commonwealth (2) in the brazier, whose inflamed complexion, comically likened here to a miniature cosmos, seems made up of meteors and discharging cannons **48–49 the meteor** i.e., the red-faced brazier

"Clubs!" when I might see from far some forty trun- 50
cheoners draw to her succor, which were the hope o' 51
the Strand, where she was quartered. They fell on; I 52
made good my place. At length they came to the 53
broomstaff to me. I defied 'em still, when suddenly a 54
file of boys behind 'em, loose shot, delivered such a 55
shower of pebbles that I was fain to draw mine honor 56
in, and let 'em win the work. The devil was amongst 57
'em, I think, surely.

PORTER These are the youths that thunder at a playhouse and fight for bitten apples, that no audience
but the tribulation of Tower Hill or the limbs of Lime- 61
house, their dear brothers, are able to endure. I have 62
some of 'em in *Limbo Patrum,* and there they are like 63
to dance these three days, besides the running ban- 64
quet of two beadles that is to come. 65

Enter Lord Chamberlain.

CHAMBERLAIN
Mercy o' me, what a multitude are here!
They grow still too; from all parts they are coming,
As if we kept a fair here! Where are these porters,
These lazy knaves? You've made a fine hand, fellows! 69
There's a trim rabble let in. Are all these 70
Your faithful friends o' the suburbs? We shall have 71
Great store of room, no doubt, left for the ladies, 72
When they pass back from the christening.

50 Clubs (The rallying cry for London apprentices to join in or stop a brawl.) **50–51 truncheoners** men armed with cudgels **52 Strand** a prosperous street of shops and residences. **fell on** made their assault **53 made . . . place** stood my ground **54 broomstaff** i.e., close quarters **55 loose shot** throwers or marksmen not attached to a particular company **56 fain** obliged **56–57 draw . . . in** i.e., withdraw from the fight **57 work** fort **61 tribulation** troublemakers, gang. **limbs** lads; here, rowdies **61–62 Limehouse** a dockyard area east of Tower Hill, a rough neighborhood **63 Limbo Patrum** resting place for the pre-Christian patriarchs who had to remain there until the coming of Christ; hence, prison. **like** likely **64 dance** kick their heels **64–65 running banquet** whipping following imprisonment (like a *banquet* or "dessert" after a meal) **69 fine hand** fine job. (Said ironically.) **70 trim** fine. (Said ironically.) **71 suburbs** areas outside London walls and hence outside its legal jurisdiction **72 store** plenty

PORTER
An 't please your honor, 73
We are but men, and what so many may do,
Not being torn a-pieces, we have done.
An army cannot rule 'em.

CHAMBERLAIN
As I live, 76
If the King blame me for 't, I'll lay ye all 77
By th' heels, and suddenly, and on your heads 78
Clap round fines for neglect. You're lazy knaves, 79
And here ye lie baiting of bombards, when 80
Ye should do service. [*A trumpet.*] Hark, the trumpets sound.
They're come already from the christening.
Go break among the press, and find a way out 83
To let the troop pass fairly, or I'll find 84
A Marshalsea shall hold ye play these two months. 85

PORTER
Make way there for the Princess!

MAN
You great fellow,
Stand close up, or I'll make your head ache.

PORTER
You i' the camlet, get up o' the rail! 88
I'll peck you o'er the pales else. *Exeunt.* 89

5.5

Enter trumpets, sounding; then two Aldermen, Lord Mayor, Garter, Cranmer, Duke of Norfolk with his marshal's staff, Duke of Suffolk, two noblemen bearing great standing bowls for the christening gifts; then four noblemen bearing a canopy, under which the Duchess of Norfolk, godmother, bearing the child richly habited in

73 An 't if it **76 rule** control **77–78 lay . . . heels** put you in the stocks or in chains **79 round** heavy **80 baiting of bombards** drinking from leathern bottles **83 press** crowd **84 troop** royal retinue
85 Marshalsea prison in Southwark. **hold ye play** keep you engaged
88 camlet a kind of fabric made with goat's hair. (Since no "crowd" is onstage, the Porter may be speaking to his audience here as though it were crowding to see the christening.) **89 peck** pitch. **pales** palings, fence

5.5. Location: London. The royal court.
s.d. Garter Garter King at Arms, a chief herald of the College of Arms

a mantle, etc., train borne by a lady; then follows the Marchioness Dorset, the other godmother, and ladies. The troop pass once about the stage, and Garter speaks.

GARTER Heaven, from thy endless goodness, send prosperous life, long, and ever happy, to the high and mighty Princess of England, Elizabeth!

Flourish. Enter King and guard.

CRANMER [*Kneeling*]
And to your royal Grace and the good Queen,
My noble partners and myself thus pray
All comfort, joy, in this most gracious lady
Heaven ever laid up to make parents happy 7
May hourly fall upon ye!

KING
Thank you, good Lord Archbishop.
What is her name?

CRANMER Elizabeth.

KING Stand up, lord.
[*Cranmer rises. The King kisses the child.*]
With this kiss take my blessing. God protect thee,
Into whose hand I give thy life.

CRANMER Amen.

KING
My noble gossips, you've been too prodigal. 13
I thank ye heartily; so shall this lady,
When she has so much English.

CRANMER Let me speak, sir,
For heaven now bids me; and the words I utter
Let none think flattery, for they'll find 'em truth.
This royal infant—heaven still move about her!— 18
Though in her cradle, yet now promises
Upon this land a thousand thousand blessings,
Which time shall bring to ripeness. She shall be—
But few now living can behold that goodness—
A pattern to all princes living with her,

7 laid up provided **13 gossips** godparents **18 still** ever

And all that shall succeed. Saba was never 24
More covetous of wisdom and fair virtue
Than this pure soul shall be. All princely graces
That mold up such a mighty piece as this is, 27
With all the virtues that attend the good,
Shall still be doubled on her. Truth shall nurse her,
Holy and heavenly thoughts still counsel her.
She shall be loved and feared. Her own shall bless her; 31
Her foes shake like a field of beaten corn, 32
And hang their heads with sorrow. Good grows with her.
In her days every man shall eat in safety
Under his own vine what he plants, and sing
The merry songs of peace to all his neighbors.
God shall be truly known, and those about her
From her shall read the perfect ways of honor 38
And by those claim their greatness, not by blood. 39
Nor shall this peace sleep with her; but as when 40
The bird of wonder dies, the maiden phoenix, 41
Her ashes new-create another heir
As great in admiration as herself, 43
So shall she leave her blessedness to one, 44
When heaven shall call her from this cloud of darkness, 45
Who from the sacred ashes of her honor
Shall starlike rise, as great in fame as she was,
And so stand fixed. Peace, plenty, love, truth, terror, 48
That were the servants to this chosen infant,
Shall then be his, and like a vine grow to him.
Wherever the bright sun of heaven shall shine,
His honor and the greatness of his name
Shall be, and make new nations. He shall flourish,
And like a mountain cedar reach his branches
To all the plains about him. Our children's children
Shall see this and bless heaven.

KING Thou speakest wonders.

24 Saba i.e., the Queen of Sheba, who visited Solomon to discover wisdom from him; see 1 Kings 10:1–10 **27 mighty piece** princely person **31 own** i.e., own people **32 beaten corn** wind-beaten grain **38 read** learn **39 greatness** nobility **40 sleep** i.e., die **41 phoenix** mythical bird believed to rise from its own ashes; a symbol of regeneration **43 great in admiration** greatly wondered at **44 she** i.e., Elizabeth. **one** i.e., King James I **45 cloud of darkness** i.e., mortal life **48 terror** quality inspiring awe

CRANMER

She shall be, to the happiness of England,
An agèd princess; many days shall see her,
And yet no day without a deed to crown it. 59
Would I had known no more! But she must die,
She must, the saints must have her; yet a virgin,
A most unspotted lily shall she pass
To th' ground, and all the world shall mourn her.

KING O Lord Archbishop,
Thou hast made me now a man! Never, before
This happy child, did I get anything. 66
This oracle of comfort has so pleased me
That when I am in heaven I shall desire
To see what this child does, and praise my Maker.
I thank ye all. To you, my good Lord Mayor,
And you, good brethren, I am much beholding; 71
I have received much honor by your presence,
And ye shall find me thankful. Lead the way, lords.
Ye must all see the Queen, and she must thank ye;
She will be sick else. This day, no man think 75
H'as business at his house; for all shall stay. 76
This little one shall make it holiday. *Exeunt.*

59 deed good deed **66 get** beget; achieve **71 beholding** beholden
75 sick unhappy **76 H'as** (that) he has. **stay** i.e., cease work

Epilogue

[*Enter the Epilogue.*]

EPILOGUE

'Tis ten to one this play can never please
All that are here. Some come to take their ease,
And sleep an act or two; but those, we fear,
We've frighted with our trumpets; so, 'tis clear,
They'll say 'tis naught. Others to hear the city 5
Abused extremely, and to cry "That's witty!"
Which we have not done neither; that I fear 7
All the expected good we're like to hear 8
For this play at this time is only in
The merciful construction of good women, 10
For such a one we showed 'em. If they smile
And say 'twill do, I know, within a while
All the best men are ours; for 'tis ill hap 13
If they hold when their ladies bid 'em clap. [*Exit.*] 14

Epilogue.
5 naught worthless **7 that** so that **8 expected good** anticipated approval, applause **10 construction** interpretation **13 ill hap** bad luck **14 hold** hold back

Date and Text

The Famous History of the Life of King Henry the Eighth was first printed in the First Folio of 1623. The text is a good one, set from a careful transcript of Shakespeare's own manuscript. The stage directions are unusually elaborate. The first recorded performance was on June 29, 1613. A letter of July 2 in that year from Sir Henry Wotton to Sir Edmund Bacon tells of a performance of "a new play, called *All Is True*, representing some principal pieces of the reign of Henry VIII." During this performance, as King Henry was arriving as a masker at the house of Cardinal Wolsey (1.4), "certain chambers [cannons] being shot off at his entry, some of the paper, or other stuff, wherewith one of them was stopped, did light on the thatch, where being thought at first but an idle smoke, and their eyes more attentive to the show, it kindled inwardly, and ran round like a train, consuming within less than an hour the whole house to the very grounds." The identification of this *All Is True* with Shakespeare's play is certain. Other accounts include a letter from Thomas Lorkin to Sir Thomas Puckering, June 1613, asserting the fire to have started "while Burbage his company were acting at the Globe the play of Henry VIII," a letter of 8 July from John Chamberlain to Sir Ralph Winwood, and an account in John Stow's *Annals* as continued by Edmund Howe (1618).

Wotton calls it a new play, and stylistic considerations confirm this characterization. The play may also have helped provide entertainment for the betrothal and marriage of James I's daughter Elizabeth to the Elector Palatine earlier in 1613, though *Henry VIII* is not listed among the many plays acted on this occasion.

On the controversy over John Fletcher's purported share in the authorship of *Henry VIII*, see the play's Introduction.

Textual Notes

These textual notes are not a historical collation, either of the early folios or of more recent editions; they are simply a record of departures in this edition from the copy text. The reading adopted in this edition appears in boldface, followed by the rejected reading from the copy text, i.e., the First Folio. Only major alterations in punctuation are noted. Changes in lineation are not indicated, nor are some minor and obvious typographical errors.

Abbreviations used:
F the First Folio
s.d. stage direction
s.p. speech prefix

Copy text: the First Folio.

1.1. 42–45 All . . . function [assigned in F to Buckingham] **47 as you guess** [assigned in F to Norfolk] **63 'a** O **69–70 that? . . . hell, the** that, . . . Hell? The **115 s.p. [and elsewhere] Wolsey** Car **120 venom** venom'd **200 Hereford** Hertford **219 Perk** Pecke **chancellor** Councellour **221 Nicholas** Michaell **226 lord** Lords

1.2. 8 s.d. [F: A noyse within crying roome for the Queene, usher'd by the Duke of Norfolke. Enter the Queene, Norfolke and Suffolke: she kneels.] [etc.] **9 s.p. [and elsewhere] Katharine** Queen **67 business** basenesse **156 feared** feare **164 confession's** Commissions **170 To gain** To **180 him** this **190 Bulmer** Blumer

1.3. s.d. Sands Sandys [elsewhere both **Sands** and **Sandys**] **13 Or** A **15 s.d.** [at. l. 16 in F] **34 oui** wee **59 wherewithal: in him** wherewithall in him; **66 [and at 1.4. s.d. and elsewhere] Guildford** Guilford

1.4. 50 s.d. [at l. 49 in F]

2.1. 18 have him **20 Perk** Pecke **86 mark** make

2.2. 1 s.p. Chamberlain [not in F]

2.3. 61 of you of you, to you

2.4. 11 s.p. Katharine [not in F] **125 s.p. Griffith** Gent. Ush **131 s.d. Exeunt** Exit **172 A** And

3.1. 3 s.p. Gentlewoman [not in F] **23 s.d. Campeius** Campian **61 your** our

3.2. 143 glad gald **172 filed** fill'd **293 Who** Whom **344 Chattels** Castles

4.1. 20 s.p. Second Gentleman 1 **34 Kimbolton** Kymmalton **55 s.p. First Gentleman** [not in F] **101 Stokesley** Stokeley

4.2. 7 think thanke

5.1. 37 time Lime **55 s.d. Exeunt** Exit [at l. 54 in F] **78 s.d.** [at l. 79 in F] **139 precipice** Precepit **140 woo** woe **157 s.p. Lovell** Gent

5.2. 4 s.d. Keeper [after "Sure you know me?" in F] **8 piece** Peere

5.3. 86, 87 s.p. Chancellor Cham **133 this** his **173 heart** hearts

5.4. 4, 27 s.p. One [not in F]

5.5. 38 ways way

Shakespeare's Sources

Shakespeare's chief source for the first four acts of *Henry VIII,* as for many of his earlier history plays, was Raphael Holinshed's *Chronicles* (1587 edition). Holinshed presented him with conflicting views of Cardinal Wolsey, however, and traces of the conflict remain in Shakespeare's play. Much of Holinshed is actually a compilation of the writings of earlier historiographers. In this case, some of Holinshed's material is from the bitterly anti-Wolseyan *Anglica Historia* (1534) of Polydore Vergil. Accordingly, Holinshed gives decidedly unfavorable interpretations of Wolsey's animosity toward the Duke of Buckingham and his unscrupulous meddling in the question of the King's marriage. Vergil was particularly distressed by the way in which Katharine had been shabbily treated; he (and Holinshed) report her speeches in her own behalf with manifest approval. Shakespeare preserves this alignment of sympathies in which Katharine is the wrongly accused wife and Wolsey the scheming Machiavel.

Other portions of Holinshed, on the other hand, derive from George Cavendish's *The Life and Death of Thomas Wolsey,* written some time around 1557 and extensively used by the chroniclers, though not separately printed until 1641. Cavendish was a gentleman usher in the household of Cardinal Wolsey from 1526 to 1530. Although he moralizes about the lesson to be learned from Wolsey's ambitious rise and sudden fall, Cavendish speaks admiringly of the Cardinal as an extraordinarily great man. He captures in minutely observed detail the magnificence of Wolsey's prosperous estate. He gives a moving portrait of Wolsey after his fall, on his sickbed and near the end, saying to a companion: "If I had served God as diligently as I have done the King, he would not have given me over in my gray hairs." This passage, borrowed verbatim by Holinshed from Cavendish, produces in turn the famous lines from Shakespeare: "Had I but served my God with half the zeal / I served my king, he would not in mine age / Have left me naked to mine enemies" (3.2.456–458).

For his fifth act, Shakespeare turned to John Foxe's *Acts*

and Monuments of Martyrs (1583 edition). Here he encountered a particularly rabid Protestant point of view, which has left its impression not only on the fifth act but on portrayals of Wolsey (whom Foxe naturally deplored) in earlier scenes. Foxe's hero, Thomas Cranmer, emerges as the victor of Shakespeare's play. Although the triumphantly Protestant ending contrasts oddly with Shakespeare's earlier manifest sympathy for Queen Katharine, the duality of attitudes is somehow plausible and perhaps even typically Elizabethan: Katharine suffered lamentably, and Henry and Wolsey treated her shabbily, but these great events did after all lead to the English Reformation and the rule of Queen Elizabeth. The ambiguity so often noted in *Henry VIII*, then, is an essential part of Shakespeare's sources, not merely because he used conflicting accounts but because many Elizabethan Englishmen necessarily felt mixed emotions toward this chapter of their past.

Shakespeare may also have read in Edward Hall's *The Union of the Two Noble and Illustre Families of Lancaster and York* (1542), and in John Speed's *History of Great Britain* (1611). In addition, he probably knew a dramatic version of the reign of Henry VIII that had appeared about eight years before, *When You See Me You Know Me* by Samuel Rowley (1603–1605).

The Third Volume of Chronicles (1587 edition)

Compiled by Raphael Holinshed

HENRY THE SEVENTH

[In his account of the reign of Henry VII, Holinshed tells a story very much like that in which a secret account of Cardinal Wolsey's great wealth is inadvertently delivered into the hands of King Henry VIII; see *Henry VIII*, 3.2.121 ff. The blunderer in this present story is Thomas Ruthall, made Bishop of Durham in 1508 by Henry VII and commissioned by him to write "a book of the whole estate of the kingdom."]

Afterwards, the King commanded Cardinal Wolsey to go to this bishop and to bring the book away with him to deliver to His Majesty. But see the mishap! That a man in all other things so provident should now be so negligent, and at that time most forget himself when, as it after fell out, he had most need to have remembered himself. For this bishop, having written two books, the one to answer the King's command and the other entreating of[1] his own private affairs, did bind them both after one sort in vellum, just of one length, breadth, and thickness, and in all points in such like proportion answering one another as the one could not by any especial note be discerned from the other, both which he also laid up together in one place of his study.

Now when the Cardinal came to demand the book due to the King, the Bishop unadvisedly commanded his servant to bring him the book bound in white vellum lying in his study in such a place. The servant, doing accordingly, brought forth one of those books so bound, being the book entreating of the state of the Bishop, and delivered the same unto his master, who, receiving it, without further consideration or looking on gave it to the Cardinal to bear unto the King. The Cardinal, having the book, went from the Bishop, and after, in his study by himself, understanding the contents thereof, he greatly rejoiced, having now occasion (which he long sought for) offered unto him to bring the Bishop into the King's disgrace.

Wherefore he went forthwith to the King, delivered the book into his hands, and briefly informed the King of the contents thereof; putting further into the King's head that if at any time he were destitute of a mass of money, he should not need to seek further therefor than to the coffers of the Bishop, who by the tenor of his own book had accounted his proper riches and substance to the value of a hundred thousand pounds. Of all which when the Bishop had intelligence . . . he was stricken with such grief of the same that he shortly through extreme sorrow ended his life at London.

Henry the Eighth

[Beginning his account of the reign of Henry VIII in 1509, Holinshed comes at length to 1519–1520 and the handing over of Tournai to the French King.]

1 entreating of dealing with

During this time remained in the French court divers young gentlemen of England, and they with the French King rode daily disguised through Paris, throwing eggs, stones, and other foolish trifles at the people; which light demeanor of a king was much discommended and jested at. And when these young gentlemen came again into England, they were all French in eating, drinking, and apparel, yea, and in French vices and brags, so that all the estates[2] of England were by them laughed at. The ladies and gentlewomen were dispraised, so that nothing by them was praised but if it were after the French turn, which after turned them to displeasure, as you shall hear. . . .

Then the King's Council caused the Lord Chamberlain to call before them divers of the privy chamber, which had been in the French court, and banished them the court for divers considerations, laying nothing particularly to their charges, and they that had offices were commanded to go to their offices. Which discharge out of court grieved sore the hearts of these young men, which were called the King's minions. . . .

The King specially rebuked Sir William Bulmer, knight, because he, being his servant sworn, refused the King's service and became servant to the Duke of Buckingham. . . .

The French King,[3] desirous to continue the friendship lately begun betwixt him and the King of England, made means unto the Cardinal that they might in some convenient place come to an interview together, that he might have further knowledge of King Henry and likewise King Henry of him. But the fame[4] went that the Cardinal desired greatly, of himself, that the two Kings might meet, who, measuring by his will what was convenient, thought it should make much with his glory if in France also at some high assembly of noblemen he should be seen in his vain pomp and show of dignity. He therefore breaketh with the King of that matter, declaring how honorable, necessary, and convenient it should be for him to gratify his friend[5] therein; and thus with his persuasions the King began to conceive an earnest desire to see the French King, and

2 estates noblemen **3 French King** i.e., Francis I **4 fame** rumor **5 his friend** i.e., Francis I

thereupon appointed to go over to Calais and so in the marches[6] of Guînes to meet with him. . . .

Herewith were letters written to all such lords, ladies, gentlemen, and gentlewomen which should give their attendance on the King and Queen, which incontinently[7] put themselves in a readiness after the most sumptuous sort. Also it was appointed that the King of England and the French King, in a camp between Ardres and Guînes, with eighteen aides, should in June next ensuing abide all comers, being gentlemen, at the tilt, at tourney, and at barriers. . . .[8]

Moreover, now that it was concluded that the Kings of England and France should meet, as ye have heard, then both the Kings committed the order and manner of their meeting, and how many days the same should continue, and what preeminence each should give to other, unto the Cardinal of York, which, to set all things in a certainty, made an instrument containing an order and direction concerning the premises by him devised and appointed.

[Holinshed prints the instrument of direction made by Cardinal Wolsey.]

The peers of the realm, receiving letters to prepare themselves to attend the King in this journey and no apparent necessary cause expressed why nor wherefore, seemed to grudge that such a costly journey should be taken in hand, to their importunate charges and expenses, without consent of the whole board of the Council. But namely[9] the Duke of Buckingham, being a man of a lofty courage but not most liberal,[10] sore repined that he should be at so great charges for his furniture forth[11] at this time, saying that he knew not for what cause so much money should be spent about the sight of a vain talk to be had and communication to be ministered of things of no importance. Wherefore he

6 marches boundaries, frontiers **7 incontinently** immediately
8 barriers military exercises named for the railings down the center of the tilting or tournament arena, on opposite sides of which the combatants rode toward one another. (The date is 1520.) **9 namely** especially
10 of a . . . liberal of great spirit but not generous **11 charges . . . forth** expenses to furnish himself for the event

sticked[12] not to say that it was an intolerable matter to obey such a vile and importunate person.

The Duke indeed could not abide the Cardinal, and specially he had of late conceived an inward malice against him for Sir William Bulmer's cause, whose trouble was only procured by the Cardinal, who first caused him to be cast in prison. Now such grievous words as the Duke thus uttered against him came to the Cardinal's ear, whereupon he cast beforehand all ways possible to have him in a trip, that he might cause him to leap headless.[13] But because he doubted[14] his friends, kinsmen, and allies, and chiefly the Earl of Surrey, Lord Admiral, which had married the Duke's daughter, he thought good first to send him somewhither out of the way lest he might cast a trump[15] in his way. There was great enmity betwixt the Cardinal and the Earl for that, on a time, when the Cardinal took upon him to check the Earl, he had like to have[16] thrust his dagger into the Cardinal.

At length there was occasion offered him to compass his purpose, by occasion of the Earl of Kildare his coming out of Ireland. For the Cardinal . . . accused him to the King of that he had not borne himself uprightly in his office in Ireland, where he was the King's lieutenant. Such accusations were framed against him, when no bribes would come, that he was committed to prison, and then by the Cardinal's good preferment the Earl of Surrey was sent into Ireland as the King's deputy in lieu of the said Earl of Kildare, there to remain rather as an exile than as lieutenant to the King, even at the Cardinal's pleasure, as he himself well perceived. . . .

Now it chanced that the Duke, coming to London with his train of men to attend the King into France, went before into Kent unto a manor place which he had there. And whilst he stayed in that country till the King set forward, grievous complaints were exhibited to him by his farmers and tenants against Charles Knevet, his surveyor,[17] for such bribing as he had used there amongst them. Whereupon the Duke

12 sticked hesitated **13 to have him . . . headless** to trip him (the Duke) up in such a way as to cause him to be beheaded **14 doubted** feared **15 trump** i.e., obstruction. (The metaphor is from card playing.) **16 check . . . he had like to have** rebuke . . . he nearly **17 surveyor** overseer

took such displeasure against him that he deprived him of his office, not knowing how that in so doing he procured his own destruction, as after appeared.

[The Emperor Charles V visits England in May 1520 to see his aunt, the Queen, "of whom ye may be sure he was most joyfully received and welcomed."]

The chief cause that moved the Emperor to come thus on land at this time was to persuade[18] that by word of mouth which he had before done most earnestly by letters; which was, that the King should not meet with the French King at any interview. For he doubted lest, if the King of England and the French King should grow into some great friendship and faithful bond of amity, it might turn him to displeasure.[19]

But now that he perceived how the King was forward on his journey, he did what he could to procure that no trust should be committed to the fair words of the Frenchmen; and that, if it were possible, the great friendship that was now in breeding betwixt the two Kings might be dissolved. And forsomuch as he knew the Lord Cardinal to be won with rewards, as a fish with a bait, he bestowed on him great gifts and promised him much more so that he would be his friend and help to bring his purpose to pass. The Cardinal . . . promised to the Emperor that he would so use the matter as his purpose should be sped.[20]

[King Henry sails from Dover in late May and early June 1520 for his meeting with King Francis I at the Field of the Cloth of Gold.]

The day of the meeting was appointed to be on the Thursday, the seventh of June, upon which day the two Kings met in the vale of Andren, accompanied with such a number of the nobility of both realms, so richly appointed in apparel and costly jewels, as chains, collars of S's, and other the like ornaments to set forth their degrees and estates, that a

18 persuade urge **19 turn him to displeasure** i.e., cause him, the Emperor, trouble and sorrow **20 as his . . . sped** so that his, the Emperor's, purpose should prosper

wonder it was to behold and view them in their order and rooms,[21] which every man kept according to his appointment.

The two Kings meeting in the field, either saluted other in most loving wise, first on horseback, and after alighting on foot eftsoons[22] embraced with courteous words, to the great rejoicing of the beholders; and after they had thus saluted each other, they went both together into a rich tent of cloth of gold there set up for the purpose, in the which they passed the time in pleasant talk, banqueting, and loving devices till it drew toward the evening, and then departed for that night, the one to Guînes, the other to Ardres.

[Holinshed gives a long description of the tilting, in which all did "right valiantly," but "the two Kings surmounted all the rest in prowess and valiantness."]

On Monday, the eighteenth of June, was such an hideous storm of wind and weather that many conjectured it did prognosticate trouble and hatred shortly after to follow between princes.

[In 1521, some months after King Henry's return to England, trouble breaks out between Wolsey and Buckingham.]

The Cardinal, boiling in hatred against the Duke of Buckingham and thirsting for his blood, devised to make Charles Knevet, that had been the Duke's surveyor and put from him[23] (as ye have heard), an instrument to bring the Duke to destruction. This Knevet, being had in examination before the Cardinal, disclosed all the Duke's life. And first he uttered that the Duke was accustomed, by way of talk, to say how he meant so to use the matter that he would attain to the crown if King Henry chanced to die without issue; and that he had talk and conference of that matter on a time with George Neville, Lord of Abergavenny, unto whom he had given his daughter in marriage; and also that he threatened to punish the Cardinal for his manifold misdoings, being without cause his mortal enemy.

21 rooms places **22 eftsoons** immediately **23 put from him** dismissed

The Cardinal, having gotten that which he sought for, encouraged, comforted, and procured[24] Knevet, with many comfortable words and great promises, that he should with a bold spirit and countenance object and lay these things to the Duke's charge, with more if he knew it when time required. Then Knevet, partly provoked with desire to be revenged and partly moved with hope of reward, openly confessed that the Duke had once fully determined to devise means how to make the King away, being brought into a full hope that he should be king by a vain prophecy which one Nicholas Hopkins, a monk of an house of the Chartreux order beside Bristol, called Henton, sometime his confessor, had opened[25] unto him.

The Cardinal, having thus taken the examination of Knevet, went unto the King and declared unto him that his person was in danger by such traitorous purpose as the Duke of Buckingham had conceived in his heart, and showed how that[26] now there is manifest tokens of his wicked pretense;[27] wherefore he exhorted the King to provide for his own surety with speed. The King, hearing the accusation enforced to the uttermost by the Cardinal, made this answer: "If the Duke have deserved to be punished, let him have according to his deserts." The Duke hereupon was sent for up to London and, at his coming thither, was straightways attached[28] and brought to the Tower by Sir Henry Marney, Captain of the Guard, the sixteenth of April. There was also attached the foresaid Chartreux monk, Master John de la Car alias de la Court, the Duke's confessor, and Sir Gilbert Perke, priest, the Duke's chancellor.[29]

After the apprehension of the Duke, inquisitions were taken in divers shires of England of him, so that by the knights and gentlemen he was indicted of high treason for certain words spoken (as before ye have heard) by the same Duke at Blechingley to the Lord of Abergavenny; and therewith was the same lord attached for concealment, and so likewise was the Lord Montacute, and both led to the Tower.

[Holinshed gives the counts in the indictment of Buckingham for high treason, including the following:]

24 procured induced **25 opened** revealed, expounded **26 showed how that** explained how **27 pretense** intent **28 attached** arrested
29 chancellor secretary

. . . the same Duke . . . said unto one Charles Knevet, esquire, after that the King had reproved the Duke for retaining William Bulmer, knight, into his service, that if he had perceived that he should have been committed to the Tower (as he doubted[30] he should have been), he would have so wrought that the principal doers therein should not have had cause of great rejoicing, for he would have played the part which his father intended to have put in practice against King Richard the Third at Salisbury, who made earnest suit to have come unto the presence of the same King Richard; which suit if he might have obtained, he, having a knife secretly about him, would have thrust it into the body of King Richard as he had made semblance to kneel down before him. And in speaking these words, he maliciously laid his hand upon his dagger and said that, if he were so evil used, he would do his best to accomplish his pretensed[31] purpose, swearing to confirm his word by the blood of our Lord.

Besides all this, the same Duke . . . at London in a place called the Rose, within the parish of St. Lawrence Poultney, in Canwick Street Ward, demanded of the said Charles Knevet, esquire, what was the talk amongst the Londoners concerning the King's journey beyond the seas? And the said Charles told him that many stood in doubt[32] of that journey, lest the Frenchmen meant some deceit towards the King. Whereto the Duke answered that it was to be feared lest it would come to pass, according to the words of a certain holy monk. "For there is," saith he, "a Chartreux monk that divers times hath sent to me, willing me to send unto him my chancellor; and I did send unto him John de la Court, my chaplain, unto whom he would not declare anything till de la Court had sworn unto him to keep all things secret and to tell no creature living what he should hear of him, except it were to me.

"And then the said monk told de la Court that neither the King nor his heirs should prosper and that I should endeavor myself to purchase the good wills of the commonalty of England, for I, the same Duke, and my blood should prosper and have the rule of the realm of England." Then said Charles Knevet, "The monk may be deceived through

30 doubted feared **31 pretensed** intended **32 doubt** fear the devil's illusion," and that it was evil to meddle with such matters. "Well," said the Duke, "it cannot hurt me," and so (saith the indictment) the Duke seemed to rejoice in the monk's words. And further, at the same time, the Duke told the said Charles that, if the King had miscarried now in his last sickness, he would have chopped off the heads of the Cardinal, of Sir Thomas Lovell, knight, and of others; and also said that he had rather die for it than to be used as he had been.

[Popular opinion blames the Cardinal for Buckingham's fall.]

I trust I may without offense say that, as the rumor then went, the Cardinal chiefly procured the death of this nobleman, no less favored and beloved of the people of this realm in that season than the Cardinal himself was hated and envied. Which thing caused the Duke's fall the more to be pitied and lamented, sith[33] he was the man of all other that chiefly went about to cross the Cardinal in his lordly demeanor and heady proceedings. But to the purpose. Shortly after that the Duke had been indicted, as before ye have heard, he was arraigned in Westminster Hall, before the Duke of Norfolk. . . . When the lords had taken their place, the Duke was brought to the bar, and upon his arraignment pleaded not guilty and put himself upon[34] his peers. Then was his indictment read, which the Duke denied to be true and, as he was an eloquent man, alleged reasons to falsify[35] the indictment, pleading the matter for his own justification very pithily and earnestly. The King's attorney, against the Duke's reasons, alleged the examinations, confessions, and proofs of witnesses.

The Duke desired that the witnesses might be brought forth. And then came before him Charles Knevet, Perke, de la Court, and Hopkins the monk of the priory of the Charterhouse beside Bath, which like a false hypocrite had induced the Duke to the treason with his false, forged prophecies. Divers presumptions[36] and accusations were

33 sith since **34 put himself upon** submitted his case to **35 falsify** confute, prove false **36 presumptions** inferences, allegations

laid unto him by Charles Knevet, which he would fain have covered.[37] The depositions were read and the deponents delivered as prisoners to the officers of the Tower.

[Buckingham is commanded to withdraw. The peers confer and find him guilty by vote of all the lords present.]

The Duke was brought to the bar sore chafing, and sweat marvelously; and after he had made his reverence, he paused awhile. The Duke of Norfolk, as judge, said: "Sir Edward, you have heard how you be indicted of high treason. You pleaded thereto not guilty, putting yourself to the peers of the realm, which have found you guilty." Then the Duke of Norfolk wept and said, "You shall be led to the King's prison and there laid on a hurdle[38] and so drawn to the place of execution, and there be hanged, cut down alive, your members cut off and cast into the fire, your bowels burnt before you, your head smitten off, and your body quartered and divided at the King's will, and God have mercy on your soul. Amen."

The Duke of Buckingham said: "My lord of Norfolk, you have said as a traitor should be said unto, but I was never any; but, my lords, I nothing malign for that you have done to me, but the eternal God forgive you my death, and I do. I shall never sue to the King for life, howbeit he is a gracious prince, and more grace may come from him than I desire. I desire you, my lords and all my fellows, to pray for me." Then was the edge of the ax turned towards him and he led into a barge. Sir Thomas Lovell desired him to sit on the cushions and carpet ordained for him. He said, "Nay, for when I went to Westminster I was Duke of Buckingham; now I am but Edward Bohun, the most caitiff[39] of the world." Thus they landed at the Temple, where received him Sir Nicholas Vaux and Sir William Sands, baronets, and led him through the city, who desired ever the people to pray for him, of whom some wept and lamented.

[Buckingham is led to the scaffold on Tower Hill, May 17, 1521.]

37 fain have covered gladly have concealed **38 hurdle** frame or sledge for dragging prisoners to execution **39 caitiff** wretched, miserable

He said he had offended the King's Grace through negligence and lack of grace, and desired all noblemen to beware by him and all men to pray for him and that he trusted to die the King's true man. Thus meekly with an ax he took his death.

[Holinshed takes this occasion to provide "A convenient collection concerning the High Constables of England, which office ceased and took end at the Duke of Buckingham above-mentioned." The present duke and his father are thus the last of the line.]

Henry Stafford . . . was High Constable of England and Duke of Buckingham. This man, raising war against Richard the Third usurping the crown, was in the first year of the reign of the said Richard . . . betrayed by his man Humphrey Banister (to whom being in distress he fled for succor) and . . . was beheaded without arraignment or judgment. . . .

Edward Stafford, son to Henry, Duke of Buckingham, being also Duke of Buckingham after the death of his father, was Constable of England, Earl of Hereford, Stafford, and Northampton, being in the first year of Henry the Seventh, in the year of our redemption 1485, restored to his father's dignities and possessions. He is termed . . . to be the flower and mirror of all courtesy. This man (as before is touched) was by Henry the Seventh restored to his father's inheritance, in recompense of the loss of his father's life.

[Some years later, in 1525, Cardinal Wolsey uses the King's determination to make war in France as his excuse for devising new and unpopular taxes.]

Wherefore by the Cardinal there was devised strange[40] commissions and sent in the end of March into every shire . . . that the sixth part of every man's substance should be paid in money or plate to the King without delay for the furniture[41] of his war. Hereof followed such cursing, weeping, and exclamation against both King and Cardinal that pity it was to hear. . . .

40 strange unprecedented **41 furniture** equipping

The Duke of Suffolk, sitting in commission about this subsidy in Suffolk, persuaded by courteous means the rich clothiers to assent thereto; but when they came home and went about to discharge and put from them their spinners, carders, fullers, weavers, and other artificers, which they kept in work aforetime, the people began to assemble in companies. . . . The rage of the people increased. . . . And herewith there assembled together after the manner of rebels four thousand men. . . .

The King then came to Westminster to the Cardinal's palace, and assembled there a great Council, in the which he openly protested that his mind was never to ask anything of his commons which might sound to the breach of his laws, wherefore he willed to know by whose means the commissions were so strictly given forth, to demand the sixth part of every man's goods.

The Cardinal excused himself and said that . . . by the consent of the whole Council it was done, and took God to witness that he never desired the hindrance of the commons, but like a true councillor devised how to enrich the King. The King indeed was much offended that his commons were thus entreated and thought it touched his honor that his Council should attempt such a doubtful matter in his name and to be denied both of the spirituality and temporality. Therefore he would no more of that trouble, but caused letters to be sent into all shires that the matter should no further be talked of; and he pardoned all them that had denied the demand openly or secretly. The Cardinal, to deliver himself of the evil will of the commons purchased by procuring and advancing of this demand, affirmed and caused it to be bruited[42] abroad that through his intercession the King had pardoned and released all things.

[Some two years later, in 1527, rumors circulate about King Henry's marriage.]

There rose a secret bruit in London that the King's confessor, Dr. Longland, and divers other great clerks had told the King that the marriage between him and the Lady Kath-

42 bruited rumored

arine, late wife to his brother Prince Arthur, was not lawful; whereupon the King should sue a divorce and marry the Duchess of Alençon, sister to the French King, at the town of Calais this summer; and that the Viscount Rochford had brought with him the picture of the said lady. The King was offended with those tales and sent for Sir Thomas Seymour, Mayor of the city of London, secretly charging him to see that the people ceased from such talk. . . .

The truth is that, whether this doubt was first moved by the Cardinal or by the said Longland, being the King's confessor, the King was not only brought in doubt whether it was a lawful marriage or no but also determined to have the case examined, cleared, and adjudged by learning, law, and sufficient authority. The Cardinal verily was put in most blame for this scruple now cast into the King's conscience for the hate he bare to the Emperor because he would not grant to him the archbishopric of Toledo, for the which he was a suitor. And therefore he did not only procure the King of England to join in friendship with the French King but also sought a divorce betwixt the King and the Queen that the King might have had in marriage the Duchess of Alençon, sister unto the French King; and, as some have thought, he travailed[43] in that matter with the French King at Amiens; but the Duchess would not give ear thereunto.

But howsoever it came about that the King was thus troubled in conscience concerning his marriage, this followed, that, like a wise and sage prince, to have the doubt clearly removed, he called together the best learned of the realm, which were of several opinions. Wherefore he thought to know the truth by indifferent judges, lest peradventure the Spaniards and other also in favor of the Queen would say that his own subjects were not indifferent[44] judges in this behalf. And therefore he wrote his cause to Rome and also sent to all the universities in Italy and France and to the great clerks of all Christendom to know their opinions, and desired the court of Rome to send into his realm a legate, which should be indifferent and of a great and profound judgment, to hear the cause debated. At whose request the whole consistory of the College of Rome sent thither

43 travailed labored **44 indifferent** impartial

Laurence Campeius, a priest cardinal, a man of great wit and experience . . . and with him was joined in commission the Cardinal of York and legate of England. . . .

The place where the cardinals should sit to hear the cause of matrimony betwixt the King and the Queen was ordained to be at the Blackfriars in London, where in the great hall was preparation made of seats, tables, and other furniture according to such a solemn session and royal appearance. The court was platted in tables and benches in manner of a consistory,[45] one seat raised higher for the judges to sit in. Then, as it were in the midst of the said judges, aloft above them three degrees high was a cloth of estate[46] hanged, with a chair royal under the same, wherein sat the King, and besides him, some distance from him, sat the Queen, and under the judges' feet sat the scribes and other officers. The chief scribe was Doctor Steevens,[47] and the caller of the court was one Cook of Winchester.

Then before the King and the judges within the court sat the Archbishop of Canterbury, Warham, and all the other bishops. . . . The judges commanded silence whilst their commission was read both to the court and to the people assembled. That done, the scribes commanded the crier to call the King by the name of "King Henry of England, come into the court," etc. With that the King answered and said, "Here." Then called he the Queen by the name of "Katharine, Queen of England, come into the court," etc.; who made no answer, but rose out of her chair.

And because she could not come to the King directly, for the distance severed between them, she went about by the court and came to the King, kneeling down at his feet, to whom she said in effect as followeth: "Sir," quoth she, "I desire you to do me justice and right and take some pity upon me, for I am a poor woman and a stranger,[48] born out of your dominion, having here no indifferent counsel and less assurance of friendship. Alas, sir, what have I offended you or what occasion of displeasure have I showed you in-

45 platted . . . consistory arranged, laid out in tables and benches according to a plan of an ecclesiastical tribunal or court of judgment **46 cloth of estate** canopy spread over a throne **47 Doctor Steevens** i.e., Stephen Gardiner, just recently appointed to a position of royal adviser in place of Doctor Pace **48 stranger** foreigner

tending thus to put me from you after this sort? I take God to my judge, I have been to you a true and humble wife, ever conformable to your will and pleasure, that never contraried or gainsaid anything thereof, and being always contented with all things wherein you had any delight, whether little or much, without grudge or displeasure. I loved for your sake all them whom you loved, whether they were my friends or enemies.

"I have been your wife these twenty years and more, and you have had by me divers children. If there be any just cause that you can allege against me, either of dishonesty[49] or matter lawful to put me from you, I am content to depart to my shame and rebuke; and if there be none, then I pray you to let me have justice at your hand. The King your father was in his time of excellent wit, and the King of Spain, my father Ferdinando, was reckoned one of the wisest princes that reigned in Spain many years before. It is not to be doubted but that they had gathered as wise counselors unto them of every realm as to their wisdoms they thought meet, who deemed the marriage between you and me good and lawful, etc. Wherefore I humbly desire you to spare me until I may know what counsel my friends in Spain will advertise[50] me to take, and if you will not, then your pleasure be fulfilled." With that she arose up, making a low curtsy to the King, and departed from thence.

The King, being advertised that she was ready to go out of the house, commanded the crier to call her again, who called her by these words: "Katharine, Queen of England, come into the court." With that, quoth Master Griffith,[51] "Madam, you be called again." "On, on," quoth she, "it maketh no matter, I will not tarry; go on your ways." And thus she departed without any further answer at that time or any other, and never would appear after in any court. The King, perceiving she was departed, said these words in effect: "Forasmuch," quoth he, "as the Queen is gone, I will in her absence declare to you all that she hath been to me as true, as obedient, and as conformable a wife as I would wish or desire. She hath all the virtuous qualities that ought to be in a woman of her dignity or in any other of a

49 dishonesty unchastity **50 advertise** advise **51 Master Griffith** the Queen's gentleman usher; see *Henry VIII*, dramatis personae

baser estate. She is also surely a noblewoman born; her conditions[52] will well declare the same."

With that, quoth Wolsey the Cardinal: "Sir, I most humbly require[53] Your Highness to declare before all this audience whether I have been the chief and first mover of this matter unto Your Majesty or no, for I am greatly suspected herein." "My Lord Cardinal," quoth the King, "I can well excuse you in this matter. Marry," quoth he, "you have been rather against me in the tempting hereof than a setter forward or mover of the same. The special cause that moved me unto this matter was a certain scrupulosity that pricked my conscience upon certain words spoken at a time when it was by the Bishop of Bayonne, the French ambassador, who had been hither sent upon the debating of a marriage to be concluded between our daughter, the Lady Mary, and the Duke of Orleans, second son to the King of France.

"Upon the resolution and determination whereof, he desired respite to advertise[54] the King his master thereof, whether our daughter Mary should be legitimate in respect of this my marriage with this woman, being sometime[55] my brother's wife. Which words, once conceived within the secret bottom of my conscience, engendered such a scrupulous doubt that my conscience was incontinently accumbered,[56] vexed, and disquieted; whereby I thought myself to be greatly in danger of God's indignation—which appeared to be (as meseemed) the rather for that He sent us no issue male, and all such issues male as my said wife had by me died incontinent[57] after they came into the world, so that I doubted[58] the great displeasure of God in that behalf.

"Thus my conscience being tossed in the waves of a scrupulous mind, and partly in despair to have any other issue than I had already by this lady now my wife, it behooved me further to consider the state of this realm and the danger it stood in for lack of a prince to succeed me. I thought it good, in release of the weighty burden of my weak conscience and also the quiet estate of this worthy realm, to attempt[59] the law therein, whether I may lawfully take an-

52 conditions personal qualities **53 require** ask **54 advertise** advise **55 sometime** formerly **56 incontinently accumbered** immediately encumbered **57 incontinent** immediately **58 doubted** feared **59 attempt** essay to engage with

other wife more lawfully, by whom God may send me more issue, in case this my first copulation was not good; without any carnal concupiscence and not for any displeasure or misliking of the Queen's person and age, with whom I would be as well contented to continue, if our marriage may stand with the laws of God, as with any woman alive.

"In this point consisteth all this doubt that we go about now to try, by the learning, wisdom, and judgment of you our prelates and pastors of all this our realm and dominions now here assembled for that purpose, to whose conscience and learning I have committed the charge and judgment according to the which I will, God willing, be right well content to submit myself and, for my part, obey the same. Wherein, after that I perceived my conscience so doubtful, I moved it in confession to you, my lord of Lincoln, then ghostly father.[60] And forsomuch as then you yourself were in some doubt, you moved me to ask the counsel of all these my lords; whereupon I moved you, my lord of Canterbury, first to have your license, inasmuch as you were metropolitan,[61] to put this matter in question. And so I did of all you, my lords; to which you granted, under your seals, here to be showed." "That is truth," quoth the Archbishop of Canterbury. After that the King rose up, and the court was adjourned until another day.

Here is to be noted that the Queen, in presence of the whole court, most grievously accused the Cardinal of untruth, deceit, wickedness, and malice, which had sown dissension betwixt her and the King her husband; and therefore openly protested that she did utterly abhor, refuse, and forsake such a judge as was not only a most malicious enemy to her but also a manifest adversary to all right and justice; and therewith did she appeal unto the Pope, committing her whole cause to be judged of him. But notwithstanding this appeal, the legates sat weekly . . . and still they assayed if they could by any means procure the Queen to call back her appeal, which she utterly refused to do. The King would gladly have had an end in the matter, but when the legates drave time[62] and determined upon no certain point, he conceived a suspicion that this was done

60 ghostly father confessor **61 metropolitan** archbishop **62 drave time** i.e., delayed matters

of purpose, that their doings might draw to none effect or conclusion. . . .

And thus this court passed from sessions to sessions and day to day, till at certain of their sessions the King sent the two cardinals to the Queen (who was then in Bridewell)[63] to persuade[64] with her by their wisdoms and to advise her to surrender the whole matter into the King's hands by her own consent and will, which should be much better to her honor than to stand to the trial of law and thereby to be condemned, which should seem much to her dishonor.

The Cardinals being in the Queen's chamber of presence,[65] the gentleman usher advertised the Queen that the Cardinals were come to speak with her. With that she rose up and, with a skein of white thread about her neck, came into her chamber of presence, where the Cardinals were attending. At whose coming, quoth she, "What is your pleasure with me?" "If it please Your Grace," quoth Cardinal Wolsey, "to go into your privy chamber, we will show you the cause of our coming." "My lord," quoth she, "if ye have anything to say, speak it openly before all these folk, for I fear nothing that ye can say against me but that I would all the world should hear and see it, and therefore speak your mind." Then began the Cardinal to speak to her in Latin. "Nay, good my lord," quoth she, "speak to me in English."

"Forsooth," quoth the Cardinal, "good madam, if it please you, we come both to know your mind how you are disposed to do in this matter between the King and you and also to declare secretly our opinions and counsel unto you; which we do only for very zeal and obedience we bear unto Your Grace." "My lord," quoth she, "I thank you for your good will, but to make you answer in your request I cannot so suddenly, for I was set among my maids at work, thinking full little of any such matter, wherein there needeth a longer deliberation and a better head than mine to make answer; for I need counsel in this case, which toucheth me so near, and for[66] any counsel or friendship that I can find in England, they are not for my profit. What think you, my lords, will any Englishman counsel me or be friend to me

63 Bridewell (At this time a house owned by the King.) **64 persuade** use persuasion **65 chamber of presence** presence chamber, reception room in a palace **66 for** as for

against the King's pleasure that is his subject?[67] Nay, forsooth. And as for my council in whom I will put my trust, they be not here; they be in Spain in my own country.

"And, my lords, I am a poor woman, lacking wit, to answer to any such noble persons of wisdom as you be in so weighty a matter. Therefore I pray you be good to me, poor woman, destitute of friends here in a foreign region, and your counsel also I will be glad to hear." And therewith she took the Cardinal by the hand and led him into her privy chamber with the other cardinal, where they tarried a season talking with the Queen.

[Some time later, the King comes to the court to hear judgment given.]

That done, the King's counsel at the bar called for judgment. With that, quoth Cardinal Campeius: "I . . . will adjourn this court for this time, according to the order of the court of Rome." And with that the court was dissolved and no more done. This protracting of the conclusion of the matter King Henry took very displeasantly. Then Cardinal Campeius took his leave of the King and returned towards Rome.

Whilst these things were thus in hand, the Cardinal of York was advised that the King had set his affection upon a young gentlewoman named Anne, the daughter of Sir Thomas Bullen, Viscount Rochford, which did wait upon the Queen. This was a great grief unto the Cardinal, as he that perceived aforehand that the King would marry the said gentlewoman if the divorce took place. Wherefore he began with all diligence to disappoint[68] that match, which, by reason of the misliking that he had to the woman, he judged ought to be avoided more than present death. While the matter stood in this state, and that the cause of the Queen was to be heard and judged at Rome by reason of the appeal which by her was put in, the Cardinal required[69] the Pope by letters and secret messengers that in any wise he should defer the judgment of the divorce till he might frame the King's mind to his purpose.

67 that is his subject who is subject to the King **68 disappoint** frustrate **69 required** requested

Howbeit he went about nothing so secretly but that the same came to the King's knowledge, who took so high displeasure with such his cloaked dissimulation that he determined to abase his degree, sith[70] as an unthankful person he forgot himself and his duty towards him that had so highly advanced him to all honor and dignity. When the nobles of the realm perceived the Cardinal to be in displeasure, they began to accuse him of such offenses as they knew might be proved against him, and thereof they made a book containing certain articles, to which divers of the King's Council set their hands. The King, understanding more plainly by those articles the great pride, presumption, and covetousness of the Cardinal, was sore moved against him; but yet kept his purpose secret for a while. . . .

In the meantime the King, being informed that all those things that the Cardinal had done by his power legantine within this realm were in the case of the praemunire and provision,[71] caused his attorney, Christopher Hales, to sue out a writ of praemunire against him, in the which he licensed him to make his attorney.[72] And further, the seventeenth of November, the King sent the two Dukes of Norfolk and Suffolk to the Cardinal's place at Westminster, who went as they were commanded; and finding the Cardinal there, they declared that the King's pleasure was that he should surrender up the Great Seal into their hands and to depart simply unto Asher, which was an house situate nigh unto Hampton Court belonging to the bishopric of Winchester. The Cardinal demanded of them their commission that gave them such authority; who answered again that they were sufficient commissioners and had authority to do no less by the King's mouth. Notwithstanding, he would in no wise agree in that behalf without further knowledge of their authority, saying that the Great Seal was delivered him by the King's person to enjoy the ministration thereof,

70 abase his degree, sith reduce his (Wolsey's) authority and lower his station, since **71 by his power . . . provision** i.e., by his power as papal legate within the realm of England came under the provisions of the assertion of papal jurisdiction in England, thus denying the ecclesiastical supremacy of the King. (A *writ of praemunire* charges the sheriff to summon a person, here Wolsey, accused of violating English law in this way.) **72 in the which . . . attorney** i.e., in which the King licensed Hales to act as his (the King's) attorney with the room[73] of the chancellor for the term of his life, whereof for his surety he had the King's letters patents.

This matter was greatly debated between them with many great words, insomuch that the Dukes were fain to depart again without their purpose, and rode to Windsor to the King and made report accordingly; but the next day they returned again, bringing with them the King's letters. Then the Cardinal delivered unto them the Great Seal and was content to depart simply, taking with him nothing but only certain provision for his house. . . . Then the Cardinal called all his officers before him and took account of them for all such stuff whereof they had charge. And in his gallery were set divers tables whereupon lay a great number of goodly rich stuff. . . .

There was laid, on every table, books reporting the contents of the same, and so was there inventories of all things, in order against the King's coming. . . . Then had he two chambers adjoining to the gallery, the one most commonly called the gilt chamber and the other the council chamber, wherein were set up two broad and long tables upon trestles, whereupon was set such a number of plate[74] of all sorts as was almost incredible. . . .

After this, in the King's Bench,[75] his matter for the praemunire being called upon, two attorneys, which he had authorized by his warrant signed with his own hand, confessed the action and so had judgment to forfeit all his lands, tenements, goods, and chattels, and to be out of the King's protection. . . .

During this Parliament was brought down to the Commons the book of articles which the Lords had put to the King against the Cardinal, the chief whereof were these:

1. First, that he without the King's assent had procured to be a legate, by reason whereof he took away the right of all bishops and spiritual persons.

2. Item, in all writings which he wrote to Rome or any other foreign prince he wrote *Ego et rex meus,* I and my King, as who would say that the King were his servant.

73 room position **74 plate** objects of precious metal **75 the King's Bench** a supreme court of common law

3. Item, that he hath slandered the Church of England in the court of Rome. . . .

4. Item, he without the King's assent carried the King's Great Seal with him into Flanders when he was sent ambassador to the Emperor.

5. Item, he without the King's assent sent a commission to Sir Gregory de Cassado, knight, to conclude a league between the King and the Duke of Ferrar without the King's knowledge.

6. Item, that he, having the French pox,[76] presumed to come and breathe on the King.

7. Item, that he caused the Cardinal's hat to be put on the King's coin.

8. Item, that he would not suffer the King's clerk of the market to sit at Saint Albans.

9. Item, that he had sent innumerable substance to Rome for the obtaining of his dignities, to the great impoverishment of the realm.

[Holinshed reports that, in the Lenten season of 1530, Wolsey is licensed to go to his diocese of York and not return south without express permission. Among those who leave his service is Thomas Cromwell, now serving the King in the suppressing of the monasteries. Wolsey is subsequently arrested for treason at Cawood by the Earl of Northumberland. On the way south he becomes very ill with dysentery.]

The next day he rode to Nottingham and there lodged that night more sick; and the next day he rode to Leicester Abbey, and by the way waxed so sick that he was almost fallen from his mule; so that it was night before he came to the Abbey of Leicester, where, at his coming in at the gates, the abbot with all his convent met him with divers torches light,[77] whom they honorably received and welcomed.

To whom the Cardinal said: "Father abbot, I am come hither to lay my bones among you." . . . And as soon as he was in his chamber he went to bed. This was on the Saturday at night, and then increased he sicker and sicker until Monday, that all men thought he would have died. So on Tuesday, Saint Andrew's Even, Master Kingston came to

76 French pox syphilis **77 light** lighted

him and bade him good morrow. . . . "Sir," quoth he, "I tarry but the pleasure of God to render up my poor soul into his hands." . . .

"Well, well, Master Kingston," quoth the Cardinal, "I see the matter how it is framed. But if I had served God as diligently as I have done the King, he would not have given me over in my gray hairs. . . ."

Then they did put him in remembrance of Christ His passion . . . and incontinent[78] the clock struck eight, and then he gave up the ghost and departed this present life; which caused some to call to remembrance how he said the day before that at eight of the clock they should lose their master.

Here is the end and fall of pride and arrogancy of men exalted by fortune to dignity; for in his time he was the haughtiest man in all his proceedings alive, having more respect to the honor of his person than he had to his spiritual profession, wherein should be showed all meekness, humility, and charity. . . .

This Cardinal, as Edmund Campian in his *History of Ireland* describeth him, was a man undoubtedly born to honor. "I think," saith he, "some prince's bastard, no butcher's son; exceeding wise, fair-spoken, high-minded; full of revenge; vicious of his body; lofty to his enemies, were they never so big; to those that accepted and sought his friendship, wonderful courteous; a ripe schoolman; thrall to affections;[79] brought abed with flattery; insatiable to get,[80] and more princely in bestowing, as appeareth by his two colleges at Ipswich and Oxenford, the one overthrown with his fall, the other unfinished, and yet as it lieth for an house of students, considering all the appurtenances, incomparable thorough Christendom . . . a great preferrer[81] of his servants . . . stout in every quarrel; never happy till this his overthrow, wherein he showed such moderation and ended so perfectly that the hour of his death did him more honor than all the pomp of his life past." . . .

This Thomas Wolsey was a poor man's son of Ipswich, in

78 incontinent immediately **79 ripe schoolman . . . affections** mature scholar in divinity; enslaved to passions **80 brought abed with flattery . . . get** i.e., debilitated by his proneness to flattery . . . acquire **81 preferrer** one who gives advancement

the county of Suffolk, and there born; and, being but a child,[82] very apt to be learned. . . .

[Holinshed describes Wolsey's career at length, including the ceremonial honors he insisted upon for himself, such as two great crosses of silver that were borne before him wherever he went. Particularly impressive is the order of procession attending his daily going in to Westminster Hall during term:]

Before him was borne first the Broad Seal of England and his cardinal's hat by a lord or some gentleman of worship, right solemnly, and as soon as he was once entered into his chamber of presence his two great crosses were there attending to be borne before him. Then cried the gentlemen ushers, going before him bareheaded, and said: "On before, my lords and masters, on before! Make way for my lord's Grace!" Thus went he down through the hall with a sergeant-of-arms before him, bearing a great mace of silver, and two gentlemen carrying two great pillars of silver. . . .

Thus in great honor, triumph, and glory he reigned a long season, ruling all things within the realm appertaining unto the King. His house was resorted to with[83] noblemen and gentlemen, feasting and banqueting ambassadors divers times, and all other right nobly. And when it pleased the King for his recreation to repair to the Cardinal's house, as he did divers times in the year, there wanted no preparations or furniture.[84] Banquets were set forth with masques and mummeries in so gorgeous a sort and costly manner that it was an heaven to behold. There wanted no dames or damosels meet or apt to dance with the maskers or to garnish the place for the time; then was there all kind of music and harmony, with fine voices both of men and children.

On a time the King came suddenly thither in a masque with a dozen maskers all in garments like shepherds made of fine cloth of gold and crimson satin paned[85] and caps of the same, with visors of good physiognomy, their hairs[86] and beards either of fine goldwire silk or black silk; having

82 being but a child even when he was still a child **83 with** by
84 furniture things provided for lavish entertainment **85 paned** bordered or lined with fur **86 hairs** wigs

sixteen torchbearers, besides their drums[87] and other persons with visors all clothed in satin of the same color. And before his entering into the hall, he came by water to the water gate without any noise, where were laid divers chambers and guns charged with shot, and at his landing they were shot off, which made such a rumble in the air that it was like thunder. It made all the noblemen, gentlemen, ladies, and gentlewomen to muse what it should mean, coming so suddenly, they sitting quiet at a solemn banquet, after this sort.[88]

First ye shall understand that the tables were set in the chamber of presence just[89] covered, and the Lord Cardinal sitting under the cloth of estate, there having all his service alone; and then was there set a lady with a nobleman, or a gentleman and a gentlewoman, throughout all the tables in the chamber on the one side, which were made and joined as it were but one table, all which order and device was done by the Lord Sands, then Lord Chamberlain to the King, and by Sir Henry Guildford, Comptroller of the King's Majesty's house. Then immediately after, the Great Chamberlain and the said Comptroller sent to look what it should mean (as though they knew nothing of the matter), who, looking out of the windows into the Thames, returned again and showed[90] him that it seemed they were noblemen and strangers that arrived at his bridge,[91] coming as ambassadors from some foreign prince.

With that quoth the Cardinal: "I desire you, because you can speak French, to take the pains to go into the hall, there to receive them according to their estates and to conduct them into this chamber, where they shall see us and all these noble personages being merry at our banquet; desiring them to sit down with us and to take part of our fare." Then went he incontinent down into the hall, whereas[92] they received them with twenty new torches and conveyed them up into the chamber with such a noise of drums and flutes as seldom had been heard the like. At their entering into the chamber, two and two together, they went directly before the Cardinal where he sat, and saluted him reverently.

87 drums drummers **88 after this sort** in this manner **89 just** appropriately **90 showed** informed **91 bridge** gangway or movable landing stage for boats **92 whereas** where

To whom the Lord Chamberlain for them said: "Sir, forasmuch as they be strangers and cannot speak English, they have desired me to declare unto you that they, having understanding of this your triumphant banquet where was assembled such a number of excellent dames, they could do no less, under support of Your Grace, but to repair hither to view as well their incomparable beauty as for to accompany them at mumchance[93] and then to dance with them; and, sir, they require[94] of Your Grace license to accomplish the said cause of their coming." To whom the Cardinal said he was very well content they should so do. Then went the maskers and first saluted all the dames, and returned to the most worthy and there opened their great cup of gold filled with crowns and other pieces of gold; to whom they set certain pieces of gold to cast at.

Thus, perusing all the ladies and gentlewomen, to some they lost and of some they won; and marking after this manner all the ladies, they returned to the Cardinal with great reverence, pouring down all their gold so left in their cup, which was above two hundred crowns. "At all!" quoth the Cardinal, and so cast the dice and wan them, whereat was made a great noise and joy. Then quoth the Cardinal to the Lord Chamberlain: "I pray you," quoth he, "that you would show[95] them that meseemeth there should be a nobleman amongst them who is more meet to occupy this seat and place than I am, to whom I would most gladly surrender the same according to my duty, if I knew him."

Then spake the Lord Chamberlain to them in French, and they rounding[96] him in the ear, the Lord Chamberlain said to my Lord Cardinal: "Sir," quoth he, "they confess that among them there is such a noble personage whom, if Your Grace can appoint him out from the rest, he is content to disclose himself and to accept your place." With that the Cardinal, taking good advisement[97] among them, at the last quoth he, "Meseemeth the gentleman with the black beard should be even he." And with that he arose out of his chair and offered the same to the gentleman in the black beard, with his cap in his hand. The person to whom he offered the chair was Sir Edward Neville, a comely knight, that much

93 mumchance a dicing game **94 require** request **95 show** inform
96 rounding whispering to **97 good advisement** careful scrutiny

more resembled the King's person in that masque than any other.

The King, perceiving the Cardinal so deceived, could not forbear laughing, but pulled down his visor and Master Neville's also and dashed out such a pleasant countenance and cheer that all the noble estates there assembled, perceiving the King to be there among them, rejoiced very much. The Cardinal eftsoons[98] desired His Highness to take the place of estate. To whom the King answered that he would go first and shift his apparel, and so departed into my Lord Cardinal's chamber and there new appareled him; in which time the dishes of the banquet were clean taken up and the tables spread again with new, clean, perfumed cloths, every man and woman sitting still until the King with all his maskers came among them again all new appareled.

Then the King took his seat under the cloth of estate, commanding every person to sit still as they did before. In came a new banquet before the King and to all the rest throughout all the tables, wherein were served two hundred divers dishes of costly devices and subtleties. Thus passed they forth the night with banqueting, dancing, and other triumphs, to the great comfort of the King and pleasant regard of the nobility there assembled. . . .

This Cardinal, as you may perceive in this story,[99] was of a great stomach,[100] for he counted himself equal with princes and by crafty suggestion gat into his hands innumerable treasure. He forced little on simony,[101] and was not pitiful, and stood affectionate[102] in his own opinion. In open presence he would lie and say untruth and was double both in speech and meaning; he would promise much and perform little. He was vicious of his body and gave the clergy evil example.

[In 1532 King Henry creates Anne Boleyn Marchioness of Pembroke. He marries her secretly on November 14. Order is given that Katharine is to be called Princess Dowager rather than Queen.]

98 eftsoons very soon afterward **99 story** history **100 stomach** haughtiness **101 forced little on simony** had few scruples about the selling of church offices **102 affectionate** obstinate

After that the King perceived his new wife to be with child, he caused all officers necessary to be appointed to her, and so on Easter Even she went to her closet openly as Queen; and then the King appointed the day of her coronation to be kept on Whitsunday[103] next following. And writings were sent to all sheriffs to certify the names of men of forty pounds to receive the order of knighthood or else to make fine. The assessment of the fine was appointed to Thomas Cromwell, Master of the King's Jewel House and councillor to the King, a man newly received into high favor. He so used the matter that a great sum of money was raised to the King's use by those fines. The matter of the Queen's appeal, whereunto she still sticked and by no means could be removed from it, was communed of[104] both in the Parliament House and also in the Convocation House, where it was so handled that many were of opinion that not only her appeal but also all other appeals made to Rome were void and of none effect; for that in ancient councils it had been determined that a cause rising in one province should be determined in the same.

This matter was opened with all the circumstances[105] to the Lady Katharine Dowager (for so was she then called), the which persisted still in her former opinion and would revoke by no means her appeal to the court of Rome. Whereupon the Archbishop of Canterbury, accompanied with the Bishops of London, Winchester, Bath, Lincoln, and divers other learned men in great number, rode to Dunstable, which is six miles from Ampthill, where the Princess Dowager lay. And there by one Doctor Lee she was cited to appear before the said Archbishop in cause of matrimony in the said town of Dunstable; and at the day of appearance, she appeared not but made default, and so she was called peremptory[106] every day fifteen days together; and at the last, for lack of appearance, by the assent of all the learned men there present she was divorced from the King and the marriage declared to be void and of none effect.

[Anne's coronation in May 1533 is an occasion of ceremonial splendor.]

103 Whitsunday the seventh Sunday after Easter **104 communed of** discussed **105 opened with all the circumstances** laid out in full detail **106 peremptory** by decree

First went gentlemen, then esquires, then knights, then the aldermen of the city in their cloaks of scarlet; after them the judges in their mantles of scarlet and coifs.[107] Then followed the Knights of the Bath, being no lords, every man having a white lace on his left sleeve; then followed barons and viscounts in their parliament robes of scarlet. After them came earls, marquesses, and dukes, in their robes of estate of crimson velvet furred with ermine, powdered according to their degrees. After them came the Lord Chancellor in a robe of scarlet open before, bordered with lettice.[108] After him came the King's chapel and the monks solemnly singing with procession; then came abbots and bishops mitered, then sergeants- and officers-of-arms; then after them went the Mayor of London with his mace, and Garter[109] in his coat of arms. Then went the Marquess Dorset in a robe of estate, which bare[110] the scepter of gold, and the Earl of Arundel, which bare the rod of ivory with the dove, both together.

Then went alone the Earl of Oxford, High Chamberlain of England, which bare the crown; after him went the Duke of Suffolk in his robe of estate also, for that day being High Steward of England, having a long white rod in his hand; and the Lord William Howard, with the rod of the marshalship; and every Knight of the Garter had on his collar of the order. Then proceeded forth the Queen in a surcoat and robe of purple velvet furred with ermine, in her hair, coif, and circlet[111] as she had the Saturday; and over her was borne the canopy by four of the Five Ports,[112] all crimson with points[113] of blue and red hanging on their sleeves; and the Bishops of London and Winchester bare up the laps[114] of the Queen's robe. The Queen's train, which was very long, was borne by the old Duchess of Norfolk; after her followed ladies, being lords' wives, which had surcoats of scarlet. . . .

When she was thus brought to the high place made in the midst of the church, between the choir and the high altar,

107 coifs close-fitting caps **108 lettice** whitish gray fur **109 Garter** Garter King at Arms, a chief herald **110 which bare** who bore **111 in her hair, coif, and circlet** with her hair unbound, in a close-fitting cap and metal headband **112 the Five Ports** the barons of the Five Cinque Ports on the English southern coast; see *Henry VIII*, 4.1.36 s.d.
113 points laces for fastening clothing **114 laps** folds or flaps

she was set in a rich chair. And after that she had rested awhile she descended down to the high altar and there prostrate[115] herself while the Archbishop of Canterbury said certain collects.[116] Then she rose, and the Bishop anointed her on the head and on the breast; and then she was led up again where, after divers orisons said, the Archbishop set the crown of Saint Edward on her head and then delivered her the scepter of gold in her right hand and the rod of ivory with the dove in the left hand; and then all the choir sung *Te Deum,*[117] etc. Which done, the Bishop took off the crown of Saint Edward, being heavy, and set on the crown made for her. Then went she to Saint Edward's shrine and there offered, after which offering done she withdrew her into a little place made for the nonce on the one side of the choir.

Now in the mean season, every duchess had put on their bonnets a coronal of gold wrought with flowers, and every marquess put on a demicoronal of gold, every countess a plain circlet of gold without flowers, and every King of Arms put on a crown of copper and gilt, all which were worn till night. When the Queen had a little reposed her, the company returned in the same order that they set forth, and the Queen went crowned, and so did the ladies aforesaid. . . . Now when she was out of the sanctuary and appeared within the palace, the trumpets played marvelous freshly. Then she was brought to Westminster Hall and so to her withdrawing chamber.

[Anne gives birth to a child some four months later, 1533.]

The seventh of September, being Sunday, between three and four of the clock in the afternoon, the Queen was delivered of a fair young lady. On which day the Duke of Norfolk came home to the christening, which was appointed on the Wednesday next following and was accordingly accomplished on the same day with all such solemn ceremonies as were thought convenient. The godfather at the font was the Lord Archbishop of Canterbury, the godmothers the old Duchess of Norfolk and the old Marchioness Dorset,

115 prostrate prostrated **116 collects** short prayers **117 Te Deum** We praise you O God. (A hymn of thanksgiving.)

widow; and at the confirmation[118] the Lady Marchioness of Exeter was godmother. The child was named Elizabeth.

[The christening is an elaborate ceremonial occasion.]

When the ceremonies and christening were ended, Garter Chief King of Arms cried aloud, "God of his infinite goodness send prosperous life and long to the high and mighty Princess of England, Elizabeth!" and then the trumpets blew. Then the Archbishop of Canterbury gave to the Princess a standing cup of gold, the Duchess of Norfolk gave to her a standing cup of gold fretted with pearl, the Marchioness of Dorset gave three gilt bowls, pounced,[119] with a cover, and the Marchioness of Exeter gave three standing bowls, graven, all gilt, with a cover. Then was brought in wafers, comfits, and hippocras[120] in such plenty that every man had as much as he would desire. Then they set forwards, the trumpets going before in the same order, towards the King's palace.

[Katharine, as Princess Dowager, lives in isolation until early 1536.]

The Princess Dowager, lying at Kimbolton, fell into her last sickness, whereof the King, being advertised, appointed the Emperor's ambassador that was ledger[121] here with him, named Eustachius Capucius, to go to visit her and to do his commendations to her and will her to be of good comfort. The ambassador with all diligence did his duty therein, comforting her the best he might; but she, within six days after, perceiving herself to wax very weak and feeble and to feel death approaching at hand, caused one of her gentlewomen to write a letter to the King commending to him her daughter and his, beseeching him to stand good father unto her, and further desired him to have some consideration of her gentlewomen that had served her

118 the confirmation a rite administered to baptized persons to confirm or strengthen the practice of the Christian faith; in more recent days, normally done after the child has been able to learn and study the articles of faith **119 pounced** embossed **120 hippocras** a spicy wine drink **121 ledger** resident

and to see them bestowed in marriage. Further, that it would please him to appoint that her servants might have their due wages and a year's wages besides. This in effect was all that she requested; and so, immediately hereupon, she departed this life the eighth of January at Kimbolton aforesaid and was buried at Peterborough. The nine-and-twentieth of January, Queen Anne was delivered of a child before her time, which was born dead.

The second edition of Raphael Holinshed's *Chronicles* was published in 1587. This selection is based on that edition, Volume 3, folios 796 and 850–939. Some proper names have been regularized: Ardres (Ard), Guînes (Guisnes), etc.

Acts and Monuments of Martyrs (1583 edition)
By John Foxe

[Foxe describes the machinations of certain Catholic members of the King's Privy Council, especially Stephen Gardiner, the Bishop of Winchester, to bring down the Protestant reforming Archbishop of Canterbury, Thomas Cranmer.]

It came into a common proverb: Do unto my lord of Canterbury displeasure or a shrewd turn, and then you may be sure to have him your friend whiles he liveth. . . .

Notwithstanding, not long after that, certain of the Council, whose names need not to be repeated, by the enticement and provocation of his ancient enemy the Bishop of Winchester and other of the same sect, attempted[1] the King against him, declaring plainly that the realm was so infected with heresies and heretics that it was dangerous to His Highness farther to permit it unreformed,[2] lest peradventure by long suffering[3] such contention should arise and ensue in the realm among his subjects that thereby might spring horrible commotions and uproars, like as in some

1 attempted tried to influence **2 permit it unreformed** permit it (Protestant heresy) to continue uncorrected **3 by long suffering** by being long tolerated

parts of Germany it did not long ago; the enormity whereof they could not impute to any so much as to the Archbishop of Canterbury, who, by his own preaching and his chaplains', had defiled the whole realm full of divers pernicious heresies. The King would needs know[4] his accusers. They answered that forasmuch as he was a councillor no man durst take upon him to accuse him, but if it would please His Highness to commit him to the Tower for a time there would be accusations and proofs enough against him. . . .

The King, perceiving their importunate suit against the Archbishop (but yet meaning not to have him wronged and utterly given over unto their hands), granted unto them that they should the next day commit him to the Tower for his trial. When night came, the King sent Sir Anthony Denny, about midnight, to Lambeth to the Archbishop, willing him forthwith to resort unto him at the court. The message done, the Archbishop speedily addressed himself[5] to the court, and coming into the gallery where the King walked and tarried for him, His Highness said: "Ah, my lord of Canterbury, I can tell you news. For divers weighty considerations, it is determined by me and the Council that you, tomorrow at nine of the clock, shall be committed to the Tower, for that you and your chaplains (as information is given us) have taught and preached and thereby sown within the realm such a number of execrable heresies that it is feared, the whole realm being infected with them, no small contention and commotions will rise thereby amongst my subjects, as of late days the like was in divers parts of Germany; and therefore the Council have requested me, for the trial of the matter, to suffer them to commit you to the Tower, or else no man dare come forth as witness in these matters, you being a councillor."

When the King had said his mind, the Archbishop kneeled down and said: "I am content, if it please Your Grace, with all my heart to go thither at Your Highness's commandment, and I most humbly thank Your Majesty that I may come to my trial, for there be that[6] have many ways slandered me, and now this way I hope to try[7] myself not worthy of such report."

4 would needs know wished to know the names of **5 addressed himself** betook himself **6 there be that** there are those who **7 try** prove

The King, perceiving the man's uprightness joined with such simplicity, said: "Oh, lord, what manner o' man be you? What simplicity is in you? I had thought that you would rather have sued to us[8] to have taken the pains to have heard you and your accusers together for your trial without any such indurance.[9] Do not you know what state you be in with the whole world and how many great enemies you have? Do you not consider what an easy thing it is to procure[10] three or four false knaves to witness against you? Think you to have better luck that way than your master Christ had? I see by it you will run headlong to your undoing if I would suffer you. Your enemies shall not so prevail against you, for I have otherwise devised with myself to keep you out of their hands. Yet notwithstanding, tomorrow when the Council shall sit and send for you, resort unto them, and if in charging you with this matter they do commit you to the Tower, require[11] of them, because you are one of them—a councillor—that you may have your accusers brought before them without any further indurance, and use for yourself as good persuasions that way as you may devise, and if no entreaty or reasonable request will serve, then deliver unto them this my ring" (which when the King delivered unto the Archbishop) "and say unto them, 'If there be no remedy, my lords, but that I must needs go to the Tower, then I revoke[12] my cause from you and appeal to the King's own person by this his token unto you all.' For," said the King then unto the Archbishop, "so soon as they shall see this my ring, they know it so well that they shall understand that I have resumed the whole cause into mine own hands and determination, and that I have discharged them thereof."

The Archbishop, perceiving the King's benignity so much to him wards,[13] had much ado to forbear tears. "Well," said the King, "go your ways, my lord, and do as I have bidden you." My lord, humbling himself with thanks, took his leave of the King's Highness for that night.

On the morrow, about nine of the clock before noon, the Council sent a gentleman usher for the Archbishop, who,

8 us i.e., me. (The royal plural.) **9 indurance** imprisonment **10 to procure** i.e., for your enemies to procure **11 require** request **12 revoke** call back, withdraw **13 to him wards** toward him

when he came to the Council chamber door, could not be let in, but of purpose (as it seemed) was compelled there to wait among the pages, lackeys, and servingmen all alone. Dr. Butts, the King's physician, resorting that way and espying how my lord of Canterbury was handled, went to the King's Highness and said: "My lord of Canterbury, if it please Your Grace, is well promoted; for now he is become a lackey or a servingman, for yonder he standeth this half hour at the Council chamber door amongst them." "It is not so," quoth the King, "I trow, nor the Council hath not so little discretion as to use the metropolitan[14] of the realm in that sort, specially being one of their own number. But let them alone," said the King, "and we shall hear more soon."

Anon the Archbishop was called into the Council chamber, to whom was alleged as before is rehearsed. The Archbishop answered in like sort as the King had advised him; and in the end, when he perceived that no manner of persuasion or entreaty could serve, he delivered them the King's ring, revoking his cause into the King's hands. The whole Council being thereat somewhat amazed, the Earl of Bedford with a loud voice, confirming his words with a solemn oath, said: "When you first began the matter, my lords, I told you what would come of it. Do you think that the King will suffer this man's finger to ache? Much more, I warrant you, will he defend his life against brabbling varlets.[15] You do but cumber[16] yourselves to hear tales and fables against him." And so, incontinently[17] upon the receipt of the King's token, they all rose and carried to the King his ring, surrendering that matter, as the order and use[18] was, into his own hands.

When they were all come to the King's presence, His Highness, with a severe countenance, said unto them: "Ah, my lords, I thought I had had wiser men of my Council than now I find you. What discretion was this in you thus to make the primate[19] of the realm, and one of you in office, to wait at the Council chamber door amongst servingmen? You might have considered that he was a councillor as well as you, and you had no such commission of me so to handle

14 metropolitan archbishop **15 brabbling varlets** quibbling, quarrelsome rascals **16 cumber** trouble, undo, confound **17 incontinently** immediately **18 use** custom, practice **19 primate** archbishop

him. I was content that you should try him as a councillor and not as a mean[20] subject. But now I well perceive that things be done against him maliciously, and if some of you might have had your minds,[21] you would have tried him to the uttermost. But I do you all to wit,[22] and protest that if a prince may be beholding unto his subject" (and so, solemnly laying his hand upon his breast, said), "by the faith I owe to God, I take this man here, my lord of Canterbury, to be of all other a most faithful subject unto us and one to whom we are much beholding, giving him great commendations otherwise." And with that, one or two of the chiefest of the Council, making their excuse, declared that, in requesting his indurance, it was rather meant for his trial and his purgation against the common fame[23] and slander of the world than for any malice conceived against him. "Well, well, my lords," quoth the King, "take him and well use him, as he is worthy to be, and make no more ado." And with that every man caught him by the hand and made fair weather of altogethers,[24] which might easily be done with that man.

Text based on *The Second Volume of the Ecclesiastical History, Containing the Acts and Monuments of Martyrs . . . newly recognized and enlarged by the author, John Foxe, 1583. . . . Printed by John Day,* pp. 1863, 1866–1867. The first edition of this work appeared in 1563.

20 mean of ordinary rank **21 minds** intents **22 do you all to wit** wish you all to know **23 fame** rumor, reputation **24 of altogethers** altogether

Further Reading

Anderson, Judith H. "Shakespeare's *Henry VIII:* The Changing Relation of Truth to Fiction." *Biographical Truth: The Representation of Historical Persons in Tudor–Stuart Writing.* New Haven, Conn.: Yale Univ. Press, 1984. Anderson examines *Henry VIII*'s treatment of its historical source material, as it exposes and explores the provocative ironies of the play's apparent subtitle, *All Is True.* Anderson claims "divorce" is not merely a central historical event in the play but a crucial metaphor for the disjunctions that exist throughout the play between private and public lives as well as between objective and subjective understandings of the truth.

Baillie, William M. "*Henry VIII:* A Jacobean History." *Shakespeare Studies* 12 (1979): 247–266. Baillie argues that in dramatizing the reign of Henry VIII Shakespeare holds a mirror up to political concerns of the time. The play's presentation of Henry's reign is designed to comment on the central political issues of James's court in 1613: concerns about state divorce, the role of a court favorite, and the limits of royal power.

Berry, Edward I. "*Henry VIII* and the Dynamics of Spectacle." *Shakespeare Studies* 12 (1979): 229–246. Berry examines the way Shakespeare blends the play's archaic tragic pattern of political falls with stylized and spectacular elements derived from the masque. The play thus reveals both a serious concern with the world of historical flux and a powerful impulse toward political idealization.

Bertram, Paul. "Henry VIII: The Conscience of the King." In *In Defense of Reading: A Reader's Approach to Literary Criticism,* ed. Reuben A. Brower and Richard Poirier. New York: E. P. Dutton, 1962. Bertram discovers the play's design in its presentation of Henry's progression from a king who merely reigns to one who effectively rules. The entire fifth act celebrates the new Henrician order and affirms a festive union of King and people that overshadows and transcends the private tragedies of Katharine and Wolsey.

Bliss, Lee. "The Wheel of Fortune and the Maiden Phoenix

of Shakespeare's *King Henry the Eighth.*" *ELH* 42 (1975): 1–25. Bliss emphasizes the disturbing political and moral realities revealed in the world of the play: Henry understands that power rather than truth or integrity succeeds and that justice is at best provisional and expedient. Cranmer's prophecy in Act 5, however, offers an alternative to the disillusioned political world of Henry's rule; it provides an ideal, hortatory portrait of what England and its ruler should be.

Cespedes, Frank V. " 'We are one in fortunes': The Sense of History in *Henry VIII.*" *English Literary Renaissance* 10 (1980): 413–438. In Cespedes's view, *Henry VIII* is above all a history play, though one suffused with irony. The play exploits the tension between the fortunate progress toward Elizabeth's reign and the unfortunate fate of the individuals whose personal tragedies lead up to that event. Throughout, Shakespeare emphasizes the disparity between what his characters and what his Jacobean audience know about the outcome of sixteenth-century English history.

Cox, John D. "*Henry the Eighth* and the Masque." *ELH* 45 (1978): 390–409. Cox examines how Shakespeare in *Henry VIII* adapted the principles of the Jacobean court masque to the popular stage. While the masque typically celebrates Jacobean kingship, the play is able to exploit and modify this adulation, exploring the ambiguities of divine right as it combines masque elements with older, popular theatrical traditions.

Felperin, Howard. "Tragical-Comical-Historical-Pastoral: *Cymbeline* and *Henry VIII.*" *Shakespearean Romance.* Princeton, N.J.: Princeton Univ. Press, 1972. *Henry VIII,* Felperin argues, enacts a pattern of secular fall and spiritual regeneration that differentiates the play from the earlier histories and relates it to the idealizing concerns of the late romances. Felperin feels that the insistent redemptive design never succeeds in firmly grounding the romance vision in history; rather it abandons history—not perfecting but distorting the world of fact in its myth of the Tudor golden age.

Foakes, R. A. "Epilogue: A Note on *King Henry VIII.*" *Shakespeare, The Dark Comedies to the Last Plays: From Satire to Celebration*. Charlottesville, Va.: The Univ. Press of Virginia, 1971. Foakes finds that in *Henry VIII* the instruments of rule are flawed and incapable of insuring justice, but that human history is redeemed by the operation of a benign providence. Henry's emergence as a capable ruler is part of a providential action in which suffering and injustice are transcended as the truth of heaven's grace is finally revealed.

Harris, Bernard. "'What's Past is Prologue': *Cymbeline* and *Henry VIII*." In *Later Shakespeare,* ed. John Russell Brown and Bernard Harris. New York: St. Martin's Press, 1967. Harris focuses on the play's final prophecy, a vision of England's past history and future security, in which Shakespeare addresses the political situation facing James I, especially the religious and economic confrontation with England's Catholic foes.

Johnson, Samuel. *Johnson on Shakespeare,* ed. Arthur Sherbo. *The Yale Edition of the Works of Samuel Johnson,* vol. 8. New Haven, Conn.: Yale Univ. Press, 1968. Johnson considers *Henry VIII* among the least successful of Shakespeare's histories; nonetheless, he admires "the splendour of its pageantry," which largely accounted for its popularity on the eighteenth-century stage, and the pathos of Katharine's fall, tenderly depicted in "some scenes which may be justly numbered among the greatest efforts of tragedy."

Kermode, Frank. "What Is Shakespeare's *Henry VIII* About?" *Durham University Journal* 40, n.s. 9 (1948): 48–55. Rpt. in *Shakespeare, the Histories: A Collection of Critical Essays,* ed. Eugene M. Waith. Englewood Cliffs, N.J.: Prentice-Hall, 1965; and in *Shakespeare's Histories: An Anthology of Modern Criticism,* ed. William A. Armstrong. Baltimore, Md.: Penguin, 1972. With Henry, as God's deputy, standing at the center of the play, Kermode sees *Henry VIII* as an anthology of literary tragedies organized around a providential theme. The falls of "Good Queen, Ambitious Prelate, Virtuous Prelate, or merely Great Man" not only exhibit individual variations on the familiar moralistic pattern of the inevitable decline from greatness but also participate together in a larger providential design that moves toward the establishment of a reformed church and Elizabeth's great reign.

Knight, G. Wilson. "*Henry VIII* and the Poetry of Conversion." *The Crown of Life: Essays in Interpretation of Shakespeare's Final Plays.* London: Oxford Univ. Press, 1947. *Henry VIII,* Knight argues, powerfully binds Shakespeare's entire dramatic achievement into a whole. In a wide-ranging essay, Knight explores the play's synthesis of the tragic, historical, and theological strands of Shakespeare's earlier plays, a synthesis that is realized in the humility and charity achieved by the fallen characters and in the play's emphasis on ceremony and ritual. In Cranmer's prophecy, the play moves beyond mere political affirmation to its transcendent vision of power and peace.

Leech, Clifford. "The Structure of the Last Plays." *Shakespeare Survey* 11 (1958): 19–30. The structures of Shakespeare's last plays, for Leech, resist any decisive closure (and deny the claims of transcendence that have been made for the romances), enacting instead cyclical patterns of flux and repetition. This is most strongly realized in *Henry VIII,* where the repeated falls from high position and the foreshadowing of future events by the action of the play declare the cyclical process of history and the inherent instability of any new order.

Leggatt, Alexander. "*Henry VIII* and the Ideal England." *Shakespeare Survey* 38 (1985): 131–143. In extending its idealizing prophecy from Elizabeth to James, Cranmer's speech, Leggatt argues, encourages an audience to set the "ideal vision against our sense of the world as it really is." For Leggatt, this double perspective enacts the historical vision of the play itself. *Henry VIII* acknowledges the tensions and contradictions of history as well as the powerful impulse to purify these, revealing the "close relationship between what we dream of and what we are."

Richmond, H. M. "Shakespeare's *Henry VIII:* Romance Redeemed by History." *Shakespeare Studies* 4 (1968): 334–349. Richmond regards *Henry VIII* as a play in which the values of the romances are tested and vindicated by history. In locating the redemptive pattern of these values in an overtly historical world, Shakespeare articulates the substantiality of the romance vision, asserting its ability to operate not merely in the exotic worlds of the other late plays but in a world of ordinary causality and circumstantial fact.

Saccio, Peter. "Henry VIII: The Supreme Head." *Shakespeare's English Kings: History, Chronicle, and Drama*. New York: Oxford Univ. Press, 1977. Saccio distinguishes between *Henry VIII* and Henry VIII—between Shakespeare's romance and historical reality. He reviews the events of Henry's reign and examines how Shakespeare reorders and reshapes the historical material into drama.

A portrait of Shakespeare from the First Folio.

THE COMPLETE POEMS AND SONNETS

THE COMPLETE POEMS AND SONNETS

The Poems

Most of Shakespeare's nondramatic poems were written early in his career. As a young man in London in the early 1590s, he did what any aspiring writer naturally would do: turned to the writing of amatory poetry, sonnets, and edifying verse narratives in the prevailing genres of the time. Here was the pathway to literary recognition and, one might hope, to the patronage of some influential and generous member of the aristocracy. Shakespeare soon found employment as an actor and writer of plays and no doubt took comfort in his success in the theatrical world; but writing plays then was somewhat like writing movie or television scripts today, often remunerative but usually anonymous. Play scripts were regarded as subliterary; when, some years later, Ben Jonson had the temerity to publish his plays as *operae,* or works, his critics were unsparing in their ridicule of one who confused "works" with "plays." Sonnets and Ovidian amatory verse, on the other hand, were generally recognized as "serious" literary forms.

Cultivated young gentlemen at the Inns of Court, purportedly studying law there but often spending a good deal of their time in literary pursuits, contributed plentifully to the vogue in sonnets, satires, love lyrics, and the like. (John Donne was such a student at the Inns of Court in the late 1590s.) Other aspiring or already recognized writers, including Sir Philip Sidney, Edmund Spenser, Christopher Marlowe, Michael Drayton, Samuel Daniel, Thomas Lodge, and, later in the 1590s, John Marston, Sir John Davies, George Chapman, and Ben Jonson, some of whom were also playwrights, made their mark by writing nondramatic poetry. The classical model provided by such poets as Ovid, Virgil, and Horace added to the sense of propriety in beginning a literary career with the writing of certain kinds of poems such as the eclogue.

Perhaps some enforced leisure in his acting and playwriting career, unwelcomely provided by severe outbreaks of the plague during warmer months in the early 1590s, gave Shakespeare added opportunity and incentive to turn to the writing of nondramatic verse. At any rate, he wrote *Venus and Adonis,* an amatory and even decorously erotic poem in the vein of Ovid, for publication in 1593, carefully seeing it through the press of his Stratford acquaintance Richard Field and assiduously dedicating it to Henry Wriothesley, the young Earl of Southampton. *The Rape of Lucrece* followed in 1594, also from Field's press and also dedicated to Southampton, the dedication on this occasion expressing an increasing sense of confidence and fondness between poet and patron. Whether Southampton substantially assisted Shakespeare in his career we do not know, but that Shakespeare had hopes from this sponsorship seems clear from his way of addressing his aristocratic friend.

Are the sonnets also addressed to Southampton? Although the identity of the friend addressed in Shakespeare's sonnets cannot be assigned with certainty, Southampton is inevitably a likely candidate—young, influential in literary circles, handsome, unmarried until 1598, belonging to a family that no doubt wished to see him settle down with the right wife and beget heirs. It may, however, be mere coincidence that his initials, H. W. (Henry Wriothesley), are the reverse of the mysterious "Mr. W. H." named in the dedication as "the only begetter" of these sonnets. Perhaps the situation described in the sonnets is not autobiographical. At any rate, many if not most of the sonnets must have been written fairly early in Shakespeare's career, when the sonnet form was in vogue. They were not published until 1609, and even then seemingly without Shakespeare's authorization or cooperation, but they were evidently circulated in manuscript among knowledgeable readers, and in fact two of them (138 and 144) made their way into print in 1599, seemingly without Shakespeare's authorization, in a volume published by William Jaggard called *The Passionate Pilgrim*. The sonnets are so extraordinarily fine that we can only wonder at Shakespeare's reluctance or indifference toward publishing, but he may have felt that they were personal, or that the sonnet vogue was past by the time he had written most of them, or that it was the gentlemanly thing to be offhand about publication. (Many of Donne's songs and sonnets were privately circulated in much the same manner some time before they were put into print.) We cannot be sure that the order of the sonnets reflects Shakespeare's final intentions in the matter, since he did not see them through the press, but the overall impression is remarkably cohesive and belies most scholarly efforts to rearrange or disintegrate them.

"The Phoenix and Turtle" and "A Lover's Complaint," published in 1601 and 1609 respectively as parts of volumes largely devoted to other materials and printed seemingly without Shakespeare's cooperation, are probably also early in date of composition, though nothing is known about the circumstances that might have produced them, and the assertion of Shakespeare's authorship is still uncertain though very likely in both cases.

Other nondramatic poems sometimes included in complete collections of Shakespeare's poetry are less certainly vouched for and have been omitted here as of too tenuous a connection to merit inclusion. William Jaggard's *The Passionate Pilgrim,* 1598, mentioned above because it printed two sonnets (138 and 144) some nine years before the sonnets were published as a group, also pirated three lyric passages from Act 4 of *Love's Labor's Lost,* published in that same year (1598). Except for minor textual variants, these texts simply reproduce material available elsewhere in the Shakespeare canon. Plainly Jaggard was capitalizing on Shakespeare's growing reputation by attributing *The Passionate Pilgrim* entirely to him, and doing so most irresponsibly, for a number of poems in the slim volume are manifestly not by Shakespeare at all. Poem 11 of the twenty or twenty-one poems in the volume (number 14 appears as one poem in the original text but is sometimes divided by modern editors) is a sonnet from Bartholomew Griffin's *Fidessa More Chaste Than Kind* (1596), and 4, 6, and 9 are so closely related to it in subject and style that they seem part of a sequence. The obvious resemblance in all four to Shakespeare's *Venus and Adonis* is probably a tribute to that poem's popularity rather than an indication of Shakespeare's authorship of these sonnets. Poems 8 and 20 first appeared in *Poems in Divers Humors,* 1598, by Richard Barnfield. The second of these was reprinted in another popular anthology, *England's Helicon* (1600), in which poem 17 of *The Passionate Pilgrim* also appears and is attributed to the author of poem 20, that is, to Barnfield. (Poem 17 was first published in Thomas Weelkes's *Madrigals,* 1597.) *England's Helicon* also printed a version of poem 19, attributing this famous lyric ("Live with me and be my love") to "Chr. Marlowe," although its Reply (signed "Ignoto") was later said to be by Sir Walter Ralegh. In any case, poem 19 is certainly not by Shakespeare.

These attributions to other poets, most of them fairly reliable, leave only 7, 10, 11, 12, 13, 15, and 18 as possible new works in *The Passionate Pilgrim* to be assigned to Shakespeare's hand. Because of that volume's unreliability, and because most of these otherwise unattributed verses are mediocre, no good reason exists to credit any of them to Shakespeare. If one poem is to be singled out for praise, the usual choice is 12:

> Crabbed age and youth cannot live together.
> Youth is full of pleasance, age is full of care;
> Youth like summer morn, age like winter weather;
> Youth like summer brave, age like winter bare.
> Youth is full of sport, age's breath is short;
>   Youth is nimble, age is lame;
> Youth is hot and bold, age is weak and cold;
>   Youth is wild, and age is tame.
> Age, I do abhor thee; youth, I do adore thee.
>   O, my love, my love is young!
> Age, I do defy thee. O, sweet shepherd, hie thee,
>   For methinks thou stays too long.

Even here we find no unequivocal sign of Shakespeare's genius.

The reliability of attribution to Shakespeare is no stronger in the case of the song, "Shall I die? Shall I fly," transcribed in a manuscript collection of miscellaneous poems probably from the late 1630s and attributed there to Shakespeare by the transcriber. The poem has been noticed before by researchers in its Bodleian Library manuscript but has been passed over in silence as an indifferent piece of work attributed to Shakespeare without authority; another manuscript in the Beinecke Library, Yale University, contains a transcription of the same poem without attribution. Manuscript anthologies, prepared for personal use by literary amateurs fond of assembling their own collection of favorite pieces, were common during the period, and the attributions in them are, for understandable reasons, not infrequently quite wrong. The general accuracy of this particular Bodleian collection is in dispute, and certainly its attributions are not above suspicion. The literary merit of "Shall I die? Shall I fly" is perhaps a matter of opinion, though current interest in it surely derives chiefly from the news media's fascination with the story of a supposed discovery of a new poem by Shakespeare (though in fact the poem had been taken cognizance of by earlier scholars) rather than from anything in the poem itself.

Because it is the kind of poem that virtually any poet of the period could have achieved, and because the attribution is so slenderly based on any reliable authority, it has been omitted here as the poems in *The Passionate Pilgrim* have been. If an editor of a "complete" Shakespeare were to include all writings attributed to Shakespeare during the Renaissance, he or she would have to consider the imposing list of so-called apocryphal plays to which his name was visibly attached, including seven plays actually included in the second printing of the Third Folio of 1664 (*The London Prodigal, The History of Thomas Lord Cromwell,* etc.) along with at least eight others. It is a tribute to Shakespeare's fame that so many works were attributed to him, including some plays now lost. At any rate, a collection of Shakespeare's poems can perhaps better indicate the range of his accomplishment in nondramatic verse if it avoids the distractions of works that are distinctly inferior and have been attributed to him only on the slenderest of authorities.

VENUS
—AND—
ADONIS

Introduction

Like most of his contemporaries, Shakespeare apparently did not regard the writing of plays as an elegant literary pursuit. He must have known that he was good at it, and he certainly became famous in his day as a playwright, but he took no pains over the publication of his plays. We have no literary prefaces for them, no indication that Shakespeare saw them through the press. Writing for the theater was rather like writing for the movies today, a profitable and even glamorous venture but subliterary. When Ben Jonson brought out his collected *Works* (mostly plays) during his lifetime, he was jeered at for pretension.

The writing of sonnets and other "serious" poetry, on the other hand, was conventionally a bid for true literary fame. Shakespeare's prefatory epistle to his *Venus and Adonis* betrays an eagerness for recognition. Deferentially he seeks the sponsorship of the Earl of Southampton, in hopes of literary prestige as well as financial support. He speaks of *Venus and Adonis* as "the first heir of my invention," as though he had written no plays earlier, and promises Southampton a "graver labor" to appear shortly. *Venus and Adonis* in 1593 and *The Rape of Lucrece* in 1594 were in fact Shakespeare's first publications. Both were carefully and correctly printed. They were probably composed between June of 1592 and May of 1594, a period when the theaters were closed because of the plague. Shakespeare's belief in their importance to his literary career is confirmed by the reports of his contemporaries. Richard Barnfield singled them out as the works most likely to assure a place for Shakespeare in "fame's immortal book." Francis Meres, in his *Palladis Tamia: Wit's Treasury,* exclaimed in 1598 that "the sweet witty soul of Ovid lives in mellifluous and honey-tongued Shakespeare: witness his *Venus and Adonis,* his *Lucrece,* his sugared sonnets among his private friends, etc." Gabriel Harvey, although preferring *Lucrece* and *Hamlet* as more pleasing to "the wiser sort," conceded that "the younger sort takes much delight in Shakespeare's *Venus and Adonis.*" John Weever and still others add further testimonials to the extraordinary reputation of Shakespeare's nondramatic poems.

As Gabriel Harvey's puritanical comment on *Venus and Adonis* suggests, this poem was regarded as amatory and even risqué. It mirrored a current vogue for Ovidian erotic poetry, as exemplified by Thomas Lodge's *Scilla's Metamorphosis,* 1589 (in which an amorous nymph courts a reluctant young man), and by Christopher Marlowe's *Hero and Leander*. This latter poem, left unfinished at Marlowe's death in 1593 and published in 1598 with a continuation by George Chapman, was evidently circulated in manuscript as were so many poems of this sophisticated sort, including Shakespeare's sonnets. Shakespeare may well have been influenced by Marlowe's tone of wryly comic detachment and sensuous grace. He may also have read Michael Drayton's *Endymion and Phoebe* (published in 1595 but written earlier), in which the erotic tradition is somewhat idealized into moral allegory. Most important, however, Shakespeare knew his Ovid, both firsthand and in Golding's English translation (1567). He appears to have combined three mythical tales from the *Metamorphoses*. The narrative outline is to be found in Venus' pursuit of Adonis (Book 10), but the bashful reluctance of the young man is more reminiscent of Hermaphroditus (Book 4) and Narcissus (Book 3). Hermaphroditus pleads youth as his reason for wishing to escape the clutches of the water nymph Salmacis, and so is transformed with her into a single body containing both sexes; Narcissus evades the nymph Echo out of self-infatuation. Shakespeare has thus drawn a composite portrait of male coyness, a subject he was to explore further in the sonnets. Such a theme was suited to a nobleman of Southampton's youth and prospects. In tone it was also well suited to the aristocratic and intellectual set who read such poetry. Shakespeare here aimed at a more refined audience than that for which he wrote plays, though his theatrical audience was generally intelligent and well-to-do. The ornate qualities of *Venus and Adonis* should be judged in the fashionable context of a sophisticated audience.

The poem is, among other things, a tour de force of stylized poetic techniques. The story itself is relatively uneventful, and the characters are static. For two-thirds of the poem, very little happens other than a series of amorous claspings from which Adonis feebly attempts to extricate himself. Even his subsequent fight with the boar and his violent death are occasions for rhetorical pathos rather than for vivid narrative description. The story is essentially a frame. Similarly, we must not expect psychological insight or meaningful self-discovery. The conventions of amatory verse do not encourage a serious interest in character. Venus and Adonis are mouthpieces for contrasting attitudes toward love. They debate a favorite courtly topic in the style of John Lyly. Both appeal to conventional wisdom and speak in *sententiae,* or aphoristic pronouncements. Venus, for example, warning Adonis of the need for caution in pursuing the boar, opines that "Danger deviseth shifts; wit waits on fear" (l. 690). Adonis, pleading his unreadiness for love, cites commonplace analogies: "No fisher but the ungrown fry forbears. / The mellow plum doth fall, the green sticks fast" (ll. 526–527). In substance, their arguments are equally conventional. Venus urges a carpe diem philosophy of seizing the moment of pleasure. "Make use of time, let not advantage slip; / Beauty within itself should not be wasted" (ll. 129–130). She bolsters her claim with an appeal to the "law of nature," according to which all living things are obliged to reproduce themselves; only by begetting can man conquer time and death. Yet however close this position may be to a major theme of the sonnets, it does not go unchallenged. Adonis charges plausibly that Venus is only rationalizing her lust: "O strange excuse, / When reason is the bawd to lust's abuse!" (ll. 791–792). His plea for more time in which to mature and prove his manliness is commendable, however much we may smile at his inability to be aroused by Venus' blandishments. Thus, neither contestant wins the argument. Venus is proved right in her fear that Adonis will be killed by the boar he hunts, but Adonis' rejection of idle lust for manly activity affirms a conventional truth. The debate is in a sense an ingeniously elaborate literary exercise, yet it also allows for reflection on contrasting views of love as sensual and spiritual, absurd and magnificent, funny and serious.

The narrator's persona is central to the ambivalence in the debate. He too speaks in *sententiae,* and his aphorisms appear to sympathize with both contestants. At times, he affirms the irresistible force of love: "What though the rose have prickles, yet 'tis plucked" (l. 574). At other times he laughs at Venus for her vacillation of mood: "Thy weal and woe are both of them extremes. / Despair and hope makes thee ridiculous" (ll. 987–988). Like Ovid's usual persona, the speaker here is both intrigued and amused by love, compelled to heed its power and yet aware of the absurdities. The result is a characteristic Ovidian blend of irony and pathos. The irony is especially evident in the delightful comic touches that undermine the potential seriousness of the action: Venus like an Amazon pulling Adonis off his mount and tucking him under one arm, pouting and blushing; Adonis' horse chasing away after a mare in heat, leaving Adonis to fend for himself; Venus fainting at the thought of the boar and pulling Adonis right on top of her, "in the very lists of love, / Her champion mounted for the hot encounter" (ll. 595–596). These devices distance us from the action and create an atmosphere of elegant entertainment. Yet the poem is also suffused with the rich pathos of sensuous emotion. The sensuousness would cloy without the ironic humor, whereas the humor would seem frivolous without the pathos.

The poem hints at moral allegory, in the manner of Ovidian mythologizing. Venus represents herself as the goddess not only of erotic passion but of eternal love conquering time and death. Because Adonis perversely spurns this ideal, Venus concludes that human beauty must perish and that man's happiness must be subject to mischance. Yet this reading is only one part of the argument and is contradicted by an opposing suggestion that Adonis is the rational principle attempting unsuccessfully to govern man's lust (the boar and Adonis' unbridled horse). These contradictions, which derive from the structure of the poem as a debate, and also from Renaissance Neoplatonism, confirm our impression that the allegory is not the true "meaning" of the poem but is part of an ambiguous view of love as both exalted and earthly, a mystery that we will never comprehend in single terms. The allegory elevates the seriousness, adding poetic dignity to what might otherwise appear to be an unabashedly erotic poem. We should not minimize the sexual teasing or fail to acknowledge our own erotic pleasure in it. Venus' repeated encounters with Adonis take the form of ingeniously varied positions, ending in coital embrace although without consummation. Adonis' passive role invites the male reader to fantasize himself in Adonis' place, being seduced by the goddess of beauty. The famous passage comparing Venus' body to a deer park with "pleasant fountains," "sweet bottom grass," and "round rising hillocks" (ll. 229–240) is graphic through the use of double entendre without being pornographic. The poem is equally explicit in its "banquet" of the five senses (ll. 433–450). This is the "naughty" Ovid of the *Ars Amatoria*.

Shakespeare's poem is an embroidery of poetic flourishes, of "conceits" or ingeniously wrought similes, of artfully constructed digressions such as the narrative of Adonis' horse, and of color symbolism. Images usually are drawn from nature (eagles, birds caught in nets, wolves, berries) or connote burning, blazing, and shining (torches, jewels). The dominant colors are red and white, usually paired antithetically: the red of the rising sun or Adonis' blushing face or Mars' ensign, the white of an alabaster hand or fresh bed linen or "ashy-pale" anger. Ironically, too, the boar's frothy-white mouth is stained with red, and Adonis' red blood blemishes his "wonted lily white." Adonis' flower, the anemone, is reddish-purple and white. A similarly balanced antithesis pervades the play's rhetorical figures, as in the symmetrical repetition of words in grammatically parallel phrases *(parison)*, or in phrases of equal length *(isocolon)*, or in inverted order *(antimetabole)*, or at the beginning and ending of a line *(epanalepsis)*, and so on. These pyrotechnics may at first seem mechanical, but they too have a place in a work of art that celebrates both the erotic and the spiritual in love. Decoration has its function and is not mere embellishment for its own sake.

Venus and Adonis

"Vilia miretur vulgus; mihi flavus Apollo Pocula Castalia plena ministret aqua."

To the RIGHT HONORABLE HENRY WRIOTHESLEY, *Earl of Southampton, and Baron of Titchfield.*

RIGHT HONORABLE,

I know not how I shall offend in dedicating my unpolished lines to your lordship, nor how the world will censure me for choosing so strong a prop to support so weak a burden; only if your honor seem but pleased, I account myself highly praised, and vow to take advantage of all idle hours, till I have honored you with some graver labor. But if the first heir of my invention prove 8 deformed, I shall be sorry it had so noble a godfather, and never after ear so barren a land, for 10 fear it yield me still so bad a harvest. I leave it to your honorable survey, and your honor to your heart's content, which I wish may always answer your own wish and the world's hopeful expectation.

Your honor's in all duty,

William Shakespeare.

Motto: Vilia miretur, etc. Let the base vulgar admire trash; may golden-haired Apollo serve me goblets filled from the Castalian spring. (Ovid, *Amores,* 1.15.35–36).
Dedication: Henry Wriothesley, Earl of Southampton (A popular and brilliant young gentleman of nineteen years, already prominent at court. Subsequent dedications by Shakespeare and others indicate that he was a genuinely devoted patron of literature throughout his life.)
8 the first . . . invention (This phrase has been variously interpreted to mean Shakespeare's first written work, his first printed work, his first "invented" work in the sense that the plots of his plays were usually not original with him, his first work independent of collaborators, or his first "literary" work, since plays were unliterary in the Elizabethan sense. The second and last are the most probable.) **10 ear** plow, cultivate

Even as the sun with purple-colored face
Had ta'en his last leave of the weeping morn, 2
Rose-cheeked Adonis hied him to the chase. 3
Hunting he loved, but love he laughed to scorn.
  Sick-thoughted Venus makes amain unto him, 5
  And like a boldfaced suitor 'gins to woo him.

"Thrice-fairer than myself," thus she began,
"The field's chief flower, sweet above compare,
Stain to all nymphs, more lovely than a man, 9
More white and red than doves or roses are:
  Nature that made thee, with herself at strife, 11
  Saith that the world hath ending with thy life. 12

"Vouchsafe, thou wonder, to alight thy steed, 13
And rein his proud head to the saddlebow. 14
If thou wilt deign this favor, for thy meed 15
A thousand honey secrets shalt thou know. 16
  Here come and sit, where never serpent hisses,
  And being set, I'll smother thee with kisses;

"And yet not cloy thy lips with loathed satiety,
But rather famish them amid their plenty,
Making them red and pale with fresh variety—
Ten kisses short as one, one long as twenty.
  A summer's day will seem an hour but short,
  Being wasted in such time-beguiling sport." 24

2 the weeping morn i.e., the goddess of the dawn, Aurora, weeping to be left by the sun god. (*Weeping* suggests the dew of morning.) **3 hied him** betook himself, hastened **5 Sick-thoughted** lovesick. **makes amain** hastens **9 Stain to** eclipsing (in beauty). **nymphs** i.e., young and beautiful women **11–12 Nature . . . life** i.e., nature strove to surpass herself in making her masterpiece, Adonis, and says that if you die the world will cease. (The story of Adonis' death, and of the anemone that springs from his blood, is a vegetation myth.) **13 Vouchsafe** deign. **alight** alight from **14 the saddlebow** the arch in or the pieces forming the front of the saddle **15 meed** reward **16 honey** i.e., sweet **24 wasted** spent

With this she seizeth on his sweating palm, 25
The precedent of pith and livelihood, 26
And, trembling in her passion, calls it balm,
Earth's sovereign salve, to do a goddess good. 28
  Being so enraged, desire doth lend her force 29
  Courageously to pluck him from his horse. 30

Over one arm the lusty courser's rein, 31
Under her other was the tender boy,
Who blushed and pouted in a dull disdain, 33
With leaden appetite, unapt to toy; 34
  She red and hot as coals of glowing fire,
  He red for shame, but frosty in desire.

The studded bridle on a ragged bough
Nimbly she fastens. O, how quick is love!
The steed is stallèd up, and even now 39
To tie the rider she begins to prove. 40
  Backward she pushed him, as she would be thrust,
  And governed him in strength, though not in lust.

So soon was she along as he was down, 43
Each leaning on their elbows and their hips.
Now doth she stroke his cheek, now doth he frown,
And 'gins to chide, but soon she stops his lips
  And kissing speaks, with lustful language broken, 47
  "If thou wilt chide, thy lips shall never open."

He burns with bashful shame; she with her tears
Doth quench the maiden burning of his cheeks.
Then with her windy sighs and golden hairs
To fan and blow them dry again she seeks.
  He saith she is immodest, blames her miss; 53
  What follows more, she murders with a kiss.

25 sweating i.e., indicative of youth; not dried with age **26 precedent** sign, promise. **pith and livelihood** sexual strength and vitality **28 sovereign** efficacious **29 enraged** ardent **30 Courageously** lustfully. **pluck** drag **31 lusty courser's** vigorous horse's **33 dull** moody, listless **34 unapt to toy** undisposed to dally amorously **39 stallèd** fastened, secured (as in a stall) **40 prove** try **43 along** lying at his side **47 broken** interrupted **53 miss** offense, misconduct

Even as an empty eagle, sharp by fast, 55
Tires with her beak on feathers, flesh, and bone, 56
Shaking her wings, devouring all in haste,
Till either gorge be stuffed or prey be gone, 58
  Even so she kissed his brow, his cheek, his chin,
  And where she ends she doth anew begin.

Forced to content, but never to obey, 61
Panting he lies and breatheth in her face.
She feedeth on the steam as on a prey,
And calls it heavenly moisture, air of grace,
  Wishing her cheeks were gardens full of flowers,
  So they were dewed with such distilling showers. 66

Look how a bird lies tangled in a net, 67
So fastened in her arms Adonis lies;
Pure shame and awed resistance made him fret, 69
Which bred more beauty in his angry eyes.
  Rain added to a river that is rank 71
  Perforce will force it overflow the bank.

Still she entreats, and prettily entreats,
For to a pretty ear she tunes her tale.
Still is he sullen, still he lours and frets,
Twixt crimson shame and anger ashy-pale.
  Being red, she loves him best; and being white, 77
  Her best is bettered with a more delight. 78

Look how he can, she cannot choose but love;
And by her fair immortal hand she swears
From his soft bosom never to remove, 81
Till he take truce with her contending tears, 82
  Which long have rained, making her cheeks all wet;
  And one sweet kiss shall pay this countless debt. 84

55 sharp by fast hungry as a result of fasting **56 Tires** tears, feeds ravenously. **on** at **58 gorge** stomach **61 content** acquiesce. **obey** i.e., answer her lust **66 So** provided that. **distilling** gently falling, in fine droplets **67 Look how** just as **69 awed** daunted, overborne **71 rank** full to overflowing **77 Being** i.e., he being **78 more** greater **81 remove** move, remove herself **82 take truce** come to terms **84 countless** beyond reckoning

Upon this promise did he raise his chin,
Like a divedapper peering through a wave, 86
Who, being looked on, ducks as quickly in.
So offers he to give what she did crave;
But when her lips were ready for his pay,
He winks and turns his lips another way. 90

Never did passenger in summer's heat 91
More thirst for drink than she for this good turn.
Her help she sees, but help she cannot get;
She bathes in water, yet her fire must burn. 94
"O, pity," 'gan she cry, "flint-hearted boy!
'Tis but a kiss I beg. Why art thou coy?

"I have been wooed, as I entreat thee now,
Even by the stern and direful god of war, 98
Whose sinewy neck in battle ne'er did bow,
Who conquers where he comes in every jar; 100
Yet hath he been my captive and my slave,
And begged for that which thou unasked shalt have.

"Over my altars hath he hung his lance,
His battered shield, his uncontrollèd crest, 104
And for my sake hath learned to sport and dance,
To toy, to wanton, dally, smile, and jest, 106
Scorning his churlish drum and ensign red,
Making my arms his field, his tent my bed. 108

"Thus he that overruled I overswayed,
Leading him prisoner in a red-rose chain.
Strong-tempered steel his stronger strength obeyed,
Yet was he servile to my coy disdain. 112
O, be not proud, nor brag not of thy might,
For mastering her that foiled the god of fight! 114

86 divedapper dabchick, a common English water bird **90 winks** shuts his eyes (and winces) **91 passenger** wayfarer **94 water** i.e., her tears. **fire** (of passion) **98 direful** inspiring dread **100 where** wherever. **jar** fight **104 uncontrollèd** unconquered, unbowed. **crest** i.e., of helmet **106 toy, wanton** dally, sport amorously **108 arms** (with a pun on "weapons") **112 coy** aloof, teasing **114 foiled** vanquished

"Touch but my lips with those fair lips of thine— 115
Though mine be not so fair, yet are they red—
The kiss shall be thine own as well as mine. 117
What seest thou in the ground? Hold up thy head.
  Look in mine eyeballs, there thy beauty lies; 119
  Then why not lips on lips, since eyes in eyes?

"Art thou ashamed to kiss? Then wink again, 121
And I will wink; so shall the day seem night.
Love keeps his revels where there are but twain;
Be bold to play, our sport is not in sight. 124
  These blue-veined violets whereon we lean
  Never can blab, nor know not what we mean. 126

"The tender spring upon thy tempting lip 127
Shows thee unripe, yet mayst thou well be tasted.
Make use of time, let not advantage slip; 129
Beauty within itself should not be wasted. 130
  Fair flowers that are not gathered in their prime
  Rot and consume themselves in little time.

"Were I hard-favored, foul, or wrinkled old, 133
Ill-nurtured, crooked, churlish, harsh in voice,
O'erworn, despisèd, rheumatic, and cold, 135
Thick-sighted, barren, lean, and lacking juice, 136
  Then mightst thou pause, for then I were not for
    thee;
  But having no defects, why dost abhor me?

115 Touch i.e., if you touch **117 thine . . . mine** i.e., mutual, shared **119 there . . . lies** i.e., (1) see your beauty reflected there (2) your beauty lies in my beholding **121 wink** close the eyes **124 not in sight** observed by no one **126 mean** intend **127 spring** growth (i.e., down) **129 advantage** opportunity **130 Beauty . . . wasted** beauty should not be wasted by being kept to itself **133 hard-favored** ugly. **foul** ugly **135 O'erworn** worn by time **136 Thick-sighted** dim-eyed

"Thou canst not see one wrinkle in my brow;
Mine eyes are gray and bright and quick in turning; 140
My beauty as the spring doth yearly grow, 141
My flesh is soft and plump, my marrow burning; 142
My smooth moist hand, were it with thy hand felt, 143
Would in thy palm dissolve, or seem to melt.

"Bid me discourse, I will enchant thine ear,
Or like a fairy, trip upon the green, 146
Or like a nymph, with long disheveled hair,
Dance on the sands, and yet no footing seen. 148
Love is a spirit all compact of fire, 149
Not gross to sink, but light, and will aspire. 150

"Witness this primrose bank whereon I lie;
These forceless flowers like sturdy trees support me. 152
Two strengthless doves will draw me through the sky, 153
From morn till night, even where I list to sport me. 154
Is love so light, sweet boy, and may it be 155
That thou shouldst think it heavy unto thee? 156

"Is thine own heart to thine own face affected? 157
Can thy right hand seize love upon thy left? 158
Then woo thyself, be of thyself rejected; 159
Steal thine own freedom and complain on theft. 160
Narcissus so himself himself forsook, 161
And died to kiss his shadow in the brook. 162

140 gray i.e., blue. **quick in turning** i.e., animated **141 as . . . grow** i.e., is perennially renewed, like spring **142 marrow** vital or essential part. **burning** sexually ardent **143 moist** (Indicative of youth and passion, as with *sweating* in l. 25.) **146 trip** dance **148 footing** footprint **149 compact** composed **150 gross** heavy. (The heavy elements, earth and water, sink; fire and air rise.) **aspire** rise **152 forceless** frail **153 doves** (Venus' chariot was depicted as being drawn by doves.) **154 list** desire **155 light** (1) rising, weightless (2) wanton **156 heavy** (1) weighty (2) troublous **157 affected** drawn by affection **158 upon thy left** i.e., by clasping the left hand **159 of** by **160 Steal . . . freedom** i.e., take your own affections captive. **on** of **161 Narcissus** a beautiful youth in classical mythology who, leaning over a pool to drink, fell in love with his reflection and stayed there until he died. He was afterward changed into a flower. (Ovid, *Metamorphoses*, 3.339–510.) **himself himself forsook** i.e., abandoned himself to a hopeless passion for himself **162 to kiss** i.e., seeking fruitlessly to kiss

"Torches are made to light, jewels to wear,
Dainties to taste, fresh beauty for the use,
Herbs for their smell, and sappy plants to bear. 165
Things growing to themselves are growth's abuse. 166
Seeds spring from seeds, and beauty breedeth beauty.
Thou wast begot; to get it is thy duty. 168

"Upon the earth's increase why shouldst thou feed,
Unless the earth with thy increase be fed?
By law of nature thou art bound to breed,
That thine may live when thou thyself art dead;
And so, in spite of death, thou dost survive,
In that thy likeness still is left alive."

By this the lovesick queen began to sweat, 175
For where they lay the shadow had forsook them,
And Titan, tirèd in the midday heat, 177
With burning eye did hotly overlook them, 178
Wishing Adonis had his team to guide, 179
So he were like him, and by Venus' side. 180

And now Adonis, with a lazy sprite, 181
And with a heavy, dark, disliking eye,
His louring brows o'erwhelming his fair sight, 183
Like misty vapors when they blot the sky,
Souring his cheeks, cries, "Fie, no more of love! 185
The sun doth burn my face; I must remove." 186

165 sappy plants sap-bearing fruit trees **166 to themselves** i.e., solely for their own use **168 get** beget, procreate **175 By this** by this time **177 Titan** the sun god. **tirèd** attired **178 overlook** look upon **179 his team** i.e., Titan's team of horses **180 So . . . him** i.e., so that he, Titan, might be in Adonis' place **181 lazy sprite** dull spirit **183 o'erwhelming** overhanging so as to cover. **sight** eyes **185 Souring his cheeks** scowling **186 remove** move

"Ay me," quoth Venus, "young, and so unkind? 187
What bare excuses mak'st thou to be gone!
I'll sigh celestial breath, whose gentle wind
Shall cool the heat of this descending sun. 190
I'll make a shadow for thee of my hairs;
If they burn too, I'll quench them with my tears.

"The sun that shines from heaven shines but warm,
And, lo, I lie between that sun and thee.
The heat I have from thence doth little harm;
Thine eye darts forth the fire that burneth me,
And were I not immortal, life were done 197
Between this heavenly and earthly sun.

"Art thou obdurate, flinty, hard as steel?
Nay, more than flint, for stone at rain relenteth. 200
Art thou a woman's son, and canst not feel
What 'tis to love, how want of love tormenteth?
O, had thy mother borne so hard a mind,
She had not brought forth thee, but died unkind. 204

"What am I, that thou shouldst contemn me this? 205
Or what great danger dwells upon my suit? 206
What were thy lips the worse for one poor kiss? 207
Speak, fair, but speak fair words, or else be mute. 208
Give me one kiss, I'll give it thee again, 209
And one for interest, if thou wilt have twain.

"Fie, lifeless picture, cold and senseless stone, 211
Well-painted idol, image dull and dead,
Statue contenting but the eye alone,
Thing like a man, but of no woman bred!
Thou art no man, though of a man's complexion, 215
For men will kiss even by their own direction." 216

187 unkind unrelenting; unnatural **190 descending** beating down **197 were done** would be undone, finished **200 relenteth** wears slowly away **204 unkind** unnaturally unrelenting, not fulfilling her natural function **205 contemn** refuse scornfully. **this** i.e., this request **206 dwells upon** attends **207 What** in what way **208 fair** fair one **209 Give** if you give **211 senseless** insensible **215 complexion** outward appearance **216 direction** inclination

This said, impatience chokes her pleading tongue,
And swelling passion doth provoke a pause.
Red cheeks and fiery eyes blaze forth her wrong; 219
Being judge in love, she cannot right her cause. 220
  And now she weeps, and now she fain would speak, 221
  And now her sobs do her intendments break. 222

Sometimes she shakes her head and then his hand, 223
Now gazeth she on him, now on the ground;
Sometimes her arms enfold him like a band. 225
She would, he will not in her arms be bound; 226
  And when from thence he struggles to be gone,
  She locks her lily fingers one in one.

"Fondling," she saith, "since I have hemmed thee here 229
Within the circuit of this ivory pale, 230
I'll be a park, and thou shalt be my deer. 231
Feed where thou wilt, on mountain or in dale;
  Graze on my lips; and if those hills be dry,
  Stray lower, where the pleasant fountains lie. 234

"Within this limit is relief enough, 235
Sweet bottom grass and high delightful plain, 236
Round rising hillocks, brakes obscure and rough, 237
To shelter thee from tempest and from rain.
  Then be my deer, since I am such a park;
  No dog shall rouse thee, though a thousand bark." 240

219 blaze forth proclaim (with a metaphorical sense of "seem to burn," "show by their flaming") **220 Being . . . cause** i.e., although goddess and hence arbiter of love, Venus cannot prevail in her own case
221 fain gladly **222 do . . . break** interrupt what she intends to say
223 his hand (i.e., not in a handshake but in a gesture of frustration)
225 like a band as in a bond or fetter **226 would** i.e., would bind him
229 Fondling foolish one **230 pale** fence (i.e., her arms; the sexual topography is continued in *fountains, bottom grass, hillocks, brakes,* etc.) **231 park** deer preserve. **deer** (with a pun on *dear*)
234 fountains (1) springs (2) breasts **235 limit** boundary. **relief** (1) pasture (2) sexual pleasure **236 bottom grass** valley grass (with an allusion to pubic hair) **237 brakes** thickets (again with sexual suggestion). **obscure** dark. **rough** shaggy, dense **240 rouse** cause to start from cover

At this Adonis smiles as in disdain,
That in each cheek appears a pretty dimple. 242
Love made those hollows, if himself were slain, 243
He might be buried in a tomb so simple, 244
  Foreknowing well, if there he came to lie,
  Why, there Love lived; and there he could not die. 246

These lovely caves, these round enchanting pits,
Opened their mouths to swallow Venus' liking. 248
Being mad before, how doth she now for wits? 249
Struck dead at first, what needs a second striking?
  Poor queen of love, in thine own law forlorn, 251
  To love a cheek that smiles at thee in scorn!

Now which way shall she turn? What shall she say?
Her words are done, her woes the more increasing;
The time is spent; her object will away,
And from her twining arms doth urge releasing.
  "Pity," she cries, "some favor, some remorse!" 257
  Away he springs and hasteth to his horse.

But, lo, from forth a copse that neighbors by, 259
A breeding jennet, lusty, young, and proud, 260
Adonis' trampling courser doth espy,
And forth she rushes, snorts, and neighs aloud.
  The strong-necked steed, being tied unto a tree,
  Breaketh his rein, and to her straight goes he. 264

242 That so that **243 Love** Cupid. **if** so that if **244 simple** unadorned **246 Love** (1) the essence of love, loveliness (2) Cupid himself **248 Opened . . . liking** i.e., looked so winsome in their dimpling that Venus was engulfed, swallowed up, by love. **liking** desire **249 how . . . wits** i.e., how may she keep her sanity now **251 in . . . forlorn** condemned to suffer under your own rule of love **257 remorse** compassion **259 copse . . . by** neighboring thicket **260 breeding** in heat. **jennet** small Spanish mare. **lusty** spirited **264 straight** straightaway

Imperiously he leaps, he neighs, he bounds,
And now his woven girths he breaks asunder.
The bearing earth with his hard hoof he wounds, 267
Whose hollow womb resounds like heaven's thunder.
  The iron bit he crusheth 'tween his teeth,
  Controlling what he was controllèd with.

His ears up-pricked, his braided hanging mane
Upon his compassed crest now stand on end; 272
His nostrils drink the air, and forth again,
As from a furnace, vapors doth he send.
  His eye, which scornfully glisters like fire,
  Shows his hot courage and his high desire. 276

Sometimes he trots, as if he told the steps, 277
With gentle majesty and modest pride;
Anon he rears upright, curvets, and leaps, 279
As who should say, "Lo, thus my strength is tried, 280
  And this I do to captivate the eye
  Of the fair breeder that is standing by."

What recketh he his rider's angry stir, 283
His flattering "Holla," or his "Stand, I say"? 284
What cares he now for curb or pricking spur?
For rich caparisons or trappings gay? 286
  He sees his love, and nothing else he sees,
  For nothing else with his proud sight agrees.

267 bearing receiving **272 compassed** arched. **crest** ridge of the neck **276 courage** passion **277 told** numbered **279 curvets** raises his forelegs and then springs with his hind legs before the forelegs reach the ground **280 As who should** as one might. **tried** tested **283 recketh he** does he care about or pay attention to. **stir** bustle **284 flattering** cajoling. **Holla** stop **286 caparisons** gaily ornamental cloth coverings for the saddle and harness

Look when a painter would surpass the life, 289
In limning out a well-proportioned steed, 290
His art with nature's workmanship at strife,
As if the dead the living should exceed, 292
So did this horse excel a common one
In shape, in courage, color, pace, and bone. 294

Round-hoofed, short-jointed, fetlocks shag and long, 295
Broad breast, full eye, small head, and nostril wide,
High crest, short ears, straight legs and passing strong, 297
Thin mane, thick tail, broad buttock, tender hide: 298
Look what a horse should have he did not lack, 299
Save a proud rider on so proud a back.

Sometimes he scuds far off, and there he stares;
Anon he starts at stirring of a feather;
To bid the wind a base he now prepares, 303
And whe'er he run or fly they know not whether; 304
For through his mane and tail the high wind sings,
Fanning the hairs, who wave like feathered wings.

He looks upon his love and neighs unto her;
She answers him as if she knew his mind.
Being proud, as females are, to see him woo her,
She puts on outward strangeness, seems unkind, 310
Spurns at his love and scorns the heat he feels, 311
Beating his kind embracements with her heels. 312

289 Look when just as when **290 limning out** portraying, drawing **292 dead** inanimate **294 bone** frame **295 fetlocks** lower part of horses' legs where the tuft of hair grows behind, just above the hoof. **shag** shaggy **297 crest** ridge of the neck. **passing** surpassingly **298 tender hide** i.e., delicate of hide, not coarse **299 Look what** whatever **303 bid the wind a base** challenge the wind to a contest. (From the children's game of prisoner's base.) **304 whe'er** whether. **whether** which of the two **310 outward strangeness** seeming coldness. **unkind** unattracted sexually, not responding to natural feeling **311 Spurns at** (1) kicks at (2) rejects, repels **312 kind** (1) affectionate, passionate (2) prompted by nature

Then, like a melancholy malcontent,
He vails his tail that, like a falling plume, 314
Cool shadow to his melting buttock lent;
He stamps and bites the poor flies in his fume. 316
His love, perceiving how he was enraged,
Grew kinder, and his fury was assuaged.

His testy master goeth about to take him, 319
When, lo, the unbacked breeder, full of fear, 320
Jealous of catching, swiftly doth forsake him, 321
With her the horse, and left Adonis there. 322
As they were mad, unto the wood they hie them, 323
Outstripping crows that strive to overfly them. 324

All swoll'n with chafing, down Adonis sits, 325
Banning his boisterous and unruly beast; 326
And now the happy season once more fits 327
That lovesick Love by pleading may be blest; 328
For lovers say the heart hath treble wrong
When it is barred the aidance of the tongue. 330

An oven that is stopped, or river stayed, 331
Burneth more hotly, swelleth with more rage;
So of concealèd sorrow may be said. 333
Free vent of words love's fire doth assuage; 334
But when the heart's attorney once is mute, 335
The client breaks, as desperate in his suit. 336

314 vails lowers **316 fume** anger **319 testy** irritated. **goeth about** makes an effort **320 unbacked** unbroken, riderless. **breeder** i.e., female in heat **321 Jealous of catching** fearful of being caught
322 horse i.e., stallion **323 As** as if. **hie them** hasten **324 overfly them** fly faster than they can run, or keep pace with them in flight
325 swoll'n with chafing puffed with anger **326 Banning** cursing
327 fits is fitting, is suited **328 Love** i.e., Venus, the goddess of love, not Cupid, as at ll. 243–246 **330 aidance** help **331 stopped** stopped up. **stayed** hindered, dammed **333 may** it may **334 love's . . . assuage** assuages love's fire **335 the heart's attorney** i.e., the tongue
336 breaks (1) goes bankrupt (2) breaks asunder, as the heart is said to break in rejected love

Thus she replies: "Thy palfrey, as he should,
Welcomes the warm approach of sweet desire.
Affection is a coal that must be cooled, 387
Else, suffered, it will set the heart on fire. 388
  The sea hath bounds, but deep desire hath none;
  Therefore no marvel though thy horse be gone.

"How like a jade he stood, tied to the tree, 391
Servilely mastered with a leathern rein!
But when he saw his love, his youth's fair fee, 393
He held such petty bondage in disdain,
  Throwing the base thong from his bending crest, 395
  Enfranchising his mouth, his back, his breast. 396

"Who sees his true love in her naked bed, 397
Teaching the sheets a whiter hue than white,
But when his glutton eye so full hath fed, 399
His other agents aim at like delight? 400
  Who is so faint that dares not be so bold
  To touch the fire, the weather being cold?

"Let me excuse thy courser, gentle boy;
And learn of him, I heartily beseech thee,
To take advantage on presented joy. 405
Though I were dumb, yet his proceedings teach thee. 406
  O, learn to love; the lesson is but plain,
  And once made perfect, never lost again." 408

387 Affection passion. **coal** ember **388 suffered** permitted to continue **391 jade** spiritless worn-out nag **393 fair fee** due reward **395 base** worthless, paltry. **bending crest** arching ridge of the neck **396 Enfranchising** freeing **397 in . . . bed** i.e., naked in her bed **399 But when** but that when **400 agents** organs, senses **405 on** of. **presented joy** joy that presents itself **406 dumb** unable to speak **408 made perfect** learned completely

"I know not love," quoth he, "nor will not know it,
Unless it be a boar, and then I chase it;
'Tis much to borrow, and I will not owe it; 411
My love to love is love but to disgrace it; 412
For I have heard it is a life in death,
That laughs and weeps, and all but with a breath. 414

"Who wears a garment shapeless and unfinished?
Who plucks the bud before one leaf put forth?
If springing things be any jot diminished, 417
They wither in their prime, prove nothing worth.
The colt that's backed and burdened being young 419
Loseth his pride and never waxeth strong.

"You hurt my hand with wringing. Let us part
And leave this idle theme, this bootless chat. 422
Remove your siege from my unyielding heart;
To love's alarms it will not ope the gate. 424
Dismiss your vows, your feignèd tears, your flattery;
For where a heart is hard they make no battery." 426

"What, canst thou talk?" quoth she. "Hast thou a
tongue?
O, would thou hadst not, or I had no hearing!
Thy mermaid's voice hath done me double wrong; 429
I had my load before, now pressed with bearing: 430
Melodious discord, heavenly tune harsh sounding,
Ear's deep sweet music, and heart's deep sore
wounding.

411 borrow assume as an obligation. **owe** have to repay **412 My . . . disgrace it** my only inclination toward love is a desire to render it contemptible, discredit it **414 all . . . breath** all in the same breath **417 springing** sprouting, immature **419 backed** broken in **422 idle** useless. **bootless** profitless **424 alarms** signals of attack **426 battery** breach in a fortified wall **429 mermaid's** siren's **430 pressed** oppressed, weighted down (making her previous burden of his coy beauty now unbearable)

"Had I no eyes but ears, my ears would love
That inward beauty and invisible; 434
Or were I deaf, thy outward parts would move 435
Each part in me that were but sensible. 436
Though neither eyes nor ears, to hear nor see,
Yet should I be in love by touching thee.

"Say that the sense of feeling were bereft me,
And that I could not see, nor hear, nor touch,
And nothing but the very smell were left me,
Yet would my love to thee be still as much;
For from the stillitory of thy face excelling 443
Comes breath perfumed that breedeth love by
smelling.

"But, O, what banquet wert thou to the taste,
Being nurse and feeder of the other four!
Would they not wish the feast might ever last,
And bid Suspicion double-lock the door, 448
Lest Jealousy, that sour unwelcome guest,
Should, by his stealing in, disturb the feast?"

Once more the ruby-colored portal opened, 451
Which to his speech did honey passage yield, 452
Like a red morn, that ever yet betokened
Wreck to the seaman, tempest to the field, 454
Sorrow to shepherds, woe unto the birds,
Gusts and foul flaws to herdmen and to herds. 456

434 That . . . invisible i.e., the unseen beauty of your voice **435 deaf** i.e., deaf as well as blind. **outward parts** i.e., tangible body **436 sensible** susceptible to sensual impressions **443 stillitory** still (used in making perfume). **excelling** exceedingly beautiful **448 Suspicion** caution against being detected **451 portal** i.e., mouth **452 honey** sweet **454 Wreck** shipwreck. (A red sun at sunrise proverbially betokens a storm.) **tempest to the field** a heavy storm that beats down the grain **456 flaws** gusts of wind

This ill presage advisedly she marketh. 457
Even as the wind is hushed before it raineth,
Or as the wolf doth grin before he barketh, 459
Or as the berry breaks before it staineth,
  Or like the deadly bullet of a gun,
  His meaning struck her ere his words begun.

And at his look she flatly falleth down,
For looks kill love, and love by looks reviveth;
A smile recures the wounding of a frown. 465
But blessèd bankrupt, that by love so thriveth! 466
  The silly boy, believing she is dead, 467
  Claps her pale cheek, till clapping makes it red;

And all amazed brake off his late intent, 469
For sharply he did think to reprehend her,
Which cunning Love did wittily prevent.
Fair fall the wit that can so well defend her! 472
  For on the grass she lies as she were slain, 473
  Till his breath breatheth life in her again.

He wrings her nose, he strikes her on the cheeks, 475
He bends her fingers, holds her pulses hard, 476
He chafes her lips; a thousand ways he seeks
To mend the hurt that his unkindness marred. 478
  He kisses her, and she, by her good will, 479
  Will never rise, so he will kiss her still. 480

457 ill presage prediction of storm. **advisedly** attentively **459 grin** bare its teeth **465 recures** cures **466 blessèd** fortunate. **that . . . thriveth** who prospers so by this gesture of love. (*Love* is sometimes emended to *loss,* or to *looks*. Venus paradoxically gains what she wants—Adonis' attention—by her fainting.) **467 silly** naive **469 amazed** perplexed, distraught. **brake** broke **472 Fair fall** good luck befall **473 as** as if **475 He . . . nose** (A standard first-aid remedy; briefly stopping the air supply can induce the patient to resume breathing.) **476 bends her fingers** (as a stimulus or test of consciousness). **holds . . . hard** takes her pulse **478 marred** caused to her detriment **479 good will** consent **480 so** provided that. **still** continually

The night of sorrow now is turned to day.
Her two blue windows faintly she upheaveth,
Like the fair sun, when in his fresh array
He cheers the morn and all the earth relieveth;
  And as the bright sun glorifies the sky,
  So is her face illumined with her eye,

Whose beams upon his hairless face are fixed,
As if from thence they borrowed all their shine.
Were never four such lamps together mixed, 489
Had not his clouded with his brow's repine; 490
  But hers, which through the crystal tears gave light,
  Shone like the moon in water seen by night.

"O, where am I?" quoth she, "in earth or heaven,
Or in the ocean drenched, or in the fire? 494
What hour is this? Or morn or weary even? 495
Do I delight to die, or life desire?
  But now I lived, and life was death's annoy; 497
  But now I died, and death was lively joy. 498

"O, thou didst kill me; kill me once again!
Thy eyes' shrewd tutor, that hard heart of thine, 500
Hath taught them scornful tricks and such disdain
That they have murdered this poor heart of mine;
  And these mine eyes, true leaders to their queen, 503
  But for thy piteous lips no more had seen. 504

489 Were never never before were **490 repine** repining, dissatisfaction **494 drenched** drowned **495 Or** either **497 death's annoy** i.e., as wretched as death **498 lively joy** i.e., as joyous as life **500 shrewd** sharp, harsh **503 leaders** guides. **queen** i.e., the heart **504 But for** were it not for. **seen** had the power of sight

"Long may they kiss each other, for this cure! 505
O, never let their crimson liveries wear! 506
And as they last, their verdure still endure, 507
To drive infection from the dangerous year!
That the stargazers, having writ on death, 509
May say the plague is banished by thy breath.

"Pure lips, sweet seals in my soft lips imprinted, 511
What bargains may I make, still to be sealing? 512
To sell myself I can be well contented,
So thou wilt buy and pay and use good dealing, 514
Which purchase if thou make, for fear of slips 515
Set thy seal manual on my wax-red lips. 516

"A thousand kisses buys my heart from me;
And pay them at thy leisure, one by one.
What is ten hundred touches unto thee? 519
Are they not quickly told and quickly gone? 520
Say for nonpayment that the debt should double,
Is twenty hundred kisses such a trouble?"

"Fair queen," quoth he, "if any love you owe me, 523
Measure my strangeness with my unripe years. 524
Before I know myself, seek not to know me. 525
No fisher but the ungrown fry forbears. 526
The mellow plum doth fall; the green sticks fast,
Or being early plucked is sour to taste.

505 they i.e., your lips. **for** in payment for, as a means of effecting **506 crimson liveries** uniforms or costumes of crimson. **wear** wear out **507 their verdure** may their fresh fragrance (Alludes to belief in the efficacy of certain herbs to ward off contagion.) **509 writ on death** predicted (by means of astrology) an epidemic of plague **511 seals . . . imprinted** stamps that have left their impression on my soft lips **512 still to be sealing** (1) to continue kissing always (2) to seal a bargain **514 So** provided that **515 slips** errors or fraudulent payment (which Venus suggests they avoid by means of a *seal manual* or seal placed on the contract of their love) **516 wax-red** (since wax would be used in sealing) **519 touches** i.e., kisses **520 told** counted **523 owe** bear **524 Measure . . . with** i.e., explain my reserve by **525 to know me** (with erotic suggestion) **526 No . . . forbears** there is no fisherman who does not throw back immature fish

"Look the world's comforter, with weary gait, 529
His day's hot task hath ended in the west;
The owl, night's herald, shrieks; 'tis very late;
The sheep are gone to fold, birds to their nest,
And coal-black clouds that shadow heaven's light
Do summon us to part and bid good night.

"Now let me say 'Good night,' and so say you;
If you will say so, you shall have a kiss."
"Good night," quoth she, and, ere he says "Adieu,"
The honey fee of parting tendered is. 538
Her arms do lend his neck a sweet embrace;
Incorporate then they seem; face grows to face; 540

Till, breathless, he disjoined, and backward drew
The heavenly moisture, that sweet coral mouth,
Whose precious taste her thirsty lips well knew,
Whereon they surfeit, yet complain on drouth. 544
He with her plenty pressed, she faint with dearth, 545
Their lips together glued, fall to the earth.

Now quick desire hath caught the yielding prey,
And gluttonlike she feeds, yet never filleth;
Her lips are conquerors, his lips obey,
Paying what ransom the insulter willeth, 550
Whose vulture thought doth pitch the price so high 551
That she will draw his lips' rich treasure dry.

And having felt the sweetness of the spoil, 553
With blindfold fury she begins to forage;
Her face doth reek and smoke, her blood doth boil, 555
And careless lust stirs up a desperate courage, 556
Planting oblivion, beating reason back, 557
Forgetting shame's pure blush and honor's wrack. 558

529 Look see how. **world's comforter** i.e., sun **538 honey** sweet. **tendered is** is given **540 Incorporate** united into one body **544 on drouth** of drought, of not having enough **545 with . . . pressed** oppressed with the plenty she bestowed on him **550 insulter** boasting conqueror **551 vulture** i.e., ravenous. **pitch** set at a certain level or point **553 spoil** plunder, conquest **555 reek** i.e., steam **556 careless** heedless **557 Planting oblivion** implanting or causing forgetfulness of all that she ought to remember **558 wrack** ruin

Hot, faint, and weary, with her hard embracing,
Like a wild bird being tamed with too much handling,
Or as the fleet-foot roe that's tired with chasing, 561
Or like the froward infant stilled with dandling, 562
He now obeys, and now no more resisteth,
While she takes all she can, not all she listeth. 564

What wax so frozen but dissolves with temp'ring 565
And yields at last to every light impression?
Things out of hope are compassed oft with vent'ring, 567
Chiefly in love, whose leave exceeds commission. 568
Affection faints not like a pale-faced coward, 569
But then woos best when most his choice is froward. 570

When he did frown, O, had she then gave over,
Such nectar from his lips she had not sucked.
Foul words and frowns must not repel a lover. 573
What though the rose have prickles, yet 'tis plucked.
Were beauty under twenty locks kept fast,
Yet love breaks through and picks them all at last. 576

For pity now she can no more detain him; 577
The poor fool prays her that he may depart. 578
She is resolved no longer to restrain him,
Bids him farewell, and look well to her heart, 580
The which, by Cupid's bow she doth protest, 581
He carries thence encagèd in his breast.

561 with chasing with being chased **562 froward** fretful **564 listeth** desires **565 temp'ring** heating and working with the fingers **567 out of** beyond. **compassed** encompassed, accomplished **568 leave exceeds commission** liberties go beyond due warrant **569 Affection** passion. **faints not** does not relent or fall back **570 choice is froward** chosen one is stubborn, obstinate **573 Foul** hostile, disagreeable **576 picks them all** (Picking a lock often has sexual meaning in Shakespeare.) **577 For pity** appealing to his sense of pity **578 fool** (An affectionate term.) **580 and look well to** i.e., and bids him take good care of **581 protest** vow, affirm

"Sweet boy," she says, "this night I'll waste in sorrow, 583
For my sick heart commands mine eyes to watch. 584
Tell me, Love's master, shall we meet tomorrow?
Say, shall we, shall we? Wilt thou make the match?"
He tells her no, tomorrow he intends
To hunt the boar with certain of his friends.

"The boar!" quoth she, whereat a sudden pale, 589
Like lawn being spread upon the blushing rose, 590
Usurps her cheek. She trembles at his tale
And on his neck her yoking arms she throws.
She sinketh down, still hanging by his neck;
He on her belly falls, she on her back.

Now is she in the very lists of love, 595
Her champion mounted for the hot encounter.
All is imaginary she doth prove, 597
He will not manage her, although he mount her; 598
That worse than Tantalus' is her annoy, 599
To clip Elysium and to lack her joy. 600

Even as poor birds, deceived with painted grapes, 601
Do surfeit by the eye and pine the maw, 602
Even so she languisheth in her mishaps,
As those poor birds that helpless berries saw. 604
The warm effects which she in him finds missing 605
She seeks to kindle with continual kissing.

583 waste spend **584 watch** stay awake **589 pale** pallor **590 lawn** fine linen **595 lists** tournament field (with erotic suggestion) **597 she doth prove** that she experiences **598 manage** control, ride (as one manages a horse) **599 Tantalus** a son of Zeus who was punished by perpetual hunger and thirst with food and drink always in sight yet untouchable. **annoy** vexation, torment **600 clip** embrace. **Elysium** blissful afterlife in classical mythology. **and** and yet **601 birds . . . grapes** (Allusion to Zeuxis, a Greek painter of the fifth century B.C., so skillful an artist that birds were said to peck at his picture of a bunch of grapes.) **602 pine the maw** starve the stomach **604 As** like. **helpless** affording no sustenance **605 warm effects** sexual response

But all in vain; good queen, it will not be.
She hath assayed as much as may be proved. 608
Her pleading hath deserved a greater fee; 609
She's Love, she loves, and yet she is not loved.
"Fie, fie," he says, "you crush me, let me go!
You have no reason to withhold me so."

"Thou hadst been gone," quoth she, "sweet boy, ere this,
But that thou toldst me thou wouldst hunt the boar.
O, be advised! Thou know'st not what it is 615
With javelin's point a churlish swine to gore,
Whose tushes, never sheathed, he whetteth still, 617
Like to a mortal butcher bent to kill. 618

"On his bow-back he hath a battle set 619
Of bristly pikes, that ever threat his foes; 620
His eyes like glowworms shine when he doth fret; 621
His snout digs sepulchers where'er he goes;
Being moved, he strikes whate'er is in his way, 623
And whom he strikes his crooked tushes slay.

"His brawny sides, with hairy bristles armed,
Are better proof than thy spear's point can enter; 626
His short thick neck cannot be easily harmed;
Being ireful, on the lion he will venter. 628
The thorny brambles and embracing bushes,
As fearful of him, part, through whom he rushes. 630

608 assayed tried. **proved** experienced, tried **609 pleading . . . fee** (A legal metaphor; she is *pleading* her own case.) **615 advised** warned **617 tushes** tusks. **still** continually **618 Like to** like. **mortal** deadly. **bent to kill** intent on killing **619 bow-back** arched back, but suggestive also of a bowman's quiver. **battle** i.e., martial array **620 ever threat** continually threaten **621 fret** i.e., gnash his teeth **623 moved** angered **626 proof** armor **628 ireful** wrathful. **venter** venture **630 As** as if

"Alas, he naught esteems that face of thine,
To which Love's eyes pays tributary gazes,
Nor thy soft hands, sweet lips, and crystal eyne, 633
Whose full perfection all the world amazes;
But having thee at vantage—wondrous dread!— 635
Would root these beauties as he roots the mead. 636

"O, let him keep his loathsome cabin still! 637
Beauty hath naught to do with such foul fiends.
Come not within his danger by thy will; 639
They that thrive well take counsel of their friends.
When thou didst name the boar, not to dissemble, 641
I feared thy fortune, and my joints did tremble. 642

"Didst thou not mark my face? Was it not white?
Sawest thou not signs of fear lurk in mine eye?
Grew I not faint, and fell I not downright? 645
Within my bosom, whereon thou dost lie,
My boding heart pants, beats, and takes no rest,
But, like an earthquake, shakes thee on my breast.

"For where Love reigns, disturbing Jealousy 649
Doth call himself Affection's sentinel,
Gives false alarms, suggesteth mutiny, 651
And in a peaceful hour doth cry 'Kill, kill!' 652
Distempering gentle Love in his desire, 653
As air and water do abate the fire. 654

633 eyne eyes **635 at vantage** at a disadvantage **636 root** root up. **mead** meadow **637 keep** occupy. **cabin** den **639 danger** i.e., zone of danger. **by thy will** intentionally **641 not to dissemble** to tell you the plain truth **642 feared** feared for **645 downright** forthwith
649 Jealousy apprehension **651 suggesteth mutiny** incites dissension **652 in a** i.e., disturbing a **653 Distempering** quenching **654 abate** extinguish

"This sour informer, this bate-breeding spy, 655
This canker that eats up Love's tender spring, 656
This carry-tale, dissentious Jealousy, 657
That sometimes true news, sometimes false doth bring,
Knocks at my heart and whispers in mine ear
That if I love thee, I thy death should fear;

"And more than so, presenteth to mine eye 661
The picture of an angry chafing boar,
Under whose sharp fangs on his back doth lie
An image like thyself, all stained with gore,
Whose blood upon the fresh flowers being shed
Doth make them droop with grief and hang the head.

"What should I do, seeing thee so indeed, 667
That tremble at th' imagination? 668
The thought of it doth make my faint heart bleed,
And fear doth teach it divination. 670
I prophesy thy death, my living sorrow,
If thou encounter with the boar tomorrow.

"But if thou needs wilt hunt, be ruled by me; 673
Uncouple at the timorous flying hare, 674
Or at the fox which lives by subtlety,
Or at the roe which no encounter dare.
Pursue these fearful creatures o'er the downs, 677
And on thy well-breathed horse keep with thy
hounds. 678

655 bate-breeding strife-breeding **656 canker** cankerworm. **spring** young shoot of a plant **657 carry-tale** spreader of (distressing) talk **661 more than so** even more than that **667–668 seeing . . . imagination** if I should actually see you dead, when merely imagining it makes me tremble **670 divination** i.e., power to prophesy **673 needs wilt** must **674 Uncouple** unleash the hounds. **flying** fleeing pursuit **677 fearful** full of fears **678 well-breathed** not easily winded, in good condition

"And when thou hast on foot the purblind hare, 679
Mark the poor wretch, to overshoot his troubles 680
How he outruns the wind and with what care 681
He cranks and crosses with a thousand doubles. 682
The many musets through the which he goes 683
Are like a labyrinth to amaze his foes. 684

"Sometimes he runs among a flock of sheep,
To make the cunning hounds mistake their smell,
And sometimes where earth-delving coneys keep, 687
To stop the loud pursuers in their yell, 688
And sometimes sorteth with a herd of deer. 689
Danger deviseth shifts; wit waits on fear. 690

"For there his smell with others being mingled,
The hot scent-snuffing hounds are driven to doubt,
Ceasing their clamorous cry till they have singled
With much ado the cold fault cleanly out. 694
Then do they spend their mouths; echo replies, 695
As if another chase were in the skies.

"By this, poor Wat, far off upon a hill, 697
Stands on his hinder legs with listening ear,
To hearken if his foes pursue him still.
Anon their loud alarums he doth hear,
And now his grief may be comparèd well
To one sore sick that hears the passing bell. 702

679 on foot in chase. **purblind** dimsighted **680 overshoot** run beyond **681 outruns the wind** i.e., leaves his scent far behind **682 cranks** twists and turns **683 musets** gaps in hedge or fence **684 amaze** bewilder **687 coneys** rabbits. **keep** dwell **688 yell** cry **689 sorteth** consorts, mingles **690 shifts** tricks. **wit waits** intelligence attends **694 cold fault** cold or lost scent **695 spend their mouths** give the cry on spotting the game **697 Wat** (A common name applied to the hare.) **702 sore** very. **passing bell** bell tolled for a person who has just died

"Then shalt thou see the dew-bedabbled wretch 703
Turn, and return, indenting with the way; 704
Each envious brier his weary legs do scratch, 705
Each shadow makes him stop, each murmur stay;
For misery is trodden on by many,
And, being low, never relieved by any.

"Lie quietly, and hear a little more.
Nay, do not struggle, for thou shalt not rise.
To make thee hate the hunting of the boar,
Unlike myself thou hear'st me moralize, 712
Applying this to that, and so to so;
For love can comment upon every woe.

"Where did I leave?" "No matter where," quoth he, 715
"Leave me, and then the story aptly ends;
The night is spent." "Why, what of that?" quoth she.
"I am," quoth he, "expected of my friends, 718
And now 'tis dark, and going I shall fall."
"In night," quoth she, "desire sees best of all.

"But if thou fall, O, then imagine this,
The earth, in love with thee, thy footing trips,
And all is but to rob thee of a kiss.
Rich preys make true men thieves; so do thy lips 724
Make modest Dian cloudy and forlorn, 725
Lest she should steal a kiss and die forsworn. 726

703 dew-bedabbled sprinkled with dew **704 indenting** zigzagging **705 envious** malicious **712 Unlike . . . moralize** i.e., contrary to the usual way of the goddess of love, you hear me point out a moral application **715 leave** leave off. (But Adonis answers with another sense, "go away from.") **718 of** by **724 Rich . . . thieves** i.e., the chance of rich spoils (*preys*) will make thieves even of honest (*true*) men **725 Dian** Diana, goddess of the moon, chastity, and the hunt. (Even Diana would fall in love with Adonis.) **cloudy** obscured with clouds; sorrowful **726 forsworn** i.e., having broken her vow as the goddess of chastity

"Now of this dark night I perceive the reason: 727
Cynthia for shame obscures her silver shine, 728
Till forging Nature be condemned of treason, 729
For stealing molds from heaven that were divine,
Wherein she framed thee, in high heaven's despite, 731
To shame the sun by day and her by night. 732

"And therefore hath she bribed the Destinies
To cross the curious workmanship of nature, 734
To mingle beauty with infirmities,
And pure perfection with impure defeature, 736
Making it subject to the tyranny
Of mad mischances and much misery;

"As burning fevers, agues pale and faint, 739
Life-poisoning pestilence and frenzies wood, 740
The marrow-eating sickness, whose attaint 741
Disorder breeds by heating of the blood,
Surfeits, impostumes, grief, and damned despair 743
Swear Nature's death for framing thee so fair. 744

"And not the least of all these maladies
But in one minute's fight brings beauty under.
Both favor, savor, hue, and qualities, 747
Whereat th' impartial gazer late did wonder, 748
Are on the sudden wasted, thawed, and done, 749
As mountain snow melts with the midday sun.

727 of for **728 Cynthia** i.e., Diana, the moon **729 forging** counterfeiting **731 she** i.e., Nature. **in . . . despite** in defiance of high heaven **732 her** i.e., the moon **734 cross** thwart. **curious** ingenious **736 defeature** disfigurement **739 As** such as **740 frenzies** seizures. **wood** mad **741 The marrow-eating sickness** (probably venereal disease; love is said to burn or melt the marrow, as in l. 142; hence the *heating of the blood* in l. 742). **attaint** infection **743 impostumes** abscesses **744 Swear . . . fair** (all these diseases) swear to kill Nature because she formed you so beautiful **747 favor** beauty of feature. **savor** sweetness of smell. **hue** (1) color (2) shape **748 impartial** i.e., uninfluenced by love. **late** lately **749 wasted** wasted away. **done** destroyed

"Therefore, despite of fruitless chastity, 751
Love-lacking vestals and self-loving nuns,
That on the earth would breed a scarcity
And barren dearth of daughters and of sons,
Be prodigal. The lamp that burns by night
Dries up his oil to lend the world his light. 756

"What is thy body but a swallowing grave,
Seeming to bury that posterity
Which by the rights of time thou needs must have,
If thou destroy them not in dark obscurity?
If so, the world will hold thee in disdain,
Sith in thy pride so fair a hope is slain. 762

"So in thyself thyself art made away, 763
A mischief worse than civil homebred strife, 764
Or theirs whose desperate hands themselves do slay,
Or butcher sire that reaves his son of life. 766
Foul cankering rust the hidden treasure frets, 767
But gold that's put to use more gold begets."

"Nay, then," quoth Adon, "you will fall again
Into your idle overhandled theme. 770
The kiss I gave you is bestowed in vain,
And all in vain you strive against the stream; 772
For, by this black-faced night, desire's foul nurse, 773
Your treatise makes me like you worse and worse. 774

"If love have lent you twenty thousand tongues,
And every tongue more moving than your own,
Bewitching like the wanton mermaids' songs, 777
Yet from mine ear the tempting tune is blown;
For know, my heart stands armèd in mine ear
And will not let a false sound enter there,

751 despite of in defiance of. **fruitless** barren **756 his** its **762 Sith** since **763 thyself art made away** i.e., your futurity is destroyed **764 mischief** evil **766 reaves** bereaves **767 cankering** consuming (like the cankerworm). **frets** eats away **770 idle** profitless **772 stream** current **773 night . . . nurse** i.e., night, the foul nourisher of evil desire **774 treatise** discourse **777 mermaids'** i.e., sirens'

With this, he breaketh from the sweet embrace
Of those fair arms which bound him to her breast
And homeward through the dark laund runs apace, 813
Leaves Love upon her back deeply distressed.
  Look how a bright star shooteth from the sky,
  So glides he in the night from Venus' eye;

Which after him she darts, as one on shore
Gazing upon a late-embarkèd friend, 818
Till the wild waves will have him seen no more, 819
Whose ridges with the meeting clouds contend.
  So did the merciless and pitchy night
  Fold in the object that did feed her sight. 822

Whereat amazed, as one that unaware 823
Hath dropped a precious jewel in the flood, 824
Or stonished as night wanderers often are, 825
Their light blown out in some mistrustful wood, 826
  Even so confounded in the dark she lay, 827
  Having lost the fair discovery of her way. 828

And now she beats her heart, whereat it groans,
That all the neighbor caves, as seeming troubled,
Make verbal repetition of her moans.
Passion on passion deeply is redoubled: 832
  "Ay me!" she cries, and twenty times "Woe, woe!"
  And twenty echoes twenty times cry so.

She marking them begins a wailing note
And sings extemporally a woeful ditty
How love makes young men thrall and old men dote, 837
How love is wise in folly, foolish witty.
  Her heavy anthem still concludes in woe, 839
  And still the choir of echoes answer so.

813 laund glade **818 late-embarkèd** having recently taken ship **819 have him seen** allow him to be seen **822 Fold in** enfold, close in **823 amazed** dazed, confused. **unaware** inadvertently **824 flood** body of flowing water **825 stonished** dismayed **826 mistrustful** causing apprehension **827 confounded** bewildered **828 the fair . . . way** i.e., the one who lighted her path. **discovery** discoverer **832 Passion** lamentation **837 thrall** captive **839 heavy** melancholy. **still** continually

"Lest the deceiving harmony should run
Into the quiet closure of my breast; 782
And then my little heart were quite undone,
In his bedchamber to be barred of rest.
  No, lady, no. My heart longs not to groan,
  But soundly sleeps, while now it sleeps alone.

"What have you urged that I cannot reprove? 787
The path is smooth that leadeth on to danger.
I hate not love but your device in love, 789
That lends embracements unto every stranger.
  You do it for increase. O strange excuse,
  When reason is the bawd to lust's abuse!

"Call it not love, for Love to heaven is fled,
Since sweating Lust on earth usurped his name,
Under whose simple semblance he hath fed 795
Upon fresh beauty, blotting it with blame; 796
  Which the hot tyrant stains and soon bereaves, 797
  As caterpillars do the tender leaves.

"Love comforteth like sunshine after rain,
But Lust's effect is tempest after sun;
Love's gentle spring doth always fresh remain,
Lust's winter comes ere summer half be done.
  Love surfeits not, Lust like a glutton dies;
  Love is all truth, Lust full of forgèd lies.

"More I could tell, but more I dare not say;
The text is old, the orator too green. 806
Therefore, in sadness, now I will away. 807
My face is full of shame, my heart of teen; 808
  Mine ears, that to your wanton talk attended,
  Do burn themselves for having so offended." 810

782 closure enclosure **787 urged** argued for. **reprove** refute **789 device** cunning, deceitful conduct **795 whose** i.e., Love's. **simple semblance** guileless appearance. **he** i.e., Lust **796 blotting** soiling **797 bereaves** spoils **806 The text** the point being explicated (like the *text* of a sermon). **green** young, unpracticed **807 in sadness** seriously, truly **808 teen** grief, vexation **810 burn themselves** blush

Her song was tedious and outwore the night,
For lovers' hours are long, though seeming short.
If pleased themselves, others, they think, delight
In suchlike circumstance, with suchlike sport.
  Their copious stories, oftentimes begun,
  End without audience and are never done.

For who hath she to spend the night withal 847
But idle sounds resembling parasits, 848
Like shrill-tongued tapsters answering every call, 849
Soothing the humor of fantastic wits? 850
  She says "'Tis so," they answer all "'Tis so,"
  And would say after her, if she said "No."

Lo here the gentle lark, weary of rest,
From his moist cabinet mounts up on high, 854
And wakes the morning, from whose silver breast 855
The sun ariseth in his majesty,
  Who doth the world so gloriously behold 857
  That cedar tops and hills seem burnished gold.

Venus salutes him with this fair good morrow:
"O thou clear god, and patron of all light, 860
From whom each lamp and shining star doth borrow
The beauteous influence that makes him bright, 862
  There lives a son that sucked an earthly mother 863
  May lend thee light, as thou dost lend to other." 864

847 withal with **848 parasits** parasites, flattering attendants **849 tapsters** waiters in taverns **850 Soothing . . . wits** i.e., complying with the whim of capricious tavern customers **854 moist cabinet** dewy dwelling, nest **855 whose silver breast** (Aurora, the dawn, is personified as a goddess bidding farewell to her lover, the sun.) **857 behold** i.e., shine upon **860 clear** bright **862 influence** a supposed flowing or streaming of an ethereal fluid from a celestial body, influencing human destiny. (An astrological term.) **863 a son** i.e., Adonis. **sucked** suckled from **864 May** who may

This said, she hasteth to a myrtle grove,
Musing the morning is so much o'erworn, 866
And yet she hears no tidings of her love.
She hearkens for his hounds and for his horn.
  Anon she hears them chant it lustily, 869
  And all in haste she coasteth to the cry. 870

And as she runs, the bushes in the way
Some catch her by the neck, some kiss her face,
Some twine about her thigh to make her stay.
She wildly breaketh from their strict embrace, 874
  Like a milch doe, whose swelling dugs do ache, 875
  Hasting to feed her fawn hid in some brake. 876

By this, she hears the hounds are at a bay, 877
Whereat she starts, like one that spies an adder
Wreathed up in fatal folds just in his way, 879
The fear whereof doth make him shake and shudder;
  Even so the timorous yelping of the hounds
  Appalls her senses and her spirit confounds.

For now she knows it is no gentle chase,
But the blunt boar, rough bear, or lion proud,
Because the cry remaineth in one place,
Where fearfully the dogs exclaim aloud.
  Finding their enemy to be so curst, 887
  They all strain court'sy who shall cope him first. 888

866 Musing wondering (that). **o'erworn** advanced **869 chant** i.e., sound **870 coasteth to** approaches **874 strict** tight **875 milch doe** female deer producing milk. **dugs** udders **876 brake** thicket **877 By this** by this time. **at a bay** i.e., faced by their quarry, which, being cornered, has turned to make its stand **879 folds** coils **887 curst** savage **888 strain court'sy** are punctiliously polite, stand upon ceremony; i.e., they hold back. **cope** cope with

This dismal cry rings sadly in her ear, 889
Through which it enters to surprise her heart, 890
Who, overcome by doubt and bloodless fear, 891
With cold-pale weakness numbs each feeling part. 892
  Like soldiers, when their captain once doth yield, 893
  They basely fly and dare not stay the field. 894

Thus stands she in a trembling ecstasy, 895
Till, cheering up her senses all dismayed,
She tells them 'tis a causeless fantasy 897
And childish error that they are afraid;
  Bids them leave quaking, bids them fear no more—
  And with that word she spied the hunted boar,

Whose frothy mouth, bepainted all with red,
Like milk and blood being mingled both together,
A second fear through all her sinews spread, 903
Which madly hurries her she knows not whither.
  This way she runs, and now she will no further,
  But back retires to rate the boar for murther. 906

A thousand spleens bear her a thousand ways; 907
She treads the path that she untreads again; 908
Her more than haste is mated with delays, 909
Like the proceedings of a drunken brain,
  Full of respects, yet naught at all respecting, 911
  In hand with all things, naught at all effecting. 912

889 dismal foreboding ill **890 surprise** assail suddenly **891 bloodless fear** i.e., fear that causes the blood to draw to the heart and desert the features, leaving one *cold, pale,* and *weak* (l. 892) **892 feeling part** bodily part and organ of sense **893 when . . . yield** once their commanding officer has yielded **894 stay the field** remain in the battlefield and stand against the onslaught **895 ecstasy** agitated state **897 them** i.e., her senses **903 sinews** nerves **906 rate** berate **907 spleens** impulses **908 untreads** retraces **909 mated** confounded, checked **911 respects** designs, considerations. **naught at all respecting** i.e., heedless **912 In hand with** busy about

Here kenneled in a brake she finds a hound, 913
And asks the weary caitiff for his master, 914
And there another licking of his wound,
'Gainst venomed sores the only sovereign plaster; 916
  And here she meets another sadly scowling,
  To whom she speaks, and he replies with howling.

When he hath ceased his ill-resounding noise,
Another flapmouthed mourner, black and grim, 920
Against the welkin volleys out his voice; 921
Another and another answer him,
  Clapping their proud tails to the ground below,
  Shaking their scratched ears, bleeding as they go.

Look how the world's poor people are amazed 925
At apparitions, signs, and prodigies,
Whereon with fearful eyes they long have gazed,
Infusing them with dreadful prophecies; 928
  So she at these sad signs draws up her breath
  And, sighing it again, exclaims on Death. 930

"Hard-favored tyrant, ugly, meager, lean,
Hateful divorce of love!"—thus chides she Death— 932
"Grim-grinning ghost, earth's worm, what dost thou
    mean 933
To stifle beauty and to steal his breath,
  Who, when he lived, his breath and beauty set
  Gloss on the rose, smell to the violet? 936

913 kenneled hiding as if in its kennel **914 caitiff** wretch **916 only sovereign plaster** best all-curing application **920 flapmouthed** having broad, hanging lips or jowls **921 welkin** sky **925 Look how** just as **928 Infusing them with** attributing to them. **prophecies** prophetic qualities **930 exclaims on** denounces **932 divorce** terminator **933 Grim-grinning** i.e., grinning like a skull. **worm** i.e., cankerworm, consumer of flowers (with the suggestion also of worms that devour corpses) **936 smell** i.e., and gave smell

"If he be dead—O no, it cannot be,
Seeing his beauty, thou shouldst strike at it! 938
O yes, it may; thou hast no eyes to see, 939
But hatefully at random dost thou hit.
Thy mark is feeble age, but thy false dart 941
Mistakes that aim and cleaves an infant's heart.

"Hadst thou but bid beware, then he had spoke, 943
And, hearing him, thy power had lost his power. 944
The Destinies will curse thee for this stroke;
They bid thee crop a weed, thou pluck'st a flower.
Love's golden arrow at him should have fled,
And not Death's ebon dart, to strike him dead. 948

"Dost thou drink tears, that thou provok'st such
weeping?
What may a heavy groan advantage thee?
Why hast thou cast into eternal sleeping
Those eyes that taught all other eyes to see?
Now Nature cares not for thy mortal vigor, 953
Since her best work is ruined with thy rigor." 954

Here overcome, as one full of despair,
She vailed her eyelids, who, like sluices, stopped 956
The crystal tide that from her two cheeks fair
In the sweet channel of her bosom dropped; 958
But through the floodgates breaks the silver rain,
And with his strong course opens them again. 960

938 Seeing i.e., that, seeing **939 no eyes** (The eye sockets of the skull of Death are empty.) **941 mark** target **943 bid beware** i.e., issued a warning of the approach of Death. **he** i.e., Adonis **944 his** its **948 ebon** ebony, black **953 cares . . . vigor** does not fear your deadly power **954 with** by **956 vailed** lowered. **who** which. **stopped** stopped up **958 channel** i.e., cleavage **960 his** its

O, how her eyes and tears did lend and borrow! 961
Her eye seen in the tears, tears in her eye,
Both crystals, where they viewed each other's sorrow, 963
Sorrow that friendly sighs sought still to dry; 964
But like a stormy day, now wind, now rain,
Sighs dry her cheeks, tears make them wet again.

Variable passions throng her constant woe,
As striving who should best become her grief. 968
All entertained, each passion labors so 969
That every present sorrow seemeth chief,
But none is best; then join they all together, 971
Like many clouds consulting for foul weather. 972

By this, far off she hears some huntsman hallow; 973
A nurse's song ne'er pleased her babe so well.
The dire imagination she did follow 975
This sound of hope doth labor to expel;
For now reviving joy bids her rejoice
And flatters her it is Adonis' voice.

Whereat her tears began to turn their tide, 979
Being prisoned in her eye like pearls in glass;
Yet sometimes falls an orient drop beside, 981
Which her cheek melts, as scorning it should pass, 982
To wash the foul face of the sluttish ground, 983
Who is but drunken when she seemeth drowned. 984

961 lend and borrow i.e., reflect each other **963 crystals** i.e., mirrors **964 friendly** i.e., consoling **968 As** as if. **who** which (passion). **become** suit **969 entertained** having been admitted **971 best** supreme **972 consulting for** cooperating to produce **973 By this** by this time. **hallow** halloo **975 follow** pursue in her thoughts **979 turn their tide** ebb **981 orient** shining. **beside** to one side **982 melts** i.e., dries. **as** as if **983 foul** dirty **984 Who . . . drowned** i.e., the sluttish earth would seem as though made drunk by her tears, which in her produce a more innocent effect of drowning

O hard-believing love, how strange it seems 985
Not to believe, and yet too credulous! 986
Thy weal and woe are both of them extremes.
Despair and hope makes thee ridiculous: 988
  The one doth flatter thee in thoughts unlikely, 989
  In likely thoughts the other kills thee quickly.

Now she unweaves the web that she hath wrought;
Adonis lives, and Death is not to blame;
It was not she that called him all to naught. 993
Now she adds honors to his hateful name:
  She clepes him king of graves and grave for kings, 995
  Imperious supreme of all mortal things. 996

"No, no," quoth she, "sweet Death, I did but jest.
Yet pardon me, I felt a kind of fear
Whenas I met the boar, that bloody beast, 999
Which knows no pity, but is still severe. 1000
  Then, gentle shadow—truth I must confess— 1001
  I railed on thee, fearing my love's decesse. 1002

"'Tis not my fault; the boar provoked my tongue.
Be wreaked on him, invisible commander. 1004
'Tis he, foul creature, that hath done thee wrong;
I did but act, he's author of thy slander. 1006
  Grief hath two tongues, and never woman yet 1007
  Could rule them both without ten women's wit."

985–986 O . . . credulous i.e., love is at once too skeptical and too credulous **988 Despair and hope** i.e., the rapid oscillation between despair and hope **989 The one** i.e., hope **993 all to naught** wholly evil **995 clepes** names, calls **996 Imperious supreme** imperial ruler **999 Whenas** when **1000 still severe** incessantly ruthless **1001 shadow** specter **1002 railed on** reviled. **decesse** decease **1004 wreaked** revenged. **invisible commander** i.e., Death, a specter that orders our final destiny **1006 act** i.e., act as agent **1007 two tongues** i.e., a double tongue, twice as loud and hard to control as a usual tongue. (Women are conventionally unable to rule their tongues in any case.)

Thus hoping that Adonis is alive,
Her rash suspect she doth extenuate; 1010
And that his beauty may the better thrive,
With Death she humbly doth insinuate; 1012
  Tells him of trophies, statues, tombs, and stories 1013
  His victories, his triumphs, and his glories.

"O Jove," quoth she, "how much a fool was I
To be of such a weak and silly mind
To wail his death who lives and must not die
Till mutual overthrow of mortal kind! 1018
  For, he being dead, with him is beauty slain,
  And, beauty dead, black chaos comes again.

"Fie, fie, fond love, thou art as full of fear 1021
As one with treasure laden, hemmed with thieves; 1022
Trifles, unwitnessèd with eye or ear, 1023
Thy coward heart with false bethinking grieves." 1024
  Even at this word she hears a merry horn,
  Whereat she leaps that was but late forlorn. 1026

As falcon to the lure, away she flies—
The grass stoops not, she treads on it so light—
And in her haste unfortunately spies
The foul boar's conquest on her fair delight;
  Which seen, her eyes, as murdered with the view, 1031
  Like stars ashamed of day, themselves withdrew; 1032

Or, as the snail, whose tender horns being hit,
Shrinks backward in his shelly cave with pain,
And there, all smothered up, in shade doth sit,
Long after fearing to creep forth again;
  So, at his bloody view, her eyes are fled
  Into the deep dark cabins of her head,

1010 rash suspect too hasty suspicion (of Death). **extenuate** excuse, make light of **1012 insinuate** ingratiate herself **1013 trophies** memorial monuments. **stories** narrates, relates **1018 mutual** i.e., universal **1021 fond** foolish **1022 hemmed with** hemmed about by **1023–1024 Trifles . . . grieves** mere trifles, not actually seen by eye or heard by ear, grieve your cowardly heart with false imaginings **1026 leaps** i.e., leaps for joy. **late** lately **1031 as** as if **1032 ashamed of** put to shame by. **withdrew** i.e., closed

Where they resign their office and their light
To the disposing of her troubled brain, 1040
Who bids them still consort with ugly night 1041
And never wound the heart with looks again— 1042
Who, like a king perplexèd in his throne, 1043
By their suggestion gives a deadly groan. 1044

Whereat each tributary subject quakes, 1045
As when the wind, imprisoned in the ground, 1046
Struggling for passage, earth's foundation shakes,
Which with cold terror doth men's minds confound.
This mutiny each part doth so surprise 1049
That from their dark beds once more leap her eyes;

And, being opened, threw unwilling light
Upon the wide wound that the boar had trenched
In his soft flank, whose wonted lily white 1053
With purple tears, that his wound wept, was drenched.
No flower was nigh, no grass, herb, leaf, or weed,
But stole his blood and seemed with him to bleed. 1056

This solemn sympathy poor Venus noteth.
Over one shoulder doth she hang her head.
Dumbly she passions, franticly she doteth; 1059
She thinks he could not die, he is not dead.
Her voice is stopped, her joints forget to bow; 1061
Her eyes are mad that they have wept till now. 1062

Upon his hurt she looks so steadfastly
That her sight, dazzling, makes the wound seem three; 1064
And then she reprehends her mangling eye,
That makes more gashes where no breach should be.
His face seems twain, each several limb is doubled;
For oft the eye mistakes, the brain being troubled.

1040 disposing direction, ordering **1041 still consort** always remain **1042 with looks** by looking **1043 Who** which, i.e., the heart **1044 By their suggestion** incited by the eyes **1045 tributary subject** i.e., subordinate part of the body **1046 wind . . . ground** (The common Elizabethan explanation of earthquakes; cf. *1 Henry IV,* 3.1.30.) **1049 surprise** attack suddenly **1053 wonted** customary **1056 But stole** that did not steal **1059 passions** shows grief **1061 forget to bow** are paralyzed (with grief) **1062 till now** before now (in a lesser cause) **1064 dazzling** being dazzled

"My tongue cannot express my grief for one,
And yet," quoth she, "behold two Adons dead!
My sighs are blown away, my salt tears gone;
Mine eyes are turned to fire, my heart to lead.
Heavy heart's lead, melt at mine eyes' red fire!
So shall I die by drops of hot desire. 1074

"Alas, poor world, what treasure hast thou lost!
What face remains alive that's worth the viewing?
Whose tongue is music now? What canst thou boast
Of things long since, or anything ensuing? 1078
The flowers are sweet, their colors fresh and trim,
But true sweet beauty lived and died with him.

"Bonnet nor veil henceforth no creature wear! 1081
Nor sun nor wind will ever strive to kiss you.
Having no fair to lose, you need not fear; 1083
The sun doth scorn you, and the wind doth hiss you.
But when Adonis lived, sun and sharp air
Lurked like two thieves, to rob him of his fair.

"And therefore would he put his bonnet on,
Under whose brim the gaudy sun would peep; 1088
The wind would blow it off and, being gone, 1089
Play with his locks. Then would Adonis weep;
And straight, in pity of his tender years, 1091
They both would strive who first should dry his tears.

"To see his face the lion walked along
Behind some hedge, because he would not fear him; 1094
To recreate himself when he hath song, 1095
The tiger would be tame and gently hear him;
If he had spoke, the wolf would leave his prey
And never fright the silly lamb that day. 1098

1074 So shall I die (Venus imagines a terrible death by melted lead.) **1078 Of . . . ensuing** past or to come **1081 Bonnet nor veil** neither hat nor veil (worn to guard a fair complexion, regarded as particularly beautiful, against the sun) **1083 fair** beauty. (Also in l. 1086.) **1088 gaudy** brilliantly shining **1089 being gone** it (the hat) being gone **1091 straight** at once **1094 would not fear** did not wish to frighten **1095 To recreate . . . song** whenever he sang for his own recreation **1098 silly** innocent

"When he beheld his shadow in the brook,
The fishes spread on it their golden gills;
When he was by, the birds such pleasure took
That some would sing, some other in their bills 1102
  Would bring him mulberries and ripe-red cherries;
  He fed them with his sight, they him with berries.

"But this foul, grim, and urchin-snouted boar, 1105
Whose downward eye still looketh for a grave, 1106
Ne'er saw the beauteous livery that he wore— 1107
Witness the entertainment that he gave. 1108
  If he did see his face, why then I know
  He thought to kiss him, and hath killed him so.

"'Tis true, 'tis true! Thus was Adonis slain:
He ran upon the boar with his sharp spear,
Who did not whet his teeth at him again, 1113
But by a kiss thought to persuade him there; 1114
  And, nuzzling in his flank, the loving swine
  Sheathed unaware the tusk in his soft groin.

"Had I been toothed like him, I must confess,
With kissing him I should have killed him first;
But he is dead, and never did he bless
My youth with his—the more am I accurst."
  With this, she falleth in the place she stood, 1121
  And stains her face with his congealèd blood.

1102 other others **1105 urchin-snouted** having a snout like a hedgehog
1106 still continually. **for a grave** i.e., as if for a grave in which to bury victims. (Compare l. 622, where the boar's snout *digs sepulchers* as it roots in the earth.) **1107 livery** i.e., outside appearance
1108 entertainment treatment, reception **1113 again** in return
1114 persuade win over, or persuade to stay **1121 place** place where

She looks upon his lips, and they are pale;
She takes him by the hand, and that is cold;
She whispers in his ears a heavy tale, 1125
As if they heard the woeful words she told;
She lifts the coffer-lids that close his eyes, 1127
Where, lo, two lamps, burnt out, in darkness lies;

Two glasses, where herself herself beheld 1129
A thousand times, and now no more reflect,
Their virtue lost, wherein they late excelled, 1131
And every beauty robbed of his effect. 1132
"Wonder of time," quoth she, "this is my spite, 1133
That, thou being dead, the day should yet be light.

"Since thou art dead, lo, here I prophesy:
Sorrow on love hereafter shall attend.
It shall be waited on with jealousy, 1137
Find sweet beginning but unsavory end,
Ne'er settled equally, but high or low, 1139
That all love's pleasure shall not match his woe. 1140

"It shall be fickle, false, and full of fraud,
Bud and be blasted in a breathing while; 1142
The bottom poison, and the top o'erstrawed 1143
With sweets that shall the truest sight beguile.
The strongest body shall it make most weak,
Strike the wise dumb and teach the fool to speak.

1125 heavy sad **1127 coffer-lids** lids covering chests of treasure, i.e., eyelids **1129 glasses** mirrors **1131 virtue** power (to see and to reflect) **1132 his** its **1133 time** i.e., the ages, human existence. **spite** torment, vexation **1137 It** love. **with** by **1139 Ne'er . . . low** i.e., (love will be) never equal between the two lovers; they will be from high and low social stations **1140 his** its **1142 blasted** blighted. **breathing while** i.e., short time **1143 The bottom** i.e., the substance, what is inside. **top** surface. **o'erstrawed** strewn over

"It shall be sparing and too full of riot, 1147
Teaching decrepit age to tread the measures; 1148
The staring ruffian shall it keep in quiet, 1149
Pluck down the rich, enrich the poor with treasures;
It shall be raging mad and silly mild, 1151
Make the young old, the old become a child.

"It shall suspect where is no cause of fear; 1153
It shall not fear where it should most mistrust;
It shall be merciful and too severe,
And most deceiving when it seems most just; 1156
Perverse it shall be where it shows most toward, 1157
Put fear to valor, courage to the coward.

"It shall be cause of war and dire events
And set dissension twixt the son and sire,
Subject and servile to all discontents, 1161
As dry combustious matter is to fire.
Sith in his prime Death doth my love destroy, 1163
They that love best their loves shall not enjoy."

By this, the boy that by her side lay killed 1165
Was melted like a vapor from her sight,
And in his blood that on the ground lay spilled
A purple flow'r sprung up, checkered with white, 1168
Resembling well his pale cheeks and the blood
Which in round drops upon their whiteness stood.

1147 sparing . . . riot i.e., both niggardly and excessive **1148 tread the measures** dance. (An inappropriate action for the old.) **1149 staring** looking savage, glaring **1151 silly** innocently **1153 is** there is **1156 just** trustworthy **1157 Perverse** stubborn, contrary. **toward** tractable **1161 Subject . . . discontents** (love will be) both the cause and the unwilling slave of every kind of dissension **1163 Sith** since **1165 By this** by this time **1168 flow'r** i.e., anemone

She bows her head, the new-sprung flower to smell,
Comparing it to her Adonis' breath,
And says within her bosom it shall dwell,
Since he himself is reft from her by death. 1174
  She crops the stalk, and in the breach appears
  Green dropping sap, which she compares to tears.

"Poor flower," quoth she, "this was thy father's
    guise— 1177
Sweet issue of a more sweet-smelling sire— 1178
For every little grief to wet his eyes; 1179
To grow unto himself was his desire, 1180
  And so 'tis thine; but know, it is as good
  To wither in my breast as in his blood.

"Here was thy father's bed, here in my breast;
Thou art the next of blood, and 'tis thy right.
Lo, in this hollow cradle take thy rest;
My throbbing heart shall rock thee day and night.
  There shall not be one minute in an hour
  Wherein I will not kiss my sweet love's flower."

Thus weary of the world, away she hies
And yokes her silver doves, by whose swift aid
Their mistress, mounted, through the empty skies 1191
In her light chariot quickly is conveyed, 1192
  Holding their course to Paphos, where their queen 1193
  Means to immure herself and not be seen.

1174 reft bereft **1177 guise** manner, way **1178 Sweet issue** i.e., you, the anemone, who are the sweet offspring **1179 For . . . eyes** i.e., to weep compassionately at every little sorrow **1180 To grow unto himself** i.e., to mature self-made and independent **1191–1192 mounted . . . conveyed** is quickly conveyed, mounted in her light chariot, through the empty skies **1193 Paphos** Venus' dwelling in Cyprus

Date and Text

On April 18, 1593, "a booke intituled, Venus and Adonis" was entered to Richard Field in the Stationers' Register, the official record book of the London Company of Stationers (booksellers and printers), and was published by him the same year. The quarto contains a dedication written by Shakespeare to the Earl of Southampton. The text seems to have been carefully supervised through the press, and based on the author's manuscript. The poem was very popular, and was reprinted nine times before Shakespeare's death. The First Folio of 1623, being limited to plays, did not include it or any other nondramatic poems. Contemporary references are numerous: Francis Meres and Richard Barnfield in 1598, Gabriel Harvey in 1598–1601, and John Weever in 1599, among others. Shakespeare probably wrote this poem shortly before its publication, since his intention was to present it to Southampton. The theaters closed from June 1592 to May 1594, giving Shakespeare a period of enforced leisure in which to write poetry.

Textual Notes

These textual notes are not a historical collation; they are simply a record of departures in this edition from the copy text. The reading adopted in this edition appears in boldface, followed by the rejected reading from the copy text, i.e., the quarto of 1593. Only major alterations in punctuation are noted. Corrections of minor and obvious typographical errors are not indicated.

Copy text: the quarto of 1593.

185 Souring So wring **304 whe'er** where **457 marketh.** marketh, **458 raineth,** raineth: **570 woos** woes **601 as** so **680 overshoot** ouer-shut **748 th'** the th' **873 twine** twin'd **1013 stories** stories, **1027 falcon** Faulcons **1031 as** are **1054 was** had

THE RAPE
OF
LUCRECE

Introduction

The Rape of Lucrece is closely related to *Venus and Adonis.* The two were published about a year apart, in 1593 and 1594, both printed by Richard Field. Both are dedicated to the young Earl of Southampton, Henry Wriothesley, whose confidence and friendship Shakespeare appears to have gained during the interim between the two poems; the dedicatory preface to *The Rape of Lucrece* expresses assurance that the poem will be accepted. Stylistically the two poems are of a piece, alike reliant on Petrarchan ornament and rhetorical showmanship, alike steeped in Ovidian pathos. Yet they are complementary rather than similar in attitude and subject. *The Rape of Lucrece* appears to be the "graver labor" promised to Southampton in the dedication of the earlier poem, a planned sequel in which love would be subjected to a darker treatment. *Venus and Adonis* is chiefly about sensual pleasure, whereas *The Rape of Lucrece* is about heroic chastity. The first poem is amatory, erotic, and amusing despite its sad end; the second is moral, declamatory, and lugubrious. As Gabriel Harvey observed (c. 1598–1601), "The younger sort takes much delight in Shakespeare's *Venus and Adonis,* but his *Lucrece* and his *Tragedy of Hamlet, Prince of Denmark* have it in them to please the wiser sort."

Harvey's pairing of this poem with *Hamlet* suggests that, to Harvey at least, Shakespeare aspires to sublime effects in *Lucrece.* For his verse pattern Shakespeare chooses the seven-line rhyme royal stanza, traditionally used for tragic expression, as in Geoffrey Chaucer's *Troilus and Criseyde* and several of the more formal *Canterbury Tales,* in John Lydgate's *The Fall of Princes* (1430–1438) and its continuation in *A Mirror for Magistrates* (1559), in Samuel Daniel's *The Complaint of Rosamond,* and others. Although Shakespeare turns to Ovid once again as his chief source, he chooses a tale of ravishment, suicide, and vengeance rather than one of titillating amatory pursuit. The story of Lucrece had gained wide currency in the ancient and medieval worlds as an exemplum of chaste conduct in women. Shakespeare seems to have known Livy's *History of Rome* (Book 1, chaps. 57–59), though he relied primarily on Ovid's *Fasti* (2, 721–852). Among later versions he may have known Chaucer's *The Legend of Good Women* and a translation of Livy in William Painter's *The Palace of Pleasure* (1566, 1575). He encountered other "complaints" in *A Mirror for Magistrates* and in Daniel's *The Complaint of Rosamond,* and it is to this well-established genre that *Lucrece* belongs. The poem had the desired effect of enhancing Shakespeare's reputation for elegant poetry; it was reprinted five times during his lifetime and was frequently admired by his contemporaries. *Venus and Adonis* was, to be sure, more popular still (it was reprinted nine times during Shakespeare's lifetime), but no one in Shakespeare's day seems to have regarded *Lucrece* as anything other than a noble work.

To understand the poem in terms of its own generic sense of form, we must recognize its conventions and not expect it to be other than what it professes to be. As in *Venus and Adonis,* plot and character are secondary. Although the story outlined in "The Argument" is potentially sensational and swift-moving, Shakespeare deliberately cuts away most of the action. We do not see Lucius Tarquinius' murder of his father-in-law and tyrannical seizure of Rome, or Collatinus' rash boasting of his wife Lucrece's virtue in the presence of the King's lustful son Sextus Tarquinius. Nor, at the conclusion of the story, do we learn much about the avenging of Lucrece's rape. Shakespeare's focus is on the attitudes of the two protagonists immediately before and after the ravishment. Even here, despite opportunities for psychological probing, Shakespeare's real interest is not in the characters themselves so much as in the social ramifications of their actions. As Coppélia Kahn has shown (in *Shakespeare Studies* 9), the rape serves as a means of examining the nature of marriage in a patriarchal society where competition for ownership and struggles for power characterize men's attitudes toward politics and sex. Using Rome as a familiar mirror for English customs, Shakespeare presents Lucrece as a heroine acting to uphold the institution of marriage. It is she who acquires the stain through being violated and she who must pay the cost of wifely duty in marriage. Like a number of Shakespeare's later heroines, such as Imogen in *Cymbeline,* Lucrece is portrayed as beautiful but not alluring, restrained even in her marriage bed. She arranges her death so as to make the most of its social implications.

Along with his interest in patriarchy and violence, Shakespeare frames the story of *The Rape of Lucrece* in terms of the political events that lead to the founding of the Roman republic. The corruption of the Tarquins raises issues about Roman values generally, and the poem ends with a strong repudiation of the old order. The villain of the poem is at once rapist and tyrant; the resolution is both a vindication of women as victims and a movement toward republicanism. To be sure, the patriarchy that has dictated the conditions of Lucrece's life and honor will remain intact in the republic; the wife is still her husband's possession, and her greatest obligation to state and family must be to ensure that the husband's honor remains unbesmirched. Nonetheless, the assumptions of Roman hierarchy have been held up to scrutiny.

Shakespeare casts his narrative in the form of a series of rhetorical disputations, each a set piece presented as a debate or as a formal declamation. The debates are built around familiar antitheses: honor versus lust, rude will versus conscience, "affection" versus reason, nobility versus baseness, and so on. Many of the images are similarly arranged in contrasting pairs: dove and owl, daylight and darkness, clear and cloudy weather, white and red. Tarquin debates with himself the reasons for and against rape; Lucrece tries to persuade him of the depravity of his course; Lucrece ponders suicide. These debates generate in turn a number of rhetorical apostrophes to marital fidelity (ll. 22–28), to the ideal of kingship as a moral example to others (ll. 610–637), to Night (ll. 764–812), to Opportunity (ll. 876–924), and to Time (ll. 925–1022). Another rhetorical formula, perhaps the most successful in the poem, is the use of structural digression. The most notable describes a painting of Troy with obvious relevance to Lucrece's sad fate: Troy is a city destroyed by a rape, Paris achieves his selfish pleasure at the expense of the public good, Sinon wins his sinister victory through deceitful appearance.

Throughout, the poem's ornament strives after heightened and elaborate effects. The comparisons, or "conceits" as the Elizabethans called them, are intentionally contrived and reliant on ingenious wordplay. Shakespeare puns on the word "will," for example, as he does in the Sonnets, where he takes advantage of his own first name being Will (see Sonnet 135), and in *Venus and Adonis* (see ll. 365, 369). In *The Rape of Lucrece,* the word is central to Shakespeare's depiction of Tarquin, as we see the ravisher holding a disputation between "frozen conscience and hot-burning will" (l. 247), forcing the locks "between her chamber and his will" (l. 302), feeding ravenously "in his will his willful eye" (l. 417), and the like. These and other passages often frame the word in a polarity of "will" and "heart," and range over numerous meanings that include inclination, desire, appetite, sexual lust, request or command, volition, pleasure, permission, good will, spontaneity. The fact that the word rhymes with "kill" and "ill" adds to its usefulness. Another kind of "conceit" found throughout *The Rape of Lucrece*—one that arises integrally from the poem's deepest concerns—is the extended military metaphor of a city under siege. Tarquin's heart beats an alarum, Lucrece's breasts are "round turrets" made pale by the assault (ll. 432–441), and, in her subsequent death, she is likened to a "late-sacked island" surrounded by rivers of her own blood (l. 1740). Elsewhere she is a house that has been pillaged, "Her mansion battered by the enemy" (ll. 1170–1171). Classical allusions are of course common, notably to the story of the rape of Philomel or Philomela (ll. 1079, 1128, etc.). Rhetorical devices of antithesis are displayed with the same ornate versatility as in *Venus and Adonis.* In a poem on a serious subject, these devices may seem overly contrived to us. We should nevertheless recognize them as conventional in the genre to which *The Rape of Lucrece* belongs. We find a similar blending of the sensuous and the moral in the sometimes grotesque conceits of the Catholic poet Robert Southwell (d. 1595) and in the later baroque paradoxes of Richard Crashaw (d. 1649). Among Shakespeare's dramatic works, *Titus Andronicus* seems closest to *The Rape of Lucrece* in its pathos, refined sensationalism, and use of classical allusion and specifically in the character of Lavinia, whose misfortunes and chaste dignity so much resemble those of Lucrece.

Throughout *The Rape of Lucrece,* we find a consciousness of the poem's own artistry. In Lucrece's tragic plight, Shakespeare explores art's ability to articulate through its various means of expression. Especially in the long passage on the painting of the fall of Troy (ll. 1366–1568), Lucrece shows an understandable anxiety about art's ability to deceive. The painting is in some ways more realistic than life itself; the figures in the painting seem to move and are so cunningly rendered that they "mock the mind" (l. 1414). The imaginary work is "Conceit deceitful" (l. 1423), able through synecdoche (using the part to represent the whole) to suggest a series of general truths lying behind the particulars that are shown. This power of art to deceive is most troublesome in the case of Sinon, the betrayer of Troy—"In him the painter labored with his skill / To hide deceit" (ll. 1506–1507)—and has succeeded with such devastating effect that the viewer cannot tell from Sinon's mild appearance that he is in fact capable of limitless evil. In his capacity for deception, Sinon is like Tarquin, the seemingly attractive courtier who has ravaged Lucrece. Art is thus capable of misrepresentation for purposes of evil; its persuasive power, its imaginative vision, can be perverted to wrong ends. Seen through such art, Rome too is at once a great source of civilization and a nation whose values are cast seriously in doubt. *The Rape of Lucrece* thus grapples with issues of serious consequence, ones that also concerned Shakespeare in his early plays (such as *Titus Andronicus*) and indeed throughout his career as dramatist.

The Rape of Lucrece

To the RIGHT HONORABLE HENRY WRIOTHESLEY,
Earl of Southampton, and Baron of Titchfield.

The love I dedicate to your lordship is without end; whereof this pamphlet without beginning is 2 but a superfluous moiety. The warrant I have of 3 your honorable disposition, not the worth of my untutored lines, makes it assured of acceptance. What I have done is yours; what I have to do is yours; being part in all I have, devoted yours. 7 Were my worth greater, my duty would show greater; meantime, as it is, it is bound to your lordship, to whom I wish long life still length- 10 ened with all happiness.

Your lordship's in all duty,

William Shakespeare.

THE ARGUMENT

Lucius Tarquinius, for his excessive pride surnamed Superbus, after he had caused his own father-in-law 2 Servius Tullius to be cruelly murdered and, contrary to the Roman laws and customs, not requiring or 4 staying for the people's suffrages, had possessed 5

Dedication.
2 without beginning i.e., beginning *in medias res,* in the middle of the action **3 moiety** part. **warrant** assurance **7 being . . . have** since you are part of everything I have done and have to do **10 still** continually

The Argument.
2 Superbus "the Proud" **4 requiring** requesting **5 suffrages** consent

himself of the kingdom, went, accompanied with his sons and other noblemen of Rome, to besiege Ardea. During which siege, the principal men of the army meeting one evening at the tent of Sextus Tarquinius, the King's son, in their discourses after supper everyone commended the virtues of his own wife; among whom Collatinus extolled the incomparable chastity of his wife Lucretia. In that pleasant 13 humor they all posted to Rome; and intending, by 14 their secret and sudden arrival, to make trial of that which everyone had before avouched, only Colla- 16 tinus finds his wife, though it were late in the night, spinning amongst her maids; the other ladies were all found dancing and reveling, or in several dis- 19 ports. Whereupon the noblemen yielded Collatinus 20 the victory and his wife the fame. At that time Sextus Tarquinius, being inflamed with Lucrece's beauty, yet smothering his passions for the present, departed with the rest back to the camp; from whence he shortly after privily withdrew himself, and was, 25 according to his estate, royally entertained and 26 lodged by Lucrece at Collatium. The same night he treacherously stealeth into her chamber, violently ravished her, and early in the morning speedeth away. Lucrece, in this lamentable plight, hastily dispatcheth messengers, one to Rome for her father, another to the camp for Collatine. They came, the one accompanied with Junius Brutus, the other with Publius Valerius; and finding Lucrece attired in mourning habit, demanded the cause of her sorrow. 35 She, first taking an oath of them for her revenge, revealed the actor and whole manner of his dealing, 37 and withal suddenly stabbed herself. Which done, with one consent they all vowed to root out the whole hated family of the Tarquins; and, bearing the dead body to Rome, Brutus acquainted the people with the doer and manner of the vile deed, with a bitter invective against the tyranny of the King,

13 pleasant merry **14 posted** hastened **16 avouched** affirmed **19–20 several disports** various pastimes **25 privily** secretly **26 estate** rank **35 habit** attire **37 actor** doer

wherewith the people were so moved that with one consent and a general acclamation the Tarquins were all exiled and the state government changed from kings to consuls.

From the besiegèd Ardea all in post, 1
Borne by the trustless wings of false desire, 2
Lust-breathèd Tarquin leaves the Roman host, 3
And to Collatium bears the lightless fire 4
Which, in pale embers hid, lurks to aspire 5
And girdle with embracing flames the waist
Of Collatine's fair love, Lucrece the chaste.

Haply that name of "chaste" unhapp'ly set 8
This bateless edge on his keen appetite, 9
When Collatine unwisely did not let 10
To praise the clear unmatchèd red and white
Which triumphed in that sky of his delight, 12
Where mortal stars, as bright as heaven's beauties, 13
With pure aspects did him peculiar duties. 14

For he the night before, in Tarquin's tent,
Unlocked the treasure of his happy state; 16
What priceless wealth the heavens had him lent
In the possession of his beauteous mate;
Reck'ning his fortune at such high proud rate 19
That kings might be espousèd to more fame,
But king nor peer to such a peerless dame.

1 Ardea a city twenty-four miles south of Rome. **post** haste **2 trustless** treacherous **3 Lust-breathèd** excited by lust **4 Collatium** a city about ten miles east of Rome. **lightless** i.e., smoldering invisibly **5 aspire** rise, i.e., break into flames **8 Haply** perchance. **unhapp'ly** (1) unhappily (2) by mischance **9 bateless** not to be blunted **10 let** forbear **12 sky** i.e., Lucrece's face **13 mortal stars** i.e., Lucrece's eyes **14 aspects** (1) looks (2) astrologically favorable position. **peculiar** exclusively for him **16 Unlocked the treasure** i.e., opened and revealed (in conversation) the riches **19 high proud** making him highly proud

O happiness enjoyed but of a few!
And, if possessed, as soon decayed and done 23
As is the morning silver melting dew
Against the golden splendor of the sun!
An expired date, canceled ere well begun. 26
  Honor and beauty in the owner's arms
  Are weakly fortressed from a world of harms.

Beauty itself doth of itself persuade 29
The eyes of men without an orator;
What needeth then apology be made
To set forth that which is so singular?
Or why is Collatine the publisher
  Of that rich jewel he should keep unknown
  From thievish ears, because it is his own?

Perchance his boast of Lucrece's sovereignty 36
Suggested this proud issue of a king; 37
For by our ears our hearts oft tainted be.
Perchance that envy of so rich a thing, 39
Braving compare, disdainfully did sting 40
  His high-pitched thoughts, that meaner men should
    vaunt 41
  That golden hap which their superiors want. 42

But some untimely thought did instigate
His all too timeless speed, if none of those. 44
His honor, his affairs, his friends, his state, 45
Neglected all, with swift intent he goes
To quench the coal which in his liver glows. 47
  O rash false heat, wrapped in repentant cold,
  Thy hasty spring still blasts and ne'er grows old! 49

23 done done with **26 date** period of time **29 of itself** by its own nature **36 sovereignty** supremacy **37 Suggested** tempted. **issue** offspring, son (i.e., Tarquin) **39 Perchance that** i.e., perhaps it was that **40 Braving compare** defying comparison **41 meaner** less nobly born **42 hap** fortune. **want** lack **44 timeless** unseemly, unseasonable **45 state** position **47 liver** (Regarded as the seat of the passions.) **49 blasts** is blighted (by cold winds)

When at Collatium this false lord arrived,
Well was he welcomed by the Roman dame,
Within whose face beauty and virtue strived
Which of them both should underprop her fame.
When virtue bragged, beauty would blush for shame;
  When beauty boasted blushes, in despite
  Virtue would stain that o'er with silver white.

But beauty, in that white entitulèd 57
From Venus' doves, doth challenge that fair field. 58
Then virtue claims from beauty beauty's red,
Which virtue gave the golden age to gild 60
Their silver cheeks, and called it then their shield,
  Teaching them thus to use it in the fight,
  When shame assailed, the red should fence the white. 63

This heraldry in Lucrece' face was seen,
Argued by beauty's red and virtue's white. 65
Of either's color was the other queen,
Proving from world's minority their right. 67
Yet their ambition makes them still to fight, 68
  The sovereignty of either being so great
  That oft they interchange each other's seat.

This silent war of lilies and of roses,
Which Tarquin viewed in her fair face's field,
In their pure ranks his traitor eye encloses, 73
Where, lest between them both it should be killed,
The coward captive vanquishèd doth yield
  To those two armies that would let him go,
  Rather than triumph in so false a foe.

57 entitulèd entitled, having a claim **58 doves** (Venus' chariot was drawn by white doves.) **challenge** claim. **field** (1) battlefield (2) the surface of the shield, where the armorial device is displayed **60 gild** i.e., cover with a blush of modesty. (Gold and red were often considered interchangeable as colors.) **63 fence** defend **65 Argued** disputed, and demonstrated **67 world's minority** the long-ago *golden age*, mentioned in l. 60 (i.e., their right is as old as the doves of Venus and the first blush) **68 still** always **73 encloses** surrounds, overwhelms

Now thinks he that her husband's shallow tongue,
The niggard prodigal that praised her so, 79
In that high task hath done her beauty wrong,
Which far exceeds his barren skill to show.
Therefore that praise which Collatine doth owe 82
  Enchanted Tarquin answers with surmise, 83
  In silent wonder of still-gazing eyes.

This earthly saint, adorèd by this devil,
Little suspecteth the false worshiper,
For unstained thoughts do seldom dream on evil;
Birds never limed no secret bushes fear. 88
So, guiltless, she securely gives good cheer 89
  And reverend welcome to her princely guest,
  Whose inward ill no outward harm expressed.

For that he colored with his high estate, 92
Hiding base sin in pleats of majesty, 93
That nothing in him seemed inordinate 94
Save sometimes too much wonder of his eye,
Which, having all, all could not satisfy;
  But, poorly rich, so wanteth in his store 97
  That, cloyed with much, he pineth still for more.

But she, that never coped with stranger eyes, 99
Could pick no meaning from their parling looks, 100
Nor read the subtle shining secrecies
Writ in the glassy margins of such books. 102
She touched no unknown baits, nor feared no hooks;
  Nor could she moralize his wanton sight 104
  More than his eyes were opened to the light. 105

79 niggard prodigal unwisely lavish yet coming too short in praise **82 doth owe** i.e., must still render, having fallen short on previous occasions **83 answers** renders. **surmise** visual contemplation **88 limed** snared with birdlime, a sticky substance placed on branches **89 securely** unsuspiciously **92 that he colored** i.e., he disguised his harmful intent **93 pleats** cunning folds, concealments **94 That** so that **97 so . . . store** feels such a craving despite the abundance **99 stranger eyes** eyes of a stranger **100 parling** speaking, conferring **102 glassy . . . books** (Refers to the custom of printing explanatory comments in book margins; cf. *Romeo and Juliet,* 1.3.87.) **104 moralize** interpret. **sight** looking **105 than** than that

He stories to her ears her husband's fame, 106
Won in the fields of fruitful Italy,
And decks with praises Collatine's high name,
Made glorious by his manly chivalry
With bruisèd arms and wreaths of victory. 110
  Her joy with heaved-up hand she doth express
  And, wordless, so greets heaven for his success.

Far from the purpose of his coming thither
He makes excuses for his being there.
No cloudy show of stormy blustering weather
Doth yet in his fair welkin once appear, 116
Till sable Night, mother of dread and fear, 117
  Upon the world dim darkness doth display
  And in her vaulty prison stows the day.

For then is Tarquin brought unto his bed,
Intending weariness with heavy sprite; 121
For, after supper, long he questionèd 122
With modest Lucrece, and wore out the night.
Now leaden slumber with life's strength doth fight,
  And everyone to rest himself betakes,
  Save thieves and cares and troubled minds that
    wakes.

As one of which doth Tarquin lie revolving 127
The sundry dangers of his will's obtaining; 128
Yet ever to obtain his will resolving,
Though weak-built hopes persuade him to abstaining.
Despair to gain doth traffic oft for gaining; 131
  And when great treasure is the meed proposed, 132
  Though death be adjunct, there's no death supposed. 133

106 stories relates **110 bruisèd arms** armor battered in combat **116 welkin** sky, i.e., appearance, face **117 sable** black **121 Intending** pretending. **sprite** spirit **122 questionèd** conversed **127 revolving** considering **128 his will's obtaining** obtaining his will **131 Despair . . . gaining** i.e., even a despairing hope often perversely undertakes to venture for gain; or, despair of success again and again changes place with a will to succeed **132 meed** reward **133 adjunct** adjoined, resultant. **supposed** thought of

Those that much covet are with gain so fond 134
That what they have not, that which they possess 135
They scatter and unloose it from their bond, 136
And so, by hoping more, they have but less;
Or, gaining more, the profit of excess 138
  Is but to surfeit, and such griefs sustain 139
  That they prove bankrupt in this poor-rich gain.

The aim of all is but to nurse the life
With honor, wealth, and ease in waning age;
And in this aim there is such thwarting strife 143
That one for all or all for one we gage: 144
As life for honor in fell battle's rage, 145
  Honor for wealth; and oft that wealth doth cost
  The death of all, and all together lost.

So that in venturing ill we leave to be 148
The things we are for that which we expect; 149
And this ambitious foul infirmity, 150
In having much, torments us with defect 151
Of that we have. So then we do neglect
  The thing we have, and all for want of wit 153
  Make something nothing by augmenting it.

Such hazard now must doting Tarquin make,
Pawning his honor to obtain his lust,
And for himself himself he must forsake. 157
Then where is truth, if there be no self-trust?
When shall he think to find a stranger just,
  When he himself himself confounds, betrays
  To slanderous tongues and wretched hateful days?

134 fond infatuated **135 what** for what **136 bond** possession **138 profit of excess** advantage of having more than enough **139 such griefs sustain** i.e., to sustain such griefs as accompany surfeit **143 And** yet **144 gage** stake, risk **145 As** such as. **fell** fierce **148 leave to be** cease being **149 expect** i.e., hope to be **150 infirmity** i.e., covetousness **151 In having much** though we have much. **defect** the imagined deficiency **153 want of wit** lack of common sense **157 for . . . forsake** i.e., he must forsake his honorable self to satisfy his lustful self

Now stole upon the time the dead of night,
When heavy sleep had closed up mortal eyes.
No comfortable star did lend his light, 164
No noise but owls' and wolves' death-boding cries.
Now serves the season that they may surprise
The silly lambs. Pure thoughts are dead and still, 167
While lust and murder wakes to stain and kill.

And now this lustful lord leapt from his bed,
Throwing his mantle rudely o'er his arm;
Is madly tossed between desire and dread;
Th' one sweetly flatters, th' other feareth harm;
But honest fear, bewitched with lust's foul charm,
Doth too too oft betake him to retire, 174
Beaten away by brainsick rude desire.

His falchion on a flint he softly smiteth, 176
That from the cold stone sparks of fire do fly;
Whereat a waxen torch forthwith he lighteth,
Which must be lodestar to his lustful eye; 179
And to the flame thus speaks advisedly: 180
"As from this cold flint I enforced this fire,
So Lucrece must I force to my desire."

Here pale with fear he doth premeditate
The dangers of his loathsome enterprise,
And in his inward mind he doth debate
What following sorrow may on this arise.
Then, looking scornfully, he doth despise
His naked armor of still-slaughtered lust, 188
And justly thus controls his thoughts unjust: 189

164 comfortable cheering, benevolent. **his** its **167 silly** helpless, defenseless **174 betake . . . retire** i.e., (honest fear) retires in confusion. **him** himself **176 falchion** curved sword **179 lodestar** the guiding polestar **180 advisedly** deliberately **188 His . . . lust** his poor defense against his own lust, which is continually being slaughtered, i.e., temporarily satiated, but never killed; or, his insatiable and vulnerable lust, which will be his only poor armor once he has committed the rape **189 justly** accurately, closely

"Fair torch, burn out thy light, and lend it not
To darken her whose light excelleth thine;
And die, unhallowed thoughts, before you blot
With your uncleanness that which is divine.
Offer pure incense to so pure a shrine.
  Let fair humanity abhor the deed
  That spots and stains love's modest snow-white weed. 196

"O shame to knighthood and to shining arms!
O foul dishonor to my household's grave! 198
O impious act, including all foul harms! 199
A martial man to be soft fancy's slave! 200
True valor still a true respect should have; 201
  Then my digression is so vile, so base, 202
  That it will live engraven in my face.

"Yea, though I die, the scandal will survive
And be an eyesore in my golden coat; 205
Some loathsome dash the herald will contrive 206
To cipher me how fondly I did dote; 207
That my posterity, shamed with the note, 208
  Shall curse my bones, and hold it for no sin
  To wish that I their father had not been.

"What win I, if I gain the thing I seek?
A dream, a breath, a froth of fleeting joy.
Who buys a minute's mirth to wail a week?
Or sells eternity to get a toy? 214
For one sweet grape who will the vine destroy?
  Or what fond beggar, but to touch the crown,
  Would with the scepter straight be strucken down? 217

196 weed garment (i.e., chastity) **198 my household's grave** memorial tomb of my forebears **199 including** encompassing **200 fancy's** love's, infatuation's **201 true respect** i.e., proper consideration for virtue **202 digression** falling away (from honor) **205 coat** coat of arms **206 dash** bar, stroke (devised by the heralds to indicate something dishonorable in the pedigree) **207 cipher** express in characters, indicate. **fondly** foolishly **208 note** stigma, the heraldic bar (l. 206) **214 toy** trifle **217 straight** at once

"If Collatinus dream of my intent,
Will he not wake and in a desperate rage
Post hither, this vile purpose to prevent? 220
This siege that hath engirt his marriage, 221
This blur to youth, this sorrow to the sage,
  This dying virtue, this surviving shame,
  Whose crime will bear an ever-during blame? 224

"O, what excuse can my invention make
When thou shalt charge me with so black a deed?
Will not my tongue be mute, my frail joints shake,
Mine eyes forgo their light, my false heart bleed? 228
The guilt being great, the fear doth still exceed;
  And extreme fear can neither fight nor fly,
  But cowardlike with trembling terror die.

"Had Collatinus killed my son or sire,
Or lain in ambush to betray my life,
Or were he not my dear friend, this desire
Might have excuse to work upon his wife,
As in revenge or quittal of such strife; 236
  But as he is my kinsman, my dear friend,
  The shame and fault finds no excuse nor end.

"Shameful it is; ay, if the fact be known, 239
Hateful it is. There is no hate in loving.
I'll beg her love. But she is not her own. 241
The worst is but denial and reproving.
My will is strong, past reason's weak removing.
  Who fears a sentence or an old man's saw 244
  Shall by a painted cloth be kept in awe." 245

220 Post hasten **221 engirt** engirdled, as in a siege **224 ever-during** everlasting **228 forgo their light** lose their power of vision **236 quittal** requital **239 fact** deed **241 she . . . own** i.e., she is not entirely independent, since she has duties to her husband **244 Who** whoever. **sentence** moral sentiment. **saw** saying, proverb **245 painted cloth** wall hanging in which moral tales and maxims were sometimes depicted. (Cf. ll. 1366–1456, where such a painted cloth is described.)

Thus, graceless, holds he disputation 246
'Tween frozen conscience and hot-burning will,
And with good thoughts makes dispensation, 248
Urging the worser sense for vantage still,
Which in a moment doth confound and kill
  All pure effects, and doth so far proceed 251
  That what is vile shows like a virtuous deed.

Quoth he, "She took me kindly by the hand
And gazed for tidings in my eager eyes,
Fearing some hard news from the warlike band
Where her belovèd Collatinus lies.
O, how her fear did make her color rise!
  First red as roses that on lawn we lay, 258
  Then white as lawn, the roses took away.

"And how her hand, in my hand being locked,
Forced it to tremble with her loyal fear!
Which struck her sad, and then it faster rocked,
Until her husband's welfare she did hear;
Whereat she smilèd with so sweet a cheer
  That had Narcissus seen her as she stood 265
  Self-love had never drowned him in the flood.

"Why hunt I then for color or excuses? 267
All orators are dumb when beauty pleadeth;
Poor wretches have remorse in poor abuses; 269
Love thrives not in the heart that shadows dreadeth. 270
Affection is my captain, and he leadeth; 271
  And when his gaudy banner is displayed,
  The coward fights and will not be dismayed. 273

246 graceless lacking in social and divine grace **248 makes dispensation** dispenses, sets aside **251 effects** impulses **258 lawn** fine white linen **265 Narcissus** youth who fell in love with his own reflection in the water (but who would have fallen in love with Lucrece if he had seen her) **267 color** pretext **269 Poor . . . abuses** i.e., only lowborn cowardly men feel remorse for their paltry misdeeds **270 shadows** i.e., the chimeras of conscience **271 Affection** passion **273 The coward** i.e., even the coward

"Then, childish fear, avaunt! Debating, die! 274
Respect and reason, wait on wrinkled age! 275
My heart shall never countermand mine eye. 276
Sad pause and deep regard beseems the sage; 277
My part is youth, and beats these from the stage.
 Desire my pilot is, beauty my prize;
 Then who fears sinking where such treasure lies?"

As corn o'ergrown by weeds, so heedful fear 281
Is almost choked by unresisted lust.
Away he steals with open listening ear,
Full of foul hope and full of fond mistrust, 284
Both which, as servitors to the unjust,
 So cross him with their opposite persuasion 286
 That now he vows a league, and now invasion. 287

Within his thought her heavenly image sits,
And in the selfsame seat sits Collatine.
That eye which looks on her confounds his wits; 290
That eye which him beholds, as more divine, 291
Unto a view so false will not incline,
 But with a pure appeal seeks to the heart, 293
 Which once corrupted takes the worser part;

And therein heartens up his servile powers, 295
Who, flattered by their leader's jocund show, 296
Stuff up his lust, as minutes fill up hours;
And as their captain, so their pride doth grow,
Paying more slavish tribute than they owe.
 By reprobate desire thus madly led,
 The Roman lord marcheth to Lucrece' bed.

274 avaunt begone **275 Respect** circumspection. **wait on** attend, accompany **276 heart** (Here, *moral sense;* cf. ll. 293 ff., where the heart is corrupted.) **277 Sad** serious, reflective **281 corn** grain **284 fond** foolish **286 cross** thwart **287 league** treaty (of peace) **290 confounds his wits** i.e., overwhelms reason with lust **291 as more divine** i.e., as representing reason **293 seeks** applies **295 servile powers** base passions, appetites. (The image is the common one of the faculties as an army: the heart as captain of the sensible soul commands all the affections to serve him. Cf. ll. 433 ff., below.) **296 jocund** sprightly

The locks between her chamber and his will,
Each one by him enforced, retires his ward; 303
But, as they open, they all rate his ill, 304
Which drives the creeping thief to some regard. 305
The threshold grates the door to have him heard;
  Night-wandering weasels shriek to see him there; 307
  They fright him, yet he still pursues his fear. 308

As each unwilling portal yields him way,
Through little vents and crannies of the place
The wind wars with his torch to make him stay
And blows the smoke of it into his face,
Extinguishing his conduct in this case; 313
  But his hot heart, which fond desire doth scorch,
  Puffs forth another wind that fires the torch.

And being lighted, by the light he spies
Lucretia's glove, wherein her needle sticks.
He takes it from the rushes where it lies, 318
And gripping it, the needle his finger pricks,
As who should say, "This glove to wanton tricks
  Is not inured. Return again in haste;
  Thou seest our mistress' ornaments are chaste."

But all these poor forbiddings could not stay him; 323
He in the worst sense consters their denial. 324
The doors, the wind, the glove, that did delay him,
He takes for accidental things of trial, 326
Or as those bars which stop the hourly dial, 327
  Who with a lingering stay his course doth let 328
  Till every minute pays the hour his debt.

303 retires his ward draws back its guard, i.e., the locking bolt
304 rate his ill chide his evil (by creaking) **305 regard** caution
307 weasels (Weasels were sometimes kept in houses as rat catchers.)
308 his fear i.e., the cause of his fear **313 conduct** conductor, i.e., his torch **318 rushes** reeds used as floor covering **323 stay** restrain
324 consters construes **326 accidental . . . trial** i.e., accidents that test his resolve, not portents **327 bars . . . dial** minute marks on a clock face at which the minute hand seems to pause slightly **328 Who** which. **his** its. **let** hinder

"So, so," quoth he, "these lets attend the time, 330
Like little frosts that sometimes threat the spring,
To add a more rejoicing to the prime, 332
And give the sneapèd birds more cause to sing. 333
Pain pays the income of each precious thing; 334
  Huge rocks, high winds, strong pirates, shelves, and
    sands 335
  The merchant fears, ere rich at home he lands."

Now is he come unto the chamber door
That shuts him from the heaven of his thought,
Which with a yielding latch, and with no more,
Hath barred him from the blessèd thing he sought.
So from himself impiety hath wrought 341
  That for his prey to pray he doth begin,
  As if the heavens should countenance his sin.

But in the midst of his unfruitful prayer,
Having solicited th' eternal power
That his foul thoughts might compass his fair fair, 346
And they would stand auspicious to the hour, 347
Even there he starts. Quoth he, "I must deflower. 348
  The powers to whom I pray abhor this fact; 349
  How can they then assist me in the act?

"Then Love and Fortune be my gods, my guide!
My will is backed with resolution.
Thoughts are but dreams till their effects be tried;
The blackest sin is cleared with absolution;
Against love's fire fear's frost hath dissolution.
  The eye of heaven is out, and misty night 356
  Covers the shame that follows sweet delight."

330 these . . . time i.e., these hindrances (like the minute marks) are part of the passage of time **332 more** greater. **prime** spring **333 sneapèd** nipped or pinched with cold **334 pays . . . of** is the price of obtaining **335 shelves** sandbars **341 So . . . wrought** impiety has so wrested him away from his true nature **346 compass** encompass, possess. **fair fair** virtuous fair one **347 they** i.e., that they, the eternal powers of heaven **348 starts** i.e., is startled, taken aback **349 fact** deed **356 out** extinguished

This said, his guilty hand plucked up the latch,
And with his knee the door he opens wide.
The dove sleeps fast that this night owl will catch.
Thus treason works ere traitors be espied.
Who sees the lurking serpent steps aside; 362
  But she, sound sleeping, fearing no such thing,
  Lies at the mercy of his mortal sting. 364

Into the chamber wickedly he stalks,
And gazeth on her yet unstainèd bed.
The curtains being close, about he walks,
Rolling his greedy eyeballs in his head.
By their high treason is his heart misled,
  Which gives the watchword to his hand full soon
  To draw the cloud that hides the silver moon. 371

Look as the fair and fiery-pointed sun, 372
Rushing from forth a cloud, bereaves our sight,
Even so, the curtain drawn, his eyes begun
To wink, being blinded with a greater light. 375
Whether it is that she reflects so bright 376
  That dazzleth them, or else some shame supposed;
  But blind they are, and keep themselves enclosed.

O, had they in that darksome prison died,
Then had they seen the period of their ill! 380
Then Collatine again by Lucrece' side
In his clear bed might have reposèd still. 382
But they must ope, this blessèd league to kill, 383
  And holy-thoughted Lucrece to their sight 384
  Must sell her joy, her life, her world's delight.

362 Who whoever **364 mortal** deadly **371 draw the cloud** i.e., draw back the bedcurtains **372 Look as** just as **375 wink** shut **376 reflects** shines **380 period** end. **ill** wrongdoing **382 clear** pure, innocent **383 league** i.e., marriage **384 to their sight** for the sake of what they (his eyes) will see

Her lily hand her rosy cheek lies under,
Cozening the pillow of a lawful kiss, 387
Who, therefore angry, seems to part in sunder,
Swelling on either side to want his bliss; 389
Between whose hills her head entombèd is;
  Where, like a virtuous monument, she lies, 391
  To be admired of lewd unhallowed eyes.

Without the bed her other fair hand was, 393
On the green coverlet, whose perfect white
Showed like an April daisy on the grass,
With pearly sweat resembling dew of night.
Her eyes, like marigolds, had sheathed their light,
  And canopied in darkness sweetly lay,
  Till they might open to adorn the day.

Her hair, like golden threads, played with her breath—
O modest wantons, wanton modesty!
Showing life's triumph in the map of death 402
And death's dim look in life's mortality. 403
Each in her sleep themselves so beautify 404
  As if between them twain there were no strife,
  But that life lived in death and death in life.

Her breasts like ivory globes circled with blue,
A pair of maiden worlds unconquerèd,
Save of their lord no bearing yoke they knew,
And him by oath they truly honorèd.
These worlds in Tarquin new ambition bred,
  Who, like a foul usurper, went about
  From this fair throne to heave the owner out.

387 Cozening cheating **389 to want his** i.e., protesting the lack of its **391 monument** effigy on a tomb **393 Without** on the outside of **402 the map of death** i.e., sleep. (*Map* means "image, picture.") **403 life's mortality** life's least-living aspect, i.e., sleep **404 Each** i.e., life and death

What could he see but mightily he noted?
What did he note but strongly he desired?
What he beheld, on that he firmly doted,
And in his will his willful eye he tired. 417
With more than admiration he admired
  Her azure veins, her alabaster skin,
  Her coral lips, her snow-white dimpled chin.

As the grim lion fawneth o'er his prey, 421
Sharp hunger by the conquest satisfied,
So o'er this sleeping soul doth Tarquin stay,
His rage of lust by gazing qualified— 424
Slacked, not suppressed, for standing by her side,
  His eye, which late this mutiny restrains, 426
  Unto a greater uproar tempts his veins.

And they, like straggling slaves for pillage fighting, 428
Obdurate vassals fell exploits effecting, 429
In bloody death and ravishment delighting,
Nor children's tears nor mothers' groans respecting,
Swell in their pride, the onset still expecting. 432
  Anon his beating heart, alarum striking,
  Gives the hot charge and bids them do their liking.

His drumming heart cheers up his burning eye,
His eye commends the leading to his hand; 436
His hand, as proud of such a dignity,
Smoking with pride, marched on to make his stand
On her bare breast, the heart of all her land;
  Whose ranks of blue veins, as his hand did scale, 440
  Left their round turrets destitute and pale.

417 will lust. **tired** (1) exhausted (2) glutted, fed ravenously. (A term from falconry.) **421 fawneth** shows delight **424 qualified** softened, abated **426 late** lately, a moment ago **428 slaves** i.e., base-born soldiers **429 fell** fierce. **effecting** i.e., on the verge of carrying out **432 pride** lust. **still** continually **436 commends** entrusts, commissions **440 scale** ascend (as in military attack)

They, mustering to the quiet cabinet 442
Where their dear governess and lady lies,
Do tell her she is dreadfully beset,
And fright her with confusion of their cries.
She, much amazed, breaks ope her locked-up eyes,
  Who, peeping forth this tumult to behold,
  Are by his flaming torch dimmed and controlled. 448

Imagine her as one in dead of night
From forth dull sleep by dreadful fancy waking,
That thinks she hath beheld some ghastly sprite,
Whose grim aspect sets every joint a-shaking.
What terror 'tis! But she, in worser taking, 453
  From sleep disturbèd, heedfully doth view
  The sight which makes supposèd terror true.

Wrapped and confounded in a thousand fears,
Like to a new-killed bird she trembling lies.
She dares not look; yet, winking, there appears 458
Quick-shifting antics, ugly in her eyes. 459
Such shadows are the weak brain's forgeries,
  Who, angry that the eyes fly from their lights, 461
  In darkness daunts them with more dreadful sights.

His hand, that yet remains upon her breast—
Rude ram, to batter such an ivory wall!— 464
May feel her heart—poor citizen!—distressed,
Wounding itself to death, rise up and fall,
Beating her bulk, that his hand shakes withal. 467
  This moves in him more rage and lesser pity
  To make the breach and enter this sweet city.

442 mustering gathering. **cabinet** i.e., heart **448 controlled** overpowered **453 taking** state of agitation **458 winking** closing the eyes **459 antics** phantoms, fantastic appearances, shapes **461 fly . . . lights** i.e., refuse to send out the beams, which enable the eyes to see **464 ram** battering ram **467 bulk** i.e., chest, breast. **that** so that

First, like a trumpet, doth his tongue begin
To sound a parley to his heartless foe, 471
Who o'er the white sheet peers her whiter chin,
The reason of this rash alarm to know,
Which he by dumb demeanor seeks to show; 474
  But she with vehement prayers urgeth still 475
  Under what color he commits this ill. 476

Thus he replies: "The color in thy face, 477
That even for anger makes the lily pale,
And the red rose blush at her own disgrace,
Shall plead for me and tell my loving tale.
Under that color am I come to scale 481
  Thy never-conquered fort; the fault is thine,
  For those thine eyes betray thee unto mine.

"Thus I forestall thee, if thou mean to chide:
Thy beauty hath ensnared thee to this night,
Where thou with patience must my will abide—
My will that marks thee for my earth's delight,
Which I to conquer sought with all my might.
  But as reproof and reason beat it dead, 489
  By thy bright beauty was it newly bred.

"I see what crosses my attempt will bring; 491
I know what thorns the growing rose defends;
I think the honey guarded with a sting; 493
All this beforehand counsel comprehends.
But will is deaf and hears no heedful friends;
  Only he hath an eye to gaze on beauty
  And dotes on what he looks, 'gainst law or duty. 497

471 a parley a summoning of the defenders to a negotiation. **heartless** spiritless, wanting courage **474 dumb demeanor** dumb show **475 urgeth** cries out to know **476 color** pretext **477 color** hue (punning on the previous line) **481 color** banner (punning on l. 476) **489 as** as soon as **491 crosses** vexations **493 think the honey** know the honey to be **497 looks** sees

"I have debated, even in my soul,
What wrong, what shame, what sorrow I shall breed,
But nothing can affection's course control 500
Or stop the headlong fury of his speed.
I know repentant tears ensue the deed, 502
  Reproach, disdain, and deadly enmity;
  Yet strive I to embrace mine infamy."

This said, he shakes aloft his Roman blade,
Which, like a falcon towering in the skies,
Coucheth the fowl below with his wings' shade, 507
Whose crooked beak threats if he mount he dies. 508
So under his insulting falchion lies 509
  Harmless Lucretia, marking what he tells
  With trembling fear, as fowl hear falcons' bells. 511

"Lucrece," quoth he, "this night I must enjoy thee.
If thou deny, then force must work my way,
For in thy bed I purpose to destroy thee.
That done, some worthless slave of thine I'll slay,
To kill thine honor with thy life's decay; 516
  And in thy dead arms do I mean to place him,
  Swearing I slew him, seeing thee embrace him.

"So thy surviving husband shall remain
The scornful mark of every open eye, 520
Thy kinsmen hang their heads at this disdain,
Thy issue blurred with nameless bastardy; 522
And thou, the author of their obloquy,
  Shalt have thy trespass cited up in rhymes
  And sung by children in succeeding times.

500 affection's passion's **502 ensue** follow upon **507 Coucheth** causes to couch, i.e., remain concealed **508 Whose** i.e., the falcon's. **he** i.e., the fowl **509 insulting** exulting in triumph **511 bells** (Falcons had bells attached to their feet.) **516 To kill . . . decay** i.e., to destroy your honor even while also taking your life **520 open eye** i.e., observer **522 issue blurred** offspring tarnished. **nameless** the father's name being unknown

"But if thou yield, I rest thy secret friend. 526
The fault unknown is as a thought unacted;
A little harm done to a great good end
For lawful policy remains enacted. 529
The poisonous simple sometimes is compacted 530
  In a pure compound; being so applied, 531
  His venom in effect is purified.

"Then, for thy husband and thy children's sake,
Tender my suit. Bequeath not to their lot 534
The shame that from them no device can take, 535
The blemish that will never be forgot,
Worse than a slavish wipe or birth hour's blot. 537
  For marks descried in men's nativity
  Are nature's faults, not their own infamy."

Here with a cockatrice' dead-killing eye 540
He rouseth up himself and makes a pause,
While she, the picture of pure piety,
Like a white hind under the gripe's sharp claws, 543
Pleads, in a wilderness where are no laws,
  To the rough beast that knows no gentle right, 545
  Nor aught obeys but his foul appetite.

526 rest remain. **friend** lover **529 For . . . enacted** is accepted as a legal expedient **530 simple** ingredient, drug. **compacted** mixed **531 pure** i.e., benign, medically efficacious **534 Tender** regard **535 device** heraldic motto **537 slavish wipe** brand with which slaves were marked. **birth hour's blot** unsightly birthmark **540 cockatrice** the basilisk, said to be hatched by a serpent from a cock's egg and to kill by its breath and the rays it emitted from its eyes **543 hind** female deer. **gripe's** vulture's, or griffin's **545 gentle right** the right that should be given to the weak and noble. (*Gentle* means both "weak" and "nobly born.")

But when a black-faced cloud the world doth threat,
In his dim mist th' aspiring mountains hiding,
From earth's dark womb some gentle gust doth get, 549
Which blow these pitchy vapors from their biding, 550
Hindering their present fall by this dividing; 551
  So his unhallowed haste her words delays, 552
  And moody Pluto winks while Orpheus plays. 553

Yet, foul night-waking cat, he doth but dally,
While in his hold-fast foot the weak mouse panteth.
Her sad behavior feeds his vulture folly, 556
A swallowing gulf that even in plenty wanteth. 557
His ear her prayers admits, but his heart granteth
  No penetrable entrance to her plaining; 559
  Tears harden lust, though marble wear with raining.

Her pity-pleading eyes are sadly fixed
In the remorseless wrinkles of his face; 562
Her modest eloquence with sighs is mixed,
Which to her oratory adds more grace.
She puts the period often from his place, 565
  And midst the sentence so her accent breaks 566
  That twice she doth begin ere once she speaks.

She conjures him by high almighty Jove,
By knighthood, gentry, and sweet friendship's oath, 569
By her untimely tears, her husband's love,
By holy human law and common troth, 571
By heaven and earth, and all the power of both,
  That to his borrowed bed he make retire 573
  And stoop to honor, not to foul desire. 574

549 doth get comes into being **550 pitchy** black. **their biding** where they hang **551 their present fall** i.e., the imminent onset of the storm **552 So . . . delays** thus her words delay his unhallowed haste **553 winks** closes his eyes. **Orpheus** husband of Eurydice who went to the underworld for her and charmed Pluto, ruler of the underworld, with his playing the lyre **556 vulture folly** ravenous lewdness and madness **557 gulf** maw, belly. **wanteth** craves insatiably **559 plaining** lamentation **562 wrinkles** i.e., frowns **565 his place** its place (in the sentence; i.e., she speaks in broken phrases) **566 accent** speech **569 gentry** nobleness of birth and breeding **571 troth** good faith **573 borrowed** lent him for the night **574 stoop** (Plays on the meanings "subject oneself," "debase oneself," and "stoop to the lure or prey" like a falcon.)

Quoth she, "Reward not hospitality
With such black payment as thou hast pretended. 576
Mud not the fountain that gave drink to thee;
Mar not the thing that cannot be amended. 578
End thy ill aim before thy shoot be ended; 579
He is no woodman that doth bend his bow 580
To strike a poor unseasonable doe. 581

"My husband is thy friend; for his sake spare me.
Thyself art mighty; for thine own sake leave me.
Myself a weakling; do not then ensnare me.
Thou look'st not like deceit; do not deceive me.
My sighs, like whirlwinds, labor hence to heave thee.
If ever man were moved with woman's moans,
Be movèd with my tears, my sighs, my groans;

"All which together, like a troubled ocean,
Beat at thy rocky and wreck-threatening heart,
To soften it with their continual motion;
For stones dissolved to water do convert. 592
O, if no harder than a stone thou art,
Melt at my tears, and be compassionate!
Soft pity enters at an iron gate.

"In Tarquin's likeness I did entertain thee.
Hast thou put on his shape to do him shame?
To all the host of heaven I complain me.
Thou wrong'st his honor, wound'st his princely name.
Thou art not what thou seem'st; and if the same, 600
Thou seem'st not what thou art, a god, a king;
For kings like gods should govern everything.

576 pretended proposed **578 amended** returned to its former purity **579 shoot** shooting, hunting **580 woodman** huntsman **581 unseasonable** in foal or not yet bearing, out of the hunting season **592 stones . . . convert** i.e., stones are worn away in time by water. **convert** change **600 if the same** i.e., if you are actually Tarquin

"How will thy shame be seeded in thine age, 603
When thus thy vices bud before thy spring?
If in thy hope thou dar'st do such outrage, 605
What dar'st thou not when once thou art a king?
O, be remembered, no outrageous thing 607
From vassal actors can be wiped away; 608
Then kings' misdeeds cannot be hid in clay. 609

"This deed will make thee only loved for fear, 610
But happy monarchs still are feared for love. 611
With foul offenders thou perforce must bear, 612
When they in thee the like offenses prove.
If but for fear of this, thy will remove; 614
For princes are the glass, the school, the book, 615
Where subjects' eyes do learn, do read, do look.

"And wilt thou be the school where Lust shall learn?
Must he in thee read lectures of such shame?
Wilt thou be glass wherein it shall discern
Authority for sin, warrant for blame,
To privilege dishonor in thy name? 621
Thou back'st reproach against long-living laud 622
And mak'st fair reputation but a bawd.

"Hast thou command? By Him that gave it thee, 624
From a pure heart command thy rebel will.
Draw not thy sword to guard iniquity,
For it was lent thee all that brood to kill. 627
Thy princely office how canst thou fulfill,
When, patterned by thy fault, foul Sin may say 629
He learned to sin, and thou didst teach the way?

603 be seeded ripen **605 in thy hope** i.e., while you are yet only heir to the kingdom **607 be remembered** bear in mind **608 vassal actors** i.e., vassals or ordinary subjects who commit crimes **609 in clay** i.e., even in death **610 loved for fear** i.e., obeyed out of fear **611 still . . . love** i.e., always are regarded with reverential awe stemming from love **612 With . . . bear** i.e., you will have to put up with others' foul offenses **614 but** only. **thy will remove** dissuade your lust **615 glass** mirror and paradigm **621 privilege** license **622 Thou back'st** you support. **laud** praise **624 Him** i.e., God **627 that brood** i.e., the progeny of evil **629 patterned** shown a precedent

"Think but how vile a spectacle it were
To view thy present trespass in another.
Men's faults do seldom to themselves appear;
Their own transgressions partially they smother. 634
This guilt would seem death-worthy in thy brother.
O, how are they wrapped in with infamies
That from their own misdeeds askance their eyes! 637

"To thee, to thee, my heaved-up hands appeal, 638
Not to seducing lust, thy rash relier. 639
I sue for exiled majesty's repeal; 640
Let him return, and flattering thoughts retire. 641
His true respect will prison false desire 642
And wipe the dim mist from thy doting eyne, 643
That thou shalt see thy state and pity mine."

"Have done," quoth he. "My uncontrollèd tide
Turns not, but swells the higher by this let. 646
Small lights are soon blown out; huge fires abide,
And with the wind in greater fury fret.
The petty streams that pay a daily debt
To their salt sovereign, with their fresh falls' haste 650
Add to his flow but alter not his taste."

"Thou art," quoth she, "a sea, a sovereign king;
And lo, there falls into thy boundless flood
Black lust, dishonor, shame, misgoverning,
Who seek to stain the ocean of thy blood.
If all these petty ills shall change thy good,
Thy sea within a puddle's womb is hearsed, 657
And not the puddle in thy sea dispersed.

634 partially showing partiality toward themselves. **smother** conceal **637 askance** avert **638 heaved-up** raised **639 thy rash relier** on which you rashly rely; or, which rashly relies on you in your present emotional state **640 repeal** recall from exile **641 and flattering thoughts retire** i.e., and let those thoughts that flatter and egg on lust go away **642 His true respect** true respect for him; or, his true judgment. **prison** imprison **643 eyne** eyes **646 let** hindrance **650 salt sovereign** i.e., the sea **657 hearsed** buried, coffined

"So shall these slaves be king, and thou their slave; 659
Thou nobly base, they basely dignified;
Thou their fair life, and they thy fouler grave;
Thou loathèd in their shame, they in thy pride.
The lesser thing should not the greater hide;
The cedar stoops not to the base shrub's foot,
But low shrubs wither at the cedar's root.

"So let thy thoughts, low vassals to thy state—"
"No more," quoth he, "by heaven, I will not hear thee.
Yield to my love; if not, enforcèd hate, 668
Instead of love's coy touch, shall rudely tear thee. 669
That done, despitefully I mean to bear thee
Unto the base bed of some rascal groom, 671
To be thy partner in this shameful doom."

This said, he sets his foot upon the light,
For light and lust are deadly enemies;
Shame folded up in blind concealing night,
When most unseen, then most doth tyrannize.
The wolf hath seized his prey, the poor lamb cries;
Till with her own white fleece her voice controlled 678
Entombs her outcry in her lips' sweet fold. 679

For with the nightly linen that she wears
He pens her piteous clamors in her head,
Cooling his hot face in the chastest tears
That ever modest eyes with sorrow shed.
O, that prone lust should stain so pure a bed! 684
The spots whereof could weeping purify, 685
Her tears should drop on them perpetually.

659 these slaves i.e., lust, dishonor, etc.; see l. 654 **668 enforcèd hate** force impelled by hatred **669 coy** gentle **671 groom** servant
678–679 Till . . . fold until, overmastering her voice with her own nightwear, he buries her outcry as though in the fold of her sweet lips. (*Fold* refers to her folded or compressed lips and to a sheepfold; hence *pens* in l. 681.) **684 prone** eager, headlong **685 could weeping** if weeping could

But she hath lost a dearer thing than life,
And he hath won what he would lose again.
This forcèd league doth force a further strife;
This momentary joy breeds months of pain;
This hot desire converts to cold disdain. 691
  Pure Chastity is rifled of her store,
  And Lust, the thief, far poorer than before.

Look as the full-fed hound or gorgèd hawk, 694
Unapt for tender smell or speedy flight, 695
Make slow pursuit, or altogether balk 696
The prey wherein by nature they delight;
So surfeit-taking Tarquin fares this night.
  His taste delicious, in digestion souring,
  Devours his will, that lived by foul devouring.

O, deeper sin than bottomless conceit 701
Can comprehend in still imagination!
Drunken Desire must vomit his receipt 703
Ere he can see his own abomination.
While Lust is in his pride, no exclamation 705
  Can curb his heat or rein his rash desire,
  Till like a jade Self-will himself doth tire. 707

And then with lank and lean discolored cheek,
With heavy eye, knit brow, and strengthless pace,
Feeble Desire, all recreant, poor, and meek, 710
Like to a bankrupt beggar wails his case. 711
The flesh being proud, Desire doth fight with Grace, 712
  For there it revels, and when that decays, 713
  The guilty rebel for remission prays. 714

691 converts changes **694 Look as** just as **695 tender smell** delicate scent **696 balk** turn away from, let slip **701 bottomless conceit** limitless imagination **703 his receipt** what it has swallowed **705 exclamation** protest **707 jade** untrained or unbroken horse **710 recreant** craven, cowed **711 Like to** like **712 proud** i.e., stubborn, willful **713 there** i.e., in the flesh. **when that decays** when the reveling in pleasure subsides **714 The guilty . . . prays** i.e., the flesh prays for forgiveness

So fares it with this faultful lord of Rome,
Who this accomplishment so hotly chased;
For now against himself he sounds this doom, 717
That through the length of times he stands disgraced.
Besides, his soul's fair temple is defaced,
  To whose weak ruins muster troops of cares
  To ask the spotted princess how she fares. 721

She says her subjects with foul insurrection 722
Have battered down her consecrated wall,
And by their mortal fault brought in subjection 724
Her immortality, and made her thrall
To living death and pain perpetual,
  Which in her prescience she controllèd still, 727
  But her foresight could not forestall their will. 728

Ev'n in this thought through the dark night he stealeth,
A captive victor that hath lost in gain, 730
Bearing away the wound that nothing healeth,
The scar that will, despite of cure, remain,
Leaving his spoil perplexed in greater pain. 733
  She bears the load of lust he left behind,
  And he the burden of a guilty mind.

He like a thievish dog creeps sadly thence;
She like a wearied lamb lies panting there.
He scowls and hates himself for his offense;
She, desperate, with her nails her flesh doth tear.
He faintly flies, sweating with guilty fear;
  She stays, exclaiming on the direful night; 741
  He runs, and chides his vanished, loathed delight.

717 sounds this doom pronounces this judgment **721 spotted princess** i.e., his contaminated soul, of whom the *temple,* l. 719, is the body **722 subjects** i.e., the senses **724 mortal** deadly **727–728 Which . . . will** i.e., she could foresee the inevitable coming of pain and death but could do nothing to prevent it **730 captive victor** i.e., Tarquin, who has triumphed over Lucrece and thus gained perpetual durance in sin **733 spoil** prey, i.e., Lucrece **741 exclaiming on** denouncing

He thence departs a heavy convertite; 743
She there remains a hopeless castaway.
He in his speed looks for the morning light;
She prays she never may behold the day.
"For day," quoth she, "night's scapes doth open lay, 747
And my true eyes have never practiced how
To cloak offenses with a cunning brow.

"They think not but that every eye can see
The same disgrace which they themselves behold;
And therefore would they still in darkness be,
To have their unseen sin remain untold.
For they their guilt with weeping will unfold, 754
And grave, like water that doth eat in steel, 755
Upon my cheeks what helpless shame I feel."

Here she exclaims against repose and rest 757
And bids her eyes hereafter still be blind. 758
She wakes her heart by beating on her breast,
And bids it leap from thence, where it may find
Some purer chest to close so pure a mind. 761
Frantic with grief thus breathes she forth her spite 762
Against the unseen secrecy of night:

"O comfort-killing Night, image of hell,
Dim register and notary of shame, 765
Black stage for tragedies and murders fell, 766
Vast sin-concealing chaos, nurse of blame! 767
Blind muffled bawd, dark harbor for defame, 768
Grim cave of death, whisp'ring conspirator
With close-tongued treason and the ravisher! 770

743 heavy convertite sad penitent **747 scapes** transgressions
754 unfold reveal **755 grave** engrave. **water** i.e., aqua fortis, nitric acid **757 exclaims against** reproaches **758 still** forever **761 close** enclose **762 spite** vexation **765 register** registrar. **notary** recorder
766 Black stage (Referring seemingly to a practice of hanging the stage with black for the performance of a tragedy.) **767 blame** evil
768 defame infamy **770 close-tongued** closemouthed, secretive of speech

"O hateful, vaporous, and foggy Night,
Since thou art guilty of my cureless crime,
Muster thy mists to meet the eastern light,
Make war against proportioned course of time; 774
Or if thou wilt permit the sun to climb
  His wonted height, yet ere he go to bed
  Knit poisonous clouds about his golden head.

"With rotten damps ravish the morning air;
Let their exhaled unwholesome breaths make sick
The life of purity, the supreme fair, 780
Ere he arrive his weary noontide prick; 781
And let thy musty vapors march so thick
  That in their smoky ranks his smothered light
  May set at noon and make perpetual night.

"Were Tarquin Night, as he is but Night's child,
The silver-shining queen he would distain; 786
Her twinkling handmaids too, by him defiled, 787
Through Night's black bosom should not peep again.
So should I have copartners in my pain;
  And fellowship in woe doth woe assuage,
  As palmers' chat makes short their pilgrimage. 791

"Where now I have no one to blush with me, 792
To cross their arms and hang their heads with mine, 793
To mask their brows and hide their infamy; 794
But I alone alone must sit and pine, 795
Seasoning the earth with showers of silver brine,
  Mingling my talk with tears, my grief with groans,
  Poor wasting monuments of lasting moans. 798

774 proportioned i.e., orderly in the regulated interchange of day and night **780 life** life-giving essence. **supreme fair** i.e., the sun **781 arrive** arrive at. **prick** mark (as on a dial) **786 queen** i.e., moon. **distain** stain, soil **787 handmaids** i.e., stars **791 palmers'** pilgrims' **792 Where** whereas **793–794 To cross . . . infamy** (Folding the arms and pulling the hat over the brows were conventional gestures of grief.) **795 I alone alone** only I alone **798 monuments** tokens, mementos

"O Night, thou furnace of foul reeking smoke!
Let not the jealous Day behold that face
Which underneath thy black all-hiding cloak
Immodestly lies martyred with disgrace! 802
Keep still possession of thy gloomy place,
  That all the faults which in thy reign are made
  May likewise be sepulchered in thy shade.

"Make me not object to the telltale Day. 806
The light will show charactered in my brow 807
The story of sweet chastity's decay, 808
The impious breach of holy wedlock vow.
Yea, the illiterate, that know not how
  To cipher what is writ in learnèd books, 811
  Will quote my loathsome trespass in my looks. 812

"The nurse, to still her child, will tell my story,
And fright her crying babe with Tarquin's name;
The orator, to deck his oratory, 815
Will couple my reproach to Tarquin's shame;
Feast-finding minstrels, tuning my defame, 817
  Will tie the hearers to attend each line,
  How Tarquin wrongèd me, I Collatine.

"Let my good name, that senseless reputation, 820
For Collatine's dear love be kept unspotted.
If that be made a theme for disputation, 822
The branches of another root are rotted, 823
And undeserved reproach to him allotted
  That is as clear from this attaint of mine 825
  As I, ere this, was pure to Collatine.

802 martyred i.e., disfigured **806 object** a thing perceived, object of gossip **807 charactered** inscribed **808 decay** ruin **811 cipher** decipher, read **812 quote** note, observe **815 deck** adorn **817 Feast-finding** searching out feasts at which to sing **820 senseless** impalpable **822–823 If . . . rotted** i.e., if my reputation comes in question then Collatine's will also be attacked **825 attaint** stain, imputation of dishonor

"O unseen shame, invisible disgrace!
O unfelt sore, crest-wounding, private scar! 828
Reproach is stamped in Collatinus' face,
And Tarquin's eye may read the mot afar, 830
How he in peace is wounded, not in war.
  Alas, how many bear such shameful blows,
  Which not themselves but he that gives them knows!

"If, Collatine, thine honor lay in me,
From me by strong assault it is bereft;
My honey lost, and I, a dronelike bee,
Have no perfection of my summer left, 837
But robbed and ransacked by injurious theft.
  In thy weak hive a wandering wasp hath crept
  And sucked the honey which thy chaste bee kept.

"Yet am I guilty of thy honor's wrack;
Yet for thy honor did I entertain him.
Coming from thee, I could not put him back,
For it had been dishonor to disdain him.
Besides, of weariness he did complain him,
  And talked of virtue. O unlooked-for evil,
  When virtue is profaned in such a devil!

"Why should the worm intrude the maiden bud?
Or hateful cuckoos hatch in sparrows' nests?
Or toads infect fair founts with venom mud?
Or tyrant folly lurk in gentle breasts? 851
Or kings be breakers of their own behests? 852
  But no perfection is so absolute
  That some impurity doth not pollute.

828 crest-wounding disgraceful to the crest, or device above the shield in one's coat of arms **830 mot** motto **837 Have . . . left** have nothing left of the honey I perfected in the summer **851 gentle** noble (in rank and temperament) **852 behests** biddings, injunctions

"The agèd man that coffers up his gold
Is plagued with cramps and gouts and painful fits,
And scarce hath eyes his treasure to behold,
But like still-pining Tantalus he sits, 858
And useless barns the harvest of his wits, 859
  Having no other pleasure of his gain
  But torment that it cannot cure his pain.

"So then he hath it when he cannot use it,
And leaves it to be mastered by his young,
Who in their pride do presently abuse it. 864
Their father was too weak, and they too strong,
To hold their cursèd-blessèd fortune long.
  The sweets we wish for turn to loathèd sours
  Even in the moment that we call them ours.

"Unruly blasts wait on the tender spring;
Unwholesome weeds take root with precious flowers;
The adder hisses where the sweet birds sing;
What virtue breeds iniquity devours.
We have no good that we can say is ours,
  But ill-annexèd Opportunity 874
  Or kills his life or else his quality. 875

"O Opportunity, thy guilt is great!
'Tis thou that execut'st the traitor's treason;
Thou sets the wolf where he the lamb may get;
Whoever plots the sin, thou 'point'st the season. 879
'Tis thou that spurn'st at right, at law, at reason;
  And in thy shady cell, where none may spy him,
  Sits Sin, to seize the souls that wander by him.

858 still-pining continually starving. **Tantalus** a son of Zeus who was punished by perpetual hunger and thirst with unreachable food and drink always in sight. (Renaissance commentators on Ovid glossed Tantalus as a usurer; hence the image of ll. 859 ff.) **859 barns** stores, as in a barn **864 presently** immediately **874 ill-annexèd** joined to the good for an evil purpose. **Opportunity** chance or circumstance **875 Or . . . quality** either destroys that good thing or else destroys its nature that makes it good **879 'point'st** appointest

"Thou makest the vestal violate her oath;
Thou blowest the fire when temperance is thawed;
Thou smother'st honesty, thou murderest troth. 885
Thou foul abettor, thou notorious bawd,
Thou plantest scandal and displacest laud. 887
  Thou ravisher, thou traitor, thou false thief,
  Thy honey turns to gall, thy joy to grief!

"Thy secret pleasure turns to open shame,
Thy private feasting to a public fast,
Thy smoothing titles to a ragged name, 892
Thy sugared tongue to bitter wormwood taste.
Thy violent vanities can never last.
  How comes it then, vile Opportunity,
  Being so bad, such numbers seek for thee?

"When wilt thou be the humble suppliant's friend,
And bring him where his suit may be obtained?
When wilt thou sort an hour great strifes to end? 899
Or free that soul which wretchedness hath chained?
Give physic to the sick, ease to the pained?
  The poor, lame, blind, halt, creep, cry out for thee,
  But they ne'er meet with Opportunity.

"The patient dies while the physician sleeps;
The orphan pines while the oppressor feeds; 905
Justice is feasting while the widow weeps;
Advice is sporting while infection breeds. 907
Thou grant'st no time for charitable deeds.
  Wrath, envy, treason, rape, and murder's rages,
  Thy heinous hours wait on them as their pages.

885 honesty chastity. **troth** honesty **887 laud** praise **892 smoothing** flattering. **ragged** faulty, irregular **899 sort** choose, appoint **905 pines** starves **907 Advice** i.e., medical advice. **sporting** taking idle pleasure

"When Truth and Virtue have to do with thee,
A thousand crosses keep them from thy aid. 912
They buy thy help; but Sin ne'er gives a fee, 913
He gratis comes; and thou art well apaid 914
As well to hear as grant what he hath said. 915
My Collatine would else have come to me
When Tarquin did, but he was stayed by thee.

"Guilty thou art of murder and of theft,
Guilty of perjury and subornation,
Guilty of treason, forgery, and shift, 920
Guilty of incest, that abomination—
An accessory by thine inclination 922
To all sins past and all that are to come,
From the creation to the general doom. 924

"Misshapen Time, copesmate of ugly Night, 925
Swift subtle post, carrier of grisly care, 926
Eater of youth, false slave to false delight,
Base watch of woes, sin's packhorse, virtue's snare! 928
Thou nursest all, and murderest all that are.
O, hear me then, injurious, shifting Time!
Be guilty of my death, since of my crime. 931

"Why hath thy servant Opportunity
Betrayed the hours thou gav'st me to repose,
Canceled my fortunes, and enchainèd me
To endless date of never-ending woes? 935
Time's office is to fine the hate of foes, 936
To eat up errors by opinion bred, 937
Not spend the dowry of a lawful bed.

912 crosses hindrances **913 buy** i.e., have to pay for **914 apaid** satisfied **915 As . . . as** both to hear and **920 shift** fraud **922 inclination** natural disposition **924 general doom** Doomsday, Day of Judgment **925 copesmate** companion, accomplice **926 post** messenger **928 watch** crier, one who announces woes **931 since of** i.e., since you are guilty of **935 date** duration **936 office is** function ideally is. **fine** punish, or put an end to **937 opinion** popular rumor

"Time's glory is to calm contending kings,
To unmask falsehood and bring truth to light,
To stamp the seal of time in agèd things,
To wake the morn and sentinel the night, 942
To wrong the wronger till he render right,
To ruinate proud buildings with thy hours,
And smear with dust their glittering golden towers;

"To fill with wormholes stately monuments,
To feed oblivion with decay of things,
To blot old books and alter their contents, 948
To pluck the quills from ancient ravens' wings, 949
To dry the old oak's sap and cherish springs, 950
To spoil antiquities of hammered steel,
And turn the giddy round of Fortune's wheel;

"To show the beldam daughters of her daughter, 953
To make the child a man, the man a child, 954
To slay the tiger that doth live by slaughter,
To tame the unicorn and lion wild,
To mock the subtle in themselves beguiled, 957
To cheer the plowman with increaseful crops, 958
And waste huge stones with little waterdrops. 959

"Why work'st thou mischief in thy pilgrimage,
Unless thou couldst return to make amends?
One poor retiring minute in an age 962
Would purchase thee a thousand thousand friends,
Lending him wit that to bad debtors lends. 964
O, this dread night, wouldst thou one hour come back,
I could prevent this storm and shun thy wrack! 966

942 sentinel stand guard over **948 blot** erase, obliterate **949 To pluck . . . wings** i.e., to end even the existence of long-lived ravens **950 springs** new growth, shoots **953 beldam** old woman **954 a child** i.e., in the second childishness of old age **957 subtle . . . beguiled** crafty who are foiled by their own cleverness **958 increaseful** fruitful **959 waste** wear away **962 retiring** returning (thereby allowing men an opportunity to undo some evil) **964 Lending . . . lends** i.e., giving the person who has made loans to poor credit risks an opportunity to reconsider **966 prevent** anticipate, forestall

"Thou ceaseless lackey to Eternity, 967
With some mischance cross Tarquin in his flight! 968
Devise extremes beyond extremity
To make him curse this cursèd crimeful night.
Let ghastly shadows his lewd eyes affright,
And the dire thought of his committed evil
Shape every bush a hideous shapeless devil.

"Disturb his hours of rest with restless trances; 974
Afflict him in his bed with bedrid groans; 975
Let there bechance him pitiful mischances,
To make him moan, but pity not his moans.
Stone him with hardened hearts harder than stones,
And let mild women to him lose their mildness,
Wilder to him than tigers in their wildness.

"Let him have time to tear his curlèd hair,
Let him have time against himself to rave,
Let him have time of Time's help to despair,
Let him have time to live a loathèd slave,
Let him have time a beggar's orts to crave, 985
And time to see one that by alms doth live
Disdain to him disdainèd scraps to give.

"Let him have time to see his friends his foes,
And merry fools to mock at him resort; 989
Let him have time to mark how slow time goes
In time of sorrow, and how swift and short
His time of folly and his time of sport;
And ever let his unrecalling crime 993
Have time to wail th' abusing of his time.

967 ceaseless lackey omnipresent attendant. (The image is of Time as a footman accompanying humanity on its journey to eternity.) **968 cross** thwart **974 trances** visions, fits **975 bedrid** bedridden **985 orts** refuse, fragments of food **989 And . . . resort** and merry fools gather (*resort*) to mock him **993 unrecalling** that may not be recalled

"O Time, thou tutor both to good and bad,
Teach me to curse him that thou taught'st this ill! 996
At his own shadow let the thief run mad,
Himself himself seek every hour to kill!
Such wretched hands such wretched blood should
spill;
For who so base would such an office have
As slanderous deathsman to so base a slave? 1001

"The baser is he, coming from a king,
To shame his hope with deeds degenerate. 1003
The mightier man, the mightier is the thing
That makes him honored or begets him hate;
For greatest scandal waits on greatest state. 1006
The moon being clouded presently is missed, 1007
But little stars may hide them when they list.

"The crow may bathe his coal-black wings in mire,
And unperceived fly with the filth away,
But if the like the snow-white swan desire,
The stain upon his silver down will stay.
Poor grooms are sightless night, kings glorious day. 1013
Gnats are unnoted wheresoe'er they fly,
But eagles gazed upon with every eye.

"Out, idle words, servants to shallow fools, 1016
Unprofitable sounds, weak arbitrators!
Busy yourselves in skill-contending schools; 1018
Debate where leisure serves with dull debaters;
To trembling clients be you mediators.
For me, I force not argument a straw, 1021
Since that my case is past the help of law.

996 that to whom **1001 slanderous** despised, contemptible. **deathsman** executioner **1003 his hope** the hope men had of him as heir to the crown **1006 waits . . . state** potentially attends those of most exalted rank **1007 presently** at once **1013 grooms** i.e., lowborn persons. **are** are like. **sightless** making things invisible; pitch dark **1016 Out** (An exclamation of disapproval.) **1018 in . . . schools** i.e., among scholars who perennially debate with words **1021 force** value. **a straw** i.e., a straw's worth

"In vain I rail at Opportunity,
At Time, at Tarquin, and uncheerful Night;
In vain I cavil with mine infamy, 1025
In vain I spurn at my confirmed despite. 1026
This helpless smoke of words doth me no right. 1027
The remedy indeed to do me good
Is to let forth my foul-defilèd blood. 1029

"Poor hand, why quiver'st thou at this decree?
Honor thyself to rid me of this shame!
For if I die, my honor lives in thee,
But if I live, thou liv'st in my defame.
Since thou couldst not defend thy loyal dame,
And wast afeard to scratch her wicked foe,
Kill both thyself and her for yielding so."

This said, from her betumbled couch she starteth,
To find some desperate instrument of death;
But this, no slaughterhouse, no tool imparteth 1039
To make more vent for passage of her breath,
Which, thronging through her lips, so vanisheth
As smoke from Etna, that in air consumes,
Or that which from dischargèd cannon fumes.

"In vain," quoth she, "I live, and seek in vain
Some happy means to end a hapless life.
I feared by Tarquin's falchion to be slain, 1046
Yet for the selfsame purpose seek a knife;
But when I feared I was a loyal wife.
So am I now.—O no, that cannot be!
Of that true type hath Tarquin rifled me. 1050

1025 cavil with raise objections to **1026 spurn at** (Literally, kick against.) **confirmed despite** unavoidable injury **1027 helpless** affording no help **1029 let . . . blood** bleed (1) as a *remedy* (l. 1028) for illness, a standard form of medical treatment (2) as a means of death **1039 no slaughterhouse** being no slaughterhouse. **imparteth** provides **1046 falchion** curved sword **1050 type** stamp; example

"O, that is gone for which I sought to live,
And therefore now I need not fear to die.
To clear this spot by death, at least I give 1053
A badge of fame to slander's livery, 1054
A dying life to living infamy.
Poor helpless help, the treasure stol'n away,
To burn the guiltless casket where it lay!

"Well, well, dear Collatine, thou shalt not know
The stainèd taste of violated troth;
I will not wrong thy true affection so
To flatter thee with an infringèd oath; 1061
This bastard graft shall never come to growth. 1062
He shall not boast who did thy stock pollute
That thou art doting father of his fruit.

"Nor shall he smile at thee in secret thought,
Nor laugh with his companions at thy state,
But thou shalt know thy interest was not bought 1067
Basely with gold, but stol'n from forth thy gate.
For me, I am the mistress of my fate,
And with my trespass never will dispense 1070
Till life to death acquit my forced offense. 1071

"I will not poison thee with my attaint, 1072
Nor fold my fault in cleanly coined excuses; 1073
My sable ground of sin I will not paint, 1074
To hide the truth of this false night's abuses.
My tongue shall utter all; mine eyes, like sluices,
As from a mountain spring that feeds a dale,
Shall gush pure streams to purge my impure tale."

1053 To clear i.e., in clearing. **spot** stain **1054 fame** good reputation. **livery** clothing or uniform worn by those in service, bearing a heraldic *badge* on the sleeve to indicate in whose service the livery is worn. (Lucrece says that the livery of shame will be partially redeemed by the badge of an honorable death.) **1061 flatter** deceive. (Lucrece will not bear a bastard child that might deceive Collatine with the thought of being the father.) **1062 graft** scion **1067 interest** claim, property **1070 with . . . dispense** never will pardon my offense. (To *dispense* is to grant dispensation.) **1071 acquit** atone for **1072 attaint** infection **1073 cleanly coined** cleverly counterfeited **1074 sable ground** dark surface on a heraldic device

By this, lamenting Philomel had ended 1079
The well-tuned warble of her nightly sorrow,
And solemn night with slow sad gait descended
To ugly hell, when, lo, the blushing morrow
Lends light to all fair eyes that light will borrow. 1083
But cloudy Lucrece shames herself to see, 1084
And therefore still in night would cloistered be.

Revealing day through every cranny spies
And seems to point her out where she sits weeping,
To whom she sobbing speaks: "O eye of eyes,
Why pry'st thou through my window? Leave thy
peeping.
Mock with thy tickling beams eyes that are sleeping.
Brand not my forehead with thy piercing light,
For day hath naught to do what's done by night." 1092

Thus cavils she with everything she sees.
True grief is fond and testy as a child, 1094
Who wayward once, his mood with naught agrees. 1095
Old woes, not infant sorrows, bear them mild. 1096
Continuance tames the one; the other wild,
Like an unpracticed swimmer plunging still,
With too much labor drowns for want of skill.

So she, deep-drenchèd in a sea of care,
Holds disputation with each thing she views,
And to herself all sorrow doth compare;
No object but her passion's strength renews, 1103
And as one shifts, another straight ensues. 1104
Sometimes her grief is dumb and hath no words,
Sometimes 'tis mad and too much talk affords.

1079 Philomel, i.e., the nightingale. Philomela was raped by her brother-in-law, Tereus, who cut out her tongue so that she could not disclose his villainy; she was changed into a nightingale. **1083 borrow** i.e., make use of that which heaven lends **1084 shames** is ashamed **1092 to do** to do with **1094 fond** foolish **1095 wayward once** i.e., once in a peevish mood **1096 them** themselves. **mild** mildly, calmly **1103 her . . . renews** renews the strength of her passion **1104 shifts** moves, yields place. **straight** at once

The little birds that tune their morning's joy
Make her moans mad with their sweet melody,
For mirth doth search the bottom of annoy; 1109
Sad souls are slain in merry company.
Grief best is pleased with grief's society.
  True sorrow then is feelingly sufficed 1112
  When with like semblance it is sympathized. 1113

'Tis double death to drown in ken of shore; 1114
He ten times pines that pines beholding food; 1115
To see the salve doth make the wound ache more;
Great grief grieves most at that would do it good; 1117
Deep woes roll forward like a gentle flood,
  Who, being stopped, the bounding banks o'erflows; 1119
  Grief dallied with nor law nor limit knows. 1120

"You mocking birds," quoth she, "your tunes entomb
Within your hollow-swelling feathered breasts,
And in my hearing be you mute and dumb.
My restless discord loves no stops nor rests; 1124
A woeful hostess brooks not merry guests. 1125
  Relish your nimble notes to pleasing ears; 1126
  Distress likes dumps, when time is kept with tears. 1127

"Come, Philomel, that sing'st of ravishment,
Make thy sad grove in my disheveled hair.
As the dank earth weeps at thy languishment,
So I at each sad strain will strain a tear 1131
And with deep groans the diapason bear; 1132
  For burden-wise I'll hum on Tarquin still, 1133
  While thou on Tereus descants better skill. 1134

1109 search probe. **annoy** grief, injury **1112 sufficed** contented
1113 sympathized matched **1114 ken** sight **1115 pines** hungers
1117 would which wishes to **1119 Who** which. **stopped** dammed up.
bounding containing, confining **1120 dallied** trifled. **nor . . . nor** neither . . . nor **1124 restless** agitated (with a pun on the musical sense of having no *stops* or *rests,* i.e., being ceaseless, without pause) **1125 brooks** enjoys **1126 Relish** (1) warble, make attractive (2) elaborate with musical ornamentation. **pleasing** capable of being pleased **1127 dumps** mournful songs **1131 strain . . . strain** melody . . . force, squeeze **1132 diapason** bass accompaniment below the melody **1133 burden-wise** in the manner of an undersong or bass (with a play on *burden* meaning "sorrow")
1134 descants better skill i.e., sing a musical elaboration in the upper register with better skill (than my bass accompaniment)

"And whiles against a thorn thou bear'st thy part 1135
To keep thy sharp woes waking, wretched I,
To imitate thee well, against my heart
Will fix a sharp knife to affright mine eye,
Who, if it wink, shall thereon fall and die. 1139
These means, as frets upon an instrument, 1140
Shall tune our heartstrings to true languishment.

"And for, poor bird, thou sing'st not in the day, 1142
As shaming any eye should thee behold, 1143
Some dark deep desert seated from the way, 1144
That knows not parching heat nor freezing cold,
Will we find out; and there we will unfold
To creatures stern sad tunes, to change their kinds. 1147
Since men prove beasts, let beasts bear gentle
minds."

As the poor frighted deer, that stands at gaze, 1149
Wildly determining which way to fly,
Or one encompassed with a winding maze,
That cannot tread the way out readily,
So with herself is she in mutiny,
To live or die which of the twain were better
When life is shamed and death reproach's debtor. 1155

1135 against a thorn (According to popular belief, the nightingale perched deliberately with a thorn against her breast to keep herself awake.) **1139 Who** which, i.e., my heart. **if it wink** i.e., if my eye should close in sleep **1140 frets** bars placed on the fingerboards of stringed instruments to regulate the fingering (with a pun on *frets* meaning "vexations") **1142 for** because. **sing'st not in the day** (One of the common errors of the time; nightingales sing both by day and by night.) **1143 As shaming** as though being ashamed that, or since you are ashamed that **1144 desert** deserted place. **seated from** situated away from **1147 kinds** natures **1149 at gaze** transfixed, bewildered **1155 death reproach's debtor** i.e., death by suicide would incur reproach

"To kill myself," quoth she, "alack, what were it
But with my body my poor soul's pollution? 1157
They that lose half with greater patience bear it
Than they whose whole is swallowed in confusion. 1159
That mother tries a merciless conclusion 1160
Who, having two sweet babes, when death takes one,
Will slay the other and be nurse to none.

"My body or my soul, which was the dearer,
When the one pure, the other made divine?
Whose love of either to myself was nearer, 1165
When both were kept for heaven and Collatine?
Ay me! The bark pilled from the lofty pine, 1167
His leaves will wither and his sap decay;
So must my soul, her bark being pilled away.

"Her house is sacked, her quiet interrupted,
Her mansion battered by the enemy,
Her sacred temple spotted, spoiled, corrupted,
Grossly engirt with daring infamy.
Then let it not be called impiety
If in this blemished fort I make some hole 1175
Through which I may convey this troubled soul. 1176

"Yet die I will not till my Collatine
Have heard the cause of my untimely death,
That he may vow, in that sad hour of mine,
Revenge on him that made me stop my breath.
My stainèd blood to Tarquin I'll bequeath,
Which by him tainted shall for him be spent,
And as his due writ in my testament. 1183

1157 But . . . pollution but to add my poor soul's pollution (through suicide) to that of my body (through the rape) **1159 confusion** ruin **1160 conclusion** experiment **1165 Whose . . . either** love of which of the two **1167 pilled** peeled, stripped off, rifled **1175 fort** i.e., body **1176 convey** let out **1183 testament** last will and testament

"My honor I'll bequeath unto the knife
That wounds my body so dishonorèd.
'Tis honor to deprive dishonored life; 1186
The one will live, the other being dead.
So of shame's ashes shall my fame be bred,
For in my death I murder shameful scorn;
My shame so dead, mine honor is new born.

"Dear lord of that dear jewel I have lost, 1191
What legacy shall I bequeath to thee?
My resolution, love, shall be thy boast,
By whose example thou revenged mayst be.
How Tarquin must be used, read it in me:
Myself, thy friend, will kill myself, thy foe,
And for my sake serve thou false Tarquin so.

"This brief abridgment of my will I make:
My soul and body to the skies and ground;
My resolution, husband, do thou take;
Mine honor be the knife's that makes my wound;
My shame be his that did my fame confound;
And all my fame that lives disbursèd be 1203
To those that live and think no shame of me.

"Thou, Collatine, shalt oversee this will.
How was I overseen that thou shalt see it! 1206
My blood shall wash the slander of mine ill;
My life's foul deed my life's fair end shall free it. 1208
Faint not, faint heart, but stoutly say 'So be it.'
Yield to my hand; my hand shall conquer thee.
Thou dead, both die, and both shall victors be."

1186 deprive take away **1191 dear jewel** i.e., chastity **1203 disbursèd** i.e., paid out as legacies **1206 overseen** deluded, taken advantage of (with quibble on *oversee,* l. 1205, i.e., attend to as an executor of an estate) **1208 My . . . free it** my life's virtuous end will atone for my life's foul deed

This plot of death when sadly she had laid,
And wiped the brinish pearl from her bright eyes,
With untuned tongue she hoarsely calls her maid, 1214
Whose swift obedience to her mistress hies; 1215
For fleet-winged duty with thought's feathers flies.
  Poor Lucrece' cheeks unto her maid seem so
  As winter meads when sun doth melt their snow.

Her mistress she doth give demure good morrow 1219
With soft slow tongue, true mark of modesty,
And sorts a sad look to her lady's sorrow, 1221
Forwhy her face wore sorrow's livery; 1222
But durst not ask of her audaciously
  Why her two suns were cloud-eclipsèd so,
  Nor why her fair cheeks over-washed with woe. 1225

But as the earth doth weep, the sun being set,
Each flower moistened like a melting eye,
Even so the maid with swelling drops 'gan wet
Her circled eyne, enforced by sympathy 1229
Of those fair suns set in her mistress' sky,
  Who in a salt-waved ocean quench their light,
  Which makes the maid weep like the dewy night.

A pretty while these pretty creatures stand, 1233
Like ivory conduits coral cisterns filling. 1234
One justly weeps; the other takes in hand 1235
No cause but company of her drops spilling. 1236
Their gentle sex to weep are often willing,
  Grieving themselves to guess at others' smarts, 1238
  And then they drown their eyes or break their hearts.

1214 untuned discordant **1215 Whose . . . hies** who in swift obedience hastens to her mistress **1219 Her** i.e., to her **1221 sorts** adapts **1222 Forwhy** because **1225 over-washed** overflowed **1229 circled** i.e., circled with red. **eyne** eyes. **enforced** compelled **1233 pretty while** considerable while **1234 conduits** (Alludes to conduit spouts and fountains shaped in the form of human figures; the women's eyes run like conduits.) **1235 takes in hand** acknowledges, entertains **1236 No . . . spilling** i.e., no cause for the shedding of teardrops other than to keep her mistress company **1238 to guess at** i.e., merely when they conjecture

For men have marble, women waxen, minds, 1240
And therefore are they formed as marble will. 1241
The weak oppressed, th' impression of strange kinds 1242
Is formed in them by force, by fraud, or skill.
Then call them not the authors of their ill,
No more than wax shall be accounted evil
Wherein is stamped the semblance of a devil.

Their smoothness, like a goodly champaign plain, 1247
Lays open all the little worms that creep; 1248
In men, as in a rough-grown grove, remain
Cave-keeping evils that obscurely sleep. 1250
Through crystal walls each little mote will peep. 1251
Though men can cover crimes with bold stern looks,
Poor women's faces are their own faults' books.

No man inveigh against the withered flower, 1254
But chide rough winter that the flow'r hath killed.
Not that devoured, but that which doth devour,
Is worthy blame. O, let it not be hild 1257
Poor women's faults, that they are so fulfilled 1258
With men's abuses. Those proud lords, to blame, 1259
Make weak-made women tenants to their shame. 1260

The precedent whereof in Lucrece view, 1261
Assailed by night with circumstances strong 1262
Of present death, and shame that might ensue 1263
By that her death, to do her husband wrong. 1264
Such danger to resistance did belong 1265
That dying fear through all her body spread; 1266
And who cannot abuse a body dead?

1240 waxen i.e., soft, impressionable **1241 will** wills, wishes **1242 The weak** i.e., when the weak are. **strange kinds** natures unlike their own **1247 champaign** level, open **1248 Lays open** reveals. **worms** reptiles, i.e., blemishes **1250 Cave-keeping** remaining concealed in caves **1251 mote** speck **1254 No man** let no man **1257 hild** held **1258 fulfilled** filled **1259 lords, to blame** lords, who are blameworthy; or, who are too much to blame (*too blame*); or, owners of blame (*lords to blame*) **1260 tenants** i.e., occupying and sharing a shame that is properly men's **1261 precedent** proof, example **1262–1263 circumstances . . . death** a situation strongly threatening immediate death **1264 By that her death** by her very death **1265 danger** i.e., the danger of being defamed by Tarquin **1266 dying** i.e., paralyzing

By this, mild patience bid fair Lucrece speak 1268
To the poor counterfeit of her complaining: 1269
"My girl," quoth she, "on what occasion break
Those tears from thee, that down thy cheeks are
  raining?
If thou dost weep for grief of my sustaining, 1272
  Know, gentle wench, it small avails my mood.
  If tears could help, mine own would do me good.

"But tell me, girl, when went"—and there she stayed
Till after a deep groan—"Tarquin from hence?"
"Madam, ere I was up," replied the maid,
"The more to blame my sluggard negligence. 1278
Yet with the fault I thus far can dispense: 1279
  Myself was stirring ere the break of day,
  And, ere I rose, was Tarquin gone away.

"But, lady, if your maid may be so bold,
She would request to know your heaviness." 1283
"O, peace!" quoth Lucrece. "If it should be told,
The repetition cannot make it less;
For more it is than I can well express,
  And that deep torture may be called a hell
  When more is felt than one hath power to tell.

"Go, get me hither paper, ink, and pen.
Yet save that labor, for I have them here.
What should I say? One of my husband's men
Bid thou be ready by and by to bear
A letter to my lord, my love, my dear.
  Bid him with speed prepare to carry it;
  The cause craves haste, and it will soon be writ."

1268 By this by this time **1269 counterfeit of her complaining** i.e., the maid, weeping like her **1272 of my sustaining** borne by me **1278 to blame** at fault **1279 dispense** give dispensation, find excuse
1283 know i.e., know the reason for

Her maid is gone, and she prepares to write,
First hovering o'er the paper with her quill.
Conceit and grief an eager combat fight; 1298
What wit sets down is blotted straight with will; 1299
This is too curious-good, this blunt and ill. 1300
  Much like a press of people at a door
  Throng her inventions, which shall go before. 1302

At last she thus begins: "Thou worthy lord
Of that unworthy wife that greeteth thee,
Health to thy person! Next vouchsafe t' afford—
If ever, love, thy Lucrece thou wilt see—
Some present speed to come and visit me.
  So, I commend me from our house in grief. 1308
  My woes are tedious, though my words are brief." 1309

Here folds she up the tenor of her woe, 1310
Her certain sorrow writ uncertainly. 1311
By this short schedule Collatine may know 1312
Her grief, but not her grief's true quality.
She dares not thereof make discovery, 1314
  Lest he should hold it her own gross abuse, 1315
  Ere she with blood had stained her stained excuse. 1316

Besides, the life and feeling of her passion
She hoards, to spend when he is by to hear her,
When sighs and groans and tears may grace the
    fashion 1319
Of her disgrace, the better so to clear her
From that suspicion which the world might bear her.
  To shun this blot, she would not blot the letter 1322
  With words, till action might become them better.

1298 Conceit thought (of what she will write). **eager** fierce **1299 wit** intellect. **blotted** canceled. **will** passion, feeling **1300 curious-good** fastidiously, studiedly phrased **1302 which . . . before** contending as to who is to enter first **1308 commend me** ask to be remembered **1309 tedious** prolonged, painful **1310 tenor** gist, summary **1311 uncertainly** i.e., not in precise detail, vaguely **1312 schedule** document, summary **1314 thereof make discovery** i.e., reveal the true extent and nature of her grief **1315 abuse** wrongdoing **1316 had stained** (1) had discolored (2) had given color or credence to. **her stained excuse** i.e., the explanation of her shame **1319 fashion** fashioning **1322 blot . . . blot** stain . . . mar

To see sad sights moves more than hear them told,
For then the eye interprets to the ear
The heavy motion that it doth behold, 1326
When every part a part of woe doth bear. 1327
'Tis but a part of sorrow that we hear.
  Deep sounds make lesser noise than shallow fords, 1329
  And sorrow ebbs, being blown with wind of words.

Her letter now is sealed, and on it writ,
"At Ardea to my lord with more than haste."
The post attends, and she delivers it, 1333
Charging the sour-faced groom to hie as fast
As lagging fowls before the northern blast. 1335
  Speed more than speed but dull and slow she deems; 1336
  Extremity still urgeth such extremes. 1337

The homely villain curtsies to her low; 1338
And, blushing on her, with a steadfast eye
Receives the scroll without or yea or no,
And forth with bashful innocence doth hie.
But they whose guilt within their bosoms lie
  Imagine every eye beholds their blame;
  For Lucrece thought he blushed to see her shame,

When, silly groom, God wot, it was defect 1345
Of spirit, life, and bold audacity.
Such harmless creatures have a true respect 1347
To talk in deeds, while others saucily 1348
Promise more speed, but do it leisurely.
  Even so this pattern of the worn-out age 1350
  Pawned honest looks but laid no words to gage. 1351

1326 heavy motion sad action **1327 every part** i.e., of the body **1329 Deep sounds** deep waters (with pun on *sounds,* i.e., inlets of the sea, and "noise") **1333 post** messenger **1335 lagging** falling behind in migratory flight **1336 Speed . . . deems** i.e., she considers even extraordinary speed too tedious and slow **1337 still** ever **1338 homely** simple and unhandsome. **villain** servant. **curtsies** bows **1345 silly** simple **1347 respect** care **1348 To talk in deeds** i.e., to express themselves in deeds only **1350 pattern . . . age** i.e., example of faithful service in the good old days **1351 Pawned . . . gage** i.e., pledged his loyalty wordlessly through honest looks

His kindled duty kindled her mistrust, 1352
That two red fires in both their faces blazed.
She thought he blushed as knowing Tarquin's lust,
And, blushing with him, wistly on him gazed. 1355
Her earnest eye did make him more amazed. 1356
  The more she saw the blood his cheeks replenish,
  The more she thought he spied in her some blemish.

But long she thinks till he return again, 1359
And yet the duteous vassal scarce is gone.
The weary time she cannot entertain, 1361
For now 'tis stale to sigh, to weep, and groan.
So woe hath wearied woe, moan tirèd moan,
  That she her plaints a little while doth stay, 1364
  Pausing for means to mourn some newer way.

At last she calls to mind where hangs a piece 1366
Of skillful painting, made for Priam's Troy, 1367
Before the which is drawn the power of Greece, 1368
For Helen's rape the city to destroy,
Threat'ning cloud-kissing Ilion with annoy, 1370
  Which the conceited painter drew so proud 1371
  As heaven, it seemed, to kiss the turrets bowed.

A thousand lamentable objects there,
In scorn of nature, art gave lifeless life. 1374
Many a dry drop seemed a weeping tear, 1375
Shed for the slaughtered husband by the wife.
The red blood reeked, to show the painter's strife, 1377
  And dying eyes gleamed forth their ashy lights
  Like dying coals burnt out in tedious nights.

1352 kindled duty i.e., blushing obeisance. **mistrust** i.e., fear of her shame being known **1355 wistly** intently **1356 amazed** embarrassed **1359 long she thinks** she thinks it long **1361 entertain** occupy **1364 stay** halt **1366 piece** picture (evidently in a tapestry) **1367 made for** depicting **1368 drawn** drawn up, arrayed. **power** army **1370 cloud-kissing Ilion** i.e., lofty-towered Troy. **annoy** harm **1371 conceited** ingenious **1374 In scorn of** i.e., defiantly rivaling. **lifeless** inanimate **1375 dry drop** i.e., drop of paint depicting a tear **1377 strife** rivalry, i.e., with Nature; also the strife depicted in the painting

There might you see the laboring pioneer 1380
Begrimed with sweat and smearèd all with dust;
And from the towers of Troy there would appear
The very eyes of men through loopholes thrust,
Gazing upon the Greeks with little lust. 1384
Such sweet observance in this work was had 1385
That one might see those far-off eyes look sad.

In great commanders grace and majesty
You might behold, triumphing in their faces;
In youth, quick bearing and dexterity; 1389
And here and there the painter interlaces
Pale cowards marching on with trembling paces,
Which heartless peasants did so well resemble 1392
That one would swear he saw them quake and
tremble.

In Ajax and Ulysses, O, what art
Of physiognomy might one behold!
The face of either ciphered either's heart; 1396
Their face their manners most expressly told.
In Ajax' eyes blunt rage and rigor rolled,
But the mild glance that sly Ulysses lent
Showed deep regard and smiling government. 1400

There pleading might you see grave Nestor stand, 1401
As 'twere encouraging the Greeks to fight,
Making such sober action with his hand
That it beguiled attention, charmed the sight.
In speech, it seemed, his beard, all silver white,
Wagged up and down, and from his lips did fly
Thin winding breath, which purled up to the sky. 1407

1380 pioneer digger of trenches and mines **1384 lust** pleasure, delight **1385 sweet observance** i.e., verisimilitude created with loving attention to detail **1389 quick** lively **1392 heartless** cowardly **1396 ciphered** showed, expressed **1400 deep . . . government** profound wisdom and the complacency arising from passions being under the command of reason **1401 pleading** making a persuasive oration **1407 purled** curled

About him were a press of gaping faces,
Which seemed to swallow up his sound advice,
All jointly listening, but with several graces, 1410
As if some mermaid did their ears entice;
Some high, some low, the painter was so nice. 1412
  The scalps of many, almost hid behind, 1413
  To jump up higher seemed, to mock the mind. 1414

Here one man's hand leaned on another's head,
His nose being shadowed by his neighbor's ear;
Here one being thronged bears back, all boll'n and red; 1417
Another, smothered, seems to pelt and swear; 1418
And in their rage such signs of rage they bear
  As, but for loss of Nestor's golden words, 1420
  It seemed they would debate with angry swords.

For much imaginary work was there, 1422
Conceit deceitful, so compact, so kind, 1423
That for Achilles' image stood his spear
Gripped in an armèd hand; himself, behind,
Was left unseen, save to the eye of mind.
  A hand, a foot, a face, a leg, a head,
  Stood for the whole to be imaginèd.

And from the walls of strong-besiegèd Troy,
When their brave hope, bold Hector, marched to field,
Stood many Trojan mothers, sharing joy
To see their youthful sons bright weapons wield;
And to their hope they such odd action yield 1433
  That through their light joy seemèd to appear,
  Like bright things stained, a kind of heavy fear.

1410 with several graces i.e., in differing attitudes **1412 Some . . . low** some tall, some short. **nice** accurate, particular **1413 scalps** heads of hair **1414 to mock the mind** (The artistic illusion deceives the mind of the viewer into thinking he sees the movement of those in the back of the crowd who are jumping higher to catch Nestor's oration.)
1417 thronged crowded. **bears** pushes. **boll'n** swollen up **1418 pelt** scold **1420 but . . . words** i.e., were it not that they would thereby miss Nestor's speech **1422 imaginary work** work of the imagination
1423 Conceit deceitful artful contrivance, techniques. **compact** economical and well composed. **kind** natural **1433 they . . . yield** they add such actions and emotions at odds with the joy

And from the strand of Dardan where they fought 1436
To Simois' reedy banks the red blood ran, 1437
Whose waves to imitate the battle sought
With swelling ridges; and their ranks began
To break upon the gallèd shore, and then 1440
  Retire again, till, meeting greater ranks,
  They join and shoot their foam at Simois' banks.

To this well-painted piece is Lucrece come,
To find a face where all distress is stelled. 1444
Many she sees where cares have carvèd some,
But none where all distress and dolor dwelled,
Till she despairing Hecuba beheld, 1447
  Staring on Priam's wounds with her old eyes,
  Which bleeding under Pyrrhus' proud foot lies.

In her the painter had anatomized 1450
Time's ruin, beauty's wrack, and grim care's reign.
Her cheeks with chaps and wrinkles were disguised; 1452
Of what she was no semblance did remain.
Her blue blood, changed to black in every vein,
  Wanting the spring that those shrunk pipes had fed, 1455
  Showed life imprisoned in a body dead.

On this sad shadow Lucrece spends her eyes, 1457
And shapes her sorrow to the beldam's woes, 1458
Who nothing wants to answer her but cries 1459
And bitter words to ban her cruel foes. 1460
The painter was no god to lend her those;
  And therefore Lucrece swears he did her wrong,
  To give her so much grief and not a tongue.

1436 strand shore **1437 Simois** river near Troy **1440 gallèd** eroded **1444 stelled** portrayed, engraved **1447 Hecuba** Queen of Troy, wife of King Priam **1450 anatomized** laid open, dissected **1452 chaps** cracks and lines in the skin. **disguised** disfigured **1455 spring** i.e., source of blood and life. **pipes** i.e., veins **1457 shadow** image, likeness **1458 shapes** likens, compares. **beldam's** old woman's **1459 wants to answer her** i.e., lacks in order to be perfectly like Lucrece in her sorrow **1460 ban** curse

"Poor instrument," quoth she, "without a sound,
I'll tune thy woes with my lamenting tongue, 1465
And drop sweet balm in Priam's painted wound,
And rail on Pyrrhus that hath done him wrong,
And with my tears quench Troy that burns so long,
  And with my knife scratch out the angry eyes
  Of all the Greeks that are thine enemies.

"Show me the strumpet that began this stir,
That with my nails her beauty I may tear.
Thy heat of lust, fond Paris, did incur 1473
This load of wrath that burning Troy doth bear.
Thy eye kindled the fire that burneth here,
  And here in Troy, for trespass of thine eye,
  The sire, the son, the dame, and daughter die.

"Why should the private pleasure of some one
Become the public plague of many moe? 1479
Let sin, alone committed, light alone 1480
Upon his head that hath transgressèd so;
Let guiltless souls be freed from guilty woe.
  For one's offense why should so many fall,
  To plague a private sin in general? 1484

"Lo, here weeps Hecuba, here Priam dies,
Here manly Hector faints, here Troilus swounds, 1486
Here friend by friend in bloody channel lies, 1487
And friend to friend gives unadvisèd wounds, 1488
And one man's lust these many lives confounds.
  Had doting Priam checked his son's desire,
  Troy had been bright with fame and not with fire."

1465 tune sing **1473 fond** doting **1479 moe** more **1480 alone committed** committed by one person alone. **light** alight **1484 in general** collectively, publicly. (Lucrece wonders why it should be necessary to punish the general public for an individual's sin.) **1486 swounds** swoons **1487 channel** gutter **1488 unadvisèd wounds** wounds they never intended for each other

Here feelingly she weeps Troy's painted woes,
For sorrow, like a heavy-hanging bell,
Once set on ringing, with his own weight goes; 1494
Then little strength rings out the doleful knell.
So Lucrece, set a-work, sad tales doth tell
To penciled pensiveness and colored sorrow; 1497
She lends them words, and she their looks doth borrow.

She throws her eyes about the painting round,
And who she finds forlorn she doth lament. 1500
At last she sees a wretched image bound, 1501
That piteous looks to Phrygian shepherds lent. 1502
His face, though full of cares, yet showed content;
Onward to Troy with the blunt swains he goes, 1504
So mild that patience seemed to scorn his woes. 1505

In him the painter labored with his skill
To hide deceit and give the harmless show 1507
An humble gait, calm looks, eyes wailing still, 1508
A brow unbent that seemed to welcome woe;
Cheeks neither red nor pale, but mingled so
That blushing red no guilty instance gave, 1511
Nor ashy pale the fear that false hearts have.

But, like a constant and confirmèd devil,
He entertained a show so seeming just, 1514
And therein so ensconced his secret evil, 1515
That jealousy itself could not mistrust 1516
False-creeping craft and perjury should thrust
Into so bright a day such black-faced storms,
Or blot with hell-born sin such saintlike forms.

1494 his its **1497 penciled** painted. **colored** painted **1500 who** whoever **1501 image** i.e., of Sinon, betrayer of Troy. **bound** onward bound **1502 piteous . . . lent** i.e., drew pitying looks from Phrygian shepherds. (Sinon deceived humble Trojans into pitying him as a deserter from the Greeks, thereby persuading them to admit the wooden horse.) **1504 blunt swains** rustic peasants **1505 patience** i.e., his patience. **scorn** make light of **1507 harmless show** outwardly harmless appearance **1508 still** continually **1511 guilty instance** symptom of guilt **1514 entertained a show** kept up an appearance **1515 ensconced** hid **1516 jealousy** suspicion. **mistrust** suspect (that)

The well-skilled workman this mild image drew
For perjured Sinon, whose enchanting story 1521
The credulous old Priam after slew; 1522
Whose words like wildfire burnt the shining glory 1523
Of rich-built Ilion, that the skies were sorry,
And little stars shot from their fixèd places,
When their glass fell wherein they viewed their faces. 1526

This picture she advisedly perused, 1527
And chid the painter for his wondrous skill,
Saying, some shape in Sinon's was abused; 1529
So fair a form lodged not a mind so ill.
And still on him she gazed, and gazing still,
Such signs of truth in his plain face she spied 1532
That she concludes the picture was belied. 1533

"It cannot be," quoth she, "that so much guile—"
She would have said "can lurk in such a look";
But Tarquin's shape came in her mind the while,
And from her tongue "can lurk" from "cannot" took.
"It cannot be" she in that sense forsook,
And turned it thus: "It cannot be, I find,
But such a face should bear a wicked mind.

"For even as subtle Sinon here is painted,
So sober-sad, so weary, and so mild,
As if with grief or travel he had fainted, 1543
To me came Tarquin armèd, so beguiled 1544
With outward honesty, but yet defiled
With inward vice. As Priam him did cherish,
So did I Tarquin; so my Troy did perish.

1521 For to represent. **enchanting** bewitching **1522 The . . . slew** subsequently brought about the slaughter of credulous old Priam **1523 wildfire** a highly inflammable mixture of tar, sulfur, grease, etc., used in war **1526 glass** mirror (i.e., rich-built Troy) **1527 advisedly** studiously **1529 some shape** i.e., the figure of some other person. **abused** slanderously portrayed **1532 plain** honest **1533 belied** falsified **1543 travel** (The quarto's *trauaile* also contains the idea of "travail," labor.) **1544 armèd** equipped, accoutered. **beguiled** concealed or disguised by guile

"Look, look, how listening Priam wets his eyes,
To see those borrowed tears that Sinon sheeds! 1549
Priam, why art thou old and yet not wise?
For every tear he falls a Trojan bleeds. 1551
His eye drops fire, no water thence proceeds;
Those round clear pearls of his, that move thy pity,
Are balls of quenchless fire to burn thy city.

"Such devils steal effects from lightless hell, 1555
For Sinon in his fire doth quake with cold,
And in that cold hot-burning fire doth dwell.
These contraries such unity do hold 1558
Only to flatter fools and make them bold. 1559
So Priam's trust false Sinon's tears doth flatter 1560
That he finds means to burn his Troy with water." 1561

Here, all enraged, such passion her assails
That patience is quite beaten from her breast.
She tears the senseless Sinon with her nails, 1564
Comparing him to that unhappy guest 1565
Whose deed hath made herself herself detest.
At last she smilingly with this gives o'er:
"Fool, fool!" quoth she, "his wounds will not be sore."

1549 borrowed counterfeited. **sheeds** sheds **1551 he** i.e., Sinon. **falls** lets fall **1555 Such devils** (The ability to weep without real tears—*effects*—was attributed to devils.) **1558–1561 These . . . water** i.e., this illusory coinciding of contraries, hot and cold, is designed to encourage and embolden fools, just as Sinon hoodwinks Priam into a false sense of security; thus false Sinon's tears lull Priam into misplaced trust, so that Sinon finds means to burn Priam's Troy by use of false tears. (*Fools*, l. 1559, can perhaps refer to Priam or to Sinon, and much of the grammar is ingeniously reversible.) **1559, 1560 flatter** encourage with false hopes **1564 senseless** inanimate; unfeeling **1565 unhappy** causing unhappiness

Thus ebbs and flows the current of her sorrow,
And time doth weary time with her complaining.
She looks for night, and then she longs for morrow,
And both she thinks too long with her remaining.
Short time seems long in sorrow's sharp sustaining; 1573
Though woe be heavy, yet it seldom sleeps, 1574
And they that watch see time how slow it creeps. 1575

Which all this time hath overslipped her thought
That she with painted images hath spent,
Being from the feeling of her own grief brought 1578
By deep surmise of others' detriment, 1579
Losing her woes in shows of discontent. 1580
It easeth some, though none it ever cured,
To think their dolor others have endured.

But now the mindful messenger, come back, 1583
Brings home his lord and other company,
Who finds his Lucrece clad in mourning black,
And round about her tear-distainèd eye 1586
Blue circles streamed, like rainbows in the sky.
These water galls in her dim element 1588
Foretell new storms to those already spent. 1589

Which when her sad-beholding husband saw,
Amazedly in her sad face he stares.
Her eyes, though sod in tears, looked red and raw, 1592
Her lively color killed with deadly cares.
He hath no power to ask her how she fares;
Both stood like old acquaintance in a trance,
Met far from home, wond'ring each other's chance. 1596

1573 in . . . sustaining when it is sustained by sharp sorrow
1574 heavy exhausting; sorrowful **1575 watch** stay awake
1578 brought made mindful **1579 surmise** conjecture, contemplation
1580 shows of discontent representations of sorrow, i.e., the painted scene of Troy's woe **1583 mindful** diligent **1586 tear-distainèd** tear-stained **1588 water galls** fragments of rainbow, secondary rainbows (foretelling stormy weather). **dim** cloudy. **element** sky, i.e., face or eye
1589 to besides **1592 sod** sodden, steeped **1596 wond'ring . . . chance** wondering about each other's fortune; or, each wondering at the chance that has brought him to the other

At last he takes her by the bloodless hand,
And thus begins: "What uncouth ill event 1598
Hath thee befall'n, that thou dost trembling stand?
Sweet love, what spite hath thy fair color spent? 1600
Why art thou thus attired in discontent? 1601
  Unmask, dear dear, this moody heaviness, 1602
  And tell thy grief, that we may give redress."

Three times with sighs she gives her sorrow fire 1604
Ere once she can discharge one word of woe. 1605
At length addressed to answer his desire, 1606
She modestly prepares to let them know
Her honor is ta'en prisoner by the foe,
  While Collatine and his consorted lords 1609
  With sad attention long to hear her words. 1610

And now this pale swan in her watery nest 1611
Begins the sad dirge of her certain ending:
"Few words," quoth she, "shall fit the trespass best,
Where no excuse can give the fault amending.
In me more woes than words are now depending, 1615
  And my laments would be drawn out too long,
  To tell them all with one poor tirèd tongue.

"Then be this all the task it hath to say:
Dear husband, in the interest of thy bed 1619
A stranger came, and on that pillow lay
Where thou wast wont to rest thy weary head;
And what wrong else may be imaginèd
  By foul enforcement might be done to me,
  From that, alas, thy Lucrece is not free.

1598 uncouth unknown, strange **1600 spite** injury. **spent** expended, taken away **1601 attired** wrapped up **1602 Unmask** reveal **1604–1605 Three . . . woe** (The metaphor is that of discharging firearms by means of a match.) **1606 addressed** prepared **1609 consorted** companion **1610 sad** serious **1611 swan** (Alludes to the belief that the swan, ordinarily without a song, sings beautifully at its own death.) **1615 depending** belonging, suspended, or pending (?) **1619 in the interest** claiming possession

"For in the dreadful dead of dark midnight,
With shining falchion in my chamber came
A creeping creature with a flaming light,
And softly cried, 'Awake, thou Roman dame,
And entertain my love! Else lasting shame 1629
  On thee and thine this night I will inflict,
  If thou my love's desire do contradict.

"'For some hard-favored groom of thine,' quoth he, 1632
'Unless thou yoke thy liking to my will,
I'll murder straight, and then I'll slaughter thee 1634
And swear I found you where you did fulfill
The loathsome act of lust, and so did kill
  The lechers in their deed. This act will be
  My fame and thy perpetual infamy.'

"With this, I did begin to start and cry;
And then against my heart he set his sword,
Swearing, unless I took all patiently,
I should not live to speak another word;
So should my shame still rest upon record,
  And never be forgot in mighty Rome
  Th' adulterate death of Lucrece and her groom. 1645

"Mine enemy was strong, my poor self weak,
And far the weaker with so strong a fear.
My bloody judge forbade my tongue to speak;
No rightful plea might plead for justice there.
His scarlet lust came evidence to swear 1650
  That my poor beauty had purloined his eyes;
  And when the judge is robbed the prisoner dies.

1629 entertain receive **1632 hard-favored** ugly **1634 straight** at once
1645 adulterate adulterous **1650 came evidence** supplied evidence

"O, teach me how to make mine own excuse!
Or at the least this refuge let me find:
Though my gross blood be stained with this abuse,
Immaculate and spotless is my mind.
That was not forced, that never was inclined
To accessory yieldings, but still pure 1658
Doth in her poisoned closet yet endure." 1659

Lo, here, the hopeless merchant of this loss, 1660
With head declined and voice dammed up with woe, 1661
With sad set eyes and wreathèd arms across,
From lips new waxen pale begins to blow 1663
The grief away that stops his answer so.
But, wretched as he is, he strives in vain;
What he breathes out his breath drinks up again.

As through an arch the violent roaring tide 1667
Outruns the eye that doth behold his haste,
Yet in the eddy boundeth in his pride
Back to the strait that forced him on so fast—
In rage sent out, recalled in rage, being past—
Even so his sighs, his sorrows, make a saw, 1672
To push grief on and back the same grief draw. 1673

Which speechless woe of his poor she attendeth, 1674
And his untimely frenzy thus awaketh: 1675
"Dear lord, thy sorrow to my sorrow lendeth
Another power; no flood by raining slaketh. 1677
My woe too sensible thy passion maketh 1678
More feeling-painful. Let it then suffice 1679
To drown one woe, one pair of weeping eyes.

1658 accessory yieldings i.e., as an accessory to crime **1659 poisoned closet** i.e., violated body **1660 merchant of this loss** i.e., owner who has sustained this loss, Collatine **1661 declined** lowered, bent down **1663 new waxen** newly turned **1667 arch** i.e., of a bridge, such as London Bridge or Clopton Bridge **1672 saw** i.e., sawlike back-and-forth motion **1673 and . . . draw** and draw the same grief back. (Collatine breathes and sighs, in and out.) **1674 Which . . . attendeth** i.e., to which speechless woe of Collatine poor Lucrece pays heed **1675 And . . . awaketh** and awakens him from his ill-timed distraction **1677 Another power** added strength. **no . . . slaketh** no flood is lessened by more rain **1678–1679 My . . . painful** your passionate grief makes my woe, already too keenly felt, even more painfully perceived

"And for my sake, when I might charm thee so, 1681
For she that was thy Lucrece, now attend me:
Be suddenly revengèd on my foe, 1683
Thine, mine, his own. Suppose thou dost defend me 1684
From what is past. The help that thou shalt lend me
Comes all too late, yet let the traitor die;
For sparing justice feeds iniquity. 1687

"But ere I name him, you fair lords," quoth she,
Speaking to those that came with Collatine,
"Shall plight your honorable faiths to me, 1690
With swift pursuit to venge this wrong of mine;
For 'tis a meritorious fair design
To chase injustice with revengeful arms.
Knights, by their oaths, should right poor ladies' harms."

At this request, with noble disposition
Each present lord began to promise aid,
As bound in knighthood to her imposition, 1697
Longing to hear the hateful foe bewrayed. 1698
But she, that yet her sad task hath not said, 1699
The protestation stops. "O, speak," quoth she, 1700
"How may this forcèd stain be wiped from me?

"What is the quality of my offense, 1702
Being constrained with dreadful circumstance? 1703
May my pure mind with the foul act dispense, 1704
My low-declinèd honor to advance? 1705
May any terms acquit me from this chance? 1706
The poisoned fountain clears itself again,
And why not I from this compellèd stain?"

1681 so i.e., in the person of my former self, still unravished
1683 suddenly quickly **1684 his own** i.e., his own worst enemy
1687 sparing too lenient. **feeds iniquity** encourages wrongdoing
1690 plight pledge **1697 imposition** injunction **1698 bewrayed** revealed, named **1699 her . . . said** had not yet finished her sad task of speaking **1700 protestation** resolution **1702 quality** nature
1703 with dreadful circumstance in a situation filled with dread
1704 with . . . dispense be able to free itself from the foul deed
1705 advance raise up **1706 terms** mitigating grounds

With this they all at once began to say
Her body's stain her mind untainted clears,
While with a joyless smile she turns away
The face, that map which deep impression bears 1712
Of hard misfortune, carved in it with tears.
"No, no," quoth she, "no dame hereafter living
By my excuse shall claim excuse's giving." 1715

Here with a sigh, as if her heart would break,
She throws forth Tarquin's name: "He, he," she says,
But more than "he" her poor tongue could not speak;
Till after many accents and delays, 1719
Untimely breathings, sick and short assays,
She utters this: "He, he, fair lords, 'tis he,
That guides this hand to give this wound to me."

Even here she sheathèd in her harmless breast
A harmful knife, that thence her soul unsheathed.
That blow did bail it from the deep unrest 1725
Of that polluted prison where it breathed.
Her contrite sighs unto the clouds bequeathed
Her wingèd sprite, and through her wounds doth fly
Life's lasting date from canceled destiny. 1729

Stone-still, astonished with this deadly deed,
Stood Collatine and all his lordly crew,
Till Lucrece' father, that beholds her bleed,
Himself on her self-slaughtered body threw,
And from the purple fountain Brutus drew 1734
The murderous knife, and, as it left the place,
Her blood, in poor revenge, held it in chase;

1712 map i.e., image **1715 By . . . giving** will be able to claim the right to offer (give) an excuse using my excuse as her precedent
1719 accents sounds expressive of emotion **1725 bail it** pay for its release **1729 Life's . . . destiny** i.e., the life that now has a perpetual existence, its subjugation to corporeal existence having been canceled
1734 Brutus Lucius Junius Brutus, whose brother had been killed by the father of the Tarquin in this poem

And bubbling from her breast, it doth divide
In two slow rivers, that the crimson blood
Circles her body in on every side,
Who, like a late-sacked island, vastly stood 1740
Bare and unpeopled in this fearful flood.
  Some of her blood still pure and red remained,
  And some looked black, and that false Tarquin
    stained.

About the mourning and congealèd face
Of that black blood a watery rigol goes, 1745
Which seems to weep upon the tainted place;
And ever since, as pitying Lucrece' woes,
Corrupted blood some watery token shows,
  And blood untainted still doth red abide,
  Blushing at that which is so putrified.

"Daughter, dear daughter," old Lucretius cries,
"That life was mine which thou hast here deprived. 1752
If in the child the father's image lies,
Where shall I live now Lucrece is unlived? 1754
Thou wast not to this end from me derived.
  If children predecease progenitors,
  We are their offspring, and they none of ours.

"Poor broken glass, I often did behold 1758
In thy sweet semblance my old age new born;
But now that fair fresh mirror dim and old
Shows me a bare-boned death by time outworn. 1761
O, from thy cheeks my image thou hast torn,
  And shivered all the beauty of my glass,
  That I no more can see what once I was!

1740 late-sacked recently pillaged. **vastly** having been desolated
1745 rigol rim of serum **1752 deprived** taken away **1754 unlived**
bereft of life **1758 glass** mirror (i.e., Lucrece, the image of her father)
1761 death death's-head, skull

"O Time, cease thou thy course and last no longer,
If they surcease to be that should survive! 1766
Shall rotten Death make conquest of the stronger
And leave the faltering feeble souls alive?
The old bees die, the young possess their hive.
Then live, sweet Lucrece, live again and see
Thy father die, and not thy father thee!"

By this, starts Collatine as from a dream,
And bids Lucretius give his sorrow place; 1773
And then in key-cold Lucrece' bleeding stream 1774
He falls, and bathes the pale fear in his face, 1775
And counterfeits to die with her a space, 1776
Till manly shame bids him possess his breath
And live to be revengèd on her death.

The deep vexation of his inward soul
Hath served a dumb arrest upon his tongue, 1780
Who, mad that sorrow should his use control,
Or keep him from heart-easing words so long,
Begins to talk; but through his lips do throng
Weak words, so thick come in his poor heart's aid, 1784
That no man could distinguish what he said.

Yet sometimes "Tarquin" was pronouncèd plain,
But through his teeth, as if the name he tore.
This windy tempest, till it blow up rain,
Held back his sorrow's tide, to make it more.
At last it rains, and busy winds give o'er;
Then son and father weep with equal strife
Who should weep most, for daughter or for wife.

1766 surcease cease **1773 give . . . place** yield him precedence in sorrowing **1774 key-cold** i.e., cold as steel **1775 pale fear** fearful pallor **1776 counterfeits to die** gives the appearance of dying. **a space** for a period of time **1780 dumb arrest** injunction to be silent **1784 thick** thickly, fast

The one doth call her his, the other his,
Yet neither may possess the claim they lay. 1794
The father says, "She's mine." "O, mine she is,"
Replies her husband. "Do not take away
My sorrow's interest. Let no mourner say 1797
He weeps for her, for she was only mine,
And only must be wailed by Collatine."

"O," quoth Lucretius, "I did give that life
Which she too early and too late hath spilled." 1801
"Woe, woe," quoth Collatine, "She was my wife,
I owed her, and 'tis mine that she hath killed." 1803
"My daughter" and "my wife" with clamors filled
The dispersed air, who, holding Lucrece' life,
Answered their cries, "my daughter" and "my wife."

Brutus, who plucked the knife from Lucrece' side,
Seeing such emulation in their woe,
Began to clothe his wit in state and pride, 1809
Burying in Lucrece' wound his folly's show. 1810
He with the Romans was esteemèd so
As silly jeering idiots are with kings, 1812
For sportive words and uttering foolish things.

But now he throws that shallow habit by, 1814
Wherein deep policy did him disguise, 1815
And armed his long-hid wits advisedly
To check the tears in Collatinus' eyes.
"Thou wrongèd lord of Rome," quoth he, "arise!
Let my unsounded self, supposed a fool, 1819
Now set thy long-experienced wit to school.

1794 possess . . . lay take possession of what they claim (since she is dead) **1797 interest** claim to possession **1801 late** recently **1803 owed** owned **1809 state** dignity **1810 folly's show** pretense of folly. (Brutus feigned madness to escape the fate of his brother; see l. 1734, note.) **1812 silly jeering idiots** i.e., innocent court jesters **1814 habit** cloak and disposition **1815 policy** cunning **1819 unsounded** unplumbed, unexplored

"Why, Collatine, is woe the cure for woe?
Do wounds help wounds, or grief help grievous deeds?
Is it revenge to give thyself a blow
For his foul act by whom thy fair wife bleeds?
Such childish humor from weak minds proceeds. 1825
  Thy wretched wife mistook the matter so
  To slay herself, that should have slain her foe.

"Courageous Roman, do not steep thy heart
In such relenting dew of lamentations,
But kneel with me and help to bear thy part
To rouse our Roman gods with invocations
That they will suffer these abominations— 1832
  Since Rome herself in them doth stand disgraced—
  By our strong arms from forth her fair streets
    chased. 1834

"Now, by the Capitol that we adore,
And by this chaste blood so unjustly stained,
By heaven's fair sun that breeds the fat earth's store, 1837
By all our country rights in Rome maintained, 1838
And by chaste Lucrece' soul that late complained
  Her wrongs to us, and by this bloody knife,
  We will revenge the death of this true wife."

This said, he struck his hand upon his breast,
And kissed the fatal knife, to end his vow;
And to his protestation urged the rest, 1844
Who, wondering at him, did his words allow. 1845
Then jointly to the ground their knees they bow,
  And that deep vow which Brutus made before
  He doth again repeat, and that they swore.

1825 humor disposition **1832 suffer** permit **1834 chased** i.e., to be chased away **1837 fat** fertile **1838 country rights** rights we have as a people **1844 protestation** resolution **1845 allow** approve

When they had sworn to this advisèd doom, 1849
They did conclude to bear dead Lucrece thence,
To show her bleeding body thorough Rome, 1851
And so to publish Tarquin's foul offense; 1852
Which being done with speedy diligence,
The Romans plausibly did give consent 1854
To Tarquin's everlasting banishment.

1849 advisèd doom considered judgment **1851 thorough** throughout
1852 publish make public **1854 plausibly** with applause

Date and Text

Shakespeare promised a "graver labor" to Southampton in his dedication of *Venus and Adonis,* 1593, and *The Rape of Lucrece* is almost surely that promised sequel. It was registered in the Stationers' Register, the official record book of the London Company of Stationers (booksellers and printers), by John Harrison on May 9, 1594, and issued that same year as "printed by Richard Field, for Iohn Harrison." The printed text was probably based on Shakespeare's manuscript. Although not quite as popular as *Venus and Adonis,* the poem was reprinted five times during Shakespeare's lifetime. Contemporaries of Shakespeare who allude favorably to the poem include W. Har and Michael Drayton in 1594, William Covell in 1595, Francis Meres in 1598, Gabriel Harvey in 1598–1601, John Weever in 1599, and others. The date of composition of the poem is well fixed between the publication of *Venus and Adonis* in 1593 and that of *The Rape of Lucrece* itself in 1594.

Textual Notes

These textual notes are not a historical collation; they are simply a record of departures in this edition from the copy text. The reading adopted in this edition appears in boldface, followed by the rejected reading from the copy text, i.e., the quarto of 1594. Only major alterations in punctuation are noted. Corrections of minor and obvious typographical errors are not indicated.

Copy text: the corrected quarto of 1594 [Q corr.] A number of corrected readings are however rejected as sophistications; see text notes below at ll. 24, 31, 50, 125, 126.

24 morning [Q uncorr.] mornings [Q corr.] **31 apology** [Q uncorr.] Apologies [Q corr.] **50 Collatium** [Q uncorr., Colatium] Colatia [Q corr.] **125 himself betakes** [Q uncorr.] themselues betake [Q corr.] **126 wakes** [Q uncorr.] wake [corr.] **555 panteth** pateth **560 wear** were **688 lose** loose [also at ll. 979 and 1158] **922 inclination** inclination. **1126 Relish** Ralish **1129 hair** heare **1249 remain** remaine. **1251 peep** peepe, **1312 schedule** Cedule **1350 this pattern of the** the pattern of this [in four copies of Q; it is uncertain which is the corrected state] **1386 far-off** farre of **1543 travel** trauaile **1544 so** to

1580 Losing Loosing **1648 forbade** forbod **1660 here** heare **1662 wreathed** wretched **1680 one woe** on woe **1713 in it** it in **1768 faltering** foultring

THE PHOENIX —AND— TURTLE

Introduction

"The Phoenix and Turtle" first appeared in a collection of poems called *Loves Martyr: Or, Rosalins Complaint* by Robert Chester (1601). This quarto volume offered various poetic exercises about the phoenix and the turtle "by the best and chiefest of our modern writers." The poem assigned to Shakespeare has been universally accepted as his and is one of his most remarkable productions. With a deceptively simple diction, in gracefully pure tetrameter quatrains and triplets, the poem effortlessly evokes the transcendental ideal of a love existing eternally beyond death. The occasion is an assembly of birds to observe the funeral rites of the phoenix and the turtle. The phoenix, legendary bird of resurrection from her own ashes, once more finds life through death in the company of the turtledove, emblem of pure constancy in affection. Their spiritual union becomes a mystical oneness in whose presence Reason stands virtually speechless. Baffled human discourse must resort to paradox in order to explain how two beings become one essence, "Hearts remote yet not asunder." Mathematics and logic are "confounded" by this joining of two spirits into a "concordant one." This paradox of oneness echoes scholastic theology and its expounding of the doctrine of the Trinity, although, somewhat in the manner of John Donne's poetry, this allusion is more a part of the poem's serious wit than its symbolic meaning. The poignant brevity of this vision is rendered all the more mysterious by our not knowing what if any human tragedy may have prompted this metaphysical affirmation.

The Phoenix and Turtle

Let the bird of loudest lay 1
On the sole Arabian tree 2
Herald sad and trumpet be, 3
To whose sound chaste wings obey. 4

But thou shrieking harbinger, 5
Foul precurrer of the fiend, 6
Augur of the fever's end, 7
To this troop come thou not near.

From this session interdict
Every fowl of tyrant wing, 10
Save the eagle, feathered king;
Keep the obsequy so strict.

Let the priest in surplice white,
That defunctive music can, 14
Be the death-divining swan, 15
Lest the requiem lack his right. 16

Title: Phoenix mythical bird that was thought to be consumed in flame and reborn in its own ashes, symbol of immortality. **Turtle** turtledove, symbol of constancy in love

1 bird . . . lay the bird (possibly the nightingale) of loudest song **2 sole Arabian tree** (The phoenix was thought to build its nest in a unique tree in Arabia.) **3 sad** solemn. **trumpet** trumpeter **4 chaste wings** i.e., the wings of the good birds that are being summoned. **obey** are obedient **5 shrieking harbinger** i.e., screech owl **6 precurrer** forerunner **7 Augur . . . end** i.e., prognosticator of death **10 fowl . . . wing** bird of prey **14 defunctive** funereal. **can** knows, has skill in **15 death-divining swan** (Alludes to the belief that the swan foresees its own death and sings when it is about to die.) **16 his right** its proper ceremony, or its proper due (referring either to the *requiem* or to the *swan*)

And thou treble-dated crow, 17
That thy sable gender mak'st 18
With the breath thou giv'st and tak'st, 19
'Mongst our mourners shalt thou go.

Here the anthem doth commence.
Love and constancy is dead;
Phoenix and the turtle fled
In a mutual flame from hence.

So they loved, as love in twain 25
Had the essence but in one,
Two distincts, division none; 27
Number there in love was slain. 28

Hearts remote yet not asunder,
Distance and no space was seen
Twixt this turtle and his queen;
But in them it were a wonder. 32

So between them love did shine, 33
That the turtle saw his right 34
Flaming in the phoenix' sight; 35
Either was the other's mine. 36

17 treble-dated i.e., living thrice as long as the normal span of life **18–19 That . . . tak'st** (Cf. *Hortus Sanitatis,* Bk. 3, sec. 34, in Seager's *Natural History in Shakespeare's Time:* "They [ravens] are said to conceive and to lay eggs at the bill. The young become black on the seventh day.") **18 sable gender** black offspring **25 So . . . as** they so loved that **27 distincts** separate or individual persons or things **28 Number . . . slain** i.e., their love, being of one essence, paradoxically renders the very concept of number meaningless; "one is no number" **32 But . . . wonder** this phenomenon, had it been seen anywhere but in them, would have seemed amazing **33 So** in such a way **34 his right** his true nature, what pertained uniquely and rightly to him; or, what was due to him **35 sight** eyes **36 mine** i.e., very own. (The phoenix and turtle are so merged in one another's identity that each contains the other's being.)

Property was thus appalled 37
That the self was not the same; 38
Single nature's double name 39
Neither two nor one was called. 40

Reason, in itself confounded, 41
Saw division grow together, 42
To themselves yet either neither, 43
Simple were so well compounded, 44

That it cried, "How true a twain 45
Seemeth this concordant one!
Love hath reason, Reason none, 47
If what parts can so remain." 48

Whereupon it made this threne 49
To the phoenix and the dove,
Co-supremes and stars of love, 51
As chorus to their tragic scene.

THRENOS

Beauty, truth, and rarity, 53
Grace in all simplicity,
Here enclosed, in cinders lie. 55

Death is now the phoenix' nest,
And the turtle's loyal breast
To eternity doth rest,

37–38 Property . . . same i.e., the very idea of a peculiar or essential quality was thus confounded by the paradoxical revelation here that each lover's identity was merged into the other's and was no longer itself **39–40 Single . . . called** i.e., their nature was at once so single and double that it could not properly be called either one or two **41–44 Reason . . . compounded** i.e., Reason, which proceeds by making discriminations between separate entities, is confounded when it beholds a paradoxical union of such entities, each at once discrete and fused into a single being, at once a simple (i.e., made of one substance) and a compound **45 it** i.e., Reason **47–48 Love . . . remain** i.e., Love, which ordinarily lacks reason, is reasonable, and Reason itself lacks reason, if two that can be disunited or parted nevertheless remain thus in union **49 threne** lamentation, funeral song (from Greek *threnos*) **51 Co-supremes** joint rulers **53 truth** constancy in love (also in l. 62) **55 enclosed** i.e., enclosed in *this urn* (l. 65)

Leaving no posterity;
'Twas not their infirmity, 60
It was married chastity. 61

Truth may seem, but cannot be; 62
Beauty brag, but 'tis not she; 63
Truth and beauty buried be. 64

To this urn let those repair
That are either true or fair;
For these dead birds sigh a prayer.

60–61 'Twas . . . chastity i.e., it was not a defect in them to leave no posterity, but an emblem of their mystical eternal trothplight
62–64 Truth . . . be i.e., fidelity and beauty as known to mortal perception are only illusory, for their ideal incarnation now lies buried with the phoenix and turtle

Date and Text

"The Phoenix and Turtle" first appeared in a volume with the following title:

> LOVES MARTYR: OR, ROSALINS COMPLAINT. *Allegorically shadowing the truth of Loue,* in the constant Fate of the Phoenix *and Turtle. . . .* by ROBERT CHESTER. . . . *To these are added some new compositions, of seuerall moderne Writers whose names are subscribed to their seuerall workes, vpon the first subiect: viz. the* Phoenix *and* Turtle.

The date 1601 appears on a separate title page. One poem is signed "William Shake-speare," others John Marston, George Chapman, and Ben Jonson.

–A LOVER'S– COMPLAINT

Introduction

Thomas Thorpe published "A Lover's Complaint" in his 1609 quarto of Shakespeare's *Sonnets,* ascribing the poem to "William Shake-speare" in its title heading (sig. K^v). The ascription must not be given too much weight, for Thorpe evidently did not have Shakespeare's authorization to publish the sonnets and may possibly have added the last two sonnets from some other source. Yet Thorpe's edition remains the only objective evidence we have, and its authority has never been convincingly refuted. The modern tendency to dismiss "A Lover's Complaint" as unworthy of Shakespeare's genius rests on subjective judgment and on stylistic "tests" that are too often proved unreliable. In fact the density of metaphor and energy of wordplay are stylistically and intellectually very much like that of his known work. The poem was never ascribed to anyone else during Shakespeare's lifetime. On balance, the evidence is in favor of his authorship, though the issue will continue to remain in doubt.

The poem's genre, the "complaint" of a forsaken maiden, is conventional, along with the pastoral setting, the catalog of the fickle lover's features, and the sententious warnings against blind passion. The poem did not add to Shakespeare's contemporary reputation. Still, it cannot safely be assigned to any other Elizabethan poet. Nor does it read like a mere effusion of Shakespeare's youth. Though written in *The Rape of Lucrece*'s seven-line rhyme royal stanza, the poem eschews Ovidian and Petrarchan conceit for an occasional richness and complexity of metaphor.

A Lover's Complaint

From off a hill whose concave womb reworded 1
A plaintful story from a sistering vale, 2
My spirits t' attend this double voice accorded, 3
And down I laid to list the sad-tuned tale; 4
Ere long espied a fickle maid full pale, 5
Tearing of papers, breaking rings a-twain, 6
Storming her world with sorrow's wind and rain.

Upon her head a platted hive of straw, 8
Which fortified her visage from the sun, 9
Whereon the thought might think sometimes it saw 10
The carcass of a beauty spent and done. 11
Time had not scythèd all that youth begun,
Nor youth all quit, but spite of heaven's fell rage 13
Some beauty peeped through lattice of seared age. 14

Oft did she heave her napkin to her eyne, 15
Which on it had conceited characters, 16
Laund'ring the silken figures in the brine
That seasoned woe had pelleted in tears, 18
And often reading what contents it bears;
As often shrieking undistinguished woe, 20
In clamors of all size, both high and low.

1 concave womb hollow-shaped hillside. **reworded** echoed **2 plaintful story** i.e., mournful sound (which turns out to be the grieving of a maiden). **sistering** neighboring **3 attend** listen to. **double** (because echoed). **accorded** inclined, consented **4 list** listen to. **sad-tuned** i.e., sung in a minor key **5 fickle** i.e., perturbed, moody **6 papers** i.e., love letters **8 platted hive** i.e., woven hat **9 fortified** protected **10 the thought** the mind; that which thinks **11 carcass** decaying lifeless remnant. **spent** consumed **13 all quit** deserted every part. **fell** deadly, cruel **14 seared** dried up **15 heave** lift. **napkin** handkerchief. **eyne** eyes **16 conceited characters** fanciful or emblematic devices **18 seasoned** (1) matured (2) salted. **pelleted** formed into small globules **20 undistinguished woe** incoherent cries of grief

Sometimes her leveled eyes their carriage ride, 22
As they did battery to the spheres intend; 23
Sometimes, diverted, their poor balls are tied 24
To th' orbèd earth; sometimes they do extend 25
Their view right on; anon their gazes lend 26
To every place at once, and, nowhere fixed, 27
The mind and sight distractedly commixed. 28

Her hair, nor loose nor tied in formal plat, 29
Proclaimed in her a careless hand of pride; 30
For some, untucked, descended her sheaved hat, 31
Hanging her pale and pinèd cheek beside; 32
Some in her threaden fillet still did bide, 33
And, true to bondage, would not break from thence,
Though slackly braided in loose negligence.

A thousand favors from a maund she drew 36
Of amber, crystal, and of beaded jet, 37
Which one by one she in a river threw,
Upon whose weeping margent she was set, 39
Like usury applying wet to wet, 40
Or monarch's hands that lets not bounty fall
Where want cries some, but where excess begs all. 42

22 her . . . ride i.e., her eyes, directed and aimed like a cannon, swiveled about as on a gun carriage **23 As . . . intend** as if they did intend to direct their fire against the heavens **24 balls** eyeballs **24–25 are . . . earth** seem fixed to the orb-shaped earth, to the ground **26 right on** straight in front of her **26–27 lend . . . once** i.e., roll distractedly everywhere **28 The mind . . . commixed** her mind and sight wildly confused or mingled **29 nor . . . nor** neither . . . nor. **in formal plat** neatly braided **30 careless . . . pride** hand careless of appearances
31 descended hung from. **sheaved** straw **32 Hanging . . . beside** hanging beside her pale cheek wasted with pining **33 threaden fillet** i.e., ribbon binding her hair **36 favors** love tokens. **maund** woven basket with handles **37 beaded jet** jet beads **39 weeping margent** moist bank (though *weeping* also applies to her) **40 usury** i.e., adding money to money; she adds tears to the river's water **42 Where . . . all** i.e., (not) where the needy cry out for some charity, but where the rich beg all the bounty there is

Of folded schedules had she many a one, 43
Which she perused, sighed, tore, and gave the flood; 44
Cracked many a ring of posied gold and bone, 45
Bidding them find their sepulchers in mud;
Found yet more letters sadly penned in blood,
With sleided silk feat and affectedly 48
Enswathed and sealed to curious secrecy. 49

These often bathed she in her fluxive eyes, 50
And often kissed, and often 'gan to tear;
Cried, "O false blood, thou register of lies, 52
What unapprovèd witness dost thou bear! 53
Ink would have seemed more black and damnèd here!"
This said, in top of rage the lines she rents, 55
Big discontent so breaking their contents. 56

A reverend man that grazed his cattle nigh— 57
Sometime a blusterer, that the ruffle knew 58
Of court, of city, and had let go by
The swiftest hours, observèd as they flew— 60
Towards this afflicted fancy fastly drew, 61
And, privileged by age, desires to know
In brief the grounds and motives of her woe.

43 schedules papers containing writing, i.e., letters **44 gave the flood** threw in the stream **45 posied** inscribed with a motto **48 sleided** separated into threads. **feat** featly, adroitly. **affectedly** lovingly
49 Enswathed . . . secrecy wrapped about (with the silk) and sealed (with wax) into careful secrecy **50 fluxive** flowing **52 blood** i.e., the blood in which the letters were written (l. 47), but with a sense also of the *blood* or passion that has played her *false*. **register** record
53 unapprovèd unconfirmed, false **55 in top of** in the height of. **rents** rends, tears **56 discontent . . . contents** (with a play of antithesis)
57 reverend aged **58 Sometime** at one time. **blusterer** boisterous fellow. **ruffle** commotion, bustle **60 swiftest hours** i.e., time of youth. **observèd as they flew** (This man has let his youth go by and disappear, but not without observing and learning from the years as they flew.) **61 fancy** i.e., amorous passion, and the person expressing it. **fastly** (1) quickly (2) in close proximity

So slides he down upon his grainèd bat, 64
And comely-distant sits he by her side, 65
When he again desires her, being sat, 66
Her grievance with his hearing to divide. 67
If that from him there may be aught applied 68
Which may her suffering ecstasy assuage, 69
'Tis promised in the charity of age.

"Father," she says, "though in me you behold 71
The injury of many a blasting hour, 72
Let it not tell your judgment I am old;
Not age, but sorrow, over me hath power.
I might as yet have been a spreading flower, 75
Fresh to myself, if I had self-applied 76
Love to myself and to no love beside.

"But, woe is me! Too early I attended 78
A youthful suit—it was to gain my grace— 79
O, one by nature's outwards so commended 80
That maidens' eyes stuck over all his face. 81
Love lacked a dwelling and made him her place; 82
And when in his fair parts she did abide,
She was new lodged and newly deified.

"His browny locks did hang in crooked curls,
And every light occasion of the wind 86
Upon his lips their silken parcels hurls. 87
What's sweet to do, to do will aptly find; 88
Each eye that saw him did enchant the mind,
For on his visage was in little drawn 90
What largeness thinks in Paradise was sawn. 91

64 So . . . bat and so he lowers himself by means of his club or staff that is worn and showing the grain **65 comely-distant** at a decorous distance **66 being** he being **67 divide** share **68 If that** if **69 ecstasy** frenzy (of grief) **71 Father** i.e., old man **72 blasting** blighting, withering **75 spreading** unfolding **76 Fresh to myself** i.e., like a flower that lives and dies unseen and unplucked **78 attended** heeded **79 grace** favor **80 nature's outwards** the physical appearance given him by nature **81 stuck over** i.e., were glued to **82 Love** Venus **86 occasion** i.e., stirring **87 Upon . . . hurls** (the wind) tosses the *silken parcels,* the curls, against his lips **88 to do will aptly find** i.e., will find a doer or an occasion **90 in little** in miniature **91 What . . . sawn** what one supposes was seen in full scale in Paradise

"Small show of man was yet upon his chin;
His phoenix down began but to appear 93
Like unshorn velvet on that termless skin 94
Whose bare outbragged the web it seemed to wear. 95
Yet showed his visage by that cost more dear; 96
And nice affections wavering stood in doubt 97
If best were as it was, or best without. 98

"His qualities were beauteous as his form, 99
For maiden-tongued he was, and thereof free; 100
Yet, if men moved him, was he such a storm 101
As oft twixt May and April is to see, 102
When winds breathe sweet, unruly though they be.
His rudeness so with his authorized youth 104
Did livery falseness in a pride of truth. 105

"Well could he ride, and often men would say,
'That horse his mettle from his rider takes. 107
Proud of subjection, noble by the sway, 108
What rounds, what bounds, what course, what stop he
makes!' 109
And controversy hence a question takes, 110
Whether the horse by him became his deed, 111
Or he his manage by th' well-doing steed. 112

93 phoenix i.e., suggesting his unique perfection (since only one phoenix, a mythical bird, exists at one time) **94 termless** indescribable; youthful **95 bare outbragged** bareness surpassed. **web** i.e., covering, the downy beard **96 cost** (1) expense (2) rich covering; i.e., his face seemed lovelier because of its rich or silken covering. **dear** (1) costly (2) lovely **97 nice affections** carefully discriminating tastes, inclinations **98 without** i.e., lacking the downy beard **99 qualities were** manner was as **100 maiden-tongued** modest of speech, soft-spoken. **free** eloquent; innocent **101 moved** i.e., to anger **102 to see** to be seen **104–105 His . . . truth** his roughness, privileged by his youth, thereby did dress falseness in a magnificent garment or concealment of truth **107 mettle** vigor and strength of spirit **108 noble by the sway** made noble by the way he's controlled **109 stop** sudden check in a horse's "career" or trial gallop at full speed. (All the terms here are terms of *manage*, l. 112, the schooling or handling of a horse.)
110 takes takes up, considers **111–112 Whether . . . steed** whether it was owing to his horsemanship that his horse acted so becomingly or whether he seemed such a good rider because he had so good a horse

"But quickly on this side the verdict went:
His real habitude gave life and grace 114
To appertainings and to ornament,
Accomplished in himself, not in his case. 116
All aids, themselves made fairer by their place, 117
Came for additions, yet their purposed trim 118
Pieced not his grace, but were all graced by him. 119

"So on the tip of his subduing tongue
All kind of arguments and question deep,
All replication prompt and reason strong, 122
For his advantage still did wake and sleep. 123
To make the weeper laugh, the laugher weep,
He had the dialect and different skill, 125
Catching all passions in his craft of will, 126

"That he did in the general bosom reign 127
Of young, of old, and sexes both enchanted,
To dwell with him in thoughts, or to remain
In personal duty, following where he haunted. 130
Consents bewitched, ere he desire, have granted, 131
And dialogued for him what he would say, 132
Asked their own wills, and made their wills obey. 133

114 habitude constitution, temperament **116 case** conditions and circumstances, e.g., the possession of so good a horse **117 place** i.e., place near to him or on his person **118 Came for additions** came in for consideration as additional graces. **purposed trim** intended function as adornment **119 Pieced** mended, augmented **122 replication** reply. **reason strong** persuasive argument **123 still** continually. **wake and sleep** i.e., work in varying moods, now actively, now insinuatingly **125 dialect** manner of expression. **different** varied, readily adaptable **126 passions** (1) passions of his hearers (2) passions incorporated into his moving speech. **craft of will** skill in persuasion **127 That** so that. **general bosom** hearts of all **130 In personal duty** i.e., like a personal servant. **haunted** frequented **131–133 Consents . . . obey** i.e., women have consented to his will before he even asked them, and have made up his love speeches to them for him, and have made themselves obey their own desires

"Many there were that did his picture get
To serve their eyes, and in it put their mind, 135
Like fools that in th' imagination set
The goodly objects which abroad they find 137
Of lands and mansions, theirs in thought assigned, 138
And laboring in more pleasures to bestow them 139
Than the true gouty landlord which doth owe them; 140

"So many have, that never touched his hand, 141
Sweetly supposed them mistress of his heart. 142
My woeful self, that did in freedom stand,
And was my own fee simple, not in part, 144
What with his art in youth, and youth in art,
Threw my affections in his charmèd power, 146
Reserved the stalk and gave him all my flower.

"Yet did I not, as some my equals did, 148
Demand of him, nor being desired yielded; 149
Finding myself in honor so forbid, 150
With safest distance I mine honor shielded. 151
Experience for me many bulwarks builded 152
Of proofs new-bleeding, which remained the foil 153
Of this false jewel, and his amorous spoil. 154

135 in it . . . mind let their minds become engrossed with it
137 objects i.e., of sight. **abroad** round about them, in the world
138 theirs . . . assigned imagining those possessions to be their own
139 laboring . . . them striving to derive more pleasure from them
140 owe own **141 So many** thus many persons, many women
142 them themselves **144 was . . . part** i.e., had total control of my own destiny, not partial control, as of land held in freehold **146 charmèd power** power to charm or cast a spell **148 my equals** i.e., of those equal to me in age and station **149 Demand . . . yielded** i.e., ask him to take me, or yield myself to him the moment he desired me to **150 in honor so forbid** forbidden by (maidenly) honor to do so (i.e., to yield at once) **151 With safest distance** by staying at a safe distance
152–153 Experience . . . new-bleeding i.e., the experience of those recently undone in love by him provided me with many defenses
153 foil dark background used to show off the brilliance of a jewel
154 this false jewel i.e., the young man. **spoil** plunder; that which is spoiled

"But, ah, who ever shunned by precedent
The destined ill she must herself assay? 156
Or forced examples, 'gainst her own content, 157
To put the by-past perils in her way? 158
Counsel may stop awhile what will not stay; 159
For when we rage, advice is often seen 160
By blunting us to make our wits more keen. 161

"Nor gives it satisfaction to our blood 162
That we must curb it upon others' proof, 163
To be forbade the sweets that seems so good 164
For fear of harms that preach in our behoof. 165
O appetite, from judgment stand aloof! 166
The one a palate hath that needs will taste, 167
Though Reason weep and cry, 'It is thy last.'

"For further I could say 'This man's untrue,' 169
And knew the patterns of his foul beguiling; 170
Heard where his plants in others' orchards grew, 171
Saw how deceits were gilded in his smiling; 172
Knew vows were ever brokers to defiling; 173
Thought characters and words merely but art, 174
And bastards of his foul adulterate heart.

156 assay learn by experience **157 forced** proffered, urged. **content** i.e., presumed happiness in love **158 To . . . way** to raise as objections (to her own love happiness) the past perils (of others) **159 stay** remain stopped forever **160 rage** i.e., in passion **161 By . . . keen** i.e., in attempting to stop us, merely making us all the more ingenious and eager **162 blood** passion **163 proof** experience **164 seems** i.e., seem **165 preach in our behoof** i.e., offer us good advice aimed at benefiting us **166 O appetite . . . aloof** i.e., beware lest passion overwhelm reason by its immediacy **167 The one** i.e., passion, *appetite*. **needs will taste** insists upon gratification **169 say . . . untrue** tell of this man's faithlessness **170 knew . . . beguiling** i.e., had examples of his treachery before me **171 plants** i.e., children illegitimately begotten. **orchards** gardens **172 gilded** given a gilded (false) surface **173 brokers** panders **174 characters and words** i.e., the written and spoken word. **art** artifice

"And long upon these terms I held my city, 176
Till thus he 'gan besiege me: 'Gentle maid,
Have of my suffering youth some feeling pity,
And be not of my holy vows afraid.
That's to ye sworn to none was ever said; 180
For feasts of love I have been called unto, 181
Till now did ne'er invite, nor never woo. 182

" 'All my offenses that abroad you see 183
Are errors of the blood, none of the mind.
Love made them not. With acture they may be, 185
Where neither party is nor true nor kind. 186
They sought their shame that so their shame did find;
And so much less of shame in me remains 188
By how much of me their reproach contains. 189

" 'Among the many that mine eyes have seen,
Not one whose flame my heart so much as warmed, 191
Or my affection put to th' smallest teen, 192
Or any of my leisures ever charmed. 193
Harm have I done to them, but ne'er was harmed;
Kept hearts in liveries, but mine own was free, 195
And reigned, commanding in his monarchy.

176 city citadel (of chastity) **180 That's** that which is **181–182 For . . . woo** I have been invited to other feasts of love before now, but never until now did I do the inviting and the wooing **183 abroad** in the world around us **185–186 With . . . kind** they may be physically performed where neither partner is faithful or truly in love **188–189 And . . . contains** i.e., and I am all the less to blame by how little their reproaches really accuse me (rather than themselves) **191 Not one . . . warmed** i.e., there is not one whose flame of passion so much as warmed my heart **192 Or . . . teen** or gave my affection the least sorrow (*teen*) **193 Or . . . charmed** or put a spell on any of my times of leisure **195 in liveries** in the uniform of a person in service, i.e., almost enslaved

" 'Look here what tributes wounded fancies sent me, 197
Of pallid pearls and rubies red as blood,
Figuring that they their passions likewise lent me 199
Of grief and blushes, aptly understood
In bloodless white and the encrimsoned mood— 201
Effects of terror and dear modesty, 202
Encamped in hearts but fighting outwardly. 203

" 'And, lo, behold these talents of their hair, 204
With twisted metal amorously impleached, 205
I have received from many a several fair, 206
Their kind acceptance weepingly beseeched, 207
With th' annexions of fair gems enriched, 208
And deep-brained sonnets that did amplify 209
Each stone's dear nature, worth, and quality.

" 'The diamond? Why, 'twas beautiful and hard,
Whereto his invised properties did tend; 212
The deep-green emerald, in whose fresh regard 213
Weak sights their sickly radiance do amend; 214
The heaven-hued sapphire and the opal blend 215
With objects manifold—each several stone, 216
With wit well blazoned, smiled or made some moan. 217

197 wounded fancies i.e., doting young women **199 Figuring** symbolizing **201 mood** mode, form, emotional state (i.e., blushing) **202 Effects** the signs or results. **dear** precious; deeply felt **203 but fighting outwardly** and only feigning resistance **204 talents** i.e., treasures, riches. (Literally, coins or valuable metal plates.) **205 impleached** intertwined **206 a several fair** different beautiful ladies **207 Their kind . . . beseeched** who have besought me with their tears to accept their gifts kindly **208 annexions** additions **209 deep-brained** intricate. **amplify** enlarge upon, go into detail about **212 Whereto . . . tend** toward which its invisible properties incline. (*Invised,* used nowhere else, is of uncertain meaning.) The young man too is beautiful and hard. **213 regard** aspect, sight **214 radiance** power of vision. (The emerald helps repair weak vision to those who look at it, just as the young man refreshes the eyes by his beauty.) **215–216 blend . . . manifold** blended with many colors (?) or, blended with (or that blends with) many objects presented to the sight (?) **217 blazoned** proclaimed, cataloged (in the accompanying sonnets)

" 'Lo, all these trophies of affections hot, 218
Of pensived and subdued desires the tender, 219
Nature hath charged me that I hoard them not,
But yield them up where I myself must render,
That is, to you, my origin and ender; 222
For these, of force, must your oblations be, 223
Since, I their altar, you enpatron me. 224

" 'O, then, advance of yours that phraseless hand, 225
Whose white weighs down the airy scale of praise! 226
Take all these similes to your own command, 227
Hallowed with sighs that burning lungs did raise; 228
What me, your minister, for you obeys, 229
Works under you; and to your audit comes 230
Their distract parcels in combinèd sums. 231

" 'Lo, this device was sent me from a nun,
Or sister sanctified, of holiest note, 233
Which late her noble suit in court did shun, 234
Whose rarest havings made the blossoms dote; 235
For she was sought by spirits of richest coat, 236
But kept cold distance, and did thence remove 237
To spend her living in eternal love. 238

218 affections passions **219 pensived** saddened. **tender** offering **222 ender** end, conclusion. (You are the source of my life and that without which I cannot live.) **223 of force** perforce. **your oblations** offerings made at the altar of love for you **224 Since . . . me** since I am the altar (on which these gifts are offered), and you are my patron saint (to whom the altar is dedicated) **225 phraseless** which no words can describe **226 weighs . . . praise** i.e., outweighs in the scales any praise that can be offered to it in airy words **227 similes** i.e., symbolic love tokens or gems accompanied by symbolic explanation in the sonnets **228 Hallowed** consecrated. **burning** i.e., hot with passion **229–230 What . . . you** i.e., whatever obeys me and is at my command as your minister or agent acting on your authority is thus yours also **230 audit** accounting **231 distract** separate **233 note** reputation **234 Which . . . shun** i.e., who recently shunned the attendance at court to which her noble rank entitled her. **suit in** attendance at **235 Whose . . . dote** i.e., whose rare gift of beauty made the young courtiers (in the blossom of their life) dote on her **236 spirits** spirited young men. **coat** coat of arms, i.e., descent **237 remove** depart **238 living** lifetime. **eternal love** love of the eternal God (i.e., she became a nun)

" 'But, O my sweet, what labor is 't to leave 239
The thing we have not, mast'ring what not strives, 240
Paling the place which did no form receive, 241
Playing patient sports in unconstrainèd gyves? 242
She that her fame so to herself contrives, 243
The scars of battle scapeth by the flight
And makes her absence valiant, not her might. 245

" 'O, pardon me, in that my boast is true! 246
The accident which brought me to her eye
Upon the moment did her force subdue, 248
And now she would the cagèd cloister fly. 249
Religious love put out religion's eye. 250
Not to be tempted, would she be immured, 251
And now to tempt all liberty procured. 252

" 'How mighty then you are, O, hear me tell!
The broken bosoms that to me belong 254
Have emptied all their fountains in my well, 255
And mine I pour your ocean all among.
I strong o'er them, and you o'er me being strong, 257
Must for your victory us all congest, 258
As compound love to physic your cold breast. 259

239–242 what . . . gyves i.e., how can it be called a difficult thing to give up something we haven't tried yet, mastering an emotion that offers no resistance, *paling,* or fencing, in the heart upon which no lover has yet made any impression, patiently pretending to endure restraints that in fact impose no restraint and that one is not obliged to endure
243 fame . . . contrives devises for herself a reputation (for renouncing love) **245 makes . . . might** i.e., shows valor only in avoiding temptation, not in confronting it directly **246 my boast** i.e., that she could resist me only by fleeing, not when she saw me **248 Upon the moment** at once **249 would . . . fly** wished to flee the locked convent
250 Religious . . . eye i.e., love of me put out love of the divine
251–252 Not . . . procured before, she wished to be shut up from temptation, but now she sought liberty to venture everything. (The quarto reads *enur'd* for *immured,* and perhaps should be *inured,* habituated.) **254 bosoms** i.e., hearts **255 well** spring, stream **257 strong** victorious **258 for** because of. **us all** i.e., my admirers and myself.
congest gather together **259 compound love** i.e., love compounded of the various loves of myself and my former loves. (*Compound* also has the suggestion of a drug.) **physic** cure

" 'My parts had power to charm a sacred nun, 260
Who, disciplined, ay, dieted in grace, 261
Believed her eyes when they t' assail begun, 262
All vows and consecrations giving place.
O most potential love! Vow, bond, nor space, 264
In thee hath neither sting, knot, nor confine, 265
For thou art all, and all things else are thine.

" 'When thou impressest, what are precepts worth 267
Of stale example? When thou wilt inflame, 268
How coldly those impediments stand forth
Of wealth, of filial fear, law, kindred, fame!
Love's arms are peace, 'gainst rule, 'gainst sense,
'gainst shame, 271
And sweetens, in the suffering pangs it bears, 272
The aloes of all forces, shocks, and fears. 273

" 'Now all these hearts that do on mine depend,
Feeling it break, with bleeding groans they pine, 275
And, supplicant, their sighs to you extend 276
To leave the battery that you make 'gainst mine, 277
Lending soft audience to my sweet design,
And credent soul to that strong-bonded oath 279
That shall prefer and undertake my troth.' 280

260 parts qualities **261 disciplined** subjected to religious discipline. **dieted** nourished, controlled **262 assail** i.e., assail her heart **264 potential** powerful **264–265 Vow . . . confine** against you vows have no strength (*sting*), bonds have no binding force (*knot*), and space is no barrier or impediment (*confine*) **267 thou impressest** you make an impression on a heart, or conscript it into your service **267–268 what . . . example** of what worth are moralistic warnings based on stale old instances **271 Love's . . . shame** i.e., love's might enforces its own peace in the teeth of reason, good sense, and decorum **272 it bears** that it (love) brings, the pangs that lovers must suffer **273 aloes** i.e., bitterness. **forces** acts of force. **shocks** clashes **275 break** i.e., break in disappointment at the threat of rejection by the woman now addressed. **bleeding groans** (Each groan was thought to cost the heart a drop of blood.) **276 supplicant** as supplicants **277 leave** leave off **279 credent** believing, trusting **280 prefer** advance. **undertake** guarantee, see through to the end

"This said, his watery eyes he did dismount, 281
Whose sights till then were leveled on my face; 282
Each cheek a river running from a fount
With brinish current downward flowed apace.
O, how the channel to the stream gave grace! 285
Who glazed with crystal gate the glowing roses 286
That flame through water which their hue encloses.

"O father, what a hell of witchcraft lies 288
In the small orb of one particular tear! 289
But with the inundation of the eyes
What rocky heart to water will not wear?
What breast so cold that is not warmèd here?
O cleft effect! Cold modesty, hot wrath, 293
Both fire from hence and chill extincture hath. 294

"For, lo, his passion, but an art of craft, 295
Even there resolved my reason into tears; 296
There my white stole of chastity I daffed, 297
Shook off my sober guards and civil fears; 298
Appear to him as he to me appears, 299
All melting; though our drops this difference bore: 300
His poisoned me, and mine did him restore.

281 dismount remove from its mount, lower (as with an artillery piece) **282 leveled on** aimed at **285 channel . . . stream** i.e., cheek to the flow of tears **286 Who** which, i.e., the stream of tears. **gate** i.e., a protective layer **288 father** i.e., the old man to whom she is talking **289 particular** single **293 cleft** twofold. **wrath** passion (the wrath of love) **294 extincture** extinguishing **295 passion** passionate wooing. **but an art** merely an artifice **296 resolved** dissolved **297 daffed** doffed, put off **298 guards** defenses. **civil** decorous, grave **299 Appear** I did appear **300 drops** i.e., tears (which here have medicinal qualities)

"In him a plenitude of subtle matter, 302
Applied to cautels, all strange forms receives, 303
Of burning blushes, or of weeping water,
Or swooning paleness; and he takes and leaves, 305
In either's aptness, as it best deceives, 306
To blush at speeches rank, to weep at woes, 307
Or to turn white and swoon at tragic shows;

"That not a heart which in his level came 309
Could scape the hail of his all-hurting aim, 310
Showing fair nature is both kind and tame; 311
And, veiled in them, did win whom he would maim. 312
Against the thing he sought he would exclaim;
When he most burnt in heart-wished luxury, 314
He preached pure maid and praised cold chastity. 315

"Thus merely with the garment of a grace 316
The naked and concealèd fiend he covered, 317
That th' unexperient gave the tempter place, 318
Which like a cherubin above them hovered. 319
Who, young and simple, would not be so lovered? 320
Ay me! I fell, and yet do question make 321
What I should do again for such a sake. 322

302 subtle matter matter capable of being variously impressed or formed **303 cautels** crafty devices **305 takes and leaves** i.e., uses one and avoids the other **306 In either's aptness** whichever is more appropriate **307 rank** gross **309 That** so that. **level** range and aim. (Continues the metaphor of siege.) **310 Could** that could. **hail** i.e., of artillery **311 Showing . . . tame** i.e., his aim being to represent his true nature as loving and docile **312 And . . . maim** and, disguised thus in kindness and docility, or in *blushes, weeping,* and *paleness* (ll. 304–305), won the heart of the woman he intended to harm **314 heart-wished luxury** deeply desired lechery **315 pure maid** as if he were an untouched virgin **316 with . . . grace** with a charming outward show or appearance (perhaps suggesting also one of the three Graces) **317 The naked . . . covered** he covered his fiendish inner self with concealment **318 inexperient** inexperienced. **place** entry **319 Which . . . hovered** who, resembling a cherub, hovered over his victims as though offering them protection **320 simple** naive. **be so lovered** surrender to a lover like him **321 question make** i.e., ask myself **322 for such a sake** for someone like him, or for the sake of falling into such pleasure—however brief

"O, that infected moisture of his eye, 323
O, that false fire which in his cheek so glowed,
O, that forced thunder from his heart did fly, 325
O, that sad breath his spongy lungs bestowed, 326
O, all that borrowed motion seeming owed, 327
Would yet again betray the fore-betrayed,
And new pervert a reconcilèd maid!" 329

323 infected infectious **325 forced** feigned. **from** that from
326 spongy lungs lungs that are spongelike (as all lungs are; perhaps with the suggestion of "blown up with flattery and pretended grief")
327 borrowed . . . owed pretended action that seemed in earnest. **owed** owned, his own **329 reconcilèd** penitent

Date and Text

A Lover's Complaint first appeared in Thomas Thorpe's 1609 edition of the sonnets. It may have been printed from the same transcript as that used to print the sonnets. The poem is not mentioned on the title page of the volume, but has its own head-title on sig. K^v: "A Louers complaint. By William Shake-speare." For the reliability of this attribution, see the Introduction to *A Lover's Complaint.*

Textual Notes

These textual notes are not a historical collation; they are simply a record of departures in this edition from the copy text. The reading adopted in this edition appears in boldface, followed by the rejected reading from the copy text, i.e., the quarto of 1609. Only major alterations in punctuation are noted. Corrections of minor and obvious typographical errors are not indicated.

Copy text: the Sonnet quarto of 1609 [Q].

7 sorrow's sorrowes, **14 lattice** lettice **37 beaded** bedded **51 'gan** gaue **95 wear** were **103 breathe** breath **112 manage** mannad'g **118 Came** Can **164 forbade** forbod **182 woo** vovv **198 pallid** palyd **204 hair** heir **205 metal** mettle **228 Hallowed** Hollowed **251 immured** enur'd **252 procured** procure **260 nun** Sunne **293 O** Or **303 strange** straing

SONNETS

Introduction

Shakespeare seems to have cared more about his reputation as a lyric poet than as a dramatist. He contributed to the major nondramatic genres of his day: to amatory Ovidian narrative in *Venus and Adonis,* to the Complaint in *The Rape of Lucrece,* to philosophical poetry in "The Phoenix and Turtle." He cooperated in the publication of his first two important poems, dedicating them to the young Earl of Southampton with a plea to him for sponsorship. To write poetry in this vein was more fashionable than to write plays, which one did mainly for money.

A poet with ambitions of this sort simply had to write a sonnet sequence. Sonneteering was the rage in England in the early and mid 1590s. Based on the sonneteering tradition of Francesco Petrarch, Sir Thomas Wyatt, and others, and gaining new momentum in 1591 with the publication of Sir Philip Sidney's *Astrophel and Stella,* the vogue ended almost as suddenly as it began, in 1596 or 1597. The sonnet sequences of this brief period bear the names of most well-known and minor poets of the day: *Amoretti* by Edmund Spenser (1595), *Delia* by Samuel Daniel (1591 and 1592), *Caelica* by Fulke Greville (not published until 1633), *Idea's Mirror* by Michael Drayton (1594), *Diana* by Henry Constable (1592), *Phyllis* by Thomas Lodge (1593), and the more imitative sequences of Barnabe Barnes, Giles Fletcher, William Percy, Bartholomew Griffin, William Smith, and Robert Tofte.

Shakespeare wrote sonnets during the heyday of the genre, for in 1598 Francis Meres, in his *Palladis Tamia: Wit's Treasury,* praised Shakespeare's "sugared sonnets among his private friends." Even though they were not printed at the time, we know from Meres's remark that they were circulated in manuscript among the cognoscenti and commanded respect. Shakespeare may actually have preferred to delay the publication of his sonnets, not through indifference to their literary worth but through a desire not to seem too professional. The "courtly makers" of the English Renaissance, those gentlemen whose chivalric accomplishments were supposed to include versifying, looked on the writing of poetry as an avocation designed to amuse one's peers or to court a lady. Publication was not quite genteel, and many such authors affected dismay when their verses were pirated into print. The young wits about London of the 1590s, whether aristocratic or not, sometimes imitated this fashion. Like young John Donne, they sought the favorable verdict of their fellow wits at the Inns of Court (where young men studied law) and professed not to care about wider recognition. Whether Shakespeare was motivated in this way we do not know, but in any event his much-sought-after sonnet sequence was not published until 1609, long after the vogue had passed. The publisher, Thomas Thorpe, seems not to have obtained Shakespeare's authorization. Two sonnets, numbers 138 and 144, had been pirated ten years earlier by William Jaggard in *The Passionate Pilgrim,* 1599, a little anthology with some poems by Shakespeare and some wrongly attributed to him. The sonnets were not reprinted until 1640, either because the sonnet vogue had passed or because Thorpe's edition had been suppressed.

The unexplained circumstances of publication have given rise to a host of vexing and apparently unanswerable questions. Probably no puzzle in all English literature has provoked so much speculation and produced so little agreement. To whom are the sonnets addressed? Do they tell a consistent story, and if so do they tell us anything about Shakespeare's life? The basic difficulty is that we cannot be sure that the order in which Thorpe published the sonnets represents Shakespeare's intention, nor can we assume that Thorpe spoke for Shakespeare when he dedicated the sonnets to "Mr. W. H." As they stand, most of the first 126 sonnets appear to be addressed in warm friendship to a handsome young aristocrat, whereas sonnets 127–152 speak of the poet's dark-haired mistress. Yet the last two sonnets, 153–154, seem unrelated to anything previous, and cast some doubt on the reliability of the ordering. Within each large grouping of the sonnets, moreover, we find evident inconsistencies: jealousies disappear and suddenly reappear, the poet bewails his absolute rejection by the friend and then speaks a few sonnets later of harmonious affection as though nothing had happened, and so on. Some sonnets are closely linked to their predecessors, some are apparently disconnected (although even here we must allow for the real possibility that Shakespeare intends juxtaposition and contrast). We cannot be sure if the friend of sonnets 1–126 is really one person or several. We can only speculate that the unhappy love triangle described in 40–42, in which the friend has usurped the poet's mistress, can be identified with the love triangle of the "Dark Lady" sonnets, 127–152. Most readers sense a narrative continuity of the whole, yet find blocks of sonnets stubbornly out of place. The temptation to rearrange the order has proved irresistible, but no alternative order has ever won acceptance. The consensus is that Thorpe's order is at times suspect, but may have more rationale than at first appears. It is, in any case, the only authoritative order we have.

No less frustrating is Thorpe's dedication "To the Only Begetter of These Ensuing Sonnets, Mr. W. H." Given the late and unauthorized publication, we cannot assume that Thorpe speaks for Shakespeare. Quite possibly he is only thanking the person who obtained the sonnets for him, making publication possible. Mundanely enough, Mr. W. H. could be William Hall, an associate of Thorpe's in the publishing business. Yet Elizabethan usage affords few instances of "begetter" in this sense of "obtainer." Recently, Donald Foster has offered new and persuasive arguments for the idea that "Mr. W. H." is only a typographical error of a common sort, and that Thorpe meant to say "Mr. W. S.," Master William Shakespeare. In this case, "begetter" would mean simply "creator." This solution has a wonderful neatness about it, but other readers have wondered if it answers the seeming contradiction that Thorpe speaks of "Mr. W. H." and "our ever-living poet" in the dedication as though they are two people. Thorpe offers to Mr. W. H. "that eternity promised by our ever-living poet," as though Mr. W. H. were the very subject of those sonnets whom Shakespeare vows to immortalize.

This interpretation of "begetter" as "inspirer" has prompted many enthusiasts to search for a Mr. W. H. in Shakespeare's life, a nobleman who befriended him. The chief candidates are two. First is the young Earl of Southampton, to whom Shakespeare had dedicated *Venus and Adonis* and *The Rape of Lucrece*. The dedication to the second of these poems bespeaks a warmth and gratitude that had been lacking in the first. The Earl's name, Henry Wriothesley, yields initials that are the reverse of W. H. If this correspondence seems unconvincing, W. H. could stand for Sir William Harvey, third husband of Mary, Lady Southampton, the young Earl's mother. Some researchers would have us believe that Shakespeare wrote the sonnets for Lady Southampton, especially those urging a young man (her son) to marry and procreate. This entire case is speculative, however, and we have no evidence that Shakespeare had any dealings whatever with Southampton after *The Rape of Lucrece*. The plain ascription "Mr. W. H." seems an oddly uncivil way for Thorpe to have addressed an earl. If meant for Southampton, the sonnets must have been written fairly early in the 1590s, for they give no hint of Southampton's later career: his courtship of Elizabeth Vernon, her pregnancy and their secret marriage in 1598, his later involvement in Essex's Irish campaign and abortive uprising against Queen Elizabeth. Those literary sleuths who stress similarities to the Southampton relationship are too willing to overlook dissimilarities.

The second chief candidate for Mr. W. H. is William Herbert, third Earl of Pembroke, to whom, along with his brother, Shakespeare's colleagues dedicated the First Folio of 1623. In 1595 Pembroke's parents were attempting to arrange his marriage with Lady Elizabeth Carey, granddaughter of the first Lord Hunsdon, who was Lord Chamberlain and patron of Shakespeare's company. In 1597 another alliance was attempted with Bridget Vere, granddaughter of Lord Burghley. In both negotiations, young Pembroke objected to the girl in question. This hypothesis requires, however, an uncomfortably late date for the sonnets, and postulates a gap in age between Shakespeare and Pembroke that would have afforded little opportunity for genuine friendship. Pembroke was only fifteen in 1595, Shakespeare thirty-one. Besides, no evidence whatever supports the claim other than historical coincidence. The common initials W. H. can be made to produce other candidates as well, such as the Lincolnshire lawyer named William Hatcliffe proposed (to no one's satisfaction) by Leslie Hotson. Hotson wants to date most of the sonnets before 1589, since Hatcliffe came to London in 1587–1588. When such speculations are constructed on the single enigmatic testimonial of the dedication by Thomas Thorpe, who may well have had no connection with Shakespeare, we are left with a case that would not be worth describing had it not captured the imagination of so many researchers.

Biographical identifications have also been proposed for the various personages in the sonnet sequence, predictably with no better success. The rival poet, with "the proud full sail of his great verse" (86), has been linked to Christopher Marlowe (who died in 1593), George Chapman, and others. The sequence gives us little to go on, other than that the rival poet possesses a considerable enough talent to intimidate the author of the sonnets and ingratiate himself with the author's aristocratic friend. No biographical circumstances even distantly resembling this rivalry have come to light. Various candidates have also been found for the "Dark Lady." One is Mary Fitton, a lady-in-waiting at court who bore a child by Pembroke in 1601. Again, we have no evidence that Shakespeare knew her, nor is he likely to have carried on an affair with one of such high rank. A. L. Rowse has proposed Emilia Lanier, wife of Alfonso Lanier and daughter of a court musician named Bassano, a woman of suitably dark complexion perhaps but whose presumed connection with Shakespeare rests only on the reported rumor that she was a mistress of Lord Hunsdon. We are left finally without knowing who any of these people were, or whether indeed Shakespeare was attempting to be biographical at all.

The same irresolution afflicts the dating of the sonnets. Do they give hints of a personal chronicle extending over some years, following Thorpe's arrangement of the sonnets or some alternative order? Sonnet 104 speaks of three years having elapsed since the poet met his friend. Are there other signposts that relate to contemporary events? A line in Sonnet 107 ("The mortal moon hath her eclipse endured") is usually linked to the death of Queen Elizabeth (known as Diana or Cynthia) in 1603, though Leslie Hotson prefers to see in it an allusion to the Spanish Armada, shaped for sea battle in a moonlike crescent when it met defeat in 1588. The newly built pyramids in Sonnet 123 remind Hotson of the obelisks built by Pope Sixtus V in Rome, 1586–1589; other researchers have discovered pyramids erected on London's streets in 1603 to celebrate the coronation of James I. As these illustrations suggest, speculative dating can be used to support a hypothesis of early or late composition. The wary consensus of most scholars is that the sonnets were written over a number of years, a large number certainly before 1598 but some perhaps later and even up to the date of publication in 1609.

However fruitless this quest for nonexistent certainties, it does at least direct us to a meaningful critical question: should we expect sonnets of this "personal" nature to be at least partly autobiographical? Shakespeare's sonnets have struck many readers as cries from the heart, voicing at times fears of rejection, self-hatred, humiliation, and at other times a serene gratitude for reciprocated affection. This power of expression may, however, be a tribute to Shakespeare's dramatic gift rather than evidence of personal involvement. Earlier sonnet sequences, both Elizabethan and pre-Elizabethan, had established a variety of artistic conventions that tended to displace biography. Petrarch's famous *Rime,* or sonnets, later collected in his *Canzoniere,* though addressed to Laura in two sequences (during her life and after her death), idealized her into the unapproachable lady worshiped by the self-abasing and miserable lover. Petrarch's imitators—Serafino Aquilano, Pietro Bembo, Ludovico Ariosto, and Torquato Tasso among the Italians, Clement Marot, Joachim du Bellay, Pierre de Ronsard, and Philippe Desportes among the French Pléiade—reworked these conventions in countless variations. In England the fashion was taken up by Sir Thomas Wyatt, the Earl of Surrey, George Gascoigne, Thomas Watson, and others. Spenser's *Amoretti* and Sidney's *Astrophel and Stella,* though inspired at least in part by real women in the poets' lives, are also deeply concerned with theories of writing poetry. Rejection of the stereotyped attitudes and relationships that had come to dominate the typical Petrarchan sonnet sequence is evidence not of biographical literalism in art but of a new insistence on lifelike emotion in art; as Sidney's muse urges him, "look in thy heart and write." Thus, both the Petrarchan and the anti-Petrarchan schools avoid biographical writing for its own sake. This is essentially true of all Elizabethan sonneteering, from Drayton's serious pursuit of Platonic abstraction in his *Idea's Mirror* to the facile chorusing of lesser sonnet writers about Diana, Phyllis, Zepheria, or Fidessa.

The "story" connecting the individual poems of an Elizabethan sonnet sequence is never very important or consistent, even when we can be sure of the order in which the sonnets were written. Dante had used prose links in his *La Vita Nuova* (c. 1282) to stress narrative continuity, and so had Petrarch, but this sturdy framework had been abandoned by the late sixteenth century. Rather than telling a chronological story, the typical Elizabethan sonnet sequence offers a thematically connected series of lyrical meditations, chiefly on love but also on poetic theory, the adversities of fortune, death, or what have you. The narrative events mentioned from time to time are not the substance of the sequence but the mere occasion for meditative reflection. Attitudes need not be consistent throughout, and the characters need not be consistently motivated like dramatis personae in a play.

Shakespeare's sonnet sequence retains these conventions of Elizabethan sonneteering and employs many archetypal situations and themes that had been explored by his predecessors and contemporaries. His emphasis on friendship seems new, for no other sequence addressed a majority of its sonnets to a friend rather than to a mistress, but even here the anti-Petrarchan quest for spontaneity and candor is in the best Elizabethan tradition of Sidney and Spenser. Besides, the exaltation of friendship over love was itself a widespread Neoplatonic commonplace recently popularized in the writings of John Lyly. Shakespeare's sequence makes use of the structural design found in contemporary models. Even though we cannot reconstruct a rigorously consistent chronological narrative from the sonnets, we can discern overall patterns out of which the poet's emotional crises arise and upon which he constructs his meditative lyrics. Certain groupings, such as the sonnets addressed to the "Dark Lady," 127–152, achieve a plausible cohesion in which the individual sonnets comment on one another through reinforcement or antithetical design and are thus enhanced by their context; a case can be made, in other words, for the order of the poems as Thorpe printed them. Even the last two sonnets, 153 and 154, have their defenders (see Michael J. B. Allen's essay in *Shakespeare Survey,*

1978). Juxtaposition is a favorite technique in Shakespeare's plays, and we must remember that he alone among the major Elizabethan sonneteers wrote for the stage.

Taking note of such considerations, we can account for most of the situations portrayed in Shakespeare's sonnets by postulating four figures: the poet-speaker himself, his friend, his mistress, and a rival poet. The order of events in this tangled relationship is not what the poet wishes to describe; instead, he touches upon this situation from time to time as he explores his own reaction to love in its various aspects.

The poet's relationship to his friend is a vulnerable one. This friend to whom he writes is aristocratic, handsome, younger than he is. The poet is beholden to this friend as a sponsor and must consider himself as subservient no matter how deep their mutual affection. Even at its happiest, their relationship is hierarchical. The poet abases himself in order to extol his friend's beauty and virtues (52–54, 105–106). He confesses that his love would be idolatry, except that the friend's goodness excels all poetic hyperbole. As the older of the two, the poet sententiously urges his young friend to marry and eternize his beauty through the engendering of children (1–17). Such a course, he argues, is the surest way to conquer devouring Time, the enemy of all earthly beauty and love. Yet elsewhere the poet exalts his own art as the surest defense against Time (55, 60, 63–65, etc.). These conclusions are nominally contradictory, offering procreation in one instance and poetry in another as the best hope for immortality, but thematically the two are obviously related. In even the happiest of the sonnets, such as those giving thanks for "the marriage of true minds" (116, 123), the consciousness of devouring Time is inescapable. If love and celebratory poetry can sometimes triumph over Time, the victory is all the more precious because it is achieved in the face of such odds.

Love and perfect friendship are a refuge for the poet faced with hostile fortune and an indifferent world. He is too often "in disgrace with fortune and men's eyes" (29), oppressed by his own failings, saddened by the facile success of opportunists (66–68), ashamed of having sold himself cheap in his own profession (110–111). If taken biographically, this could mean that Shakespeare was not happy about his career as actor and playwright, but the motif makes complete sense in the sonnet sequence without resort to biography. A biographical reading also raises the question of homosexual attraction, as urged recently anew by Joseph Pequigney in his *Such Is My Love* (University of Chicago Press, 1985). The bawdy reference in Sonnet 20.12 to the friend's possession of "one thing to my purpose nothing" would seem to militate against the idea of a consummated homosexual relationship, while conversely many sonnets (such as 138) do point to the poet's consummation with his mistress. Still, the bond between poet and friend is extraordinarily strong. The poet is pathetically dependent on his friend. Occasional absences torture him with the physical separation, even though he realizes that pure love of the spirit ought not to be hampered by distance or time (43–51). The absence is especially painful when the poet must confess his own disloyalty (117–118). The chronology of these absences cannot be worked out satisfactorily, but the haunting theme of separation is incessant, overwhelming. By extension it includes the fear of separation through death (71–73, 126). The concern with absence is closely related to the poet's obsession with devouring Time.

All the poet's misfortunes would be bearable if love were constant, but his dependency on the aristocratic friend leaves him at the mercy of that friend's changeable mood. The poet must not complain when his well-born friend entertains a rival poet (78–86) or forms other emotional attachments, even with the poet's own mistress (40–42). These disloyalties evoke outbursts of jealousy. The poet vacillates between forgiveness and recrimination. Sometimes even his forgiveness is self-loathing, in which the poet confesses he would take back the friend on any terms (93–95). At times the poet grovels, conceding that he deserves no better treatment (57–58), but at other times his stored-up resentment bursts forth (93–95). The poet's fears, though presented in no clear chronological order, run the gamut from a fatalistic sense that rejection will come one day (49) to an abject and bitter final farewell (87). Sometimes he is tormented by jealousy (61), sometimes by self-hate (88–89).

The sonnets addressed to the poet's mistress, the "Dark Lady," similarly convey fear, self-abasement, and a panicky awareness of loss of self-control. In rare moments of happiness, the poet praises her dark features as proof of her being a real woman, not a Petrarchan goddess (130). Too often, however, her lack of ideal beauty reminds the poet of his irrational enchantment (148–150). She is tyrannous, disdainful, spiteful, disloyal, a "female evil" (144) who has tempted away from the poet his better self, his friend. The poet is distressed not so much by her perfidy as by his own self-betrayal; he sees bitterly that he offends his nobler reason by his attachment to the rebellious flesh. He worships what others abhor, and perjures himself by swearing to what he knows to be false (150–152). His only hope for escape is to punish his flesh and renounce the vanity of all worldly striving (146), but this solution evades him as he plunges helplessly back into the perverse enslavement of a sickened appetite.

This sketch of only some themes of the sequence may suggest the range and yet the interconnection of Shakespeare's meditations on love, friendship, and poetry. Patterns are visible, even if the exact chronology (never important in the Elizabethan sonnet sequence) cannot be determined. This patterning is equally evident in matters of versification and imagery. The sonnets are written throughout in the "Shakespearean" or English form, *abab cdcd efef gg*. (Number 126, written entirely in couplets, is an exception, perhaps because it was intended as the envoy to the series addressed to the poet's friend.) This familiar sonnet form, introduced by Wyatt and developed by Sidney, differs markedly from the octave-sestet division of the Petrarchan, or Italian, sonnet. The English form of three quatrains and a concluding couplet lends itself to a step-by-step development of idea and image, culminating in an epigrammatic two-line conclusion that may summarize the thought of the preceding twelve lines or give a sententious interpretation of the images developed up to this point. Sonnet 7 pursues the image of the sun at morning, noon, and evening through three quatrains, one for each phase of the day, and then in the couplet "applies" the image to the friend's unwillingness to beget children. Sonnet 29 moves from resentment of misfortune to a rejoicing in the friend's love, and rhetorically mirrors this sudden elevation of mood in the image of the lark "at break of day arising / From sullen earth." Shakespeare's rhetorical and imagistic devices exploit the sonnet structure he inherited and perfected, and remind us again of the strong element of convention and artifice in these supremely "personal" sonnets. The recurring images—the canker on the rose, the pleading of a case at law, the seasonal rhythms of summer and winter, the alternations of day and night, the harmonies and dissonances of music—also testify to the artistic unity of the whole and to the artist's extraordinary discipline in evoking a sense of helpless loss of self-control.

Sonnets

To the Only Begetter of These Ensuing Sonnets

Mr. W. H.

All Happiness and That Eternity Promised
by Our Ever-living Poet
Wisheth the Well-wishing Adventurer in Setting Forth

T. T.

1

From fairest creatures we desire increase,
That thereby beauty's rose might never die,
But as the riper should by time decease,
His tender heir might bear his memory; 4
But thou, contracted to thine own bright eyes,
Feed'st thy light's flame with self-substantial fuel,
Making a famine where abundance lies,
Thyself thy foe, to thy sweet self too cruel. 8
Thou that art now the world's fresh ornament
And only herald to the gaudy spring,
Within thine own bud buriest thy content,
And, tender churl, mak'st waste in niggarding. 12
  Pity the world, or else this glutton be,
  To eat the world's due, by the grave and thee.

1 • 1 increase procreation **3 as** just as, while **4 bear his memory** i.e., immortalize him by bearing his features **5 contracted** engaged, espoused **6 self-substantial** of your own substance **10 only** unique. **herald to** messenger of **11 thy content** (1) that which is contained in you; potential fatherhood (2) contentment **12 mak'st . . . niggarding** squander your substance by being miserly. (An oxymoron, like *tender churl,* youthful old miser.) **14 the world's due** i.e., the offspring you owe to posterity. **by . . . thee** (consumed) by death and by your willfully remaining childless

2

When forty winters shall besiege thy brow
And dig deep trenches in thy beauty's field,
Thy youth's proud livery, so gazed on now,
Will be a tattered weed, of small worth held. 4
Then being asked where all thy beauty lies,
Where all the treasure of thy lusty days,
To say within thine own deep-sunken eyes
Were an all-eating shame and thriftless praise. 8
How much more praise deserved thy beauty's use
If thou couldst answer, "This fair child of mine
Shall sum my count and make my old excuse,"
Proving his beauty by succession thine. 12
  This were to be new made when thou art old,
  And see thy blood warm when thou feel'st it cold.

2 • 2 trenches i.e., wrinkles. **field** (1) meadow (2) battlefield (3) heraldic background **4 weed** garment (with a play on a *weed* growing in *beauty's field,* l. 2) **6 lusty** (1) vigorous (2) lustful **7 deep-sunken** i.e., with age **8 all-eating shame** shameful gluttony, and one that would consume you with shame. **thriftless praise** (1) praise of extravagance (2) idle praise **9 deserved . . . use** would the proper investment and employment of your beauty deserve **11 sum . . . excuse** even my account and make amends (for growing old, or for consuming beauty during my life) in my old age **12 thine** i.e., derived from you **13 were** would be

3

Look in thy glass, and tell the face thou viewest
Now is the time that face should form another,
Whose fresh repair if now thou not renewest
Thou dost beguile the world, unbless some mother. 4
For where is she so fair whose uneared womb
Disdains the tillage of thy husbandry?
Or who is he so fond will be the tomb
Of his self-love, to stop posterity? 8
Thou art thy mother's glass, and she in thee
Calls back the lovely April of her prime;
So thou through windows of thine age shalt see,
Despite of wrinkles, this thy golden time. 12
  But if thou live remembered not to be,
  Die single, and thine image dies with thee.

3 • 1 glass mirror **3 fresh repair** youthful condition **4 beguile** cheat. **unbless some mother** withhold the happiness of childbearing from some woman **5 uneared** untilled, uncultivated **6 husbandry** cultivation (with obvious suggestion of "playing the husband") **7 fond** foolish. **will be** i.e., that he will be **9 thy mother's glass** the image of your mother **11 windows of thine age** i.e., eyes dimmed by advancing years **13 remembered not to be** in such a way as not to be remembered, without children

4

Unthrifty loveliness, why dost thou spend
Upon thyself thy beauty's legacy?
Nature's bequest gives nothing, but doth lend,
And being frank she lends to those are free. 4
Then, beauteous niggard, why dost thou abuse
The bounteous largess given thee to give?
Profitless usurer, why dost thou use
So great a sum of sums, yet canst not live? 8
For having traffic with thyself alone,
Thou of thyself thy sweet self dost deceive.
Then how, when Nature calls thee to be gone,
What acceptable audit canst thou leave? 12
  Thy unused beauty must be tombed with thee,
  Which, usèd, lives th' executor to be.

4 • 1 Unthrifty (1) prodigal (2) unavailing **4 frank** liberal, bounteous. **are free** who are generous **7 use** (1) use up (2) fail to invest for profit. (See Sonnet 6.5 and note.) **8 live** (1) have a livelihood (2) live in your posterity **9 traffic** commerce. (The commercial and financial metaphor hints at sexual self-fascination.) **10 deceive** cheat **13 unused** (1) unemployed (2) not invested for profit **14 lives** would live (in your son)

5

Those hours, that with gentle work did frame
The lovely gaze where every eye doth dwell,
Will play the tyrants to the very same
And that unfair which fairly doth excel; 4
For never-resting Time leads summer on
To hideous winter and confounds him there,
Sap checked with frost and lusty leaves quite gone,
Beauty o'ersnowed and bareness everywhere. 8
Then, were not summer's distillation left
A liquid prisoner pent in walls of glass,
Beauty's effect with beauty were bereft,
Nor it nor no remembrance what it was. 12
But flowers distilled, though they with winter meet,
Leese but their show; their substance still lives sweet.

5 • 1 frame make **2 gaze** object of gazes **3 play . . . to** oppress **4 unfair** make unlovely. **fairly** (1) in beauty (2) truly, honestly **6 confounds** destroys **7 lusty** vigorous **9 summer's distillation** distilled perfume of flowers **10 walls of glass** glass containers **11 with . . . bereft** would be lost along with beauty itself **12 Nor it nor no** (leaving behind) neither it (beauty) nor any **14 Leese** lose. **still** (1) notwithstanding (2) always

6

Then let not winter's ragged hand deface
In thee thy summer ere thou be distilled.
Make sweet some vial; treasure thou some place
With beauty's treasure ere it be self-killed. 4
That use is not forbidden usury
Which happies those that pay the willing loan;
That's for thyself to breed another thee,
Or ten times happier, be it ten for one. 8
Ten times thyself were happier than thou art,
If ten of thine ten times refigured thee;
Then what could death do, if thou shouldst depart,
Leaving thee living in posterity? 12
  Be not self-willed, for thou art much too fair
  To be death's conquest and make worms thine heir.

6 • 1 ragged rough **3 vial** (with suggestion of a womb). **treasure** enrich **5 use** lending money at interest **6 happies** makes happy. **pay . . . loan** willingly borrow on these terms and repay the loan **7 That's . . . thee** i.e., such would be the case if you were to sire a child like you **8 Or . . . one** i.e., or indeed the happy mother (of l. 6) would be ten times happier were she to bear you ten children instead of one. (*Ten for one* alludes to the highest legal rate of interest, one for ten.) **9 Ten . . . art** i.e., ten children of yours would be a tenfold blessing and would make you happier **10 refigured** duplicated, copied **13 self-willed** (1) obstinate (2) bequeathed to self

7

Lo, in the orient when the gracious light
Lifts up his burning head, each under eye
Doth homage to his new-appearing sight,
Serving with looks his sacred majesty; 4
And having climbed the steep-up heavenly hill,
Resembling strong youth in his middle age,
Yet mortal looks adore his beauty still,
Attending on his golden pilgrimage; 8
But when from highmost pitch, with weary car,
Like feeble age, he reeleth from the day,
The eyes, 'fore duteous, now converted are
From his low tract and look another way. 12
So thou, thyself outgoing in thy noon,
Unlooked on diest, unless thou get a son.

7 • 1 orient east. **light** i.e., sun **2 under** earthly **9 pitch** highest point (as of a falcon's flight before it attacks). **car** chariot (of the sun god) **11 converted** turned away **12 tract** course **14 get** beget

8

Music to hear, why hear'st thou music sadly?
Sweets with sweets war not, joy delights in joy.
Why lov'st thou that which thou receiv'st not gladly,
Or else receiv'st with pleasure thine annoy? 4
If the true concord of well-tunèd sounds,
By unions married, do offend thine ear,
They do but sweetly chide thee, who confounds
In singleness the parts that thou shouldst bear. 8
Mark how one string, sweet husband to another,
Strikes each in each by mutual ordering,
Resembling sire and child and happy mother
Who, all in one, one pleasing note do sing; 12
Whose speechless song, being many, seeming one,
Sings this to thee: "Thou single wilt prove none."

8 • 1 **Music to hear** i.e., you whom it is music to hear. **sadly** gravely; without joy **4 thine annoy** what annoys you **6 married** i.e., harmonized **7–8 who . . . bear** you who destroy, by playing a single part only, the harmony (i.e., marriage) that you should sustain **9 sweet husband** i.e., paired, as on the double strings of the lute, one string vibrating sympathetically to the other **10 each in each** i.e., with double resonance, sounding mutually **13 Whose** i.e., the strings'. **being . . . one** i.e., making harmony out of several voices **14 Thou . . . none** (Alludes to the proverb, "One is no number." The single person who dies without posterity leaves nothing of himself behind.)

9

Is it for fear to wet a widow's eye
That thou consum'st thyself in single life?
Ah, if thou issueless shalt hap to die,
The world will wail thee like a makeless wife; 4
The world will be thy widow and still weep
That thou no form of thee hast left behind,
When every private widow well may keep,
By children's eyes, her husband's shape in mind. 8
Look what an unthrift in the world doth spend
Shifts but his place, for still the world enjoys it;
But beauty's waste hath in the world an end,
And, kept unused, the user so destroys it. 12
  No love toward others in that bosom sits
  That on himself such murd'rous shame commits.

9 • 3 issueless without offspring **4 makeless** mateless, i.e., widowed **5 still** constantly, always **7 private** individual, as distinguished from the whole world **8 By** by means of **9 Look what** whatever. **unthrift** spendthrift **10 his** its. **enjoys** uses, keeps in circulation **12 user** i.e., he who should use it (with a suggestion of a *usurer* who is miserly)

10

For shame, deny that thou bear'st love to any,
Who for thyself art so unprovident!
Grant, if thou wilt, thou art beloved of many,
But that thou none lov'st is most evident; 4
For thou art so possessed with murd'rous hate
That 'gainst thyself thou stick'st not to conspire,
Seeking that beauteous roof to ruinate
Which to repair should be thy chief desire. 8
O, change thy thought, that I may change my mind!
Shall hate be fairer lodged than gentle love?
Be, as thy presence is, gracious and kind,
Or to thyself at least kindhearted prove: 12
  Make thee another self, for love of me,
  That beauty still may live in thine or thee.

10 • 6 thou stick'st you scruple **9 thought** intention. **change my mind** no longer believe as I have until now **11 presence** appearance, bearing

11

As fast as thou shalt wane, so fast thou grow'st
In one of thine from that which thou departest;
And that fresh blood which youngly thou bestow'st
Thou mayst call thine when thou from youth
convertest. 4
Herein lives wisdom, beauty, and increase;
Without this, folly, age, and cold decay.
If all were minded so, the times should cease
And threescore year would make the world away. 8
Let those whom Nature hath not made for store,
Harsh, featureless, and rude, barrenly perish;
Look whom she best endowed she gave the more,
Which bounteous gift thou shouldst in bounty cherish. 12
She carved thee for her seal, and meant thereby
Thou shouldst print more, not let that copy die.

11 • 1–2 thou grow'st . . . departest i.e., you become, through a child of your own, what you cease to be in yourself **3 youngly** in youth **4 thou . . . convertest** you change from youth (to old age) **7 minded so** sharing your intention (to have no children). **times** succeeding generations **8 year** years **9 for store** as a source of supply **10 Harsh** hard-favored. **featureless** having no attractive features or appearance. **rude** rudely fashioned **11 Look whom** whomever **13 seal** stamp from which impressions are made

12

When I do count the clock that tells the time,
And see the brave day sunk in hideous night;
When I behold the violet past prime,
And sable curls all silvered o'er with white; 4
When lofty trees I see barren of leaves
Which erst from heat did canopy the herd,
And summer's green, all girded up in sheaves,
Borne on the bier with white and bristly beard, 8
Then of thy beauty do I question make
That thou among the wastes of time must go,
Since sweets and beauties do themselves forsake
And die as fast as they see others grow; 12
  And nothing 'gainst Time's scythe can make defense
  Save breed, to brave him when he takes thee hence.

12 • 1 tells (1) announces (2) counts **2 brave** splendid **4 sable** black **6 erst** formerly **7 girded** bundled **8 bier** i.e., harvest cart (but with suggestion of funeral bier). **beard** i.e., the tufted grain (but suggesting also a dead man laid out for burial) **9 do . . . make** I discuss with myself **14 breed** offspring. **brave him** defy Time

13

O, that you were yourself! But, love, you are
No longer yours than you yourself here live.
Against this coming end you should prepare,
And your sweet semblance to some other give. 4
So should that beauty which you hold in lease
Find no determination; then you were
Yourself again after yourself's decease,
When your sweet issue your sweet form should bear. 8
Who lets so fair a house fall to decay,
Which husbandry in honor might uphold
Against the stormy gusts of winter's day
And barren rage of death's eternal cold? 12
  O, none but unthrifts! Dear my love, you know
  You had a father; let your son say so.

13 • 1 yourself i.e., your eternal self, not vulnerable to Time's decay **2 here** i.e., here on earth **3 Against** in anticipation of **6 determination** end **10 husbandry** careful management (with a pun on "being a husband")

14

Not from the stars do I my judgment pluck,
And yet methinks I have astronomy,
But not to tell of good or evil luck,
Of plagues, of dearths, or seasons' quality; 4
Nor can I fortune to brief minutes tell,
'Pointing to each his thunder, rain, and wind,
Or say with princes if it shall go well
By oft predict that I in heaven find. 8
But from thine eyes my knowledge I derive,
And, constant stars, in them I read such art
As truth and beauty shall together thrive
If from thyself to store thou wouldst convert. 12
Or else of thee this I prognosticate:
Thy end is truth's and beauty's doom and date.

14 • 1 judgment pluck derive conclusions **2 have astronomy** am skilled in astrology **4 seasons' quality** i.e., what the weather of the seasons will be like **5 fortune . . . tell** i.e., foretell events to the precise minute **6 'Pointing** appointing, assigning. **each** each minute. **his** its **7 Or . . . well** or say if things will go well for certain rulers **8 oft predict** frequent predictions **10–11 read . . . As** gather such learning as, in effect, that **12 store** replenishment (through the begetting of children). **convert** turn **14 doom and date** limit of duration, destruction

15

When I consider every thing that grows
Holds in perfection but a little moment,
That this huge stage presenteth naught but shows
Whereon the stars in secret influence comment; 4
When I perceive that men as plants increase,
Cheerèd and checked even by the selfsame sky,
Vaunt in their youthful sap, at height decrease,
And wear their brave state out of memory; 8
Then the conceit of this inconstant stay
Sets you most rich in youth before my sight,
Where wasteful Time debateth with Decay
To change your day of youth to sullied night; 12
  And all in war with Time for love of you,
  As he takes from you I engraft you new.

15 • 2 Holds in perfection maintains its prime **3 stage** i.e., the world **6 Cheerèd and checked** (1) urged on, nourished, and held back, starved (2) applauded and hissed **7 Vaunt** boast, exult. **sap** vigor. **at height decrease** i.e., no sooner reach full maturity but they (humans) start to decline **8 brave** splendid. **out of memory** i.e., until forgotten **9 conceit** notion. **inconstant stay** mutable duration **11 wasteful . . . Decay** i.e., Time and Decay contend to see who can ruin you fastest, or join forces to do so, debating between them the best procedure **13 all in war** I, fighting with might and main **14 engraft you new** renew you by grafting, infusing new life into you (by means of my verse)

16

But wherefore do not you a mightier way
Make war upon this bloody tyrant, Time,
And fortify yourself in your decay
With means more blessèd than my barren rhyme? 4
Now stand you on the top of happy hours,
And many maiden gardens yet unset
With virtuous wish would bear your living flowers,
Much liker than your painted counterfeit. 8
So should the lines of life that life repair
Which this time's pencil, or my pupil pen,
Neither in inward worth nor outward fair
Can make you live yourself in eyes of men. 12
To give away yourself keeps yourself still,
And you must live, drawn by your own sweet skill.

16 • 4 barren (1) unable to produce offspring (2) poetically sterile **6 unset** (1) unplanted (2) unimpregnated **7 virtuous wish** desire that is still chaste **8 liker** more resembling you. **painted** rendered by art (including poetry), artificial. **counterfeit** portrait **9 lines of life** lineage, i.e., children (whose lineaments are more lifelike than lines of verse or of a portrait) **10 this time's pencil** a portraiture done in this present age. **pupil** apprenticed, inexpert **11 fair** beauty **13 give away yourself** i.e., beget children. **keeps** preserves

17

Who will believe my verse in time to come
If it were filled with your most high deserts?
Though yet, heaven knows, it is but as a tomb
Which hides your life and shows not half your parts. 4
If I could write the beauty of your eyes
And in fresh numbers number all your graces,
The age to come would say, "This poet lies;
Such heavenly touches ne'er touched earthly faces." 8
So should my papers, yellowed with their age,
Be scorned like old men of less truth than tongue,
And your true rights be termed a poet's rage
And stretchèd meter of an antique song. 12
But were some child of yours alive that time,
You should live twice, in it and in my rhyme.

17 • 3 yet as yet **4 parts** qualities **6 numbers** verses **10 of . . . tongue** more garrulous than truthful **11 rage** exaggerated inspiration **12 stretchèd meter** overstrained poetry, poetic license

18

Shall I compare thee to a summer's day?
Thou art more lovely and more temperate.
Rough winds do shake the darling buds of May,
And summer's lease hath all too short a date. 4
Sometimes too hot the eye of heaven shines,
And often is his gold complexion dimmed;
And every fair from fair sometimes declines,
By chance or nature's changing course untrimmed. 8
But thy eternal summer shall not fade
Nor lose possession of that fair thou ow'st;
Nor shall Death brag thou wanderest in his shade,
When in eternal lines to time thou grow'st. 12
So long as men can breathe or eyes can see,
So long lives this, and this gives life to thee.

18 • 4 lease allotted time. **date** duration **5 eye** i.e., sun **7 fair from fair** beautiful thing from beauty **8 untrimmed** stripped of ornament and beauty **10 fair thou ow'st** beauty you own **12 lines** i.e., of poetry. **to . . . grow'st** you become incorporated into time, engrafted upon it **14 this** i.e., this sonnet

19

Devouring Time, blunt thou the lion's paws,
And make the earth devour her own sweet brood;
Pluck the keen teeth from the fierce tiger's jaws,
And burn the long-lived phoenix in her blood; 4
Make glad and sorry seasons as thou fleet'st,
And do whate'er thou wilt, swift-footed Time,
To the wide world and all her fading sweets.
But I forbid thee one most heinous crime: 8
O, carve not with thy hours my love's fair brow,
Nor draw no lines there with thine antique pen;
Him in thy course untainted do allow
For beauty's pattern to succeeding men. 12
  Yet, do thy worst, old Time. Despite thy wrong,
  My love shall in my verse ever live young.

19 • 4 phoenix legendary bird reputed to live for hundreds of years and then be consumed alive (*in her blood*) in its own ashes from which it is then reborn **5 sorry** i.e., miserable, uncomfortable. **thou fleet'st** you fleet, hurry **10 antique** (1) old (2) antic, capricious, fantastic
11 untainted (1) unhit in tilting (2) unsullied

20

A woman's face with Nature's own hand painted
Hast thou, the master-mistress of my passion;
A woman's gentle heart, but not acquainted
With shifting change, as is false women's fashion; 4
An eye more bright than theirs, less false in rolling,
Gilding the object whereupon it gazeth;
A man in hue, all hues in his controlling,
Which steals men's eyes and women's souls amazeth. 8
And for a woman wert thou first created,
Till Nature, as she wrought thee, fell a-doting,
And by addition me of thee defeated,
By adding one thing to my purpose nothing. 12
But since she pricked thee out for women's pleasure,
Mine be thy love and thy love's use their treasure.

20 • 1 with . . . hand i.e., without cosmetics **2 master-mistress** i.e., both master and mistress, male and female. **passion** love **4 as . . . fashion** as is the way with women, who are false by nature **5 rolling** i.e., roving **6 Gilding** causing to shine brightly **7 A man . . . controlling** one who has a manly appearance, and has power over all other appearances (suggesting too that he captivates all beholders, and that his *hue* is womanly as well as manly) **10 fell a-doting** fell infatuatedly in love with you, and so went mildly crazy **11 defeated** defrauded, deprived **12 to my purpose nothing** out of line with my wishes **13 pricked** designated (with bawdy suggestion; the *thing* in l. 12 is a phallus). **for women's pleasure** to give (sexual) pleasure to women **14 and . . . treasure** i.e., and let women enjoy the profits of love's *use* (usury) as their treasure (with bawdy suggestion that the lover is to use the *treasure* of their bodies)

21

So is it not with me as with that muse,
Stirred by a painted beauty to his verse,
Who heaven itself for ornament doth use
And every fair with his fair doth rehearse, 4
Making a couplement of proud compare
With sun and moon, with earth and sea's rich gems,
With April's firstborn flowers, and all things rare
That heaven's air in this huge rondure hems. 8
O, let me, true in love, but truly write,
And then, believe me, my love is as fair
As any mother's child, though not so bright
As those gold candles fixed in heaven's air. 12
Let them say more that like of hearsay well;
I will not praise that purpose not to sell.

21 • 1 muse i.e., poet **2 Stirred** inspired. **painted** artificial, created by cosmetics **3 Who . . . use** i.e., who does not scruple to invoke heaven itself as an ornament of praise for his mistress **4 every . . . rehearse** compares his lady fair with every lovely thing **5 Making . . . compare** joining (her) in proud comparison **8 rondure** sphere. **hems** encloses, encircles **12 gold candles** i.e., stars. (The trite and exaggerated metaphor is of the sort the poet hopes to eschew.) **13 like . . . well** like to deal in secondhand or trite expressions **14 I will . . . sell** i.e., I, who do not intend to sell as a merchant might, will accordingly not indulge in extravagant and empty praise

22

My glass shall not persuade me I am old
So long as youth and thou are of one date;
But when in thee Time's furrows I behold,
Then look I death my days should expiate. 4
For all that beauty that doth cover thee
Is but the seemly raiment of my heart,
Which in thy breast doth live, as thine in me.
How can I then be elder than thou art? 8
O, therefore, love, be of thyself so wary
As I, not for myself, but for thee will,
Bearing thy heart, which I will keep so chary
As tender nurse her babe from faring ill. 12
  Presume not on thy heart when mine is slain;
  Thou gav'st me thine, not to give back again.

22 • 1 glass mirror **2 of one date** of an age, i.e., young **4 look I** I foresee. **expiate** end **6 seemly** becoming **10 will** i.e., will take wary care of myself for your sake **11 Bearing** since I bear. **chary** carefully **13 Presume not on** do not expect to receive back

23

As an unperfect actor on the stage
Who with his fear is put beside his part,
Or some fierce thing replete with too much rage,
Whose strength's abundance weakens his own heart, 4
So I, for fear of trust, forget to say
The perfect ceremony of love's rite,
And in mine own love's strength seem to decay,
O'ercharged with burden of mine own love's might. 8
O, let my books be then the eloquence
And dumb presagers of my speaking breast,
Who plead for love and look for recompense
More than that tongue that more hath more expressed. 12
  O, learn to read what silent love hath writ.
  To hear with eyes belongs to love's fine wit.

23 • 1 unperfect one who has not learned his lines **2 beside** out of **3 Or . . . rage** i.e., or some wild animal overfilled with ungovernable rage **4 heart** courage **5 for . . . trust** mistrusting myself. **forget** forget how **9 books** (Possibly refers to the sonnets, or to *Venus and Adonis* and *The Rape of Lucrece*, or more generally the works of the persona poet.) **10 dumb presagers** silent messengers or presenters **12 more hath more expressed** has more often or more fully said more **14 fine wit** sharp intelligence

24

Mine eye hath played the painter and hath stelled
Thy beauty's form in table of my heart;
My body is the frame wherein 'tis held,
And perspective it is best painter's art. 4
For through the painter must you see his skill
To find where your true image pictured lies,
Which in my bosom's shop is hanging still,
That hath his windows glazèd with thine eyes. 8
Now see what good turns eyes for eyes have done:
Mine eyes have drawn thy shape, and thine for me
Are windows to my breast, wherethrough the sun
Delights to peep, to gaze therein on thee. 12
Yet eyes this cunning want to grace their art:
They draw but what they see, know not the heart.

24 • 1 played acted the part of. **stelled** fixed, installed; or possibly steeled, i.e., engraved. (The quarto reads *steeld*.) **2 table** tablet, wooden panel used for painting **3 frame** (1) picture frame (2) bodily frame **4 perspective** an artist's method of producing a distorted picture that looks right only from an oblique point of view; or a painter's technique used to produce the illusion of distance, one thing seeming to lie behind another; or an optical device for bringing images to the painter's eye **5 For . . . skill** i.e., you must look through the eyes of me, the skillful painter **7 bosom's shop** i.e., heart **8 his** its. **glazèd** fitted with glass, paned. (The friend, looking at the poet's portrait of him engraved in the poet's heart, sees into that heart.) **13 this cunning want** lack this skill. **grace** enhance **14 know not** do not perceive the thoughts of. (The poet cannot see into the heart of the friend.)

25

Let those who are in favor with their stars
Of public honor and proud titles boast,
Whilst I, whom fortune of such triumph bars,
Unlooked-for joy in that I honor most. 4
Great princes' favorites their fair leaves spread
But as the marigold at the sun's eye,
And in themselves their pride lies burièd,
For at a frown they in their glory die. 8
The painful warrior famousèd for fight,
After a thousand victories once foiled,
Is from the book of honor rasèd quite,
And all the rest forgot for which he toiled. 12
  Then happy I, that love and am beloved
  Where I may not remove nor be removed.

25 • 3 of from **4 Unlooked-for** (1) unexpectedly (2) out of the public eye. **that** that which **5 their . . . spread** i.e., flourish, blossom, prosper **6 But** only **7 lies burièd** i.e., will die with the ending of their brief glory **8 a frown** (1) a prince's frown (2) a cloud obscuring the sun **9 painful** enduring much, striving. **famousèd** renowned. **fight** (Reads *worth* in the 1609 quarto; some editors retain, and emend *quite* in l. 11 to *forth.*) **11 rasèd** erased **12 the rest** i.e., his *thousand victories* **14 remove** i.e., be unfaithful. **removed** i.e., removed from favor

26

Lord of my love, to whom in vassalage
Thy merit hath my duty strongly knit,
To thee I send this written embassage
To witness duty, not to show my wit— 4
Duty so great, which wit so poor as mine
May make seem bare, in wanting words to show it,
But that I hope some good conceit of thine
In thy soul's thought, all naked, will bestow it; 8
Till whatsoever star that guides my moving
Points on me graciously with fair aspect,
And puts apparel on my tattered loving
To show me worthy of thy sweet respect. 12
Then may I dare to boast how I do love thee;
Till then not show my head where thou mayst
prove me.

26 • 1 vassalage allegiance **4 witness** bear witness to **6 wanting** lacking **7 good conceit** good conception, or favorable opinion **8 all naked** (Modifies *Duty.*) **bestow** give lodging to **9 moving** life and deeds **10 aspect** influence (as of a star) **14 prove** test

27

Weary with toil, I haste me to my bed,
The dear repose for limbs with travel tirèd;
But then begins a journey in my head,
To work my mind when body's work's expirèd. 4
For then my thoughts, from far where I abide,
Intend a zealous pilgrimage to thee,
And keep my drooping eyelids open wide,
Looking on darkness which the blind do see; 8
Save that my soul's imaginary sight
Presents thy shadow to my sightless view,
Which, like a jewel hung in ghastly night,
Makes black night beauteous and her old face new. 12
  Lo, thus by day my limbs, by night my mind,
  For thee and for myself no quiet find.

27 • 2 travel (with connotation also of *travail;* spelled *trauaill* in the quarto) **5 from far** i.e., far away from you **6 Intend** direct, set out upon **9 Save** except **10 thy shadow** the image of you

28

How can I then return in happy plight
That am debarred the benefit of rest?
When day's oppression is not eased by night,
But day by night, and night by day, oppressed? 4
And each, though enemies to either's reign,
Do in consent shake hands to torture me,
The one by toil, the other to complain
How far I toil, still farther off from thee. 8
I tell the day, to please him, thou art bright
And dost him grace when clouds do blot the heaven;
So flatter I the swart-complexioned night,
When sparkling stars twire not, thou gild'st th' even. 12
  But day doth daily draw my sorrows longer,
  And night doth nightly make grief's strength seem
    stronger.

28 • 4 But . . . oppressed i.e., but experiencing sleeplessness at night and fatigue during the day **6 consent** i.e., mutual agreement **7 the other to complain** i.e., the night by causing me to complain **10 And . . . heaven** i.e., and that you shine in place of the sun when the sun is overclouded **11 So flatter I** similarly I gratify. **swart** dark **12 When . . . even** i.e., by saying that, when sparkling stars do not twinkle or peep out, you make bright the evening

29

When, in disgrace with fortune and men's eyes,
I all alone beweep my outcast state,
And trouble deaf heaven with my bootless cries,
And look upon myself and curse my fate, 4
Wishing me like to one more rich in hope,
Featured like him, like him with friends possessed,
Desiring this man's art and that man's scope,
With what I most enjoy contented least; 8
Yet in these thoughts myself almost despising,
Haply I think on thee, and then my state,
Like to the lark at break of day arising
From sullen earth, sings hymns at heaven's gate; 12
  For thy sweet love remembered such wealth brings
  That then I scorn to change my state with kings.

29 • 3 bootless useless **4 look upon myself** consider my predicament **5 more rich in hope** with better prospects of success **6 Featured** formed, i.e., having good looks. **like him, like him** like a second man, like a third **7 art** literary skill (?) **scope** range of powers **8 most enjoy** possess the most **10 state** state of mind **14 change** exchange

30

When to the sessions of sweet silent thought
I summon up remembrance of things past,
I sigh the lack of many a thing I sought,
And with old woes new wail my dear time's waste. 4
Then can I drown an eye, unused to flow,
For precious friends hid in death's dateless night,
And weep afresh love's long since canceled woe,
And moan th' expense of many a vanished sight. 8
Then can I grieve at grievances foregone,
And heavily from woe to woe tell o'er
The sad account of fore-bemoanèd moan,
Which I new pay as if not paid before. 12
  But if the while I think on thee, dear friend,
  All losses are restored and sorrows end.

30 • 1 sessions (The metaphor is that of a court of law, continued in *summon up,* l. 2.) **3 sigh** sigh for **4 new . . . waste** lament anew the wasting of precious time or time's erosion of those things held precious **5 unused to flow** not prone to weep **6 dateless** endless **7 canceled** paid in full (by grieving) **8 expense** loss **9 grievances foregone** sorrows past **10 heavily** sadly. **tell** count **11 The sad . . . moan** the distressing total of previously-uttered laments

31

Thy bosom is endearèd with all hearts,
Which I by lacking have supposèd dead,
And there reigns love and all love's loving parts,
And all those friends which I thought burièd. 4
How many a holy and obsequious tear
Hath dear religious love stol'n from mine eye
As interest of the dead, which now appear
But things removed that hidden in thee lie! 8
Thou art the grave where buried love doth live,
Hung with the trophies of my lovers gone,
Who all their parts of me to thee did give;
That due of many now is thine alone. 12
  Their images I loved I view in thee,
  And thou, all they, hast all the all of me.

31 • 1 endearèd with all hearts (1) beloved by all (2) made dear to me by representing and including those I have loved **2 lacking** not having **3 parts** attributes **5 obsequious** suitable to mourning **6 religious** dutiful **7 interest** that which is rightfully due. **which** who **8 But . . . lie** i.e., no more than absent persons (now dead) whose best qualities are to be found concealed in you **10 lovers** loved ones, friends **11 parts** shares **12 That due of many** that which was the due of many **13 I loved** which I loved **14 all they** (you) who comprise all of them

32

If thou survive my well-contented day
When that churl Death my bones with dust shall cover,
And shalt by fortune once more re-survey
These poor rude lines of thy deceasèd lover, 4
Compare them with the bettering of the time,
And though they be outstripped by every pen,
Reserve them for my love, not for their rhyme,
Exceeded by the height of happier men. 8
O, then vouchsafe me but this loving thought:
"Had my friend's Muse grown with this growing age,
A dearer birth than this his love had brought
To march in ranks of better equipage; 12
  But since he died and poets better prove,
  Theirs for their style I'll read, his for his love."

32 • 1 my . . . day i.e., the day of my death, which will content me well **3 fortune** chance **4 rude** unpolished. **lover** friend **5 bettering** i.e., improved writing, greater cultural sophistication **7 Reserve** preserve. **rhyme** i.e., poetic skill **8 height** superiority, highest achievement. **happier** more gifted **9 vouchsafe me but** deign to bestow on me just **11 dearer birth** i.e., better poem, better artistic creation **12 of better equipage** i.e., more finely wrought verse **13 better prove** turn out to be superior

33

Full many a glorious morning have I seen
Flatter the mountaintops with sovereign eye,
Kissing with golden face the meadows green,
Gilding pale streams with heavenly alchemy; 4
Anon permit the basest clouds to ride
With ugly rack on his celestial face,
And from the forlorn world his visage hide,
Stealing unseen to west with this disgrace. 8
Even so my sun one early morn did shine
With all-triumphant splendor on my brow.
But out, alack! He was but one hour mine;
The region cloud hath masked him from me now. 12
  Yet him for this my love no whit disdaineth;
  Suns of the world may stain when heaven's sun
    staineth.

33 • 1 Full very **5 Anon** soon afterward. **basest** darkest; also, far below the royal glory of the sun in dignity and in altitude **6 rack** mass of cloud scudding before the wind **12 region** of the upper air **14 Suns** i.e., great men (with a pun on *sons of the world,* mortal men). **stain** grow dim, be obscured, soiled. **staineth** is clouded over

34

Why didst thou promise such a beauteous day
And make me travel forth without my cloak,
To let base clouds o'ertake me in my way,
Hiding thy bravery in their rotten smoke? 4
'Tis not enough that through the cloud thou break,
To dry the rain on my storm-beaten face,
For no man well of such a salve can speak
That heals the wound and cures not the disgrace. 8
Nor can thy shame give physic to my grief;
Though thou repent, yet I have still the loss.
Th' offender's sorrow lends but weak relief
To him that bears the strong offense's cross. 12
  Ah, but those tears are pearl which thy love sheeds,
  And they are rich and ransom all ill deeds.

34 • 3 To only to **4 bravery** finery. **rotten smoke** foul vapors **8 disgrace** i.e., the scar, the disfigurement caused by his friend's neglect or harsh treatment; the *loss* mentioned in l. 10 **9 shame** repentance for the wrong done. **physic** remedy **12 cross** affliction **13 sheeds** sheds

35

No more be grieved at that which thou hast done.
Roses have thorns, and silver fountains mud,
Clouds and eclipses stain both moon and sun,
And loathsome canker lives in sweetest bud. 4
All men make faults, and even I in this,
Authorizing thy trespass with compare,
Myself corrupting, salving thy amiss,
Excusing thy sins more than thy sins are. 8
For to thy sensual fault I bring in sense—
Thy adverse party is thy advocate—
And 'gainst myself a lawful plea commence.
Such civil war is in my love and hate 12
  That I an accessary needs must be
  To that sweet thief which sourly robs from me.

35 • 3 stain dim, obscure **4 canker** cankerworm **6 Authorizing** sanctioning, justifying. **compare** comparisons (as in this sonnet) **7 Myself . . . amiss** i.e., excusing your misdeed, thereby bringing blame on myself **8 Excusing . . . are** i.e., going further to excuse your sins than they warrant **9 sensual** pertaining to the flesh. **sense** pertaining to the rational faculty (i.e., I reason away your fleshly offenses with sophistical justifications) **10 Thy . . . advocate** I who profess to be your accuser find myself instead pleading your case **13 That . . . be** that I am compelled (by my love) to be a guilty accomplice

36

Let me confess that we two must be twain,
Although our undivided loves are one;
So shall those blots that do with me remain,
Without thy help, by me be borne alone. 4
In our two loves there is but one respect,
Though in our lives a separable spite,
Which though it alter not love's sole effect,
Yet doth it steal sweet hours from love's delight. 8
I may not evermore acknowledge thee,
Lest my bewailèd guilt should do thee shame,
Nor thou with public kindness honor me
Unless thou take that honor from thy name. 12
But do not so; I love thee in such sort
As, thou being mine, mine is thy good report.

36 • 1 twain parted **3 blots** defects, stains of dishonor **5 but one respect** i.e., a mutual regard, singleness of attitude **6 separable spite** spiteful separation **7 sole** unique **9 not evermore** nevermore. **acknowledge** admit my acquaintance with **12 Unless . . . from** without consequent loss of honor to **13 in such sort** in such a way **14 As** that. **report** reputation

37

As a decrepit father takes delight
To see his active child do deeds of youth,
So I, made lame by Fortune's dearest spite,
Take all my comfort of thy worth and truth. 4
For whether beauty, birth, or wealth, or wit,
Or any of these all, or all, or more,
Entitled in thy parts do crownèd sit,
I make my love engrafted to this store. 8
So then I am not lame, poor, nor despised,
Whilst that this shadow doth such substance give
That I in thy abundance am sufficed
And by a part of all thy glory live. 12
  Look what is best, that best I wish in thee.
  This wish I have; then ten times happy me!

37 • 3 made lame handicapped in life. **dearest** most bitter **4 of** in, from **5 wit** intelligence **7 Entitled . . . sit** sit enthroned in first place among your qualities **8 I make . . . store** I add my love to this abundance (and thereby flourish by drawing on their strength) **10 shadow** idea (in the Platonic sense). **substance** actuality **13 Look what** whatever

38

How can my Muse want subject to invent
While thou dost breathe, that pour'st into my verse
Thine own sweet argument, too excellent
For every vulgar paper to rehearse? 4
O, give thyself the thanks, if aught in me
Worthy perusal stand against thy sight,
For who's so dumb that cannot write to thee,
When thou thyself dost give invention light? 8
Be thou the tenth Muse, ten times more in worth
Than those old nine which rhymers invocate;
And he that calls on thee, let him bring forth
Eternal numbers to outlive long date. 12
  If my slight Muse do please these curious days,
  The pain be mine, but thine shall be the praise.

38 • 1 want . . . invent lack something to write about **2 that** you who **3 Thine . . . argument** yourself as subject **4 vulgar paper** common piece of writing. **rehearse** recite, repeat **5 in me** of my writing **6 stand against** meet **7 dumb** silent, lacking in subject **12 numbers** verses. **date** duration **13 curious** critical **14 pain** labor

39

O, how thy worth with manners may I sing,
When thou art all the better part of me?
What can mine own praise to mine own self bring?
And what is 't but mine own when I praise thee? 4
Even for this let us divided live,
And our dear love lose name of single one,
That by this separation I may give
That due to thee which thou deserv'st alone. 8
O absence, what a torment wouldst thou prove,
Were it not thy sour leisure gave sweet leave
To entertain the time with thoughts of love,
Which time and thoughts so sweetly dost deceive, 12
  And that thou teachest how to make one twain
  By praising him here who doth hence remain!

39 • 1 with manners decently, becomingly **4 mine own** i.e., praise of myself **5 Even for** precisely because of **6 name** reputation
11 entertain pass, occupy **12 dost deceive** (you) do beguile away
13 that were it not that. **make one twain** i.e., divide one beloved person into two **14 praising him here** i.e., invoking his presence here through my praising of him

40

Take all my loves, my love, yea, take them all;
What hast thou then more than thou hadst before?
No love, my love, that thou mayst true love call;
All mine was thine before thou hadst this more. 4
Then if for my love thou my love receivest,
I cannot blame thee for my love thou usest;
But yet be blamed, if thou this self deceivest
By willful taste of what thyself refusest. 8
I do forgive thy robbery, gentle thief,
Although thou steal thee all my poverty;
And yet love knows it is a greater grief
To bear love's wrong than hate's known injury. 12
  Lascivious grace, in whom all ill well shows,
  Kill me with spites; yet we must not be foes.

40 • 1 all my loves (1) all those whom I love (2) all the love I have. (The young man addressed has taken away the poet's mistress.) **3 No . . . call** i.e., any love more than you had already—my complete affection—cannot be called true love **5 my love . . . my love** love of me . . . her whom I love **6 for** because. **thou usest** you enjoy (sexually) **7 this self** i.e., this other self of yours, the poet. (Often emended to *thyself*.) **8 willful taste** i.e., sensual enjoyment. **thyself** i.e., your true self (?) **10 steal . . . poverty** take for your own the poor little that I have **12 known** undisguised **13 Lascivious grace** i.e., you who are gracious even in your lasciviousness

41

Those pretty wrongs that liberty commits
When I am sometimes absent from thy heart,
Thy beauty and thy years full well befits,
For still temptation follows where thou art. 4
Gentle thou art, and therefore to be won;
Beauteous thou art, therefore to be assailed;
And when a woman woos, what woman's son
Will sourly leave her till she have prevailed? 8
Ay me, but yet thou mightst my seat forbear,
And chide thy beauty and thy straying youth,
Who lead thee in their riot even there
Where thou art forced to break a twofold truth: 12
  Hers, by thy beauty tempting her to thee,
  Thine, by thy beauty being false to me.

41 • 1 pretty minor; sportive. **liberty** licentiousness **3 befits** (The subject is *wrongs*, l. 1.) **4 still** constantly **9 seat** place, that which belongs to me (i.e., my mistress) **11 Who** which. **riot** debauchery **12 twofold truth** i.e., her plighted love and your plighted friendship

42

That thou hast her, it is not all my grief,
And yet it may be said I loved her dearly;
That she hath thee is of my wailing chief,
A loss in love that touches me more nearly. 4
Loving offenders, thus I will excuse ye:
Thou dost love her because thou know'st I love her,
And for my sake even so doth she abuse me,
Suff'ring my friend for my sake to approve her. 8
If I lose thee, my loss is my love's gain,
And, losing her, my friend hath found that loss;
Both find each other, and I lose both twain,
And both for my sake lay on me this cross. 12
But here's the joy: my friend and I are one.
Sweet flattery! Then she loves but me alone.

42 • 3 is . . . chief is chief cause of my lamentation **7 abuse** betray, wrong **8 Suff'ring** allowing. **approve** try, test (in a sexual sense) **9 my love's** hers whom I love, my mistress's **10 losing her** i.e., I losing her **12 for my sake** out of love for me. **cross** torment **14 flattery** gratifying deception

43

When most I wink, then do mine eyes best see,
For all the day they view things unrespected;
But when I sleep, in dreams they look on thee,
And, darkly bright, are bright in dark directed. 4
Then thou, whose shadow shadows doth make bright,
How would thy shadow's form form happy show
To the clear day with thy much clearer light,
When to unseeing eyes thy shade shines so! 8
How would, I say, mine eyes be blessèd made
By looking on thee in the living day,
When in dead night thy fair imperfect shade
Through heavy sleep on sightless eyes doth stay! 12
All days are nights to see till I see thee,
And nights bright days when dreams do show
thee me.

43 • 1 wink close my eyes in sleep **2 unrespected** unnoticed, unregarded; not deserving notice **4 And . . . directed** and, able to see in the darkness, are directed toward your brightness in the dark **5 whose . . . bright** whose image makes darkness bright **6 thy shadow's form** the substance of the shadow, i.e., your presence. **form happy show** make a gladdening sight **8 unseeing eyes** i.e., closed eyes of the dreamer **11 imperfect** unsubstantial, indistinct as in a dream **12 stay** linger, dwell **13 All . . . to see** all days are gloomy to behold **14 me** to me

44

If the dull substance of my flesh were thought,
Injurious distance should not stop my way;
For then despite of space I would be brought,
From limits far remote, where thou dost stay. 4
No matter then although my foot did stand
Upon the farthest earth removed from thee;
For nimble thought can jump both sea and land
As soon as think the place where he would be. 8
But, ah, thought kills me that I am not thought,
To leap large lengths of miles when thou art gone,
But that, so much of earth and water wrought,
I must attend time's leisure with my moan, 12
Receiving naught by elements so slow
But heavy tears, badges of either's woe.

44 • 1 dull heavy **4 limits** regions, bounds. **where** i.e., to the place where **6 farthest earth removed** that part of the earth farthest removed **8 he** i.e., thought **9 ah, thought** ah, the thought **11 so . . . wrought** i.e., I, compounded to such an extent of the heavier elements, earth and water. (The lighter elements are fire and air.) **12 attend time's leisure** i.e., wait until time has leisure to reunite us **13 by** from **14 badges** signs, tokens. **either's** i.e., both earth's and water's, because the earth is heavy and the sea is salt and wet, both like tears

45

The other two, slight air and purging fire,
Are both with thee, wherever I abide;
The first my thought, the other my desire,
These present-absent with swift motion slide. 4
For when these quicker elements are gone
In tender embassy of love to thee,
My life, being made of four, with two alone
Sinks down to death, oppressed with melancholy; 8
Until life's composition be recured
By those swift messengers returned from thee,
Who even but now come back again, assured
Of thy fair health, recounting it to me. 12
  This told, I joy; but then no longer glad,
  I send them back again and straight grow sad.

45 • 1 other two i.e., of the four elements discussed in Sonnet 44. **slight** insubstantial. **purging** purifying **4 present-absent** now here and immediately gone **7 life** living body. **two alone** i.e., earth and water **8 melancholy** a humor thought to be induced by an excess of earth and water **9 composition** proper balance among the four elements. **recured** restored **10 swift messengers** i.e., fire and air, thought and desire **14 straight** straightway

46

Mine eye and heart are at a mortal war
How to divide the conquest of thy sight;
Mine eye my heart thy picture's sight would bar,
My heart mine eye the freedom of that right. 4
My heart doth plead that thou in him dost lie—
A closet never pierced with crystal eyes—
But the defendant doth that plea deny
And says in him thy fair appearance lies. 8
To 'cide this title is impanelèd
A quest of thoughts, all tenants to the heart,
And by their verdict is determinèd
The clear eye's moiety and the dear heart's part, 12
  As thus: mine eye's due is thy outward part,
  And my heart's right thy inward love of heart.

46 • 1 mortal deadly **2 conquest** spoils. **thy sight** the sight of you **3 Mine . . . bar** i.e., my eye would issue an order prohibiting my heart from enjoying the sight of your picture **4 My . . . right** i.e., my heart would deny to my eye the privilege of looking on your picture **6 closet** small private room **9 'cide** decide **10 quest** inquest, jury **12 moiety** portion **13 mine . . . part** i.e., the eye gets the mere appearance of the young man only (since the jury is composed entirely of those who are loyal to the heart, its *tenants*)

47

Betwixt mine eye and heart a league is took,
And each doth good turns now unto the other.
When that mine eye is famished for a look,
Or heart in love with sighs himself doth smother, 4
With my love's picture then my eye doth feast
And to the painted banquet bids my heart;
Another time mine eye is my heart's guest
And in his thoughts of love doth share a part. 8
So, either by thy picture or my love,
Thyself, away, are present still with me;
For thou not farther than my thoughts canst move,
And I am still with them and they with thee; 12
  Or, if they sleep, thy picture in my sight
  Awakes my heart to heart's and eye's delight.

47 • 1 a league is took an agreement is reached **3 When that** when
4 Or heart or when my heart. **himself** itself **5 With** i.e., on **6 painted banquet** i.e., visual feast, perhaps an actual picture of the friend
12 still constantly

48

How careful was I, when I took my way,
Each trifle under truest bars to thrust,
That to my use it might unusèd stay
From hands of falsehood, in sure wards of trust! 4
But thou, to whom my jewels trifles are,
Most worthy comfort, now my greatest grief,
Thou best of dearest and mine only care,
Art left the prey of every vulgar thief. 8
Thee have I not locked up in any chest,
Save where thou art not—though I feel thou art—
Within the gentle closure of my breast,
From whence at pleasure thou mayst come and part; 12
  And even thence thou wilt be stol'n, I fear,
  For truth proves thievish for a prize so dear.

48 • 1 took my way set out on my journey **2 truest** most trusty **3 to my use** for my own use and profit **3–4 stay From** remain out of **4 hands of falsehood** the hands of thieves **5 to** compared to **6 worthy** valuable. **grief** anxiety, cause of sorrow (i.e., because of your absence and likeliness of being stolen) **8 vulgar** common **12 part** depart **14 truth** i.e., even honesty itself

49

Against that time, if ever that time come,
When I shall see thee frown on my defects,
Whenas thy love hath cast his utmost sum,
Called to that audit by advised respects; 4
Against that time when thou shalt strangely pass
And scarcely greet me with that sun, thine eye,
When love, converted from the thing it was,
Shall reasons find of settled gravity— 8
Against that time do I ensconce me here
Within the knowledge of mine own desart,
And this my hand against myself uprear
To guard the lawful reasons on thy part. 12
  To leave poor me thou hast the strength of laws,
  Since why to love I can allege no cause.

49 • 1 Against in anticipation of **3 Whenas** when. **cast . . . sum** added up the sum total. (The metaphor is from closing accounts on a dissolution of partnership.) **4 advised respects** careful consideration
5 strangely as a stranger **8 of settled gravity** for a dignified reserve or continued coldness (?) of sufficient weight (?) **9 ensconce** fortify, shelter **10 desart** i.e., deserving, such as it is. (This quarto spelling of desert, *desart,* indicates the rhyme with *part.*) **11 this . . . uprear** I raise my own hand (as a witness) against my own interest **12 To . . . part** i.e., to testify in behalf of the lawful reasons on your side of the case
14 Since . . . cause since I can urge no lawful cause why you should love me

50

How heavy do I journey on the way,
When what I seek, my weary travel's end,
Doth teach that ease and that repose to say,
"Thus far the miles are measured from thy friend!" 4
The beast that bears me, tired with my woe,
Plods dully on, to bear that weight in me,
As if by some instinct the wretch did know
His rider loved not speed being made from thee. 8
The bloody spur cannot provoke him on
That sometimes anger thrusts into his hide,
Which heavily he answers with a groan,
More sharp to me than spurring to his side; 12
For that same groan doth put this in my mind:
My grief lies onward and my joy behind.

50 • 1 heavy sadly **2–4 When . . . friend** i.e., when the ease and repose I seek at journey's end will merely remind me that I have gone so many miles from my friend **8 speed being made** (1) speed that is made (2) speed when he is being carried

51

Thus can my love excuse the slow offense
Of my dull bearer when from thee I speed:
From where thou art why should I haste me thence?
Till I return, of posting is no need. 4
O, what excuse will my poor beast then find
When swift extremity can seem but slow?
Then should I spur, though mounted on the wind;
In wingèd speed no motion shall I know. 8
Then can no horse with my desire keep pace;
Therefore desire, of perfect'st love being made,
Shall neigh—no dull flesh—in his fiery race.
But love, for love, thus shall excuse my jade: 12
Since from thee going he went willful slow,
Towards thee I'll run, and give him leave to go.

51 • 1 love affection. **slow offense** offense consisting in slowness **2 my dull bearer** i.e., the horse **4 posting** riding swiftly **6 swift extremity** extreme swiftness **8 In . . . know** even at the speed of flight I won't perceive the motion at all, won't feel as though I'm moving **11 Shall . . . race** i.e., shall neigh proudly in its fire-swift race, since it, composed like fire of a lighter element, is not held back by the heavy flesh. (See Sonnet 45.) **12 for love** for love's sake. **jade** nag **14 go** walk, as contrasted with running

52

So am I as the rich whose blessèd key
Can bring him to his sweet up-lockèd treasure,
The which he will not every hour survey,
For blunting the fine point of seldom pleasure. 4
Therefore are feasts so solemn and so rare,
Since, seldom coming, in the long year set,
Like stones of worth they thinly placèd are,
Or captain jewels in the carcanet. 8
So is the time that keeps you as my chest,
Or as the wardrobe which the robe doth hide,
To make some special instant special blest,
By new unfolding his imprisoned pride. 12
  Blessèd are you whose worthiness gives scope,
  Being had, to triumph, being lacked, to hope.

52 • 1 as the rich like the rich man **4 For blunting** lest he blunt. **fine** delicate; splendid. **seldom pleasure** pleasure sparingly enjoyed **5 feasts** feast days. **solemn** ceremonious, festive. **rare** excellent; uncommon **8 captain** principal. **carcanet** necklace of jewels **9 as** like **12 his** its. **pride** splendor, proud treasure **13–14 gives . . . hope** gives me opportunity, when you are with me, to rejoice, and when you are away from me, to hope for reunion

53

What is your substance, whereof are you made,
That millions of strange shadows on you tend?
Since everyone hath, every one, one shade,
And you, but one, can every shadow lend. 4
Describe Adonis, and the counterfeit
Is poorly imitated after you;
On Helen's cheek all art of beauty set,
And you in Grecian tires are painted new. 8
Speak of the spring and foison of the year;
The one doth shadow of your beauty show,
The other as your bounty doth appear,
And you in every blessèd shape we know. 12
  In all external grace you have some part,
  But you like none, none you, for constant heart.

53 • 2 strange (1) exotic (2) not belonging to you. **tend** attend, wait upon **3 shade** shadow (as cast by the sun) **4 And . . . lend** and yet you, being only one person, can cast all sorts of shadowy images or reflections (such as Adonis, Helen, etc.) **5 Adonis** beautiful youth beloved of Venus. **counterfeit** likeness, portrait **7–8 On . . . new** set forth the entire art used to beautify the cheek of Helen of Troy, and the result will be a portrait of you in Grecian attire or headdress **9 foison** abundance, i.e., autumn **14 But . . . heart** but in the matter of constancy you resemble no one and no one can resemble you

54

O, how much more doth beauty beauteous seem
By that sweet ornament which truth doth give!
The rose looks fair, but fairer we it deem
For that sweet odor which doth in it live. 4
The canker blooms have full as deep a dye
As the perfumèd tincture of the roses,
Hang on such thorns, and play as wantonly
When summer's breath their maskèd buds discloses. 8
But, for their virtue only is their show,
They live unwooed and unrespected fade,
Die to themselves. Sweet roses do not so;
Of their sweet deaths are sweetest odors made. 12
  And so of you, beauteous and lovely youth,
  When that shall vade, by verse distills your truth.

54 • 2 By by means of. **truth** (1) constancy (2) substance, reality **5 canker blooms** dog roses (outwardly attractive, but not as sweetly scented as the damask rose). **dye** tincture **7 wantonly** sportively **8 discloses** causes to open **9 for** because. **their show** in their appearance **10 unrespected** unregarded **11 to themselves** i.e., without profit to others **12 Of . . . made** i.e., perfumes are made from the crushed petals of these roses **13 of you** (1) distilled from you (2) with regard to you. **lovely** (1) lovable (2) handsome **14 When . . . truth** when your physical beauty fades, your true substance will be distilled and preserved by (my) verse. (See Sonnet 5.) **vade** (1) fade (2) go away

55

Not marble nor the gilded monuments
Of princes shall outlive this powerful rhyme,
But you shall shine more bright in these contents
Than unswept stone besmeared with sluttish time. 4
When wasteful war shall statues overturn,
And broils root out the work of masonry,
Nor Mars his sword nor war's quick fire shall burn
The living record of your memory. 8
'Gainst death and all-oblivious enmity
Shall you pace forth; your praise shall still find room
Even in the eyes of all posterity
That wear this world out to the ending doom. 12
  So, till the judgment that yourself arise,
  You live in this, and dwell in lovers' eyes.

55 • 3 these contents i.e., the contents of my poems written in praise of you **4 Than unswept stone** than in a memorial stone that has been left unswept, unattended. **with sluttish time** by neglectful time **5 wasteful** laying waste **6 broils** uprisings, battles **7 Nor Mars his sword** neither Mars' sword (shall destroy) **9 all-oblivious enmity** i.e., oblivion, at enmity with everything **12 That . . . doom** that will last from now till doomsday. (*That* refers to *eyes*.) **13 till . . . arise** until the Judgment Day when you will arise from the dead

56

Sweet love, renew thy force; be it not said
Thy edge should blunter be than appetite,
Which but today by feeding is allayed,
Tomorrow sharpened in his former might. 4
So, love, be thou; although today thou fill
Thy hungry eyes even till they wink with fullness,
Tomorrow see again, and do not kill
The spirit of love with a perpetual dullness. 8
Let this sad interim like the ocean be
Which parts the shore where two contracted new
Come daily to the banks, that, when they see
Return of love, more blest may be the view; 12
  As call it winter, which being full of care
  Makes summer's welcome thrice more wished,
    more rare.

56 • 1 love i.e., the spirit of love. (The friend is not directly mentioned in this sonnet.) **2 edge** keenness. **should blunter be** is blunter. **appetite** lust, craving **3 but** only for **4 his** its **6 wink** shut **9 sad interim** i.e., the period of love's abatement or absence **10 parts the shore** separates the shores. **contracted new** newly betrothed **11 banks** shores **12 love** the loved one **13 As** just as appropriately

57

Being your slave, what should I do but tend
Upon the hours and times of your desire?
I have no precious time at all to spend,
Nor services to do, till you require. 4
Nor dare I chide the world-without-end hour
Whilst I, my sovereign, watch the clock for you,
Nor think the bitterness of absence sour
When you have bid your servant once adieu. 8
Nor dare I question with my jealous thought
Where you may be, or your affairs suppose,
But, like a sad slave, stay and think of naught
Save where you are how happy you make those. 12
So true a fool is love that in your will,
Though you do anything, he thinks no ill.

57 • 1 tend attend **5 world-without-end** interminable **6 my . . . you** watch the clock for you, my sovereign **7 Nor think** nor dare I think **9 question with** (1) debate with (2) seek to know by means of **10 suppose** make conjectures about **11 sad** sober **13 true** (1) constant (2) utter. **will** desire. (This word, which is capitalized in the 1609 quarto, is regarded by some as a pun on Shakespeare's first name; see Sonnet 135.)

58

That god forbid that made me first your slave
I should in thought control your times of pleasure,
Or at your hand th' account of hours to crave,
Being your vassal, bound to stay your leisure! 4
O, let me suffer, being at your beck,
Th' imprisoned absence of your liberty,
And, patience-tame to sufferance, bide each check,
Without accusing you of injury. 8
Be where you list, your charter is so strong
That you yourself may privilege your time
To what you will; to you it doth belong
Yourself to pardon of self-doing crime. 12
  I am to wait, though waiting so be hell,
  Not blame your pleasure, be it ill or well.

58 • 3 th' account . . . crave should crave an accounting of how you spend your time **4 stay** await **6 Th' imprisoned . . . liberty** i.e., the lack of freedom I suffer in being absent from you, arising from (*of*) your freedom and free behavior **7 And . . . check** and, trained to endure any suffering, let me put up with each rebuke **9 list** please. **charter** privilege **10 privilege** authorize **12 self-doing** committed by yourself **13 am to** must

59

If there be nothing new, but that which is
Hath been before, how are our brains beguiled,
Which, laboring for invention, bear amiss
The second burden of a former child! 4
O, that record could with a backward look,
Even of five hundred courses of the sun,
Show me your image in some antique book,
Since mind at first in character was done! 8
That I might see what the old world could say
To this composèd wonder of your frame;
Whether we are mended, or whe'er better they,
Or whether revolution be the same. 12
O, sure I am the wits of former days
To subjects worse have given admiring praise.

59 • 1 that everything **3–4 laboring . . . child** i.e., striving to give birth to a new creation, merely miscarry with the repetition of something created before **5 record** memory, especially memory preserved in writing **6 courses . . . sun** years **8 Since . . . done** since thought was first expressed in writing **10 composèd wonder** wonderful composition **11 mended** improved. **whe'er** whether **12 revolution . . . same** i.e., the revolving of the ages brings only repetition **13 wits** i.e., poets

60

Like as the waves make towards the pebbled shore,
So do our minutes hasten to their end;
Each changing place with that which goes before,
In sequent toil all forwards do contend. 4
Nativity, once in the main of light,
Crawls to maturity, wherewith being crowned,
Crookèd eclipses 'gainst his glory fight,
And Time that gave doth now his gift confound. 8
Time doth transfix the flourish set on youth
And delves the parallels in beauty's brow,
Feeds on the rarities of nature's truth,
And nothing stands but for his scythe to mow. 12
  And yet to times in hope my verse shall stand,
  Praising thy worth, despite his cruel hand.

60 • 3 changing place with replacing **4 In . . . contend** one after another all struggle onward **5 Nativity** i.e., the newborn infant. **once** (1) no sooner (2) formerly. **main** main body, expanse. (The child is seen as dwelling in the main or ocean of light.) **7 Crookèd** perverse, malignant **8 confound** destroy **9 transfix the flourish** pierce through and destroy the decoration or embellishment, i.e., physical beauty **10 delves the parallels** digs the wrinkles, furrows **11 Feeds . . . truth** consumes the most precious things created by the fidelity of nature **12 but . . . mow** i.e., that can escape the mowing of Time's scythe **13 times in hope** times to come

61

Is it thy will thy image should keep open
My heavy eyelids to the weary night?
Dost thou desire my slumbers should be broken
While shadows like to thee do mock my sight? 4
Is it thy spirit that thou send'st from thee
So far from home into my deeds to pry,
To find out shames and idle hours in me,
The scope and tenor of thy jealousy? 8
O, no, thy love, though much, is not so great;
It is my love that keeps mine eye awake,
Mine own true love that doth my rest defeat,
To play the watchman ever for thy sake. 12
For thee watch I whilst thou dost wake elsewhere,
From me far off, with others all too near.

61 • 4 shadows images (but also suggesting spirits) **8 The scope . . . jealousy** the aim and purport of your suspicion (probably modifying *shames and idle hours*) **13 watch** stay awake. **wake** revel

62

Sin of self-love possesseth all mine eye,
And all my soul, and all my every part;
And for this sin there is no remedy,
It is so grounded inward in my heart. 4
Methinks no face so gracious is as mine,
No shape so true, no truth of such account;
And for myself mine own worth do define,
As I all other in all worths surmount. 8
But when my glass shows me myself indeed,
Beated and chapped with tanned antiquity,
Mine own self-love quite contrary I read;
Self so self-loving were iniquity. 12
'Tis thee, myself, that for myself I praise,
Painting my age with beauty of thy days.

62 • 5 Methinks it seems to me **7 for myself** (1) by my own reckoning (2) for my own pleasure **8 As** (1) inasmuch as (2) as if. **other** others **9 indeed** i.e., as I actually am **10 Beated** battered, weather-beaten. **tanned antiquity** i.e., leathery old age **12 Self . . . iniquity** i.e., it would be wicked for the self to love such an aged and unattractive self **13 thee, myself** i.e., you, with whom I identify myself. **for** as **14 days** i.e., youth

63

Against my love shall be, as I am now,
With Time's injurious hand crushed and o'erworn;
When hours have drained his blood and filled his brow
With lines and wrinkles; when his youthful morn 4
Hath traveled on to age's steepy night,
And all those beauties whereof now he's king
Are vanishing or vanished out of sight,
Stealing away the treasure of his spring; 8
For such a time do I now fortify
Against confounding age's cruel knife,
That he shall never cut from memory
My sweet love's beauty, though my lover's life. 12
His beauty shall in these black lines be seen,
And they shall live, and he in them still green.

63 • 1 Against anticipating the time when. **love** beloved **2 crushed and o'erworn** creased and worn threadbare (like a long-used garment) **5 steepy** precipitous, i.e., descending swiftly toward death **9 For such a time** (Parallel in construction with *Against* in l. 1.) **fortify** raise works of defense **10 confounding** destroying **11 That** so that **12 though** i.e., though he cut **13 black** (1) inscribed in ink (2) the opposite of fair or beautiful **14 green** i.e., as in springtime and youth

64

When I have seen by Time's fell hand defaced
The rich proud cost of outworn buried age;
When sometime lofty towers I see down-razed
And brass eternal slave to mortal rage; 4
When I have seen the hungry ocean gain
Advantage on the kingdom of the shore,
And the firm soil win of the watery main,
Increasing store with loss and loss with store; 8
When I have seen such interchange of state,
Or state itself confounded to decay,
Ruin hath taught me thus to ruminate:
That Time will come and take my love away. 12
  This thought is as a death, which cannot choose
  But weep to have that which it fears to lose.

64 • 1 fell cruel **2 The rich . . . age** i.e., those monuments that were the product of proud wealth and magnificent outlay in times now past and forgotten **3 sometime** formerly **4 brass . . . rage** i.e., seemingly indestructible brass subdued to the destructive power of mortality **7 of** at the expense of **8 Increasing . . . store** i.e., one gaining as the other loses, and losing as the other gains **9 state** condition **10 state** pomp, greatness; condition in the abstract. **confounded to decay** destroyed to the point of being in ruins **12 love** beloved **13 which cannot choose** (Modifies *thought.*) **14 to have** i.e., because it now has

65

Since brass, nor stone, nor earth, nor boundless sea,
But sad mortality o'ersways their power,
How with this rage shall beauty hold a plea,
Whose action is no stronger than a flower? 4
O, how shall summer's honey breath hold out
Against the wrackful siege of battering days,
When rocks impregnable are not so stout,
Nor gates of steel so strong, but Time decays? 8
O fearful meditation! Where, alack,
Shall Time's best jewel from Time's chest lie hid?
Or what strong hand can hold his swift foot back?
Or who his spoil of beauty can forbid? 12
O, none, unless this miracle have might,
That in black ink my love may still shine bright.

65 • 1 Since i.e., since there is neither **2 But** but that. **o'ersways** overrules **3 with this rage** against this destructive force (the *mortal rage* of 64.4). **hold** maintain (as in a legal action) **4 action** case (in law) **6 wrackful** destructive **7 stout** sturdy, impregnable **8 decays** brings about their decay **10 from Time's chest** i.e., away from being deposited by Time in his repository of forgetfulness **12 spoil** despoliation, ravaging

66

Tired with all these, for restful death I cry:
As, to behold desert a beggar born,
And needy nothing trimmed in jollity,
And purest faith unhappily forsworn, 4
And gilded honor shamefully misplaced,
And maiden virtue rudely strumpeted,
And right perfection wrongfully disgraced,
And strength by limping sway disablèd, 8
And art made tongue-tied by authority,
And folly doctorlike controlling skill,
And simple truth miscalled simplicity,
And captive good attending captain ill. 12
Tired with all these, from these would I be gone,
Save that, to die, I leave my love alone.

66 • 1 all these i.e., the following **2 As** for instance, namely. **desert** i.e., those who have merit, as contrasted with *needy nothing* in the next line, those insignificant persons who deserve nothing, or those who in beggarly worthlessness squander what little they have on *jollity* or finery **4 unhappily forsworn** evilly betrayed **5 gilded** golden, splendid (not here suggesting mere appearance of splendor) **7 right** true. **disgraced** banished from favor **8 limping sway** halting leadership **9 art** literature, learning. **made tongue-tied** i.e., censored, stifled **10 doctorlike** assuming a learned bearing. **controlling** dominating, curbing **11 simplicity** foolishness, naivete **12 attending** waiting on, subordinated to **14 to die** in dying

67

Ah, wherefore with infection should he live,
And with his presence grace impiety,
That sin by him advantage should achieve
And lace itself with his society? 4
Why should false painting imitate his cheek
And steal dead seeing of his living hue?
Why should poor beauty indirectly seek
Roses of shadow, since his rose is true? 8
Why should he live, now Nature bankrupt is,
Beggared of blood to blush through lively veins,
For she hath no exchequer now but his,
And, proud of many, lives upon his gains? 12
O, him she stores, to show what wealth she had
In days long since, before these last so bad.

67 • 1 wherefore why. **with infection** i.e., with the world's ills as enumerated in the preceding sonnet. **he** i.e., the poet's friend **3 That . . . achieve** with the result that sin should flourish by his means **4 lace . . . society** (1) adorn itself with his company (2) weave its way into his company **6 dead seeing of** lifeless appearance from **7 poor** inferior. **indirectly** imitatively, or falsely **8 Roses of shadow** i.e., painted roses, cosmetically applied **9–10 now . . . veins** i.e., seeing as Nature is bankrupt through supplying him all her arts, and is therefore now destitute of healthy blood to make red the veins **11 For** since. **exchequer** i.e., treasury of natural beauty **12 proud** i.e., though proudly boasting. **gains** endowments **13 stores** preserves, keeps in store **14 last** i.e., recent days, the present

68

Thus is his cheek the map of days outworn,
When beauty lived and died as flowers do now,
Before these bastard signs of fair were born,
Or durst inhabit on a living brow; 4
Before the golden tresses of the dead,
The right of sepulchers, were shorn away
To live a second life on second head;
Ere beauty's dead fleece made another gay. 8
In him those holy antique hours are seen
Without all ornament, itself and true,
Making no summer of another's green,
Robbing no old to dress his beauty new; 12
And him as for a map doth Nature store,
To show false Art what beauty was of yore.

68 • 1 map picture, image **3 bastard . . . fair** i.e., cosmetics **4 inhabit** dwell **6 The right of** rightly belonging in. (Wigs were made of dead persons' hair.) **8 gay** lovely, gaudy **9 holy antique hours** blessed ancient times **10 all** any **13 store** preserve

69

Those parts of thee that the world's eye doth view
Want nothing that the thought of hearts can mend;
All tongues, the voice of souls, give thee that due,
Utt'ring bare truth, even so as foes commend. 4
Thy outward thus with outward praise is crowned,
But those same tongues that give thee so thine own
In other accents do this praise confound
By seeing farther than the eye hath shown. 8
They look into the beauty of thy mind,
And that, in guess, they measure by thy deeds;
Then, churls, their thoughts, although their eyes were
kind,
To thy fair flower add the rank smell of weeds. 12
But why thy odor matcheth not thy show,
The soil is this, that thou dost common grow.

69 • 2 Want lack. **mend** improve upon **3 the voice of souls** i.e., uttering heartfelt conviction. **give thee that due** allow that as your due **4 Utt'ring . . . commend** i.e., thus saying what even your enemies would concede to be the bare truth **5 outward praise** the kind of praise suited to mere outward qualities **6 thine own** your due **7 In other accents** in other terms and with another emphasis. **confound** confute, destroy **10 in guess** at a guess **12 To . . . weeds** i.e., to the flower of your outward beauty they contrastingly suggest something putrid within **13 odor** i.e., reputation **14 soil** (1) blemish, fault (2) origin, source, ground. **common** stale, vulgar (like a weed)

70

That thou are blamed shall not be thy defect,
For slander's mark was ever yet the fair;
The ornament of beauty is suspect,
A crow that flies in heaven's sweetest air. 4
So thou be good, slander doth but approve
Thy worth the greater, being wooed of time,
For canker vice the sweetest buds doth love,
And thou present'st a pure unstainèd prime. 8
Thou hast passed by the ambush of young days,
Either not assailed, or victor being charged;
Yet this thy praise cannot be so thy praise
To tie up envy evermore enlarged. 12
  If some suspect of ill masked not thy show,
  Then thou alone kingdoms of hearts shouldst owe.

70 • 1 defect fault **2 mark** target **3 The . . . suspect** i.e., beauty is always attended by suspicion (*suspect*), as though suspicion were a necessary ornament to beauty **5 So** provided that. **approve** prove **6 being . . . time** i.e., since you are courted by the world **7 canker vice** i.e., slander that is like the cankerworm **8 unstainèd prime** unspotted youth (like the pure unspoiled flower that attracts the cankerworm) **9 ambush . . . days** i.e., temptations of youth **10 being charged** when you were assailed **11 so** sufficiently **12 To . . . enlarged** i.e., as to silence malice, which is always at liberty **13 If . . . show** if some suspicion (*suspect*) of illdoing did not partly obscure your outward attractiveness **14 owe** own

71

No longer mourn for me when I am dead
Than you shall hear the surly sullen bell
Give warning to the world that I am fled
From this vile world, with vilest worms to dwell. 4
Nay, if you read this line, remember not
The hand that writ it, for I love you so
That I in your sweet thoughts would be forgot
If thinking on me then should make you woe. 8
O, if, I say, you look upon this verse
When I perhaps compounded am with clay,
Do not so much as my poor name rehearse,
But let your love even with my life decay, 12
  Lest the wise world should look into your moan
  And mock you with me after I am gone.

71 • 2 bell a passing bell for one who has died, rung once for each year of that person's life **8 on** of, about. **make** cause **10 compounded** mingled **11 rehearse** repeat **12 even with** at the same time as **14 with** because of, for loving

72

O, lest the world should task you to recite
What merit lived in me that you should love
After my death, dear love, forget me quite;
For you in me can nothing worthy prove, 4
Unless you would devise some virtuous lie
To do more for me than mine own desert,
And hang more praise upon deceasèd I
Than niggard truth would willingly impart. 8
O, lest your true love may seem false in this,
That you for love speak well of me untrue,
My name be buried where my body is,
And live no more to shame nor me nor you. 12
For I am shamed by that which I bring forth,
And so should you, to love things nothing worth.

72 • 1 recite tell **7 hang** (as in hanging trophies on a funeral monument) **10 untrue** untruly **11 My name be** let my name be **12 nor . . . nor** neither . . . nor **13 that . . . forth** (Perhaps a deprecatory reference to the author's acting and writing of plays, but more probably his verse or his written work generally.) **14 should you** i.e., you ought to be ashamed

73

That time of year thou mayst in me behold
When yellow leaves, or none, or few, do hang
Upon those boughs which shake against the cold,
Bare ruined choirs, where late the sweet birds sang. 4
In me thou seest the twilight of such day
As after sunset fadeth in the west,
Which by and by black night doth take away,
Death's second self, that seals up all in rest. 8
In me thou seest the glowing of such fire
That on the ashes of his youth doth lie,
As the deathbed whereon it must expire,
Consumed with that which it was nourished by. 12
This thou perceiv'st, which makes thy love more strong,
To love that well which thou must leave ere long.

73 • 4 choirs those areas of churches where the service is sung, here viewed as in ruins and resembling the arched shape of bare trees. **late** lately **8 seals** closes **10 That** as. **his** (1) its (2) his

74

But be contented when that fell arrest
Without all bail shall carry me away;
My life hath in this line some interest,
Which for memorial still with thee shall stay. 4
When thou reviewest this, thou dost review
The very part was consecrate to thee.
The earth can have but earth, which is his due;
My spirit is thine, the better part of me. 8
So then thou hast but lost the dregs of life,
The prey of worms, my body being dead,
The coward conquest of a wretch's knife,
Too base of thee to be rememberèd. 12
The worth of that is that which it contains,
And that is this, and this with thee remains.

74 • 1 be contented do not be distressed. **that fell arrest** i.e., death. **fell** cruel **3 line** verse. **interest** legal concern, right, or title **4 still** always **5 reviewest this** see this again (and view it with a critical eye) **6 part was** part (of me) that was. **consecrate** dedicated solemnly (as in a religious service) **7 his** its **11 The coward . . . knife** i.e., the cowardly conquest that even such a poor wretch as Mortality, or Death, can make with his scythe **12 of . . . rememberèd** to be remembered by you **13–14 The worth . . . remains** the only worth of my body is the spirit it contains—i.e., this verse, which will remain with you

75

So are you to my thoughts as food to life,
Or as sweet-seasoned showers are to the ground.
And for the peace of you I hold such strife
As twixt a miser and his wealth is found: 4
Now proud as an enjoyer, and anon
Doubting the filching age will steal his treasure;
Now counting best to be with you alone,
Then bettered that the world may see my pleasure; 8
Sometimes all full with feasting on your sight
And by and by clean starvèd for a look;
Possessing or pursuing no delight
Save what is had or must from you be took. 12
  Thus do I pine and surfeit day by day,
  Or gluttoning on all, or all away.

75 • 1 as food to life what food is to life **2 sweet-seasoned** of the sweet season, i.e., spring **3 of you** to be found in loving you **6 Doubting** suspecting, fearing that. **filching** thieving **7 counting** (1) thinking it (2) reckoning, like a miser **8 bettered** made happier, better pleased. **see my pleasure** i.e., see me with you, enjoying your company **10 clean** completely, absolutely. **a look** (1) a glimpse of you (2) an exchange of glances **12 from you** (Modifies both verbs, *had* and *must be took*.) **13 pine and surfeit** starve and overeat **14 Or . . . or** either . . . or. **all away** i.e., all food being taken away

76

Why is my verse so barren of new pride?
So far from variation or quick change?
Why with the time do I not glance aside
To newfound methods and to compounds strange? 4
Why write I still all one, ever the same,
And keep invention in a noted weed,
That every word doth almost tell my name,
Showing their birth and where they did proceed? 8
O, know, sweet love, I always write of you,
And you and love are still my argument;
So all my best is dressing old words new,
Spending again what is already spent. 12
For as the sun is daily new and old,
So is my love still telling what is told.

76 • 1 pride ornament **2 quick change** fashionable innovation **3 time** way of the world, fashion **4 compounds strange** literary inventions, or perhaps compound words, neologisms **5 still all one** continually one way **6 invention** literary creation. **noted weed** familiar garment **8 where** whence **10 still** always. **argument** subject, theme **14 telling** (1) retelling (2) counting over. (Continuing the financial wordplay of *Spending* and *spent* in l. 12.)

77

Thy glass will show thee how thy beauties wear,
Thy dial how thy precious minutes waste;
The vacant leaves thy mind's imprint will bear,
And of this book this learning mayst thou taste. 4
The wrinkles which thy glass will truly show
Of mouthèd graves will give thee memory;
Thou by thy dial's shady stealth mayst know
Time's thievish progress to eternity. 8
Look what thy memory cannot contain
Commit to these waste blanks, and thou shalt find
Those children nursed, delivered from thy brain,
To take a new acquaintance of thy mind. 12
These offices, so oft as thou wilt look,
Shall profit thee and much enrich thy book.

77 • 1 glass mirror. **wear** wear away **2 dial** sundial **3 vacant leaves** blank pages. (Apparently these lines accompanied the gift of a book of blank pages, a memorandum book.) **thy mind's imprint** i.e., your reflections and ideas, to be set down in the memorandum book **4 this learning** i.e., mental profit derived from reflecting and keeping a journal, as explained in ll. 9 ff. **6 mouthèd** all-devouring, gaping. **memory** reminder **7 shady stealth** slow progress of the shadow on the dial **9 Look what** whatever **10 waste blanks** blank pages **11 nursed** i.e., preserved and matured. **delivered from** having been produced by **12 take . . . of** i.e., provide fresh insight to, be freshly remembered by **13 offices** duties (of meditation and reflection) **14 and . . . book** i.e., and you will set down your reflections in the memorandum book, where they will profit you

78

So oft have I invoked thee for my Muse
And found such fair assistance in my verse
As every alien pen hath got my use,
And under thee their poesy disperse. 4
Thine eyes, that taught the dumb on high to sing
And heavy ignorance aloft to fly,
Have added feathers to the learnèd's wing
And given grace a double majesty. 8
Yet be most proud of that which I compile,
Whose influence is thine and born of thee.
In others' works thou dost but mend the style,
And arts with thy sweet graces gracèd be; 12
But thou art all my art, and dost advance
As high as learning my rude ignorance.

78 • 2 fair favorable **3 As** that. **alien pen** i.e., other poet. **got my use** adopted my practice **4 under thee** i.e., with you as their muse or patron; under your influence. **disperse** circulate **5 on high** aloud **6 aloft to fly** i.e., to get off the ground **7 added . . . wing** i.e., enabled learned poets to fly higher still. (A falconry metaphor; birds could be given extra wing feathers.) **8 And . . . majesty** and have added to the majesty of poets already capable of it **9 compile** compose, write **10 influence** inspiration (with suggestion of astrological meaning) **11 mend the style** correct or improve the style (but with a suggestion of repairing the point of a writing quill or stylus, continuing the metaphor of *pen*) **12 arts** learning, literary culture **13 advance** lift up

79

Whilst I alone did call upon thy aid,
My verse alone had all thy gentle grace,
But now my gracious numbers are decayed
And my sick Muse doth give another place. 4
I grant, sweet love, thy lovely argument
Deserves the travail of a worthier pen,
Yet what of thee thy poet doth invent
He robs thee of and pays it thee again. 8
He lends thee virtue, and he stole that word
From thy behavior; beauty doth he give,
And found it in thy cheek; he can afford
No praise to thee but what in thee doth live. 12
  Then thank him not for that which he doth say,
  Since what he owes thee thou thyself dost pay.

79 • 3 numbers verse **4 give another place** yield place to another **5 thy lovely argument** the theme of your lovable qualities **6 travail** labor **7–8 Yet . . . again** i.e., yet whatever a poet under your patronage discovers as a literary subject concerning you he merely robs from you and gives you back your own again **11 afford** offer to pay

80

O, how I faint when I of you do write,
Knowing a better spirit doth use your name,
And in the praise thereof spends all his might
To make me tongue-tied, speaking of your fame! 4
But since your worth, wide as the ocean is,
The humble as the proudest sail doth bear,
My saucy bark, inferior far to his,
On your broad main doth willfully appear. 8
Your shallowest help will hold me up afloat,
Whilst he upon your soundless deep doth ride;
Or, being wrecked, I am a worthless boat,
He of tall building and of goodly pride. 12
Then if he thrive and I be cast away,
The worst was this: my love was my decay.

80 • 1 faint grow weak, falter **2 better spirit** i.e., rival poet, whom the speaker admires **5 wide . . . is** as wide as is the ocean **6 as** as well as **8 main** ocean. **willfully** perversely, boldly, in spite of all **10 soundless** unfathomable **11 wrecked** shipwrecked **12 tall building** i.e., sturdy construction. **pride** splendor **13 cast away** (1) shipwrecked (2) abandoned **14 decay** ruin

81

Or I shall live your epitaph to make,
Or you survive when I in earth am rotten,
From hence your memory death cannot take,
Although in me each part will be forgotten. 4
Your name from hence immortal life shall have,
Though I, once gone, to all the world must die;
The earth can yield me but a common grave,
When you entombèd in men's eyes shall lie. 8
Your monument shall be my gentle verse,
Which eyes not yet created shall o'erread,
And tongues to be your being shall rehearse
When all the breathers of this world are dead. 12
You still shall live—such virtue hath my pen—
Where breath most breathes, even in the mouths
of men.

81 • 1 Or whether **3 hence** (1) this poetry (2) the earth (also in l. 5) **4 in . . . part** every quality of mine (as distinguished from the poetry) **5 from hence** (1) from this poetry (2) henceforth **11 to be** i.e., of persons yet unborn. **rehearse** recite **12 breathers** living people. **this world** this present time **13 virtue** power

82

I grant thou wert not married to my Muse,
And therefore mayst without attaint o'erlook
The dedicated words which writers use
Of their fair subject, blessing every book. 4
Thou art as fair in knowledge as in hue,
Finding thy worth a limit past my praise,
And therefore art enforced to seek anew
Some fresher stamp of the time-bettering days. 8
And do so, love; yet when they have devised
What strainèd touches rhetoric can lend,
Thou, truly fair, wert truly sympathized
In true plain words by thy true-telling friend; 12
  And their gross painting might be better used
  Where cheeks need blood; in thee it is abused.

82 • **2 attaint** blame, discredit. **o'erlook** look at, peruse **3 dedicated** devoted (with suggestion of *dedicatory*). **writers** i.e., other writers **4 blessing every book** i.e., you bestowing favor thus on the writings of others **5 hue** complexion, appearance **6 a limit** an extent **8 Some . . . days** some more recent and current literary product of this culturally advanced age **11 wert truly sympathized** would be faithfully matched and described **13 gross** extravagantly flattering. **painting** (The imagery sees flattering praise as a kind of cosmetic.) **14 abused** misused, misapplied

83

I never saw that you did painting need,
And therefore to your fair no painting set;
I found, or thought I found, you did exceed
The barren tender of a poet's debt; 4
And therefore have I slept in your report,
That you yourself, being extant, well might show
How far a modern quill doth come too short,
Speaking of worth, what worth in you doth grow. 8
This silence for my sin you did impute,
Which shall be most my glory, being dumb;
For I impair not beauty, being mute,
When others would give life and bring a tomb. 12
There lives more life in one of your fair eyes
Than both your poets can in praise devise.

83 • 2 fair beauty. **set** applied **4 barren tender** paltry offering. **debt** payment **5 slept . . . report** been neglectful in writing praisingly of you **6 That** because, so that. **extant** still alive and much in the public eye **7 modern** commonplace **7–8 doth . . . grow** comes too short, in describing your worth, of the actual worth that flourishes in you **9–10 This . . . dumb** you imputed my silence to sinfulness when in fact it will prove most to my credit **11 being mute** (Modifies *I*.) **12 a tomb** i.e., an inadequate monument that conceals lifelessly rather than enhancing **14 both your poets** i.e., (probably,) I and the rival poet

84

Who is it that says most which can say more
Than this rich praise—that you alone are you,
In whose confine immurèd is the store
Which should example where your equal grew? 4
Lean penury within that pen doth dwell
That to his subject lends not some small glory;
But he that writes of you, if he can tell
That you are you, so dignifies his story. 8
Let him but copy what in you is writ,
Not making worse what nature made so clear,
And such a counterpart shall fame his wit,
Making his style admirèd everywhere. 12
You to your beauteous blessings add a curse,
Being fond on praise, which makes your praises worse.

84 • 1–2 Who . . . praise what extravagant writer of praise can say more than this in way of praise. **which** who **3–4 In . . . grew** i.e., in whose person are contained all those rich qualities that would be needed as a model to produce again your equal in beauty **5–6 Lean . . . glory** i.e., it is a poor piece of writing indeed that does not confer at least some glory on its subject **8 so** sufficiently, thus **10 clear** glorious **11 counterpart** copy, likeness. **fame** endow with fame **13 curse** (1) defect in character (2) burden for those seeking to praise you **14 Being fond** doting. **which . . . worse** (1) which encourages false flattery (2) which makes all praises seem inadequate in comparison to you

85

My tongue-tied Muse in manners holds her still,
While comments of your praise, richly compiled,
Reserve thy character with golden quill
And precious phrase by all the Muses filed. 4
I think good thoughts whilst other write good words,
And like unlettered clerk still cry "Amen"
To every hymn that able spirit affords
In polished form of well-refinèd pen. 8
Hearing you praised, I say " 'Tis so, 'tis true,"
And to the most of praise add something more;
But that is in my thought, whose love to you,
Though words come hindmost, holds his rank before. 12
Then others for the breath of words respect,
Me for my dumb thoughts, speaking in effect.

85 • 1 in . . . still i.e., politely remains silent **2 comments . . . compiled** eulogies of you composed in fine language **3 Reserve thy character** i.e., store up praise of you in their writings. (The quarto reading, *Reserne* [i.e., *Reserve*] *their Character,* might mean "preserve their own writing.") **golden** aureate, affected **4 precious** affected. **filed** polished **5 other** others **6 unlettered clerk** illiterate assistant to a priest. **still cry "Amen"** i.e., continually give my approval **7 hymn** i.e., praising verse. **that able spirit** i.e., the rival poet (and others like him). **affords** provides **10 most** utmost **11 that . . . thought** i.e., that which I add is added silently **12 holds . . . before** considers its place to be before all others **13 Then . . . respect** then take notice of others for what they say **14 speaking in effect** i.e., which convey what speech would say

86

Was it the proud full sail of his great verse,
Bound for the prize of all-too-precious you,
That did my ripe thoughts in my brain inhearse,
Making their tomb the womb wherein they grew? 4
Was it his spirit, by spirits taught to write
Above a mortal pitch, that struck me dead?
No, neither he, nor his compeers by night
Giving him aid, my verse astonishèd. 8
He, nor that affable familiar ghost
Which nightly gulls him with intelligence,
As victors of my silence cannot boast;
I was not sick of any fear from thence. 12
But when your countenance filled up his line,
Then lacked I matter; that enfeebled mine.

86 • 1 his i.e., an unidentified rival poet's **2 prize** capture, booty (as in a seized cargo vessel) **3 inhearse** coffin up **5 spirits** i.e., literary ancestors or contemporaries (with a suggestion also of daemons) **6 pitch** height. (A term from falconry.) **dead** i.e., dumb, silent **7 compeers by night** spirits (see l. 5) visiting and aiding the poet in his dreams or nighttime reading **8 astonishèd** struck dumb **9 ghost** spirit (as in ll. 5 and 7) **10 gulls** misleads, gorges. **intelligence** information, ideas **12 of** with **13 countenance filled up** (1) approval repaired any defect in (2) beauty served as subject for **14 lacked I matter** I had nothing left to write about

87

Farewell! Thou art too dear for my possessing,
And like enough thou know'st thy estimate.
The charter of thy worth gives thee releasing;
My bonds in thee are all determinate. 4
For how do I hold thee but by thy granting,
And for that riches where is my deserving?
The cause of this fair gift in me is wanting,
And so my patent back again is swerving. 8
Thyself thou gav'st, thy own worth then not knowing,
Or me, to whom thou gav'st it, else mistaking;
So thy great gift, upon misprision growing,
Comes home again, on better judgment making. 12
  Thus have I had thee as a dream doth flatter,
  In sleep a king, but waking no such matter.

87 • 1 dear precious **2 like** likely, probably. **estimate** value **3 charter of** privilege derived from. **releasing** i.e., release from obligations of love **4 determinate** ended, expired. (A legal term, as throughout this sonnet.) **8 patent** charter granting rights of monopoly; hence, privilege. **swerving** returning (to you) **10 mistaking** i.e., overvaluing **11 upon misprision growing** arising out of error **12 on . . . making** on your forming a more accurate judgment

88

When thou shalt be disposed to set me light
And place my merit in the eye of scorn,
Upon thy side against myself I'll fight
And prove thee virtuous, though thou art forsworn. 4
With mine own weakness being best acquainted,
Upon thy part I can set down a story
Of faults concealed, wherein I am attainted,
That thou in losing me shall win much glory. 8
And I by this will be a gainer too;
For, bending all my loving thoughts on thee,
The injuries that to myself I do,
Doing thee vantage, double-vantage me. 12
  Such is my love, to thee I so belong,
  That for thy right myself will bear all wrong.

88 • 1 set me light make light of me, value me slightingly **3 Upon thy side** supporting your case (also *Upon thy part* in l. 6) **7 concealed** not publicly known. **attainted** dishonored **8 That** so that. **losing** i.e., separating from (with a suggestion of *loosing*, setting free, the quarto spelling) **12 vantage** advantage

89

Say that thou didst forsake me for some fault,
And I will comment upon that offense;
Speak of my lameness, and I straight will halt,
Against thy reasons making no defense. 4
Thou canst not, love, disgrace me half so ill,
To set a form upon desirèd change,
As I'll myself disgrace, knowing thy will.
I will acquaintance strangle and look strange, 8
Be absent from thy walks, and in my tongue
Thy sweet belovèd name no more shall dwell,
Lest I, too much profane, should do it wrong
And haply of our old acquaintance tell. 12
  For thee against myself I'll vow debate,
  For I must ne'er love him whom thou dost hate.

89 • 1 Say assert, claim **2 comment** enlarge **3 Speak . . . halt** i.e., if you ascribe to me any kind of handicap, I immediately will limp to show that you are right. (*Halt* also has the suggestion of ceasing to object, remaining silent.) **4 reasons** charges, arguments **5 disgrace** discredit **6 To . . . change** to provide a pretext for (in the interest of justifying) your change of affection, and to set it in proper order **7 As . . . disgrace** as I will disfigure and depreciate myself **8 acquaintance strangle** put an end to familiarity (with you). **strange** like a stranger **9 walks** haunts **12 haply** perchance **13 vow debate** declare hostility, quarrel

90

Then hate me when thou wilt; if ever, now;
Now, while the world is bent my deeds to cross,
Join with the spite of fortune, make me bow,
And do not drop in for an after-loss. 4
Ah, do not, when my heart hath scaped this sorrow,
Come in the rearward of a conquered woe;
Give not a windy night a rainy morrow,
To linger out a purposed overthrow. 8
If thou wilt leave me, do not leave me last,
When other petty griefs have done their spite,
But in the onset come; so shall I taste
At first the very worst of fortune's might, 12
  And other strains of woe, which now seem woe,
  Compared with loss of thee will not seem so.

90 • 2 bent determined. **cross** thwart **4 drop . . . after-loss** crushingly add to my sorrow at some future time **5–6 when . . . woe** i.e., follow with an attack after I have overcome my present misfortune. **in the rearward of** behind. (A military metaphor.) **7 windy, rainy** (Suggestive of sighs and tears.) **8 linger out** protract. **purposed** intended, inevitable **11 in the onset** at the outset **13 strains** kinds

91

Some glory in their birth, some in their skill,
Some in their wealth, some in their body's force,
Some in their garments, though newfangled ill,
Some in their hawks and hounds, some in their horse; 4
And every humor hath his adjunct pleasure,
Wherein it finds a joy above the rest.
But these particulars are not my measure;
All these I better in one general best. 8
Thy love is better than high birth to me,
Richer than wealth, prouder than garments' cost,
Of more delight than hawks or horses be;
And having thee, of all men's pride I boast— 12
  Wretched in this alone, that thou mayst take
  All this away and me most wretched make.

91 • 3 newfangled ill fashionably unattractive **4 horse** horses **5 humor** disposition, temperament. **his** its. **adjunct** corresponding **7 measure** standard (of happiness) **8 better** surpass, improve upon **10 prouder** more an object of pride **12 of . . . boast** I boast of having the equivalent of all that is a source of pride in other men

92

But do thy worst to steal thyself away,
For term of life thou art assurèd mine,
And life no longer than thy love will stay,
For it depends upon that love of thine. 4
Then need I not to fear the worst of wrongs,
When in the least of them my life hath end;
I see a better state to me belongs
Than that which on thy humor doth depend. 8
Thou canst not vex me with inconstant mind,
Since that my life on thy revolt doth lie.
O, what a happy title do I find,
Happy to have thy love, happy to die! 12
  But what's so blessèd-fair that fears no blot?
  Thou mayst be false, and yet I know it not.

92 • 1 But do i.e., but even if you do **2 term of life** i.e., my lifetime **5–6 Then . . . end** i.e., I need not fear what most men would call the worst of misfortunes, since the seemingly lesser misfortune—loss of your friendship—would prove fatal to me **7–8 I see . . . depend** i.e., I see that I am happier than most men whose happiness ends when they are cast from favor, since my very existence will cease when I am cast from favor, and thus end my misery. **humor** whim, fancy **10 Since . . . lie** since if you desert me it will cost me my life **11 happy title** right to be thought happy; fortunate legal right of ownership **13 that fears** as to fear **14 Thou . . . not** i.e., my worst fate would be to lose your affection without knowing it, and thereby live on in an unloved state, unreleased by the death that certainty of your desertion would bring

93

So shall I live, supposing thou art true,
Like a deceivèd husband; so love's face
May still seem love to me, though altered new,
Thy looks with me, thy heart in other place. 4
For there can live no hatred in thine eye,
Therefore in that I cannot know thy change.
In many's looks the false heart's history
Is writ in moods and frowns and wrinkles strange, 8
But heaven in thy creation did decree
That in thy face sweet love should ever dwell;
Whate'er thy thoughts or thy heart's workings be,
Thy looks should nothing thence but sweetness tell. 12
How like Eve's apple doth thy beauty grow,
If thy sweet virtue answer not thy show!

93 • 1 So (Continues the thought of Sonnet 92.) **supposing** I supposing (incorrectly) **2 face** appearance **3 new** to something new **5 For** since **6 in . . . change** I won't be able to detect your changed affection from your looks **8 moods** moody looks. **strange** unfriendly **14 answer . . . show** does not conform with your outward appearance

94

They that have power to hurt and will do none,
That do not do the thing they most do show,
Who, moving others, are themselves as stone,
Unmovèd, cold, and to temptation slow, 4
They rightly do inherit heaven's graces
And husband nature's riches from expense;
They are the lords and owners of their faces,
Others but stewards of their excellence. 8
The summer's flower is to the summer sweet,
Though to itself it only live and die,
But if that flower with base infection meet,
The basest weed outbraves his dignity. 12
For sweetest things turn sourest by their deeds;
Lilies that fester smell far worse than weeds.

94 • 1 and . . . none i.e., and do not willfully try to do hurt **2 show** i.e., show themselves capable of; or, seem to do **4 cold** dispassionate
5 inherit (1) receive through inheritance (2) enjoy, make use of
6 husband carefully manage, preserve. **expense** waste, expenditure
7 They . . . faces i.e., they are completely masters of themselves and of the qualities that appear in them **8 but stewards** merely custodians or dispensers **10 it only** alone it **12 outbraves his dignity** surpasses in show its worth **14 Lilies . . . weeds** (This line appears in the anonymous play *Edward III,* usually dated before 1595 and attributed in part by some editors to Shakespeare.)

95

How sweet and lovely dost thou make the shame
Which, like a canker in the fragrant rose,
Doth spot the beauty of thy budding name!
O, in what sweets dost thou thy sins enclose! 4
That tongue that tells the story of thy days,
Making lascivious comments on thy sport,
Cannot dispraise but in a kind of praise;
Naming thy name blesses an ill report. 8
O, what a mansion have those vices got
Which for their habitation chose out thee,
Where beauty's veil doth cover every blot,
And all things turns to fair that eyes can see! 12
Take heed, dear heart, of this large privilege;
The hardest knife ill used doth lose his edge.

95 • 2 canker cankerworm that destroys buds and leaves **3 name** reputation **6 sport** amours **8 blesses** graces **12 all . . . fair** either (1) makes all things beautiful (the object of *veil*), or (2) all things become beautiful **14 his** its

96

Some say thy fault is youth, some wantonness;
Some say thy grace is youth and gentle sport;
Both grace and faults are loved of more and less;
Thou mak'st faults graces that to thee resort. 4
As on the finger of a thronèd queen
The basest jewel will be well esteemed,
So are those errors that in thee are seen
To truths translated and for true things deemed. 8
How many lambs might the stern wolf betray,
If like a lamb he could his looks translate!
How many gazers mightst thou lead away,
If thou wouldst use the strength of all thy state! 12
  But do not so; I love thee in such sort
  As, thou being mine, mine is thy good report.

96 • 1 wantonness amorousness **2 gentle sport** gentlemanlike amorousness **3 of more and less** by high and low **4 Thou . . . resort** you convert into graces the faults that attend you **8 translated** transformed **9 stern** cruel **11 away** astray **12 the strength . . . state** the full power at your command—i.e., your wealth, charm, and social rank **13–14 But . . . report** (The same couplet ends Sonnet 36.)

97

How like a winter hath my absence been
From thee, the pleasure of the fleeting year!
What freezings have I felt, what dark days seen!
What old December's bareness everywhere! 4
And yet this time removed was summer's time,
The teeming autumn, big with rich increase,
Bearing the wanton burden of the prime,
Like widowed wombs after their lords' decease. 8
Yet this abundant issue seemed to me
But hope of orphans and unfathered fruit,
For summer and his pleasures wait on thee,
And, thou away, the very birds are mute; 12
  Or, if they sing, 'tis with so dull a cheer
  That leaves look pale, dreading the winter's near.

97 • 5 time removed time of separation **6 big** pregnant **7 the wanton . . . prime** the fruit or offspring of wanton spring, i.e., the crops planted in springtime **9 issue** offspring **10 hope of orphans** orphaned hope **11 his** its. **wait on thee** attend on you, are at your disposal **13 with . . . cheer** in so melancholy a fashion

98

From you have I been absent in the spring,
When proud-pied, April dressed in all his trim,
Hath put a spirit of youth in everything,
That heavy Saturn laughed and leapt with him. 4
Yet nor the lays of birds nor the sweet smell
Of different flowers in odor and in hue
Could make me any summer's story tell,
Or from their proud lap pluck them where they grew. 8
Nor did I wonder at the lily's white,
Nor praise the deep vermilion in the rose;
They were but sweet, but figures of delight
Drawn after you, you pattern of all those. 12
  Yet seemed it winter still, and, you away,
  As with your shadow I with these did play.

98 • 2 proud-pied gorgeously multi-colored. **trim** finery **4 That** so that. **Saturn** (A planet associated with melancholy, *heavy*.) **5 nor the lays** neither the songs **6 different flowers** flowers differing **7 any summer's story** i.e., any pleasant story **8 proud lap** i.e., the earth **11 but sweet . . . delight** mere sweetness, mere delightful forms or emblems **12 after** resembling **14 shadow** image, portrait. **these** i.e., the flowers

99

The forward violet thus did I chide:
"Sweet thief, whence didst thou steal thy sweet that
 smells,
If not from my love's breath? The purple pride
Which on thy soft cheek for complexion dwells 4
In my love's veins thou hast too grossly dyed."
The lily I condemnèd for thy hand,
And buds of marjoram had stol'n thy hair;
The roses fearfully on thorns did stand, 8
One blushing shame, another white despair;
A third, nor red nor white, had stol'n of both
And to his robbery had annexed thy breath,
But, for his theft, in pride of all his growth 12
A vengeful canker eat him up to death.
 More flowers I noted, yet I none could see
 But sweet or color it had stol'n from thee.

99 • 1 forward early, and presumptuous. (This sonnet has fifteen lines, the first being introductory.) **2 thy sweet** your scent **3 pride** splendor **5 grossly** obviously and heavily **6 for thy hand** i.e., because it has stolen its whiteness from your hand **7 And . . . hair** i.e., and I condemned the buds of marjoram for having stolen your hair. **buds of marjoram** (These are dark purple red or auburn, and it may be that the reference is to color, although marjoram is noted for its sweet scent.) **8 on thorns did stand** grew on thorny stems (with a suggestion of being apprehensive) **9 shame** i.e., red for shame **10 nor red** neither (purely) red **11 to . . . annexed** to this robbery had added the robbery of **12 But, for** although, in punishment for. **in pride . . . growth** in his prime **13 canker eat** cankerworm ate **15 But** except. **sweet** scent (as in l. 2)

100

Where art thou, Muse, that thou forgett'st so long
To speak of that which gives thee all thy might?
Spend'st thou thy fury on some worthless song,
Dark'ning thy pow'r to lend base subjects light? 4
Return, forgetful Muse, and straight redeem
In gentle numbers time so idly spent;
Sing to the ear that doth thy lays esteem
And gives thy pen both skill and argument. 8
Rise, resty Muse, my love's sweet face survey,
If Time have any wrinkle graven there;
If any, be a satire to decay,
And make Time's spoils despisèd everywhere. 12
Give my love fame faster than Time wastes life;
So thou prevent'st his scythe and crooked knife.

100 • 3 fury poetic inspiration **4 Dark'ning** debasing **5 straight** straightway **6 gentle numbers** noble verses. **idly** foolishly **7 lays** songs **8 argument** subject **9 resty** inactive, inert **10 If** to see if **11 If any** if there are any. **satire to** satirist of, here one composing a satire on Time as a despoiler **12 spoils** acts of destruction, ravages **13 faster** (1) more quickly (2) more firmly **14 thou prevent'st** you forestall, thwart. **crooked knife** curved blade

101

O truant Muse, what shall be thy amends
For thy neglect of truth in beauty dyed?
Both truth and beauty on my love depends;
So dost thou too, and therein dignified. 4
Make answer, Muse. Wilt thou not haply say,
"Truth needs no color with his color fixed,
Beauty no pencil, beauty's truth to lay;
But best is best, if never intermixed"? 8
Because he needs no praise, wilt thou be dumb?
Excuse not silence so, for 't lies in thee
To make him much outlive a gilded tomb
And to be praised of ages yet to be. 12
  Then do thy office, Muse; I teach thee how
  To make him seem, long hence, as he shows now.

101 • 1 what . . . amends what reparation will you make **3–4 Both . . . dignified** i.e., both faith and beauty depend on my love for their proper appreciation and recognition, and you, my Muse, depend for your very office and dignity on that same function **5 haply** perhaps **6 no . . . fixed** no artificial color (with suggestion of *pretense*) added to its natural and permanent color or hue **7 pencil** paint brush. **lay** apply color to, as with a brush **8 intermixed** adulterated **9 dumb** silent **12 of** by **13 office** function **14 long hence** long in the future. **shows** appears

102

My love is strengthened, though more weak in seeming;
I love not less, though less the show appear.
That love is merchandized whose rich esteeming
The owner's tongue doth publish everywhere. 4
Our love was new and then but in the spring
When I was wont to greet it with my lays,
As Philomel in summer's front doth sing
And stops her pipe in growth of riper days. 8
Not that the summer is less pleasant now
Than when her mournful hymns did hush the night,
But that wild music burdens every bough
And sweets grown common lose their dear delight. 12
Therefore like her I sometimes hold my tongue,
Because I would not dull you with my song.

102 • 1 seeming outward appearance **3 merchandized** degraded by being treated as a thing of sale. **esteeming** valuation **4 publish** announce, advertise **6 wont . . . lays** accustomed to salute it (our love) with my song **7 Philomel** the nightingale. **front** forehead, beginning **8 stops her pipe** stops singing. **riper** i.e., those of late summer and autumn **11 But . . . music** i.e., but because a profusion of wild birds' singing. (Refers to other poets.) **burdens** weighs down (but with a musical sense as well; a *burden* is a chorus) **14 dull** surfeit

103

Alack, what poverty my Muse brings forth,
That, having such a scope to show her pride,
The argument all bare is of more worth
Than when it hath my added praise beside. 4
O, blame me not if I no more can write!
Look in your glass, and there appears a face
That overgoes my blunt invention quite,
Dulling my lines and doing me disgrace. 8
Were it not sinful then, striving to mend,
To mar the subject that before was well?
For to no other pass my verses tend
Than of your graces and your gifts to tell; 12
  And more, much more, than in my verse can sit
  Your own glass shows you when you look in it.

103 • 1 poverty poor stuff **2 pride** splendor **3 argument all bare** subject alone, unadorned **5 no more can write** i.e., cannot go beyond what you yourself are, cannot excel my own poverty of invention **6 glass** mirror **7 overgoes** surpasses. **blunt invention** unpolished style, writing **8 Dulling** i.e., making dull by comparison **11 pass** purpose, issue **13 sit** reside

104

To me, fair friend, you never can be old,
For, as you were when first your eye I eyed,
Such seems your beauty still. Three winters cold
Have from the forests shook three summers' pride, 4
Three beauteous springs to yellow autumn turned
In process of the seasons have I seen,
Three April perfumes in three hot Junes burned,
Since first I saw you fresh, which yet are green. 8
Ah, yet doth beauty, like a dial hand,
Steal from his figure and no pace perceived.
So your sweet hue, which methinks still doth stand,
Hath motion, and mine eye may be deceived, 12
For fear of which, hear this, thou age unbred:
Ere you were born was beauty's summer dead.

104 • 4 pride splendor **6 process** the progression **9 dial hand** watch hand **10 his figure** (1) the dial's numeral (2) the friend's shape. **and . . . perceived** i.e., imperceptibly **11 hue** appearance, complexion. **still doth stand** remains motionless, unaltered **13 of which** i.e., that my eye may be deceived. (The poet, though wishing to believe that his friend never can be old, concedes that this is a deception.) **unbred** not yet born

105

Let not my love be called idolatry,
Nor my belovèd as an idol show,
Since all alike my songs and praises be
To one, of one, still such, and ever so. 4
Kind is my love today, tomorrow kind,
Still constant in a wondrous excellence;
Therefore my verse, to constancy confined,
One thing expressing, leaves out difference. 8
"Fair, kind, and true" is all my argument,
"Fair, kind, and true" varying to other words;
And in this change is my invention spent,
Three themes in one, which wondrous scope affords. 12
  Fair, kind, and true have often lived alone,
  Which three till now never kept seat in one.

105 • 2 show appear **3 Since** (1) simply because, or (2) since it can be said in my defense that **4 still** always **8 difference** variety of other literary subjects; any kind of diversity that detracts from the young man's constancy (including any suggestion of quarreling or fluctuation of mood) **11 this change** variations on this theme. **invention** inventiveness. **spent** expended **13 alone** separately (in different people) **14 kept seat** resided; sat enthroned

106

When in the chronicle of wasted time
I see descriptions of the fairest wights,
And beauty making beautiful old rhyme
In praise of ladies dead and lovely knights, 4
Then, in the blazon of sweet beauty's best,
Of hand, of foot, of lip, of eye, of brow,
I see their antique pen would have expressed
Even such a beauty as you master now. 8
So all their praises are but prophecies
Of this our time, all you prefiguring;
And, for they looked but with divining eyes,
They had not skill enough your worth to sing. 12
For we, which now behold these present days,
Have eyes to wonder, but lack tongues to praise.

106 • 1 wasted past, used up **2 wights** persons **3 beauty** (1) beauty of style and language (2) beauty of the persons described **5 blazon** i.e., glorification, cataloguing of qualities. (A heraldic metaphor.) **7 see** perceive (that). **their** i.e., of antique poets. **would have expressed** wished to express **8 master** possess, control **11 for** because. **divining** guessing or predicting as to the future **13 For we** for even we **14 praise** i.e., praise you worthily, sufficiently

107

Not mine own fears nor the prophetic soul
Of the wide world dreaming on things to come
Can yet the lease of my true love control,
Supposed as forfeit to a confined doom. 4
The mortal moon hath her eclipse endured
And the sad augurs mock their own presage;
Incertainties now crown themselves assured
And peace proclaims olives of endless age. 8
Now with the drops of this most balmy time
My love looks fresh, and Death to me subscribes,
Since, spite of him, I'll live in this poor rhyme,
While he insults o'er dull and speechless tribes; 12
And thou in this shalt find thy monument,
When tyrants' crests and tombs of brass are spent.

107 • 1–2 soul . . . world collective consciousness of humanity **3 yet** now. **lease** term, allotted time. **control** set a limit to **4 Supposed . . . doom** i.e., though imagined to be destined to expire after a limited term **5 mortal moon** (Probably a reference to Queen Elizabeth, ill or deceased, most probably to her death in 1603; she was known as Diana, Cynthia, etc.) **6 And . . . presage** and the solemn prophets of disaster now mock their earlier predictions **7 Incertainties . . . assured** uncertainties have triumphantly given way to certainties **8 olives** (Conventionally associated with peace, and probably pointing here to King James VI's resolutions of war with Spain and strife in Ireland.) **of endless age** i.e., without foreseen end **9 with the drops** i.e., healed as though by a balmy dew. (Balm was employed in the coronation ceremony for James in 1603, as in all such coronations.) **10 subscribes** yields **12 insults** triumphs **14 crests** trophies adorning a tomb. **spent** expended, wasted away

108

What's in the brain that ink may character
Which hath not figured to thee my true spirit?
What's new to speak, what now to register,
That may express my love or thy dear merit? 4
Nothing, sweet boy; but yet, like prayers divine,
I must each day say o'er the very same,
Counting no old thing old—thou mine, I thine—
Even as when first I hallowed thy fair name. 8
So that eternal love in love's fresh case
Weighs not the dust and injury of age,
Nor gives to necessary wrinkles place,
But makes antiquity for aye his page, 12
  Finding the first conceit of love there bred
  Where time and outward form would show it dead.

108 • 1 character write **2 figured** revealed, represented. **true** constant **3 register** record **7 Counting . . . thine** i.e., dismissing no old truth as out of date or shopworn, such as the truth that you are mine and I yours **8 hallowed** (As in "hallowed be thy name" from the Lord's Prayer.) **9 fresh case** new exterior and circumstance **10 Weighs not** is unconcerned about **11 place** consideration, primacy **12 aye** ever. **page** servant, subordinate **13 the first . . . love** i.e., the first conception of love, experienced as though for the first time. **there** (1) in you (2) in my verse. **bred** generated **14 would** try to, wish to

109

O, never say that I was false of heart,
Though absence seemed my flame to qualify.
As easy might I from myself depart
As from my soul, which in thy breast doth lie. 4
That is my home of love; if I have ranged,
Like him that travels I return again,
Just to the time, not with the time exchanged,
So that myself bring water for my stain. 8
Never believe, though in my nature reigned
All frailties that besiege all kinds of blood,
That it could so preposterously be stained
To leave for nothing all thy sum of good; 12
For "nothing" this wide universe I call
Save thou, my rose; in it thou art my all.

109 • 2 flame passion. **qualify** temper, moderate **5 ranged** traveled, wandered **7 Just** punctual. **the time . . . the time** the exact hour . . . the period of separation. **exchanged** changed **8 So . . . stain** i.e., so that I myself provide the means (my tears) of excusing my absence, of washing away the stain **10 blood** temperament, sensual nature **12 for** in exchange for

110

Alas, 'tis true, I have gone here and there
And made myself a motley to the view,
Gored mine own thoughts, sold cheap what is most
dear,
Made old offenses of affections new; 4
Most true it is that I have looked on truth
Askance and strangely. But, by all above,
These blenches gave my heart another youth,
And worse essays proved thee my best of love. 8
Now all is done, have what shall have no end.
Mine appetite I nevermore will grind
On newer proof, to try an older friend,
A god in love, to whom I am confined. 12
Then give me welcome, next my heaven the best,
Even to thy pure and most most loving breast.

110 • 2 motley jester, fool. **to the view** in the eyes of the world **3 Gored** wounded **4 Made . . . new** i.e., repeated old offenses or made offense against old friendships in forming new attachments **5 truth** constancy **6 Askance and strangely** disdainfully, obliquely and at a distance. **by all above** by heaven **7 blenches** swervings **8 essays** experiments (in friendship) **9 Now all** now that all that. **have what . . . end** take what is eternal (my friendship) **10 grind** whet, sharpen **11 newer proof** further experiment, experience. **try** test **12 A god** godlike **13 next my heaven** i.e., you, who are to me second only to heaven itself

111

O, for my sake do you with Fortune chide,
The guilty goddess of my harmful deeds,
That did not better for my life provide
Than public means which public manners breeds. 4
Thence comes it that my name receives a brand,
And almost thence my nature is subdued
To what it works in, like the dyer's hand.
Pity me then, and wish I were renewed, 8
Whilst, like a willing patient, I will drink
Potions of eisel 'gainst my strong infection;
No bitterness that I will bitter think,
Nor double penance, to correct correction. 12
  Pity me then, dear friend, and I assure ye
  Even that your pity is enough to cure me.

111 • 2 guilty goddess goddess responsible for **3 life** livelihood **4 Than . . . breeds** i.e., than providing me a means of livelihood that depends on catering to the public. (A probable reference to Shakespeare's career as an actor.) **5 receives a brand** is disgraced (through prejudice against my occupation) **7 like the dyer's hand** (The dyer's hand is stained by the dye it handles, just as the poet's nature is almost overpowered by the medium in which he works—the language of poetry and, more particularly, the theater.) **8 renewed** restored to what I was by nature, cleansed **10 eisel** vinegar, used as an antiseptic against the plague and also as an agent for removing stains **11 No bitterness** i.e., there is no bitterness **12 Nor . . . correction** i.e., nor will I think it bitter to undertake a twofold penance in order to correct what must be corrected
14 Even that your pity that very pity of yours

112

Your love and pity doth th' impression fill
Which vulgar scandal stamped upon my brow;
For what care I who calls me well or ill,
So you o'ergreen my bad, my good allow? 4
You are my all the world, and I must strive
To know my shames and praises from your tongue;
None else to me, nor I to none alive,
That my steeled sense or changes right or wrong. 8
In so profound abysm I throw all care
Of others' voices, that my adder's sense
To critic and to flatterer stoppèd are.
Mark how with my neglect I do dispense: 12
You are so strongly in my purpose bred
That all the world besides methinks are dead.

112 • 1 th' impression fill efface the scar **2 vulgar scandal** i.e., notoriety (for being an actor?) **4 So you o'ergreen** provided that you cover as with green growth. **allow** approve **5 my all the world** everything to me **7–8 None . . . wrong** i.e., no one else but you affects my fixed and hardened sensibilities, whether for better or for worse **9 In so profound** into such a deep **10 Of** about. **voices** i.e., criticism. **adder's sense** i.e., deaf ears **11 critic** fault-finder **12 Mark . . . dispense** i.e., see how I excuse my disregard of the opinion of others **13 You . . . bred** i.e., you are so nurtured in my thoughts and are such a powerful influence over my intentions

113

Since I left you, mine eye is in my mind,
And that which governs me to go about
Doth part his function and is partly blind,
Seems seeing, but effectually is out; 4
For it no form delivers to the heart
Of bird, of flower, or shape, which it doth latch;
Of his quick objects hath the mind no part,
Nor his own vision holds what it doth catch; 8
For if it see the rud'st or gentlest sight,
The most sweet-favor or deformedst creature,
The mountain or the sea, the day or night,
The crow or dove, it shapes them to your feature. 12
  Incapable of more, replete with you,
  My most true mind thus maketh mine eye untrue.

113 • 1 mine . . . mind i.e., I'm guided by my mind's eye **2 that . . . about** i.e., my physical sight **3 part** divide. **his** its, i.e., the physical eye's (also in ll. 7 and 8) **4 Seems seeing** seems to be seeing. **effectually** in reality. **out** out of commission, ineffectual **5 heart** (Here portrayed as capable of receiving sense impressions and of consciousness, as in Sonnet 47.) **6 latch** catch or receive the sight of **7 Of . . . part** i.e., the mind, attuned to its inner eye, takes no part in the fleeting and lively (*quick*) things seen by the physical sight **8 Nor . . . holds** i.e., nor does the eye itself retain. **catch** i.e., see glimpsingly **9 For . . . sight** for whether it see the most uncouth or most gracious sight **10 sweet-favor** sweet-featured **12 shapes . . . feature** makes them resemble you

114

Or whether doth my mind, being crowned with you,
Drink up the monarch's plague, this flattery?
Or whether shall I say mine eye saith true,
And that your love taught it this alchemy, 4
To make of monsters and things indigest
Such cherubins as your sweet self resemble,
Creating every bad a perfect best
As fast as objects to his beams assemble? 8
O, 'tis the first, 'tis flattery in my seeing,
And my great mind most kingly drinks it up;
Mine eye well knows what with his gust is greeing,
And to his palate doth prepare the cup. 12
  If it be poisoned, 'tis the lesser sin
  That mine eye loves it and doth first begin.

114 • 1, 3 Or whether (Indicates alternative possibilities.) **1 crowned with you** elevated by possession of you **2 the monarch's . . . flattery** this pleasing delusion to which all monarchs are prone **4 your love** my love of you. **alchemy** science of transmuting base metals **5 indigest** chaotic, formless **6 cherubins** angelic forms (suggesting the youth and beauty of the friend) **7 Creating** creating out of **8 his beams** its (the eye's) gaze **9 'tis . . . seeing** my eye is flattering my mind (see ll. 1–2) **11 what . . . greeing** what agrees with the mind's taste **12 to** to suit **13–14 'tis . . . it** i.e., it extenuates the eye's sinful deed (of misleading the mind) that it first drinks in the poison itself **14 doth first begin** i.e., tastes of the poison first, like an official taster sampling food before it is given to the king

115

Those lines that I before have writ do lie,
Even those that said I could not love you dearer;
Yet then my judgment knew no reason why
My most full flame should afterwards burn clearer. 4
But reckoning Time, whose millioned accidents
Creep in twixt vows and change decrees of kings,
Tan sacred beauty, blunt the sharp'st intents,
Divert strong minds to th' course of altering things— 8
Alas, why, fearing of Time's tyranny,
Might I not then say, "Now I love you best,"
When I was certain o'er incertainty,
Crowning the present, doubting of the rest? 12
Love is a babe; then might I not say so,
To give full growth to that which still doth grow.

115 • 5 reckoning Time (1) Time, which we reckon up (2) Time, that makes a reckoning. **millioned** numbered in the millions **6 twixt vows** i.e., between the making of vows and their fulfillment **7 Tan** darken, i.e., coarsen. **sacred** deserving worship **8 to . . . things** i.e., into the current that flows toward decay of all things **9 fearing of** fearing **10 Might . . . say** i.e., wasn't it understandable for me to say then, when I wrote *Those lines* (l. 1) **11 certain o'er incertainty** i.e., certain of my love's perfection then, as contrasted with the uncertainty of the future **12 Crowning** glorifying. **doubting of** fearing **13 then might . . . so** i.e., therefore it was wrong of me to say, "Now I love you best" (l. 10) **14 To give** thereby attributing

116

Let me not to the marriage of true minds
Admit impediments. Love is not love
Which alters when it alteration finds,
Or bends with the remover to remove. 4
O, no, it is an ever-fixèd mark
That looks on tempests and is never shaken;
It is the star to every wandering bark,
Whose worth's unknown, although his height be taken. 8
Love's not Time's fool, though rosy lips and cheeks
Within his bending sickle's compass come;
Love alters not with his brief hours and weeks,
But bears it out even to the edge of doom. 12
If this be error and upon me proved,
I never writ, nor no man ever loved.

116 • 2 Admit concede that there might be, allow consideration of. (An echo of the marriage service.) **3 alteration** i.e., in age, beauty, affection, health, circumstance **4 Or . . . remove** or inclines to inconstancy simply because the person loved is inconstant **5 mark** seamark, conspicuous object distinguishable at sea as an aid to navigation **8 Whose . . . taken** whose value is beyond estimation, although its altitude above the horizon can be determined (for purposes of navigation) **9 fool** plaything, laughingstock **10 his** i.e., Time's (also in l. 11). **bending** curved. **compass** range **12 bears . . . doom** endures or holds out to the very Day of Judgment

117

Accuse me thus: that I have scanted all
Wherein I should your great deserts repay,
Forgot upon your dearest love to call,
Whereto all bonds do tie me day by day; 4
That I have frequent been with unknown minds,
And given to time your own dear-purchased right;
That I have hoisted sail to all the winds
Which should transport me farthest from your sight. 8
Book both my willfulness and errors down,
And on just proof surmise accumulate;
Bring me within the level of your frown,
But shoot not at me in your wakened hate; 12
Since my appeal says I did strive to prove
The constancy and virtue of your love.

117 • 1 scanted come short in **3 upon . . . call** i.e., to pay my respects to your love, or to invoke your aid **5 frequent** familiar. **unknown minds** strangers of no consequence **6 given . . . right** squandered your rights in me on temporary matters and alliances **8 should** would **9 Book . . . down** record both my willful faults and errors **10 on . . . accumulate** to sure proof add surmise, suspicion **11 level** point-blank range, aim **13 appeal** legal appealing of the case. **I . . . prove** my intention was to test

118

Like as to make our appetites more keen
With eager compounds we our palate urge,
As to prevent our maladies unseen
We sicken to shun sickness when we purge: 4
Even so, being full of your ne'er-cloying sweetness,
To bitter sauces did I frame my feeding
And, sick of welfare, found a kind of meetness
To be diseased ere that there was true needing. 8
Thus policy in love, t' anticipate
The ills that were not, grew to faults assured,
And brought to medicine a healthful state
Which, rank of goodness, would by ill be cured. 12
  But thence I learn, and find the lesson true,
  Drugs poison him that so fell sick of you.

118 • 1 Like as just as **2 eager compounds** pungent, bitter concoctions. **urge** stimulate, prompt **3 As** just as. **prevent** anticipate, forestall. **unseen** not yet physically manifested **4 sicken . . . sickness** induce a kind of sickness, purging (i.e., evacuation of stomach or bowel), in order to ward off greater sickness **5 Even so** in just the same way **6 bitter sauces** i.e., other loves, undesirable in comparison with you. **frame** adapt, direct **7 sick of welfare** surfeited and made ill by health and happiness (in love). **meetness** suitability **8 ere . . . needing** before there was any real necessity for it **9 policy** shortsighted calculation. **anticipate** forestall **10 assured** actual **11 to medicine** to a state of needing medical care **12 rank of goodness** gorged and sickened by good health **14 Drugs . . . you** i.e., the cure is worse than the disease. **so** thus

119

What potions have I drunk of siren tears,
Distilled from limbecks foul as hell within,
Applying fears to hopes and hopes to fears,
Still losing when I saw myself to win! 4
What wretched errors hath my heart committed,
Whilst it hath thought itself so blessèd never!
How have mine eyes out of their spheres been fitted
In the distraction of this madding fever! 8
O, benefit of ill! Now I find true
That better is by evil still made better;
And ruined love, when it is built anew,
Grows fairer than at first, more strong, far greater. 12
So I return rebuked to my content,
And gain by ills thrice more than I have spent.

119 • 1 siren tears i.e., deceitful tears of a seductive woman. (The poet seems to speak of an affair like that with the Dark Lady in Sonnets 127–152.) **2 limbecks** vessels used in distillation. **foul as hell within** i.e., possessing an inner ugliness and evil contrasted with a beautiful and seductive appearance **3 Applying . . . fears** i.e., trying vainly to control my wild hopes with a sense of fear and to assuage my fears with hope **4 Still** always. **saw myself** vainly expected **6 so blessèd never** never before so fortunate **7 How . . . fitted** how my eyes have popped out in convulsive fit **8 distraction** frenzy. **madding** maddening

120

That you were once unkind befriends me now,
And for that sorrow which I then did feel
Needs must I under my transgression bow,
Unless my nerves were brass or hammered steel. 4
For if you were by my unkindness shaken
As I by yours, you've passed a hell of time,
And I, a tyrant, have no leisure taken
To weigh how once I suffered in your crime. 8
O, that our night of woe might have remembered
My deepest sense how hard true sorrow hits,
And soon to you, as you to me then, tendered
The humble salve which wounded bosoms fits! 12
But that your trespass now becomes a fee;
Mine ransoms yours, and yours must ransom me.

120 • 1 befriends gives me friendly advice **2–3 for . . . bow** i.e., realizing the sorrow I felt from your unkindness, I must now give up my unkindness to you **4 nerves** sinews **6 hell of** hellish **7 have . . . taken** have not taken the opportunity **8 weigh** consider. **in your crime** i.e., from your unkindness. (If I suffered so, I should realize you've suffered too from my unkindness.) **9 that** would that. **our night of woe** the dark and woeful time of our earlier estrangement. **remembered** reminded **10 sense** consciousness, apprehension **11 And . . . tendered** i.e., and would that I had quickly offered to you, as you did to me **12 humble salve** i.e., apology and remorse. **which . . . fits** which is just what wounded hearts need **13 that your trespass** that unkindness of yours. **fee** payment, compensation **14 ransoms** redeems, excuses

121

'Tis better to be vile than vile esteemed
When not to be receives reproach of being,
And the just pleasure lost which is so deemed
Not by our feeling but by others' seeing. 4
For why should others' false adulterate eyes
Give salutation to my sportive blood?
Or on my frailties why are frailer spies,
Which in their wills count bad what I think good? 8
No, I am that I am, and they that level
At my abuses reckon up their own.
I may be straight though they themselves be bevel.
By their rank thoughts my deeds must not be shown, 12
Unless this general evil they maintain:
All men are bad, and in their badness reign.

121 • 1 vile esteemed (to be) considered vile **2 When . . . being** when not to be vile receives the reproach of vileness. (It's just as bad, or even worse, to be unjustly accused of wickedness as to be truly wicked.) **3–4 And . . . seeing** and to lose justifiable pleasure because its justification has to depend not on our feelings but on the censorious attitudes of others **5 false adulterate eyes** i.e., the eyes of those whose own wickedness prompts them to misconstrue my innocent love **6 Give . . . blood** i.e., greet me, in my lusty merriment, with familiarity and with a knowing wink of the eye **7 Or . . . spies** or why should there be more faulty persons spying on my fleshly indulgences **8 in their wills** i.e., by the measure of their prurient, licentious minds **9 am that** am what. **level** (1) aim (2) guess **10 abuses** misdoings. **reckon up their own** i.e., merely enumerate their own misdeeds **11 bevel** out of square, crooked **12 rank** ugly, foul. **shown** viewed, interpreted **14 reign** i.e., prosper

122

Thy gift, thy tables, are within my brain
Full charactered with lasting memory,
Which shall above that idle rank remain
Beyond all date, even to eternity— 4
Or at the least, so long as brain and heart
Have faculty by nature to subsist;
Till each to razed oblivion yield his part
Of thee, thy record never can be missed. 8
That poor retention could not so much hold,
Nor need I tallies thy dear love to score;
Therefore to give them from me was I bold,
To trust those tables that receive thee more. 12
To keep an adjunct to remember thee
Were to import forgetfulness in me.

122 • 1 tables writing tablet, memorandum book **2 charactered** written. **with** by **3 that idle rank** i.e., the relative unimportance of that memorandum book (as compared with the memory itself) **6 faculty . . . subsist** natural power to survive **7 each** i.e., brain and heart. **razed oblivion** obliterating forgetfulness. (*Razed,* effaced, destroyed, and *rased,* erased, scraped away, often mean much the same thing.) **his** its **8 missed** lost. (The poet is apologizing for having given away or lost a memorandum book written by the friend.) **9 retention** i.e., the book, an instrument for retaining memoranda. **so much** i.e., as much as is in my memory **10 tallies** sticks notched to serve for reckoning. (The notebook is such a mere *tally.*) **score** reckon **11 to . . . me** i.e., to give away the writing tablet. **bold** i.e., bold in taking the liberty **12 those tables** i.e., those of memory. **receive thee more** retain more of you **13 adjunct** aid **14 Were** would be. **import** imply, impute

123

No, Time, thou shalt not boast that I do change.
Thy pyramids built up with newer might
To me are nothing novel, nothing strange;
They are but dressings of a former sight. 4
Our dates are brief, and therefore we admire
What thou dost foist upon us that is old,
And rather make them born to our desire
Than think that we before have heard them told. 8
Thy registers and thee I both defy,
Not wondering at the present nor the past,
For thy records and what we see doth lie,
Made more or less by thy continual haste. 12
  This I do vow and this shall ever be:
  I will be true, despite thy scythe and thee.

123 • 2 pyramids (May refer to obelisks or other structures erected in Rome in 1586 or in London in 1603.) **3 nothing** not at all **4 dressings . . . sight** reconstructions in new form of things from the past **5 dates** life spans **7 make . . . desire** consider them newly created to our liking and reinvented by us **8 told** reckoned, told about **9 registers** visual records, monuments **10 wondering** marveling **11 doth lie** deceives us **12 Made more or less** i.e., raised one minute and ruined the next (by Time), and alternately overvalued and undervalued by us

124

If my dear love were but the child of state,
It might for Fortune's bastard be unfathered,
As subject to Time's love or to Time's hate,
Weeds among weeds, or flowers with flowers gathered. 4
No, it was builded far from accident;
It suffers not in smiling pomp, nor falls
Under the blow of thrallèd discontent,
Whereto th' inviting time our fashion calls. 8
It fears not Policy, that heretic,
Which works on leases of short-numbered hours,
But all alone stands hugely politic,
That it nor grows with heat nor drowns with showers. 12
To this I witness call the fools of Time,
Which die for goodness, who have lived for crime.

124 • 1 love i.e., love for you. **but** merely. **child of state** result of (your) rank or power; or, of changing circumstance **2 for . . . unfathered** i.e., be declared to have no father or source other than (your) good fortune **3 As** i.e., and accordingly regarded as **4 Weeds . . . gathered** i.e., either despised as worthless like a weed or cherished like a flower, as Fortune dictates **5 accident** chance, fortune **6 It . . . pomp** i.e., it does not lessen or weaken in circumstances of pomp and finery **6–7 nor . . . discontent** nor does it weaken under the blows of adversity, turning melancholy. **thrallèd** enslaved, oppressed **8 Whereto . . . calls** i.e., to which the temptations of our present age expose all of us; or, which the age invites us to regard as fashionable **9 Policy, that heretic** cunning expediency, false to the spirit of love **10 Which . . . hours** i.e., which thinks only shortsightedly of short-term gain and makes only short-term commitments **11 hugely politic** i.e., prudent in a long-term sense **12 nor . . . heat** i.e., neither flourishes only in good times. **showers** i.e., adversity **13 witness call** call to witness. **fools** playthings, laughing-stocks. (See Sonnet 116.) **14 Which . . . crime** i.e., those who have lived evilly and then attempt to repent at their deaths or to die in a good cause

125

Were 't aught to me I bore the canopy,
With my extern the outward honoring,
Or laid great bases for eternity,
Which proves more short than waste or ruining? 4
Have I not seen dwellers on form and favor
Lose all, and more, by paying too much rent,
For compound sweet forgoing simple savor,
Pitiful thrivers, in their gazing spent? 8
No, let me be obsequious in thy heart,
And take thou my oblation, poor but free,
Which is not mixed with seconds, knows no art
But mutual render, only me for thee. 12
  Hence, thou suborned informer! A true soul
  When most impeached stands least in thy control.

125 • 1 Were 't . . . canopy i.e., would it be anything to me if I did public homage as one honors great persons by carrying over their heads a cloth of state as they go in procession **2 With . . . honoring** honoring the external by means of external action **3 laid . . . eternity** laid foundations for supposedly lasting monuments **5 dwellers on** those who insist fulsomely upon (with pun on the idea of "tenants"). **form and favor** (1) courtly etiquette and the achieving of status through influence (2) figure and face **6 Lose all, and more** i.e., lose all their wealth, and then go into debt. **by . . . rent** i.e., by overdoing their obligations to mere ceremony **7 For . . . savor** i.e., foregoing wholesome sincerity for the sake of obsequious flattery **8 Pitiful thrivers** i.e., those thriving only in pitiful or worthless gains. **in . . . spent** i.e., starved merely by ceremonial observance **9 obsequious** (1) courtly (2) devoted **10 oblation** offering. **free** freely offered **11 seconds** inferior matter, adulterants. **art** artifice **12 render** exchange **13 suborned informer** perjured witness, the envious one who has charged the poet with self-interested flattery **14 impeached** accused

126

O thou, my lovely boy, who in thy power
Dost hold Time's fickle glass, his sickle hour;
Who hast by waning grown, and therein show'st
Thy lovers withering as thy sweet self grow'st; 4
If Nature, sovereign mistress over wrack,
As thou goest onwards, still will pluck thee back,
She keeps thee to this purpose, that her skill
May Time disgrace and wretched minutes kill. 8
Yet fear her, O thou minion of her pleasure!
She may detain, but not still keep, her treasure.
Her audit, though delayed, answered must be,
And her quietus is to render thee. 12

126 • 1 (This sonnet is made up of six couplets.) **2 Time's . . . hour** i.e., Time's hourglass by which we are constantly betrayed and the hour of final reckoning when all is cut down by Time's sickle (? The line may be corrupt.) **3 by waning grown** grown more youthful as age increases. **show'st** i.e., show by way of contrast with yourself **5 wrack** ruin. (Nature is mistress over decay because of her power of restoration.) **6 onwards** i.e., in life's journey **7 to** for **8 and . . . kill** i.e., and render powerless the passing of the minutes **9 minion** darling; slave **10 She . . . treasure** i.e., Nature may keep and restore you for a time, but Time will ultimately triumph. **still** always **11 Her audit** i.e., the proverbial paying of one's debt to Nature through death; also, Nature's account to Time. **answered** settled **12 quietus** discharge, quittance. **render** surrender

127

In the old age black was not counted fair,
Or if it were, it bore not beauty's name;
But now is black beauty's successive heir,
And beauty slandered with a bastard shame. 4
For since each hand hath put on nature's power,
Fairing the foul with art's false borrowed face,
Sweet beauty hath no name, no holy bower,
But is profaned, if not lives in disgrace. 8
Therefore my mistress' eyes are raven black,
Her brows so suited, and they mourners seem
At such who, not born fair, no beauty lack,
Sland'ring creation with a false esteem. 12
Yet so they mourn, becoming of their woe,
That every tongue says beauty should look so.

127 • 1 old age olden times. **black** darkness of hair and eyes. **fair** (1) beautiful (2) light-complexioned **2 it. . . name** i.e., it was not called so **3 now . . . heir** i.e., nowadays black has been named lawful successor to the title of beauty **4 beauty** i.e., blonde beauty. **slandered . . . shame** i.e., declared illegitimate, created artificially by cosmetics **5 put on** assumed **6 Fairing the foul** making the ugly beautiful. **borrowed face** i.e., cosmetics **7 no name . . . bower** no reputation or pride of family, and no sacred abode **8 profaned** i.e., scorned, and violated by those who use cosmetics. **if not** or even **10 so suited** decked out in the same color and for the same reason **11 At** for. **no beauty lack** i.e., nonetheless make themselves attractive **12 Sland'ring . . . esteem** i.e., dishonoring nature by a false reputation for beauty **13 they** i.e., my mistress's eyes. **becoming of** gracing, or being graced by

128

How oft, when thou, my music, music play'st
Upon that blessèd wood whose motion sounds
With thy sweet fingers when thou gently sway'st
The wiry concord that mine ear confounds, 4
Do I envy those jacks that nimble leap
To kiss the tender inward of thy hand,
Whilst my poor lips, which should that harvest reap,
At the wood's boldness by thee blushing stand! 8
To be so tickled, they would change their state
And situation with those dancing chips
O'er whom thy fingers walk with gentle gait,
Making dead wood more blest than living lips. 12
  Since saucy jacks so happy are in this,
  Give them thy fingers, me thy lips to kiss.

128 • 2 wood keys of the spinet or virginal. **motion** mechanism **3 thou gently sway'st** you gently control **4 wiry concord** harmony produced by strings. **confounds** i.e., pleasurably overwhelms **5 jacks** (Literally, upright pieces of wood fixed to the key-lever and fitted with a quill that plucks the strings of the virginal; here used of the keys, and with a pun on *jacks* in the sense of "common fellows," as in l. 13.) **8 by** beside; or with. (The poet stands beside the lady as she plays, blushing to his very lips; and he blushes in vexation at the *jacks'* boldness with her hand.) **9 they** i.e., my lips **13 jacks** (with a pun on "knaves, fellows" as in l. 5)

129

Th' expense of spirit in a waste of shame
Is lust in action; and, till action, lust
Is perjured, murderous, bloody, full of blame,
Savage, extreme, rude, cruel, not to trust, 4
Enjoyed no sooner but despisèd straight,
Past reason hunted, and no sooner had
Past reason hated, as a swallowed bait
On purpose laid to make the taker mad; 8
Mad in pursuit, and in possession so;
Had, having, and in quest to have, extreme;
A bliss in proof, and proved, a very woe;
Before, a joy proposed; behind, a dream. 12
All this the world well knows; yet none knows well
To shun the heaven that leads men to this hell.

129 • 1–2 Th' expense . . . action lust being consummated is the expenditure or dissipation of vital energy in an orgy of shameful extravagance and guilt. (*Spirit* also suggests "sperm.") **2 till action** until it achieve consummation **3 blame** (1) guilt (2) recrimination **4 rude** brutal. **to trust** to be trusted **5 straight** immediately **6 Past reason** madly, intemperately **11 in proof** while experienced. **proved** i.e., afterward **12 Before** in prospect

130

My mistress' eyes are nothing like the sun;
Coral is far more red than her lips' red;
If snow be white, why then her breasts are dun;
If hairs be wires, black wires grow on her head. 4
I have seen roses damasked, red and white,
But no such roses see I in her cheeks;
And in some perfumes is there more delight
Than in the breath that from my mistress reeks. 8
I love to hear her speak, yet well I know
That music hath a far more pleasing sound.
I grant I never saw a goddess go;
My mistress, when she walks, treads on the ground. 12
And yet, by heaven, I think my love as rare
As any she belied with false compare.

130 • 1 nothing not at all **3 dun** dull grayish brown, mouse-colored **5 damasked** mingled red and white **8 reeks** issues as smell **11 go** walk **13 rare** extraordinary and unique **14 she** woman. **belied** misrepresented. **compare** comparison

131

Thou art as tyrannous, so as thou art,
As those whose beauties proudly make them cruel;
For well thou know'st to my dear doting heart
Thou art the fairest and most precious jewel. 4
Yet, in good faith, some say that thee behold
Thy face hath not the power to make love groan;
To say they err I dare not be so bold,
Although I swear it to myself alone. 8
And, to be sure that is not false I swear,
A thousand groans, but thinking on thy face,
One on another's neck, do witness bear
Thy black is fairest in my judgment's place. 12
  In nothing art thou black save in thy deeds,
  And thence this slander, as I think, proceeds.

131 • 1 tyrannous pitiless and domineering. **so as thou art** even as you are (dark, not considered handsome) **3 dear** fond **9 to be sure** as proof. **false I** false that I **10 but thinking on** when I do no more than think of **11 One . . . neck** one rapidly after another **12 black** dark complexion. **my judgment's place** i.e., my opinion **14 this slander** (See ll. 5–6.) **proceeds** originates

132

Thine eyes I love, and they, as pitying me,
Knowing thy heart torment me with disdain,
Have put on black, and loving mourners be,
Looking with pretty ruth upon my pain. 4
And truly not the morning sun of heaven
Better becomes the gray cheeks of the east,
Nor that full star that ushers in the even
Doth half that glory to the sober west 8
As those two mourning eyes become thy face.
O, let it then as well beseem thy heart
To mourn for me, since mourning doth thee grace,
And suit thy pity like in every part. 12
Then will I swear beauty herself is black,
And all they foul that thy complexion lack.

132 • 1 as as if **2 Knowing . . . torment** knowing that your heart torments **4 ruth** pity **6 becomes** adorns. **cheeks** i.e., clouds **7 that full star** the evening star, Hesperus, i.e., Venus. **even** evening **8 Doth** i.e., lends. **sober** somber, subdued in color **9 mourning** (Spelled *morning* in the quarto, suggesting a pun on l. 5.) **10 beseem** suit **12 suit thy pity like** dress your pity alike, make it alike and consistent. **in every part** i.e., in the heart as well as the eyes **14 And . . . that** and that all those are ugly who

133

Beshrew that heart that makes my heart to groan
For that deep wound it gives my friend and me!
Is 't not enough to torture me alone,
But slave to slavery my sweet'st friend must be? 4
Me from myself thy cruel eye hath taken,
And my next self thou harder hast engrossed.
Of him, myself, and thee I am forsaken—
A torment thrice threefold thus to be crossed. 8
Prison my heart in thy steel bosom's ward,
But then my friend's heart let my poor heart bail;
Whoe'er keeps me, let my heart be his guard;
Thou canst not then use rigor in my jail. 12
And yet thou wilt; for I, being pent in thee,
Perforce am thine, and all that is in me.

133 • 1 Beshrew i.e., a plague upon **2 it** i.e., *that heart* (l. 1), the cruel heart of the Dark Lady **4 slave to slavery** enslaved to slavery itself, to a slavish infatuation **6 And . . . engrossed** i.e., and you have put my dearest friend, my other self, under even greater restraint. **engrossed** (1) driven into obsession (2) bought up wholesale **8 crossed** thwarted, afflicted **9 Prison** imprison. **steel bosom's ward** the prison cell of your hard heart **10 bail** set free by taking its place **11 keeps** has custody of. **his guard** my friend's guardhouse **12 rigor** harshness. **my jail** i.e., my heart, where my friend is kept (and where I can protect him from your harsh authority) **13 pent** shut up **14 and all** along with everything

134

So, now I have confessed that he is thine,
And I myself am mortgaged to thy will,
Myself I'll forfeit, so that other mine
Thou wilt restore to be my comfort still. 4
But thou wilt not, nor he will not be free,
For thou art covetous and he is kind;
He learned but surety-like to write for me
Under that bond that him as fast doth bind. 8
The statute of thy beauty thou wilt take,
Thou usurer, that putt'st forth all to use,
And sue a friend came debtor for my sake;
So him I lose through my unkind abuse. 12
  Him have I lost, thou hast both him and me;
  He pays the whole, and yet am I not free.

134 • 2 will (1) wishes (2) fleshly desire **3 so . . . mine** provided that my other self, my friend **5 will not** does not wish to **7 surety-like** as security, as guarantor. **write** sign the bond, endorse (suggesting that the friend has taken the poet's place with the mistress) **8 that bond . . . bind** that mortgage or bond (of sexual enslavement) that now binds him as securely as it does me **9 statute** a usurer's security or amount of money secured under his bond. **take** call in, invoke. (The lady will exact the full forfeiture specified in the mortgage as the amount to which her beauty entitles her.) **10 use** (1) usury (2) sexual pleasure **11 sue** (with suggestion also of "woo"). **came** i.e., who became **12 my unkind abuse** your ill-usage and unkind deceiving (of me) **14 pays** (with sexual suggestion)

135

Whoever hath her wish, thou hast thy Will,
And Will to boot, and Will in overplus;
More than enough am I that vex thee still,
To thy sweet will making addition thus. 4
Wilt thou, whose will is large and spacious,
Not once vouchsafe to hide my will in thine?
Shall will in others seem right gracious,
And in my will no fair acceptance shine? 8
The sea, all water, yet receives rain still
And in abundance addeth to his store;
So thou, being rich in Will, add to thy Will
One will of mine, to make thy large Will more. 12
  Let no unkind no fair beseechers kill;
  Think all but one, and me in that one Will.

135 • 1 Will (This and the following sonnet and Sonnet 143 ring changes on the word *will*—sexual desire, temper, passion, and the poet's name; possibly also the friend's name. The word can also suggest the sexual organs, male and female.) **3 vex** (by unwelcome wooing). **still** continually **6 hide . . . thine** (with sexual suggestion) **7 will in others** others' will **10 his** its **13 Let . . . kill** let no unkind word kill any who seek your favors; or, *Let "no" unkind,* etc., do not kill your wooers with the word "no" **14 Think . . . Will** i.e., think all your wooers and their wills to be but one, all comprised in me

136

If thy soul check thee that I come so near,
Swear to thy blind soul that I was thy Will,
And will, thy soul knows, is admitted there;
Thus far for love my love suit, sweet, fulfill. 4
Will will fulfill the treasure of thy love,
Ay, fill it full with wills, and my will one.
In things of great receipt with ease we prove
Among a number one is reckoned none. 8
Then in the number let me pass untold,
Though in thy store's account I one must be;
For nothing hold me, so it please thee hold
That nothing me, a something, sweet, to thee. 12
  Make but my name thy love, and love that still,
  And then thou lovest me for my name is Will.

136 • 1 check rebuke. **come so near** i.e., come so near the truth about you (in my previous sonnet); with suggestion of physical nearness also **2 blind** unperceptive **4 fulfill** grant **5 fulfill the treasure** fill full the treasury (with sexual suggestion) **6 my will** (suggesting "my penis"). **one** one of them **7 receipt** capacity (suggesting profligacy) **8 one . . . none** (A variant of the common saying "one is no number.") **9 untold** uncounted **10 in . . . account** in your (huge) inventory (of lovers) **11–12 For . . . thee** i.e., consider me too insignificant to think of, provided that you deign to hold insignificant me to you, my sweet, thereby making me something of worth. (*Something* is sexually suggestive.) **13 my name** i.e., "will," that is, desire. **still** continually **14 for** because

137

Thou blind fool, Love, what dost thou to mine eyes
That they behold and see not what they see?
They know what beauty is, see where it lies,
Yet what the best is take the worst to be. 4
If eyes corrupt by overpartial looks
Be anchored in the bay where all men ride,
Why of eyes' falsehood hast thou forgèd hooks,
Whereto the judgment of my heart is tied? 8
Why should my heart think that a several plot
Which my heart knows the wide world's common
place?
Or mine eyes seeing this, say this is not,
To put fair truth upon so foul a face? 12
In things right true my heart and eyes have erred,
And to this false plague are they now transferred.

137 • 1 Love Cupid, portrayed as blind **2 see not** do not comprehend **3 lies** resides **4 Yet . . . be** yet take the worst for the best **5 corrupt by overpartial looks** corrupted by doting and frankly prejudiced gazing **6 Be . . . ride** have brought me to anchor in a bay used by everyone (with sexual suggestion of a wanton woman) **7 Why . . . hooks** why have you, Love, fashioned snares out of my eyes' delusion **9 think . . . plot** think that to be a private field, i.e., that woman to be the exclusive property of one man **10 knows** knows to be. **common place** (1) a commons, a common pasture (2) a woman's body that is open, promiscuous **11 Or** i.e., or why should. **not** not so **14 false plague** (1) plague of judging falsely (2) false woman

138

When my love swears that she is made of truth
I do believe her, though I know she lies,
That she might think me some untutored youth,
Unlearnèd in the world's false subtleties. 4
Thus vainly thinking that she thinks me young,
Although she knows my days are past the best,
Simply I credit her false-speaking tongue;
On both sides thus is simple truth suppressèd. 8
But wherefore says she not she is unjust?
And wherefore say not I that I am old?
O, love's best habit is in seeming trust,
And age in love loves not to have years told. 12
Therefore I lie with her, and she with me,
And in our faults by lies we flattered be.

138 • 1 (A version of this sonnet appears in *The Passionate Pilgrim.*) **truth** fidelity, constancy **2 believe** i.e., pretend to believe **5 vainly thinking** acting as though I thought **7 Simply** pretending to be foolish. **credit** give credence to **9 unjust** unfaithful **11 habit** demeanor (with, however, a suggestion of *garb,* i.e., something put on). **seeming trust** apparent fidelity **12 age in love** an aging person in love, or, in matters of love. **told** (1) counted (2) told **13 lie with** deceive (with sexual pun) **14 And . . . be** and so by lies we flatteringly deceive ourselves about our moral lapses

139

O, call not me to justify the wrong
That thy unkindness lays upon my heart;
Wound me not with thine eye but with thy tongue;
Use power with power and slay me not by art. 4
Tell me thou lov'st elsewhere, but in my sight,
Dear heart, forbear to glance thine eye aside;
What need'st thou wound with cunning when thy might
Is more than my o'erpressed defense can bide? 8
Let me excuse thee: "Ah, my love well knows
Her pretty looks have been mine enemies,
And therefore from my face she turns my foes,
That they elsewhere might dart their injuries." 12
  Yet do not so; but since I am near slain,
  Kill me outright with looks and rid my pain.

139 • 1 call ask. **justify** i.e., condone something actually taking place under my eyes **2 unkindness** i.e., flagrant infidelity **3 with thine eye** i.e., with a roving eye. (See ll. 5–6.) **4 with power** i.e., candidly, directly. **art** artifice, cunning **7 What** why **8 bide** abide, withstand **11 foes** i.e., the *pretty looks* or wanton glances of l. 10 **13 near** nearly **14 rid** end. (*Rid my pain* also suggests "satiate my craving.")

140

Be wise as thou art cruel; do not press
My tongue-tied patience with too much disdain,
Lest sorrow lend me words, and words express
The manner of my pity-wanting pain. 4
If I might teach thee wit, better it were,
Though not to love, yet, love, to tell me so,
As testy sick men, when their deaths be near,
No news but health from their physicians know. 8
For if I should despair, I should grow mad,
And in my madness might speak ill of thee.
Now this ill-wresting world is grown so bad,
Mad slanderers by mad ears believèd be. 12
  That I may not be so, nor thou belied,
  Bear thine eyes straight, though thy proud heart
    go wide.

140 • 4 The manner . . . pain the nature of my pain, on which you bestow no pity **5 wit** wisdom, prudence **6 Though . . . so** even though you don't love me, yet, love, to tell me that you do **8 know** i.e., hear **11 ill-wresting** misinterpreting in an evil sense. **bad** bad (that) **13 so** i.e., a *mad slanderer*. **belied** slandered **14 wide** astray. (The image is from archery.)

141

In faith, I do not love thee with mine eyes,
For they in thee a thousand errors note;
But 'tis my heart that loves what they despise,
Who in despite of view is pleased to dote. 4
Nor are mine ears with thy tongue's tune delighted,
Nor tender feeling to base touches prone,
Nor taste, nor smell, desire to be invited
To any sensual feast with thee alone. 8
But my five wits nor my five senses can
Dissuade one foolish heart from serving thee,
Who leaves unswayed the likeness of a man,
Thy proud heart's slave and vassal wretch to be. 12
Only my plague thus far I count my gain,
That she that makes me sin awards me pain.

141 • 2 errors flaws in beauty **4 Who . . . view** which (i.e., the heart), in spite of what the eyes see **6 Nor . . . prone** nor (is) my delicate sense of touch inclined toward carnal contact (with you) **9 my five wits** (neither) my five intellectual senses, i.e., the common sense, imagination, fancy, estimation (judgment), and memory **11 Who . . . man** i.e., which heart abandons the proper government of my person, leaving me the mere likeness of a man **13 thus far** to the following extent **14 That . . . pain** i.e., that the sin brings with it its own punishment and contrition, thus presumably shortening my torment after death (with a suggestion in *pain* of "sexual pleasure"; see Sonnet 139)

142

Love is my sin, and thy dear virtue hate,
Hate of my sin, grounded on sinful loving.
O, but with mine compare thou thine own state,
And thou shalt find it merits not reproving; 4
Or, if it do, not from those lips of thine,
That have profaned their scarlet ornaments
And sealed false bonds of love as oft as mine,
Robbed others' beds' revenues of their rents. 8
Be it lawful I love thee as thou lov'st those
Whom thine eyes woo as mine importune thee.
Root pity in thy heart, that when it grows
Thy pity may deserve to pitied be. 12
  If thou dost seek to have what thou dost hide,
  By self-example mayst thou be denied.

142 • 1–2 Love . . . loving i.e., my sin is to love you, and your best virtue is to hate—hate that sin in me, the sin of loving you. (The bitter paradox here is that hatred of sin must be virtue, and yet the lady is herself deeply implicated in this sin; her hatred is more a disdainful rejection of the poet's love than a noble virtue.) **4 it** i.e., my state **6–7 That . . . mine** i.e., that have forsworn themselves in love as often as my lips. (The *scarlet ornaments* are lips and also red wax used to seal documents; they *seal* with a kiss.) **8 Robbed . . . rents** i.e., and committed adultery with other women's husbands. (The metaphor is of income-yielding estates, *revenues,* whose *rents* or payments made by tenants are not properly paid; the husband does not pay what is owed to the wife in terms of marital affection and producing children.) **9–10 Be . . . thee** i.e., I am as justified in loving you and imploring you with my eyes as you are in pursuing other men. (*Be it lawful* is a legal phrase meaning "let it be considered lawful that.") **12 deserve** make you deserving **13 what . . . hide** what you withhold, i.e., pity

143

Lo, as a careful huswife runs to catch
One of her feathered creatures broke away,
Sets down her babe and makes all swift dispatch
In pursuit of the thing she would have stay, 4
Whilst her neglected child holds her in chase,
Cries to catch her whose busy care is bent
To follow that which flies before her face,
Not prizing her poor infant's discontent; 8
So runn'st thou after that which flies from thee,
Whilst I, thy babe, chase thee afar behind;
But if thou catch thy hope, turn back to me,
And play the mother's part: kiss me, be kind. 12
So will I pray that thou mayst have thy Will,
If thou turn back and my loud crying still.

143 • 1 careful distressed, full of cares, busy. **huswife** housewife **5 holds her in chase** chases after her **7 flies** flees **8 Not prizing** disregarding **13 Will** (See Sonnets 135, 136.) **14 still** hush, make quiet

144

Two loves I have, of comfort and despair,
Which like two spirits do suggest me still:
The better angel is a man right fair,
The worser spirit a woman colored ill. 4
To win me soon to hell, my female evil
Tempteth my better angel from my side,
And would corrupt my saint to be a devil,
Wooing his purity with her foul pride. 8
And whether that my angel be turned fiend
Suspect I may, yet not directly tell;
But being both from me, both to each friend,
I guess one angel in another's hell. 12
  Yet this shall I ne'er know, but live in doubt
  Till my bad angel fire my good one out.

144 • 1 (This sonnet appears, somewhat altered, in *The Passionate Pilgrim.*) **2 suggest** urge, offer counsel, tempt. **still** continually **4 ill** i.e., dark of complexion **11 from me** away from me. (The poet suspects they are together.) **both . . . friend** friends to each other **12 I . . . hell** I suspect that she (the evil angel) has him in her power (i.e., her sexual embracement; *hell* is slang for the pudenda) **14 fire . . . out** drive out my good angel, stop seeing him (with the suggestion of driving him out of the lady's sexual body as one would use fire and smoke to drive an animal out of its burrow, and with the further suggestion that the *fire* is venereal disease. *Bad angel* also hints at bad coinage driving out good money.)

145

Those lips that Love's own hand did make
Breathed forth the sound that said "I hate"
To me that languished for her sake;
But when she saw my woeful state, 4
Straight in her heart did mercy come,
Chiding that tongue that ever sweet
Was used in giving gentle doom,
And taught it thus anew to greet: 8
"I hate" she altered with an end,
That followed it as gentle day
Doth follow night, who like a fiend
From heaven to hell is flown away. 12
"I hate" from hate away she threw,
And saved my life, saying "not you."

145 • 1 (This sonnet is in eight-syllable meter.) **5 Straight** at once **7 used . . . doom** accustomed to passing a mild sentence **13 "I hate" . . . threw** i.e., she separated the phrase "I hate" from the hatred I feared it expressed, from hateful meaning

146

Poor soul, the center of my sinful earth,
Thrall to these rebel powers that thee array,
Why dost thou pine within and suffer dearth,
Painting thy outward walls so costly gay? 4
Why so large cost, having so short a lease,
Dost thou upon thy fading mansion spend?
Shall worms, inheritors of this excess,
Eat up thy charge? Is this thy body's end? 8
Then, soul, live thou upon thy servant's loss,
And let that pine to aggravate thy store;
Buy terms divine in selling hours of dross;
Within be fed, without be rich no more. 12
So shalt thou feed on Death, that feeds on men,
And Death once dead, there's no more dying then.

146 • 1 sinful earth body **2 Thrall to** (One of several conjectures; the quarto repeats *My sinfull earth* from l. 1.) **rebel powers** i.e., rebellious flesh. **array** dress, clothe **4 outward walls** i.e., the body, decked out in finery, cosmetics, etc. **5 so short a lease** (because we are lent the *mansion* of our body for so short a time) **6 mansion** dwelling, i.e., the body **8 thy charge** that on which you have expended so much, and that was put in your *charge* or custody **9 thy servant's** i.e., the body's **10 that . . . store** the body starve to increase your stock of riches **11 Buy . . . dross** i.e., purchase eternal life in return for giving up (selling) mere hours of wasteful pleasure; arrange *terms* that only God can provide

147

My love is as a fever, longing still
For that which longer nurseth the disease,
Feeding on that which doth preserve the ill,
Th' uncertain sickly appetite to please. 4
My reason, the physician to my love,
Angry that his prescriptions are not kept,
Hath left me, and I desperate now approve
Desire is death, which physic did except. 8
Past cure I am, now reason is past care,
And frantic-mad with evermore unrest;
My thoughts and my discourse as madmen's are,
At random from the truth vainly expressed; 12
  For I have sworn thee fair and thought thee bright,
  Who art as black as hell, as dark as night.

147 • 1 still always **3 preserve the ill** sustain the illness **4 uncertain** finicky **7 desperate** in despair. **approve** demonstrate, show by experience that **8 Desire . . . except** (that) desire, which the advice of medicine (i.e., reason) proscribed, proves fatal **9 care** medical care. (The line is an inversion of the proverb, "things past cure are past care," i.e., don't worry about what can't be helped. Reason, the physician, has ceased to care for his patient.) **10 evermore** constant and increasing **12 vainly** to no sensible purpose

148

O me, what eyes hath love put in my head,
Which have no correspondence with true sight!
Or, if they have, where is my judgment fled,
That censures falsely what they see aright? 4
If that be fair whereon my false eyes dote,
What means the world to say it is not so?
If it be not, then love doth well denote
Love's eye is not so true as all men's "no." 8
How can it? O, how can love's eye be true,
That is so vexed with watching and with tears?
No marvel then though I mistake my view;
The sun itself sees not till heaven clears. 12
O cunning love, with tears thou keep'st me blind,
Lest eyes well-seeing thy foul faults should find.

148 • 4 censures judges **7 love** i.e., the self-deceiving nature of my love. **denote** indicate, demonstrate (that) **8 eye** (with a pun on *ay,* yes) **10 vexed** troubled. **watching** remaining awake **11 mistake my view** err in what I see

149

Canst thou, O cruel, say I love thee not,
When I against myself with thee partake?
Do I not think on thee when I forgot
Am of myself, all tyrant for thy sake? 4
Who hateth thee that I do call my friend?
On whom frown'st thou that I do fawn upon?
Nay, if thou lour'st on me, do I not spend
Revenge upon myself with present moan? 8
What merit do I in myself respect
That is so proud thy service to despise,
When all my best doth worship thy defect,
Commanded by the motion of thine eyes? 12
  But, love, hate on, for now I know thy mind:
  Those that can see thou lov'st, and I am blind.

149 • 2 partake take part (against myself) **3 think on thee** put consideration of you foremost **3–4 when . . . sake** when I am tyrannously neglectful of, or oblivious of, myself and my best interests on your behalf. **forgot** forgotten **7 spend** vent **8 present moan** immediate suffering **9 respect** value **10 thy . . . despise** as to think it demeaning to serve you **11 all my best** all that is best in me. **defect** insufficiency **14 Those . . . blind** i.e., you scorn one who loves you in a blind passion, in defiance of reason, and are drawn instead to those who worship your looks only

150

O, from what power hast thou this powerful might
With insufficiency my heart to sway?
To make me give the lie to my true sight
And swear that brightness doth not grace the day? 4
Whence hast thou this becoming of things ill,
That in the very refuse of thy deeds
There is such strength and warrantise of skill
That, in my mind, thy worst all best exceeds? 8
Who taught thee how to make me love thee more,
The more I hear and see just cause of hate?
O, though I love what others do abhor,
With others thou shouldst not abhor my state. 12
If thy unworthiness raised love in me,
More worthy I to be beloved of thee.

150 • 2 With insufficiency by means of all your shortcomings. **sway** rule **3 give the lie to** accuse flatly of lying **4 And . . . day** i.e., and swear that what is so is not so, that what is fair and beautiful is not fair and beautiful since you are dark **5 becoming . . . ill** i.e., ability to show ill things in a becoming light **6 in . . . deeds** in the most debased of your actions **7 warrantise of skill** warrant or assurance of expertise **12 state** i.e., condition of being helplessly in love

151

Love is too young to know what conscience is;
Yet who knows not conscience is born of love?
Then, gentle cheater, urge not my amiss,
Lest guilty of my faults thy sweet self prove. 4
For, thou betraying me, I do betray
My nobler part to my gross body's treason;
My soul doth tell my body that he may
Triumph in love; flesh stays no farther reason, 8
But, rising at thy name, doth point out thee
As his triumphant prize. Proud of this pride,
He is contented thy poor drudge to be,
To stand in thy affairs, fall by thy side. 12
  No want of conscience hold it that I call
  Her "love" for whose dear love I rise and fall.

151 • 1 too young (Love is personified as the young Cupid.) **2 conscience** guilty knowing, carnal knowledge (playing on *conscience,* "moral sense," in l. 1) **3 urge** stress, invoke. **amiss** sin **5 betraying** (1) exposing (2) leading into temptation **6 nobler part** i.e., soul **8 stays** awaits. **reason** reasoning talk **9 rising** (with bawdy suggestion of erection, continued in *point, Proud, stand, fall*) **10 triumphant prize** spoils to be enjoyed in victory. **Proud of** swelling with. **pride** splendor; erection **12 stand** (1) serve, undertake business (2) be erect. **fall** (as in battle; with sexual suggestion of detumescence) **13 want** lack

152

In loving thee thou know'st I am forsworn,
But thou art twice forsworn, to me love swearing;
In act thy bed-vow broke, and new faith torn
In vowing new hate after new love bearing. 4
But why of two oaths' breach do I accuse thee,
When I break twenty? I am perjured most,
For all my vows are oaths but to misuse thee,
And all my honest faith in thee is lost; 8
For I have sworn deep oaths of thy deep kindness,
Oaths of thy love, thy truth, thy constancy,
And, to enlighten thee, gave eyes to blindness,
Or made them swear against the thing they see; 12
  For I have sworn thee fair. More perjured eye,
  To swear against the truth so foul a lie!

152 • 1 forsworn i.e., faithless to my vows of love (perhaps marriage vows) **3 act** sexual act. **bed-vow** marriage vows to your husband **3–4 new . . . bearing** i.e., a new contract of fidelity is torn up by your swearing hatred toward me to whom you have only recently professed love. (Or the *new faith* that is torn up may be that which the lady has sworn to the friend.) **7 but to misuse** merely to misrepresent; or, deceive **8 And . . . lost** i.e., and by loving you I forfeit all claim to integrity **11 And . . . blindness** i.e., and, to invest you with brightness, I made my eyes testify to things they did not see **13 eye** (with a pun on *I*)

153

Cupid laid by his brand and fell asleep.
A maid of Dian's this advantage found,
And his love-kindling fire did quickly steep
In a cold valley-fountain of that ground; 4
Which borrowed from this holy fire of Love
A dateless lively heat, still to endure,
And grew a seething bath, which yet men prove
Against strange maladies a sovereign cure. 8
But at my mistress' eye Love's brand new-fired,
The boy for trial needs would touch my breast;
I, sick withal, the help of bath desired,
And thither hied, a sad distempered guest, 12
But found no cure. The bath for my help lies
Where Cupid got new fire—my mistress' eyes.

153 • 1 (This sonnet and the following seemingly have no direct connection with those preceding. They are adaptations of epigrams in the *Palatine Anthology,* Greek poems of the fifth century translated into Latin in the sixteenth century.) **brand** torch **2 maid** attendant virgin, votaress. **Dian** Diana, goddess of chastity **4 of that ground** i.e., nearby **6 dateless** endless, eternal. **still** always **7 grew** became. **seething bath** spring of hot medicinal waters. **yet** even today. **prove** discover to be **8 sovereign** efficacious **9 new-fired** having been reignited **10 for trial** by way of test **11 withal** from it **12 hied** hastened. **distempered** sick. (The bath is suggestive of the sweating cure for venereal disease.)

154

The little love god lying once asleep
Laid by his side his heart-inflaming brand,
Whilst many nymphs that vowed chaste life to keep
Came tripping by; but in her maiden hand 4
The fairest votary took up that fire
Which many legions of true hearts had warmed,
And so the general of hot desire
Was, sleeping, by a virgin hand disarmed. 8
This brand she quenchèd in a cool well by,
Which from Love's fire took heat perpetual,
Growing a bath and healthful remedy
For men diseased; but I, my mistress' thrall, 12
Came there for cure, and this by that I prove:
Love's fire heats water, water cools not love.

154 • 7 general inspirer and commander, i.e., Cupid **9 by** nearby **11 Growing** becoming **12 thrall** slave, bondman **13 cure** (with suggestion of treatment for venereal disease, as in 153.7–14). **this** i.e., the following proposition. **that** i.e., my coming, which failed to cure me

Date and Text

On May 20, 1609, "Thomas Thorpe Entred for his copie vnder thandes of master Wilson and master Lownes Warden a Booke called Shakespeares sonnettes." In the same year appeared the following volume:

> SHAKE-SPEARES SONNETS. Neuer before Imprinted. AT LONDON By *G. Eld* for *T. T.* and are to be solde by *Iohn Wright*, dwelling at Christ Church gate. 1609.

Some copies of this same edition are marked to be sold by William Aspley rather than John Wright; evidently Thorpe had set up two sellers to distribute the volume. The sonnets were not reprinted until John Benson's rearranged edition of 1640, possibly because the first edition had been suppressed or because sonnets were no longer in vogue. The 1609 edition may rest on a transcript of Shakespeare's sonnets by someone other than the author, and the edition itself is marred by misprints, though Thorpe was a reputable printer. Clearly the sonnet sequence was not supervised through the press as were *Venus and Adonis* and *The Rape of Lucrece*. All the evidence suggests that it was obtained without Shakespeare's permission from a manuscript that had been in private circulation (as we know from Francis Meres's 1598 allusion, in his *Palladis Tamia: Wit's Treasury*, to Shakespeare's "sugared sonnets among his private friends"). Two sonnets, 138 and 144, had appeared in 1599 in *The Passionate Pilgrim*. On questions of dating and order of the sonnets, see the Introduction to *Sonnets* in this volume.

Textual Notes

These textual notes are not a historical collation; they are simply a record of departures in this edition from the copy text. The reading adopted in this edition appears in boldface, followed by the rejected reading from the copy text, i.e., the quarto of 1609. Only major alterations in punctuation are noted. Corrections of minor and obvious typographical errors are not indicated.

Copy text: the quarto of 1609 [Q].

2.14 cold could **6.4 beauty's** beautits **8.10 Strikes** Strike **12.4 all** or **13.7 Yourself** You selfe **15.8 wear** were **17.12 meter** miter **18.10 [and elsewhere] lose** loose **19.3 jaws** yawes **20.2 Hast** Haste **22.3 furrows** forrwes **23.6 rite** right **23.14 with** wit **wit** wiht **24.1 stelled** steeld **25.9 fight** worth **26.12 thy** their [also at 27.10, 35.8 (twice), 37.7, 43.11, 45.12, 46.3, 46.8, 46.13, 46.14, 69.5, 70.6, 85.3, 128.11, 128.14] **27.2 travel** trauaill **28.12 gild'st** guil'st **28.14 strength** length **31.8 thee** there **34.2 travel** trauaile **34.12 cross** losse **38.2 pour'st** poor'st **38.3 too** to **41.7 woos** woes **41.8 she** he **42.10 losing** loosing **44.13 naught** naughts **45.9 life's** liues **46.9 'cide** side **46.12 the** he **47.2 other.** other, **47.4 smother,** smother; **47.11 not** nor **50.6 dully** duly **51.10 perfect'st** perfects **55.1 monuments** monument **56.3 [and elsewhere] today** too daie **58.7 patience-tame to sufferance,** patience tame, to sufferance **59.6 hundred** hundreth **59.11 whe'er** where **61.14 off** of **too** to **62.10 chapped** chopt **65.12 of** or **69.3 due** end **72.1 lest** least [also at l. 9 and elsewhere] **73.4 ruined** rn'wd **choirs** quiers **76.7 tell** fel **77.1 wear** were **77.10 blanks** blacks **83.7 too** to **85.3 Reserve** Reserne **88.8 losing** loosing **90.11 shall** stall **91.9 better** bitter **93.5 there** their **98.11 were** weare **99.4 dwells** dwells? **99.9 One** Our **102.8 her** his **106.12 skill** still **111.1 with** wish **112.14 are** y'are **113.6 latch** lack **113.14 mine eye** mine **118.5 ne'er-cloying** nere cloying **118.10 were not, grew** were, not grew **119.4 losing** loosing **126.8 minutes** mynuit **127.2 were** weare **127.10 brows** eyes **129.9 Mad** Made **129.11 proved, a** proud and **132.9 mourning** morning **138.12 to have** t' haue **140.5 were** weare **144.6 side** [adopted from *The Passionate Pilgrim*] sight **144.9 fiend** [adopted from *The Passionate Pilgrim*] finde **146.2 Thrall to** My sinfull earth **147.7 approve** approoue. **153.14 eyes** eye

Index of Sonnet First Lines

Further Reading

Venus and Adonis

Dubrow, Heather. "'Upon Misprision Growing': *Venus and Adonis.*" *Captive Victors: Shakespeare's Narrative Poems and Sonnets.* Ithaca and London: Cornell Univ. Press, 1987. Dubrow explores the poem's formal strategies of characterization. Focusing mainly on Venus, Dubrow argues that Shakespeare transforms the Ovidian mythological poem into a mode "conducive to the creation of complex characters and to the evocation of complex responses to them."

Hulse, Clarke. *Metamorphic Verse: The Elizabethan Minor Epic,* pp. 143–175. Princeton, N.J.: Princeton Univ. Press, 1981. Hulse examines the "iconographic" technique in *Venus and Adonis* that enables Shakespeare to hold "conflicting attitudes towards love in an aesthetic balance." The poem is structured like a formal debate in which one set of images alternates with another without any resolution of the contradiction and with unity provided only "by the repetition of the image itself."

Kahn, Coppélia. "Self and Eros in *Venus and Adonis.*" *Centennial Review* 4 (1976): 351–371; Rev. and rpt. in *Man's Estate: Masculine Identity in Shakespeare.* Berkeley, Los Angeles, and London: Univ. of California Press, 1981. Kahn views Adonis' rejection of Venus as "a *rite de passage* in reverse": instead of forging an adult sexual identity, Adonis flees from the possibility of intimacy, regressing into narcissistic isolation. His narcissism masks a deep desire for dependence, a wish ultimately fulfilled in his transformation into a flower that Venus nurtures as her child.

Keach, William. "*Venus and Adonis.*" *Elizabethan Erotic Narrative.* New Brunswick, N.J.: Rutgers Univ. Press, 1977. Examining Shakespeare's alterations of Ovid's version of the story, Keach finds "an antithetical, bipartite structure" in *Venus and Adonis* that organizes the poem's "tragic parody of the Platonic doctrine that love is the desire for beauty."

Muir, Kenneth. "*Venus and Adonis:* Comedy or Tragedy?" *Shakespeare the Professional, and Related Studies.* Totowa, N.J.: Rowman and Littlefield, 1973. Finding that the poem's fundamental ambivalence extends even to its "mingling of wit and seriousness," Muir sees *Venus and Adonis* neither as praise of chastity nor a paean to sensuality, but as a self-consciously Ovidian poem, imaginatively engaged with both Venus and Adonis and equally dismissive of Neoplatonic and Puritan arguments for "the denial of the flesh."

Rabkin, Norman. *Shakespeare and the Common Understanding,* pp. 150–162. New York: Free Press, 1967. Rabkin argues that the poem explores contradictions and unresolved tensions between spiritual and sensual love: Adonis' idealized conception of love's purity is juxtaposed with Venus' emphasis on love as sensual desire. The poem's provocative ambivalence mirrors the paradoxical treatment of love found in Shakespeare's plays.

The Rape of Lucrece

Allen, D. C. "Some Observations on *The Rape of Lucrece.*" *Shakespeare Survey* 15 (1962): 89–98. Allen argues for the predominance of Christian over classical perspectives in the poem, a view implicitly critical of Lucrece, whose actions, he finds, are largely motivated by her "love of pagan honour." Allen suggests that the poem invites an allegorical reading that confirms this harsh view of Lucrece's fate, despite the sympathy aroused for her plight.

Donaldson, Ian. " 'A Theme for Disputation': Shakespeare's Lucrece." *The Rapes of Lucretia: A Myth and Its Transformations.* Oxford: Clarendon Press, 1982. Donaldson's book considers the interpretations and transformations of the Lucrece story from Ovid to Giraudoux, and his account of Shakespeare's treatment focuses on the poem's movement between the conflicting ethical demands of Roman and Christian perspectives on the action.

Dubrow, Heather. "'Full of Forged Lies': *The Rape of Lucrece.*" *Captive Victors: Shakespeare's Narrative Poems and Sonnets.* Ithaca and London: Cornell Univ. Press, 1987. Dubrow probes the poem's elaborate rhetorical surface to discover Shakespeare's "preoccupation with the moral and psychological issues expressed through—or even raised by—such adornment."

Hulse, Clarke. *Metamorphic Verse: The Elizabethan Minor Epic,* pp. 175–194. Princeton, N.J.: Princeton Univ. Press, 1981. Hulse argues for the importance of pictorial elements in the poem in establishing the poem's characteristic "movement between incident and analysis." In the tapestry of the fall of Troy, Lucrece sees the analogy between the Trojan fate and her rape, enabling her to recognize her innocence and to demand her revenge through her own vivid portrayal of her suffering.

Kahn, Coppélia. "The Rape in Shakespeare's *Lucrece.*" *Shakespeare Studies* 9 (1976): 45–72. The focus of Kahn's essay is on the complex moral, social, and psychological ramifications of Lucrece's rape. The rigid structure of Rome's patriarchal society, where chastity is the "only value which gives meaning to her as a Roman wife," determines her tragic fate. Only by her death can she recreate her "ideal self" and restore Collatine's honor.

Miola, Robert S. "*The Rape of Lucrece*: Rome and Romans." *Shakespeare's Rome.* Cambridge and New York: Cambridge Univ. Press, 1983. Focusing on the poem's imagery of Lucrece herself as a city under attack by a barbarian, Miola sees the poem as part of Shakespeare's ongoing exploration of Rome and Romans, and he finds in Lucrece's fate—a suicide chosen as an act of Roman honor and piety—the origins of Shakespeare's disillusioned scrutiny of Roman values.

Vickers, Nancy J. "'The Blazon of Sweet Beauty's Best': Shakespeare's *Lucrece.*" In *Shakespeare and the Question of Theory,* ed. Patricia Parker and Geoffrey Hartman. London and New York: Methuen, 1985. Vickers examines the language of praise in the poem to discover the limits and dangers of a descriptive rhetoric that "displays" women as part of an aggressive rivalry between men. Her analysis reveals the complex relationship of the poem to its own insight, as it exposes the disturbing implications of rhetorical competition and yet "remains embedded in the descriptive rhetoric it undercuts."

The Phoenix and Turtle

Alvarez, A. "William Shakespeare: 'The Phoenix and the Turtle.'" In *Interpretations: Essays on Twelve English Poems*, ed. John Wain. London: Routledge and Kegan Paul, 1955. Alvarez offers a close and detailed reading of the logical, philosophical, and linguistic complexities of "The Phoenix and Turtle" that reveals the "stringent logic" of the poem's paradoxical presentation of mysterious love.

Ellrodt, Robert. "An Anatomy of 'The Phoenix and the Turtle.'" *Shakespeare Survey* 15 (1962): 99–110. Ellrodt's thorough account of the poem's symbolism and philosophical assumptions leads him to recognize the "originality of Shakespeare's handling of the Phoenix theme" and his sobering awareness that "truth may seem but cannot be," for "Love and Constancy are dead."

Empson, William. "'The Phoenix and the Turtle.'" *Essays in Criticism* 16 (1966): 147–153. Empson suggests that Shakespeare's poem must be understood in terms of its appearance in an anthology by Robert Chester designed to celebrate the knighting of Sir John Salusbury. He examines the genesis of the anthology as well as the relationship of Shakespeare's poem to the other poems included in the celebratory collection.

Garber, Marjorie. "Two Birds with One Stone: Lapidary Re-Inscription in 'The Phoenix and Turtle.'" *The Upstart Crow* 5 (1984): 5–19. Garber sees the poem as triumphing over its conventional subject matter and the restrictions of its occasion through the "highly self-conscious formal structure" and the fusion of elegy and epithalamion that permit its witty subversion of its own formal and logical authority.

Matchett, William H. "*The Phoenix and the Turtle*": *Shakespeare's Poem and Chester's "Loues Martyr."* The Hague and Paris: Mouton; New York: Humanities Press, 1965. Matchett provides a patient analysis of the poem's language and structure before turning to the poem's literary and historical contexts. He sees the poem as a political allegory about Elizabeth (the Phoenix) and Essex (the Turtle) and finds its terms of praise qualified by the elegiac quality of the threnos and the "insistence" of the final line.

A Lover's Complaint

Jackson, MacD. P. *Shakespeare's "A Lover's Complaint": Its Date and Authenticity*. Auckland, N.Z.: Univ. of Auckland Press, 1965. By examining the poem's vocabulary, phrasing, imagery, stylistic mannerisms, and subject matter, Jackson's thirty-nine-page pamphlet affirms Shakespeare's authorship.

Muir, Kenneth. "'A Lover's Complaint': A Reconsideration." In *Shakespeare 1564–1964: A Collection of Modern Essays By Various Hands,* ed. Edward A. Bloom. Providence, R.I.: Brown Univ. Press, 1964. Muir considers the question of authorship and concludes, on the basis of stylistic as well as bibliographic indications, that the poem was written by Shakespeare, probably sometime near 1600. He also provides an account of the poem's paired thematic concerns: "the difficulty of distinguishing between appearance and reality" and "the battle of the sexes."

Warren, Roger. "'A Lover's Complaint,' *All's Well,* and the Sonnets." *Notes and Queries* n.s. 17 (1970): 130–132. Warren finds verbal echoes of the sonnets and *All's Well That Ends Well* in "A Lover's Complaint," which leads him to posit a connection "in Shakespeare's mind (and perhaps in date of composition) between the Helena/Bertram relationship and the lovely but deceitful boy of both sonnets and poem."

Sonnets

Booth, Stephen. *An Essay on Shakespeare's Sonnets*. New Haven, Conn.: Yale Univ. Press, 1969. Booth sees the sonnets as being "multiply ordered" by a variety of formal patterns, and he traces their function and interaction as they structure the reader's experience of the poems.

_______, ed. *Shakespeare's Sonnets, Edited with Analytic Commentary*. New Haven, Conn.: Yale Univ. Press, 1977. Booth's edition includes almost 400 pages of commentary on the diction, syntax, idiom, and background of individual sonnets, focusing on the "fusions by which incompatible and contradictory truths are voiced simultaneously."

Fineman, Joel. *Shakespeare's Perjured Eye: The Invention of Poetic Subjectivity in the Sonnets*. Berkeley, Los Angeles, and London: Univ. of California Press, 1986. In this dense and provocative study of the sonnets, Fineman finds in Shakespeare's complex response to the Renaissance poetry of praise a profound disruption of its idealizing strategies, dependent upon the recognition of a divided self-consciousness and permitting the development of "a genuinely new poetic subjectivity."

Herrnstein, Barbara, ed. *Discussions of Shakespeare's Sonnets*. Boston: D. C. Heath, 1964. The collection includes nineteen essays, ranging from John Benson's preface to the 1640 edition of Shakespeare's poems to an essay by C. L. Barber written in 1960, encompassing a wide variety of critical responses "to the themes, attitudes, and experiences which the poems reflect, to their value as literary achievements and to their characteristics as poetic art."

Hubler, Edward, ed. *The Riddle of Shakespeare's Sonnets*. New York: Basic Books, 1962. Hubler provides a text of the sonnets, plus essays by Northrop Frye, Leslie A. Fiedler, Stephen Spender, and R. P. Blackmur. Hubler also includes his own "Shakespeare's Sonnets and the Commentators" and Oscar Wilde's "The Portrait of Mr. W. H." (1895).

Krieger, Murray. *A Window to Criticism: Shakespeare's Sonnets and Modern Poetics*. Princeton, N.J.: Princeton Univ. Press, 1964. Rejecting both mimetic and formalistic critical approaches, Krieger argues for a "contextualism" that reveals, through his supple reading of individual sonnets, the ways in which Shakespeare's poetry is both a "window" and "mirror," at once opening out to an historical existence and reflecting the "insistent" reality of the aesthetic object itself: "word and thing—indeed word and world—are made one."

Landry, Hilton, ed. *New Essays on Shakespeare's Sonnets.* New York: AMS, 1976. Landry's collection of nine specially commissioned essays includes studies by Winifred Nowottny on the sonnets' "form and style," W. G. Ingram on the poems' "internal poetic organization," Anton M. Pirkhofer on their "dramatic character," and Landry's own "defense" of the sonnets against the criticism of John Crowe Ransom and Yvor Winters.

Leishman, J. B. *Themes and Variations in Shakespeare's Sonnets.* New York: Hillary House, 1961. Leishman examines the central themes and strategies of organization in the sonnets and their sources in the classical and Renaissance literary traditions available to Shakespeare.

Melchiori, Giorgio. *Shakespeare's Dramatic Meditations: An Experiment in Criticism.* Oxford: Clarendon Press, 1976. Melchiori's subtle analysis of sonnets 20, 94, 121, 129, and 146, focusing on the poems' linguistic, literary, and socio-historical resources, reveals them as "meditations *in action,*" dramatic engagements with the contradictions and unresolved tensions of their originating idea or emotion.

Muir, Kenneth. *Shakespeare's Sonnets.* London and Boston: George Allen and Unwin, 1979. Muir's sensible introduction to the sonnets includes a discussion of their date, the text, and the sonnet order, as well as a consideration of their relation to the sonnet tradition and an essay examining the themes and attitudes of the sequence.

Pequigney, Joseph. *Such Is My Love: A Study of Shakespeare's Sonnets.* Chicago: Univ. of Chicago Press, 1985. Pequigney's interpretation focuses on the drama of human desire articulated by Shakespeare's sonnet sequence, usefully differentiating Renaissance conventions of friendship from the erotic (including homoerotic) relations he finds delineated in the poems.

Contributors

DAVID BEVINGTON, Phyllis Fay Horton Professor of Humanities at the University of Chicago, is editor of *The Complete Works of Shakespeare* (Scott, Foresman, 1980) and of *Medieval Drama* (Houghton Mifflin, 1975). His latest critical study is *Action Is Eloquence: Shakespeare's Language of Gesture* (Harvard University Press, 1984).

DAVID SCOTT KASTAN, Professor of English and Comparative Literature at Columbia University, is the author of *Shakespeare and the Shapes of Time* (University Press of New England, 1982).

JAMES HAMMERSMITH, Associate Professor of English at Auburn University, has published essays on various facets of Renaissance drama, including literary criticism, textual criticism, and printing history.

ROBERT KEAN TURNER, Professor of English at the University of Wisconsin–Milwaukee, is a general editor of the New Variorum Shakespeare (Modern Language Association of America) and a contributing editor to *The Dramatic Works in the Beaumont and Fletcher Canon* (Cambridge University Press, 1966–).

JAMES SHAPIRO, who coedited the bibliographies with David Scott Kastan, is Assistant Professor of English at Columbia University.

✣

JOSEPH PAPP, one of the most important forces in theater today, is the founder and producer of the New York Shakespeare Festival, America's largest and most prolific theatrical institution. Since 1954 Mr. Papp has produced or directed all but one of Shakespeare's plays—in Central Park, in schools, off and on Broadway, and at the Festival's permanent home, The Public Theater. He has also produced such award-winning plays and musical works as *Hair, A Chorus Line, Plenty,* and *The Mystery of Edwin Drood,* among many others.

THE COMPLETE WORKS OF WILLIAM SHAKESPEARE

Volume I

Love's Labor's Lost
The Comedy of Errors
The Two Gentlemen of Verona
Henry VI, Parts One, Two, and Three
Richard III

Volume II

The Taming of the Shrew
The Merchant of Venice
Romeo and Juliet
King John
A Midsummer Night's Dream
Richard II
Much Ado about Nothing

Volume III

Henry IV, Part One
Henry IV, Part Two
The Merry Wives of Windsor
Hamlet
As You Like It
Henry V

Volume IV

Julius Caesar
Twelfth Night
Troilus and Cressida
All's Well that Ends Well
Measure for Measure
Othello

Volume V

King Lear
Macbeth
Antony and Cleopatra
Pericles
Cymbeline
Coriolanus

Volume VI

Timon of Athens
Titus Andronicus
The Tempest
The Winter's Tale
Henry VIII
The Complete Poems and Sonnets